Cost Accounting: Traditions and Innovations

JESSE T. BARFIELD
Loyola University—New Orleans

CECILY A. RAIBORN
Loyola University—New Orleans

MICHAEL R. KINNEY
Texas A&M University

Australia · Canada · Mexico · Singapore · Spain · United Kingdom · United States

Cost Acounting: Traditions and Innovations, 4e by Jesse T. Barfield, Cecily A. Raiborn, and Michael R. Kinney

Vice-President/Team Director: Dave Shaut
Acquisitions Editor: Sharon Oblinger
Developmental Editor: Leslie Kauffman, Litten Editing and Production, Inc.
Marketing Manager: Larry Qualls
Production Editor: Kelly Keeler
Manufacturing Coordinator: Doug Wilke
Internal Design: A Small Design Studio/Ann Small
Cover Design: Jennifer Lambert
Cover Photograph: © Paul Steel/The Stock Market
Photo Manager: Cary Benbow
Production House: Litten Editing and Production, Inc.
Compositor: GGS Information Services
Printer: Quebecor World

Printed in the United States of America
1 2 3 4 5 03 02 01 00

For more information contact South-Western, 5101 Madison Road, Cincinnati, Ohio, 45227 or find us on the Internet at http://www.swcollege.com

For permission to use material from this text or product, contact us by

- **telephone: 1-800-730-2214**
- **fax: 1-800-730-2215**
- **Web: http://www.thomsonrights.com**

Library of Congress Cataloging-in-Publication Data

Barfield, Jesse T.
Cost accounting: traditions and innovations / Jesse T. Barfield, Cecily A. Raiborn, Michael R. Kinney.--4th ed.
p. cm.
Includes indexes.
ISBN 0-324-02645-5 (alk. paper)
1. Cost accounting. I. Raiborn, Cecily A. II. Kinney, Michael R. III. Title.

HF5686.C8 B2758 2000
657'.42--dc21 00-061260

This book is printed on acid-free paper.

Brief Contents

Contents

Preface

Today accounting graduates must possess knowledge of the interrelated areas of cost and management accounting. Cost accounting is used to determine the cost of manufacturing products and/or providing services in organizations involved in a conversion process. Conversion includes transforming raw materials into finished goods, general ledger data into financial statements, or ideas into architectural drawings. Product and service costs are needed for internal management decisions and for inventory and cost of goods sold valuations on external financial statements. Cost accounting is part of management accounting, which provides managers with quantitative and qualitative information for planning, controlling, evaluating performance, and making decisions. Thus, management accounting is applicable in all organizations regardless of the degree to which they engage in conversion processes.

Because of overlapping job functions, growth in information technology, and institution of new production methods that require the availability of more nontraditional information, cost and management accounting are becoming increasingly indistinguishable. Therefore, this text covers traditional product costing methods as well as innovative topics such as cost management systems, accounting as part of organizational strategy, global cost management practices, quality costs, and balanced scorecards for business organizations.

WHO WILL BENEFIT FROM THIS BOOK?

This book is written for students who wish to become professional accountants and to obtain professional certifications such as Certified Management Accountant (CMA), Certified Public Accountant (CPA), Certified Financial Manager (CFM), and/or Certified Internal Auditor (CIA). The text offers a thorough but concise presentation of the essential issues of cost and management accounting for use in a one- or two-semester course in a college accounting program. Typically, students will have taken Principles of Accounting or Financial Accounting before taking Cost Accounting.

STRUCTURE

The text's chapter sequence reflects both curriculum characteristics and a pedagogical format that will greatly aid in learning. Because many universities stress product cost computations in the first (or only) cost accounting course, product costing techniques (job order, process, spoilage, joint, and standard) are covered in Chapters 5 through 10. Variance analysis is included in Chapter 10 with standard costing, even though standard costing is a product costing or planning topic and variance analysis is a management control and performance evaluation topic.

Part 1 (Chapters 1 and 2) provides an overview of cost/management accounting, the current business environment, and cost management systems. Part 2 (Chapters 3 through 10) discusses methods of product costing, accounting for product shrinkage and expansion, quality as a means of reducing product and service defects, and treatment of joint process costs. These chapters constitute the traditional cost accounting focus on determining cost for use in valuation on financial statements. Parts 3 through 5 (Chapters 11 through 21) concentrate on managerial information needs and processes. These chapters are divided into the areas of planning and controlling (Chapters 11 through 15), decision making (Chapters 16 through 18), and evaluating performance (Chapters 19 through 21).

The chapter sequence is just one of the many ways in which the topics may be covered; other potential sequences are provided in the preface to the Instructor's Manual. Assuming that basic definitions have been covered, each chapter is written in a fairly stand-alone fashion. Because the end-of-chapter materials predominantly relate to the information within the chapter, an instructor wishing to vary the sequence of chapters should find little difficulty in assigning end-of-chapter material. If a problem in one chapter includes a significant use of another chapter's material, it is so designated in the heading to the problem. (For example, a standard costing problem may also be designated as a process costing problem.)

Each chapter contains an "Introducing" and "Revisiting" segment about a real organization. These vignettes have been selected to illustrate all types of organizations (domestic/international, profit/not-for-profit, large/small, and manufacturing/ service). Although a real organization's data is not (for competitive reasons) used in chapter numerical computations, in-chapter examples utilize comparable data for an illustrative company similar to the one discussed in the chapter vignettes. Through these chapter openers and closures, students are shown how the chapter topics affect businesses on a daily basis.

To reinforce the real-world perspective and maintain student interest, all chapters contain boxed "News Note" examples from the current business press featuring up-to-date applications of text concepts in real-world situations. These "Notes" are keyed with headings as being primarily related to one of the following areas: ethics, general business, international, or quality. There are approximately three to five "notes" per chapter.

CHANGES IN THE FOURTH EDITION

Because of the inclusion of innovative topics, student orientation, readability, and real-world applications, the previous editions of this text were very well received. The fourth edition continues these positive features, improving upon them by increasing their coverage as well as that of multinational businesses and modern global business techniques. This edition also incorporates suggestions from users and reviewers for organizational and pedagogical changes (explained in an upcoming section).

The following changes to the fourth edition of *Cost Accounting: Traditions and Innovations* increase the text's teachability and real-world focus and enhance the student's comprehension and intellectual skills. The Accounting Education Change Commission (in its "Position Statement Number One: Objectives of Education for Accountants") has been instrumental in providing guidance on improving and expanding each edition's pedagogical features. The AECC has indicated that it is essential for accounting graduates to possess strong communication, intellectual, and interpersonal skills, as well as to understand professional ethics and make value-based judgments.

Pedagogy

To encourage students to improve their communication and intellectual skills, we have again expanded the quantity of essay and "logic" problems in end-of-chapter materials, the student study guide, and the test bank. Some end-of-chapter items in each chapter make use of concepts or require information from business disciplines outside the field of accounting. The international and service dimensions of business have been more heavily integrated in the chapters, illustrative examples, and end-of-chapter materials. Such inclusions reflect the ever-increasing global expansion of business enterprises and the diminished quantity of manufacturing in the United States. Approximately 40 percent of the end-of-chapter materials are newly added or modified; some of these items reflect real-world situations. An attempt has been made to provide at least two exercises and/or problems for each key concept in the chapter.

Organization

The revised organizational structure streamlines chapter materials as well as reduces redundancy within this course and between it and other business courses. Additionally, the new structure includes a significant amount of new material that emphasizes the changing nature of cost/management accounting activities.

Chapter 1 introduces the disciplines of financial, cost, and management accounting. The chapter also addresses the issue of the global environment of business. Included in this chapter are many of the strategy aspects provided in Chapter 2 of the third edition, such as how organizational strategy is the underlying linkage for all business activities.

Chapter 2 is the previous edition's Chapter 15. The placement of this chapter at the front of the text reflects the view that knowledge of the cost management system is integral to a successful global business. This chapter discusses the emergence of cost management systems and how they should be developed, implemented, and maintained as continuous feedback systems for communicating and using information for all managerial functions.

Chapter 3 combines the third edition's Chapters 4 and 5. This chapter reduces the emphasis on terminology and focuses instead on the elements of product and service cost. The discussion of overhead allocation using predetermined rates in this chapter sets the stage for the use of activity-based management and activity-based costing topics (Chapter 4).

Chapter 5 contains the job order costing details that were covered in the third edition's Chapter 7. Chapters 6 and 7 are revisions of the previous edition's Chapters 8 and 9 on process costing and spoilage. Chapter 8 on quality is a revision of the previous edition's Chapter 3. It was moved to highlight the impact on spoilage reduction that quality methodologies can make. Chapters 9 through 13 (joint products, standard costing, variable costing and cost-volume-profit, relevant costing, and master budgeting) are revisions of the previous edition's Chapters 10 through 14. Chapter 12 on relevant costing has an extensive discussion of outsourcing.

Chapters 13 and 14 are the budgeting chapters. Chapter 14 on capital budgeting was moved forward from its previous placement as Chapter 18.

Chapter 15 discusses a variety of financial management topics, including management of fixed costs, cost control for noninventory costs, activity-based budgeting, and cash management. These topics reflect the increased emphasis that organizations must place on monitoring and controlling operations in an ever more competitive world. Many of these topics were covered in less detail in various locations in the third edition; others of them, such as activity-based budgeting and cash management issues, are new to this edition.

Chapter 16 illustrates innovative inventory management techniques such as life-cycle costing, target and kaizen costing, value engineering, and theory of constraints. Chapter 17 on emerging business practices is a new chapter that includes the changing workplace, open book management, environmental management systems, and enterprise resource planning (ERP).

Chapter 18 (Responsibility Accounting and Transfer Pricing) is a revision of the third edition's Chapter 19. Chapter 18 also includes discussion of Japanese responsibility accounting structures such as pseudomicroprofit centers and real microprofit centers. Because of the tie to transfer pricing, service department allocations have been moved to this chapter from their placement in Chapter 5 in the previous edition.

Chapters 19 through 21 discuss performance measurement and rewards. Chapter 19 discusses EVA (economic value added) and MVA (market value added) as emerging methods of evaluating organizational financial performance. Chapter 20 includes expanded coverage of determining nonfinancial measurements and the use of the balanced scorecard as a tool for evaluating long-run performance.

End-of-Chapter Materials

The authors have included a variety of end-of-chapter items that ask students to obtain information from the Web. These Internet-related items are designated with an icon. In some instances, students must utilize a search engine to find companies or topics related to the question. In other situations, a specific URL has been provided. Web sites do, however, change over time, so faculty are cautioned to attempt to access specific sites to make certain that the information is still available. Help in this regard can also be obtained from the book's Web site.

The previous edition's ethics and quality questions have been replaced with a new section called "Reality Check." This change was implemented so that additional types of questions related to Internet activities, current events, and innovative topics could be included.

STYLE

This text is extremely student-oriented and integrates procedural methods with the conceptual and behavioral aspects of information that help students solve real-world problems. The authors have endeavored to make the text highly readable and to provide numerous examples, models, and illustrations of real-world applicability. Topical coverage is current and reflects issues being used in today's dynamic business organizations.

Features in the text (such as learning objectives, opening and closing vignettes, news notes, chapter summaries, demonstration problems, and a full range of end-of-chapter materials) have been designed to promote the learning process, provide a high student interest level, and make the text a valuable student resource. The inclusion of quality concepts, international business considerations, discussions of diverse types of organizations, and the "Reality Check" end-of-chapter materials reinforces the applied nature of the text and assists faculty to make the course information more relevant to students.

INSTRUCTOR SUPPORT MATERIALS

A comprehensive instructor support package is provided for this text.

Instructor's Manual This manual (developed by Dale L. Flesher at the University of Mississippi) contains sample syllabi, terminology glossaries, and lecture outline summaries. Masters for over 100 teaching transparencies are included at the end of this volume; these masters provide additional perspectives on text materials or reflect some PowerPoint presentation slides rather than duplicate text exhibits.

Solutions Manual This volume, prepared by the authors, has been independently reviewed and checked for accuracy. It contains solutions to all numerical end-of-chapter materials and to many non-numerical items. Discussion points are provided for many of the "Reality Check" items. This volume also contains a copy of the Student Check Figures.

Solution Transparency Acetates Over 300 acetates are provided from the solutions manual for all numerical end-of-chapter materials.

Test Bank The test bank has been prepared by J. David Fred of Indiana University South Bend and contains over one thousand multiple-choice, short exercise, and short discussion questions with related solutions. It has been updated from the third edition to include approximately 25 percent new materials. Five to ten new problems have been added to each chapter. Also, the level of difficulty (easy, medium, difficult) is now identified for each question.

ExamView Testing Software—Computerized Testing Software This supplement contains all of the questions in the printed test bank. This program is an easy-to-use test creation software compatible with Microsoft Windows. Instructors can add or edit questions, instructions, and answers, and select questions (randomly or numerically) by previewing them on the screen. Instructors can also create and administer quizzes online, whether over the Internet, a local area network (LAN), or a wide area network (WAN).

PowerPoint Teaching Transparency Slides PowerPoint files (prepared by Margaret A. Houston of Wright State University) are available on disk and provide entertaining and informative graphics and text for full-color, electronic presentations.

Videos This text is accompanied by a series of videos, *BusinessLink*, that depict key management accounting concepts including activity-based costing, product costing, and total quality management. These videos feature companies such as Archway Cookies, World Gym, and Symbios Logic. A student workbook is available to accompany these videos.

NEW! Web Resource This text's supporting Web site at **http://barfield.swcollege.com** provides downloadable versions of key instructor supplements, as well as on-line quizzes, virtual tours, crossword puzzle terminology quizzes, Excel® templates to solve selected EOC problems, links to other cost accounting resources, and updates on URL cites in the text.

STUDENT SUPPORT MATERIALS

The student support materials are equally comprehensive and are designed to help students to learn on their own—a factor stressed by the Accounting Education Change Commission.

Student Study Guide This study guide (prepared by Alan D. Campbell of Saint Leo University) is a chapter-by-chapter manual that allows students, through independent review and self-examination, to gain additional exposure and reinforce the materials detailed in the text. The study guide contains chapter overviews, detailed chapter notes, and self-test questions. The study guide includes approximately 30 percent new materials.

Student Check Figures For instructors who wish to provide students with answers to end-of-chapter materials, this list has been prepared by the authors from the solutions contained in the solutions manual.

Student Solutions Manual This supplement provides complete solutions to alternate end-of-chapter exercises and problems.

Spreadsheet Templates Prepared by Michael Blue of Bloomsburg University, this package allows students to solve icon-designated end-of-chapter exercises and problems using Excel®.

Cases in Cost Management: A Strategic Emphasis, 2nd edition Written by John Shank, this book provides thirty-five proven cases that focus on strategic decision making. The cases help develop the ability to apply the concepts of managerial cost analysis in strategic decision making and give particular attention to such topics as ABC, ABM, value chain, and target cost.

Readings and Issues in Cost Management, 2nd edition Written by James Reeve, this book provides articles on topics such as TQM, employee empowerment, reengineering, and short-cycle management. The book presents not only cost management concepts but also the way managers use cost information for decision making.

Excel® Applications for Cost Accounting Written by Gaylord Smith, this text-software package provides 51 spreadsheet problems that reinforce cost accounting concepts. The problems incorporate formula development and model-building skills that may be used in a variety of accounting applications.

THOMSON LEARNING CUSTOM PUBLISHING

The process is simple. The options many. The results rewarding.

Custom publishing from Thomson Learning is an opportunity to take your favorite text and make it even better by adding your personal touch. We realize that courses vary and instructors use textbooks differently. So, custom publishing lets you build your own text or supplement to suit your own curriculum. This exciting option allows you to assemble, in a single book, all of your preferred materials—content from Thomson's huge library of printed material and our online digital database, as well as notes, supplements, articles, study guides . . . you name it. You can determine the length, sequence of materials, and even the cover design. In the end, you have a custom text or supplement of exceptional quality that's exactly what you want. Best of all, your Thomson custom sales rep coordinates our team of experts who make your custom text an easy and rewarding experience. We call our program *The Perfect Course.* Ask your rep for details.

Your custom text can include:

- Market-leading content from thousands of textbooks, books, and study guides from the *Thomson Learning family of imprints* (including Brooks/Cole, Course Technology, Delmar, Heinle & Heinle, South-Western, and Wadsworth publishers)
- Your original materials including your class handouts
- Out-of-print books and chapters
- Journal articles
- University or school materials
- Materials from other publishers*

*Materials not owned by Thomson may not always be available for use. Please consult your Custom Publishing Representative or Custom Editor to discuss options in securing permission for usage.

Ask your Custom Representative or Custom Editor about other possibilities.

Find out more. It's as easy as a call to your Custom Sales Rep at 800.355.9983, or visit us at **http://www.custom.thomsonlearning.com**

ACKNOWLEDGEMENTS

We would like to thank all the people who have helped us during the revision of this text. The constructive comments and suggestions made by the following reviewers were instrumental in developing, rewriting, reorganizing, and improving the quality, readability, and student orientation of the fourth edition of *Cost Accounting: Traditions and Innovations.*

Vidya N. Awasthi
Seattle University

Richard J. Campbell
University of Rio Grande

Kay C. Carnes
Gonzaga University

Henry H. Davis
Eastern Illinois University

Dale Flesher
University of Mississippi

J. David Fred
Indiana University South Bend

Jan Richard Heier
Auburn University at Montgomery

Dick Houser
Northern Arizona University

Margaret A. Houston
Wright State University

Phillip A. Jones, Sr.
University of Richmond

Celina L. Jozsi
University of South Florida

Robert Kee
University of Alabama

Jenice J. Prather-Kinsey
University of Missouri—Columbia

Robert L. Putnam
University of Tennessee at Martin

Special mention must be given to Margaret Gagne at Marist College for her hard work as problem checker and to Lorretta Palagi for obtaining all the necessary permissions. In addition, use of materials from the Institute of Management Accountants, the American Institute of CPAs, the various periodical publishers, and the featured organizations have contributed significantly to making this text a truly useful learning tool for the students. Many kudos must be given to Leslie Kauffman, our developmental editor, at Litten Editing and Production; she has been a pleasure to work with and has taken numerous situations in stride and with encouraging words. The authors also need to thank all the people at South-Western College Publishing (Sharon Oblinger, acquisitions editor; Larry Qualls, marketing manager; Kelly Keeler, production editor) and those at Litten Editing and Production (Malvine Litten and Denise Morton) who have helped us on this project. Lastly, sincere gratitude goes to our families and friends who provided unending support and encouragement during this process.

Jesse Barfield
Cecily Raiborn
Mike Kinney

PART 1

Overview

CHAPTER ONE

Introduction to Cost and Management Accounting in a Global Business Environment

CHAPTER TWO

Introduction to Cost Management Systems

CHAPTER 1

Introduction to Cost and Management Accounting in a Global Business Environment

LEARNING OBJECTIVES

After completing this chapter, you should be able to answer the following questions:

1 How do financial and management accounting relate to each other?

2 How does cost accounting relate to financial and management accounting?

3 What is the role of a code of ethics in guiding the behaviors of an organization's global workforce?

4 What factors have influenced the globalization of businesses and why have these factors been significant?

5 What are the primary factors and constraints that influence an organization's strategy and why are these factors important?

6 How does an organization's competitive environment impact its strategy and how might an organization respond to competition?

7 How does the accounting function impact an organization's ability to successfully achieve its strategic goals and objectives?

8 Why is a company segment's mission affected by product life cycle?

9 What is the value chain and why is it important in managing a business?

INTRODUCING

ABN AMRO Bank

http://www.abnamro.com

The Netherlands-based bank, ABN AMRO, was formed in 1990 when Algemene Bank Nederland merged with Amsterdam-Rotterdam Bank. Following the merger, ABN AMRO has established itself as a global bank with operations in 76 countries and territories including the United States, where the bank has a 16% share of the Midwest market. ABN AMRO's global expansion was driven initially by mergers but more recently by innovative web-based delivery of products and services.

By traditional measures (such as its $505 billion in assets and its capital position), ABN AMRO is the largest bank in Holland, the fourth largest in Europe, and the eighth largest in the world. ABN AMRO's core lending business is solid. Over half of ABN AMRO's revenues come from Dutch clients—a very stable source of business that includes such companies as Royal Dutch Shell, Philips Electronics, and Unilever.

ABN AMRO formulated an identity statement in 1992 to reflect its corporate aspirations: "ABN AMRO Bank is a long-established, solid, multi-faceted bank of international reputation and standing. We will strive to fulfill the bank's ambition in being a frontrunner in value-added banking, both on a local and worldwide level. . . ." The corporate values statement was formalized in 1997, although the values have been important priorities since the bank was established in the 1800s. The four values forming the basis of the bank's activities are integrity, teamwork, respect, and professionalism. Bank managers believe that the values need to be formalized even though they are and should be self-evident. The formalization provides external parties criteria by which the bank can be assessed. ABN AMRO perceives its corporate identity and values as the underlying tenets of the organization.

SOURCE: **www.abnamro.com/profile**; Chris Costanzo, "ABN AMRO Says Web Will Anchor Its Expansion," *American Banker* (December 9, 1999), p. 16.

ABN AMRO is successfully pursuing a corporate identity as a "bank of international reputation and standing." ABN AMRO was ranked as the fifth largest commercial and savings bank and the seventy-third largest corporation in the 1999 Fortune Global 500. The corporation (with its foreign subsidiaries and affiliates) is comprised of over 3,500 branches and offices in 76 countries and territories across five continents. Although international trade was once confined to extremely large corporations such as ABN AMRO, the explosion of World Wide Web usage has enabled any business with the right infrastructure capabilities and the necessary funds for Web site development to market its products and services around the world.

Organizations operating globally face three primary challenges. First, managers must understand factors influencing international business markets so they can identify locations in which the company has the strengths and desire to compete. Second, managers must devise a long-term plan to achieve organizational goals. Third, the company must devise information systems that keep operations consistent with its plans and goals.

This chapter introduces cost accounting and describes the global environment of business, international market structures, trade agreements, e-commerce, and legal and ethical considerations. It addresses the importance of strategic planning and links strategy creation and implementation to the accounting information system. The chapter discussion applies equally well to large and small profit-seeking businesses, and most discussion is appropriate for not-for-profit and governmental entities.

INTRODUCTION TO COST ACCOUNTING

To manage a diverse, international banking organization, ABN AMRO's leaders need monetary and nonmonetary information that helps them to analyze and solve problems by reducing uncertainty. Accounting, often referred to as the language of business, provides much of that necessary information. Accounting language has two primary "variations": financial accounting and management accounting. Cost accounting is a bridge between financial and management accounting.

Accounting information addresses three different functions: (1) providing information to external parties (stockholders, creditors, and various regulatory bodies) for investment and credit decisions; (2) estimating the cost of products produced and services provided by the organization; and (3) providing information useful to internal managers who are responsible for planning, controlling, decision making, and evaluating performance. Financial accounting is designed to meet external information needs and to comply with generally accepted accounting principles. Management accounting attempts to satisfy internal information needs and to provide product costing information for external financial statements. The primary differences between these two accounting disciplines are given in Exhibit 1–1.

Financial accounting must comply with the generally accepted accounting principles (currently established by the Financial Accounting Standards Board [FASB], a private-sector body). The information used in financial accounting is typically historical, quantifiable, monetary, and verifiable. These characteristics are essential to the uniformity and consistency needed for external financial statements. Financial accounting information is usually quite aggregated and related to the organization as a whole. In some cases, a regulatory agency such as the Securities and Exchange Commission (SEC) or an industry commission (such as banking or insurance) may mandate financial accounting practices. In other cases, financial accounting information is required for obtaining loans, preparing tax returns, and understanding how well or poorly the business is performing.

By comparison, management accounting provides information for internal users. Because managers are often concerned with individual parts or segments of the business rather than the whole organization, management accounting information commonly addresses such individualized concerns rather than the "big picture" of financial accounting. Management accounting is not required to adhere to generally accepted accounting principles in providing information for managers' internal purposes. It is, however, expected to be flexible in serving management's needs

EXHIBIT 1–1

Financial and Management Accounting Differences

	Financial Accounting	Management Accounting
Primary users	External	Internal
Primary organizational focus	Whole (aggregated)	Parts (segmented)
Information characteristics	Must be • Historical • Quantitative • Monetary • Verifiable	May be • Current or forecasted • Quantitative or qualitative • Monetary or nonmonetary • Timely and, at a minimum, reasonably estimated
Overriding criteria	Generally accepted accounting principles	Situational relevance (usefulness)
	Consistency	Benefits in excess of costs
	Verifiability	Flexibility
Recordkeeping	Formal	Combination of formal and informal

and to be useful to managers' functions. A related criterion is that information should be developed and provided only if the cost of producing that information is less than the benefit of having it. This is known as cost-benefit analysis. These two criteria, though, must be combined with the financial accounting information criteria of verifiability, uniformity, and consistency, because all accounting documents and information (whether internal or external) must be grounded in reality rather than whim.

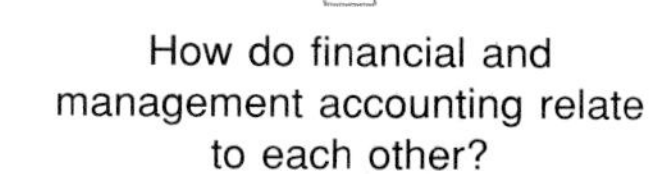

1 How do financial and management accounting relate to each other?

The objectives and nature of financial and management accounting differ, but all accounting information tends to rely on the same basic data system and set of accounts. The accounting system provides management with a means by which costs are accumulated from input of materials through the production process until completion and, ultimately, to cost of goods sold. Although technology has improved to the point that a company can have different accounting systems designed for different purposes, some companies still rely on a single system to supply the basic accounting information. The single system typically focuses on providing information for financial accounting purposes, but its informational output can be adapted to meet most internal management requirements.

Relationship of Financial and Management Accounting to Cost Accounting

How does cost accounting relate to financial and management accounting?

cost accounting

Cost accounting is defined as "a technique or method for determining the cost of a project, process, or thing. . . . This cost is determined by direct measurement, arbitrary assignment, or systematic and rational allocation."[1] The appropriate method of determining cost depends on the circumstances that generate the need for information. Various costing methods are illustrated throughout the text.

Central to a cost accounting system is the process for tracing various input costs to an organization's outputs (products or services). This process uses the traditional accounting form of recordkeeping—general and subsidiary ledger accounts. Accounts containing cost and management accounting information include those dealing with sales, procurement (materials and plant assets), production and inventory, personnel, payroll, delivery, financing, and funds management.[2] Not all cost information is

This manufacturer of televisions must use cost accounting techniques to determine financial statement valuations for product inventory and cost of goods sold.

[1] Institute of Management Accountants (formerly National Association of Accountants), *Statements on Management Accounting Number 2: Management Accounting Terminology* (Montvale, N.J.: NAA, June 1, 1983), p. 25.

[2] With reference to accounts, this text will focus primarily on the set of accounts that depicts the internal flow of costs.

reproduced on the financial statements, however. Correspondingly, not all financial accounting information is useful to managers in performing their daily functions.

Cost accounting creates an overlap between financial accounting and management accounting. Cost accounting integrates with financial accounting by providing product costing information for financial statements and with management accounting by providing some of the quantitative, cost-based information managers need to perform their tasks. Exhibit 1–2 depicts the relationship of cost accounting to the larger systems of financial and management accounting. None of the three areas should be viewed as a separate and exclusive "type" of accounting. The boundaries of each are not clearly and definitively drawn and, because of changing technology and information needs, are becoming increasingly blurred.

EXHIBIT 1–2

Accounting Information System Components and Relationships

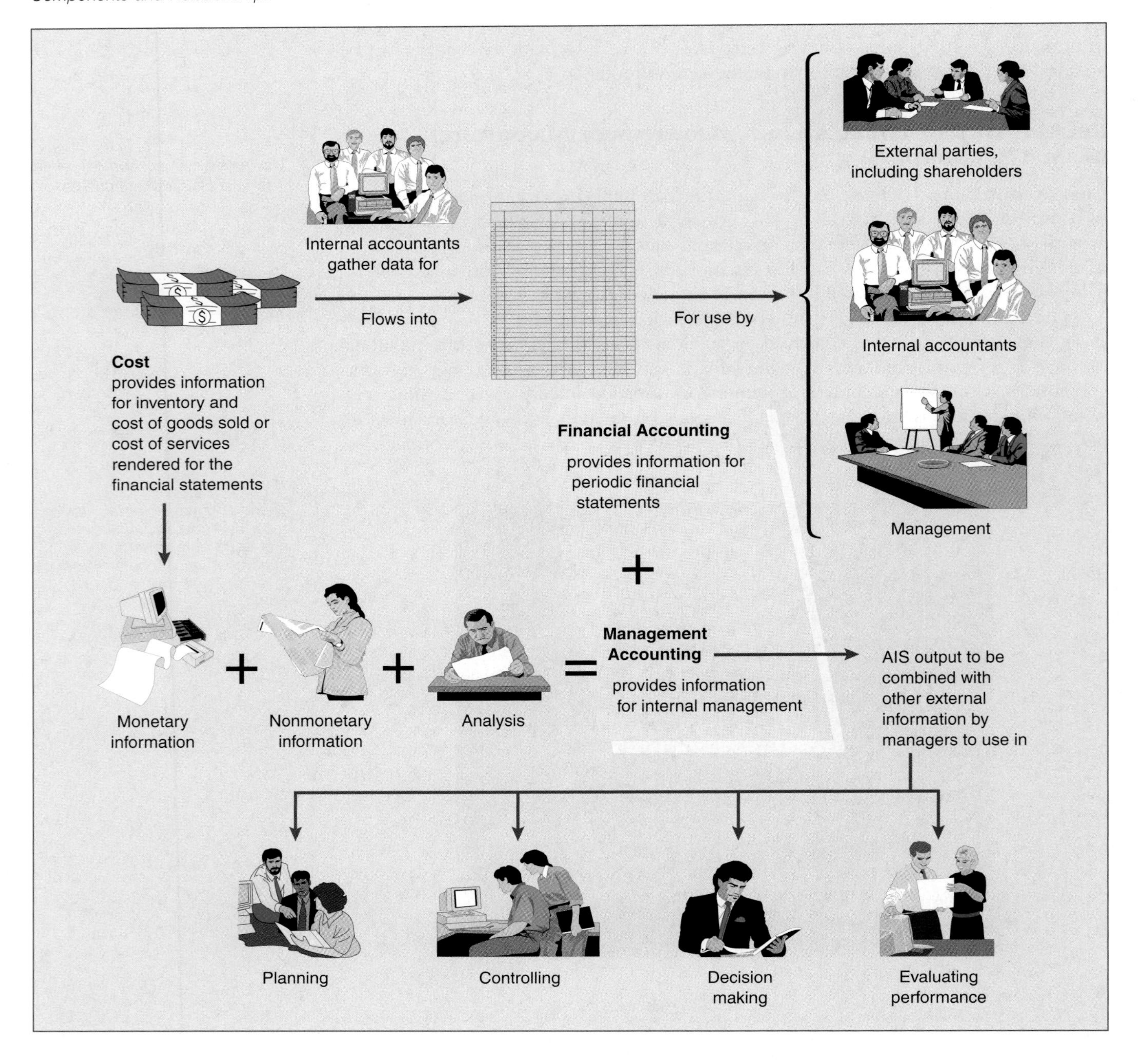

The cost accounting overlap causes the financial and management accounting systems to articulate or be joined together to form an informational network. Because these two systems articulate, accountants must understand how cost accounting provides costs for financial statements and supports management information needs. Organizations that do not manufacture products may not require elaborate cost accounting systems. However, even service companies need to understand how much their services cost so that they can determine whether it is cost-effective to be engaged in particular business activities.

Management and Cost Accounting Standards

Management accountants can use different costs and different information for different purposes, because their discipline is not required to adhere to generally accepted accounting principles when providing information for managers' internal use. In the United States, financial accounting standards are established by the Financial Accounting Standards Board (FASB), a private-sector body. No similar board exists to define universal management accounting standards. However, a public-sector board called the Cost Accounting Standards Board (CASB) was established in 1970 by the U.S. Congress to promulgate uniform cost accounting standards for defense contractors and federal agencies.

The CASB produced 20 cost accounting standards (of which one has been withdrawn) from its inception until it was terminated in 1980. The CASB was recreated in 1988 as an independent board of the Office of Federal Procurement Policy. The board's objectives are to

- Increase the degree of uniformity in cost accounting practices among government contractors in like circumstances;
- Establish consistency in cost accounting practices in like circumstances by each individual contractor over time; and
- Require contractors to disclose their cost accounting practices in writing.[3]

Although CASB standards do not constitute a comprehensive set of rules, compliance is required for companies bidding on or pricing cost-related contracts for the federal government.

An organization important to the practice of management and cost accounting is the Institute of Management Accountants, or the IMA. The IMA is a voluntary membership organization of accountants, finance specialists, academics, and others. It sponsors two major certification programs: Certified Management Accountant (CMA) and Certified in Financial Management (CFM). The IMA also issues directives on the practice of management and cost accounting called *Statements on Management Accounting*, or SMAs. The SMAs, unlike the pronouncements of the CASB, are not legally binding standards, but they undergo a rigorous developmental and exposure process that ensures their wide support.

An organization similar to the IMA is the Society of Management Accountants of Canada, which also issues guidelines on the practice of management accounting. These Management Accounting Guidelines (MAGs), like the SMAs, are not requirements for organizational accounting, but are merely suggestions.

Although the IMA, Cost Accounting Standards Board, and Society of Management Accountants of Canada have been instrumental in standards development, much of the body of knowledge and practice in management accounting has been provided by industry practice and economic and finance theory. Thus, no "official" agency publishes generic management accounting standards for all companies, but there is wide acceptance of (and, therefore, authority for) the methods presented in the text. The development of cost and management accounting standards and

[3] Robert B. Hubbard, "Return of the Cost Accounting Standards Board," *Management Accounting* (October 1990), p. 56.

practices indicates that management accountants are interested and involved in professional recognition. Another indication of this movement is the adoption of ethics codes by both the IMA and the various provincial societies in Canada.

3

What is the role of a code of ethics in guiding the behaviors of an organization's global workforce?

Ethics for Management Accountant Professionals

Because of the pervasive nature of management accounting and the organizational level at which many management accountants work, the IMA believed that some guidelines were necessary to help its members with ethical dilemmas. Thus, *Statement on Management Accounting* 1C, *Standards of Ethical Conduct for Management Accountants*, was adopted in June 1983. These standards are in the areas of competence, confidentiality, integrity, and objectivity. The IMA Code of Ethics is reproduced in Exhibit 1–3.

EXHIBIT 1-3

Standards of Ethical Conduct for Management Accountants

COMPETENCE

Practitioners of management accounting and financial management have responsibility to:

- Maintain an appropriate level of professional competence by ongoing development of their knowledge and skills.
- Perform their professional duties in accordance with relevant laws, regulations, and technical standards.
- Prepare complete and clear reports and recommendations after appropriate analyses of relevant and reliable information.

CONFIDENTIALITY

Practitioners of management accounting and financial management have responsibility to:

- Refrain from disclosing confidential information acquired in the course of their work except when authorized, unless legally obligated to do so.
- Inform subordinates as appropriate regarding the confidentiality of information acquired in the course of their work and monitor their activities to assure the maintenance of that confidentiality.
- Refrain from using or appearing to use confidential information acquired in the course of their work for unethical or illegal advantage either personally or through third parties.

INTEGRITY

Practitioners of management accounting and financial management have responsibility to:

- Avoid actual or apparent conflicts of interest and advise all appropriate parties of any potential conflict.
- Refrain from engaging in any activity that would prejudice their ability to carry out their duties ethically.
- Refuse any gift, favor, or hospitality that would influence or would appear to influence their actions.
- Refrain from either actively or passively subverting the attainment of the organization's legitimate and ethical objectives.
- Recognize and communicate professional limitations or other constraints that would preclude responsible judgment or successful performance of an activity.
- Communicate unfavorable as well as favorable information and professional judgments or opinions.
- Refrain from engaging in or supporting any activity that would discredit the profession.

OBJECTIVITY

Practitioners of management accounting and financial management have responsibility to:

- Communicate information fairly and objectively.
- Disclose fully all relevant information that could reasonably be expected to influence an intended user's understanding of the reports, comments, and recommendations presented.

SOURCE: http://www.imanet.org/content/Abou...cle_of_Ethics/Ethical-standards.htm. May 1, 2000, 10:30 a.m., *Statements on Management Accounting Number 1C: Standards of Ethical Conduct for Management Accountants* (Montvale, N.J.: NAA, June 1, 1983). Copyright by Institute of Management Accountants (formerly National Association of Accountants), Montvale, N.J.

Accountants have always been regarded as individuals of conviction, trust, and integrity. The most important of all the standards listed are those designated under integrity. These statements reflect honesty of character and embody the essence and intent of U.S. laws and moral codes. Standards of integrity should be foremost in business dealings on individual, group, and corporate levels.

To summarize, cost accounting allows organizations to determine a reliable and reasonable measurement of "costs" and "benefits." These costs and benefits may relate to particular products, customers, divisions, or other objects. Much of this text is dedicated to discussing the various methods, tools, and techniques used in cost accounting. However, before providing that discussion, the balance of this chapter and Chapter 2 provide important descriptive information about trends in business today, as well as information about important practices widely used by managers. This descriptive information will establish a context for understanding the practice of cost accounting in the contemporary organization. One of the big influences on current business practices is globalization.

THE GLOBAL ENVIRONMENT OF BUSINESS

Most businesses participate in the **global economy**, which encompasses the international trade of goods and services, movement of labor, and flows of capital and information.[4] The world has essentially become smaller through improved technology and communication abilities as well as trade agreements that promote the international movement of goods and services among countries. Exhibit 1–4 provides the results of a survey of Fortune 1000 executives about the primary factors that encourage the globalization of business. Currently, the evolution of Web-based technology is dramatically affecting international business.

4

What factors have influenced the globalization of businesses and why have these factors been significant?

global economy

E-Commerce

Electronic commerce (**e-commerce**) is any business activity that uses the Internet and World Wide Web to engage in financial transactions. But e-commerce had its beginnings in two important events that occurred before a computer was even developed: (1) the introduction of wireless money transfers in 1871 by Western Union and (2) the introduction in 1914 of the first consumer charge card. These inventions alone, however, were not enough to produce global opportunities for business.

e-commerce

EXHIBIT 1–4

Factors Driving Business Globalization

Factor	Percentage Indicating Factor as Primary in Globalization Trend
Technology	43%
Competition	29%
The Economy	21%
Better Communications	17%
Need for New Markets/Growth	13%
Deregulation	11%
Access to Information	9%
Legislation	7%
Ease of Entering New Market	5%

SOURCE: Deloitte & Touche LLP, *Survey of American Business Leaders: Information Technology* (November 1996), pp. 1–11. Reprinted with permission from Deloitte & Touche.

[4] Paul Krugman, Peddling Prosperity, quoted by Alan Farnham in "Global—or Just Globaloney," Fortune (June 27, 1994), p. 98.

Web sites of manufacturers and retailers worldwide can be accessed by potential customers 24 hours a day. Businesses and consumers can view products and the way they work or fit together on computer or television screens. Customers can access product information and order and pay for their choices without picking up the phone or leaving home or the office. In the world of banking and financial services, bills can be paid, balances accessed, loans and insurance obtained, and stocks traded.

Some of the numerous positives and negatives of having e-commerce capability are provided in Exhibit 1–5. In some cases, a seller's positive may be a buyer's negative: the ability to accumulate, use, reuse, and instantaneously transmit customer information "can, if not managed carefully, diminish personal privacy."[5]

But the current drawbacks to e-commerce will not stop the ever-increasing usage of this sales and purchasing medium. More and more merchants will develop sites that are easy and safe to use by customers but that inhibit hackers from causing internal problems. The rapid expansion of e-commerce illustrates the success of its positives and necessitates the correction of its negatives.

Trade Agreements

economic integration

Encouragement of a global economy has been fostered not only by e-commerce but also by government and business leaders worldwide who have made economic integration a paramount concern. **Economic integration** refers to creating multicountry markets by developing transnational rules that reduce the fiscal and physical barriers to trade as well as encourage greater economic cooperation among countries. Most economic integration occurs through the institution of trade agreements allowing consumers the opportunity to choose from a significantly larger selection of goods than that previously available. Many of these agreements encompass a limited number of countries in close geographic proximity, but the General Agreement on Tariffs and Trade (GATT) involves over 100 nations worldwide.

Trade agreements have created access to more markets with vast numbers of new customers, new vendor sources for materials and labor, and opportunities for new production operations. In turn, competitive pressures from the need to meet or beat prices and quality of international competitors force organizations to focus on cost control, quality improvements, rapid time-to-market, and dedicated customer service. The accompanying News Note on page 12 reveals an interesting outcome from the North American Free Trade Agreement. As companies become more globally competitive, consumers' choices are often made on the bases of price, quality, access (time of availability), and design rather than on whether the goods were made domestically or in another country.

Globalization Considerations

There is no question that globalization is occurring and at a remarkably rapid rate. But operating in foreign markets may create situations that vary dramatically from those found only in domestic markets. Considerations about risk, legal standards, and ethical behaviors can be vastly dissimilar between and among different foreign markets.

RISK CONSIDERATIONS

Numerous risks exist in any business environment. But when a business decides to enter markets outside its domicile, it needs to carefully evaluate the potential risks. Some of the risks depend on the level of economic development of the country in which operations are being considered; these risks often include political and

[5] W. J. Clinton and A. Gore, Jr., *A Framework for Global Electronic Commerce* (http://www.iitf.nist.gov/eleccomm/ecomm.htm, April 4, 1999), p. 12.

EXHIBIT 1–5

The Realities of E-Commerce

	Merchant	Customer
Positives:		
• Convenience and efficiency	No downtime Real-time accumulation of customer and product/service data Ease of updating product/service information Ease of obtaining feedback on customer satisfaction or providing customer service Comparative ease of business start-up Ease of access to new markets Ease of instantaneous communication	Around-the-clock availability for product information and purchases Access to international merchants Ease of use Ease of comparison shopping Ease of providing feedback Ease of gaining information on products/services from other companies or individuals Ability to receive instantaneous communications from merchants
• Cost savings	Staff, paperwork, and inventory reduction No need for around-the-clock staffing to take orders Less expensive to testmarket new products Lower transaction costs, such as those related to errors or electronic data interchange Wide dissemination of information at nominal incremental cost (after start-up) Inexpensive method of document transfer Ability to use site as an employment recruiting tool	Access is local rather than long-distance Rapid access to on-line technical support
Negatives:		
• Privacy	Lack of standardized international privacy policies Theft of passwords or exploitation of unprotected connections to take over Web sites and corporate computers	Questionable ability to obtain redress if personal information is used improperly Theft of passwords, credit card numbers, etc., allowing unauthorized purchases
• Legality	Lack of international laws governing transactions Questionable ability to ensure intellectual property protection Difficulty of assessing compliance with tax regulations in all business jurisdictions	Questionable ability to obtain redress if decisions are made on inaccurate or incomplete information
• Costs	Cost of Web site development (including need for multiple languages), maintenance, and security (including firewalls and data encryption) Potential for internal network shutdown from e-mail complaints, such as those related to inappropriate advertising Losses due to fraudulent sales	Cost of "distraction time" from Net surfing Possibility of purchasing from a fraudulent business or a business that will not correct problems, such as damaged merchandise Possibility of purchasing counterfeit goods
• Other	Potential for sites to be accessed by improper parties (e.g., minors) Some products/services may be too complex for e-commerce (e.g., health care)	Poor customer service due to merchant's inability to manage increased e-commerce Difficulty in using site Difficulty in finding specific site, product, or service

NEWS NOTE  INTERNATIONAL

Taking Business South

Among chief executives, Phillip Martin is unique. He runs a conglomerate that does everything from making auto parts to running casinos. And he is a real chief, as in chief of the Mississippi Band of Choctaw Indians. Over the past 30 years, he has helped to bring a wealth of jobs within the border of the 25,000-acre Choctaw reservation.

The profits from Chief Martin's enterprises have given the Choctaws employment opportunities they never had before, and they have elected to send low-skilled work south and bring higher-paying jobs to their community. So, like so many other U.S. CEOs, Martin has taken business to Mexico. Chahta Enterprise is the first Native American-owned company to leave the reservation and take a giant step into the global economy.

"We started in this business competing with the Japanese, but now all our competition is coming from Mexico," says the 73-year-old chief. Mr. Martin says the North American Free Trade Agreement meant that Chahta had to join the migration south or lose its automobile industry contracts. The Choctaws opened a factory in Sonora, Mexico, in 1998, and its 1,400 employees—none Choctaws—assemble wire harnesses for Ford Motor Co. A second Chahta plant in Mexico, making car-stereo components, is scheduled to open in late 1999.

Chahta had to invest more than $1 million to build a factory that met Ford's price and quality demands. A typical employee at the Mexican plant makes $6 per day for work that would cost $7 to $12 per hour in Mississippi. The Sonora plant manager explains how the economics of the auto industry forced the Choctaws to relocate in Mexico: a door lock electrical cluster that Ford paid $65 to $70 for in 1994 now sells for $50. And car makers keep pounding away for every penny that Chahta, and all other suppliers, can reduce costs. But going south has benefited the Choctaw Nation. Chahta's 1999 Mexican operations were expected to gross over $100 million, which will be used to fund other investments to create jobs in tribal schools and in the hotels, casinos, and golf courses that dot the reservation in Mississippi as well as an American Greetings Co. printing operation.

SOURCE: Adapted from Joel Millman, "Choctaw Chief Leads His Mississippi Tribe into the Global Market," *The Wall Street Journal* (July 23, 1999), p. B1.

currency risks. Political risks include the potential for expropriation or nationalization of assets and the potential for change in business, legal or tax treatment under new political leadership.

Currency risks can cause widely unpredictable results. For example, ABN AMRO acquired 40 percent of Banco Real, Brazil, for $2.1 billion; Brazil's currency devaluation three months after the purchase caused two situations. First, depending on the depth of the recession, there may be a significant level of loans that "go bad." But, second, the devaluation made the acquisition much less expensive for ABN AMRO.[6]

Risks relating to cultural differences are more subtle. The business must assess whether product names and slogans will translate correctly, whether gender issues (such as female supervisors) will create labor problems, and whether products reflect the lifestyles or product preferences of different global customers. To illustrate this latter point, consider that diet cola comprises about 25 percent of all Coca-Cola and PepsiCo beverage brands sold in the United States. However, these companies, which have just begun selling diet colas in India, forecast a maximum long-term market share of only 3 percent of that country's sales. Diet foods are a new concept in a country where malnutrition was a recent phenomenon. "There is a deep-seated feeling that anything labeled 'diet' is meant for a sick person, such as a diabetic or someone with heart problems."[7]

http://www.coca-cola.com
http://www.PepsiCo.com

Exhibit 1–6 provides numerous considerations in a business risk framework. These items must be evaluated whether a business is operating domestically or internationally. The difference in the evaluation process is often the greater depth of

[6] Deborah Orr, "Dutch Colonizers," *Forbes* (June 14, 1999), p. 119.
[7] Miriam Jordan, "Debut of Rival Diet Colas in India Leaves a Bitter Taste," *The Wall Street Journal* (July 21, 1999), p. B1.

EXHIBIT 1–6

A Business Risk Framework

Strategic Risks—Risks that relate to doing the wrong thing.

Environment Risks:
- Natural and manmade disasters
- Political/country
- Laws and regulations
- Industry
- Competitors
- Financial markets

Organization Risks:
- Corporate Objectives and Strategies: planning; resource allocation; monitoring; mergers, acquisitions, and divestitures; joint ventures and alliances
- Leadership: vision, judgment, succession planning, tone at the top
- Management: accountability, authority, responsibility
- Corporate Governance: ethics, reputation, values, fraud and illegal acts
- Investor/Creditor Relations
- Human Resources: performance rewards, benefits, workplace environment, diversity

Operating Risks—Risks that relate to doing the right things the wrong way.
- Workforce: hiring, knowledge and skills, development and training, size, safety
- Suppliers: outsourcing; procurement practices; availability, price, and quality of suppliers' products and services
- Physical Plant: capacity, technology/obsolescence
- Protection: physical plant and other tangible assets, knowledge and other intellectual property
- Products and Services: development, quality, pricing, cost, delivery, consumer protection, technology/obsolescence
- Customers: needs, satisfaction, credit
- Regulatory Compliance: employment, products and services, environmental, antitrust laws

Financial Risks—Risks that relate to losing financial resources or incurring unacceptable liabilities.
- Capital/Financing: availability, interest rates, creditworthiness
- Investing: cash availability, securities, receivables, inventories, derivatives
- Regulatory Compliance: securities law, taxation

Information Risks—Risks that relate to inaccurate or irrelevant information, unreliable systems, and inaccurate or misleading reports.
- Information Systems: reliability, sufficiency, protection, technology
- Strategic Information: relevance and accuracy of measurements, availability, assumptions
- Operating Information: relevance and accuracy of measurements, availability, regulatory reporting
- Financial Information: relevance and accuracy of measurements, accounting, budgets, taxation, financial reporting, regulatory reporting

SOURCE: Deloitte & Touche LLP, *Perspectives on Risk* (New York: 1997), pp. 12, 24, 25. Reprinted with permission from Deloitte & Touche.

knowledge necessary and the greater potential for change when operating in foreign markets. The corporate implications of many of these items can be minimized or exploited depending on the business's ability to respond to change and to manage uncertainty.

LEGAL CONSIDERATIONS

Domestic and international laws and treaties can significantly affect how an organization legally obtains new business, reduces costs, or conducts operating activities. Laws represent codified societal rules and can change as the society for which they are established changes. For example, Communism's fall resulted in new laws promoting for-profit businesses in the former Soviet Union. Britain, in the face of budget troubles, changed its laws to allow privatization of some utility companies. China, in pursuit of a more open international trade position, altered its laws to allow some foreign banks (including ABN AMRO) to have full-fledged branches in Beijing. These examples represent a small proportion of how laws regarding business activities change as society changes.

NEWS NOTE  INTERNATIONAL

Unacceptable Rebates

In July 1999, the European Union's executive body, the European Commission, conducted raids to examine documents and gather evidence . . . that could lead to a full-blown antitrust action against Coca-Cola. The raids focused on suspicions that Coke was illegally using rebates to enhance its market share—charges Coke denied. In Europe, the company outsells PepsiCo Inc. and other rivals in soft-drink sales by vast margins. For instance, in Germany, Coke's share of the soft-drink market is 55%, compared to Pepsi's 5%.

The raids focused on rebates to distributors. Such rebates aren't necessarily illegal in the 15-nation EU, but EU authorities say they can be illegal in some cases if paid by companies that dominate their markets. In the Coke case, the commission is looking for evidence that the U.S. company stifled competition with several types of rebates. Among them are rebates on sales that boost Coke's market share at the expense of rivals and rebates given to distributors who agree to sell the full range of Coke products or stop buying from competitors.

SOURCE: Brandon Mitchener and Betsy McKay, "EU Raids Coca-Cola's European Offices on Suspicions of Illegal Use of Rebates," *The Wall Street Journal* (July 22, 1999), p. A4.

Most government regulations seek to encourage an environment in which businesses can succeed. As indicated in the accompanying News Note, regulatory agencies monitor business practices for activities detrimental to healthy commerce.

Many early U.S. laws relating to business were concerned with regulating certain industries on which the public depended, such as telecommunications, utilities, airlines, and trucking. With substantial deregulation, American laws are now more concerned with issues such as fair disclosure of corporate information, product safety, and environmental protection. Companies might even be held "liable for human rights abuses against indigenous people in foreign countries, even if the companies are not directly involved" if the abuses took place near company operations.[8] Freeport-McMoRan Copper & Gold and Unocal Corp. both have been sued in the United States because of alleged military abuses in, respectively, Indonesia and Myanmar.

http://www.fcx.com
http://www.Unocal.com

Organizations are becoming more active in defining responsible corporate behavior, and this trend is likely to continue. Irresponsible behavior tends to invite an increase in governmental monitoring and regulation. For example, after many American companies were found to have given bribes in connection with business activities, the United States passed the **Foreign Corrupt Practices Act (FCPA)** in 1977. This law prohibits U.S. corporations from offering or giving bribes (directly or indirectly) to foreign officials to influence those individuals (or cause them to use their influence) to help businesses obtain or retain business. The act is directed at payments that cause officials to act in a way specified by the firm rather than in a way prescribed by their official duties.

Foreign Corrupt Practices Act (FCPA)

ETHICAL CONSIDERATIONS

ethical standard

In contrast to laws, **ethical standards** represent beliefs about moral and immoral behaviors. Because beliefs are inherently personal, some differences in moral perspectives exist among all individuals. However, the moral perspective is generally more homogeneous within a given society than it is across societies. In a business context, ethical standards are norms for individual conduct in making decisions and engaging in business transactions. Also, many professions have established ethical standards for their practitioners such as those promulgated by the IMA.

[8] Stewart Yerton, "World Will Watch Lawsuits' Outcome," [New Orleans] *The Times-Picayune* (May 11, 1997), p. F-1.

In general, ethical standards for business conduct are higher in most industrialized and economically developed countries than in less developed countries. But the standards and their enforcement vary greatly from one industrialized country to another. Thus, because of the tremendous variations, companies should develop internal norms for conduct (such as a code of ethics) to ensure that certain behaviors are consistent in all of its geographical operating segments. There must also be respect for local customs and traditions if they do not violate the accepted ethical and legal standards of the company and its domicile country. One cannot categorize all business practices as either ethical or unethical; there must be a *moral free space*[9] that allows managers and employees to make decisions within the bounds of reason. The accompanying News Note about Texas Instruments (TI) addresses this issue.

http://www.ti.com

It is important for an organization to have and support a code of conduct that promotes integrity of behavior at all organizational levels. Companies can use a variety of methods to communicate corporate ethical values to all employees. For instance, in 1997, Lockheed Martin developed an interactive board game featuring Scott Adams' Dilbert character and a multitude of potential, practical ethical challenges to be addressed by employee teams. Texas Instruments uses an alternative method, an ethical "quick test" for its employees facing an ethical decision:

http://www.lmco.com

- Is the action legal?
- Does it comply with our values?
- If you do it, will you feel bad?
- How will it look in the newspaper?
- If you know it's wrong, don't do it!
- If you're not sure, ask.
- Keep asking until you get an answer.[10]

ETHICS **NEWS NOTE**

Addressing Ethical Challenges at TI

"Ethical questions face businesspeople every day, especially when a company is involved in worldwide markets," said Carl Skooglund, former TI vice president and director of ethics. The challenge is "to provide tools to our employees so that they can make the tough, quick decisions on the fly, on the firing line. And, make them correctly. There are two elements to making decisions and taking action on behalf of an organization: (1) a clear understanding of the organization's values, principles, and ethical expectations and (2) sound personal judgment and appropriate choices."

TI has adopted a three-level approach to ethical integrity on a global level. The first level asks whether there is compliance with all legal requirements on a local level. The second level addresses whether there are local business practices or requirements that will impact interactions with other parts of the world. The third level asks whether some business practices need to be adapted to fit local laws and customers of a specific locale. What may be believed to be proper in one country may not migrate well to another. And, on what basis can universal standards be defined that apply to TI employees everywhere?

Today, no rulebook or library of policies is going to guide ethical actions. "They must be guided by a shared understanding of basic values and principles of integrity. And they must be supported by resources that will help people to recognize when the caution lights should come on and to know where they can seek expert advice quickly. TI's reputation is completely in our hands, to be enhanced or damaged by the nature of our actions," concluded Skooglund.

SOURCE: Texas Instruments, "Ethics in the Global Market," http://www.ti.com/corp/docs/company/citizen/ethics/market.shtml (August 13, 1999).

[9] Thomas Donaldson, "Values in Tension: Ethics Away from Home," *Harvard Business Review* (September–October 1996), p. 56.
[10] Texas Instruments, "The TI Ethics Quick Test," http://www.ti.com/corp/docs/company/citizen/ethics/quicktest.shtml (August 13, 1999).

The high quality of international competition today requires managers to develop systematic, disciplined approaches to running their organizations. As shown in Exhibit 1–2, managers have four primary functions to execute in which accounting information is consumed. These functions are planning, controlling, decision making, and evaluating performance. The first function, planning, requires management to develop a road map that lays out the future course for operations. This road map also serves an important role in the design of the organization's accounting and control systems.

ORGANIZATIONAL STRATEGY

5

What are the primary factors and constraints that influence an organization's strategy and why are these factors important?

mission statement

In responding to the challenges of e-commerce and globalization, managers must consider the organization's mission and, correspondingly, the underlying strategy that links its mission to actual activities. An organization's **mission statement** should (1) clearly state what the organization wants to accomplish and (2) express how that organization uniquely meets its targeted customers' needs with its products and services. As indicated in the following News Note, a mission statement should be an organizational road map.

http://www.Hibernia.com

The mission statement may, and most likely should, be modified over time. Not adapting the mission statement probably means the organization is stagnating and not facing the ever-changing business environment. For instance, Hibernia Corporation's mission statement in 1994 was "to be recognized by 1996 as the best provider of financial services throughout Louisiana." By 1997, the mission statement was "By 1999, we will be recognized by our customers, employees, and shareholders as the best financial services company in each of our markets."[11] Only three years yet a dramatic difference: the corporation had engaged in multiple bank merger opportunities outside Louisiana and was looking for more.

planning

Translating the organization's mission into the specific activities and resources needed for achievement is called **planning**. The long-term, dynamic plan that in-

NEWS NOTE  GENERAL BUSINESS

Where Are We Going?

Imagine yourself driving down a dark road. You have no idea where you are going, let alone how you are going to get there. To your dismay, a storm crops up, rain pelting the window so hard you can barely see anything outside. You may decide to stop the car and just sit there. Moving on or parked, you are going nowhere fast.

One of the main reasons for writing a mission statement is to develop a road map showing management where the company should be going and giving general directions for how to get there. In addition to the mission statement, strategic plans should be developed that give detailed information about specific roads the company should travel to arrive at its mission destination.

When defining organization objectives, mission statements should reflect the environment in which the organization operates as well as the competencies and competitive advantages that the organization possesses. A good mission statement says clearly and exactly what an organization expects to accomplish. Many companies have eloquently stated missions, but they often neglect one of the most important characteristics of a solid mission statement: the objectives must be measurable. To know where you are on the road, you need mile markers. To know where you are going, you need signs and landmarks. Unless a company has specific measurement standards, it will not be able to determine if it has achieved its mission.

SOURCE: James A. Bailey, "Measuring Your Mission," *Management Accounting* (December 1996), pp. 44–45. Copyright Institute of Management Accountants, Montvale, N.J.

[11] Hibernia Corporation, 1994 and 1997 annual reports.

dicates how the organizational goals and objectives will be fulfilled through satisfaction of customer needs or wants reflects **strategy**. Strategy can also be defined as:

strategy

> *the art of creating value. It provides the intellectual frameworks, conceptual models, and governing ideas that allow a company's managers to identify opportunities for bringing value to customers and for delivering value at a profit. In this respect, strategy is the way a company defines its business and links together the only two resources that really matter in today's economy: knowledge and relationships or an organization's competencies and its customers.*[12]

An organization's strategy tries to match its internal skills and resources to the opportunities found in the external environment.[13] Small organizations may have a single strategy, while large organizations often have an overall entity strategy as well as individual strategies for each business unit (such as a division). The business units' strategies should flow from the overall strategy to ensure that effective and efficient resource allocations are made, an overriding corporate culture is developed, and organizational direction is enhanced. For instance, at ABN AMRO, the Netherlands Division strategy is to position the bank as a provider of integrated banking and insurance products; the strategy for Central/Eastern Europe is strong internal growth and selective acquisition; and the strategy for Asia/Pacific is to raise the profitability of core corporate banking activities.

Exhibit 1–7 provides a checklist of questions that help indicate whether an organization has a comprehensive strategy in place. Small businesses may need to substitute "product lines" for "business segments" in answering the questions.

EXHIBIT 1–7

Does Your Organization Have a Good Strategy?

1. Who are your five most important competitors?
2. Is your firm more or less profitable than these firms?
3. Do you generally have higher or lower prices than these firms, for equivalent product/service offerings? Is this difference due mainly to the mix of customers, to different costs, or to different requirements for profit?
4. Do you have higher or lower relative costs than your main competitors? Where in the cost structure (for example, cost of raw materials, cost of product, cost of selling, cost of distributing, cost of advertising and marketing) are the differences most pronounced?
5. [What are] the different business segments which account for 80 percent of your profits? [You will probably find that you are in many more segments than you thought and that their profit variability is much greater than you thought.] If you cannot define the segments that constitute 80 percent of your total profits, you need to conduct a detailed product line profitability review.
6. In each of the business segments defined above, how large are you relative to the largest of your competitors? Are you gaining or losing relative market share?
7. In each of your important business segments, what are your customers' and potential customers' most important purchase criteria?
8. How do you and your main competitors in each segment rate on these market purchase criteria?
9. What are the main strengths of the company as a whole, based on aggregating customers' views of your firm in the segments that comprise most of your profits? What other competencies do you believe the firm has, and why do they seem to be not appreciated by the market?
10. Which are your priority segments and where is it most important to the firm as a whole that you gain market share? How confident are you that you will achieve this, given that other firms may have targeted the same segments for share gain? What is your competitive advantage in these segments and how sure are you that this advantage is real rather than imagined? (If you are not gaining relative market share, the advantage is probably illusory.)

SOURCE: *The Financial Times Guide to Management and Finance* (London: Financial Times/Pearson Education Limited, 1994), p. 359. Reprinted with permission.

[12] Richard Normann and Rafael Ramirez, "From Value Chain to Value Constellation: Designing Interactive Strategy," *Harvard Business Review* (July–August 1993), p. 65.
[13] Thomas S. Bateman and Scott A. Snell, *Management: Building Competitive Advantage* (Chicago: Irwin, 1996), p. 117.

INFLUENCES ON ORGANIZATIONAL STRATEGY

Because each organization is unique, even those in the same industries employ different strategies that are feasible and likely to be successful. Exhibit 1–8 provides a model of the major factors that influence an organization's strategy. These factors include organizational structure, core competencies, organizational constraints, organizational culture, and environmental constraints.

Organizational Structure

An organization is composed of people, resources other than people, and commitments that are acquired and arranged to achieve specified goals and objectives.

EXHIBIT 1–8

Factors Influencing Organizational Strategy

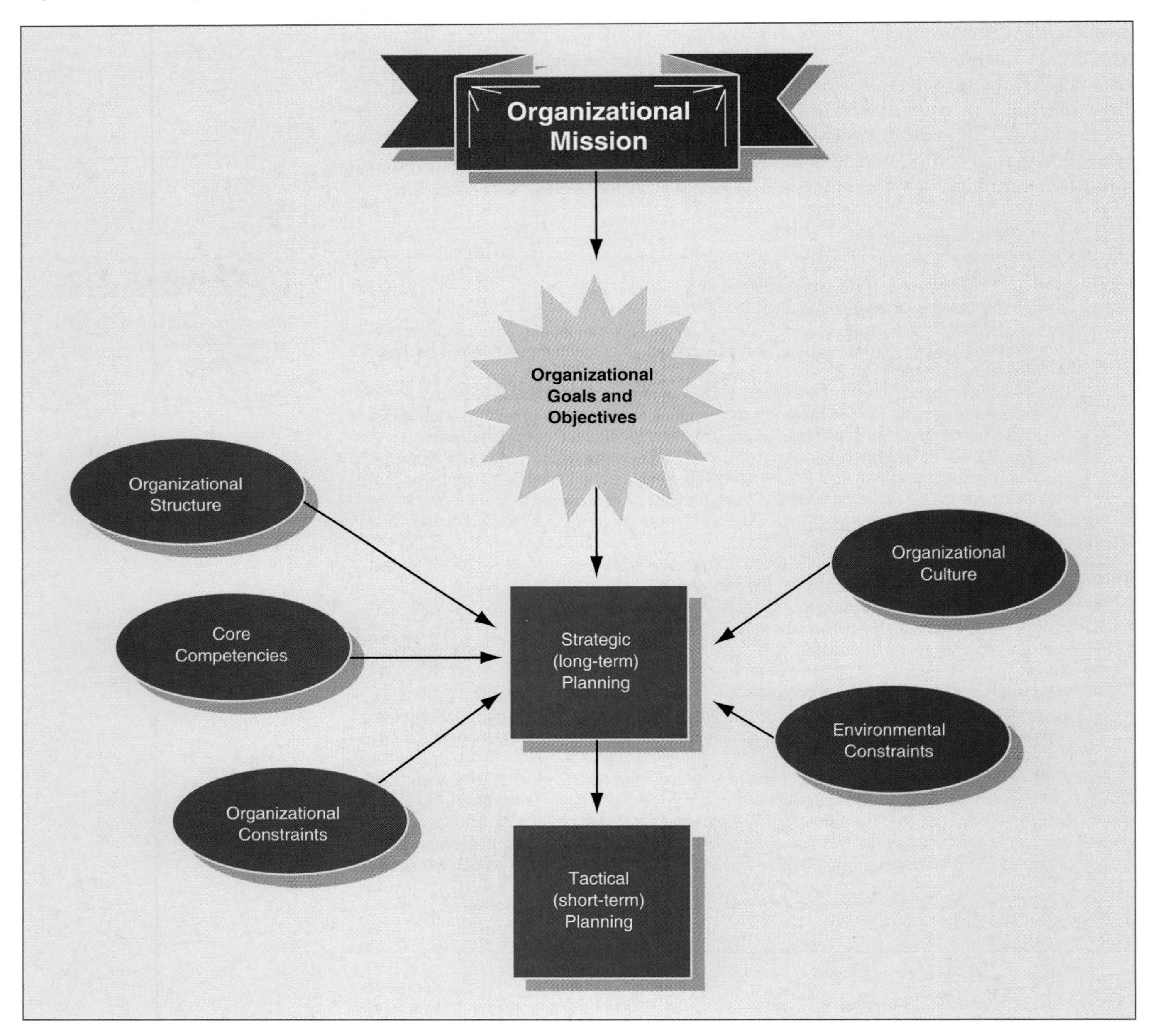

Goals are desired results expressed in qualitative terms. For example, a typical goal of profit-oriented firms is to maximize shareholder wealth. Goals are also likely to be formulated for other major stakeholders, such as customers, employees, and suppliers. In contrast, **objectives** are quantitatively expressed results that can be achieved during a pre-established period or by a specified date. Objectives should logically be used to measure progress in achieving goals. For example, one of ABN AMRO's goals is to become a leading bank in the euro. In pursuit of that goal, the bank established an objective of having all of its systems euro-compatible by January 1, 1999, when the euro was introduced. The objective was achieved at tremendous cost, but management believes that ABN AMRO's new ability to offer harmonized banking services throughout Euroland will be worth the investment.[14]

goal

objective

An organization's structure normally evolves from its mission, goals, and managerial personalities. **Organizational structure** reflects the way in which authority and responsibility for making decisions is distributed in an organization. **Authority** refers to the right (usually by virtue of position or rank) to use resources to accomplish a task or achieve an objective. **Responsibility** is the obligation to accomplish a task or achieve an objective.

organizational structure
authority

responsibility

A continuum of feasible structures reflects the extent of authority and responsibility of managers and employees. At one end of the continuum is **centralization**, where top management retains all authority for making decisions. Centralized firms often have difficulty diversifying operations because top management might lack the necessary and critical industry-specific knowledge. The people who deal directly with the issues (whether problems or opportunities), have the most relevant information, and can best foresee the decision consequences are not making the decisions.

centralization

At the other end of the continuum is **decentralization**, in which the authority for making decisions is distributed to many organizational personnel, including lower-level managers and, possibly, line employees. In today's fast-changing and competitive operating environment, implementation of a decentralized organizational structure in a large firm is almost imperative and typically cost-beneficial. However, for decentralization to work effectively, there must be employee **empowerment**, which means that people are given the authority and responsibility to make their own decisions about their work. A decision to decentralize is also a decision to use responsibility accounting, which is discussed in Chapter 18.

decentralization

empowerment

Most organizations operate at some point on the continuum other than at either of the ends. Thus, a top management decision might be the location of a new division, while the ongoing operating decisions of that division might lie with the new division manager. Long-term strategic decisions for the division might be made by the division manager in conjunction with top management.

Core Competencies

In addition to organizational structure, an organization's strategy is influenced by its core competencies. A **core competency** is any critical function or activity in which one organization seeks a higher proficiency than its competitors, making it the root of competitiveness and competitive advantage. "Core competencies are different for every organization; they are, so to speak, part of an organization's personality."[15] Technological innovation, engineering, product development, and after-sale service are some examples of core competencies. The Japanese electronics industry is viewed as having a core competency in miniaturization of electronics. MCI and Disney believe they have core competencies, respectively, in communications and entertainment. The accompanying News Note further examines core competencies.

core competency

http://www.wcom.com
http://www.disney.go.com

[14] ABN AMRO Holding N.V., *Annual Report 1998*, pp. 18–19.
[15] Peter F. Drucker, "The Information Executives Truly Need," *Harvard Business Review* (January–February 1995), p. 60.

NEWS NOTE  GENERAL BUSINESS

Finding Core Competencies

Core competencies are the combination of attributes that make an organization's products/services different and, more importantly, make customers want to buy those products/services. Organizations compete for customers, revenue, market share, etc., with products/services that meet customers' needs. Accordingly, without core competencies, organizations cannot compete.

Identifying core competencies involves research of a representative sample of customers (retailers), their customers (consumers), suppliers, and other industry experts. Ask questions about what attributes differentiate the organization's products/services over those of competitors. Follow up answers to questions with more questions; then explore for the underlying core products/services that differentiate. The unique combination of knowledge, special skills, proprietary technologies, and/or unique operating methods will be identified.

While some organizations compete for current core competencies, smart organizations also compete for core competencies that can gain them competitive advantage in the future. How fast can the organization acquire and develop these core competencies and at what cost? A company's ability to successfully find and integrate these future core competencies will determine its ability to deliver future products/services, their future scope, the degree of differentiation, the costs, and the price the market will pay.

SOURCE: Adapted from interview with Maurice Greaver, "Strategic Outsourcing," http://www.outsourcing.com/howandwhy/interviews/greaver/main/htm (August 14, 1999).

http://www.Rolls-Royce.com

But core competencies are likely to change over time. Consider that Rolls-Royce plc, once one of the most respected names in luxury automobiles, sold its motorcar division in 1972. Company management decided its priority should be products resulting from its core gas-turbine technologies. Thus, the company began focusing on civilian and military aircraft engines and power generation and improving its service, parts, and repair business. Business boomed for Rolls-Royce: in 1987, RR engines were used on only six types of civil airframes; in 1999, they were used on 30 types, deployed in 37 of the top 50 airlines.[16]

Organizational Constraints

Numerous organizational constraints may affect a firm's strategy options. In almost all instances, these hindrances are short-term because they can be overcome by existing business opportunities. Two common organizational constraints involve monetary capital and intellectual capital. Decisions to minimize or eliminate each of these constraints can be analyzed using capital budgeting analysis, which is covered in Chapter 14.

MONETARY CAPITAL

Strategy implementation generally requires a monetary investment, and all organizations are constrained by the level and cost of available capital. Although companies almost always can acquire additional capital through borrowings or equity sales, management should decide whether (1) the capital could be obtained at a reasonable cost and (2) a reallocation of existing capital would be more effective and efficient.

INTELLECTUAL CAPITAL

intellectual capital

Another potentially significant constraint on strategy is the level of the firm's intellectual capital (IC). Many definitions exist for IC, but all have a common thread of intangibility. **Intellectual capital** reflects the "invisible" assets that provide distinct intrinsic organizational value but which are not shown on balance sheets.

[16] Robert T. Scott, "Rolls Chief Has Profits Flying High," [New Orleans] *The Times-Picayune* (April 27, 1999), pp. C-1, 10.

One expansion of the definition is that IC encompasses human, structural, and relationship capital.[17] Human capital is reflected in the knowledge and creativity of an organization's personnel and is a source of strategic innovation and renewal. Human capital may provide, at least until adopted by others, the company a core competency.

Structural capital, such as information systems and technology, allows human capital to be used. Structural capital "doesn't go home at night or quit and hire on with a rival; it puts new ideas to work; and it can be used again and again to create value, just as a die can stamp out part after part."[18] Acquiring new technology is one way to create new strategic opportunities by allowing a company to do things better or faster—assuming that the company has trained its human capital in the use of that technology.

Relationship capital reflects ongoing interactions between the organization and its customers and suppliers. These relationships should be, respectively, profitable and cost-beneficial. In many respects, the customer element of relationship capital is the most valuable part of an organization's intellectual capital: without customers to purchase products and services, an organization would have no need to employ human or structural capital.

Organizational Culture

Going global, implementing employee empowerment, and investing in new forms of capital are all decisions that require organizational change. An organization's ability to change depends heavily on its organizational culture.

organizational culture

Organizational culture is the set of basic assumptions about the organization, its goals, and its business practices. Culture describes an organization's norms in internal and external, as well as formal and informal, transactions.

> *Culture refers to the values, beliefs, and attitudes that permeate a business. If strategy defines where a company wants to go, culture determines how—maybe whether—it gets there. Every business has some kind of culture, just because it's an organization of human beings. But most businesses never give the topic a second thought. Their culture is to do things the way they always have or the way everybody else does them.*
>
> *A few companies, by contrast, have explicit, highly distinctive cultures—strong, focused cultures that stick out from the crowd like the Grateful Dead at a marching-band convention. [For example, Southwest Airlines is] famous for its wild and woolly—not to say manic—culture. Everybody at Southwest, from CEO Herb Kelleher to the newest gate attendant, pitches in to make sure that customers have a good time and that airplanes get unloaded and reloaded and back in the air fast."*[19]

http://www.iflyswa.com

Organizational culture is heavily influenced by the culture of the nation in which the organization is domiciled, the extent of diversity in the workforce, and the personal styles and philosophies of the top management team. These variables play a significant role in determining whether the communication system tends to be formal or informal, whether authority is likely to be centralized or decentralized, whether relations with employees tend to be antagonistic or cooperative, and how control systems are designed and used. Like many of the other influences on organizational strategy, organizational culture can change over time. In most cases, however, culture is more likely to change due to new management rather than because existing managers changed their style.

[17] Thomas A. Stewart, *Intellectual Capital* (New York: Currency/Doubleday, 1999), pp. 75–77.
[18] Thomas A. Stewart, "Your Company's Most Valuable Asset: Intellectual Capital," *Fortune* (October 3, 1994), pp. 71–72.
[19] John Case, "Corporate Culture," *Inc.* (November 1996), pp. 46–47.

Environmental Constraints

environmental constraint

A final factor affecting strategy is the environment in which the organization operates. An **environmental constraint** is any limitation on strategy brought about by external differences in culture, competitive market structures, fiscal policy (such as taxation structures), laws, or political situations. Because an organization's management cannot directly control environmental constraints, these factors tend to be long-run rather than short-run.

http://www.walmart.com

Wal-Mart provides an excellent example of the influence of environmental constraints on organizational strategy. Wal-Mart first entered Europe in 1997 by purchasing a chain of German retail stores. Germany, unfortunately, is known for high labor costs, surly employees, and a variety of arcane restrictions about zoning, pricing, and operating hours. Wal-Mart had to discontinue its "Ten-Foot Rule" requiring employees to speak to customers within ten feet of them and encouraging employees to be customer friendly. Some stores do not bag purchases because the practice is unheard of in Germany. But the company cannot refund customers the price difference on an item sold elsewhere for less because it is illegal in Germany. Nor can the associates receive Wal-Mart stock options because they are difficult and expensive to grant under German law.[20]

RESPONSES TO COMPETITION

6

How does an organization's competitive environment impact its strategy and how might an organization respond to competition?

differentiation strategy

An organization operating in a competitive market structure may choose to avoid competition through differentiation or cost leadership.[21] A company choosing a **differentiation strategy** distinguishes its product or service from that of competitors by adding enough value (including quality and/or features) that customers are willing to pay a higher price. Differentiation is often related to the product or service, distribution system, or advertising. The accompanying News Note illustrates a slightly different version of differentiation strategy: including substantially fewer features and charging higher prices!

NEWS NOTE

GENERAL BUSINESS

Less Costs More??

For $675 a night, guests at the Meridian Club, on a private island in the Caribbean, get a room with no television, no radio, no telephone and no air conditioning—"almost like a motel room," says JoAnn Setzer, of Sacramento, California.

Call it downscale deluxe, and call it trendy. Ms. Setzer isn't complaining; she visits Meridian every year. And many well-heeled tourists apparently have similar tastes. These days, some of the most sought-after resorts are those that charge a whole lot but offer next to nothing in the way of amenities and nothing at all when it comes to technological innovations.

Deliberately distancing themselves from the far more numerous luxury hotels that boast every possible creature comfort and convenience, these spartan resorts proudly specialize in the experience of . . . *nada*.

Such resorts insist that simplicity is part of an industrywide trend in travel. But travel-industry consultants warn that the tactic is risky. The demand for less-is-more luxury is small, they say, and suited for only a few, mostly older resorts rather than a chain.

SOURCE: Adapted from Lisa Miller, "Stifling Heat, No Room Service . . . and Sky-High Prices," *The Wall Street Journal* (June 27, 1997), p. B1.

[20] Jeremy Kahn, "Wal-Mart Goes Shopping in Europe," *Fortune* (June 7, 1999), pp. 105ff.
[21] Michael Porter, *Competitive Advantage: Creating and Sustaining Superior Performance* (New York: Free Press, 1985), p. 17.

cost leadership

Competition may also be avoided by establishing a position of **cost leadership**, that is, by becoming the low-cost producer/provider and, thus, being able to charge low prices that emphasize cost efficiencies. In this strategy, competitors cannot compete on price and must differentiate their products/services from the cost leader.

confrontation strategy

In today's business environment, maintaining a competitive advantage by avoiding competition can be difficult. Within a short time, competitors are generally able to duplicate the factors that originally provided the competitive advantage. For many companies, the future key to success may be to confront competition by identifying and exploiting temporary opportunities for advantage. In a **confrontation strategy**, an organization tries to differentiate its products/services by introducing new features or tries to develop a price leadership position by dropping prices even though competitors will rapidly bring out equivalent products and match price changes.[22] Although potentially necessary, a confrontation strategy is, by its very nature, less profitable for companies than differentiation or cost leadership.

business intelligence (BI) system

To assess all of the varying internal and external factors that affect strategic planning, an organization needs to have a well-designed **business intelligence (BI) system**. This system represents the "formal process for gathering and analyzing information and producing intelligence to meet decision-making needs."[23] A BI system requires knowledge of markets, technologies, and competitors, as shown in Exhibit 1–9.

In addition to the need for information about external influences, the BI system should provide management comprehensive information about internal functions and processes, including organizational strengths and constraints.[24] Information provided by this system will be of great importance in helping managers perform their organizational functions, especially strategic and tactical planning.

EXHIBIT 1–9

Levels of Intelligence Gathering

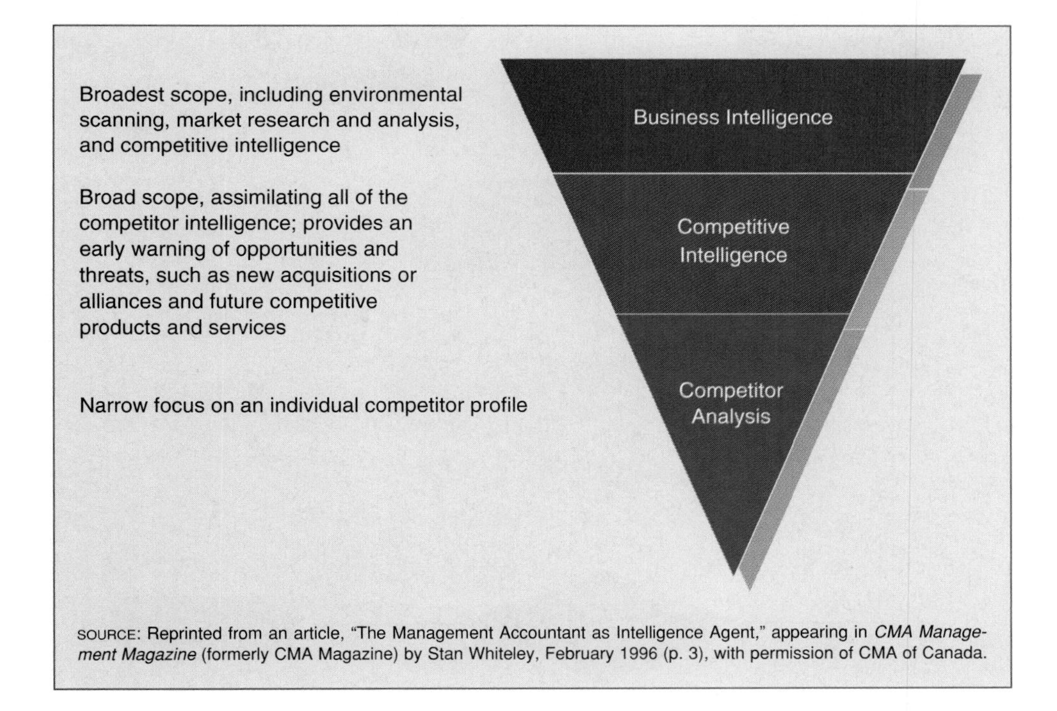

SOURCE: Reprinted from an article, "The Management Accountant as Intelligence Agent," appearing in *CMA Management Magazine* (formerly CMA Magazine) by Stan Whiteley, February 1996 (p. 3), with permission of CMA of Canada.

[22] Robin Cooper, *When Lean Enterprises Collide* (Boston: Harvard Business School Press, 1995), p. 11.

[23] "U.S. Companies Slow to Develop Business Intelligence," *Deloitte & Touche Review* (October 16, 1995), p. 1.

[24] For more information, see the Society of Management Accountants of Canada's *Management Accounting Guideline 39: Developing Comprehensive Competitor Intelligence*.

ROLE OF ACCOUNTING IN ORGANIZATIONS

7

How does the accounting function impact an organization's ability to successfully achieve its strategic goals and objectives?

When setting strategy, managers must consider the opportunities and threats provided by the entity's customers, competition, and environment and must analyze those opportunities and threats relative to the entity's strengths and weaknesses. Such an analysis is the first part of the model shown in Exhibit 1–10. Next, management must consider the impact the selected strategies will have on organizational stakeholders. In a profit-oriented business, strategies should promote a primary goal of profit generation so that customers are served effectively, shareholders can obtain wealth maximization, employees can retain their jobs and increase their personal human capital, and creditors can be paid. Therefore, management must consider the financial implications of its chosen strategies.

Profitability is typically achieved by delivering to customers the products and services they desire, on time, and at reasonable prices. Profit measurement is one function of the accounting information system. To best assess financial implications of organizational strategies, detailed, short-term tactical plans should be prepared in the form of a budget. If the projected financial results are unacceptable, management will revise either the objectives or the strategies selected to achieve those objectives.

Although the financial accounting system is extremely important in assessing current or projected profitability, that system does not provide all the information needed by management to make decisions. "Exclusive focus on the financial results and budgets does not encourage managers to invest and build for longer-

EXHIBIT 1–10

The Planning Process

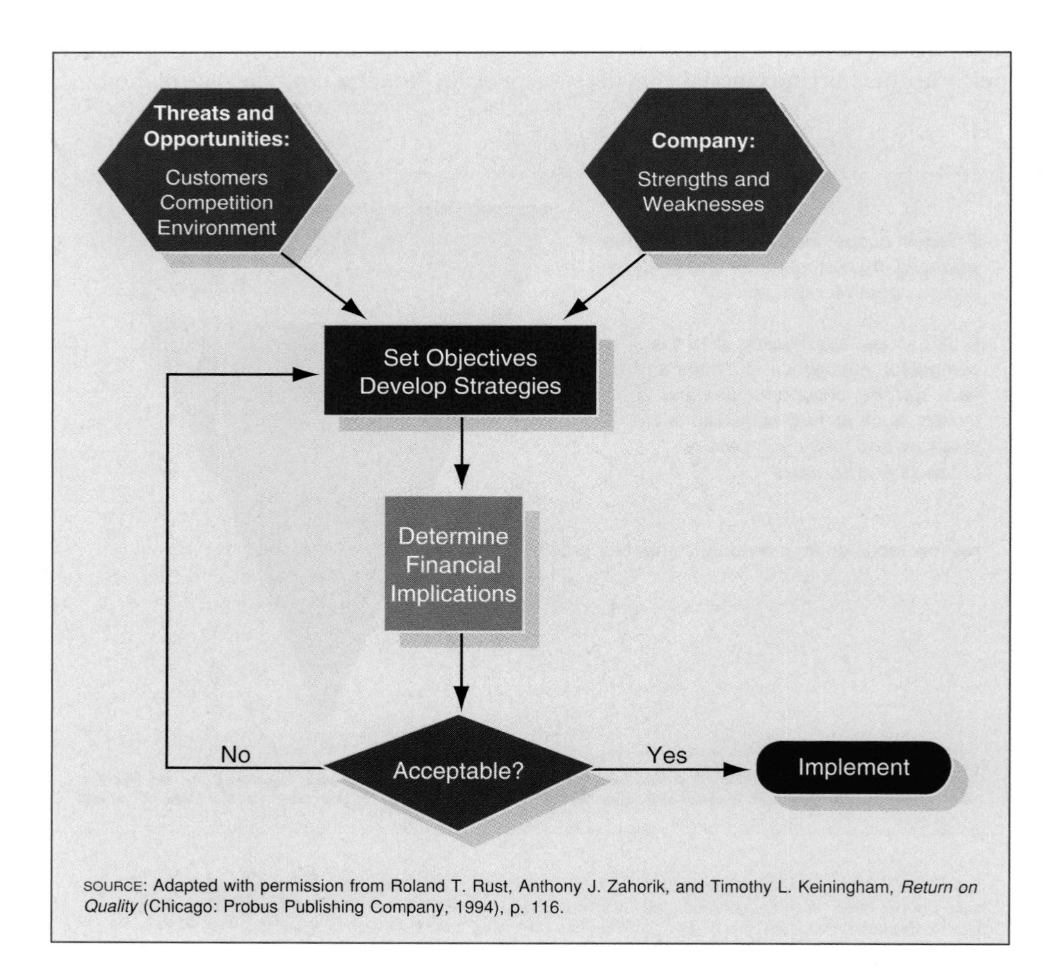

SOURCE: Adapted with permission from Roland T. Rust, Anthony J. Zahorik, and Timothy L. Keiningham, *Return on Quality* (Chicago: Probus Publishing Company, 1994), p. 116.

term competitive advantage."[25] Also, according to noted management author Peter Drucker:

> *The standard concepts and tools of [traditional financial reporting] are inadequate to control operations because all they provide is a view of the skeleton of a business. What's needed is a way to examine the soft tissue.*
>
> *Financial accounting, balance sheets, profit-and-loss statements, allocations of costs, etc., are an X-ray of the enterprise's skeleton. But in as much as the diseases we most commonly die from—heart disease, cancer, Parkinson's—do not show in a skeletal X-ray, a loss of market standing and failure to innovate do not register in the accountant's figures until the damage is done.*[26]

Organizations now have the technological capabilities to easily expand data collection activities to satisfy both external and internal information requirements. Accounting information is often a primary basis for making strategic decisions and for measuring and evaluating managerial efficiency and effectiveness. To provide the correct management incentives, accounting measurements should be tied to the established mission. In large organizations, an individual segment (or division) may pursue one of three generic organizational missions: build, hold, or harvest, as defined in Exhibit 1–11.

Segments with a build mission require the most strategic planning because they are to be operated for the long run. Segments with a harvest mission require little strategic planning; their role is to generate cash, and at some point, they will probably be sold or spun off as other company segments begin to mature.

Segment mission is directly related to the **product life cycle** or the sequential stages that a product passes through from idea conception until discontinuation of the product. The five stages of the product life cycle are design and development, introduction, growth, maturity, and decline. The build mission is appropriate for products that are in the early stages of the product life cycle, and the harvest mission is appropriate for products in the final stages of the life cycle. Accordingly, long-term performance measures are more appropriate for build missions, and shorter-term performance measures are more appropriate for harvest missions. For example, increase in market share would be a long-term measure, while annual profitability would be a short-term measure.

8

Why is a company segment's mission affected by product life cycle?

product life cycle

EXHIBIT 1–11

Generic Strategic Missions

- **Build**—This mission implies a goal of increased market share, even at the expense of short-term earnings and cash flow. A business unit that follows this mission is expected to be a net user of cash; that is, the cash flow from its current operations would usually be insufficient to meet its capital investment needs. Business units with "low market share" in "high-growth industries" typically pursue a build mission.
- **Hold**—This mission is geared to the protection of the business unit's market share and competitive position. The cash outflows for a business unit that follows this mission generally equal the cash inflows. Businesses with "high market share" in "high-growth industries" typically pursue a hold mission.
- **Harvest**—The harvest mission implies a goal of maximizing short-term earnings and cash flow, even at the expense of market share. A business unit that follows the harvest mission is a net supplier of cash. Businesses with "high market share" in "low-growth industries" typically pursue a harvest mission.

SOURCE: Vijay Govindarajan and John K. Shank, "Strategic Cost Management: Tailoring Controls to Strategies," *The Journal of Cost Management* (Fall 1992). © 1992 Warren Gorham & Lamont. Reprinted with permission of RIA.

[25] Michael Goold and John Quinn, *Strategic Control: Milestones for Long-Term Performance* (London: The Economics Books Ltd/Hutchison, 1990); cited in Tony Barnes, *Kaizen Strategies for Successful Leadership* (London: Pitman Publishing, 1996), p. 135.
[26] "Drucker on Soft Tissue Metrics," *Datamation* (September 1, 1994), p. 64.

Additionally, the measurement system will need to be modified when an organization begins to empower its employees and use work teams. Group (rather than individual) performance will need to be assessed, and nonfinancial measures are often more appropriate than financial ones to make this assessment. Accounting can help derive the new measurements, tie them to organizational goals and objectives, and integrate them with an organizational pay-for-performance plan.

The degree of decentralization must reflect consideration of, among other things, how rapidly decisions need to be made, the willingness of upper management to allow subordinates to make potentially poor decisions, and the level of training required so that workers can understand and evaluate the consequences of their decisions. Decisions should be made only after comparing implementation costs (such as employee training) with expected benefits (such as better communication, more rapid decisions, and higher levels of employee skills).

In evaluating core competencies, an organization must analyze its activities and compare them to internal or external benchmark measurements. Some comparison metrics will often relate to costs: how does the cost of making a product or performing a service internally compare to the price of external acquisition? To make fair comparisons, a company must be reasonably certain of the validity of its costs. Unfortunately, a recent survey of over 200 financial and operating executives in North America showed that less than half of the respondents were confident of their cost data. They wanted "more accurate, timely, and detailed information from their systems."[27] To help provide such information, some companies use activity-based costing, which is discussed in Chapter 4.

In assessing alternative strategies that require substantial monetary investments (such as investing in new technology or opening a foreign production facility), managers compare the investment's costs and benefits. Often, as with other strategic decisions, cost details may be more attainable than benefit details. Managers, aided by financial personnel, must then make quantitative estimates of the investment's qualitative benefits (for instance, allowing the company to be the first to bring a product or service to market). The accompanying News Note addresses the significance of estimating future benefits from investments.

http://www.gm.com

From an accounting standpoint, there is frequently a mismatch in the timing of costs and benefits. Costs are recorded and recognized in the early years of many strategic decisions, whereas benefits created by these decisions are either recognized in later years or possibly not at all because they are nonmonetary in nature. For example, financial accounting does not recognize the qualitative organizational benefits of faster delivery time, customer satisfaction, and more rapid development time for new products. Consequently, measurement methods other than traditional financial accounting ones are necessary to help managers better evaluate the strategic implications of organizational investments.

strategic resource management (SRM)

Strategic resource management (SRM) involves the organizational planning for deployment of resources to create value for customers and shareholders. Key attributes in the success of SRM are the management of information and of change in responding to threats and opportunities. SRM is concerned with the following issues:[28]

- how to deploy resources to support strategies;
- how resources are used in, or recovered from, change processes;
- how customer value and shareholder value will serve as guides to the effective use of resources; and
- how resources are to be deployed and redeployed over time.

[27] Mary Lee Geishecker, "New Technologies Support ABC," *Management Accounting* (March 1996), p. 44.
[28] Adapted from W. P. Birkett, "Management Accounting and Knowledge Management," *Management Accounting* (November 1995), pp. 44–48.

GENERAL BUSINESS NEWS NOTE

Less Time Means More Profits

General Motors Corp. said sophisticated new computer and digital-imaging tools are expected to cut product-development costs as much as $200 million for a given global car or truck program. Because of these tools, GM is making substantial progress in one of the core arenas of competition in the auto industry. An auto maker's capacity to develop new cars and trucks quickly can give it an edge in responding to swings in customer demand. In the 1990s, for example, GM's inability to move quickly left it way behind in various high-profit truck segments. And savings on engineering and tooling costs translate directly into profit.

Central to GM's transformation is the adoption of "an integrated portfolio of computer math-based tools." This means that all of the various design and manufacturing activities use the same software package, which turns every aspect of a vehicle into digital and mathematical models. GM is spending about $1 billion a year on this sort of computing.

GM uses these tools to take a vehicle design from a designer's initial computer-screen pen strokes all the way into production. This saves money by eliminating the need for physical models, cutting down engineering changes, reducing lead times 50 percent for ordering production tooling, and making it possible to solve manufacturing problems in "virtual" factories instead of real ones. GM now takes about 24 months from design until the start of production, down from 42 months in 1994.

SOURCE: Adapted from Robert L. Simison, "GM Turns to Computers to Cut Development Costs," *The Wall Street Journal* (October 12, 1998), p. B4.

These areas cannot be measured by financial accounting because they often relate to nonmonetary benefits. Thus, management accounting provides the necessary estimates to help managers address these issues and focus on strategic objectives.

9

What is the value chain and why is it important in managing a business?

value chain

The foundation of SRM is the **value chain** (supply chain), or the set of processes that convert inputs into products and services for the firm's customers. As shown in Exhibit 1–12, the value chain includes both internal and supplier processes. Managers can use the value chain to determine which activities create customer value as reflected in product/service prices and, thus, revenues earned. By reducing or eliminating activities that add no value within the value chain, firms can become more efficient and effective.

For their contributions to the value chain, employees earn compensation and suppliers earn revenues. Successful firms will gain the cooperation of everyone in the value chain and communicate a perspective that today's competition is between value chains more so than between individual businesses. Once this concept is accepted, members of the value chain become aware that information must be shared among all entities in the value chain.

The arrows in Exhibit 1–12 indicate information flows that provide the key linkages between managing resources and managing change in a business. Managers, as the agents of change, must understand internal organizational processes, external markets (customers), available and visionary technologies, current and future competitors, and operating environments. This knowledge helps managers to respond proactively to new market opportunities and to competitors' actions. Much of the information required by managers comes from the business intelligence system (which includes the accounting information system) discussed earlier in this chapter.

One of the most significant challenges of managing an organization is balancing the short-run and long-run demands for resources. Resources include all organizational assets, including people. In the contemporary business environment, managers must be able to balance short-term and long-term considerations as well as recognize and prioritize strategic resource needs. In addition, managers must be careful to structure strategic initiatives such that they allow flexibility in day-to-day

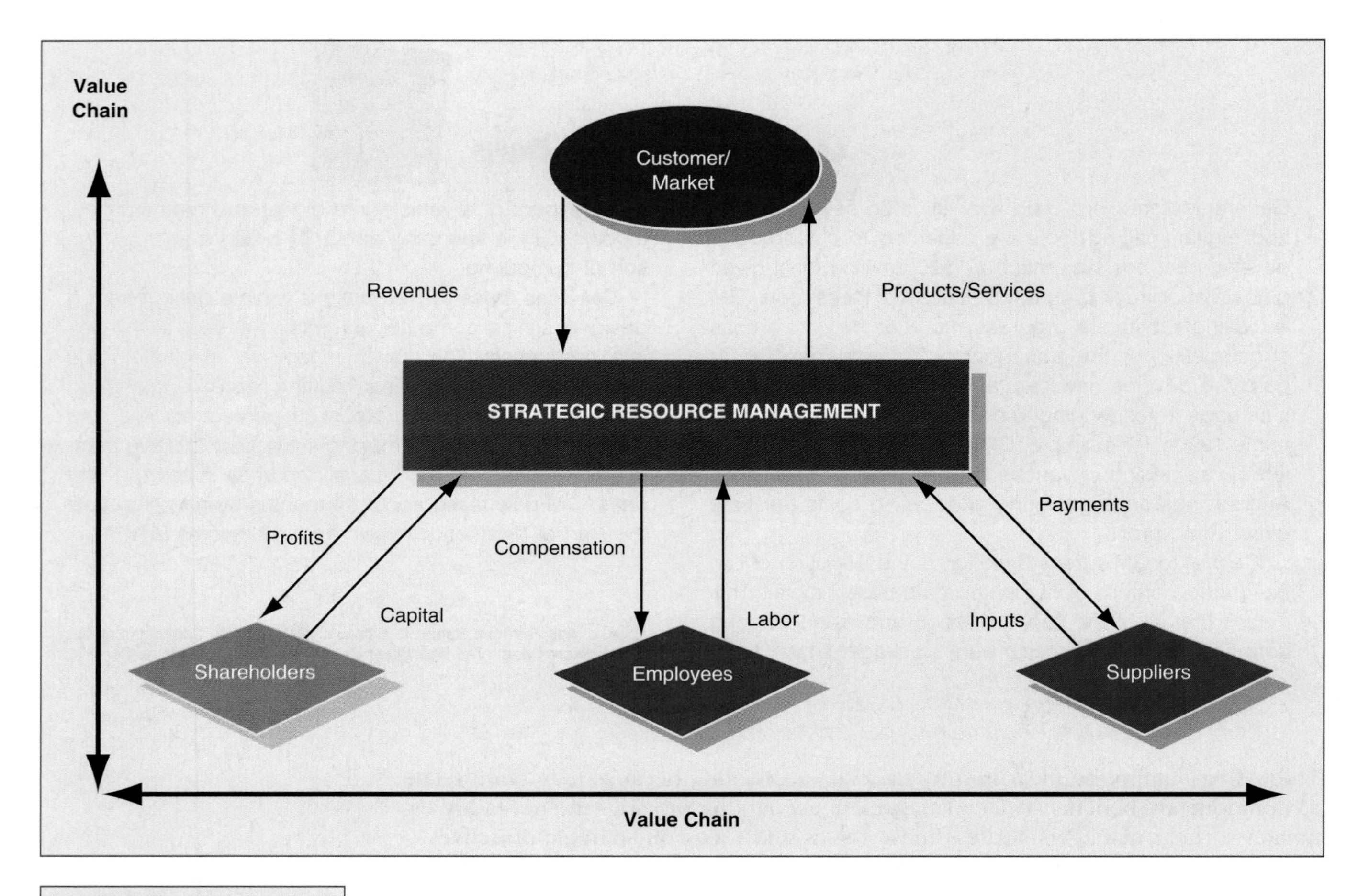

EXHIBIT 1-12

The Value Chain and Strategic Resource Management

management. Stated another way, in making long-term commitments of resources, managers must consider how those commitments affect short-term management of resources. Information is the key to successfully analyzing and resolving all of these decision situations—and much of that information is provided by an organization's accounting system.

REVISITING ABN AMRO Bank

http://www.abnamro.com

ABN AMRO sees itself as a prominent universal banking group with a strong international focus. Its strength lies on the one hand in its extensive, worldwide network of branches and subsidiaries with highly qualified staff and, on the other hand, in the integrated delivery of banking services to all customer segments through every available channel of distribution. Embedded in the organization is a corporate culture based on the four corporate values (integrity, teamwork, respect, and professionalism) that guide daily activities.

In its quest to provide value-added services to clients, the bank has a virtual product for corporations willing to outsource their accounts receivables operations. In effect, the bank's service would start by generating the invoice for the client and end with dunning its customers, if it came to that.

Other new cash management products include IntelliTracs, an interactive, automated payments tracking system, and Facet, a global system that enables correspondent banks to initiate faster and more accurate payment transactions from anywhere in the world. Both products use cutting-edge technology, keeping the bank abreast of other leading global banks.

Three important policy support divisions at ABN AMRO are Planning & Control, Financial Accounting, and Management Accounting. The P&C area is responsible for formulating corporate strategy and objectives, translating these into financial plans, and engaging in investor relations. Financial Accounting compiles, analyzes, and provides financial information to group management in respect to domestic and international operations as well as preparing financial statements. Management Accounting responsibilities include developing and implementing instruments for analyzing product, customer and distribution channel profitability, engaging in medium- and long-range planning and budgeting, offering organizational advice, supporting strategic planning, conducting operations research, and providing policy support advice.

ABN AMRO has retail banking operations in 23 countries. The bank intends to expand in these markets using the Internet. In Europe, web-based expansion will be more important than in other markets because defensive governments have frequently blocked the bank's merger-based expansion strategy. To ensure the Internet gets deployed effectively throughout its markets, ABN AMRO has formed a team with responsibility for examining Web plans on a case-by-case basis. The approach offers "a disconnect from the yearly budget approval process," said a senior executive of the bank. The disconnect ensures the Internet expansion strategy will not wither on the vine for want of resources.

SOURCE: **www.abnamro.com/profile**; ABN AMRO Holding N.V., *Annual Report 1998*; Chris Costanzo, "ABN AMRO Says Web Will Anchor Its Expansion," *American Banker* (December 9, 1999), p. 16.

CHAPTER SUMMARY

Accounting information addresses three different functions: (1) providing information to external parties (stockholders, creditors, and various regulatory bodies) for investment and credit decisions; (2) estimating the cost of products produced and services provided by the organization; and (3) providing information useful to internal managers who are responsible for planning, controlling, decision making, and evaluating performance. Financial accounting is designed to meet external information needs and to comply with generally accepted accounting principles. Management accounting attempts to satisfy internal information needs and to provide product costing information for external financial statements.

Cost accounting creates an overlap between financial accounting and management accounting. Cost accounting integrates with financial accounting by providing product costing information for financial statements and with management accounting by providing some of the quantitative, cost-based information managers need to perform their tasks.

Most companies must now adapt to operating in a globally competitive environment. E-commerce is taking hold and is certain to be the norm of the future. Governments have established trade arrangements (including the General Agreement on Tariffs and Trade, European Union, and North American Free Trade Agreement) to reduce tariff barriers and foster global competition. Although an open global business environment provides new opportunities, it often creates greater risks (strategic, operating, financial, and information) and requires knowledge of and adherence to differing legal requirements. Additionally, the ethical norms may vary by location, but a solid corporate code of ethics should help a company operate in a consistent, moral way throughout the world.

Organizational strategy should be based on a mission statement that indicates what the organization wants to accomplish and how it will meet customer needs. Goals and objectives should flow from that statement. Strategy options may be constrained by numerous factors. How the organization is structured provides some constraints on who within the entity has authority and responsibility for tasks. The core competencies of an organization dictate internal strengths and capabilities and, thus, help indicate appropriate business functions to outsource. Strategy may also be constrained by the level of capital (monetary or intellectual) available to the organization. Organizational culture provides a foundation for normal business practices and protocol for interactions among employees, managers, customers, suppliers, and the public. Lastly, environmental factors such as market structures, government regulations, and national cultures may help or hinder strategic options. A business intelligence system can help management understand the factors that influence the organization's choice of strategies.

Accounting provides important information for an organization's management. Strategic resource management links organizational strategy to resource deployment. SRM's key focus is the value chain, or the string of activities that convert organizational inputs into outputs. The accounting information system is comprised of the cost, financial, and management accounting functions—all of which provide essential information that supports strategic resource management.

KEY TERMS

authority (p. 19)
business intelligence (BI) system (p. 23)
centralization (p. 19)
confrontation strategy (p. 23)
core competency (p. 19)
cost accounting (p. 5)
cost leadership strategy (p. 23)
decentralization (p. 19)
differentiation strategy (p. 22)
e-commerce (p. 9)
economic integration (p. 10)
empowerment (p. 19)
environmental constraint (p. 22)
ethical standards (p. 14)
Foreign Corrupt Practices Act (FCPA) (p. 14)
global economy (p. 9)
goals (p. 19)
intellectual capital (p. 20)
mission statement (p. 16)
objectives (p. 19)
organizational culture (p. 21)
organizational structure (p. 19)
planning (p. 16)
product life cycle (p. 25)
responsibility (p. 19)
strategic resource management (SRM) (p. 26)
strategy (p. 17)
value chain (p. 27)

QUESTIONS

1. Discuss how financial, cost, and managerial accounting interface. Is one more important than another? Discuss the rationale for your answer.
2. Flexibility is said to be the hallmark of modern management accounting, whereas standardization and consistency describe financial accounting. Explain why the focus of these two accounting systems differs.
3. Is cost accounting a subset of management accounting or is management accounting a subset of cost accounting? Why?
4. Why would operating in a global (rather than a strictly domestic) marketplace create a need for additional information for management? Discuss some of the additional information you think managers would need and why such information would be valuable.
5. Discuss the validity of the following statement, "Only large companies (such as those that are publicly held and listed on a major stock exchange) have the opportunity to operate in a global marketplace."

6. Would you purchase products from Internet sources? Why or why not? If you have purchased from the Internet, did you experience any problems? If so, what were they and were they easily eliminated?
7. The AICPA has introduced CPA WebTrust to reduce or eliminate some problems related to engaging in e-commerce. Use the Internet to prepare a short discussion about WebTrust. What organizations are included in the WebTrust index?
8. Why are economic trade agreements so important to the globalization of business?
9. Use the Internet to find two businesses that have benefited and two businesses that have been disadvantaged by NAFTA. Briefly discuss the situations of each of these four businesses.
10. Use the Internet to find how the euro has impacted businesses in the last six months.
11. What political and cultural issues might affect an American (or a Canadian) company considering opening a business in Russia?
12. Use the Internet to find five domestic companies that have introduced in foreign countries what you would consider "radically" different products than those sold domestically. Discuss why these differences might exist. (*Hint:* Food and drink companies are good candidates for this question.)
13. Select a category of risk from Exhibit 1–6. Briefly explain some differences in the risks that would be experienced for the listed factors between your country and another selected country.
14. How do government regulations affect planning processes in the business organizations in your country?
15. Why should businesses concern themselves with a clean environment when it might be substantially less expensive to pollute, thus making their products cheaper for consumers?
16. Compare and contrast legal and ethical standards.
17. Use the Internet to find three companies that have been indicted for or convicted of violating the Foreign Corrupt Practices Act. In what countries were these companies offering bribes? Do you think the American companies believed that, without bribery, they could not have operated on a "level playing field?" Discuss your response.
18. What factors impede the development of an international code of ethics for profit-oriented businesses? Do you believe these factors can be overcome through the passage of laws? Discuss the rationale for your answer.
19. Why is a code of ethics a necessity in any organization?
20. Use the Internet to find the ethics codes for three businesses. How do these codes differ? Which do you think is better and why?
21. Why is a mission statement important to an organization?
22. Select three large, publicly held companies in the same industry. Use the Internet to access their Web sites and find a mission statement for each. How do these mission statements differ and how are they similar? Assuming that you are the president of a new company in this industry, write a mission statement for your company.
23. What is organizational strategy? Why would each organization have a unique strategy or set of strategies?
24. Are the financial implications of strategic planning more important in a business than in a not-for-profit organization? Why or why not?
25. Distinguish between goals and objectives. What goals do you hope to achieve by taking this course? What objectives can you establish to measure the degree to which you achieve these stated goals?
26. Differentiate between authority and responsibility. Can you have one without the other? Explain.

27. In what types of organizations or under what organizational conditions would centralization be a more useful structure than decentralization? Would decentralization be more useful than centralization?

28. Use the Internet to find three companies that have recently changed their organizational structures. How were the companies restructured and what reasons were given for the change?

29. If you were Dean of your College, how would you more fully empower your students relative to their college studies?

30. What is a core competency and how do core competencies impact the feasible set of alternative organizational strategies?

31. "If an organization can borrow money or sell stock, it does not have a capital constraint." Is this statement true or false? Discuss the rationale for your answer.

32. Differentiate between human, structural, and relationship forms of intellectual capital. Which do you believe is more important in each of the following organizations: a start-up software development company, a car dealership, a university, a hospital, and Coca-Cola? Provide reasons for your answers.

33. How can a change in governmental laws or regulations create a strategic opportunity for an organization? Give an example.

34. Define each of the strategies an organization may pursue to avoid competition, and discuss the benefits of each type of strategy.

35. Why would a useful business intelligence system contain substantial information about an organization's competitors?

36. What are the three generic segment missions and how are these missions related to the concept of product life cycle?

37. What is strategic resource management? Why is financial accounting an insufficient information source for strategic resource management?

38. What is the value chain of an organization and how does it interface with strategic resource management?

EXERCISES

39. *(Terminology)* Match the following lettered items on the left with the appropriate numbered description on the right.

a. Authority
b. Centralization
c. Core competency
d. Decentralization
e. Empowerment
f. Goal
g. Mission
h. Objective
i. Planning
j. Responsibility

1. A target expressed in quantitative terms
2. The right to use resources to accomplish something
3. An expression of an organization's future path
4. A process that an organization does better than other organizations
5. A desired result, expressed qualitatively
6. A situation in which all decisions are made by top management
7. The obligation to accomplish something
8. A situation in which employees are allowed to make decisions about their work
9. The process of determining long-term and short-term strategies
10. A situation in which many decisions are made by subordinate managers

40. *(Terminology)* Match the following lettered items on the left with the appropriate numbered description on the right.

a. Business intelligence system
b. Differentiation
c. E-commerce
d. Economic integration
e. Ethical standard
f. Intellectual capital
g. Organizational culture
h. Organizational structure
i. Strategy
j. Value chain

1. An organization's intangible assets of skill, knowledge, and information
2. A belief about moral and immoral behavior
3. The long-term plan related to organizational goals and objectives
4. The way in which authority and responsibility are distributed in an organization
5. The basic assumptions about an organization, its goals, and its practices
6. A strategy based on differentiating products or services from those of competitors
7. The source of information about external competitors and markets
8. The processes of an organization and its suppliers to convert inputs into products and services structure
9. The process of using the Internet to buy and sell goods
10. The process of creating multi-country markets

41. *(Accounting information)* You are the owner and manager of a small auto repair shop that does routine maintenance, major repairs, and body work. Business is good, and your monthly financial statements show that your shop is consistently profitable. Cash flow is becoming a small problem, however, and you may need to take out a loan from the bank. You have also been receiving customer complaints about time delays and price increases.

a. What accounting information do you think is most important to take with you to discuss a possible loan with your banker?
b. What accounting information do you think is most important in ascertaining the business activities of your repair shop in regard to addressing time delays and price increases? What about nonaccounting information?
c. Can the various information in parts (a) and (b) be gathered from the accounting records directly? Indirectly? If not at all, where would you need to look for such information?

42. *(Globalization)* The 1996 annual report of Callaway Golf Company (headquartered in California) was slightly untraditional in that the opening "letter" to shareholders was given not only in English, but also in German, French, Spanish, Japanese, and Chinese.

http://www.Callaway.com

a. Discuss the costs and benefits of a U.S.-based company taking the time to provide such translations.
b. What additional information would you want to have to assess how such translations are related to Callaway's strategic plans?

43. *(E-commerce)* A new aspect of e-commerce is home management services. Andersen Consulting predicts that "the market for on-line orders of food, household goods, and services will mushroom from $100 million in 1997 to $57 billion or more by 2007."[29]

http://andersenconsulting.com

[29] Jane Hodges, "On the Web, It's Slow Food," *Fortune* (October 26, 1998), p. 262.

You own a grocery store in downtown San Francisco and have decided to allow on-line customer orders and provide delivery.

a. What problems could arise from the on-line ordering? How would you and your staff solve these issues?

b. What problems could arise from the delivery process? How would you and your staff solve these issues?

44. *(E-commerce)* It is predicted that e-commerce will help speed the process of a single European market by forming "eZones" or "regions of Internet commerce between cross-border constituencies."[30] Use library and Internet resources to gather information and write a short description on how e-commerce has affected European market harmonization.

45. *(Trade agreements)* You have been appointed to a business advisory group in your country to consider the implementation of the NAFTA. What issues relative to implementation concern you and why?

46. *(Business risks)* You have just been promoted to manage a branch location of a regional bank.

a. Provide three examples of the strategic, operating, financial, and information risks that your organization faces.

b. What might you do to minimize the impacts of each of these risks?

47. *(Mission)* Obtain a copy of your college's mission statement. Draft a mission statement for this class that supports the college's mission statement.

a. How does your mission statement reflect the goals and objectives of the college's mission statement?

b. How can you measure the successful accomplishment of your college's objectives?

http://www.homedepot.com

48. *(Strategy)* You are the manager of the local Home Depot store. What are the five factors that you believe to be most critical to the success of your organization? How would these factors influence your store's strategy?

49. *(Strategy)* You are the manager of a small restaurant in your hometown.

a. What information would you want to have in making the decision whether to add chicken fajitas and Boston clam chowder to your menu?

b. Why would each of the above information items be significant?

50. *(Empowerment)* Early this year, you started a house-cleaning service and now have 20 customers. Because of other obligations (including classes), you have had to hire three employees.

a. What types of business activities would you empower these employees to handle and why?

b. What types of business activities would you keep for yourself and why?

51. *(Core competencies)* As a team, make a list of the core competencies of your college or university and explain why you believe these items to be core competencies. Make appointments with the dean, one vice president, and, if possible, the president of your college or university, and without sharing your list, ask these individuals what they believe the core competencies to be and why. Prepare a written or video presentation that summarizes, compares, and contrasts all the lists. Share copies of your presentation with all the individuals you contacted.

52. *(Intellectual capital)* Use library and Internet resources to research the inclusion of intellectual capital measurement at Skandia, a Swedish financial services company. Write a short paper describing the company's IC measurement process.

http://www.Skandia.com

[30] Robert F. Randall, "Internet Will Speed Europe Market Harmonization," *Strategic Finance* (May 1999), p. 20.

53. *(Organizational culture)* Southwest Airlines is known for its "wacky" organizational culture. Use library and Internet resources to research this culture and write a brief paper about how you believe the culture has impacted Southwest's strategy and organizational profitability.

http://www.iflyswa.com

54. *(Competition strategy)* Choose a company that might utilize each of the following strategies relative to its competitors and discuss the benefits that might be realized from that strategy. Indicate the industry in which the company does business and the company's primary competitors.

- **a.** Differentiation
- **b.** Cost leadership
- **c.** Confrontation

55. *(Value chain)* You are the management accountant for a manufacturer of breakfast cereals. You've been asked to prepare a presentation that will illustrate the company's value chain.

- **a.** What activities or types of companies would you include in the upstream (supplier) part of the value chain?
- **b.** What internal activities would you include in the value chain?
- **c.** What activities or types of companies would you include in the downstream (distribution and retailing) part of the value chain?

56. *(Organizational accountants)* Use library and Internet resources to find how the jobs of management accountants have changed in the last 10 years.

- **a.** Prepare a "then vs. now" comparison.
- **b.** What five skills do you believe are the most important for management accountants to possess? Discuss the rationale for your choices.

CASES

57. *(E-commerce)* Competition in your industry is becoming fierce and you decide to begin selling on-line. Select one of the following industries and research the benefits and problems of e-commerce by a company in that industry. One article is suggested as a starting point for each industry.

- **a.** Banking [Paul Beckett, "American Express Starts Online Bank, An Increasingly Competitive Business," *The Wall Street Journal* (July 23, 1999)].
- **b.** Brokerage [Shawn Tully, "Will the Web Eat Wall Street?" *Fortune* (August 2, 1999)].
- **c.** Automobile sales [Fara Warner, "Priceline.com, AutoNations Team Up to Offer Online Car-Buying Service," *The Wall Street Journal* (July 28, 1999)].

58. *(Mission statement)* You have owned Lee Construction for 15 years and employ 100 employees. Business has been profitable, but you are concerned that the locale in which your business is based may soon experience a downturn in growth. One way you have decided to help prepare for such an event is to engage in a higher level of strategic planning, beginning with a mission statement for your company. (*Note:* The December 1996 *Management Accounting* article "Measuring Your Mission" may provide a useful starting point.)

- **a.** How does a mission statement add strength to the strategic planning process?
- **b.** Who should be involved in developing a mission statement and why?
- **c.** What factors should be considered in the development of a mission statement? Why are these factors important?
- **d.** Prepare a mission statement for Lee Construction and discuss how your mission statement will provide benefits to tactical (in addition to strategic) planning.

59. *(Benefits of successful planning)* Successful business organizations appear to be those that have clearly defined long-range goals and a well-planned strategy to reach those goals. These successful organizations understand their markets as well as the internal strengths and weaknesses of the organizations. These organizations take advantage of this knowledge to grow (through internal development or acquisitions) in a consistent and disciplined manner.

a. Discuss the need for long-range goals for business organizations.

b. Discuss how long-range goals are set.

c. Define the concepts of strategic planning and management control. Discuss how they relate to each other and contribute to progress toward the attainment of long-range goals. *(CMA adapted)*

http://www.dell.com

60. *(Strategy)* Dell Computer Co. has a straightforward business strategy: "Eliminate middlemen and don't build PCs until you have firm orders in hand."[31]

a. Dell is gaining a large European market share using its uniquely American strategy. Provide some reasons why a U.S. strategy might *not* be accepted by overseas customers.

b. Dell once tried to enter the retail sales market instead of relying on direct sales. Research Dell's attempt at a different strategic approach and discuss its outcome.

61. *(Strategy)* Select a major company in a well-known industry. Use library, Internet, and other resources to answer as completely as possible the questions in Exhibit 1–7 about the company you have chosen.

62. *(Organizational constraints)* Four common organizational constraints involve monetary capital, intellectual capital, technology, and organizational structure. Additionally, the environment in which the organization operates may present one or more types of constraints (cultural, fiscal, legal/regulatory, or political).

a. Discuss whether each of these constraints might or might not be influential in the following types of organizations:

1. City Hall in a major metropolitan city
2. a franchised quick-copy business
3. a newly opened firm of attorneys, all of whom recently graduated from law school
4. an international oil exploration and production company

Explain the rationale for each of your answers.

b. For each of the previously listed organizations, discuss your perceptions of which of the constraints would be most critical and why.

c. For each of the previously listed organizations, discuss your perceptions of whether human or structural capital would be most important and why.

63. *(Organizational culture)* The United States provides an ethnically, racially, and culturally diverse workplace. It has been argued that this plurality may be a competitive handicap for U.S. businesses. For example, communicating may be difficult because some workers do not speak English, motivating workers may be complicated because workers have diverse work ethics, and work scheduling may be difficult because of differing religions and ethnic holidays. It has been argued that Japan has a competitive advantage because its population is much more homogeneous.

a. What are the advantages of a pluralistic society in the global marketplace?

b. On balance, does America's plurality give it a competitive advantage or place it at a competitive disadvantage? Discuss.

64. *(Competition)* You recently received a very large inheritance and have decided to buy an existing business or open a new business. Given your interests, you have narrowed your choices to the following:

[31] Silvia Ascarelli, "Dell Finds U.S. Strategy Works in Europe," *The Wall Street Journal* (February 3, 1997).

- Purchase the existing cable company in your regional area.
- Purchase an airline that operates in most areas of the country.
- Open a plant to manufacture and sell hot-sauce domestically and in Central and South America.
- Buy franchises for and open 15 locations of a fast-food restaurant in areas of the former Soviet Union.

a. Discuss the competitive influences that will impact each of your potential businesses.
b. How would the tactics of product/service differentiation, cost leadership, or confrontation work in each of your potential businesses?
c. What would be the most critical factors for each of your potential businesses?
d. Which business would you open and why?

65. *(Value chain)* Strategic alliances are important parts of the value chain. In many organizations, suppliers are beginning to provide more and more input into customer activities.

a. In the United States, when would a strategic alliance be considered illegal?
b. What would you perceive to be the primary reasons for pursuing a strategic alliance?
c. You are the manager of a catalog company that sells flowers and plants. With whom would you want to establish strategic alliances? What issues might you want to specify prior to engaging in the alliance?

REALITY CHECK

66. Many individuals do not shop on-line because of the risk of theft of passwords, credit card numbers, and so forth. Do you believe that this risk is a significant one? Discuss the rationale for your answer.

67. You are a senior manager at a large domestic firm. All senior managers and the board of directors are scheduled for a meeting next week to discuss the opportunities for e-business. The CEO has asked you to be prepared to start the discussion by developing questions that should be addressed before embarking on such a strategy. Categorize your questions as follows:

a. executive focus on strategy and risks
b. customers
c. products and services
d. value chain
e. competition
f. business processes and technology
g. regulatory and tax environment

68. The Foreign Corrupt Practices Act (FCPA) prohibits U.S. firms from giving bribes in foreign countries, although giving bribes is customary in some countries and non-U.S. companies operating in foreign countries may not be similarly restricted. Thus, adherence to the FCPA could make competing with non-U.S. firms more difficult in foreign countries.

Do you think that bribery should be considered so ethically repugnant to Americans that companies are asked to forego a foreign custom and, hence, the profits that could be obtained through observance of the custom? Prepare both a pro and a con position for your answer, assuming you will be asked to defend one position or the other.

69. As chief legal officer in a well-respected company making lifesaving drugs, Alistair had been asked by his board of directors to look into rumors of price-fixing in the firm's European offices. His board has a very strong ethics policy and especially wary of price-fixing, bribery, kick-backs, and other unethical activities that can plague overseas operations.

After conducting detailed interviews in Europe for several months, Alistair was satisfied that the rumors were groundless. As one of the European managers said, "There's no issue here." But, he added, "if you really want something to investigate, look into the Bosnia contract."

Over the months, Alistair kept hearing about "the Bosnia contract." So when he had finished his report on the price-fixing rumors, he decided to delve into the other matter. The contract, he discovered, had been ordinary in almost every respect: A major relief organization had contracted with his company to supply one million inexpensive kits of medicine for delivery into the war-torn regions of Bosnia. Like most such contracts with charitable organizations, it contained hardly any profit for his firm.

What he found strange, however, was the payment of an extraordinarily large commission to a Romanian distributor to deliver the kits deep into Bosnia. Seeking out the executive in his own firm who had negotiated the contract, he had one question in mind: Was this a bribe?

Yes and no, said the executive. According to the Romanian distributor, the backs of the delivery trucks were loaded with the kits—and the glove compartments were stuffed with cash. That way, when the drivers were stopped at roadblocks set up by local militia units operating all across Bosnia, they could pay whatever was demanded and continue their journey. In the past, he noted, drivers without cash had been taken from their trucks and shot. For the kits to be delivered, this was a cost of doing business.

Alistair felt sure that none of the money had flowed back to the executive, whose only motive was to get the kits delivered. And by this time, the deliveries had already been made. Yet Alistair still faced a dilemma. Should he draft a separate report to the board on this most unorthodox contract—possibly causing great harm to the executive who had negotiated it or embarrassment to the relief organization, which was aware of the commission? Or should he keep silent? Everything in Alistair's background with his company told him that this contract was not the way to do business. Bribery, he knew, was simply unacceptable to the board, who felt strongly that once that barrier was breached, there would be no stopping the shakedowns in the future.

But everything in his makeup as a compassionate being told him that providing medicine for the wounded was of overriding importance and that the normal ethics of commerce didn't apply in a war zone.

What should Alistair do?

70. "Few trends could so thoroughly undermine the very foundation of our free society," writes Milton Friedman in *Capitalism and Freedom*, "as the acceptance by corporate officials of a social responsibility other than to make as much money for their shareholders as possible."

a. Discuss your reactions to this quote from a legal standpoint.

b. Discuss your reactions to this quote from an ethical standpoint.

c. How would you resolve any conflicts that exist between your two answers?

71. Mission statements are supposed to indicate what an organization does and why it exists. Some of them, however, are simply empty words, with little or no substance and with few people using them to guide activities.

a. Why does an organization need a mission statement? Or does it?

b. How might a mission statement help an organization in its pursuit of ethical behavior from employees?

c. How might a mission statement help an organization in its pursuit of production of high-quality products and provision of high levels of customer service?

72. Intellectual capital is extremely important to the longevity of an organization. There are, however, "intellectual capital pirates" who make their livings from stealing.

a. Assume that you have made several popular recordings. These recordings are being pirated overseas. Discuss how you view these intellectual capital pirates and what (if anything) should be done to them.

b. Copying a computer software program is also intellectual capital piracy. Do you perceive any difference between this type of copying and the copying of recordings? Discuss the rationale for your answer.

73. Accounting has a long history of being an ethical profession. In recent years, however, some companies have asked their accountants to help "manage earnings."

a. What does it mean to "manage earnings"?

b. List several companies that have been accused of "managing earnings."

c. Who is more likely to be involved in such a situation: the financial accountant or the management accountant? Why?

d. Do you believe that "managing earnings" is ethical? Discuss the rationale for your answer.

CHAPTER

2

Introduction to Cost Management Systems

LEARNING OBJECTIVES

After completing this chapter, you should be able to answer the following questions:

1. Why do organizations have management control systems?
2. What is a cost management system and what are its primary goals?
3. What major factors influence the design of a cost management system?
4. Why should one consider organizational form, structure, and culture when designing a cost management system?
5. How do the internal and external operating environments impact the cost management system?
6. What three groups of elements affect the design of a cost management system and how are these elements used?
7. How is gap analysis used in the implementation of a cost management system?

INTRODUCING Motorola, Inc.

http://www.mot.com

When times are tough, some people eat their seed corn. Motorola managers are planting theirs.

Despite recent struggles in businesses such as cellular phones and satellites, this big electronics company is boosting efforts in basic research that might not pay off for several years. Motorola's initiative is not yet in the league of such companies as International Business Machines Corp. or Lucent Technologies, but it is taking the company in some unusual directions.

The biggest breakthrough so far has been organizational. This past November, Motorola combined separate research groups for wireless communications, chips, and other products into a single corporate entity called Motorola Labs. The goal was to reduce duplication, spend funds more efficiently, and develop ideas faster.

Surprisingly, the move didn't mean cost savings; after looking at other big companies' research arms, Motorola officials concluded they were spending too little. "We discovered there's a relatively steady proportion spent on research: about one percent of prior-year revenues. We were a little below that," recalls Dennis Robertson, Motorola's chief technology officer.

Motorola began loosening the spending spigot. The one percent goal, with Motorola's 1998 revenue of $30 billion, would be $300 million a year. While Robertson didn't give precise figures, he said Motorola is getting close to the target.

There is an old adage that declares "you have to spend money to make money." The adage expresses the idea that revenues cannot be produced without first incurring costs. Motorola managers have recognized the necessity of incurring costs to realize revenues by increasing expenditures on research and development with the expectation that an increase in revenues will follow. However, the managers have also recognized that costs must be contained for the relationships among costs, revenues, and profits to be satisfactory—a large amount of costs cannot be incurred to produce a modest amount of revenue. Motorola managers acted to contain costs when they created Motorola Labs "to spend funds more efficiently. . . ."

http://www.ibm.com
http://www.lucent.com

A fundamental concern managers have in executing their duties is how their actions affect costs incurred, and benefits received, by their employers. Ultimately, most models applied by managers reduce to a comparative analysis of costs versus benefits. Financial experts, especially accountants, bear the primary responsibility for providing managers with information about measurements of costs and benefits.

In Chapter 1, the differences and similarities among the disciplines of financial, management, and cost accounting were discussed. Cost accounting was shown to play a role in both internal and external reporting. Also, the linkages between cost accounting and the specific managerial functions of planning, controlling, decision making, and performance evaluation were shown.

Cost accounting practices are increasingly being scrutinized by financial experts who hope to improve the relevance of the information they provide to managers and external parties. As shown in Exhibit 2–1, cost accounting has recently become the top financial function target for reengineering according to a 1998 membership survey of the Institute of Management Accountants. Because a given cost accounting system is typically cast in two separate, often competing, roles, and because the financial reporting role often dominates the management role, cost accounting information is frequently found to be of limited value to managers.

EXHIBIT 2-1

Which Finance Functions Are You Reengineering?

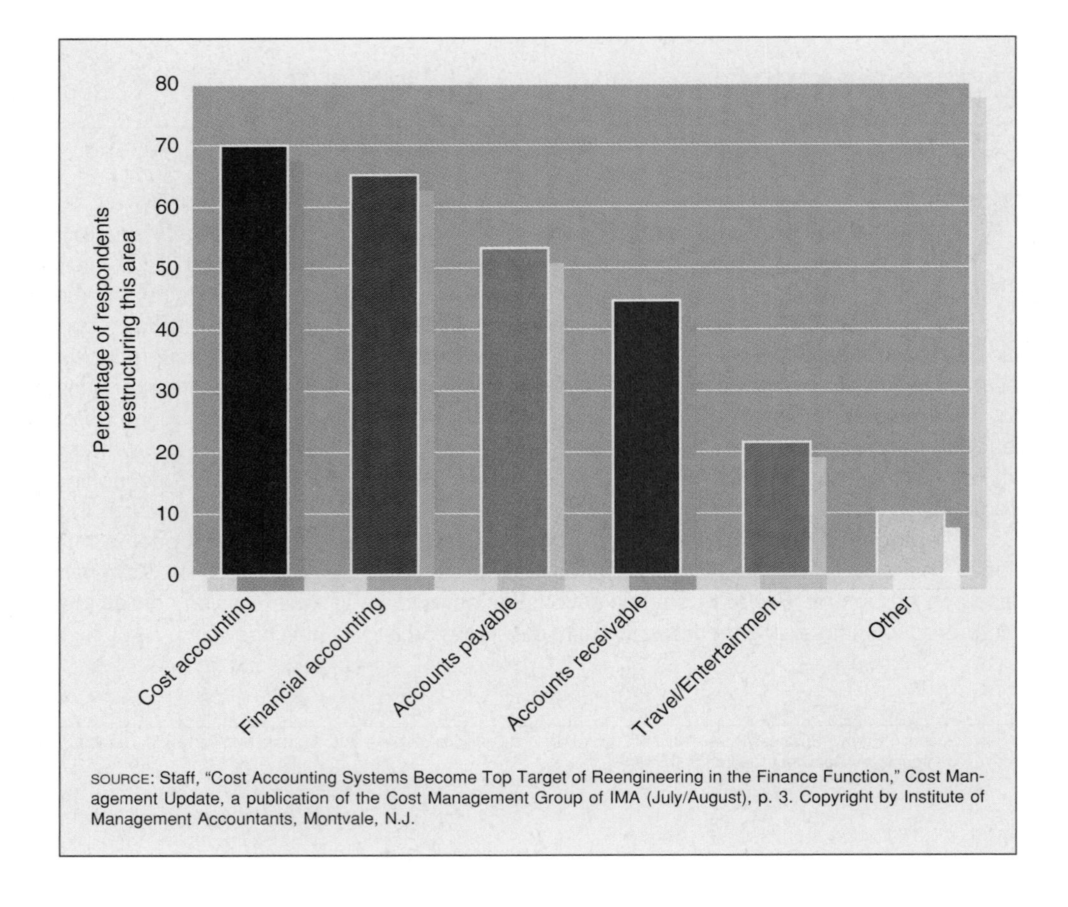

SOURCE: Staff, "Cost Accounting Systems Become Top Target of Reengineering in the Finance Function," Cost Management Update, a publication of the Cost Management Group of IMA (July/August), p. 3. Copyright by Institute of Management Accountants, Montvale, N.J.

The problem is that the dictates of financial reporting are very different from those of strategic cost management. For financial reporting purposes, cost information can be highly aggregated, historical, and must be consistent with GAAP. In contrast, the cost information required for management purposes may be segmented, current, and relevant for a particular purpose. Consequently, the cost information provided by the financial reporting system is of little value for cost management purposes.[1]

1 Why do organizations have management control systems?

In redesigning cost accounting systems, the general internal use of information and the specific application of information to manage costs are getting increased attention. This chapter discusses concepts and approaches to designing information systems that support the internal use of accounting and other information to manage costs. The perspective taken is that a cost management system is an integral part of an organization's overall management information and control systems. An emphasis is placed on the main factors that determine the structure and success of a cost management system, the factors that influence the design of such a system, and the elements that comprise the system.

The next section provides a broad introduction to management information and control systems. It offers a foundation and context for understanding the roles of the cost management system.

INTRODUCTION TO MANAGEMENT INFORMATION AND CONTROL SYSTEMS

2 What is a cost management system and what are its primary goals?

A cost management system is part of an overall management information and control system. Exhibit 2–2 illustrates the types of information needed in an organization

[1] Robin Cooper and Regine Slagmulder, "Strategic Cost Management: Introduction to Enterprise-wide Cost Management," *Management Accounting* (August 1998), p. 17.

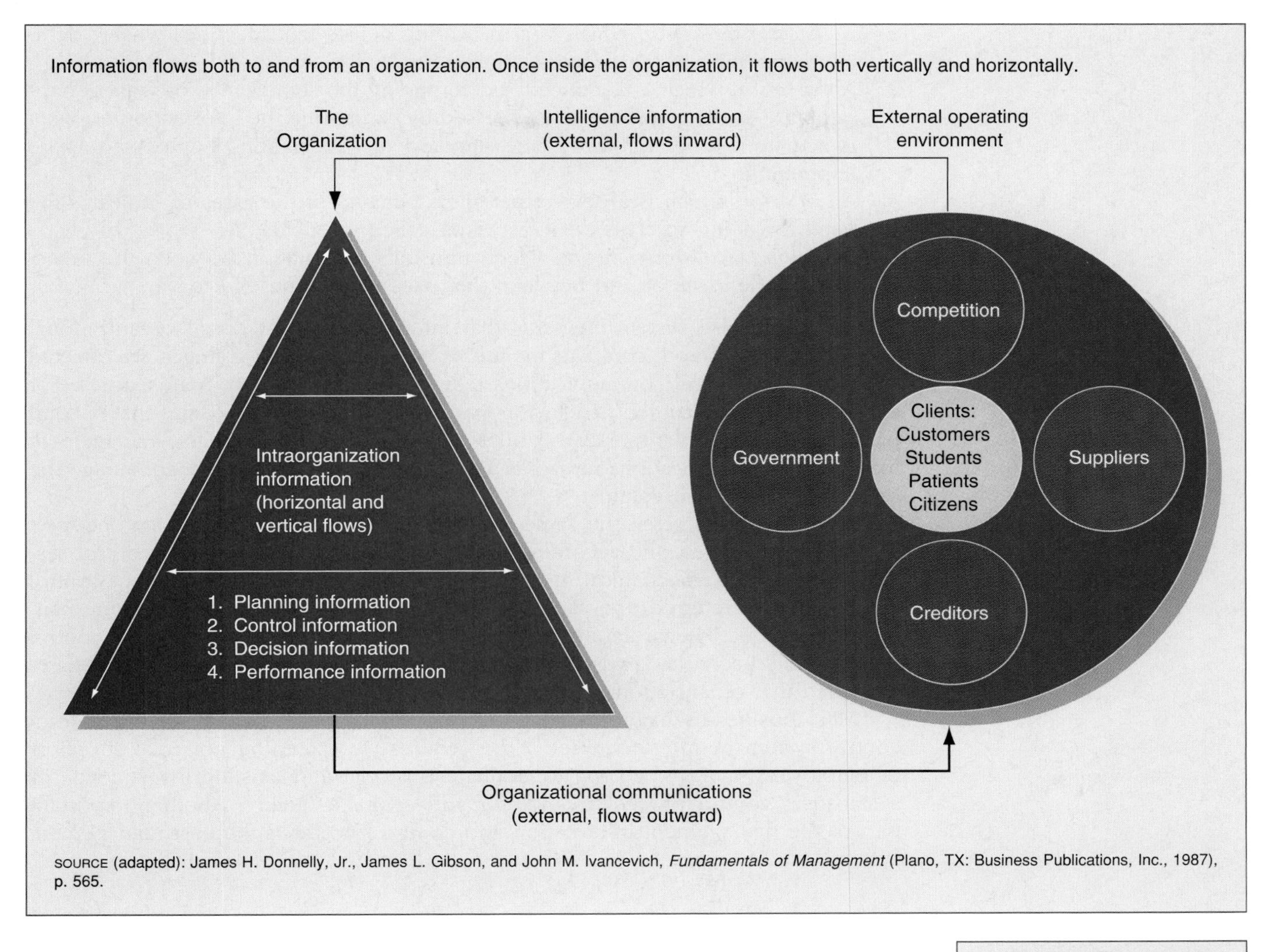

SOURCE (adapted): James H. Donnelly, Jr., James L. Gibson, and John M. Ivancevich, *Fundamentals of Management* (Plano, TX: Business Publications, Inc., 1987), p. 565.

EXHIBIT 2–2

Information Flows and Types of Information

for individuals to perform their managerial functions. The exhibit also demonstrates the demand from external parties for information from the firm. A **management information system (MIS)** is a structure of interrelated elements that collects, organizes, and communicates data to managers so they may plan, control, make decisions, and evaluate performance. A MIS emphasizes satisfying internal demands for information rather than external demands. In most modern organizations, the MIS is computerized for ease of access to information, reliability of input and processing, and ability to simulate outcomes of alternative situations.

management information system (MIS)

As Exhibit 2–2 illustrates, the accounting personnel are charged with the task of providing information to interested external parties such as creditors, the government (for mandatory reporting to the Internal Revenue Service, Securities and Exchange Commission, and other regulatory bodies), and suppliers, in regard to payments and purchases. External intelligence is also gathered from these parties as well as from competitors. Managers use internally and externally generated information to govern their organizations.

Because one of the managerial functions requiring information is control, the MIS is part of the **management control system (MCS)**. As illustrated in Exhibit 2–3, a control system has the following four primary components:

management control system (MCS)

1. A *detector* or *sensor*, which is a measuring device that identifies what is actually happening in the process being controlled.
2. An *assessor*, which is a device for determining the significance of what is happening. Usually, significance is assessed by comparing the information on what is actually happening with some standard or expectation of what should be happening.
3. An *effector*, which is a device that alters behavior if the assessor indicates the need for doing so. This device is often called "feedback."
4. A *communications network*, which transmits information between the detector and the assessor and between the assessor and the effector.[2]

It is through these system elements that information about actual organizational ocurrences is gathered, comparisons are made against plans, changes are effected when necessary, and communications take place among appropriate parties. For example, source documents (detectors) gather information about sales that is compared to the budgets (assessor). If sales revenues are below budget, management may issue (communications network) a variance report (effector) to encourage the sales staff to increase volume.

However, even given the same information, different managers may interpret it differently and respond accordingly. In this respect, a management control system is not merely mechanical, it requires judgment. Thus, a management control system may be referred to as a black box: an operation whose exact nature cannot be observed.[3] Regardless of the specific actions taken, a management control system should serve to guide organizations in designing and implementing strategies such that organizational goals and objectives are achieved.

Most businesses have a variety of control systems in place. For example, a control system may reflect a set of procedures for screening potential suppliers or employees, a set of criteria to evaluate potential and existing investments, or a statistical control process to monitor and evaluate quality. Another important part of the management information and control systems is the cost management system.

EXHIBIT 2-3

Elements of a Control System

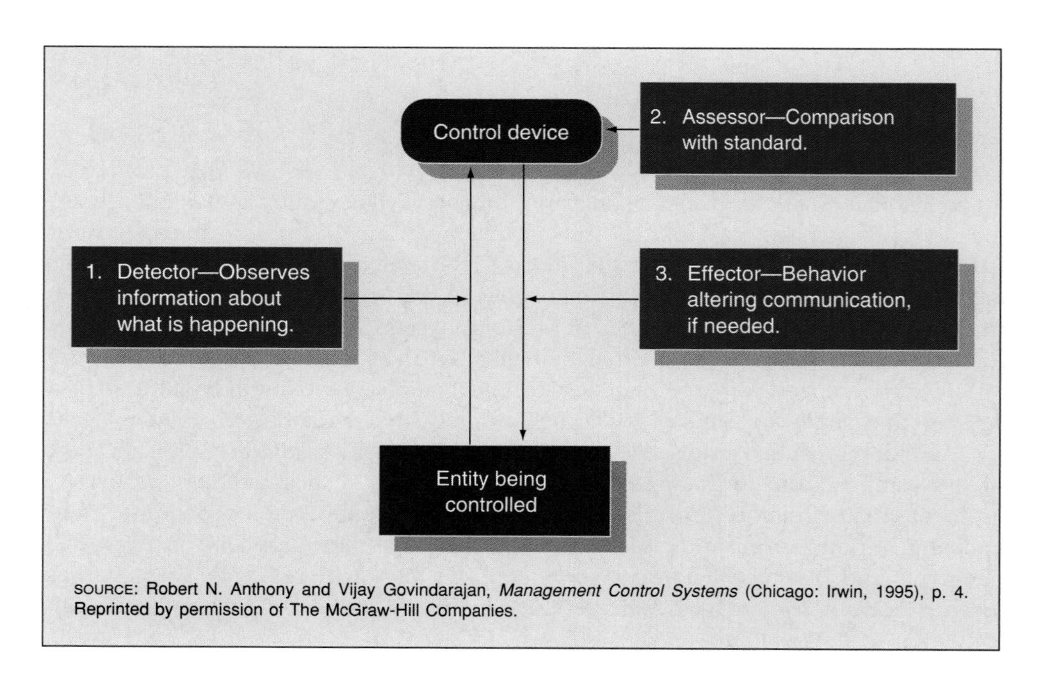

SOURCE: Robert N. Anthony and Vijay Govindarajan, *Management Control Systems* (Chicago: Irwin, 1995), p. 4. Reprinted by permission of The McGraw-Hill Companies.

[2] Robert N. Anthony and Vijay Govindarajan, *Management Control Systems* (Chicago: Irwin, 1995), p. 3.
[3] Ibid., p. 6.

DEFINING A COST MANAGEMENT SYSTEM

3

What major factors influence the design of a cost management system?

cost management system (CMS)

A **cost management system (CMS)** consists of a set of formal methods developed for planning and controlling an organization's cost-generating activities relative to its short-term objectives and long-term strategies. Business entities face two major challenges: achieving profitability in the short run and maintaining a competitive position in the long run. An effective cost management system must provide managers the information needed to meet both of these challenges.

Exhibit 2–4 summarizes the differences in the information requirements for organizational success in the short run and long run. The short-run requirement is that revenues exceed costs—the organization must make efficient use of its resources relative to the revenues that are generated. Specific cost information is needed and must be delivered in a timely fashion to an individual who is in a position to influence the cost. Short-run information requirements are often described as relating to operational management.

Meeting the long-run objective, survival, depends on acquiring the right inputs from the right suppliers, selling the right mix of products to the right customers, and using the most appropriate channels of distribution. These decisions require only periodic information that is reasonably accurate. Long-run information requirements are often described as relating to strategic management.

The information generated from the CMS should benefit all functional areas of the entity. Thus, the system should integrate the areas shown in Exhibit 2–5 and should "improve the quality, content, relevance, and timing of cost information that managers use for short-term and long-term decision making."[4]

cost driver

Crossing all functional areas, a cost management system can be viewed as having six primary goals: (1) develop reasonably accurate product costs, especially through the use of **cost drivers** (activities that have direct cause-and-effect relationships with costs); (2) assess product/service life-cycle performance; (3) improve understanding of processes and activities; (4) control costs; (5) measure performance; and (6) allow the pursuit of organizational strategies.

First and foremost, a CMS should provide the means to develop accurate product or service costs. This requires that the system be designed to use cost driver information to trace costs to products and services. The system does not have to be the most accurate, but it should match benefits of additional accuracy with expenses of achieving additional accuracy. Traceability has been made easier by improved information technology, including bar coding.

EXHIBIT 2–4

Dual Focus of Cost Management System

	Short Run	Long Run
Objective	Organizational efficiency	Survival
Focus	Specific costs: • manufacturing • service • marketing • administration	Cost categories: • customers • suppliers • products • distribution channels
Important characteristics of information	Timely Accurate Highly specific Short-term	Periodic Reasonably accurate Broad focus Long-term

SOURCE: Adapted from: Robin Cooper and Regine Slagmulder, "Operational Improvement and Strategic Costing," *Management Accounting* (September 1998), pp. 12–13.

[4] Steven C. Schnoebelen, "Integrating an Advanced Cost Management System into Operating Systems (Part 2)," *Journal of Cost Management* (Spring 1993), p. 60.

EXHIBIT 2-5

An Integrated Cost Management System

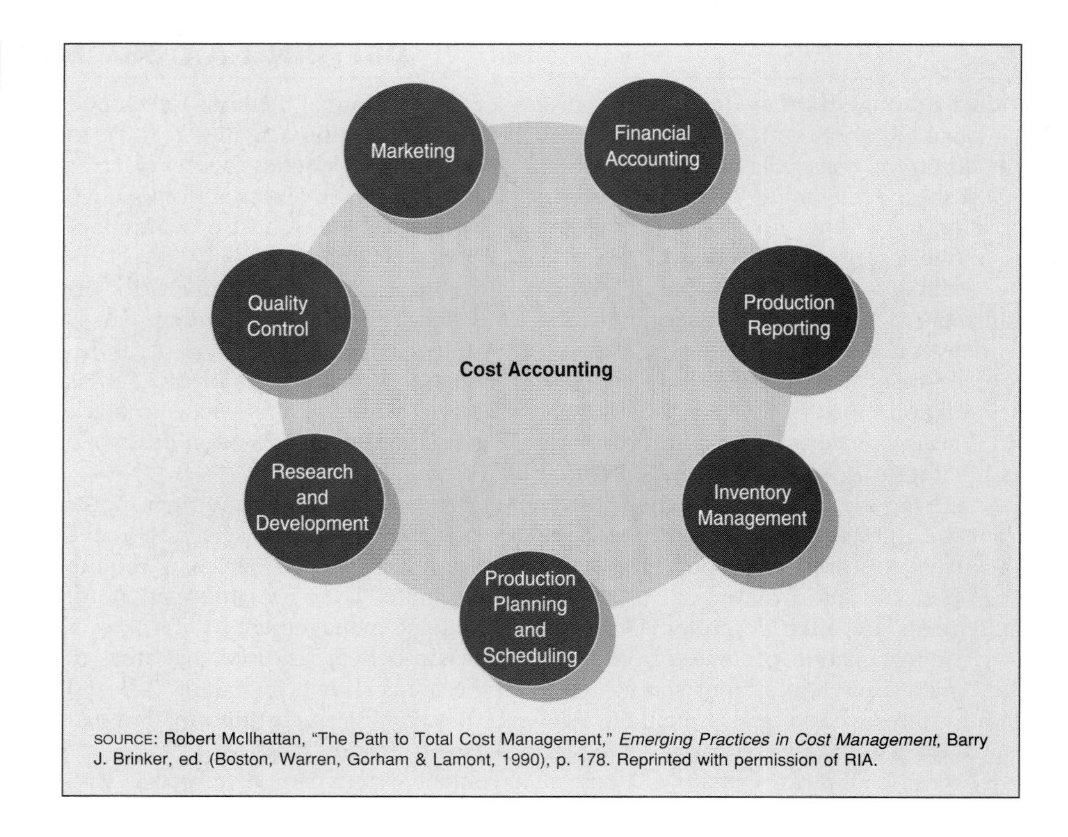

SOURCE: Robert McIlhattan, "The Path to Total Cost Management," *Emerging Practices in Cost Management*, Barry J. Brinker, ed. (Boston, Warren, Gorham & Lamont, 1990), p. 178. Reprinted with permission of RIA.

The product/service costs generated by the cost management system are the input to managerial processes. These costs are used to plan, prepare financial statements, assess individual product/service profitability and period profitability, establish prices for cost-plus contracts, and create a basis for performance measurements. If the input costs generated by the CMS are not reasonably accurate, the output of the preceding processes will be inappropriate for control and decision-making purposes.

Although product/service profitability may be calculated periodically as a requirement for external reporting, the financial accounting system does not reflect life-cycle information. The cost management system should provide information about the life-cycle performance of a product or service. Without life-cycle information, managers will not have a basis to relate costs incurred in one stage of the life cycle to costs and profitability of other stages. For example, managers may not recognize that strong investment in the development and design stage could provide significant rewards in later stages by minimizing costs of engineering changes and potential quality-related costs. Further, if development/design cost is not traced to the related product or service, managers may not be able to recognize organizational investment "disasters."

A cost management system should help managers comprehend business processes and organizational activities. Only by understanding how an activity is accomplished and the reasons for cost incurrence can managers make cost-beneficial improvements in the production and processing systems. Managers of a company desiring to implement new technology or production systems must recognize what costs and benefits will flow from such actions; these assessments can be made only if the managers understand how the processes and activities will differ after the change.

The original purpose of a cost accounting system was to control costs. This is still an important function of cost management systems given the current global competitive environment. A cost can be controlled only when the related activity

Financial accounting requires that research and development costs be expensed when incurred. However, because these costs are essential to any resulting product, a cost management system would trace them to that product as part of life-cycle costing.

is monitored, the cost driver is known, and the information is available. For example, if units are spoiled in a process, the CMS should provide information on spoilage quantity and cost rather than "burying" that information in other cost categories. Additionally, the cost management system should allow managers to understand the process so that the underlying causes of the spoilage can be determined. Armed with this information, managers can compare the costs of fixing the process with the benefits to be provided.

The information generated from a cost management system should help managers measure and evaluate performance. The measurements may be used to evaluate human or equipment performance or to evaluate future investment opportunities. As indicated in the accompanying News Note, one of the critical decisions managers must make involves trade-offs between long-run strategic benefits and short-run operational benefits.

GENERAL BUSINESS **NEWS NOTE**

A Little Pain Now for a (Potential) Big Gain Later

Amazon.com, Inc., posted a $138 million net loss for the second quarter of 1999 and warned that future results would be affected by heavy spending on bigger warehouses. It followed this up with the assertion that three new strategic initiatives—on-line auctions, toy sales, and electronic sales—were off to brisk starts.

The latest results mark yet another quarter in which the Seattle-based on-line merchant has pursued brand building and rapid revenue growth at the expense of near-term profitability. For the quarter, revenue nearly tripled to $314.4 million from the year-earlier $116 million. Amazon noted that total customer accounts grew to 10.7 million as of June 30, up 2.3 million from the March 31 tally. However, even with the huge growth in revenues, the loss posted for the second quarter exceeded the total revenues generated in the same quarter for the prior year.

In a conference call with investors, CEO Jeff Bezos cautioned: "We're new to these businesses. I can guarantee you we won't operate as efficiently in the near term as we would like." That means ordering more inventory than needed and building warehouses before they are fully needed. That can affect profit margins, according to Bezos, but he defended it as the right choice for Amazon's long-term growth.

SOURCE: George Anders, "Amazon Posts $138 Million Loss but Sales Surge," *The Wall Street Journal* (July 22, 1999), p. B6. Permission conveyed through the Copyright Clearance Center.

Lastly, to maintain a competitive position in an industry, a firm must generate the information necessary to define and implement its organizational strategies. As discussed in Chapter 1, strategy is the link between an organization's goals and objectives and the operational activities executed by the organization. In the current global market, firms must be certain that such a linkage exists. Information provided by a CMS enables managers to perform strategic analyses on issues such as determining core competencies and organizational constraints from a cost-benefit perspective and assessing the positive and negative financial and nonfinancial factors of strategic and operational plans. The News Note about Amazon.com illustrates how managers must consider trade-offs between the benefits of incurring costs for short-term and long-term benefits. Thus, the cost management system is essential to the generation of information for effective strategic resource management.

Because the world of business competition is dynamic, and creative managers are constantly devising new business practices and innovative approaches to competition, a cost management system must be dynamic. The following section discusses the issues affecting the design and ongoing development of cost management systems in a continually evolving organization.

DESIGNING A COST MANAGEMENT SYSTEM

In designing and revising a cost management system, managers and accountants must be attuned to the unique characteristics of their firms. A generic cost management system cannot be "pulled off the shelf" and applied to any organization. Each firm warrants a cost management system that is tailored to its situation. However, some overriding factors are important in designing a cost management system. These factors are depicted in Exhibit 2–6 and are described in this section.

Organizational Form, Structure, and Culture

4

Why should one consider organizational form, structure, and culture when designing a cost management system?

organizational form

An entity's legal nature reflects its **organizational form**. Selecting the organizational form is one of the most important decisions business owners make. This choice affects the costs of raising capital, operating the business (including taxation issues), and, possibly, litigating. The available organizational form alternatives have increased remarkably in recent years.

The most popular form for large, publicly traded businesses is the corporation. However, smaller businesses or cooperative ventures between large businesses also use general partnerships, limited partnerships, limited liability partnerships (LLPs), and limited liability companies (LLCs). These latter two forms have recently emerged due to new federal, state, and international legislation. Both the LLP and LLC provide more protection for a partner's personal assets than a general partnership in the event of litigation that leads to firm liquidation. Accordingly, LLPs and LLCs may offer better control for legal costs than general partnerships.

Organizational form also helps determine who has the statutory authority to make decisions for the firm. In a general partnership, all partners are allowed to make business decisions as a mere incidence of ownership. Alternatively, in a corporation, individual shareholders must act through a board of directors who, in turn, typically rely on professional managers. This ability to "centralize" authority is regarded as one of the primary advantages of the corporate organizational form and, to some extent, is available in limited partnerships, LLPs, and LLCs.

Once the organizational form is selected, top managers are responsible for creating a structure that is best suited to achieving the firm's goals and objectives. Organizational structure, introduced in Chapter 1, refers to how authority and responsibility for decision making are distributed in the entity.[5] Top managers make

[5] Organizational structure is discussed in detail in Chapter 1 and later in this chapter.

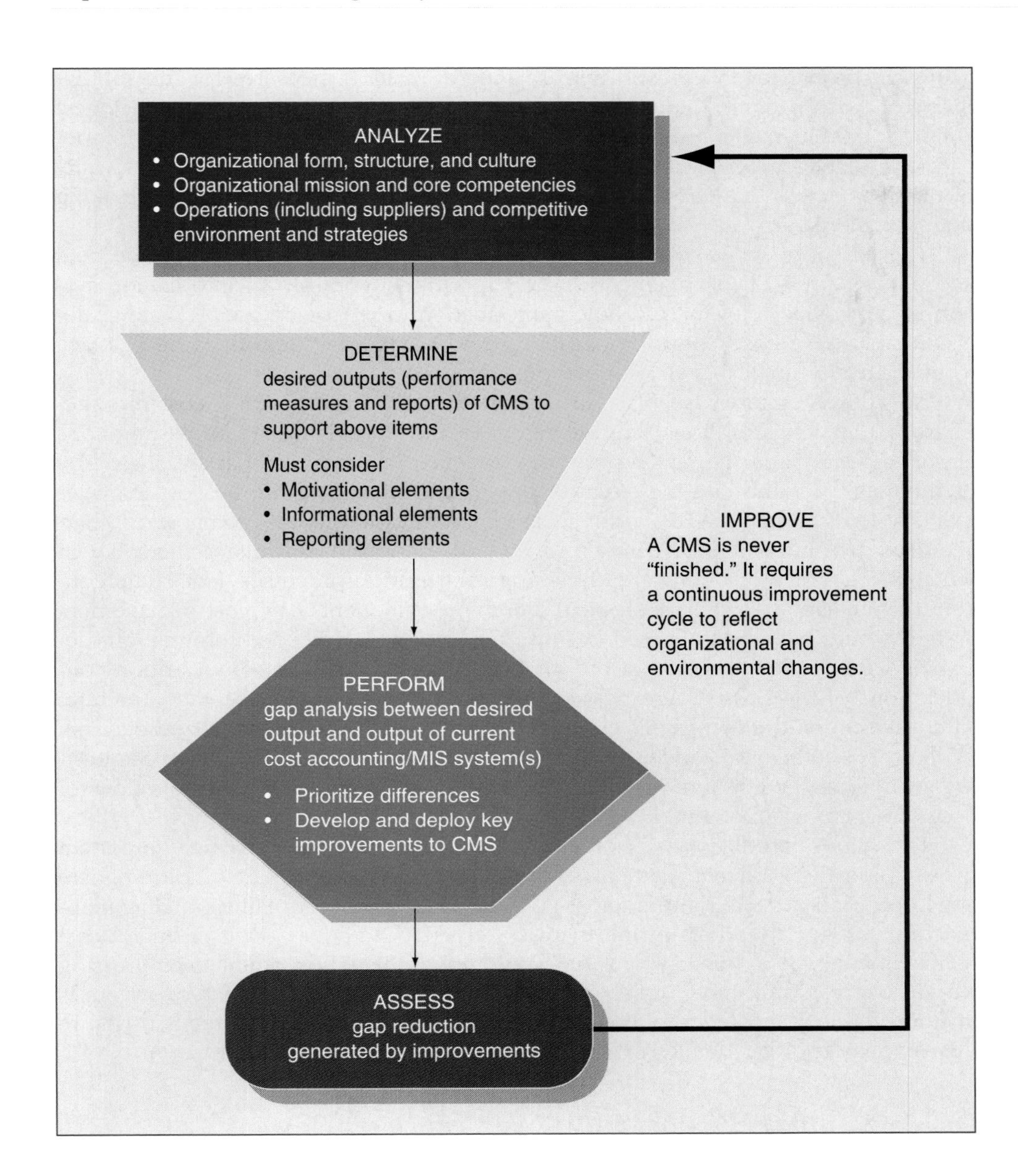

EXHIBIT 2-6

Design of a Cost Management System

judgments about how to organize subunits and the extent to which authority will be decentralized. Although the current competitive environment is conducive to strong decentralization, top managers usually retain authority over operations that can be performed more economically centrally because of economies of scale. For example, financing, personnel, and certain accounting functions may be maintained "at headquarters" rather than being delegated to organizational subunits.

In designing the organizational structure, top managers normally will try to group subunits either geographically or by similar missions or natural product clusters. These aggregation processes provide effective cost management because of proximity or similarity of the units under a single manager's control.

For example, relative to similarity of mission, Chapter 1 introduced three generic missions (build, harvest, and hold) for business subunits. Subunits pursuing a "build" mission are using more cash than they are generating. Such subunits are investing cash with an expectation of future returns. At the other extreme, subunits pursuing a "harvest" mission are expected to generate excess cash and have a much shorter investment horizon. If one manager were responsible for subunits that represented both build and harvest missions, it would be difficult for top management to design proper incentives and performance evaluation measures for the subunit manager or to evaluate his or her cost management effectiveness and efficiency. Different cost management tools are used for different subunit missions. If a specific cost management tool is to be applied to an entire subunit but there is a mix of missions across that subunit's components, there is greater potential for making poor decisions.

The extent to which managers decentralize also determines who will be held accountable for cost management and organizational control. An information system must provide relevant and timely information to persons who are making decisions that have cost control implications, and a control system must be in place to evaluate the quality of those decisions.

An entity's culture also plays an important role in setting up a cost management system. Organizational culture refers to the underlying set of assumptions about the entity and the goals, processes, practices, and values that are shared by its members. To illustrate the effect of organizational culture on the cost management system, consider AT&T prior to its divestiture. It was an organization characterized by "bureaucracy, centralized control, nepotism, a welfare mentality in which workers were 'taken care of,' strong socialization processes, [and] little concern for efficiency. . . ."[6] In such a culture, the requirements of a cost management system would have been limited because few individuals needed information, decisions were made at the top of the organization, and cost control was not a consideration because costs were passed on to customers through the rate structure. After divestiture, the company's culture changed to embrace decentralized decision making, cost efficiency, and individual responsibility and accountability. Supporting such a changed culture requires different types, quantities, and distributions of cost management information.

http://www.att.com

The values-based aspects of organizational culture are also extremely important in assessing the cost management system. For example, one part of Birmingham Steel Corporation's mission statement is "to be the lowest-cost, highest-quality manufacturer of steel products in the markets served."[7] Without a well designed cost management system, Birmingham Steel could not evaluate how well it is progressing toward the accomplishment of that mission. Thus, the cost management system is instrumental in providing a foundation for companies with an organizational culture that emphasizes total quality management.

http://www.birsteel.com

Organizational Mission and Core Competencies

Knowledge of the organization's mission and core competencies is a key consideration in the design of a cost management system. The mission provides a long-term goal toward which the organization wishes to move. If the mission that the entity wishes to achieve is unknown, it does not matter what information is generated by the cost management system—or any other information system!

As discussed in Chapter 1, in pursuing the business mission, companies may avoid or confront competition. For example, companies may try to avoid competition by attempting to be more adept in some way than other entities. The generic paths a company may take to avoid competition include differentiation and cost leadership.[8]

In the current global environment, it is often difficult to maintain a competitive advantage under either a differentiation or cost leadership strategy. Competitors are becoming skilled at duplicating the specific competencies that gave rise to the original competitive advantage. For many companies, the key to success in the future may be to confront competition by identifying and exploiting temporary

[6] Thomas S. Bateman and Scott A. Snell, *Management Building Competitive Advantage* (Chicago: Irwin, 1996), p. 268.
[7] Birmingham Steel Corporation, *1995 Annual Report*, p. 1.
[8] Michael Porter, *Competitive Advantage: Creating and Sustaining Superior Performance* (New York: Free Press, 1985), p. 17.

opportunities for advantage. In a confrontation strategy, companies "still try to differentiate their products by introducing new features, or try to develop a price leadership position by dropping prices, . . . [but, the companies] assume that their competitors will rapidly bring out products that are equivalent and match any price changes."[9] Although it may be necessary, a confrontation strategy is, by its very nature, less profitable for companies than differentiation or cost leadership.

Exhibit 2–7 shows how the strategy of the firm, together with the life-cycle stages of products, determines what a firm must do well to be successful at any point in time. This exhibit illustrates how the information requirements of managers change over time as the life cycle evolves and, thus, are dependent upon the strategy being pursued.

The globalization of markets has created, in many industries, competition among equals. Today, many firms are capable of delivering products and services that are

EXHIBIT 2–7

Strategy and Life-Cycle Stage Determine Critical Organizational Activities

Product Strategy	LIFE-CYCLE STAGE			
	Introduction	Growth	Maturity	Decline
Differentiation				
	Product R&D and design are critical. Establish presence in market and product distinctiveness.	Strengthen distinctive product competencies and formalize product support structure. Marketing is critical.	Exploit competitive advantage. Maintain heavy product marketing emphasis.	Divest/spin off operations early. Relate service to new products.
Cost Leadership				
	Process R&D and design are critical. Manage high costs present with low volume.	Quickly determine product cost structure and viability. Establish or increase market share and/or distribution channels.	Make no major product changes. Standardization is critical.	Manage, reduce, and control costs. Reduce capacity and evaluate low-cost alternatives (e.g., make, outsource, shutdown).
Confrontation				
	Minimize product development time. Design to facilitate process flexibility.	Establish market leadership and reliability. Provide distribution for quick delivery.	Refine product manufacturability and process reliability. Increase and innovate distribution efforts.	Develop existing distribution network for new products. Emphasize exceptional service options.

SOURCE: B. Douglas Clinton and Aaron H. Graves, "Product Value Analysis: Strategic Analysis Over the Entire Product Life Cycle," *Journal of Cost Management* (May/June 1999), p. 23. © 1999 Warren Gorham & Lamont. Reprinted with permission of RIA.

[9] Robin Cooper, *When Lean Enterprises Collide* (Boston: Harvard Business School Press, 1995), p. 11.

http://www.ingersoll-rand.com
http://www.csfb.com

qualitatively and functionally equivalent. Without being able to distinguish one competitor's products from those of another based on quality or functionality, the consumer's focus switches to price. In turn, price-based competition changes the internal focus to costs. One industry currently particularly affected by price-based competition is communication. The accompanying News Note illustrates the shift to an intensive internal focus on costs.

Clarification of mission can be served by identifying the organization's core competencies, which are dimensions of operations that are key to an organization's survival. Most organizations would consider timeliness, quality, customer service, efficiency and cost control, and responsiveness to change as five critical competencies. Once managers have gained consensus on an entity's core competencies, the cost management system can be designed to (1) gather information related to measurement of those items and (2) generate output about those competencies in forms that are useful to interested parties.

5

How do the internal and external operating environments impact the cost management system?

Competitive Environment and Strategies

cost structure

Once the organizational "big picture" has been established, managers can assess internal specifics related to the design of a cost management system. A primary consideration is the firm's cost structure. Traditionally, **cost structure** has been defined in terms of how costs change relative to changes in production or sales volume.

As firms have become increasingly dependent on automated technology, it has become more difficult to control costs through sales and production. Many technology costs are associated with plant, equipment, and infrastructure investments that provide the capacity to produce goods and services. Higher proportions of these costs exist in industries that depend on technology for competing on the bases of quality and price. Manufacturing and service firms have aggressively adopted advanced technology. The data shown in Exhibit 2–8 reveal the effects of technology on the efficiency of particular industries.[10] Sales per employee traditionally has been viewed as a measure of organizational productivity. Technology acquisition and employee training are now regarded as principal sources of productivity improvement.

NEWS NOTE  GENERAL BUSINESS

How Do You Raise Profits without Raising Prices?

At a town meeting with employees early in 1999, AT&T Corp.'s chief financial officer, Daniel E. Somers, was asked if the company was through with its battle to cut costs. "No, we're not," Somers recalls answering. "We think of costs the way we used to think of price. It's something we're constantly working on."

It's not just high-tech companies fighting this battle. Ingersoll-Rand Co., of Woodcliff Lake, N.J., saw its average selling price for products from door locks to industrial pumps increase just under 1 percent in 1998, after no increase in 1997. "In all of our business plans, we really don't count on price to increase our profits," said David W. Devonshire, Ingersoll-Rand's chief financial officer. "We really rely on what we're doing on the cost side."

"Raising prices was just an easier way of making money than all of the other things you could think of," says Roseanne M. Cahn, economist at Credit Suisse First Boston. "This is now getting into manager's psyches, that you do not have pricing power and guess what, you have to do something else to make money."

SOURCE: Darren McDermott, "Cost-Consciousness Beats 'Pricing Power,'" *The Wall Street Journal* (May 3, 1999), p. A1. Permission conveyed through the Copyright Clearance Center.

[10] These data are not adjusted for inflation.

EXHIBIT 2-8

Average Sales (in thousands) per Employee by Industry

Industry	YEAR 1978	1998	Percentage Increase
Agriculture and forestry	$ 37	$100	270%
Air transportation	67	166	248%
Computers	47	259	551%
Grocery stores	85	143	168%
Hotels and motels	21	51	243%
Mining	80	102	128%
Petroleum refining	265	710	268%
Pharmaceuticals	66	270	409%
Plastics	59	141	239%
Restaurants	40	44	110%
Steel works	85	327	385%
Telephone and telegraph	68	208	306%
Textiles	54	127	235%
Trucking	66	157	238%

SOURCE: COMPUSTAT (an electronic financial data source published by Standard and Poors).

The cost management implications of this shift in cost structure are significant. Most importantly, because most technology costs are not susceptible to short-run control, cost management efforts are increasingly directed toward the longer term. Also, managing costs is increasingly a matter of capacity management: high capacity utilization (if accompanied by high sales volumes) allows a firm to reduce its per-unit costs in pursuing a cost leadership strategy.

A second implication of the changing cost structure is the firm's flexibility to respond to changing short-term conditions. As the proportion of costs relating to technology investment increases, a firm has less flexibility to take short-term actions that would reduce costs with no long-term adverse consequences.[11]

In pursuing either a differentiation or cost leadership strategy, the management of high technology costs requires beating competitors to the market with new products. The importance of timeliness is illustrated in the following quote:

> *There are numerous innovations which have maximized a market window to achieve phenomenal success—Polaroid is a case in point. Equally, there have been numerous high-quality products that arrived too late, either because the market had been acquired by a competitor, or because the need no longer existed. By the time Head began to produce oversized tennis racquets, Prince had cornered the market.*[12]

http://www.polaroid.com

Being first to market may allow a company to set a price that leads to a large market share, which, in turn, may lead to an industry position of cost leader. Alternatively, the leading edge company may set a product price that provides a substantial per-unit profit for all sales generated before competitors are able to offer alternative products. Rapid time-to-market requires fast development of new products and services.

Time-to-market is critical in the high-tech industry because profitability depends on selling an adequate number of units at an acceptable price. Because the price per unit has been falling steadily for years, getting a new product to the market late can be disastrous. The risk is described by Richard O'Brien, an economist for Hewlett-Packard in the following quote:[13]

http://hewlett-packard.com

[11] Many of the new fixed costs would be regarded as "committed" rather than "discretionary." See Chapter 15 for additional details.

[12] Simon Cooper, "There Is No Point Putting a Wind Spoiler on the Back of a Turtle" *CMA Magazine* (February 1996), p. 4.

[13] Darren McDermott, "Cost Consciousness Beats 'Pricing Power,'" *The Wall Street Journal* (May 3, 1999), p. A1.

"Product life cycles keep shrinking. If you can't get to market on time, you will have missed your chance because the price point will have moved."

Reducing time-to-market is one way a company can cut costs. Exhibit 2–9 lists other ways, most of which are associated with the earlier stages of the product life cycle. Thus, as has been previously mentioned, product profitability is largely determined by an effective design and development process.

Getting products to market quickly and profitably requires a compromise between the advantages of product innovation and superior product design. Rapid time-to-market may mean that a firm incurs costs associated with design flaws (such as the costs of engineering changes) that could have been avoided if more time had been allowed for the product's development. Also, if a flawed product is marketed, costs will likely be incurred for returns, warranty work, or customer "bad will" regarding the firm's reputation for product quality.

Time-to-market is important because of the competitive advantages it offers and because of compressed product life cycles. Both of these factors have a significant effect on cost management systems, as discussed in the accompanying News Note.

http://www.honda.com

Another aspect of an organization's operating environment is supplier relations. Many companies that have formed strategic alliances with suppliers have found such relationships to be effective cost control mechanisms. For example, by involving suppliers early in the design and development stage of new products, a better design for manufacturability will be achieved and the likelihood of meeting cost targets will be improved. Additionally, if information systems of customers and suppliers are linked electronically, the capabilities and functions of systems must be considered in designing the CMS.

Another operating environment consideration in the design of a cost management system is the need to integrate the organization's current information systems. The "feeder" systems (such as payroll, inventory valuation, budgeting, and costing) that are in place should be evaluated to answer the following questions:

- What data are being gathered and in what form?
- What outputs are being generated and in what form?
- How do the current systems interact with one another and how effective are those interactions?

EXHIBIT 2–9

Actions to Substantially Reduce Product Costs

- Develop new production processes
- Capture learning curve and experience effects
- Increase capacity utilization
- Use focused factory arrangement
  - — reduces coordination costs
- Design for manufacturability
  - — reduces assembly time
  - — reduces training costs
  - — reduces warranty costs
  - — reduces required number of spare parts
- Design for logistical support
- Design for reliability
- Design for maintainability
- Adopt advanced manufacturing technologies
  - — reduces inventory levels
  - — reduces required production floor space
  - — reduces defects, rework and quality costs

SOURCE: Adapted from Gerald I. Susman, "Product Life Cycle Management," *Journal of Cost Management* (Summer 1989), pp. 8–22.

INTERNATIONAL **NEWS NOTE**

Can a David Survive Among the Goliaths?

Honda Motor Co.'s ability to shave more savings from its manufacturing operations will be one of the keys to the company's drive to prove that an automaker doesn't have to be huge to survive, says the company's president.

Honda's go-it-alone strategy challenges industry wisdom that bigger is better and that a manufacturing scale of at least four million vehicles a year is needed to defray the cost of developing technologies such as environmentally friendly engines. Instead, Honda wants to remain small but double its efficiency level.

"Who says you have to be a member of the four million club to survive?" asks Honda's president, Hiroyuki Yoshino. "If you spend small, then you don't have to sell a lot to be profitable."

Yoshino says staying ahead of the competition to come up with cleaner gasoline engines and zero-emission "green car" power sources, such as fuel cells, is vital to Honda's survival. But equally important, he says, will be the ability to design cars and standardize manufacturing tools to eliminate costly retooling for model changeovers and new-product launches, and thus give Honda the agility and flexibility to meet sudden shifts in consumer tastes.

The company is experimenting with new manufacturing methods at its Canadian assembly line for minivans and introducing some of those methods at its facilities in Japan. In the next several years, Honda "should become capable of halving the time and cost for a new-model introduction," asserts Masaki Iwai, Honda's senior managing director, which he believes would lower the bar for turning a profit.

SOURCE: Norihiko Shirouzu, "Honda Bucks Industry Wisdom, Aiming to Be Small and Efficient," *The Wall Street Journal* (July 9, 1999), p. A12. Permission conveyed through the Copyright Clearance Center.

- Is the current chart of accounts appropriate for the cost management information desired?
- What significant information issues (such as yield, spoilage, and cycle time) are not currently being addressed by the information system, and could those issues be integrated into the current feeder systems?

With knowledge of the preceding information, management must analyze the cost-benefit trade-offs that relate to the design of the cost management system. As the costs of gathering, processing, and communicating information decrease, or as the quantity and intensity of competition increase, more sophisticated cost management systems are required. Additionally, as companies focus on customer satisfaction and expand their product or service offerings, more sophisticated cost management systems are needed. In these conditions, the generation of "better" cost information is essential to long-run organizational survival and short-run profitability.

Even with appropriate information systems in place, there is no guarantee that managers will make decisions consistent with organizational strategies. Proper incentives and reporting systems must be incorporated into the CMS for managers to make appropriate decisions. This is the subject of the following section.

ELEMENTS OF A COST MANAGEMENT SYSTEM

6

What three groups of elements affect the design of a cost management system and how are these elements used?

A cost management system is composed of three primary elements: motivational elements, information elements, and reporting elements. These elements are detailed in Exhibit 2–10. The elements as a whole must be internally consistent, and the individually selected elements must be consistent with the strategies and missions of the subunits. Different aspects of these elements may be used for different purposes. For example, numerous measures of performance can be specified, but only certain measures will be appropriate for specific purposes.

EXHIBIT 2–10

Cost Management System Elements

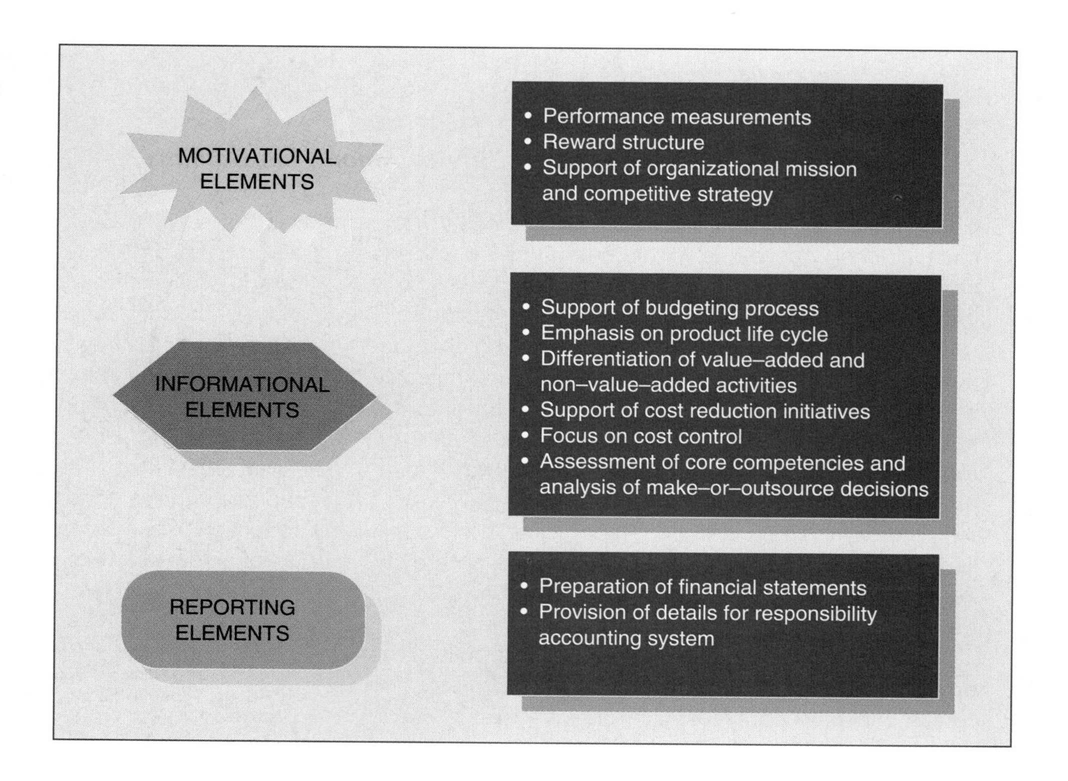

Motivational Elements

Performance measurements are chosen so as to be consistent with organizational goals and objectives and to "drive" managers toward designated achievements. These measurements, which are discussed in depth in Chapters 20 and 21, may be quantitative or nonquantitative, financial or nonfinancial, and short-term or long-term. For example, if a subunit is expected to generate a specified dollar amount of profit for the year, the performance measure has been set to be quantitative, financial, and short-term. A longer-term performance measure might be an average increase in profit or change in stock price over a five-to-ten-year period.

Today, performance measures and rewards are designed not only to motivate employees and managers to act in the best interest of the organization but also to help recruit and retain qualified employees. These roles are illustrated in the accompanying News Note.

The performance measurement system should encourage managers to act in the best interest of the organization and its subunits and to support organizational missions and competitive strategies. Once defined, the nature of the criteria used to measure performance should be linked to the organizational incentive system because, as implied in the News Note, "you get what you measure." This linkage sends the message to managers that they will be rewarded in line with the quality of their organizational and subunit decisions and, thereby, their contributions to achieving the organizational missions.

http://www.aon.com

In addition to performance measures, different forms of rewards have different incentive effects and can reflect different time orientations. In general, longer-term incentives encourage managers to be more long-term oriented in their decisions, while short-term incentives encourage managers to be focused on the near future.

To illustrate, cash is the most obvious reward for short-term performance. All managers receive some compensation in cash for paying living expenses. However, once a manager receives a cash reward, its value is not dependent on future performance. In contrast, a stock option that is not exercisable until a future time

GENERAL BUSINESS  NEWS NOTE

What's in It for Me?

Aon Consulting's 1998 America at Work Survey of 1,800 employees measures critical factors that employees weigh when making employment decisions. Results of the survey support both sides of the retention equation. On the intrinsic or environmental side, opportunities for learning and growth top the list of reasons for employees to stay with their employers. On the extrinsic or more tangible side, meaningful rewards and recognition of performance are highly correlated with employee commitment. In fact, salary and benefits are viewed as two of the most important factors affecting employment decisions.

Traditionally, compensation systems have been designed to attract, retain, motivate, and reward employees by being externally competitive and internally equitable. Unquestionably, these are noble intentions. However, the actual plan design that's in place at many organizations was originally conceived in the 1950s, when the world of work looked very different from what it does today. It was a time when fairness was defined as "sameness," when employment was for a lifetime, and when following procedure was far more critical to success than innovation and gaining competitive advantage.

Today, compensation systems must support the mission and culture of the organization and communicate to employees what is important, why they are important, and what their role is in ensuring the ongoing viability of the organization. Compensation systems are incredibly powerful communication tools to apply to a workforce looking for answers to the fundamental questions, "Why am I here?" "What am I contributing?" and "How (well) am I being recognized for my contribution?" Basically, if employees feel good about the answers to those questions, they stay; if they don't, they go.

SOURCE: Valerie L. Williams and Jennifer E. Sunderland, "New Pay Programs Boost Retention," *Workforce* (May 1999), pp. 36–40. Permission conveyed through the Copyright Clearance Center.

provides a manager with an incentive to be more concerned about long-term performance. The ultimate value of the stock option is determined in the future when the option is exercised, rather than on the date it is received. Thus, the option's value is related more to long-term than to short-term organizational performance.

Performance rewards for top management may consist of both short-term and long-term incentives. Normally, a major incentive is performance-based pay that is tied to the firm's stock price. The rewards for subunit managers should be based on the specific subunit's mission. Managers of subunits charged with a "build" mission should receive long-term incentives. These managers need to be concerned about long-term success and be willing to make short-term sacrifices for long-term gains.

Alternatively, managers of subunits charged with a "harvest" mission must be more oriented to the short term. These subunits are expected to squeeze out as much cash and profit as possible from their operations. Accordingly, incentives should be in place to encourage these managers to have a short-term focus in decision making.

profit sharing

Profit sharing refers to compensation that is contingent on the level of organizational profit generated. This type of pay is a powerful incentive and is now used in virtually every U.S. industry. Today's companies experiment with a variety of incentives as a "carrots" to induce employees and managers to act in the best interest of customers and shareholders. As indicated in the following News Note, not all of these efforts are successful.

http://www.knoll.de

Selection of performance measurements and the reward structure is important because managers evaluate decision alternatives based on how the outcomes may impact the selected performance (measurement and reward) criteria. Because higher performance equals a larger reward, the cost management system must have specified performance "yardsticks" and provide measurement information to the appropriate individuals for evaluation purposes. Performance measurement is meaningful only in a comparative or relative sense. Typically, current performance is assessed relative to past or expected performance or, as illustrated in the following News Note, relative to peers.

NEWS NOTE  ETHICS

Show Me the Money!

Dave Kerr knew his sales team's compensation plan just wasn't working the way it should. For one thing, star salespeople weren't bringing home substantially more money than the lowest performers. But even slower sellers, who were favored by the imbalance in the system, weren't really happy. "No one thought their quota was fair," says Kerr, director of strategic planning for Knoll Pharmaceuticals in Mount Olive, New Jersey. "We spent too much time setting, managing, and adjudicating complaints about the quotas—it was just a massive, unproductive effort every four months."

So in 1996 Kerr went to the extreme and dumped the quota system for all 600 of Knoll's field salespeople. Today, Knoll's incentive compensation plan is based on comparing performance of reps against that of their colleagues, so they're not selling in a vacuum. Here's how it works. Incentive money is put into a companywide pool that grows or shrinks with the company's earnings. Reps can earn a larger or smaller share of the pool depending on both the absolute volume growth and the percentage of volume growth for individual products. Relative payments are determined in advance. For example, the top seller might make three times the average; the lowest performing seller might earn nothing; and the average seller would make an average amount. "What makes the plan more fair," Kerr says, "is that employees are measured only against those with similar sales potential."

SOURCE: Tricia Campbell, "Quashing the Quota System," *Sales & Marketing Management* (July 1999), p. 89. Permission conveyed through the Copyright Clearance Center.

Informational Elements

The accounting function in an organization is expected to support managers in the areas of planning, controlling, decision making, and performance evaluation. These roles converge in a system designed for cost management. Relative to the planning role, the cost management system should provide a sound foundation for the financial budgeting process.

Budgets provide both a specification of expected achievement as well as a benchmark against which to compare actual performance. A CMS, like a traditional cost accounting system, should be able to provide the financial information needed for budget preparation. But, in addition, a well designed CMS will disclose the cost drivers for activities so that more useful simulations of alternative scenarios can be made. The same system can highlight any activities that have a poor cost-benefit relationship so that these activities can be reduced or eliminated. This helps reduce budget preparation time. "By reducing the length of the budgeting cycle and making the process more efficient, the informational benefit of semiannual or quarterly budgeting may become practical."[14]

As firms find it more difficult to maintain a competitive advantage, they must place greater emphasis on managing the product life cycle. In such an environment, firms often use innovative tools, many of which are discussed in later chapters, to provide information relevant to assessing their competitive positions. As discussed earlier in this chapter, most actions available to managers to control costs are concentrated in the earliest stages of the product life cycle. Accordingly, information relevant to managing costs must be focused on decisions made during those stages—that information will be provided by a well designed and integrated cost management system.

The life cycle of many products will become shorter as firms become more and more adept at duplicating their competitors' offerings. In the future, managers

[14] Steven C. Schnoebelen, "Integrating an Advanced Cost Management System Into Operating Systems (Part 2)," *Journal of Cost Management* (Spring 1993), p. 63.

will confront the fact that products will spend less time in the maturity stage of the product life cycle. In this competitive environment, firms will be forced to find ways to continue to squeeze out cash from their mature products to support development of new products. Additionally, the future will place greater emphasis on a firm's ability to adapt to changing competitive conditions. Flexibility will be an important organizational attribute and will cause managers to change the emphasis of control systems as shown in Exhibit 2–11.

To provide information relevant to product design and development, the accounting information system must be able to relate resource consumption and cost to alternative product and process designs. Computer simulation models are useful in relating products to activities.[15] In addition to focusing information on the front end of the product life cycle, the capital spending is becoming an increasingly important tool in cost management, especially relative to new technology acquisition decisions. Decisions made with regard to capital investments affect the future cost structure of firms and, hence, the extent to which short-term actions can effect a change in the level of total costs.

Lastly, the system should produce cost information with minimal distortions from improper or inaccurate allocations, or from improper exclusions. Improper exclusions usually relate to the influence of financial accounting, such as the mandate to expense product development or distribution costs. If the system minimizes these cost distortions, the cost assignments are more relevant for control purposes and for internal decision making.

The information required to support decisions depends on the unique situational factors of the firm and its subunits. The information system must enable the decision maker to evaluate how alternative decision choices would impact the items that are used to measure and evaluate the decision maker's performance.

Techniques such as relevant costing, quality cost management, job order and process costing, and cost-volume-profit analysis, discussed in later chapters, relate to the role of cost information in decision making. Many decisions involve comparing the benefit received from some course of action (such as serving a given customer) to the costs of the action (costs of providing services). Only if the cost data contain minimal distortion can managers make valid cost-benefit assessments.

EXHIBIT 2–11

Shift in Control Emphasis in Future Competitive Environment

	From		To
Strategic Focus	Achieving financial results: sales, costs, and profits	→	Achieving operational objectives: low cost, quality, sales mix, on-time delivery, and capacity usage
Product Sales Partnerships	Submitting bids and taking orders	→	Developing and creating sales opportunities
Budgeting	Developing annual plans	→	Ongoing planning and frequent budget revisions
Culture	Meeting project expectations	→	Learning and improving upon processes

SOURCE: Ralph E. Drtina and Gary A. Monetti, "Controlling Flexible Business Strategies," *Journal of Cost Management* (Fall 1995), pp. 42–49. © 1995 Warren Gorham & Lamont. Reprinted with permission of RIA.

[15] Using computer models is an element of process cost management. For more details, see "Process Cost Management," by Thomas G. Greenwood and James M. Reeve in the *Journal of Cost Management* (Winter 1994), pp. 4–19.

Reporting Elements

The reporting elements of a cost management system refer to methods of providing information to persons in evaluative roles. First and foremost, the CMS must be effective in generating fundamental financial statement information including inventory valuation and cost of sales information. This information is not necessarily the same as that being used for internal planning, control, decision making, or performance evaluation. But, if the feeder systems to the CMS have been appropriately integrated and the system itself designed to minimize distortions, there should be little difficulty generating an "external" product or service cost.

responsibility accounting system

In addition to financial statement valuations, the reporting elements of the cost management system must address internal needs of a **responsibility accounting system**. This system provides information to top management about the performance of an organizational subunit and its manager.[16] For each subunit, the responsibility accounting system separately tracks costs and, if appropriate, revenues.

Performance reports are useful only to the extent that the measured performance of a given manager or subunit can be compared to a meaningful baseline. The normal baseline is a measure of expected performance. Expected performance can be denoted in financial terms, such as budgetary figures, or in nonfinancial terms, such as throughput, customer satisfaction measures, lead time, capacity utilization, and research and development activities. By comparing expected and actual performance, top managers are able to determine which managers and subunits performed according to expectations and which exceeded or failed to meet expectations. Using this information that has been processed and formulated by the cost management system, top managers link decisions about managerial rewards to performance. Exhibit 2–12 demonstrates a typical performance measurement system that gathers data from four perspectives: internal, innovation, customer, and stockholder.

The movement toward decentralization has increased the importance of an effective reporting system. With decentralization, top managers must depend on the reporting system to keep all organizational subunits aligned with their subunit missions and organizational goals and objectives. A cost management system is not designed to "cut" costs. It exists to ensure that a satisfactory yield (revenue) is realized from the incurrence of costs. Accordingly, cost management begins with an understanding that different costs are incurred for different purposes. Some costs are incurred to yield immediate benefits; others are expected to yield benefits in the near or distant future.

EXHIBIT 2–12

Performance Evaluation from Multiple Perspectives

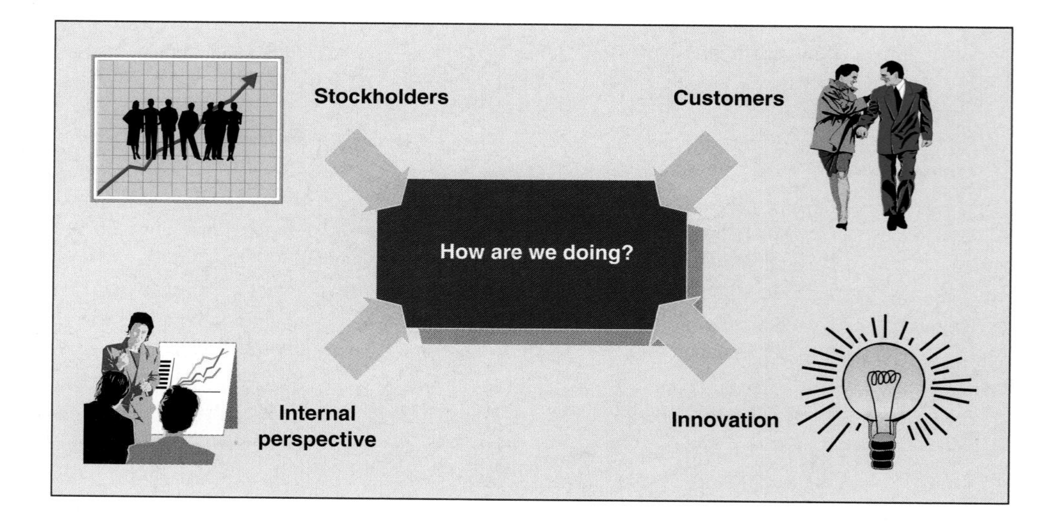

[16] Responsibility accounting concepts are discussed in detail in Chapters 18 through 21.

Only by linking costs to activities and activities to strategies can the yield on costs be understood. Thus, to achieve effective cost management, it is useful to start by sorting organizational activities according to their strategic roles. This logic suggests that organizational management is made easier by breaking down operations into subunits. By so doing, top managers can assign responsibility and accountability for distinct subunit missions to a particular manager. In turn, by creating the proper incentives for each subunit manager, top management will have set the stage for each subunit manager to act in the best interest of the overall organization. This linkage is the start of a process that focuses a specific subunit manager's attention on a set of costs and activities that uniquely relates to the subunit's organizational mission.

For subunit managers to effectively manage costs, each must be provided with relevant information. Because the nature and time horizon of decisions made by managers vary across subunits, each manager requires unique information. Accountants face the task of providing information to each subunit manager that is tailored to the particular context. In addition to information about decision alternatives, managers need to know how the alternatives are likely to impact their expected rewards.

The role of a reporting system is to compare benchmark performance to actual performance for each manager. On the basis of this comparison, the relative rewards of subunit managers are determined. Accordingly, this comparison is a key source of motivation for subunit managers to act in the best interest of the organization.

Optimal organizational performance is realized only if there is consistency for each subunit across the elements of motivation, information, and reporting. Managers of subunits with a "build" mission need information tailored to their competitive strategies and focused on the early stages of the product life cycle. Their incentives to manage costs need to be relatively long-term, and their reward structures should emphasize success in the areas of product development and design and market share growth. Alternatively, subunit managers of mature businesses need information that pertains more to short-term competition. Their reward and reporting structures should emphasize near-term profit and cash flow.

One of the evolving challenges in today's business environment is the management of activities across an entire supply chain. Competition is prevalent among supply or "value" chains as well as individual businesses. Thus, future financial specialists will develop only cost management systems that include activities not occurring within single firms but occurring within a supply chain and involving several firms.

Since most businesses have a CMS in place, most CMS design and implementation issues relate to modifications in cost management systems. The modification of existing systems is discussed next.

CMS IMPLEMENTATION

7

How is gap analysis used in the implementation of a cost management system?

Once the organization and its subunits have been structured and the elements of the cost management system determined, the current information system(s) should be evaluated. A gap analysis is necessary to compare the information that is needed to the information that is currently available, or to determine how well desired information outputs coincide with current outputs. Any difference represents a "gap" to be overcome.

In many situations, it is impossible to eliminate all system gaps in the short term, potentially because of software or hardware capability or availability. Methods of reducing or eliminating the gaps, including all related technical requirements and changes to existing feeder systems, should be specified in detail. These details should be expressed, qualitatively and quantitatively, in terms of costs and benefits.

In the event of limited resources, top management may then prioritize the differences as to which gap issues to address and in which order. As system implementation proceeds, management should assess the effectiveness of the improvements and determine the need for other improvements. Once the CMS has been established, previously identified gaps may become irrelevant or may rise in rank of priority. Only through continuous improvement efforts can the cost management system provide an ongoing, viable network of information to users.

Technology's impact on cost management system design and implementation is significant. With advancements in technology, it is becoming possible to link the feeder systems of a company into a truly integrated cost management system.

enterprise resource planning (ERP)

Enterprise resource planning (ERP) systems are packaged business software systems that allow companies to (1) automate and integrate the majority of their business processes, (2) share common data and practices across the entire enterprise, and (3) produce and access information in a real-time environment.[17] The ERP software often involves 30 separate modules that collect data from individual processes in the firm (sales, shipping, distribution, etc.) and assemble that data in a form accessible by all managers. ERP is discussed in detail in Chapter 17.

REVISITING Motorola, Inc.

http://www.mot.com

The consolidation of Motorola's separate research programs into Motorola Labs is already starting to pay dividends. The consolidation has made it possible for Motorola to tweak a single innovation for several products. A new semiconductor for sending video signals, for example, works in both an experimental wireless phone and a set-top box for interactive TV. The chip's key elements are also used in a device for fingerprint identification on computer keyboards, soon to be a product, that eliminates the need for passwords.

Other efforts are more speculative. With DNA, Motorola researchers are trying to exploit the attractions of pairs of organic acids, using the links to lay down patterns of chip circuitry. The effort reflects management's interest in moving Motorola into biotechnology; the labs intend to use DNA to help map genetic sequences to find abnormalities that could lead to diseases.

In looking for new ways to make wireless networks more efficient, Motorola scientists developed a computer program that mimics a city full of roaming pager and cellphone users. The permutations are virtually infinite: a supercomputer using the software, working at 100 billion instructions per second, can create only about 10 seconds of a real-time simulation in an hour of number crunching. But the software has led to design improvements that can cut dropped cellular calls by 50 percent, Motorola researchers say.

Motorola also is building an enormous internal library of maps and related materials to help decision making in construction projects. The system will include information such as how many pumps a gas station will have, what payment systems it will use, and how fuel will be stored and mixed. These industry "road maps" could be the foundation of a future design and consulting business, the company says.

SOURCE: Quentin Hardy, "Business Brief—Motorola, Inc.: Wireless Divisions to Add 1,400 Workers by Year-End," *The Wall Street Journal* (June 17, 1999), p. B6. Permission conveyed through the Copyright Clearance Center.

[17] Win G. Jordan and Kip R. Krumwiede, "ERP Implementers Beware!" *Cost Management Update* (March 1999), pp. 1–4.

CHAPTER SUMMARY

As first discussed in Chapter 1, cost accounting's role in management accounting is to provide information for managers' planning, controlling, decision-making, and performance evaluation needs. This chapter discusses the role of accountants and accounting information in developing a formal system of cost management.

A cost management system is a subpart of a firm's information and control systems. A management information system is a structure that organizes and communicates data to managers. Control systems exist to guide organizations in achieving their goals and objectives. They have four primary components: detectors, assessors, effectors, and a communications network.

A cost management system consists of a set of formal methods developed for planning and controlling an organization's cost-generating activities relative to its goals and objectives. This system serves multiple purposes: to develop product costs, assess product/service profitability, improve understanding of how processes affect costs, facilitate cost control, measure performance, and implement organizational strategies.

It is not feasible to simply adopt a generic, "off-the-shelf" cost management system. As in the design of any control system, managers must be sensitive to the unique aspects of their organizations. Three factors that specifically should be taken into account in designing a control system are the organizational form, structure, and culture; organizational mission and critical success factors; and the competitive environment.

A cost management system's design is based on elements from three groups of management control tools. The selected elements of the system should be internally consistent and be consistent with the missions of the individual subunits. The three groups of control tools are motivational elements, informational elements, and reporting elements.

The motivational elements exist to provide managers the incentive to take the actions that are in the best interest of their subunits and the overall organization. Managers are motivated to do the right thing when the rewards they receive for their efforts are linked to the quality of decisions they make on behalf of the organization and their specific subunits.

The informational elements provide managers with relevant data. Accountants play a primary role in information management and are charged with maintaining an information system that is useful in performance measurement of managers and subunits and in making managerial decisions. To compete in the global environment, firms are developing new techniques to provide information relevant to assessing their competitive positions.

The reporting elements exist to provide information regarding managerial performance. For accounting, this is sometimes referred to as the "scorekeeping" role. A responsibility accounting system provides information to top management about the performance of an organizational subunit and its manager.

Gap analysis is the key to identifying differences (gaps) between the ideal cost management system and the existing system. By prioritizing the order in which gaps are to be closed, managers can proceed in an orderly manner with updating the cost management system. Because business processes are constantly evolving, the cost management system must be continuously evaluated and updated so that it provides the information and motivation that managers currently require.

APPENDIX

Cost Management System Conceptual Design Principles

"In 1986, Computer Aided Manufacturing-International, Inc. (CAM-I) formed a consortium of progressive industrial organizations, professional accounting firms, and government agencies to define the role of cost management in the new advanced manufacturing environment."[18] One outcome of this consortium was a conceptual framework of principles (listed in Exhibit 2–13) for designing a cost management system. If a CMS provides the suggested information relating to costs, performance measurements, and investment management, that system will be relevant to management's decision-making needs. Although compatible with existing cost accounting systems, the set of principles as a whole suggests a radical departure from traditional practices. The practices focus management attention on organizational activities, product life cycles, integrating cost management and performance measurement, and integrating investment management and strategic management.

EXHIBIT 2–13

CMS Conceptual Design Principles

Cost Principles

- Identify costs of non-value-added activities to improve use of resources.
- Recognize holding costs as a non-value-added activity traceable directly to a product.
- Significant costs should be directly traceable to management reporting objectives.
- Separate cost centers should be established for each homogeneous group of activities consistent with organizational responsibility.
- Activity-based cost accumulation and reporting will improve cost traceability.
- Separate bases for allocations should be developed to reflect causal relations between activity costs and management reporting objectives.
- Costs should be consistent with the requirement to support life-cycle management.
- Technology costs should be assigned directly to products.
- Actual product cost should be measured against target cost to support elimination of waste.
- Cost-effective approaches for internal control should be developed as a company automates.

Performance Measurement Principles

- Performance measures should establish congruence with a company's objectives.
- Performance measures should be established for significant activities.
- Performance measures should be established to improve visibility of cost drivers.
- Financial and nonfinancial activities should be included in the performance measurement system.

Investment Management Principles

- Investment management should be viewed as more than the capital budgeting process.
- Investment management decisions should be consistent with company goals.
- Multiple criteria should be used to evaluate investment decisions.
- Investments and attendant risks should be considered interrelated elements of an investment strategy.
- Activity data should be traceable to the specific investment opportunity.
- Investment management decisions should support the reduction or elimination of non-value-added activities.
- Investment management decisions should support achieving target cost.

SOURCE: Callie Berliner and James A. Brimson, eds., *Cost Management for Today's Advanced Manufacturing* (Boston: Harvard Business School Press, 1988), pp. 13–18. Reprinted by permission of Harvard Business School Press. Copyright 1988 by CAM-1.

[18] Berliner and Brimson, *Cost Management*, p. vii.

KEY TERMS

cost driver (p. 45)
cost management system (CMS) (p. 45)
cost structure (p. 52)
enterprise resource planning (ERP) (p. 62)
management control system (MCS) (p. 43)
management information system (MIS) (p. 43)
organizational form (p. 48)
profit sharing (p. 57)
responsibility accounting system (p. 60)

QUESTIONS

1. Why must a company spend money to make money? What do you predict would occur to a company's revenues if that company achieved its objective of incurring annual operating costs of $0?
2. Why are so many companies presently redesigning their cost accounting systems?
3. How can a company evaluate whether it is effectively managing its costs?
4. Why is an effective management information system a key element of an effective management control system?
5. What is a control system? What purpose does a control system serve in an organization?
6. Why would an organization have multiple control systems in place?
7. Why does an effective cost management system necessarily have both a short-term and long-term focus?
8. Why would management be willing to accept somewhat inaccurate costs from the cost management system? What sacrifices would be necessary to obtain more accurate costs?
9. List some examples of costs that a cost management system might treat differently for internal and external purposes. Why would these treatments be appropriate?
10. How can an integrated cost management system help managers understand and evaluate the effectiveness and efficiency of business processes?
11. Is cost reduction the primary purpose of a cost management system? Discuss the rationale for your answer.
12. Why is it not possible for a cost management system to simply be "pulled off the shelf"?
13. How does the choice of organizational form influence the design of a firm's cost management system?
14. What information could be generated from a cost management system that would help an organization manage its core competencies?
15. Describe characteristics of organizations in which centralized control would be effective and those in which decentralized control would be effective.
16. Would you prefer to work as an employee in an organization that had centralized or decentralized control? Discuss the reasons for your answer.
17. List five types of cost management information that would be most useful to an organizational subunit that was engaged in a (a) build, (b) harvest, or (c) hold mission.
18. Discuss ways in which organizational culture could be used as a control mechanism.
19. Compare the description in the chapter of AT&T prior to divestiture with the former Soviet Union prior to perestroika. How has the culture of each of these entities changed over time? How would these changes affect the types of information needed by managers/leaders?

20. Why would a cost management system, within a company pursuing confrontational competition, be required to provide information about competitors?
21. How does the life-cycle stage of a product influence the nature of information that is required to successfully manage costs of that product?
22. In the present highly competitive environment, why has cost management risen to such a high level of concern while price management has declined in importance?
23. What do you believe the core competencies of your college or university to be? Why did you choose these?
24. Why can "dollar sales per employee" be viewed as a measure of organizational productivity? What actions can managers take to increase productivity?
25. Give three examples of industries in which time-to-market is critical. Give three examples of industries in which time-to-market is almost irrelevant. Discuss the reasons for importance or lack thereof in each industry.
26. Why is the supply chain, or value chain, becoming an increased focus of cost management systems?
27. What are feeder systems and why are they important in the design of a cost management system?
28. Which is most important in the design of a cost management system: motivational elements, informational elements, or reporting elements? Discuss the rationale for your answer.
29. "A firm cannot be successful unless short-term profits are achieved." Is this statement true or false? Why?
30. Provide three examples from your academic career of the truthfulness of the statement "you get what you measure."
31. Why do companies measure their performance from a variety of perspectives (e.g., shareholder, customer) rather than a single perspective?
32. What is gap analysis, and what role does it play in the implementation of a cost management system?
33. *(Appendix)* What was CAM-I and why was it organized?

EXERCISES

34. *(Cost management and strategy)* Assume that you are a financial analyst and you have just been handed a 2000 financial report of Firm X, a large, global pharmaceutical firm. The company competes in both traditional pharmaceutical products and the evolving biotechnology products. Also assume that you have been given the following data on the pharmaceutical industry.

	Firm X	Industry Average
Sales	$5.0 billion	$1.2 billion
Net income	$1.3 billion	$0.12 billion
Advertising	$0.1 billion	$0.2 billion
Research and development	$0.4 billion	$0.3 billion
New investment in facilities	$0.5 billion	$0.3 billion

Given the above data, evaluate the cost management performance of Firm X.

35. *(Cost management system benefits)* Consider the following excerpt regarding advertising agencies:

http://www.isba.org.uk

The latest study on advertising agency performance from the Incorporated Society of British Advertisers found that agencies are failing to provide adequate service, to develop trusting relationships, be innovative, be efficient, control costs, and keep their promises. Agency staff are difficult to reach, planners are lack-

ing when it comes to monitoring and evaluating advertising, creatives still do not listen to advertisers' concerns or understand their target markets, and production departments fail to deliver value for money or meet budgets. On a grander scale, the majority of advertisers do not feel that their agencies provide competent advice on business and marketing issues.

SOURCE: Ruth Nicholas, "Survey Finds Ad Agency Still Failing Clients." From an original article in the 3 June 1999 issue of *Marketing* with the permission of Haymarket Business Publications Ltd.

Given the problems plaguing advertising agencies, discuss how an integrated cost management system could help individual ad agencies become more competitive.

36. *(Organizational form)* As a team of three, or as individuals, write a paper that compares and contrasts the corporate, general partnership, limited partnership, LLP, and LLC forms of business. At a minimum, include in your discussion issues related to the following: formation, capital generation, managerial authority and responsibility, taxation, ownership liability, and implications for success in mission and objectives.

37. *(Cost management and organizational culture)* Use Internet resources to compare and contrast the organizational cultures and operating performance of any two firms in the same industry. Following are possible pairs to compare.

1. Delta Air Lines and Southwest Airlines (http://www.delta-air.com and http://www.southwest.com)
2. Exxon and Royal Dutch Shell (http://www.exxon.com and http://www.shell.com)
3. Nordstrom's and Wal-Mart (http://www2.nordstrom.com and http://www.walmart.com)
4. Haggar and Levi-Strauss (http://www.haggar.com and http://www.levi.com)
5. IBM and Dell Computer (http://www.ibm.com and http://www.dell.com)

In your discussion, address the following questions:

a. Which of the pair is the better operating performer?
b. Do you believe that organizational culture has any relationship to the differences in operations?

38. *(Organizational strategy)* Use Internet resources to find a company (regardless of where they are domiciled) whose managers have chosen to (a) avoid competition through differentiation, (b) avoid competition through cost leadership, and (c) confront competitors head-on. Prepare an analysis of each of these company's strategies and discuss your perception of how well that strategy has worked.

39. *(Cost management and organizational objectives)* In a team of three, prepare an oral presentation discussing how accounting information can (a) help and (b) hinder an organization's progress toward its mission and objectives. Be sure to differentiate between the effects of what you perceive as "traditional" versus "nontraditional" accounting information.

40. *(Organizational culture)* Write a paper describing the organizational culture at a job you have held or at the college or university that you attend. Be sure to include a discussion of the value system and how it was communicated to new employees or new students.

41. *(Cost management and strategy change)* The following excerpt illustrates a strategy change by Corel, the software company.

http://www.corel.com
http://www.novell.com

Corel's problems originated four years ago when the company purchased the WordPerfect word-processing software from Novell Inc. and started waging war with Microsoft for the top retail sales spot in packaged office suites. Within months of the $124 million acquisition, Corel transformed the moribund

WordPerfect into the centerpiece of a rival to Microsoft's Office package, which included a word processor, a spreadsheet, graphics software, and a personal organizer. For two months in 1995, Corel's package edged out Microsoft's in retail sales.

But the early success was deceptive. Corel sacrificed profit for market share by marketing its office suite at about half the retail price of Microsoft's Office. Meanwhile, Corel's aggressive advertising campaign, including title sponsorship of the women's professional tennis tour and national television commercials in the United States, drained the company's meager resources. When Microsoft introduced its own upgraded Office 97 suite, the battle was over.

To reverse its fortunes, Corel is slashing costs. . . . For instance, it is spending much less than before to attract new office-software customers.

SOURCE: Adapted from Julian Beltrame, "Corel Stages Comeback from Battle with Microsoft—Cost Cutting, Refocusing on Corel Products Move Company Into the Black," *The Wall Street Journal* (August 9, 1999), p. B4.

Corel's change in cost management has resulted in the company's return to profitable operations. The change in cost management resulting in "slashing costs" implies that the company has changed its strategy. Discuss how the firm's strategy might have changed such that the firm's new strategy would be consistent with the change in cost management that is described in the article.

CASES

http://www.kpmgconsulting.com

42. *(Information and cost management)* Consider the following excerpt about customer communication.

Companies worldwide lose millions of dollars each year because they fail to communicate with customers and suppliers. These and other supply chain inefficiencies are pointed out in the results of two surveys issued by KPMG Consulting, a part of KPMG Peat Marwick LLP.

"Most companies think they're more efficient than they really are," said Thomas Wilde of KPMG. "It's either too painful to make the necessary organizational changes to become more efficient, or the benefits are not clear to them."

Supplier and customer involvement is essential to efficient supply chain management, yet 29% of companies report their suppliers have no involvement in their inventory management, according to the survey. Another 22% of companies report no involvement from their customers when planning manufacturing requirements. "It's as if a tire company just guessed at the number it needed to manufacture every year, without talking to auto manufacturers first," said Steven Y. Gold, KPMG partner.

The problem is particularly acute in consumer markets. While 96% of retailers share information with customers/suppliers, 79% are using outdated modes of communication, such as paper or fax.

SOURCE: Anonymous, "Companies Lose Millions by Ignoring Customers in Supply Chain Forecasting and Inventory Control," *Cost Management Update 87* (May 1998), p. 3.

Select a major manufacturing company in your area. For this company, prepare a table identifying specific ways in which an improved system of communications with suppliers and customers could result in specific cost savings for the manufacturing firm, its suppliers, or its customers. Organize your table in three columns as follows.

Specific Information to Be Obtained	Information Source	Specific Cost to Be Reduced

43. *(Alternative cost management strategies)* Robert L. Wehling, Procter & Gamble's senior vice president for advertising and market research, would like to wean Americans off coupons.

http://www.pg.com

His relentless cost-control efforts, which P&G began in the manufacturing area in 1993, have led to moves to eliminate couponing, increase print advertising, and curb growth in P&G's marketing spending.

In fact, fewer than 2% of the 291.9 billion coupons that companies distributed in 1995 were redeemed. . . .

P&G has been plowing back savings from cost-cutting initiatives into lowering prices on most of its 300 brands. Since 1992–93, the list prices on P&G brands, excluding coffee, have declined by $1 billion. Prices on diapers and detergents have particularly declined.

In February, P&G eliminated all promotional coupons in three New York state markets—in a test that many industry watchers doubted could be successfully expanded nationwide because coupons are such an integral part of American consumers' psyche.

Until P&G came along, no company had risked eliminating all coupons in a big geographical market, despite the growing consensus among major marketers that coupons are expensive and turn brand-loyal customers into bargain hunters who select brands based on short-term price promotions.

P&G spent $3.3 billion in 1995 on advertising. Its popular brand names include Tide, Vicks, Cover Girl, and Pampers.

SOURCE: Raju Narisetti, "P&G Ad Chief Plots Demise of the Coupon," *The Wall Street Journal* (April 17, 1996) pp. B1, B5A. Permission conveyed through the Copyright Clearance Center.

a. What costs and benefits did P&G likely consider in its decision to discontinue the use of coupons to promote its products?
b. What is P&G's apparent market strategy in deciding to lower prices? Explain.
c. What risks should P&G take into account before discontinuing the use of coupons nationwide?

44. *(Cost management and customer service)* The following excerpt illustrates how one company experienced negative fallout due to cost-cutting measures.

In Digital Equipment Corp.'s 1994 reorganization, its second in as many years, the company eliminated hundreds of sales and marketing jobs in its health-industries group, which had been bringing in $800 million of annual revenue by selling computers to hospitals and other health-care providers worldwide.

Digital says it cut [costs and positions] because it had to act fast. It was losing about $3 million a day, and its cost of sales was much higher than that of its rivals. Robert B. Palmer, the chief executive officer of the Maynard, Massachusetts, company, saw across-the-board cuts in all units, regardless of profitability, as the way to go. . . .

But in the health-industries group, the cutbacks imposed unexpected costs. Digital disrupted longstanding ties between its veteran salespeople and major customers by transferring their accounts to new sales divisions. It also switched hundreds of smaller accounts to outside distributors without notifying the customers.

At the industry's annual conference, "I had customers coming up to me and saying, 'I haven't seen a Digital sales rep in nine months. Whom do I talk to now?' " recalls Joseph Lesica, a former marketing manager in the group who resigned last year. "That really hurt our credibility. I was embarrassed."

Resellers of Digital computers, who account for most of its health-care sales, also complained about diminished technology and sales support. "There were months when you couldn't find anybody with a Digital badge," complains an official at one former reseller who had been accustomed to Digital sales reps accompanying him on customer calls. "They walked away from large numbers of clients." Adds Richard Tarrant, chief executive of IDX Systems Corp., a Burlington, Vermont, reseller that used to have an exclusive arrangement with Digital, "Now, they're just one of several vendors we use."

Many Digital customers turned to International Business Machines Corp. [IBM] and Hewlett-Packard Co., and so did some employees of Digital's downsized health-care group. Lesica says some laid-off workers went to Hewlett-Packard and quickly set about bringing Digital clients with them. "That's another way [Digital] shot itself in the foot," he says.

SOURCE: Alex Markels and Matt Murray, "Call It Dumbsizing: Why Some Companies Regret Cost-Cutting," *The Wall Street Journal* (May 4, 1996), pp. A1, A6. Permission conveyed through the Copyright Clearance Center.

a. What is the implied mission (build, hold, or harvest) of the health-industries group of Digital? Explain.
b. Describe the circumstances in which "across-the-board" cuts in spending represent a rational approach to cost management.
c. When Digital decided to cut costs, what were the apparent criteria used to determine which costs to cut?
d. How could a better, integrated cost management system have helped Digital avoid the adverse effects of its cost-cutting efforts?

45. *(Cost management: short-term vs. long-term)* Flatland Metals Co. produces steel products for a variety of customers. One division of the company is Residential Products Division, created in the late 1940s. Since that time, this division's principal products have been galvanized steel components used in garage door installations. The division has been continuously profitable since 1950, and in 1996, it generated profits of $10 million on sales of $300 million.

However, over the past ten years, growth in the division has been slow; profitability has become stagnant, and few new products have been developed, although the garage door components market has matured. The president of the company, John Stamp, has asked his senior staff to evaluate the operations of the Residential Products Division and to make recommendations for changes that would improve its operations. The staff uncovered the following facts:

- Tracinda Green, age 53, has been president of the division for the past fifteen years.
- Green receives a compensation package that includes a salary of $175,000 annually plus a cash bonus based on achievement of the budgeted level of annual profit.
- Growth in sales in the residential metal products industry has averaged 12 percent annually over the past decade. Most of the growth has occurred in ornamental products used in residential privacy fencing.
- Nationally, the division's market share in the overall residential metal products industry has dropped from 12 percent to 7 percent during the past ten years and has dropped from 40 percent to 25 percent for garage door components.
- The division maintains its own information systems. The systems in use today are mostly the same systems that were in place fifteen years ago; however, some of the manual systems have been computerized (e.g., payroll, accounts payable, accounting).
- The division has no customer service department. A small sales staff solicits and takes orders by phone from national distribution chains.
- The major intra-division communication tool is the annual operating budget. No formal statements have been prepared in the division regarding strategies, mission, values, goals and objectives, or identifying core competencies.

Given the introductory paragraphs and the facts from the staff of the company's president, identify the major problems in the Residential Products Division and develop recommendations to address the problems you have identified.

46. *(Cost management and profitability)* The following excerpt deals with Nordstrom's cost-cutting efforts.

http://www2.nordstrom.com

Nordstrom's Inc., a retailing-industry laggard in profits, has been undergoing an effort to cut costs. But can the department store chain do that while maintaining its famously obsessive level of customer service?

"The biggest challenge is to keep the culture in the organization while making the necessary changes for the new millennium," says Jennifer Black, president and analyst at Black & Co. in Portland, Oregon.

The good news is that Nordstrom's lags so far behind the industry's most efficient and profitable department store operators that it can cut a lot of costs without gutting the sales staff. "There is so much at this company that hasn't been done," Black says. "They've only skimmed the surface."

For instance, May Department Stores Co., based in St. Louis, boasts a 12.5% operating margin, while Nordstrom's was among retailing's lowest, at 5.6% for 1998. Nordstrom's certainly has opportunity for improvement. Its sales per square foot of store space, at $382 for 1998, are the envy of the industry. May's sales per square foot were just $201.

But inefficient operations have prevented Nordstrom's from boosting its bottom line, despite its higher sales. Becoming efficient requires Nordstrom's family, which owns a controlling 35 percent stake in the company, to embrace change at what has been an insular operation. So far, the family is talking the talk. "Nothing is sacred," says 36-year-old William Nordstrom.

SOURCE: Calmetta Y. Coleman, "Nordstrom's Tries to Cut Costs While Maintaining Service—Retailer Consolidates Operations That Have Weighed on Its Bottom Line," *The Wall Street Journal* (April 8, 1999) p. B4. Permission conveyed through the Copyright Clearance Center.

a. What is Nordstrom's strategy as implied by the discussion in the news article?

b. Given your answer to part (a), discuss how, as a paid consultant to Nordstrom's, you would go about developing a plan to recommend cost management changes at the company.

47. *(Cost management and product life cycle)* Ford Motor Co. reported a 58 percent drop in its fourth-quarter profits as a result of the heavy costs of launching new vehicles. And officials predicted that similar costs will continue to depress earnings through the first half of this year.

http://www.fordvehicles.com

Ford launched its Taurus sedan, its biggest-selling car, in the fourth quarter, while preparing for the debut of its F-series pickup trucks. The two vehicle lines account for sales of more than one million vehicles each year.

In the first half of 1996, Ford also plans to introduce a new version of its Escort small car, another of Ford's top sellers.

"The time to make changes is when you are strong," said David McCammon, Ford's vice president of finance. He said the automaker still managed to finish 1995 with $12.4 billion in cash despite a drop in full-year reported profit of 22%.

SOURCE: Adapted from Oscar Suris, "Ford's Net Declined 58 Percent in Fourth Period," *The Wall Street Journal* (February 1, 1996) pp. A3–A4.

a. Why would Ford's reported profits for 1995 have dropped because of the launching of new vehicles?

b. How would Ford's reported profit have differed if the company had used life-cycle costing techniques to account for the costs of launching new products?

c. Explain what McCammon meant when he said, "The time to make changes is when you are strong."

(continued)

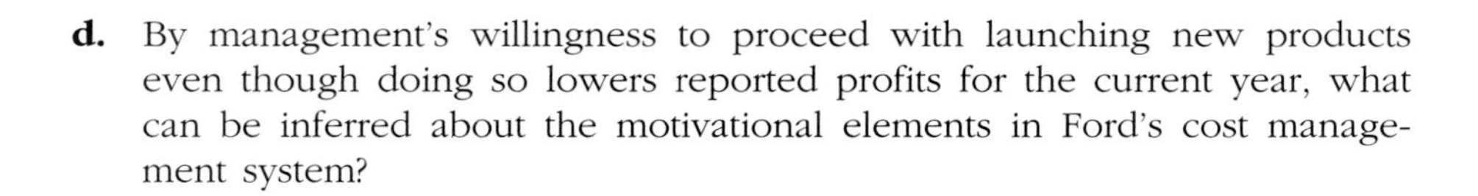

d. By management's willingness to proceed with launching new products even though doing so lowers reported profits for the current year, what can be inferred about the motivational elements in Ford's cost management system?

REALITY CHECK

48. A joke making the rounds in Philadelphia-area doctors' lounges goes like this:

Leonard Abramson, chief executive officer of U.S. Healthcare Inc., the big health-maintenance company, dies and goes to heaven, where he tells God what a great place it is. "Don't get too comfortable," God advised, "You're only approved for a three-day stay."

That's the kind of cost control that the messianic Abramson understands. In the past two years, U.S. Healthcare has slashed the fees it pays to specialists and hospitals by 12 percent to 20 percent and sometimes more, these providers say. In the past year, it has cut members' days in hospitals by 11 percent. Increasingly, it asks specialists and hospitals to assume the financial risk for procedures that cost more than anticipated.

U.S. Healthcare is widely considered one of the country's toughest HMO companies and one of the most innovative. It keeps 30 cents of every premium dollar to pay for salaries, marketing, administration and shareholder dividends, nearly 10 cents more than the industry average. It zealously tracks the performance of doctors and hospitals, paying more to those whose quality scores are high. It is earning robust profits—up 99 percent in the past 24 months—while rocking the tradition-bound, health-care markets along the East Coast.

"Unless you change the culture of the community you're working in, you're not changing health care," Abramson declares.

In the health-care community, U.S. Healthcare has both staunch supporters and critics. Consider the following additional information:

- Last year, Abramson earned $9.8 million in salary, bonuses, and stock options. Critics suggest this is excessive pay and takes resources that could otherwise have been applied to benefit patients. Abramson says, in a free market economy, large rewards flow to those who provide superior performance.
- Critics claim U.S. Healthcare selects service providers based on price rather than quality.
- The company pays doctors to take training courses, such as one in breast cancer screening techniques.
- The company has an information system that allows it to rank hospitals according to infection rates of urology patients, by the length of stay for coronary-bypass surgery, or by the number of babies delivered by Cesarean. The company shows the comparative data to its service providers and uses it as leverage in negotiations.
- The company is increasingly using performance-based pay contracts for its service providers.
- All of U.S. Healthcare's HMOs have earned three-year accreditation from the National Committee for Quality Assurance; this is the best performance of any U.S. managed-care company.

Examine the preceding information and discuss your opinion as to whether U.S. Healthcare is applying an ethical approach to the management of healthcare costs. Where possible, use concepts presented in the chapter to defend your position.

49. [John] Strazzanti is president of Com-Corp Industries, a $13 million, 100-employee metal-stamping shop he incorporated in Cleveland in 1980. He'd started out as a machine operator with a tool-and-die manufacturer, rapidly climbing the ladder to become general manager of another stamping company. Along the way, he didn't just dream about what he'd change if he were a company president. He figured out ways to make his dreams a reality.

[Dateline Cleveland, 1977] Packie Presser was vice president of the notoriously demanding local chapter of the teamsters' union. The chapter controlled a metal-stamping plant where Strazzanti had just been promoted from floor supervisor to general manager. Strazzanti recalls:

Two coworkers marched into my office. It was a hot summer day; they had had a few beers at lunch and were fired up. They worked hard in the warehouse and saw the engineers working in the air-conditioning and getting paid a lot more. They didn't think it was fair and wanted more money. I knew I was in a no-win situation. If I told them I thought they were being paid fairly, that's what they expected; they were going to argue, and they weren't going to be happy with the results. If I gave them more money, I was being unfair to everybody else.

So I took out a legal pad and I told them to write down whatever they wanted to be paid. Thirty days from that date, they would get that pay—with one caveat. During the 30 days, I would shop for replacements for them. If I could get highly qualified people to work for anything less than that number, they would have to take a hike. They asked for time to think about it and never came back with a number.

A lot of these guys think that if a company fills an order for a million dollars, it earns a million dollars in profit. I realized that if workers understood how a company earned a profit and how it had to be competitive, a lot of the resentment between managers and employees could be eliminated. And they needed to understand that if they improved their job skills, they could receive a higher wage.

SOURCE: Anonymous, "If I Were President. . . ," *Inc.* (April 1995) pp. 56–61. Permission conveyed through the Copyright Clearance Center.

a. How does the sharing of information in an organization contribute to the empowerment of employees in a decentralized organizational structure to enhance their performance and that of the organization?

b. In a decentralized organization, how does the sharing of information allow employees to better understand their organizational roles relative to the roles of others?

c. In a decentralized organization, how does quality control depend on widespread distribution of information?

50. The motivational elements of a cost management system are integral to the success of cost management goals. It is understood that the stronger the individual incentive to manage costs correctly, the greater is the likelihood that a given manager will act to manage costs effectively.

Currently, many employers provide fringe benefits to their employees that may provide a significant social benefit but that do not necessarily provide the strongest incentive to effectively manage costs. A significant employee benefit of this type is employer-provided health care. Discuss whether employers have an ethical responsibility to their employees, and to society, to provide health coverage to their employees, given that other forms of compensation that provide more powerful incentives could be offered to employees instead of health coverage.

Systems and Methods of Product Costing

CHAPTER 3

Organizational Cost Flows

LEARNING OBJECTIVES

After completing this chapter, you should be able to answer the following questions:

1. How are costs classified and why are such classifications useful?
2. How does the conversion process occur in manufacturing and service companies?
3. What assumptions do accountants make about cost behavior and why are these assumptions necessary?
4. How are the high-low method and least squares regression analysis (Appendix) used in analyzing mixed costs?
5. What product cost categories exist and what items compose those categories?
6. Why and how are overhead costs allocated to products and services?
7. What causes underapplied or overapplied overhead and how is it treated at the end of a period?
8. How is cost of goods manufactured calculated?

INTRODUCING **Wisconsin Film & Bag**

Wisconsin Film & Bag (WF&B), headquartered in Shawano, Wisconsin, is a custom manufacturer of high-quality polyethylene bags and film for a variety of packaging applications such as food, electronics, and other manufactured products. WF&B serves a market niche that requires Manufactured to Order quality products. The company focuses on "time-sensitive," low-volume orders including smaller, lighter gauge bags (bakery bags, parts bags, and specialized packaging bags) from which most large competitors shy away.

WF&B's ability to produce a broad range of polyethylene products, low overhead, short lead times, production efficiencies, and "in-line" bag-making capabilities competitively position the company and enhance its potential to acquire new customers.

The company's success in the last several years can be attributed to its service to customers—ranging from short lead times, quick responses to requests for quotations, flexible manufacturing and scheduling, immediate problem solving by customer service representatives, to training of distributor sales representatives by WF&B employees.

Raw materials consist primarily of prime and offgrade low-density and linear low-density polyethylene resin pellets. Management splits purchases among suppliers to ensure competitive pricing and stable supply during times of shortage. Approximately 50 percent of WF&B's annual requirements are purchased from a variety of vendors under long-term contract.

WF&B has two plants: one in Shawano, Wisconsin, and the other in Hartland, Wisconsin. The Shawano plant operates two 12-hour shifts, 363 days annually. Each production line is comprised of a machine operator and each shift includes a lead operator, an extruder technician and a quality control specialist. WF&B's plant layout and parallel production lines allow it to achieve a high degree of workforce flexibility, thus avoiding unnecessary use of manpower and excess material handling.

SOURCE: Corporate Headquarters, Wisconsin Film & Bag, 3100 E. Richmond Street, Shawano, WI 54166.

Every product or service has costs for material, labor, and overhead associated with it. **Cost** reflects the monetary measure of resources given up to attain an objective such as acquiring a good or service. However, like many other words, the term *cost* must be defined more specifically before "the cost" can be determined. Thus, a preceding adjective is generally used to specify the type of cost being considered. Different definitions for the term *cost* are used in different situations for different purposes. For example, the value presented on the balance sheet for an asset is an **unexpired cost**, but the portion of an asset's value consumed or sacrificed during a period is presented as an expense or **expired cost** on the income statement.

cost

unexpired cost
expired cost

Before being able to effectively communicate information to others, accountants must clearly understand the differences among the various types of costs, their computations, and their usage. This chapter provides the terminology that is necessary to understand and articulate cost and management accounting information. The chapter also presents cost flows and accumulation in a production environment.

Costs are commonly defined based on the objective or information desired and in terms of their relationship to the following four items: (1) time of incidence (e.g., historical or budgeted), (2) reaction to changes in activity (e.g., variable, fixed, or mixed), (3) classification on the financial statements (e.g., unexpired or expired), and (4) impact on decision making (e.g., relevant or irrelevant). These categories are not mutually exclusive; a cost may be defined in one way at one time and in another way at a different time. The first three cost classifications are discussed in this chapter. Costs related to decision making are covered at various points throughout the text.

COST CLASSIFICATIONS ON THE FINANCIAL STATEMENTS

1

How are costs classified and why are such classifications useful?

The balance sheet and income statement are two financial statements prepared by a company. The balance sheet is a statement of unexpired costs (assets) and equities (liabilities and owners' capital); the income statement is a statement of revenues and expired costs (expenses and losses). The concept of matching revenues and expenses on the income statement is central to financial accounting. The matching concept provides a basis for deciding when an unexpired cost becomes an expired cost and is moved from an asset category to an expense or loss category.

Expenses and losses differ in that expenses are intentionally incurred in the process of generating revenues, and losses are unintentionally incurred in the context of business operations. Cost of goods sold and expired selling and administrative costs are examples of expenses. Costs incurred for damage related to fires, for abnormal production waste, and for the sale of a machine at below book value are examples of losses.

product cost

period cost

Costs can also be classified as either product or period costs. **Product costs** are related to making or acquiring the products or providing the services that directly generate the revenues of an entity; **period costs** are related to other business functions such as selling and administration.

inventoriable cost

direct material

direct labor

Product costs are also called **inventoriable costs** and include the cost of direct material, direct labor, and overhead. Any readily identifiable part of a product (such as the clay in a vase) is a **direct material**. Direct material includes raw materials, purchased components from contract manufacturers, and manufactured subassemblies. **Direct labor** refers to the time spent by individuals who work specifically on manufacturing a product or performing a service. At WF&B, the people handling the polyethylene material for storage bags are considered direct labor and their wages are direct labor costs. Any factory or production cost that is indirect to the product or service and, accordingly, does not include direct material and direct labor is **overhead**. This cost element includes factory supervisors' salaries, depreciation on the machines producing plastic food storage bags, and insurance on the production facilities. The sum of direct labor and overhead costs is referred to as **conversion cost**.

overhead

conversion cost

Direct material, direct labor, and overhead are discussed in depth later in the chapter. Precise classification of some costs into one of these categories may be difficult and judgment may be required in the classification process.

Period costs are generally more closely associated with a particular time period rather than with making or acquiring a product or performing a service. Period costs that have future benefit are classified as assets, whereas those deemed to have no future benefit are expensed as incurred. Prepaid insurance on an administration building represents an unexpired period cost; when the premium period passes, the insurance becomes an expired period cost (insurance expense). Salaries paid to the sales force and depreciation on computers in the administrative area are also period costs.

distribution cost

Mention must be made of one specific type of period cost: distribution. A **distribution cost** is any cost incurred to warehouse, transport, or deliver a product or service. Although distribution costs are expensed as incurred, managers should remember that these costs relate directly to products and services and should not adopt an "out-of-sight, out-of-mind" attitude about these costs simply because they have been expensed for financial accounting purposes. Distribution costs must be planned for in relationship to product/service volume, and these costs must be controlled for profitability to result from sales. Thus, even though distribution costs are not technically considered part of product cost, they can have a major impact on managerial decision making.[1]

[1] The uniform capitalization rules (unicap rules) of the Tax Reform Act of 1986 caused many manufacturers, wholesalers, and retailers to expand the types and amounts of nonproduction-area costs that are treated as product costs for tax purposes. The unicap rules require that distribution costs for warehousing be considered part of product cost, but not distribution costs for marketing and customer delivery. The rationale for such treatment is that such warehousing costs are incidental to production or acquisition.

THE CONVERSION PROCESS

2

How does the conversion process occur in manufacturing and service companies?

In general, product costs are incurred in the production or conversion area and period costs are incurred in all nonproduction or nonconversion areas.[2] To some extent, all organizations convert (or change) inputs into outputs. Inputs typically consist of material, labor, and overhead. The output of a conversion process is usually either products or services. Exhibit 3–1 compares the conversion activities of different types of organizations. Note that many service companies engage in a high degree of conversion. Firms of professionals (such as accountants, architects, attorneys, engineers, and surveyors) convert labor and other resource inputs (material and overhead) into completed jobs (audit reports, building plans, contracts, blueprints, and property survey reports).

Firms that engage in only low or moderate degrees of conversion can conveniently expense insignificant costs of labor and overhead related to conversion. The savings in clerical cost from expensing outweigh the value of any slightly improved information that might result from assigning such costs to products or services. For example, when employees open shipping containers, hang clothing on racks, and tag merchandise with sales tickets, a labor cost for conversion is incurred. Retail clothing stores, however, do not try to attach the stockpeople's wages to inventory; such labor costs are treated as period costs and are expensed when they are incurred.

In contrast, in high-conversion firms, the informational benefits gained from accumulating the material, labor, and overhead costs of the output produced significantly exceed the clerical accumulation costs. For instance, to immediately expense labor costs incurred for workers constructing a building would be inappropriate; these costs are treated as product costs and inventoried as part of the cost of the construction job until the building is completed.

manufacturer

For convenience, a **manufacturer** is defined as any company engaged in a high degree of conversion of raw material input into other tangible output. Manufacturers typically use people and machines to convert raw material to output that has substance and can, if desired, be physically inspected. A **service company** refers to a firm engaged in a high or moderate degree of conversion using a significant amount of labor. A service company's output may be tangible (an architectural drawing) or intangible (insurance protection) and normally cannot be inspected prior to use. Service firms may be profit-making businesses or not-for-profit organizations.

service company

EXHIBIT 3–1

Degrees of Conversion in Firms

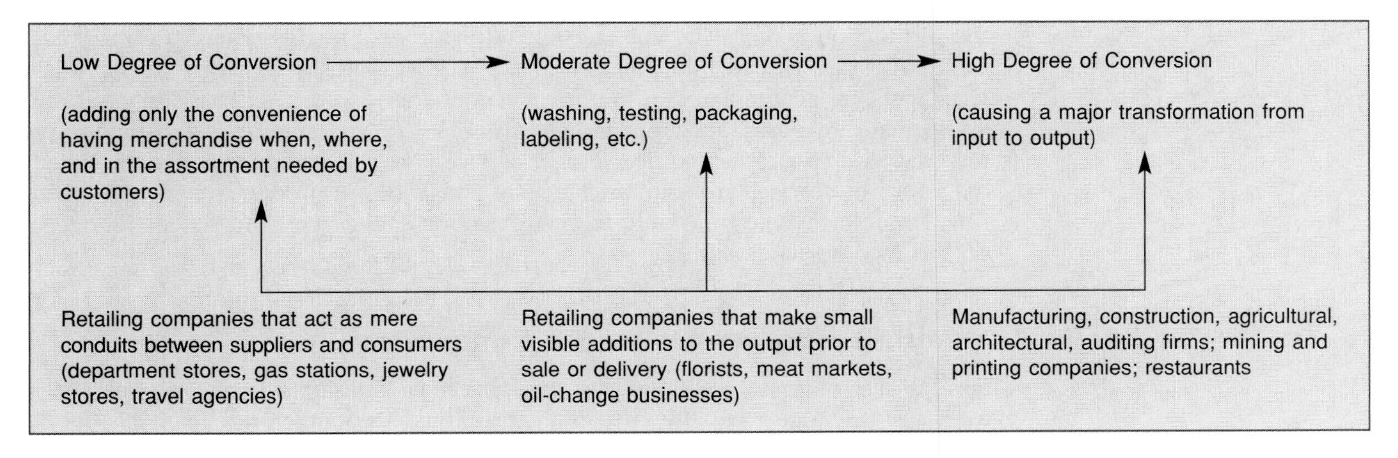

[2] It is less common, but possible, for a cost incurred outside the production area to be in direct support of production and, therefore, considered a product cost. An example of this situation is the salary of a product cost analyst who is based at corporate headquarters; this cost is part of overhead.

Firms engaging in only low or moderate degrees of conversion ordinarily have only one inventory account (Merchandise Inventory). In contrast, manufacturers normally use three inventory accounts: (1) Raw Material Inventory, (2) Work in Process Inventory (for partially converted goods), and (3) Finished Goods Inventory. Service firms will have an inventory account for the supplies used in the conversion process and may have a Work in Process Inventory account, but these firms do not normally have a Finished Goods Inventory account because services typically cannot be warehoused. If collection is yet to be made for a completed service engagement, the service firm has a receivable from its client instead of Finished Goods Inventory.

Retailers versus Manufacturers/Service Companies

Retail companies purchase goods in finished or almost finished condition; thus those goods typically need little, if any, conversion before being sold to customers. Costs associated with such inventory are usually easy to determine, as are the valuations for financial statement presentation.

In comparison, manufacturers and service companies engage in activities that involve the physical transformation of inputs into, respectively, finished products and services. The materials or supplies and conversion costs of manufacturers and service companies must be assigned to output to determine cost of inventory produced and cost of goods sold or services rendered. Cost accounting provides the structure and process for assigning material and conversion costs to products and services.

Exhibit 3–2 compares the input–output relationships of a retail company with those of a manufacturing/service company. This exhibit illustrates that the primary difference between retail companies and manufacturing/service companies is the absence or presence of the area labeled "the production center." This center involves the conversion of raw material to final products. Input factors flow into the production center and are transformed and stored there until the goods or services are completed. If the output is a product, it can be warehoused and/or displayed until it is sold. Service outputs are directly provided to the client commissioning the work.

As mentioned previously, the time, effort, and cost of conversion in a retail business are not as significant as they are in a manufacturing or service company. Thus, although a retailer could have a department (such as one that adds store name labels to goods) that might be viewed as a "mini" production center, most often, retailers have no designated "production center."

Exhibit 3–2 reflects an accrual-based accounting system in which costs flow from the various inventory accounts on the balance sheet through (if necessary) the production center. The cost accumulation process begins when raw materials or supplies are placed into production. As work progresses on a product or service, costs are accumulated in the firm's accounting records. Accumulating costs in appropriate inventory accounts allows businesses to match the costs of buying or manufacturing a product or providing a service with the revenues generated when the goods or services are sold. At the point of sale, these product/service costs will flow from an inventory account to cost of goods sold or cost of services rendered on the income statement.

Manufacturers versus Service Companies

Several differences in accounting for production activities exist between a manufacturer and a service company. A manufacturer must account for raw materials, work in process, and finished goods to maintain control over the production process. An accrual accounting system is essential for such organizations so that the total production costs can be accumulated as the goods flow through the manufacturing

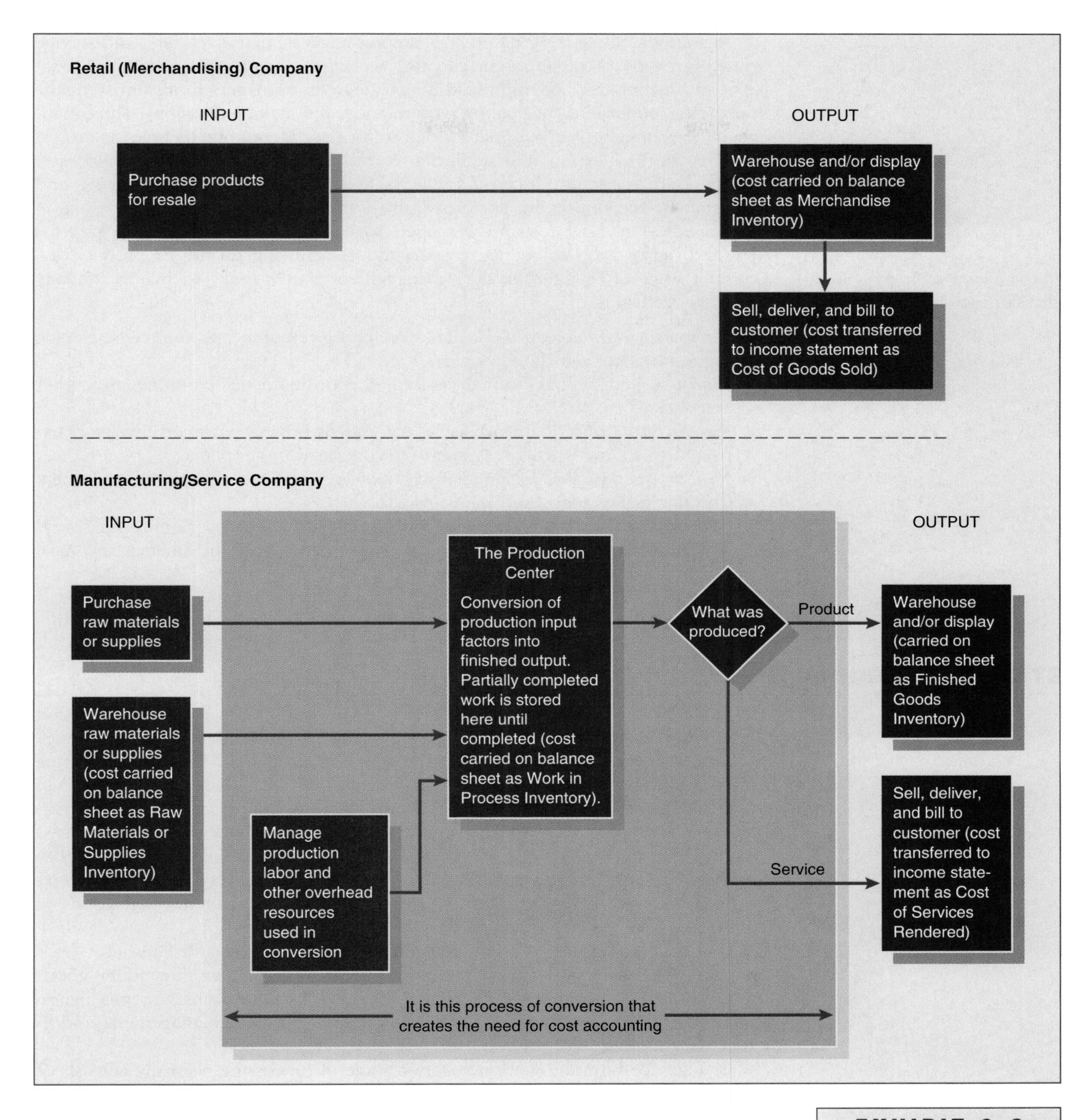

EXHIBIT 3-2

Business Input/Output Relationships

process. On the other hand, most service firms need only to keep track of their work in process (incomplete jobs). Such accounting is acceptable because service firms normally have few, if any, materials costs other than supplies for work not started. As mentioned earlier, because services generally cannot be warehoused, costs of finished jobs are usually transferred immediately to the income statement to be matched against job revenues, rather than being carried on the balance sheet in a finished goods account.

Despite the accounting differences among retailers, manufacturers, and service firms, each type of organization can use cost and management accounting concepts and techniques, although in different degrees. Managers in all firms engage in planning, controlling, evaluating performance, and making decisions. Thus, management accounting is appropriate for all firms. Cost accounting techniques are essential to all firms engaged in significant conversion activities. In most companies, managers are constantly looking for ways to reduce costs; cost accounting and management accounting are used extensively in this pursuit.

Regardless of how costs are classified, managers are continuously looking for new and better ways to reduce costs without sacrificing quality or productivity. Consider some of DaimlerChrysler's management plans to save $3 billion annually in various activities:

http://www.daimler chrysler.com

- *Advanced technologies:* Eliminate overlapping research into fuel cells, electric cars, and advanced diesel engines.
- *Finance:* Reduce back-office costs and coordinate tax planning and other activities.
- *Purchasing:* Consolidate parts and equipment buying. DaimlerChrysler is expected to follow Chrysler's system of working with suppliers.
- *Joint production:* Build Daimler sport-utility vehicles at a plant in Austria where Chrysler makes Jeeps and minivans.
- *New products:* Possibly cooperate on future products, such as minivans.
- *New markets:* Cooperate in emerging markets such as Latin America and Asia, perhaps with joint ventures.[3]

STAGES OF PRODUCTION

The production or conversion process can be viewed in three stages: (1) work not started (raw materials), (2) work in process, and (3) finished work. Costs are associated with each processing stage. The stages of production in a manufacturing firm and some costs associated with each stage are illustrated in Exhibit 3–3. In the first stage of processing, the cost incurred reflects the prices paid for raw materials and/or supplies. As work progresses through the second stage, accrual-based accounting requires that labor and overhead costs related to the conversion of raw materials or supplies be accumulated and attached to the goods. The total costs incurred in stages 1 and 2 equal the total production cost of finished goods in stage 3.

Cost accounting uses the Raw Material, Work in Process, and Finished Goods Inventory accounts to accumulate the processing costs and assign them to the goods produced. The three inventory accounts relate to the three stages of production shown in Exhibit 3–3 and form a common database for cost, management, and financial accounting information.

In a service firm, the work-not-started stage of processing normally consists of the cost of supplies needed to perform the services (Supplies Inventory). When supplies are placed into work in process, labor and overhead are added to achieve finished results. Determining the cost of services provided is extremely important in both profit-oriented service businesses and not-for-profit entities. For instance, architectural firms need to accumulate the costs incurred for designs and models of each project, and hospitals need to accumulate the costs incurred by each patient during his or her hospital stay.

[3] Gregory White and Brian Coleman, "Chrysler, Daimler Focus on Value of Stock," *The Wall Street Journal* (September 21, 1998), p. A3.

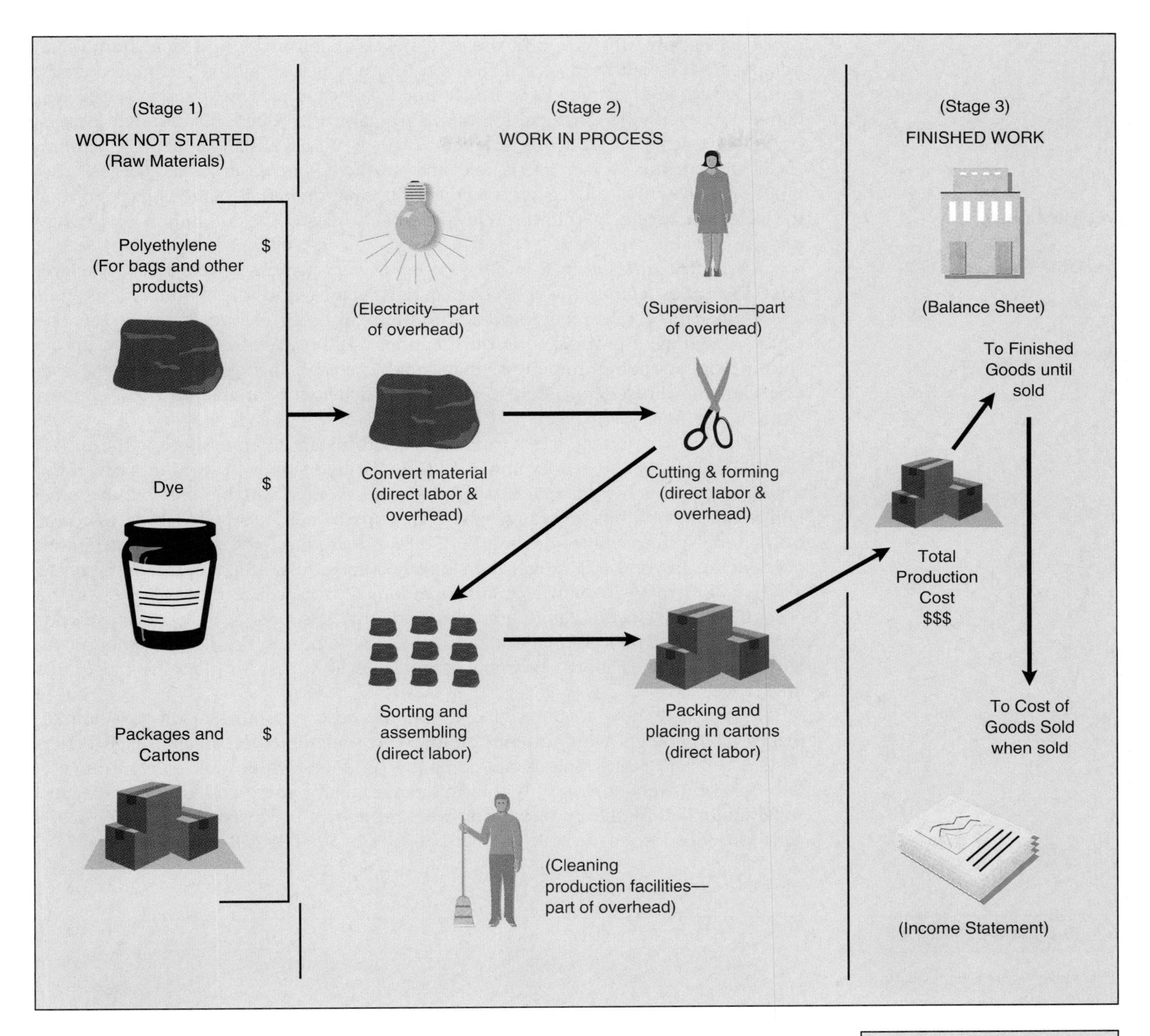

EXHIBIT 3–3

Stages and Costs of Production

COST REACTIONS TO CHANGES IN ACTIVITY

3

What assumptions do accountants make about cost behavior and why are these assumptions necessary?

Accountants describe a given cost's behavior pattern according to the way its *total* cost (rather than its unit cost) reacts to changes in a related activity measure. Every cost in an organization will change if activity levels are shifted to extremes or if the time span is long enough. However, a total cost may be observed to behave within a period in relation to limited changes in an associated activity measure. Activity measures include production, service and sales volumes, hours of machine time used, pounds of material moved, and number of purchase orders sent. To properly identify, analyze, and use cost behavior information, a time frame must be specified to indicate how far into the future a cost should be examined, and a particular range of activity must be assumed. For example, the standard-sized container of polyethylene material for WF&B to make a production run might increase by $1 next year but by $5 by the year 2010. If WF&B's management is planning for next year, the $1 increase is relevant but the $5 increase is not. The assumed range of activity that reflects the company's normal operating range is referred to as the **relevant range**. Within the relevant range, the two most common cost behaviors are variable and fixed.

relevant range

variable cost

A cost that varies in total in direct proportion to changes in activity is a **variable cost**. Examples include the costs of materials, wages, and sales commissions. Variable costs can be extremely important in the total profit picture of a company, because every time a product is produced and/or sold or a service is rendered and/or sold, a corresponding amount of that variable cost is incurred. Because the total cost varies in direct proportion to changes in activity, a variable cost is a constant amount per unit.

Although accountants view variable costs as linear, economists view these costs as curvilinear as shown in Exhibit 3–4. The cost line slopes upward at a given rate until a range of activity is reached in which the average variable cost rate becomes fairly constant. Within this range, the firm experiences benefits such as discounts on material prices, improved worker skill and productivity, and other operating efficiencies. Beyond this range, the slope becomes quite steep as the entity enters a range of activity in which certain operating factors cause the average variable cost to increase. In this range, the firm finds that costs rise rapidly due to worker crowding, equipment shortages, and other operating inefficiencies. Although the curvilinear graph is more correct, it is not as easy to use in planning or controlling costs.

To illustrate how to determine a variable cost, assume that Smith Company makes lawnmowers with batteries attached to start them electrically. Each battery costs a constant $8 as long as the company produces within the relevant range of 0 to 3,000 mowers annually. Within this range, total battery cost can be calculated as $8 multiplied by the number of mowers produced. For instance, if 2,500 mowers were produced, total variable cost of batteries is $20,000 ($8 × 2,500 mowers).

EXHIBIT 3–4

Economic Representation of a Variable Cost

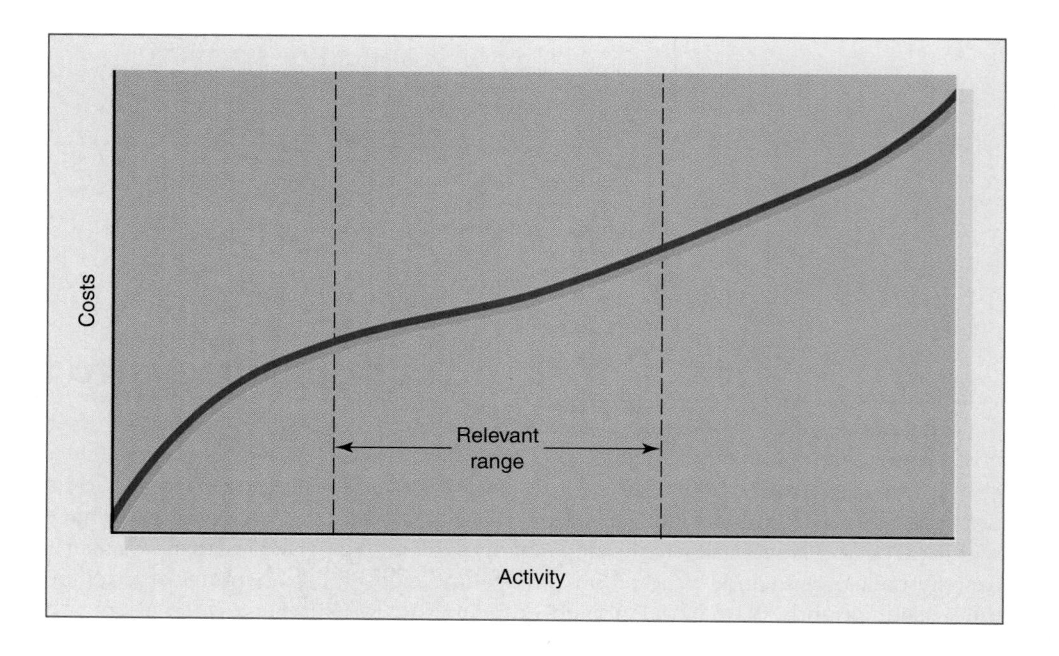

If the firm advances to a new relevant range and makes between 3,001 units and 7,000 mowers annually, the new unit cost would drop to $6. Total battery cost for making, for example, 5,800 mowers annually would be $34,800 ($6 × 5,800 mowers).

In contrast, a cost that remains constant in total within the relevant range of activity is considered a **fixed cost**. Many fixed costs are incurred to provide a firm with production capacity. Fixed costs include salaries (as opposed to wages), depreciation (other than that computed under the units-of-production method), and insurance. On a per-unit basis, a fixed cost varies inversely with changes in the level of activity: the per-unit fixed cost decreases with increases in the activity level, and increases with decreases in the activity level. If a greater proportion of capacity is used, then fixed costs per unit are lower.

fixed cost

To illustrate how to determine the total and unit amounts of a fixed cost, suppose that Smith Company rents for $12,000 annually manufacturing facilities in which its operating relevant range is 0 to 8,000 mowers annually. However, if Smith Company wants to produce between 8,001 and 12,000 mowers, it can rent an adjacent building for an additional $4,000, thus making the annual total fixed rent $16,000 in that higher capacity range.

If the firm produces fewer than 8,001 mowers, its total fixed annual facility rental cost is $12,000. Unit fixed cost can be found by dividing $12,000 by the number of units produced. For instance, if 6,000 units were made, the fixed facility rental cost per mower would be $2 ($12,000 ÷ 6,000 mowers).

If Smith Company rents the second facility, then total fixed rent would be $16,000 for this new relevant range of 8,001 to 12,000 mowers annually. Suppose that Smith made 10,000 mowers in a given year. The unit fixed cost for facilities rental can be calculated as $1.60 ($16,000 ÷ 10,000 mowers). The respective total cost and unit cost definitions for variable and fixed cost behaviors are presented in Exhibit 3–5.

Consider the following excerpt regarding automobile manufacturing costs and prices:

> *The ultimate culprit [of widely fluctuating costs and, therefore, prices of cars], explains [Bill] Pochiluk [a partner at PriceWaterhouse Coopers LLP], is the auto industry's excess capacity. When the manufacturers can't sell as many vehicles as they can build, the fixed costs of the assembly plants drive up the cost of each vehicle. Thus, the automakers use incentives so they can sell more cars, and thus keep production up and unit costs down.*[4]

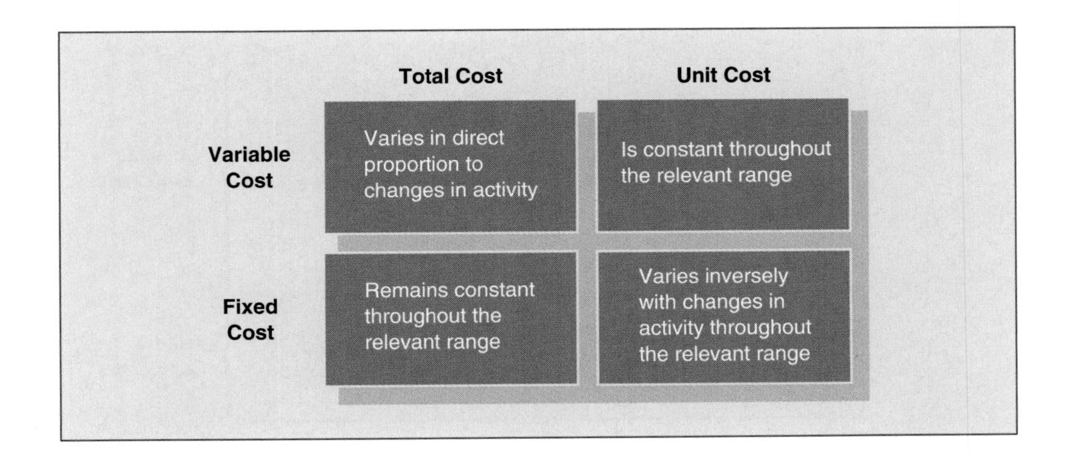

EXHIBIT 3-5

Comparative Total and Unit Cost Behavior Definitions

[4] Al Haas, "Falling Prices Make It a Vintage Year for Used-Car Buying," *The (New Orleans) Times-Picayune* (July 3, 1998), p. F1.

In the long run, however, even fixed costs will not remain constant. Business will increase or decrease sufficiently that production capacity may be added or sold. Alternatively, management may decide to "trade" fixed and variable costs for one another. For example, if WF&B installed new more highly computerized equipment, that decision would generate an additional fixed cost for depreciation and eliminate the variable cost of some hourly production workers.

If WF&B decided to outsource its data processing support function, the company might be able to trade its fixed costs of depreciation of data processing equipment and personnel salaries for a variable cost based on transaction volume. Whether variable costs are traded for fixed or vice versa, a shift in costs from one type of cost behavior to another changes the basic cost structure of a company and can have a significant impact on profits.

mixed cost

Other costs exist that are not strictly variable or fixed. For example, a **mixed cost** has both a variable and a fixed component. On a per-unit basis, a mixed cost does not fluctuate in direct proportion to changes in activity nor does it remain constant with changes in activity. An electric bill that is computed as a flat charge for basic service (the fixed component) plus a stated rate for each kilowatt-hour of usage (the variable component) is an example of a mixed cost. Exhibit 3–6 shows a graph for Grand Polymers' electricity charge from its power company, which consists of $500 per month plus $0.018 per kilowatt-hour (kwh) used. In a month when Grand Polymers uses 80,000 kwhs of electricity, its total electricity bill is $1,940 [$500 + ($0.018 × 80,000)]. If 90,000 kwhs are used, the electricity bill is $2,120.

step cost

Another type of cost shifts upward or downward when activity changes by a certain interval or "step." A **step cost** can be variable or fixed. Step variable costs have small steps and step fixed costs have large steps. For example, a water bill computed as $0.002 per gallon for up to 1,000 gallons, $0.003 per gallon for 1,001 to 2,000 gallons, $0.005 per gallon for 2,001 to 3,000 gallons, is an example of a step variable cost. In contrast, the salary cost for an airline ticket agent who can serve 3,500 customers per month is $3,200 per month. If airline volume increases from 10,000 customers to 12,800 customers, the airline will need four ticket agents rather than three. Each additional 3,500 passengers will result in an additional step fixed cost of $3,200.

Understanding the types of behavior exhibited by costs is necessary to make valid estimates of total costs at various activity levels. Although all costs do not

EXHIBIT 3-6

Graph of a Mixed Cost

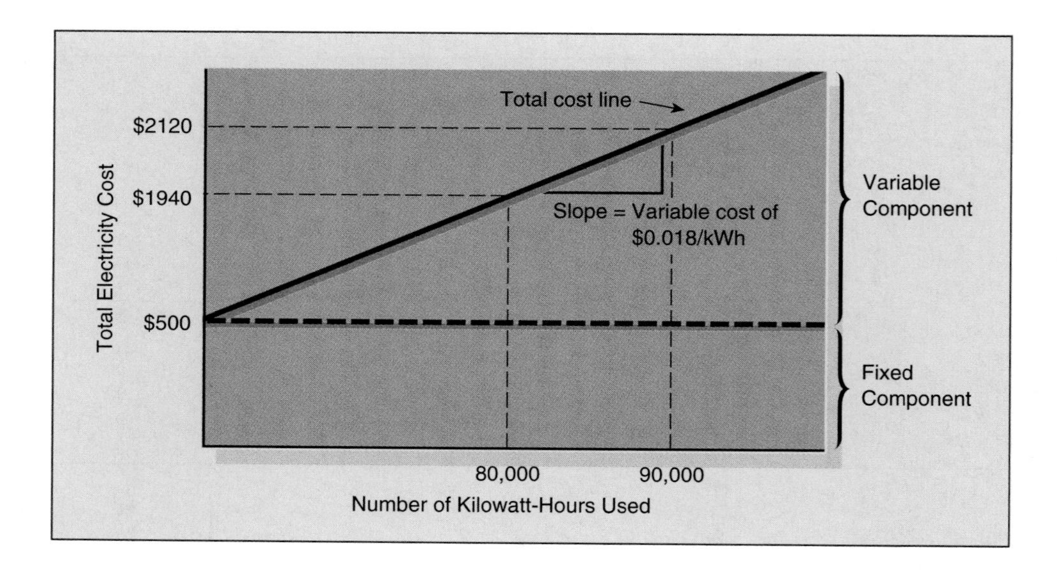

conform strictly to the aforementioned behavioral categories, the categories represent the types of cost behavior typically encountered in business. Cost accountants generally separate mixed costs into their variable and fixed components so that the behavior of these costs is more readily apparent. When step variable or step fixed costs exist, accountants must choose a specific relevant range of activity that will allow step variable costs to be treated as variable and step fixed costs to be treated as fixed.

By separating mixed costs into their variable and fixed components and by specifying a relevant range for step costs, accountants force all costs into either variable or fixed categories as an approximation of true cost behavior. Assuming a variable cost to be constant per unit and a fixed cost to be constant in total within the relevant range can be justified for two reasons. First, the assumed conditions approximate reality and, if the company operates only within the relevant range of activity, the cost behaviors selected are appropriate. Second, selection of a constant per-unit variable cost and a constant total fixed cost provides a convenient, stable measurement for use in planning, controlling, and decision making.

To make these generalizations about variable and fixed costs, accountants can use predictors for cost changes. A **predictor** is an activity measure that, when changed, is accompanied by consistent, observable changes in a cost item. However, simply because the two items change together does not prove that the predictor causes the change in the other item. For instance, assume that every time the mosquito control truck sprays in a particular neighborhood, the local high school principal wears a black dress. If this is consistent, observable behavior, you can use the mosquito truck spraying incident to predict that the principal will wear her black dress—but the spraying does not cause the principal to wear that black dress!

predictor

In contrast, a predictor that has a direct cause and effect relation to a cost is called a **cost driver**. For example, production volume has a direct effect on the total cost of raw material used and can be said to "drive" that cost. Thus, production volume can be used as a valid predictor of that cost. In most situations, the cause–effect relationship is less clear because costs are commonly caused by multiple factors. For example, factors including production volume, material quality, worker skill levels, and level of automation affect quality control costs. Although determining which factor actually caused a specific change in a quality control cost may be difficult, any of these factors could be chosen to predict that cost if confidence exists about the factor's relationship with cost changes. To be used as a predictor, the factor and the cost need only change together in a foreseeable manner.

cost driver

Traditionally, a single predictor has been used to predict all types of costs. Accountants and managers, however, are realizing that single predictors do not necessarily provide the most reasonable forecasts. This realization has caused a movement toward activity-based costing (Chapter 4), which uses different cost drivers to predict different costs. Production volume, for instance, would be a valid cost driver for the cost of standard-sized containers of polyethylene material, but the number of vendors used might be a more realistic driver for WF&B's purchasing department costs.[5]

Separating Mixed Costs

As discussed earlier in this chapter, accountants assume that costs are linear rather than curvilinear. Because of this assumption, the general formula for a straight line

[5] Using multiple cost drivers for illustrative purposes in the text would be unwieldy. Therefore, except when topics such as activity-based costing are being discussed, examples will typically make use of a single cost driver.

can be used to describe any type of cost within a relevant range of activity. The straight-line formula is

$$y = a + bX$$

where y = total cost (dependent variable)

a = fixed portion of total cost

b = unit change of variable cost relative to unit changes in activity

X = activity base to which y is being related (the predictor, cost driver, or independent variable)

If a cost is entirely variable, the a value in the formula will be zero. If the cost is entirely fixed, the b value in the formula will be zero. If a cost is mixed, it is necessary to determine formula values for both a and b.

4

How are the high-low method and least squares regression analysis (Appendix) used in analyzing mixed costs?

high-low method

outlier

HIGH-LOW METHOD

The **high-low method** analyzes a mixed cost by first selecting two observation points in a data set: the highest and lowest levels of activity, if these points are within the relevant range. Activity levels are used because activities cause costs to change and not the reverse. Occasionally, operations may occur at a level outside the relevant range (a rush special order may be taken that requires excess labor or machine time) or distortions might occur in a normal cost within the relevant range (a leak in a water pipe goes unnoticed for a period of time). Such nonrepresentative or abnormal observations are called **outliers** and should be disregarded when analyzing a mixed cost.

Next changes in activity and cost are determined by subtracting low values from high values. These changes are used to calculate the b (variable unit cost) value in the $y = a + bX$ formula as follows:

$$b = \frac{\text{Cost at High Activity Level} - \text{Cost at Low Activity Level}}{\text{High Activity Level} - \text{Low Activity Level}}$$

$$= \frac{\text{Change in the Total Cost}}{\text{Change in Activity Level}}$$

The b value is the unit variable cost per measure of activity. This value is multiplied by the activity level to determine the amount of total variable cost contained in total cost at either (high or low) level of activity. The fixed portion of a mixed cost is then found by subtracting total variable cost from total cost.

Total mixed cost changes with changes in activity. The change in the total mixed cost is equal to the change in activity times the unit variable cost; the fixed cost element does not fluctuate with changes in activity.

Exhibit 3–7 illustrates the high-low method using machine hours and utility cost information for the Cutting and Mounting Department of the Indianapolis Division of Alexander Polymers International. Information was gathered for the eight months prior to setting the predetermined overhead rate for 2001. During 2000, the department's normal operating range of activity was between 4,500 and 9,000 machine hours per month. For the Cutting and Mounting Department, the March observation is an outlier (substantially in excess of normal activity levels) and should not be used in the analysis of utility cost.

One potential weakness of the high-low method is that outliers may be inadvertently used in the calculation. Estimates of future costs calculated from a line drawn using such points will not be indicative of actual costs and probably are not good predictions. A second weakness is that this method considers only two data

EXHIBIT 3–7

Analysis of Mixed Cost

The following machine hours and utility cost information is available:

Month	Machine Hours	Utility Cost	
January	4,800	$192	
February	9,000	350	
March	11,000	390	*Outlier*
April	4,900	186	
May	4,600	218	
June	8,900	347	
July	5,900	248	
August	5,500	231	

STEP 1: Select the highest and lowest levels of activity within the relevant range and obtain the costs associated with those levels. These levels and costs are 9,000 and 4,600 hours, and $350 and $218, respectively.

STEP 2: Calculate the change in cost compared to the change in activity.

	Machine Hours	Associated Total Cost
High activity	9,000	$350
Low activity	4,600	218
Changes	4,400	$132

STEP 3: Determine the relationship of cost change to activity change to find the variable cost element.

$$b = \$132 \div 4{,}400 \text{ MH} = \$0.03 \text{ per machine hour}$$

STEP 4: Compute total variable cost (TVC) at either level of activity.

High level of activity: TVC = $0.03(9,000) = $270
Low level of activity: TVC = $0.03(4,600) = $138

STEP 5: Subtract total variable cost from total cost at the associated level of activity to determine fixed cost.

High level of activity: a = $350 − $270 = $80
Low level of activity: a = $218 − $138 = $80

STEP 6: Substitute the fixed and variable cost values in the straight-line formula to get an equation that can be used to estimate total cost at any level of activity within the relevant range.

$$y = \$80 + \$0.03X$$

where X = machine hours

points. A more precise method of analyzing mixed costs is least squares regression analysis, which is presented in the Appendix at the end of this chapter.

COMPONENTS OF PRODUCT COST

5

What product cost categories exist and what items compose these categories?

Product costs are related to the products or services that generate an entity's revenues. These costs can be separated into three components: direct material, direct labor, and production overhead.[6] A **direct cost** is one that is distinctly traceable

direct cost

[6] This definition of product cost is the traditional one and is referred to as *absorption cost*. Another product costing method, called variable costing, excludes the fixed overhead component. Absorption and variable costing are compared in Chapter 11.

cost object

indirect cost

to a specified cost object. A **cost object** is anything of interest or useful informational value, such as a product, service, department, division, or territory. Costs that must be allocated or assigned to a cost object using one or more predictors or cost drivers are called **indirect** (or common) **costs**. Different cost objects may be designated for different decisions. As the cost object changes, the costs that are direct and indirect to it may also change. For instance, if a production division is specified as the cost object, the production division manager's salary is direct. If, instead, the cost object is a sales territory and the production division operates in more than one territory, the production division manager's salary is indirect.

Direct Material

Any readily identifiable part of a product is called a direct material. Direct material costs theoretically should include the cost of all materials used in the manufacture of a product or performance of a service. However, some material costs are not conveniently or practically traceable from an accounting standpoint. Such costs are treated and classified as indirect costs. For example, in producing gallon-sized kitchen storage bags (see Exhibit 3–3), the polyethylene raw material, dye to highlight the bag zippers, and packaging for the bags are all costs for the materials needed in production. Because the dye cost is not easily traceable or monetarily significant to WF&B's production cost, this cost may be classified and accounted for as an indirect material and included as part of overhead.

In a service business, direct materials are often insignificant or may not be easily traced to a designated cost object. For instance, in a telephone company, the department responsible for new customer hook-ups could be designated as a cost object. Although the cost of preprinted application forms might be significant enough to trace directly to this department, the cost of other departmental supplies (such as pens, paper, and paperclips) might be relatively inconvenient to trace and thus would be treated as overhead.

Managers usually try to keep the cost of raw materials at the lowest price possible within the context of satisfactory quality. However, as indicated in the following News Note on page 91, enlightened businesspeople are now more often taking a longer run view that considers the economic health of their raw material suppliers.

Direct Labor

Direct labor refers to the individuals who work specifically on manufacturing a product or performing a service. Another perspective of direct labor is that it directly adds value to the final product or service. The chef preparing the meals at the local restaurant and the dental hygienist at the dental clinic represent direct labor workers.

Direct labor cost consists of wages or salaries paid to direct labor employees. Such wages and salaries must also be conveniently traceable to the product or service. Direct labor cost should include basic compensation, production efficiency bonuses, and the employer's share of Social Security and Medicare taxes. In addition, if a company's operations are relatively stable, direct labor cost should include all employer-paid insurance costs, holiday and vacation pay, and pension and other retirement benefits.[7]

As with materials, some labor costs that theoretically should be considered direct are treated as indirect. The first reason for this treatment is that specifically tracing the particular labor costs to production may be inefficient. For instance,

[7] Institute of Management Accountants (formerly National Association of Accountants), *Statements on Management Accounting Number 4C: Definition and Measurement of Direct Labor Cost* (Montvale, N.J.: NAA, June 13, 1985), p. 4.

GENERAL BUSINESS  NEWS NOTE

Showing Concern for Suppliers

As farmers saw hog prices plunge to Depression-era lows this winter, they felt as if salt were being rubbed into their wounds. For even as they were losing heavily, somebody down the line—big meat packers or supermarket chains—seemed to be getting rich on pigs. The price of pork at the supermarket was staying about as high as ever.

"These big companies are essentially saying, 'Your goods are worth $20—we'll pay you $4,' " says Tom Dewig, a local businessman. "That's what our farmers are going through."

At his meat shop, Mr. Dewig rushed to a monitor each morning to check the price of hogs, unable to believe his eyes. "We'd sit there and look at the thing and say, 'It can't go any lower.' But it did," he says, shaking his head. "The next day, we'd say, 'It can't go any lower.' But, it did again."

Mr. Dewig had always said that no hog should sell for less than 30 cents a pound. So when the market price dipped into the mid-20s in September and October, he continued paying farmers 30, knowing that even at that price, he could profit handily. By Halloween, though, the price farmers could get elsewhere was down almost to 20 cents. Mr. Dewig finally broke his rule and started paying less than 30 cents. "I lowered my standards," he says.

When the market fell to the teens, Mr. Dewig set himself a new floor: 20 cents a pound. But then, in mid-December, prices briefly dipped below 10 cents a pound—about a 60-year low—and Mr. Dewig lowered his standards again. Still, on a day when [another] plant was offering farmers 11.5 cents a pound, Mr. Dewig offered a nickel more.

For his hog-farmer neighbors, the above-market prices Dewig paid helped ease both losses and resentment. "He's fair," says Ray Rexing, who has sold hogs to Mr. Dewig since 1970.

Mr. [Joe] Knapp is of two minds. Mr. Dewig "understands we're losing our a— and he's making money faster than he can rake it in," the farmer says. But the next moment, he recalls the losses Mr. Dewig himself took two or three years ago when hog farmers were doing well, and calls him a "dang good guy."

SOURCE: Carl Quintanilla, "Hog Raiser's Pain Puts an Old-Style Butcher on the Knife-Edge," *The Wall Street Journal* (March 24, 1999), pp. A1, A8.

fringe benefit costs should be treated as direct labor cost, but many companies do not have stable workforces that would allow a reasonable estimate of fringe benefit costs. Alternatively, the time, effort, and cost of such tracing might not be worth the additional accuracy it would provide. Thus, the treatment of employee fringe benefits as indirect costs is often based on clerical cost efficiencies.

Second, treating certain labor costs as direct may result in erroneous information about product or service costs. Assume that WF&B employs 20 workers in its cutting room, and that these workers are paid $8 per hour and time and a half ($12) for overtime. One week, the employees worked a total of 1,000 hours (or 200 hours of overtime) to complete all production orders. Of the total employee labor payroll of $8,800, only $8,000 (1,000 hours × $8 per hour) would be classified as direct labor cost. The remaining $800 (200 hours × $4 per hour) would be considered overhead. If the overtime cost were assigned to products made during the overtime hours, these products would appear to have a labor cost 50 percent greater than items made during regular working hours. Because scheduling of particular production runs is random, the items completed during overtime hours should not be forced to bear overtime charges. Therefore, costs for overtime or shift premiums are usually considered overhead rather than direct labor cost and are allocated among all units.

There are, however, some occasions when costs such as overtime should not be considered overhead. If a customer requests a job to be scheduled during overtime hours or is in a rush and requests overtime to be worked, overtime or shift premiums should be considered direct labor and be attached to the job that created the costs. Assume that, in July, the purchasing agent for People's Seafood Stores ordered a large shipment of gallon-sized freezer bags to be delivered in

Workers who specifically work on a product should be classified as direct labor and their wages can be assigned, without any allocation method, to production.

three days for a local seafood festival. To produce this order, WF&B workers had to work overtime. People's Seafood Stores' bill for the shipment should reflect the overtime charges.

Because people historically performed the majority of production activity, direct labor once represented a primary production cost. Now, in highly automated work environments, direct labor often comprises less than 10 to 15 percent of total manufacturing cost. Soon, managers may find that almost all direct labor cost is replaced with a new production cost—the cost of robots and other fully automated machinery. Consider the accompanying News Note regarding the diminished cost and size of direct labor in the era of high technology.

6

Why and how are overhead costs allocated to products and services?

Overhead

Overhead is any factory or production cost that is indirect to manufacturing a product or providing a service and, accordingly, does not include direct material and direct labor. Overhead does include indirect material and indirect labor as well as any and all other costs incurred in the production area.[8] As direct labor has become a progressively smaller proportion of product cost in recent years, overhead has become progressively larger and merits much greater attention than in the past. The following comments reflect these fundamental changes in the way manufacturing is conducted:

> *Automation, technology and computerization have shifted costs, making the typical manufacturing process less labor intensive and more capital intensive. This shift has changed the cost profile of many industries. No longer do direct materials and labor costs make up the major portion of total product cost. Instead, overhead, which is shared by many products and services, is the dominant cost.*[9]

[8] Another term used for overhead is *burden*. Although this is the term under which the definition appears in SMA No. 2, *Management Accounting Terminology*, the authors believe that this term is unacceptable because it connotes costs that are extra, unnecessary, or oppressive. Overhead costs are essential to the conversion process, but simply cannot be traced directly to output.

[9] Sidney J. Baxendale and Michael J. Spurlock, "Does Activity-Based Cost Management Have Any Relevance for Electricity?" *Public Utilities Fortnightly* (July 15, 1997), p. 32.

INTERNATIONAL  **NEWS NOTE**

Firms See High-Wage Germany in A New Light

They're still talking about it. The roof-raising ceremony for Motorola's new $110-million cellular-telephone factory in Germany [in 1998] was one of a kind.

But how typical is Motorola with its big investment in Germany? Isn't this the land of the fading economic miracle? The place where consumer demand is flat on its back, and where no one can agree on how to bring down unemployment hovering near the double digits? Is Motorola crazy to bet on Germany? German manufacturing labor costs may be the highest in the world—more than $31 an hour, or nearly twice the U.S. figure—and people here may regularly disappear for the world's longest vacations and sick leaves. You can't lay off thousands here in one fell swoop.

Consider Varta, a big German maker of batteries. Until last year, it was making small, rechargeable "button-cell" batteries at a big plant in Singapore, a city-state known for its disciplined work force and other competitive strengths. That plant had seven production lines and employed about 500 people.

But in 1995—way too early to be influenced by the current Asian financial upheavals—Varta decided to move its button-cell operation back home to Germany. Here, according to board member Wout van der Kooij, Varta has been able to set up far more modern machinery and, beginning this year, is able to produce 50% more batteries than in Singapore in a tenth the space. Only 70 Germans will be needed to run the plant.

"If you need to pay only 70 people, then the high wage cost of Germany is not relevant anymore," Van der Kooij said. "What is relevant," he said, "is Germany's technological infrastructure: the host of skilled electrochemical engineers and related technicians available on the job market. Electrochemists are virtually nonexistent in Southeast Asia," Van der Kooij said. But with their abundance here in Germany, Varta could install its state-of-the-art equipment, confident of maintaining it, repairing it and buying needed supplies without ever leaving the company's own backyard.

Because the German working class tends to be so well-educated, [Norbert] Quinkert [Motorola Country Manager] said, "Motorola's existing cell-phone factory here has higher productivity than the company's other such plants in China, Scotland, and Illinois. The only bad mark Motorola's German plant gets," he said, "is for its high direct labor costs—but labor accounts for only 2% of the total cost of manufacturing a cellular phone."

SOURCE: Mary Williams Walsh, "Firms See High-Wage Germany in a New Light," *Los Angeles Times—Sunday Home Edition* (April 12, 1998), p. D1.

Overhead costs are either variable or fixed based on their behavior in response to changes in production volume or some other activity measure. Variable overhead includes the costs of indirect material, indirect labor paid on an hourly basis (such as wages for forklift operators, material handlers, and others who support the production, assembly, and/or service process), lubricants used for machine maintenance, and the variable portion of factory electricity charges. Depreciation calculated using either the units-of-production or service life method is also a variable overhead cost; this depreciation method reflects a decline in machine utility based on usage rather than time passage and is appropriate in an automated plant.

Fixed overhead comprises costs such as straight-line depreciation on factory plant assets, factory license fees, and factory insurance and property taxes. Fixed indirect labor costs include salaries for production supervisors, shift superintendents, and plant managers. The fixed portion of factory mixed costs (such as maintenance and utilities) is also part of fixed overhead. An example of fixed overhead for a professional sports team is depreciation of arena seating. The accompanying News Note on page 94 discusses a trend in cost management that does not sit too well with some sports fans.

http://www.nba.com
http://www.nba.com/magic
http://www.nfl.com/redskins

One important overhead cost is the amount spent on quality. Quality is a managerial concern on two general levels. First, product or service quality from the consumer perspective is an important consideration because consumers want the best quality they can find for the money. Second, managers are concerned about production process quality because higher process quality leads to greater

NEWS NOTE  QUALITY

Stadium Squeeze Play

At a time when most indoor arenas are spending millions of dollars on a slew of upgrades, from cigar bars to gourmet chow, one aspect of the fan experience is quietly shrinking: seat size. Indeed, many sports patrons are being stuffed into chairs that are about as wide as a computer keyboard, or the average coach-class airplane seat.

And it's only getting worse. A new basketball and hockey arena that's being built in Atlanta will be state-of-the-art in all respects except one: seats that could be as narrow as 18 inches in some places. Another, Denver's Pepsi Center, plans to jam in up to 30% more seats per row.

For their part, National Basketball Association teams and stadium officials say they're simply trying to keep pace with the soaring player salaries and construction costs. At today's ticket prices, one general-admission seat can generate $1 million in revenue over a facility's lifetime, experts say. "If the Orlando Magic hadn't renovated its arena to fit an additional 2,000 seats four years ago," says team executive Pat Williams, "the Magic would have had to hike ticket prices to an untenable level."

"I know some longtime fans will never get over it," Mr. Williams says, "But without the extra seats we would have been priced out of business."

"It's like a sardine can," says a longtime Washington Redskins fan who has season tickets at the team's new Jack Kent Cooke Stadium in suburban Maryland. "It's good to have someone you love sitting next to you."

Back in Portland, Jerry Nothman, a former season ticket holder, didn't like his new basketball arena seat. Arena officials say it's possible some fans might have wound up in narrower chairs when the team moved there in 1995. But they insist that the average seat size is still pretty much the same.

But Mr. Nothman isn't buying it. And he's not buying season tickets anymore, either. Last year, he declined to renew them for the first time in 22 years. "It was insulting," he says. "I don't mind sitting on a wooden bench for $7, but if someone is going to charge me $60, I expect a certain comfort level."

SOURCE: Sam Walker, "Stadium Squeeze Play," *The Wall Street Journal* (March 26, 1999), pp. W1, W4. Permission conveyed through the Copyright Clearance Center.

customer satisfaction through minimizing production cycle time, cost, and defects. Both levels of quality generate costs that often total 20 to 25 percent of sales.[10] The two categories of quality costs are the cost of control and the cost of failure to control.

The cost of control includes prevention and appraisal costs. Prevention costs are incurred to improve quality by precluding product defects and dysfunctional processing from occurring. Amounts spent on implementing training programs, researching customer needs, and acquiring improved production equipment are prevention costs. Amounts incurred for monitoring or inspection are called appraisal costs; these costs compensate for mistakes not eliminated through prevention.

The second category of quality costs is failure costs, which may be internal (such as scrap and rework) or external (such as product returns caused by quality problems, warranty costs, and complaint department costs). Expenditures made for prevention will minimize the costs that will be incurred for appraisal and failure. Quality costs are discussed in greater depth in Chapter 8.

In manufacturing, quality costs may be variable in relation to the quantity of defective output, step fixed with increases at specific levels of defective output, or fixed. Rework cost approaches zero if the quantity of defective output is also nearly zero. However, these costs would be extremely high if the number of defective parts produced were high. In contrast, training expenditures are set by management and might not vary regardless of the quantity of defective output produced in a given period.

[10] "Measuring the Cost of Quality Takes Creativity" *(Grant Thornton) Manufacturing Issues* (Spring 1991), p. 1.

ACCUMULATION AND ALLOCATION OF OVERHEAD

Direct material and direct labor are easily traced to a product or service. Overhead, on the other hand, must be accumulated over a period and allocated to the products manufactured or services rendered during that time. **Cost allocation** refers to the assignment of an indirect cost to one or more cost objects using some reasonable basis. This section of the chapter discusses underlying reasons for cost allocation, use of predetermined overhead rates, separation of mixed costs into variable and fixed elements, and capacity measures that can be used to compute predetermined overhead rates.

cost allocation

Why Overhead Costs Are Allocated

Many accounting procedures are based on allocations. Cost allocations can be made over several time periods or within a single time period. For example, in financial accounting, a building's cost is allocated through depreciation charges over its useful or service life. This process is necessary to fulfill the matching principle. In cost accounting, production overhead costs are allocated within a period through the use of predictors or cost drivers to products or services. This process reflects application of the cost principle, which requires that all production or acquisition costs attach to the units produced, services rendered, or units purchased.

Overhead costs are allocated to cost objects for three reasons: (1) to determine a full cost of the cost object, (2) to motivate the manager in charge of the cost object to manage it efficiently, and (3) to compare alternative courses of action for management planning, controlling, and decision making.[11] The first reason relates to financial statement valuations. Under generally accepted accounting principles (GAAP), "full cost" must include allocated production overhead. In contrast, the assignment of nonfactory overhead costs to products is not normally allowed under GAAP.[12] The other two reasons for overhead allocations are related to internal purposes and, thus, no hard-and-fast rules apply to the overhead allocation process.

Regardless of why overhead costs are allocated, the method and basis of the allocation process should be rational and systematic so that the resulting information is useful for product costing and managerial purposes. Traditionally, the information generated for satisfying the "full cost" objective was also used for the second and third objectives. However, because the first purpose is externally focused and the others are internally focused, different methods can be used to provide different costs for different needs.

Predetermined Overhead Rates

In an **actual cost system**, actual direct material and direct labor costs are accumulated in Work in Process Inventory as the costs are incurred. Actual production overhead costs are accumulated separately in an Overhead Control account and are assigned to Work in Process Inventory at the end of a period or at completion of production.

actual cost system

The use of an actual cost system is generally considered to be less than desirable because all production overhead information must be available before any cost allocation can be made to products or services. For example, the cost of products and services produced in May could not be calculated until the May electricity bill is received in June.

[11] Institute of Management Accountants, *Statements on Management Accounting Number 4B: Allocation of Service and Administrative Costs* (Montvale, N.J.: NAA, June 13, 1985), pp. 9–10.

[12] Although potentially unacceptable for GAAP, certain nonfactory overhead costs must be assigned to products for tax purposes.

normal cost system

predetermined overhead rate

An alternative to an actual cost system is a **normal cost system**, which uses actual direct material and direct labor costs and a predetermined overhead (OH) rate or rates. A **predetermined overhead rate** (or overhead application rate) is a budgeted and constant charge per unit of activity that is used to assign overhead cost from an Overhead Control account to Work in Process Inventory for the period's production or services.

Three primary reasons exist for using predetermined overhead rates in product costing. First, a predetermined rate allows overhead to be assigned during the period to the goods produced or services rendered. Thus, a predetermined overhead rate improves the timeliness (though it reduces the precision) of information.

Second, predetermined overhead rates compensate for fluctuations in actual overhead costs that are unrelated to activity. Overhead may vary monthly because of seasonal or calendar factors. For example, factory utility costs may be highest in the summer. If monthly production were constant and actual overhead were assigned to production, the increase in utilities would cause product cost per unit to be higher in the summer than in the rest of the year. If a company produced 3,000 units of its sole product in each of the months of April and July but utilities were $600 in April and $900 in July, then the average actual utilities cost per unit for April would be $0.20 ($600 ÷ 3,000 units) and $0.30 ($900 ÷ 3,000) in July. Although one such cost difference may not be significant, numerous differences of this type could cause a large distortion in unit cost.

Third, predetermined overhead rates overcome the problem of fluctuations in activity levels that have no impact on actual fixed overhead costs. Even if total production overhead were the same for each period, changes in activity would cause a per-unit change in cost because of the fixed cost element of overhead. If a company incurred $600 utilities cost in each of October and November but produced 3,750 units of product in October and 3,000 units of product in November, its average actual unit cost for utilities would be $0.16 ($600 ÷ 3,750 units) in October but $0.20 ($600 ÷ 3,000 units) in November. Although one such overhead cost difference caused by fluctuation in production activity may not be significant, numerous differences of this type could cause a large distortion in unit cost. Use of an annual, predetermined overhead rate would overcome the variations demonstrated by the examples above through application of a uniform rate of overhead to all units produced throughout the year.

To calculate a predetermined OH rate, divide the total budgeted overhead cost at a specific activity level by the related activity level for a specific period:

$$\text{Predetermined OH Rate} = \frac{\text{Total Budgeted OH Cost at a Specified Activity Level}}{\text{Volume of Specified Activity Level}}$$

Overhead cost and its related activity measure are typically budgeted for one year "unless the production/marketing cycle of the entity is such that the use of a longer or shorter period would clearly provide more useful information."[13] For example, the use of a longer period would be appropriate in a company engaged in activities such as constructing ships, bridges, or high-rise office buildings.

A company should use an activity base that is logically related to overhead cost incurrence. The activity base that may first be considered is production volume, but this base is reasonable if the company manufactures only one type of product or renders only one type of service. If multiple products or services exist, a summation of production volumes cannot be made to determine "activity" because of the heterogeneous nature of the items.

To most effectively allocate overhead to heterogeneous products, a measure of activity must be determined that is common to all output. The activity base

[13] Institute of Management Accountants, *Statements on Management Accounting Number 2G: Accounting for Indirect Production Costs* (Montvale, N.J.: NAA, June 1, 1987), p. 11.

should be a cost driver that directly causes the incurrence of overhead costs. Direct labor hours and direct labor dollars have been commonly used measures of activity; however, the deficiencies caused by using these bases are becoming more apparent as companies become increasingly automated. Using direct labor to allocate overhead costs in automated plants results in extremely high overhead rates because the costs are applied over a smaller number of labor hours (or dollars). In automated plants, machine hours may be more appropriate for allocating overhead than either direct labor base. Other traditional measures include number of purchase orders and product-related physical characteristics such as tons or gallons. Additionally, innovative new measures for overhead allocation include number or time of machine setups, number of parts, quantity of material handling time, and number of product defects.

APPLYING OVERHEAD TO PRODUCTION

The predetermined overhead rates are used throughout the year to apply overhead to Work in Process Inventory. Overhead may be applied as production occurs, when goods or services are transferred out of Work in Process Inventory, or at the end of each month. Under real-time systems in use today, overhead is frequently applied continuously. **Applied overhead** is the amount of overhead assigned to Work in Process Inventory as a result of incurring the activity that was used to develop the application rate. Application is made using the predetermined rate(s) and the actual level(s) of activity.

applied overhead

Overhead can be recorded either in separate accounts for actual and applied overhead or in a single account. If actual and applied accounts are separated, the applied account is a contra account to the actual overhead account and is closed against it at year-end. The alternative, more convenient, recordkeeping option is to maintain one general ledger account that is debited for actual overhead costs and credited for applied overhead. This method is used throughout the text.

Additionally, overhead may be recorded in a single overhead account or in separate accounts for the variable and fixed components. Exhibit 3–8 presents the alternative overhead recording possibilities.

If separate rates are used to apply variable and fixed overhead, the general ledger would most commonly contain separate variable and fixed overhead accounts. When separate accounts are used, mixed costs must be separated into their variable and fixed components or assigned to either the variable or fixed overhead general ledger account. Because overhead costs in an automated factory represent an ever larger part of product cost, the benefits of separating costs according to their behavior are thought to be greater than the time and effort expended to make that separation.

EXHIBIT 3–8

Cost Accounting System Possibilities for Manufacturing Overhead

Separate Accounts For Actual & Applied and For Variable & Fixed

VOH Actual: XXX |

VOH Applied: | YYY

FOH Actual: XX |

FOH Applied: | YY

Combined Accounts For Actual & Applied; Separate Accounts For Variable & Fixed

VOH: Actual XXX | Applied YYY

FOH: Actual XX | Applied YY

Combined Account For Actual & Applied and For Variable & Fixed

Manufacturing Overhead: Total actual XXX, XX | Total applied YYY, YY

Regardless of the number (combined or separate) or type (plantwide or departmental) of predetermined overhead rates used, actual overhead costs are debited to the appropriate overhead general ledger account(s) and credited to the various sources of overhead costs. Applied overhead is debited to Work in Process Inventory and credited to the overhead general ledger account(s). Actual activity causes actual overhead costs to be incurred and overhead to be applied to Work in Process Inventory. Thus, actual and applied overhead costs are both related to actual activity, and only by actual activity are they related to each other.

Assume that during March 2001, the Cutting and Mounting Department incurs 5,000 machine hours. Actual variable and fixed overhead costs for the month were $10,400 and $7,300, respectively. Assume also that applied variable overhead for March is $10,000 (5,000 × $2.00) and applied fixed overhead is $7,150 (5,000 × $1.43). The journal entries to record actual and applied overhead for March 2001 are

Variable Manufacturing Overhead	10,400	
Fixed Manufacturing Overhead	7,300	
Various Accounts		17,700
To record actual manufacturing overhead.		
Work in Process Inventory	17,150	
Variable Manufacturing Overhead		10,000
Fixed Manufacturing Overhead		7,150
To apply variable and fixed manufacturing overhead to WIP.		

underapplied overhead

overapplied overhead

At year-end, actual overhead will differ from applied overhead and the difference is referred to as underapplied or overapplied overhead. **Underapplied overhead** means that the overhead applied to Work in Process Inventory is less than actual overhead; **overapplied overhead** means that the overhead applied to Work in Process Inventory is greater than actual overhead. Underapplied or overapplied overhead must be closed at year-end because a single year's activity level was used to determine the overhead rate(s).

7

What causes underapplied or overapplied overhead and how is it treated at the end of a period?

DISPOSITION OF UNDERAPPLIED AND OVERAPPLIED OVERHEAD

Disposition of underapplied or overapplied overhead depends on the significance of the amount involved. If the amount is immaterial, it is closed to Cost of Goods Sold. When overhead is underapplied (debit balance), an insufficient amount of overhead was applied to production and the closing process causes Cost of Goods Sold to increase. Alternatively, overapplied overhead (credit balance) reflects the fact that too much overhead was applied to production, so closing overapplied overhead causes Cost of Goods Sold to decrease. To illustrate this entry, note that the Cutting and Mounting Department has an overhead credit balance at year-end of $40,000 in Manufacturing Overhead as presented in the upper left section of Exhibit 3–9; we first assume this amount to be immaterial for *illustrative purposes*. The journal entry to close overapplied overhead that is assumed to be immaterial is

Manufacturing Overhead	40,000	
Cost of Goods Sold		40,000

If the amount of underapplied or overapplied overhead is significant, it should be allocated among the accounts containing applied overhead: Work in Process Inventory, Finished Goods Inventory, and Cost of Goods Sold. A significant amount of underapplied or overapplied overhead means that the balances in these accounts are quite different from what they would have been if actual overhead costs had been assigned to production. Allocation restates the account balances to conform more closely to actual historical cost as required for external reporting by generally accepted accounting principles. Exhibit 3–9 uses assumed data for the Cutting and Mounting Department to illustrate the proration of overapplied overhead among the necessary accounts; had the amount been underapplied, the accounts debited

EXHIBIT 3-9

Proration of Overapplied Overhead

Manufacturing Overhead		Account Balances	
Actual	$220,000	Work in Process Inventory	$ 45,640
Applied	260,000	Finished Goods Inventory	78,240
Overapplied	$ 40,000	Cost of Goods Sold	528,120

1. Add balances of accounts and determine proportional relationships:

	Balance	Proportion	Percentage
Work in Process	$ 45,640	$45,640 ÷ $652,000	7
Finished Goods	78,240	$78,240 ÷ $652,000	12
Cost of Goods Sold	528,120	$528,120 ÷ $652,000	81
Total	$652,000		100

2. Multiply percentages times overapplied overhead amount to determine the amount of adjustment needed:

	Account %	×	Overapplied OH	=	Adjustment Amount
Work in Process	7	×	$40,000	=	$ 2,800
Finished Goods	12	×	$40,000	=	$ 4,800
Cost of Goods Sold	81	×	$40,000	=	$32,400

3. Prepare journal entry to close manufacturing overhead account and assign adjustment amount to appropriate accounts:

Manufacturing Overhead	40,000	
Work in Process Inventory		2,800
Finished Goods Inventory		4,800
Cost of Goods Sold		32,400

and credited in the journal entry would be the reverse of that presented for overapplied overhead. A single overhead account is used in this illustration.

Theoretically, underapplied or overapplied overhead should be allocated based on the amounts of applied overhead contained in each account rather than on total account balances. Use of total account balances could cause distortion because they contain direct material and direct labor costs that are not related to actual or applied overhead. In spite of this potential distortion, use of total balances is more common *in practice* for two reasons. First, the theoretical method is complex and requires detailed account analysis. Second, overhead tends to lose its identity after leaving Work in Process Inventory, thus making more difficult the determination of the amount of overhead in Finished Goods Inventory and Cost of Goods Sold account balances.

ALTERNATIVE CAPACITY MEASURES

One primary cause of underapplied or overapplied overhead is a difference in budgeted and actual costs. Another cause is a difference in the level of activity or capacity chosen to compute the predetermined overhead and the actual activity incurred. **Capacity** refers to a measure of production volume or some other activity base. Alternative measures of activity include theoretical, practical, normal, and expected capacity.

capacity

The estimated maximum potential activity for a specified time is the **theoretical capacity**. This measure assumes that all factors are operating in a technically and humanly perfect manner. Theoretical capacity disregards realities such as machinery breakdowns and reduced or stopped plant operations on holidays. Choice of this level of activity provides a probable outcome of a material amount of underapplied overhead cost.

theoretical capacity

practical capacity

normal capacity

expected capacity

Reducing theoretical capacity by ongoing, regular operating interruptions (such as holidays, downtime, and start-up time) provides the **practical capacity** that could be achieved during regular working hours. Consideration of historical and estimated future production levels and the cyclical fluctuations provides a **normal capacity** measure that encompasses the long run (5 to 10 years) average activity of the firm. This measure represents a reasonably attainable level of activity, but will not provide costs that are most similar to actual historical costs. Thus, many firms use expected annual capacity as the selected measure of activity. **Expected capacity** is a short-run concept that represents the anticipated activity level of the firm for the upcoming period, based on projected product demand. It is determined during the budgeting process conducted in preparation of the master budget for that period. The process for preparing the master budget is presented in Chapter 13. If actual results are close to budgeted results (in both dollars and volume), this measure should result in product costs that most closely reflect actual costs and, thus, an immaterial amount of underapplied or overapplied overhead.[14]

ACCUMULATION OF PRODUCT COSTS—ACTUAL COST SYSTEM

Product costs can be accumulated using either a perpetual or a periodic inventory system. In a perpetual inventory system, all product costs flow through Work in Process Inventory to Finished Goods Inventory and, ultimately, to Cost of Goods Sold. The perpetual system continuously provides current information for financial statement preparation and for inventory and cost control. Because the costs of maintaining a perpetual system have diminished significantly as computerized production, bar coding, and information processing have become more pervasive, this text assumes that all companies discussed use a perpetual system.

The Midwestern Polyethylene Products Corporation is used to illustrate the flow of product costs in a manufacturing organization. The April 1, 2001, inventory account balances for Midwestern were as follows: Raw Material Inventory (all direct), $73,000; Work in Process Inventory, $145,000; and Finished Goods Inventory, $87,400. Midwestern uses separate variable and fixed accounts to record the incurrence of overhead. In this illustration, actual overhead costs are used to apply overhead to Work in Process Inventory. However, an additional, brief illustration applying predetermined overhead in a normal cost system is presented in the section following the current illustration. The following transactions keyed to the journal entries in Exhibit 3–10 represent Midwestern's activity for April.

During the month, Midwestern's purchasing agent bought $280,000 of direct materials on account (entry 1), and the warehouse manager transferred $284,000 of materials into the production area (entry 2). Production wages for the month totaled $530,000, of which $436,000 was for direct labor (entry 3). April salaries for the production supervisor was $20,000 (entry 4). April utility cost of $28,000 was accrued; analyzing this cost indicated that $16,000 was variable and $12,000 was fixed (entry 5). Supplies costing $5,200 were removed from inventory and placed into the production process (entry 6). Also, Midwestern paid $7,000 for April's property taxes on the factory (entry 7), depreciated the factory assets $56,880 (entry 8), and recorded the expiration of $3,000 of prepaid insurance on the factory assets (entry 9). Entry 10 shows the application of actual overhead to Work in Process Inventory for, respectively, variable and fixed overhead for Midwestern during April. During April, $1,058,200 of goods were completed and transferred to

[14] Except where otherwise noted in the text, expected annual capacity has been chosen as the basis to calculate the predetermined fixed manufacturing overhead rate because it is believed to be the most prevalent practice. This choice, however, may not be the most effective for planning and control purposes as is discussed further in Chapter 10 with regard to standard cost variances.

EXHIBIT 3-10

Midwestern Polyethylene Products Corporation—April 2001 Journal Entries

	Debit	Credit
(1) Raw Materials Inventory	280,000	
Accounts Payable		280,000
To record cost of direct materials purchased on account.		
(2) Work in Process Inventory	284,000	
Raw Materials Inventory		284,000
To record direct materials transferred to production.		
(3) Work in Process Inventory	436,000	
Variable Overhead Control	94,000	
Salaries & Wages Payable		530,000
To accrue factory wages for direct and indirect labor.		
(4) Fixed Overhead Control	20,000	
Salaries & Wages Payable		20,000
To accrue production supervisors salaries.		
(5) Variable Overhead Control	16,000	
Fixed Overhead Control	12,000	
Utilities Payable		28,000
To record mixed utility cost in its variable and fixed amounts.		
(6) Variable Overhead Control	5,200	
Supplies Inventory		5,200
To record supplies used.		
(7) Fixed Overhead Control	7,000	
Cash		7,000
To record payment for factory property taxes for the period.		
(8) Fixed Overhead Control	56,880	
Accumulated Depreciation—Equipment		56,880
To record depreciation on factory assets for the period.		
(9) Fixed Overhead Control	3,000	
Prepaid Insurance		3,000
To record expiration of prepaid insurance on factory assets.		
(10) Work in Process Inventory	214,080	
Variable Overhead Control		115,200
Fixed Overhead Control		98,880
To record the application of actual overhead costs to Work in Process Inventory.		
(11) Finished Goods Inventory	1,058,200	
Work in Process Inventory		1,058,200
To record the transfer of work completed during the period.		
(12) Accounts Receivable	1,460,000	
Sales		1,460,000
To record the selling price of goods sold on account during the period.		
(13) Cost of Goods Sold	1,054,000	
Finished Goods Inventory		1,054,000
To record cost of goods sold for the period.		

Finished Goods Inventory (entry 11). Sales of $1,460,000 on account were recorded during the month (entry 12); the goods that were sold had a total cost of $1,054,000 (entry 13). An abbreviated presentation of the cost flows is shown in selected T-accounts in Exhibit 3–11.

EXHIBIT 3–11

Selected T-Accounts for Midwestern Polyethylene Products Corporation

Raw Materials Inventory

Beg. bal.	73,000	(2)	284,000
(1)	280,000		
End. bal.	69,000		

Variable Overhead Control

(3)	94,000	(10)	115,200
(5)	16,000		
(6)	5,200		

Work in Process Inventory

Beg. bal.	145,000	(11)	1,058,200
(2) DM	284,000		
(3) DL	436,000		
(10) OH	214,080		
End. bal.	20,880		

Fixed Overhead Control

(4)	20,000	(10)	98,880
(5)	12,000		
(7)	7,000		
(8)	56,880		
(9)	3,000		

Finished Goods Inventory

Beg. bal.	87,400	(13) CGS	1,054,000
(11) CGM	1,058,200		
End. bal.	91,600		

Cost of Goods Sold

(13) CGS	1,054,000		

COST OF GOODS MANUFACTURED AND SOLD

8

How is cost of goods manufactured calculated?

cost of goods manufactured

The T-accounts in Exhibit 3–11 provide detailed information about the cost of materials used, goods transferred from work in process, and goods sold. This information is needed to prepare financial statements. Because most managers do not have access to the detailed accounting records, they need to have the flow of costs and the calculation of important income statement amounts presented in a formalized manner. Therefore, a schedule of **cost of goods manufactured** (CGM) is prepared as a preliminary step to the determination of cost of goods sold (CGS).[15] CGM is the total production cost of the goods that were completed and transferred to Finished Goods Inventory during the period. This amount is similar to the cost of net purchases in the cost of goods sold schedule for a retailer.

Formal schedules of cost of goods manufactured and cost of goods sold are presented in Exhibit 3–12 using the amounts shown in Exhibits 3–10 and 3–11. The schedule of cost of goods manufactured starts with the beginning balance of Work in Process (WIP) Inventory and details all product cost components. The cost of materials used in production during the period is equal to the beginning balance of Raw Materials Inventory plus raw materials purchased minus the ending balance of Raw Materials Inventory. If Raw Materials Inventory includes both direct and indirect materials, the cost of direct material used is assigned to WIP Inventory and the cost of indirect materials used is included in variable overhead. Because direct labor cannot be warehoused, all charges for direct labor during the period are part of WIP Inventory. Variable and fixed overhead costs are added to direct material and direct labor costs to determine total manufacturing costs.

Beginning Work in Process Inventory cost is added to total current period manufacturing costs to obtain a subtotal amount that can be referred to as "total costs to account for." The value of ending WIP Inventory is calculated (through techniques discussed later in the text) and subtracted from the subtotal to provide the cost of goods manufactured during the period. The schedule of cost of

[15] A service business prepares a schedule of cost of services rendered.

EXHIBIT 3–12

Cost of Goods Manufactured and Cost of Goods Sold Schedules

MIDWESTERN POLYETHYLENE PRODUCTS CORPORATION
Schedule of Cost of Goods Manufactured
For the Month Ended April 30, 2001

Beginning balance of Work in Process, 4/1/01			$ 145,000
Manufacturing costs for the period:			
Raw materials (all direct):			
Beginning balance	$ 73,000		
Purchases of materials	280,000		
Raw materials available	$353,000		
Ending balance	69,000		
Total raw materials used		$284,000	
Direct labor		436,000	
Variable overhead:			
Indirect labor	$ 94,000		
Utilities	16,000		
Supplies	5,200	115,200	
Fixed overhead:			
Supervisor's salary	$ 20,000		
Utilities	12,000		
Factory property taxes	7,000		
Factory asset depreciation	56,880		
Factory insurance	3,000	98,880	
Total current period manufacturing costs			934,080
Total costs to account for			$1,079,080
Ending work in process, 4/30/01			(20,880)
Cost of goods manufactured			$1,058,200

MIDWESTERN POLYETHYLENE PRODUCTS CORPORATION
Schedule of Cost of Goods Sold
For the Month Ended April 30, 2001

Beginning Finished Goods, 4/1/01	$ 87,400
Cost of Goods Manufactured	1,058,200
Cost of Goods Available for Sale	$1,145,600
Ending Finished Goods, 4/30/01	(91,600)
Cost of Goods Sold	$1,054,000

goods manufactured is usually prepared only as an internal schedule and is not provided to external parties.

In the schedule of cost of goods sold, cost of goods manufactured is added to the beginning balance of Finished Goods (FG) Inventory to find the cost of goods available for sale during the period. The ending FG Inventory is calculated by multiplying a physical unit count times a unit cost. If a perpetual inventory system is used, the actual amount of ending FG Inventory can be compared to that which should be on hand based on the finished goods account balance recorded at the end of the period. Any differences can be attributed to losses that might have arisen from theft, breakage, evaporation, or accounting errors. Ending Finished Goods Inventory is subtracted from the cost of goods available for sale to determine cost of goods sold.

ACCUMULATION OF PRODUCT COSTS—NORMAL COST SYSTEM

In a normal cost system, only entry 10, which applies overhead to WIP Inventory, is different from that presented in Exhibit 3–10. Assume, for the purpose of illustrating what happens using a normal cost system, that the predetermined variable overhead rate is $2.40 per machine hour, that the predetermined fixed overhead rate is $2.04 per machine hour and that 48,000 machine hours were incurred by Midwestern in April. These statistics are used to exactly match the information in the actual cost illustration above and for simplifying the illustration by precluding the presence of under- or overapplied overhead for April at Midwestern.

However, predetermined overhead most often does not match actual overhead. Monthly under- or overapplied overhead that does occur is accumulated and disposed of at year-end in the manner described earlier in this chapter. In a normal cost system, entry 10 of Exhibit 3–10 is the only entry that is different from its counterpart in an actual cost system because, instead of applying actual overhead, predetermined overhead is applied to WIP Inventory. Although the numbers appear to be the same amounts in this simplified case as in the original entry 10, the manner in which they are derived is entirely different (and in a realistic setting, the dollar amounts are virtually always different). In a normal cost setting, the credits to the variable and fixed overhead accounts are calculated as follows:

Variable overhead credit = $2.40 × 48,000 machine hours
= $115,200

Fixed overhead credit = $2.06 × 48,000 machine hours
= $ 98,880

The debit to WIP Inventory is the sum of these two credits:

WIP Inventory debit = $115,200 + $98,880 = $214,080

The complete entry follows:

		Debit	Credit
10)	Work in Process Inventory	214,080	
	Variable Overhead Control		115,200
	Fixed Overhead Control		98,880
	To record the application of *predetermined* overhead costs to WIP Inventory.		

Some accountants prefer to streamline the presentation of the Schedule of Cost of Goods Manufactured and Sold when perpetual inventory accounting is used. Such an alternative is presented in Exhibit 3–13; in addition, the use of normal costing supports condensing the overhead presentation further.

EXHIBIT 3-13

Cost of Goods Manufactured and Cost of Goods Sold Schedules

MIDWESTERN POLYETHYLENE PRODUCTS CORPORATION
Schedule of Cost of Goods Manufactured
For the Month Ended April 30, 2001

Beginning balance of Work in Process, 4/1/01		$ 145,000
Manufacturing costs for the period:		
Total raw materials used	$284,000	
Direct labor	436,000	
Variable overhead applied	115,200	
Fixed overhead applied	98,880	
Total current period manufacturing costs		934,080
Total costs to account for		$1,079,080
Ending Work in Process, 4/30/01		(20,880)
Cost of goods manufactured		$1,058,200

(continued)

EXHIBIT 3–13

(Concluded)

MIDWESTERN POLYETHYLENE PRODUCTS CORPORATION Schedule of Cost of Goods Sold For the Month Ended April 30, 2001	
Beginning Finished Goods, 4/1/01	$ 87,400
Cost of Goods Manufactured	1,058,200
Cost of Goods Available for Sale	$1,145,600
Ending Finished Goods, 4/30/01	(91,600)
Cost of Goods Sold	$1,054,000

REVISITING

Wisconsin Film & Bag

Wisconsin Film & Bag has grown 500 percent since Jack Riopelle, president and chief operating officer, helped purchase the firm in 1993. The workforce has expanded from 43 employees in 1993 to 285 employees in 1999 currently. At that time WF&B annual sales exceed $30 million.

WF&B's vision statement is as follows:

Wisconsin Film & Bag will become the standard by which our competitors measure themselves. We intend to be known as the company people want to work for, buy from and sell to. This will be accomplished by achieving the following:

1. *We will maintain a consistent attitude toward employee involvement and incorporate unconditional integrity in all interactions with customers, suppliers, employees, shareholders and the community.*
2. *We are committed to sustained, profitable growth with a dedication toward excellence in quality, service and creativity. We will also commit human and capital resources to improve our quality, control costs, and expand our capabilities to meet our customers' needs.*
3. *We will strive for preferred vendor status from each of our customers and universal respect from all our competitors.*
4. *We will become an industry leader by making environmentally conscious decisions in everything we do.*

There is much evidence that the firm is progressing toward this vision. Not only has the firm grown at a fast pace, but it has also tried to be a good environmental neighbor and a good citizen.

The firm's first repelletizer, which repelletizes production scrap and purchased film scrap, was installed in May 1995. This has allowed the firm to reuse its own internally generated scrap and to use purchased scrap from outside sources, saving over $100,000 annually in raw material cost for production of "non-food-grade" products.

When WF&B recently opened its Hartland, Wisconsin facility, it had trouble staffing manufacturing operations because Western Waukesha County is a white-collar community. So the firm tapped into the area's long-term unemployed, providing assistance in locating competent day care, reliable transportation, and training in life skills such as reading a ruler, using a calculator, looking someone in the eyes while talking, and budgeting paychecks. New employees receive company T-shirts so they're dressed the same as the old-timers. WF&B assigns a 24-hour "Retention Specialist" to each new hire to help resolve personal issues.

In 1999, WF&B received two awards: "Employer of the Year" from the Private Industry Council of Waukesha-Ozaukee-Washington counties and one of the 15 "Exemplary Employers" in the State of Wisconsin at the Sixth Annual Governor's Employment and Training Conference.

SOURCE: Corporate Headquarters—Wisconsin Film & Bag, 3100 E. Richmond Street, Shawano, WI 54166.

CHAPTER SUMMARY

This chapter presents a variety of definitions and classifications of cost.

Historical, replacement, and budgeted costs are typically associated with time. Historical costs are used for external financial statements; replacement and budgeted costs are more often used by managers in conducting their planning, controlling, and decision-making functions.

Variable, fixed, mixed, and step costs describe cost behavior within the context of a relevant range. Total variable cost varies directly and proportionately with changes in activity; variable costs are constant on a per-unit basis. Costs that remain constant in total, regardless of changes in activity, are fixed. On a per-unit basis, fixed costs vary inversely with activity changes. Mixed costs contain both a variable and fixed component and are usually separated (using the high-low method or least squares regression analysis) into these components for product costing and management's uses. Step costs can be variable or fixed, depending on the size of the "step" change (small or large, respectively) that occurs relative to the change in activity. Accountants select a relevant range that allows step variable costs to be treated as variable and step fixed costs to be treated as fixed.

For financial statements, costs are either considered unexpired and reported on the balance sheet as assets, or expired and reported on the income statement as expenses or losses. Costs may also be viewed as product or period costs. Product costs are inventoried and include direct material, direct labor, and manufacturing overhead. When the products are sold, these costs expire and become cost of goods sold expense. Period costs are incurred outside the production area and are usually associated with the functions of selling, administrating, and financing.

Costs are also said to be direct or indirect relative to a cost object. The material and labor costs of production that are physically and conveniently traceable to products are direct costs. All other costs incurred in the production area are indirect and are referred to as manufacturing overhead.

The extensive activity required to convert raw materials into finished goods distinguishes manufacturers and service companies from retailers. This conversion process necessitates that all factory costs be accumulated and reported as product costs under accrual accounting.

A predetermined overhead rate is calculated by dividing the upcoming period's budgeted overhead costs by a selected level of activity. (Budgeted overhead costs at various levels of activity are shown on a flexible budget, which is discussed in Chapter 10 on standard costing.) Predetermined overhead rates eliminate the problems caused by delays in obtaining actual cost data, make the overhead allocation process more effective, and allocate a uniform amount of overhead to goods or services based on related production efforts.

The activity base chosen to compute a predetermined overhead rate should be logically related to cost changes and be a direct causal factor of that cost (a cost driver) rather than simply a predictor. Units of output are a valid measure only if the company produces a single product.

When a company uses a predetermined overhead rate, underapplied or overapplied overhead results at the end of the year. This amount (if insignificant) should be closed to Cost of Goods Sold or (if significant) allocated among Work in Process Inventory, Finished Goods Inventory, and Cost of Goods Sold.

An internal management report, known as the cost of goods manufactured schedule, traces the flow of costs into the production area and through conversion into finished goods. This report provides the necessary information to prepare the cost of goods sold section of a manufacturer's income statement.

APPENDIX

Plantwide versus Departmental Overhead Application Rates

The Indianapolis Division of Alexander Polymers International is used to illustrate the calculation of a single, plantwide overhead application rate. This division contains two departments (Cutting and Mounting, and Packaging). At the end of 2000, division management budgets its 2001 activity level at 75,000 machine hours and manufacturing overhead costs at $399,750. If a plantwide predetermined overhead application rate is calculated on per machine hour:

$$\text{Plantwide OH Rate} = \frac{\text{Total Budgeted OH Cost at a Specific Activity Level}}{\text{Volume of Specified Activity Level}}$$

$$= \frac{\$399{,}750}{75{,}000 \text{ MH}}$$

$$= \$5.33$$

Although a single plantwide overhead rate can be computed, such a process is frequently not adequate. In most companies, work is performed differently in different departments or organizational units. For example, although machine hours may be an appropriate activity base in a highly automated department, direct labor hours (DLHs) may be better for assigning overhead in a labor-intensive department. In the quality control area, number of defects may provide the best allocation base. Thus, because homogeneity is more likely within a department than among departments, separate departmental rates are generally thought to provide managers more useful information than plantwide rates.

Exhibit 3–14 presents the calculations of separate departmental and plantwide overhead rates for the Indianapolis Division of Alexander Polymers International. The Cutting and Mounting Department is highly automated and, therefore, uses machine hours as its overhead cost driver. In contrast, the Packaging Department is more labor intensive and uses DLHs.

Least Squares Regression Analysis

least squares regression analysis
dependent variable

Least squares regression analysis is a statistical technique that analyzes the relationship between dependent and independent variables. Least squares is used to develop an equation that predicts an unknown value of a **dependent variable**

EXHIBIT 3–14

Departmental versus Plantwide Overhead Rates

	Cutting and Mounting	Packaging
Budgeted annual overhead	$240,100	$159,650
Budgeted annual direct labor hours (DLHs)	5,400	20,600
Budgeted annual machine hours (MHs)	70,000	5,000

Departmental overhead rates:
Cutting and Mounting (automated): $240,100 ÷ 70,000 MHs = $3.43 per MH
Packaging (manual): $159,650 ÷ 20,600 DLHs = $7.75 per DLH

Total plantwide overhead = $240,100 + $159,650 = $399,750
Plantwide overhead rate (using DLHs): $399,750 ÷ 26,000 DLHs = $15.375 per DLH
Plantwide overhead rate (using MHs): $399,750 ÷ 75,000 MHs = $5.33 per MH

independent variable

(cost) from the known values of one or more **independent variables** (activity). When multiple independent variables exist, least squares regression also helps to select the independent variable that is the best predictor of the dependent variable. For example, managers can use least squares to decide whether machine hours, direct labor hours, or pounds of material moved best explain and predict changes in a specific overhead cost.[16]

simple regression

multiple regression

Simple regression analysis uses one independent variable to predict the dependent variable. Simple linear regression uses the $y = a + bX$ formula for a straight line. In **multiple regression**, two or more independent variables are used to predict the dependent variable. All examples in this appendix use simple regression and assume that a linear relationship exists between variables so that each one-unit change in the independent variable produces a constant unit change in the dependent variable.[17]

regression line

The least squares method mathematically fits the best possible regression line to observed data points. A **regression line** is any line that goes through the means (or averages) of the independent and dependent variables in a set of observations. Numerous straight lines can be drawn through any set of data observations, but most of these lines would provide a poor fit. Least squares regression analysis finds the line of "best fit" for the observed data.

This line of best fit is found by predicting the a and b values in a straight-line formula using the actual activity and cost values (y values) from the observations. The equations necessary to compute b and a values using the method of least squares are as follows[18]:

$$b = \frac{\sum xy - n(\bar{x})(\bar{y})}{\sum x^2 - n(\bar{x})^2}$$

$$a = \bar{y} - b\bar{x}$$

where

$\bar{x}$ = mean of the independent variable
$\bar{y}$ = mean of the dependent variable
n = number of observations

Using the Cutting and Mounting Department data for the Indianapolis Division of Alexander Polymers International (presented in the chapter in Exhibit 3–7 and excluding the March outlier), the following calculations can be made:

x	y	xy	x^2
4,800	$ 192	$ 921,600	23,040,000
9,000	350	3,150,000	81,000,000
4,900	186	911,400	24,010,000
4,600	218	1,002,800	21,160,000
8,900	347	3,088,300	79,210,000
5,900	248	1,463,200	34,810,000
5,500	231	1,270,500	30,250,000
43,600	$1,772	$11,807,800	293,480,000

[16] Further discussion of finding independent variable(s) that best predict the value of the dependent variable can be found in most textbooks on statistical methods treating regression analysis under the headings of dispersion, coefficient of correlation, coefficient of determination, or standard error of the estimate.
[17] Curvilinear relationships between variables also exist. For example, quality defects (dependent variable) tend to increase at an increasing rate in relationship to machinery age (independent variable).
[18] These equations are derived from mathematical computations beyond the scope of this text, but which are found in many statistics books. The symbol $\sum$ means "the summation of."

The mean of x ($\bar{x}$) is 6,228.57 (43,600 ÷ 7) and the mean of y ($\bar{y}$) is \$253.14 (\$1,772 ÷ 7). Thus,

$$b = \frac{11{,}807{,}800 - 7(6{,}228.57)(\$253.14)}{293{,}480{,}000 - 7(6{,}228.57)(6{,}228.57)}$$

$$= \frac{\$770{,}898.53}{21{,}914{,}410.29}$$

$$= \$0.035$$

$$a = \$253.14 - \$0.035\ (6{,}228.57)$$

$$= \$35.14$$

Thus, the b (variable cost) and a (fixed cost) values for the department's utility costs are \$0.035 and \$35.14, respectively.

By using these values, predicted costs (y_c values) can be computed for each actual activity level. The line that is drawn through all of the y_c values will be the line of best fit for the data. Because actual costs do not generally fall directly on the regression line and predicted costs naturally do, there are differences between these two costs at their related activity levels. It is acceptable for the regression line not to pass through any or all of the actual observation points because the line has been determined to mathematically "fit" the data.

KEY TERMS

actual cost system (p. 95)
applied overhead (p. 97)
capacity (p. 99)
conversion cost (p. 78)
cost (p. 77)
cost allocation (p. 95)
cost driver (p. 87)
cost object (p. 90)
cost of goods manufactured (p. 102)
dependent variable (p. 107)
direct cost (p. 89)
direct labor (p. 78)
direct material (p. 78)
distribution cost (p. 78)
expected capacity (p. 100)
expired cost (p. 77)
fixed cost (p. 85)
high-low method (p. 88)
historical cost (p. 98)
independent variable (p. 108)
indirect cost (p. 90)
inventoriable cost (p. 78)
least squares regression analysis (p. 107)
manufacturer (p. 79)
mixed cost (p. 86)
multiple regression (p. 108)
normal capacity (p. 100)
normal cost system (p. 96)
outlier (p. 88)
overapplied overhead (p. 98)
overhead (p. 78)
period cost (p. 78)
practical capacity (p. 100)
predetermined overhead rate (p. 96)
predictor (p. 87)
product cost (p. 78)
regression line (p. 108)
relevant range (p. 84)
service company (p. 79)
simple regression (p. 108)
step cost (p. 86)
theoretical capacity (p. 99)
underapplied overhead (p. 98)
unexpired cost (p. 77)
variable cost (p. 84)

SOLUTION STRATEGIES

Predetermined Overhead Rate

$$\text{Predetermined OH Rate} = \frac{\text{Total Budgeted Overhead Cost}}{\text{Total Budgeted Level of Volume or Activity}}$$

(Can be separate variable and fixed rates or a combined rate)

High-Low Method

(Using assumed amounts)

	(Independent Variable) Activity	(Dependent Variable) Associated Total Cost	−	Total Variable Cost (Rate × Activity)	=	Total Fixed Cost
"High" level	14,000	$18,000	−	$11,200	=	$6,800
"Low" level	9,000	14,000	−	7,200	=	6,800
Differences	5,000	$ 4,000				

$0.80 variable cost per unit of activity

Least Squares Regression Analysis

The equations necessary to compute b and a values using the method of least squares are as follows:

$$b = \frac{\Sigma xy - n(\bar{x})(\bar{y})}{\Sigma x^2 - n(\bar{x})^2}$$

$$a = \bar{y} - b\bar{x}$$

where

$\bar{x}$ = mean of the independent variable

$\bar{y}$ = mean of the dependent variable

n = number of observations

Underapplied and Overapplied Overhead

Overhead Control	XXX	
Various accounts		XXX
Actual overhead is debited to the overhead general ledger account.		
Work in Process Inventory	YYY	
Overhead Control		YYY
Applied overhead is debited to WIP and credited to the overhead general ledger account.		

A debit balance in Manufacturing Overhead at the end of the period is underapplied overhead; a credit balance is overapplied overhead. The debit or credit balance in the overhead account is closed at the end of the period to CGS or prorated to WIP, FG, and CGS.

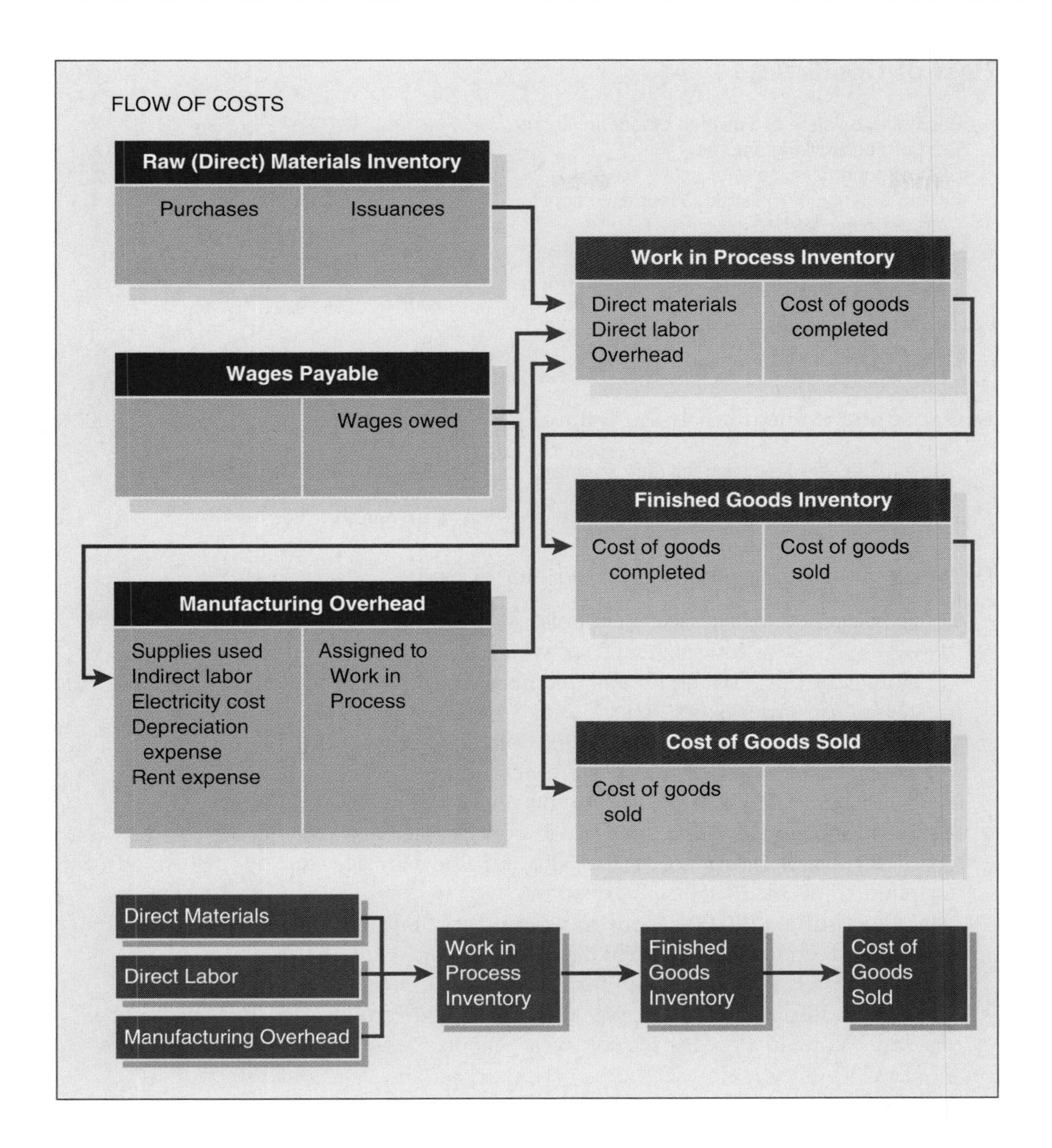

Cost of Goods Manufactured

Beginning balance of Work in Process Inventory			$XXX
Manufacturing costs for the period:			
Raw materials (all direct):			
Beginning balance	$XXX		
Purchases of materials	XXX		
Raw materials available for use	$XXX		
Ending balance	(XXX)		
Direct materials used		$XXX	
Direct labor		XXX	
Variable overhead		XXX	
Fixed overhead		XXX	
Total current period manufacturing costs			XXX
Total costs to account for			$XXX
Ending balance of Work in Process Inventory			(XXX)
Cost of goods manufactured			$XXX

Cost of Goods Sold

Beginning balance of Finished Goods Inventory	$XXX
Cost of goods manufactured	XXX
Cost of goods available for sale	$XXX
Ending balance of Finished Goods Inventory	(XXX)
Cost of goods sold	$XXX

DEMONSTRATION PROBLEM

BagsSoStrong Company had the following account balances as of August 1, 2001:

Raw Materials (direct and indirect) Inventory	$ 9,300
Work in Process Inventory	14,000
Finished Goods Inventory	18,000

During August, the company incurred the following factory costs:

- Purchased $82,000 of raw materials on account.
- Issued $90,000 of raw materials, of which $67,000 were direct to the product.
- Factory payroll of $44,000 was accrued; $31,000 was for direct labor and the rest was for supervisors.
- Utility costs were accrued at $3,500; of these costs, $800 were fixed.
- Property taxes on the factory were accrued in the amount of $1,000.
- Prepaid insurance of $800 on factory equipment expired in August.
- Straight-line depreciation on factory equipment was $20,000.
- Predetermined overhead of $62,500 ($28,000 variable and $34,500 fixed) was applied to Work in Process Inventory.
- Goods costing $170,000 were transferred to Finished Goods Inventory.
- Sales on account totaled $350,000.
- Cost of goods sold was $175,000.
- Selling and administrative costs were $140,000 (credit "Various Accounts").
- Ending Work in Process Inventory is $3,300.

Required:

a. Journalize the transactions for August.
b. Prepare a schedule of cost of goods manufactured for August using normal costing.
c. Prepare an income statement, including a detailed schedule of cost of goods sold.

Solution to Demonstration Problem

a. (1)	Raw Materials Inventory	82,000	
	Accounts Payable		82,000
(2)	Work in Process Inventory	67,000	
	Variable Overhead Control	23,000	
	Raw Materials Inventory		90,000
(3)	Work in Process Inventory	31,000	
	Fixed Overhead Control	13,000	
	Salaries and Wages Payable		44,000
(4)	Variable Overhead Control	2,700	
	Fixed Overhead Control	800	
	Utilities Payable		3,500

		Debit	Credit
(5)	Fixed Overhead Control	1,000	
	Property Taxes Payable		1,000
(6)	Fixed Overhead Control	800	
	Prepaid Insurance		800
(7)	Fixed Overhead Control	20,000	
	Accumulated Depreciation—Factory Equipment		20,000
(8)	Work in Process Inventory	62,500	
	Variable Overhead Control		28,000
	Fixed Overhead Control		34,500
(9)	Finished Goods Inventory	171,200	
	Work in Process Inventory		171,200
(10)	Accounts Receivable	350,000	
	Sales		350,000
(11)	Cost of Goods Sold	175,000	
	Finished Goods Inventory		175,000
(12)	Selling & Administrative Expenses	140,000	
	Various Accounts		140,000

b.

BAGSSOSTRONG
Cost of Goods Manufactured Schedule
For Month Ended August 31, 2001

Balance of Work in Process Inventory, 8/1/01			$ 14,000
Manufacturing costs for the period:			
Raw materials:			
Beginning balance		$ 9,300	
Purchases of materials		82,000	
Raw materials available		$91,300	
Indirect materials used	$23,000		
Ending balance	1,300	(24,300)	
Total direct materials used		$67,000	
Direct labor		31,000	
Variable overhead		28,000	
Fixed overhead		34,500	
Total current period manufacturing costs			160,500
Total costs to account for			$174,500
Balance of Work in Process Inventory, 8/31/01			(3,300)
Cost of goods manufactured*			$171,200

*During August, factory overhead was overapplied by $1,200. Underapplied or overapplied overhead is accumulated throughout the year and disposed of at year end.

c.

BAGSSOSTRONG
Income Statement
For the Month Ended August 31, 2001

Sales		$350,000
Cost of Goods Sold		
Finished Goods, 8/1/01	$ 18,000	
Cost of Goods Manufactured	171,200	
Cost of Goods Available	$189,200	
Finished Goods, 8/31/01	(13,000)	
Cost of Goods Sold		(176,200)
Gross Margin		$173,800
Selling & Administrative Expenses		(140,000)
Income from Operations		$ 33,800

QUESTIONS

1. Distinguish among the cost accounting uses of historical costs, replacement costs, and budgeted costs.
2. How does a company determine its relevant range of activity? Of what use to managers is the concept of a relevant range of activity?
3. Why is a cost referred to as variable if it remains constant per unit for all volume levels within the relevant range?
4. Would it be true that fixed costs will never change in an organization? Explain the rationale for your answer.
5. What is the difference between a variable and a mixed cost, given that each changes in total with changes in activity levels?
6. How do predictors and cost drivers differ? Why is such a distinction important?
7. The high-low method of analyzing mixed costs uses only two observation points: the high and the low points of activity. Are these always the best points for prediction purposes? Why or why not?
8. Relative to a set of data observations, what is an outlier? Why is it inappropriate to use outliers to determine the cost formula for a mixed cost?
9. What is a product cost? What types of costs are included in product costs for retailers, manufacturers, and service companies?
10. What is a period cost? What types of costs are included in period costs for retailers, manufacturers, and service companies?
11. Are all product costs unexpired costs and all period costs expired costs? Explain.
12. How is the concept of a direct cost related to that of a cost object?
13. Why are some material and labor costs that should, in theory, be considered direct costs instead accounted for as indirect costs?
14. What is the process of conversion and why does this process create a need for cost accounting?
15. What inventory accounts are shown on the balance sheet of a manufacturer and what information is contained in each of these accounts?
16. Is allocation of manufacturing overhead to products necessary for external reporting purposes? Internal purposes? Provide explanations for your answers.
17. Compare and contrast a normal cost system and an actual cost system. Relative to an actual cost system, what are the advantages associated with the use of a normal cost system? What are the disadvantages?
18. Discuss the reasons a company would use a predetermined overhead rate rather than apply actual overhead to products or services.
19. When a normal cost system is used, how are costs removed from a single Manufacturing Overhead account and charged to Work in Process Inventory?
20. What recordkeeping options are available to account for overhead costs in a normal cost system? Which would be easiest? Which would provide the best information and why?
21. If overhead was materially underapplied for a year, how would it be treated at year-end? Why is this treatment appropriate?
22. What factors can cause overhead to be underapplied or overapplied? Are all of these factors controllable by management? Why or why not?
23. Why can it be said that the cost of goods manufactured schedule shows the flow of production costs in a manufacturing company?
24. Why is the amount of cost of goods manufactured different from the amount of cost of goods sold? Could there be a situation in which these amounts are equal? If so, explain.
25. *(Appendix)* Why are departmental overhead rates more useful for managerial decision making than plantwide rates? Separate variable and fixed rates rather than total rates?

26. *(Appendix)* Why would regression analysis provide a more accurate cost formula for a mixed cost than the high-low method?

27. Using the Internet, find an article about costs. List and define as many different types of costs from the article as you can.

EXERCISES

28. *(Terminology)* Match the following lettered terms on the left with the appropriate numbered description on the right.

a. Budgeted cost
b. Direct cost
c. Distribution cost
d. Expired cost
e. Fixed cost
f. Inventoriable cost
g. Period cost
h. Product cost
i. Variable cost

1. An expense or loss
2. A cost that remains constant on a per-unit basis
3. A cost associated with a specific cost object
4. Direct material, direct labor, and manufacturing overhead
5. Product cost
6. A cost that varies inversely on a per-unit basis with changes in activity
7. A cost primarily associated with the passage of time rather than production activity
8. An expected future cost
9. A cost of transporting a product

29. *(Cost classifications)* Indicate whether each item listed below is a variable (V), fixed (F), or mixed (M) cost and whether it is a product or service (PT) cost or a period (PD) cost. If some items have alternative answers, indicate the alternatives and the reasons for them.

a. Wages of forklift operators who move finished goods from a central warehouse to the loading dock.
b. Paper towels used in factory restrooms.
c. Insurance premiums paid on the headquarters of a manufacturing company.
d. Columnar paper used in an accounting firm.
e. Cost of labels attached to shirts made by a company.
f. Wages of factory maintenance workers.
g. Property taxes on a manufacturing plant.
h. Salaries of secretaries in a law firm.
i. Freight costs of acquiring raw materials from suppliers.
j. Cost of wax to make candles.
k. Cost of radioactive material used to generate power in a nuclear power plant.

30. *(Company type)* Indicate whether each of the following terms is associated with a manufacturing (Mfg.), a retailing or merchandising (Mer.), or a service (Ser.) company. There can be more than one correct answer for each term.

a. Prepaid rent
b. Merchandise inventory
c. Cost of goods sold
d. Sales salaries expense
e. Finished goods inventory
f. Depreciation—factory equipment
g. Cost of services rendered
h. Auditing fees expense
i. Direct labor wages

31. *(Degrees of conversion)* Indicate whether each of the following types of organizations is characterized by a high, low, or moderate degree of conversion.

a. Bakery in a grocery store
b. Convenience store
c. Christmas tree farm
d. Textbook publisher
e. Sporting goods retailer
f. Auto manufacturer
g. Cranberry farm
h. Custom print shop
i. Italian restaurant
j. Concert ticket seller

32. *(Cost behavior)* O'Malley Company produces baseball caps. The company incurred the following costs to produce 2,000 caps last month:

Cardboard for the bills	$ 1,200
Cloth materials	2,000
Plastic for headband straps	1,500
Straight-line depreciation	1,800
Supervisors' salaries	4,800
Utilities	900
Total	$12,200

a. What did each cap component cost on a per-unit basis?
b. What is the probable type of behavior that each of the costs exhibits?
c. The company expects to produce 2,500 caps this month. Would you expect each type of cost to increase or decrease? Why? Why can't the total cost of 2,500 caps be determined?

33. *(Cost behavior)* The Hudson Company manufactures high-pressure garden hoses. Costs incurred in the production process include a rubber material used to make the hoses, steel mesh used in the hoses, depreciation on the factory building, and utilities to run production machinery. Graph the most likely cost behavior for each of these costs and show what type of cost behavior is indicated by each cost.

34. *(Total cost determination with mixed cost)* Heathcliff Accounting Services pays $400 per month for a tax software license. In addition, variable charges average $15 for every tax return the firm prepares.

a. Determine the total cost and the cost per unit if the firm expects to prepare the following number of tax returns in March 2000:
  1. 150
  2. 300
  3. 600

b. Why does the cost per unit change in each of the three cases above?

35. *(High-low method)* Information about Brightman Corporation's utility cost for the first six months of 2001 follows. The company's cost accountant wants to use the high-low method to develop a cost formula to predict future charges and believes that the number of machine hours is an appropriate cost driver.

Month	Machine Hours	Utility Expense
January	68,000	$1,220
February	62,000	1,172
March	66,300	1,014
April	64,000	1,195
May	67,500	1,300
June	62,500	1,150

a. What is the cost formula for utility expense?
b. What would be the budgeted utility cost for September 2001 if 64,750 machine hours are projected?

36. *(High-low method)* The Evanstonian builds tabletop replicas of some of the most famous lighthouses in North America. The company is highly automated and, thus, maintenance cost is a significant organizational expense. The company's owner has decided to use machine hours as a basis for predicting maintenance costs and has gathered the following data from the prior eight months of operations:

Number of Machine Hours	Maintenance Costs
3,000	$980
4,500	690
8,000	510
7,000	600
6,000	550
9,000	440
3,500	840
5,500	600

a. Using the high-low method, determine the cost formula for maintenance costs.
b. What aspect of the estimated equation is bothersome? Provide an explanation for this situation.
c. Within the relevant range, can the formula be reliably used to predict maintenance costs? Can the a and b values in the cost formula be interpreted as fixed and variable costs? Why or why not?

37. *(Predictors and cost drivers; team activity)* Accountants often use factors that change in a consistent pattern with costs to explain or predict cost behavior.
a. As a team of three or four, select factors to predict or explain the behavior of the following costs:
  1. Salesperson's travel expenses
  2. Raw material costs at a pizza restaurant
  3. Paper costs in a College of Business
  4. Maintenance costs for a lawn service company
b. Prepare a presentation of your chosen factors that also addresses whether the factors could be used as cost drivers in addition to predictors.

38. *(Direct vs. indirect costs)* Babin Cutlery Inc. manufactures kitchen knives. Following are some costs incurred in the factory in 2000 for knife production:

Material Costs:	
Stainless steel	$400,000
Equipment oil and grease	8,000
Plastic and fiberglass for handles	15,000
Wooden knife racks for customer storage	9,200
Labor Costs:	
Equipment operators	$200,000
Equipment mechanics	50,000
Factory supervisors	118,000

a. What is the direct material cost for 2000?
b. What is the direct labor cost for 2000?
c. What are the indirect material and total indirect labor overhead costs for 2000?

39. *(Direct vs. indirect costs)* Midwestern State University's College of Business has five departments: Accounting, Finance, Management, Marketing, and Decision Sciences. Each department chairperson is responsible for the department's budget preparation. Indicate whether each of the following costs incurred in the Marketing Department is direct or indirect to the department:

a. Chairperson's salary
b. Cost of computer time of campus mainframe used by members of the department
c. Marketing faculty salaries
d. Cost of equipment purchased by the department from allocated state funds
e. Cost of travel by department faculty paid from externally generated funds contributed directly to the department
f. Cost of secretarial salaries (secretaries are shared by the entire college)
g. Depreciation allocation of the college building cost for the number of offices used by department faculty
h. Cost of periodicals/books purchased by the department

40. *(Labor cost classification)* House & Home Inc. produces a variety of household products. The firm operates 24 hours per day with three daily work shifts. The first-shift workers receive "regular pay." The second shift receives a 10 percent pay premium, and the third shift receives a 20 percent pay premium. In addition, when production is scheduled on weekends, the firm pays an overtime premium of 50 percent (based on the pay rate for first-shift employees). Labor premiums are included in overhead. The August 2001 factory payroll is as follows:

Total wages for August for 18,000 hours	$168,000
Normal hourly wage for Shift #1 employees	$8
Total regular hours worked, split evenly among the three shifts	15,000

a. How many overtime hours were worked in August?
b. How much of the total labor cost should be charged to direct labor? To overhead?
c. What amount of overhead was for second- and third-shift premiums? For overtime premiums?

41. *(Product and period costs)* Alexander Company incurred the following costs in August 2000:

- Paid a six-month premium for insurance of company headquarters, $12,000.
- Paid three months of property taxes on its factory building, $7,500.
- Paid a $40,000 bonus to the company president.
- Accrued $10,000 of utility costs, of which 30 percent was for the headquarters and the remainder for the factory.

a. What expired period cost is associated with the August information?
b. What unexpired period cost is associated with the August information?
c. What product cost is associated with the August information?
d. Discuss why the product cost cannot be described specifically as expired or unexpired in this situation.

42. *(Essay)* A portion of the costs incurred by business organizations is designated as direct labor cost. As used in practice, the term *direct labor cost* has a wide variety of meanings. Unless the meaning intended in a given context is clear, misunderstanding and confusion are likely to ensue. If a user does not understand the elements included in direct labor cost, erroneous interpretations of the numbers may occur and could result in poor management decisions.

In addition to understanding the conceptual definition of direct labor cost, management accountants must understand how direct labor cost should be measured.

Write a paper that discusses the following issues:

a. Distinguish between direct labor and indirect labor.
b. Discuss why some nonproductive labor time (such as coffee breaks, personal time) can be and often is treated as direct labor, whereas other nonproductive time (such as downtime or training) is treated as indirect labor.

c. Following are labor cost elements that a company has classified as direct labor, manufacturing overhead, or either direct labor or manufacturing overhead, depending on the situation.

- *Direct labor:* Included in the company's direct labor are cost production efficiency bonuses and certain benefits for direct labor workers such as FICA (employer's portion), group life insurance, vacation pay, and workers' compensation insurance.
- *Manufacturing overhead:* Included in the company's overhead are costs for wage continuation plans in the event of illness, the company-sponsored cafeteria, the personnel department, and recreational facilities.
- *Direct labor or manufacturing overhead:* Included in the "situational" category are maintenance expense, overtime premiums, and shift premiums.

Explain the rationale used by the company in classifying the cost elements in each of the three presented categories.

d. The two aspects of measuring direct labor costs are (1) the quantity of labor effort that is to be included, that is, the types of hours that are to be counted; and (2) the unit price by which each of these quantities is multiplied to arrive at a monetary cost. Why are these considered separate and distinct aspects of measuring labor cost? *(CMA adapted)*

43. *(Predetermined overhead rate)* Walton Company has developed a monthly overhead cost formula of $2,760 + $4 per direct labor hour for 2000. The firm's 2000 expected annual capacity is 24,000 direct labor hours, to be incurred evenly each month. Two direct labor hours are required to make one unit of the company's product.

a. Determine the total overhead to be applied to each unit of product in 2000.

b. Prepare journal entries to record the application of overhead to Work in Process Inventory and the incurrence of $10,430 of actual overhead in a month in which 1,850 direct labor hours were worked.

44. *(Overhead application)* Brooke & Associates applies overhead at a combined rate for fixed and variable overhead of 175 percent of professional labor costs. During the first three months of 2000, the following professional labor costs and actual overhead costs were incurred:

Month	Professional Labor Cost	Actual Overhead
January	$270,000	$480,000
February	247,500	427,800
March	255,000	450,000

a. How much overhead was applied to the services provided each month by the firm?

b. What was underapplied or overapplied overhead for each of the three months and for the quarter?

45. *(Underapplied or overapplied overhead)* At the end of 2000, Schmitt Corporation has the following account balances:

Manufacturing Overhead (credit)	$ 20,000
Work in Process Inventory	128,000
Finished Goods Inventory	32,000
Cost of Goods Sold	240,000

a. Prepare the necessary journal entry to close the overhead account if the balance is considered immaterial.

b. Prepare the necessary journal entry to close the overhead account if the balance is considered material.

c. Which method do you feel is more appropriate for the company and why?

46. *(Underapplied or overapplied overhead)* Hume Company uses a normal cost system. At year-end, the balance in the manufacturing overhead control account is a $50,000 debit. Information concerning relevant account balances at year-end is as follows:

	Work in Process	Finished Goods	Cost of Goods Sold
Direct materials	$20,000	$ 40,000	$ 60,000
Direct labor	10,000	20,000	25,000
Factory overhead	20,000	40,000	50,000
	$50,000	$100,000	$135,000

a. What overhead rate was used during the year?
b. Provide arguments to be used for deciding whether to prorate the balance in the overhead account at year-end.
c. Prorate the overhead account balance based on the relative balances of the appropriate accounts.
d. Prorate the overhead account balance based on the relative overhead components of the appropriate account balances.
e. Identify some possible reasons why the company had a debit balance in the overhead account at year-end.

47. *(CGM and CGS)* Holiday Products Company had the following inventory balances at the beginning and end of March 2000:

	March 1, 2000	March 31, 2000
Raw Materials Inventory	$12,000	$16,000
Work in Process Inventory	68,000	84,000
Finished Goods Inventory	32,000	24,000

All raw materials are direct to the production process. The following information is also available about March manufacturing costs:

Cost of raw materials used	$128,000
Direct labor cost	162,000
Factory overhead	116,000

a. Calculate the cost of goods manufactured for March.
b. Determine the cost of goods sold for March.

48. *(Cost of services rendered)* The following information is related to the Perrrfect Veterinary Clinic for April 2001, the firm's first month in operation:

Veterinarian salaries for April	$12,000
Assistants' salaries for April	4,200
Medical supplies purchased in April	1,800
Utilities for month (80 percent related to animal treatment)	900
Office salaries for April (20 percent related to animal treatment)	2,600
Medical supplies on hand at April 30	800
Depreciation on medical equipment for April	600
Building rental (70 percent related to animal treatment)	700

Compute the cost of services rendered.

49. *(CGM and CGS)* Cathy's Custom Clocks' August 2001 cost of goods sold was $2,300,000. August 31 work in process was 40 percent of the August 1 work in process. Overhead was 225 percent of direct labor cost. During August, $768,500 of direct materials were purchased. Other August information follows:

Inventories	August 1, 2001	August 31, 2001
Direct materials	$ 30,000	$42,000
Work in process	90,000	?
Finished goods	125,000	98,000

a. Prepare a schedule of the cost of goods sold for August.
b. Prepare the August cost of goods manufactured schedule.
c. What was the amount of direct production costs incurred in August?
d. What was the amount of conversion costs incurred in August?

50. *(Financial statement classifications)* Cajun Airboats purchased a plastics extruding machine for $100,000 to make boat hulls. During its first operating year, the machine produced 5,000 units and depreciation was calculated to be $12,500 on the machine. The company sold 4,000 of the hulls.
a. What part of the $100,000 machine cost is expired?
b. Where would each of the amounts related to this machine appear on the financial statements?

51. *(Appendix–Least squares)* Below are data on number of shipments received and the cost of receiving reports for Pacific Supply Company for the first seven weeks of 2000:

Number of Shipments Received	Cost of Receiving Report
100	$175
87	162
80	154
70	142
105	185
115	200
120	202

a. Using the least squares method, develop the equation for predicting weekly receiving report costs based on the number of shipments received.
b. What is the predicted amount of receiving report costs for a month (assume a month is exactly four weeks) in which 390 shipments are received?

52. *(Appendix–Least squares)* Tom's Charters operates a fleet of powerboats in Fort Myers, Florida. Tom wants to develop a cost formula for labor costs (a mixed cost). He has gathered the following data on labor costs and two potential predictive bases: number of charters and gross receipts:

Month	Labor Costs	Number of Charters	Gross Receipts
January	$16,000	10	$ 12,000
February	18,400	14	18,000
March	24,000	22	26,000
April	28,400	28	36,000
May	37,000	40	60,000
June	56,000	62	82,000
July	68,000	100	120,000
August	60,000	90	100,000
September	48,000	80	96,000

Using the least squares method, develop a labor cost formula using each prediction base.

PROBLEMS

53. *(Cost behavior)* Officestuff Ink makes stationery sets. In an average month, the firm produces 200,000 boxes of stationery; each box contains 50 pages of stationery and 40 envelope sets. Production costs are incurred for paper, ink, glue, and boxes. The company manufactures this product in batches of 500 boxes of a specific stationery design. The following data have been extracted from the company's accounting records for April 2000:

Cost of paper for each batch	$10
Cost of ink and glue for each batch	1
Cost of 500 boxes for each batch	32
Direct labor for producing each batch	16
Labor costs for each batch design	40

Overhead charges total $20,400 per month; these are considered fully fixed for purposes of cost estimation.

a. What is the cost per box of stationery based on average production volume?

b. If sales volume increases to 300,000 boxes per month, what will be the cost per box (assuming that cost behavior patterns remain the same as in April)?

c. If sales are 300,000 boxes per month but the firm does not want the cost per box to exceed its current level [based on part (a) above], what amount can the company pay for labor design costs, assuming all other costs are the same as April levels?

d. Assume that Officestuff Ink is now able to sell, on average, each box of stationery at a price of $5. If the company is able to increase its volume to 300,000 boxes per month, what sales price per box will generate the same gross margin that the firm is now achieving on 200,000 boxes per month?

e. Would it be possible to lower total costs by producing more boxes per batch, even if the total volume of 200,000 is maintained? Explain.

54. *(Cost behavior)* A company's cost structure may contain numerous different cost behavior patterns. Below are descriptions of several different costs; match these to the appropriate graphs. On each graph, the vertical axis represents cost and the horizontal axis represents level of activity or volume.

Identify, by letter, the graph that illustrates each of the following cost behavior patterns. Graphs can be used more than once.

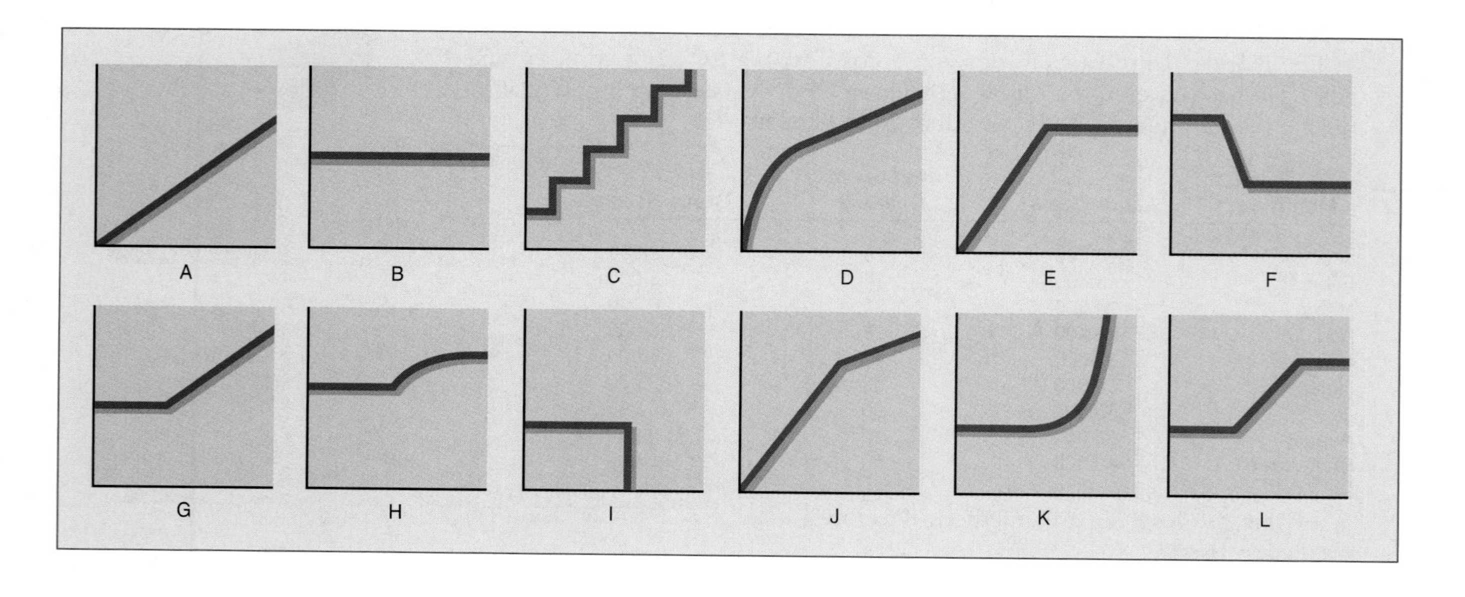

1. Cost of raw materials, where the cost decreases by $0.06 per unit for each of the first 150 units purchased, after which it remains constant at $2.75 per unit.
2. City water bill, which is computed as follows:

First 750,000 gallons or less	$1,000 flat fee
Next 15,000 gallons	$0.002 per gallon used
Next 15,000 gallons	$0.005 per gallon used
Next 15,000 gallons	$0.008 per gallon used
Etc.	Etc.

3. Rent on a factory building donated by the city, where the agreement provides for a fixed-fee payment, unless 250,000 labor hours are worked, in which case no rent needs to be paid.
4. Cost of raw materials used.
5. Electricity bill—a flat fixed charge of $250 plus a variable cost after 150,000 kilowatt-hours are used.
6. Salaries of maintenance workers if one maintenance worker is needed for every 1,000 hours or less of machine time.
7. Depreciation of equipment using the straight-line method.
8. Rent on a factory building donated by the county, where the agreement provides for a monthly rental of $100,000 less $1 for each labor hour worked in excess of 200,000 hours. However, a minimum rental payment of $20,000 must be made each month.
9. Rent on a machine that is billed at $1,000 for up to 500 hours of machine time. After 500 hours of machine time, an additional charge of $1 per hour is paid up to a maximum charge of $2,500 per period. *(AICPA adapted)*

55. *(Cost classifications)* Donald Trumpett is a house painter who incurred the following costs during June 2001 when he painted four houses. He spent $1,000 on paint, $50 on mineral spirits, and $100 on brushes. He also bought two pairs of coveralls for $50 each; he wears coveralls only while he works. During the first week of June, Donald placed a $60 ad for his business in the classifieds. He had to hire an assistant for one of the painting jobs; the assistant was paid $12 per hour and worked 25 hours.

Being a very methodical person, Donald kept detailed records of his mileage to and from each painting job. His average operating cost per mile for his van is $0.32. He found a $15 receipt in his van for a metropolitan map that he purchased in June. The map is used as a part of contact file for referral work and for bids that he has made on potential jobs. He also had $15 in receipts for bridge tolls ($1 per trip) for a painting job he did across the river.

Near the end of June, Donald decided to go camping, and he turned down a job on which he had bid $2,800. He called the homeowner long distance (at a cost of $1.60) to explain his reasons for declining the job.

Using the headings below, indicate how each of the June costs incurred by Donald would be classified. Assume that the cost object is a house-painting job.

Type of Cost	Variable	Fixed	Direct	Indirect	Period	Product

56. *(Analyzing mixed costs)* Frances' Dairy determined that the total overhead rate for costing purposes is $6.70 per cow per day (referred to as an "animal day"). Of this, $6.30 is the variable portion. Cost information for two levels of monthly activity within the relevant range follow:

	4,000 Animal Days	6,000 Animal Days
Overhead cost:		
Indirect materials	$ 6,400	$ 9,600
Indirect labor	14,000	20,000
Maintenance	2,600	3,400
Utilities	2,000	3,000
All other	3,800	5,400

a. Determine the fixed and variable values for each of the above overhead items and determine the total overhead cost formula.

b. Assume that the total overhead rate is based on expected annual capacity. What is this level of activity for the company?

c. Determine expected overhead costs at the expected annual capacity.

d. If the company raises its expected capacity by 3,000 animal days above the present level, calculate a new total overhead rate for product costing.

57. *(High-low; least squares regression)* Andrews Company manufactures insulated windows. The firm has encountered a problem in budgeting repairs and maintenance. The cost is apparently a mixed cost and varies most directly with machine hours worked. However, management does not know the exact relationship between machine hours and repairs and maintenance. The following data have been gathered from recent operations and may help describe the relationship:

Month	Machine Hours	Repairs and Maintenance
May	1,400	$ 9,000
June	1,700	9,525
July	2,000	10,900
August	1,900	10,719
September	2,300	11,670
October	2,700	13,154
November	2,500	13,000
December	2,200	11,578

a. How can you tell from the data that repairs and maintenance is a mixed cost?

b. Use the high-low method to estimate a cost formula for repairs and maintenance.

c. Use least squares regression to estimate a cost formula for repairs and maintenance.

d. Does the answer to part (b) or (c) provide the better estimate of the relationship between repairs and maintenance costs and machine hours? Why?

58. *(Mixed costs and predetermined overhead rates; two bases)* King-O'Brien Enterprises makes fiberglass swimming pools in a two-department process: Production and Installation. Production is highly automated and machine hours are used as the basis for allocating departmental overhead. Installation is labor intensive and uses direct labor hours to apply overhead. Cost information for various activity levels follows for each department:

	ACTIVITY IN MACHINE HOURS (MHs)		
	Low 3,000	4,000	High 5,000
Production overhead costs:			
Variable	$12,150	$16,200	$20,250
Fixed	7,950	7,950	7,950
Total	$20,100	$24,150	$28,200

	ACTIVITY IN DIRECT LABOR HOURS (DLHs)		
	Low 1,000	2,000	High 3,000
Installation overhead costs:			
Variable	$14,250	$28,500	$42,750
Fixed	6,150	6,150	6,150
Total	$20,400	$34,650	$48,900

Each pool is estimated to require 500 machine hours in Production and 250 hours of direct labor in Installation. Expected annual capacity is 120 pools. The company plans to produce and install 10 pools next month.

a. Compute the variable and fixed values in the formula $y = a + bX$ for each department.

b. Prepare a budget for next month's variable, fixed, and total overhead costs for each department assuming expected production is 10 pools.

c. Calculate the predetermined total overhead cost to be applied to each pool scheduled for production in the coming month if expected annual capacity is used to calculate the predetermined overhead rates.

59. *(Journal entries)* Ballyhoo Rags makes evening dresses. The following information has been gathered from the company records for 2001, the first year of company operations. Work in Process Inventory at the end of 2001 was $25,500.

Direct material purchased on account	$330,000
Direct material issued to production	294,000
Direct labor payroll accrued	215,000
Indirect labor payroll accrued	62,000
Factory insurance expired	2,500
Factory utilities paid	14,300
Depreciation on factory equipment recorded	21,700
Factory rent paid	84,000
Sales on account	958,000

The company's gross profit rate for the year was 35 percent.

a. Compute the cost of goods sold for 2001.

b. What was the total cost of goods manufactured for 2001?

c. If net income was $60,300, what were total selling and administrative expenses for the year?

d. Prepare journal entries to record the flow of costs for the year, assuming the company uses a perpetual inventory system.

60. *(Journal entries)* Mundell Company applies overhead at the rate of $4 per direct labor hour. The following transactions occurred during April 2000:

1. Direct material issued to production, $160,000.
2. Direct labor cost paid, 35,000 hours at $16 per hour.
3. Indirect labor cost accrued, 7,500 hours at $9 per hour.
4. Depreciation on factory assets recorded, $37,200.
5. Supervisors' salaries paid, $15,000.
6. Indirect materials issued to production, $9,000.
7. Goods costing $840,000 were completed and transferred to finished goods.

a. Prepare journal entries for the above transactions using a single overhead account and assuming the Raw Materials Inventory account contains only direct materials.

b. If Work in Process Inventory had a beginning balance of $55,620, what is the ending balance?

c. Was overhead underapplied or overapplied for the month? By how much?

61. *(CGM and CGS)* VitalStrength Inc. began business in October 2000. The firm makes an exercise machine for home and gym use. Below are data taken from the firm's accounting records that pertain to its first year of operations.

Direct material purchased on account	$213,000
Direct material issued to production	192,000
Direct labor payroll accrued	114,000
Indirect labor payroll paid	45,300
Factory insurance expired	2,700
Factory utilities paid	8,900
Factory depreciation recorded	18,700
Ending Work in Process Inventory (48 units)	32,000
Ending Finished Goods Inventory (30 units)	45,600
Sales on account ($1,060 per unit)	212,000

a. How many units did the company sell in its first year? How many units were completed in the first year?
b. What was the cost of goods manufactured?
c. What was the per-unit cost of goods manufactured?
d. What was cost of goods sold in the first year?
e. What was the company's first-year gross margin?

62. *(Product and period costs, CGM and CGS)* At the beginning of August 2001, Brennan Corporation had the following account balances:

Raw Materials Inventory (both direct and indirect)	$ 8,000
Work in Process Inventory	13,000
Finished Goods Inventory	5,000

During August, the following transactions took place.

1. Raw materials were purchased on account, $75,000.
2. Direct materials ($21,200) and indirect materials ($2,500) were issued to production.
3. Factory payroll consisted of $50,000 for direct labor employees and $7,000 for indirect labor employees.
4. Office salaries totaled $21,100 for the month.
5. Utilities of $8,700 were accrued; 70 percent of the utilities cost is for the factory area.
6. Depreciation of $9,000 was recorded on plant assets; 80 percent of the depreciation is related to factory machinery and equipment.
7. Rent of $12,000 was paid on the building. The factory occupies 60 percent of the building.
8. At the end of August, the Work in Process Inventory balance was $8,300.
9. At the end of August, the balance in Finished Goods Inventory was $8,900.

Brennan uses an *actual* cost system and debits actual overhead costs incurred to Work in Process.

a. Determine the total amount of product cost (cost of goods manufactured) and period cost incurred during August 2001.
b. Compute the cost of goods sold for August 2001.
c. What level of August sales would have generated net income of $27,700?

63. *(CGM and CGS)* Catherine's Collectibles produces objets d'art. The company's Raw Materials Inventory account includes the costs of both direct and indirect materials. Account balances for the company at the beginning and end of July 2000 are shown below.

	July 1, 2000	July 31, 2000
Raw Materials Inventory	$23,300	$17,400
Work in Process Inventory	36,600	30,000
Finished Goods Inventory	18,000	26,200

During the month, Catherine's Collectibles purchased $85,000 of raw materials; direct materials used during the period amounted to $68,000. Factory payroll costs for July were $91,300 of which 85 percent was related to direct labor. Overhead charges for depreciation, insurance, utilities, and maintenance totaled $81,200 for July.

a. Prepare a schedule of cost of goods manufactured.
b. Prepare a schedule of cost of goods sold.

64. *(Plant vs. department OH rates)* Bass Fine Furniture has two departments: Fabrication and Finishing. Fabrication is composed of 2 workers and 25 machines, and Finishing has 25 workers and 3 machines. One of the company's products passes through both departments and uses the following quantities of direct labor and machine time:

	Fabrication	Finishing
Machine hours	8.00	0.15
Direct labor hours	0.02	2.00

Following are the budgeted overhead costs and volumes for each department for the upcoming year:

	Fabrication	Finishing
Estimated overhead	$624,240	$324,000
Estimated machine hours	72,000	9,300
Estimated direct labor hours	4,800	48,000

a. What is the plantwide rate for overhead application based on machine hours for the upcoming year? How much overhead will be assigned to each unit using this rate?
b. The company's auditors inform Bass that it would be more appropriate to use machine hours as the application base in Fabrication and direct labor hours in Finishing. What would the rates be for each department? How much overhead would have been assigned to each unit of product using departmental rates?

CASE

65. *(Missing data)* The Hurlstone Company suffered major losses in a fire on April 18, 2000. In addition to destroying several buildings, the blaze destroyed the company's work in process for an entire product line. Fortunately, the company was insured. However, the company needs to substantiate the amount of the claim. To this end, the company has gathered the following information that pertains to production and sales of the affected product line:

1. The company's sales for the first 18 days of April amounted to $230,000. Normally, this product line generates a gross profit equal to 30 percent of sales.
2. Finished Goods Inventory was $29,000 on April 1 and $42,500 on April 18.
3. On April 1, Work in Process Inventory was $48,000.
4. During the first 18 days of April, the company incurred the following costs:

Direct materials used	$76,000
Direct labor	44,000
Manufacturing overhead applied	42,000

a. Determine the value of Work in Process Inventory that was destroyed by the fire.

b. What other information might the insurance company require? How would management determine or estimate this information?

REALITY CHECK

66. An extremely important and expensive variable cost per employee is health care provided by the employer. This cost is expected to rise each year as more and more expensive technology is used on patients and as the costs of that technology are passed along through the insurance company to the employer. One simple way to reduce these variable costs is to cut back on employee insurance coverage.

a. Discuss the ethical implications of reducing employee health care coverage to cut back on the variable costs incurred by the employer.

b. Assume that you are an employer with 600 employees. You are forced to cut back on some insurance benefits. Your coverage currently includes the following items: mental health coverage, long-term disability, convalescent facility care, nonemergency but medically necessary procedures, dependent coverage, and life insurance. Select the two you would eliminate or dramatically reduce and provide reasons for your selections.

c. Prepare a plan that might allow you to "trade" some variable employee health care costs for a fixed or mixed cost.

67. *Outsourcing is a frequently used method of cost cutting or of eliminating organizational activities that are not viewed as core competencies. However, outsourcing also creates new costs and, sometimes, new problems.*

Some companies have found themselves locked into long-term contracts with outside suppliers that are no longer competitive. Indeed, multimillion-dollar technology-outsourcing contracts are often so complex that companies are hiring consultants at very high fees simply to evaluate the proposals.

SOURCE: John A. Byrne, "Has Outsourcing Gone Too Far?" *Business Week* (April 1, 1996), p. 27.

a. Discuss some benefits and drawbacks to outsourcing the following activities: (1) finance function, (2) data-processing function, and (3) travel arrangements.

b. How might outsourcing of manufacturing functions affect the (1) prevention, (2) appraisal, and (3) failure costs of a company?

c. What effect might outsourcing of each of the activities in part (a) have on an organization's corporate culture?

68. Frequently, corporations issue forecasts of earnings for the upcoming year. Such forecasts require estimations of both costs and revenues. Search the Internet for a discussion of a revision in the earnings forecast of any company. Relative to the original forecast, did the revision indicate earnings would be higher or lower? Discuss the reasons given for the revision in the forecasted earnings.

69. Global Tool & Die Maker is bidding on a contract with the government of Manatuka. The contract is a cost-plus situation, with an add-on profit margin of 50 percent. Direct material and direct labor are expected to total $15 per unit. Variable overhead is estimated at $4 per unit. Total fixed overhead to produce the 50,000 units needed by the government is $1,400,000. By acquiring the machinery and supervisory support needed to produce the 50,000 units, Global Tool will obtain the actual capacity to produce 80,000 units.

a. Should the price bid by Global Tool include a fixed overhead cost of $28 per unit or $17.50? How were these two amounts determined? Which of these two amounts would be more likely to cause Global Tool to obtain the contract? Why?

b. Assume that Global Tool set a bid price of $54.75 and obtained the contract. After producing the units, Global Tool submitted an invoice to the government of Manatuka for $3,525,000. The minister of finance for the country requests an explanation. Can you provide one?

c. Global Tool uses the excess capacity to produce an additional 30,000 units while making the units for Manatuka. These units are sold to another buyer. Is it ethical to present a $3,525,000 bill to Manatuka? Discuss.

d. Global Tool does not use the excess capacity while making the units for Manatuka. However, several months after that contract was completed, the company begins production of additional units. Was it ethical to present a $3,525,000 bill to Manatuka? Discuss.

e. Global Tool does not use the excess capacity because no other buyer exists for units of this type. Was it ethical to make a bid based on a fixed overhead rate per unit of $54.75? Discuss.

CHAPTER 4

Activity-Based Cost Systems for Management

LEARNING OBJECTIVES

After completing this chapter, you should be able to answer these questions:

1
What is the focus of activity-based management?

2
Why do non-value-added activities cause costs to increase unnecessarily?

3
Why must cost drivers be designated in an activity-based costing system?

4
How does activity-based costing differ from a traditional cost accounting system?

5
How does the installation of an activity-based costing system affect behavior?

6
What is attribute-based costing and how does it extend activity-based costing?

7
When is activity-based costing appropriate in an organization?

INTRODUCING

Carrier Corporation

http://www.carrier.com

Carrier, a United Technologies' company, is the world's largest manufacturer of air conditioning and heating products. Competition is intense, however, and among its six largest competitors, Carrier is the only one that is not Japanese owned. The director of cost improvement for Carrier's worldwide operations notes that Carrier's customers demand "a wide range of products that have unquestionable quality and include state-of-the-art features. Further, they expect these products to be delivered when needed, at a competitive price."

As the industry leader, Carrier strives to maintain its dominant position through innovative product design (product differentiation), high-quality low-cost manufacturing (zero defects and cost leadership), and time-based competition. To achieve these objectives, Carrier has implemented a series of improvement initiatives, including just-in-time, product and process standardization, strategic outsourcing, supply chain management, target costing, and performance measurement. Complexity reduction is a common goal among each of these initiatives. These changes instituted by Carrier were in response to both internal and external challenges.

While Carrier's manufacturing environment was changing dramatically at the plant level, its parent company, United Technologies, continued to emphasize financial reporting and control at the corporate level and placed relatively little emphasis on developing modern cost management systems for its manufacturing plants. Therefore, the manufacturing plants lacked the cost management information that was needed to support the improvement initiatives adequately and profitability suffered. "The intense competition, coupled with ever increasing customer demands, had made it difficult to maintain adequate profit margins on many products. Accordingly, Carrier's North American Operations profitability had dropped significantly below historical levels."

Carrier needed what it describes as a set of "enablers," or tools, to support the development of cost-effective product designs and manufacturing processes. Activity-based cost management (ABCM) was selected as the enabler that provides the necessary financial and activity information. Following its implementation, ABCM has been used by Carrier to quantify the benefits of redesigning plant layouts, using common parts, outsourcing, strengthening supplier and customer relationships, and developing alternative product designs. In some cases, even though management knows intuitively how to improve its operations, until the improvements are quantified they are not acted on.

SOURCE: Dan W. Swenson, "Managing Costs through Complexity Reduction at Carrier Corporation," *Strategic Finance* (April 1998), pp. 20–28.

Carrier Corporation, like many other manufacturers, recognized that its accounting reports were not providing managers with the information and details needed to make good business decisions in a global economy. This flaw was caused, in part, by the company's traditional overhead allocation system that was in use. The traditional system discussed in Chapter 3 is geared to satisfy external reporting requirements, but often does a less than adequate job of meeting management needs. Carrier investigated its cost accounting system and found that some basic changes were necessary. Management concluded that overhead allocations using a minimal number of rates and cost drivers did not provide realistic information for managerial functions.

This chapter presents topics that are at the forefront of managerial accounting literature and result from the intensely competitive nature of the global economy. First, the chapter presents the reasons that companies now focus on value-added and non-value-added activities, and explains how activities (rather than volume measures) can be used to determine product and service costs and to measure performance. Then, basics of activity-based costing, as well as some criticisms of this technique, are discussed and illustrated.

ACTIVITY-BASED MANAGEMENT

1

What is the focus of activity-based management?

Product cost determination, although specifically designated as an accounting function, is a major concern of all managers. For example, product costs affect decisions on corporate strategy (Is it profitable to be in this particular market?), marketing (How should this product be priced?), and finance (Should investments be made in additional plant assets to manufacture this product?). In theory, what a product or service costs to produce or perform would not matter if enough customers were willing to buy that product or service at a price high enough to cover costs and provide a reasonable profit margin. In reality, customers purchase something only if it provides acceptable value for the price being charged.

Management, then, should be concerned about whether customers perceive an equitable relationship between selling price and value. Activity-based management focuses on the activities incurred during the production or performance process as a way to improve the value received by a customer and the resulting profit achieved by providing this value. The concepts covered by activity-based management are shown in Exhibit 4–1 and are discussed in this and other chapters. These concepts help companies to produce more efficiently, determine costs more accurately, and control and evaluate performance more effectively. A primary component of activity-based management is **activity analysis**, which is the process of studying activities to classify them and to devise ways of minimizing or eliminating non-value-added activities.

activity analysis

2

Why do non-value-added activities cause costs to increase unnecessarily?

Value-Added versus Non-Value-Added Activities

activity

In a business context, an **activity** is defined as a repetitive action performed in fulfillment of business functions. If one takes a black-or-white perspective, activities are either value-added or non-value-added. A value-added (VA) activity increases the worth of a product or service to a customer and is one for which the customer is willing to pay. Alternatively, a non-value-added (NVA) activity increases the time spent on a product or service but does not increase its worth. Non-value-added activities are unnecessary from the perspective of the customer, which means they

EXHIBIT 4–1

The Activity-Based Management Umbrella

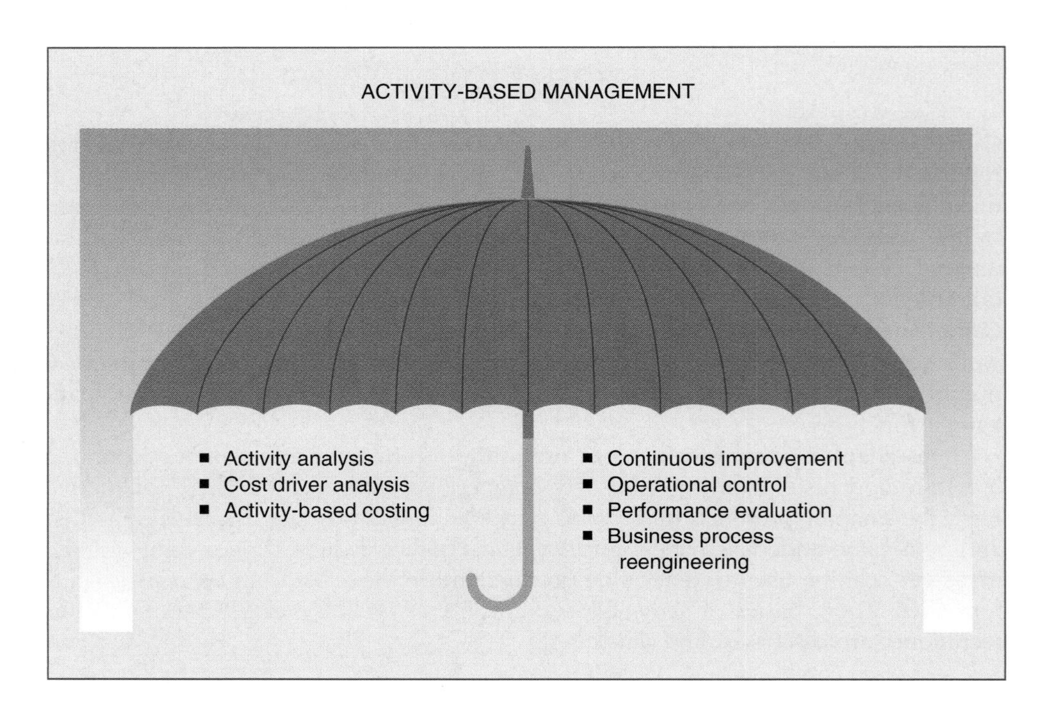

create costs that can be eliminated without affecting the market value or quality of the product or service.

Businesses also experience significant non-value-added time and activities. Some NVA activities are essential to business operations, but customers would not willingly choose to pay for these activities. These activities are known as **business-value-added activities**. For instance, companies must prepare invoices as documentation for sales and collections. Customers know this activity must occur, that it creates costs, and that product selling prices must be set to cover the costs of this activity. However, because invoice preparation adds no direct value to products and services, customers would prefer not to have to pay for this activity.

business-value-added activity

In striving to manage the relationship between price charged to and value received by the customer, firms are increasingly turning to their suppliers for help. The accompanying News Note indicates how electronics manufacturers depend on their suppliers not only for efficient and effective delivery of necessary components but also for the ideas that lead to new generations of products.

To help in activity analysis, managers should first identify organizational processes. "Processes include production, distribution, selling, administration, and other company functions. A company should define a process before it attempts to associate related activities to the defined process. Processes should not be forced or defined to fit activities; activities should fit processes."[1] Processes are commonly horizontal in nature (across organizational functions) and overlap multiple functional areas. For example, any production process also affects engineering, purchasing, warehousing, accounting, personnel, and marketing.

For each distinct process, a **process map** (or detailed flowchart) should be prepared that indicates every step that goes into making or doing something. All steps and all affected areas must be included, not just the obvious ones. For example, storing newly purchased parts would not be on a typical list of "Steps in Making Product X," but when materials and supplies are purchased, they are commonly stored until needed. Storage uses facilities that cost money and time is

process map

http://www.ibm.com

QUALITY **NEWS NOTE**

Sorting Suppliers for Competitive Advantage

Supplier evaluation programs have never been more important in the electronics industry. Electronics Original Equipment Manufacturers (OEMs) are relying on suppliers not only to supply parts, but to develop new technologies that OEMs will need for future products. With new product development time for some equipment being six months or less, and with life cycles being two years or less for many products, reliance on suppliers will continue to grow.

In recent years, IBM has reduced its number of suppliers, aggregating more business with fewer suppliers. To determine which suppliers to use and how much business to give each, IBM evaluates them on price, quality, delivery, and technology. However, each criterion is weighted differently depending on the commodity that the supplier produces.

"We base the technology rating on what's going on in the supplier's lab," says Gene Richter, chief procurement officer. "Is the supplier going to be the first to be qualified on a 1 gigabit DRAM, or the last? Does the supplier offer a full breadth of memory products or only one narrow niche? Is the supplier going to be the leader in the next generation in new technology? It can be very subjective. It's hard to sort the top three, but it's easy to tell the top three from the bottom three," says Richter.

SOURCE: James Carbone, "Evaluation Programs Determine Top Suppliers," *Purchasing* (November 18, 1999), pp. 31–35.

[1] Charles D. Mecimore and Alice T. Bell, "Are We Ready for Fourth-Generation ABC?" *Management Accounting* (January 1995), p. 24.

required to move the items in and out, resulting in labor costs. Each process map is unique and based on the results of a management and employee team's study.

value chart

Once the process map has been developed, a **value chart** can be constructed that identifies the stages and time spent in those stages from beginning to end of a process. Time can be consumed in four general ways: processing (or service), inspection, transfer, and idle. The actual time that it takes to perform the functions necessary to manufacture the product or perform the service is the **processing** (or **service**) **time**; this quantity of time is value-added. Performing quality control results in **inspection time**, whereas moving products or components from one place to another constitutes **transfer time**. Lastly, storage time and time spent waiting at a production operation for processing are **idle time**. Inspection time, transfer time, and idle time are all non-value-added. Thus, the **cycle** (or **lead**) **time** from the receipt of an order to completion of a product or performance of a service is equal to value-added processing time plus non-value-added time.

processing (service) time

inspection time

transfer time

idle time

cycle (lead) time

Although viewing inspection time and transfer time as non-value-added is theoretically correct, few companies can completely eliminate all quality control functions and all transfer time. Understanding the non-value-added nature of these functions, however, should help managers strive to minimize such activities to the extent possible. Thus, companies should view value-added and non-value-added activities as occurring on a continuum and concentrate on attempting to eliminate or minimize those activities that add the most time and cost *and* the least value.

Exhibit 4–2 illustrates a value chart for a chemical product made by Titan Chemical. Note the excessive time consumed by simply storing and moving materials. Value is added to products only during the times that production actually occurs; thus, Titan Company's entire production sequence has only 5.5 days of value-added time.

EXHIBIT 4–2

Value Chart for Titan Chemical

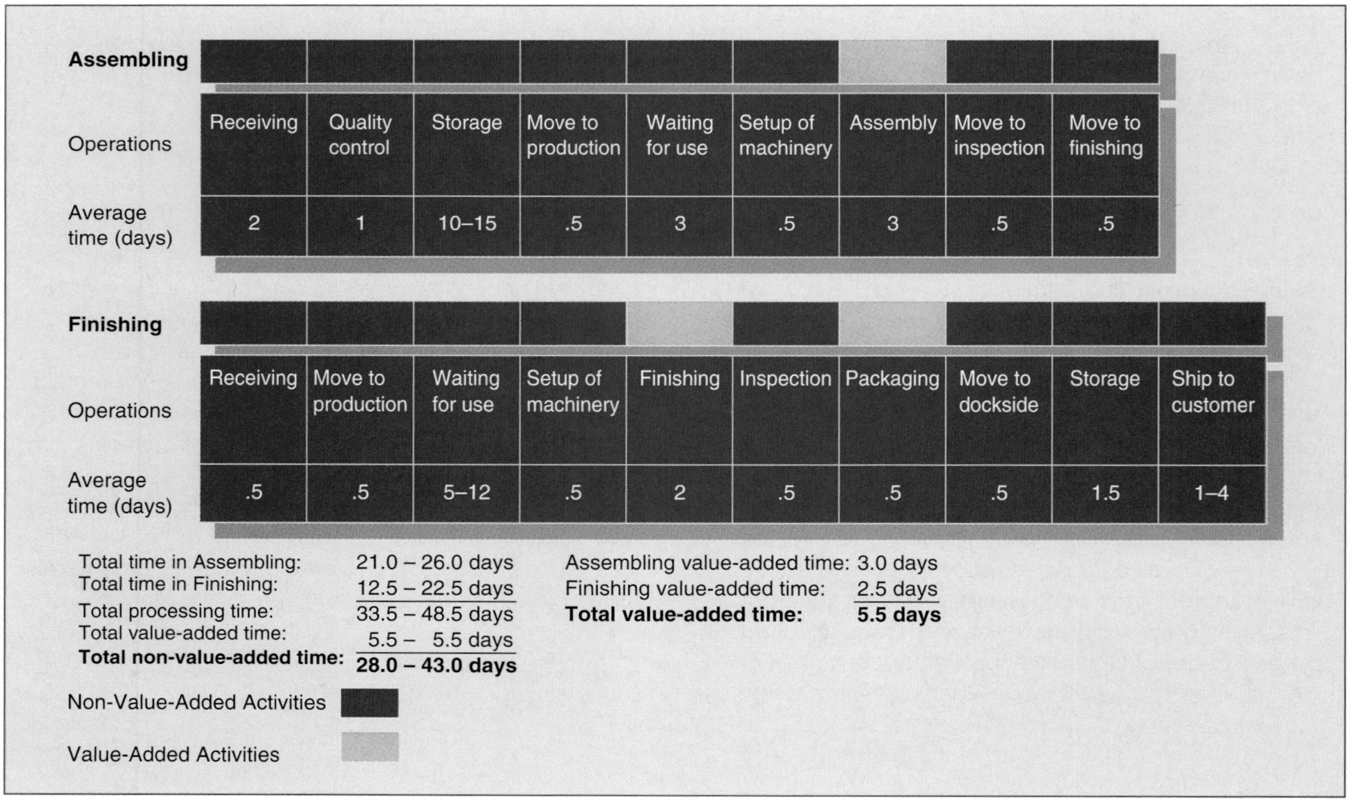

Assembling

Operations	Receiving	Quality control	Storage	Move to production	Waiting for use	Setup of machinery	Assembly	Move to inspection	Move to finishing
Average time (days)	2	1	10–15	.5	3	.5	3	.5	.5

Finishing

Operations	Receiving	Move to production	Waiting for use	Setup of machinery	Finishing	Inspection	Packaging	Move to dockside	Storage	Ship to customer
Average time (days)	.5	.5	5–12	.5	2	.5	.5	.5	1.5	1–4

Total time in Assembling:	21.0 – 26.0 days
Total time in Finishing:	12.5 – 22.5 days
Total processing time:	33.5 – 48.5 days
Total value-added time:	5.5 – 5.5 days
Total non-value-added time:	**28.0 – 43.0 days**

Assembling value-added time:	3.0 days
Finishing value-added time:	2.5 days
Total value-added time:	**5.5 days**

Non-Value-Added Activities (dark)

Value-Added Activities (light)

In some instances, a company may question whether the time spent in packaging is value-added. Packaging is essential for some products but unnecessary for others and, because packaging takes up about a third of the U.S. landfills and creates a substantial amount of cost, companies and consumers are beginning to focus their attention on reducing or eliminating packaging.

Manufacturing Cycle Efficiency

manufacturing cycle efficiency (MCE)

Dividing value-added processing time by total cycle time provides a measure of efficiency referred to as **manufacturing cycle efficiency (MCE)**. (A service company would compute service cycle efficiency by dividing actual service time by total cycle time.) If a company's production time were 3 hours and its total cycle time were 24 hours, its manufacturing cycle efficiency would be 12.5 (3 ÷ 24) percent.

Although the ultimate goal of 100 percent efficiency can never be achieved, typically, value is added to the product only 10 percent of the time from receipt of the parts until shipment to the customer. Ninety percent of the cycle time is waste. A product is much like a magnet. The longer the cycle time, the more the product attracts and creates cost.[2]

A just-in-time manufacturing process seeks to achieve substantially higher efficiency by producing components and goods at the precise time they are needed by either the next production station or the consumer. Thus, a significant amount of idle time (especially in storage) is eliminated. Raising MCE can also be achieved by installing and using automated technology, such as flexible manufacturing systems.

In a retail environment, cycle time relates to the length of time from ordering an item to selling that item. Non-value-added activities in retail include shipping time from the supplier, receiving delays for counting merchandise, and any storage time between receipt and sale. In a service company, cycle time refers to the time between the service order and service completion. All time spent on activities that are not actual service performance or are nonactivities (such as delays in beginning a job) are considered non-value-added for that job.

Non-value-added activities can be attributed to systemic, physical, and human factors. For example, systemic causes could include a processing requirement that products be manufactured in large batches to minimize setup cost or that service jobs be taken in order of urgency. Physical factors contribute to non-value-added activities because, in many instances, plant and machine layout do not provide for the most efficient transfer of products. This factor is especially apparent in multistory buildings in which receiving and shipping are on the ground floor, but storage and production are on upper floors. People may also be responsible for non-value-added activities because of improper skills or training or the need to be sociable.

Attempts to reduce non-value-added activities should be directed at all of these causes, but it is imperative that the "Willie Sutton" rule be applied. This rule is named for the bank robber who, when asked why he robbed banks, replied, "That's where the money is." The NVA activities that create the most costs should be the ones that management concentrates its efforts on reducing or eliminating. The system must be changed to reflect a new management philosophy regarding performance measures and determination of product cost. Physical factors must be changed as much as possible to eliminate layout difficulties and machine bottlenecks, and people must accept and work toward total quality control. Focusing attention on eliminating non-value-added activities should cause product/service quality to increase, and cycle time and cost to decrease.

[2] Tom E. Pryor, "Activity Accounting: The Key to Waste Reduction," *Accounting Systems Journal* (Fall 1990), p. 38.

Although constructing value charts for every product or service would be time consuming, a few such charts can quickly indicate where a company is losing time and money through non-value-added activities. Using amounts such as depreciation on storage facilities, wages for employees who handle warehousing, and the cost of capital on working capital funds tied up in stored inventory can provide an estimate of the amount by which costs could be reduced through the elimination of non-value-added activities.

COST DRIVER ANALYSIS

Why must cost drivers be designated in an activity-based costing system?

Companies engage in many activities that consume resources and, thus, cause costs to be incurred. All activities have cost drivers, defined in Chapter 3 as the factors having direct cause–effect relationships to a cost. Many cost drivers may be identified for an individual business unit. For example, cost drivers for factory insurance are number of employees; value of property, plant, and equipment; and number of accidents or claims during a specified time period. Cost drivers affecting the entire plant include inventory size, physical layout, and number of different products produced. Cost drivers are classified as volume-related (such as machine hours) and non-volume-related, which generally reflect the incurrence of specific transactions (such as setups, work orders, or distance traveled).

A greater number of cost drivers can be identified than should be used for cost accumulation or activity elimination. Management should limit the cost drivers selected to a reasonable number and ascertain that the cost of measuring a driver does not exceed the benefit of using it. A cost driver should be easy to understand, directly related to the activity being performed, and appropriate for performance measurement.

Costs have traditionally been accumulated into one or two cost pools (total factory overhead or variable and fixed factory overhead), and one or two drivers (direct labor hours and/or machine hours) have been used to assign costs to products. These procedures cause few, if any, problems for financial statement preparation. However, the use of single cost pools and single drivers may produce illogical product or service costs for internal managerial use in complex production (or service) environments.

Exhibit 4–3 indicates how activity analysis is combined with cost driver analysis to create a tool for managing costs. While cost driver analysis identifies the activities causing costs to be incurred, the activity analysis highlights activities that are not value-adding and can be targeted for elimination to reduce costs and product prices.

cost driver analysis

unit-level costs

To reflect the more complex environments, the accounting system must first recognize that costs are created and incurred because their drivers occur at different levels.[3] This realization necessitates using **cost driver analysis**, which investigates, quantifies, and explains the relationships of drivers and their related costs. Traditionally, cost drivers were viewed only at the unit level; for example, how many hours of labor or machine time did it take to produce a product or render a service? These drivers create **unit-level costs**, meaning that they are caused by the production or acquisition of a single unit of product or the delivery of a single unit of service. Other drivers and their costs are incurred for broader-based categories or levels of activity. These broader-based activity levels have successively wider scopes of influence on products and product types. The categories are classified as batch, product or process, and organizational or facility levels. Examples of the kinds of costs that occur at the various levels are given in Exhibit 4–4.

[3] This hierarchy of costs was introduced by Robin Cooper in "Cost Classification in Unit-Based and Activity-Based Manufacturing Cost Systems," *Journal of Cost Management* (Fall 1990), p. 6.

EXHIBIT 4–3

ABC Data and Cost Management

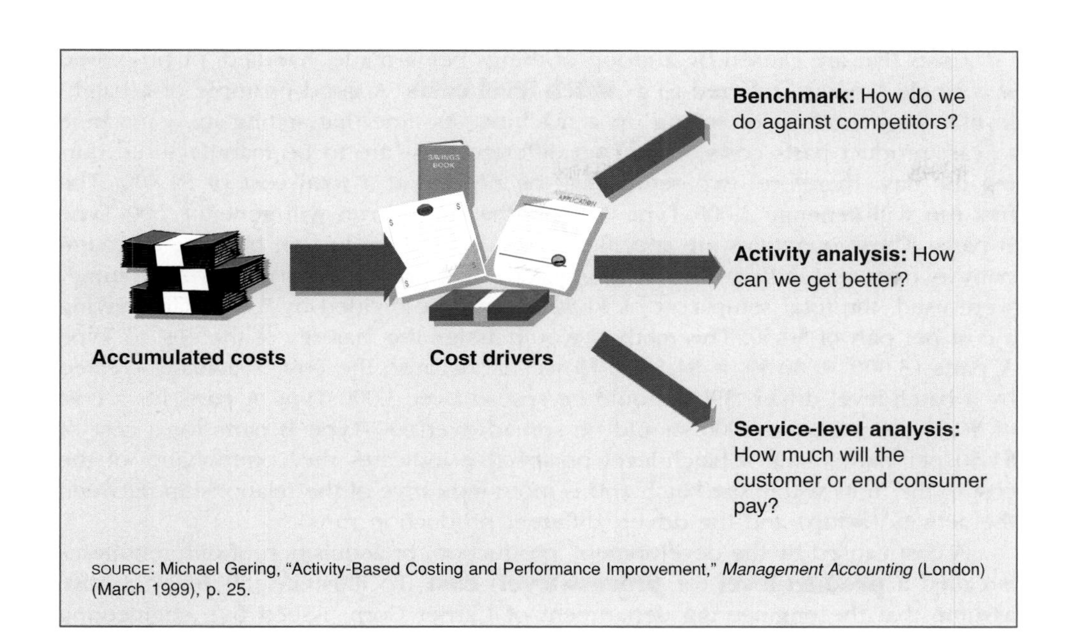

SOURCE: Michael Gering, "Activity-Based Costing and Performance Improvement," *Management Accounting* (London) (March 1999), p. 25.

EXHIBIT 4–4

Levels of Costs

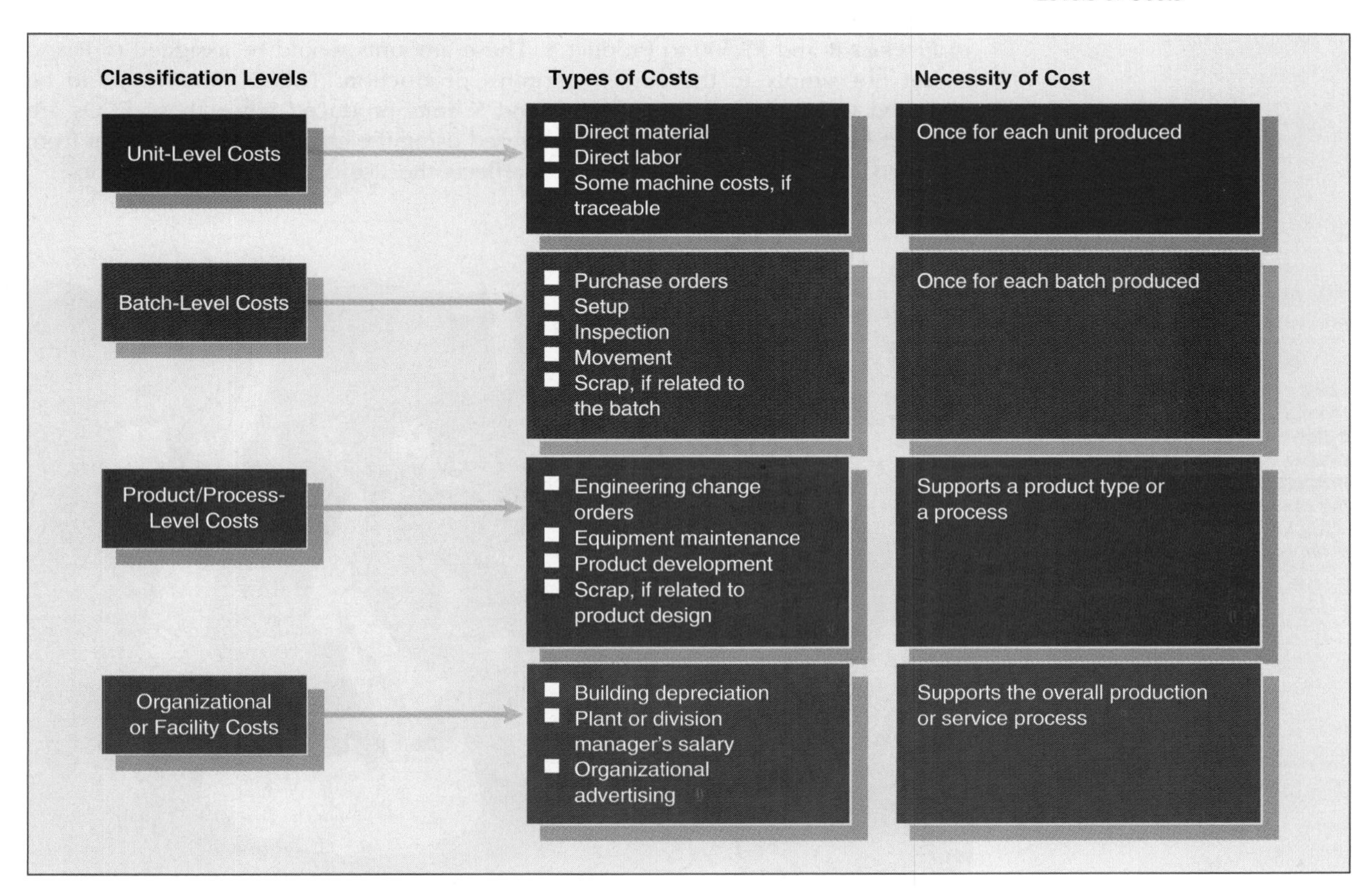

batch-level cost

Costs that are caused by a group of things being made, handled, or processed at a single time are referred to as **batch-level costs**. A good example of a batch-level cost is the cost of setting up a machine. Assume that setting up a machine to cast product parts costs $900. Two different parts are to be manufactured during the day; therefore, two setups will be needed at a total cost of $1,800. The first run will generate 3,000 Type A parts; the second run will generate 600 Type B parts. These quantities are specifically needed for production because the company is on a just-in-time production system. If a unit-based cost driver (volume) were used, the total setup cost of $1,800 would be divided by 3,600 parts, giving a cost per part of $0.50. This method would assign the majority of the cost to Type A parts (3,000 × $0.50 = $1,500). However, because the cost is actually created by a batch-level driver, $900 should be spread over 3,000 Type A parts for a cost of $0.30 per part and $900 should be spread over 600 Type B parts for a cost of $1.50 per part. Using a batch-level perspective indicates the commonality of the cost to the units within the batch and is more indicative of the relationship between the activity (setup) and the driver (different production runs).

product-level (process-level) cost

A cost caused by the development, production, or acquisition of different items is called a **product-level** (or **process-level**) **cost**. To illustrate this level of cost, assume that the engineering department of Carrier Corp. issued five engineering change orders (ECOs) during May. Of these ECOs, four related to Product R, one related to Product S, and none related to Product T. Each ECO costs $7,500 to issue. During May, the company produced 1,000 units of Product R, 1,500 units of Product S, and 5,000 units of Product T. If ECO costs were treated as unit-level costs, the total ECO cost of $37,500 would be spread over the 7,500 units produced at a cost per unit of $5. However, this method inappropriately assigns $25,000 of ECO cost to Product T, which had no engineering change orders issued for it! Using a product/process-level driver (number of ECOs) for ECO costs would assign $30,000 of costs to Product R and $7,500 to Product S. These amounts would be assigned to R and S, but not simply to the current month's production. The ECO cost should be allocated to all current and future R and S units produced while these ECOs are in effect because the products manufactured using the changed design benefit from the costs of the ECOs. This allocation reflects the use of a life-cycle concept.

This plant bottles several different types of juices. The costs of the gallon of orange juice and the plastic jug are unit-level costs. The setup cost of filling the vat with orange juice is a batch-level cost. The cost of developing each juice recipe is a process-level cost. And, finally, the cost of depreciation on the equipment and building is an organizational-level cost.

Certain costs at the organizational level are incurred for the singular purpose of supporting continuing facility operations. These **organizational-level costs** are common to many different activities and products or services and can be prorated to products only on an arbitrary basis. Although organizational-level costs theoretically should not be assigned to products at all, some companies attach them to goods produced or services rendered because the amounts are insignificant relative to all other costs.

organizational-level cost

Accountants have traditionally (and incorrectly) assumed that if costs did not vary with changes in production at the unit level, those costs were fixed rather than variable. In reality, batch, product/process, and organizational level costs are all variable, but they vary for reasons other than changes in production volume. Therefore, to determine a valid estimate of product or service cost, costs should be accumulated at each successively higher level of costs. Because unit, batch, and product/process level costs are all associated with units of products (merely at different levels), these costs can be summed at the product level to match with the revenues generated by product sales. Organizational-level costs are not product related, thus they should only be subtracted in total from net product revenues.

Exhibit 4–5 illustrates how costs collected at the unit, batch, and product/process levels can be used to generate a total product cost. Each product cost would be multiplied by the number of units sold and that amount of cost of goods sold would be subtracted from total product revenues to obtain a product line profit or loss item. These computations would be performed for each product line and summed to determine net product income or loss from which the unassigned organizational-level costs would be subtracted to find company profit or loss for internal management use. In this model, the traditional distinction (discussed in Chapter 3) between product and period costs can be and is ignored. The emphasis is on refining product profitability analysis for internal management purposes, rather than for external financial statements. Because the product/period cost distinction required by generally accepted accounting principles is not recognized, the model presented in Exhibit 4–5 is not currently acceptable for external reporting.

Data for a sample manufacturing company with three products are presented in Exhibit 4–6 to illustrate the difference in information that would result from recognizing multiple cost levels. Before recognizing that some costs were incurred at the batch, product, and organizational level, the company accumulated and allocated its factory overhead costs among its three products on a machine hour (MH) basis. Each product requires one machine hour, but Product D is a low-volume, special-order line. As shown in the first section of Exhibit 4–6, cost information indicated that Product D was a profitable product. After analyzing its activities, the company began capturing costs at the different levels and assigning them to products based on appropriate cost drivers. The individual details for this overhead assignment are not shown, but the final assignments and resulting product profitability figures are presented in the second section of Exhibit 4–6. This more refined approach to assigning costs shows that Product D is actually unprofitable.

Costs are incurred because firms engage in a variety of activities, and these activities consume company resources. Accountants have traditionally used a transaction basis to accumulate costs and, additionally, have focused on the cost incurred rather than the source of the cost. However, managers now believe that the "conventional transaction-driven system is costly to administer, fails to control costs, and usually yields erroneous product cost data."[4]

Traditional cost allocations tend to subsidize low-volume, specialty products by misallocating overhead to high-volume, standard products. This problem occurs because costs of the extra activities needed to make specialty products are assigned

[4] Richard J. Schonberger, "World-Class Performance Management," in Peter B. B. Turney, ed., *Performance Excellence in Manufacturing and Service Organizations* (Sarasota, Fla.: American Accounting Association, 1990), p. 1.

EXHIBIT 4-5

Determining Product Profitability and Company Profit

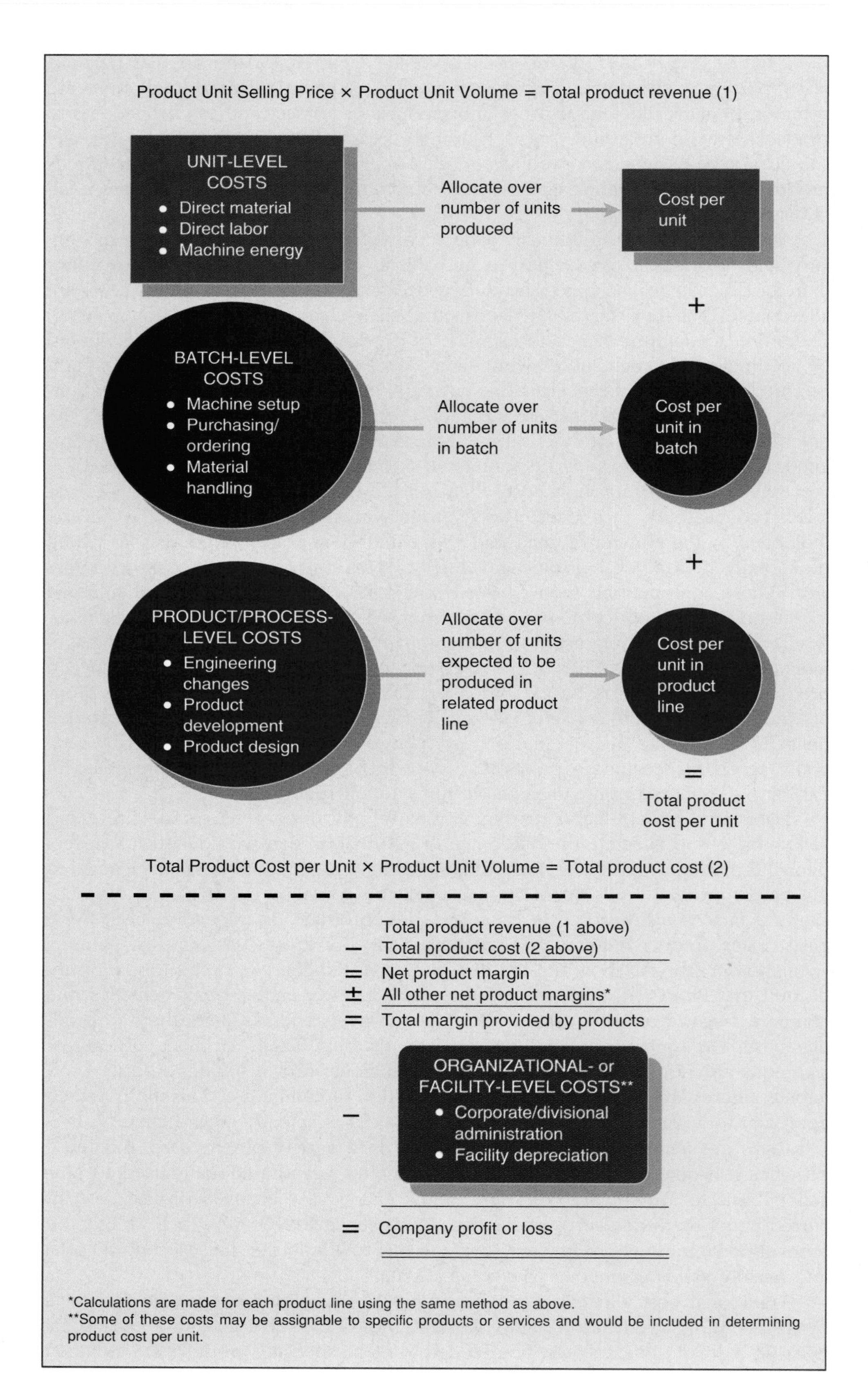

Total overhead cost = $1,505,250
Total machine hours = 111,500
Overhead rate per machine hour = $13.50

	PRODUCT C (5,000 UNITS)		PRODUCT D (1,500 UNITS)		PRODUCT E (105,000 UNITS)		
	Unit	**Total**	**Unit**	**Total**	**Unit**	**Total**	**Total**
Product revenue	$50.00	$250,000	$45.00	$67,500	$40.00	$4,200,000	$4,517,500
Product costs							
Direct	$20.00	100,000	$20.00	$30,000	$ 9.00	$ 945,000	
OH per MH	13.50	67,500	13.50	20,250	13.50	1,417,500	
Total	$33.50	$167,500	$33.50	$50,250	$22.50	$2,362,500	(2,580,250)
Net income		$ 82,500		$17,250		$1,837,500	$1,937,250

	PRODUCT C (5,000 UNITS)		PRODUCT D (1,500 UNITS)		PRODUCT E (105,000 UNITS)		
	Unit	**Total**	**Unit**	**Total**	**Unit**	**Total**	**Total**
Product revenue	$50	$250,000	$45	$ 67,500	$40	$4,200,000	$4,517,500
Product costs							
Direct	$20	100,000	$20	$ 30,000	$ 9	$ 945,000	
Overhead							
Unit level	8	40,000	12	18,000	6	630,000	
Batch level	9	45,000	19	28,500	3	315,000	
Product level	3	15,000	15	22,500	2	210,000	
Total	$40	$200,000	$66	$ 99,000	$20	$2,100,000	(2,399,000)
Product line income or (loss)		$ 50,000		$(31,500)		$2,100,000	$2,118,500
Organizational-level costs							(181,250)
Net income							$1,937,250

EXHIBIT 4-6

Product Profitability Analysis

using the one or very few drivers of traditional costing—and usually these drivers are volume based. Interestingly, as long ago as 1954, William J. Vatter noted that "[j]ust as soon as cost accounting is found inadequate for the needs it is supposed to meet, just as soon as cost accounting does not provide the data which management must have, cost accounting will either change to meet those needs or it will be replaced with something else."[5] The time has come for cost accounting to change by utilizing new bases on which to collect and assign costs. Those bases are the activities that drive or create the costs.

ACTIVITY-BASED COSTING

4

How does activity-based costing differ from a traditional cost accounting system?

Recognizing that several levels of costs exist, accumulating costs into related cost pools, and using multiple cost drivers to assign costs to products and services are the three fundamental components of activity-based costing (ABC). ABC is a cost accounting system that focuses on the various activities performed in an organization and collects costs on the basis of the underlying nature and extent of those activities. This costing method focuses on attaching costs to products and services based on the activities conducted to produce, perform, distribute, or support those products and services. The accompanying News Note illustrates use of ABC at the U.S. Postal Service.

[5] William J. Vatter, "Tailor-Making Cost Data for Specific Uses," in L. S. Rosen, ed., *Topics in Managerial Accounting* (Toronto: McGraw-Hill Ryerson Ltd., 1954), p. 194.

NEWS NOTE  GENERAL BUSINESS

Paying the Postman

The U.S. Postal Service (USPS) is a unique federal entity in several respects. First, the USPS, in essence, operates in a manner similar to many private sector companies. The USPS provides a variety of services, generates revenue from these services, and incurs costs and expenses as a result of its operations. Second, the USPS is unique in that it is open to private sector competition. Competition includes companies such as Federal Express, United Parcel Service, Mail Boxes, Etc., and a host of other similar companies. Few other governmental agencies or departments operate in a similar business environment.

Retailers as well as USPS competitors have long accepted credit cards as payments for goods and services. Moreover, new technologies are beginning to lead to a "cashless" world. Customers are seeking convenience and value, while businesses are striving for increased sales and guaranteed payment. Given the competitive forces facing the USPS and the rapid pace at which new technologies are becoming available, USPS management realized that it had to use innovative business methods to maintain and increase its market share against the competition and provide increased value to its customers while ensuring cost effectiveness.

Based on this evaluation of its position in the marketplace, the USPS engaged Coopers and Lybrand (C&L)* to conduct activity-based cost studies of its key revenue collection processes for a national credit card and debit card program. To obtain an understanding of the cash, check, and credit/debit card activities, C&L reviewed USPS data and procedure manuals, interviewed USPS headquarters staff, and conducted telephone surveys of front window supervisors and district office accounting personnel. Using an activity-based cost modeling approach, C&L defined the cash and check process in terms of the activities that link together to make the processes.

In summarizing its findings, C&L reported that, "Credit and debit card processing costs are relatively high at the moment due to the normal impact of process start-up, low initial volume and high initial implementation costs. However, as volumes continue to grow, projected credit and debit card costs can become competitive with current cash and check processing costs.

*now PricewaterhouseCoopers

SOURCE: Terrell L. Carter, Ali M. Sedaghat, and Thomas D. Williams, "How ABC Costs Changed the Post Office," *Strategic Finance* (February 1998), pp. 20–36.

http://www.usps.com
http://www.fedex.com
http://www.ups.com
http://www.mbe.com

Managers in many manufacturing companies are concerned about the product costing information being provided by the traditional cost accounting systems. The general consensus is that product costs currently being developed are useful in preparing financial statements, but are often of limited use for management decision making. Activity-based costing, on the other hand, is useful in companies having the following characteristics:

1. the production or performance of a wide variety of products or services;
2. high overhead costs that are not proportional to the unit volume of individual products;
3. significant automation that has made it increasingly more difficult to assign overhead to products using the traditional direct labor or machine-hour bases;
4. profit margins that are difficult to explain; and
5. hard-to-make products that show big profits and easy-to-make products that show losses.[6]

Companies having the above characteristics may want to reevaluate their cost systems and implement activity-based costing.

5

How does the installation of an activity-based costing system affect behavior?

activity center

Two-Step Allocation

After being recorded in the general ledger and subledger accounts, costs are accumulated in activity center cost pools. An **activity center** is a segment of the production or service process for which management wants a separate report of

[6] Robin Cooper, "You Need a New Cost System When . . . ," *Harvard Business Review* (January–February 1989), pp. 77–82.

the costs of activities performed. In defining these centers, management should consider the following issues: geographical proximity of equipment, defined centers of managerial responsibility, magnitude of product costs, and a need to keep the number of activity centers manageable. Costs having the same driver are accumulated in pools reflecting the appropriate level of cost incurrence (unit, batch, or product/process). The fact that a relationship exists between a cost pool and a cost driver indicates that, if the cost driver can be reduced or eliminated, the related cost should also be reduced or eliminated.

Gathering costs in pools reflecting the same cost drivers allows managers to recognize cross-functional activities in an organization. In the past, some companies may have accumulated overhead in smaller-than-plantwide pools, but this accumulation was typically performed on a department-by-department basis. Thus, the process reflected a vertical-function approach to cost accumulation. But production and service activities are horizontal by nature. A product or service flows through an organization, affecting numerous departments as it goes. Using a cost driver approach to develop cost pools allows managers to more clearly focus on the various cost impacts created in making a product or performing a service than was possible traditionally.

After accumulation, costs are allocated out of the activity center cost pools and assigned to products and services by use of a second driver. These drivers are often referred to as activity drivers. An **activity driver** measures the demands placed on activities and, thus, the resources consumed by products and services. An activity driver selected often indicates an activity's output. The process of cost assignment is the same as the overhead application process illustrated in Chapter 3. Exhibit 4–7 illustrates this two-step process of tracing costs to products and services in an ABC system.

activity driver

EXHIBIT 4–7

Tracing Costs in an Activity-Based Costing System

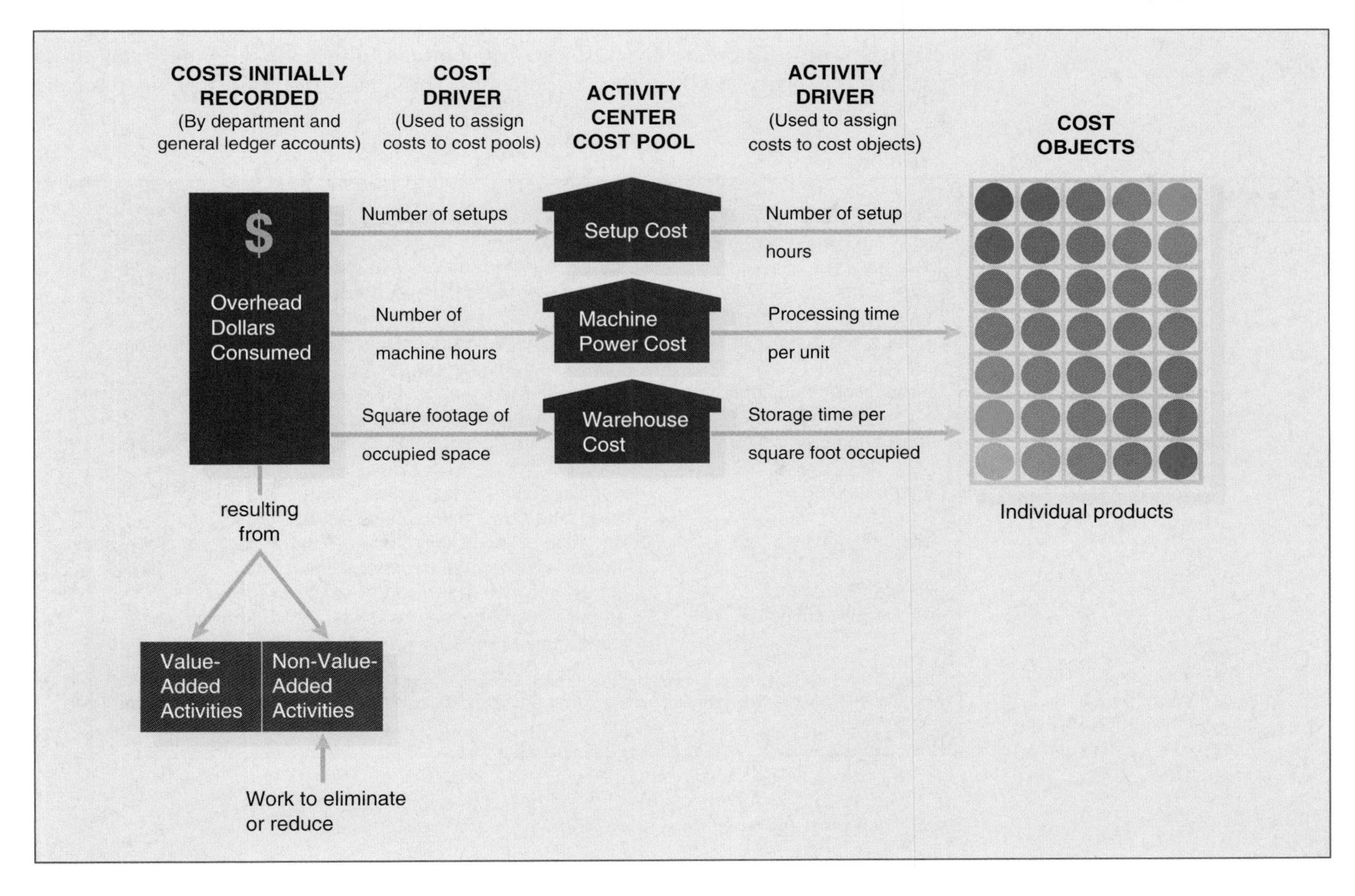

As noted in Exhibit 4–7, the cost drivers for the collection stage may differ from the activity drivers used for the allocation stage because some activity center costs are not traceable to lower levels of activity. Costs at the lowest (unit) level of activity should be allocated to products by use of volume- or unit-based drivers. Costs incurred at higher (batch and product/process) levels may also be allocated to products by use of volume-related drivers, but the volume measure should include only those units associated with the batch or the product/process—not total production or service volume. Exhibit 4–8 provides some common drivers for various activity centers.

Activity-Based Costing Illustrated

An ABC example is shown in Exhibit 4–9. Information is gathered about the activities and costs for a factory maintenance department. Costs are then assigned to specific products based on activities. This department allocates its total personnel cost among the three activities performed in that department based on the number of employees in those areas. This allocation reflects the fact that occurrences of a specific activity, rather than volume of production or service, are indicative of work performed in the department.

This company manufactures Product Z, which is a rather complex unit with relatively low demand. The cost allocated to Product Z with the activity-based costing system is 132 percent higher than the cost allocated with the traditional allocation system ($1.564 versus $0.675)!

Discrepancies in costs between traditional and activity-based costing methods are not uncommon. Activity-based costing systems indicate that significant resources are consumed by low-volume products and complex production operations. Studies have shown that, after the implementation of activity-based costing, the costs of high-volume, standard products have often been too high and, using ABC, have declined anywhere from 10 to 30 percent. Low-volume, complex specialty product costs tend to increase from 100 to 500 percent, although in some cases these costs have risen by 1,000 to 5,000 percent![7] Thus, activity-based costing typically

EXHIBIT 4-8

Activity Drivers

Activity Center	Activity Drivers
Accounting	Reports requested; dollars expended
Personnel	Job change actions; hiring actions; training hours; counseling hours
Data processing	Reports requested; transactions processed; programming hours; program change requests
Production engineering	Hours spent in each shop; job specification changes requested; product change notices processed
Quality control	Hours spent in each shop; defects discovered; samples analyzed
Plant services	Preventive maintenance cycles; hours spent in each shop; repair and maintenance actions
Material services	Dollar value of requisitions; number of transactions processed; number of personnel in direct support
Utilities	Direct usage (metered to shop); space occupied
Production shops	Fixed per-job charge; setups made; direct labor; machine hours; number of moves; material applied

SOURCE: Michael D. Woods, "Completing the Picture: Economic Choices with ABC," *Management Accounting* (December 1992), p. 54. Reprinted from *Management Accounting*. Copyright by Institute of Management Accountants, Montvale, N.J.

[7] Peter B. B. Turney, *An Introduction to Activity-Based Costing* (ABC Technologies, Inc., 1990), video.

Factory Maintenance Department: The company's conventional system assigns the personnel costs of this department to products using direct labor hours (DLHs); the department has 9 employees and incurred $450,000 of personnel costs in the current year or $50,000 per employee. Expected DLHs are 200,000.

ABC ALLOCATION

Stage 1
Trace costs from general ledger and subsidiary ledger accounts to activity center pools according to number of employees:

- Regular maintenance—uses 5 employees; $250,000 is allocated to this activity; second-stage allocation to be based on machine hours (MHs)
- Preventive maintenance—uses 2 employees; $100,000 is allocated to this activity; second-stage allocation to be based on number of setups
- Repairs—uses 2 employees; $100,000 is allocated to this activity; second-stage allocation is based on number of machine starts

Stage 2
Allocate activity center cost pools to products using cost drivers chosen for each cost pool.

2001 activity of second-stage drivers: 500,000 MHs; 5,000 setups; 100,000 machine starts

Step 1: Allocate costs per unit of activity of second-stage cost drivers.

- Regular maintenance—$250,000 ÷ 500,000 MHs = $0.50 per MH
- Preventive maintenance—$100,000 ÷ 5,000 setups = $20 per setup
- Repairs—$100,000 ÷ 100,000 machine starts = $1 per machine start

Step 2: Allocate costs to products using quantity of second-stage cost drivers consumed in making these products. The following quantities of activity are relevant to Product Z: 30,000 MHs; 30 setups; 40 machine starts; and 3,000 DLHs out of a total of 200,000 DLHs in 2001. Ten thousand units of Product Z were manufactured during 2001.

ABC Allocation to Product Z = (30,000 × $0.50) + (30 × $20) + (40 × $1) = $15,640 for 10,000 units or $1.564 per unit

Traditional Allocation to Product Z = $450,000 ÷ 200,000 DLHs = $2.25 per DLH; (3,000 × $2.25) = $6,750 for 10,000 units or $0.675 per unit

EXHIBIT 4–9

Illustration of Activity-Based Costing Allocation

shifts a substantial amount of overhead cost from standard, high-volume products to premium special-order, low-volume products, as shown in Exhibit 4–10. The ABC costs of moderate products and services (those that are neither extremely simple nor complex, nor produced in extremely low or high volumes) tend to remain approximately the same as the costs calculated using traditional costing methods.

Although the preceding discussion addresses costs normally considered product costs, activity-based costing is just as applicable to service department costs. Many companies use an activity-based costing system to allocate corporate overhead costs to their revenue-producing units based on the number of reports, documents, customers, or other reasonable measures of activity.

Short-Term and Long-Term Variable Costs

Short-term variable costs increase or decrease corresponding with changes in the volume of activity. Costs that do not move in relation to volume have conventionally been accepted as fixed. "Generally [however], as a business expands, costs tend to be far more variable than they should be, and when it contracts, they are far more fixed than they should be."[8] Professor Robert Kaplan of Harvard University considers the ability of "fixed" costs to change under the "Rule of One," which means that possessing or using more than one unit of a resource is evidence that

[8] B. Charles Ames and James D. Hlavacek, "Vital Truths About Managing Your Costs," *Harvard Business Review* (January–February 1990), p. 145.

EXHIBIT 4–10

Traditional versus ABC Overhead Allocations

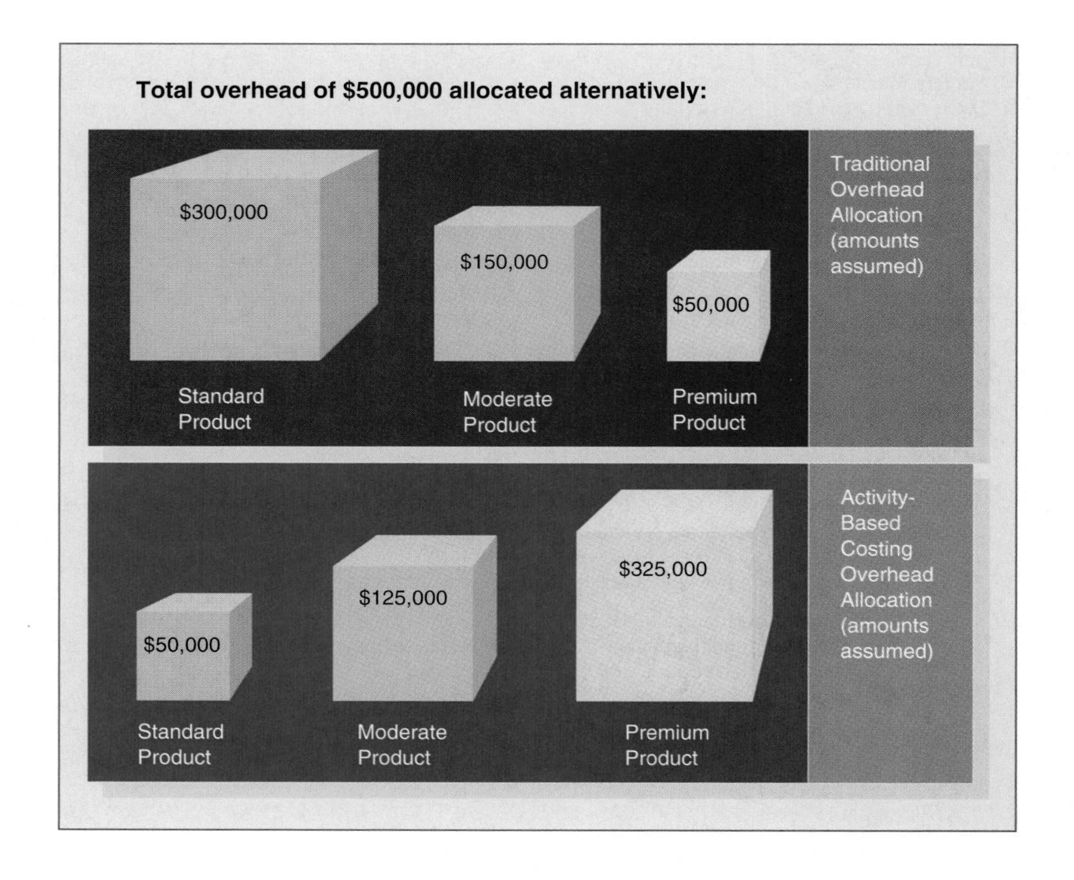

long-term variable cost

the resource is variable.[9] Because of this logic, many people have come to view fixed costs as **long-term variable costs**, for which suitable (usually non-volume-related) cost drivers simply need to be identified.

product variety
product complexity
process complexity

Two significant cost drivers that cause long-term variable costs to change, but which traditionally have been disregarded, are product variety and product complexity. **Product variety** refers to the number of different types of products made; **product complexity** refers to the number of components included in a product; **process complexity** refers to the number of processes through which a product flows. These items create additional overhead (such as warehousing, purchasing, setups, and inspections), so long-term variable costs tend to increase as the number and types of products increase. Therefore, managers should use these cost drivers in applying ABC.

Attribute-Based Costing

6

What is attribute-based costing and how does it extend activity-based costing?

attribute-based costing (ABC II)

Attribute-based costing (ABC II), an extension of activity-based costing, employs detailed cost–benefit analyses relating to information on customer needs (in terms of performance attributes of a product such as reliability, durability, responsiveness, and so forth) and the costs of the incremental improvements necessary to obtain these attributes. ABC II employs planned costs rather than past costs because, as discussed earlier, such a high percentage of a product's life-cycle costs are locked in during the product's development stage. The approach focuses on satisfying customer needs by searching for the optimum enhancement of customer utility through comparisons of alternatives for attribute enhancements relative to the costs of producing those enhancements.[10]

[9] Patrick L. Romano, "Activity Accounting: An Update—Part 2," *Management Accounting* (June 1989), p. 63.
[10] For additional information, see Mike Walker, "Attribute Based Costing," *Australian Accountant* (March 1992), pp. 42–45.

DETERMINING WHETHER ABC IS APPROPRIATE

7

When is activity-based costing appropriate in an organization?

A vital loss of information may occur in an accounting system that ignores activity and cost relationships. Not every accounting system using direct labor or machine hours as the cost driver is providing inadequate or inaccurate cost information. However, some general clues may alert managers to the need to review the cost data being provided by a conventional accounting system. Some of these clues are more relevant to manufacturing entities, but others are equally appropriate for both manufacturing and service businesses. Consider the following:

> *For a given organization, is it likely that ABC will produce costs that are significantly different from those that are generated with conventional accounting, and does it seem likely that those costs will be "better"? The factors involved here include:*
> - *the number and diversity of products or services produced,*
> - *the diversity and differential degree of support services used for different products,*
> - *the extent to which common processes are used,*
> - *the effectiveness of current cost allocation methods,*
> - *and the rate of growth of period costs.*
>
> *If information that is considered "better" is generated by ABC, will the new information change the dependent decisions made by the management? The factors involved here are:*
> - *management's freedom to set prices,*
> - *the ratio of period costs to total costs,*
> - *strategic considerations,*
> - *the climate and culture of cost reduction in the company,*
> - *and the frequency of analysis that is desirable or necessary.*[11]

Two primary underlying assumptions that companies must consider before adopting ABC are that the costs in each cost pool are (1) driven by homogeneous activities and (2) strictly proportional to the activity.[12] If these assumptions are met, the following circumstances may indicate a need to consider using activity-based costing.

With Product Variety and Product Complexity

http://www.hallmark.com
http://www.pg.com

Product variety is commonly associated with a need to consider activity-based costing. Products may be variations of the same product line (such as Hallmark's different types of greeting cards), or they may be in numerous product families (such as Procter & Gamble's detergents, diapers, fabric softeners, and shampoos). In either case, product additions cause numerous overhead costs to increase.

mass customization

In the quest for product variety, many companies are striving for **mass customization** of products through the use of flexible manufacturing systems. Such personalized production can often be conducted at a relatively low cost. Although such customization may please some customers, it does have some drawbacks. First, there may simply be too many choices. For instance, at GE Fanuc (a Charlottesville, Virginia, manufacturer), customers had to look through several 4-inch-thick binders of components to design a custom-made product—an extremely time-consuming project.[13] Nissan reportedly had 87 different varieties of steering wheels, but customers did not want many of them and disliked having to choose from so many

http://gefanuc.com
http://www.nissanmotors.com

[11] T. L. Estrin, Jeffrey Kantor, and David Albers, "Is ABC Suitable for Your Company?" *Management Accounting* (April 1994), p. 40.
[12] Harold P. Roth and A. Faye Borthick, "Are You Distorting Costs by Violating ABC Assumptions?" *Management Accounting* (November 1991), pp. 39–40.
[13] B. Joseph Pine, "Customers Don't Want Choices," *The Wall Street Journal* (April 18, 1994), p. A12.

options.[14] Second, mass customization creates a tremendous opportunity for errors. And third, most companies have found that customers, given the wide variety of choices, typically make selections from a rather small percentage of the total. At Toyota, investigation of purchases revealed that 20 percent of the product varieties accounted for 80 percent of the sales.[15] This 20:80 ratio is a fairly common one and is referred to as the **Pareto principle**, after the Italian economist Vilfredo Pareto.[16]

Pareto principle

Companies with complex products, services, or processes may want to investigate ways to reduce that complexity. Management may want to review the design of the company's products and processes to standardize them and reduce the number of different components, tools, and processes required. Products should be designed to consider the Pareto principle and take advantage of commonality of parts. An analysis of components will generally reveal that 20 percent of the components are used in 80 percent of the products. If this is the case, then companies need to consider two other factors. First, are the remaining components used in key products? If so, could equal quality be achieved by using the more common parts? If not, can the products be sold for a premium price to cover the costs associated with the use of low-volume components? Second, are the parts specified for use in products purchased by important customers who are willing to pay a premium price for the products? If so, the benefits from the complexity may be worth the cost. However, would customers be equally satisfied if more common parts were used and the product price were reduced? Complexity is acceptable only if it is value-added from the customer's point of view.

Process complexity may develop over time, or it may exist because of a lack of sufficient planning in product development. Processes are complex when they create difficulties for the people attempting to perform production operations (physical straining, awkwardness of motions, or wasted motions) or for the people using manufacturing machinery (multiple and/or detailed setups, lengthy transfer time between machine processes, recalibration of instruments, and so on). Process complexity reflects numerous non-value-added activities and thus causes time delays and cost increases.

A company can employ simultaneous engineering to reduce both product and process complexity. **Simultaneous** (or **concurrent**) **engineering** refers to the continuous involvement of all primary functions and personnel contributing to a product's origination and production from the beginning of a project. Multifunctional teams design the product by considering customer expectations, vendor capabilities, parts commonality, and production process compatibility. Such an integrated design effort is referred to as a design-for-manufacturability approach. Simultaneous engineering helps companies to shorten the time-to-market for new products and minimize complexity and cost.

simultaneous (concurrent) engineering

Many traditional cost systems are not designed to account for information such as how many different parts are used in a product, so management cannot identify products made with low-volume or unique components. Activity-based costing systems are flexible and can gather such details so that persons involved in reengineering efforts have information about relationships among activities and cost drivers. Armed with these data, reengineering efforts can be focused on the primary causes of process complexity and on the causes that create the highest levels of waste.

[14] B. Joseph Pine II, Bart Victor, and Andrew C. Boynton, "Making Mass Customization Work," *Harvard Business Review* (September–October 1993), p. 110.

[15] Ibid, p. 108.

[16] Pareto found that about 85 percent of Milan's wealth was held by about 15 percent of the people. The term *Pareto principle* was coined by Joseph Juran in relationship to quality problems. Juran found that a high proportion of such problems were caused by a small number of process characteristics (the vital few), whereas the majority of process characteristics (the trivial many) accounted for only a small proportion of quality problems.

With Lack of Commonality in Overhead Costs

Certain products and services create substantially more overhead costs than others. Although some of these additional overhead costs may be caused by product variety or product/process complexity, others may be related to support services. For example, some products require significant levels of advertising; some use high cost distribution channels; and some necessitate the use of high-technology machinery. "A software distribution company, for example, discovered that a supposedly profitable high-margin product was generating so many calls to its help line that it was actually a money loser. Dropping that one product improved company profitability by nearly 10%."[17] If only one or two overhead pools are used, overhead related to specific products will be spread over all products. The result will be increased costs for products that are not responsible for the increased overhead.

With Problems in Current Cost Allocations

If a company has undergone one or more significant changes in its products or processes (such as increased product variety or business process reengineering), managers and accountants need to investigate whether the existing cost system still provides a reasonable estimate of product or service cost. Many companies that have automated their production processes have experienced large reductions in labor and large increases in overhead costs. In such companies, using direct labor as an overhead allocation base produces extraordinarily high application rates. Prior to the introduction of ABC at Harris Semiconductor Sector, the overhead application rate per area ranged from 800 to 1,800 percent of the direct labor costs. This process resulted in 90 to 95 percent of all costs being allocated on a "mere 5–10 percent (i.e., direct labor costs) of the cost base."[18] Products made using automated equipment tend to be charged an insufficient amount of overhead, whereas products made using high proportions of direct labor tend to be overcharged.

Traditional cost allocations also generally emphasize the assignment of product costs to products at the same time the majority of period costs are expensed as incurred. Activity-based costing recognizes that some period costs (such as R&D and distribution) may be distinctly and reasonably associated with specific products and thus should be traced and allocated to those products. This recognition changes the traditional view of product versus period cost. And, as indicated in the News Note on page 150, ABC information can be used, with diplomacy, to evaluate customer profitability.

With Changes in Business Environment

A change in a company's competitive environment may also require better cost information. Increased competition may occur for several reasons: (1) other companies have recognized the profit potential of a particular product or service, (2) the product or service has become cost-feasible to make or perform, or (3) an industry has been deregulated. If many new companies are competing for old business, the best estimate of product or service cost must be available to management so that profit margins and prices can be reasonably set.

Changes in management strategy can also signal a need for a new cost system. For example, if management wants to begin new operations, the cost system must be capable of providing information on how costs will change. Confirming management's view of costs to the traditional variable versus fixed classifications may not allow such information to be effectively developed. Viewing costs as short-term

[17] Srikumar S. Rao, "True Cost," *Financial World* (September 25, 1995), pp. 62–63.

[18] Christopher R. Dedera, "Harris Semiconductor ABC: Worldwide Implementation and Total Integration," *Journal of Cost Management* (Spring 1996), p. 44.

NEWS NOTE  GENERAL BUSINESS

Measuring Customers to Manage Profits

Activity-based costing differs from conventional costing in that it uses cost drivers to assign costs. By understanding the overhead that a particular customer or product really uses, ABC pinpoints customer profitability in a way that conventional accounting cannot.

The first shock comes when customers or products previously believed to be profitable are shown to consume more resources than the revenue that they generate.

Take for example the owner of a chain of pharmaceutical companies who wanted to reprice his products. He focused on assigning the transaction and holding costs associated with each product and used ABC to put in place a quick but fairly accurate system. Not surprisingly many small items generated costs well out of line with the accounting system and the Christmas break was used to reprice the items in the warehouse and on his shelves. Unfortunately, the new pricing was not well received; the business underwent a shock and his management team spent the next four months back-peddling with their customers.

Big changes, whether they are performed inside or across the boundaries of the organization, require careful diplomacy. Knowing the costs of your products sets a target. Implementing that target requires careful steps.

In big companies this usually requires the input of various players, of multifunctional teams that negotiate joint solutions with suppliers and customers. Often this leads to dramatic solutions that no one party would have reached on its own—standard packaging, availability of forecasts, more frequent deliveries, cheaper materials for noncritical parts.

ABC provides the tools to negotiate these solutions. By negotiating what the customer is prepared to pay for, we are able to minimize total costs across the entire value chain and add value for the final user.

SOURCE: Michael Gering, "Activity-Based Costing and the Customer," *Management Accounting* (London) (April 1999), pp. 26–27.

variable versus long-term variable focuses on cost drivers and on the changes the planned operations will have on activities and costs.

continuous improvement

Continuous improvement recognizes the concepts of eliminating non-value-added activities to reduce cycle time, making products (or performing services) with zero defects, reducing product costs on an ongoing basis, and simplifying products and processes. Activity-based costing, by promoting an understanding of cost drivers, allows the non-value-added activities to be identified and their causes eliminated or reduced.

CRITICISMS OF ACTIVITY-BASED COSTING

Realistically assessing new models and accounting approaches for what they can help managers accomplish is always important. However, no currently existing accounting technique or system will provide management with exact cost information for every product or with the information needed to make consistently perfect decisions. Activity-based costing, although it typically provides better information than was generated under the traditional overhead allocation process, is not a panacea for all managerial concerns. The following are some of this method's shortcomings.

First, ABC requires a significant amount of time and, thus, cost to implement. If implementation is to be successful, substantial support is needed throughout the firm. An environment for change must be created that requires overcoming a variety of individual, organizational, and environmental barriers. Individual barriers are typically related to (1) fear of the unknown or shift in status quo, (2) potential loss of status, or (3) a necessity to learn new skills. Organizational barriers are often related to "territorial," hierarchical, or corporate culture issues. Environmental barriers are often built by employee groups (including unions), regulatory agencies, or other stakeholders of interest.

To overcome these barriers, a firm must first recognize that these barriers exist; second, investigate their causes; and, third, communicate information about the "what," "why," and "how" of ABC to all concerned parties. Top management must be involved with and support the implementation process. Lack of commitment or involvement by top management will make any meaningful progress slow and difficult. Additionally, employees and managers must be educated in some nontraditional techniques that include new terminology, concepts, and performance measurements. Assuming that top management supports the changes in the internal accounting system and that employees are educated about the system, additional time will be required to analyze the activities taking place in the activity centers, trace costs to those activities, and determine the cost drivers.

Another problem with ABC is that it does not conform specifically with generally accepted accounting principles (GAAP). ABC would suggest that some nonproduct costs (such as those in research and development) be allocated to products, whereas certain other traditionally designated product costs (such as factory building depreciation) not be allocated to products. Therefore, most companies have used ABC for internal reporting, while continuing to maintain their general and subsidiary ledger accounts and prepare their external financial statements on the basis of a more "traditional" system—requiring two product costing systems and causing even more costs to be incurred. As ABC systems become more widely accepted, more companies may choose to refine how ABC and GAAP determine product cost to make those definitions more compatible and, thereby, eliminate the need for two costing systems.

One final criticism that has been leveled at activity-based costing is that it does not promote total quality management (TQM) and continuous improvement. Dr. H. Thomas Johnson (the Retzlaff Professor of Quality Management at Portland State University) has issued the following cautions:

> *The decade of the 1970s ushered in a new competitive environment—call it the global economy—in which accounting information is not capable of guiding companies toward competitiveness and long-term profitability.*
>
> *Activity-based prescriptions for improved competitiveness usually entail steps that lead to selling more or doing less of what should not be sold or done in the first place. Indeed, activity-based cost information does nothing to change old remote-control, top-down management behavior. Simply because improved cost information becomes available, a company does not change its commitment to mass-produce output at high speed, to control costs by encouraging people to manipulate processes, and to persuade customers to buy output the company has produced to cover its costs. American businesses will not become long-term global competitors until they change the way managers think. No cost information, not even activity-based cost management information, will do that.*[19]

Companies attempting to implement ABC as a cure-all for product failures, volume declines, or financial losses will quickly recognize that Professor Johnson is correct. However, companies can implement ABC and its related management techniques in support of and in conjunction with TQM, JIT, or any of the other world-class methodologies. Companies doing so will provide the customer with the best variety, price, quality, service, and lead time of which they are capable. Not coincidentally, they should find their businesses booming. Activity-based costing and activity-based management are effective in supporting continuous improvement, short lead times, and flexible manufacturing by helping managers to

- identify and monitor significant technology costs;
- trace many technology costs directly to products;
- promote increase in market share;

[19] H. Thomas Johnson, "It's Time to Stop Overselling Activity-Based Concepts," *Management Accounting* (September 1992), pp. 31, 33.

- identify the cost drivers that create or influence cost;
- identify activities that do not contribute to perceived customer value (i.e., non-value-added activities or waste);
- understand the impact of new technologies on all elements of performance;
- translate company goals into activity goals;
- analyze the performance of activities across business functions;
- analyze performance problems; and
- promote standards of excellence.

In summary, ABC is an improved cost accounting tool that helps managers know how the score is kept so that they can play the game more competitively.

REVISITING Carrier Corporation

http://www.carrier.com

The American Productivity and Quality Center (APQC) and the Consortium for Advanced Manufacturing International (CAM-I) recently sponsored a study to benchmark best practices in the installation and use of activity-based cost management systems. Seven hundred and fifty manufacturing and service organizations were invited to participate in the study, and 166 responded by completing a 20-page survey instrument.

The survey results and telephone interviews were then used to select 15 "best practice" companies. The best practice companies were selected based on their ABCM system's maturity, the breadth of their ABCM applications, the extent of their system's integration, and their level of success with ABCM.

Carrier Corporation participated in the survey and was selected as one of the best practice companies. Carrier currently has more than a dozen manufacturing sites located throughout the world, and it was Carrier's McMinville, Tenn., manufacturing plant that was identified as the best practice site.

Carrier's complexity reduction program along with its other improvement initiatives have combined to produce tangible results. For example, the firm has eliminated some product lines, moved subassemblies to point of use, outsourced some conversion operations, outsourced product lines, and created a greater understanding of how complexity affects costs. But more work needs to be done for Carrier to maintain its competitive edge. In the current competitive environment, Carrier is striving to better understand cost behavior and the steps the company can take to maintain its position as the world's largest manufacturer of air conditioning and heating products. Even though Carrier's management believes that product and process complexity hurts profitability, it needs hard financial data. ABCM provides Carrier managers the information they need to make difficult decisions.

SOURCE: Dan W. Swenson, "Managing Costs through Complexity Reduction at Carrier Corporation," *Strategic Finance* (April 1998), pp. 20–28.

CHAPTER SUMMARY

Significant changes have taken place in the business environment. These changes have caused concern about the reliability of cost information generated by a system primarily intended to provide product costs for external financial statements.

To make profits given the present competitive environment and consumer focus on product price and quality, businesses must find ways to minimize costs. Costs can be reduced without reducing quality by decreasing the number of non-value-added organizational activities. Process mapping can be performed to see all the VA and NVA activities that take place in the production of a product or the performance of a service. Value is added to products only during the times when processing (manufacturing company), performance (service company), or display (retail company) is actually taking place. Inspection time, transfer time, and idle time all add to cycle time and cost, but not to value. The proportion of total cycle time spent in value-added processing is referred to as manufacturing cycle efficiency.

A third category of activities, known as business-value-added activities, also exists. Although not wanting to pay for these activities, customers know the activities are necessary expenses incurred by a business to conduct operations.

In addition to activity analysis, activity-based management is also concerned with finding and selecting activity cost pools and identifying the set of cost drivers that best represents the firm's activities and are the underlying causes of costs. Management should first investigate activities that reflect the major and most significant processes conducted by the company. These activities normally overlap several functional areas and occur horizontally across the firm's departmental lines.

A new method of cost assignment, more compatible with the increased high-technology environment in which business operates, is activity-based costing (ABC). ABC assigns costs to products on the basis of the types and quantities of activities that must be performed to create those products. This costing system accumulates costs for activity centers in multiple cost pools at a variety of levels (unit, batch, product, and organizational) and then allocates these costs using multiple cost drivers (both volume- and non-volume-related). Thus, costs are assigned more accurately, and managers can focus on controlling activities that cause costs rather than trying to control the costs that result from the activities. The use of activity-based costing should provide a more realistic picture of actual production cost than has traditionally been available.

Product variety and process complexity often cause a business's costs to increase because of increases in non-value-added activities. Simultaneous engineering (using multifunctional teams) can help firms to accelerate the time-to-market of new products and reduce the complexity and costs of these new products and the processes by which they are made.

KEY TERMS

activity (p. 132)
activity analysis (p. 132)
activity center (p. 142)
activity driver (p. 143)
attribute-based costing (ABC II) (p. 146)
batch-level cost (p. 138)
business-value-added activity (p. 133)
continuous improvement (p. 150)
cost driver analysis (p. 136)
cycle (lead) time (p. 134)
idle time (p. 134)
inspection time (p. 134)
long-term variable cost (p. 146)
manufacturing cycle efficiency (MCE) (p. 135)
mass customization (p. 147)
organizational-level cost (p. 139)
Pareto principle (p. 148)
process complexity (p. 146)
process map (p. 133)
processing (service) time (p. 134)
product complexity (p. 146)
product-level (process-level) cost (p. 138)
product variety (p. 146)
simultaneous (concurrent) engineering (p. 148)
transfer time (p. 134)
unit-level cost (p. 136)
value chart (p. 134)

SOLUTION STRATEGIES

Manufacturing Cycle Efficiency

Cycle Time = Processing Time + Inspection Time + Transfer Time + Idle Time

MCE = Value-Added Processing Time ÷ Total Cycle Time

Activity-Based Costing

1. Determine the activity centers of the organization.
2. Determine departmental activities and efforts needed to conduct those activities, that is, the cost drivers.
3. Determine departmental resources consumed in conducting activities and allocate costs of these resources to activity centers based on the cost drivers.
4. Determine activities needed to manufacture products or provide revenue-producing services, that is, the activity drivers.
5. Allocate costs to products and services based on activities and cost drivers involved.

DEMONSTRATION PROBLEM

Pierre Press prepares two versions of gourmet cookbooks: One is paperback and the other is hand-sewn and leather bound. Management is considering publishing only the higher quality book. The firm assigns its $500,000 of overhead to the two types of books. The overhead is composed of $200,000 of utilities and $300,000 of quality control inspectors' salaries. Some additional data follow:

	Paperback	Leather Bound
Revenues	$1,600,000	$1,400,000
Direct costs	$1,250,000	$600,000
Production (units)	500,000	350,000
Machine hours	42,500	7,500
Inspections	2,500	12,500

Required:

a. Compute the overhead cost that should be allocated to each type of cookbook using cost drivers appropriate for each type of overhead cost.

b. The firm has used machine hours to allocate overhead in the past. Should Pierre Press stop producing the paperback cookbooks? Explain why management was considering this action and what its decision should be.

Solution to Demonstration Problem

a.

	Paperback	Leather Bound	Total
Machine hours	42,500	7,500	50,000
Rate per MH ($200,000 ÷ 50,000)	× $4	× $4	× $4
Utility cost	$170,000	$ 30,000	$200,000
Number of inspections	2,500	12,500	15,000
Rate per inspection ($300,000 ÷ 15,000)	× $20	× $20	× $20
Quality inspection cost	$ 50,000	$250,000	$300,000
Total traceable overhead costs	$220,000	$280,000	$500,000

b. Income calculation using machine hours to allocate utilities and inspection hours to allocate inspectors' salaries to products:

Using the traditional cost driver (machine hours), the following results had been achieved, given a $10 charge ($500,000 ÷ 50,000) per MH:

	Paperback	Leather Bound
Revenue	$1,600,000	$1,400,000
Direct costs	$1,250,000	$ 600,000
Overhead	425,000	75,000
Total costs	$1,675,000	$ 675,000
Margin	$ (75,000)	$ 725,000

The reason paperbacks were erroneously thought to be unprofitable was caused by the method of allocating overhead. The firm should continue producing paperbacks as shown in the following calculations.

	Paperback	Leather Bound
Revenue	$1,600,000	$1,400,000
Direct costs	$1,250,000	$ 600,000
Overhead	220,000	280,000
Total costs	$1,470,000	$ 880,000
Margin	$ 130,000	$ 520,000

QUESTIONS

1. What is activity-based management (ABM) and what are the specific management tools that fall beneath the ABM umbrella?
2. Define value-added activities and non-value-added activities. Compare and give three examples of each type.
3. Why are value-added activities defined from a customer viewpoint?
4. What management opportunity is associated with identifying the non-value-added activities in a production process?
5. In a televised football game, what activities are value added? What activities are non-value-added? Would everyone agree with your choices? Why or why not?
6. How is a process map used to identify opportunities for cost savings?
7. What is manufacturing cycle efficiency? What would its value be in an optimized manufacturing environment and why?
8. What is a cost driver and how is it used? Give four examples of cost drivers.
9. Do cost drivers exist in a traditional accounting system? Are they designated as such? How, if at all, does the use of cost drivers differ between a traditional accounting system and an activity-based costing system?
10. What is activity analysis and how is it used in concert with cost driver analysis to manage costs?
11. What is activity-based costing? How does it differ from traditional product costing approaches?
12. Why do the more traditional methods of overhead assignment "overload" standard, high-volume products with overhead costs, and how does ABC improve overhead assignments?
13. What characteristics of a company would generally indicate that activity-based costing might improve product costing?
14. Why does activity-based costing require that costs be aggregated at different levels?
15. List the benefits of activity-based costing. How could these reduce costs?
16. Traditional costing systems often differentiate between fixed and variable costs. How does the ABC philosophy address fixed and variable costs?

17. How does attribute-based costing extend the concept of activity-based costing?

18. Are all companies likely to benefit to an equal extent from adopting ABC? Discuss.

19. Significant hurdles are often encountered in adopting ABC including a large time commitment. What specific activities associated with ABC adoption require large investments of time?

EXERCISES

20. *(Terminology)* Match the following lettered terms on the left with the appropriate numbered description on the right.

a. Activity driver	**1.** Non-value-added use of time
b. Cost driver analysis	**2.** Cost explained well by traditional cost drivers
c. Cycle time	**3.** Driver of some costs
d. Idle time	**4.** Time from receipt of order to delivery of product
e. Long-term variable cost	**5.** Cost not usually assigned to products under ABC
f. Mass customization	**6.** Personalized production
g. Product complexity	**7.** Establishing cost causality
h. Organizational-level cost	**8.** Measure of activity demand
i. Unit-level cost	**9.** Indicator of activities and their time
j. Value chart	**10.** Costs traditionally known as fixed

21. *(Terminology)* Match the following lettered terms on the left with the appropriate numbered description on the right.

a. Activity analysis	**1.** Setup cost
b. Activity-based costing	**2.** A costing system that uses multiple cost drivers
c. Attribute-based costing	**3.** A process of involving all affected personnel from the beginning of a project
d. Batch-level cost	**4.** An approach to associate costs with activities
e. Manufacturing cycle efficiency	**5.** A tool to find the cost of product features
f. Non-value-added activity	**6.** A flowchart indicating all steps in producing a product or performing a service
g. Process map	**7.** Idle time, transfer time, or storage time
h. Research and development	**8.** Actual production time divided by total cycle time
i. Simultaneous engineering	**9.** Product/process level cost
j. Value-added activity	**10.** Something that increases worth of a product or service

22. *(Activity analysis)* Conveyance Systems is investigating the costs of schedule changes in its factory. Following is a list of the activities, estimated times, and average costs required for a single schedule change.

Activity	Estimated Time	Average Cost
Review impact of orders	30 min–2 hrs	$ 300
Reschedule orders	15 min–24 hrs	800
Lost sales		
Unreliable customer service		
Reschedule production orders	15 min–1 hr	75
Contact production supervisor	5 min	5
Stop production and change over		
Generate paperwork to return materials		
Return and locate material (excess inventory)	20 min–6 hrs	1,500
Generate new production paperwork	15 min–4 hrs	500
Change routings		
Change bill of materials		
Change procurement schedule	10 min–8 hrs	2,100
Purchase orders		
Inventory		
Collect paperwork from the floor	15 min	75
Review new line schedule	15 min–30 min	100
Overtime premiums	3 hrs–10 hrs	1,000
Total		$6,455

a. Which of the above, if any, are value-added activities?
b. What is the cost driver in this situation?
c. How can the cost driver be controlled and the activities eliminated?

23. *(Cycle time and MCE)* The following functions are performed in making salad dressing at A-1 Toppings.

Function	Time (Minutes)
Receiving ingredients	45
Moving ingredients to stockroom	15
Storing ingredients in stockroom	3,600
Moving ingredients from stockroom	15
√ Mixing ingredients	30
√ Cooking ingredients	90
√ Bottling ingredients	90
Moving bottled dressing to warehouse	20
Storing bottled dressing in warehouse	5,040
Moving bottled dressing from warehouse to trucks	30

a. Calculate the cycle time of this manufacturing process.
b. Calculate the manufacturing cycle efficiency of this process.
c. What could A-1 Toppings do to improve its MCE?

24. *(Identifying cost drivers)* The Fast Lane is a highly automated, fast-food restaurant that relies on sophisticated, computer-controlled equipment to prepare and deliver food to customers. Operationally and organizationally, the restaurant operates like other major franchise fast-food restaurants. Determine whether each of the following costs are unit level (U), batch level (B), product/process level (P), or organizational level (O).
a. Store manager's salary
b. Frozen french fries
c. Napkins
d. Oil for the deep-fat fryer
e. Maintenance of the restaurant building
f. Wages of employees who clear and clean tables
g. Electricity expense for the pizza oven
h. Property taxes
i. Depreciation on kitchen equipment
j. Refrigeration of raw materials

25. *(Cost drivers)* For each of the following important costs in manufacturing companies, identify a cost driver and explain why it is appropriate.

a. Equipment maintenance
b. Building utilities
c. Computer operations
d. Quality control
e. Material handling
f. Material storage
g. Factory depreciation
h. Setup cost
i. Engineering changes
j. Advertising expense
k. Freight costs for materials

26. *(Cost allocation using cost drivers)* Peterson Wholesale has an in-house legal department whose activities fall into one of three major categories. Recently, operating costs in the department have risen dramatically. Management has decided to implement an activity-based costing system to help control costs and charge in-house users for the legal services provided. The principal expense in the legal department is professional salaries, and the estimated cost of professional salaries associated with each activity follow:

Reviewing supplier or customer contracts	(Contracts)	$400,000
Reviewing regulatory compliance issues	(Regulation)	250,000
Court actions	(Court)	350,000

Management has determined that the appropriate cost allocation base for Contracts is the number of pages in the contract reviewed; for Regulation, the allocation base is the number of reviews; and for Court, the allocation base is professional hours. For 2001, the legal department reviewed 20,000 pages of contracts, responded to 500 regulatory review requests, and logged 3,000 professional hours in court.

a. Determine the allocation rate for each activity in the legal department.
b. What amount would be charged to a producing department that had 1,000 pages of contracts reviewed, made 15 regulatory review requests, and consumed 250 professional hours in court services during the year?
c. How can the developed rates be used for evaluating output relative to cost incurred in the legal department? What alternative does the firm have to maintaining an internal legal department and how might this choice affect costs?

27. *(Activity-based costing)* Management at Cooper Steel Co. has decided to institute a pilot activity-based costing project in its eight-person purchasing department. Annual departmental costs are $790,000. Because finding the best supplier takes the majority of effort in the department, most of the costs are allocated to this area.

Activity	Allocation Measure	Number of People	Total Cost
Find best suppliers	Number of telephone calls	5	$500,000
Issue purchase orders	Number of purchase orders	2	200,000
Review receiving reports	Number of receiving reports	1	90,000

During the year, the purchasing department made 250,000 telephone calls, issued 25,000 purchase orders, and reviewed 15,000 receiving reports. Many purchase orders are received in a single shipment.

One product manufactured by Cooper Steel required the following purchasing department activities: 235 telephone calls, 70 purchase orders, and 22 receipts.

a. What amount of purchasing department cost should be assigned to this product?

b. If 300 units of the product are manufactured during the year, what is the purchasing department cost per unit?

28. *(Product profitability)* Lawn Management Systems (LMS) manufactures two products: lawnmowers and garden tractors. Lawnmowers are relatively simple to produce and are made in large quantities. Garden tractors must be more customized to individual wholesale customer specifications. LMS sells 50,000 lawnmowers and 10,000 garden tractors annually. Revenues and costs incurred for each product are as follows:

	Lawnmowers	Garden Tractors
Revenue	$8,000,000	$8,800,000
Direct material	2,000,000	1,800,000
Direct labor	1,200,000	4,000,000
Overhead	?	?

Labor is paid $20 per hour, manufacturing overhead totals $2,210,000, and administrative expenses equal $1,612,000.

a. Calculate the profit (loss) on each product if overhead and administrative expenses are assigned to the products using a direct labor hour base.

b. Calculate the profit (loss) on each product if overhead is assigned to products using a direct labor hour base but administrative expenses are deducted from total company income rather than being allocated to products.

c. Does your answer in part (a) or part (b) provide the better representation of the profit contributed by each product? Explain.

29. *(Value chart)* You are the new controller of a small shop that manufactures special-order desk nameplate stands. As you review the records, you find that all the orders are shipped late, the average process time for any order is three weeks, and the time actually spent in production operations is two days. The president of the company has called you in to discuss missed delivery dates. Prepare an oral presentation for the executive officers in which you address the following:

a. Possible causes of the problem.

b. How a value chart could be used to address the problem.

30. *(Controlling overhead)* Industrial Paints Inc. has engaged you to help the company analyze and update its costing and pricing practices. The company product line has changed over time from general paints to specialized marine coatings. Although some large orders are received, the majority of business is now generated from products designed and produced in small lot sizes to meet specifically detailed environmental and technical requirements.

The company has experienced tremendous overhead growth, including costs in customer service, production scheduling, inventory control, and laboratory work. Factory overhead has essentially doubled since the shift in product lines. Management believes that large orders are being penalized and small orders are receiving favorable cost (and therefore selling price) treatment.

a. Indicate why the shift in product lines would have caused such major increases in overhead.

b. Is it possible that management is correct in its belief about the costs of large and small orders? If so, why?

c. Write a memo to management suggesting how it might change the cost accounting system to reflect the changes in the business.

31. *(Traditional vs. ABC methods)* Many companies now recognize that their cost systems are inadequate in the context of today's powerful global competition. Managers in companies selling multiple products are making important product decisions based on distorted cost information, because most cost systems designed in the past focused on inventory measurement. To elevate the level of management information, current literature suggests that companies should have as many as three cost systems for (1) inventory measurement, (2) operational control, and (3) activity-based costing.

a. Discuss why the traditional cost information system, originally developed for valuing inventory, distorts product cost information.

b. Identify the purpose and characteristics of each of the following cost systems:

1. Inventory measurement

2. Activity-based costing

c. Describe the benefits that management can obtain from using activity-based costing.

d. List the steps that a company using a traditional cost system would take to implement activity-based costing. *(CMA adapted)*

PROBLEMS

32. *(Identifying non-value-added activities)* Stacy Kroger is planning to build a concrete walkway for her home during her annual vacation. She has prepared the following schedule of how her time on the project will be allocated:

Purchase materials	4 hours
Obtain rental equipment	2 hours
Remove sod and level site	10 hours
Build forms for concrete	12 hours
Mix and pour concrete into forms	5 hours
Level concrete and smooth	2 hours
Let dry	24 hours
Remove forms from concrete	1 hour
Return rental tools	1 hour
Clean up	2 hours

a. Identify the value-added activities. How much total time is value-added?

b. Identify the non-value-added activities. How much total time is spent performing non-value-added activities?

c. Calculate the manufacturing cycle efficiency.

33. *(Activity analysis; MCE)* Southern Living constructs log cabin vacation houses in the Tennessee mountains for customers. As the company's consultant, you developed the following value chart:

Operations	Average Number of Days
Receiving materials	2
Storing materials	4
√ Measuring and cutting materials	3
Handling materials	7
Setting up and moving scaffolding	6
√ Assembling materials	7
√ Building fireplace	9
√ Pegging logs	4
√ Cutting and framing doors and windows	3
√ Sealing joints	4
Inspecting property (county inspectors)	3

a. What are the value-added activities and their total time?

b. What are the non-value-added activities and their total time?

c. Calculate the manufacturing cycle efficiency of the process.
d. Prepare a one-minute presentation explaining the difference between value-added and non-value-added activities.

34. *(Activity-based costing)* Patio Solutions makes umbrellas, gazebos, and lawn chairs. The company uses a traditional overhead allocation scheme and assigns overhead to products at the rate of $10 per direct labor hour. In 2000, the company produced 100,000 umbrellas, 10,000 gazebos, and 30,000 lawn chairs and incurred $2,000,000 of manufacturing overhead costs. The cost per unit for each product group in 2000 was as follows:

	Umbrellas	Gazebos	Lawn Chairs
Direct material	$ 4.00	$ 40.00	$ 4.00
Direct labor	6.00	45.00	15.00
Overhead	8.00	60.00	20.00
Total	$18.00	$145.00	$39.00

Because profitability has been lagging and competition has been getting more keen, Patio Solutions is considering implementing an activity-based costing system for 2001. In analyzing the 2000 data, management determined that all $2,000,000 of factory overhead could be assigned to four basic activities: quality control, setups, material handling, and equipment operation. Data from 2000 on the costs associated with each of the four activities follows:

Quality Control	Setups	Material Handling	Equipment Operation	Total Costs
$100,000	$100,000	$300,000	$1,500,000	$2,000,000

Management determined that the following allocation bases and total 2000 volumes for each allocation base could have been used for ABC:

Activity	Base	Volume
Quality control	Number of units produced	140,000
Setups	Number of setups	1,000
Material handling	Pounds of material used	2,000,000
Equipment operation	Number of machine hours	1,000,000

Volume measures for 2000 for each product and each allocation base were as follows:

	Umbrellas	Gazebos	Lawn Chairs
Number of units	100,000	10,000	30,000
Number of setups	200	400	400
Pounds of material	400,000	1,000,000	600,000
Number of machine hours	200,000	400,000	400,000

a. For 2000, determine the total overhead allocated to each product group using the traditional allocation based on direct labor hours.
b. For 2000, determine the total overhead that would have been allocated to each product group if activity-based costing were used. Compute the cost per unit for each product group.
c. Patio Solutions has a policy of setting selling prices based on product costs. How would the sales prices using activity-based costing differ from those obtained using the traditional overhead allocation?

35. *(Activity-based costing)* Williams Components Company manufactures two products. Following is a production and cost analysis for each product for the year 2000.

Cost Component	Product A	Product B	Both Products	Cost
Units produced	10,000	10,000	20,000	
Raw materials used (units)				
X	50,000	50,000	100,000	$ 800,000
Y		100,000	100,000	$ 200,000
Labor hours used				
Department 1:				$ 681,000
Direct labor ($375,000)	20,000	5,000	25,000	
Indirect labor				
Inspection	2,500	2,500	5,000	
Machine operations	5,000	10,000	15,000	
Setups	200	200	400	
Department 2:				$ 462,000
Direct labor ($200,000)	5,000	5,000	10,000	
Indirect labor				
Inspection	2,500	5,000	7,500	
Machine operations	1,000	4,000	5,000	
Setups	200	400	600	
Machine hours used				
Department 1	5,000	10,000	15,000	$ 400,000
Department 2	5,000	20,000	25,000	$ 800,000
Power used (kw-hours)				$ 400,000
Department 1			1,500,000	
Department 2			8,500,000	
Other activity data:				
Building occupancy				$1,000,000
Purchasing				$ 100,000
Number of purchase orders				
Material X			200	
Material Y			300	
Square feet occupied				
Purchasing			10,000	
Power			40,000	
Department 1			200,000	
Department 2			250,000	

Roberto Lopez, the firm's cost accountant, has just returned from a seminar on activity-based costing. To apply the concepts he has learned, he decides to analyze the costs incurred for Products A and B from an activity basis. In doing so, he specifies the following first and second allocation processes:

FIRST STAGE: ALLOCATIONS TO DEPARTMENTS

Cost Pool	Cost Object	Activity Allocation Base
Power	Departments	Kilowatt-hours
Purchasing	Materials	Number of purchase orders
Building occupancy	Departments	Square feet occupied

SECOND STAGE: ALLOCATIONS TO PRODUCTS

Cost Pool	Cost Object	Activity Allocation Base
Departments:		
Indirect labor	Products	Hours worked
Power	Products	Machine hours
Machinery-related	Products	Machine hours
Building occupancy	Products	Machine hours
Materials:		
Purchasing	Products	Materials used

SOURCE: From Harold P. Roth and A. Faye Borthick, "Getting Closer to Real Product Costs," *Management Accounting* (May 1989), pp. 28–33. Reprinted from *Management Accounting*. Copyright by Institute of Management Accountants, Montvale, N.J.

a. Determine the total overhead for Williams Components Company.
b. Determine the plantwide overhead rate for the company, assuming the use of direct labor hours.
c. Determine the cost per unit of Product A and Product B, using the overhead application rate found in part (b).
d. Using the step-down approach, determine the cost allocations to departments (first-stage allocations). Allocate in the following order: building occupancy, purchasing, and power.
e. Using the allocations found in part (d), determine the cost allocations to products (second-stage allocations).
f. Determine the cost per unit of Product A and Product B using the overhead allocations found in part (e).

36. *(Using ABC to set price)* The budgeted manufacturing overhead costs of Garage Door Company for 2001 are as follows:

Type of Cost	Cost Amount
Electric power	$ 500,000
Work cells	3,000,000
Material handling	1,000,000
Quality control inspections	1,000,000
Product runs (machine setups)	500,000
Total budgeted overhead costs	$6,000,000

For the last five years, the cost accounting department has been charging overhead production costs based on machine hours. The estimated budgeted capacity for 2001 is 1,000,000 machine hours.

Jason Tracy, president of Garage Door, recently attended a seminar on activity-based costing. He now believes that ABC results in more reliable cost data that, in turn, will give the company an edge in pricing over its competitors. On the president's request, the production manager provided the following data regarding expected 2001 activity for the cost drivers of the preceding budgeted overhead costs.

Type of Costs	Activity Drivers
Electric power	100,000 kilowatt-hours
Work cells	600,000 square feet
Material handling	200,000 material moves
Quality control inspections	100,000 inspections
Product runs (machine setups)	50,000 product runs

Linda Ryan, the VP of marketing, received an offer to sell 5,000 doors to a local construction company. Linda asks the head of cost accounting to prepare cost estimates for producing the 5,000 doors. The head of cost accounting accumulated the following data concerning production of 5,000 doors:

Direct material cost	$100,000
Direct labor cost	$300,000
Machine hours	10,000
Direct labor hours	15,000
Electric power—kilowatt-hours	1,000
Work cells—square feet	8,000
Number of material handling moves	100
Number of quality control inspections	50
Number of product runs (setups)	25

SOURCE: Adapted from Nabil Hassa, Herbert E. Brown, and Paul M. Saunders, "Management Accounting Case Study: Beaver Window Inc.," *Management Accounting Campus Report* (Fall 1990). Copyright Institute of Management Accountants, Montvale, N.J.

a. What is the predetermined overhead rate if the traditional measure of machine hours is used?

(continued)

b. What is the manufacturing cost per door as presently accounted for?
c. What is the manufacturing cost per door under the proposed ABC method?
d. If the two cost systems will result in different cost estimates, which cost accounting system is preferable as a pricing base and why?

37. *(Activity driver analysis and decision making)* High Plains Manufacturing Products is concerned about its ability to control factory labor-related costs. The company has recently finished an analysis of these costs for 2001. Following is a summary of the major categories of labor costs identified by High Plain's accounting department:

Category	Amount
Base wages	$42,000,000
Health care benefits	7,000,000
Payroll taxes	3,360,000
Overtime	5,800,000
Training	1,250,000
Retirement benefits	4,600,000
Workers' compensation	800,000

Listed below are some of the potential cost drivers identified by the company for labor-related costs, along with their 2001 volume levels.

Potential Activity Driver	2001 Volume Level
Average number of factory employees	1,400
Number of new hires	200
Number of regular labor hours worked	2,100,000
Number of overtime hours worked	192,000
Total factory wages	$47,800,000
Volume of production in units	8,000,000
Number of production process changes	400
Number of production schedule changes	250

a. For each cost pool, determine the cost per unit of the activity driver using the activity driver that you believe has the closest relationship to the cost pool.
b. Based on your judgments and calculations in part (a), which activity driver should receive the most attention from company managers in their efforts to control labor-related costs? How much of the total labor-related cost is attributable to this activity driver?
c. In the contemporary environment, many firms are asking their employees to work record levels of overtime. What activity driver does this practice suggest is a major contributor to labor-related costs? Explain.

38. *(Activity-based costing and pricing)* Covington Community Hospital has found itself under increasing pressure to be accountable for the charges it assesses its patients. Its current pricing system is ad hoc, based on pricing norms for the geographical area, and it only explicitly considers direct costs for surgery, medication, and other treatments. Covington's controller has suggested that the hospital try to improve its pricing policies by seeking a tighter relationship between costs and pricing. This approach would make prices for services less arbitrary. As a first step, the controller has determined that most costs can be assigned to one of three cost pools. The three cost pools follow along with the estimated amounts and activity drivers.

Activity Center	Amount	Activity Driver	Quantity
Professional salaries	$900,000	Professional hours	30,000 hours
Building costs	450,000	Square feet used	15,000 sq. ft.
Risk management	320,000	Patients served	1,000 patients

The hospital provides service in three broad categories. The services are listed below with their volume measures for the activity centers.

Service	Professional Hours	Square Feet	Number of Patients
Surgery	6,000	1,200	200
Housing patients	20,000	12,000	500
Outpatient care	4,000	1,800	300

a. Determine the allocation rates for each activity center cost pool.
b. Allocate the activity center costs to the three services provided by the hospital.
c. What bases might be used as cost drivers to allocate the service center costs among the patients served by the hospital? Defend your selections.

39. *(Determining product cost)* Belton Furniture Corporation has identified activity centers to which overhead costs are assigned. The cost pool amounts for these centers and their selected activity drivers for 2000 are as follows.

Activity Centers	Costs	Activity Drivers
Utilities	$300,000	60,000 machine hours
Scheduling and setup	273,000	780 setups
Material handling	640,000	1,600,000 pounds of material

The company's products and other operating statistics follow:

	PRODUCTS		
	A	B	C
Direct costs	$80,000	$80,000	$90,000
Machine hours	30,000	10,000	20,000
Number of setups	130	380	270
Pounds of material	500,000	300,000	800,000
Number of units produced	40,000	20,000	60,000
Direct labor hours	32,000	18,000	50,000

a. Determine unit product cost using the appropriate cost drivers for each of the products.
b. Before it installed an ABC system, the company used a conventional costing system and allocated factory overhead to products using direct labor hours. The firm operates in a competitive market and product prices were set at cost plus a 20 percent markup.
   1. Calculate unit costs based on conventional costing.
   2. Determine selling prices based on unit costs for conventional costing and for ABC costs.
c. Discuss the problems related to setting prices based on conventional costing and explain how ABC improves the information.

CASES

40. *(Product complexity)* Tektronix Inc. is a world leader in the production of electronic test and measurement instruments. The company experienced almost uninterrupted growth through the 1980s, but in the 1990s, the low-priced end of the Portables Division product line was challenged by an aggressive low-price strategy of several Japanese competitors. These Japanese companies set prices 25 percent below Tektronix's prevailing prices. To compete, the division needed to reduce costs and increase customer value by increasing operational efficiency.

Steps were taken to implement just-in-time delivery and scheduling techniques, a total quality control program, and people involvement techniques that moved responsibility for problem solving down to the operating level of the division. The results of these changes were impressive: substantial reductions in cycle time, direct labor hours per unit, and inventory levels as well as increases in output dollars per person per day and operating income. The cost accounting system was providing information, however, that did not seem to support the changes.

Total overhead cost for the division was $10,000,000; of this, part (55%) seemed to be related to materials and the remainder (45%) to conversion. Material-related costs pertain to procurement, receiving, inspection, stockroom personnel, etc. Conversion-related costs pertain to direct labor, supervision, and process-related engineering. All overhead was applied on the basis of direct labor.

The division decided to concentrate efforts on revamping the application system for material-related overhead. Managers believed the majority of material overhead (MOH) costs were related to the maintenance and handling of each different part number. Other types of MOH costs were costs due to the value of parts, absolute number of parts, and each use of a different part number.

At this time, the division used 8,000 different parts and in extremely different quantities. For example, annual usage of one part was 35,000 units; usage of another part was only 200 units. The division decided that MOH costs would decrease if a smaller number of different parts were used in the products.

SOURCE: Adapted from Michael A. Robinson, ed., *Cases from Management Accounting Practice*, No. 5 (Montvale, N.J.: National Association of Accountants, 1989), pp. 13–17. Copyright by Institute of Management Accountants (formerly National Association of Accountants), Montvale, N.J.

a. Give some reasons that materials overhead (MOH) would decrease if parts were standardized.

b. Using the numbers given above, develop a cost allocation method for MOH to quantify and communicate the strategy of parts standardization.

c. Explain how the use of the method developed in part (b) would support the strategy of parts standardization.

d. Is any method that applies the entire MOH cost pool on the basis of one cost driver sufficiently accurate for complex products? Explain.

e. Are MOH product costing rates developed for management reporting appropriate for inventory valuation for external reporting? Why or why not?

41. *(Activity-based costing)* Kendall Corporation manufactures several different types of printed circuit boards; however, two of the boards account for the majority of the company's sales. The first of these boards, a television (TV) circuit board, has been a standard in the industry for several years. The market for this type of board is competitive and, therefore, price sensitive. Kendall plans to sell 65,000 of the TV circuit boards in 2000 at a price of $150 per unit. The second high-volume product, a personal computer (PC) circuit board, is a recent addition to Kendall's product line. Because the PC board incorporates the latest technology, it can be sold at a premium price; the 2000 plans include the sale of 40,000 PC boards at $300 per unit.

Kendall's management group is meeting to discuss strategies for 2000, and the current topic of conversation is how to spend the sales and promotion dollars for next year. The sales manager believes that the market share for the TV board could be expanded by concentrating Kendall's promotional efforts in this area. In response to this suggestion, the production manager said, "Why don't you go after a bigger market for the PC board? The cost sheets that I get show that the contribution from the PC board is more than double the contribution from the TV board. I know we get a premium price for the PC board; selling it should help overall profitability."

Kendall uses a standard cost system, and the following data apply to the TV and PC boards.

	TV Board	PC Board
Direct material	$80	$140
Direct labor	1.5 hours	4 hours
Machine time	0.5 hours	1.5 hours

Variable factory overhead is applied on the basis of direct labor hours. For 2000, variable factory overhead is budgeted at $1,120,000, and direct labor hours are estimated at 280,000. The hourly rates for machine time and direct labor are $10 and $14, respectively. Kendall applies a material handling charge at 10 percent of material cost; this material handling charge is not included in variable factory overhead. Total 2000 expenditures for materials are budgeted at $10,600,000.

Ed Welch, Kendall's controller, believes that before the management group proceeds with the discussion about allocated sales and promotional dollars to individual products, it might be worthwhile to look at these products on the basis of the activities involved in their production. As he explained to the group, "Activity-based costing integrates the cost of all activities, known as cost drivers, into individual product costs rather than including these costs in overhead pools." Welch has prepared the following schedule to help the management group understand this concept.

Budgeted Cost		Cost Driver	Annual Activity for Cost Driver
Material overhead:			
Procurement	$ 400,000	Number of parts	4,000,000 parts
Production scheduling	220,000	Number of boards	110,000 boards
Packaging and shipping	440,000	Number of boards	110,000 boards
	$1,060,000		
Variable overhead:			
Machine setup	$ 446,000	Number of setups	278,750 setups
Hazardous waste disposal	48,000	Pounds of waste	16,000 pounds
Quality control	560,000	Number of inspections	160,000 inspections
General supplies	66,000	Number of boards	110,000 boards
	$1,120,000		

Budgeted Cost		Cost Driver	Annual Activity for Cost Driver
Manufacturing:			
Machine insertion	$1,200,000	Number of parts	3,000,000 parts
Manual insertion	4,000,000	Number of parts	1,000,000 parts
Wave soldering	132,000	Number of boards	110,000 boards
	$5,332,000		

	REQUIRED PER UNIT	
	TV Board	PC Board
Parts	25	55
Machine insertions of parts	24	35
Manual insertions of parts	1	20
Machine setups	2	3
Hazardous waste	0.02 lb.	0.35 lb.
Inspections	1	2

"Using this information," Welch explained, "we can calculate an activity-based cost for each TV board and each PC board and then compare it to the standard cost we have been using. The only cost that remains the same for both cost methods is the cost of direct materials. The cost drivers will replace the direct labor, machine time, and overhead costs in the standard cost."

a. Identify at least four general advantages associated with activity-based costing.

b. On the basis of standard costs, calculate the total contribution expected in 2000 for Kendall Corporation's
 1. TV board.
 2. PC board.

c. On the basis of activity-based costs, calculate the total contribution expected in 2000 for Kendall Corporation's
 1. TV board.
 2. PC board.

d. Explain how the comparison of the results of the two costing methods may impact the decisions made by Kendall Corporation's management group. *(CMA adapted)*

42. *(Activity-based costing)* Miami Valley Architects Inc. provides a wide range of engineering and architectural consulting services through its three branch offices in Columbus, Cincinnati, and Dayton. The company allocates resources and bonuses to the three branches based on the net income reported for the period. The following presents the results of 2001 performance ($ in thousands).

	Columbus	Cincinnati	Dayton	Total
Sales	$1,500	$1,419	$1,067	$ 3,986
Less: Direct labor	(382)	(317)	(317)	(1,016)
Direct material	(281)	(421)	(185)	(887)
Overhead	(710)	(589)	(589)	(1,888)
Net income	$ 127	$ 92	$ (24)	$ 195

Overhead items are accumulated in one overhead pool and allocated to the branches based on direct labor dollars. For 2001, this predetermined overhead rate was $1.859 for every direct labor dollar incurred by an office. The overhead pool includes rent, depreciation, taxes, and so on, regardless of which office incurred the expense. This method of accumulating costs forces the offices to absorb a portion of the overhead incurred by other offices.

Management is concerned with the results of the 2001 performance reports. During a review of the overhead, it became apparent that many items of overhead are not correlated to the movement in direct labor dollars as previously assumed. Management decided that applying overhead based on activity-based costing and direct tracing, where possible, should provide a more accurate picture of the profitability of each branch.

An analysis of the overhead revealed that the following dollars for rent, utilities, depreciation, taxes, and so on, could be traced directly to the office that incurred the overhead ($ in thousands).

	Columbus	Cincinnati	Dayton	Total
Direct overhead	$180	$270	$177	$627

Activity pools and activity drivers were determined from the accounting records and staff surveys as follows:

Activity Pools		Activity Driver	# OF ACTIVITIES BY LOCATION Columbus	Cincinnati	Dayton
General Administration	$ 409,000	Direct Labor $	382,413	317,086	317,188
Project Costing	48,000	# of Timesheet Entries	6,000	3,800	3,500
Accounts Payable/Receiving	139,000	# of Vendor Invoices	1,020	850	400
Accounts Receivable	47,000	# of Client Invoices	588	444	96
Payroll/Mail Sort & Delivery	30,000	# of Employees	23	26	18
Personnel Recruiting	38,000	# of New Hires	8	4	7
Employee Insurance Processing	14,000	Insurance Claims Filed	230	260	180
Proposals	139,000	# of Proposals	200	250	60
Sales Meetings/Sales Aids	202,000	Contracted Sales	1,824,439	1,399,617	571,208
Shipping	24,000	# of Projects	99	124	30
Ordering	48,000	# of Purchase Orders	135	110	80
Duplicating Costs	46,000	# of Copies Duplicated	162,500	146,250	65,000
Blueprinting	77,000	# of Blueprints	39,000	31,200	16,000
	$1,261,000				

a. What overhead costs should be assigned to each branch based on activity-based costing concepts?

b. What is the contribution of each branch before subtracting the results obtained in part (a)?

c. What is the profitability of each branch office using activity-based costing?

d. Evaluate the concerns of management regarding the traditional costing technique currently used. *(IMA adapted)*

43. *(Activity-based costing and pricing)* Joey Lutz owns and manages a commercial cold-storage warehouse. He stores a vast variety of perishable goods for his customers. Historically, he has charged customers using a flat rate of $0.04 per pound per month for goods stored. His cold-storage warehouse has 100,000 cubic feet of storage capacity.

In the past two years, Lutz has become dissatisfied with the profitability of the warehouse operation. Despite the fact that the warehouse remains relatively full, revenues have not kept pace with operating costs. Recently, Lutz approached his accountant, Jill Green, about using activity-based costing to improve his understanding of the causes of costs and revise the pricing formula. Green has determined that most costs can be associated with one of four activities. Those activities and their related costs, volume measures, and volume levels for 2001 follow:

Activity	Cost	Monthly Volume Measure
Send/receive goods	$6,000	Weight in pounds—500,000
Store goods	4,000	Volume in cubic feet—80,000
Move goods	5,000	Volume in square feet—5,000
Identify goods	2,000	Number of packages—500

SOURCE: Adapted from Harold P. Roth and Linda T. Sims, "Costing for Warehousing and Distribution," *Management Accounting* (August 1991), pp. 42–45. Reprinted from *Management Accounting.* Copyright by Institute of Management Accountants, Montvale, N.J.

a. Based on the activity cost and volume data, determine the amount of cost assigned to the following customers, whose goods were all received on the first day of last month.

Customer	Weight of Order	Cubic Feet	Square Feet	Number of Packages
Jones	40,000	3,000	300	5
Hansen	40,000	2,000	200	20
Assad	40,000	1,000	1,000	80

b. Determine the price to be charged to each customer under the existing pricing plan.
c. Determine the price to be charged using ABC, assuming Lutz would base the price on the cost determined in part (a) plus a markup of 40 percent.
d. How well does Lutz's existing pricing plan capture the costs incurred to provide the warehouse services? Explain.

REALITY CHECK

44. Many manufacturers are deciding to no longer service small retailers. For example, some companies have policies to serve only customers who purchase $10,000 or more of products from the companies annually. The companies defend such policies on the basis that they allow the companies to better serve their larger outlet, which handle more volume and more diverse product lines.
a. Relate the concepts in the chapter to the decision of manufacturers to drop small customers.
b. Are there any ethical implications of eliminating groups of customers that may be less profitable than others?
c. Does activity-based costing adequately account for all costs that are related to a decision to eliminate a particular customer base? (*Hint:* Consider opportunity costs such as those related to reputation.)

45. *Evidence suggests that ABM implementations are more likely to succeed in more open organizations. The ground is especially fertile for companies that have a stated interest in becoming world-class competitors and have backed these ambitions up with other initiatives. ABM dovetails with these initiatives, and they reinforce each other. A clear commitment from top management is also essential.*

SOURCE: Helen Thorne and Bruce Gurd, "Some Human Aspects of Implementing Activity-Based Management," *Journal of Cost Management* (Fall 1995), p. 51.

a. What are some of the "other initiatives" to which the article would be referring?
b. How might activity-based management and activity-based costing help a company in its quest to achieve world-class status?
c. Would it be equally important to have top management support if a company was instituting activity-based costing rather than activity-based management? Justify your answer.
d. Assume you are a member of top management in a large organization. Do you think implementation of ABM or ABC would be more valuable? Explain the rationale for your answer.

46. As the chief executive officer of a large corporation, you have made a decision after discussion with production and accounting personnel to implement activity-based management concepts. Your goal is to reduce cycle time and, thus, costs. A primary way to accomplish this goal is to install highly automated equipment in your plant, which would then displace approximately 60 percent of your workforce. Your company is the major employer in the area of the country where it is located.
a. Discuss the pros and cons of installing the equipment from the perspective of your (1) stockholders, (2) employees, and (3) customers.
b. How would you explain to a worker that his or her job is non-value-added?
c. What alternatives might you have that could accomplish the goal of reducing cycle time but not create economic havoc for the local area?

CHAPTER 5

Job Order Costing

LEARNING OBJECTIVES

After completing this chapter, you should be able to answer the following questions:

1
How do job order and process costing systems and how do actual, normal, and standard costing valuation methods differ?

2
In what production situations is a job order costing system appropriate and why?

3
What constitutes a "job" from an accounting standpoint?

4
What purposes are served by the primary documents used in a job order costing system?

5
What journal entries are used to accumulate costs in a job order costing system?

6
How do technological changes impact the gathering and use of information in job order costing systems?

7
How are standard costs used in a job order costing system?

8
How does information from a job order costing system support management decision making?

INTRODUCING

Aker Gulf Marine

http://www.akermaritime.no/

Aker Gulf Marine, AGM, is known throughout the Gulf Coast oil and gas industry as a small firm that executes big projects—very big projects. Situated on the shore of the Gulf of Mexico near the city of Corpus Christi, Texas, AGM builds offshore oil rigs, often in cooperative ventures with other firms.

AGM serves as a contractor to the major firms that extract oil and gas from the Gulf of Mexico and other offshore locations. At any particular time, the company will have several projects in progress. Like most contractors, AGM gets business from the oil producers only when it is the successful bidder on construction contracts. The reputation of the company as an innovative, high-quality producer is often a factor in the ability of the company to win contracts.

AGM's expertise is in engineering and converting various stock metal materials into mammoth integrated structures often weighing thousands of tons. For example, a recently completed project, nicknamed "Mars" and contracted by Shell Oil, required AGM to build a system to anchor a floating oil platform in 3,000 feet of water. The massive platform, is designed to accommodate 106 workers and 24 well slots. The anchoring system consists of 12 "tendons" each 28 inches in diameter and one-half mile in length. The system is engineered to withstand 140-mph winds and 70-foot waves. Combined, the platform and anchoring system weigh over 36,000 tons. The Mars platform connects to a pipeline that moves the oil 116 miles to shore in southern Louisiana.

As a builder of offshore oil production equipment, AGM has several significant constraints in its operations. For example, because completed projects must be floated to their permanent locations, AGM must have its production facilities located on a deep-water channel with access to the Gulf. Also, because the projects are physically very large, most production occurs in the open air, with little protection from the weather, including hurricanes and other adverse weather conditions. Finally, the completed projects must be assembled on location in the open ocean. The installation process exposes the various components to the risks of adverse weather and seas.

SOURCE: Anonymous, "Offshore Technology—Mars Shell Oil Field Project—Gulf of Mexico," http://www.offshore-technology.com/projects/mars/index.html.

At AGM and other custom manufacturers, most business is conducted through a process of competitive bidding. In this process, a company must accurately estimate the costs of making products associated with each contract. Competitive bidding is complicated by the nature of custom manufacturing—each bid may involve unique products. For example, at AGM the only common aspects of all products are the materials used and the conversion processes. Because each bid/order is substantially different from all others, contract pricing and cost control cannot be based on an accounting system that aggregates costs across contracts. Thus, AGM uses job order costing to accumulate the costs of each job (contract) separately from all other jobs.

A primary role for cost accounting is to determine the cost of an organization's products or services. Just as various methods (first-in, first-out; last-in, first-out; average; specific identification) exist to determine inventory valuation and cost of goods sold for a retailer, different methods are available to value inventory and calculate product cost in a manufacturing or service environment. The method chosen depends on the product or service and the company's conversion processes. A cost flow assumption is required for processes in which costs cannot be identified with and attached to specific units of production.

This chapter is the first of a sequence of chapters that will present methods of product costing. The chapter first distinguishes between two primary costing systems (job order and process) and then discusses three methods of valuation that can be used within these systems (actual, normal, and standard). The remainder of the chapter focuses on the job order costing system, such as that used by AGM.

METHODS OF PRODUCT COSTING

1

How do job order and process costing systems, and how do actual, normal, and standard costing valuation methods differ?

Before the cost of products can be computed, a determination must be made about (1) the product costing system and (2) the valuation method to be used. The product costing system defines the cost object and the method of assigning costs to production. The valuation method specifies how product costs will be measured. Companies must have both a cost system and a valuation method; six possible combinations exist as shown in Exhibit 5–1.[1]

Costing Systems

job order costing system

Job order and process costing are the two primary cost systems. A **job order costing system** is used by entities that make (perform) relatively small quantities or distinct batches of identifiable, unique products (services). For example, job order costing is appropriate for a publishing company that produces educational textbooks, an accountant who prepares tax returns, an architectural firm that designs commercial buildings, and a research firm that performs product development studies. In each instance, the organization produces tailor-made goods or services that conform to specifications designated by the purchaser of those goods or services. Services in general are typically user specific, so job order costing systems are commonly used in such businesses. In these various settings, the word "job" is synonymous with engagement, project, and contract.

process costing system

The other primary product costing system, a **process costing system**, is used by entities that produce large quantities of homogeneous goods. Process costing is appropriate for companies that mass manufacture products such as bricks, gasoline, detergent, and breakfast cereal. The output of a single process in a mass manufacturing situation is homogeneous; thus, within a given period, one unit of output cannot be readily identified with specific input costs. This characteristic of process

EXHIBIT 5–1

Costing Systems and Inventory Valuation

COST ACCUMULATION SYSTEM	METHOD OF VALUATION: Actual	Normal	Standard
JOB ORDER	Actual DM Actual DL Actual OH (assigned to job after end of period)	Actual DM Actual DL OH applied using predetermined rates at completion of job or end of period (predetermined rates times actual input)	Standard DM and/or Standard DL OH applied using predetermined rates when goods are completed or at end of period (predetermined rates times standard input)
PROCESS	Actual DM Actual DL Actual OH (assigned to job after end of period using FIFO or weighted average cost flow)	Actual DM Actual DL OH applied using predetermined rates (using FIFO or weighted average cost flow)	Standard DM Standard DL Standard OH using predetermined rates (will always be FIFO cost flow)

[1] A third and fourth dimension (cost accumulation and cost presentation) are also necessary in this model. These dimensions relate to the use of absorption or variable costing and are covered in Chapter 12.

costing systems makes a cost flow assumption necessary. Cost flow assumptions provide a means for accountants to assign costs to products without regard for the actual physical flow of units. Process costing systems (covered in Chapters 6 and 7) allow the use of either a weighted average or FIFO cost flow assumption.

The accompanying News Note discusses a small enterprise that manufactures custom golf clubs. This firm is different from most of the companies that mass manufacture clubs. Although the individual featured in the News Note would likely use a job order costing system, most firms in the industry would appropriately use process costing.

http://www.fortunebrands.com

Valuation Methods

The three valuation methods shown in Exhibit 5–1 are actual, normal, and standard costing. A company using the actual costs of direct materials, direct labor, and overhead to determine work in process inventory cost is employing an actual cost system. Service businesses that have few customers and/or low volume, such as some advertising agencies or consulting firms, may use an actual cost system. However, because of the reasons discussed in Chapter 3, many companies modify actual cost systems by using predetermined overhead rates rather than actual overhead costs. This combination of actual direct materials and direct labor costs with predetermined overhead rates is called a *normal cost system*. If the predetermined rate is substantially equivalent to what the actual rate would have been for an annual period, its use provides acceptable and useful costs.

Companies using either job order or process costing may employ standards (or predetermined benchmarks) for costs to be incurred and/or quantities to be used. In a standard cost system, unit norms or standards are developed for direct material and direct labor quantities and/or costs. Overhead is applied to production using a predetermined rate that is considered the standard. These standards can then be used to plan for future activities and cost incurrence and to value inventories. Both actual and standard costs are recorded in the accounting records to provide an essential element of cost control—having norms against which actual costs of operations can be compared. A standard cost system allows companies to quickly recognize deviations or variances from normal production costs and to correct problems resulting from excess usage and/or costs. Actual costing systems do not provide this benefit, and normal costing systems cannot provide it in relation to materials and labor.

GENERAL BUSINESS NEWS NOTE

Puttering around Building Golf Clubs

It's the start of the Greater Greensboro Chrysler Classic, and the pros are practicing at the Forest Oaks Country Club driving range when Tim West arrives to hawk his wares.

Measured by money alone, Mr. West is a bit player in the burgeoning $6 billion golf equipment market. Most of his rivals deliver products for industry titans such as Fortune Brands Inc. Mr. West, in contrast, is an independent representing start-ups and other tiny companies that can't afford to pay endorsements. With no expense account he must rely on guile, persuasion, and his "Book of Love," a meticulously maintained notebook in which he records players' preferences, down to such details as the no-rib grip favored by John Daly or a club-shaft weight down to the gram.

On the road, he uses the book to build custom clubs from scratch, usually in one of the machine-shop trailers that follow the tour and are subsidized by big equipment makers. "I love machines," he says assembling a hybrid while hunched over a pot of smelly glue.

SOURCE: Adapted from Christopher Cooper, "Even Golf Pros Need Help, and Tim West Tries Hard to Give It—He Persuades Them to Test New Gear That May Offer That Always-Needed Edge," *The Wall Street Journal* (May 28, 1998), p. A1.

Because the use of predetermined overhead rates is more common than the use of actual overhead costs, this chapter addresses a job order/normal cost system and describes some job order/standard cost combinations.[2]

JOB ORDER COSTING SYSTEM

2

In what production situations is a job order costing system appropriate and why?

job

3

What constitutes a "job" from an accounting standpoint?

Product costing is concerned with (1) cost identification, (2) cost measurement, and (3) product cost assignment. In a job order costing system, costs are accumulated individually on a per-job basis. A **job** is a single unit or group of units identifiable as being produced to distinct customer specifications.[3] Each job is treated as a unique cost entity or cost object. Costs of different jobs are maintained in separate subsidiary ledger accounts and are not added together or commingled in those ledger accounts.

The logic of separating costs for individual jobs is shown by the example given in Exhibit 5–2. Assume Island Marine (a builder of offshore oil production equipment) produced three products in March: a production platform, a barge designed to deliver offshore products to their installation sites, and an assembly of components built by other firms into a completed oil rig. The quantity of resources used for each project is clearly unique. Each product required a different amount of material and different conversion operations. Because each contract is distinctive, the costs of those products cannot logically be averaged—a unique cost must be determined for each contract.

Exhibit 5–2 provides the Work in Process Inventory control and subsidiary ledger accounts for Island Marine's product costing system. The usual production costs of direct material, direct labor, and overhead are accumulated for each contract. Actual direct material and direct labor costs are combined with an overhead cost that is computed as a predetermined overhead rate multiplied by some actual cost driver (such as direct labor hours, cost or quantity of materials used, or number of material requisitions). Normal cost valuation is used because, although actual direct material and direct labor costs are fairly easy to identify and associate with a particular job, overhead costs are usually not traceable to specific jobs and must be allocated to production. For example, Island Marine's March utility costs are related to all jobs worked on during that month. Accurately determining which jobs created the need for a given amount of water, heat, or electricity would be almost impossible.

To ensure the proper recording of costs, the amounts appearing in the subsidiary ledger accounts are periodically compared with and reconciled to the Work in Process Inventory control account in the general ledger. This reconciliation is indicated by the equality of the assumed ending balances of the subsidiary ledger accounts with the WIP Inventory control account in Exhibit 5–2.

http://www.seagate.com
http://www.compaq.com

The output of any job can be a single unit or multiple similar or dissimilar units. With multiple outputs, a unit cost can be computed only if the units are similar or if costs are accumulated for each separate unit (such as through an identification number). For example, Seagate Technology produces compact disk drives to the specifications of a variety of companies including Compaq. Seagate can determine the cost per disk drive for each company by accumulating the costs per batch of homogeneous products in different production runs and treating each production run as a separate job. In such cases, production costs of each job batch can be commingled because the units within the batch are not distinguishable and the total cost can be averaged over the number of units produced in the batch to

[2] Although actual overhead may be assigned to jobs, such an approach would be less customary because total overhead would not be known until the period was over, causing an unwarranted delay in overhead assignment. Activity-based costing can increase the validity of tracing overhead costs to specific products or jobs.

[3] To eliminate the need for repetition, *units* should be read to mean either products or services because job order costing is applicable to both manufacturing and service companies. For the same reason, *produced* can mean *manufactured* or *performed*.

EXHIBIT 5–2

Separate Subsidiary Ledger Accounts for Jobs

GENERAL LEDGER

Work in Process Inventory Control

Direct materials (actual)	XXX	Transferred to finished goods (could also be next department)	XXX
Direct labor (actual)	XXX		
Overhead (predetermined rate × actual activity)	XX		
Ending balance	2,548,000		

SUBSIDIARY LEDGER

Job #301 Exxon Platform

Direct materials (actual)	XXX	
Direct labor (actual)	XXX	
Overhead (predetermined rate × actual activity)	XX	
Ending balance	1,417,000	

Job #318 Delivery Barge

Direct materials (actual)	XXX	
Direct labor (actual)	XXX	
Overhead (predetermined rate × actual activity)	XX	
Ending balance	319,000	

Job #541 Rig Assembly

Direct materials (actual)	XX	
Direct labor (actual)	XXX	
Overhead (predetermined rate × actual activity)	XX	
Ending balance	812,000	

determine a cost per unit. If the output consists of dissimilar units for which individual cost information is not gathered, no cost per unit can be determined although it is still possible to know the total job cost.

JOB ORDER COSTING: DETAILS AND DOCUMENTS

A job can be categorized by the stage of its production cycle. There are three stages of production: (1) contracted for but not yet started, (2) in process, and (3) completed.[4]

4

What purposes are served by the primary documents used in a job order costing system?

[4] In concept, there could be four categories. The third and fourth categories would distinguish between products completed but not sold and products completed and sold. However, the usual case is that firms using a job order costing system produce only products for which there is a current demand. Consequently, there is usually no inventory of finished products that await sale.

Because a company using job order costing is making products according to user specifications, jobs might occasionally require unique raw material. Thus, some raw material may not be acquired until a job is under contract and it is known that production will occur. The raw material acquired, although often separately distinguishable and related to specific jobs, is accounted for in a single general ledger control account (Raw Material Inventory) with subsidiary ledger backup. The material may, however, be designated in the storeroom and possibly in the subsidiary records as being "held for use in Job XX." Such designations should keep the material from being used on a job other than the one for which it was acquired.

Material Requisitions

5

What journal entries are used to accumulate costs in a job order costing system?

material requisition form

When material is needed to begin a job, a **material requisition form** (shown in Exhibit 5–3) is prepared so that the material can be released from the warehouse and sent to the production area. This source document indicates the types and quantities of materials to be placed into production or used to perform a service job. Such documents are usually prenumbered and come in multiple-copy sets so that completed copies can be maintained in the warehouse, in the department, and with each job. Completed material requisition forms are important for a company's audit trail because they provide the ability to trace responsibility for material cost and to verify the flow of material from the warehouse to the department for the job receiving the material. These forms release warehouse personnel from further responsibility for issued materials and assign responsibility to the requisitioning department. Although hardcopy material requisition forms may still be used, it is increasingly common for this document to exist only electronically.

When material is issued, its cost is released from Raw Material Inventory, and if direct to the job, is sent to Work in Process Inventory. If the Raw Material Inventory account also contains indirect material, the costs of these issuances are assigned to Manufacturing Overhead. Thus, the journal entry will be as follows:

Work in Process Inventory (if direct)	XXX	
Manufacturing Overhead (if indirect)	XXX	
Raw Material Inventory		XXX

EXHIBIT 5–3

Material Requisition Form

Date ____________ No. 341
Job Number ____________ Department ____________
Authorized by ____________ Issued by ____________
Received by ____________ Inspected by ____________

Item No.	Part No.	Description	Unit of Measure	Quantity Required	Quantity Issued	Unit Cost	Total Cost

When the first direct material associated with a job is issued to production, that job moves to the second stage of its production cycle—being in process. When a job enters this stage, cost accumulation must begin using the primary accounting document in a job order system—the job order cost sheet (or job cost record).

Job Order Cost Sheet

The source document that provides virtually all financial information about a particular job is the **job order cost sheet**. The set of job order cost sheets for all uncompleted jobs comprises the Work in Process Inventory subsidiary ledger. Total costs contained on the job order cost sheets for all uncompleted jobs should reconcile to the Work in Process Inventory control account balance in the general ledger as shown in Exhibit 5–2.

job order cost sheet

The top portion of a job order cost sheet includes a job number, a description of the task, customer identification, various scheduling information, delivery instructions, and contract price. The remainder of the form details actual costs for material, labor, and applied overhead. The form also might include budgeted cost information, especially if such information is used to estimate the job's selling price or support a bid price. In bid pricing, budgeted and actual costs should be compared at the end of a job to determine any deviations from estimates. Like the material requisition form, the job cost sheet exists only electronically in many companies today.

Exhibit 5–4 illustrates a job order cost sheet for Island Marine. The company has contracted to produce a floating hull that will serve as a platform for an offshore oil rig. All of Island Marine's job order cost sheets include a section for budgeted data so that budget-to-actual comparisons can be made for planning and control purposes. Direct material and direct labor costs are assigned and posted to jobs as work on the job is performed. Direct material information is gathered from the material requisition forms, and direct labor information is found on employee time sheets or employee labor tickets. (Employee time sheets are discussed in the next section.)

Overhead is applied to production at Island Marine based on departmental rates. Each department may have more than one rate. For example, in the Cutting & Forming Department, the overhead rates for 2000 are as follows:

Labor-related costs: $25 per direct labor hour
Machine-related costs: $45 per machine hour

Employee Time Sheets

An **employee time sheet** (Exhibit 5–5, page 181) indicates for each employee the jobs worked on and the direct labor time consumed. These time sheets are most reliable if the employees fill them in as the day progresses. Work arriving at an employee station is accompanied by a tag or bar code specifying its job order number. The time work is started and stopped are noted on the time sheet.[5] These time sheets should be collected and reviewed by supervisors to ensure that the information is as accurate as possible.

employee time sheet

The time sheet shown in Exhibit 5–5 is appropriate only if employees are asked to record their time and work manually. The time sheet information is the same as that which would be recorded if a computer were used to track employee tasks, as is the norm in larger businesses. In fact, larger businesses today use electronic time-keeping software. Employees simply swipe an employee ID card and a job

[5] Alternatives to daily time sheets are job time tickets that supervisors give to employees as they are assigned new jobs and supervisors' records of which employees worked on what jobs for what period of time. The latter alternative is extremely difficult if a supervisor is overseeing a large number of employees or if employees are dispersed through a large section of the plant.

Job Number 323

Customer Name and Address:

Dolphin Petroleum Co.
9901 La. Freeway
New Orleans, LA

Description of Job:

Hull for floating rig
Per specifications in bid agreement #913
dated 2/01/00

Contract Agreement Date: *3/25/00*
Scheduled Starting Date: *6/5/00*
Agreed Completion Date: *7/01/01*
Actual Completion Date:
Delivery Instructions: *Floating: ICW at New Orleans*

Contract Price *$21,000,000*

CUTTING & FORMING

DIRECT MATERIALS (EST. $6,140,000)			DIRECT LABOR (EST. $1,100,000)			OVERHEAD BASED ON # OF LABOR HOURS (EST. $500,000)			OVERHEAD BASED ON # OF MACHINE HOURS (EST. $750,000)		
Date	**Source**	**Amount**	**Date**	**Source**	**Amount**	**Date**	**Source**	**Amount**	**Date**	**Source**	**Amount**

WELDING & ASSEMBLY
(SAME FORMAT AS ABOVE BUT WITH DIFFERENT OH RATES)

PAINTING & FINISHING
(SAME FORMAT AS ABOVE BUT WITH DIFFERENT OH RATES)

SUMMARY (THOUSANDS OF DOLLARS)

	CUTTING & FORMING Actual	CUTTING & FORMING Budget	WELDING & ASSEMBLY Actual	WELDING & ASSEMBLY Budget	PAINTING & FINISHING Actual	PAINTING & FINISHING Budget
Direct materials		*$6,140*		*$1,200*		*$ 400*
Direct labor		*1,100*		*2,100*		*700*
Overhead (labor)		*500*		*400*		*450*
Overhead (machine)		*750*		*520*		*370*
Totals		*$8,490*		*$4,220*		*$1,920*

Final Costs:	Actual	Budget
Cutting & Forming		*$ 8,490*
Welding & Assembly		*4,220*
Painting & Finishing		*1,920*
Totals		*$14,630*

EXHIBIT 5-4

Island Marine's Job Order Cost Sheet

card through a reader when they switch from one job to another. This software allows labor costs to be accumulated by job and department.

In highly automated factories, employee time sheets may not be extremely useful or necessary documents because of the low proportion of direct labor cost to total cost. However, machine time can be tracked through the use of machine clocks or counters in the same way as human labor. As jobs are transferred from one machine to another, the clock or counter can be reset to mark the start and

For Week Ending ____________________

Department ____________________

Employee Name ____________________

Employee ID No. ____________________

Type of Work		Job Number	Start Time	Stop Time	Day (circle)	Total Hours
Code	Description					
					M T W Th F S	
					M T W Th F S	
					M T W Th F S	
					M T W Th F S	
					M T W Th F S	
					M T W Th F S	

Employee Signature

Supervisor's Signature (for overtime)

EXHIBIT 5-5

Employee Time Sheet

stop times. Machine times can then be equated to employee-operator time. Another convenient way to track employee time is through bar codes that can be scanned as products pass through individual workstations. At one large Midwest plumbing manufacturer, for example, a bar coding system was implemented for time-and-attendance and shop-floor control systems. "In less than two years, the company eliminated eleven different forms that were used when time and inspection data were recorded manually. Inspector efficiency improved by 10 to 12 percent, in part because the inspector never touched a piece of paper other than a bar code label."[6]

Transferring employee time sheet (or alternative source document) information to the job order cost sheet requires a knowledge of employee labor rates. Wage rates are found in employee personnel files. Time spent on the job is multiplied by the employee's wage rate, and the amounts are summed to find total direct labor cost for the period. The summation is recorded on the job order cost sheet. Time sheet information is also used for payroll preparation; the journal entry to record the information is

Work in Process Inventory (if direct)	XXX	
Manufacturing Overhead (if indirect)	XXX	
Salaries and Wages Payable		XXX

After these uses, time sheets are filed and retained so they can be referenced if necessary for any future information needs. If total actual labor costs for the job differ significantly from the original estimate, the manager responsible for labor cost control may be asked to clarify the reasons underlying the situation. In addition, if a job is to be billed at cost plus a specified profit margin (a **cost-plus contract**), the number of hours worked may be audited by the buyer. This situation is quite common and especially important when dealing with government contracts. Therefore,

cost-plus contract

[6] Thomas Tyson, "The Use of Bar Coding in Activity-Based Costing, *Journal of Cost Management* (Winter 1991), pp. 52–53.

hours not worked directly on the contracted job cannot be arbitrarily or incorrectly charged to the cost-plus job without the potential for detection. Last, time sheets provide information on overtime hours. Under the Fair Labor Standards Act, overtime must generally be paid at a time-and-a-half rate to all nonmanagement employees when they work more than 40 hours in a week.

Overhead

Overhead costs can be substantial in manufacturing and service organizations. As indicated in the following News Note, the ability to estimate and correctly apply overhead is a major factor in the relative success of custom producers. As suggested by the News Note, activity-based costing, presented in Chapter 4, can be effectively used in a custom job production environment.

Actual overhead incurred during production is included in the Manufacturing Overhead control account. If actual overhead is applied to jobs, the cost accountant will wait until the end of the period and divide the actual overhead incurred in each designated cost pool by a related measure of activity or cost driver. Actual overhead would be applied to jobs by multiplying the actual overhead rate by the actual measure of activity associated with each job.

More commonly, overhead is applied to jobs using one or more annualized predetermined overhead application rates. Overhead is assigned to jobs by multiplying the predetermined rate by the actual measure of the activity base that was incurred during the period for each job. This method is normal costing.

NEWS NOTE  GENERAL BUSINESS

High Tech Is High Overhead

A few years ago, an aerospace manufacturer of high-precision aircraft components was approached by one of its customers who was looking for additional machine capacity to support an overload situation in the customer's site. What an opportunity to sell excess machine hours and reap a great reward! The sales and manufacturing managers were all set to bid a rate to the customer, when the new controller stepped in and said, "Wait, before you bid, let me review the numbers." A little surprised, the managers gave the controller a couple of days to look at the bid.

The manufacturer was a large job shop with a variety of machine-shop-type equipment, ranging from simple drill presses to extremely complex high-precision finishing machines. Job costing used direct labor dollars as the overhead allocation base, and although the manufacturing overhead rate for the plant was now almost 300 percent of direct labor, nobody had questioned how jobs had been priced in the past. Pricing was, simply, the number of direct labor hours, times the direct labor rate, plus overhead at the 300 percent rate, plus 20 percent for administrative expense, plus a further fee representing expected profit, normally 12 percent of cost. Therefore, in this case, direct labor of $21.25 per hour was grossed up to provide a manufacturing rate including overhead of $85 per direct labor hour.

The reality of the situation was, however, that the customer was not buying the average shop. The customer wanted to buy specific, high-precision finishing machines to complete work started in its own facility. What the controller sensed in the situation was that the normal pricing model might not work in this case. His approach to analyzing the opportunity was to take each machine and trace to it as best he could the actual resources consumed by the equipment including supplies, electricity, maintenance, setup, tools and fixtures, space, quality control, scheduling, material handling, etc. He still had to add some cost for management and shared facilities. Much to his horror, he discovered that the real cost of the machines ranged from $225 to as much as $350 per operating hour. Astonishingly, not one machine had an hourly cost lower than the proposed selling price.

Prices based on the revised higher level rates per machine were quoted to the customer, and most were accepted.

SOURCE: Reprinted from an article appearing in CMA Management Magazine (formerly CMA Magazine) by Murray A. Best, CMA, with permission of CMA Canada.

When predetermined rates are used, overhead is applied at the end of the period or at completion of production, whichever is earlier. Overhead is applied at the end of each period so that the Work in Process Inventory account contains costs for all three product elements (direct material, direct labor, and overhead). Overhead is applied to Work in Process Inventory at completion so that a proper product cost can be transferred to Finished Goods Inventory. The journal entry to apply overhead follows.

Work in Process Inventory	XXX	
Manufacturing Overhead		XXX

Completion of Production

When a job is completed, its total cost is transferred to Finished Goods Inventory.

Finished Goods Inventory	XXX	
Work in Process Inventory		XXX

Job order cost sheets for completed jobs are removed from the WIP subsidiary ledger and become the subsidiary ledger for the Finished Goods Inventory control account. When a job is sold, the cost contained in Finished Goods Inventory for that job is transferred to Cost of Goods Sold.

Cost of Goods Sold	XXX	
Finished Goods Inventory		XXX

Such a cost transfer presumes the use of a perpetual inventory system, which is common in a job order costing environment because goods are generally easily identified and tracked.

Job order cost sheets for completed jobs are kept in a company's permanent files. A completed job order cost sheet provides management with a historical summary about total costs and, if appropriate, the cost per finished unit for a given job. The cost per unit may be helpful for planning and control purposes as well as for bidding on future contracts. If a job was exceptionally profitable, management might decide to pursue additional similar jobs. If a job was unprofitable, the job order cost sheet may provide indications of areas in which cost control was lax. Such areas are more readily identifiable if the job order cost sheet presents the original, budgeted cost information.

Unlike the case of a retailer or wholesaler, most businesses that use job order costing have little finished goods inventory. Because they build custom products, only when a specific customer contracts for a particular service or product does production occur. Then, on completion, the costs of the product or service may flow immediately to Cost of Goods Sold.

JOB ORDER COSTING AND TECHNOLOGY

6

How do technological changes impact the gathering and use of information in job order costing systems?

The trend in job order costing is to automate the data collection and data entry functions required to support the accounting system. By automating recordkeeping functions, not only are production employees relieved of that burden, but the electronically stored data can be accessed to serve many purposes. For example, the data from a completed job can be used as inputs for projecting the costs that are the bases for setting bid prices on future jobs. Regardless of whether the data entry process is automated, virtually all product costing software contains a job costing module, even very inexpensive off-the-shelf programs. And as indicated in the accompanying News Note, there is a significant role for public accountants in vending software to smaller manufacturing firms.

NEWS NOTE  GENERAL BUSINESS

Middle Market Manufacturing Going "Soft" for CPAs

The market for selling technology products and consulting services to middle-market manufacturers is as abundant as Mike Meyers's chest hair in the latest Austin Powers movie, but some observers of this niche industry doubt that many practitioners will capitalize on it.

Major middle-market accounting software vendors—Great Plains, Sage, SBT, Solomon and Epicor—are rapidly adding manufacturing capabilities to their core accounting technologies. And they are looking to their reseller channels, whose makeup is often as much as 30 percent CPAs, for help in reaching that market.

The move is both fueling and being fueled by middle-market manufacturers' expanding technology appetite. "Five years ago, a manufacturer had to be $20 million a year [in revenues] to automate, now the $5 million-a-year companies are automating and doing so rapidly with the right partners," said Jim Kent of the Kent Group, an Andover-based reseller of Macola, an established manufacturing software specialist.

"There's a huge opportunity for CPAs to work with manufacturers who want their manufacturing and accounting systems to work together," said David Lahey, president of Lahey Financial Systems, which expects to expand dramatically by virtue of now being sold exclusively by SBT and its reseller channel.

Lahey, whose company has been developing manufacturing software since 1984, claims that most mid-market manufacturers have not in the past focused on accounting software and now they're being forced to take on integrated, multiple-application programs. "They're being forced to play catch-up and CPAs are a logical party to help them deal with systems that directly integrate accounting and manufacturing solutions," he explained.

Brian Sittley, president of Productivity Management, a South Bend, Ind., reseller of SBT, said the manufacturing industry technology consulting opportunity is particularly keen for CPAs well versed in cost accounting.

SOURCE: John Covaleski, "Manufacturing Niche May Be Too Hairy for CPAs," *Accounting Today* (July 26–August 8, 1999), pp. 22, 28. © Faulkner & Gray, republished with permission.

intranet

http://www.greatplains.com
http://www.us.sage.com
http://www.sbt.com
http://www.solomon.com
http://www.macola.com
http://www.lfscorp.com

Within many companies, intranets are being created to manage the information pertaining to jobs. An **intranet** is a mechanism for sharing information and delivering data from corporate databases to the local-area network (LAN) desktops. Intranets use Web technology and are restricted networks that can enhance communication and distribute information.[7] Exhibit 5–6 provides an illustration of the types of information that can be accessed on an intranet.

As shown in Exhibit 5–6, much information relevant to managing the production of a particular job is available on-line to managers. From contract information and technical specifications to cost budgets, actual costs incurred, and stage of production measurements, data are instantly available to managers. As data input functions are automated, the data available on the Intranet become more and more up to the minute, or real time. Chapter 17 addresses more fully the automation and integration of information systems.

In any job order costing system, the individual job is the focal point. The next section presents a comprehensive job order costing situation using information from Island Marine, the company introduced earlier.

JOB ORDER COSTING ILLUSTRATION

Island Marine sets bid prices based on its costs. Over the long term, the company has a goal of realizing a gross profit equal to 25 percent of the bid price. This level of gross profit is sufficient to generate a reasonable profit after covering selling and administrative costs. In more competitive circumstances, such as when the company has too much unused capacity, bid prices may be set lower to increase the likelihood

[7] Lawrence Barkowski, "Intranets for Projects and Cost Management in Manufacturing," *Cost Engineering* (June 1999), p. 33.

EXHIBIT 5–6

Project Management Site Content

Project Management Library
- ❑ Instructions on how to use the project intranet site
- ❑ Project manager manuals
- ❑ Policy and procedure manuals
- ❑ Templates and forms
- ❑ Project management training exercises

General Project Information
- ❑ Project descriptions
- ❑ Photos of project progress
- ❑ Contract information
- ❑ Phone and e-mail directories
- ❑ Project team rosters
- ❑ Document control logs
- ❑ Scope documents
- ❑ Closure documents
- ❑ Links to project control tools
- ❑ Links to electronic document retrieval systems

Technical Information
- ❑ Drawing logs
- ❑ Detailed budgets and physical estimates
- ❑ Specifications
- ❑ Bill of materials by department
- ❑ Punch lists
- ❑ Links to drawing databases

Management Information
- ❑ Meeting minutes
- ❑ Daily logs
- ❑ Project schedules
- ❑ Task and resource checklists
- ❑ Shutdown and look-ahead reports
- ❑ Work-hour estimates
- ❑ Change notices
- ❑ Labor hours worked
- ❑ Earned value

Financial Information
- ❑ Project cost sheet
- ❑ Funding requests for each cost account
- ❑ Cash flow projections and budgets
- ❑ Original cost budgets and adjustments
- ❑ Contract status reports
- ❑ Departmental budget reports
- ❑ Links to mainframe sessions for requisitions and purchase order tracking
- ❑ Companywide financial statements

SOURCE: Lawrence Barkowski, "Intranets for Project and Cost Management in Manufacturing," *Cost Engineering* (June 1999), p. 36. Reprinted with permission of AACE International, 209 Prairie Ave., Suite 100, Morgantown, WV 25601 USA. Internet: http://www.aacei.org. E-mail: info@aacei.org.

of successful bids. If the company has little unused capacity, it may set bid prices somewhat higher so that the likelihood of successfully bidding on too many contracts is reduced.

To help in establishing the bid price on the hull for the floating platform, Island Marine's cost accountant provided the vice president of sales with the budgeted cost information shown earlier in Exhibit 5–4. The vice president of sales believed that a bid price slightly above normal levels was possible because of the noncompetitive nature of this particular market. Accordingly, the vice president set the sales price to yield a gross margin of roughly 30.3 percent [($21,000,000 − $14,630,000) ÷ $21,000,000]. This sales price was agreed to by the customer in a contract dated March 25, 2000. Island Marine's managers scheduled the job to begin on June 5, 2000, and to be completed by July 1, 2001. The job is assigned the number 323 for identification purposes.

The following journal entries illustrate the flow of costs for the Cutting & Forming Department of Island Marine during June 2000. Work on several contracts including Job #323 was performed in Cutting & Forming during that month. In entries 1, 2, and 4 that follow, separate WIP inventory accounting is shown for costs related to Job #323 and to other jobs. In practice, the Work in Process control account for a given department would be debited only once for all costs assigned to it. The details for posting to the individual job cost records would be presented in the journal entry explanations. *All amounts are shown in thousands of dollars.*

1. During June 2000, material requisition forms #340–355 indicated that $2,925 of raw materials were issued from the warehouse to the Cutting & Forming Department. This amount included $1,982 of direct materials used on Job #323 and $723 of direct materials used on other jobs. The remaining $120 of raw materials issued during June were indirect materials.

Work in Process Inventory—Cutting & Forming (Job #323)	1,982	
Work in Process Inventory—Cutting & Forming (other jobs)	723	
Manufacturing Overhead—Cutting & Forming (indirect materials)	120	
Raw Material Inventory		2,825
To record direct and indirect materials issued per requisitions during June.		

2. The June time sheets and payroll summaries for the Cutting & Forming Department nonsalaried workers were used to trace direct and indirect labor to that department. Total labor cost for the Cutting & Forming Department for June was $417. Job #323 required $310 of direct labor cost combining the two biweekly pay periods in June. The remaining jobs in process required $45 of direct labor cost, and indirect labor cost for the month totaled $32.

Work in Process Inventory—Cutting & Forming (Job #323)	310	
Work in Process Inventory—Cutting & Forming (other jobs)	45	
Manufacturing Overhead—Cutting & Forming (indirect labor)	32	
Wages Payable		387
To record wages associated with Cutting & Forming during June.		

3. The Cutting & Forming Department incurred overhead costs in addition to indirect materials and indirect labor during June. Factory building and equipment depreciation of $65 was recorded for April. Insurance on the factory building ($12) for the month had been prepaid and had expired. The $88 bill for June factory utility costs was received and would be paid in July. Repairs and maintenance costs of $63 were paid in cash. Overhead costs of $27 for items such as supplies used, supervisors' salaries, and so forth were incurred; these costs are credited to "Various accounts" for illustrative purposes. The following entry summarizes the accumulation of these other actual overhead costs for June.

Manufacturing Overhead—Cutting & Forming	255	
Accumulated Depreciation		65
Prepaid Insurance		12
Utilities Payable		88
Cash		63
Various accounts		27
To record actual overhead costs of the Cutting & Forming Department during June exclusive of indirect materials and indirect nonsalaried labor.		

4. Island Marine prepares financial statements at month end. To do so, Work in Process Inventory must include all production costs: direct material, direct labor, and overhead. The company allocates overhead to the Cutting & Forming Work in Process Inventory based on two predetermined overhead rates: $25 per direct labor hour and $45 per machine hour. In June the employees committed 6,200 hours of direct labor time to Job #323, and 3,000 machine hours were consumed on that job. The other jobs worked on during the month received total applied overhead of $88,000 [1,000 direct labor hours (assumed) × $25 plus 1,400 machine hours (assumed) × $45].

Work in Process Inventory—Cutting & Forming (Job #323)	290	
Work in Process Inventory—Cutting & Forming (other jobs)	88	
Manufacturing Overhead—Cutting & Forming		378
To apply overhead to Cutting & Forming work in process for June using predetermined application rates.		

Notice that the amount of actual overhead for June ($120 + $32 + $255 = $407) in the Cutting & Forming Department is not equal to the amount of overhead applied to that department's Work in Process Inventory ($378). This $29 difference is the underapplied overhead for the month. Because the predetermined rates were based on annual estimates, differences in actual and applied overhead accumulate during the year. Underapplied or overapplied overhead will be closed at year-end (as shown in Chapter 3) to either Cost of Goods Sold (if the amount is immaterial) or to Work in Process Inventory, Finished Goods Inventory, and Cost of Goods Sold (if the amount is material).

The preceding entries for the Cutting & Forming Department would be similar to the entries made in each of the other departments of Island Marine. Direct material and direct labor data are posted to each job order cost sheet frequently (usually daily); entries are posted to the general ledger control accounts for longer intervals (usually monthly).

Job #323 will be executed by three departments of Island Marine. Other jobs accepted by the company may involve a different combination of departments, and different conversion operations within departments. In this company, jobs flow consecutively from one department to the next. In other types of job shops, different departments may work on the same job concurrently. Similar entries for Job #323 are made throughout the production process, and Exhibit 5–7 shows the cost sheet at the job's completion. Note that direct material requisitions, direct labor cost, and applied overhead shown previously in entries 1, 2, and 4 are posted on the job cost sheet. Other entries are not detailed.

When the job is completed, its costs are transferred to Finished Goods Inventory. The journal entries related to completion and sale are as follows:

Finished Goods Inventory—Job #323	14,283	
Work in Process Inventory—Cutting & Forming		8,289
Work in Process Inventory—Welding & Assembly		4,153
Work in Process Inventory—Painting & Finishing		1,841
Cost of Goods Sold—Job #323	14,283	
Finished Goods Inventory—Job #323		14,283
Accounts Receivable—Dolphin Petroleum Co.	21,000	
Sales		21,000

The completed job order cost sheet can be used by managers in all departments to determine how well costs were controlled. Overall, costs were below the budgeted level. The Cutting & Forming Department experienced lower costs than budgeted in all categories except machine-related overhead. In the Welding & Assembly Department, actual direct material costs were well below budget. However, direct labor costs were above budget and this caused labor-related overhead to be above budget. Machine-related overhead was significantly below budget. Painting and Finishing costs, overall, were significantly below budget. Only machine-related overhead exceeded the budgeted amount. Summarizing, costs were well controlled on this job, because total actual costs were substantially below the budgeted amounts (approximately 2.37 percent below budget).

In the remainder of the chapter, the use of job order costing data to support management decision making and improve cost control is discussed. The next section discusses how standard costs, rather than actual costs, can be used to improve cost management.

JOB ORDER COSTING USING STANDARD COSTS

7

How are standard costs used in a job order costing system?

The Island Marine example illustrates the use of actual historical cost data for direct material and direct labor in a job order costing system. However, using actual direct material and direct labor costs may cause the costs of similar units to fluctuate from period to period or job to job because of changes in component costs. Use of

Job Number 323

Customer Name and Address:

Dolphin Petroleum Co.
9901 La. Freeway
New Orleans, LA

Description of Job:

Hull for floating rig
Per specifications in bid agreement #913
dated 2/01/00

Contract Agreement Date: *3/25/00*
Scheduled Starting Date: *6/5/00*
Agreed Completion Date: *7/01/01*
Actual Completion Date:
Delivery Instructions: *Floating: ICW at New Orleans*

Contract Price *$21,000,000*

CUTTING & FORMING

DIRECT MATERIALS (EST. $6,140,000)			DIRECT LABOR (EST. $1,100,000)			OVERHEAD BASED ON # OF LABOR HOURS (EST. $500,000)			OVERHEAD BASED ON # OF MACHINE HOURS (EST. $750,000)		
Date	**Source**	**Amount**	**Date**	**Source**	**Amount**	**Date**	**Source**	**Amount**	**Date**	**Source**	**Amount**
6/30	MR #340 MR #355	$1,982	6/30	payroll	$310	6/30	payroll	$155	6/30	Machine hour meters	$135

WELDING & ASSEMBLY
(SAME FORMAT AS ABOVE BUT WITH DIFFERENT OH RATES)

PAINTING & FINISHING
(SAME FORMAT AS ABOVE BUT WITH DIFFERENT OH RATES)

SUMMARY (THOUSANDS OF DOLLARS)

	CUTTING & FORMING Actual	CUTTING & FORMING Budget	WELDING & ASSEMBLY Actual	WELDING & ASSEMBLY Budget	PAINTING & FINISHING Actual	PAINTING & FINISHING Budget
Direct materials	*$6,056*	*$6,140*	*$1,134*	*$1,200*	*$ 380*	*$ 400*
Direct labor	*1,010*	*1,100*	*2,120*	*2,100*	*650*	*700*
Overhead (labor)	*460*	*500*	*420*	*400*	*430*	*450*
Overhead (machine)	*763*	*750*	*479*	*520*	*381*	*370*
Totals	*$8,289*	*$8,490*	*$4,153*	*$4,220*	*$1,841*	*$1,920*

Final Costs:	Actual	Budget
Cutting & Forming	*$ 8,289*	*$ 8,490*
Welding & Assembly	*4,153*	*4,220*
Painting & Finishing	*1,841*	*1,920*
Totals	*$14,283*	*$14,630*

EXHIBIT 5-7

Island Marine's Completed Job Order Cost Sheet

standard costs for direct material and direct labor can minimize the effects of such cost fluctuations in the same way that predetermined rates do for overhead costs.

standard cost system

A **standard cost system** determines product cost by using, in the inventory accounts, predetermined norms for prices and/or quantities of component elements. After production is complete, the standard production cost is compared to the actual production cost to determine the efficiency of the production process. A difference between the actual quantity, price, or rate and its related standard is called a **variance**.

variance

Standards can be used in a job order system only if a company typically engages in jobs that produce fairly similar products. One type of standard job order costing system uses standards only for input prices of material and/or rates for labor. This process is reasonable if all output relies on basically the same kinds of material and/or labor. If standards are used for price or rate amounts only, the debits to Work in Process Inventory become a combination of actual and standard information: actual quantities at standard prices or rates.

Jones Brothers, a house-painting company located in Indiana, illustrates the use of price and rate standards. Management has decided that, because of the climate, one specific brand of paint (costing $30 per gallon) is the best to use. Painters employed by the company are paid $12 per hour. These two amounts can be used as price and rate standards for Jones Brothers. No standards can be set for the quantity of paint that will be used on a job, or the amount of time the job will require, because those items will vary with the quantity and texture of wood on the structure and the size of the structure being painted.

Assume that Jones Brothers paints a house requiring 50 gallons of paint and 80 hours of labor time. The standard paint and labor costs, respectively, are $1,500 (50 × $30) and $960 (80 × $12). Assume Jones Brothers bought the paint when it was on sale, so the actual price paid was $27 per gallon or a total of $1,350. Comparing this price to the standard results in a $150 favorable material price variance (50 gallons at $3 per gallon). If the actual labor rate paid to painters was $11 per hour, there would be an $80 favorable (80 hours at $1 per hour) labor rate variance.

Other job order companies produce output that is homogeneous enough to allow standards to be developed for both quantities and prices for material and labor. Such companies usually use distinct production runs for numerous similar products. In such circumstances, the output is homogeneous for each run, unlike the heterogeneous output of Jones Brothers.

Green Manufacturing, Inc., is a job order manufacturer that uses both price and quantity material and labor standards. Green manufactures wooden flower boxes that are retailed through several chains of garden supply stores. The boxes are contracted for on a job order basis, because the retailing chains tend to demand changes in style, color, and size with each spring gardening season. Green produces the boxes in distinct production runs each month for each retail chain. Price and quantity standards for direct material and direct labor have been established and are used to compare the estimated and actual costs of monthly production runs for each type of box produced.

The standards set for boxes sold to Mountain Gardens are as follows:

8 linear feet of 1" × 10" redwood plank at $0.60 per linear foot
1.4 direct labor hours at $9 per direct labor hour

In June, 2,000 boxes were produced for Mountain Gardens. Actual wood used was 16,300 linear feet, which was purchased at $0.58 per linear foot. Direct labor employees worked 2,700 hours at an average labor rate of $9.10.

From this information, it can be concluded that Green used 300 linear feet of redwood above the standard quantity for the job [16,300 − (8 × 2,000)]. This usage causes an unfavorable material quantity variance of $180 at the $0.60 standard price ($0.60 × 300 linear feet). The actual redwood used was purchased at $0.02 below the standard price per linear foot, which results in a $326 ($0.02 × 16,300) favorable material price variance.

The actual DLHs used were 100 less than standard [2,700 − (1.4 hours × 2,000)], which results in a favorable labor quantity variance of $900 ($9 standard rate × 100 hours). The work crew earned $0.10 per hour above standard, which translates to a $270 unfavorable labor rate variance ($0.10 × 2,700). A summary of variances follows:

Direct material quantity variance	$ 180	unfavorable
Direct material price variance	(326)	favorable
Direct labor quantity variance	(900)	favorable
Direct labor rate variance	270	unfavorable
Net variance (cost less than expected)	$(776)	favorable

From a financial perspective, Green controlled its total material and labor costs well on the Mountain Garden job.

Variances can be computed for actual-to-standard differences regardless of whether standards have been established for both quantities and prices or for prices/rates only. Standard costs for material and labor provide the same types of benefits as predetermined overhead rates: more timely information and comparisons against actual amounts.

A predetermined overhead rate is, in essence, a type of standard. It establishes a constant amount of overhead assignable as a component of product cost and eliminates any immediate need for actual overhead information in the calculation of product cost. More is presented on standards and variances in Chapter 10.

Standard cost job order systems are reasonable substitutes for actual or normal costing systems as long as the standard cost systems provide managers with useful information. Any type of product costing system is acceptable in practice if it is effective and efficient in serving the company's unique production needs, provides the information desired by management, and can be implemented at a cost that is reasonable when compared to the benefits to be received. These criteria apply equally well to both manufacturers and service companies.

JOB ORDER COSTING TO ASSIST MANAGERS

8

How does information from a job order costing system support management decision making?

Managers are interested in controlling costs in each department as well as for each job. Actual direct material, direct labor, and factory overhead costs are accumulated in departmental accounts and are periodically compared to budgets so that managers can respond to significant deviations. Transactions must be recorded in a consistent, complete, and accurate manner to have information on actual costs available for periodic comparisons. Managers may stress different types of cost control in different types of businesses.

The major difference in job order costing for a service organization and a manufacturing firm is that most service organizations use an insignificant amount of materials relative to the value of labor for each job. In such cases, direct material may be treated (for the sake of convenience) as part of overhead rather than accounted for separately. A few service organizations, such as in the medical industry, may use some costly materials.

Accountants in some service companies may trace only direct labor to jobs and allocate all other production costs. These cost allocations may be accomplished most effectively by using a predetermined rate per direct labor hour, or per direct labor dollar. Other cost drivers may also be used as possible overhead allocation bases.

Knowing the costs of individual jobs allows managers to better estimate future job costs and establish realistic bids and selling prices. The use of budgets and standards in a job order costing system provides information against which actual costs can be compared at regular time intervals for control purposes. These comparisons can also furnish some performance evaluation information. The following two examples demonstrate the usefulness of job order costing to managers.

Custom Systems: An Illustration of Job Costing Information

Custom Systems is an engineering firm that specializes in concrete structures. The firm has a diverse set of clients and types of jobs. Josh Bradley is the founder and president. Mr. Bradley wants to know which clients are the most profitable and which

Periodically comparing actual to budgeted costs for a job will help managers engage in ongoing cost control activities. Waiting to make such a comparison until job completion provides information that can impact future jobs, but not the one just finished.

are the least profitable. To determine this information, he requested a breakdown of profits per job measured on both a percentage and an absolute dollar basis.

Mr. Bradley discovered that the company did not maintain records of costs per client-job. Costs had been accumulated only by type—travel, entertainment, and so forth. Ms. Tobias, the sales manager, was certain that the largest profits came from the company's largest accounts. A careful job cost analysis found that the largest accounts contributed the most revenue to the firm, but the smallest percentage and absolute dollars of incremental profits. Until the president requested this information, no one had totaled the costs of recruiting each client or the travel, entertainment, and other costs associated with maintaining each client.

A company that has a large number of jobs that vary in size, time, or effort may not know which jobs are responsible for disproportionately large costs. Job order costing can assist in determining which jobs are truly profitable and can help managers to better monitor costs. As a result of the cost analysis, Mr. Bradley changed the company's marketing strategy. The firm began concentrating its efforts on smaller clients who were located closer to the primary office. These efforts caused profits to substantially increase because significantly fewer costs were incurred for travel and entertainment. A job order costing system was implemented to track the per-period and total costs associated with each client. Unprofitable accounts were dropped, and account managers felt more responsibility to monitor and control costs related to their particular accounts.

Monihan's Boatworks

Monihan's Boatworks manufactures three types of boats to customer specifications.[8] Before job order costing was instituted, the managers had no means of determining

[8] This example is based on an article by Leonard A. Robinson and Loudell Ellis Robinson, "Steering a Boat Maker Through Cost Shoals," *Management Accounting* (January 1983), pp. 60–66.

the costs associated with the production of each type of boat. When a customer provided yacht specifications and asked what the selling price would be, managers merely estimated costs in what they felt was a reasonable manner. In fact, during the construction process, no costs were assigned to Work in Process Inventory; all production costs were sent to Finished Goods Inventory.

After implementing a job order costing system, Monihan's Boatworks had better control over its inventory, better inventory valuations for financial statements, and better information with which to prevent part stockouts (not having parts in inventory) and production stoppages. The job order costing system provided managers with information on what work was currently in process and at what cost. From this information, they were better able to judge whether additional work could be accepted and when current work would be completed. Because job order costing assigns costs to Work in Process Inventory, balance sheet figures were more accurate. As material was issued to production, the use of material requisition forms produced inventory records that were more current and reflective of raw material quantities on hand. Finally, the use of a job order costing system gave managers an informed means by which to estimate costs and more adequately price future jobs.

Whether an entity is a manufacturer or service organization that tailors its output to customer specifications, company management will find that job order costing techniques will help in the managerial functions. This cost system is useful for determining the cost of goods produced or services rendered in companies that are able to attach costs to specific jobs. As product variety increases, the size of production lots for many items shrinks, and job order costing becomes more applicable. Custom-made goods may become the norm rather than the exception in an environment that relies on flexible manufacturing systems and computer-integrated manufacturing.

REVISITING Aker Gulf Marine

http://www.akermaritime.no/

Aker Gulf Marine is a relatively young firm having been established in 1991. The firm is typical of many new businesses formed today in that it is a partnership of two larger, older firms: Aker Maritime and Peter Kiewit Sons' Inc. AGM is a successful company competing in a cyclical industry. To keep operations profitable and functioning near capacity, the company must continually find ways to differentiate itself from competitors.

To successfully bid projects, the firm must carefully monitor and control costs. In part, this requires managers to achieve high levels of quality, minimize waste and scrapped materials, utilize recycled materials, and maintain a clean, safe work environment. Safety is a crucial issue both from a cost and personnel perspective because risks of injury to employees is inherently high in rig construction. The company has implemented several successful programs to involve employees in safety and quality training.

AGM has also invested heavily in capital equipment to leverage technology. Recently the firm built a facility to house certain production operations, such as painting, that are sensitive to weather effects. Also, the company has built a massive, specialized lifting device that dominates the Corpus Christi Bay skyline. This lifting device is capable of moving 4,800-ton product components from the land-based construction yard to the firm's dockage on the intracoastal waterway.

Today, AGM's products can be found offshore in the Gulf of Mexico, West Africa, and South America.

SOURCES: Discussions with company personnel; Anonymous, "Aker Gulf Marine," http://www.hartpub.com/wallmaps/rampow/aker.htm.

CHAPTER SUMMARY

A cost accounting system should be compatible with the manufacturing environment in which it is used. Job order costing and process costing are two traditional cost accounting systems. Job order costing is used in companies that make a limited quantity of products or provide a limited number of services uniquely tailored to customer specifications. This system is especially appropriate and useful for many service businesses, such as advertising, legal, and architectural firms. Process costing is appropriate in production situations in which large quantities of homogeneous products are manufactured on a continuous flow basis.

A job order costing system considers the "job" as the cost object for which costs are accumulated. A job can consist of one or more units of output, and job costs are accumulated on a job order cost sheet. Job order cost sheets for uncompleted jobs serve as the Work in Process Inventory subsidiary ledger. Cost sheets for completed jobs not yet delivered to customers constitute the Finished Goods Inventory subsidiary ledger, and cost sheets for completed and sold jobs compose the Cost of Goods Sold subsidiary ledger.

In an actual or a normal cost job order system, direct material and direct labor are traced, respectively, using material requisition forms and employee time sheets, to individual jobs in process. Service companies may not attempt to trace direct material to jobs, but instead consider the costs of direct material to be part of overhead. Tracing is not considered necessary when the materials cost is insignificant in relation to the job's total cost.

Technology is playing an increasing role in aiding the management of jobs and in tracking job costs. Even basic accounting software typically has a job costing module. By automating the data entry processes, more accurate and timely data are gathered and employees are relieved of the recurring burden of logging data. The latest technology being adopted in job shops is project management software. These programs allow operational and financial data about jobs to be shared throughout the firm. Intranets are being created to facilitate the dissemination of this information.

In an actual cost system, actual overhead is assigned to jobs. More commonly, however, a normal costing system is used in which overhead is applied using one or more predetermined overhead rates multiplied by the actual activity base(s) incurred. Overhead is applied to Work in Process Inventory at the end of the month or when the job is complete, whichever is earlier.

Standard costing can be utilized in a job shop environment. Standards may be established both for the quantities of production inputs and the prices of those inputs. By using standard costs rather than actual costs, managers have a basis for evaluating the efficiency of operations. Differences between actual costs and standard costs are captured in variance accounts. By analyzing the variances, managers gain an understanding of the factors that cause costs to differ from the expected amounts. Standard costing is most easily adopted in job shops that routinely produce batches of similar products.

Job order costing assists management in planning, controlling, decision making, and evaluating performance. It allows managers to trace costs associated with specific current jobs to better estimate costs for future jobs. Additionally, managers using job order costing can better control the costs associated with current production, especially if comparisons with budgets or standards are used. Attachment of costs to jobs is also necessary to price jobs that are contracted on a cost-plus basis. Last, because costs are accumulated by jobs, managers can more readily determine which jobs or types of jobs are most profitable to the organization.

KEY TERMS

cost-plus contract (p. 181)
employee time sheet (p. 179)
intranet (p. 184)
job (p. 176)
job order cost sheet (p. 179)
job order costing system (p. 174)
material requisition form (p. 178)
process costing system (p. 174)
standard cost system (p. 188)
variance (p. 188)

SOLUTION STRATEGIES

Basic Journal Entries in a Job Order Costing System

	Debit	Credit
Raw Material Inventory	XXX	
Accounts Payable		XXX
To record the purchase of raw materials.		
Work in Process Inventory—Dept. (Job #)	XXX	
Manufacturing Overhead	XXX	
Raw Material Inventory		XXX
To record the issuance of direct and indirect materials requisitioned for a specific job.		
Work in Process Inventory—Dept. (Job #)	XXX	
Manufacturing Overhead	XXX	
Wages Payable		XXX
To record direct and indirect labor payroll for production employees.		
Manufacturing Overhead	XXX	
Various accounts		XXX
To record the incurrence of actual overhead costs. (Account titles to be credited must be specified in an actual journal entry.)		
Work in Process Inventory—Dept. (Job #)	XXX	
Manufacturing Overhead		XXX
To apply overhead to a specific job. (This may be actual OH or OH applied using a predetermined rate. Predetermined OH is applied at job completion or end of period, whichever is earlier.)		
Finished Goods Inventory (Job #)	XXX	
Work in Process Inventory		XXX
To record the transfer of completed goods from WIP to FG.		
Accounts Receivable	XXX	
Sales		XXX
To record the sale of goods on account.		
Cost of Goods Sold	XXX	
Finished Goods Inventory		XXX
To record the cost of the goods sold.		

DEMONSTRATION PROBLEM

Advanced Exploration is a newly formed firm that conducts marine research in the Gulf of Mexico for contract customers. Organizationally, the firm is composed of two departments: Offshore Operations and Lab Research. The Offshore Operations

Department is responsible for gathering test samples and drilling operations on the ocean floor. The Lab Research Department is responsible for analysis of samples and other data gathered by Offshore Operations.

In its first month of operations (March 2001), Advanced Exploration obtained contracts for three research projects:

Job 1: Drill, collect, and analyze samples from 10 sites for a major oil company.
Job 2: Collect and analyze samples for specific toxins off the coast of Louisiana for the U.S. government.
Job 3: Evaluate 12 existing offshore wells for the presence of oil seepage for a major oil company.

Advanced Exploration contracts with its customers on a cost-plus basis; that is, the price charged is equal to costs plus a profit equal to 10 percent of costs. The firm uses a job order costing system based on normal costs. Overhead is applied in the Offshore Operations Department at the predetermined rate of $2,000 per hour of research vessel use (RVH). In the Lab Research Department, overhead is applied at the predetermined rate of $45 per professional labor hour (PLH). For March 2001, significant transactions are summarized here:

1. Materials and test components were purchased on account: $110,000.
2. Materials were requisitioned for use in the three research projects by the Offshore Operations Department (all of these materials are regarded as direct): Job #1—$40,000; Job #2—$28,000; and Job #3—$10,000. Materials were issued to the Lab Research Department: Job #1—$8,000; Job #2—$6,000; and Job #3—$4,500.
3. The time sheets and payroll summaries indicated the following direct labor costs were incurred:

	Offshore Operations	Lab Research
Job #1	$60,000	$56,000
Job #2	50,000	20,000
Job #3	45,000	16,000

4. Indirect research costs were incurred in each department:

	Offshore Operations	Lab Research
Labor	$120,000	$10,000
Utilities/Fuel	290,000	5,000
Depreciation	330,000	80,000

5. Overhead was applied based on the predetermined overhead rates in effect in each department. Offshore Operations had 360 RVHs (170 RVHs on Job #1; 90 RVHs on Job #2; and 100 RVHs on Job #3), and Lab Research worked 2,300 PLHs (1,400 PLHs on Job #1; 500 PLHs on Job #2; and 400 PLHs on Job #3) for the year.
6. Job #1 was completed and cash was collected for the agreed-on price of cost plus 10 percent. At the end of the month, Jobs #2 and #3 were only partially complete.
7. Any underapplied or overapplied overhead is assigned to Cost of Goods Sold.

Required:

a. Record the journal entries for transactions 1 through 7.
b. As of the end of March 2001, determine the total cost assigned to Jobs #2 and #3.

Solution to Demonstration Problem

a. 1. Raw Material Inventory	110,000	
Accounts Payable		110,000
To record purchase of materials.		

	Debit	Credit
2. WIP Inventory—Offshore Operations (Job #1)	40,000	
WIP Inventory—Offshore Operations (Job #2)	28,000	
WIP Inventory—Offshore Operations (Job #3)	10,000	
Raw Material Inventory		78,000
To record requisition and issuance of materials to Offshore Operations.		
WIP Inventory—Lab Research (Job #1)	8,000	
WIP Inventory—Lab Research (Job #2)	6,000	
WIP Inventory—Lab Research (Job #3)	4,500	
Raw Material Inventory		18,500
To record requisition and issuance of materials to Lab Research.		
3. WIP Inventory—Offshore Operations (Job #1)	60,000	
WIP Inventory—Offshore Operations (Job #2)	50,000	
WIP Inventory—Offshore Operations (Job #3)	45,000	
Wages Payable		155,000
To record direct labor costs for Offshore Operations.		
WIP Inventory—Lab Research (Job #1)	56,000	
WIP Inventory—Lab Research (Job #2)	20,000	
WIP Inventory—Lab Research (Job #3)	16,000	
Wages Payable		92,000
To record direct labor costs for Lab Research.		
4. Research Overhead—Offshore Operations	740,000	
Research Overhead—Lab Research	95,000	
Wages Payable		130,000
Utilities/Fuel Payable		295,000
Accumulated Depreciation		410,000
To record indirect research costs.		
5. WIP Inventory—Offshore Operations (Job #1)	340,000	
WIP Inventory—Offshore Operations (Job #2)	180,000	
WIP Inventory—Offshore Operations (Job #3)	200,000	
Research Overhead—Offshore Operations		720,000
To record application of research overhead.		
WIP Inventory—Lab Research (Job #1)	63,000	
WIP Inventory—Lab Research (Job #2)	22,500	
WIP Inventory—Lab Research (Job #3)	18,000	
Research Overhead—Lab Research		103,500
To record application of research overhead.		
6. Finished Goods Inventory*	567,000	
WIP Inventory—Offshore Operations		440,000
WIP Inventory—Lab Research		127,000
To record completion of Job #1.		
Cash	623,700	
Research Revenues**		623,700
To record sale of Job #1.		
Cost of Goods Sold	567,000	
Finished Goods Inventory		567,000
To record cost of sales for Job #1.		
7. Cost of Goods Sold	11,500	
Research Overhead—Lab Research	8,500	
Research Overhead—Offshore Operations		20,000
To assign underapplied and overapplied overhead to cost of goods sold.		

*Job #1 costs = $40,000 + $8,000 + $60,000 + $56,000 + $340,000 + $63,000 = $567,000

**Revenue, Job #1 = $567,000 × 1.10 = $623,700

b.

	Job #2	Job #3
Direct material—Offshore Operations	$ 28,000	$ 10,000
Direct labor—Offshore Operations	50,000	45,000
Research overhead—Offshore Operations	180,000	200,000
Direct material—Lab Research	6,000	4,500
Direct labor—Lab Research	20,000	16,000
Research overhead—Lab Research	22,500	18,000
Totals	$306,500	$293,500

QUESTIONS

1. When a company produces custom products to the specifications of its customers, why should it not aggregate costs across customer orders to determine the prices to be charged?
2. What production conditions are necessary for a company to use job order costing?
3. What is the alternative to the use of a job order costing system? In what type of production environment would this alternative costing system be found?
4. Identify the three valuation methods discussed in the chapter. What are the differences among these methods?
5. In a job order costing system, what is a job?
6. What are the three stages of production of a job? Of what use is cost information pertaining to completed jobs?
7. What are the principal documents used in a job order costing system and what are their purposes?
8. Why is the material requisition form an important document in a company's audit trail?
9. What is a job order cost sheet, and what information does it contain? How do job order cost sheets relate to control accounts for Work in Process, Finished Goods, and Cost of Goods Sold?
10. Of what use to management are job order cost sheets? Why do some job order cost sheets contain columns for both budgeted and actual costs?
11. "Because the costs of each job are included in the job order cost sheet, they do not need to be recorded in the general ledger." Is this statement true or false, and why?
12. Which document in a job order costing system would show the amount of overtime worked by a specific individual? Explain.
13. Is an actual overhead application rate better than a predetermined overhead rate? Why or why not?
14. What creates underapplied or overapplied overhead when applying overhead to jobs?
15. What is the principal difference in job order costing between service and manufacturing firms?
16. How is the cost of goods sold determined in a company that uses job order costing?
17. How are the advancement of technology and the development of new software affecting the accounting function in job order costing systems?
18. Many software companies produce custom programs for computerized accounting applications. Search the Internet and find two or more companies that make software for job order costing (job costing). Read the ads and descriptions of the job order costing software and identify five of the most important capabilities (or modules) that the software company offers. Write one

to two pages describing how these modules might be used in a company that custom manufactures robotic equipment used in manufacturing applications.

19. What differences exist between job order costing based on actual costs and job order costing based on standard costs? Why would a company use a standard cost job order system?

20. If a company produces a given type of product only one time, will standard costing be as useful as if the company continually produces the same type of product? Explain.

21. How does a firm use information on "variances" in a standard costing system to control costs?

22. How can the implementation of a job order costing system help improve managerial decision making?

EXERCISES

23. *(Classifying)* For each of the following firms, determine whether it is more likely to use job order or process costing. This firm

- **a.** does custom printing.
- **b.** manufactures paint.
- **c.** is involved in landscape architecture.
- **d.** is an automobile repair shop.
- **e.** provides public accounting services.
- **f.** manufactures hair spray and hand lotion.
- **g.** is a hospital.
- **h.** cans vegetables and fruits.
- **i.** designs custom software.
- **j.** provides property management services for a variety of real estate developments.

24. *(Journal entries)* Olson Inc. produces custom-made floor tiles. During June 2001, the following information was obtained relating to operations and production:

1. Direct material purchased on account, $85,000.
2. Direct material issued to jobs, $81,900.
3. Direct labor hours incurred, 1,700. All direct factory employees were paid $18 per hour.
4. Actual factory overhead costs incurred for the month totaled $41,100. This overhead consisted of $9,000 of supervisory salaries, $17,500 of depreciation charges, $3,600 of insurance, $6,250 of indirect material, and $4,750 of utilities. Salaries, insurance, and utilities were paid in cash, and indirect material was removed from the supplies account.
5. Overhead is applied to production at the rate of $25 per direct labor hour. The beginning balances of Raw Material Inventory and Work in Process Inventory were $4,150 and $11,150, respectively. The ending balance in Work in Process Inventory was $2,350.

- **a.** Prepare journal entries for the above transactions.
- **b.** Determine the balances in Raw Material Inventory and Work in Process Inventory at the end of the month.
- **c.** Determine the cost of the goods completed during June. If 5,000 similar units were completed, what was the cost per unit?
- **d.** What is the amount of underapplied or overapplied overhead at the end of June?

25. *(Journal entries; cost flows)* U Store It produces customized storage buildings that serve the midwest U.S. market. For February 2001, the company incurred the following costs:

Direct material purchased on account		$19,000
Direct material used for jobs		
Job #217	$11,200	
Job #218	1,800	
Other jobs	13,400	26,400
Direct labor costs for month		
Job #217	$ 2,600	
Job #218	3,500	
Other jobs	4,900	11,000
Actual overhead costs for February		18,900

The February beginning balance in Work in Process Inventory was $4,200, which consisted of $2,800 for Job #217 and $1,400 for Job #218. The February beginning balance in Direct Material Inventory was $12,300.

Actual overhead is applied to jobs on the basis of direct labor cost. Job #217 was completed and transferred to finished goods during February. It was then sold for cash at 140 percent of cost.

a. Prepare journal entries to record the above information.

b. Determine the February ending balance in Work in Process Inventory and the amount of the balance related to Job #218.

26. *(Cost flows)* Custom Landscapes began operations on March 1, 2001. Its Work in Process Inventory account on March 31 appeared as follows:

Work in Process Inventory

Direct material	554,400	Cost of completed jobs	??
Direct labor	384,000		
Applied overhead	345,600		

The company applies overhead on the basis of direct labor cost. Only one job was still in process on March 31. That job had $132,600 in direct material and $93,600 in direct labor cost assigned to it.

a. What was the predetermined overhead application rate?

b. How much cost was transferred out for jobs completed during March?

27. *(Normal versus actual costing)* For fiscal year 2001, Lazlow Metalworks estimated it would incur total overhead costs of $1,200,000 and work 40,000 machine hours. During January 2001, the company worked exclusively on one job, Job #1211. It incurred January costs as follows:

Direct material usage		$121,000
Direct labor (1,400 hours)		30,800
Manufacturing overhead:		
Rent	$11,200	
Utilities	15,200	
Insurance	32,100	
Labor	15,500	
Depreciation	23,700	
Maintenance	10,800	
Total OH		108,500

Machine hours worked in January: 3,400

a. Assuming the company uses an actual cost system, compute the January costs assigned to Job #1211.

b. Assuming the company uses a normal cost system, compute the January costs assigned to Job #1211.

c. What is the major factor driving the difference between your answers in parts (a) and (b)?

28. *(Cost flows)* Integrated Solutions manufactures hardware for local-area networks. The firm applies overhead to jobs at a rate of 120 percent of direct labor cost. On December 31, 2001, a flood destroyed many of the firm's computerized cost records. Only the following information for 2001 was available from the records:

Direct Material Inventory

Beg. bal.	6,150	
Purchases	?	?
	2,050	

Work in Process Inventory

Beg. bal.	14,000	
Direct mat.	?	?
Direct labor	45,000	
Overhead		
	12,000	

Finished Goods Inventory

Beg. bal.	22,500	
Goods completed	?	342,500
	21,000	

Cost of Goods Sold

?	

As the accountant of Integrated Solutions, you must find the following:

a. Cost of goods sold for the year.
b. Cost of goods completed during the year.
c. Cost of direct material used during the year.
d. Amount of applied factory overhead during the year.
e. Cost of direct material purchased during the year.

29. *(Departmental overhead rates)* Ashford Paving Company uses a predetermined overhead rate to apply overhead to jobs, and the company employs a job order costing system. Overhead is applied to jobs in the Mixing Department based on the number of machine hours used, whereas Paving Department overhead is applied on the basis of direct labor hours. In December 2000, the company estimated the following data for its two departments for 2001:

	Mixing Department	Paving Department
Direct labor hours	1,000	3,500
Machine hours	7,500	1,500
Budgeted overhead cost	$60,000	$98,000

a. Compute the predetermined overhead rate that should be used in each department of the Ashford Paving Company.
b. Job #116 was started and completed during March 2001. The job cost sheet shows the following information:

	Mixing Department	Paving Department
Direct material	$5,800	$700
Direct labor cost	$60	$525
Direct labor hours	12	60
Machine hours	80	22

c. Compute the overhead applied to Job #116 for each department and in total.
d. If the company had computed a companywide rate for overhead rather than departmental rates, do you feel that such a rate would be indicative of the actual overhead cost of each job? Explain.

30. *(Job cost and pricing)* Jason Hart is an attorney who employs a job order costing system related to his client engagements. Hart is currently working on a case for Janice Keene. During the first four months of 2001, Hart logged 85 hours on the Keene case.

In addition to direct hours spent by Hart, his secretary has worked 14 hours typing and copying 126 pages of documents related to the Keene case. Hart's secretary works 160 hours per month and is paid a salary of $1,800 per month. The average cost per copy is $0.04 for paper, toner, and machine rental. Telephone charges for long-distance calls on the case totaled $165.50. Last, Hart has estimated that total office overhead for rent, utilities, parking, and so on, amount to $7,200 per month and that, during a normal month, he is at the office 120 hours.

a. Hart feels that his time, at a minimum, is worth $40 per hour, and he wishes to cover all direct and allocated indirect costs related to a case. What minimum charge per hour (rounded to the nearest dollar) should Hart charge Keene? (*Hint:* Include office overhead.)

b. All the hours that Hart spends at the office are not necessarily billable hours. In addition, Hart did not take into consideration certain other expenses such as license fees, country club dues, automobile costs, and other miscellaneous expenses, when he determined the amount of overhead per month. Therefore, to cover nonbillable time as well as other costs, Hart feels that billing each client for direct costs plus allocated indirect costs plus 50 percent margin on his time and overhead is reasonable. What will Hart charge Keene in total for the time spent on her case?

31. *(Underapplied or overapplied overhead)* For 2001, Ainsworth Rafter Co. applied overhead to jobs using a predetermined overhead rate of $23.20 per machine hour. This rate was derived by dividing the company's total budgeted overhead of $556,800 by the 24,000 machine hours anticipated for the year.

At the end of 2001, the company's manufacturing overhead control account had debits totaling $562,600. Actual machine hours for the year totaled 24,900.

a. How much overhead should be debited to Work in Process Inventory for 2001?

b. Is overhead underapplied or overapplied and by how much?

c. Job #47 consumed 750 machine hours during 2001. How much overhead should be assigned to this job for the year?

d. Describe the disposition of the underapplied or overapplied overhead determined in part (b).

32. *(Assigning costs to jobs)* Westside Racing uses a job order costing system in which overhead is applied to jobs at a predetermined rate of $2.20 per direct labor dollar. During April 2001, the company spent $13,900 on direct labor related to Job #344. In addition, the company incurred direct material costs of $24,800 on this job during the month. Budgeted factory overhead for the company for the year was $660,000.

a. Give the journal entry to apply overhead to all jobs if April's total direct labor cost was $30,100.

b. How much overhead from part (a) was assigned to Job #344?

c. If Job #344 had a balance of $14,350 on April 1, what was the balance on April 30?

d. Demonstrate how the company arrived at the predetermined overhead rate. Include the amount of budgeted direct labor costs for the year in your answer.

33. *(Assigning costs to jobs, cost flows)* Martha's Interiors, an interior decorating firm, uses a job order costing system and applies overhead to jobs using a predetermined rate of 60 percent of direct labor cost. At the beginning of June

2002, Job #918 was the only job in process. Costs of Job #918 included direct material of $16,500, direct labor of $2,400, and applied overhead of $1,440. During June, the company began work on Jobs #919, #920, and #921 and purchased and issued $34,700 of direct material. Direct labor cost for the month totaled $12,600. Job #920 had not been completed at the end of June, and its direct material and direct labor charges were $6,700 and $1,300, respectively. All the other jobs were completed in June.

a. What was the total cost of Job #920 as of the end of June 2002?
b. What was the cost of goods manufactured for June 2002?
c. If actual overhead for June was $8,700, was the overhead underapplied or overapplied for the month? By how much?

34. *(Assigning costs to jobs)* Ace Show is an advertising consultant. Recently, he has been working with his accountant to develop a formal accounting system. His accountant has suggested the use of a job order costing system to simplify costing procedures. During September, Ace and his staff worked on jobs for the following companies:

	Angston Company	Westside Manufacturing	Randall Inc.
Direct material cost	$4,500	$8,100	$9,600
Direct labor cost	$1,800	$9,450	$20,250
Number of ads designed	5	10	15

Ace is able to trace direct material to each job because most of the cost associated with material is related to photography and duplicating. The accountant has told Joe that a reasonable charge for overhead, based on previous information, is $55 per direct labor hour. The normal labor cost per hour is $45.

a. Determine the total cost for each of the advertising accounts for the month.
b. Determine the cost per ad developed for each client.
c. Ace has been charging $4,500 per ad developed. What was his net income for the month, if actual overhead for the month was $40,000?
d. Do you have any suggestions for Ace about the way he bills his clients for developing ads?

35. *(Standard costing)* Corner Kopy, Inc., incurred the following direct material costs in November 2002 for high-volume routine print jobs:

Actual unit purchase price	$0.015 per sheet
Quantity purchased in November	480,000 sheets
Quantity used in November	480,000 sheets
Standard quantity allowed for good production	460,000 sheets
Standard unit price	$0.017 per sheet

Calculate the material price variance and the material quantity variance.

36. *(Standard costing)* Carolina Mfg. uses a standard cost system. The company experienced the following results related to direct labor in December 2002:

Actual hours worked	45,500
Actual direct labor rate	$9.25
Standard hours allowed for production	44,200
Standard direct labor rate	$9.75

a. Calculate the total actual payroll.
b. Determine the labor rate variance.
c. Determine the labor quantity variance.

37. *(Standard costing)* Gone To The Birds employs a job order costing system based on standard costs. For one of its products, a small teak-rimmed concrete bird bath (Product No. 17), the standard costs per unit are as follows:

Direct material	$10
Direct labor	18
Manufacturing overhead	15

a. Record the journal entry for the transfer of direct material into production for 800 units of Product No. 17.

b. Compute the total cost assigned to the 800 units of Product No. 17, and record the journal entry to recognize the completion of the 800 units.

c. Record the journal entries associated with the sale of the 800 units of Product No. 17 for $44,300.

38. *(Cost control)* Baltimore Fabricated Steel Products Company produces a variety of steel drums that are used as storage containers for various chemical products. One of the products the firm produces is a 55-gallon drum. In the past year, the company produced this drum on four separate occasions for four different customers. Some financial details of each of the four orders follow.

Date	Job No.	Quantity	Bid Price	Budgeted Cost	Actual Cost
Jan. 17	2118	30,000	$150,000	$120,000	$145,000
Mar. 13	2789	25,000	125,000	100,000	122,000
Oct. 20	4300	40,000	200,000	160,000	193,000
Dec. 3	4990	35,000	175,000	140,000	174,000

Baltimore Fabricated Steel Products Company uses a job order costing system and obtains jobs based on competitive bidding. For each project, a budget is developed. As the controller of the company, write a memo to company management describing any problems that you perceive in the data presented and steps to be taken to eliminate the recurrence of these problems.

39. *(Production and marketing environment) When it comes to tortillas, Americans and Mexicans have distinctly different tastes. Americans are content to purchase mass-produced, prepackaged tortillas from their local grocery stores. Regional and national brands dominate sales. In Mexico, more than 95 percent of all tortillas are sold in little shops licensed by the government. These outlets, many grinding tortillas on hand-powered conveyor belts, are virtual monopolies in their neighborhoods, with a captive market that so far has resisted modern sales efforts.*

Assume that you are involved in developing a strategy for your employer, a U.S. food company, to produce tortillas. You are considering competing in both the United States and Mexico. Write a brief report recommending how your company should produce and market tortillas in each country. Also, describe the product costing system that you would recommend for each country.

SOURCE: Adapted from Joel Millman, "Mexican Tortilla Firms Stage U.S. Bake-Off," *The Wall Street Journal* (May 10, 1996), p. A6.

40. *(Cost manipulation) Excel Communications is a direct sales marketer of long-distance phone services. The company earns revenues by selling long-distance services to new subscribers. The company is preparing to "go public" through an initial public offering (IPO) of its stock. As with any IPO, the trick for an investment analyst is to determine the value of the stock.*

One of the controversial valuation issues for Excel is how to treat the costs the firm incurs to obtain subscribers. Excel defers a large portion of the costs it incurs to sign up new subscribers—$85 million in the first two months of 1996 alone. Excel amortizes these costs and revenue over 12 months as a way to "appropriately match revenues and expenses."

SOURCE: Adapted from Jeff D. Opdyke, "Excel's Accounting Methods Raise Red Flags Among IPO Watchers," *The Wall Street Journal* (May 8, 1996), p. T2.

Put yourself into the position of a stock analyst. Write a report for your investor clientele explaining the effect of Excel's accounting methods on its level of reported net income. Be sure to include a discussion of whether this accounting method provides a fair picture of the firm's "economic earnings."

41. *(Cost management) A focus on the customer may lead companies to join forces with erstwhile competitors. "If a customer is looking for a solution to a business problem, then it's quite common for us to work together with a competitor to find that exact solution," says Jim Mavel, CEO and president of Scan-Optics, Inc., a $57 million Manchester, Connecticut, firm that manufactures and supports high-performance scanners, develops software, and offers professional services. "We also sometimes bid against that firm for other projects at the same time."*

http://www.scsinc.com

In some cases, as part of a prearranged deal, Scan-Optics will win a contract and subcontract with a competitor that vied for, but lost, that same deal. In rarer cases, Scan-Optics incorporates a competitor's products or services into a bid for work the competitor is also seeking.

In what may be a glimpse of the complicated business relationships of the future, a company could find itself serving as competitor, supplier, customer, and partner to another firm on an given day, says Barry Nalebuff, Yale University School of Management professor.

In today's complex, intertwined economy, the business-as-war, winner-take-all mindset doesn't cut it, says Nalebuff. Better to get a piece of the pie, he says, than no portion at all.

SOURCE: Harvey Meyer, "My Enemy, My Friend," *Journal of Business Strategy* (Sept.–Oct. 1998), p. 42. © Faulkner & Gray, reprinted with permission.

a. How does the contemporary use of joint ventures and other cooperative arrangements with other firms add complexity to the accounting function for a business managing its costs?

b. Why is it necessary for managers and accountants not to look only inside the firm to manage costs, but to also look outside the firm?

PROBLEMS

42. *(Journal entries)* Sunny Day Awning Company installs awnings on residential and commercial structures. The company had the following transactions for February 2002:

- Purchased $440,000 of building (raw) material on account.
- Issued $370,000 of building (direct) material to jobs.
- Issued $60,000 of building (indirect) material for use on jobs.
- Accrued wages payable of $594,000, of which $474,000 could be traced directly to particular jobs.
- Applied overhead to jobs on the basis of 60 percent of direct labor cost.
- Completed jobs costing $666,000. For these jobs, revenues of $824,000 were collected.

Make all appropriate journal entries for the above transactions. (*Hint:* There is no finished goods inventory.)

43. *(Journal entries)* Canton Refrigeration uses a job order costing system based on actual costs. The following transactions relate to a single period in which the beginning Direct Material Inventory was $10,000, Work in Process Inventory was $25,000, and Finished Goods Inventory was $21,000.

- Direct material purchases on account were $70,000.
- Direct labor cost for the period totaled $75,500 for 8,000 direct labor hours.
- Actual overhead costs were $72,000.

- Actual overhead is applied to production based on direct labor hours.
- The ending inventory of Direct Material Inventory was $3,000.
- The ending inventory of Work in Process Inventory was $10,500.
- Of the goods finished during the period, goods costing $95,000 were sold for $133,000.

Prepare all journal entries for the above transactions and determine the ending balance in Finished Goods Inventory.

44. *(Journal entries, assigning costs to jobs)* Alpha Mechanical uses a job order costing system. On September 1, 2002, the company had the following account balances:

Raw Material Inventory	$ 332,400
Work in Process Inventory	1,056,300
Cost of Goods Sold	4,732,000

Work in Process Inventory is the control account for the job cost subsidiary ledger. On September 1, the three accounts in the job cost ledger had the following balances:

Job #75	$593,200
Job #78	316,800
Job #82	146,300

The following transactions occurred during September:

Sept. 1 Purchased $940,000 of raw material on account.

4 Issued $950,000 of raw material as follows: Job #75, $43,800; Job #78, $227,800; Job #82, $396,600; Job #86, $256,200; indirect material, $25,600.

15 Prepared and paid the factory payroll for Sept. 1–15 in the amount of $368,500. Analysis of the payroll for Sept. 1–15 reveals the following information as to where labor effort was devoted:

Job #75	4,430 hours	$ 44,300
Job #78	11,160 hours	111,600
Job #82	12,150 hours	121,500
Job #86	5,540 hours	55,400
Indirect wages		35,700

16 Alpha Mechanical applies manufacturing overhead to jobs at a rate of $7.50 per direct labor hour each time the payroll is made.

16 Job #75 was completed and accepted by the customer and billed at a selling price of cost plus 25 percent.

20 Paid the following monthly factory bills: utilities, $17,200; rent, $38,300; and accounts payable (accrued in August), $91,000.

24 Purchased raw material on account, $412,000.

25 Issued raw material as follows: Job #78, $74,400; Job #82, $108,300; Job #86, $192,500; and indirect material, $27,200.

30 Recorded additional factory overhead costs as follows: depreciation, $206,500; expired prepaid insurance, $35,100; and accrued taxes and licenses, $13,000.

30 Recorded the gross salaries and wages for the factory payroll for Sept. 16–30 of $357,200. Analysis of the payroll follows:

Job #78	8,840 hours	$ 88,400
Job #82	11,650 hours	116,500
Job #86	11,980 hours	119,800
Indirect wages		32,500

30 Applied overhead for the second half of the month to jobs.

a. Prepare journal entries for the transactions for September 2002.
b. Use T-accounts to post the information from the journal entries in part (a) to the job cost subsidiary accounts and to general ledger accounts.
c. Reconcile the September 30 balances in the subsidiary ledger with the Work in Process Inventory account in the general ledger.
d. Determine the amount of underapplied or overapplied overhead for September.

45. *(Journal entries, cost flows)* Specialty Components began 2002 with three jobs in process:

	TYPE OF COST			
Job No.	**Direct Material**	**Direct Labor**	**Overhead**	**Total**
247	$ 77,200	$ 91,400	$ 34,732	$ 203,332
251	176,600	209,800	79,724	466,124
253	145,400	169,600	64,448	379,448
Totals	$399,200	$470,800	$178,904	$1,048,904

During 2002, the following transactions occurred:

1. The firm purchased and paid for $532,000 of raw material.
2. Factory payroll records revealed the following:

- Indirect labor incurred was $54,000.
- Direct labor incurred was $602,800 and was associated with the jobs as follows:

Job No.	Direct Labor Cost
247	$ 17,400
251	8,800
253	21,000
254	136,600
255	145,000
256	94,600
257	179,400

3. Material requisition forms issued during the year revealed the following:

- Indirect material issued totaled $76,000.
- Direct material issued totaled $468,400 and was associated with jobs as follows:

Job No.	Direct Material Cost
247	$ 14,400
251	6,200
253	16,800
254	103,200
255	119,800
256	72,800
257	135,200

4. Overhead is applied to jobs on the basis of direct labor cost. Management budgeted overhead of $240,000 and total direct labor cost of $600,000 for 2002. Actual total factory overhead costs (including indirect labor and indirect material) for the year were $244,400.
5. Jobs #247 through #255 were completed and delivered to customers, C.O.D. The revenue on these jobs was $2,264,774.

a. Prepare journal entries for all of the above events.
b. Determine ending balances for jobs still in process.
c. Determine cost of jobs completed, adjusted for underapplied or overapplied overhead.

46. *(Simple inventory calculation)* Production data for the first week in November 2002 for Illinois Lighting were as follows:

WORK IN PROCESS INVENTORY

	Job No.	Material	Labor	Machine Time (Overhead)
Nov. 1	411	$950	18 hours	25 hours
1	412	620	5 hours	15 hours
7	417	310	4 hours	8 hours

Finished Goods Inventory, Nov. 1: $11,900
Finished Goods Inventory, Nov. 7: $ 0

MATERIAL RECORDS

	Inv. 11/1	Purchases	Issuances	Inv. 11/7
Aluminum	$4,150	$49,150	$29,350	$?
Steel	6,400	13,250	17,100	$?
Other	2,900	11,775	12,950	$?

Direct labor hours worked: 340. Labor cost is $15 per direct labor hour. Machine hours worked: 600; Job #411, 175 hours; Job #412, 240 hours; and Job #417, 185 hours.

Overhead for first week in November:	
Depreciation	$ 4,500
Supervisor salaries	7,200
Indirect labor	4,175
Insurance	1,400
Utilities	1,125
Total	$18,400

Overhead is charged to production at a rate of $30 per machine hour. Underapplied or overapplied overhead is treated as an adjustment to Cost of Goods Sold at year-end. (All company jobs are consecutively numbered, and all work not in ending Finished Goods Inventory has been completed and sold.)

a. Calculate the value of beginning Work in Process Inventory.

b. What is the value at the end of November of (1) the three material accounts, (2) Work in Process Inventory, and (3) Cost of Goods Sold?

47. *(Job cost sheet analysis)* As a candidate for a cost accounting position with Global Construction, you have been asked to take a quiz to demonstrate your knowledge of job order costing. Global's job order costing system is based on normal costs and overhead is applied based on direct labor cost. The following records pertaining to May have been provided to you:

Job No.	Direct Material	Direct Labor	Applied Overhead	Total Cost
167	$ 17,703	$ 6,920	$ 7,960	$ 32,583
169	54,936	7,240	8,328	70,504
170	1,218	2,000	2,300	5,518
171	154,215	28,500	43,700	226,415
172	28,845	2,200	2,532	33,577

To explain the missing job number, you are informed that Job #168 had been completed in April. You are also told that Job #167 was the only job in process at the beginning of May. At that time, the job had been assigned $12,900 for direct material and $3,600 for direct labor. At the end of May, Job #171 had not been completed; all others had. You are to provide answers to the following questions:

a. What is the predetermined overhead rate used by Global Construction?
b. What was the total cost of beginning Work in Process Inventory?
c. What were total direct manufacturing costs incurred for May?
d. What was cost of goods manufactured for May?

48. *(Departmental rates)* The Houston Custom Tile Corporation has two departments: Mixing and Drying. All jobs go through each department, and the company uses a job order costing system. The company applies overhead to jobs based on labor hours in Mixing and on machine hours in Drying. In December 2001, corporate management estimated the following production data for 2002 in setting its predetermined overhead rates:

	Mixing	Drying
Machine hours	7,200	104,000
Direct labor hours	88,000	12,400
Departmental overhead	$374,000	$494,000

Two jobs completed during 2002 were #2296 and #2297. The job order cost sheets showed the following information about these jobs:

	Job #2296	Job #2297
Direct material cost	$4,875	$6,300
Direct labor hours—Mixing	425	510
Machine hours—Mixing	40	45
Direct labor hours—Drying	20	23
Machine hours—Drying	110	125

Direct labor workers are paid $9 per hour in the Mixing Department and $22 per hour in Drying.

a. Compute the predetermined overhead rates used in Mixing and Drying for 2002.
b. Compute the direct labor cost associated with each job for both departments.
c. Compute the amount of overhead assigned to each job in each department.
d. Determine the total cost of Jobs #2296 and #2297.
e. Actual data for 2002 for each department follow. What is the amount of underapplied or overapplied overhead for each department for the year ended December 31, 2002?

	Mixing	Drying
Machine hours	7,400	106,800
Direct labor hours	86,400	12,600
Overhead	$362,000	$512,000

49. *(Comprehensive)* In May 2002, Aztec Construction Company was the successful bidder on a contract to build a pedestrian overpass in Flagstaff, Arizona. The firm utilizes a job order costing system, and this job was assigned Job #515. The contract price for the overpass was $450,000. The owners of Aztec Construction agreed to a completion date of December 15, 2002, for the contract. The firm's engineering and cost accounting departments estimated the following costs for completion of the overpass: $120,000 for direct material, $135,000 for direct labor, and $81,000 for overhead.

The firm began work on the overpass in August. During August, direct material cost assigned to Job #515 was $30,900 and direct labor cost associated with Job #515 was $47,520. The firm uses a predetermined overhead rate of 60 percent of direct labor cost. Aztec Construction also worked on several other jobs during August and incurred the following costs:

Direct labor (including Job #515)	$252,000
Indirect labor	27,900
Administrative salaries and wages	19,800
Depreciation on construction equipment	13,200
Depreciation on office equipment	3,900
Client entertainment (on accounts payable)	5,550
Advertising for firm (paid in cash)	3,300
Indirect material (from supplies inventory)	9,300
Miscellaneous expenses (design related; to be paid in the following month)	5,100
Accrued utilities (for office, $900; for construction, $2,700)	3,600

During August, Aztec Construction completed several jobs that had been in process before the beginning of the month. These completed jobs generated $312,000 of revenues for the company. The related job cost sheets showed costs associated with those jobs of $214,500. At the beginning of August, Aztec Construction had Work in Process Inventory of $135,900.

a. Prepare a job order cost sheet for Job #515, including all job details, and post the appropriate cost information for August.

b. Prepare journal entries for the above information.

c. Prepare a Schedule of Cost of Goods Manufactured for August for Aztec Construction Company.

d. Assuming the company pays income tax at a 40 percent rate, prepare an income statement for August.

50. *(Comprehensive)* Enforcer Inc. designs and manufactures perimeter fencing for large retail and commercial buildings. Each job goes through three stages: design, production, and installation. Three jobs were started and completed during the first week of May 2002. There were no jobs in process at the end of April 2002. Information for the three departments for the first week in May follows:

	DEPARTMENT		
Job #2019	**Design**	**Production**	**Installation**
Direct labor hours	100	NA	70
Machine hours	NA	90	NA
Direct labor cost	$10,200	$ 4,250	$1,260
Direct material	$ 1,200	$14,550	$1,300
Job #2020	**Design**	**Production**	**Installation**
Direct labor hours	85	NA	80
Machine hours	NA	300	NA
Direct labor cost	$8,670	$ 7,450	$1,440
Direct material	$1,025	$33,600	$4,600
Job #2021	**Design**	**Production**	**Installation**
Direct labor hours	90	NA	410
Machine hours	NA	120	NA
Direct labor cost	$9,180	$ 2,950	$1,900
Direct material	$2,200	$29,000	$1,300

Overhead is applied using departmental rates. Design and Installation use direct labor cost as the base, with rates of 40 and 90 percent, respectively. Production uses machine hours as the base, with a rate of $15 per hour.

Actual overhead in the Design Department for the month was $12,200. Actual overhead costs for the Production and Installation Departments were $7,200 and $3,850, respectively.

a. Determine the overhead to be applied to each job. By how much is the overhead underapplied or overapplied in each department? For the company?

b. Assume no journal entries have been made to Work in Process Inventory. Make all necessary entries to both the subsidiary ledger and general ledger accounts.

c. Calculate the total cost for each job.

51. *(Standard costing)* One of the products made by Factory Logistics is a robotic conveyor system. A single model (Model No. 89) accounts for approximately 60 percent of the company's annual sales. Because the company has produced and expects to continue to produce a significant quantity of this model, the company uses a standard costing system to account for Model No. 89 production costs. The company has a separate plant that is strictly dedicated to Model No. 89 production. The standard costs to produce a single unit follow:

Direct material (7,000 pounds)	$14,000
Direct labor 430 hours at $20.00 per hour	8,600
Overhead	19,000
Total standard cost	$41,600

For the 200 units of Model No. 89 produced in 2002, the actual costs were

Direct material (1,500,000 pounds)	$2,900,000
Direct labor (89,200 hours)	1,739,400
Overhead	3,700,000
Total actual cost	$8,339,400

a. Compute a separate variance between actual and standard cost for direct material, direct labor, and manufacturing overhead for the Model No. 89 units produced in 2002.

b. Is the direct material variance found in part (a) driven primarily by the price per pound difference between standard and actual or the quantity difference between standard and actual? Explain.

52. *(Standard costing)* Trailer Solutions uses a job order costing system. During July 2002, the company worked on two production runs of the same product, a trailer hitch component. These units were included in Jobs #918 and #2002. Job #918 consisted of 1,200 units of the product, and Job #2002 contained 2,000 units. The hitch components are made from 1/2" sheet metal. Because the trailer hitch component is a product that is routinely produced for one of Trailer Solution's long-term customers, standard costs have been developed for its production. The standard cost of material for each unit is $4.50; each unit contains six pounds of material. The standard direct labor time per unit is six minutes for workers earning a rate of $20 per hour. The actual costs recorded for each job were as follows:

	Direct Material	Direct Labor
Job #918	(7,500 pounds) $5,250	(130 hours) $2,470
Job #2002	(11,800 pounds) 9,440	(230 hours) 4,255

a. What is the standard cost of each trailer hitch component?

b. What was the total standard cost assigned to each of the jobs?

c. Compute the variances for direct material and for direct labor for each job.

d. Why should variances be computed separately for each job rather than for the aggregate annual trailer hitch component production?

CASES

53. *(Comprehensive; job cost sheet)* The Big Plains Construction Company builds bridges. For the months of October and November 2001, the firm worked exclusively on a bridge spanning the Niobrara River in northern Nebraska. The firm is organized into two departments. The Precast Department builds structural elements of the bridges in temporary plants located near the construction sites. The Construction Department operates at the bridge site and assembles the precast structural elements. Estimated costs for the Niobrara River Bridge for the Precast Department were $150,000 for direct labor, $310,500 for direct material, and $110,000 for overhead. For the Construction Department, estimated costs for the Niobrara River Bridge were $160,000 for direct labor, $50,000 for direct material, and $160,000 for overhead. Overhead is applied on the last day of each month. Overhead application rates for the Precast and Construction Departments are $18 per machine hour and 100 percent of direct labor cost, respectively.

TRANSACTIONS FOR OCTOBER

Oct. 1	$150,000 of material was purchased (on account) for the Precast Department to begin building structural elements. All of the material issued to production, $130,000, was considered direct.
5	Utilities were installed at the bridge site at a total cost of $15,000.
8	Rent was paid for the temporary construction site housing the Precast Department, $4,000.
15	Bridge support pillars were completed by the Precast Department and transferred to the construction site.
20	$30,000 of machine rental expense was incurred by the Construction Department for clearing the bridge site and digging foundations for bridge supports.
24	Additional material costing $285,000 was purchased on account.
31	The company paid the following bills for the Precast Department: utilities, $7,000; direct labor, $45,000; insurance, $6,220; and supervision and other indirect labor costs, $7,900. Departmental depreciation was recorded, $15,200. The company also paid bills for the Construction Department: utilities, $2,300; direct labor,$16,300; indirect labor, $5,700; and insurance, $1,900. Departmental depreciation was recorded on equipment, $8,750.
31	A check was issued to pay for the material purchased on October 1 and October 24.
31	Overhead was applied to production in each department; 2,000 machine hours were worked in the Precast Department in October.

TRANSACTIONS FOR NOVEMBER

Nov. 1	Additional structural elements were transferred from the Precast Department to the construction site. The Construction Department incurred a cash cost of $5,000 to rent a crane.
4	$200,000 of material was issued to the Precast Department. Of this amount, $165,000 was considered direct.
8	Rent of $4,000 was paid in cash for the temporary site occupied by the Precast Department.
15	$85,000 of material was issued to the Construction Department. Of this amount, $40,000 was considered direct.
18	Additional structural elements were transferred from the Precast Department to the construction site.
24	The final batch of structural elements was transferred from the Precast Department to the construction site.
29	The bridge was completed.
30	The company paid final bills for the month in the Precast Department: utilities $15,000; direct labor, $115,000; insurance, $9,350; and supervision and other indirect labor costs, $14,500. Depreciation was recorded, $15,200. The company also paid bills for the Construction Department: utilities, $4,900; direct labor, $134,300; indirect labor, $15,200; and insurance, $5,400. Depreciation was recorded on equipment, $18,350.
30	Overhead was applied in each department. The Precast Department recorded 3,950 machine hours in November.
30	The company billed the state of Nebraska for the completed bridge at the contract price of $1,550,000.

a. Prepare all necessary journal entries for the preceding transactions. For purposes of this problem, it is not necessary to transfer direct material and direct labor from one department into the other.

b. Post all entries to T-accounts.

c. Prepare a job order cost sheet, which includes estimated costs, for the construction of the bridge.

54. *(Comprehensive)* Young Stuff is a manufacturer of furnishings for infants and children. The company uses a job order cost system. Young Stuff's Work in Process Inventory on April 30, 2002, consisted of the following jobs:

Job No.	Items	Units	Accumulated Cost
CBS102	Cribs	20,000	$ 900,000
PLP086	Playpens	15,000	420,000
DRS114	Dressers	25,000	1,570,000

The company's finished goods inventory, carried on a FIFO basis, consists of five items:

Item	Quantity and Unit Cost	Total Cost
Cribs	7,500 units @ $ 64	$ 480,000
Strollers	13,000 units @ $ 23	299,000
Carriages	11,200 units @ $102	1,142,400
Dressers	21,000 units @ $ 55	1,155,000
Playpens	19,400 units @ $ 35	679,000
		$3,755,400

Young Stuff applies factory overhead on the basis of direct labor hours. The company's factory overhead budget for the year ending May 31, 2002, totals $4,500,000, and the company plans to expend 600,000 direct labor hours during this period. Through the first 11 months of the year, a total of 555,000 direct labor hours were worked, and total factory overhead amounted to $4,273,500.

At the end of April, the balance in Young Stuff's Material Inventory account, which includes both raw material and purchased parts, was $668,000. Additions to and requisitions from the material inventory during May included the following:

	Raw Material	Parts Purchased
Additions	$242,000	$396,000
Requisitions:		
Job #CBS102	51,000	104,000
Job #PLP086	3,000	10,800
Job #DRS114	124,000	87,000
Job #STR077 (10,000 strollers)	62,000	81,000
Job #CRG098 (5,000 carriages)	65,000	187,000

During May, Young Stuff's factory payroll consisted of the following:

Job No.	Hours	Cost
CBS102	12,000	$122,400
PLP086	4,400	43,200
DRS114	19,500	200,500
STR077	3,500	30,000
CRG098	14,000	138,000
Indirect	3,000	29,400
Supervision		57,600
		$621,100

The jobs that were completed in and the unit sales for May follow:

Job No.	Items	Quantity Completed
CBS102	Cribs	20,000
PLP086	Playpens	15,000
STR077	Strollers	10,000
CRG098	Carriages	5,000

Items	Quantity Shipped
Cribs	17,500
Playpens	21,000
Strollers	14,000
Dressers	18,000
Carriages	6,000

a. Describe when it is appropriate for a company to use a job order costing system.

b. Calculate the dollar balance in Young Stuff's Work in Process Inventory account as of May 31, 2002.

c. Calculate the dollar amount related to the playpens in Young Stuff's Finished Goods Inventory as of May 31, 2002.

d. Explain the treatment of underapplied or overapplied overhead when using a job order costing system. *(CMA adapted)*

55. *(Missing amounts)* Downstream Manufacturing Company realized too late that it had made a mistake locating its controller's office and its electronic data processing system in the basement. Because of the spring thaw, the Mississippi River overflowed on May 2 and flooded the company's basement. Electronic data storage was beyond retrieval, and the company had not provided off-site storage of data. Some of the paper printouts were located but were badly faded and only partially legible. On May 3, when the river subsided, company accountants were able to assemble the following factory-related data from the debris and from discussions with various knowledgeable personnel. Data about the following accounts were found:

- Raw Material (includes indirect material) Inventory: Balance April 1 was $4,800.
- Work in Process Inventory: Balance April 1 was $7,700.
- Finished Goods Inventory: Balance April 30 was $6,600.
- Total company payroll cost for April was $29,200.
- Accounts payable balance April 30 was $18,000.
- Indirect material used in April cost $5,800.
- Other nonmaterial and nonlabor overhead items for April totaled $2,500.

Payroll records, kept at an across-town service center that processes the company's payroll, showed that April's direct labor amounted to $18,200 and represented 4,400 labor hours. Indirect factory labor amounted to $5,400 in April.

The president's office had a file copy of the production budget for the current year. It revealed that the predetermined manufacturing overhead application rate is based on planned annual direct labor hours of 50,400 and expected factory overhead of $151,200.

Discussion with the factory superintendent indicated that only two jobs remained unfinished on April 30. Fortunately, the superintendent also had copies of the job cost sheets that showed a combined total of $2,400 of direct material and $4,500 of direct labor. The direct labor hours on these jobs totaled 1,072. Both of these jobs had been started during the current period.

A badly faded copy of April's Cost of Goods Manufactured and Sold schedule showed cost of goods manufactured was $48,000, and the April 1 Finished Goods Inventory was $8,400.

The treasurer's office files copies of paid invoices chronologically. All invoices are for raw material purchased on account. Examination of these files revealed that unpaid invoices on April 1 amounted to $6,100; $28,000 of purchases had been made during April; and $18,000 of unpaid invoices existed on April 30.

a. Calculate the cost of direct material used in April.
b. Calculate the cost of raw material issued in April.
c. Calculate the April 30 balance of Raw Material Inventory.
d. Determine the amount of underapplied or overapplied overhead for April.
e. What is the Cost of Goods Sold for April?

REALITY CHECK

56. One of the main points of using a job order costing system is to achieve profitability by charging a price for each job that is proportionate to the related costs. The fundamental underlying concept is that the buyer of the product should be charged a price that exceeds all of the costs related to the job contract—thus the price reflects the cost.

However, there are settings in which the price charged to the consumer does not reflect the costs incurred by the vendor to serve that customer. This is the situation in a recent case heard by the U.S. Supreme Court. The case involves the University of Wisconsin, which charges all students a user fee, then redistributes these fees to student organizations.

The purpose of collecting the fee is to ensure that money is available to support diversity of thought and speech in student organizations. Even unpopular causes were supported so that the students would hear many voices. In total, the fee subsidized about 125 student groups. However, a group of students filed suit claiming that students should not be required to fund causes that are inconsistent with their personal beliefs.

a. In your opinion, how would diversity of thought be affected if a student were allowed to select the organizations that would receive the student's user fee (e.g., as with dues)?
b. Is the University of Wisconsin treating its students ethically by charging them to support student organizations that conflict with students' personal beliefs?

57. In 1995, British steelmaker Ispat purchased Kazakhstan's largest steel plant:

http://www.inland.com

Little known outside the steel world, Ispat has in recent months assumed a new visibility—as an example of Western companies' problems in the former Soviet Union. Hundreds of its employees come to work drunk; its biggest customer is broke; and Chechen gunmen have been spotted prowling the plant's perimeter, threatening suppliers and hitting customers up for bribes. Despite all their experience in the developing world, the Ispat officials at Karmet "are up against problems we never dreamed about," says Lakshmi Mittal, the company's chairman.

Since arriving, Ispat has ladled out $11 million for back pay, $31 million to repay debts to raw material suppliers, and $75 million to begin rebuilding the crumbling plant. Overall, the company has pledged to pay $450 million over the next four years, plus an additional $550 million for new technology.

Because the company is the first Karmet owner in years to have any money, it was quickly viewed as a soft target. The local union is seeking a 75% increase in workers' pay, and a Temirtau child-care center is hitting up plant managers for more money.

Soon after Ispat arrived, a man claiming to represent a society for the blind asked the company for donations. If Ispat would donate steel, he said, the society could resell it and raise money. After the company agreed, 68 other societies for the blind turned up. "Karmet in 1995 was not a steel plant. It was looked upon more as a social institution," says Arabinda Tripathy, Ispat's personnel director.

So, Ispat embarked on an ambitious goal—to teach its workers about capitalism. Senior managers get a weeklong course, beginning with the basics of how a market economy works and progressing to discuss how profits are calculated.

SOURCE: Kyle Pope, "Saga on the Steppes: A Steelmaker Built Up By Buying Cheap Mills Finally Meets Its Match," *The Wall Street Journal* (May 2, 1996), pp. A1, A6. Reprinted by permission of *The Wall Street Journal,* © 1996 Dow Jones & Company, Inc. All rights reserved worldwide. Permission conveyed through the Copyright Clearance Center.

a. How would the quality considerations in the Temirtau, Kazakhstan, steel plant be fundamentally different from quality considerations in a more developed nation?

b. Should the ethical standards of conduct be different for managers in the Temirtau plant than in other plants operated by Ispat? Explain.

58. From William J. Fife Jr., chairman of Giddings & Lewis Inc.:

http://www.giddings.com

"The labor content of a product today is probably less than 15%. So, I don't care how much I cut [direct] labor, it's not going to get to the bottom line. We have to get at overhead costs."

Today, U.S. firms have some of the highest overhead burdens of all global companies. Much of the higher overhead cost is associated with the tiered management structures prevalent in the United States. The layers of white-collar managers create a tremendous cost disadvantage. The redundant layers of management are associated with the traditional notion that employees need to be supervised to maintain productivity and control quality.

SOURCE: Adapted from Thane Peterson, "Can Corporate America Get Out From Under Its Overhead?" *Business Week* (May 18, 1992), p. 102.

a. With appropriate training of blue-collar workers in American industry, how can layers of white-collar managers be eliminated and productivity and quality increased?

b. How does the traditionally hostile relationship between white-collar managers and blue-collar workers place American firms at a disadvantage in the global market relative to countries that have traditionally fostered cooperation among all employees?

59. *Cyclemakers Group of Washdyke near Timaru (New Zealand) is lifting its profile locally and overseas in the cycling world through its custom-built bike service.*

Although the prospect of sitting astride a 10-speed may not be everyone's idea of relaxation, at least now they can dictate their choice of seat—or for that matter, their choice of frame, wheels, gears, and the other bits and pieces that Cyclemakers imports from the major branded overseas manufacturers. The company has built simulators so people can try out a range of configurations to see what measurements suit. They can then choose from an enormous range of components of varying sizes and prices including the color and style of the paint job.

"We're doing it at a price not much greater than an off-the-peg production bike because we use a computerised system. The idea has proven very successful here and in Australia. It's not a large percentage of business yet but has provided a lot at the top end," says Bryan Jackson, managing director.

SOURCE: "Boosting Bike Sales," *NZ Business* (November 1992), p. 33. NZ Business is published by Profile Publishing Ltd., P.O. Box 5544, Auckland, New Zealand; www.profile.co.nz.

a. Why would Cyclemakers be able to produce custom-made bicycles for almost the same cost as mass-produced ones?

b. Would you expect the quality of the custom-produced bicycles to be higher or lower than the mass-produced ones? Discuss the rationale for your answer.

c. Why would the custom-made bicycles "provide a lot at the top end" (show a high profit margin)?

60. Two types of contracts are commonly used when private firms contract to provide services to governmental agencies: cost-plus and fixed-price contracts. The cost-plus contract allows the contracting firm to recover the costs associated with providing the product or service plus a reasonable profit. The fixed-price contract provides for a fixed payment to the contractor. When a fixed-price contract is used, the contractor's profits will be based on its ability to control costs relative to the price received.

http://www.atk.com

A *Wall Street Journal* article announced that, in May 1996, Alliant Techsystems Inc. was being investigated for the way that it accounted for its government contracts. Specifically, the company was being investigated because of suspicions that costs related to fixed-price government contracts were being shifted to cost-plus government contracts.

SOURCE: Andy Pasztor, "Alliant Unit Is Said to Face Criminal Probe," *The Wall Street Journal* (May 3, 1996), pp. A3, A6.

a. Why would a company that conducts work under both cost-plus and fixed-price contracts have an incentive to shift costs from the fixed-price to the cost-plus contracts?

b. From an ethical perspective, do you feel such cost shifting is ever justified? Explain.

CHAPTER

6

Process Costing

LEARNING OBJECTIVES

After completing this chapter, you should be able to answer the following questions:

1
How is process costing different from job order costing?

2
Why are equivalent units of production used in process costing?

3
How are equivalent units of production determined using the weighted average and FIFO methods of process costing?

4
How are unit costs and inventory values determined using the weighted average and FIFO methods of process costing?

5
How can standard costs be used in a process costing system?

6
Why would a company use a hybrid costing system?

7
(Appendix) What alternative methods can be used to calculate equivalent units of production?

INTRODUCING

Lumina Candles & Art

http://www.borsheimarts.com/lumina/about.htm

Kelly Borsheim started Lumina Candles & Art, a home-based business located in Cedar Creek, Texas, in the early 1990s. While working for a photo lab in college in the 1980s, Kelly had supplemented her income by selling fine art photography and shooting occasional wedding jobs. This led to an abiding interest in art, and she would later attend art school.

A friend, Jamshid, gave Kelly a beeswax honeycomb candle that she still has. Kelly decided to find out what it took to make one. She started making and selling only a few natural candles, later adding colors a few at a time to test the market.

Even though she was still working 60 hours a week at the photo lab, Kelly continued to develop the candle and art business. She left the photo industry in 1995 and, in the following year, another friend, Mark, showed Kelly how the Internet worked. He also gave her a basic HTML lesson along with a list of sources for teaching herself how to do more. In May 1996, she launched her Web site. Although she still sells beeswax candles via local shows, she now relies mainly on the Internet for customers.

In making candles, Lumina uses two different processes. One process is used to make hand-rolled 100 percent beeswax candles and the other process is used to make solid beeswax candles, natural or scented, in molds. Either process produces a variety of shapes, sizes, and colors of candles.

The company must account for the direct material, direct labor, and manufacturing overhead for each production run of candles. The hand-rolled candle process is more labor intensive. Direct material includes beeswax, nontoxic and odorless aniline dyes, essential oils, and wicks.

SOURCE: Lumina Candles & Art Web site: http://www.borsheimarts.com/lumina/about.htm

At Lumina Candles & Art (Lumina), the primary products are manufactured in a continuous flow process, and each unit of output is identical to each other unit. Because Lumina production differs so dramatically from the products made by a company tailoring unique products to individual customer specifications as described in Chapter 5, the two companies' product costing systems also differ.

Job order costing is appropriate for companies making products or providing services in limited quantities that conform to customer specifications. In contrast, Lumina uses process costing to accumulate and assign costs to units of production. This costing method is also used by manufacturers of candy products, bricks, gasoline, paper, and food products, among many other types of firms.

1

How is process costing different from job order costing?

Both job order and process costing systems accumulate costs by cost component in each production department. However, the two systems assign costs to departmental output differently. In a job order system, costs are assigned to specific jobs and then to the units composing the job. Process costing uses an averaging technique to assign the costs directly to the units produced during the period. In both costing systems, unit costs are transferred as goods are moved from one department to the next so that a total production cost can be accumulated.

This chapter presents process costing procedures and illustrates the weighted average and FIFO methods of calculating unit cost in a process costing system. These methods differ only in the treatment of beginning inventory units and costs. Once unit cost is determined, total costs are assigned to the units transferred out of a department and to that department's ending inventory. The chapter also illustrates a standard cost process costing system, which is an often-used simplification of the FIFO process costing system.

INTRODUCTION TO PROCESS COSTING

Assigning costs to units of production is an averaging process. In the easiest possible situation, a product's actual unit cost is found by dividing a period's departmental production costs by that period's departmental production quantity. This average is expressed by the following formula:

$$\text{Unit Cost} = \frac{\text{Sum of Production Costs}}{\text{Production Quantity}}$$

Peter Longmore describes the overall simplicity of the process costing process in the following excerpt:

> *Process costing is applicable to production involving a continuous process resulting in a high volume of identical or almost identical units of output. While there are a number of complexities attached to process costing, the basic idea involves nothing more than calculating an average cost per unit. As such, the technique is divisible into 3 stages: (1) Measure the productive output in a period. (2) Measure the cost incurred in the period. (3) Calculate the average cost by spreading the total cost across the total output.*[1]

The Numerator

The formula numerator is obtained by accumulating departmental costs incurred in a single period. Because most companies make more than one type of product, costs must be accumulated by product within each department. Costs can be accumulated by using different Work in Process Inventory accounts for each product and for each department through which that product passes. Alternatively, costs can be accumulated using departmental Work in Process Inventory control accounts that are supported by detailed subsidiary ledgers containing specific product information.

Cost accumulation in a process costing system differs from that in a job order costing system in two ways: (1) the *quantity* of production for which costs are accumulated at any one time, and (2) the *cost object* to which the costs are assigned. Suppose that Lumina occasionally contracts to hand-make four-foot candles for special religious occasions. For these orders, the company would use job order costing. The direct material and direct labor costs associated with each four-foot candle would be accumulated and assigned directly to the buyer's job. After each job is completed, the total material, labor, and allocated overhead costs are known and job cost can be determined.

In contrast, for its traditional candles, Lumina would use a process costing system to accumulate periodic costs for each department and each product. Because a variety of sizes, colors, and scents of candles are manufactured each period, the costs assignable to each type of product must be individually designated and attached to the specific production runs. These costs are then assigned to the units worked on during the period.

Exhibit 6–1 presents the source documents used to make initial cost assignments to production departments during a period. Costs are reassigned at the end of the period (usually each month) from the departments to the units produced. As goods are transferred from one department to the next, the related departmental production costs are also transferred. When products are complete, their costs are transferred from Work in Process Inventory to Finished Goods Inventory.

As in job order costing, the direct material and direct labor components of product cost present relatively few problems for cost accumulation and assignment.

[1] Peter Longmore, "Process Costing Demystified," *Accountancy* (October 1994), p. 88.

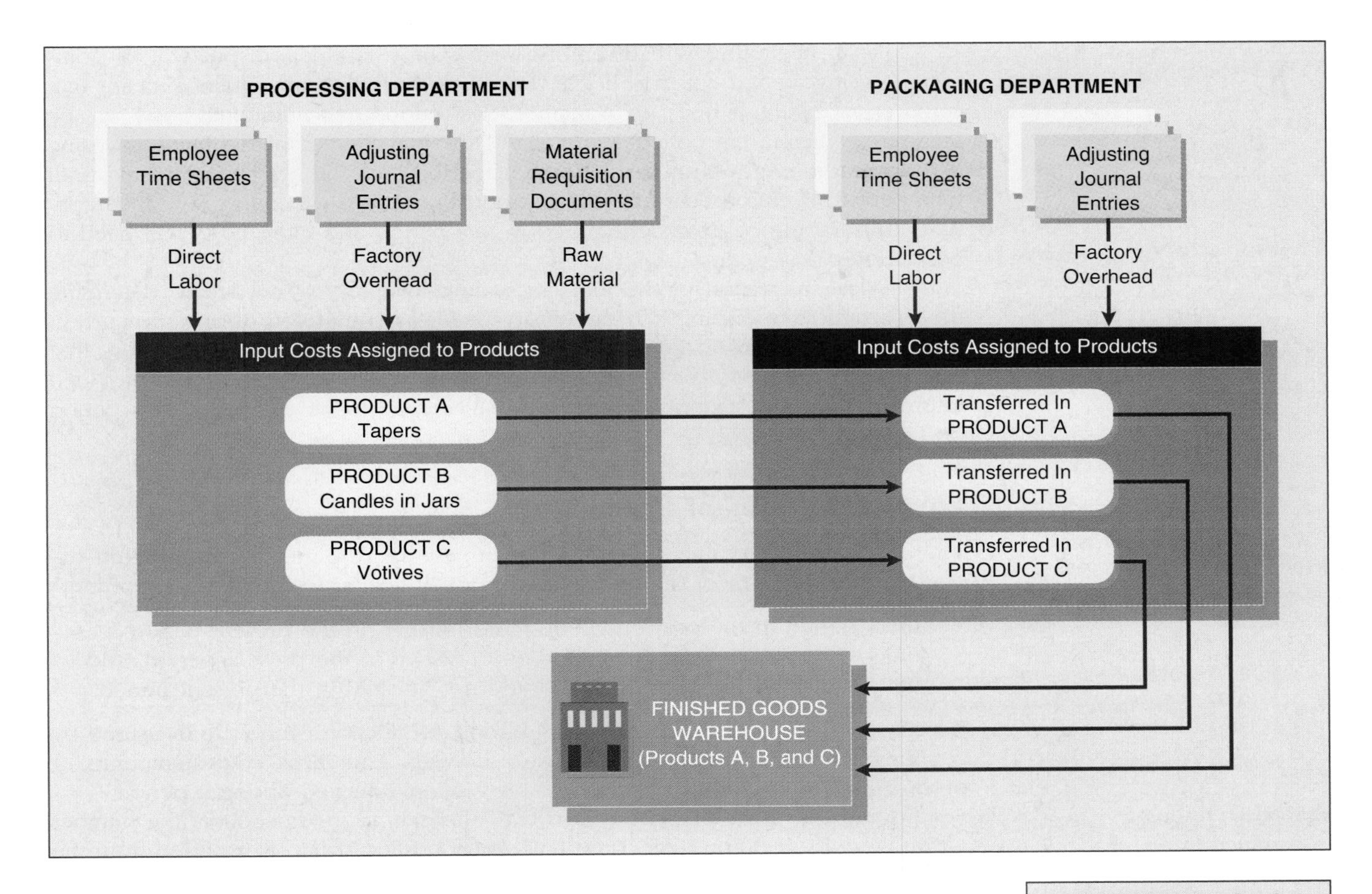

EXHIBIT 6-1

Cost Flows and Cost Assignment

Direct material cost can be measured from material requisition slips; direct labor can be determined from employee time sheets and wage rates for the period.

In contrast, overhead is indirectly assigned to output. If total overhead costs are relatively constant from period to period and production volume is relatively steady over time, actual overhead costs provide a fairly uniform production cost and may be used for product costing. If such conditions do not exist, using actual overhead for product costing would result in fluctuating unit costs and, therefore, predetermined application rates are more appropriate.

In both job order costing and process costing systems, firms may change the definitions of cost pools or adopt new schemes for assigning overhead costs to production. Such changes may be desirable as managers find new ways to structure production activities and develop new management methods. The changes in management practices create challenges for accountants in creating accounting systems that provide useful information to managers.

The Denominator

The denominator in the unit cost formula represents total departmental production for the period. If all units were 100 percent complete at the end of each accounting period, units could simply be counted to obtain the denominator. But in most production processes, Work in Process (WIP) Inventory exists, which consists of partially completed units. Any partially completed ending inventory of the current period becomes the partially completed beginning inventory of the next period. Process costing assigns costs to both fully and partially completed units by mathematically converting partially completed units to equivalent whole units.

Units in beginning WIP Inventory were started last period, but will be completed during the current period. This two-period production sequence means that some costs for these units were incurred last period and additional costs will be incurred in the current period. Additionally, the partially completed units in ending WIP Inventory were started in the current period, but will not be completed until next period. Therefore, current period production efforts on ending WIP Inventory units cause some costs to be incurred in this period and more costs will need to be incurred next period.

Physical inspection of the units in ending inventory is needed to determine the proportion of ending WIP Inventory that was completed during the current period. The mathematical complement to this proportion represents the work that needs to be completed next period. Inspection at the end of last period provided information on the proportion of work that needed to be completed this period on beginning inventory.

2

Why are equivalent units of production used in process costing?

Equivalent Units of Production

The physical flow of units through a department and the manufacturing effort expended in a department during a period normally occur in the following order:

- units started in the previous period and finished in the present period,
- units started in the present period and finished in the present period, and
- units started in the present period and not finished in the present period.

Because of these mixed manufacturing efforts, production cannot be measured by counting whole units. Accountants use a concept known as equivalent units of production to measure the quantity of production achieved during a period.

equivalent units of production

Equivalent units of production (EUP) are an approximation of the number of whole units of output that could have been produced during a period from the actual effort expended during that period. EUPs are calculated by multiplying the number of actual but incomplete units produced by the respective percentage degree of completion. The following simple example indicates how equivalent units are calculated.

Assume the cooking department of a company had no beginning inventory in November. During November, the department worked on 220,000 units: 200,000 units were completed and 20,000 units were 40 percent complete at the end of the period. The EUP for the period are 208,000 [(200,000 × 100%) + (20,000 × 40%)].

WEIGHTED AVERAGE AND FIFO PROCESS COSTING METHODS

3

How are equivalent units of production determined using the weighted average and FIFO methods of process costing?

The two methods of accounting for cost flows in process costing are (1) weighted average and (2) FIFO. These methods relate to the manner in which cost flows are assumed to occur in the production process. In a very general way, these process costing approaches can be related to the cost flow methods used in financial accounting.

In a retail business, the weighted average method is used to determine an average cost per unit of inventory. This cost is computed by dividing the total cost of goods available by total units available. Total cost and total units are found by adding purchases to beginning inventory. Costs and units of the current period are not distinguished in any way from those on hand at the end of the prior period. In contrast, the FIFO method of accounting for merchandise inventory separates goods by when they were purchased and at what cost. The costs of beginning inventory are the first costs sent to Cost of Goods Sold; units remaining in the ending inventory are assigned costs based on the most recent purchase prices.

The use of these methods for costing the production of a manufacturing firm is similar to their use by a retailer. The **weighted average method** computes a single average cost per unit of the combined beginning inventory and current period production. The **FIFO method** separates beginning inventory and current period production and their costs so that a current period cost per unit can be calculated. The denominator used in the cost formula to determine unit cost differs depending on which of the two methods is used.[2]

weighted average method

FIFO method

In almost all cases, some direct material must be introduced at the start of a production process or there would be no need for labor or overhead to be incurred. For example, to make its various products, Lumina introduces wax at the start of a process. Any material added at the start of production is 100 percent complete throughout the process *regardless* of the percentage of completion of labor and overhead.

Most production processes require multiple direct materials. Additional materials may be added at any point or even continuously during processing. A material, such as a box, may even be added at the end of processing. During the production process, the product is 0 percent complete as to the box although other materials may be complete and some labor and overhead may have been incurred.

The production flow for candles shown in Exhibit 6–2 visually illustrates the need for separate EUP computations for each cost component. The material "wax" is 100 percent complete at any point in the process after the start of production; no additional wax is added later in production. When enough labor and overhead have been added to melt the wax and reach the 20 percent completion point, additional materials (coloring and scent) are added. Prior to 20 percent completion, these materials were 0 percent complete; after the 20 percent point, these materials are 100 percent complete. The wick is added at the 50 percent completion point, and the candles are packaged when processing is 99 percent finished, after

EXHIBIT 6–2

Candle Manufacturing Process—Production Department

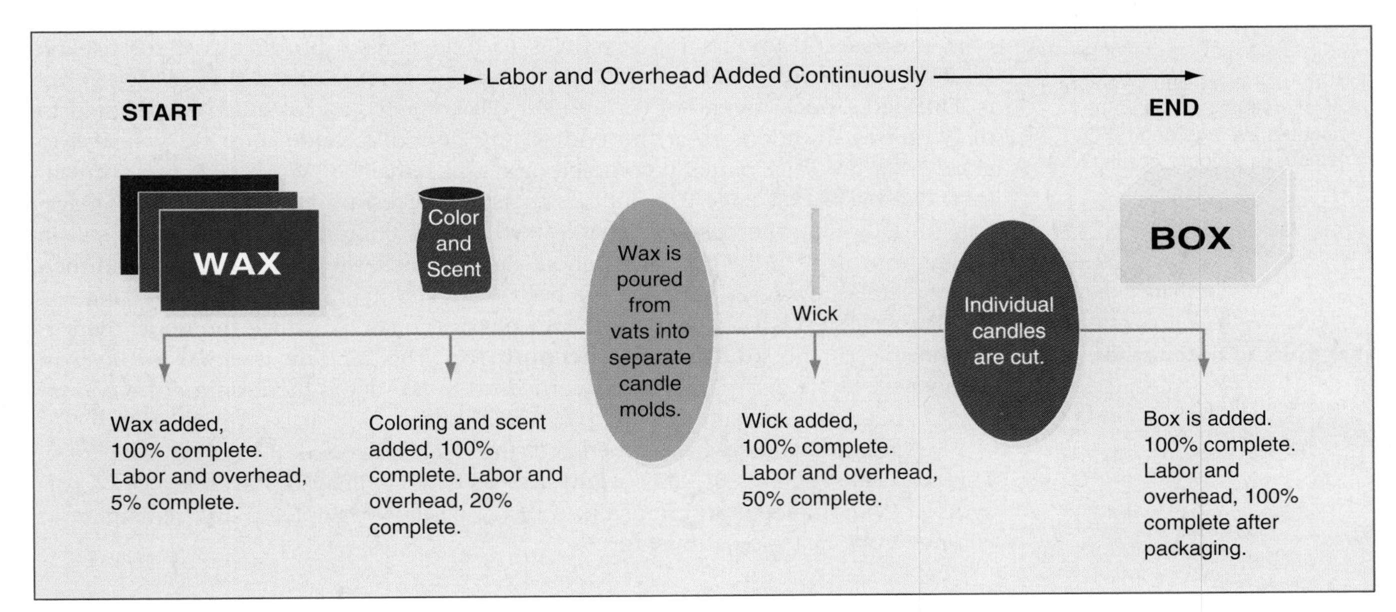

[2] Note that the term *denominator* is used here rather than equivalent units of production. Based on its definition, EUPs are related to current period productive activity. Thus, for any given set of production facts, there is only one true measure of equivalent units produced—regardless of the cost flow assumption used—and that measure is FIFO EUP. However, this fact has been obscured over time due to continued references to the "EUP" computation for weighted average. Thus, the term *EUP* has taken on a generic use to mean "the denominator used to compute the unit cost of production for a period in a process costing system." We use EUP in this generic manner throughout the discussion of process costing.

which the candles are 100 percent complete. Thus, boxes are 0 percent complete throughout production; when the candles are packaged, the product is complete and is transferred to the finished goods warehouse or directly to customers.

If 8,000 candles are assumed to be 75 percent complete as to labor and overhead at the end of a period, those candles would be 100 percent complete as to wax, coloring and scent, and wicks, and 0 percent complete as to boxes. The EUP calculations would indicate that there are 8,000 EUPs for wax, coloring and scent, and wicks, and 0 EUPs for boxes. The labor and overhead (conversion) components of cost would have an equivalency of 6,000 candles, because the product is 75 percent complete and labor and overhead are added continuously during the process.[3]

When overhead is applied on a direct labor basis, or when direct labor and overhead are added to the product at the same rate, a single percentage of completion estimate can be made and used for both conversion cost components. However, because cost drivers other than direct labor are increasingly being used to apply overhead costs, single computations for "conversion EUP" will be made less often. For example, the cost driver for the utilities portion of overhead cost may be machine hours; the cost driver for the materials handling portion of overhead cost may be pounds of material. The increased use of multiple cost pools and/or activity-based costing concepts makes it less likely that the degrees of completion for the direct labor and overhead components of processing will be equal. The accompanying News Note (page 225) discusses a European view of process costing.

The calculation of equivalent units of production requires that a process cost flow method be specified. A detailed example of the calculations of equivalent units of production and cost assignment for each of the cost flow methods is presented in the next section.

EUP CALCULATIONS AND COST ASSIGNMENTS

4

How are unit costs and inventory values determined using the weighted average and FIFO methods of process costing?

One purpose of any costing system is to determine a product cost for use on financial statements. When goods are transferred from Work in Process Inventory to Finished Goods Inventory (or another department), a cost must be assigned to those goods. In addition, at the end of any period, a value must be assigned to goods that are only partially complete and still remain in Work in Process Inventory. Exhibit 6–3 on page 226 outlines the steps necessary in a process costing system to determine the costs assignable to the units completed and to those still in ending inventory at the end of a period. Each of these steps is discussed, and then a complete example is provided for both weighted average and FIFO costing.

total units to account for

The first step is to calculate the total physical units for which the department is responsible or the **total units to account for**. This amount is equal to the total number of whole and partial units worked on in the department during the current period: beginning inventory units plus units started.

Second, determine what happened to the units to account for during the period. This step also requires the use of physical units. Units may fit into one of two categories: (1) completed and transferred or (2) partially completed and remaining in ending Work in Process Inventory.[4]

[3] Although the same number of equivalent units results for wax, coloring and scent, and wicks, and for labor and overhead, separate calculations of unit cost may be desirable for each component. These separate calculations would give managers more information for planning and control purposes. Managers must weigh the costs of making separate calculations against the benefits from having the additional information. For illustrative purposes, however, single computations will be made when cost components are at equal percentages of completion.

[4] A third category (spoilage/breakage) does exist. It is assumed at this point that such happenings do not occur. Chapter 7 covers accounting for spoilage in process costing situations.

INTERNATIONAL **NEWS NOTE**

Costing Is a Three-Step Process

Besides control and budgeting, costing is essential to the managerial accounting activities in a company. Costing relates to how many expenses were used up by a product, a product group, a particular activity, or a set of business activities.

. . . Profits that are disclosed in financial statements are of the most aggregate nature. While segmental profits can provide detailed information for the external analyst, management often wants to identify the factors contributing to company profits with much greater accuracy. Deriving product cost and comparing it with the prices charged is such a detailed analysis. The difference of these two, called contribution, gives insights into the profitability of the company's various activities.

First, one has to separate product cost from period cost. Second, direct product costs are allocated to the individual products, whereas indirect costs are allocated to cost centers. Third, indirect costs are attributed from the center to the products according to their usage. The sum of direct and allocated indirect cost forms the product cost.

Costing has a strong tradition in manufacturing. Thus, costing procedures typically recognize selling, general and administrative expenses (SG&A) as period costs that are not attributable to individual products or product groups. Product costs are principally expenses for material, labor, and machinery (in the form of depreciation). Other product costs might include expenses as various as light, heating, insurance, waste, and so on.

Having separated product from period cost, one can tackle the second step of allocating direct cost to a product or any other cost object subject to managerial analysis. Direct costs are expenses incurred uniquely for a particular product.

This is quite obviously the case for material bills, but international differences exist in the treatment of labor. While Anglo-American systems treat labor other than supervisory, as a direct cost, continental European practice often regards all labor cost as indirect. This is due to the different regulatory practices, reflecting the lower flexibility that continental labor law permits. For convenience reasons, direct material also includes a surcharge for the administrative cost of material handling.

The third step of costing—attribution of indirect cost—is the most important for achieving accuracy. All indirect costs, sometimes referred to as overhead, are first allocated to cost pools. Cost pools can be areas of decision making (responsibility centers), service departments, or simple physical entities such as machines. A cost pool absorbs all those costs that vary with a certain cost driver (activity measure); it is this cost driver that reflects the services rendered to a product.

SOURCE: Chris Higson, "Counting the Cost," *Financial Times* (November 17, 1995), Mastering Management—Part 4(4), p. iv. Reprinted with permission from *Financial Times*.

At this point, verify that the total units for which the department was accountable are equal to the total units that were accounted for. If these amounts are not equal, any additional computations will be incorrect.

Third, use either the weighted average or FIFO method to determine the equivalent units of production for each cost component. If all materials are at the same degree of completion, a single materials computation can be made. If multiple materials are used and are placed into production at different points, multiple EUP calculations may be necessary for materials. If overhead is based on direct labor or if these two factors are always at the same degree of completion, a single EUP can be computed for conversion. If neither condition exists, separate EUP schedules must be prepared for labor and overhead.[5]

[5] As discussed in Chapter 4, overhead can be applied to products using a variety of traditional (direct labor hours or machine hours) or nontraditional (such as number of machine setups, pounds of material moved, and/or number of material requisitions) bases. The number of equivalent unit computations that need to be made results from the number of different cost pools and overhead allocation bases established in a company. Some highly automated manufacturers may not have a direct labor category. The quantity of direct labor may be so nominal that it is included in a conversion category and not accounted for separately.

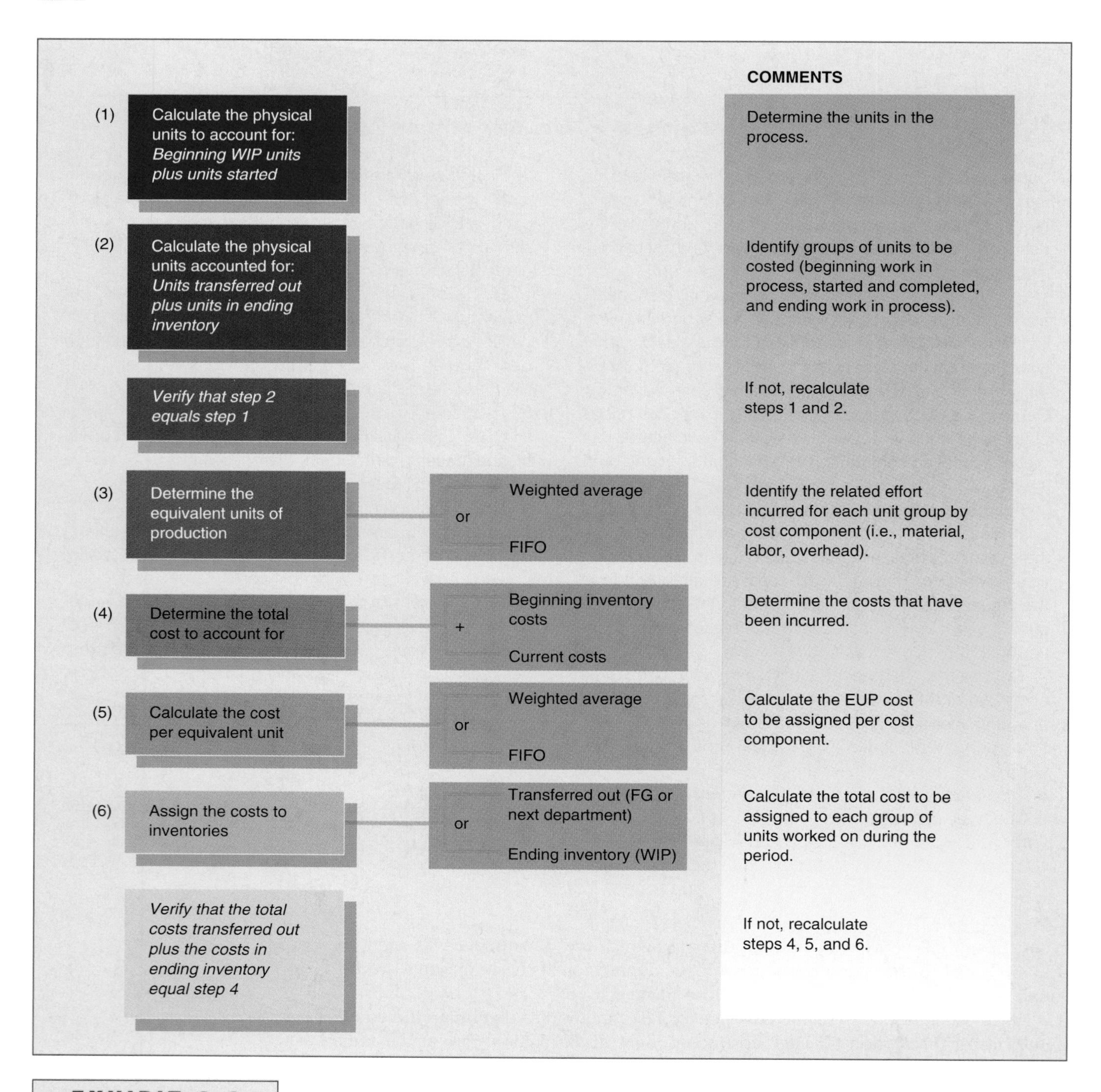

EXHIBIT 6-3

Steps in Process Costing

total cost to account for

Fourth, find the **total cost to account for**, which includes the balance in Work in Process Inventory at the beginning of the period plus all current costs for direct material, direct labor, and overhead.

Fifth, compute the cost per equivalent unit for each cost component using either the weighted average or FIFO equivalent units of production calculated in step 3.

Sixth, use the costs computed in step 5 to assign costs from the production process to the units completed and transferred and to the units remaining in ending Work in Process Inventory.

The Decorative Waxes Company is used to demonstrate the steps involved in the computation of equivalent units of production and cost assignment for both methods of process costing. The Decorative Waxes Company makes a variety of sizes and types of candles. One candle made by the Decorative Waxes Company is three inches wide and six inches tall. The company views the manufacturing process of this product as a single department with a single direct material: wax. The company treats the costs of coloring, scent, and wicks as overhead, and candles are not packaged. Because the wax is added at the start of processing, all inventories are 100 percent complete as to material as soon as processing has begun. Labor and overhead are assumed to be added at the same rate throughout the production process. Exhibit 6–4 presents information for April 2000 regarding the candle maker's production inventories and costs.

Although figures are given for both candles transferred and in ending inventory, providing both of these figures is not essential. The number of candles remaining in ending inventory on April 30 can be calculated by subtracting the candles that were completed and transferred during the period from the total candles to account for. Alternatively, the number of candles transferred can be computed as the total candles to account for minus the candles in ending inventory.

The Decorative Waxes Company information is used to illustrate each step listed in Exhibit 6–3.

Weighted Average Method

STEP 1: CALCULATE THE TOTAL UNITS TO ACCOUNT FOR

Candles in beginning inventory	25,000
Candles started during current period	510,000
Candles to account for	535,000

STEP 2: CALCULATE THE TOTAL UNITS ACCOUNTED FOR

Candles completed and transferred	523,000
Candles in ending WIP inventory	12,000
Candles accounted for	535,000

The items detailed in this step indicate the categories to which costs will be assigned in the final step. The number of candles accounted for in step 2 equals the number of candles to account for in step 1.

STEP 3: DETERMINE THE EQUIVALENT UNITS OF PRODUCTION

The weighted average EUP computation uses the number of whole candles in beginning inventory and the number of candles started and completed during the

EXHIBIT 6–4

Production and Cost Information—April 1, 2000

Candles in beginning inventory (40% complete as to labor and overhead or conversion)			25,000
Candles started during current period			510,000
Candles completed and transferred to finished goods			523,000
Candles in ending inventory (80% complete as to labor and overhead or conversion)			12,000
Costs of beginning inventory:			
Direct material	$ 42,650		
Direct labor	1,400		
Overhead	15,752	$ 59,802	
Current period costs:			
Direct material	$433,500		
Direct labor	75,777		
Overhead	263,913	$773,190	

units started and completed

period. (**Units started and completed** during a period equals the total units completed during the current period minus the units in beginning inventory.[6]) For the Decorative Waxes Company, the candles started and completed in April are 498,000 (523,000 − 25,000). Ending inventory is 100 percent complete as to material, because all material is added at the start of production. The ending inventory is 80 percent complete as to labor and overhead (conversion); one EUP computation can be made because these cost elements are assumed to be added at the same rate throughout the production process. The weighted average computation for equivalent units of production is as follows[7]:

	DM	Conversion (Labor & Overhead)
Beginning inventory (whole candles)	25,000	25,000
Candles started and completed	498,000	498,000
Ending inventory (whole candles × % complete)	12,000	9,600
Equivalent units of production	535,000	532,600

STEP 4: DETERMINE THE TOTAL COST TO ACCOUNT FOR

The total cost to account for equals beginning inventory cost plus current period costs. Note that information is provided in Exhibit 6–4 on the cost for each element of production—direct material, direct labor, and overhead. Production costs can be determined from the departmental Work in Process Inventory accounts and their subsidiary details. These costs come from transfers of direct material from the storeroom, incurrence of direct labor, and either actual or applied overhead amounts. The sum of direct labor and overhead costs is the conversion cost. For the Decorative Waxes Company, the total cost to account for is $832,992.

	DM	DL	OH	Total
Beginning inventory costs	$ 42,650	$ 1,400	$ 15,752	$ 59,802
Current period costs	433,500	75,777	263,913	773,190
To account for	$476,150	$77,177	$279,665	$832,992

Total cost is assigned to the goods transferred to Finished Goods Inventory (or, alternatively, to the next department) and to ending Work in Process Inventory in relation to the whole units or equivalent whole units contained in each category.

STEP 5: CALCULATE THE COST PER EQUIVALENT UNIT OF PRODUCTION

A cost per equivalent unit of production must be computed for each cost component for which a separate calculation of EUP is made. Under the weighted average method, the costs of beginning inventory and the current period are summed for each cost component and averaged over that component's weighted average equivalent units of production. This calculation for unit cost for each cost component at the end of the period is shown below:

$$\text{Unit Cost} = \frac{\text{Beginning Inventory Cost} + \text{Current Period Cost}}{\text{Weighted Average Equivalent Units of Production}}$$

$$= \frac{\text{Total Cost Incurred}}{\text{Total Equivalent Units of Effort}}$$

[6] Units started and completed can also be computed as the units started during the current period minus the units not finished (or the units in ending inventory).

[7] Different approaches exist to compute equivalent units of production and unit costs under weighted average and FIFO. The models presented in this chapter represent the computations that we have found to be the most readily understood and that best assist students in a clear and unambiguous reconciliation of these two methods. However, two other valid and commonly used approaches for computing and reconciling weighted average and FIFO equivalent units of production and unit costs are presented in the Appendix to this chapter.

This computation divides total cost by total units—the common weighted average approach that produces an average component cost per unit. Because labor and overhead are at the same degree of completion, their costs can be combined and shown as a single conversion cost per equivalent unit. The Decorative Waxes Company's weighted average calculations for cost per EUP for material and conversion are shown below:

	Direct Material	+	Conversion	=	Total
Beginning inventory costs	$ 42,650		$ 17,152		$ 59,802
Current period costs	433,500		339,690		773,190
Total cost per component	$476,150		$356,842		$832,992
Divided by EUP (step 3)	535,000		532,600		
Cost per EUP	$0.89		$0.67		$1.56

The amounts for the product cost components (material and conversion) are summed to find the total production cost for all whole candles completed during April. For the Decorative Waxes Company, this cost is $1.56.

STEP 6: ASSIGN COSTS TO INVENTORIES

This step assigns total production costs to units of product. Cost assignment in a department involves determining the cost of (1) the goods completed and transferred during the period and (2) the units in ending Work in Process Inventory.

Using the weighted average method, the cost of goods transferred is found by multiplying the total number of units transferred by a cost per unit that combines all the costs of the components or the total cost per EUP. Because this method is based on an averaging technique that combines both prior and current period work, it does not matter in which period the transferred units were started. All units and all costs have been commingled. The total cost transferred for the Decorative Waxes Company for April is $815,880 ($1.56 × 523,000).

Ending WIP Inventory cost is calculated based on the equivalent units of production for each cost component. The equivalent units of production for each component are multiplied by the component cost per unit computed in step 5. The cost of ending inventory using the weighted average method (using the previously determined equivalent units) is as follows:

Ending inventory	
Direct material (12,000 × $0.89)	$10,680
Conversion (9,600 × $0.67)	6,432
Total cost of ending inventory	$17,112

The total costs assigned to units transferred and units in ending inventory must equal the total cost to account for. For the Decorative Waxes Company, total cost to account for (step 4) was determined as $832,992, which equals transferred cost ($815,880) plus cost of ending Work in Process Inventory ($17,112).

The steps just discussed can be combined into a **cost of production report**. This document details all manufacturing quantities and costs, shows the computation of cost per EUP, and indicates the cost assignment to goods produced during the period. Exhibit 6–5 shows the Decorative Waxes Company's cost of production report using the weighted average method.

cost of production report

FIFO Method

Steps 1 and 2 are the same for the FIFO method as for the weighted average method because these two steps involve the use of physical units.

EXHIBIT 6–5

Cost of Production Report for the Month Ended April 30, 2000 (Weighted Average Method)

PRODUCTION DATA		EQUIVALENT UNITS OF PRODUCTION	
	Whole Units	Direct Material	Conversion
Beginning inventory	25,000*	25,000	10,000
Candles started	510,000		
Candles to account for	535,000		
Beginning inventory completed	25,000	0	15,000
Started and completed	498,000	498,000	498,000
Candles completed	523,000		
Ending WIP inventory	12,000**	12,000	9,600
Candles accounted for	535,000	535,000	532,600

COST DATA	Total	Direct Material	Conversion
Costs in beginning inventory	$ 59,802	$ 42,650	$ 17,152
Current period costs	773,190	433,500	339,690
Total cost to account for	$832,992	$476,150	$356,842
Divided by EUP		535,000	532,600
Cost per EUP	$1.56	$0.89	$0.67

COST ASSIGNMENT		
Transferred (523,000 × $1.56)		$815,880
Ending inventory		
Direct material (12,000 × $0.89)	$10,680	
Conversion (12,000 × 80% × $0.67)	6,432	17,112
Total cost accounted for		$832,992

*Fully complete as to material; 40% complete as to conversion.
**Fully complete as to material; 80% complete as to conversion.

STEP 3: DETERMINE THE EQUIVALENT UNITS OF PRODUCTION

Under FIFO, the work performed last period is *not* commingled with work of the current period. The EUP schedule for FIFO is

	DM	Conversion
Candles in beginning inventory completed in the current period	0	15,000
Candles started and completed	498,000	498,000
Ending inventory (whole candles × % complete)	12,000	9,600
Equivalent units of production	510,000	522,600

Under FIFO, only the work performed on the beginning inventory during the current period is shown in the EUP schedule; this work equals the whole units in beginning inventory times (1 − the percentage of work done in the prior period). No additional material is needed in April to complete the 25,000 candles in the beginning inventory. Because beginning inventory was 40 percent complete as to labor and overhead, the company needs to do 60 percent of the conversion work on the goods in the current period or the equivalent of 15,000 candles (25,000 × 60%).

Except for the different treatment of units in beginning inventory, the remaining figures in the FIFO EUP schedule are the same as for the weighted average method. Thus, the only EUP difference between the two methods is equal to the number of candles in beginning inventory times the percentage of work performed in the prior period, as shown below:

	DM	Conversion
FIFO EUP	510,000	522,600
Beginning inventory (25,000 units × % work done in prior period: 100% material, 40% conversion)	25,000	10,000
WA EUP	535,000	532,600

STEP 4: DETERMINE THE TOTAL COST TO ACCOUNT FOR

This step is the same as it was under the weighted average method; the total cost to account for is $832,992.

STEP 5: CALCULATE THE COST PER EQUIVALENT UNIT OF PRODUCTION

Because cost determination is based on equivalent units of production, different results will be obtained for the weighted average and FIFO methods. The calculations for cost per equivalent unit reflect the difference in quantity that each method uses for beginning inventory. The EUP calculation for FIFO ignores work performed on beginning inventory during the prior period; therefore, the FIFO cost computation per EUP also ignores prior period costs and uses only costs incurred in the current period. The FIFO cost per EUP calculation is shown here:

	Direct Material	+	Conversion	=	Total
Current period costs	$433,500		$339,690		$773,190
Divided by EUP (step 3)	510,000		522,600		
Cost per EUP	$0.85		$0.65		$1.50

It is useful to recognize the difference between the two total cost computations. The weighted average total cost of $1.56 is the average total cost of each candle completed during April, regardless of when production was begun. The FIFO total cost of $1.50 is the total cost of each candle produced (both started and completed) during the period. The $0.06 difference is caused by the difference in treatment of beginning work in process costs.

STEP 6: ASSIGN COSTS TO INVENTORIES

The FIFO method assumes that the units in beginning inventory are the first units completed during the current period and, thus, are the first units transferred. The remaining units transferred during the period were both started and completed in the current period. As shown in the cost of production report in Exhibit 6–6, the two-step computation needed to determine the cost of goods transferred distinctly presents this FIFO logic.

The first part of the cost assignment for units transferred relates to the units that were in beginning inventory. These units had the cost of material and some labor and overhead costs applied at the start of the period. These costs were not included in the cost per EUP calculations in step 5. The costs to finish these units were incurred in the current period. To determine the total cost of producing the units in beginning inventory, the beginning inventory costs are added to the current period costs that were needed to complete the goods. Next, the cost of the units started and completed in the current period is computed using current period costs. This cost assignment process for the Decorative Waxes Company, which had a

EXHIBIT 6-6

Cost of Production Report for Month Ended April 30, 2000 (FIFO Method)

PRODUCTION DATA		EQUIVALENT UNITS OF PRODUCTION	
	Whole Units	Direct Material	Conversion
Beginning inventory	25,000*		
Candles started	510,000		
Candles to account for	535,000		
Beginning inventory completed	25,000	0	15,000
Started and completed	498,000	498,000	498,000
Candles completed	523,000		
Ending inventory	12,000**	12,000	9,600
Candles accounted for	535,000	510,000	522,600

COST DATA	Total	Direct Material	Conversion
Costs in beginning inventory	$ 59,802		
Current period costs	773,190	$433,500	$339,690
Total cost to account for	$832,992		
Divided by EUP		510,000	522,600
Current period cost per EUP	$1.50	$0.85	$0.65

COST ASSIGNMENT		
Transferred		
Beginning inventory costs	$59,802	
Cost to complete:		
Conversion (15,000 × $0.65)	9,750	$ 69,552
Started and completed (498,000 × $1.50)		747,000
Total cost transferred		$816,552
Ending inventory		
Direct material (12,000 × $0.85)	$10,200	
Conversion (9,600 × $0.65)	6,240	16,440
Total cost accounted for		$832,992

*Fully complete as to material; 40% complete as to conversion.
**Fully complete as to material; 80% complete as to conversion.

beginning April inventory of 25,000 candles and transferred 523,000 candles during the month is as follows:

Transferred	
(1) Beginning inventory (prior period costs)	$ 59,802
Completion of beginning inventory:	
Direct material (0 × $0.85)	0
Conversion (25,000 × 60% × $0.65)	9,750
Total cost of beginning inventory transferred	$ 69,552
(2) Candles started and completed (498,000 × $1.50)	747,000
Total cost transferred	$816,552

The beginning inventory was 100 percent complete as to wax at the beginning of April; therefore, no additional costs for wax need to be added during the period. Conversion at the start of the month was only 40 percent complete, so 60 percent of the labor and overhead (or 15,000 equivalent units) is added during April at current period costs. The candles started and completed are costed at the total current period FIFO cost of $1.50, because these candles were fully manufactured during the current period.[8]

The process of calculating the FIFO cost of ending Work in Process Inventory is the same as under the weighted average method. Ending work in process cost using FIFO is as follows:

Ending inventory	
Direct material (12,000 × $0.85)	$10,200
Conversion (9,600 × $0.65)	6,240
Total cost of ending inventory	$16,440

The total cost of the candles transferred ($816,552) plus the cost of the candles in ending inventory ($16,440) equals the total cost to be accounted for ($832,992).

Summary journal entries and T-accounts for the Decorative Waxes Company for April are given in Exhibit 6–7 on next page. It is assumed that 520,000 candles were sold on account for $3.00 per candle and that a perpetual FIFO inventory system is in use. Assume that the Decorative Waxes Company began April with no Finished Goods Inventory. Weighted average amounts are shown where they would differ from FIFO.

PROCESS COSTING IN A MULTIDEPARTMENT SETTING

Most companies have multiple, rather than single, department processing facilities. In a multidepartment-processing environment, goods are transferred from a predecessor department to a successor department. For example, if the candles at the Decorative Waxes Company were boxed by the dozen, the company's manufacturing activities could be viewed as occurring in two departments: Processing and Packaging.

Manufacturing costs *always* follow the physical flow of goods. Therefore, the costs of the completed units of predecessor departments are treated as input material costs in successor departments. Such a sequential treatment requires the use of an additional cost component element called "transferred-in" or "prior department cost." This element always has a percentage of completion factor of 100 percent, because the goods would not have been transferred out of the predecessor department if they had not been fully complete. The transferred-in element is handled the same as any other cost element in the calculations of EUP and cost per EUP.

A successor department might add additional raw materials to the units transferred in or might simply provide additional labor with the corresponding incurrence of overhead. Anything added in the successor department requires its own cost element column for calculating equivalent units of production and cost per equivalent unit (unless the additional elements have the same degree of completion, in which case they can be combined).

[8] Because of FIFO's two-step process to determine cost of units transferred, a question exists as to how to calculate a per-unit cost for the units that were in beginning inventory and those that were started and completed in the current period. The resolution of this question is found in the use of either the strict or the modified FIFO method.

If strict FIFO is used, beginning inventory units are transferred out at their total completed cost; the units started and completed during the current period are transferred at a separate and distinct current period cost. For the Decorative Candle Company, use of strict FIFO means that the 25,000 candles in beginning inventory are transferred at a cost per unit of $2.78 ($69,552 ÷ 25,000). The candles started and completed in April are transferred at the current period cost of $1.50 (computed in step 5). If strict FIFO is used, the costs of these two groups should be reported separately and not added together to get a total transferred cost.

However, unless the difference between the unit costs of beginning inventory units and of units started and completed is significant, there is no need to maintain the distinction. The costs of the two groups can be combined and averaged over all of the units transferred in a process known as the modified FIFO method. For the Decorative Waxes Company, modified FIFO assigns an average cost of $1.56 per candle ($816,552 ÷ 523,000) to all candles transferred from the department. Modified FIFO allows the next department or Finished Goods Inventory to account for all units received during the period at the same cost per unit. This method is useful when products are processed through several departments so that the number of separate unit costs to be accounted for does not become excessive.

EXHIBIT 6–7

Process Costing Journal Entries and T-Accounts

	Debit	Credit
1. Work in Process Inventory	433,500	
Raw Material Inventory		433,500
To record issuance of materials to production (Exhibit 6–4).		
2. Work in Process Inventory	75,777	
Wages Payable		75,777
To accrue wages for direct labor (Exhibit 6–4).		
3. Manufacturing Overhead	263,913	
Various accounts		263,913
To record actual overhead costs (Exhibit 6–4).		
4. Work in Process Inventory	263,913	
Manufacturing Overhead		263,913
To apply actual overhead to production.		
5. Finished Goods Inventory	816,552	
Work in Process Inventory		816,552
To transfer cost of completed candles to finished goods (Exhibit 6–6). (Entry would be for $815,880 if weighted average were used—Exhibit 6–5.)		
6. Cost of Goods Sold	812,052	
Finished Goods Inventory		812,052
To transfer cost of goods sold, using strict FIFO:		
First 25,000 units $ 69,552		
Remaining 495,000 units at $1.50 742,500		
$812,052		
(Entry would be for $811,200 if weighted average were used: 520,000 × $1.56.)		
7. Accounts Receivable	1,560,000	
Sales		1,560,000
To record sales on account (520,000 candles × $3.00).		

Work in Process Inventory

Beginning balance	59,802	Cost of goods manufactured	816,552
Direct material	433,500		
Direct labor	75,777		
Applied overhead	263,913		
Ending balance	16,440		

Finished Goods Inventory

Beginning balance	0	Cost of goods sold	812,052
Cost of goods manufactured	816,552		
Ending balance (3,000 @ $1.50)	4,500		

Cost of Goods Sold

April CGS	812,052		

Hershey Kisses®, like most other food products, are manufactured in a plant that uses process costing. Costs for chocolate, melting, and shaping would be accumulated in the first department. The Kisses would then be transferred to a second department to be wrapped and bagged in packages of various sizes.

Occasionally, successor departments might change the unit of measure used in predecessor departments. For example, when the Decorative Waxes Company produces candles, the measure in the Processing Department would be number of candles; the measure in the Packaging Department would be number of boxes of a dozen candles.

The demonstration problem at the end of the chapter provides a complete example of predecessor and successor department activities.

PROCESS COSTING WITH STANDARD COSTS

5

How can standard costs be used in a process costing system?

Companies may prefer to use standard rather than actual historical costs for inventory valuation purposes. Actual costing requires that a new production cost be computed each production period. Once a production process is established, however, the "new" costs are often not materially different from the "old" costs, so standards for each cost element can be developed and used as predetermined cost benchmarks to simplify the costing process and eliminate periodic cost recomputations. Standards do need to be reviewed (and possibly revised) at a minimum of once per year to keep the amounts current.

Calculations for equivalent units of production for standard process costing are identical to those of FIFO process costing. Unlike the weighted average method, the emphasis of both standard costing and FIFO are on the measurement and control of current production and current period costs. The weighted average method commingles units and costs of the prior period with those of the current period. This commingling reduces the emphasis on current effort that standard costing is intended to represent and measure.

The use of standard costs allows material, labor, and overhead variances to be measured during the period. To show the differences between using actual and standard process costing, the Decorative Waxes Company example is continued. The company's April production and standard cost information is given in Exhibit 6–8. The beginning inventory cost data have been restated from the original to reflect standard costs and to demonstrate the effect of consistent use of standard costs over successive periods. Beginning inventory consisted of 25,000 units that were fully complete as to material and 40 percent complete as to conversion. Therefore, the standard cost of beginning inventory is as follows:

Material (25,000 × 100% × $0.86)	$21,500
Labor (25,000 × 40% × $0.15)	1,500
Overhead (25,000 × 40% × $0.48)	4,800
Total	$27,800

Exhibit 6–9 presents the cost of production report using the Decorative Waxes Company's standard cost information.[9]

When a standard cost system is used, inventories are stated at standard rather than actual costs. Summary journal entries for the Decorative Waxes Company's April production, assuming a standard cost FIFO process costing system and amounts from Exhibit 6–9, are as follows:

1. WIP Inventory is debited for $438,600: the standard cost ($428,280) of material used to complete 498,000 units that were started in April plus the standard cost ($10,320) for the material used to produce ending work in process. Raw Material Inventory is credited for the actual cost of the material withdrawn during April ($433,500).

Work in Process Inventory	438,600	
Raw Material Inventory		433,500
Direct Material Variance		5,100
To record issuance of material at standard and variance from standard.		

EXHIBIT 6–8

Production and Cost Data (Standard Costing)

Production Data

Beginning inventory (100%, 40%)	25,000
Units started	510,000
Ending inventory (100%, 80%)	12,000

Standard Cost of Production

Direct material	$0.86
Direct labor	0.15
Overhead	0.48
Total	$1.49

Equivalent Units of Production (repeated from Exhibit 6–6):

	DM	Conversion
BI (candles × % not complete at start of period)	0	15,000
Candles started and completed	498,000	498,000
EI (candles × % complete at end of period)	12,000	9,600
Equivalent units of production	510,000	522,600

[9] Total material, labor, and overhead variances are shown for the Decorative Waxes Company in Exhibit 6–9. More detailed variances are presented in Chapter 10 on standard costing. Additionally, variances from actual costs must be closed at the end of a period. If the variances are immaterial, they can be closed to Cost of Goods Sold; otherwise, they should be allocated among the appropriate inventory accounts and Cost of Goods Sold.

EXHIBIT 6-9

Cost of Production Report for Month Ended April 30, 2000 (Standard Costing)

COSTS TO BE ACCOUNTED FOR

	Direct Material	Direct Labor	Overhead	Total
Total costs				
BWIP (at standard)	$ 21,500	$ 1,500	$ 4,800	$ 27,800
Current period (actual)	433,500	75,777	263,913	773,190
(1) Total	$455,000	$77,277	$268,713	$800,990

COST ASSIGNMENT (AT STANDARD)

	Direct Material	Direct Labor	Overhead	Total
Transferred				
BI cost*	$ 21,500	$ 1,500	$ 4,800	$ 27,800
Cost to complete				
DL (15,000 × $0.15)		2,250		
OH (15,000 × $0.48)			7,200	
Total cost to complete				9,450
Started and completed				
DM (498,000 × $0.86)	428,280			
DL (498,000 × $0.15)		74,700		
OH (498,000 × $0.48)			239,040	
Total started and completed				742,020
Ending inventory				
DM (12,000 × $0.86)	10,320			
DL (9,600 × $0.15)		1,440		
OH (9,600 × $0.48)			4,608	
Total WIP ending				16,368
(2) Total standard cost assigned	$460,100	$79,890	$255,648	$795,638
Variances from actual (1 − 2)*	(5,100)	(2,613)	13,065	5,352
Total costs accounted for	$455,000	$77,277	$268,713	$800,990

NOTE: Favorable variances are shown in parentheses.
*Beginning work in process is carried at standard costs rather than actual. Therefore, no portion of the variance is attributable to BWIP. Any variance that might have been associated with BWIP was measured and identified with the prior period.

2. WIP Inventory is debited for the standard cost of labor allowed based on the equivalent units produced in April. The EUPs for the month reflect the production necessary to complete the beginning inventory (15,000 candles) plus the candles started and completed (498,000) plus the work performed on the ending inventory candles (9,600) or a total of 522,600 EUP. Multiplying this equivalent production by the standard labor cost per candle of $0.15 gives a total of $78,390.

Work in Process Inventory	78,390	
Wages Payable		75,777
Direct Labor Variance		2,613
To accrue direct labor cost, assign it to WIP Inventory at standard, and record direct labor variance.		

3. Actual factory overhead incurred in April is $263,913.

Manufacturing Overhead	263,913	
Various accounts		263,913
To record actual overhead cost for April.		

4. WIP Inventory is debited for the standard cost of overhead based on the EUPs produced in April. Because labor and overhead are consumed at the same rate,

equivalent production is the same as in entry 2: 522,600 EUPs. Multiplying the EUPs by the standard overhead application rate of $0.48 per candle gives $250,848.

Work in Process Inventory	250,848	
Manufacturing Overhead Variance	13,065	
Manufacturing Overhead		263,913
To apply overhead to WIP Inventory and record the overhead variance.		

5. Finished Goods Inventory is debited for the total standard cost ($779,270) of all 523,000 candles completed during the month ($1.49 × 523,000).

Finished Goods Inventory	779,270	
Work in Process Inventory		779,270
To transfer standard cost of completed candles to FG Inventory.		

A standard costing system eliminates the need to be concerned about differentiating between the per-unit cost of the beginning inventory units that were completed and the per-unit cost of the units started and completed in the current period. All units flowing out of a department are costed at the standard or "normal" production cost for each cost component: direct material, direct labor, and overhead. Thus, recordkeeping is simplified and variations from the norm are highlighted in the period of incurrence. Standard cost systems are discussed in depth in Chapter 10.

Standard costing not only simplifies the cost flows in a process costing system, but it also provides a useful tool to control costs. By developing standards, managers have a benchmark against which actual costs can be compared. Variances serve to identify differences between the benchmark (standard) cost and the actual cost. By striving to control variances, managers control costs. Managers should also compare their firm's costs to costs incurred by other firms.

HYBRID COSTING SYSTEMS

6

Why would a company use a hybrid costing system?

hybrid costing system

Many companies are now able to customize what were previously mass-produced items. In such circumstances, neither job order nor process costing techniques are perfectly suited to attach costs to output. Thus, companies may choose to use a **hybrid costing system** that is appropriate for their particular processing situation. A hybrid costing system combines certain characteristics of a job order system and a process costing system. A hybrid system would be used, for example, in a manufacturing environment in which various product lines have different direct materials, but similar processing techniques.

To illustrate the need for hybrid systems, assume you order an automobile with the following options: leather seats, a Bose stereo system and compact disk player, cruise control, and pearlized paint. The costs of all options need to be traced specifically to your car, but the assembly processes for all the cars produced by the plant are similar. The job order costing feature of tracing direct materials to specific jobs is combined with the process costing feature of averaging labor and overhead costs over all homogeneous production to derive the total cost of the automobile you ordered. It would not be feasible to try to use a job order costing system to trace labor or overhead cost to your car individually, and it would be improper to average the costs of your options over all the cars produced during the period. The accompanying News Note reflects a build-to-order approach in the automobile industry.

GENERAL BUSINESS  NEWS NOTE

Computer Techniques for Car Production

Toyota Motor Corp. announced in 1999 that it would soon begin producing the Camry Solara coupe to customer order in just five days, and it would do the same for other models starting later in that year. The announcement surprised an industry that typically requires 30 to 60 days to produce a custom order.

The Toyota announcement raises two questions. First, will the automobile industry, which now predominantly follows a "make to stock" model in North America, change to "make to order," which is more common in Europe and in Japan? Second, will Toyota gain a significant competitive advantage by making this transition first?

This is a serious question, and the personal-computer industry shows why. By making and delivering personal computers to order, Dell Computer catapulted itself from a crowded field to become an industry leader. In just a few years, Dell picked up more than six percentage points in market share.

But until now, no major manufacturer was prepared to offer quick custom-order delivery. Some visionaries envisioned a 15-day car, but no one thought it was just around the corner. There is plenty of skepticism about whether Toyota can achieve a five-day car without making unacceptable compromises in flexibility and total delivery lead time. Toyota's announcement, however, leaves little room for doubt about the company's strategy. It was not a trial balloon but a confident statement of intent.

How much of a competitive advantage can Toyota gain from a five-day car? The Dell success story offers an interesting parallel, although Dell sells directly to customers while Toyota will continue to sell through dealers. Even so, Toyota can derive savings from a build-to-order strategy, as it can help dealers drive down retail inventories.

SOURCE: Jeffrey Bodenstab, "An Automaker Tries the Dell Way," *The Wall Street Journal* (August 30, 1999), p. A26. Permission conveyed through the Copyright Clearance Center.

http://www.toyota.com
http://www.dell.com

A hybrid costing system is appropriate for companies producing items such as furniture, clothing, or jam. In each instance, numerous kinds of raw materials could be used to create similar output. A table may be made from oak, teak, or mahogany; a blouse may be made from silk, cotton, or polyester; and jam may be made from peach, strawberries, or marmalade. The material cost for a batch run would need to be traced separately, but the production process of the batch is repetitive.

Hybrid costing systems allow accounting systems to portray more accurately the actual type of manufacturing activities in which companies are engaged. Job order costing and process costing are two ends of a continuum and, as is typically the case for any continuum, neither end is necessarily the norm. As flexible manufacturing increases, so will the use of hybrid costing systems.

REVISITING

Lumina Candles & Art

http://www.borsheimarts.com/lumina.htm

Beeswax is one of nature's useful and fragrant gifts. It takes about 160,000 bees to produce 60 pounds of honey that only yield about one pound of beeswax. Naturally fragrant beeswax is dripless, burns cleaner, and lasts longer than petroleum-based waxes. Beeswax candles also burn without creating smoke. To demonstrate how long a beeswax candle can last, Kelly Borsheim timed an eight-inch pillar candle that, after 60 hours, still had greater than half remaining. At that point, she discontinued timing it.

Lumina Candles & Art is somewhat of a diversified home-based business. Not only does the company provide all the supplies and instructions needed to make beeswax candles, but Kelly also creates award-winning artistic sculptures and paintings. In addition, Kelly provides art lessons in creating both sculpture and painting.

Kelly Borsheim is devoted to helping aspiring candle makers and artists succeed, not only in their production of beautiful works but also in their success as business people. For example, the Lumina Candles & Art Web site provides a section entitled "Tips on How to Start Your Own Candle Business." The Web site also includes other sections on effective management and marketing for candle and art business ventures.

SOURCE: Lumina Candles & Art Web site: http://www.borsheimarts.com/lumina.htm

CHAPTER SUMMARY

Process costing is an averaging method used to assign costs to output in manufacturing situations producing large quantities of homogeneous products. A process costing system may use either the weighted average or FIFO method to compute equivalent units of and assign costs to production. The difference between the two methods lies solely in the treatment of the work performed in the prior period on the beginning work in process inventory.

Under the weighted average method, work performed in the prior period is combined with current period work and the total costs are averaged over all units. Using the FIFO method, work performed in the last period on beginning work in process inventory is not commingled with current period work, nor are costs of beginning work in process added to current period costs to derive unit production cost. With FIFO, current period costs are divided by current period production to generate a unit production cost related entirely to work actually performed in the current period.

Six steps must be taken when deriving and assigning product cost under a process costing system:

1. Calculate the total number of physical units to account for.
2. Calculate the physical units accounted for by tracing the physical flow of units. This step involves identifying the groups to which costs are to be assigned (transferred out of or remaining in ending inventory).
3. Determine the number of equivalent units of production, either on the weighted average or FIFO basis, for each cost component. The cost components include transferred-in (if multidepartmental), direct material, direct labor, and overhead. In cases of multiple materials having different degrees of completion, each material is considered a separate cost component. If overhead is applied on a direct labor basis or is incurred at the same rate as direct labor, labor and overhead can be combined as one cost component and referred to as "conversion."
4. Determine the total cost to account for, which is the sum of beginning inventory costs and all production costs incurred for the current period.
5. Calculate the cost per equivalent unit of production for each cost component.
6. Assign the costs to the units transferred and the units in ending work in process inventory. The method of cost assignment depends on whether weighted average or FIFO costing is used. The total of the costs assigned to units transferred and to units in ending work in process inventory must equal the total cost to account for.

The FIFO method of process costing can be combined with standard costs so that a "normal" production cost is assigned each period to equivalent units of output. This technique allows managers to quickly recognize and investigate significant deviations from normal production costs.

Hybrid costing systems allow companies to combine the characteristics of both job order and process costing systems. Direct material or direct labor that is related to a particular batch of goods can be traced to those specific goods using job order costing. Cost components that are common to numerous batches of output are accounted for using process costing techniques.

APPENDIX

Alternative Calculations of Weighted Average and FIFO Methods

7

What alternative methods can be used to calculate equivalent units of production?

Various methods are used to compute equivalent units of production under the weighted average and FIFO methods. One of the most common variations is the following EUP calculation for weighted average:

Units transferred (whole units)
\+ Ending work in process (equivalent units)
= Weighted average EUP

Once the weighted average EUP figure is available, the FIFO equivalent units can be quickly derived by subtracting the equivalent units in beginning work in process inventory that had been produced in the previous period:

Weighted average EUP
− Beginning work in process (equivalent units)
= FIFO EUP

This computation is appropriate for the following reason: The weighted average method concentrates on the units that were completed during the period as well as the units that were started but not completed during the period. Unlike FIFO, the weighted average method does not exclude the equivalent units that were in beginning inventory. Thus, to convert from weighted average to FIFO, simply remove the equivalent units produced in the previous period from beginning work in process.

The Decorative Waxes Company's April production data presented in the chapter are repeated here to illustrate these alternative calculations for the weighted average and FIFO methods.

Candles in beginning work in process (100% complete as to material; 40% complete as to conversion costs)	25,000
Candles started during the month	510,000
Candles completed during the month	523,000
Candles in ending work in process (100% complete as to material; 80% complete as to conversion costs)	12,000

Using these data, the EUPs are computed as follows:

	DM	Conversion
Candles transferred	523,000	523,000
+ Ending work in process equivalent units (12,000 candles × 100% and 80% complete)	12,000	9,600
= **Weighted average EUP**	535,000	532,600
− Beginning work in process equivalent units produced in previous period (25,000 candles × 100% and 40% complete)	(25,000)	(10,000)
= **FIFO EUP**	510,000	522,600

The distinct relationship between the weighted average and FIFO costing models can also be used to derive the equivalent units of production calculations. This method begins with the total number of units to account for in the period. From this amount, the EUPs to be completed next period are subtracted to give the weighted average EUP. Next, as in the method shown above, the equivalent units completed in the prior period (the beginning Work in Process Inventory) are deducted to give the FIFO equivalent units of production. Using the Decorative Waxes Company data, these computations are as follows:

	DM	Conversion
Total units to account for	535,000	535,000
− EUP to be completed next period (ending inventory × % not completed: 12,000 × 0%; 12,000 × 20%)		(2,400)
= **Weighted average EUP**	535,000	532,600
− EUP completed in prior period (beginning inventory × % completed last period: 25,000 × 100%; 25,000 × 40%)	(25,000)	(10,000)
= **FIFO EUP**	510,000	522,600

These alternative calculations can either be used to confirm answers found by using beginning inventory units, units started and completed, and ending inventory units or as a shortcut to initially compute equivalent units of production.

KEY TERMS

cost of production report (p. 229)
equivalent units of production (EUP) (p. 222)
FIFO method (of process costing) (p. 223)
hybrid costing system (p. 238)
total cost to account for (p. 226)
total units to account for (p. 224)
units started and completed (p. 228)
weighted average method (of process costing) (p. 223)

SOLUTION STRATEGIES

Steps in Process Costing Computations

1. Compute the total units to account for (in physical units):

Beginning inventory in physical units
\+ Units started (or transferred in) during period

2. Compute units accounted for (in physical units):

Units completed and transferred
\+ Ending inventory in physical units

3. Compute equivalent units of production per cost component:

a. Weighted average

Beginning inventory in physical units
\+ Units started and completed*
\+ (Ending inventory × % complete)

b. FIFO

(Beginning inventory × % not complete at start of period)
+ Units started and completed*
+ (Ending inventory × % complete)

*Units started and completed = (Units transferred − Units in beginning inventory).

4. Compute total cost to account for:

Costs in beginning inventory
+ Costs of current period

5. Compute cost per equivalent unit per cost component:

a. Weighted average

Cost of component in beginning inventory
+ Cost of component for current period
= Total cost of component
÷ EUP for component

b. FIFO

Cost of component for current period
÷ EUP for component

6. Assign costs to inventories:

a. Weighted average

(1) Transferred:
Units transferred × (Total cost per EUP for all components)

(2) Ending inventory:
EUP for each component × Cost per EUP for each component

b. FIFO

(1) Transferred:
Beginning inventory costs
+ (Beginning inventory × % not complete at beginning of period for each component × Cost per EUP for each component)
+ (Units started and completed × Total cost per EUP for all components)

(2) Ending inventory:
EUP for each component × Cost per EUP for each component

DEMONSTRATION PROBLEM

The Sporting Bag Company manufactures golf bags in a two-department process: Assembly and Finishing. The Assembly Department uses weighted average costing; the cost driver for overhead in this department is unrelated to direct labor. The Finishing Department adds the hardware to the assembled bags and uses FIFO costing. Overhead is applied to the bags in this department on a direct labor basis. During June, the following production data and costs have been gathered:

ASSEMBLY DEPARTMENT: UNITS

Beginning work in process (100% complete for material; 40% complete for labor; 30% complete for overhead)	250
Units started	8,800
Ending work in process (100% complete for material; 70% complete for labor; 90% complete for overhead)	400

ASSEMBLY DEPARTMENT: COSTS

	Material	Direct Labor	Overhead	Total
Beginning inventory	$ 3,755	$ 690	$ 250	$ 4,695
Current	100,320	63,606	27,681	191,607
Totals	$104,075	$64,296	$27,931	$196,302

FINISHING DEPARTMENT: UNITS

Beginning work in process (100% complete for transferred-in; 15% complete for material; 40% complete for conversion)	100
Units transferred in	8,650
Ending work in process (100% complete for transferred-in; 30% complete for material; 65% complete for conversion)	200

FINISHING DEPARTMENT: COSTS

	Transferred-In	Direct Material	Conversion	Total
Beginning inventory	$ 2,176	$ 30	$ 95	$ 2,301
Current	188,570	15,471	21,600	225,641
Totals	$190,746	$15,501	$21,695	$227,942

Required:

a. Prepare a cost of production report for the Assembly Department.
b. Prepare a cost of production report for the Finishing Department.

Solution to Demonstration Problem

a.

	Whole Units	EQUIVALENT UNITS OF PRODUCTION		
		Direct Material	Direct Labor	Overhead
Beginning inventory	250	250	100	75
Units started	8,800			
Units to account for	9,050			
BWIP completed	250	0	150	175
Started and completed	8,400	8,400	8,400	8,400
Units completed	8,650			
Ending inventory	400	400	280	360
Units accounted for	9,050			
Weighted average EUP		9,050	8,930	9,010

COST DATA

	Whole Units	Direct Material	Direct Labor	Overhead
	Total			
BWIP costs	$ 4,695	$ 3,755	$ 690	$ 250
Current period costs	191,607	100,320	63,606	27,681
Total costs	$196,302	$104,075	$ 64,296	$27,931
Divided by EUP		9,050	8,930	9,010
Cost per EUP	$21.80	$11.50	$7.20	$3.10

COST ASSIGNMENT

Transferred out (8,650 × $21.80)		$188,570
Ending inventory		
Direct material (400 × $11.50)	$4,600	
Direct labor (280 × $7.20)	2,016	
Overhead (360 × $3.10)	1,116	7,732
Total cost accounted for		$196,302

b.

	Whole Units	EQUIVALENT UNITS OF PRODUCTION: Transferred-In	Direct Material	Conversion
Beginning inventory	100			
Units started	8,650			
Units to account for	8,750			
BWIP completed	100	0	85	60
Started and completed	8,450	8,450	8,450	8,450
Units completed	8,550			
Ending inventory	200	200	60	130
Units accounted for	8,750			
FIFO EUP		8,650	8,595	8,640

COST DATA

	Total	Transferred-In	Direct Material	Conversion
BWIP costs	$ 2,301			
Current period costs	225,641	$188,570	$15,471	$21,600
Total costs	$227,942			
Divided by EUP		8,650	8,595	8,640
Cost per EUP	$26.10	$21.80	$1.80	$2.50

COST ASSIGNMENT

Transferred out		
Beginning inventory cost	$2,301	
Cost to complete:		
Transferred-in (0 × $21.80)	0	
Direct material (85 × $1.80)	153	
Conversion (60 × $2.50)	150	$ 2,604
Started and completed (8,450 × $26.10)		220,545
Ending inventory		
Transferred-in (200 × $21.80)	$4,360	
Direct material (60 × $1.80)	108	
Conversion (130 × $2.50)	325	4,793
Total cost accounted for		$227,942

QUESTIONS

1. What are the typical characteristics of a company that should employ a process costing system?
2. Why is the process of assigning costs to products essentially an averaging process?
3. How are job order and process costing similar? How do they differ?
4. Why are equivalent units of production used as an output measure in process costing? In your answer, be sure to address the problems created by partially completed inventories.
5. What creates the difference between weighted average and FIFO equivalent units of production? Which EUP calculation more accurately portrays the actual flow of units through a manufacturing process and why?
6. Why is it necessary to calculate separate equivalent units of production for each cost component of a product? Are there times when separate EUP schedules are not necessary and, if so, why?
7. How are units "started and completed" in the current period calculated? Is this figure used in both weighted average and FIFO cost assignment? Why or why not?
8. In which of the six basic steps used in process costing are physical units used and in which are equivalent units of production used? Are there steps in which neither physical nor equivalent units are used? Why or why not?
9. How is the unit cost for each cost component assigned to the units produced during the current period under (a) the weighted average method and (b) the FIFO method?
10. What is the purpose of the cost of production report? How would such a report assist accountants in making journal entries for a period?
11. Would it be correct to subtract the cost computed for EWIP from the total costs to account for as a shortcut to determine the cost of goods transferred out? If you answered yes, is there a risk in doing this?
12. Why does the "Transferred Out" section of the FIFO method cost of production report include multiple computations, whereas the same section for the weighted average report only includes one computation?
13. How does process costing in a multidepartmental manufacturing environment differ from that of a single-department manufacturing environment? Why does this difference exist?
14. Why are the EUP calculations made for standard process costing the same as the EUP calculations for FIFO process costing?
15. How are inventories accounted for under a standard process costing system? What information is provided to management when inventories are accounted for in this manner?
16. What is a hybrid costing system? Under what circumstances is the use of such a system appropriate?

17. Find five companies, in different industries, on the Internet that you believe use process costing. Name these companies, provide their Web addresses, indicate what products they make, and discuss why you believe they use process costing.

EXERCISES

18. *(EUP; weighted average)* Newton Quiches uses a weighted average process costing system. All material is added at the start of the production process. Direct labor and overhead are added at the same rate throughout the process. Newton's records indicate the following production for October 2000:

Beginning inventory (70% complete as to conversion)	120,000 units
Started during October	170,000 units
Completed during October	260,000 units

Ending inventory for October is 20 percent complete as to conversion.

a. What are the equivalent units of production for direct material?

b. What are the equivalent units of production for labor and overhead?

19. *(EUP; FIFO)* Assume that Newton Quiches in Exercise 18 uses the FIFO method of process costing.

a. What are the equivalent units of production for direct material?

b. What are the equivalent units of production for labor and overhead?

20. *(EUP; weighted average & FIFO)* McArthur Corporation makes toy metal soldiers in a one-department production process. All metal is added at the beginning of the process. Paint for the figures and the plastic bags for packaging are considered indirect materials. The following information is available relative to September 2000 production activities:

Beginning inventory:	75,000 figures (60% complete as to labor; 85% complete as to overhead)
Started into production:	metal for 250,000 figures, which were cast during the month
Ending inventory:	30,000 figures (70% complete as to labor; 90% complete as to overhead)

a. Compute the EUP for direct material, direct labor, and overhead using weighted average process costing.

b. Compute the EUP for direct material, direct labor, and overhead using FIFO process costing.

c. Reconcile the calculations in parts (a) and (b).

21. *(Cost per EUP; weighted average)* Flickering Figurines manufactures wax figurines. In October 2000, company production is 26,800 equivalent units for direct material, 24,400 equivalent units for labor, and 21,000 equivalent units for overhead. During October, direct material and conversion costs incurred are as follows:

Direct material	$ 78,880
Direct labor	122,400
Overhead	42,600

Beginning inventory costs for October were $14,920 for direct material, $36,200 for labor, and $9,900 for overhead. What is the weighted average cost per equivalent unit for the cost components for October?

22. *(Cost per EUP; FIFO)* Assume that Flickering Figurines in Exercise 21 had 3,600 EUP for direct material in October's beginning inventory, 4,000 EUP for direct labor, and 3,960 EUP for overhead. What was the FIFO cost per equivalent unit for direct material, labor, and overhead for October?

23. *(Cost per EUP; weighted average & FIFO)* Garden Edges manufactures concrete garden border sections. May 2001 production and cost information are as follows:

WA EUP:	Direct material	40,000 sections
	Direct labor	38,000 sections
	Overhead	37,500 sections
FIFO EUP:	Direct material	30,000 sections
	Direct labor	31,000 sections
	Overhead	33,000 sections
BI costs:	Direct material	$ 5,300
	Direct labor	1,580
	Overhead	3,630
Current period costs:	Direct material	$13,500
	Direct labor	8,680
	Overhead	21,120

All material is added at the beginning of processing.

a. What is the total cost to account for?

b. Using weighted average process costing, what is the cost per equivalent unit for each cost component?

c. Using FIFO process costing, what is the cost per equivalent unit for each cost component?

d. How many units were in beginning inventory and at what percentage of completion was each cost component?

24. *(EUP; cost per EUP; weighted average)* TakeThat manufactures canisters of mace. On August 1, 2001, the company had 4,800 units in beginning Work in Process Inventory that were 100 percent complete as to canisters, 60 percent complete as to other materials, 10 percent complete as to direct labor, and 20 percent complete as to overhead. During August, TakeThat started 22,500 units into the manufacturing process. Ending Work in Process Inventory included 3,600 units that were 100 percent complete as to canisters, 30 percent complete as to other materials, 25 percent complete as to direct labor, and 30 percent complete as to overhead.

Cost information for the month follows:

Beginning inventory:	Canisters	$ 8,175
	Other direct materials	3,393
	Direct labor	1,212
	Overhead	1,038
August costs:	Canisters	$39,600
	Other direct materials	20,148
	Direct labor	61,812
	Overhead	43,734

Prepare a schedule showing TakeThat's August 2001 computation of weighted average equivalent units of production and cost per equivalent unit.

25. *(EUP; cost per EUP; FIFO)* ReallyRoll makes skateboards and uses a FIFO process costing system. The company began April 2001 with 1,000 boards in process that were 70 percent complete as to material and 85 percent complete as to conversion. During the month, 3,800 additional boards were started. On April 30, 800 boards were still in process (60 percent complete as to material and 70 percent complete as to conversion). Cost information for April 2001 is as follows:

Beginning inventory costs:	Direct material	$13,181
	Conversion	6,732
Current period costs:	Direct material	$71,064
	Conversion	29,309

a. Calculate EUP for each cost component using the FIFO method.

b. Calculate cost per EUP for each cost component.

26. *(Cost assignment; weighted average)* Thomson Co. uses weighted average process costing. The company's cost accountant has determined the following production and cost per EUP information for January 2001:

Units transferred out during month	256,000
Units in ending inventory (100% complete as to direct material; 80% complete as to direct labor; 95% complete as to overhead)	37,000
Direct material cost per EUP	$3.75
Direct labor cost per EUP	$4.96
Overhead cost per EUP	$5.10

a. What is the cost of the goods transferred during January?

b. What is the cost of the goods in ending inventory at January 31, 2001?

c. What is the total cost to account for during January?

27. *(Cost assignment; FIFO)* In November 2000, Walker Corporation computed its costs per equivalent unit under FIFO process costing as follows:

Raw material	$12.75
Packaging	1.50
Direct labor	6.42
Overhead	3.87

The raw material is added at the start of processing. Packaging is added at the end of the production process immediately before the units are transferred to the finished goods warehouse.

Beginning inventory cost was $513,405 and consisted of:

- $344,520 raw material cost for 27,000 EUP,
- $95,931 direct labor cost for 14,850 EUP, and
- $72,954 overhead cost for 18,900 EUP.

Walker transferred a total of 185,000 units to finished goods during November, which left 16,000 units in ending inventory. The EI units were 20 percent complete as to direct labor and 35 percent complete as to overhead.

a. What percentage complete were the beginning inventory units as to raw material? Packaging? Direct labor? Overhead?
b. What was the total cost of the completed beginning inventory units?
c. What was the cost of the units started and completed in November?
d. What was the cost of November's ending inventory?

28. *(EUP; cost per EUP; cost assignment; FIFO & weighted average)* Berne Company mass produces miniature speakers for portable CD players. The following T-account presents the firm's cost information for February 2001:

Work in Process Inventory

2/1 Direct material cost in BI	$ 1,027	
2/1 Conversion cost in BI	588	
Feb. DM received	11,682	
Feb. DL incurred	2,513	
Feb. OH applied to production	1,257	

The company had 400 units in process on February 1. These units were 40 percent complete as to material and 30 percent complete as to conversion. During February, the firm started 1,500 units and ended the month with 150 units still in process. The units in ending WIP Inventory were 20 percent complete as to material and 70 percent complete as to conversion.

a. Compute the unit costs for February under the FIFO method for direct material and for conversion.
b. Compute the unit costs for February under the weighted average method for direct material and for conversion.
c. Determine the total costs transferred to Finished Goods Inventory during February using the FIFO method.

29. *(EUP; weighted average & FIFO; two departments)* Jones Metals has two processing departments, Fabrication and Assembly. Metal is placed into production in the Fabrication Department, where it is cut, formed, or ground into various components. These components are transferred to Assembly, where they are welded, polished, and hot-dip galvanized with sealant. The production data follow for these two departments for March 2001:

Fabrication	
Beginning WIP inventory (100% complete as to material; 45% complete as to conversion)	5,000
Units started during month	39,000
Ending WIP inventory (100% complete as to material; 80% complete as to conversion)	6,800

Assembly	
Beginning WIP inventory (0% complete as to sealant; 15% complete as to conversion)	1,500
Units started during month	?
Ending WIP inventory (100% complete as to sealant; 75% complete as to conversion)	4,600

a. Determine the equivalent units of production for each cost component for each department under the weighted average method.
b. Determine the equivalent units of production for each cost component for each department under the FIFO method.

30. *(Standard process costing; variances)* DiskCity Products manufactures 3.5-inch preformatted computer disks and uses a standard process costing system. All material is added at the start of production, and labor and overhead are incurred equally throughout the process. The standard cost of one disk is as follows:

Direct material	$0.13
Direct labor	0.02
Overhead	0.11
Total cost	$0.26

The following production and cost data are applicable to April 2001:

Beginning inventory (45% complete)	17,000 units
Started in April	130,000 units
Ending inventory (65% complete)	14,400 units
Current cost of direct material	$18,400
Current cost of direct labor	2,598
Current cost of overhead	15,000

a. What cost is carried as the April beginning balance of Work in Process Inventory?
b. What cost is carried as the April ending balance of Work in Process Inventory?
c. What cost is transferred to Finished Goods Inventory for April?
d. Using the FIFO method, what are the total direct material, direct labor, and overhead variances for April?

31. *(Standard process costing)* Tico Company uses a standard FIFO process costing system to account for its tortilla manufacturing process. The tortillas are packaged and sold by the dozen. The company has set the following standards for production of each one-dozen package:

Direct material—ingredients	$0.35
Direct material—package	0.05
Direct labor	0.07
Overhead	0.13
Total cost	$0.60

On June 1, the company had 7,200 individual tortillas in process; these were 100 percent complete as to ingredients, 0 percent complete as to the packaging, and 30 percent complete as to labor and overhead. One hundred forty-four thousand tortillas were started during June and 147,960 were finished. The ending inventory was 100 percent complete as to ingredients, 0 percent complete as to the packaging, and 60 percent complete as to labor and overhead.

a. What were the equivalent units of production for June?

b. What was the cost of the packages transferred to Finished Goods Inventory during June?

c. What was the cost of the ending Work in Process Inventory for June?

32. *(Hybrid costing)* Carolina Coats makes casual coats (one size fits most). Each coat goes through the same conversion process, but three types of fabric (Dacron, denim, or cotton) are available. The company uses a standard costing system, and standard costs for each type of coat follow:

	Dacron	Denim	Cotton
Material (5 yards)	$10	$ 5	$12
Direct labor (2 hours)	12	12	12
Overhead (based on 1.5 machine hours)	9	9	9
Total	$31	$26	$33

Material is added at the start of production. In March 2001, there was no beginning Work in Process Inventory and 1,500 coats were started into production. Of these, 200 were Dacron, 600 were denim, and 700 were cotton. At the end of March, 300 jackets (50 Dacron, 100 denim, and 150 cotton) were not yet completed. The stage of completion for each cost component for the 300 unfinished jackets is as follows:

Material	100% complete
Direct labor	25% complete
Overhead	35% complete

a. Determine the total cost of the coats completed and transferred to Finished Goods Inventory.

b. Determine the total cost of the coats in ending Work in Process Inventory.

PROBLEMS

33. *(EUP; weighted average & FIFO)* Patio Company produces outdoor brooms. On April 30, 2001, the firm had 3,600 units in process that were 70 percent complete as to material, 40 percent complete as to direct labor, and 30 percent complete as to overhead. During May, 186,000 brooms were started. Records indicate that 184,200 units were transferred to Finished Goods Inventory in May. Ending units in process were 40 percent complete as to material, 25 percent complete as to direct labor, and 10 percent complete as to overhead.

a. Calculate the physical units to account for in May.

b. How many units were started and completed during May?

c. Determine May's EUP for each category using the weighted average method.

d. Determine May's EUP for each category using the FIFO method.

e. Reconcile your answers to parts (c) and (d).

34. *(EUP; weighted average & FIFO)* The Midwest Coal Company mines and processes coal that is sold to four power plants in central Pennsylvania. The company employs a process costing system to assign production costs to the coal it processes. For the third week in March 2001, the firm had a beginning Work in Process Inventory of 50,000 tons of ore that were 100 percent complete as to material and 30 percent complete as to conversion. During the week, an additional 200,000 tons of ore were started in process. At the end of the week, 35,000 tons remained in Work in Process Inventory and were 70 percent complete as to material and 60 percent complete as to conversion.

For the third week in March:

a. Compute the total units to account for.
b. Determine how many units were started and completed.
c. Determine the equivalent units of production using the weighted average method.
d. Determine the equivalent units of production using the FIFO method.

35. *(Weighted average)* Frankfurt Products manufactures an electronic language translator. The device can translate seven languages in either direction. Analysis of beginning Work in Process Inventory for February 2001 revealed the following:

800 Units	Percent Complete	Cost Incurred
Material	45	$ 8,700
Direct labor	65	3,800
Overhead	40	6,600
Total beginning WIP		$19,100

During February, Frankfurt Products started production of another 3,800 translators and incurred $85,380 for material, $23,560 for direct labor, and $65,720 for overhead. On February 28, the company had 400 units in process (70 percent complete as to material, 90 percent complete as to direct labor, and 80 percent complete as to overhead).

a. Prepare a cost of production report for February using the weighted average method.
b. Journalize the February transactions.
c. Prepare T-accounts to represent the flow of costs for Frankfurt Products for February. Use "XXX" where amounts are unknown and identify what each unknown amount represents.

36. *(Weighted average)* Alt Enterprises manufactures belt buckles in a single-step production process. To determine the proper valuations for inventory balances and Cost of Goods Sold, you have obtained the following information for August 2001:

	Whole Units	Cost of Material	Cost of Labor
Beginning work in process	400,000	$ 400,000	$ 630,000
Units started during period	2,000,000	2,600,000	3,990,000
Units transferred to finished goods	1,800,000		

Beginning inventory units were 100 percent complete as to material, but only 80 percent complete as to labor and overhead. The ending inventory units were 100 percent complete as to material and 50 percent complete as to conversion. Overhead is applied to production at the rate of 60 percent of direct labor cost.

a. Prepare a schedule to compute equivalent units of production by cost component assuming the weighted average method.
b. Determine the unit production costs for material and conversion.
c. Calculate the costs assigned to completed units and ending inventory for August 2000.

37. *(Weighted average)* You have just been hired as the cost accountant for Sun Valley Micro, a producer of personal computer cases. This position has been vacant for one month. John Amos, manager of the firm's tax department, has performed some computations for last month's information; however, he confesses to you that he doesn't remember a great deal about cost accounting.

In the production process, materials are added at the beginning of production and overhead is applied to each product at the rate of 70 percent of direct labor cost. There was no Finished Goods Inventory at the beginning of July. A review of the firm's inventory cost records provides you with the following information:

	Units	DM Cost	DL Cost
Work in Process 7/1/00			
(70% complete as to labor and overhead)	100,000	$ 750,000	$ 215,000
Units started in production	1,300,000		
Costs for July		4,850,000	3,265,000
Work in Process 7/31/00			
(40% complete as to labor and overhead)	400,000		

At the end of July, the cost of Finished Goods Inventory was determined to be $124,033.

a. Prepare schedules for July 2000, to compute the following:
 1. Equivalent units of production using the weighted average method.
 2. Unit production costs for material, labor, and overhead.
 3. Cost of Goods Sold.

b. Prepare the journal entries to record the July transfer of completed goods and the July cost of goods sold. *(CPA adapted)*

38. *(FIFO cost per EUP)* The following information has been gathered from the records of Jack's Snacks for August 2001. The firm makes a variety of snacks; the information presented here is for a cashew and dried mango mix. Materials are added at the beginning of processing; overhead is applied on a direct labor basis. The mix is transferred to a second department for packaging. Jack's uses a FIFO process costing system.

Beginning WIP inventory (40% complete as to conversion)	5,000 pounds
Mix started in August	90,400 pounds
Ending WIP inventory (70% complete as to conversion)	4,000 pounds
Materials cost incurred in August	$415,840
Conversion costs incurred in August	$106,030

Beginning inventory cost totaled $13,875. For August 2001, compute the following:

a. Equivalent units of production by cost component.
b. Cost per equivalent unit by cost component.
c. Cost of mix transferred to the packaging department in August.
d. Cost of August's ending inventory.

39. *(Cost assignment; FIFO)* Green Seasons Processors is a contract manufacturer for the Delectable Dressing Company. Green Seasons uses a FIFO process costing system to account for the production of its salad dressing. All ingredients are added at the start of the process. Delectable provides reusable vats to Green Seasons for the completed product to be shipped to Delectable for bottling so Green Seasons incurs no packaging costs. April 2001 production and cost information for Green Seasons Processors is as follows:

Gallons of dressing in beginning inventory	37,000
Gallons transferred out during April	243,000
Gallons of dressing in ending inventory	23,500
Costs of beginning inventory:	
Direct material	$ 181,300
Direct labor	45,695
Overhead	50,320
Costs incurred in April:	
Direct material	$1,131,435
Direct labor	452,976
Overhead	770,133

The beginning and ending inventories had the following degrees of completion each for labor and overhead:

	Beginning Inventory	Ending Inventory
Direct labor	35%	25%
Overhead	60%	30%

a. How many gallons of dressing ingredients were started in April?
b. What is the total cost of the completed beginning inventory?
c. What is the total cost of goods completed during April?
d. What is the average cost per gallon of all goods completed during April?
e. What is the cost of April's ending WIP inventory?

40. *(Weighted average & FIFO)* In a single-process production system, the Cleopatra Corporation produces press-on fingernails. For October 2000, the company's accounting records reflected the following:

Beginning Work in Process Inventory (100% complete as to material; 30% complete as to direct labor; 60% complete as to overhead)	6,000 units
Units started during the month	45,000 units
Ending Work in Process Inventory (100% complete as to material; 40% complete as to direct labor; 70% complete as to overhead)	10,000 units

Cost Component	Beginning Inventory	October
Material	$4,980	$45,000
Direct labor	450	21,600
Overhead	3,180	33,300

a. For October, prepare a cost of production report assuming the company uses the weighted average method.
b. For October, prepare a cost of production report assuming the company uses the FIFO method.

41. *(FIFO; second department)* Bixby Company makes porcelain kitchen sinks in a process requiring operations in three separate departments: Molding, Curing, and Finishing. Materials are first introduced in the molding operation and additional material is added during the curing process. The following information is available for the Curing Department for May 2001:

Beginning WIP Inventory (degree of completion: transferred-in, 100%; direct material, 80%; direct labor, 40%; overhead, 30%)	8,000 units
Transferred-in from Molding	40,000 units
Ending WIP Inventory (degree of completion: transferred-in, 100%; direct material, 70%; direct labor, 50%; overhead, 40%)	4,000 units
Transferred to Finishing	? units

Cost Component	Beginning Inventory	Current Period
Transferred-in	$66,000	$320,000
Direct material	24,960	161,600
Direct labor	6,720	85,600
Overhead	3,580	43,200

Prepare, in good form, a cost of production report for the Curing Department for May 2001. *(CPA adapted)*

42. *(Two departments; weighted average)* The Best of the Season Corporation makes plastic Christmas trees in two departments: Cutting and Boxing. In the Cutting Department, wire wrapped with green "needles" is placed into production at the beginning of the process and is cut to various lengths depending on the size of the trees being made at that time. The "branches" are then transferred to the Boxing Department where the lengths are separated into the necessary groups to make a tree. These are then placed in boxes and immediately sent to Finished Goods.

The following data are available related to the October 2000 production in each of the two departments:

	Units	PERCENT OF COMPLETION		
		Transferred-in	Material	Conversion
Cutting Department				
Beginning inventory	9,000	N/A	100	30
Started in process	35,000			
Ending inventory	3,600	N/A	100	70
Boxing Department				
Beginning inventory	2,500	100	0	55
Transferred-in	?			
Ending inventory	1,200	100	0	60

COSTS	Transferred-in	Material	Conversion
Cutting Department			
Beginning inventory	N/A	$13,250	$ 5,550
Current period	$52,750	80,290	
Boxing Department			
Beginning inventory	$ 9,608	$ 0	$ 550
Current period	?	12,510	20,660

a. Prepare a cost of production report for the Cutting Department assuming a weighted average method.

b. Using the data developed from part (a), prepare a cost of production report for the Boxing Department, also using the weighted average method.

43. *(Cost flows: multiple departments)* Sharp Corporation produces accent stripes for automobiles in 50-inch rolls. Each roll passes through three departments (Striping, Adhesion, and Packaging) before it is ready for shipment to automobile dealers and detailing shops. Product costs are tracked by department and assigned using a process costing system. Overhead is applied to production in each department at a rate of 60 percent of the department's direct labor cost. The following information pertains to departmental operations for June 2001:

Work in Process—Striping

Beginning	$20,000	
DM	90,000	
DL	80,000	
Overhead	?	
Ending	$17,000	

Work in Process—Adhesion

Beginning	$70,000	
Transferred-in	?	
DM	60,000	$480,000
DL	?	
Overhead	?	
Ending	$20,000	

Work in Process—Packaging

Beginning	$150,000	
Transferred-in	?	
DM	?	
DL	?	
Overhead	90,000	
Ending	$ 90,000	

Finished Goods

Beginning	$185,000	
CGM	830,000	$720,000
Ending	?	

a. What was the cost of goods transferred from the Striping Department to the Adhesion Department for the month?

b. How much direct labor cost was incurred in the Adhesion Department? How much overhead was assigned to production in the Adhesion Department for the month?

c. How much direct material cost was charged to products passing through the Packaging Department?

d. Prepare the journal entries for all interdepartmental transfers of products and the cost of the units sold during June 2001.

44. *(Comprehensive; two departments)* Safe-N-Sound makes a backyard fencing system for pet owners in a two-stage production system. In Process 1, wood is cut and assembled into six-foot fence sections. In Process 2, the sections are pressure treated to resist the effects of weather and then coated with a wood preservative. The following production and cost data are available for March 2001 (units are six-foot fence sections):

Units	Cutting Process	Pressure Process
Beginning WIP Inventory (March 1)	1,300	900
Complete as to material	80%	0%
Complete as to conversion	75%	60%
Units started in March	4,800	?
Units completed in March	?	4,500
Ending WIP Inventory (March 31)	1,100	?
Complete as to material	40%	0%
Complete as to conversion	20%	40%
Costs		
Beginning WIP Inventory		
Transferred-in		$ 4,725
Material	$ 2,130	0
Conversion	3,175	1,674
Current		
Transferred-in		$?
Material	$ 8,800	4,995
Conversion	12,735	13,560

a. Prepare EUP schedules for both the cutting and pressure processes. Use the FIFO method.

b. Determine the cost per equivalent unit for the cutting process assuming a FIFO method.

c. Assign costs to goods transferred and to inventory in the cutting process on a FIFO basis.

d. Transfer the FIFO costs to the pressure process. Determine cost per EUP on a modified FIFO basis. (See footnote 8, page 233.)

e. Assign costs to goods transferred and to inventory in the pressure process on a modified FIFO basis.

f. Assuming there was no beginning or ending inventory of Finished Goods Inventory for March, what was Cost of Goods Sold for March?

45. *(Standard process costing)* HealthySight is a manufacturer of high-quality lenses for sunglasses and ski goggles. HealthySight uses a standard process costing system and carries inventories at standard. In May 2001, the following data were available:

	Standard Cost of 1 Unit
Direct material	$ 4.50
Conversion	12.50
Total manufacturing cost	$17.00

Beginning WIP Inventory	10,000 units (100% DM; 70% conversion)
Started in May	180,000 units
Completed in May	160,000 units
Ending WIP Inventory	? units (100% DM; 60% conversion)

Actual costs for May	
Direct material	$ 781,000
Conversion	2,045,000
Total actual cost	$2,826,000

a. Prepare an equivalent units of production schedule.
b. Prepare a cost of production report and assign costs to goods transferred and to inventory.
c. Calculate and label the variances and charge them to Cost of Goods Sold.

46. *(Multiproduct; hybrid costing)* Be-At-Ease Industries manufactures a series of three models of molded plastic chairs: standard (can be stacked), deluxe (with arms), and executive (with arms and padding); all are variations of the same design. The company uses batch manufacturing and has a hybrid costing system.

Be-At-Ease has an extrusion operation and subsequent operations to form, trim, and finish the chairs. Plastic sheets are produced by the extrusion operation, some of which are sold directly to other manufacturers. During the forming operation, the remaining plastic sheets are molded into chair seats and the legs are added; the standard model is sold after this operation. During the trim operation, the arms are added to the deluxe and executive models and the chair edges are smoothed. Only the executive model enters the finish operation where the padding is added. All of the units produced receive the same steps within each operation.

The July production run had a total manufacturing cost of $898,000. The units of production and direct material costs incurred were as follows:

	Units Produced	Extrusion Materials	Form Materials	Trim Materials	Finish Materials
Plastic sheets	5,000	$ 60,000			
Standard model	6,000	72,000	$24,000		
Deluxe model	3,000	36,000	12,000	$ 9,000	
Executive model	2,000	24,000	8,000	6,000	$12,000
	16,000	$192,000	$44,000	$15,000	$12,000

Manufacturing costs applied during July were as follows:

	Extrusion Operation	Form Operation	Trim Operation	Finish Operation
Direct labor	$152,000	$60,000	$30,000	$18,000
Factory overhead	240,000	72,000	39,000	24,000

a. For each product produced by Be-At-Ease during July, determine the
  1. Unit cost.
  2. Total cost.
  Be sure to account for all costs incurred during the month, and support your answer with appropriate calculations.
b. Without prejudice to your answer in part (a), assume that 1,000 units of the deluxe model remained in Work in Process Inventory at the end of the month. These units were 100 percent complete in the trim operation. Determine the value of the 1,000 units of the deluxe model in Be-At-Ease's Work in Process Inventory at the end of July. *(CMA adapted)*

CASE

47. *(WA and FIFO)* Rainbow Paints makes quality paint sold at premium prices in one production department. Production begins with the blending of various chemicals, which are added at the beginning of the process, and ends with the canning of the paint. Canning occurs when the mixture reaches the 90 percent stage of completion. The gallon cans are then transferred to the Shipping Department for crating and shipment. Labor and overhead are added continuously throughout the process. Factory overhead is applied at the rate of $3 per direct labor hour.

Prior to May, when a change in the process was implemented, work in process inventories were insignificant. The change in process enables greater production but results in large amounts of work in process. The company has always used the weighted average method to determine equivalent production and unit costs. Now, production management is considering changing from the weighted average method to the first-in, first-out method.

The following data relate to actual production during May:

Costs for May

Work in process inventory, May 1	
Direct material—chemicals	$ 45,600
Direct labor ($10 per hour)	6,250
Factory overhead	1,875
Current month	
Direct material—chemicals	$228,400
Direct material—cans	7,000
Direct labor ($10 per hour)	35,000
Factory overhead	10,500

Units for May (Gallons)

Work in process inventory, May 1 (25% complete)	4,000
Sent to Shipping Department	20,000
Started in May	21,000
Work in process inventory, May 31 (80% complete)	5,000

a. Prepare a cost of production report for each cost element for May using the weighted average method.

b. Prepare a cost of production report for each cost element for May using the FIFO method.

c. Discuss the advantages and disadvantages of using the weighted average method versus the FIFO method, and explain under what circumstances each method should be used. *(CMA adapted)*

REALITY CHECK

48. The term *total cost to account for* has been used in this chapter and in another setting earlier in the text. Find that earlier reference to this term and write a brief report explaining whether or not the term is being used consistently in both places.

49. The weighted average and FIFO methods generally result in approximately the same unit costs because costs do not usually vary dramatically from period to period. Discuss some reasons for exceptions to this observation.

50. Cost accountants use the concept of equivalent units of production (EUP) to measure actual production for a period in a process costing environment. Write a memo describing what EUP measures and why it is necessary to use EUP to determine actual production for a period.

51. Search the Internet to identify a vendor of process costing software. Read the on-line literature provided by the vendor regarding the software. Then, briefly describe the major features of the software in the areas of product costing, cost budgeting, and cost control.

52. In a team of three or four people, choose a company whose mass production process you would like to learn. Use the library, the Internet, and (if possible) personal resources to gather information. Prepare a visual representation (similar to Exhibit 6–2) of that production process. In this illustration, indicate the approximate percentage of completion points at which various materials are added and where/how labor and overhead flow into and through the process. Assume that 1,000 units of product are flowing through your production process and are now at the 60 percent completion point as to labor. Prepare a written explanation about the quantity of direct material equivalent units that are included in the 1,000 units. Also explain how much overhead activity and cost have occurred and why the overhead percentage is the same as or different from the percentage of completion for labor.

53. Find a Web site or current professional article discussing developments in the pharmaceutical/medical devices industry. Read the materials on that site about evolving practices in the industry to improve cost effectiveness of operations. Discuss how the industry's new practices will affect process costing in the pharmaceutical industry. Which cost pools (direct material, direct labor, manufacturing overhead) will be affected by the emerging practices? Also, address whether any of the evolving practices would be better served by life cycle costing.

54. Find the Web page for Agile Software. Provide its Web address and discuss the nature of this Internet-based software and how it can affect cost accounting practices in industries that manufacture complex products.

CHAPTER 7

Special Production Issues: Lost Units and Accretion

LEARNING OBJECTIVES

After completing this chapter, you should be able to answer the following questions:

1
What is an accepted quality level and how does it relate to zero tolerance for errors and defects?

2
Why do lost units occur in manufacturing processes?

3
How do normal and abnormal losses of units differ and how is each treated in an EUP schedule?

4
How are the costs of each type of loss assigned?

5
How are rework costs of defective units treated?

6
How are losses treated in a job order costing system?

7
How does accretion of units affect the EUP schedule and costs per unit?

8
What is the cost of quality products?

INTRODUCING General Electric Company

http://www.ge.com

Thomas Alva Edison invented the first successful incandescent light bulb in 1879. Shortly thereafter, General Electric (GE) began providing power and lighting up America and the world. General Electric Company was formed in 1892 through a merger of Edison Electric Light Company and Thomson-Houston Company.

Today, GE is the world's largest diversified services company as well as a provider of high-quality, high-technology industrial and consumer products. While maintaining world-class leadership in its beginnings in providing power systems and electric lighting, the company has expanded into many areas. A few examples include aircraft engines, medical systems, financial services, television broadcasting, and transportation systems. GE consists of more than three dozen businesses operating in 100 companies around the globe. Although widely diverse, GE businesses are also highly familial and share information, resources, technology, and intellectual capital.

GE's sharing among all its businesses includes:

1. a common operating system and a social architecture characterized by boundaryless behavior,
2. a common leadership development system,
3. one set of common values, and
4. four common initiatives—globalization, product services, e-business, and Six Sigma quality.

Six Sigma is a quality management term used to define a process for eliminating variation and, therefore, eliminating defects. Statistically, Six Sigma quality means improving manufacturing quality to six standard deviations from the specification limit. This translates to a rate of 3.4 defects out of a million items processed. GE is absolutely committed to delivering flawless products and services to its customers.

At GE, the Six Sigma initiative is in its fifth year—its fifth trip through the operating system. From a standing start in 1996, with no financial benefit to the company, it has flourished to the point where it provided more than $2 billion in benefits in 1999, with much more to come this decade.

SOURCES: General Electric Company Web site, http://www.ge.com (June 2000); Robert Buderi, "The Six Sigma Approach Revs Up," *Upside* (May 2000), p. 50.

Unlike the General Electric (GE) processes that have been subjected to zero-defect tolerance, most companies tolerate some level of defects by establishing an **accepted quality level (AQL)** for their production or service processes. AQL is the maximum limit for the number of defects or errors in a process. If the percentage of defects or errors is less than the AQL, the company considers that it has performed at an acceptable quality level.

1

What is an accepted quality level and how does it relate to zero tolerance for errors and defects?

accepted quality level (AQL)

Companies viewed as having world-class status in a particular endeavor seek to continuously tighten the accepted quality level. Thus, producing goods with zero defects and performing services with zero errors are laudable goals and ones toward which domestic and foreign companies are striving.

The examples in Chapter 6 assumed that all units to be accounted for have either been transferred or are in ending work in process inventory; however, almost every process produces some units that are spoiled or do not meet production specifications. Phenomena in the production process also may cause the total units accounted for to be less than the total units to account for. In other situations (unrelated to spoiled units), the addition or expansion of materials after the start of the process may cause the units accounted for to be greater than those to be accounted for originally or in a previous department.

This chapter covers these more complex issues of process costing. Spoiled and defective units, reworking of defective units, and accretion require adjustments to the equivalent units of production (EUP) schedule and cost assignments made at the end of a period. The last section of this chapter discusses controlling quality so that only a minimal number of inferior goods are produced.

LOSS OF UNITS

Why do lost units occur in manufacturing processes?

shrinkage

http://www.starbucks.com
http://www.siratechnologies.com

Few, if any, processes combine material, labor, and overhead with no loss of units. Some of these losses, such as evaporation, leakage, or oxidation, are inherent in the production process. For example, when Starbucks roasts coffee beans, approximately 20 percent of the original weight is lost from water evaporation. This situation results in **shrinkage**. Modifying the production process to reduce or eliminate the causes of shrinkage may be difficult, impossible, or simply not cost beneficial.

Spoilage of some food products occurs simply by exposure to the atmosphere wherever perishable foods are processed or stored. In this regard, Louisiana State University and SIRA Technologies have developed a new monitoring system for meat that can enable meat processors and food retailers to better regulate the safety requirements for storage and prevent loss of reputation and revenue from selling meat containing harmful bacteria. The technology uses a bar code treated with antibodies that are sensitive to virulent strains of bacteria.[1] As discussed in the accompanying News Note, spoilage of meats and other perishable foods awaiting customer purchases in supermarkets can be further prevented by covering refrigeration cases each night.

At other times, errors in the production process (either by humans or machines) cause a loss of units through rejection at inspection for failure to meet appropriate quality standards or designated product specifications. Whether these lost units are

NEWS NOTE  QUALITY

Closing the Curtain on Contaminants

It is estimated that 75% of the supermarkets in North America are closed to the public for 6 to 8 hours at night. With little effort, these supermarkets could claim dollars that are lost during the stores' closed hours from unnecessary energy consumption and premature spoilage of many perishable products.

Open refrigerated display cases are the best way for retailers to present fresh merchandise to consumers. Unfortunately, these cases are also open to the effects of heat and UV radiation from the store environment.

There is often a misconception that the refrigerated air escapes from the display case. However, heat or warm air is actually drawn toward the colder air, raising the temperatures in the display case; this causes merchandise to warm up and compressors to operate more frequently.

More frequent compressor operation and exposed products must be tolerated so that consumers can shop freely, but when the store is closed, simple steps can be taken to reduce store energy consumption and extend product shelf life with ideal cold temperatures.

To solve this problem, an efficient temperature barrier is needed between the opening of the display case and the store interior. The ideal thermal barrier arrangement must have several qualities to be effective in increasing store profit:

- Reasonable cost and quick initial payback period;
- Simple and quick to put in operation;
- No interference with customer access to fresh merchandise when the store is open;
- No disturbance to the cosmetic appearance of the store;
- Durable commercial quality;
- Hygienic (will not rust or attract dust, mold, and mildew);
- Simple, quick cleaning maintenance that can be done when cleaning the case; and
- Effective in the reflection of heat and UV radiation.

A vertical rolling curtain permanently attached to the top of the display was agreed upon as the simplest and easiest to use arrangement. To adapt to this arrangement, a 99% pure aluminum heat-reflective fabric was developed. To provide strength to the woven aluminum fabric and eliminate oxidation, it is coated with a thin, transparent film.

SOURCE: Staff, "The Big Cover-Up in the Refrigeration Case," *Air Conditioning, Heating, and Refrigeration News* (April 3, 2000), pp. 27ff.

[1] Ginger Koloszyc, "New Bar-Code Technology Detects Meat Spoilage," *Stores* (October 1998), p. 72.

considered defective or spoiled depends on their ability to be economically re-worked. **Economically reworked** means that (1) the unit can be reprocessed to a sufficient quality level to be salable through normal distribution channels and (2) incremental rework cost is less than incremental revenue from the sale of re-worked units. A **defective unit** can be economically reworked, but a **spoiled unit** cannot. An inspector in the company making the product determines which are defective and which are spoiled.

economically reworked

defective unit
spoiled unit

To illustrate the difference between defective and spoiled units, assume you order blackened redfish at a restaurant. You are now the control inspector. If the redfish brought to you is barely blackened, it is a defective unit because the chef can cook it longer to bring it up to "product specifications." The incremental revenue is the selling price of the redfish; the incremental cost is a few moments of the chef's time. However, if the fish brought to you is blackened to a cinder, it is a spoiled unit because it cannot be reworked. Therefore, a newly cooked blackened redfish would have to be provided.

A **normal loss** of units falls within a tolerance level expected during production. Management creates a range of tolerance of spoiled units specified by the accepted quality level, as mentioned in the beginning of this chapter. If a company had set its quality goal as 98 percent of goods produced, the company would have been expecting a normal loss of 2 percent. Any loss in excess of the AQL is an **abnormal loss**. Thus, the difference between normal and abnormal loss is merely one of degree and is determined by management.

3

How do normal and abnormal losses of units differ and how is each treated in an EUP schedule?

normal loss
abnormal loss

A variety of methods can be used to account for units lost during production. Selection of the most appropriate method depends on two factors: (1) the cause of the decrease and (2) management expectations regarding lost units. Understanding why units decreased during production requires detailed knowledge of the manufacturing process. Management's expectations are important to determine the acceptable loss quantities from defects, spoilage, or shrinkage as well as the revenue and cost considerations of defective and spoiled units.

TYPES OF LOST UNITS

In developing the product design, manufacturing process, and product quality, management selects a combination of material, labor, and overhead from the wide resource spectrum available. This combination is chosen to provide the lowest long-run cost per unit and to achieve the designated product specifications—including those for quality. In making this resource combination choice, managers recognize that, for most combinations, some degree of production error may occur that will result in lost units. Given the resource choices made by management, the quantity or percentage of lost units to be generated in a given period or production run should be reasonably estimable. This estimate is the normal loss because it is planned for and expected. Normal loss is usually calculated on the basis of good output or actual input.

Some companies may estimate the normal loss to be quite high because the lowest cost material, labor, or overhead support is chosen. For example, assume that Scrape Manufacturing Ltd. chooses to install the least advanced, lowest cost machinery for production purposes because its workers do not have the educational or technological skills to handle the more advanced equipment. The installed equipment may have fewer quality checks and, thus, produce more spoiled units than the more advanced equipment. Scrape's managers have decided that the costs of upgrading worker skills were greater than the cost of lost units.

Another reason for high estimated normal losses relates not to the resources chosen, but to a problem inherent in the product design or in the production process. In other cases, based on cost-benefit analysis, managers may find that a problem would cost more to eliminate than to tolerate. For example, assume a machine malfunctions once every 100 production runs and improperly blends ingredients. The machine processes 50,000 runs each year and the ingredients in each run cost $10. Correcting the problem has been estimated to cost $20,000 per year. Spoilage cost is $5,000 per year (500 spoiled batches × $10 worth of ingredients) plus a minimal amount of overhead costs. If company employees are aware of the malfunction and catch every improperly blended run, accepting the spoilage is less expensive than correcting the problem.

If, alternatively, the spoiled runs are allowed to leave the plant, they may create substantial quality failure costs in the form of dissatisfied customers and/or salespeople who might receive the spoiled product. Managers in world-class companies should be aware that the estimate of the cost to develop a new customer is $50,000, five times as much as the estimated cost of keeping an existing one.[2] In making their cost-benefit analysis, managers must be certain to quantify all the costs (both direct and indirect) involved in spoilage problems.

An abnormal loss is a loss in excess of the normal, predicted tolerance limits. Thus, when an abnormal loss occurs, so does a normal loss (unless zero defects have been set as the AQL). Abnormal losses generally arise because of human or machine error during the production process. For example, if the tolerances on one of a company's production machines were set incorrectly, a significant quantity of defective products might be produced before the error was noticed. Because abnormal losses result from nonrandom, special adverse conditions and actions, they are more likely to be preventable than some types of normal losses.

Realistically, units are lost in a production process at a specific point. However, accounting for lost units requires that the loss be specified as being either continuous or discrete. For example, the weight loss in roasting coffee beans and the relatively continual breakage of fragile glass ornaments can be considered **continuous losses** because they occur fairly uniformly throughout the production process.

continuous loss

discrete loss

In contrast, a **discrete loss** is assumed to occur at a specific point. Examples of discrete losses include adding the wrong amount of vinegar to a recipe for salad dressing or attaching a part to a motor upside down. The units are only deemed lost and unacceptable when a quality check is performed. Therefore, regardless of where in the process the units were truly "lost," the loss point is always deemed to be an inspection point. Thus, units that have passed an inspection point should be good units (relative to the specific characteristics inspected), whereas units that have not yet passed an inspection point may be good or may be defective/spoiled.

Control points can be either built into the system or performed by inspectors. The former requires an investment in prevention costs; the latter results in appraisal costs. Both are effective, but prevention is often more efficient because acceptable quality cannot be inspected into a product; it must be a part of the production process. Investments to prevent lost units may relate either to people or machines. (Prevention costs and appraisal costs are formally defined in Chapter 8.)

In determining how many quality control inspection points (machine or human) to install, management must weigh the costs of having more inspections against the savings resulting from (1) not applying additional material, labor, and overhead to products that are already spoiled or defective (direct savings) and (2) the reduction or elimination of internal and external failure costs (indirect savings). Quality control points should always be placed before any bottlenecks in the production system so that the bottleneck resource is not used to process already defective/spoiled units. Additionally, a process that generates a continuous defect/spoilage loss requires a quality control point at the end of production; otherwise, some defective/spoiled units would not be found and would be sent to customers, creating external failure costs. (Failure costs are formally defined in Chapter 8.)

[2] Peter L. Grieco, Jr., "World-Class Customers," *Executive Excellence* (February 1996), p. 10.

ACCOUNTING FOR LOST UNITS

4

How are the costs of each type of loss assigned?

The method of accounting for the cost of lost units depends on whether the loss is considered normal or abnormal and whether the loss occurred continuously in the process or at a discrete point. Exhibit 7–1 summarizes the accounting for the cost of lost units.

The traditional method of accounting for normal losses is simple. Normal loss cost is considered a product cost and is included as part of the cost of the good units resulting from the process. Thus, the cost of the loss is inventoried in Work in Process and Finished Goods Inventories and expensed only when the good units are sold. This treatment has been considered appropriate because normal losses have been viewed as unavoidable costs in the production of good units. If the loss results from shrinkage caused by the production process, such as the weight loss of roasting coffee beans, this treatment seems logical.

Alternatively, consider the company producing fragile scientific lenses: If the company allows for losses by virtue of the level at which some acceptable quality was set, then management will not receive valuable information about the cost of quality losses. In contrast, if the same company were to institute a zero-defect policy, there would by definition be no "normal" loss. All losses would be outside the tolerance specifications for acceptable quality.

method of neglect

The costs of normal shrinkage and normal *continuous* losses are handled through the **method of neglect**, which simply excludes the spoiled units in the equivalent units schedule. Ignoring the spoilage results in a smaller number of equivalent units of production (EUP) and, by dividing production costs by a smaller EUP, raises the cost per equivalent unit. Thus, the cost of lost units is spread proportionately over the good units transferred and those remaining in Work in Process Inventory.

Alternatively, the cost of normal, *discrete* losses is assigned only to units that have passed the inspection point. Such units should be good units (relative to the inspected characteristic), whereas the units prior to this point may be good or may be defective/spoiled. Assigning loss costs to units that may be found to be defective/spoiled in the next period would not be reasonable.

EXHIBIT 7–1

Continuous versus Discrete Losses

Type	Assumed to Occur	May Be	Cost Handled How?	Cost Assigned To?
Continuous	Uniformly throughout process	Normal	Absorbed by all units in ending inventory and transferred out on an EUP basis	Product
		or		
		Abnormal	Written off as a loss on an EUP basis	Period
Discrete	At inspection point or at end of process	Normal	Absorbed by all units past inspection point in ending inventory and transferred out on an EUP basis	Product
		or		
		Abnormal	Written off as a loss on an EUP basis	Period

Regardless of whether defects/spoilage occur in a continuous or discrete fashion, the cost of abnormal losses should be accumulated and treated as a loss in the period in which those losses occurred. This treatment is justified by the cost principle discussed in financial accounting. The cost principle allows only costs that are necessary to acquire or produce inventory to attach to it. All unnecessary costs are written off in the period in which they are incurred. Because abnormal losses are not necessary to the production of good units and the cost is avoidable in the future, any abnormal loss cost is regarded as a period cost. This cost should be brought to the attention of the production manager who should then investigate the causes of the loss to determine how to prevent future similar occurrences. Abnormal loss cost is always accounted for on an equivalent unit basis.

ILLUSTRATIONS OF LOST UNITS

To best understand how to account for a process that creates lost goods, it is helpful to know the answers to the following questions:

1. What is the process flow?
2. Where is material added during the process?
3. How are labor and overhead applied? (This answer is usually "Continuously," but not necessarily at the same rate.)
4. At what stage of completion was the beginning inventory and what is the ending inventory?
5. Where are the quality control inspection points?
6. How do defective/spoiled units occur? (Continuously or discretely?)

Impervious Inc. is used to illustrate several alternative situations regarding the handling of lost units in a process costing environment. Impervious produces a high-tech, very durable, nonfade (once color pigment is added) paint base material—hereafter simply referred to as paint—for appliances and equipment. The paint is produced in a single department and then sold to appliance and equipment manufacturers. All materials are added at the start of the process, and conversion costs are applied uniformly throughout the production process. Recyclable containers are provided by buyers and, therefore, are not a cost to Impervious. The company uses the FIFO method of calculating equivalent units.

Spoilage in the production of CD-ROMs can occur from a wide variety of causes and at numerous points in the production process. Because spoilage tends to be machine-related, quality checks are built into the production system and are often performed robotically. However, the final quality control analysis is performed by a replication operator.

Situation 1—Normal Loss Only; Loss Occurs Throughout Production Process (Continuous)

During processing, the paint is mechanically blended and cooked, resulting in a normal loss from shrinkage. Mechanical malfunctions sometimes occur and, when they do, cause some spoilage. Any decrease of 10 percent or less of the gallons placed into production for a period is considered normal. The April 2000 data for Impervious are given below:

GALLONS		
Beginning inventory (60% complete)		2,000
Started during month		15,000
Gallons completed and transferred		13,200
Ending inventory (75% complete)		2,500
Lost gallons (normal)		1,300
COSTS		
Beginning inventory:		
Material	$ 15,000	
Conversion	1,620	$ 16,620
Current period:		
Material	$102,750	
Conversion	19,425	
		122,175
Total costs		$138,795

To visualize the manufacturing process for Impervious, a flow diagram can be constructed. Such a diagram provides distinct, definitive answers to all of the questions asked at the beginning of this section.

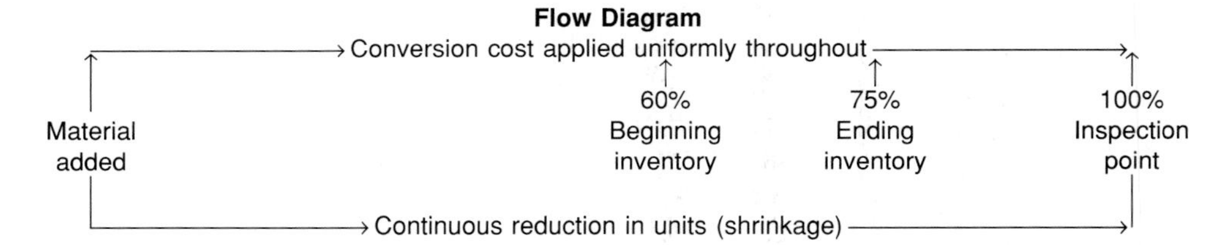

The steps discussed in Chapter 6 on process costing are followed to determine the units accountable for, units accounted for, equivalent units of production, costs accountable for, cost per equivalent unit, and cost assignment. These steps are presented in the cost of production report shown in Exhibit 7–2.

The department is accountable for 17,000 gallons of paint: 2,000 gallons in beginning inventory plus 15,000 gallons started into processing during April. Only 15,700 gallons (13,200 completed and 2,500 in ending inventory) are accounted for prior to considering the processing loss. The 1,300 lost gallons are included in the schedule of gallons accounted for to balance to the total 17,000 gallons, but these gallons are not extended into the computation of equivalent units of production. Using the method of neglect, these gallons simply "disappear" in the EUP schedule. Thus, the cost per equivalent gallon of the remaining good production of the period is higher for each cost component.

Had the lost gallons been used in the denominator of the cost per EUP computation, the cost per EUP would have been smaller, and the material cost per unit would have been $6.85 ($102,750 ÷ 15,000). Because the lost units do not appear in the cost assignment section, their costs must be assigned only to good production. The use of the lower cost per EUP would not allow all of the costs to be accounted for in Exhibit 7–2.

EXHIBIT 7-2

Cost of Production Report for Month Ended April 30, 2000 (FIFO method) (Normal continuous shrinkage)

PRODUCTION DATA		EQUIVALENT UNITS	
	Whole Units	Material	Conversion
Beginning inventory (100%; 60%)	2,000		
Gallons started	15,000		
Gallons to account for	17,000		
Beginning inventory completed (0%; 40%)	2,000	0	800
Gallons started and completed	11,200	11,200	11,200
Total gallons completed	13,200		
Ending inventory (100%; 75%)	2,500	2,500	1,875
Normal shrinkage	1,300		
Gallons accounted for	17,000	13,700	13,875

COST DATA	Total	Material	Conversion
Beginning inventory costs	$ 16,620		
Current costs	122,175	$102,750	$19,425
Total costs	$138,795		
Divided by EUP		13,700	13,875
Cost per FIFO EUP	$8.90	$7.50	$1.40

COST ASSIGNMENT		
Transferred:		
Beginning inventory	$16,620	
Cost to complete: Conversion (800 × $1.40)	1,120	
Total cost of beginning inventory	$17,740	
Started and completed (11,200 × $8.90)	99,680	
Total cost of gallons transferred		$117,420
Ending inventory:		
Material (2,500 × $7.50)	$18,750	
Conversion (1,875 × $1.40)	2,625	21,375
Total costs accounted for		$138,795

Accounting for normal, continuous shrinkage (or defects/spoilage) is the easiest of the types of lost unit computations. There is, however, a theoretical problem with this computation when a company uses weighted average process costing. The units in ending Work in Process Inventory have lost unit cost assigned to them in the current period and will have lost unit cost assigned *again* in the next period. But, even with this flaw, this method provides a reasonable measure of unit cost if the rate of spoilage is consistent from period to period.

Situation 2—Normal Spoilage Only; Spoilage Determined at Final Inspection Point in Production Process (Discrete)

This example uses the same basic cost and unit information given above for Impervious Inc. except that no shrinkage occurs. Instead, the paint is inspected at the end of the production process. Any spoiled gallons are removed and discarded at inspection; a machine malfunction or an improper blending of a batch of paint usually causes spoilage. Any spoilage of 10 percent or less of the gallons placed into production during the period is considered normal. A production flow diagram is shown at the top of the next page.

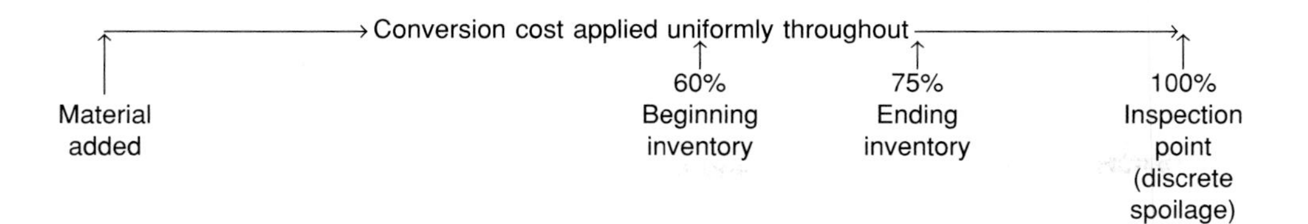

In this situation, the spoiled gallons of product are included in the equivalent unit schedule. Because the inspection point is at 100 percent completion, all work has been performed on the spoiled gallons and all costs have been incurred to produce those gallons. By including the spoiled gallons at 100 percent completion in the EUP schedule, cost per gallon reflects the cost that *would have been incurred* had all production been good production.

Cost of the spoiled gallons is assigned solely to the completed units. Because ending Work in Process Inventory has not yet passed the inspection point, this inventory may contain its own normal spoilage, which will be detected next period. The cost of production report for Situation 2 is shown in Exhibit 7–3.

Situation 3—Normal Spoilage Only; Spoilage Determined During Production Process (Discrete)

In this example, Impervious Inc. inspects the paint when the conversion process is 50 percent complete. The only difference between this example and the previous one is that, for April, the ending Work in Process Inventory has passed the inspection point. Because of this difference, spoilage cost must be allocated to both the gallons transferred and to ending inventory. Although the ending inventory *could* become spoiled during the remainder of processing, it is either highly unlikely or the cost

EXHIBIT 7–3

Cost of Production Report for Month Ended April 30, 2000 (FIFO method) (Normal discrete spoilage)

PRODUCTION DATA		EQUIVALENT UNITS	
	Whole Units	Material	Conversion
Beginning inventory (100%; 60%)	2,000		
Gallons started	15,000		
Gallons to account for	17,000		
Beginning inventory completed (0%; 40%)	2,000	0	800
Gallons started and completed	11,200	11,200	11,200
Total gallons completed	13,200		
Ending inventory (100%; 75%)	2,500	2,500	1,875
Normal spoilage (100%; 100%)	1,300	1,300	1,300
Gallons accounted for	17,000	15,000	15,175

COST DATA	Total	Material	Conversion
Beginning inventory costs	$ 16,620		
Current costs	122,175	$102,750	$19,425
Total costs	$138,795		
Divided by EUP		15,000	15,175
Cost per FIFO EUP	$8.13	$6.85	$1.28

(continued)

EXHIBIT 7-3

(Concluded)

COST ASSIGNMENT

Transferred:		
Beginning inventory	$16,620	
Cost to complete: Conversion (800 × $1.28)	1,024	
Total cost of beginning inventory	$17,644	
Started and completed (11,200 × $8.13)	91,056	
Normal spoilage (1,300 × $8.13)*	10,569	
Total cost of gallons transferred (13,200 × $9.04)**		$119,269
Ending inventory:		
Material (2,500 × $6.85)	$17,125	
Conversion (1,875 × $1.28)	2,400	19,525
Total costs accounted for (off due to rounding)		$138,794

*All spoilage cost is assigned to the units transferred.
**For convenience and clerical efficiency, modified FIFO is used. Otherwise, spoilage would have to be allocated to beginning WIP and units started and completed. The $9.04 figure is also computed as the sum of the $8.24 cost [($17,644 + $91,056) ÷ 13,200] per good EUP plus another $0.80. This $0.80 is the spoilage cost ($10,569) divided by the 13,200 good units transferred.

is so minimal that Impervious cannot justify the need for an end-of-process inspection. The flow diagram for this situation follows:

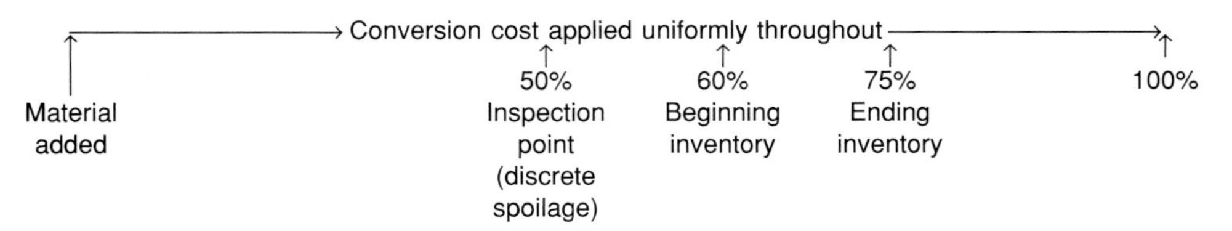

Using the same data as in the two previous situations, Exhibit 7–4 provides the cost per gallon and cost assignment for this situation. Spoiled gallons are extended in the EUP schedule at the inspection point degree of completion (100 percent for material and 50 percent for conversion) and affect the cost per gallon. As in Situation 2, the resulting cost per gallon reflects what the cost would have been had all the gallons produced been good output. Total cost of the spoiled goods is calculated by multiplying the component cost per gallon by the EUP for each cost component. Total spoilage cost is then prorated based on the EUP for each cost component between gallons transferred and gallons in ending inventory.

Situation 4—Abnormal Shrinkage (Continuous or Discrete); Some Normal Shrinkage (Continuous)

The final example of Impervious Inc. assumes that normal spoilage cannot exceed 5 percent of the gallons placed into production. Additionally, as in Situation 1, the unit reduction is assumed to occur from shrinkage. The quality control inspection point is at the end of processing. Because 15,000 gallons were started in April, the maximum allowable normal shrinkage is 750 gallons (15,000 × 5%). Because the total reduction in units in April was 1,300 gallons, 550 gallons are considered abnormal shrinkage. Exhibit 7–5 presents the cost of production report for Situation 4.

The approach presented for Situation 4 has one inequity. A portion of the normal shrinkage is automatically allocated to abnormal shrinkage because the calculation of EUP allows for the "disappearance" of the normal shrinkage. Cost per gallon is then computed based on the equivalent units of production. This approach

EXHIBIT 7–4

Cost of Production Report for Month Ended April 30, 2000 (FIFO method) (Normal discrete spoilage)

PRODUCTION DATA

	Whole Units	EQUIVALENT UNITS Material	Conversion
Beginning inventory (100%; 60%)	2,000		
Gallons started	15,000		
Gallons to account for	17,000		
Beginning inventory completed (0%; 40%)	2,000	0	800
Gallons started and completed	11,200	11,200	11,200
Total gallons completed	13,200		
Ending inventory (100%; 75%)	2,500	2,500	1,875
Normal spoilage (100%; 50%)	1,300	1,300	650
Gallons accounted for	17,000	15,000	14,525

COST DATA

	Total	Material	Conversion
Beginning inventory costs	$ 16,620		
Current costs	122,175	$102,750	$19,425
Total costs	$138,795		
Divided by EUP		15,000	14,525
Cost per FIFO EUP	$8.19	$6.85	$1.34

COST ASSIGNMENT

Transferred:		
From beginning inventory	$ 16,620	
Cost to complete: Conversion (800 × $1.34)	1,072	
Total cost of beginning inventory	$ 17,692	
Started and completed (11,200 × $8.19)	91,728	
Cost prior to proration of spoilage	$109,420	
Normal spoilage*	8,051	
Total cost of gallons transferred		$117,471
Ending inventory:		
Material (2,500 × $6.85)	$ 17,125	
Conversion (1,875 × $1.34)	2,513	
Cost prior to proration of spoilage	$ 19,638	
Normal spoilage*	1,725	
Total cost of ending inventory		21,363
Total costs accounted for (off due to rounding)		$138,834

*Proration of normal spoilage is as follows:

	Material EUP	Material %	Conversion EUP	Conversion %
Gallons started and completed**	11,200	82	11,200	86
Ending work in process	2,500	18	1,875	14
	13,700	100	13,075	100

Given the above relative EUP percentages, proration of spoilage costs is

Material (1,300 × $6.85)	$8,905
Conversion (650 × $1.34)	871
Cost of normal spoilage to be prorated	$9,776

**The gallons in beginning WIP were not included in this calculation because beginning WIP was 100% complete as to material and 60% complete as to conversion. Thus, this inventory was beyond the inspection point (50%) and no spoilage cost should be assigned to it.

(continued)

EXHIBIT 7–4

(Concluded)

	Material	Conversion	Total
Gallons started and completed:			
0.82 × $8,905	$7,302		
0.86 × $ 871		$749	$8,051
Ending work in process:			
0.18 × $8,905	1,603		
0.14 × $ 871		122	1,725
Total allocations	$8,905	$871	$9,776

EXHIBIT 7–5

Cost of Production Report for Month Ended April 30, 2000 (FIFO method) (Abnormal shrinkage; normal continuous shrinkage)

PRODUCTION DATA		EQUIVALENT UNITS	
	Whole Units	Material	Conversion
Beginning inventory (100%; 60%)	2,000		
Gallons started	15,000		
Gallons to account for	17,000		
Beginning inventory completed (0%; 40%)	2,000	0	800
Gallons started and completed	11,200	11,200	11,200
Total gallons completed	13,200		
Ending inventory (100%; 75%)	2,500	2,500	1,875
Normal shrinkage	750		
Abnormal shrinkage (100%; 100%)	550	550	550
Gallons accounted for	17,000	14,250	14,425
COST DATA	**Total**	**Material**	**Conversion**
Beginning inventory costs	$ 16,620		
Current costs	122,175	$102,750	$19,425
Total costs	$138,795		
Divided by EUP		14,250	14,425
Cost per FIFO EUP	$8.56	$7.21	$1.35

COST ASSIGNMENT

Transferred:		
From beginning inventory	$16,620	
Cost to complete: Conversion (800 × $1.35)	1,080	
Total cost of beginning inventory	$17,700	
Started and completed (11,200 × $8.56)	95,872	
Total cost of gallons transferred		$113,572
Ending inventory:		
Material (2,500 × $7.21)	$18,025	
Conversion (1,875 × $1.35)	2,531	20,556
Abnormal loss (550 × $8.56)		4,708
Total costs accounted for (off due to rounding)		$138,836

is justified on the basis of expediency as long as the amount of the allocation of normal shrinkage to abnormal shrinkage is not considered significant.

Situation 4 is used to illustrate the journal entries necessary to account for shrinkage or spoilage. These entries are as follows:

Work in Process Inventory	122,175	
Raw Material Inventory		102,750
Wages Payable (and/or other appropriate accounts)		19,425
To record current period costs.		
Finished Goods Inventory	113,572	
Work in Process Inventory		113,572
To record cost transferred from the department.		
Loss from Abnormal Spoilage	4,708	
Work in Process Inventory		4,708
To remove cost of abnormal spoilage from Work in Process Inventory.		

The accounts debited and credited in the first journal entry would be the same for Situations 1, 2, and 3. The dollar amount of the second entry would change for each of Situations 1, 2, and 3 to reflect the appropriate "cost transferred" figure shown in the respective cost of production report. The third journal entry given is made only when abnormal defects/spoilage occurs.

All illustrations to this point have used FIFO process costing. If the weighted average method were used, the difference would appear (as discussed in Chapter 6) only in the treatment of beginning inventory and its related costs. Lost units would be handled as illustrated in each exhibit shown for Situations 1 through 4. Exhibit 7–6 illustrates the weighted average method for the data used in Exhibit 7–5.

EXHIBIT 7-6

Cost of Production Report for Month Ended April 30, 2000 (Weighted average method) (Abnormal shrinkage; normal continuous shrinkage)

PRODUCTION DATA		**EQUIVALENT UNITS**	
	Whole Units	**Material**	**Conversion**
Beginning inventory (100%; 60%)	2,000	2,000	1,200
Gallons started	15,000		
Gallons to account for	17,000		
Beginning inventory completed (0%; 40%)	2,000	0	800
Gallons started and completed	11,200	11,200	11,200
Total gallons completed	13,200		
Ending inventory (100%; 75%)	2,500	2,500	1,875
Normal spoilage	750		
Abnormal spoilage (100%; 100%)	550	550	550
Gallons accounted for	17,000	16,250	15,625

COST DATA	**Total**	**Material**	**Conversion**
Beginning inventory costs	$ 16,620	$ 15,000	$ 1,620
Current costs	122,175	102,750	19,425
Total costs	$138,795	$117,750	$21,045
Divided by EUP		16,250	15,625
Cost per FIFO EUP	$8.60	$7.25	$1.35

COST ASSIGNMENT		
Transferred (13,200 × $8.60)		$113,520
Ending inventory:		
Material (2,500 × $7.25)	$18,125	
Conversion (1,875 × $1.35)	2,531	20,656
Abnormal loss (550 × $8.60)		4,730
Total costs accounted for (off due to rounding)		$138,906

A summary of the treatment of various types of lost units in a process costing system is shown in Exhibit 7–7.

EXHIBIT 7–7

Summary of Handling Lost Units in a Process Costing System

	NORMAL	ABNORMAL
CONTINUOUS	Do not include equivalent lost units in EUP schedule. Units effectively "disappear"; unit costs of good production are increased.	Must include equivalent lost units in EUP schedule. Assign cost to lost units and charge as loss of period.
DISCRETE	Must include equivalent lost units in EUP schedule. Assign cost to lost units. Determine point of ending work in process: a. if before inspection point, assign cost of lost units only to units transferred. b. if after inspection point, prorate cost of spoiled units between units transferred and units in ending inventory.	Must include equivalent lost units in EUP schedule. Assign cost to lost units and charge as loss of period.

DEFECTIVE UNITS

5

How are rework costs of defective units treated?

The preceding examples have all presumed that the lost units were valueless. However, some goods that do not meet quality specifications are merely defective rather than spoiled, and thus have value. Such units are either reworked to meet product specifications or sold as irregulars. Rework cost is a product or period cost depending on whether the rework is considered to be normal or abnormal.

If the rework is normal and actual costing is used, the rework cost is added to the current period's work in process costs for good units and assigned to all units completed. In companies using predetermined overhead application rates, normal rework costs should be estimated and included as part of the estimated factory overhead cost used in computing the overhead application rates. In this way, the overhead application rate will be large enough to cover rework costs. When actual rework costs are incurred, they are assigned to the Manufacturing Overhead account.

If rework is abnormal, the costs should be accumulated and assigned to a loss account. The units are included in the EUP schedule for the period and only actual production (not rework) costs will be considered in determining unit cost.[3]

Reworked units may be irregular and have to be sold at less than the normal selling price. The production costs of irregular items should be transferred to a special inventory account and not commingled with the production costs of good units. When the net realizable value (selling price minus cost to rework and sell) is less than total cost, the difference is referred to as a deficiency. If the number of defective units is normal, the deficiency should be treated as part of the production cost of good units. If some proportion of the defective units is considered an abnormal loss, that proportion of the deficiency should be written off as a period cost.

[3] If the company is using a standard costing system, then standard costs will be considered when determining unit costs.

Accounting for defective units is illustrated by the July 2000 manufacturing data of Impervious Inc. During July, the company produced 17,900 good gallons and 100 defective gallons of paint. The 100 gallons were considered defective because the traditional neutral color of the product was, instead, slightly yellow. Total production costs other than rework were $160,200. The 100 defective gallons can be reworked at a total cost of $140 (or $1.40 per gallon) by mixing the defective gallons with a chemical lightening additive. The cost of the additive itself is only $0.07 per gallon, so all rework costs are assumed to be related to direct labor. The chemical additive is also gaseous and will cause no increase in the number of gallons of the paint. Entries for defective units are shown in Exhibit 7–8. This exhibit uses this information to show a variety of circumstances involving defective goods.

EXHIBIT 7–8

Entries for Defective Units

Good production: 17,900 gallons
Defects: 100 gallons
Cost of production other than rework: $160,200
Cost of rework: $140 or $1.40 per gallon

1. Rework is normal; actual costing is used; reworked gallons can be sold at normal selling price

Work in Process Inventory	140	
Wages Payable		140

Cost per acceptable gallon = $8.91 ($160,340 ÷ 18,000)

2. Rework is normal; predetermined OH rate is used (rework estimated); reworked gallons can be sold at normal selling price

Manufacturing Overhead	140	
Wages Payable		140

Cost per acceptable gallon = $8.90 ($160,200 ÷ 18,000)

3. Rework is abnormal; reworked gallons can be sold at normal selling price

Loss from Defects	140	
Wages Payable		140

Cost per acceptable gallon = $8.90 ($160,200 ÷ 18,000)

4. Reworked gallons are irregular; can only be sold for $7; actual costing is used

Normal production cost ($8.90 × 100)	$ 890
Cost of rework	140
Total cost of defective units	$1,030
Total sales value of defective units (100 × $7)	700
Total deficiency	$ 330

If defects are normal:

Inventory—Defects	700	
Work in Process Inventory	140	
Wages Payable		140
Work in Process Inventory		700

The deficiency ($330) remains with the good units; cost per acceptable gallon is $8.92: [($160,200 + $140 − $700) ÷ 17,900]

If defects are abnormal:

Inventory—Defects	700	
Loss from Defects	330	
Wages Payable		140
Work in Process Inventory		890

The deficiency is assigned as a period loss; cost per acceptable gallon is $8.90: [($160,200 − $890) ÷ 17,900]

DEFECTS/SPOILAGE IN JOB ORDER COSTING

6

How are losses treated in a job order costing system?

The previous examples are related to spoilage issues in a process costing environment. In a job order situation, the accounting treatment of spoilage depends on two issues: (1) Is spoilage generally incurred for most jobs or is it specifically identified with a particular job? (2) Is the spoilage normal or abnormal?

Generally Anticipated on All Jobs

net cost of normal spoilage

If normal spoilage is anticipated on all jobs, the predetermined overhead application rate should include an amount for the **net cost of normal spoilage**, which is equal to the cost of spoiled work less the estimated disposal value of that work. This approach assumes that spoilage is naturally inherent and unavoidable in the production of good products, and its estimated cost should be proportionately assigned among the good products produced.

Assume that Impervious produces a special paint for manufacturers. Each production run is considered a separate job because each manufacturer indicates the particular paint specifications it requires. Regardless of the job, there is always some shrinkage because of the mixing process. In computing the predetermined overhead rate related to the custom paints, the following estimates are made:

Overhead costs other than spoilage		$121,500
Estimated spoilage unit cost	$10,300	
Sales of improperly mixed paints to foreign distributors	(4,300)	6,000
Total estimated overhead		$127,500
Estimated gallons of production during the year		÷ 150,000
Predetermined overhead rate per gallon		$0.85

During the year, Impervious Inc. accepted a job (#38) from General Electric to manufacture 500 gallons of paint. Direct material cost for this job was $4,660, direct labor cost totaled $640, and applied overhead was $425 ($0.85 × 500 gallons), giving a total cost for the job of $5,725. Impervious Inc. put 500 gallons of paint into production. Five gallons (or 1 percent) of the paint became defective during the production process when a worker accidentally added a thickening agent meant for another job into a container of the paint. The actual cost of the defective mixture was $57.25 (0.01 × $5,725) and it can be sold for $22. The entry below is made to account for the actual defect cost:

Disposal Value of Defective Work	22.00	
Manufacturing Overhead	35.25	
Work in Process Inventory—Job #38		57.25
To record disposal value of defective work incurred on Job #38 for General Electric.		

The estimated cost of spoilage was originally included in determining the predetermined overhead rate. Therefore, as actual defects or spoilages occur, the disposal value of the nonstandard work is included in an inventory account (if salable), and the net cost of the normal nonstandard work is charged to the Manufacturing Overhead account as is any other actual overhead cost.

Specifically Identified with a Particular Job

If defects or spoilages are not generally anticipated, but are occasionally experienced on specific jobs *because of job-related characteristics*, the estimated cost should *not* be included in setting the predetermined overhead application rate. Because the cost of defects/spoilage attaches to the job, the disposal value of such goods reduces the cost of the job that created those goods. If no disposal value exists for the defective/spoiled goods, that cost remains with the job that caused the defects/spoilage.

Assume that Impervious did not typically experience spoilage in its production process. The company's predetermined overhead would have been calculated as $0.81 per gallon ($121,500 ÷ 150,000). Thus, the total cost for the General Electric job would have been $5,705 [$4,660 + $640 + ($0.81 × 500)]. Five gallons of the batch were thickened somewhat greater than normal at the request of General Electric. After checking the stirability of the special paint, General Electric rejected the five gallons and changed the formula slightly. The five gallons could be sold for $22; this amount would reduce the cost of the General Electric job as shown in the following entry:

Disposal Value of Defective Work	22	
Work in Process Inventory—Job #38		22
To record disposal value of defective work incurred on Job #38 for General Electric.		

The production cost of any new mixture will be assigned a new job number.

Abnormal Spoilage

The cost of abnormal losses (net of any disposal value) should be written off as a period cost. The following entry assumes that Impervious normally anticipates some lost units on its custom orders and that the estimated cost of those units was included in the development of a predetermined overhead application rate. Assume that on Job #135, the cost of defective units was $198, but that $45 of disposal value was associated with those units. Of the remaining $153 of cost, $120 was related to normal defects and $33 was related to abnormal defects.

Disposal Value of Defective Work	45	
Manufacturing Overhead	120	
Loss from Abnormal Spoilage	33	
Work in Process Inventory—Job #135		198
To record reassignment of cost of defective and spoiled work on Job #135.		

The first debit represents the defective goods' disposal value; the debit to Manufacturing Overhead is for the net cost of normal spoilage. The debit to Loss from Abnormal Spoilage is for the portion of the net cost of spoilage that was not anticipated in setting the predetermined application rate.

ACCRETION

7

How does accretion of units affect the EUP schedule and costs per unit?

accretion

Accretion refers to an increase in units or volume because of the addition of material or to factors (such as heat) that are inherent in the production process.[4] For example, adding soybean derivative to beef in preparing packages of hamburger causes the pounds of product to increase just as including pasta increases the volume of a casserole.

If materials are added in a single department, the number of equivalent units computed for that department compensates for this increase from the beginning to the end of processing. When accretion occurs in successor departments in a multidepartment process, the number of units transferred into the department and the related cost per unit must be adjusted. For instance, assume that one paint made by Impervious Inc. requires processing in two departments. Department 2 adds a compound to increase the scratch-resistant properties of the mixture produced in Department 1. The gallons of compound added increase the total gallons of mixture that were transferred out of Department 1 and decrease the transferred-in cost per unit.

The production of this heavy-duty paint is used to illustrate the accounting for accretion of units in a successor department. Department 1 mixes the primary paint

[4] Not all additions of material in successor departments cause an increase in units. Adding bindings to books in a second department does not increase the number of books printed and transferred from the prior department. When the material added in a successor department does not increase the number of units, it is accounted for as shown in Chapter 6.

ingredients in large vats and sends the mixture to Department 2, which adds the scratch-resistant compound and remixes the paint. The paint is poured into 50-gallon containers that are shipped to buyers. Spoilage occurs in Department 2 when too much scratch-resistant compound is added to the paint mixture. The spoilage is detected when the mixture is transferred from the vats to the containers. Spoilage is never containerized. Spoilage is considered normal as long as it does not exceed 1 percent of the gallons transferred into Department 2 from Department 1.

December production information for Department 2 is given below. For this product, assume that Impervious Inc. uses weighted average process costing. The units in beginning inventory were 100 percent complete as to the compound, 0 percent complete as to the container, and 25 percent complete as to conversion costs. Ending inventory is 100 percent complete as to the compound, 0 percent complete as to the container, and 70 percent complete as to conversion.

Gallons in beginning inventory	1,000
Gallons transferred in	21,000
Gallons of compound added	5,000
Gallons in ending inventory	1,200
Units completed (50-gallon containers)	512

Note that the measure for completed production is containers rather than gallons. Because each container represents 50 gallons, the actual gallons completed are 25,600 (50 × 512). To handle this change in measuring units, either the incoming gallons must be reported as containers or the completed containers must be reported as gallons. The cost of production report for December (Exhibit 7–9) is prepared using gallons as the measurement unit, and assumed cost information is supplied in the exhibit.

Several items need to be noted about Exhibit 7–9. First, the number of spoiled gallons was determined by subtracting the total gallons completed plus the gallons in ending inventory from the total gallons for which the department was responsible. Because spoilage was less than 1 percent of the gallons transferred into Department 2, it was all considered normal. Second, the $197,100 cost transferred from Department 1 was related to 22,000 gallons of mixture: the gallons in beginning inventory plus those transferred during the period. Thus, the original cost of each gallon was approximately $8.96 ($197,100 ÷ 22,000). With the addition of the compound in Department 2, the transferred-in cost per gallon declined to $7.30.

EXHIBIT 7-9

Department 2 Cost of Production Report for the Month Ended December 31, 2000 (Weighted average method)

PRODUCTION DATA		EQUIVALENT UNITS			
	Whole Units	Transferred-In	Compound	Container	Conversion
Beginning inventory (100%; 100%; 0%; 25%)	1,000	1,000	1,000	0	250
Transferred-in (gals.)	21,000				
Compound added (gals.)	5,000				
Gallons to account for	27,000				
BI completed	1,000	0	0	1,000	750
Started and completed	24,600	24,600	24,600	24,600	24,600
Total gallons completed	25,600				
Ending inventory (100%; 100%; 0%; 7%)	1,200	1,200	1,200	0	840
Normal spoilage	200	200	200	0	200
Gallons accounted for	27,000	27,000	27,000	25,600	26,640

(continued)

COST DATA		**EQUIVALENT UNITS**			
	Total	**Transferred-In**	**Compound**	**Container**	**Conversion**
BI costs	$ 8,415	$ 7,385	$ 840	$ 0	$ 190
Current costs	331,455	189,715	22,110	99,840	19,790
Total costs	$339,870	$197,100	$22,950	$99,840	$19,980
Divided by EUP		27,000	27,000	25,600	26,640
Cost per EUP	$12.80	$7.30	$0.85	$3.90	$0.75

COST ASSIGNMENT		
Transferred:		
Cost of good units (25,600 × $12.80)	$327,680	
Cost of spoilage:		
Transferred-in (200 × $7.30)	1,460	
Compound (200 × $0.85)	170	
Conversion (200 × $0.75)	150	
Total cost transferred		$329,460
Ending inventory:		
Transferred-in (1,200 × $7.30)	$ 8,760	
Compound (1,200 × $0.85)	1,020	
Conversion (840 × $0.75)	630	10,410
Total costs accounted for		$339,870

EXHIBIT 7-9

(Concluded)

Third, spoilage is assignable only to the completed units because the ending inventory has not yet reached the discrete point of inspection (transference to containers). Finally, the average cost of each 50-gallon container completed is approximately $643.48 ($329,460 ÷ 512).

CONTROLLING QUALITY TO MINIMIZE LOST UNITS

8

What is the cost of quality products?

Up to this point, the chapter has focused on how to account for lost units in the production process. The fact is, if there were no lost units (from shrinkage, defects, or spoilage), there would be no need to account for them. The control aspect in quality control requires knowledge of three questions in addition to the six questions posed earlier in the chapter:

1. What do the lost units actually cost?
2. Why do the lost units occur?
3. How can the lost units be controlled?

Many companies find it difficult—if not impossible—to answer the question of what lost units (or the lack of quality) cost. A direct cause of part of this difficulty is the use of the traditional method of assigning the cost of normal losses to the good units produced. By excluding lost units from the extensions in the equivalent units schedule, the cost of those units is effectively "buried" and hidden in magnitude from managers. In a job order costing environment, if the cost of lost units is included in calculating the predetermined overhead rate, that cost is also being hidden and ignored. In service organizations, the cost of "lost units" may be even more difficult to determine because those lost units are, from a customer viewpoint, poor service. After such service, the customer simply may not do business with the organization again. Such an opportunity cost is not processed by the accounting system. Thus, in all instances, a potentially significant dollar amount is unavailable for investigation as to its planning, controlling, and decision-making ramifications.

As to the second question, managers may be able to pinpoint the reasons for lost units or poor service but may also have two perspectives of those reasons that instinctively allow for a lack of control. First, managers may believe that the cause creates only a "minimal" quantity of lost units; such a mind-set creates the predisposition for an "accepted quality level" with some tolerance for error. These error tolerances are built into the system and become justifications for problems. Production is "graded on a curve" that allows for a less-than-perfect result.

Incorporating error tolerances into the production/performance system and combining such tolerances with the method of neglect results in managers not being provided with the information necessary to determine how much spoilage cost is incurred by the company. Therefore, although believing that the quantity and cost of lost units are "minimal," the managers do not have historical or even estimated accounting amounts on which to base such a conclusion. By becoming aware of the costs, managers could make more informed decisions about whether to ignore the costs or try to correct their causes.

In other instances, managers may believe that the quantity of lost units is uncontrollable. In some cases, this belief is accurate. For example, the shrinkage of coffee beans during roasting is virtually uncontrollable as is the sticking of small amounts of candy bar coating to candy molds during processing. The frequency of problems such as these is not large. Process analysis has proven that the cost of attempting to correct this production defect would be significantly greater than the savings resulting from the correction. But in most production situations and almost every service situation, the cause of lost units or poor service is controllable. Managers should determine the cause of the problem and institute corrective action.

Defects and spoiled units were originally controlled through a process of inspecting goods or, in the case of service organizations, through surveying customers. These control methods are known as appraisal techniques. Now companies are deciding that if quality is built into the process, fewer inspections or surveys will be needed because defects/spoilage and poor service will be minimized. This involves prevention techniques. The goal, then, is prevention of defects or errors rather than output inspection or observation. Preventing defects and errors requires that managers discover the root cause of the defect or error. The accompanying News Note discusses root cause analysis.

As discussed in Chapter 8, companies implementing quality programs to minimize defects/spoilage or poor service often employ a tool called statistical process control (SPC) to analyze their processes to determine whether any situations are "out of control." SPC uses graphs and/or control charts to understand and reduce fluctuations in processes until they are under control.

SPC requires that those persons or machines involved in problem areas select a relevant measure of performance and track that performance measurement over time. The resulting control chart provides information on the circumstances existing when a problem arises. Analyzing this chart in relation to the benchmark or standard and to the amount of variation expected in a stable (controlled) process provides process control information that lets the company improve its performance.

SPC allows the individuals involved with the process to become the quality control monitoring points and helps to eliminate the need for separate quality inspections. Thus, the "accepted quality level" can be raised, and the defects can be significantly reduced. Consider what can happen to a firm that aspires to deliver parts with zero defects when reading the News Note on page 282 about the experiences of Fraen Corp.

http://www.fraen.com
http://www.aimcoinc.com

QUALITY  NEWS NOTE

Analyzing Root Causes

How much time, effort, and money do companies lose dealing with problems that continually resurface and disrupt the organization? This is known as the "price of nonconformance"—the failure to identify a problem's root cause, fix the process, measure results, and follow up.

Estimates of the price of nonconformance are as much as 25 to 40% of operating costs. However, by focusing on the process—not the people—organizations can correct the underlying causes of problems so they don't recur.

By preventing the recurrence of errors in service delivery or manufacturing processes, significant improvements in both productivity and quality are assured. By eliminating nonconformance in the system through zero defects and anticipating and preventing errors prior to process implementation, significant cost savings may be realized to positively impact the organization's profit margin. With an understanding of the environment necessary to create quality, organizations will identify solutions to costly, recurring problems.

The implementation of a system process improvement model . . . utilizing step-by-step root cause analysis will create an effective continuous quality improvement culture in an organization. Utilizing a step-by-step root cause analysis process, organizations can improve product quality, improve service quality, reduce operating costs, and impact operating profits positively.

The "root cause" is the reason for a nonconformance within a process. It is the underlying cause of a problem, not just the apparent cause. It is a focus on the process, not the people.

The root cause is a factor that, when changed or eliminated, will eliminate the nonconformance and prevent the problem. It is about designing prevention solutions into how work is done. Prevention solutions are not about reworking, redesigning, modifying, or fixing things; they are not about correction. Prevention solutions are about determining why the rework was required, why we must redesign the product, and why we must fix the item. It is about determining how to keep the problem from ever occurring again. It is about designing prevention into the process.

Root cause analysis is a formal, structured, disciplined approach to problem solving. Many root cause analysis processes have been developed to approach problem solving: some have three steps, some four, some six, or as many as 12 steps in the process.

Simply, root cause analysis is a systematic process of defining the problem, gathering and prioritizing data about the nonconformance, analyzing solutions to the problem, and evaluating the benefits versus the cost-effectiveness of all available prevention options.

SOURCE: Charles C. Handley, "Quality Improvement through Root Cause Analysis," *Hospital Material Management Quarterly* (May 2000), pp. 74–75. Originally published and copyrighted by APICS–The Educational Society for Resource Management, © 1999 APICS International Conference Proceedings.

The process of developing, implementing, and interpreting an SPC system requires a firm grasp on statistics and is well beyond the scope of this text. However, cost and management accountants must recognize the usefulness of such a tool in determining why problems occur. This knowledge allows cost and management accountants to better track the costs flowing into the problem areas, estimate the opportunity costs associated with the problems, and perform a more informed cost-benefit analysis about problem correction.

In conclusion, the important managerial concern regarding spoilage is in controlling it rather than accounting for spoilage costs. Quality control programs can be implemented to develop ideas on product redesign for quality, determine where quality control problems exist, decide how to measure the costs associated with those problems, and assess how to correct the problems. If quality is defined in an organization as zero lost units (excepting those caused by inherent shrinkage), all defects/spoilage will be accounted for as an abnormal cost of production or service. Such accounting would mean that defect/spoilage costs would no longer be hidden from managerial eyes through the use of the method of neglect discussed earlier in the chapter.

NEWS NOTE  QUALITY

Keeping an "Eye" on Things

When a small company is trying to make the leap to big contender, it needs all the help it can get. Fraen Corp. of Reading, MA, was intent on becoming a major supplier of precision machined parts, and had finally found its opportunity: a multinational corporation needed a massive quantity of electronic component fasteners. Fraen, which employed around 175 workers, felt it could deliver, but wanted to make itself stand out from its larger competitors. It offered the corporation zero defects per million parts, 100% inspection.

The corporation accepted. Before this contract, Fraen produced around 500,000 parts/week. With the new job, it would be shipping out 8 million parts. Higher volume meant that quality control would also have to be upgraded, especially since Fraen offered zero defects. The upgrade would be considerable: "We had no system—just people," explained David Cohen, Fraen's former quality manager, and now director of business development. "[The workers] would go to the machines and check parts on a regular basis, at a predetermined frequency, and record the information by hand on a piece of paper."

Fraen began investigating different inspection technologies, and also accepting bids with solutions and quotes. The company was approached by Advanced Inspection and Measurement (AIM, Niantic, CT), a manufacturer of contact and noncontact inspection systems. AIM proposed two video inspection systems, each incorporating a parts feeder and a set of three cameras that visually inspect parts and send the information to an adjoining PC, which then sends the data to a mother computer that determines part quality. Fraen decided to purchase two systems from AIM and set the systems up in a cleanroom to begin inspecting the constant flow of parts.

There was little or no training involved in learning how to operate the systems. Fraen hired two workers to run the machines, both of whom had no previous training in running video inspection systems. Both workers readily learned the operation. Cohen said that if the company had not purchased the vision inspection systems, it would have had to hire an additional 20 people to help with inspection. In addition, the systems provided real-time data, allowing Fraen to fine-tune its process.

The company, however, did not anticipate how statistically overwhelming 100% inspection could be. "Transitioning the factory from sampling parts and measuring via statistical sampling, to 100% inspection and having all of the data from every piece from every machine every day was a challenge, because you had an enormous amount of data all of a sudden," Cohen said. "We fill up a CD-ROM each week with data, so figuring out what to do with all of that and how to manage it was pretty difficult." Fraen eventually hired a full-time analyst to manage the information.

The investment was well worth the effort, according to Cohen. The two systems enabled Fraen to provide its customers with zero defects. As a result, the company purchased six more systems, as well as additional production machinery and a new facility. "We're actively pursuing high-volume jobs because of those systems, and word has gotten out about our quality," Cohen concluded. "We established ourselves as a player against people who otherwise would have buried us."

SOURCE: Samantha Hoover, "Visual Inspection System Keeps Up with Production Leap," *Quality* (March 1999), pp. 46ff.

REVISITING General Electric Company

http://www.ge.com

In the initial stages of Six Sigma, GE's efforts consisted of training more than 100,000 people in its science and methodology and focusing thousands of "projects" on improving efficiency and reducing variances from its internal operations—from industrial factories to financial services back rooms.

From there, the company's operating system steered the initiative into design engineering to prepare future generations of customer-interactive processes of the financial services businesses. Medical Systems used it to open up a commanding technology lead in several diagnostic platforms and has achieved dramatic sales increases and customer satisfaction improvements. By 1999, GE had undertaken 20,000 quality initiatives resulting in an average 80 percent error reduction.

Every GE product business and financial service activity is using Six Sigma in its product design and fulfillment processes. A growing number of Six Sigma projects are now under way for customers, many on customer premises.

In 1996, GE's CEO, Jack Welch, rang the opening bell at the New York stock exchange celebrating the 100th anniversary of the Dow Jones Index. His presence was significant, because GE is the only company on the original index that is still on the list. GE became the first company in the world to exceed $200 billion market capitalization, and in 1998 it crossed the $100 billion mark in revenue.

Given the above, is it surprising that GE was named "America's Most Admired Corporation" in 2000 for the third year in a row?

SOURCES: General Electric Company Web site, http://www.ge.com (June 2000); Staff, "GE: Lighting the Way," *Machine Design* (September 23, 1999), pp. 123–129; Geoffrey Colvin, "America's Most Admired Companies," *Fortune* (February 21, 2000), pp. 108, 110.

CHAPTER SUMMARY

This chapter covers the accounting treatment for shrinkage, defective and spoiled units, and accretion of units in a process costing system. Management typically specifies a certain level of shrinkage/defects/spoilage that will be tolerated as normal if a loss of units is commonly anticipated. If lost units exceed that expectation, the excess is considered an abnormal loss. Normal losses are product costs, and abnormal losses are period costs.

To account for the cost of lost units, the location of the loss within the process must be known in addition to knowing whether the quantity of lost units is normal or abnormal. If the loss point is continuous, the period's good production absorbs the cost of the lost units. This treatment is handled in the cost of production report by not extending the lost units to the equivalent units columns. If the loss point is discrete, lost units are included in the EUP schedule at their unit equivalency at the quality control point. If ending inventory has reached the inspection point, the cost of the lost units is allocated both to units transferred from the department and units in ending inventory. If ending inventory has not yet reached the quality control inspection point, the lost unit cost attaches only to the units transferred.

In a job order costing system, the cost of anticipated defects/spoilage is estimated and included in setting the predetermined overhead rate. This approach allows expected cost of lost units to be assigned to all jobs. When lost units occur, any disposal value of those units is carried in a separate inventory account; the net cost of defects/spoilage is debited to Manufacturing Overhead. If lost units do not generally occur in a job order system, any normal defects/spoilage associated with a specific job is carried as part of that job's cost; the disposal value of such units reduces the cost of the specific job.

Treatment of the rework cost for defective units depends on whether the rework is normal or abnormal. If rework is normal, the cost is considered to be a product cost and either (1) increases actual costs in the cost schedule or (2) is considered in setting an overhead application rate and charged to overhead when incurred. If rework is abnormal, the cost is assigned to the period as a loss.

Adding material to partially completed units may increase the number of units. If the material addition occurs in a successor department, a new transferred-in cost per unit must be calculated using the increased number of units. If units of measure change between the start and end of production, a consistent measuring unit must be used in the cost of production report to properly reflect production of the period.

Accounting for spoiled and defective units is essential when total quality does not exist. The traditional methods of accounting for spoilage often "bury" the cost of poor quality by spreading that cost over good output. Managers should attempt to compute the costs of spoiled or defective units and search for ways to improve product quality, reduce product cost, and increase the company's competitive market position.

KEY TERMS

abnormal loss (p. 263)
accepted quality level (AQL) (p. 261)
accretion (p. 277)
continuous loss (p. 264)
defective unit (p. 263)
discrete loss (p. 264)
economically reworked (p. 263)
method of neglect (p. 265)
net cost of normal spoilage (p. 276)
normal loss (p. 263)
shrinkage (p. 262)
spoiled unit (p. 263)

SOLUTION STRATEGIES

Lost units are *always* shown with other whole units under "Units accounted for" in the cost of production report.

Continuous Normal Loss

1. Lost units are *not* extended to EUP schedule.
2. All good production (both fully and partially completed) absorbs the cost of the lost units through higher per-unit costs.

Continuous Abnormal Loss

1. All units are appropriately extended to EUP schedule.
2. Cost of lost units is assigned as a period loss.

Discrete Normal Loss

1. Normal loss is appropriately extended to EUP schedule.
2. Determine whether ending inventory has passed an inspection point.
   a. If no, cost of lost units is assigned only to the good production that was transferred.
   b. If yes, cost of lost units is prorated between units in ending WIP Inventory and units transferred out based on (1) (weighted average) total costs contained in each category prior to proration, or (2) (FIFO) current costs contained in each category prior to proration.

Discrete Abnormal Loss

1. All units are appropriately extended to EUP schedule.
2. Cost of lost units is assigned as a period loss.

Normal Rework

1. *(Actual cost system)* Add rework costs to original material, labor, and overhead costs and spread over all production.
2. *(Normal and standard cost systems)* Include cost of rework in estimated overhead when determining standard application rate. Assign actual rework costs to Manufacturing Overhead.

Abnormal Rework

Accumulate rework costs separately and assign as a period loss.

Accretion in Successor Departments

An increase in units requires that the per-unit transferred-in cost be reduced in the successor department based on the new, larger number of units.

DEMONSTRATION PROBLEM

Maura Nobile & Company incurs spoilage continuously throughout the manufacturing process. All materials are added at the beginning of the process, and the inspection point is at the end of the production process. April 2000 operating statistics are as follows:

Pounds			
Beginning inventory (75% complete)			2,000
Started in April			10,000
Completed and transferred			9,500
Ending inventory (70% complete)			1,000
Normal spoilage			900
Abnormal spoilage			?
Costs			
Beginning inventory			
Material	$117,780		
Conversion	47,748	$ 165,528	
Current period			
Materials	$546,000		
Conversion	325,500	871,500	
Total costs		$1,037,028	

Required:

a. Prepare a cost of production report using the weighted average method.

b. Prepare a cost of production report using the FIFO method.

c. Using the information from part (b), prepare the journal entry to recognize the abnormal loss from spoilage.

Solution to Demonstration Problem

a.

MAURA NOBILE & COMPANY
Cost of Production Report
(Continuous spoilage—normal & abnormal; weighted average method)
For the Month Ended April 30, 2000

PRODUCTION DATA		EQUIVALENT UNITS	
	Whole Units	Material	Conversion
Beginning inventory (100%; 75%)	2,000	2,000	1,500
+ Pounds started	10,000		
= Pounds to account for	12,000		
Beginning inventory completed (0%; 25%)	2,000	0	500
+ Pounds started and completed	7,500	7,500	7,500
= Total pounds completed	9,500		
+ Ending inventory (100%; 70%)	1,000	1,000	700
+ Normal spoilage	900		
+ Abnormal spoilage (100%; 100%)	600	600	600
= Pounds accounted for	12,000	11,100	10,800

(continued)

COST DATA

	Total	Material	Conversion
Beginning inventory costs	$ 165,528	$117,780	$ 47,748
Current costs	871,500	546,000	325,500
Total costs	$1,037,028	$663,780	$373,248
Divided by EUP		11,100	10,800
Cost per WA EUP	$94.36	$59.80	$34.56

COST ASSIGNMENT

Transferred (9,500 × $94.36)		$ 896,420
Ending inventory:		
Material (1,000 × $59.80)	$59,800	
Conversion (700 × $34.56)	24,192	83,992
Abnormal loss (600 × $94.36)		56,616
Total costs accounted for		$1,037,028

b.

MAURA NOBILE & COMPANY
Cost of Production Report
(Continuous spoilage—normal & abnormal; FIFO method)
For the Month Ended June 30, 2000

PRODUCTION DATA

	Whole Units	EQUIVALENT UNITS Material	Conversion
Beginning inventory (100%; 75%)	2,000	2,000	1,500
+ Pounds started	10,000		
= Pounds to account for	12,000		
Beginning inventory completed (0%; 25%)	2,000	0	500
+ Pounds started and completed	7,500	7,500	7,500
= Total pounds completed	9,500		
+ Ending inventory (100%; 70%)	1,000	1,000	700
+ Normal spoilage	900		
+ Abnormal spoilage (100%; 100%)	600	600	600
= Pounds accounted for	12,000	11,100	9,300

COST DATA

	Total	Material	Conversion
Beginning inventory costs	$ 165,528		
Current costs	871,500	$546,000	$325,500
Total costs	$1,037,028		
Divided by EUP		9,100	9,300
Cost per FIFO EUP	$95	$60	$35

COST ASSIGNMENT

Transferred:		
From beginning inventory	$165,528	
Cost to complete: Conversion (500 × $35)	17,500	
Total cost of beginning inventory	$183,028	
Started and completed (7,500 × $95)	712,500	
Total cost of pounds transferred		$ 895,528
Ending inventory:		
Material (1,000 × $60)	$ 60,000	
Conversion (700 × $35)	24,500	84,500
Abnormal loss (600 × $95)		57,000
Total costs accounted for		$1,037,028

c.	Loss from Abnormal Spoilage	57,000	
	Work in Process Inventory		57,000
	To remove cost of abnormal spoilage from Work in Process Inventory account.		

QUESTIONS

1. Explain the meaning of an accepted quality level and discuss it in relation to a zero tolerance for defects or errors approach.
2. Differentiate among shrinkage, spoilage, and defects.
3. What are some reasons a company would set a "tolerated" loss level? How might such a level be set?
4. List five examples (similar to the blackened redfish illustration in the text) in which a unit would be considered (a) defective and (b) spoiled.
5. What is the difference between a normal and an abnormal loss?
6. Why would abnormal losses be more likely to be preventable than some types of normal losses?
7. How does a continuous loss differ from a discrete loss?
8. When does a discrete loss actually occur? When is it assumed to occur for accounting purposes? Why are these not necessarily at the same point?
9. Why is the cost of an abnormal loss considered a period cost? How is its cost removed from Work in Process Inventory?
10. What is meant by the term *method of neglect*? When is this method used?
11. How does use of the method of neglect affect the cost of good production in a period?
12. In a job order costing system, spoilage may be incurred in general for all jobs or it may be related to a specific job. What differences do these circumstances make in the treatment of spoilage?
13. In a production process, what is accretion? How does it affect the cost of the units transferred in from a predecessor department?
14. The Mixing Department of Leeward Company transferred 100,000 gallons of material to the Baking Department during July. The cost per gallon transferred out shown on Mixing's cost of production report was $2.50. On Baking's cost of production report for the same period, the cost per gallon for material transferred in was $2.00. Why might the cost have changed?
15. How are costs of reworking defective units treated if the defects are considered normal? Abnormal?
16. A company has an AQL for defects of 5 percent of units started during the period. Current period loss was 3 percent. Why should management attempt to measure the cost of this loss rather than simply include it as part of the cost of good production?
17. How do statistical process control techniques contribute to the control of spoilage costs?
18. Search the Internet for a company that has a zero tolerance for defects policy and report on the results of the company's efforts to reach its goals.

EXERCISES

19. *(Terminology)* Match the following lettered terms on the left with the appropriate numbered definition on the right.

a. Abnormal loss
b. Acceptable quality level
c. Accretion
d. Defective unit
e. Economically reworked
f. Method of neglect
g. Normal loss
h. Spoiled unit

1. Allowing the production of spoiled units to increase the cost of good production
2. Decreases the transferred-in cost per unit
3. Results from having defective production greater than the AQL
4. A unit that is discarded on inspection
5. A unit that can be reworked
6. An expected decline in units in the production process
7. Additional processing that results in net incremental revenue
8. Maximum limit below which the frequency of defects in a process is accepted as normal

20. *(Cost-benefit analysis)* Alfred Carlson, plant manager at WEBOXALL Company, is investigating spoilage created by a machine that prints packing boxes for TVs and other large, fragile items. At the beginning of each production run, 50 boxes are misprinted either because of miscoloration or misalignment. These boxes must be destroyed. The variable production cost per box is $6.00. The machine averages 200 setups for production runs each year.

A regulator is available that will correct the problem. Alfred is trying to decide whether to purchase the regulator.

a. At what cost for the regulator would the benefit of acquisition not exceed the cost? What other factors should Alfred consider in addition to the purchase price of the regulator?

b. If each setup produces an average of 500 boxes, what is the increased cost per good box that is caused by the spoiled units?

c. WEBOXALL Company runs 12 batches per year for Springtime Corporation, which makes very specialized equipment in limited quantities. Thus, each batch contains only 20 boxes. If WEBOXALL Company is passing its spoilage cost on to customers based on batch costs, might Springtime Corporation be willing to buy the regulator for WEBOXALL Company if the regulator costs $3,300? Justify your answer.

d. Why are the cost-per-box answers in parts (b) and (c) so different?

21. *(Normal vs. abnormal spoilage; WA)* Jacksonville Plastics uses a weighted average process costing system for its production process in which all material is added at the beginning of production. Company management has specified that the normal loss cannot exceed 7 percent of the units started in a period. All losses are caused by shrinkage. March processing information follows:

Beginning inventory (10% complete—conversion)	8,000 units
Started during March	60,000 units
Completed during March	53,000 units
Ending inventory (60% complete—conversion)	10,000 units

a. How many total units are there to account for?

b. How many units should be treated as normal loss?

c. How many units should be treated as abnormal loss?

d. What are the equivalent units of production for direct material? For conversion?

22. *(EUP computations; normal and abnormal loss)* The Atlanta Division of Southeastern Paint produces environmental paints in processes in which spoilage takes place on a continual basis. Management considers normal spoilage to be 0.5 percent or less of gallons of material placed into production. The following operating statistics are available for June 2000 for the paint BMZ:

Beginning inventory (20% complete as to material; 30% complete as to conversion)	8,000 gallons
Started during June	180,000 gallons
Ending inventory (60% complete as to material; 70% complete as to conversion)	4,000 gallons
Spoiled	1,400 gallons

a. How many gallons were transferred out?
b. How much normal spoilage occurred?
c. How much abnormal spoilage occurred?
d. What are the FIFO equivalent units of production for materials? For conversion costs?
e. How are costs associated with the normal spoilage handled?
f. How are costs associated with the abnormal spoilage handled?

23. *(EUP computation; normal and abnormal loss; FIFO)* Arkansas Foods manufactures corn meal in a continuous, mass-production process. Corn is added at the beginning of the process. Losses are few and occur only when foreign materials are found in the corn meal. Inspection occurs at the 95 percent completion point as to conversion.

During May, a machine malfunctioned and dumped salt into 18,000 pounds of corn meal. This abnormal loss occurred when conversion was 70 percent complete on those pounds of product. The error was immediately noticed, and those pounds of corn meal were pulled from the production process. An additional 1,000 pounds of meal were detected as unsuitable at the inspection point. These lost units were considered well within reasonable limits. May production data are shown below:

Beginning work in process (85% complete)	50,000 pounds
Started during the month	425,000 pounds
Ending work in process (25% complete)	10,000 pounds

a. Determine the number of equivalent units for direct material and for conversion assuming a FIFO cost flow.
b. If the costs per equivalent unit are \$2.50 and \$4.50 for direct material and conversion, respectively, what is the cost of ending inventory?
c. What is the cost of abnormal loss? How is this cost treated in May?

24. *(EUP computation; normal and abnormal loss; cost per EUP; FIFO)* CandleSticks uses a FIFO process costing system to account for its candle production process. Wax occasionally forms imperfectly in molds and, thus, spoilage is viewed as continuous. The accepted quality level is good output of 92 percent of the pounds of wax placed in production. All wax is entered at the beginning of the process. March 2001 data follow:

Beginning inventory (30% complete as to conversion)	9,000 pounds
Started during month	30,000 pounds
Transferred	31,500 pounds
(315,000 candles; 10 wax candles are obtained from a pound of wax)	
Ending inventory (20% complete as to conversion)	5,400 pounds
Loss	? pounds

The following costs are associated with March production:

Beginning inventory:		
Material	$3,600	
Conversion	2,700	$ 6,300
Current period:		
Material	$9,207	
Conversion	8,964	18,171
Total costs		$24,471

a. Prepare the production data segment of CandleSticks' cost of production report for March 2001.
b. Compute the cost per equivalent unit for each cost component.
c. Assign March costs to the appropriate units.

25. *(Cost assignment; WA)* CushionRide manufactures automobile springs. Its production equipment is fairly old, and one bad unit is typically produced for every 20 good units. The bad units cannot be reworked and must be discarded. Spoilage is determined at an end-of-process inspection point. CushionRide uses a weighted average process costing system and adds all material at the beginning of the process. The following data have been gathered from the accounting records for January 2001:

Beginning inventory (60% complete as to conversion)	4,000 units
Units started	20,000 units
Ending inventory (30% complete as to conversion)	3,000 units
Good units completed	20,000 units

	Material	Conversion	Total
Beginning inventory	$ 12,492	$ 9,927	$ 22,419
Current period	112,548	63,000	175,548
Total costs	$125,040	$72,927	$197,967

a. Prepare an EUP schedule.
b. Determine the cost of the normal spoilage and allocate that cost to the appropriate inventory.

26. *(Normal discrete spoilage; WA)* The Potato Division of Global Foods Company processes potatoes. In the process, raw potatoes are sequentially cleaned, skinned, cooked, and canned. Spoilage amounting to less than 12 percent of the total pounds of potatoes that are introduced to the cleaning operation is considered normal (in this case, normal spoilage is to include the weight of the potato peels). Inspection occurs when the products are 50 percent complete. Information that follows pertains to operations in the Potato Division for January 2000:

Beginning WIP inventory (30% complete)	500,000 pounds
Started	13,500,000 pounds
Transferred	11,400,000 pounds
Ending WIP inventory (40% complete)	750,000 pounds

a. Compute the amount of spoilage in January. How much of the spoilage was normal?
b. Compute the equivalent units of production assuming the weighted average method is used.
c. Prepare a memo explaining why you might expect some (1) accretion in the canning operation and (2) some shrinkage other than the weight of the peels in one or more of the operations.

27. *(Rework)* Auto Luster Inc. manufactures two-gallon tubs of car polish for body shops. The company uses an actual cost, process costing system. All material is added at the beginning of production; labor and overhead are incurred evenly through the process. Defective units are identified through inspection at the end of the production process. The following information is available for August 2001:

Beginning inventory (30% complete as to conversion)	750 units
Started during month	17,250 units
Completed during month	15,000 units
Defective units (100% complete as to conversion)	1,800 units
Ending inventory (70% complete as to conversion)	1,200 units

Actual August production costs (including those for beginning inventory) were \$126,000 for direct material and \$40,572 for conversion. In addition, the rework cost to bring the 1,800 units up to specifications was \$3,150 for material and \$1,323 for conversion.

a. Determine the equivalent units of production using the weighted average method.

b. Assume that the rework is normal. Determine the cost per good unit for direct material and conversion.

c. Assume that the rework is normal. How would the rework cost be handled in a normal (rather than actual) costing system?

d. Assume that the rework is abnormal. Determine the cost per good unit for direct material and conversion. How is the rework cost recorded for financial statement purposes?

28. *(Controlling losses)* For each of the following types of production losses or poor service, indicate whether prevention (P) or appraisal (A) techniques would provide the most effective control mechanism. Explain why you made your choice.

a. Putting pages in upside down in a book.
b. Bolting the wrong parts together.
c. Shrinkage from cooking.
d. Breaking glasses when they are being boxed.
e. Paying an account payable twice.
f. Bringing the wrong meal to a restaurant customer.

PROBLEMS

29. *(Shrinkage; WA)* Department 1 of Super Patties cooks ground beef for hamburger patties. The patties are then transferred to Department 2 where they are placed on buns, boxed, and frozen. The accepted level of shrinkage in Department 1 is 10 percent of the pounds started. Super Patties uses a weighted average process costing system and has the following production and cost data for Department 1 for May 2001:

Beginning inventory (80% complete as to conversion)	1,000 pounds
Started	125,000 pounds
Transferred to Department 2 (550,000 patties)	110,000 pounds
Ending inventory (30% complete as to conversion)	3,000 pounds
Beginning inventory cost of ground beef	\$ 1,020
May cost of ground beef	\$106,710
Beginning inventory conversion cost	\$ 195
May conversion cost	\$ 27,630

a. What is the total shrinkage (in pounds)?

b. How much of the shrinkage is classified as normal? How is it treated for accounting purposes?

c. How much of the shrinkage is classified as abnormal? How is it treated for accounting purposes?

(continued)

d. What is the total cost of the patties transferred to Department 2? Cost of ending inventory? Cost of abnormal spoilage?

e. How might Super Patties reduce its shrinkage loss? How, if at all, would your solution(s) affect costs?

30. *(Discrete spoilage; WA)* Angelique Inc. makes stuffed angels in a mass-production process. Cloth and stuffing are added at the beginning of the production process; the angels are packaged in sky-blue boxes at the end of production. Conversion costs for the highly automated process are incurred evenly throughout processing. The angels are inspected at the 95 percent completion point prior to being boxed. Defective units of more than 1 percent of the units started is considered abnormal.

The company uses a weighted average process costing system. June 2001 production and cost data for Angelique Inc. follow:

Beginning inventory (40% complete as to conversion)	5,000
Started	70,000
Ending inventory (70% complete as to conversion)	6,000
Total defective units	400
Beginning inventory cloth and stuffing cost	$ 21,900
Beginning inventory conversion cost	$ 7,680
June cloth and stuffing cost	$315,600
June box cost	$ 75,460
June conversion cost	$270,404

a. How many units were completed in June?

b. How many of the defective units are considered a normal loss? An abnormal loss?

c. What is the per-unit cost of the completed units? What would the per-unit cost of the completed units have been if the 400 units had been good units at their same stages of completion at the end of the period?

d. What is the total cost of ending inventory?

31. *(Normal and abnormal discrete spoilage; WA)* Brendan Tools manufactures one of its products in a two-department process. A separate Work in Process account is maintained for each department, and Brendan Tools uses a weighted average process costing system. The first department is Molding; the second is Grinding. At the end of production in Grinding, a quality inspection is made and then packaging is added. Overhead is applied in the Grinding Department on a machine-hour basis. Production and cost data for the Grinding Department for August 2000 follow:

Production Data

Beginning inventory (complete: labor, 30%; overhead, 40%)	2,000 units
Transferred-in from Molding	49,800 units
Normal spoilage (discrete—found at the end of processing during quality control)	650 units
Abnormal spoilage (found at end of processing during quality control)	350 units
Ending inventory (complete: labor, 40%; overhead, 65%)	1,800 units
Transferred to finished goods	? units

Cost Data

Beginning inventory:		
Transferred-in	$ 6,050	
Material (label and package)	0	
Direct labor	325	
Overhead	750	$ 7,125
Current period:		
Transferred-in	$149,350	
Material (label and package)	11,760	
Direct labor	23,767	
Overhead	50,932	235,809
Total cost to account for		$242,934

a. Prepare a cost of production report for the Grinding Department for August.
b. Prepare the journal entry to dispose of the cost of abnormal spoilage.

32. *(Normal and abnormal spoilage; WA)* Big Stone Furniture produces breakfast tables in a two-department process: Cutting/Assembly and Lamination. Varnish is added in the Lamination Department when the goods are 60 percent complete as to overhead. Spoiled units are found on inspection at the end of production. Spoilage is considered discrete.

PRODUCTION DATA FOR APRIL 2000

Beginning inventory (80% complete as to labor, 70% complete as to overhead)	2,000 units
Transferred in during month	14,900 units
Ending inventory (40% complete as to labor, 20% complete as to overhead)	3,000 units
Normal spoilage (found at final quality inspection)	200 units
Abnormal spoilage (found at 30% completion as to labor and 15% as to overhead; the sanding machine was misaligned and scarred the tables)	400 units
The remaining units were transferred to finished goods.	

COST DATA FOR APRIL 2000

Beginning Work in Process Inventory:		
Prior department costs	$ 15,020	
Varnish	1,900	
Direct labor	4,388	
Overhead	11,044	$ 32,352
Current period costs:		
Prior department costs	$137,080	
Varnish	14,030	
Direct labor	46,000	
Overhead	113,564	310,674
Total costs to account for		$343,026

Determine the proper disposition of the April costs for the Lamination Department using the weighted average method; include journal entries.

33. *(Normal and abnormal discrete spoilage; FIFO)* Use the Big Stone Furniture information from Problem 32. Determine the proper disposition of the April costs of the Lamination Department using the FIFO method; include journal entries.

34. *(Normal and abnormal discrete spoilage; FIFO)* Reagan Company produces hinges. Completed hinges are inspected at the end of production. Any spoilage in excess of 2 percent of the completed units is considered abnormal. Material is added at the start of production. Labor and overhead are incurred evenly throughout production.

Reagan's May 2001 production and cost data follow:

Beginning inventory (50% complete)	5,600
Units started	74,400
Good units completed	70,000
Ending inventory (1/3 complete)	7,500

	Material	Conversion	Total
Beginning inventory	$ 6,400	$ 1,232	$ 7,632
Current period	74,400	31,768	106,168
Total	$80,800	$33,000	$113,800

Calculate the equivalent units schedule, prepare a FIFO cost of production report, and assign all costs.

35. *(Normal and abnormal discrete spoilage; WA)* Use the Reagan Company data as given in Problem 34. Prepare a May 2001 cost of production report using the weighted average method.

36. *(Cost assignment)* Data below summarize operations for GreenerGrass Company for March 2001. The company makes five-gallon containers of weed killer/fertilizer. All material is added at the beginning of the process.

COSTS

	Material	Conversion	Total
Beginning inventory	$ 30,000	$ 3,600	$ 33,600
Current period	885,120	335,088	1,220,208
Total costs	$915,120	$338,688	$1,253,808

UNITS

Beginning inventory (30% complete-conversion)	6,000 units
Started	180,000 units
Completed	152,000 units
Ending inventory (70% complete-conversion)	20,000 units
Normal spoilage	4,800 units

Spoilage is detected at inspection when the units are 60 percent complete.

a. Prepare an EUP schedule using the weighted average method.

b. Determine the cost of goods transferred out, ending inventory, and abnormal spoilage.

37. *(Cost assignment)* Patio Products employs a weighted average process costing system for its products. One product passes through three departments (Molding, Assembly, and Finishing) during production. The following activity took place in the Finishing Department during May 2001:

Units in beginning inventory	4,200
Units transferred in from Assembly	42,000
Units spoiled	2,100
Good units transferred out	33,600

The equivalent units and the costs per equivalent unit of production for each cost factor are as follows:

Cost of prior departments	$5.00
Raw material	1.00
Conversion	3.00
Total cost per EUP	$9.00

Raw material is added at the beginning of processing in Finishing without changing the number of units being processed. Work in Process Inventory was 70 percent complete as to conversion on May 1 and 40 percent complete as to conversion on May 31. All spoilage was discovered at final inspection. Of the total units spoiled, 1,680 were within normal limits.

a. Calculate the equivalent units of production.

b. Determine the cost of units transferred out of Finishing.

c. Determine the cost of ending Work in Process Inventory.

d. The portion of the total transferred-in cost associated with beginning Work in Process Inventory amounted to $18,900. What is the current period cost that was transferred in from Assembly to Finishing?

e. Determine the cost associated with abnormal spoilage for the month. How would this amount be accounted for? *(CMA adapted)*

38. *(Comprehensive; weighted average)* Harper Company produces brooms. Department 1 winds and cuts straw into broom heads and transfers these to Department 2 where the broom head is bound and attached to a handle. Straw is added at the beginning of the first process, and the handle is added at the end of the second process.

Normal losses in Department 1 should not exceed 5 percent of the units started; losses are determined at an inspection point at the end of the production process. The AQL in Department 2 is 10 percent of the broom heads transferred in; losses are found at an inspection point located 70 percent of the way through the production process.

The following production and cost data are available for October 2001.

PRODUCTION RECORD (IN UNITS)

	Dept. 1	Dept. 2
Beginning inventory	6,000	3,000
Started or transferred in	150,000	?
Ending inventory	18,000	15,000
Spoiled units	9,000	6,000
Transferred out	?	111,000

COST RECORD

	Dept. 1	Dept. 2
Beginning inventory:		
Preceding department	n/a	$ 6,690
Material	$ 3,000	0
Conversion	2,334	504
Current period:		
Preceding department	n/a	230,910*
Material	36,000	740
Conversion	208,962	52,920

*This is not the amount derived from your calculations. Use this amount so that you do not carry forward any possible cost errors from Department 1.

The beginning and ending inventory units in Department 1 are, respectively, 10 percent and 60 percent complete as to conversion. In Department 2, the beginning and ending units are, respectively, 40 percent and 80 percent complete as to conversion.

Using the weighted average method, create a cost of production report for each department for October 2001.

39. *(Comprehensive; FIFO)* Use the information for Harper Company from Problem 38 to prepare a FIFO cost of production report for each department for October 2001.

40. *(Comprehensive; WA and FIFO)* Andaman Company mines salt in southern Florida. Approximately 30 percent of the mined salt is processed into table salt. Andaman Company uses a process costing system for the table salt operation. Processing takes place in two departments. Department 1 uses FIFO costing, and Department 2 uses weighted average. The cost of the processed salt transferred from Department 1 to Department 2 is averaged over all the units transferred.

Salt is introduced into the process in Department 1. Spoilage occurs continuously through the department and normal spoilage should not exceed 10 percent of the units started; a unit is 50 pounds of salt.

Department 2 packages the salt at the 75 percent completion point; this material does not increase the number of units processed. A quality control inspection takes place when the goods are 80 percent complete. Spoilage should not exceed 5 percent of the units transferred in from Department 1.

The following production and cost data are applicable to Andaman Company's table salt operations for July 2001:

DEPARTMENT 1 PRODUCTION DATA		
Beginning inventory (65% complete)	5,000	
Units started	125,000	
Units completed	110,000	
Units in ending inventory (40% complete)	14,000	

DEPARTMENT 1 COST DATA		
Beginning inventory:		
Material	$ 7,750	
Conversion	11,500	$ 19,250
Current period:		
Material	$190,400	
Conversion	393,225	583,625
Total costs to account for		$ 602,875

DEPARTMENT 2 PRODUCTION DATA		
Beginning inventory (90% complete)	40,000	
Units transferred in	110,000	
Units completed	120,000	
Units in ending inventory (20% complete)	22,500	

DEPARTMENT 2 COST DATA		
Beginning inventory:		
Transferred-in	$204,000	
Material	120,000	
Conversion	21,600	$ 345,600
Current period:		
Transferred-in	$568,500*	
Material	268,875	
Conversion	55,395	892,770
Total costs to account for		$1,238,370

*This may not be the same amount determined for Department 1; ignore any difference and use this figure.

a. Compute the equivalent units of production in each department.

b. Determine the cost per equivalent unit in each department and compute the cost transferred out, cost in ending inventory, and cost of spoilage (if necessary).

41. *(Defective units and rework)* Hoffus Corporation produces plastic pipe and accounts for its production process using weighted average process costing. Material is added at the beginning of production. The company applies overhead to products using machine hours. Hoffus Corporation used the following information in setting its predetermined overhead rate for 2000:

Expected overhead other than rework	$425,000
Expected rework costs	37,500
Total expected overhead	$462,500
Expected machine hours for 2000	50,000

During 2000, the following production and cost data were accumulated:

Total good production completed	2,000,000 feet of pipe
Total defects	40,000 feet of pipe
Ending inventory (35% complete)	75,000 feet of pipe

Total (beginning inventory and current period) cost of direct material	$3,750,000
Total (beginning inventory and current period) cost of conversion	$5,650,000
Cost of reworking defects	$ 37,750

Hoffus Corporation sells pipe for $3.50 per foot.

a. Determine the overhead application rate for 2000.

b. Determine the cost per pipe-foot for production in 2000.

c. Assume that the rework is normal and those units can be sold for the regular selling price. How will Hoffus Corporation account for the $37,750 of rework cost?

d. Assume that the rework is normal, but the reworked pipe is irregular and can only be sold for $2.50 per foot. Prepare the journal entry to establish the inventory account for the reworked pipe. What is the total cost per unit for the good output completed?

e. Assume that 20 percent of the rework is abnormal and that all reworked output is irregular and can be sold for only $2.50 per foot. Prepare the journal entry to establish the inventory account for the reworked pipe. What is the total cost per foot for the good output completed during 2000?

42. *(Job order costing; rework)* Argonne Rigging manufactures pulley systems to customer specifications and uses a job order system. A recent order from Michaels Company was for 10,000 pulleys, and the job was assigned number BA468. The job cost sheet for #BA468 revealed the following:

WIP—JOB #BA468

Direct material	$20,400	
Direct labor	24,600	
Overhead	18,400	
Total	$63,400	

Final inspection of the 10,000 pulleys revealed that 230 of the pulleys were defective. In correcting the defects, an additional $950 of cost was incurred ($250 for direct material and $700 for direct labor). After the defects were cured, the pulleys were included with the other good units and shipped to the customer.

a. Assuming the rework costs are normal but specific to this job, show the journal entry to record incurrence of the rework costs.

b. Assuming the company has a predetermined overhead rate that includes normal rework costs, show the journal entry to record incurrence of the rework costs.

c. Assuming the rework costs are abnormal, show the journal entry to record incurrence of the rework costs.

CASE

43. *(Normal and abnormal spoilage; WA)* Grand Monde Company manufactures various lines of bicycles. Because of the high volume of each type of product, the company employs a process cost system using the weighted average method to determine unit costs. Bicycle parts are manufactured in the Molding Department and transferred to the Assembly Department where they are partially assembled. After assembly, the bicycle is sent to the Packing Department.

Cost-per-unit data for the 20-inch dirt bike has been completed through the Molding Department. Annual cost and production figures for the Assembly Department are presented at the top of the next page.

PRODUCTION DATA

Beginning inventory (100% complete as to transferred-in; 100% complete as to assembly material; 80% complete as to conversion)	3,000 units
Transferred in during the year (100% complete as to transferred-in)	45,000 units
Transferred to Packing	40,000 units
Ending inventory (100% complete as to transferred-in; 50% complete as to assembly material; 20% complete as to conversion)	4,000 units

COST DATA

	Transferred-In	Direct Material	Conversion
Beginning inventory	$ 82,200	$ 6,660	$ 11,930
Current period	1,237,800	96,840	236,590
Totals	$1,320,000	$103,500	$248,520

Damaged bicycles are identified on inspection when the assembly process is 70 percent complete; all assembly material has been added at this point of the process. The normal rejection rate for damaged bicycles is 5 percent of the bicycles reaching the inspection point. Any damaged bicycles above the 5 percent quota are considered to be abnormal. All damaged bikes are removed from the production process and destroyed.

a. Compute the number of damaged bikes that are considered to be
   1. a normal quantity of damaged bikes.
   2. an abnormal quantity of damaged bikes.

b. Compute the weighted average equivalent units of production for the year for
   1. bicycles transferred in from the Molding Department.
   2. bicycles produced with regard to assembly material.
   3. bicycles produced with regard to assembly conversion.

c. Compute the cost per equivalent unit for the fully assembled dirt bike.

d. Compute the amount of the total production cost of $1,672,020 that will be associated with the following items:
   1. Normal damaged units
   2. Abnormal damaged units
   3. Good units completed in the Assembly Department
   4. Ending Work in Process Inventory in the Assembly Department

e. Describe how the applicable dollar amounts for the following items would be presented in the financial statements:
   1. Normal damaged units
   2. Abnormal damaged units
   3. Completed units transferred to the Packing Department
   4. Ending Work in Process Inventory in the Assembly Department

f. Determine the cost to Grand Monde Company of normal spoilage. Discuss some potential reasons for spoilage to occur in this company. Which of these reasons would you consider important enough to correct and why? How might you attempt to correct these problems? *(CMA adapted)*

REALITY CHECK

44. AudioSpectrum produces complex printed circuits for stereo amplifiers. The circuits are sold primarily to major component manufacturers, and any production overruns are sold to small manufacturers at a substantial discount. The small manufacturer segment appears to be very profitable because the basic operating budget assigns all fixed expenses to production for the major manufacturers, the only predictable market.

A common product defect that occurs in production is a "drift," caused by failure to maintain precise heat levels during the production process. Rejects from the 100 percent testing program can be reworked to acceptable levels if the defect is drift. However, in a recent analysis of customer complaints, Andrew Hill, the cost accountant, and the quality control engineer have ascertained that normal rework does not bring the circuits up to standard. Sampling shows that about one-half of the reworked circuits fail after extended, high-volume amplifier operation. The incidence of failure in the reworked circuits is projected to be about 10 percent over one to five years of operation.

Unfortunately, there is no way to determine which reworked circuits will fail because testing does not detect this problem. The rework process could be changed to correct the problem, but the cost-benefit analysis for the suggested change in the rework process indicates that it is not practicable. AudioSpectrum's marketing analyst feels that this problem will have a significant impact on the company's reputation and customer satisfaction if it is not corrected. Consequently, the board of directors would interpret this problem as having serious negative implications for the company's profitability.

Hill has included the circuit failure and rework problem in his report for the upcoming quarterly meeting of the board of directors. Due to the potential adverse economic impact, Hill has followed a long-standing practice of highlighting this information.

After reviewing the reports to be presented, the plant manager and her staff were upset and indicated to the controller that he should control his people better. "We can't upset the board with this kind of material. Tell Hill to tone that down. Maybe we can get it by this meeting and have some time to work on it. People who buy those cheap systems and play them that loud shouldn't expect them to last forever."

The controller called Hill into his office and said, "Andrew, you'll have to bury this one. The probable failure of reworks can be referred to briefly in the oral presentation, but it should not be mentioned or highlighted in the advance material mailed to the board."

Hill feels strongly that the board will be misinformed on a potentially serious loss of income if he follows the controller's orders. Hill discussed the problem with the quality control engineer, who simply remarked, "That's your problem, Andrew."

a. Discuss the ethical considerations that Andrew Hill should recognize in deciding how to proceed in this matter.

b. Explain what ethical responsibilities should be accepted in this situation by

- **1.** The controller.
- **2.** The quality control engineer.
- **3.** The plant manager and her staff.

c. What should Andrew Hill do in this situation? Explain your answer.

(CMA adapted)

45. Every job has certain requirements, and quality is defined by meeting those requirements. In some cases, however, people make decisions to override requirements. In a team of three or four, choose four requirements for your class (or for a job held by one of you). Prepare a memo that would explain to your teacher (or your boss) the following:

a. The requirements you have chosen and why you think the teacher (boss) made those requirements.

b. The conditions under which your team would decide to override the requirements.

(continued)

c. Why you believe that overriding the requirements would be appropriate in the conditions you have specified.

d. The potential for problems that may arise by overriding the requirements.

46. Use library, Internet, or personal resources to find three companies that instituted workforce education programs and, thereby, reduced the number of lost units. Prepare a five- to seven-minute oral presentation about your companies' programs and their benefits.

47. All world-class models (TQM, JIT, ABM, and theory of constraints) advocate improving throughput as a way to improve quality and minimize defects. Prepare a report for the board of directors of a company for which you are the newly appointed controller explaining why increasing throughput is linked to quality improvements and reduction of defects.

48. In accounting for spoilage, consideration should be given to how well the approach chosen to measure spoilage supports management's efforts to improve quality. Prepare a memo explaining how selecting a method to measure and account for spoilage can either assist or hinder management's efforts to improve quality.

http://www.zerodefect.com

49. The following is an excerpt from the Web site of Zero Defects, an electronics manufacturing service provider:

At Zero Defects, we have never believed that perfection is too much for our clients to expect. For over 15 years, the world's leading electronics companies have relied on us to provide legendary service and manufacture faultless products. When we say faultless, we mean much more than you might think. To us perfection means:

- *Delivering 100% usable product on time, every time.*
- *Providing service that meets and exceeds every expectation.*
- *Manufacturing each component in the most cost-effective way possible.*
- *Meeting your exact specifications and customizing any part of our production line to do so.*
- *Keeping costs at a bare minimum through tight internal controls and volume buying power.*
- *Providing and standing by detailed quotations and schedules.*
- *Preventing environmental damage through safe manufacturing and recycling programs.*

[SOURCE: Staff, Zero Defects Web site, http://www.zerod.com/index.htm, (June 15, 2000).]

Write a report briefly discussing this excerpt. Compare and contrast the approach explained in the excerpt with the traditional notion of only undertaking an action for which there is an expected net benefit using cost-benefit analysis.

50. Find three companies on the Internet (other than GE, the company featured in this chapter) that are using Six Sigma. Briefly discuss the results they have experienced from using it.

CHAPTER 8

Implementing Quality Concepts

LEARNING OBJECTIVES

After completing this chapter, you should be able to answer the following questions:

1. Why is the emphasis on quality in business unlikely to decline?
2. What is quality and from whose viewpoint should it be evaluated?
3. What primary characteristics comprise product quality and service quality?
4. Why do companies engage in benchmarking?
5. Why is total quality management significant and what conditions are necessary to yield its benefits?
6. What types of quality costs exist and how are those costs related?
7. How is cost of quality measured?
8. Why does a company need both a strategically based management accounting system and a financial accounting system?
9. How can quality be instilled as part of an organization's culture?

INTRODUCING

Solectron Corporation

http://www.solectron.com

Solectron Corporation is the first company in the history of the Malcolm Baldrige National Quality Award program to have won that award twice (in 1991 and 1997). Solectron, which was founded in 1977 as a solar energy company, has received 200 quality and service awards from its customers. The company now provides customized electronics products, services, and solutions for original equipment manufacturers such as International Business Machines, Hewlett-Packard Co., Motorola, Inc., Polaroid Corporation, and Cisco Systems, Inc.

Solectron has more than 31,000 associates in 21 worldwide manufacturing facilities that encompass more than 6 million square feet. During the past seven years, the company has averaged a 53 percent compound annual growth rate. Revenues for the fiscal year 1998 were $5.3 billion. When Solectron opened a New Product Introduction center just outside of Tokyo, it became the first United States–based electronics manufacturing services company to establish a manufacturing presence in Japan.

How does a company reach such quality heights? Rich Allen, director of quality at Solectron, believes the company's quality culture began with founder and former CEO, Winston Chen. Chen left IBM to start an American company that could and would manufacture high-quality products in the United States, and that focused on giving customers exactly what they wanted. Chen noted that the quality principles being applied in Japan at the time were not being utilized in the United States. On the other hand, the innovations being used in the United States were not being applied in foreign countries as well as they could be. So Chen combined the innovative approaches currently applied quite well in the United States with some of the Japanese quality practices such as poka-yoke techniques, kaizen techniques, seven-step continuous improvement processes, and SPC tools, and saw how they fit and applied to the company. Then Solectron started doing grassroots training while implementing those quality programs in almost every manufacturing area.

Rich Allen commented that "the most important thing was not to let the tools disappear or filter out. With most quality programs, people don't understand that if you really don't reinforce and continually modify it to make it work for you, it just goes away. Then, what you have is a quality program-of-the month. We've never had that. What we said was, 'This is what we're going to do, and we're going to make it work.'"

SOURCES: Holly Ann Suzik, "Solectron Tells Its Tale," *Business and Management Practices,* Responsive Database Services, Inc. (Vol. 38, April 1999), pp. 53ff; Scott Thurm, "Some Manufacturers Prosper by Facilitating Rise of 'Virtual' Firm," *The Wall Street Journal* (August 18, 1998), pp. A1, A6; PR Newswire, "Solectron Becomes First U.S.-Based EMS Company to Open Design and Manufacturing Center in Japan," *PR Newswire Association Inc.* (April 1, 1999), Financial News section; Todd Wallack, "Solectron to Expand," *The Boston Herald* (April 2, 1999), Finance section, p. 31.

Managers at Solectron Corporation and numerous other entities recognize that high quality is a fundamental organizational strategy for competing in a global economy. Businesses, both domestic and foreign, are scrambling to attract customers and to offer more choices to satisfy customer wants and needs than in the past. Competition usually brings out the best in companies and international competition has evoked even greater quality in company products and services.

Consumers are more aware of the greater variety of product choices. However, because they usually have limited funds and must make trade-offs among price, quality, service, and promptness of delivery, customers have a limited set of options. Even so, consumers are taking advantage of the enhanced extent of their options for quality, price, service, and lead time as afforded by the Internet and advanced technology.

Ready access, now being geometrically accelerated by the Internet, to multinational vendors has motivated producers to improve product quality and customer service. Consumers are delighted with their access to higher quality products and services and are thereby encouraged to enhance this access. Vendors are encouraged by the success of firms that delight customers and have adopted more dynamic

1

Why is the emphasis on quality in business unlikely to decline?

http://www.ibm.com
http://www.hewlett-packard.com
http://www.mot.com
http://www.polaroid.com
http://www.cisco.com

approaches to continuously improving the product, process, and service quality for their customers.

This chapter discusses issues such as benchmarking, total quality management, quality costs, quality cost measurement, and a cost management system as a support for quality initiatives. Because quality affects costs, accountants understand the long-run trade-offs involved between higher and lower product/service quality.

Many managers have realized that current expenditures on quality improvements may be more than regained through future cost reductions and sales volume increases. These improvements will benefit the firm now and in the future; thus, their costs should not be viewed as expenses or losses, but rather as recoverable investments with the potential for profit generation.

WHAT IS QUALITY?

2

What is quality and from whose viewpoint should it be evaluated?

To improve its product or service quality, an organization must agree on a definition of the term. Originally, after the Industrial Revolution helped manufacturers to increase output and decrease cost, quality was defined as conformity to designated specifications. Conformity determination was left to quality control inspectors. The late Dr. W. Edwards Deming, famous expert on quality control, defined quality as "the pride of workmanship."[1] On a less individualized basis, Philip Crosby (another noted quality expert) defines quality as "conformance to requirements."[2] This definition was adopted by the American Society for Quality Control, which also defines requirements as follows: "Requirements may be documented as specifications, product descriptions, procedures, policies, job descriptions, instructions, purchase/service orders, etc., or they may be verbal. Requirements must be measurable or they are not valid."[3] The following remarks stress conformity to requirements, but explain that conformity must be judged by customers.

> *Quality is not what the planning and producing individuals may think or wish it to be. It is exactly what exists in the mind of the customer when he or she receives and personally appraises the product or service. This includes the internal customer, recipient of internal support service or work in process, as well as the external customer. In short, the meaning of quality is directly related to customer satisfaction; it is still best defined as "conformance to customer requirements." Any other definition for quality leaves too much room for interpretation and bias, making it impossible to work with.*[4]

quality

Thus, a fairly all-inclusive definition of **quality** is the summation of all the characteristics of a product or service that influence its ability to meet the stated or implied needs of the person acquiring it. Quality must be viewed from the perspective of the user rather than the provider and relates to both performance and value. This quality perspective arose because of increased competition, public interest in product safety, and litigation relative to products and product safety. The responsibility for quality is not simply a production issue; it has become a company profitability and longevity issue. The following News Note dramatizes the importance of competition. All entity processes (production, procurement, distribution, finance, and promotion) are involved in quality improvement efforts. Therefore, the two related perspectives of quality reflect the (1) totality of internal processes that generate a product or service and (2) customer satisfaction with that product or service.

http://www.packardbell.com
http://www.nec-global.com

[1] Rafael Aguayo, *Dr. Deming* (New York: Simon & Schuster, 1990), p. xi.
[2] Philip B. Crosby, *Quality Is Free* (New York: New American Library, 1979), p. 15.
[3] American Society for Quality Control, *Finance, Accounting and Quality* (Milwaukee, WI: ASQC, 1990), p. 3.
[4] Jack Hagan, *Management of Quality* (Milwaukee, WI: ASQC, 1994), p. 18. © 1994 American Society for Quality Control. Reprinted with permission.

QUALITY  NEWS NOTE

Packard Bell to End Operations in the United States

Packard Bell NEC Inc., once a leader in the home PC market, has become its latest casualty as consumers snap up cheaper offerings from competitors and turn their backs on a company with perceived quality problems.

The Packard Bell name and 1,600 jobs ceased to exist in the United States at the end of 1999, after the Sacramento-based company failed to meet performance goals set by its Tokyo-based parent, NEC Corp., spokesman Ron Fuchs said.

The pullout closed an era of rapid U.S. decline for Packard Bell NEC, once the largest domestic maker of personal computers, but only No. 6 by summer 1999, according to researcher Dataquest. The company lost $650 million in 1998 and was on track to lose $150 million, despite increased demand for its products.

"From our point of view . . . we made a lot of progress this year, but when all is said and done, we missed our commitment to shareholders by $50 million," Fuchs said. "We've got some great products, but it's more niche products than it is volume products, and we don't think we're in the environment to survive in the low end of the PC side of the business when computers are going for $499, $399."

SOURCE: The Associated Press, "Packard Bell to End Operations in U.S.," *The Wall Street Journal* (November 4, 1999), pp. C-1, C-3. Permission conveyed through the Copyright Clearance Center.

Production View of Quality

Productivity is measured by the quantity of good output generated from a specific amount of input during a time period. Any factor that either slows down (or stops) a production process or causes unnecessary work (redundancy) hinders productivity. Activity analysis can be used to highlight such factors. As explained in Chapter 4, the various repetitive actions performed in making a product or providing a service can be classified in value-added (VA) and non-value-added (NVA) categories. Value-added activities increase the worth of the product or service to the customer; non-value-added activities consume time and costs but add no value for the consumer. Minimizing or eliminating non-value-added activities increases productivity and reduces costs.

Three important NVA process activities include storing products for which there is little immediate demand, moving materials unnecessarily, and having unscheduled production interruptions. Another non-value-added activity is caused by supplier quality problems: having to inspect incoming components. To minimize or eliminate this NVA activity, some companies require their suppliers to provide only zero-defect components. To ensure compliance with this requirement, companies may do quality audits of their vendors.

Factors causing production redundancy include the need to reprocess, rework, replace, and repair those items that did not conform to specifications. The quality of the product design, materials used, and production process largely determine the product's failure rate, longevity, and breakage tendencies. Further, the amount of waste, rework, and scrap generated by production efforts is related to production process quality.

Production technology, worker skill and training, and management programs can help significantly to control the production process quality. If the impediments to good production are reduced or eliminated, increases in productivity and higher quality products can be expected. Some techniques that increase productivity and enhance quality include having suppliers preinspect materials for quality, having employees monitor and be responsible for their own output, and fitting machinery for mistake-proof operations.

All attempts to reduce variability and defects in products reflect the implementation of **quality control (QC)**. QC places the primary responsibility for the quality

quality control (QC)

of a product or service at the source—the maker or provider. Many companies use **statistical process control (SPC)** techniques to analyze where fluctuations occur in the process. SPC is based on the theory that a process has natural (common cause) variations over time, but that "errors," which can result in defective goods or poor service, are typically produced at points of uncommon (nonrandom or special cause) variations. Often these variations are eliminated after the installation of computer-integrated manufacturing systems, which have internal controls to evaluate deviations and sense production problems.

statistical process control (SPC)

To analyze the process variations, various types of **control charts** have been developed by recording the occurrences of some specified measure(s) of performance at preselected points in a process. Charts, such as the one shown in Exhibit 8–1, graph actual process results and indicate upper and lower control limits. For example, a process is considered to be "in" or "out of" control (i.e., stable or unstable) depending on whether the results remain within established limits and do not form telltale patterns that reflect some nonrandom or special-cause variation. In effect, SPC charts make use of the principle of "management by exception" by requiring that workers respond to occurrences greater than some predetermined limit or that form nonrandom, telltale patterns.

control chart

The charts must be prepared consistently and accurately for an intelligent analysis to be made about out-of-control conditions. Although development and use of such charts is outside the scope of this text, the management accountant is directly involved in selecting appropriate performance measures and helping to interpret the charts. Often the measures selected to prepare control charts are nonfinancial, such as number of defective parts, amount of waste created, and time taken to complete a task. Selection of performance measures to investigate quality is further discussed in Chapters 19 and 20. In effect, using SPC causes a process to "talk" to workers about what is occurring in the process. If workers "listen," they can sometimes prevent potential product defects and process malfunctions from ever happening.

Consumer View of Quality

3

What primary characteristics comprise product quality and service quality?

Every customer who acquires a product or service receives a set of characteristics encompassing a range of features, such as convenience, promptness in delivery, warranty, credit availability, and packaging. The consumer's view of quality reflects more than whether the product or service delivers as it was intended, its rate of failure, or the probability of purchasing a defective unit. The customer perceives quality as

EXHIBIT 8–1

Control Chart

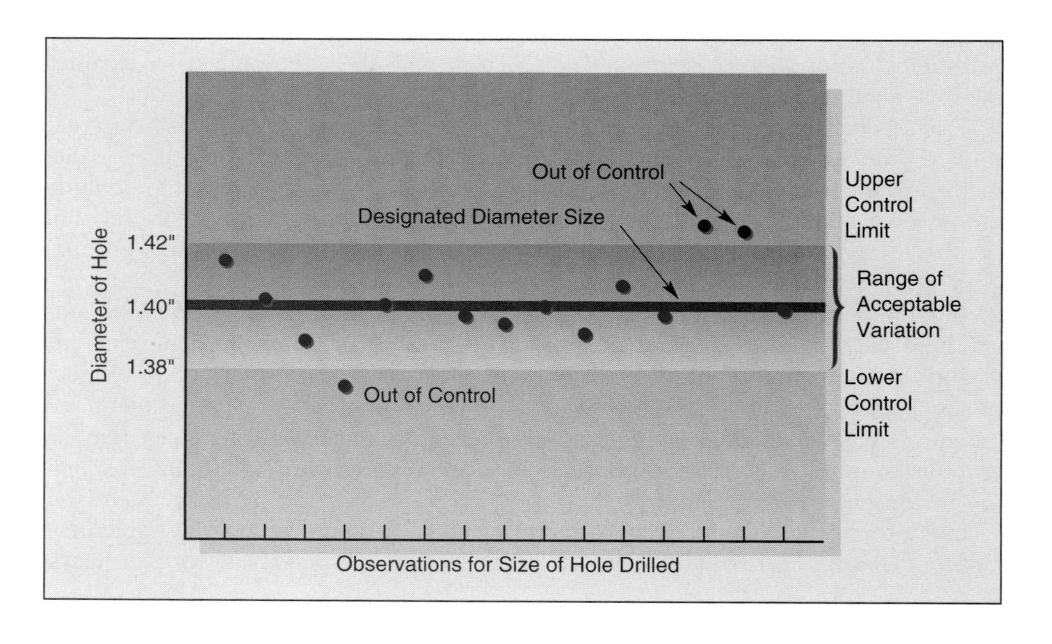

a product's or service's ability to meet and satisfy all specified needs. When high-quality producers dominate a market, entering companies must understand both their own customers' quality expectations and their competitors' quality standards.

Exhibit 8–2 provides eight characteristics that would commonly be included in any customer's definition of product quality. An important difference exists between the first six and the last two characteristics: level of objectivity. The first six characteristics can be reasonably evaluated through objective methods, whereas the last two are strictly subjective. Thus, the first six are much more susceptible to control by an organization than the other two.

Note that the "product" of some companies such as hotels, hospitals, and accounting firms is itself a service. With some imagination, one can identify most if not all, of these eight product quality characteristics in the "service" provided by the company. For example, a hotel providing rooms with computer and fax hookups or a continental breakfast could be considered "features" by the Marriott chain. Additionally, Marriott could consider the ability to provide quiet rooms for guests as high "performance."

http://www.marriott.com

Service quality reflects the manner in which a company's product or service is delivered to the customer and also has some common characteristics (Exhibit 8–3). Some firms use outside assessors to evaluate the level of service provided, as indicated in the News Note on page 308.

Not all customers can afford the same grade of product or service. **Grade** refers to one of the many levels that a product or service may have as related to the inclusion or exclusion of characteristics to satisfy needs, especially price. Customers try to maximize their satisfaction within the context of their willingness and ability to pay. They view a product or service as a **value** when it meets the highest number of their needs at the lowest possible cost (cost includes purchase price plus the costs of operating, maintaining, and disposing of an item). Thus, although customers may have a collective vision of what constitutes "high quality," some of

grade

value

EXHIBIT 8–2

Characteristics of Product Quality

1. Performance—relates to a product's primary operating characteristics
2. Features—describes the secondary characteristics that supplement a product's basic function
3. Reliability—addresses the probability of a product's likelihood of performing properly within a specified period of time
4. Conformance—relates to the degree to which preestablished standards are matched by the product's performance and features
5. Durability—measures a product's economic and technical life
6. Serviceability—measures the ease with which the product is repaired
7. Aesthetics—relates to a product's appeal to the senses
8. Perceived quality—relates to image, brand names, and other indirect measures of quality

SOURCE: Reprinted from "What Does 'Product Quality' Really Mean?" by David Garvin, *Sloan Management Review* (Fall 1984), pp. 25–43 by permission of publisher. Copyright 1984 by the Sloan Management Review Association. All rights reserved.

EXHIBIT 8–3

Characteristics of Service Quality

1. Reliability—the ability to provide what was promised, dependably and accurately
2. Assurance—the knowledge and courtesy of employees, and their ability to convey trust and confidence
3. Tangibles—the physical facilities and equipment, and the appearance of personnel
4. Empathy—the degree of caring and individual attention provided to customers
5. Responsiveness—the willingness to help customers and provide prompt service

SOURCE: A. Parasuraman, Leonard L. Berry, and Valarie Zeithaml, "Perceived Service Quality as a Customer-Based Performance Measure: An Empirical Examination of Organizational Barriers Using an Extended Service Quality Model," *Human Resource Management* 30(3) (Fall 1991), pp. 335–364. Reprinted by permission of John Wiley & Sons, Inc.

NEWS NOTE  QUALITY

Undercover with a Hotel Spy—He Checks to See If Bellhops Are Hopping

J. C. Schaefer unscrews a light bulb from a bedside lamp in the posh Windsor Court Hotel and begins violently whacking it against the bedspread. He shakes the light bulb to make sure the filament inside is broken and then carefully screws it back into the lamp.

Mr. Schaefer isn't your average hotel guest. In fact, he isn't even J. C. Schaefer. His real name is David Richey, and he's a hotel spy who uses a variety of aliases to check out luxury hotels all over the world.

Over two days, he'll employ an extensive bag of tricks to see if the Windsor Court—rated last year as the top hotel in the world in a Conde Nast Traveler magazine poll—is as good as its reputation. The "burnt-out light bulb" test is one of the toughest. Only 11% of hotels tested by Mr. Richey's Chevy Chase, Maryland, firm, Richey International, detect the burnt-out bulb on the housekeeping staff's first pass.

Some 2,000 hotels around the world pay Mr. Richey to check them out. The Windsor Court is a member of Preferred Hotels & Resorts Worldwide, a group of 120 independent luxury hotels that share a common reservations system. Preferred requires that all its hotels meet at least 80% of its standards in a test conducted annually by Richey International. In 1998, Preferred expelled three hotels that twice failed the test and then didn't take the necessary steps to improve their scores, says Robert Cornell, a Preferred Hotels senior vice president.

SOURCE: Adapted from Neal Templin, "Undercover with a Hotel Spy—He Checks to See If Bellhops Are Hopping," *The Wall Street Journal* (May 12, 1999), p. B1.

http://www.preferredhotels.com

them may choose to accept a lower grade of product or service because it satisfies their functional needs at a lower cost. Note that high quality is a more encompassing concept than "high grade." Someone with 20 minutes left for lunch may find more "value" in a fast-food hamburger than going to a sit-down restaurant for sirloin steak.

To illustrate the difference between quality and grade, assume Sally Smith is in the market for a new car. She needs the car to travel to and from work, run errands, and go on vacation and has determined that reliability, gas mileage, safety, and comfort are features that are most important to her. She may believe the Lexus to be the highest quality of car available, but her additional needs are that the car be within her price range and that repair parts and maintenance be readily available and within her budget. Thus, she will search for the highest quality product that maximizes her set of quality-characteristic preferences within the grade she can afford.

Disney has long been viewed as "best-in-class" in equipment maintenance. Other organizations, regardless of the industry they are in, can use process benchmarking to compare their maintenance activities against this world-class leader.

Customers often make quality determinations by comparing a product or service to an ideal level of a characteristic rather than to another product or service of the same type or in the same industry. For example, Sam Hill frequently stays at Marriott hotels on business trips. On a recent trip, he called a car rental agency to arrange for a car. Sam may compare the quality of service he received from the car rental agency with the high-quality service he typically receives from Marriott rather than how well another car rental company served him in the past. Sam is unconcerned that car rental agency employees may not have had the same customer satisfaction training as Marriott employees or that the Marriott corporate culture is dedicated to high quality, while the car rental agency may not have yet made such a commitment. This type of comparison, when formalized in organizations, is called competitive benchmarking.

BENCHMARKING

4

Why do companies engage in benchmarking?

benchmarking

Benchmarking means investigating, comparing, and evaluating a company's products, processes, and/or services against either those of competitors or companies believed to be the "best in class." Such comparisons allow a company to understand another's production and performance methods, so that the interested company can identify its strengths and weaknesses. Because each company has its own unique philosophy, products, and people, "copying" is neither appropriate nor feasible. Therefore, a company should attempt to imitate those ideas that are readily transferable but, more importantly, to upgrade its own effectiveness and efficiency by improving on methods used by others. There are codes of conduct that have been established for benchmarking activities. These codes address issues such as equal exchange of information, restricted use of learned data, avoidance of antitrust issues and illegalities, and interorganizational courtesy.[5]

results benchmarking

There are two types of benchmarking: results and process. In **results benchmarking**, the end product or service is examined using a process called "reverse engineering" and the focus is on product/service specifications and performance results. Results benchmarking helps companies determine which other companies are "best in class." For example, Chrysler has tear-down facilities located at its product development centers. Information gathered in these facilities helps the company focus on its competitors and promote better interaction among engineering, design, and manufacturing. By studying design differences between its own and its competitors' products, the firm seeks vital information to support quality improvements.[6] However, if benchmarking involves making an exact replica of another's product, ethical and legal considerations are at issue.

http://www.gm.com
http://www.chryslercorp.com
http://www.fordvehicles.com

Although benchmarking against direct competitors is necessary, it creates the risk of becoming stagnant. To illustrate, General Motors, Chrysler, and Ford historically competitively benchmarked among themselves and, over time, their processes became similar. But then import competition arrived, which had totally different—and better—processes. It was like three club tennis players who all had similar levels of skill and who knew each other's games inside and out—and then Pete Sampras walked on the court.[7]

process benchmarking

http://www.ab.com

For this reason, additional comparisons should be made against companies that are the best in a specific characteristic rather than necessarily the best in a specific industry. Focusing on how the best-in-class companies achieve their results is called **process benchmarking**. It is in this arena that noncompetitor benchmarking is extremely valuable. Some examples of U.S. companies that are recognized as world-class leaders in certain disciplines are Allen-Bradley (flexible manufacturing),

[5] Barbara Ettorre, "Ethics, Anti-Trust and Benchmarking," *Management Review* (June 1993), p. 13.
[6] Paul A. Stergar and James H. Cypher, "Teardown Keeps Chrysler Focused on the Competition," *Cost Management Insider's Report* (June 1995), pp. 12–13.
[7] Beth Enslow, "The Benchmarking Bonanza," *Across the Board* (April 1992), p. 20.

http://www.americanexpress.com
http://www.disney.go.com
http://www.fedex.com/us/
http://www.llbean.com

American Express (billing and collection), Disney (equipment maintenance), Federal Express (worker training), and L. L. Bean (distribution and logistics).[8]

It is against companies such as these as well as their international counterparts that others should benchmark. The process of implementing benchmarking is detailed in Exhibit 8–4. Some companies have more steps and others have fewer, but all have a structured approach. Once the negative gap analysis is made, everyone in the firm is expected to work both toward closing that gap and toward becoming a best-in-class organization.

Through benchmarking, companies are working to improve their abilities to deliver high-quality products from the perspectives of both how the products are made and how the customer perceives them. Integrating these two perspectives requires involvement of all organizational members in the implementation of a total quality management system.

EXHIBIT 8–4

Steps in Benchmarking

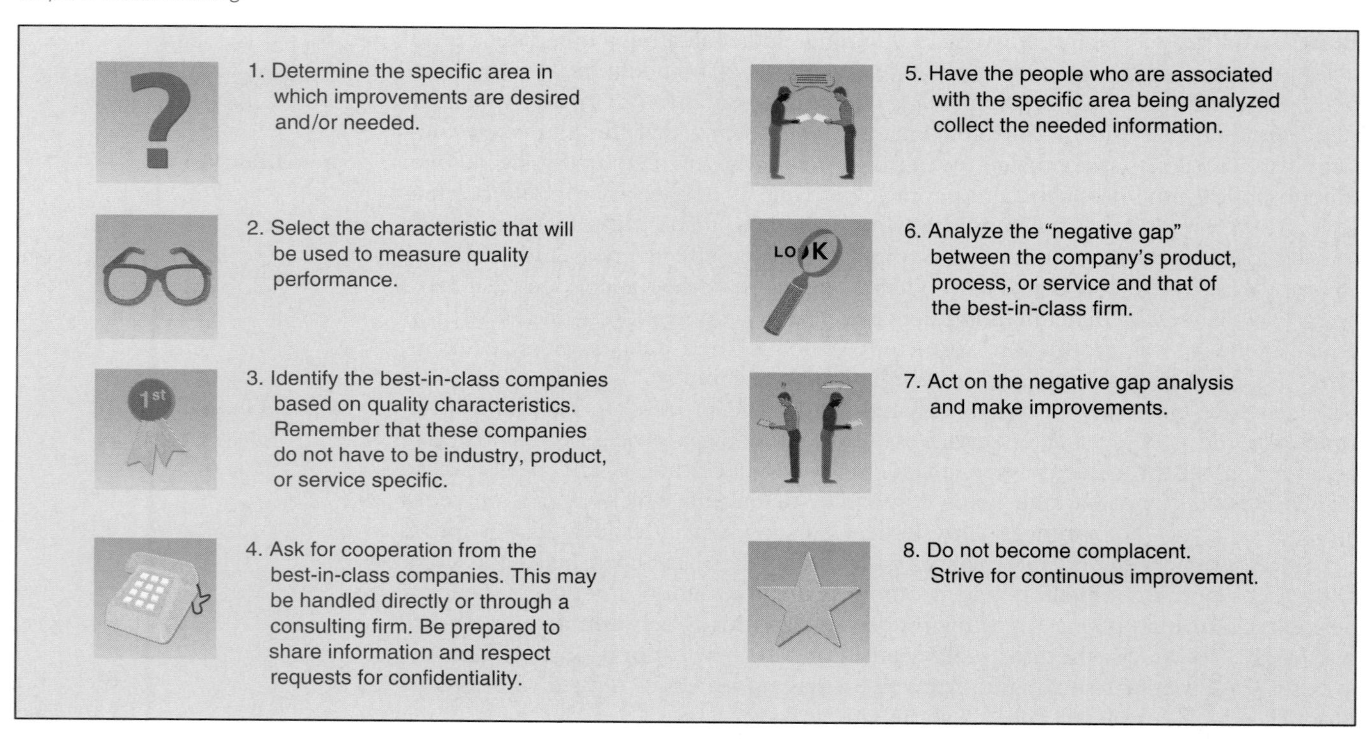

TOTAL QUALITY MANAGEMENT

5

Why is total quality management significant and what conditions are necessary to yield its benefits?

total quality management (TQM)

Total quality management (TQM) is a "management approach of an organization, centered on quality, based on the participation of all its members and aiming at long-term success through customer satisfaction, and benefits to all members of the organization and to society."[9] Thus, TQM has three important tenets:

1. It necessitates an internal managerial system of planning, controlling, and decision making for continuous improvement.
2. It requires participation by everyone in the organization.
3. It focuses on improving goods and services from the customer's point of view.

[8] "America's World-Class Champs," *Business Week* (November 30, 1992), pp. 74–75.
[9] ISO 8402, *Total Quality Management* (Geneva: ISO, 1994), definition 3.7.

The Quality System

The total quality movement requires the implementation of a system that provides information about the quality of processes so managers can plan, control, evaluate performance, and make decisions for continuous improvement. Consideration of quality has not historically been part of the planning process. More often it involved an after-the-fact measurement of errors because a certain level of defects was simply tolerated as part of the "natural" business process. Action was not triggered until a predetermined error threshold was exceeded.

In contrast, a total quality system should be designed to promote a reorientation of thinking from an emphasis on inspection to an emphasis on prevention, continuous improvement, and building quality into every process and product. This reorientation should indicate any existing quality problems so that managers can set goals and identify methods for quality improvements. The system should also be capable (possibly through the use of statistical methods) of measuring quality and providing feedback on quality improvements. Last, the system should encourage teamwork in the quality improvement process. In other words, the system should move an organization away from product inspection (finding and correcting problems at the end of the process) to proactive quality assurance (building quality into the process so that problems do not occur).

Employee Involvement

TQM recognizes that all organizational levels share the responsibility for product/service quality. These new interactions among employee levels are changing the way managers do their jobs. Upper-level management must be involved in the quality process, develop an atmosphere that is conducive to quality improvements, set an example of commitment to TQM, provide constructive feedback about opportunities for improvement, and provide positive feedback when improvements are made. Workers should believe they are part of the process of success, not the creators of problems. Encouraging employee suggestions and training workers to handle multiple job functions help improve efficiency and quality. At Solectron, for example, multifunctional work teams are commonly used to facilitate effective problem solving. The following News Note on page 312 discusses some U.K. companies' use of employee suggestion plans as an integral part of this continuous improvement process.

Product/Service Improvement

Total quality management focuses attention on the relationship between the internal production/service process and the external customer. This approach has designated consumer expectations as the ultimate arbiter of satisfaction. Therefore, TQM requires that companies first know who their customers are.

In analyzing their customers, companies may want to stop serving some groups of customers based on cost-benefit analyses. Some customers simply cost more than they add in revenues and/or other benefits to the organization. Each revenue dollar does not contribute equally to organizational profitability because the cost to serve different customers may be unequal.

The concept that shedding one or more sets of customers would be good for business is difficult to believe at first, but most organizations have some clients who drain, rather than improve, those organizations' ability to provide quality products and service. Managers should be attuned to customers whose costs exceed their benefits and send them elsewhere. By doing this, the company can focus its attention on its worthy customers and make itself attractive to new worthwhile customers.

After identifying who its value-adding customers are, a company must then understand what those customers want. The primary characteristics currently desired

NEWS NOTE  INTERNATIONAL

Suggestions are Power

Have your employees come up with any good suggestions lately? At Triple 'A' Animal Hotel & Care Centre near Washington, Tyne and Wear, 28 members of staff dream up more than 1,200 ideas a year. Not all of these are implemented but that's not the point, says finance manager Michael Brown. "We believe all ideas are good ideas. It doesn't matter whether or not we can act on them all."

But for every Triple 'A,' there are many more companies where the staff suggestion box simply gathers dust. Moribund suggestion schemes, says Alex Bryson, a researcher in employee involvement at the Policy Studies Institute, result from poor planning and inadequate employer commitment. "Staff need to feel that their ideas will be viewed constructively and taken seriously. When introduced in isolation or into a company with no culture of employee involvement, suggestion schemes have no impact," he claims. Angela Baron, policy advisor at the Institute of Personnel and Development agrees. "If employees don't believe their organisation is really committed to a suggestion scheme, then it just won't work."

What works, argues Dave Jackson, managing director of organisational change consultants Novius, are schemes that are integral to the organization's approach to continuous improvement. "Schemes need a very high level of commitment from the top but often work best when they are run by the employees themselves," he insists. The "Sir Gestion" scheme run by employees at credit card services company Credit Card Sentinel is a good example. There, the scheme is administered by employee volunteers who decide which ideas to implement. All suggestions are rewarded with gifts or money prizes. Cost-saving ideas are rewarded with a proportion of the money saved.

Car rental firm Avis attributes the success of its PIPS (Practical Ideas Profitable Solutions) scheme to ensuring employees remain involved with the progress of their ideas. Where possible, the people who come up with the ideas are encouraged to implement them. Director of Training Ian Jarvis stresses: "It is built into our Spirit of Avis program, which includes other forms of employee involvement and recognition."

SOURCE: Staff, "It's Time to Acknowledge the Power of Suggestion," *Management Today* (London; February 1998), p. 13.

http://www.avis.com

by customers appear to be quality, value, and "good" service. Good service is an intangible; it means different things to different people. But most customers would agree that it is reflective of the interaction between themselves and organizational employees. Frequently, only service quality separates one product from its competition. Solectron implements customer-focus teams and measurement techniques through its customer-satisfaction index process to learn what customers want and need. All Solectron customers have an associated customer-focus team that essentially works for them and with them and ensures that everything happens as intended. Customers grade the firm weekly with letter grades A through D in five categories:

- *Quality.* How well did the product work when you got it?
- *Delivery.* Did the product get delivered to your delivery target?
- *Communications.* Grade us anyway you want, in your understanding of our ability to communicate effectively.
- *Responsiveness or service ability.* Do we make you feel good as a customer? Do we treat you well?
- *Technology.* Are we actually moving ahead in the technology arena?[10]

The only acceptable grades for Solectron are A and A−. They are the ones above 95 percent. Any grades that are a B or less automatically demand a formal corrective action.[11]

[10] Holly Ann Suzik, "Solectron Tells Its Tale," *Quality* (April 1999), pp. 53ff.
[11] Ibid.

Poor service can be disastrous. Data indicate that "70 percent of customers stop doing business with companies because of perceived rude or indifferent behavior by an employee—over three times the total for price or product quality (20 percent)."[12] Although instituting "customer service" programs can improve a company's image, such programs should not be taken to the extreme. As noted above, some customers are not cost beneficial. For instance, consider those who demand exorbitant service yet are not willing to pay the related price.

A company can increase its product and service quality by investing in **prevention costs**, which prevent product defects that result from dysfunctional processing. Amounts spent on improved production equipment, training, and engineering and product modeling are considered prevention costs. Complementary to prevention costs are **appraisal costs**, which represent costs incurred for monitoring and compensate for mistakes not eliminated through prevention activities. Both of these types of costs will cause a reduction in **failure costs**. These costs represent internal losses, such as scrap or rework, and external losses, such as warranty work, customer complaint departments, litigation, or defective product recalls.

prevention cost

appraisal cost

failure cost

The results of TQM indicate that increasing the amounts spent on prevention should decrease the amounts spent or incurred for appraisal and failure costs—resulting in an overall decline in costs. Also, by eliminating non-value-added activities and installing technologically advanced equipment, productivity and quality will increase.

Lower costs mean that the company can contain (or reduce) selling prices; customers, pleased with the higher quality at the same (or lower) price, perceive they have received value and will buy more. These factors create larger company profits that can be reinvested in research and development activities to generate new high-quality products or services. Or the profits can be used to train workers to provide even higher quality products and services than are currently available. This cycle of benefit will continue in a company that is profitable and secure in its market share—two primary goals of an organization.

The Quality Goal

Any quality program should seek to meet the following three objectives:

1. The organization should achieve and sustain the quality of the product or service produced so as to continuously meet the purchaser's stated or implied needs.
2. The organization should give its own management confidence that the intended quality level is being achieved and sustained.
3. The organization should give the purchaser confidence that the intended quality level is, or will be, achieved in the delivered product or service. When contractually required, this assurance may involve agreed demonstration requirements.[13]

The embodiment of TQM in the United States is the Malcolm Baldrige National Quality Award. This award focuses attention on management systems, processes, consumer satisfaction, and business results as the tools required to achieve product and service excellence. There are five categories of entrants: manufacturing, service, small business, education, and health-care organizations. To win the award, applicants must show excellence in the seven categories shown in Exhibit 8–5.

Corporate America has accepted the Baldrige award because it represents excellence. Products and services of companies winning the award are regarded as some of the best in the world. Such recognition invigorates workers and delights all stakeholders, and has caused the entire national economy to be strengthened by the enhanced awareness of and attention to quality and its benefits.

[12] Scott J. Simmerman, "Improving Customer Loyalty," *Business & Economic Review* (April–June 1992), p. 4.
[13] A. Faye Borthick and Harold P. Roth, "Will Europeans Buy Your Company's Products?" *Management Accounting* (July 1992), pp. 28–29.

EXHIBIT 8-5

Baldrige Award 1999 Criteria for Performance Excellence

1999 Categories/Items		Point Values
1 Leadership		**125**
1.1 Organizational Leadership	85	
1.2 Public Responsibility and Citizenship	40	
2 Strategic Planning		**85**
2.1 Strategy Development	40	
2.2 Strategy Deployment	45	
3 Customer and Market Focus		**85**
3.1 Customer and Market Knowledge	40	
3.2 Customer Satisfaction and Relationships	45	
4 Information and Analysis		**85**
4.1 Measurement of Organizational Performance	40	
4.2 Analysis of Organizational Performance	45	
5 Human Resource Focus		**85**
5.1 Work Systems	35	
5.2 Employee Education, Training, and Development	25	
5.3 Employee Well-Being and Satisfaction	25	
6 Process Management		**85**
6.1 Product and Service Processes	55	
6.2 Support Processes	15	
6.3 Supplier and Partnering Processes	15	
7 Business Results		**450**
7.1 Customer Focused Results	115	
7.2 Financial and Market Results	115	
7.3 Human Resource Results	80	
7.4 Supplier and Partner Results	25	
7.5 Organizational Effectiveness Results	115	
TOTAL POINTS		**1000**

SOURCE: "Malcolm Baldrige National Quality Award 1999 Award Criteria," U.S. Department of Commerce, Technology Administration, National Institute of Standards and Technology, Washington, DC.

Japan's equivalent of the Malcolm Baldrige National Quality Award is the Deming prize. This award, named for the late W. Edwards Deming, has even more rigorous requirements than do those for the Baldrige award. Globally, the quality movement has progressed to the point that certain quality standards have been set, although these are not at the level of either the Baldrige award or the Deming prize. These standards are discussed in the appendix to this chapter.

TYPES OF QUALITY COSTS

6

What tyes of quality costs exist and how are those costs related?

As mentioned in the previous section, the TQM philosophy indicates that total costs will decline, rather than increase, as quality improvements are made in an organization. Thus, total quality management also includes the idea that it is the *lack* of high quality that is expensive. Understanding the types and causes of quality costs can help managers prioritize improvement projects and provide feedback that supports and justifies improvement efforts.

Two types of costs comprise the total quality cost of a firm: (1) cost of quality compliance or assurance and (2) cost of noncompliance or quality failure. The cost of compliance equals the sum of prevention and appraisal costs. Compliance cost expenditures are incurred to reduce or eliminate the present and future costs of failure; thus, they are proactive on management's part. Furthermore, effective investments in prevention costs can even minimize the costs of appraisal. The cost of noncompliance results from production imperfections and is equal to internal and external failure costs. Exhibit 8–6 presents specific examples of each type of quality cost.

Information about production quality or lack thereof is contained in inspection reports, SPC control charts, and customer returns or complaints. Information about quality costs, on the other hand, is only partially contained in the accounting records and supporting documentation. Historically, quality costs have not been given separate recognition in the accounting system.

EXHIBIT 8–6

Types of Quality Costs

COSTS OF COMPLIANCE		COSTS OF NONCOMPLIANCE	
Prevention Costs	**Appraisal Costs**	**Internal Failure Costs**	**External Failure Costs**
Employees: ▪ Hiring for quality ▪ Providing training and awareness ▪ Establishing participation programs *Customers:* ▪ Surveying needs ▪ Researching needs ▪ Conducting field trials *Machinery:* ▪ Designing to detect defects ▪ Arranging for efficient flow ▪ Arranging for monitoring ▪ Incurring preventive maintenance ▪ Testing and adjusting equipment ▪ Fitting machinery for mistake-proof operations *Suppliers:* ▪ Arranging for quality ▪ Educating suppliers ▪ Involving suppliers *Product Design:* ▪ Developing specifications ▪ Engineering and modeling ▪ Testing and adjusting for conformity, effective and efficient performance, durability, ease of use, safety, comfort, appeal, and cost	*Before Production:* ▪ Receiving inspection *Production Process:* ▪ Monitoring and inspecting ▪ Keeping the process consistent, stable, and reliable ▪ Using procedure verification ▪ Automating *During and After Production:* ▪ Conducting quality audits *Information Process:* ▪ Recording and reporting defects ▪ Measuring performance *Organization:* ▪ Administering quality control department	*Product:* ▪ Reworking ▪ Having waste ▪ Storing and disposing of waste ▪ Reinspecting rework *Production Process:* ▪ Reprocessing ▪ Having unscheduled interruptions ▪ Experiencing unplanned downtime	*Organization:* ▪ Staffing complaint departments ▪ Staffing warranty claims departments *Customer:* ▪ Losing future sales ▪ Losing reputation ▪ Losing goodwill *Product:* ▪ Repairing ▪ Replacing ▪ Reimbursing ▪ Recalling ▪ Handling litigation *Service:* ▪ Providing unplanned service ▪ Expediting ▪ Serving after purchase

In most instances, the cost of quality is "buried" in a variety of general ledger accounts. For instance, Work in Process Inventory and Finished Goods Inventory contain costs for rework, scrap, preventive maintenance, and other overhead items; marketing/advertising expense contains costs for product recalls, image improvements after poor products were sold, and surveys to obtain customer information; personnel costs include training dollars; and engineering department costs include funds spent for engineering design change orders and redesign. Because quality costs are buried, managers have no idea how large or pervasive those costs are and, therefore, have little incentive to reduce them.

Because the accounting records are commonly kept primarily to serve requirements of financial accounting, the behavior of quality costs relative to changes in activity as well as the appropriate drivers for these costs must be separately developed or estimated for quality management purposes. The need to estimate quality costs makes it essential for the management accountant to be involved in all activities from system design to cost accumulation of quality costs.

In determining the cost of quality, actual or estimated costs are identified for each item listed in Exhibit 8–6. If these costs were plotted on a graph, they would appear similar to the cost curves shown in Exhibit 8–7. If the firm spends larger amounts on prevention and appraisal costs, the number of defects is lower and the costs of failure are smaller. If less is spent on prevention and appraisal, the number of defects is greater and failure costs are larger. The external failure costs curve begins moving toward vertical when customers encounter a certain number of defects. The ultimate external failure cost is reached when customers will no longer buy a given product or any other products made by a specific firm because of perceived poor quality work.

A system in which quality costs are readily available or easily determined provides useful information to managers trying to make spending decisions by pinpointing areas having the highest cost-benefit relationships. Additionally, quality cost information will indicate how a shift in one or more curves will affect the others.

Exhibit 8–8 shows where in the production–sales cycle quality costs are usually incurred. An information feedback loop should be in effect to link the types and causes of failure costs to future prevention costs. Alert managers and employees continuously monitor failures to discover their causes and adjust prevention activities to close the gaps that allowed the failures to occur. These continuous rounds of action, reaction, and action are essential to continuous improvement initiatives. The accompanying News Note discusses how GM tracks defect problems.

EXHIBIT 8–7

Relationships among Quality Costs

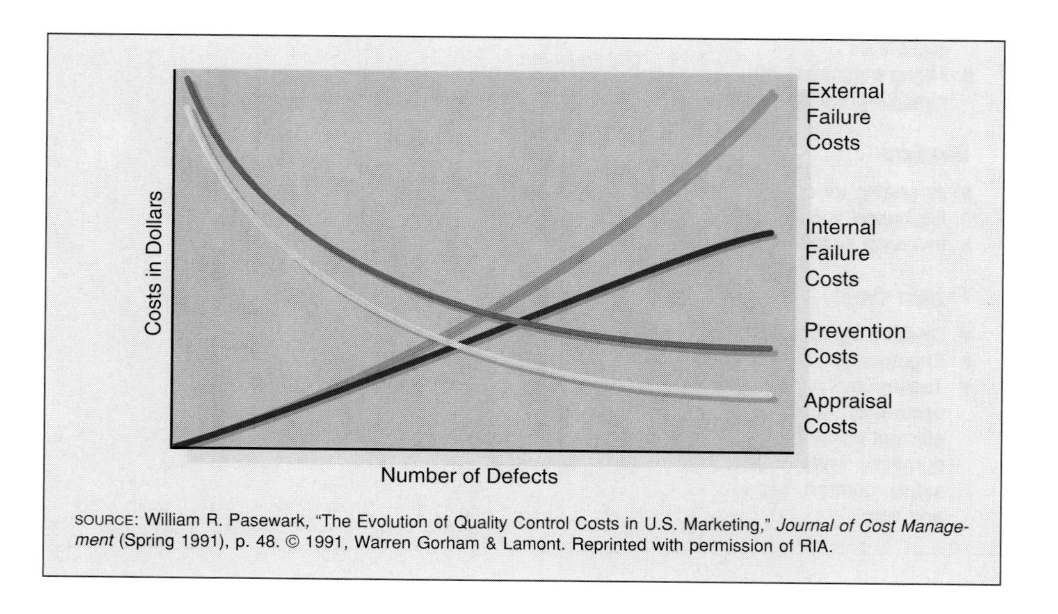

SOURCE: William R. Pasewark, "The Evolution of Quality Control Costs in U.S. Marketing," *Journal of Cost Management* (Spring 1991), p. 48. © 1991, Warren Gorham & Lamont. Reprinted with permission of RIA.

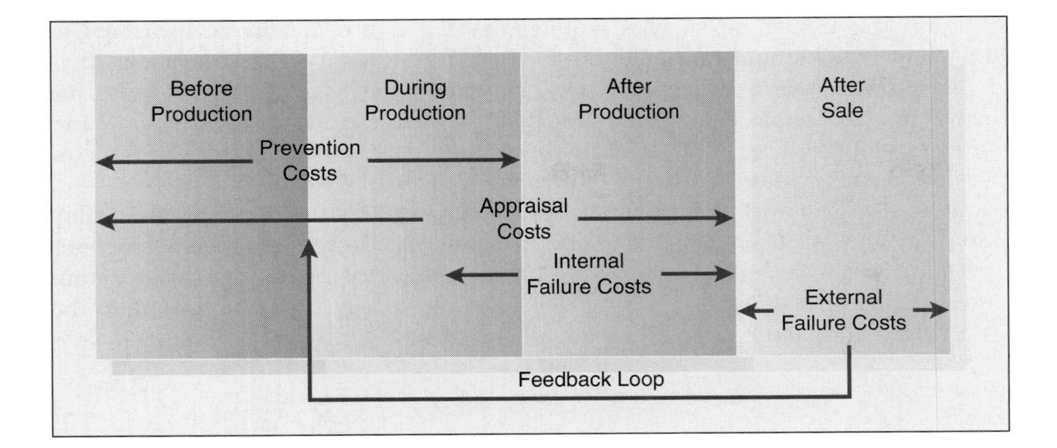

EXHIBIT 8–8

Time-Phased Model for Quality Costs

QUALITY  NEWS NOTE

CDC Tactics Used to Attack Auto Problems

General Motors executives were impressed in 1997 when doctors from the federal Centers for Disease Control and Prevention took just days to trace a hepatitis outbreak among Michigan schoolchildren to a load of bad strawberries from Mexico.

The auto executives, under orders to slash more than $1 billion from GM's annual repair bill for cars under warranty, figured the CDC's methods for tracking down disease-carrying fruit might offer some useful lessons. They adapted the CDC's epidemiological system to the industrial task of debugging cars and trucks.

Under GM's old way of handling warranty problems, word of breakdowns would filter up, with no consistent reporting rules, as dealers billed the manufacturer. It might take months for GM to find the source of a problem and correct it.

Adapting the CDC's approach to its own needs, GM standardized reporting of breakdowns across its dealer network and began tracking warranty repairs using samples of a few thousand vehicles for each vehicle model. Sophisticated computerized statistical models inspired by the CDC highlight emerging trends.

Newly discovered outbreaks [of warranty problems] are tagged with red dots and then, when a solution is put in place, with yellow dots. "If we can get it while the trail is still warm . . . we can usually get to the root cause within 24 hours," Mr. [Don] Mitchell [GM's warranty chief] says. The "first-time kill rate," or share of problems solved the first time, is 96%, he says.

In October 1998, the system revealed a surge in complaints that air conditioners on a range of brand-new cars and minivans were blowing hot air. Within three days, GM engineers had isolated the problem in the compressors and shipped samples of the defective parts to the supplier that made them. There, engineers traced the problem to a drilling machine that periodically clogged with metal shavings and made holes that were too big. Though the problem affected only about six of every 10,000 compressors, the equipment was retooled to prevent it from recurring. Problem-free output began within 10 days of GM's initial detection of the problem.

SOURCE: Adapted from Gregory L. White, "GM Takes Advice from Disease Sleuths to Debug Cars," *The Wall Street Journal* (April 8, 1999), pp. B1–B4.

MEASURING THE COST OF QUALITY

7

How is cost of quality measured?

Theoretically, if prevention and appraisal costs were prudently incurred, failure costs would become zero. However, prevention and appraisal costs would still be incurred to achieve zero failure costs. Thus, total quality costs can never be zero. This is not to disregard the knowledge that the benefits of increased sales and greater efficiency should exceed all remaining compliance quality costs. In this sense, the cost of compliance quality is free. Management should analyze the quality cost relationships and spend money for quality in ways that will provide the greatest benefit. Such an analysis requires that the cost of quality be measured to the extent possible and practical and the benefits of quality costs be estimated.

pareto analysis

Pareto analysis is a technique used to separate the "vital few" from the "trivial many." The technique is a widely used tool that has repeatedly shown that 20 to 30 percent of the items in a set of items accounts for 70 to 80 percent of the cost or values (e.g., inventory, donors to charity, sources of defects).

It is also one way management can decide where to concentrate its quality prevention cost dollars. This technique classifies the causes of process problems according to impact on an objective. For example, a company that makes computers might subclassify its warranty claim costs for the past year according to the type of product failure as follows:

Cost by Type of Failure

Model	Monitor	CPU	Printer	Keyboard	Total Dollars
Alpha	$15,000	$16,000	$12,000	$ 3,000	$ 46,000
Beta	10,000	15,000	7,000	3,000	35,000
All others	6,000	9,000	3,000	5,000	23,000
Total	$31,000	$40,000	$22,000	$11,000	$104,000

Model	Dollars	Percent of Total	Cumulative % Total
Alpha	$ 46,000	44	44
Beta	35,000	34	78
All others	23,000	22	100
Total	$104,000	100	

Listing the total failure costs of all models in descending order of magnitude indicates that models Alpha and Beta account for 78 percent of total warranty cost claims. Also, the largest single source of warranty claims cost is caused by problems with CPUs. Therefore, management should focus efforts on further analysis on what causes models Alpha and Beta, and the CPUs on all models, to generate the greatest warranty claims costs. This knowledge will permit management to devote the appropriate portion of its prevention efforts to minimizing or eliminating these specific problems. This kind of analysis should be conducted sufficiently often for trends to be detected quickly and adjustments to be made rapidly. For example, Marriott uses Pareto analysis to prioritize service problems and, thus, focus on where to devote the majority of its problem-solving efforts.

A company desiring to engage in TQM and continuous improvement should record and report its quality costs separately so that managers can plan, control, evaluate, and make decisions about the activities that cause those costs. However, just having quality cost information available does not enhance quality. Managers and workers must consistently and aggressively use the information as a basis for creatively and intelligently advancing quality.

A firm's chart of accounts can be expanded to accommodate either separate tracing or allocating quality costs to new accounts. Exhibit 8–9 lists some suggested accounts that will help management focus on quality costs. Opportunity costs, including lost future sales and a measure of the firm's loss of reputation, are also associated with poor quality. Although opportunity costs are real and may be estimated, they are not recorded in the accounting system because they do not result from specific transactions.

If a firm has a database management system, transactions can simply be coded so that reports can be generated without expanding the chart of accounts. Coding permits quality transaction types and amounts to be accessible and a cost of quality report such as the one shown in Exhibit 8–10 (which uses assumed numbers) can be generated. Two important assumptions underlie this exhibit report: stable production

EXHIBIT 8-9

New Quality Accounts

Prevention Costs	**Appraisal Costs**
Quality Training	Quality Inspections
Quality Participation	Procedure Verifications
Quality Market Research	Measurement Equipment
Quality Technology	Test Equipment
Quality Product Design	
Internal Failure Costs	**External Failure Costs**
Reworking Products	Complaints Handling
Scrap and Waste	Warranty Handling
Storing and Disposing Waste	Repairing and Replacing Returns
Reprocessing	Customer Reimbursements
Rescheduling and Setup	Expediting

and a monthly reporting system. If wide fluctuations in production or service levels occur, period-to-period comparisons of absolute amounts may not be appropriate. Amounts may need to be converted to percentages to have any valid meaning. Additionally, in some settings (such as a just-in-time environment), a weekly reporting system would be more appropriate because of the need for continuous monitoring.

EXHIBIT 8-10

Cost Of Quality Report

	Cost of Current Period	Cost of Prior Period	Percent Change from Prior Period	Current Period Budget	Percent Change from Budget
Prevention Costs					
Quality training	$ 5,800	$ 5,600	+4	$ 6,000	−3
Quality participation	8,200	8,400	−2	8,000	+4
Quality market research	9,900	7,700	+29	11,000	−10
Quality technology	9,600	10,800	−11	15,000	−36
Quality product design	16,600	12,200	+36	16,500	+1
Total	$ 50,100	$ 44,700	+12	$56,500	−11
Appraisal Costs					
Quality inspections	$ 3,300	$ 3,500	−6	$ 3,000	+10
Procedure verifications	1,200	1,400	−14	1,500	−20
Measurement equipment	2,700	3,000	−10	3,200	−16
Test equipment	1,500	1,200	+25	1,500	0
Total	$ 8,700	$ 9,100	−4	$ 9,200	−5
Internal Failure Costs					
Reworking products	$ 8,500	$ 8,300	+0.2	N/A*	
Scrap and waste	2,200	2,400	−8	N/A	
Storing and disposing waste	4,400	5,700	−23	N/A	
Reprocessing	1,800	1,600	+13	N/A	
Rescheduling and setup	900	1,200	−25	N/A	
Total	$ 17,800	$ 19,200	−7		
External Failure Costs					
Complaints handling	$ 5,800	$ 6,200	−6	N/A	
Warranty handling	10,700	9,300	+15	N/A	
Repairing and replacing returns	27,000	29,200	−8	N/A	
Customer reimbursements	12,000	10,700	+12	N/A	
Expediting	1,100	1,300	−15		
Total	$ 56,600	$ 56,700	+0		
Total quality costs	$133,200	$129,700	+3	$65,700	+103

*TQM advocates planning for zero defects; therefore, zero failure costs would be included in the budget.

Exhibit 8–11 provides formulas for calculating an organization's total quality cost, using the prevention, appraisal, and failure categories. Some amounts used in these computations are, by necessity, estimates. It is better for businesses to use reasonable estimates than to ignore the costs because of a lack of verifiable or precise amounts. Consider the following April 2000 operating information for the Jing USA Company:

Defective units (D)	2,500	Units reworked (Y)	1,200
Profit for good unit (P_1)	$25	Profit for defective unit (P_2)	$15
Cost to rework defective unit (r)	$5	Units returned (D_r)	400
Cost of return (w)	$8	Prevention cost (K)	$40,000
Appraisal cost (A)	$7,200		

Substituting these values into the formulas provided in Exhibit 8–11 provides the following results:

$$Z = (D - Y)(P_1 - P_2) = (2{,}500 - 1{,}200)(\$25 - \$15) = \$13{,}000$$
$$R = (Y)(r) = (1{,}200)(\$5) = \$6{,}000$$
$$W = (D_r)(w) = (400)(\$8) = \$3{,}200$$
$$F = Z + R + W = \$13{,}000 + \$6{,}000 + \$3{,}200 = \$22{,}200 \text{ total failure cost}$$
$$T = K + A + F = \$40{,}000 + \$7{,}200 + \$22{,}200 = \$69{,}400 \text{ total quality cost}$$

EXHIBIT 8–11

Formulas for Calculating Total Quality Cost

Calculating Lost Profits

Profit Lost by Selling Units as Defects = (Total Defective Units − Number of Units Reworked) × (Profit for Good Unit − Profit for Defective Unit)

$$Z = (D - Y)(P_1 - P_2)$$

Calculating Total Internal Costs of Failure

Rework Cost = Number of Units Reworked × Cost to Rework Defective Unit

$$R = (Y)(r)$$

Calculating Total External Costs of Failure

Cost of Processing Customer Returns = Number of Units Returned × Cost of a Return

$$W = (D_r)(w)$$

Total Failure Cost = Profit Lost by Selling Units as Defects + Rework Cost + Cost of Processing Customer Returns + Cost of Warranty Work + Cost of Product Recalls + Cost of Litigation Related to Products + Opportunity Cost of Lost Customers

$$F = Z + R + W + PR + L + O$$

Calculating the Total Quality Cost

Total Quality Cost = Total Compliance Cost + Total Failure Cost

$$T = (\text{Prevention Cost} + \text{Appraisal Cost}) + \text{Total Failure Cost}$$

$$T = K + A + F$$

Prevention and appraisal costs are total estimated amounts; no formulas are appropriate. As the cost of prevention rises, the number of defective units should decline. Additionally, as the cost of prevention rises, the cost of appraisal should decline; however, appraisal cost should never become zero.

SOURCE: Adapted from James T. Godfrey and William R. Pasewark, "Controlling Quality Costs," *Management Accounting* (March 1988), p. 50. Reprinted from *Management Accounting.* Copyright by Institute of Management Accountants, Montvale, NJ.

Of the total quality cost of $69,400, Jing USA Company managers will seek to identify the causes of the $22,200 failure costs and work to eliminate them. The results may also affect the planned amounts of prevention and appraisal costs for future periods.

High quality allows a company to improve current profits, either through lower costs or, if the market will bear, higher prices. But management is often more interested in business objectives other than short-run profits. An example of an alternative, competing objective is that of increasing the company's market share. Indeed, if increasing market share were an objective, management could combine the strategies of increasing quality while lowering prices to attract a larger market share. Giving greater attention to prevention and appraisal activities increases quality, with the result that overall costs decline and productivity increases. Lower costs and greater productivity support lower prices that, in turn, often stimulate demand. Greater market share, higher long-run profits, and, perhaps, even greater immediate profits result.

OBTAINING INFORMATION FROM THE COST MANAGEMENT SYSTEM

8

Why does a company need both a strategically based management accounting system and a financial accounting system?

Today's business strategy of focusing on customers and quality requires a firm to manage organizational costs so that a reasonable value-to-price relationship can be achieved. Although prices are commonly set in reference to the competitive market rather than being based on costs, companies lacking appropriate cost management skills cannot expect to succeed in the long run. Thus, it can be said that organizations need to engage in strategic cost management (SCM).

SCM can be viewed as the use of management accounting information for the purpose(s) of setting and communicating organizational strategies; establishing, implementing, and monitoring the success of methods to accomplish the strategies; and assessing the level of success in meeting the promulgated strategies.[14] Thus, an organization's management accounting system should accumulate and report information related to organizational success in meeting or exceeding customer needs and expectations as well as quality-related goals and objectives. Managers can analyze and interpret such information to plan and control current activities and to make decisions about current and long-term future courses of action, including expansion of the company's market base and/or technology installation.

In designing a management accounting system, consideration must be given to cost accumulation and process measurement activities. Costs that are accumulated for financial accounting purposes may be inadequate for strategy-based decisions. For example, financial accounting requires that research and development costs be expensed as incurred. However, a product's cost is largely determined during design. Design has implications for its perceived value, the complexity and variety of components required for the product's production, its manufacturability, and its durability and likelihood of failure. Consequently, strategy-based cost management would suggest that design cost be accumulated as part of product cost. This cost does not need to appear on the financial accounting statements, but it needs to exist for decision-making purposes in the management accounting system.

In contrast, financial accounting accumulates all production costs as inventoriable and does not distinguish whether they add value to the customer. A strategically based cost management system differentiates costs that add value from those that do not so that managers and employees can work to reduce the non-value-added costs and enhance continuous improvement.

Another example of the abilities of a strategically based management accounting system is in the area of process. Financial accounting is monetarily based and,

[14] The term *strategic cost management* was coined by Professors John K. Shank and Vijay Govindarajan of Dartmouth College. A full discussion of the concept is provided in their book, *Strategic Cost Management* (New York: The Free Press, 1993).

therefore, does not directly measure nonfinancial organizational activities. However, as indicated earlier in the chapter, many activities critical to success in a quality-oriented, global marketplace are related to time—a nonmonetary characteristic. A useful management accounting system ensures availability of information related to nonmonetary occurrences (such as late deliveries or defect rates). Such information can be translated into financial terms, if desired, to objectively analyze its significance to the company's profitability.

Finally, financial accounting reflects a short-term perspective of operating activity. An organizational goal of continuous improvement is not short term; it is uninterrupted into the long run. Gathering monetary information and forcing it into a particular annual period of time does not necessarily provide managers with a clear indication of how today's decisions will affect the organization's long-run financial success. For example, not investing in research and development would cause a company's short-run profitability to improve, but could be disastrous in the long run.

Thus, a strategically based management accounting system reports a greater number of the costs and benefits of organizational activities. Having this information in a form designed to meet managerial needs allows managers to make informed assessments of the company's performance in the value chain, of its position of competitive advantage (or disadvantage), and of its progress toward organizational goals.

QUALITY AS AN ORGANIZATIONAL CULTURE

9

How can quality be instilled as part of an organization's culture?

Quality, propelled by changing customer needs and better competition, must be viewed as a moving target; therefore, TQM is inseparable from the concept of continuous improvement. Higher and higher performance standards must be set for everyone in the organization (not just the production people) to provide the sense of working toward a common goal. This philosophy is expressed in the accompanying observations regarding a new basic focus for success:

> *[Consultants Michael Treacy and Fred Wiersema] show that it's not the company with the best product that's going to win—or in other markets, the company with the lowest costs or the one with the best total solution to a customer's problem. Whatever a company does to create customer value, it's not how well it performs today that matters in the long run but how good it is at learning to do it better.*[15]

The behavior of managers and employees comprise the basis for TQM. Consistent and committed top management leadership is the catalyst for moving the company culture toward an *esprit de corps* in which all individuals, regardless of rank or position, are obsessed with exceeding customer expectations. Such an attitude should also permeate everything a company does, including customer relations, marketing, research and development, product design, production, and information processing. Management can effectively induce change in its organizational culture by providing an environment in which employees know the company cares about them, is responsive to their needs, and will appreciate and reward excellent results. This knowledge goes a long way in motivating employees toward greater cooperation and making them feel trusted, respected, and comfortable. Such employees are more likely to treat customers in a similar manner.

The firm must empower employees to participate fully in the quest for excellence by providing the means by which employees gain pride, satisfaction, and

[15] Tom Richman, "What Does Business Really Want from Government?" *The State of Small Business* (1995), p. 96.

substantive involvement. Encouragement, training, job enhancement, and the proper working environment and tools are what managers must provide. The work environment in the new corporate culture involves the effective use of teams in the appropriate settings. Employees should be recognized with praise and rewarded for being involved in team problem solving, contributing ideas for improvement, acting as monitors of their own work, and sharing their knowledge and enthusiastic attitudes with their colleagues. The true importance of empowerment is discussed in the following remarks:

> *Making employees more involved in and responsible for their work activities increases the value of those individuals not only to the organization, but also to themselves and to society as a whole. The organizational benefits gained from empowerment are that employees have a sense of ownership of and work harder toward goals they have set for themselves. Thus, employee involvement automatically promotes a higher degree of effort on the part of the work force. We avoid the basis of the Marxist critique of capitalism: the exploitation and subsequent alienation and rebellion of the worker. Problems will be solved more quickly and, therefore, the cost of errors will be reduced.*[16]

With its focus on process and customers, TQM is founded on one very obvious and simple principle: Do the right things right the first time, all the time, on time and continuously improve. The accompanying News Note discusses this notion, and adds another dimension: bottom-line viability.

The heart of this principle is zero defects now and in the future. For example, a non-TQM production policy statement might read: "Do not allow defective

GENERAL BUSINESS **NEWS NOTE**

Getting It Right Produces Profits

We all know the value of "doing things right the first time." We have learned from experience that going back to fix things just doesn't make business sense (and often never happens anyway once a program or system is implemented). So, why do we continue to hear stories about projects gone bad—schedules over-run and budgets over-spent?

The other night, as I listened to a presentation about yet another example of such a case, my blood began to boil! As the speaker discussed the trials and tribulations of a current product development project, a number of issues were raised by people in the audience about the long-term viability and stability of the product being developed. Would the product survive? Could it be expanded and improved? Would the ultimate customer (the taxpayer in this case) be satisfied with what was being delivered?

The speaker shuffled a bit and was obviously nervous —"Well, actually, they hadn't really focused too much on that; they were really just focused on getting the project done, on time, on budget"—their measure of success!

After all, quality is about both the "process" and the "product"—doing things right to end up with a product that is worth delivering. We all complain about the increased international competition and customer demands for better value, so why aren't we successful at meeting these challenges? If we are going to remain competitive, we need to do something about the quality of our process. It doesn't make any sense to deliver high-quality products that nobody wants or that don't provide a measurable business benefit. We must follow a high-quality process that ensures that what we are doing is valuable and will result in a product that provides value to both the *customer* and the *business*.

SOURCE: Reprinted from an article, "Quality and Productivity: 'Quality and Do-It-Right, First Time' Has to Include Bottom-Line Viability," appearing in CMA Management Magazine (formerly CMA Magazine), by Pamela Hollington, March 1997 (p. 33), with permission of CMA Canada.

[16] Cecily Raiborn and Dinah Payne, "TQM: Just What the Ethicist Ordered," *Journal of Business Ethics* (Vol. 15, No. 9, 1996), p. 969.

production to be greater than one percent of total production." In contrast, total quality management would have the policy statement: "We will achieve zero-defect production." It follows that management's responsibility is to provide employees with the training, equipment, and quality of materials and other resources to meet this objective.

Exhibit 8–12 depicts the quality continuum along which companies move toward achieving world-class status. This continuum indicates that, at the most basic level of quality assurance, a company simply inspects to find defective products or monitors employees and surveys customers after the fact to find poor service. Implementing a variety of quality control techniques in the system to eliminate the possibilities of defective products or poor service means that the company has become quality conscious.

When the company's (or a division of the company's) quality system has progressed to a high level of development, the company (or division) may choose to compete against others for formal quality recognition. Finally, when the concept of quality has become a distinct element of the organizational culture and tolerances for defective products or poor service are set at zero percent, the company has achieved world-class status and can be viewed as the benchmark for others. But achieving world-class status does not mark an ending point. TQM is not a static concept; when one problem has been solved, another one is always waiting for a solution.

EXHIBIT 8–12

Quality Continuum

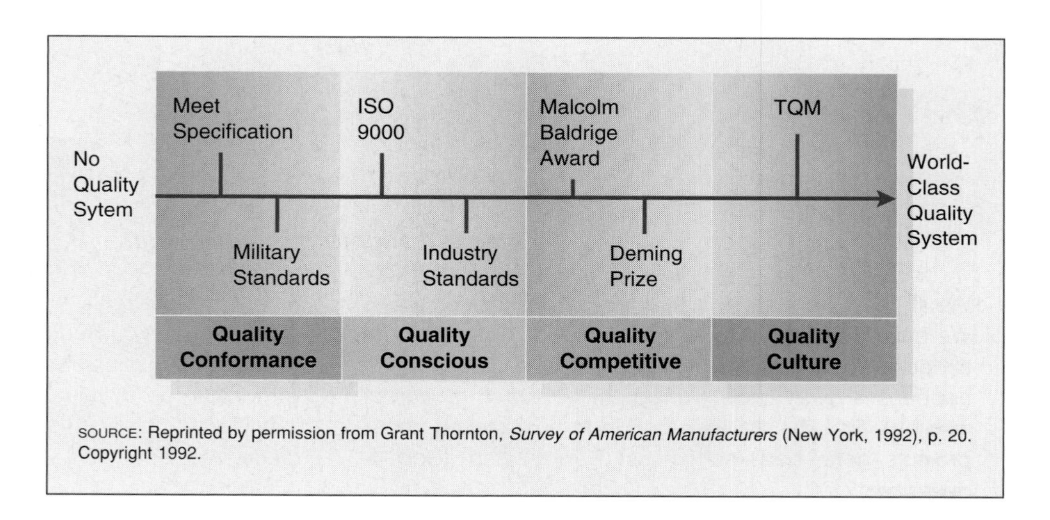

SOURCE: Reprinted by permission from Grant Thornton, *Survey of American Manufacturers* (New York, 1992), p. 20. Copyright 1992.

REVISITING Solectron Corporation

http://www.solectron.com

Solectron's *vision* is [to] "Be the best and continuously improve." This vision statement reflects the company's unceasing efforts to refine its business and its processes. The firm's *mission* allows it to maintain successful partnerships with its customers and suppliers as a global provider of total design, supply chain and manufacturing solutions. The mission statement is as follows:

Our mission is to provide worldwide responsiveness to our customers by offering the highest quality, lowest total cost, customized, integrated, design, supply chain and manufacturing solutions through long-term partnerships based on integrity and ethical business practices.

Dr. Chen's vision in the 1970s and 1980s was to revitalize U.S. manufacturing competitiveness by making Solectron a world-class electronics manufacturing company setting an example for others to follow. His approach to achieving this vision was to benchmark Japanese manufacturing companies and combine American innovation with Japanese techniques. Dr. Chen used The Five S's to achieve that vision:

Seiri—Orderliness
Put things in order
Store all materials and information in an orderly fashion at all times
Tidy
Ready for use
Organized according to frequency
A place for everything and everything in its place

Seiton—Arrange Properly
Distinguish between those things that are needed and not needed
Keep only needed materials at the job site
Throw away all unneeded items immediately

Seisou—Cleanliness
Problems are more visible when everything is neat and clean
Find minor defects while "sweeping clean"

Seiketsu—Always Clean
Clean tools, equipment and job site immediately after use
Equipment that is kept clean runs better

Shitsuke—Discipline
Follow what has been decided daily
Follow standard procedure

SOURCE: "About Solectron," Solectron Corporation Web site, http://www.solectron.com/about/mission/html (October 13, 1998), home page.

CHAPTER SUMMARY

Continuous quality improvement is essential to survival in the global marketplace. Quality is defined as conformity to requirements as judged by customers. Total quality management is a system involving all company personnel in the pursuit of a continuous improvement process that exceeds customer expectations.

The shared planning and decision making among personnel required by TQM is changing the way people perform their jobs. Enhanced technology in hardware, production processes, and management systems has made the new quality initiatives possible. Consumers are aware of greater variety by type and quality of products, and they discriminate in their purchases with regard to price, quality, service, and lead time. This intensified competition has motivated producers to adopt a more dynamic attitude about quality improvement and has heightened the use of competitive benchmarking to close any performance gaps.

Quality compliance costs include the costs of prevention and appraisal. These costs are incurred to reduce or eliminate the current costs of quality failure and to continuously improve in the future. Noncompliance costs are separated into internal and external failure costs.

The number of good units generated during a period measures productivity. Improving quality essentially increases productivity because quality improvement works to remove factors that slow down or halt the production process or that require production redundancy. Eliminating non-value-added activities also increases productivity.

The Malcolm Baldrige National Quality Award focuses attention on management systems, processes, and consumer satisfaction as the tools to achieve excellence. Winning this award is an indication that a company's products or services are among the nation's best. Such an accomplishment invigorates employees and enhances a company's reputation with all stakeholders.

Theoretically, quality can be said to be free if its benefits exceed its costs. However, management should still measure quality costs so that managers have specific information to plan, control, evaluate, and make decisions in a continuous improvement environment.

Strategically based cost management views management accounting as a means of assisting managers to set and communicate organizational strategies and to establish and monitor methods of accomplishing the intended results of those strategies. This type of cost management system differs from financial accounting by taking a longer range perspective, including an alternative view of product costs. For instance, a strategically based cost management system would include research and development costs in total product cost, but would exclude costs of activities that create no value in the value chain.

APPENDIX

International Quality Standards

Most large companies view their markets on an international, rather than a domestic, basis. To compete effectively in a global environment, companies must recognize and be willing to initiate compliance with a variety of standards outside their domestic borders. Standards are essentially the international language of trade; they are formalized agreements that define the various contractual, functional, and technical requirements that assure customers that products, services, processes, and/or systems do what they are expected to do.

ISO 9000

A primary international guideline for quality standards is the **ISO 9000** series. In 1987, the International Organization for Standardization, based in Geneva, Switzerland, developed a comprehensive list of quality standards known as the ISO 9000 series. The series of three compliance standards (ISO 9001, 9002, and 9003) and two guidance standards (ISO 9000 and 9004) resulted from discussions among quality standards boards of 91 countries. These directives are written in a general manner and prescribe the generic design, material procurement, production, quality control, and delivery procedures necessary to achieve quality assurance. These directives are not product standards and do not imply that companies using them have better products than competitors. The standards articulate what must be done to assure quality, but management must decide how to meet the standards. Exhibit 8–13 indicates the coverage of each of the five standards.

ISO 9000 registration is required for regulated products to be sold in the European Union. Unfortunately, there is no international organization to administer the program. Thus, companies seeking ISO certification have to qualify under an internationally accepted registration program that is administered by a national registrar. Examples of such registrars in the United States and Great Britain are, respectively, Underwriters Laboratories and the British Standards Institution.

After an internal review, a company deciding that it can meet the standards may apply for ISO registration. To be registered, a company must first submit to a quality audit by a third-party reviewer. A **quality audit** involves a review of product design activities (not performed for individual products), manufacturing processes and controls, quality documentation and records, and management quality policy and philosophy. After registration, teams visit the company biannually to monitor compliance.

quality audit

Although registration costs are high, certified companies believe the benefits are even higher. Internally, certification helps ensure higher process consistency and quality and should help to reduce costs. Externally, ISO 9000 certified companies have an important distinguishing characteristic from their noncertified competitors. Additionally, certified companies are listed in a registry of "approved" suppliers, which should increase business opportunities. The cost-benefit relationships of the quality system must be measured, documented, and reported under ISO 9000—all jobs for management accountants.

EXHIBIT 8-13

Content of ISO 9000 Standards

Standard #	Content
9000	Provides guidelines selection and use of the entire ISO standard series and explains basic quality terms and ideas; covers documentation, organizational quality objectives and responsibilities, process assurance, and management review and audit of the quality system.
9001	Covers requirements for conformance during product design, production, installation, and servicing; is applicable to architectural, engineering, construction, and manufacturing companies.
9002	Provides a model for assuring quality when only production and installation conformance is required; is applicable to companies in which product requirements are stated relative to established designs or specifications (such as chemical, foods, and pharmaceutical companies); ISO 9002 differs from ISO 9001 only because ISO 9001 includes the design function, whereas ISO 9002 does not.
9003	Provides a model for assuring quality when only final inspection and testing conformance is required; is applicable to companies (or internal organizational units) that inspect and test the products they supply (such as laboratories).
9004	Provides guidelines related to a company's internal quality management and developing and implementing a quality system; discusses the technical, administrative, and human factors that affect product and service quality.

ISO standards are not required to do business in the United States, but should be explored for possible implementation even by companies that do not sell overseas because of the operational and competitive benefits. And if a company's competitors are in compliance with and registered under ISO standards, good business sense would reveal the necessity of becoming ISO certified.

ISO 14000

In 1996, the International Organization for Standardization issued the **ISO 14000** series, which provides criteria for an effective environmental management system. The standards in this series are designed to support a company's environmental protection and pollution prevention goals in balance with socioeconomic needs. One part of the series, ISO 14001, establishes requirements for certification or self-declaration regarding a firm's environmental management system.

KEY TERMS

appraisal cost (p. 313)
benchmarking (p. 309)
control chart (p. 306)
failure cost (p. 313)
grade (p. 307)
ISO 9000 (p. 326)
ISO 14000 (p. 327)
Pareto analysis (p. 318)
prevention cost (p. 313)
process benchmarking (p. 309)
quality (p. 304)
quality audit (p. 326)
quality control (QC) (p. 305)
results benchmarking (p. 309)
statistical process control (SPC) (p. 306)
total quality management (TQM) (p. 310)
value (p. 307)

SOLUTION STRATEGIES

Total Quality Costs = Costs of Compliance + Costs of Noncompliance

- Costs of Compliance: Prevention Costs, Appraisal Costs
- Costs of Noncompliance: Internal Failure Costs, External Failure Costs

Costs of noncompliance are inversely related to the costs of compliance and are a direct result of the number of defects.

Dimensions of product quality include:

- Conformity to specifications
- Effective and efficient performance
- Durability
- Ease of use
- Safety
- Comfort of use
- Appeal

Cost of Quality Formulas

Profit Lost by Selling Units as Defects = (Total Defective Units − Number of Units Reworked) × (Profit for Good Unit − Profit for Defective Unit)

$$Z = (D - Y)(P_1 - P_2)$$

Rework Cost = Number of Units Reworked × Cost to Rework Defective Unit

$$R = (Y)(r)$$

Cost of Processing Customer Returns = Number of Defective Units Returned × Cost of a Return

$$W = (D_r)(w)$$

Total Failure Cost = Profit Lost by Selling Units as Defects + Rework Cost + Cost of Processing Customer Returns + Cost of Warranty Work + Cost of Product Recalls + Cost of Litigation Related to Products + Opportunity Cost of Lost Customers

$$F = Z + R + W + PR + L + O$$

Total Quality Cost = Total Compliance Cost + Total Failure Cost

$$T = (\text{Prevention Cost} + \text{Appraisal Cost}) + \text{Total Failure Cost}$$

$$T = K + A + F$$

DEMONSTRATION PROBLEM

Scott Company's quality report for October 2000 showed the following information:

Total defective units	2,000
Number of units reworked	1,400
Number of customer units returned	650
Profit for a good unit	$38
Profit for a defective unit	$22
Cost to rework a defective unit	$7
Cost to process a returned unit	$10
Total prevention cost	$27,000
Total appraisal cost	$16,000
Litigation related to product failure	$70,000

The company also estimated an opportunity cost of lost customers of $50,000 while the litigation was being settled.

Required:

Compute the following:

a. Profit lost by selling unreworked defects
b. Total rework cost
c. Cost of processing customer returns
d. Total failure cost
e. Total quality cost

Solution to Demonstration Problem

a. $Z = (D - Y)(P_1 - P_2) = (2{,}000 - 1{,}400)(\$38 - \$22) = \$9{,}600$
b. $R = (Y)(r) = (1{,}400)(\$7) = \$9{,}800$
c. $W = (D_r)(w) = (650)(\$10) = \$6{,}500$
d. $F = Z + R + W + L + O = \$9{,}600 + \$9{,}800 + \$6{,}500 + \$70{,}000 + \$50{,}000 = \$145{,}900$
e. $T = K + A + F = \$27{,}000 + \$16{,}000 + \$145{,}900 = \$188{,}900$

QUESTIONS

1. Why are high-quality products and services so important in today's global business environment?
2. Is the quality movement likely to fade away? Discuss the reasons for your conclusion.
3. What is meant by the term *quality*? In defining quality, from what two perspectives can a definition be formulated? Why are both important?
4. In conducting activity analyses, the presence of certain activities indicates low production process quality. List five of these activities.
5. What variables can management manipulate to improve production process quality? How will these changes improve product quality?
6. How can statistical process control techniques be used to evaluate the quality of a production process?
7. What are the eight characteristics that comprise product quality from the consumer's perspective? What are the five characteristics that comprise service quality from the customer's perspective? How do these sets differ?
8. Locate a product that is well described on the Internet. Discuss how that product exemplifies the eight product quality characteristics.

9. "If a company has a high-quality manufacturing process, customers will naturally view the output of that process as high quality." Explain why this statement is true or false.
10. You, your parents, and Bill Gates are all in the market for a new residence. Would each of you define "high quality" the same way? In making a choice of residence, would each of you assess the same things? Why or why not?

11. Define benchmarking. Describe the two types of benchmarking presented in the chapter.
12. Use the Internet to find a company that has engaged in benchmarking. Describe the type of benchmarking used and the benefits and costs of the company's experience.
13. How does benchmarking allow a company to evaluate the quality of its processes?
14. Describe the eight steps in benchmarking that can be used to improve a specific production process.
15. What is TQM? What are the three important tenets of TQM and why are they important?
16. Why is TQM significant? What must a company do to make it work?
17. Use the Internet or other resources to find a company that has recently experienced quality problems. Discuss that company's problems and indicate what costs were incurred, why these costs were incurred, and how the costs should be classified (prevention, appraisal, internal failure, and external failure).
18. What is the Malcolm Baldrige National Quality Award? What are the categories of entrants? What are the award criteria categories?
19. What are the two types of costs that comprise the total quality cost of a firm? What are the two subtypes within each type? Given the trade-off between the two main types of quality costs, is quality ever free? Explain.
20. What constructive adjustments can management make based on information learned from a company's internal and external failures?
21. What are the sources of information for product quality costs within a firm (both financial and nonfinancial)?
22. In the production–sales cycle, what are the four time phases in which quality costs are incurred? How are these costs interrelated through the phases?
23. How can Pareto analysis help focus managerial efforts in reducing the costs of quality-related problems?
24. Describe some additional accounts that can be added to financial records to attempt to better capture the costs of quality in the accounting records. Provide some examples of costs contained in the specified accounts.
25. How does strategic cost management link information to corporate strategies?

26. Use the Internet to find five companies that have a "quality culture." Compare and contrast these cultures.
27. What are the four stages or levels on the quality continuum? Where is TQM located on the continuum?
28. *(Appendix)* Why do countries establish quality standards? Why is it desirable to have a common set of global quality standards?
29. *(Appendix)* What role is served by the International Organization for Standardization?
30. *(Appendix)* What is a quality audit?

EXERCISES

31. *(Terminology)* Match the following lettered terms on the left with the appropriate numbered description on the right.

a. Appraisal cost	**1.** Method to rank causes of variation in a process
b. Benchmarking	**2.** Review of product design, manufacturing processes and controls, quality documentation, and records
c. Control chart	**3.** Technique to identify uncommon variations or errors in a process
d. Grade	
e. Pareto analysis	
f. Quality	
g. Quality audit	
h. Quality control	

i. Statistical process control
j. Value

4. Cost incurred for monitoring and compensating for mistakes
5. Graphical method of documenting when a process is in or out of control
6. One combination of different product or service characteristics included to satisfy different customer needs
7. Process of investigating how other firms conduct business
8. Effect of meeting or exceeding customer needs
9. Product or service characteristic relating to meeting the most customer needs at the lowest price
10. Policy and/or practice designed to eliminate poor quality

32. *(True/false)* Mark each of the following statements as true or false and explain why the false statements are incorrect.
a. The total quality cost is the sum of prevention cost plus failure cost.
b. Traditional accounting systems have separate accounts to capture quality costs.
c. Pareto analysis is used to help managers identify areas in which to focus quality-improvement efforts.
d. As the number of defective products manufactured rises, internal failure costs also rise, but external failure costs are expected to decline.
e. Higher quality yields lower profits but higher productivity.
f. Total quality management focuses on production processes rather than customer satisfaction.
g. Results benchmarking relies only on comparisons to firms within the same industry.
h. SPC control charts are used to plot the costs of quality over time.
i. Appraisal cost is used to monitor and correct mistakes.
j. Quality is free.

33. *(Control chart)* Pareto Pizza's has recently hired several college students to work part time making pizzas. Angelo Pareto, the owner, has a policy of putting 36 slices of pepperoni on a pizza, but (given diversity in size) he sometimes puts on between 34 and 38. After observing the students for a few days, Angelo gathered the following data on number of pepperoni slices:

11:00 a.m. to 5:00 p.m.
13 pizzas were made containing the following number of pepperoni slices: 35, 37, 41, 33, 36, 36, 35, 39, 44, 37, 36, 36, 35

5:00 p.m. to 11:00 p.m.
25 pizzas were made containing the following number of pepperoni slices: 35, 37, 41, 42, 36, 39, 44, 43, 44, 37, 48, 36, 35, 40, 39, 41, 29, 36, 36, 42, 45, 44, 37, 36, 36

a. Prepare a control chart for pepperoni slices.
b. What information does the chart provide Angelo?

34. *(Quality characteristics)* Prepare a five-by-eight matrix of the five characteristics of service quality (horizontal axis) and the eight characteristics of product quality (vertical axis). Place a checkmark in the matrix where there is an approximate match in characteristics on both axes. Prepare a brief oral presentation for your classmates explaining the common quality characteristics in your matrix.

35. *(Definition of quality; quality characteristics)* In a team of three, role-play the following individuals who are visiting a car dealership in your community: (1) a 19-year-old college student, (2) a young married man/woman with two children, and (3) an elderly man/woman (postretirement age). Each of you is interested in purchasing a new automobile.

a. How do each of you define quality in an automobile? Explain the reasons for your differences.

b. What vehicle characteristics are important to all of you? Which vehicle characteristics are unique to each of you?

36. *(Cost of quality)* Bronson's BronzeWorks has gathered the following data on its quality costs for 1999 and 2000:

Defect Prevention Costs	**1999**	**2000**
Quality training	$8,000	$9,500
Quality technology	6,000	8,000
Quality production design	4,000	9,000
External Failure Costs		
Warranty handling	$15,000	$10,000
Customer reimbursements	11,000	7,200
Customer returns handling	7,000	4,000

a. Compute the percentage change in the two quality cost categories from 1999 to 2000.

b. Write a brief explanation for the pattern of change in the two categories.

37. *(Cost of quality)* Sparticus Electronics' accounting system reflected the following costs related to quality for 1999 and 2000:

	1999	**2000**
Customer refunds for poor product quality	$24,000	$18,000
Fitting machines for mistake-proof operations	8,400	12,800
Supply-line management	8,000	10,000
Disposal of waste	44,000	36,000
Quality training	28,000	30,000
Litigation claims	72,000	56,000

a. Which of these are costs of compliance and which are costs of noncompliance?

b. Calculate the percentage change in each cost and for each category.

c. Discuss the pattern of the changes in the two categories.

38. *(Cost of quality)* Mathes Company wants to determine its cost of quality. The company has gathered the following information from records pertaining to August 2000:

Defective units	2,500
Units reworked	600
Defective units returned	200
Appraisal costs	$6,800
Cost per unit for rework	$6
Prevention costs	$25,000
Profit per good unit produced and sold	$30
Profit per defective unit sold	$20
Cost per unit for customer returns	$5
Cost of warranty work	$2,500

Compute the following:

a. Lost profits from selling defective work

b. Total costs of failure

c. Total quality cost

39. *(Cost of quality)* Alpine Sunglasses Company has gathered the following information pertaining to quality costs of production for June 2000 of heavy-duty sunglasses for skiing:

Total defective units	300
Number of units reworked	190
Number of units returned	50
Total prevention cost	$12,000
Total appraisal cost	$6,000
Per-unit profit for defective units	$10
Per-unit profit for good units	$28
Cost to rework defective units	$8
Cost to handle returned units	$5

Using these data, calculate the following:

a. Total cost to rework
b. Profit lost from not reworking all defective units
c. Cost of processing customer returns
d. Total failure costs
e. Total quality cost

40. *(Cost of quality)* Klein Computers is evaluating its quality control costs for 2000 and preparing plans and budgets for 2001. The 2000 quality costs incurred in the CPU Division follow:

Prevention costs	$150,000
Appraisal costs	50,000
Internal failure costs	175,000
External failure costs	50,000
Total	$425,000

Prepare a memo to the company president on the following issues:

a. Which categories of quality costs would be affected by the decision to spend $750,000 on new computer chip-making equipment (to replace an older model)? Why?
b. If projected external failure costs for 2001 can be reduced 60 percent (relative to 2000 levels) by either spending $25,000 more on appraisal or $40,000 more on prevention, why would the firm opt to spend the $40,000 on prevention rather than the $25,000 on appraisal?

41. *(Control of quality costs; team activity)* The following summary numbers have been taken from a quality cost report of North Carolina Fine Furniture Inc., for 2000. The firm manufactures a variety of Early American furniture products.

Prevention costs	$2,500,000
Appraisal costs	1,500,000
Internal failure costs	1,500,000
External failure costs	500,000
Total quality costs	$6,000,000

The company is actively seeking to identify ways to reduce total quality costs. The company's current strategy is to increase spending in one or more quality cost categories in hopes of achieving greater spending cuts in other quality cost categories. In a team of three or four individuals, prepare an oral presentation to answer the following questions:

a. Which spending categories are most susceptible to control by managers? Why?
b. Why is it more logical for the company to increase spending in the prevention cost and appraisal cost categories than in the failure cost categories?
c. Which cost category is the most likely target for spending reductions? Explain.
d. How would the adoption of a TQM philosophy affect the focus in reducing quality costs?

42. *(Quality information system; team activity)* Your company is interested in developing information about quality, but has a traditional accounting system that does not provide such information directly. In a three- or four-person team, prepare a set of recommendations about how to improve the company's information system to eliminate or reduce this deficiency. In your recommendations, also explain in what areas management would have the most difficulty satisfying its desire for more information about quality and why these areas were chosen.

http://www.toyota.com

43. *(Supplier quality)* Assume that Toyota paid for a full-page advertisement in *The Wall Street Journal.* The ad did not tout Toyota products nor was it in reference to year-end earnings or a new stock issuance. Instead, the ad was to inform readers that "buying quality parts is not a foreign idea to us." The ad named Toyota suppliers and identified their locations. Prepare a brief essay to answer the following questions.

a. Why would Toyota want other companies to know what suppliers it uses?
b. Do you think this advertisement had any benefit for Toyota itself? Discuss the rationale for your answer.

44. *(Differences from benchmarks)* For a benchmark, assume that the average firm incurs quality costs in the following proportions:

Prevention	25%
Appraisal	25%
Internal failure	25%
External failure	25%
Total costs	100%

With a partner, explain why the following industries might be inclined to have a spending pattern on quality costs that differs from the benchmark:

a. Pharmaceutical company
b. Department store
c. Computer manufacturer
d. Used car retailer
e. Lawn service company

PROBLEMS

45. *(Pareto analysis)* Leading Edge Computers has identified the following failure costs during 2000:

	COST OF TYPE OF FAILURE				
Model	**CPU**	**Internal Drive**	**External Drive**	**All Other**	**Total**
Laptop	$ 8,000	$ 7,000	$ 5,000	$ 3,000	$23,000
Desktop	7,000	6,000	12,000	5,000	30,000
Mini	3,000	1,000	8,000	3,000	15,000
Total	$18,000	$14,000	$25,000	$11,000	$68,000

a. Rearrange the rows in descending order of magnitude based on the total dollars column and prepare a table using Pareto analysis with the following headings:

Model	Dollars	Percentage of Total	Cumulative Percentage of Total

b. Which models account for almost 80 percent of all failure costs?

c. Focusing on the models identified in part (b), prepare a table using Pareto analysis to identify the types of failure causing the majority of failure costs. (*Hint:* Rearrange the cost of failure types in descending order of magnitude.) Use the following headings for your table:

Failure Type	Dollars	Percentage of Total	Cumulative Percentage of Total

d. Describe the problem areas for which to seek preventive measures first. How, if at all, does this answer reflect the concept of leverage?

46. *(Pareto analysis)* Select Refrigerators has identified the following warranty costs during 2000 according to the type of product failure as follows:

Model	Electrical	Motor	Structural	Mechanical	Dollars
Chic	$25,000	$27,000	$15,000	$ 5,000	$ 72,000
Elegant	28,000	32,000	26,000	6,000	92,000
All others	8,000	15,000	6,000	9,000	38,000
Total	$61,000	$74,000	$47,000	$20,000	$202,000

a. Rearrange the rows in descending order of magnitude based on the total dollars column and prepare a table using Pareto analysis with the following headings:

Model	Dollars	Percentage of Total	Cumulative Percentage of Total

b. Which model(s) account for the vast proportion of all failure costs? Discuss.
c. Devise a plan to address prioritizing projects regarding development of preventive measures based on the findings in the Pareto analysis you just conducted for Select Refrigerators.

47. *(Cost of quality)* Lampposts-R-Us, Ltd., manufactures hardwood lampposts for the discriminating homeowner. The firm produced 3,000 lampposts during its first year of operations. At year-end, there was no inventory of finished goods. The company sold 2,700 through regular market channels (some after rework), but 300 units were so defective that they had to be sold as scrap. For this first year, the firm spent $30,000 on prevention costs and $15,000 on quality appraisal. There were no customer returns. An income statement for the year follows.

Sales: Regular channel	$270,000	
Scrap	12,000	$282,000
Cost of goods sold:		
Original production costs	$150,000	
Rework costs	22,000	
Quality prevention and appraisal	45,000	(217,000)
Gross margin		$ 65,000
Selling and administrative expenses (all fixed)		(90,000)
Net loss		$ (25,000)

a. Compute the total profits lost by the company in its first year of operations by selling defective units as scrap rather than selling the units through regular channels.
b. Compute the total failure costs for the company in its first year.
c. Compute total quality costs incurred by the company in its first year.
d. What evidence indicates the firm is dedicated to manufacturing and selling high-quality products?

48. *(Cost of quality)* ClearTone makes portable telephones, and produced 20,000 phones during 2000, its first year of operations. It sold all it produced that first year but 500 phones had a particular defect. Of these, 200 were reworked and sold through regular channels at the original price while the rest were sold as "seconds" without rework. In 2000, ClearTone spent $25,000 for prevention measures and $18,000 on appraisal. Following is ClearTone's 2000 income statement. ClearTone is a partnership; thus, no income taxes are presented on the income statement.

Regular sales (19,700 units)	$1,970,000	
Sales of seconds (300 units)	21,000	$1,991,000
Cost of goods sold:		
Original production costs	$ 800,000	
Rework costs (200 units)	2,000	
Prevention and appraisal costs	43,000	(845,000)
Gross margin		$1,146,000
Selling and administrative expenses (all fixed)		(600,000)
Net income		$ 546,000

a. Compute the total revenue lost by ClearTone in its first year of operations by selling defective units as seconds rather than reworking the units and selling them at the regular price.
b. Compute the total failure costs for the company in 2000.
c. Compute total quality costs incurred by the company in 2000.
d. What evidence indicates the firm is dedicated to manufacturing and selling high-quality products?

49. *(Cost of quality)* Golf courses are demanding in their quest for high-quality carts because of the critical need for lawn maintenance. Ride-in-Style manufactures golf carts and is a recognized leader in the industry for quality products. In recent months, company managers have become more interested in trying to quantify the costs of quality in the company. As an initial effort, the company was able to identify the following 2000 costs, by categories that are associated with quality:

Prevention Costs	
Quality training	$15,000
Quality technology	50,000
Quality circles	32,000
Appraisal Costs	
Quality inspections	$18,000
Test equipment	14,000
Procedure verifications	9,000
Internal Failure Costs	
Scrap and waste	$ 6,500
Waste disposal	2,100
External Failure Costs	
Warranty handling	$ 9,500
Customer reimbursements/returns	7,600

Managers were also aware that in 2000, 250 of the 8,000 carts that were produced had to be sold as scrap. These 250 carts were sold for $80 less profit per unit than "good" carts. Also, the company incurred rework costs amounting to $6,000 to sell 200 other carts through regular market channels.

a. Using these data, find Ride-in-Style's 2000 expense for the following:
  1. Lost profits from scrapping the 250 units
  2. Total failure costs
  3. Total quality costs
b. Assume that the company is considering expanding its existing full 5-year warranty to a full 7-year warranty in 2001. How would such a change be reflected in quality costs?

50. *(Cost of quality)* Tanks-a-Lot Ltd. is very aware that its scuba diving tanks must be of high quality to maintain its reputation of excellence and safety. You have been retained as a consultant by the company and have suggested that quantifying the costs of quality would be important to an understanding of and management of quality. Your experience as a cost accountant helped you determine the following year 2000 costs of quality from the company's accounting records:

Prevention Costs	
Foolproofing machinery	$10,000
Quality training	30,000
Educating suppliers	22,000
Appraisal Costs	
Quality inspections	$12,000
Recording defects	9,000
Procedure verifications	6,000
Internal Failure Costs	
Waste disposal	$ 4,500
Unplanned downtime	1,400
External Failure Costs	
Warranty handling	$ 6,400
Customer reimbursements/returns	5,100

You also determined that 1,200 of the 100,000 tanks made in 2000 had to be sold as scrap for $70 less profit per tank than the nondefective tanks. Tanks-a-Lot also incurred $4,000 of rework costs that had been buried in overhead (in addition to the failure costs presented above) in producing the tanks sold at the regular price.

a. Tanks-a-Lot management has asked you to determine the year 2000 "costs" of the following:
   1. Lost profits from scrapping the 1,200 units
   2. Total failure costs
   3. Total quality costs

b. Assume that the company is considering expanding its existing full 2-year warranty to a full 3-year warranty in 2001. How would such a change be reflected in quality costs?

REALITY CHECK

51. Use the Internet to find four definitions of quality.

a. Compare and contrast each of the four definitions, with specific emphasis on whether the definition is conformity or customer oriented.

b. Assume that you are the manager of (1) a copy store and (2) a kitchen blender manufacturer. Prepare definitions of quality to distribute to your employees and discuss how you would measure service/product adherence to those definitions.

52. Institutions of higher education have a variety of internal and external customers. Use a team of three or four individuals to answer the following.

a. List three internal and two external customers of a college or university.

b. How would each of the constituents from part (a) define quality of product or service? Do any of these views conflict and, if so, how?

c. Are a college or university's internal customers as important as external customers? Explain the rationale for your answer.

53. By building quality into the process, rather than making quality inspections at the end of the process, certain job functions (such as that of quality control inspector) can be eliminated. Additionally, the installation of automated equipment to monitor product processing could eliminate some line worker jobs.

In a nation with fairly high unemployment, would employers attempting to implement valid quality improvements that resulted in employee terminations be appreciated or condemned? Discuss your answer from the standpoint of a variety of concerned constituencies, including the consumers who purchase the company's products.

54. Assume that you are in charge of a social service agency that provides counseling services to welfare families. The agency's costs have been increasing with no corresponding increase in funding. In an effort to implement some cost reductions, you implement the following ideas:

1. Counselors are empowered to make their own decisions about the legitimacy of all welfare claims.
2. To emphasize the concept of "do it right the first time," counselors are told not to review processed claims at a later date.
3. To discourage "out-of-control" conditions, an upper and lower control limit of 5 minutes is set on a standard 15-minute time for consultations.

Discuss the ethics as well as the positive and negative effects of each of the ideas listed.

55. Sometimes a company, in its efforts to reduce costs, might also reduce quality.

a. What kinds of costs could be reduced in an organization that would almost automatically lower product/service quality?

b. If quality improvements create cost reductions, why would cost reductions not create quality improvements?

c. Are there instances in which cost reductions would create quality improvements?

56. *Increasing numbers of U.S. businesses have been seeking to comply with the ISO 9000 standards simply because of real or perceived market forces. Some of the most commonly given reasons for seeking ISO 9000 registration or compliance follow:*

- *"Our customers are demanding it, often by putting ISO 9000 into contracts."*
- *"Our customers say they will treat ISO 9000-registered suppliers preferentially."*
- *"Our competitors are achieving registration, so we must also."*
- *"We need to improve quality; ISO 9000 seems like a practical, no-nonsense, and internationally accepted approach."*
- *"Our customers demand quality; ISO 9000 registration makes a statement about our commitment to quality."*
- *"Our European divisions already have ISO 9000 registration, and they are putting pressure on us to conform."*
- *"Our industry seems to be moving toward ISO 9000."*

The rapid growth of ISO 9000 implementation shows that the forces of the marketplace (whether the direct forces at work in regulated industries or the indirect ones that govern the free markets) are an effective influence in getting companies to adopt standards and, more importantly, to use them to improve their processes.

SOURCE: Stanley A. Marash and Donald W. Marquardt, "Quality Standards and Free Trade," *Quality Progress* (May 1994), p. 29.

a. Why do you think customers are insisting that suppliers meet ISO 9000 standards?

b. Does meeting ISO 9000 standards mean that a supplier's products or services are superior to those of competitors? Elaborate on what such conformance means.

c. Why would the fact that a supplier's industry is moving toward ISO 9000 motivate the supplier to seek registration?

d. How would complying with ISO 9000 help a company improve quality?

57. Find the Web page for Collins Printed Circuits of Rockwell Avionics. What products does this company make? How does the company use statistical process controls to control the quality of output? What is the role of the firm's group testing lab in controlling quality?

58. Find The Benchmarking Exchange on the Internet. What are the top five business processes that are currently the focus of benchmarking by members of The Benchmarking Exchange? Why have benchmarking processes related to managing human resources remained so highly ranked?

http://www.delta-air.com

59. *Just how tired were Delta Air Lines Capt. Roscoe McMillan and his crew last Wednesday when he diverted his Atlanta-to-Tokyo flight to Portland, Oregon, and called it a day? Too tired, in his judgment, based on more than 30 years as a Delta pilot, to continue safely with the 14-hour journey to Narita International Airport, according to what the captain told Delta officials. The problem: Two of the other pilots couldn't sleep in the aircraft's controversial new berths, and based on earlier experience, Capt. McMillian figured he couldn't either.*

Capt. McMillan, who has a perfect flying record and a reputation for being outspoken, has been campaigning against the bunks from the start. In a recent posting on the pilots' union private Web site, he wrote of the new setup: "I think it stinks."

Delta adopted the new berths as part of a redesign of its international service. Among other things, the new bunks allow for more seats, which Delta says will translate into $40 million in additional revenue from the five altered planes over the next five years. Shortly after the incident, the Air Line Pilots Association filed a grievance and lodged a complaint over the issue of the berths with the FFA.

SOURCE: Adapted from Martha Branigan, "This Is Your Captain: Prepare for Landing, It's Time for My Nap," *The Wall Street Journal* (April 15, 1999), p. A1.

a. Who are the stakeholders in this situation? What do you think are the ethical issues?

b. If you were asked by Delta and the pilots union to mediate this issue, what are the facts you might need to determine?

c. What are the economic benefits and risks that should concern an airline in such a case?

d. What are the issues that should concern the pilots and the union?

60. *In a move that clears the way for a wave of high-tech interactive gadgets in cars and trucks, five of the world's biggest automakers announced they are pursuing a common wiring standard for new vehicles. General Motors Corp., Ford Motor Co., DaimlerChrysler AG, Toyota Motor Corp., and Renault SA said they signed a memorandum of agreement to develop an industrywide standard so their new vehicles can accommodate the array of communications and entertainment equipment being developed for the auto industry. Additional automakers are expected to sign onto the agreement in coming months, industry executives said.*

http://www.daimlerchrysler.com
http://www.renault.com

SOURCE: Jeffrey Ball, "Five of the World's Top Auto Makers Agree to Develop Technology Standard," *The Wall Street Journal* (April 28, 1999), p. B6.

a. What are some advantages to an automaker of having a single industry quality standard?

b. What are some advantages to automaker customers of having a single industry quality standard?

c. How would a nation benefit if all major companies in an industry were to subscribe to a single quality standard?

61. *Words of wisdom from Dennis K. Pawley, retired manufacturing chief of the former Chrysler Corp. and now a management consultant, are as follows:*

1. *"The biggest reason companies fail is a failure to reflect. They become egotistical."*

2. *"If it ain't broke, break it."*

3. *"Heroes exist in a company because of a lack of a system."*

4. *"It's easy to be process-centered when things are going good. But when things go bad, that's the real test."*

5. *D×V×F > R. Translation: (Dissatisfaction with the status quo) × (Vision of the future) × (Courage to take the first steps) must be greater than (Resistance to change).*

SOURCE: Jeffrey Ball, "Your Career Matters: A Car Veteran Explains Why IPC = (A + W + P − I) × S," *The Wall Street Journal* (June 8, 1999), p. B1. Permissions conveyed through the Copyright Clearance Center.

In your own words, compose a brief explanation of what you think Mr. Pawley meant by each of the "words of wisdom."

http://www.sony.com

62. *Several years ago, Sony Corp., the consumer electronics and entertainment giant, halted shipments of its much-ballyhooed 18-inch digital satellite dish system following a rash of consumer complaints. The problems, which involved television picture reception, were said to have included the appearance of horizontal green lines and images freezing motionless on the screen.*

"We estimate that only 2.5% of our consumers have experienced the problems, but we're taking the matter seriously," said a Sony spokesman.

SOURCE: Adapted from Jeffrey A. Trachtenberg, "Sony Confirms It Halted Sales of Satellite Dish," *The Wall Street Journal* (September 7, 1995), p. B1.

a. Do you think admitting the product was defective hurt or helped Sony's reputation?

b. Discuss the costs and benefits of halting sales?

c. Use the Internet to find an example of a company that has continued to sell its product in spite of complaints and other negative feedback about quality. What have been the results?

CHAPTER 9

Cost Allocation for Joint Products and By-Products

LEARNING OBJECTIVES

After completing this chapter, you should be able to answer the following questions:

1. How are the outputs of a joint process classified?
2. At what point in a joint process are joint products identifiable?
3. What management decisions must be made before a joint process is begun?
4. How are joint costs allocated to products?
5. How are by-products treated in accounting systems?
6. How should not-for-profit organizations account for joint costs?

INTRODUCING

Buckhead Beef Company

http://www.buckheadbeef.com

Buckhead Beef Company, headquartered in Atlanta, is the largest provider of Certified Angus Beef™ in the United States. Howard Halpern cofounded the company in 1983, and the company currently has revenues approaching $300 million.

Approximately 75 percent of Buckhead Beef's sales are select, choice, and prime grades of steak. The rest of the company's sales are pork, veal, lamb, game meats and birds, provisions, deli meats, and seafood.

Buckhead's truck fleet delivers products to customers in the southeastern and northeastern states, and through a distribution center in Puerto Rico, serves the Caribbean market. In addition, however, through the company's steakhouse accounts, it achieves nationwide distribution. Customers also include hotels, country clubs, upscale retail outlets, and a small number of prestigious, well-established grocery stores.

The company's strength results, to some extent, from combining the expertise of an in-house cut shop with the efficiency of a large-scale distributor. Buckhead uses energy-efficient equipment in its USDA inspected plant and a state-of-the-art computerized bar coding system. This system allows the company to track products from the time they are processed at the packing plant to the time they are aged, portion-cut, vacuum-packed, and delivered to customers. The bar codes contain information on cost per pound and historical data such as production line and packaging date. Restaurant managers are particularly delighted with this technology. Buckhead has an open-book policy with its customers and sells on a true cost-plus basis.

SOURCE: Adapted from Bob Swientek, "A Cut Above," *Prepared Foods* (October 1998), Rising Stars feature section. Reprinted with permission of Cahners Business Information.

Almost every company produces and sells more than one type of product. Although companies may engage in multiple production processes to manufacture a variety of products, they may also engage in a single process to simultaneously generate various different outputs such as those of Buckhead Beef and its customers (meat processors cut, segment, process, and package meats from a side of beef). In a like manner, the refining of crude oil may produce gasoline, motor oil, heating oil, and kerosene. A single process in which one product cannot be manufactured without producing others is known as a **joint process**. Such processes are common in the extractive, agricultural, food, and chemical industries. The costs incurred for materials, labor, and overhead during a joint process are referred to as the **joint cost** of the production process.

joint process

joint cost

This chapter discusses joint processes, their related product outputs, and the accounting treatment of joint cost. Outputs of a joint process are classified based on their revenue-generating ability, and joint cost is allocated only to the primary products of a joint process, using either a physical or monetary measure. Although joint cost allocations are necessary to determine financial statement valuations, such allocations should not be used in internal decision making.[1]

Joint costs may also be incurred in service businesses and not-for-profit organizations. Such costs in these organizations are often for advertisements that publicize different product lines or locations, or ads for different purposes, such as public service information and requests for donations. Joint costs of not-for-profit firms are covered in the last section of this chapter.

[1] Sometimes, correct pricing of a product depends on knowledge of the full cost of making the product, particularly when contractual agreements require cost-plus pricing. Joint cost allocation is also necessary to the valuation of products, estimation of product line profitability, and (in some cases) determination of product selling price.

OUTPUTS OF A JOINT PROCESS

1

How are the outputs of a joint process classified?

joint product

A joint process simultaneously produces more than one product line. The product categories resulting from a joint process that have a sales value are referred to as (1) joint products, (2) by-products, and (3) scrap. **Joint products** are the *primary* outputs of a joint process; each joint product individually has substantial revenue-generating ability. Joint products are the primary reason management undertakes the production process yielding them. These products are also called *primary products, main products,* or *coproducts.*

Joint products do not necessarily have to be totally different products; the definition of joint products has been extended to include similar products of differing quality that result from the same process. For example, when an oil refinery processes petroleum into gasoline, the outputs will all have been derived from petroleum, but different grades will have more octane and other characteristics based on the extent and types of additional processing.

by-product
scrap

In contrast, **by-products** and **scrap** are incidental outputs of a joint process. Both are salable, but their sales values alone would not be sufficient for management to justify undertaking the joint process. For example, donut hole cutouts are a by-product of the donut-making process. Scrap may be generated in the setup stage. Contractors may tear out old fixtures, cupboards, etc., in remodeling a home. Such items are often resold to other contractors.[2]

waste

By-products are viewed as having a higher sales value than scrap. A final output from a joint process is **waste**, which is a residual output that has no sales value. A normal amount of waste may create a production cost that cannot be avoided in some industries. Alternatively, many companies have learned either to minimize their production waste by changing their processing techniques or to reclassify waste as a by-product or scrap through selling it to generate some minimal amount of revenue.

A company may change a product classification over time because of changes in technology, consumer demand, or ecological factors. Some products originally classified as by-products are reclassified as joint products, whereas some joint products are reduced to the by-product category. Even products originally viewed as scrap or waste may be upgraded to a joint product status. Years ago, for example, the sawdust and chips produced in a lumber mill were considered waste and discarded. These items are now processed further to produce particleboard used in making inexpensive furniture. Therefore, depending on the company, sawdust and chips may be considered a joint product or a by-product. Sometimes a by-product will be accidentally discovered by good fortune. An interesting example is found in the Internet revolution in the News Note on page 345.

http://www.bestfoods.com
http://www.genmills.com
http://www.nestle.com
http://www.perrier.com
http://www.tropicana.com

Classification of joint process output is based on the judgment of company managers, normally after considering the relative sales values of the outputs. Classifications are unique to each company engaged in the joint process. For example, Lazy-K Ranch and Sterling Steers Ltd. each engage in the same joint production process that produces three outputs: meats, bone, and hide. Lazy-K Ranch classifies all three outputs as joint products, whereas Sterling Steers Ltd. classifies meats and hide as joint products; bone is regarded as a by-product. These classifications could have resulted from the fact that Lazy-K Ranch has the facilities to process bone beyond the joint process, but Sterling Steers does not have such facilities. Further processing endows bone with a substantially higher sales value per unit than selling bone as it exits the joint process.

[2] Recycling is a related issue. Now, about 75 percent of a car's weight can be recycled. (Nissan is close to recycling 90 percent.) Companies are working to similarly recycle waste of other products.

GENERAL BUSINESS  NEWS NOTE

Can You Believe It?

E-commerce infomediaries are finding that as they mend broken supply chains, one by-product is aggregated purchase data that have never been available before.

Such is the case with Instill Corp., (http://www.instill.com) which provides an e-marketplace for the food-services industry. Last week the company added a new service called Instill Market Intelligence, which offers subscriptions to the purchase data generated by buyers on its systems.

Who is willing to pay its six-figure price tag? Some of the world's largest food manufacturers, including Bestfoods, General Mills, Nestle, Perrier, Schreiber, and Tropicana.

These vendors have never had access to data about the amount of product being purchased by restaurants and other food-services outlets, such as hospitals. That's because sales in the industry are handled by thousands of regional distributors, making it difficult to get an accurate, aggregated view of purchase data—not just shipment figures—across the manufacturer's segments, categories, and products.

Access to that data will now let manufacturers, such as Bestfoods, better manage production, plan new products, and market and sell existing products to the best-suited buyers, according to T.C. Chatterjee, senior business manager at Bestfoods.

"For the first time, we are able to support sales and marketing efforts based on actual operator purchases," said Trevor Farrell, customer supply-chain manager at Schreiber Foods Inc., another Instill subscriber.

"Using the data to standardize the industry is an absolute must as a first step in a fragmented industry," said Forrester Research Inc. (http://www.forrester.com) analyst Bruce Temkin. "To sell the data back to manufacturers is a big win. Over time, distributors will be forced to operate in a more competitive environment, and you'll see more dynamic pricing."

Food manufacturers have long had market-share data from in-store supermarket sales via data providers such as IRI or Neilsen. But in the food-services area, they have relied on educated guesses as to how their products stack up against competitors.

SOURCE: Richard Karpinski, "Infomediary Repackages Sales Data for Vendors," *Internetweek* (September 27, 1999), p. 8.

THE JOINT PROCESS

2

At what point in a joint process are joint products identifiable?

Joint products are typically produced in companies using mass production processes and, thus, a process costing accounting method.[3] The outputs of a corn processing plant, for example, may include corn on the cob and whole-kernel corn (joint products), partial corn kernels (by-product) used for corn meal and grits, inferior kernels (scrap) for sale to producers of animal food, and husks, corn silk, and cobs (waste) that are discarded. Exhibit 9–1 illustrates the output of such a joint process.

split-off point

The point at which joint process outputs are first identifiable as individual products is called the **split-off point**. A joint process may have one or more split-off points, depending on the number and types of output produced. Output may be sold at the split-off point if a market exists for products in that condition. Alternatively, some or all of the products may be processed further after exiting the joint process.

Joint cost includes all costs incurred up to the split-off point for direct material, direct labor, and overhead. Joint cost is allocated, at the split-off point, to only the joint products because these products are the reason that management undertook the production process. Allocation is necessary because of the *cost principle.* Joint cost is a necessary and reasonable cost of producing the joint products and, therefore, should be attached to them. Although necessary for valuation purposes

[3] For simplicity, Chapters 6 and 7 on process costing included examples of only single-product processes.

EXHIBIT 9–1

Illustration of Joint Process Output

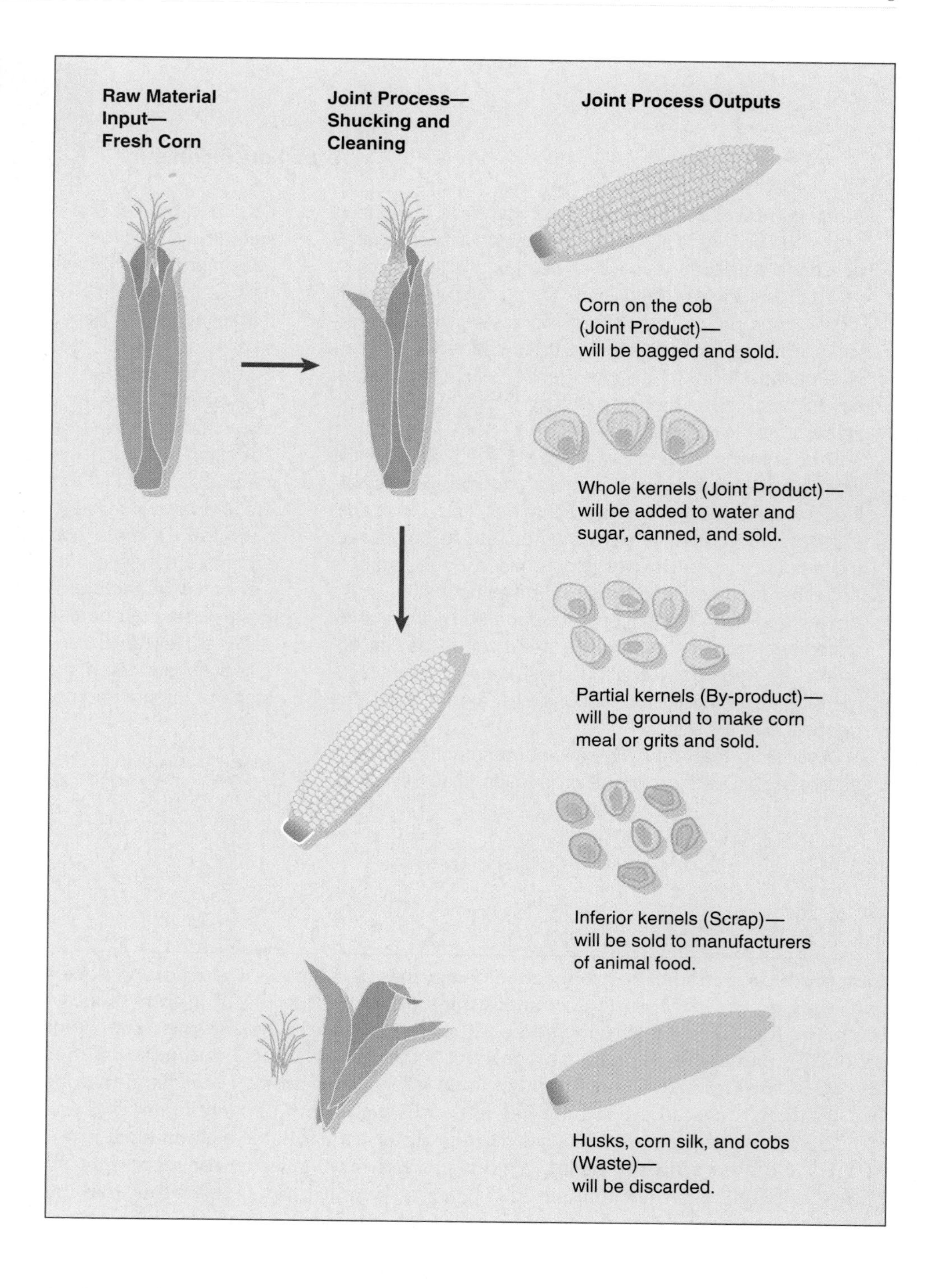

for financial statements, the joint cost allocation to joint products is, however, not relevant to decision making. Once the split-off point is reached, the joint cost has already been incurred and is a **sunk cost** that cannot be changed regardless of what future course of action is taken.

sunk cost

If any of the joint process outputs are processed further, additional costs after split-off will be incurred. Any costs after split-off are assigned to the separate products for which those costs are incurred. Exhibit 9–2 depicts a joint process with multiple split-off points and the allocation of costs to products. For simplicity, all output of this joint process is considered primary output; there are no by-products, scrap, or waste. Note that some of the output of Joint Process One (joint products B and C) becomes part of the direct material for Joint Process Two. The joint cost allocations will follow products B and C into Joint Process Two for accounting purposes, but these allocated costs should not be used in making decisions about further processing in that department or in Department Four. Such decisions should be made *only after* considering whether the expected additional revenues from further processing are greater than the expected additional costs of further processing.

EXHIBIT 9–2

Model of a Joint Process

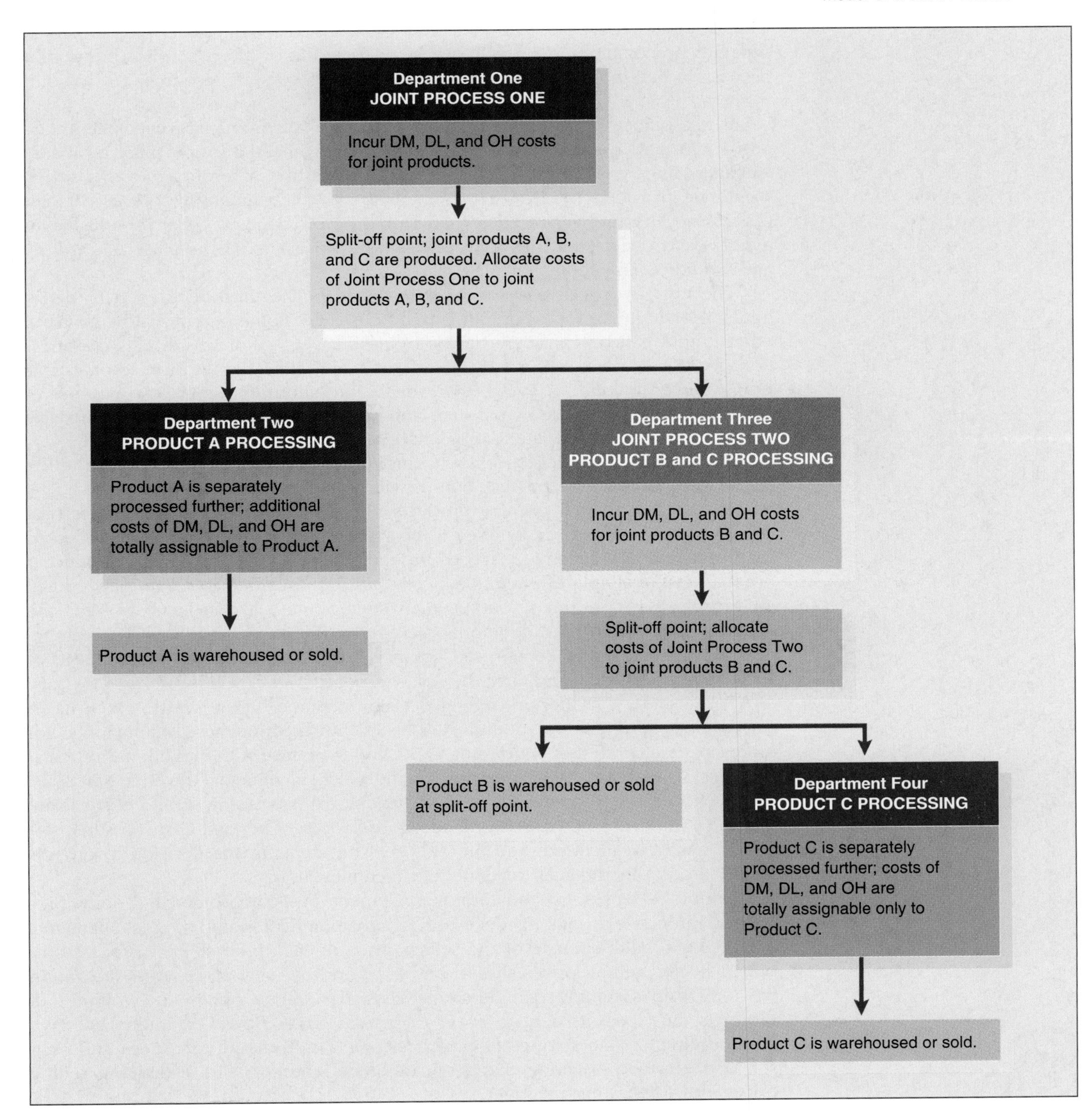

MANAGEMENT DECISIONS REGARDING JOINT PROCESSES

What management decisions must be made before a joint process is begun?

Certain decisions need to be made by company managers before committing resources to a joint production process. First, total expected revenues from the sale of the joint process output must be estimated and compared to total expected processing costs of the output. If the revenues are expected to exceed the costs, management must then consider other potential costs. Because the joint process results in a "basket" of products, managers must be aware that some of the joint process output may require additional processing to make it salable. Once joint process costs have been incurred, they become sunk costs regardless of whether the output is salable at the end of the joint process or at what amount. Thus, management must consider total joint costs plus expected separate processing and/or selling costs incurred at or after the end of the joint process in making the decision about whether to commit resources to the joint process.

If total anticipated revenues from the "basket" of products exceed the anticipated joint and separate costs, the second management decision must be made. Managers must compare the net income from this use of resources to that which would be provided by all other alternative uses of company resources. If joint process net income were greater than would be provided by other uses, management would decide that this joint production process is the best use of capacity and would begin production.

The next two decisions are made at split-off. The third decision is to determine how the joint process output is to be classified. Some output will be primary; other output will be considered to be by-product, scrap, or waste. This classification decision is necessary for the joint cost to be allocated, because *joint cost is only assigned to joint products.* However, before allocation, joint cost may be reduced by the value of the by-products and scrap. Determination of by-product and scrap value is discussed later in the chapter.

The fourth decision is the most complex. Management must decide whether any (or all) of the joint process output will be sold at split-off or whether it will be processed further. If primary products are marketable at split-off, further processing should only be undertaken if the value added to the product, as reflected by the incremental revenue, exceeds the incremental cost. If a primary product is not marketable at split-off, additional costs *must* be incurred to make that product marketable. For nonprimary output, management must also estimate whether the incremental revenue from additional processing will exceed additional processing cost. If there is no net benefit, the nonmarketable output should be disposed of without further processing after the split-off point.

To illustrate a further-processing decision, assume that a whole turkey has a selling price of $0.18 per pound at split-off, but the minimum selling price for turkey parts after further processing is $0.23 per pound. If the additional processing cost is less than $0.05 per pound, the $0.05 incremental revenue ($0.23 − $0.18) exceeds the incremental cost, and additional processing should occur. Note that the joint cost is not used in this decision process. The joint cost is a sunk cost after it has been incurred, and the only relevant items in the decision to process further are the incremental revenue and incremental cost.

Exhibit 9–3 presents the four management decision points in a joint production process. In making decisions at any potential point of sale, managers must have a valid estimate of the selling price of each type of joint process output. Expected selling prices should be based on both cost and market factors. In the long run, assuming that demand exists, the selling prices and volumes of products must be sufficient to cover their total costs. However, immediate economic influences on setting selling prices, such as competitors' prices and consumers' sensitivity to price changes, cannot be ignored when estimating selling prices and forecasting revenues.

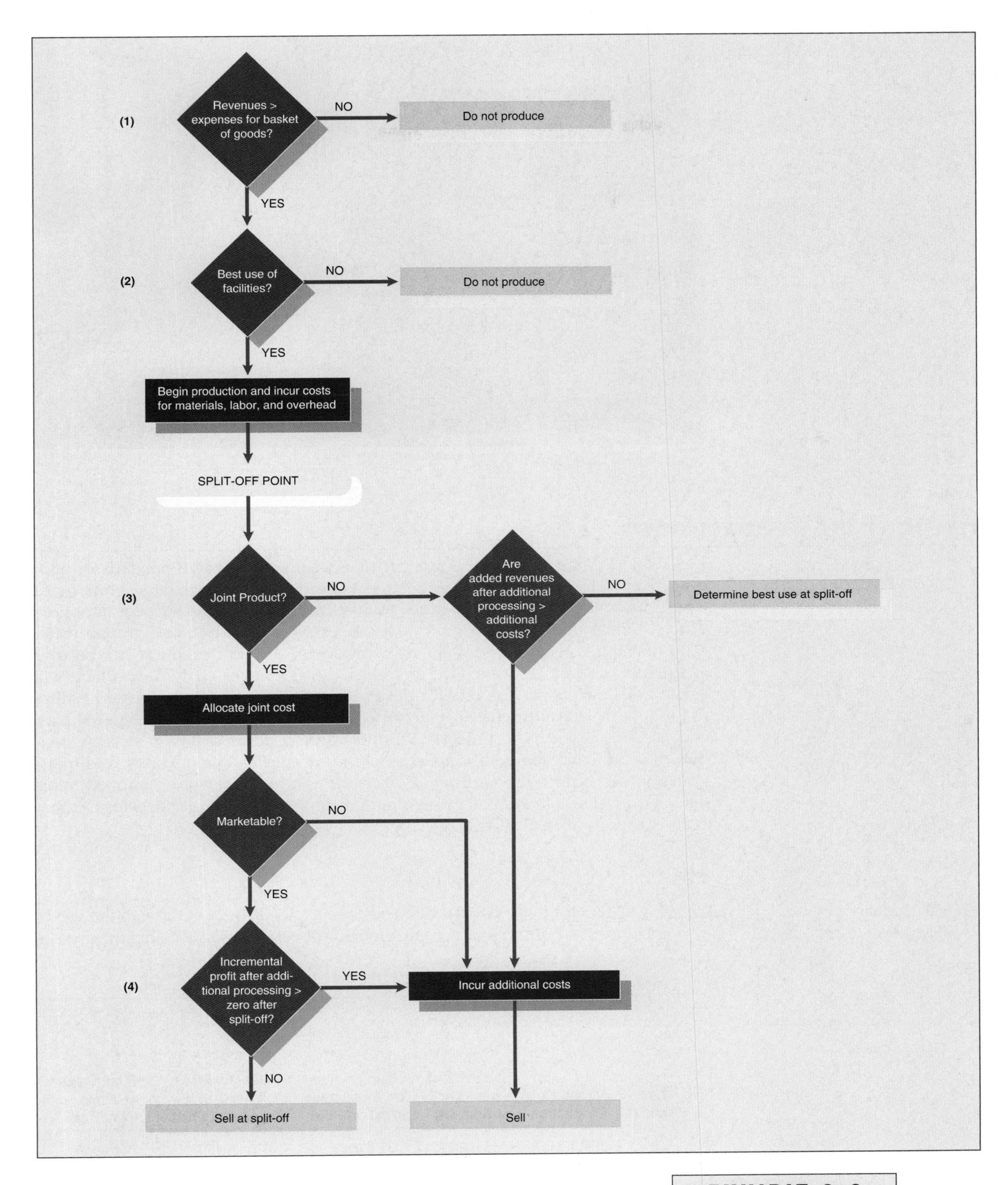

EXHIBIT 9–3

Decision Points in a Joint Production Process

Melted wax can be made into scented or unscented candles as well as into candles of different sizes and shapes, with or without a container. The cost of getting the wax to this stage is a joint cost that should be allocated among the types of products to be manufactured.

ALLOCATION OF JOINT COST

4

How are joint costs allocated to products?

Delectable Edibles Company is used to demonstrate alternative methods of allocating joint processing cost. Because the consumer market for large portions of large farm animals is limited, Delectable Edibles processes sides of beef into three distinct primary products during a joint process: steaks, roasts, and ground meat. (The remaining parts are considered by-products.) All joint products can be sold at split-off. Alternatively, each beef product can be processed further, which will create additional separate costs for the products. Steaks can be processed further to produce steak sandwiches; roasts can be processed further to make special cuts; and ground meat can be processed further to be used as part of a sausage mixture. Certain marketing and disposal costs for advertising, commissions, and transportation are incurred regardless of when the products are sold. Assumed information on Delectable Edibles' processing operations and joint products for October 2000 is presented in Exhibit 9–4.

Physical Measure Allocation

physical measurement allocation

An easy, objective way to prorate joint cost at the split-off point is through the use of a physical measure. **Physical measurement allocation** uses a common physical

EXHIBIT 9–4

Basic Joint Cost Information

Joint processing cost for period: $5,400,000

(1) Joint Products	(2) Tons of Production	(3) Sales Price per Ton at Split-Off	(4) Selling Cost per Ton Regardless of When Sold	(5) Separate Cost per Ton if Processed Further	(6) Final Sales Price per Ton
Steaks	3,800	$2,800	$200	$100	$3,200
Roasts	2,400	1,800	100	100	2,100
Ground	2,800	1,200	50	60	1,500

characteristic of the joint products as the proration base. All joint products must be measurable by the same characteristic, such as

- tons of ore in the mining industry,
- linear board feet in the lumber milling industry,
- barrels of oil in the petroleum refining industry,
- tons of meat, bone, and hide in the meat packing or processing industry, or
- number of computer chips in the semiconductor industry.

Using physical measurement allocation, Delectable Edibles' $5,400,000 of joint cost is assigned as shown in Exhibit 9–5. For Delectable Edibles, physical measurement allocation would assign a cost of approximately $600 ($5,400,000 ÷ 9,000 tons) per ton of beef, regardless of type.

Physical measurement allocation treats each unit of output as equally desirable and assigns the same per-unit cost to each. Also, unlike monetary measures, physical measures provide an unchanging yardstick of output.[4] A ton of output produced from a process 10 years ago is the same measurement as a ton produced from that process today. Physical measures are useful in allocating joint cost to products that have extremely unstable selling prices. These measures are also necessary in rate-regulated industries that use cost to determine selling prices. For example, assume that a rate-regulated company has the right to set selling price at 20 percent above cost. It is circular logic to allocate joint cost based on selling prices that were set based on cost to produce the output.

A major disadvantage of allocating joint cost based on a physical measure is that the method ignores the revenue-generating ability of individual joint products. Products that weigh the most or that are produced in the largest quantity will receive the highest proportion of joint cost allocation—regardless of their ability to bear that cost when they are sold. In the case of Delectable Edibles, each ton of ground has been assigned a cost of $600. However, computations will demonstrate that ground generates the lowest gross profit of the three joint products and yet is being assigned the same joint cost per ton as the more desirable steaks and roasts.

Monetary Measure Allocation

All commonly used allocation methods employ a process of proration. Because of the simplicity of the physical measure allocation process, a detailed proration

EXHIBIT 9–5

Joint Cost Allocation Based on Physical Measurement

Cost per Physical Measure = Total Joint Cost ÷ Total Units of Physical Measurement
= $5,400,000 ÷ 9,000 tons = $600

Joint Product	Cost per Ton	Total per Ton	Allocated Cost
Steaks	3,800	$600	$2,280,000
Roasts	2,400	600	1,440,000
Ground	2,800	600	1,680,000
Total	9,000		$5,400,000

[4] There are occasional exceptions to the belief that physical measures provide an unchanging yardstick of output. To illustrate, many grocery products have been downsized in recent years. For example, coffee was formerly sold in one-pound containers; now it is customarily sold in 13-ounce packages.

scheme was unnecessary. However, the following steps can be used to prorate joint cost to joint products in the more complex monetary measure allocations:

1. Choose a monetary allocation base.
2. List the values that comprise the base for each joint product.
3. Sum the values in step 2 to obtain a total value for the list.
4. Divide each individual value in step 2 by the total in step 3 to obtain a numerical proportion for each value. The sum of these proportions should total 1.00 or 100 percent.[5]
5. Multiply the joint cost by each proportion to obtain the amount to be allocated to each product.
6. Divide the prorated joint cost for each product by the number of equivalent units of production for each product to obtain a cost per EUP for valuation purposes.

The primary benefit of monetary measure allocations over physical measure allocations is that the former recognizes the relative ability of each product to generate a profit at sale.[6] A problem with monetary measure allocations is that the basis used is not constant or unchanging. Because of fluctuations in general and specific price levels, a dollar's worth of output today is different from a dollar's worth of output from the same process five years ago. However, accountants customarily ignore price level fluctuations when recording or processing data; in effect, this particular flaw of monetary measures is not usually viewed as significant.

Three of the many monetary measures that can be used to allocate joint cost to primary output are presented in this text. These measures are sales value at split-off, net realizable value at split-off, and approximated net realizable value at split-off.

SALES VALUE AT SPLIT-OFF

sales value at split-off allocation

The **sales value at split-off allocation** assigns joint cost to joint products based solely on the relative sales values of the products at the split-off point. Thus, to use this method, all joint products must be marketable at split-off. Exhibit 9–6 shows how Delectable Edibles' joint cost is assigned to production using the sales value at split-off allocation method. Under this method, the low selling price per ton of ground, relative to the other joint products, results in a lower allocated cost per ton than resulted from the physical measure allocation technique. This process uses a weighting technique based on both quantity produced and selling price of production.

EXHIBIT 9–6

Joint Cost Allocation Based on Sales Value at Split-Off

Joint Product	Tons	Selling Price	Revenue	Decimal Fraction	Joint Cost	Amount Allocated	Cost per Ton
Steaks	3,800	$2,800	$10,640,000	0.58	$5,400,000	$3,132,000	$824.21
Roasts	2,400	1,800	4,320,000	0.24	5,400,000	1,296,000	540.00
Ground	2,800	1,200	3,360,000	0.18	5,400,000	972,000	347.14
Total	9,000		$18,320,000	1.00		$5,400,000	

[5] Using decimal fractions often requires rounding. Greater precision can be obtained by simply dividing each step 2 value by the step 3 value, leaving the result in the calculator, and multiplying that resulting value by the total joint cost.

[6] Monetary measures are more reflective of the primary reason a joint process is undertaken: profit. Physical base allocations are sometimes of dubious value because they are based on the flawed assumption that all physical units are equally desirable.

NET REALIZABLE VALUE AT SPLIT-OFF

net realizable value at split-off allocation

The **net realizable value at split-off allocation** method assigns joint cost based on the joint products' proportional net realizable values at the point of split-off. Net realizable value (NRV) is equal to product sales revenue at split-off minus any costs necessary to prepare and dispose of the product. This method requires that all joint products be marketable at the split-off point, and it considers the additional costs that must be incurred at split-off to realize the estimated sales revenue. The costs at split-off point for Delectable Edibles' products are shown in the fourth column of Exhibit 9–4. The net realizable value of each product is computed by subtracting the cost at split-off from the selling price at split-off. The $5,400,000 joint cost is then assigned based on each product's relative proportion of total net realizable value (Exhibit 9–7). This method provides an allocated product cost that considers the disposal costs that would be necessitated if the product were to be sold at split-off.

APPROXIMATED NET REALIZABLE VALUE AT SPLIT-OFF

approximated net realizable value at split-off allocation

incremental separate cost

Often, some or all of the joint products are not salable at the split-off point. For these products to be sold, additional processing must take place after split-off, causing additional costs to be incurred. Because of this lack of marketability at split-off, neither the sales value nor the net realizable value approach can be used. **Approximated net realizable value at split-off allocation** requires that a *simulated* net realizable value at the split-off point be calculated.[7] This approximated value is computed on a per-product basis as final sales price minus incremental separate costs. **Incremental separate costs** refers to all costs that are incurred between the split-off point and the point of sale. The approximated net realizable values are then used to distribute joint cost proportionately. An underlying assumption of this method is that the incremental revenue from further processing is equal to or greater than the incremental cost of further processing and selling. Approximated net realizable values at split-off are determined for each product processed by Delectable Edibles using the information in Exhibit 9–4.

Joint Products	Final Selling Price per Ton	Separate Costs per Ton after Split-Off	Approximated Net Realizable Value at Split-Off
Steaks	$3,200	$300	$2,900
Roasts	2,100	200	1,900
Ground	1,500	110	1,390

Further processing should be undertaken only if the incremental revenues will exceed the incremental costs.[8] These computations are shown on the next page.

EXHIBIT 9–7

Joint Cost Allocation Based on Net Realizable Value at Split-Off

Joint Product	Tons	Unit Net Realizable Value per Ton	Total Net Realizable Value	Decimal Fraction	Joint Cost	Amount Allocated	Cost per Ton
Steaks	3,800	$2,600	$ 9,880,000	0.57	$5,400,000	$3,078,000	$810.00
Roasts	2,400	1,700	4,080,000	0.24	5,400,000	1,296,000	540.00
Ground	2,800	1,150	3,220,000	0.19	5,400,000	1,026,000	366.43
Total	9,000		$17,180,000	1.00		$5,400,000	

[7] Another name for this method is the "artificial net realizable value at split-off allocation."

[8] Because some products will not be processed further, the approximated NRV at split-off method sometimes cannot be used by itself and is combined with the NRV at split-off method to form a hybrid method.

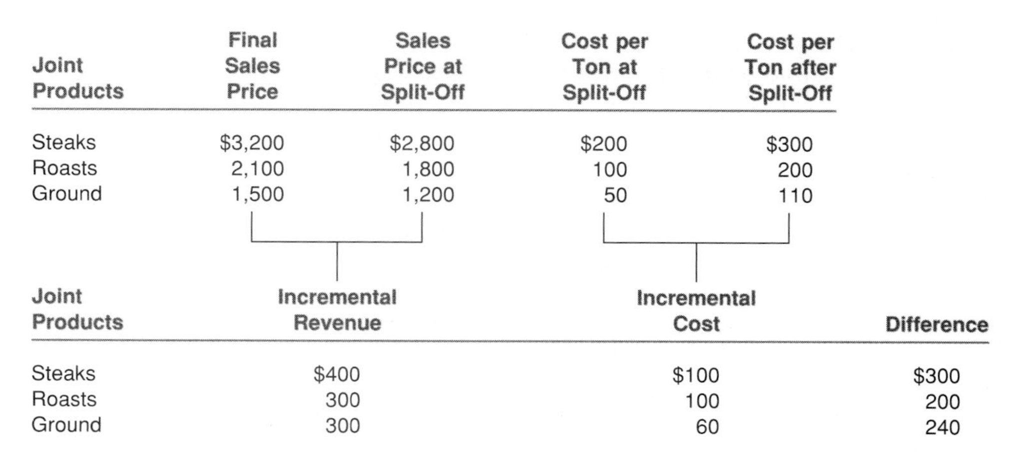

Joint Products	Final Sales Price	Sales Price at Split-Off	Cost per Ton at Split-Off	Cost per Ton after Split-Off
Steaks	$3,200	$2,800	$200	$300
Roasts	2,100	1,800	100	200
Ground	1,500	1,200	50	110

Joint Products	Incremental Revenue	Incremental Cost	Difference
Steaks	$400	$100	$300
Roasts	300	100	200
Ground	300	60	240

The previous information shows that Delectable Edibles will be better off if all of the joint products are processed further than if they are sold at split-off. For all products, the incremental revenues from further processing exceed the incremental costs beyond split-off. The same conclusion can be reached by comparing the net realizable values at split-off with the approximated net realizable values at split-off, as follows:

Joint Products	Net Realizable Value at Split-Off	Approximated Net Realizable Value at Split-Off	Difference
Steaks	$2,600	$2,900	$300
Roasts	1,700	1,900	200
Ground	1,150	1,390	240

The decisions made about further processing affect the values used to allocate joint cost in the approximated net realizable sales value method. If one or more products will not be processed further because it is uneconomical to do so, the value base used for allocation of joint cost will be a mixture of actual and approximated net realizable values at split-off. Products that will not be processed further will be valued at their actual net realizable values at split-off; products that will be processed further are valued at approximated net realizable values at split-off. However, using a mixed base is unnecessary in this case because all products are to be processed further. Delectable Edibles' $5,400,000 joint cost is allocated among the products as shown in Exhibit 9–8.

Each of the physical and monetary measures discussed allocates a different amount of joint cost to joint products and results in a different per-unit cost for each product. Each method has advantages and disadvantages. For most companies, approximated net realizable value at split-off provides the best joint cost assignment. This method is the most flexible in that no requirements exist about similar

EXHIBIT 9–8

Joint Cost Allocation Based on Approximated Net Realizable Value at Split-Off

Joint Products	Tons	Approximated Net Realizable Value per Ton	Total Approximated Net Realizable Value	Decimal Fraction	Joint Cost	Amount Allocated	Cost per Ton
Steaks	3,800	$2,900	$11,020,000	0.57	$5,400,000	$3,078,000	$810.00
Roasts	2,400	1,900	4,560,000	0.23	5,400,000	1,242,000	517.50
Ground	2,800	1,390	3,892,000	0.20	5,400,000	1,080,000	385.71
Total	9,000		$19,472,000	1.00		$5,400,000	

measurement bases (pounds, tons, etc.) or actual marketability at split-off. It is, however, more complex than the other methods, because estimations must be made about additional processing costs and potential future sales values.

The values obtained from the approximated net realizable value at split-off allocation method are used to illustrate cost flows in a joint cost environment. Delectable Edibles has four production departments: (1) Meat Processing, (2) Steak Filleting Production (using selected cuts of steak), (3) Marinating Cuts Production (using roasts), and (4) Sausage Production (using ground). Work performed in each of the second, third, and fourth departments creates finished products that have been further processed beyond the split-off point. All of the rest of the production in the Meat Processing Department, referred to as First Cuts, Roasts, and Ground, is sold immediately at the split-off point. Delectable Edibles uses FIFO costing and had the following finished goods inventories at the beginning of April:

Filet mignon	260 tons @ $900 per ton	$234,000
Marinated cuts	280 tons @ $580 per ton	162,400
Sausage	300 tons @ $420 per ton	126,000

During April, the company incurred separate costs for Filets, Marinated Cuts, and Sausage of $186,000, $122,000, and $83,406, respectively. All of the products started into processing in April were also completed during that month. The company sold the following quantities of products in April:

Product	Quantity	Sales Price per Ton	Total Sales Price (Cash)
First cut steaks	1,794 tons	$2,800	$ 5,023,200
Roasts	1,160 tons	1,800	2,088,000
Ground	1,260 tons	1,200	1,512,000
Filet mignon	1,986 tons	3,400	6,752,400
Marinated cuts	1,220 tons	2,200	2,684,000
Sausage	1,500 tons	1,500	2,250,000
Totals	8,920		$20,309,600

The April 2000 journal entries for Delectable Edibles Company are shown in Exhibit 9–9 on page 356. The ending balances of Delectable Edibles' three finished goods accounts are computed as follows:

	TONS		
	Filets	**Marinated Cuts**	**Sausage**
Beginning inventory	260	280	300
Tons completed (assumed)	2,006	1,240	1,540
Tons available	2,266	1,520	1,840
Tons sold	1,986	1,220	1,500
Ending inventory	280	300	340
× FIFO unit costs	$ 902.72[a]	$ 615.89[b]	$ 439.87[c]
EI valued at FIFO costs	$252,762	$184,767	$149,556

[a]($186,000 ÷ 2,006 tons) + $810.00 allocated joint cost = $902.72
[b]($122,000 ÷ 1,240 tons) + $517.50 allocated joint cost = $615.89
[c]($83,406 ÷ 1,540 tons) + $385.71 allocated joint cost = $439.87 (rounded)

These ending inventory unit values represent approximate actual costs of production.

Prorating joint cost provides necessary inventory valuations for manufacturing companies. However, the allocation process may be influenced by the net realizable values of the other possible outputs of a joint process—by-products and scrap.

EXHIBIT 9–9

Journal Entries for April 2000

	Account	Debit	Credit
(1)	Work in Process Inventory—Meat Processing	5,400,000	
	Supplies Inventory		185,714
	Wages Payable		3,900,000
	Manufacturing Overhead		1,314,286
	To record joint process costs incurred in April 2000; credit amounts are assumed.		
(2)	Work in Process Inventory—Filets	1,624,860	
	Work in Process Inventory—Marinated Cuts	641,700	
	Work in Process Inventory—Sausage	594,000	
	Work in Process Inventory—Meat Processing		2,860,560
	To allocate some of the joint cost incurred in Meat Processing to other departments for filleting, marinating, and making sausage.		
(3)	Work in Process Inventory—Filets	186,000	
	Work in Process Inventory—Marinated Cuts	122,000	
	Work in Process Inventory—Sausage	83,406	
	Various accounts		391,406
	To record separate costs for further processing incurred in the Filets, Marinated Cuts, and Sausage Production Departments.		
(4)	Finished Goods Inventory—First Cuts	1,453,140	
	Finished Goods Inventory—Roasts	600,300	
	Finished Goods Inventory—Ground	486,000	
	Finished Goods Inventory—Filets	1,810,860	
	Finished Goods Inventory—Marinated Cuts	763,700	
	Finished Goods Inventory—Sausage	677,400	
	Work in Process Inventory—Meat Processing		2,539,440
	Work in Process Inventory—Filets		1,810,860
	Work in Process Inventory—Marinating		763,700
	Work in Process Inventory—Sausage		677,400
	To transfer 9,000 tons of meats to finished goods status: (1,794 tons of First Cuts × $810.00), (1,160 tons of Roasts × $517.50), (1,260 tons of Ground × $385.714), (2,006 tons of Filets—$1,624,860 + $186,000), (1,240 tons of marinated cuts—$641,700 + $122,000), and (1,500 tons of sausage—$594,000 + $83,400).		
(5)	Cash	20,309,600	
	Sales		20,309,600
	To record cash sales.		
(6)	Cost of Goods Sold	5,726,721	
	Finished Goods Inventory—First Cuts		1,453,140
	Finished Goods Inventory—Roasts		600,300
	Finished Goods Inventory—Ground		486,000
	Finished Goods Inventory—Filets		1,792,098
	Finished Goods Inventory—Marinated Cuts		741,333
	Finished Goods Inventory—Sausage		653,850
	To record cost of goods sold on a FIFO basis.		
(7)	Selling Expenses	1,132,000	
	Cash		1,132,000
	To record selling expenses ($200 × 3,780) + ($100 × 2,380) + ($50 × 2,760). (Actual costs are assumed to equal estimated selling costs shown in Exhibit 9–4.)		

ACCOUNTING FOR BY-PRODUCTS AND SCRAP

5

How are by-products treated in accounting systems?

Because the distinction between by-products and scrap is one of degree, these categories have been discussed together by presenting several of the many treatments found in practice. The appropriate choice of method depends on the magnitude of the net realizable value of the by-products/scrap and the need for additional processing after split-off. As the sales value of the by-product/scrap increases, so does the need for inventory recognition. Sales value of the by-products/scrap is generally recorded under either the (1) net realizable value approach or (2) realized value approach. These approaches are discussed in the following sections using additional data for Ballad Beef Company, which considers cow hooves (sold as dog chews) as a by-product. Data for April 2000 are shown in Exhibit 9–10.

EXHIBIT 9–10

April 2000 Data for By-Product

Total processing for month: 9,000 tons of beef

Cow hooves (by-product) included in production: 25,000 pounds
Selling price of cow hooves: $1 per pound
Processing costs per pound of cow hooves: $0.10 for labor and $0.05 for overhead
Net realizable value per pound of cow hooves: $0.85

Net Realizable Value Approach

net realizable value approach

Use of the **net realizable value** (or offset) **approach** requires that the net realizable value of the by-product/scrap be treated as a reduction in the joint cost of manufacturing primary products. This method is normally used when the net realizable value of the by-product or scrap is expected to be significant.

Under the net realizable value approach, an inventory value is recorded that equals the selling price of the by-product/scrap produced minus the related processing, storing, and disposing costs. Any income remaining after covering these costs is used to reduce the joint cost of the main products. Any loss generated by the by-product/scrap is added to the cost of the main products. The credit for this Work in Process Inventory debit may be to one of two accounts. First, under the indirect method, Cost of Goods Sold for the joint products is reduced when the by-product/scrap is generated and joint products are sold:

Work in Process Inventory—Cow hooves	21,250	
Cost of Goods Sold—Main Products		21,250

When additional costs are incurred:

Work in Process Inventory—Cow hooves	3,750	
Various accounts		3,750

When by-product is completed:

Finished Goods Inventory—Cow hooves	25,000	
Work in Process Inventory—Cow hooves		25,000

When by-product is sold:

Cash (or Accounts Receivable)	25,000	
Finished Goods Inventory—Cow hooves		25,000

This technique may result in a slight mismatching of costs if by-products are created in a different period from when joint products are sold. Also, inventory values for the main products will be slightly overstated.

Alternatively, under the direct method, the work in process (WIP) joint cost of the primary products is reduced by the net realizable value of the by-product/scrap produced. Reducing WIP joint cost causes the costs of the primary products to be lowered for both cost of goods sold and inventory purposes. Thus, the only change in the preceding journal entries would be on the date the by-product was generated. The direct approach journal entry at that time is

Work in Process Inventory—Cow hooves	21,250	
Work in Process Inventory—Main Products		21,250

The major advantage of the direct approach is timing. The reduction in main products' joint cost is accomplished simultaneously with production of the main products. The disadvantage of this approach is that it is less conservative than waiting to record revenues until the by-product or scrap is actually sold, as does the realized value approach presented in the next section.

By-products and scrap may have sales potential beyond that currently known to management. Although reducing joint cost by the net realizable value of by-products/scrap is the traditional method of accounting for these goods, it is not necessarily the best method for managerial decision making.

Financial accounting methods used are frequently not geared toward providing information useful to management of by-products. By-products can be treated as either having no assignable cost or as having costs equal to their net sales value. However, in cases in which management considers the by-product to be a moderate source of income, the accounting and reporting methods used should help managers monitor production and further processing of the by-product and make effective decisions regarding this resource.[9]

The net realizable value method does not indicate the sales dollars, expenses, or profits from the by-product/scrap and, thus, does not provide sufficient information to induce management to maximize the inflows from by-product/scrap disposal.

Realized Value Approach

realized value approach

Under the **realized value** (or other income) **approach**, no value is recognized for the by-products/scrap until they are sold. This method is the simplest approach to accounting for by-products/scrap. Several reporting techniques can be used with the realized value approach. One presentation shows total sales of the by-product/scrap on the income statement under an "Other Revenue" caption. Costs of additional processing or disposal of the by-product/scrap are included with the cost of producing the main products. This presentation provides little useful information to management because the costs of producing the by-products/scrap are not matched with the revenues generated by those items.

For the Ballad Beef Company, the entries under the "Other Revenue" method are as follows when labor and overhead costs are incurred:

Work in Process Inventory—Joint Products	2,500	
Manufacturing Overhead	1,250	
Various accounts		3,750
To record the labor cost of grinding and of overhead charges to WIP Inventory for cow hooves (all included in the cost of joint products).		

At point of sale:

Cash (or Accounts Receivable)	25,000	
Other Revenue		25,000
To record sale of cow hooves.		

[9] Advances in technology and science have turned many previous "scrap" items or "by-products" into demand products. Management should not ignore the significance of such products and should seek new uses or markets for them.

Another presentation shows by-product/scrap revenue on the income statement net of additional costs of processing and disposal. This method presents the net by-product revenue as an enhancement of net income in the period of sale under an "Other Income" caption. Such a presentation allows management to recognize the dollar benefit added to company income by managing the costs and revenues related to the by-products/scrap. The entries for the processing and sale of the by-products/scrap under this method for the Ballad Beef Company are as follows when labor and overhead costs are incurred:

Work in Process Inventory—Cow hooves	3,750	
Various accounts		3,750
To record the labor cost of grinding and of overhead charges for cow hooves; this assumes that overhead charges are applied to WIP (with a corresponding credit to Manufacturing Overhead included in the various accounts).		

At point of sale:

Cash (or Accounts Receivable)	25,000	
Work in Process Inventory—Cow hooves		3,750
Other Income		21,250
To record sale of cow hooves net of processing/disposal costs.		

Because the "Other Income" method matches by-product/scrap revenue with related storage, further processing, transportation, and disposal costs, this method provides detailed information on financial responsibility and accountability for disposition, provides better control, and may improve performance. Managers are more apt to look for new or expanded sales potential because the net benefits of doing so are shown directly on the income statement.

Other alternative presentations include showing the realized value from the sale of the by-product/scrap as (1) an addition to gross margin, (2) a reduction of the cost of goods manufactured, or (3) a reduction of the cost of goods sold. The major advantage of these simplistic approaches is that of clerical efficiency.

Regardless of whether a company uses the net realizable value or the realized value approach, the specific method used to account for by-product/scrap should be established before the joint cost is allocated to the primary products. Exhibit 9–11 presents four comparative income statements using different methods of accounting for by-product income for the Ballad Beef Company. Some assumed amounts have been included to provide complete income statements.

EXHIBIT 9–11

Comparative Income Statement By-Product Presentations

(a) Net Realizable Approach: Reduce CGS			(b) Net Realizable Approach: Reduce CGM		
Sales		$6,200,000	Sales		$6,200,000
Cost of goods sold			Cost of goods sold		
Beginning FG	$ 400,000		Beginning FG	$ 400,000	
CGM	3,600,000		CGM ($3,600,000 − $21,250)	3,578,750	
CGA	$4,000,000		CGA	$3,978,750	
Ending FG	(380,000)		Ending FG [assumed to be smaller than under (a)]	(377,690)	(3,601,060)
Unadjusted CGS	$3,620,000		Gross margin		$2,598,940
NRV of by-product	(21,250)	(3,598,750)	Operating expenses		(2,600,000)
Gross margin		$2,601,250			
Operating expenses		(2,600,000)			
Income from principal operations		$ 1,250	Loss from principal operations		$ (1,060)
Other income			Other income		
Commissions		80,000	Commissions		80,000
Income before income taxes		$ 81,250	Income before income taxes		$ 78,940

(continued)

(c) Net Realized Value Approach: Increase Revenue

Sales		$6,200,000
Other revenue		
By-product sales		25,000
Total revenue		$6,225,000
Cost of goods sold		
Beginning FG	$ 400,000	
CGS (main products)	3,600,000	
CGS (processing by-product)	3,750	
CGA	$4,003,750	
Ending FG	(380,000)	(3,623,750)
Gross margin		$2,601,250
Operating expenses		(2,600,000)
Income from principal operations		$ 1,250
Other income		
Commissions		80,000
Income before income taxes		$ 81,250

(d) Net Realized Value Approach: Present as Other Income

Sales		$6,200,000
Cost of goods sold		
Beginning FG	$ 400,000	
CGM	3,600,000	
CGA	$4,000,000	
Ending FG	(380,000)	(3,620,000)
Gross margin		$2,580,000
Operating expenses		(2,600,000)
Loss from principal operations		$ (20,000)
Other income		
Commissions	$ 80,000	
By-product sales (NRV)	21,250	101,250
Income before income taxes		$ 81,250

EXHIBIT 9-11

(Concluded)

By-products, scrap, and waste are created in all types of businesses, not just manufacturing. Managers may not see the need to determine the cost of these secondary types of products. However, as discussed in Chapters 7 and 8, the importance of cost of quality information has only recently been recognized. Many companies are becoming aware of the potential value of scrap as a substantial source of revenue and are devoting time and attention to exploiting it. Sometimes old dreams of using scrap take on new energy as technology progresses. The accompanying News Note on page 361 is an example.

BY-PRODUCTS OR SCRAP IN JOB ORDER COSTING

Although joint products normally are not associated with job order costing systems, these systems may have by-products or scrap. Either the realized value approach or the net realizable value approach can be used with regard to the timing of recognition of the value of by-product/scrap.

The value of by-product/scrap in a job order system is appropriately credited to either manufacturing overhead or to the specific jobs in process. The former account is credited if by-product/scrap value is generally created by a significant proportion of all jobs undertaken. In contrast, if only a few or specific jobs generate a substantial amount of by-product/scrap, then individual jobs should be credited with the value because they directly generated the by-product/scrap.

To illustrate, assume that Versatile Foods occasionally prepares special meat-based foods for several large institutional clients. Recently, the company received an order for 20,000 beef patties from the Crestview Senior High School. As the patties are prepared, some scrap meat is generated. During October 2000, Versatile Foods sold $250 of scrap meat to the Canine Catering Corporation. The entry to record the sale, using the realized value approach, is

Cash	250	
Manufacturing Overhead		250

In contrast, assume that Versatile Foods Company seldom has salable scrap on its jobs. However, during October 2000, Versatile Foods contracted with the Green

QUALITY  **NEWS NOTE**

Get a Load of This!

Two of our most pressing concerns are the development of alternatives to our heavy reliance on fossil fuels and nuclear power, and what to do with the waste that we continue to generate in ever increasing amounts.

Working on the "where there's muck, there's brass" principle, three power stations in the eastern counties of England have taken this to a logical conclusion. Bernard Matthews and producers of his ilk have an awful lot of poultry, which in turn produce copious amounts of waste. This waste has traditionally been ploughed in as manure but the storage and spreading is a messy business. Waterways may become polluted with run-off from fields treated in this way. Given that animals are relatively inefficient converters of the energy in their foodstuff into meat, there is, so far, untapped energy in their manure. Much of the energy still present can be released by burning the stuff.

The technology is not exactly radical and has been refined with each new station built. (Italy is the only other country in on the "poultry power" act.) Its environmentally friendly credentials are good, producing less of the gases that contribute to acid rain compared to burning coal, gas or oil. Although the greenhouse gas CO_2 is released, this is not an additional load to the atmosphere, as it represents gas absorbed during photosynthesis by the plants which then became foodstuff or bedding for the poultry.

Together, the three stations have a power output of just under 65 megawatts (65 million watts). This would satisfy the electricity demand of a town the size of Nottingham. The power output is modest compared to the 1,000 MW plus of an average coal-fired or nuclear power station, but is not a bad return on 3/4 million tons of poultry waste each year. An ash by-product is marketed as a fertilizer, making the whole enterprise even more economically viable.

Despite the "green" credentials and a secure, plentiful supply of poultry litter, we are unlikely to see many more poultry waste power stations built. This is not because of the cost of building them or any political considerations, but for an altogether more pragmatic reason. The stench of burning poultry manure is not even an acquired taste. Think of the "country smell" that townies find so abhorrent and then imagine it a hundred times worse. Give me a nuclear power station in my backyard any day.

SOURCE: Anonymous, "Poultry Poo," www.zyworld.com/frncs/Poultry_Poo (December 31, 1999) p. 1.

Cove Convalescent Centers to prepare 25,000 frozen chicken croquettes. Specific raw material had to be acquired for the job because Versatile Foods normally does not process chicken. Thus, all raw material costs will be charged directly to the Green Cove Convalescent Centers. As the chicken is prepared for the order, some scraps are generated that can be sold to the Chicken Soup Cannery for $375. Because the cost of the material is directly related to this job, the sale of the scrap from that raw material also relates to the specific job. Under these circumstances, the production of the scrap is recorded (using the net realizable value approach) as follows:

Scrap Inventory—Chicken	375	
Work in Process Inventory—Green Cove Centers		375

In this case, the net realizable value approach is preferred because of the timing of recognition. To affect the specific job cost that caused an unusual incidence and amount of scrap, it may be necessary to recognize the by-product/scrap on production; otherwise, the job may be completed before a sale of the by-product/scrap can be made.

Manufacturing processes frequently create the need to allocate costs. However, some costs incurred in service businesses and not-for-profit organizations may be allocated among product lines, organizational locations, or types of activities performed by the organizations.

JOINT COSTS IN SERVICE AND NOT-FOR-PROFIT ORGANIZATIONS

6

How should not-for-profit organizations account for joint costs?

Service and not-for-profit organizations may incur joint costs for advertising multiple products, printing multipurpose documents, or holding multipurpose events. For example, not-for-profit entities often issue brochures containing information about the organization, its purposes, and its programs; simultaneously, these documents make an appeal for funds.

If a service business decides to allocate a joint cost, either a physical or monetary allocation base can be chosen. Joint costs in service businesses often relate to advertisements rather than to processes. For example, a local bicycle and lawnmower repair company may advertise a sale and list all store locations in a single newspaper ad. The ad cost could be allocated equally to all locations or be based on sales volume for each location during the period of the sale. Alternatively, a grocery delivery service may deliver several customers' orders on the same trip. The cost of the trip could be allocated based on the number of bags or the pounds of food delivered for each customer.

Service businesses may decide that allocating joint costs is not necessary. Not-for-profit organizations, however, are required under the American Institute of Certified Public Accountants (AICPA) Statement of Position (SOP) 98-2 to allocate joint costs among the activities of fundraising, accomplishing an organizational program, or conducting an administrative function.[10] A major purpose of SOP 98-2 is to ensure that external users of financial statements are able to clearly determine amounts spent by the organization for various activities—especially fundraising. Thus, SOP 98-2 provides guidance on allocating and reporting these costs.

http://www.arthurandersen.com

[10] AICPA Accounting Standards Executive Committee, *Statement of Position 98-2: Accounting for Costs of Activities of Not-for-Profit Organizations and State and Local Governmental Entities That Include Fund Raising* (effective for years beginning on or after December 15, 1998).

REVISITING Buckhead Beef Company

http://www.buckheadbeef.com

To ensure customer satisfaction, Buckhead Beef employs Executive Chef Ray Farmer to assist clients. Also, about one-third of the company's 50-person sales team have culinary degrees.

Howard Halpern says of his company, "We are the back of the house for our customers who trust us to buy the right animal from the right part of the country and then to handle it properly. We either hold the meat to age it properly or send it to our cut shop for further processing."

Such is the role of Buckhead's skilled meat cutters. Managers at the company attribute their success in recruiting and training quality employees to wages above industry standards, offering a career not just a job, an impressive safety record, and antidrug and antiharassment policies.

The company also enjoys strong ties to its suppliers by treating its packers as partners. Buckhead buys truckload volumes of carcasses and boxed beef on contract, spot buying, and price programs. This keeps costs lower.

Halpern proudly discussed Buckhead's significant investment in 1998 in a special high-quality process for preparing beef when he said, "Last year we instituted a dry-aging process, which improves the flavor, juiciness and tenderness of our steaks up to 50%."

Buckhead Beef was chosen as an official supplier to the 1996 Atlanta Olympic Games. It was honored with an Atlanta 100 Award for the highest one-year growth from Arthur Andersen. The company was also recognized with the 1996 and 1997 National Beef Backer Award from the National Cattleman's Beef Association.

SOURCE: Adapted from Bob Swientek, "A Cut Above," *Prepared Foods* (October 1998), Rising Stars feature section; and Barbara Young-Huguenin, "Aged to Perfection," *The National Provisioner* (1998).

CHAPTER SUMMARY

Multiple products from a joint process are defined (based on market value) as joint products, by-products, and scrap. A residual product that has no market value is called waste. Joint process cost is allocated solely to joint products. However, before the allocation is made, the joint cost may be reduced by the net realizable value of by-products and/or scrap. Costs incurred after the split-off point(s) are traced directly to the products with which those costs are associated.

A multiple product setting has four decision points: (1) two before the joint process is started, (2) at a split-off point, and (3) after a split-off point. At any of these points, management should consider further processing only if it believes that the incremental revenues from proceeding will exceed the incremental costs of proceeding. How joint cost was allocated is irrelevant to these decisions because the joint cost is considered sunk and, therefore, unrecoverable.

All the commonly used techniques for allocating joint process cost to the joint products use proration. Allocation bases are classified as either physical or monetary. Physical measures provide an unchanging yardstick of output over time and treat each unit of product as equally desirable. Monetary measures, because of inflation, are a changing yardstick of output over time, but these measures consider the different market values of the individual joint products.

The realized value approach to accounting for by-products and scrap ignores the value of such output until it is sold. At that time, either revenue is recorded or by-product/scrap selling price is used to reduce the joint cost of production. Alternatively, when by-products or scrap are generated, the net realizable value of the by-products/scrap at the split-off point can be recorded in a special inventory account, and the production cost of the primary products can be reduced. Additional processing costs for the by-product/scrap are debited to the special inventory account. Regardless of the approach used, if joint cost is to be reduced by the value of the by-product/scrap, the method and value to be used must be determined before allocating the net joint processing cost to the primary products.

Joint costs can also be incurred in service businesses and not-for-profit organizations for some types of processes or for things such as communications instruments (brochures, media advertisements) that serve multiple purposes. Service businesses may allocate joint costs if they so desire. Not-for-profits must allocate joint costs among fundraising, program, and/or administrative activities based on some reasonable measure, such as percentage of space or time.

KEY TERMS

approximated net realizable value at split-off allocation (p. 353)
by-product (p. 344)
incremental separate cost (p. 353)
joint cost (p. 343)
joint process (p. 343)
joint product (p. 344)
net realizable value approach (p. 357)
net realizable value at split-off allocation (p. 353)
physical measurement allocation (p. 350)
realized value approach (p. 358)
sales value at split-off allocation (p. 352)
scrap (p. 344)
split-off point (p. 345)
sunk cost (p. 346)
waste (p. 344)

SOLUTION STRATEGIES

Allocation of Joint Cost

Joint cost is allocated only to joint products; however, joint cost can be reduced by the value of by-product/scrap before the allocation process begins.

For physical measure allocations: Divide joint cost by the products' total physical measurements to obtain a cost per unit of physical measure.

For monetary measure allocation:

1. Choose an allocation base.
2. List the values that comprise the allocation base for each joint process.
3. Sum the values in step 2.
4. Calculate the decimal fraction of value of the base to the total of all values in the base. The decimal fractions so derived should add to 100 percent or 1.00.
5. Multiply the total joint cost to be allocated by each of the decimal fractions to separate the total cost into prorated parts.
6. Divide the prorated joint cost for each product by the number of equivalent units of production for each product to obtain a cost per EUP for valuation purposes.

Allocation bases, measured at the split-off point, by which joint cost is prorated to the joint products include the following:

Type of Measure	Allocation Base
Physical output	Physical measurement of units of output (e.g., tons, feet, barrels, liters)
Monetary:	Currency units of value:
Sales value	Revenues of the several products
Net realizable value	Net realizable value of the several joint products
Approximated net realizable value	Approximated net realizable value of the several joint products (may be a hybrid measure)

DEMONSTRATION PROBLEM

Rolling Meadow Farms incurred $65,000 of production cost in 2000 in a joint process to grow a crop with two joint products, Alpha and Beta. The following are data related to 2000 operations:

(1) Joint Products	(2) Tons of Production	(3) Sales Price per Ton at Split-Off	(4) Per Ton Separate Costs if Sold at Split-Off	(5) Per Ton Separate Costs if Processed Further	(6) Per Ton Final Sales Price
Alpha	45	$ 950	$ 50	$236	$1,450
Beta	20	1,200	110	200	1,600

Required:

a. Allocate the joint process cost to Alpha and Beta using tons as the allocation base.

b. Allocate the joint process cost to Alpha and Beta using the sales values at split-off.

c. Allocate the joint process cost to Alpha and Beta using the net realizable values at split-off.

d. Allocate the joint process cost to Alpha and Beta using the approximated net realizable values at split-off.

Solution to Demonstration Problem

a. $65,000 ÷ 65 tons = $1,000 per ton

Product	Tons of Production	Cost per Ton	Allocation of Joint Cost
Alpha	45	$1,000	$45,000
Beta	20	1,000	20,000
Total	65		$65,000

b.

Product	Tons of Production	Sales Price at Split-Off	Sales Value	Decimal Fraction	Joint Cost	Allocation of Joint Cost
Alpha	45	$ 950	$42,750	0.64	$65,000	$41,600
Beta	20	1,200	24,000	0.36	65,000	23,400
Total	65		$66,750	1.00		$65,000

c.

Product	Tons of Production	Per Ton NRV at Split-Off	Total NRV at Split-Off	Decimal Fraction	Joint Cost	Allocation of Joint Cost
Alpha	45	$ 900	$40,500	0.65	$65,000	$42,250
Beta	20	1,090	21,800	0.35	65,000	22,750
Total	65		$62,300	1.00		$65,000

d.

Product	Tons of Production	Per Ton Approximated NRV	Total Approximated NRV	Decimal Fraction	Joint Cost	Allocation of Joint Cost
Alpha	45	$1,164	$52,380	0.67	$65,000	$43,550
Beta	20	1,290	25,800	0.33	65,000	21,450
Total	65		$78,180	1.00		$65,000

QUESTIONS

1. What is a joint production process? If managers wanted to produce only one of the main outputs of a joint process, could they? Explain. Give several examples of joint processes.

2. What are joint products, by-products, and scrap? How do they differ? Which of these product categories provides the greatest incentive or justification to produce?

3. How does management determine into which category to classify each type of output from a joint process? Is this decided before or after production?

4. When do the multiple products of a joint process gain separate identity? Does the joint process stop there?

5. How are separate costs distinguished from joint costs?

6. To which type of joint process output is joint cost allocated? Why? Is all of the joint process cost allocated to that type of output?

7. What are the decision points associated with multiple products? By what criteria would management assess whether to proceed at each point?

8. What is cost allocation and why is it necessary in a joint process? Can you think of any other situations in which accountants allocate costs?

9. What are the two primary methods used to allocate joint cost to joint products? Compare the advantages and disadvantages of each.

10. Why is it sometimes necessary to use approximated rather than actual net realizable values at split-off to allocate joint cost? How is this approximated value calculated?

11. Describe two common approaches used to account for by-products. Which do you think is best and why?

12. When are by-product or scrap costs considered in setting the predetermined overhead rate in a job order costing system? When are they not considered?

13. Why must not-for-profit organizations allocate joint costs among fundraising, program, and administrative activities?

14. Go to the Internet and find a discussion about the number of potential outputs of a peanut crop. Report your findings along with examples. Examine the relationship of your findings to accounting for joint products, by-products, and scrap.

EXERCISES

15. *(Terminology)* Match the following lettered terms on the left with the appropriate numbered description on the right.

a. Approximated sales value at split-off method
b. By-product
c. Incremental separate costs
d. Joint cost
e. Joint process
f. Joint product
g. Monetary measure allocation
h. Net realizable value
i. Physical measure allocation
j. Proration
k. Realized value approach
l. Sales value at split-off method
m. Scrap
n. Split-off point
o. Sunk cost
p. Waste

1. Proration of joint cost on nonmonetary basis
2. Proration of joint cost on basis of dollar values
3. Calculation employed by all commonly used allocation methods
4. Cost incurred to produce several products at the same time in one process
5. Residual output with no sales value
6. Production process yielding more than one product
7. Output that has sales value less than that of a by-product
8. Proration of joint cost on the basis of relative sales values of joint products at split-off
9. Material, labor, and overhead incurred in a joint process
10. Additional costs incurred between split-off point and sale
11. A cost that cannot change, no matter what course of future action is taken
12. Incidental output with value greater than scrap
13. Primary output of a joint process
14. Point at which outputs first become identifiable as individual products
15. A method that does not recognize by-product value until sale
16. Selling price less costs to complete and dispose

16. *(Joint process decision making)* Andrew Berwick has been asked by his aged aunt to take over the family butcher shop. Andrew has learned that you are majoring in accounting—he majored in art—and asks you to help him understand the butcher shop business. He wants you to do the following:

a. Explain, in nontechnical terms, what questions about joint processes someone who manages a butcher shop must answer. Also, indicate the points in a joint process at which these questions should be addressed.

b. Describe, in your own words, the proper managerial use of a joint cost; also, describe whether a joint cost may be used inappropriately and the basis on which you think a particular use is inappropriate.

c. Compare and contrast the various categories of outputs generated by a joint process.

17. *(Physical and sales value allocations)* Scott Community College runs two noncredit evening programs. During 2000, the following operating data were generated:

	Small Business Management	Introduction to Internet
Class hours taught	4,000	2,000
Hourly tuition	$5	$15

The general ledger accounts show $37,000 for direct instructional costs and $5,000 for overhead associated with these two programs. The Board of Trustees wants to know the cost of each program.

a. Determine the cost of each program using a physical measurement base.

b. Determine the cost of each program using the sales value at split-off method.

c. Make a case for each allocation method from parts (a) and (b).

18. *(Physical measure allocation)* Patterson Chemical Company uses a joint process to manufacture two chemicals. During October 2000, the company incurred $12,000,000 of joint production cost in producing 12,000 tons of Chemical A and 8,000 tons of Chemical B (a ton is equal to 2,000 pounds). Joint cost incurred by the company is allocated on the basis of tons of chemicals produced. Patterson Chemical is able to sell Chemical A at the split-off point for $0.50 per pound, or the chemical can be processed further at a cost of $1,500 per ton and then sold for $1.50 per pound. There is no opportunity for the company to further process Chemical B.

a. What amount of joint cost is allocated to Chemical A and to Chemical B?

b. If Chemical A is processed further and then sold, what is the incremental effect on Patterson Chemical Company's net income? Should the additional processing be performed?

19. *(Allocation of joint cost)* Nova Scotia Fish Processors produces three products from a common input: fish, fish oil, and fish meal. For June 2001, the firm produced the following average quantities of each product from each pound of fish processed:

Product	Obtained from Each Pound of Fish
Fish	8 ounces
Fish oil	4 ounces
Fish meal	2 ounces
Total	14 ounces

Note that 2 ounces of each pound (1 pound = 16 ounces) of fish processed is waste that has no market value. In June, the firm processed 50 tons of fish (one ton is equal to 2,000 pounds). Joint cost amounted to $95,200. On average, each pound of fish sells for $3; each pound of fish oil sells for $4; and each pound of fish meal sells for $2.

a. Allocate the joint cost using weight as the basis.

b. Allocate the joint cost using sales value as the basis.

c. Discuss the advantages and disadvantages of your answers to parts (a) and (b).

20. *(Sales value allocation)* Elsie Dairy produces milk and sour cream from a joint process. During May, the company produced 120,000 quarts of milk and 160,000 pints of sour cream. Sales value at split-off point was $50,000 for the milk and $110,000 for the sour cream. The milk was assigned $21,600 of the joint cost.

a. Using the sales value at split-off approach, what was the total joint cost for May?

b. Assume, instead, that the joint cost was allocated based on units (quarts) produced. What was the total joint cost incurred in May?

21. *(Net realizable value allocation)* Galaxy Communications is a broadband network and television company. The firm has three service groups: Communications, News, and Entertainment. Joint production costs (costs incurred for facilities, administration, and other) for May 2000 were $12,000,000. The revenues and separate production costs of each group for May follow:

	Communications	News	Entertainment
Revenues	$18,000,000	$15,000,000	$95,000,000
Separate costs	17,000,000	8,000,000	55,000,000

a. What amounts of joint cost are allocated to each service group using the net realizable value approach? Compute the profit for each group after the allocation.

b. What amount of joint cost is allocated to each service group if the allocation is based on revenues? Compute the profit for each group after the allocation.

c. Assume you are head of the Communications Group. Would the difference in allocation bases create significant problems for you when you report to Galaxy Communications' board of directors? Develop a short presentation to make to the board if the allocation base in part (b) is used to determine group relative profitability. Be certain to discuss important differences in revenues and cost figures between the Communications and Entertainment groups.

22. *(Approximated net realizable value method)* Avignon Parfum Compagnie makes three products that can either be sold, or processed further and then sold. The cost associated with the Avignon joint process is $120,000.

Product	Units of Output	Sales Prices at Split-Off	Separate Costs after Split-Off	Final Sales Price
Product 1	7,500	$3.00	$1.00	$4.25
Product 2	10,000	2.00	0.50	3.00
Product 3	12,500	2.00	0.75	3.00

Per unit, Product 1 weighs 3 ounces, Product 2 weighs 2 ounces, and Product 3 weighs 3 ounces. Assume that all additional processing is undertaken.

a. Allocate the joint cost based on the units of output, weight, and approximated net realizable values at split-off.

b. Assume all products are additionally processed and completed. At the end of the period, the inventories are as follows: Product 1, 500 units; Product 2, 1,000 units; Product 3, 1,500 units. Determine the values of the inventories based on answers obtained in part (a).

23. *(Processing beyond split-off and cost allocations)* Planetary Products has a joint process that makes three products. Joint cost for the process is $30,000.

Product	Units of Output	Per Unit Selling Price at Split-Off	Incremental Processing Costs	Final Sales Price
Sun	5,000	$2.00	$1.50	$3.00
Moon	10,000	1.00	2.00	6.00
Mars	250	1.50	0.20	1.80

Sun, Moon, and Mars weigh 10 pounds, 6 pounds, and 2 pounds, respectively.

a. Determine which products should be processed beyond the split-off point.

b. Determine whether Mars should be treated as a by-product. Allocate the joint processing cost based on units produced, weight, and approximated net realizable value at split-off. Use the net realizable value method in accounting for any by-products.

24. *(Sell or process further)* A certain joint process yields two joint products, A and B. The joint cost for May 2001 is $20,000, and the sales value of the output at split-off is $120,000 for Product A and $100,000 for Product B. Management is trying to decide whether to process the products further. If the products are processed beyond split-off, the final sales value will be $180,000 for Product A and $140,000 for Product B. The additional costs of processing are expected to be $40,000 for A and $34,000 for B.

a. Should management process the products further? Show computations.

b. Were any revenues and/or costs irrelevant to the decision? If so, what were they and why were they irrelevant?

25. *(Processing beyond split-off)* Crews Cannery makes three products in a single joint process. For 2000, the firm processed all three products beyond the split-off point. The following data are generated for the year:

Joint Product	Final Revenues	Incremental Separate Costs
Candied peaches	$62,000	$26,000
Peach jelly	74,000	38,000
Peach jam	27,000	15,000

Analysis of 2000 market data reveals that these three products could have been sold at split-off for $40,000, $40,000, and $10,000, respectively.

a. Evaluate, based on hindsight, management's production decisions in 2000.

b. How much additional profit could the company have generated in 2000 with a better ability to forecast prices?

26. *(Net realizable value method)* Ankara Processing produces three seafood products in a single process. The joint cost is $32,000.

Product	Units Produced	Unit Costs at Split-Off	Selling Price
X	9,000	$0.75	$4.00
Y	10,000	1.00	4.25
Z	1,000	0.10	0.50

a. Allocate the joint cost based on net realizable value at split-off. If necessary, use the net realizable value method for accounting for any by-products.

b. Determine the value of the inventory, assuming the following finished goods inventories:

Product	Units
X	600
Y	900
Z	54

27. *(By-product accounting method selection)* Your company engages in joint processes that produce significant quantities and types of by-products. You have been requested by the chairman of your company's board of directors to give a report to the board regarding making a good choice of accounting methods for by-products. Develop a set of criteria for making such a choice and provide reasons why each of the criteria has been selected. On the basis of your criteria, along with any additional assumptions you may wish to provide about the nature of your company, recommend a particular method of accounting for by-products and explain why you consider it to be better than the alternatives.

28. *(Monetary measure allocation)* Marianna Realty has two operating divisions: Leasing and Sales. In March 2001, the firm spent $100,000 for general company promotions (as opposed to advertisements promoting specific properties). Sally Savoie, the corporate controller, is now faced with the task of fairly allocating the promotion costs to the two operating divisions.

Sally has reduced the potential bases for allocating the promotion costs to two alternatives: the expected revenue to be generated from the promotions for each division, or the expected profit to be generated from the promotions in each division.

The promotions are expected to have the following effects on the two divisions:

	Leasing	Sales
Increase in revenue	$800,000	$1,600,000
Increase in net income before allocated promotion costs	150,000	100,000

a. Allocate the total promotion costs to the two divisions using change in revenue.
b. Allocate the total promotion costs to the two divisions using change in net income before joint cost allocation.
c. Which of the two approaches is most appropriate? Explain.

29. *(By-products and cost allocation)* Bayshore Manufacturing has a joint process that yields three products: M, N, and O. The company allocates the joint cost to the products on the basis of pounds of output. A particular joint process run cost $115,000 and yielded the following output by weight:

Product	Weight in Pounds
M	4,800
N	13,000
O	4,200

The run also produced by-products having a total net realizable value of $15,000. The company records by-product inventory at the time of production. Allocate the joint cost to the joint products.

30. *(Sell or process further)* Midwest Clothing produces three products (precut fabrics for hats, shirts, and pants) from a joint process. Joint cost is allocated on the basis of relative sales value at split-off. Rather than sell the products at split-off, the company has the option to complete each of the products. Information related to these products is shown below:

	Hats	Shirts	Pants	Total
Number of units produced	5,000	8,000	3,000	16,000
Joint cost allocated	$87,000	?	?	$180,000
Sales values at split-off point	?	?	$40,000	$300,000
Additional costs of processing further	$13,000	$10,000	$39,000	$62,000
Sales values after all processing	$150,000	$134,000	$105,000	$389,000

a. What amount of joint cost should be allocated to the Shirts and Pants products?
b. What are the sales values at split-off for Hats and Shirts?
c. Which products should be processed further? Show computations.
d. If 4,000 Shirts are processed further and sold for $67,000, what is gross profit on the sale?

31. *(By-products and cost allocation)* Bergen Productions produced two different movies from the same original footage (joint products). The company also generated revenue from admissions paid by fans touring the movie production set. Bergen regards the net income from tours as a by-product of movie production. The firm accounts for this income as a reduction in the joint cost before that joint cost is allocated to movies. The following information pertains to the two movies:

Products	Total Receipts	Separate Costs
Movie 1	$ 4,000,000	$ 2,400,000
Movie 2	27,000,000	18,600,000
Tours	300,000	140,000

The joint cost incurred to produce the two movies was $8,000,000. Joint cost is allocated based on net realizable value.

a. How much of the joint cost is allocated to each movie?
b. How much profit was generated by each movie?

32. *(Accounting for by-products)* Clark Textiles Company manufactures various wood products that yield sawdust as a by-product. The only costs associated with the sawdust are selling costs of $6 per ton sold. The company accounts for sales of sawdust by deducting sawdust's net realizable value from the major product's cost of goods sold. Sawdust sales in 2000 were 12,000 tons at $40 each. If Clark Textiles changes its method of accounting for sawdust sales to show the net realizable value as other revenue (presented at the bottom of the income statement), how would its gross margin be affected?

33. *(Accounting for by-products)* A by-product produced from processing potatoes into the joint products of frozen potato patties and potatoes for dehydration is potato skins. Potato skins can be sold to restaurants for use in preparing appetizers. The additional processing and disposal costs associated with such by-product sales are $0.30 per pound of skins. During May 2001, Homestead Potato Processors produced and sold 45,000 pounds of potato skins for $23,850. In addition, joint cost for its dehydrated potatoes and frozen potato patties totaled $60,000, and 80 percent of all joint production was sold for $79,000. Nonfactory operating expenses for May were $7,600.

a. Prepare an income statement for Homestead Potato Processors if sales of the by-product are shown as other revenue and its additional processing and disposal costs are shown as additional cost of goods sold of the joint products.
b. Prepare an income statement for Homestead Potato Processors if the net realizable value of the by-product is shown as other income.
c. Prepare an income statement for Homestead Potato Processors if the net realizable value of the by-product is subtracted from the joint cost of the main products.
d. Which of the above presentations do you think would be most helpful to managers and why?

34. *(Accounting for by-products)* Thompson EDP provides computing services for its commercial clients. Records for clients are maintained on both computer files and paper files. After 7 years, the paper records are sold for recycling material. The net realizable value of the recycled paper is treated as a reduction to operating overhead. Data pertaining to operations for 2000 follow:

Estimated operating overhead	$400,500
Estimated CPU time (hours)	35,000
Estimated net realizable value of recycled paper	$20,400
Actual operating overhead	$399,500
Actual CPU time	34,200
Actual net realizable value of recycled paper	$19,588

a. What was the company's estimated predetermined overhead rate?
b. What journal entry should the company make to record the sale of the recycled paper?
c. What was the company's underapplied or overapplied overhead for 2000?

35. *(Accounting for scrap)* Elegant Mosaics restores antique stained glass windows. Regardless of the job, there is always some breakage or improper cuts. This scrap can be sold to amateur stained glass hobbyists. The following estimates are made in setting the predetermined overhead rate for 2001:

Overhead costs other than breakage		$128,600
Estimated cost of scrap	$8,800	
Estimated sales value of scrap	(2,400)	6,400
Total estimated overhead		$135,000

Elegant Mosaics expects to incur approximately 15,000 direct labor hours during 2001.

One job that Elegant Mosaics worked on during 2001 was a stained glass window of a family crest; the job took 63 hours. Direct materials cost $420; direct labor is invoiced at $20 per hour. The actual cost of the scrap on this job was $55; this scrap was sold for $18.

a. What predetermined overhead rate was set for 2001?
b. What was the cost of the family crest stained glass window?
c. What journal entry is made to record the cost and selling value of the scrap from the family crest stained glass window?

36. *(Scrap, job order costing)* Escambia Architects offers a variety of architectural services for its commercial construction clients. For each major job, architectural models of the completed structures are built for use in presentations to clients. The firm tracks all costs using a job order costing system. At the completion of the job, the architectural models can be sold to an arts and crafts retailer. The firm uses the realized value method of accounting for the sale of the models. The sales value of each model is credited to the cost of the specific job for which the model was built. During 2001, the model for the Barney Building was sold for $4,500.

a. Using the realized value approach, give the entry to record the sale.
b. Independent of your answer to part (a), assume instead that the sales value of the models is not credited to specific jobs. Give the entry to account for the sale of the Barney Building model.

37. *(Net realizable value versus realized value)* Indicate whether each item listed below is associated with the (1) realized value approach or (2) the net realizable value approach.

a. Has the advantage of better timing
b. Ignores value of by-product/scrap until it is sold
c. Is simpler
d. Is used to reduce the cost of main products when by-products are produced
e. Credits either cost of goods sold of main products or the joint cost when the by-product inventory is recorded
f. Presents proceeds from sale of by-products as other revenue or other income
g. Is appropriate if the by-product's net realizable value is small
h. Is less conservative
i. Is the most clerically efficient
j. Should be used when the by-product's net realizable value is large

38. *(Not-for-profit, program, and support cost allocation)* The Grand Rapids Opera Company is preparing a small pamphlet that will provide information on the types of opera, opera terminology, and storylines of some of the more well-known operas. In addition, there will be a request for funds to support the opera company at the end of the brochure. The company has tax-exempt status and operates on a not-for-profit basis.

The cost of designing and printing 100,000 copies of the pamphlet is $360,000. One page out of ten is devoted to soliciting funding; however, 98% of the time spent in the design stage was on developing and writing the opera information.

a. If space is used as the allocation measure, how much of the pamphlet's cost should be assigned to program activities? To fundraising activities?

b. If design time is used as the allocation measure, how much of the pamphlet's cost should be assigned to program activities? To fundraising activities?

PROBLEMS

39. *(Journal entries)* Madeleine Products uses a joint process to make two main products: Elegance (a perfume) and Sooosoft (a skin lotion). Two departments, Mixing and Cooking, are used, but the products do not become separable until they have been through the cooking process. After cooking, the perfume is removed from the vats and bottled without further processing. The residue remaining in the vats is then blended with aloe and lanolin to become the lotion.

In the Mixing Department, these costs were incurred during October 2000:

Direct material	$28,000
Direct labor	7,560
Manufacturing overhead applied	4,250

In the Cooking Department, costs incurred during October 2000, before separation of the joint products, were

Direct material	$6,100
Direct labor	2,150
Manufacturing overhead applied	3,240

In that same month, the Cooking Department incurred separable costs for each of the products as follows:

Elegance perfume (bottles only)	$2,120
Sooosoft lotion:	
Direct material	1,960
Direct labor	3,120
Manufacturing overhead applied	4,130

Neither department had beginning Work in Process Inventory balances, and all work started in October was completed in that month. The joint costs are allocated to perfume and lotion on the basis of approximated net realizable values at split-off. For October, the approximated net realizable values at split-off were $158,910 for perfume and $52,970 for lotion.

a. Prepare journal entries for the Mixing and Cooking Departments for October 2000.

b. Determine the joint cost allocated to, and the total cost of, Elegance and Sooosoft.

c. Diagram the flow of costs for Madeleine Products for these two products.

40. *(Joint cost allocation; by-product; income determination)* St. Louis Bank & Trust has two main service lines: commercial checking and credit cards. As a by-product of these two main services, the firm also generates some revenue from selling antitheft and embezzlement insurance. Joint costs for producing the two main services include expenses for facilities, legal support, equipment, record keeping, and administration. The joint service cost incurred during June 2000 was $800,000.

These costs are to be allocated on the basis of total revenues generated from each main service.

The following table presents the results of operations and revenues for June:

Service	Number of Accounts	Total Revenues
Commercial checking	3,000	$1,897,500
Credit cards	7,000	1,402,500
Theft insurance	6,500	65,000

Management accounts for the theft insurance on a realized value basis. When commissions on theft insurance are received, management has elected to present the proceeds as a reduction in the Cost of Services Rendered for the main services.

Separate costs for the two main services for June were $250,000 and $180,000, respectively, for checking accounts and credit cards.

a. Allocate the joint cost.

b. Determine the income for each main service and the company's overall gross margin for June 2000.

41. *(Joint cost allocation; scrap)* Washington Filaments produces cloth products for hotels. The company buys the fabric in 60-inch-wide bolts. In the first process, the fabric is set up, cut, and separated into pieces. Setup can either be for robes and bath towels or for hand towels and washcloths.

During July, the company set up and cut 3,000 robes and 6,000 bath towels. Because of the irregular pattern of the robes, scrap is produced in the process and is sold to various institutions (prisons, hospitals, etc.) for rags at $1.25 per pound. July production and cost data for Washington Filaments are as follows:

Fabric used, 12,500 feet at $1.91 per foot	$23,875
Labor, joint process	$6,000
Overhead, joint process	$5,900
Pounds of scrap produced	1,800

Washington Filaments assigns the joint processing cost to the robes and towels based on approximated net realizable value at split-off. The final selling prices for robes and bath towels are $20 and $11 per unit, respectively. Costs after split-off are $8.40 and $2.30, respectively, for the robes and the towels. The selling price of the scrap is treated as a reduction of joint cost.

a. Determine the joint cost to be allocated to the joint products for July.

b. How much joint cost is allocated to the robes in July? To the bath towels? Prepare the journal entry necessary at the point of split-off.

c. What amount of cost for robes is transferred to Finished Goods Inventory for July? What amount of cost for towels is transferred to Finished Goods Inventory for July?

42. *(Joint products; by-product)* Valley Mangoes runs a fruit-packing business in southern California. The firm buys mangoes by the truckload in season. The fruit is then separated into three categories according to its condition. Group 1 is suitable for selling as is to supermarket chains and specialty gift stores. Group 2 is suitable for slicing and bottling in light syrup to be sold to supermarkets. Group 3 is considered a by-product and is sold to another company that processes it into jelly. The firm has two processing departments: (1) Receiving and Separating and (2) Slicing and Bottling.

A particular truckload cost the company $1,500 and yielded 1,500 mangoes in Group 1, 2,000 mangoes in Group 2, and 500 mangoes in Group 3. The labor to separate the fruit into categories was $300, and the company uses a predetermined overhead application rate of 50 percent of direct labor cost. Only Group 2 has any significant additional processing cost, estimated at $220, but each group has boxing and delivery costs as follows:

Group 1	$150
Group 2	220
Group 3	50

The final sales revenue of Group 1 is $3,000, of Group 2 is $1,500, and of Group 3 is $450.

a. Determine the sum of the material, labor, and overhead costs associated with the joint process.

b. Allocate the total joint cost using the approximated net realizable value at split-off method, assuming that the by-product is recorded when realized and is shown as other income on the income statement.

c. Prepare the entries for parts (a) and (b) assuming that the by-product is sold for $450 and that all costs were incurred as estimated.

d. Allocate the total joint cost using the approximated net realizable value at split-off method, assuming that the by-product is recorded using the net realizable value approach and that the joint cost is reduced by the net realizable value of the by-product.

e. Prepare the entries for parts (a) and (d), assuming that the estimated realizable value of the by-product is $400.

43. *(Process costing; joint cost allocation; by-product)* Romano's Hair Salon provides hair styling services and sells a variety of cosmetic and hair-care products. The firm also generates some revenue from the sale of hair, which is periodically swept from the floor of the styling salon.

The net realizable value of hair is accounted for as a reduction in the joint cost assigned to the Styling Services and Cosmetic Products. Hair sells for $6 per pound. The cost of packaging the hair is $0.50 per pound, and selling costs of the hair are $0.30 per pound. The following information is available for 2001 on the inventory of Cosmetic Products (the firm does not produce these products; they are purchased):

Beginning inventory	$ 35,000
Ending inventory	21,500
Purchases	181,350

Joint cost is to be allocated to Styling Services and Cosmetic Products based on approximated net realizable values (revenues less separate costs). For 2001, total revenues were $753,000 from Styling Services and $289,000 from Cosmetic Products. The following joint costs were incurred:

Rent	$36,000
Insurance	23,800
Utilities	3,000

Separate costs were as follows:

	Styling Services	Cosmetic Products
Labor	$431,000	$24,000
Supplies	98,000	700
Equipment depreciation	65,000	1,200
Administration	113,000	3,700

For the year, 2,510 pounds of hair were collected and sold.

a. What is the total net realizable value of hair that is applied to reduce the joint cost assigned to Styling Services and to Cosmetic Products?

b. What is the joint cost to be allocated to Styling Services and Cosmetic Products?

c. What is the approximated pretax realizable value of each main product or service for 2001?

d. How much joint cost is allocated to each main product or service?

e. Determine the net income produced by each main product or service.

44. *(Joint cost allocation; by-product)* The Farmers' Delight Company produces tomato paste and tomato sauce from a joint process. In addition, second-stage processing of the tomato sauce creates a residue mixture of tomato peels and seeds (simply referred to as P&S) as a by-product. P&S is sold for $0.08 per gallon to Pavlov's Doggy Products for that company's use in Canine Delight Chow. Distribution expenses for P&S total $110.

In May 2000, 140,000 pounds of tomatoes are processed in the first department; the cost of this input is $44,200. An additional $33,700 is spent on conversion costs. There are 56,000 gallons of output from Department 1. Thirty percent of the output is transferred as tomato paste to Department 2, and 70 percent of the output is transferred to Department 3. Of the input to Department 3, 20 percent will result in P&S and 80 percent will result in tomato sauce. Joint cost is allocated to tomato paste and sauce on the basis of approximated net realizable values at split-off.

The tomato paste in Department 2 is processed at a total cost of $9,620; the tomato sauce in Department 3 is processed at a total cost of $6,450. The net realizable value of P&S is accounted for as a reduction in the separate processing costs in Department 3. Selling prices per gallon are $5.25 and $3.45 for tomato paste and tomato sauce, respectively.

a. How many gallons leaving Department 1 are sent to Department 2 for further processing? To Department 3?

b. How many gallons leave Department 3 as P&S? As tomato sauce?

c. What is the net realizable value of P&S?

d. What is the total approximated net realizable value of the tomato paste? The tomato sauce?

e. What amount of joint cost is assigned to each main product?

f. If 85 percent of the final output of each main product is sold during May and Farmers' Delight had no beginning inventory of either product, what is the value of the ending inventory of tomato paste and tomato sauce?

45. *(By-product/joint product journal entries)* Missouri Grain Agriculture is a 5,000-acre wheat farm. The growing process yields two principal products: wheat and straw. Wheat is sold for $3.50 per bushel (assumes a bushel of wheat weighs 60 pounds). Without further processing, the straw sells for $30 per ton (a ton equals 2,000 pounds). If the straw is processed further, it is baled and then sells for $45 per ton. In 2001, total joint cost to the split-off point (harvest) was $175 per acre.

The farm produced 70 bushels of wheat per acre and 1 ton of straw per acre. If all of the straw were processed further, processing costs (baling) for the straw would amount to $50,000.

Prepare the 2001 journal entries for straw, if straw is:

a. transferred to storage at sales value as a by-product without further processing, with a corresponding reduction of wheat's production costs.

b. further processed as a by-product and transferred to storage at net realizable value, with a corresponding reduction of the manufacturing costs of wheat.

c. further processed and transferred to finished goods, with joint cost being allocated between wheat and straw based on relative sales value at the split-off point. *(CPA adapted)*

CASE

46. *(Ending inventory valuation; joint cost allocation)* Gainesville Meat Packers experienced the operating statistics in the following table for its joint meat cutting process during March 2000, its first month of operations. The costs of the joint process were direct material, $20,000; direct labor, $11,700; and overhead, $5,000. Products X, Y, and Z are main products; B is a by-product. The company's policy is to recognize the net realizable value of any by-product inventory at split-off and reduce the total joint cost by that amount. Neither the main products nor the by-product require any additional processing or disposal costs, although management may consider additional processing.

Products	Weight in Pounds	Sales Value at Split-Off	Units Produced	Units Sold
X	4,300	$66,000	3,220	2,720
Y	6,700	43,000	8,370	7,070
Z	5,400	11,200	4,320	3,800
B	2,300	2,300	4,600	4,000

a. Calculate the ending inventory values of each joint product based on (1) relative sales value and (2) pounds.

b. Discuss the advantages and disadvantages of each allocation base for (1) financial statement purposes and (2) decisions about the desirability of processing the joint products beyond the split-off point.

REALITY CHECK

47. Use the Internet to find five examples of businesses that engage in joint processes. For each of these businesses, describe the following:

a. The various outputs classified as joint products, by-products, scrap, or waste.

b. Your recommendation of the most appropriate methods of allocating joint costs to the output you have described in part (a). Express, in nontechnical terms, your justification for each of your recommendations.

48. *Some waste, scrap, or by-product materials have little value. In fact, many such materials represent liabilities for companies because the materials require companies to incur significant disposal costs. Alternatively, some companies have historically found "cheap" ways to dispose of such materials. For example, between 1991 and 1994, Borden Chemicals and Plastics shipped mercury-laden-waste to Thor Chemicals' plant at Cato Ridge, South Africa. Borden maintains that the material—spent mercuric chloride catalysts—was not hazardous waste and that it expected Thor to recycle it. According to the EPA, little or none of the material was recycled. Greenpeace says Borden's barrels are leaking at the Thor site. Thor has settled a civil suit brought by families of employees whose exposure to the waste allegedly killed them. Greenpeace says the settlement exceeded $9 million. More litigation has ensued.*

SOURCE: Andrea Foster, "Borden Faces Criminal Charges in Waste Dumping Case," *Chemical Week* (February 3–10, 1999), p. 16.

a. Comment on whether this method of disposing of industrial waste is a "cheap" alternative.

b. Discuss the ethical and legal implications of disposing of industrial waste in this manner.

c. What actions can people take to reduce these kinds of incidents?

d. Ethically, what obligation does the vendor/manufacturer of these industrial materials have to the industrial consumer of the materials?

49. Find the Web site for Buckhead Beef on the Internet. On its Web site, the company provides much information regarding its philosophies, product lines, strategy, production, and distribution systems. Review the information provided. Then, discuss how an operating environment, such as that at Buckhead in which there are many joint production processes, creates unique opportunities for new product innovation. Also, discuss the characteristics of employees that would be important in such an environment.

50. Search the Internet for associations that promote the sale of beef or pork products. One or more of the associations will provide information on the many applications of beef and pork by-products. Review these materials and write a brief summary of how various by-products of beef or pork production benefit many other industries.

CHAPTER

10

Standard Costing

LEARNING OBJECTIVES

After completing this chapter, you should be able to answer the following questions:

1 Why are standard cost systems used?

2 How are standards for material, labor, and overhead set?

3 What documents are associated with standard cost systems and what information do those documents provide?

4 How are material, labor, and overhead variances calculated and recorded?

5 What are the benefits organizations derive from standard costing and variance analysis?

6 How will standard costing be affected if a company uses a single conversion element rather than the traditional labor and overhead elements?

7 (Appendix) How do multiple material and labor categories affect variances?

INTRODUCING

Commerce Bancorp

http://www.commerceonline.com

Let's face it: Almost no one likes banks. If it isn't the fees, it's the long lines or the short hours or the surly tellers.

Now, walk into any branch of Commerce Bancorp, a community lender based in Cherry Hill, New Jersey: Free checking. Free money orders. Weekday teller service from 7:30 in the morning to 8 at night. And branch service with real tellers on weekends and holidays—even a few hours on Sunday.

Commerce takes the basic service and branding concepts found at fast-food giants—right down to the big red "C" in front of each branch, evoking the golden arches—and applies them to its branches. It keeps long hours. It moves teller lines by reducing many teller functions to one-touch keystrokes, making deposit receipts almost as easy as supersizing an Extra Value Meal. It even has bathrooms in each branch. Is this any way to run a bank in the year 2000?

Yes, says Vernon W. Hill II, the founder, president and chairman of Commerce—who is 55 and also owns a string of Burger King outlets. At a time when polls suggest service in America is hitting all time lows—not just at banks, but at telephone companies, airlines and department stores, too—Mr. Hill is showing that good service can be good business.

Commerce wants to be a growth retailer such as Nordstrom or Starbucks. It will open 30 branches this year, bringing its total to about 150, and no other bank comes close to that rate of openings. "Great retailers get great not by buying somebody and trying to fix them," says Mr. Hill, waving a copy of "Built from Scratch," the Home Depot corporate history. "Great retailers get great by developing a model and using it to grow."

America's rush into the suburbs was in full swing in 1967 when Mr. Hill graduated from the University of Pennsylvania's Wharton School. He settled in southern Jersey, where towns burgeoned with refugees from the surrounding cities of Philadelphia, Trenton, N.J., and Wilmington, Del. American strip culture was booming, and Mr. Hill formed a property company that tapped the torrid growth by developing roadside outlets for retailers.

One of his biggest customers was McDonald's. Fast-food outlets are built to strict specifications covering the outside and interior of each unit. Mr. Hill copied them in 1973, when he kept a promise to his banker father and launched his own bank with a branch in Marlton, N.J. That was the first of dozens of branches he would build and operate during the next two decades.

Today, Mr. Hill still builds all his own branches to look like burger joints. Besides the ubiquitous "C" signs, each has the same open, glass-heavy architecture, the same red-black-and-gray design, the same carpet, desks and blinds. He believes this sends a message of consistent, dependable service. "A Home Depot is a Home Depot no matter where you go," he says.

SOURCE: Jathon Sapsford, "Local McBanker: A Small Chain Grows by Borrowing Ideas from Burger Joints—Jersey's Commerce Bancorp Stretches Hours, Cuts Fees to Build Volume—The Catch: Lower Interest," *The Wall Street Journal* (May 17, 2000), p. A1. Permission conveyed through Copyright Clearance Center.

The adoption of retail chain store strategies in banking has allowed Commerce Bancorp to implement a unique banking strategy—standardized service delivered at low cost. Because the bank has a high volume of repetitive transactions, it can develop standards for costs and other performance criteria to ensure consistent service.[1] Cost accountants can provide feedback to managers by comparing dimensions of actual service to predetermined measures. Without a predetermined performance measure, there is no way to know what level of performance is expected. And, without making a comparison between the actual result and the predetermined measure, there is no way to know whether expectations were met and no way for managers to exercise control.

http://www.burgerking.com
http://www.nordstrom.com
http://www.starbucks.com
http://www.mcdonalds.com
http://www.homedepot.com

[1] For instance, in 1999 Commerce had 3.9 million teller transactions, 1.5 million ATM transactions, and 1.1 million check card transactions. SOURCE: Jathon Sapsford, "Local McBanker: A Small Chain Grows by Borrowing Ideas from Burger Joints—Jersey's Commerce Bancorp Stretches Hours, Cuts Fees to Build Volume—The Catch: Lower Interest," *The Wall Street Journal* (May 17, 2000), p. A1.

Organizations develop and use standards for almost all tasks. For example, businesses set standards for employee sales expenses; hotels set standards for housekeeping tasks and room service delivery; casinos set standards for revenue to be generated per square foot of playing space. Because of the variety of organizational activities and information objectives, no single performance measurement system is appropriate for all situations. Some systems use standards for prices, but not for quantities; other systems (especially in service businesses) use labor, but not material, standards.

This chapter discusses a traditional standard cost system that provides price and quantity standards for each cost component: direct material (DM), direct labor (DL), and factory overhead (OH). Discussion is provided on how standards are developed, how variances are calculated, and what information can be gained from detailed variance analysis. Journal entries used in a standard cost system are also presented. The appendix expands the presentation by covering the mix and yield variances that can arise from using multiple materials or groups of labor.

DEVELOPMENT OF A STANDARD COST SYSTEM

1

Why are standard cost systems used?

standard cost

Although standard cost systems were initiated by manufacturing companies, these systems can also be used by service and not-for-profit organizations. In a standard cost system, both standard and actual costs are recorded in the accounting records. This dual recording provides an essential element of cost control: having norms against which actual operations can be compared. Standard cost systems make use of **standard costs**, which are the budgeted costs to manufacture a single unit of product or perform a single service. Developing a standard cost involves judgment and practicality in identifying the material and labor types, quantities, and prices as well as understanding the kinds and behaviors of organizational overhead.

A primary objective in manufacturing a product is to minimize unit cost while achieving certain quality specifications. Almost all products can be manufactured with a variety of inputs that would generate the same basic output and output quality. The input choices that are made affect the standards that are set.

Some possible input resource combinations are not necessarily practical or efficient. For instance, a work team might consist only of craftspersons or skilled workers, but such a team might not be cost beneficial if there were a large differential in the wage rates of skilled and unskilled workers. Or, although providing high-technology equipment to an unskilled labor population is possible, to do so would not be an efficient use of resources, as indicated in the following situation:

> *A company built a new $250 million computer-integrated, statistical process controlled plant to manufacture a product whose labor cost was less than 5% of total product cost. Unfortunately, 25% of the work force was illiterate and could not handle the machines. The workers had been hired because there were not enough literate workers available to hire. When asked why the plant had been located where it was, the manager explained: "Because it has one of the cheapest labor costs in the country."*[2]

Once management has established the desired output quality and determined the input resources needed to achieve that quality at a reasonable cost, quantity and price standards can be developed. Experts from cost accounting, industrial engineering, personnel, data processing, purchasing, and management are assembled to develop standards. To ensure credibility of the standards and to motivate people to operate as close to the standards as possible, involvement of managers and workers whose performance will be compared to the standards is vital. The discussion of the standard setting process begins with material.

[2] Thomas A. Stewart, "Lessons from U.S. Business Blunders," *Fortune* (April 23, 1990), pp. 128, 129.

Material Standards

2

How are standards for material, labor, and overhead set?

The first step in developing material standards is to identify and list the specific direct materials used to manufacture the product. This list is often available on the product specification documents prepared by the engineering department prior to initial production. In the absence of such documentation, material specifications can be determined by observing the production area, querying of production personnel, inspecting material requisitions, and reviewing the cost accounts related to the product. Three things must be known about the material inputs: types of inputs, quantity of inputs used, and quality of inputs used. The accompanying News Note indicates how standards can be developed for a private club.

In making quality decisions, managers should seek the advice of materials experts, engineers, cost accountants, marketing personnel, and suppliers. In most cases, as the material grade rises, so does cost; decisions about material inputs usually attempt to balance the relationships of cost, quality, and projected selling prices with company objectives. The resulting trade-offs affect material mix, material yield, finished product quality and quantity, overall product cost, and product salability. Thus, quantity and cost estimates become direct functions of quality decisions. Given the quality selected for each component, physical quantity estimates of weight, size, volume, or some other measure can be made. These estimates can be based on results of engineering tests, opinions of managers and workers using the material, past material requisitions, and review of the cost accounts.

Specifications for materials, including quality and quantity, are compiled on a **bill of materials**. Even companies without formal standard cost systems develop bills of materials for products simply as guides for production activity. When converting quantities on the bill of materials into costs, allowances are often made for normal waste of components.[3] After the standard quantities are developed,

bill of material

GENERAL BUSINESS NEWS NOTE

Chef Provides Menu for Cost Control

Although some private clubs have attempted to fully computerize their purchasing and inventory operations to accurately measure food and beverage costs, only a few have succeeded. Most have found that the cost of additional technology and staff needed to process all purchases through the system, maintain perpetual inventory information, handle requisitions and transfers for all items, update ingredient costing and recipes, and analyze computer-generated data outweighs the potential cost savings derived from full automation.

Many other factors can also get in the way of accurately measuring food and beverage costs at a private club. Banquets and special club events, buffets, employee meals, wine by the glass, variable bartender pours, yield factors, and waste all combine to make the derivation of an accurate food cost percentage almost impossible in a small operation. And in the world of food and beverage, club volumes are generally very small. There just isn't enough sales volume to justify sophisticated and costly measurement. But members still want the information.

To satisfy member requests, partial computerization can provide valuable data with a minimal investment. Most commonly this is achieved through the use of a "standard cost" module in the POS (point of sale) system. Simply put, the menu is costed by the chef, costs are assigned to each menu item (along with the price), and cost margin reports are produced with a theoretical food cost for each item, menu group, and dining area, by meal period and range of dates. This simplified plan can be an effective method of measuring menu item costs and sales margins.

SOURCE: William A. Boothe, Jr., "Taking a New Approach to Information Management for Clubs: Part III of III," *Club Management* (St. Louis, May/June 1998), pp. 101–107.

[3] Although such allowances are often made, they do not result in the most effective use of a standard cost system. Problems arising from their inclusion are discussed later in this chapter.

prices for each component must be determined. Prices should reflect desired quality, quantity discounts allowed, and freight and receiving costs. Although not always able to control prices, purchasing agents can influence prices. These individuals are aware of alternative suppliers and attempt to choose suppliers providing the most appropriate material in the most reasonable time at the most reasonable cost. The purchasing agent also is most likely to have expertise about the company's purchasing habits. Incorporating this information in price standards should allow a more thorough analysis by the purchasing agent at a later time as to the causes of any significant differences between actual and standard prices.

When all quantity and price information is available, component quantities are multiplied by unit prices to obtain the total cost of each component. (Remember, the price paid for the material becomes the cost of the material.) These totals are summed to determine the total standard material cost of one unit of product.

Labor Standards

Development of labor standards requires the same basic procedures as those used for material. Each production operation performed by either workers (such as bending, reaching, lifting, moving material, and packing) or machinery (such as drilling, cooking, and attaching parts) should be identified. In specifying operations and movements, activities such as cleanup, setup, and rework are considered. All unnecessary movements by workers and of material should be disregarded when time standards are set. Exhibit 10–1 indicates that a manufacturing worker's day is not spent entirely in productive work.

EXHIBIT 10–1

Where Did the Day Go?

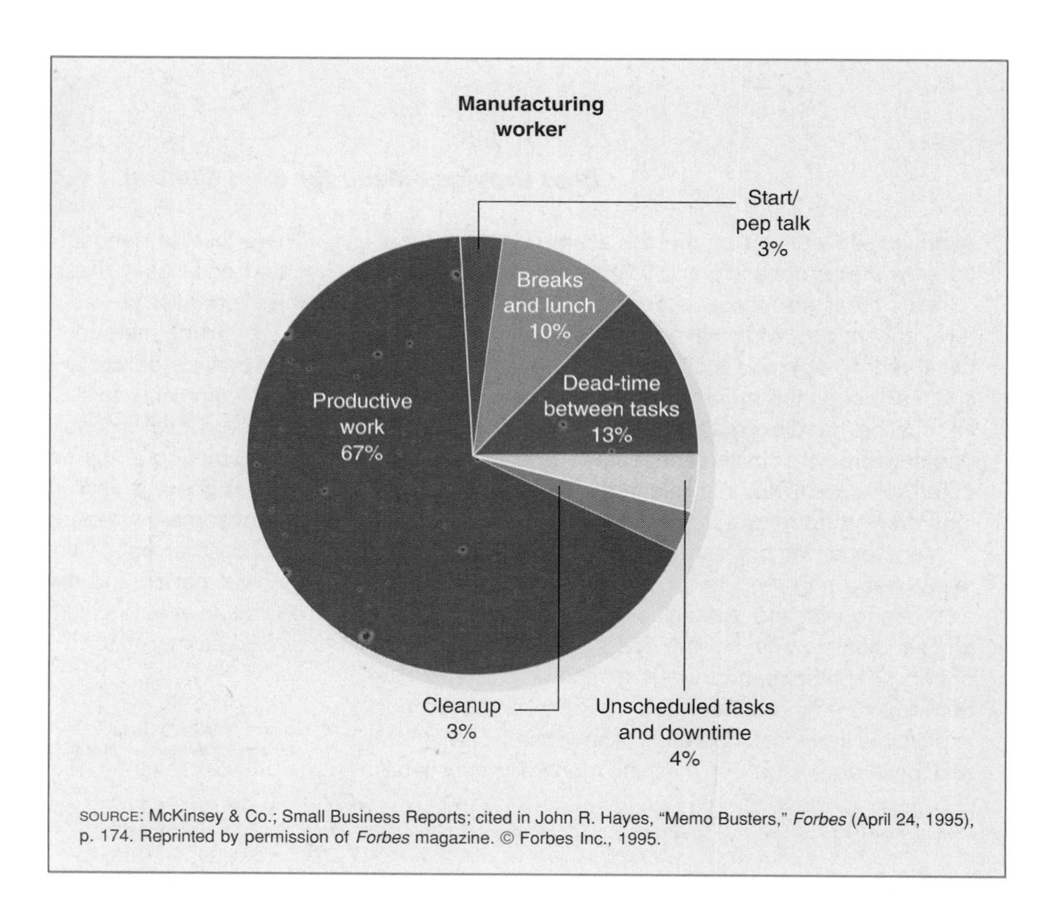

SOURCE: McKinsey & Co.; Small Business Reports; cited in John R. Hayes, "Memo Busters," *Forbes* (April 24, 1995), p. 174. Reprinted by permission of *Forbes* magazine. © Forbes Inc., 1995.

Although standards are commonly thought of as being used in manufacturing situations, many service businesses determine staffing levels based on the standard labor time needed to help a customer. Additionally, Intercity's train schedules are based on the standard time to go from point to point.

To develop usable standards, quantitative information for each production operation must be obtained. Time and motion studies may be performed by the company; alternatively, times developed from industrial engineering studies for various movements can be used.[4] A third way to set a time standard is to use the average time needed to manufacture a product during the past year. Such information can be calculated from employees' past time sheets. A problem with this method is that historical data may include inefficiencies. To compensate, management and supervisory personnel normally make subjective adjustments to the available data.

After all labor tasks are analyzed, an **operations flow document** can be prepared that lists all operations necessary to make one unit of product (or perform a specific service). When products are manufactured individually, the operations flow document shows the time necessary to produce one unit. In a flow process that produces goods in batches, individual times cannot be specified accurately.

operations flow document

3

What documents are associated with standard cost systems and what information do those documents provide?

Labor rate standards should reflect the employee wages and the related employer costs for fringe benefits, FICA (Social Security), and unemployment taxes. In the simplest situation, all departmental personnel would be paid the same wage rate as, for example, when wages are job specific or tied to a labor contract. If employees performing the same or similar tasks are paid different wage rates, a weighted average rate (total wage cost per hour divided by the number of workers) must be computed and used as the standard. Differing rates could be caused by employment length or skill level.

Overhead Standards

Overhead standards are simply the predetermined factory overhead application rates discussed in Chapters 3 and 4. To provide the most appropriate costing information, overhead should be assigned to separate cost pools based on the cost drivers, and allocations to products should be made using different activity drivers.

[4] In performing internal time and motion studies, observers need to be aware that employees may engage in "slowdown" tactics when they are being clocked. The purpose of such tactics is to establish a longer time as the standard, which would make employees appear more efficient when actual results are measured. Or employees may slow down simply because they are being observed and want to be sure they are doing the job correctly.

standard cost card

After the bill of materials, operations flow document, and predetermined overhead rates per activity measure have been developed, a **standard cost card** is prepared. This document (shown in Exhibit 10–2) summarizes the standard quantities and costs needed to complete one product or service unit.

Data for Parkside Products are used to illustrate the details of standard costing.[5] Parkside manufactures several products supporting outdoor recreation including an unassembled picnic table. The bill of materials, operations flow document, and standard cost card for the picnic table appear, respectively, in Exhibits 10–2 through 10–4.

For ease of exposition, it is assumed that the company applies overhead using only two companywide rates: one for variable overhead and another for fixed overhead.

Data from the standard cost card are then used to assign costs to inventory accounts. Both actual and standard costs are recorded in a standard cost system, although it is the standard (rather than actual) costs of production that are debited to Work in Process Inventory.[6] Any difference between an actual and a standard cost is called a variance.

EXHIBIT 10–2

Parkside Products' Bill of Materials for Picnic Table

Product: Picnic Table
Product # 017
Date Established: June 30, 2000

COMPONENT ID#	QUANTITY REQUIRED	DESCRIPTION	COMMENTS
L-04	2	2" × 6" × 12'	Pressure treated
L-07	1	2" × 10" × 12'	Pressure treated
P-13	2	Tubular frame	Predrilled red/green finish
P-19	16	2.5" × 5/16" bolts	Includes nuts and flat washers
P-21	8	5" × 3/8" bolts	Includes nuts and flat washers
F-33	1 pint	Oil-based paint	Red or green
P-100	1	1-Gallon zippable plastic bag	For packaging bolts
I-09	1	Assembly instructions	18 Pages w/pictures

[5] Data for the picnic table illustration are adapted from: Michael Umble and Elizabeth J. Umble, "How to Apply the Theory of Constraints' Five-Step Process of Continuous Improvement," *Journal of Cost Management* (September/October 1998), pp. 4–14.
[6] The standard cost of each cost element (direct material, direct labor, variable overhead, and fixed overhead) is said to be applied to the goods produced. This terminology is the same as that used when overhead is assigned to inventory based on a predetermined rate.

EXHIBIT 10–3

Parkside Products' Operations Flow Document for Picnic Table

Product: Picnic Table
Product # 017
Date Established: June 30, 2000

Operation ID#	Department	Standard Time	Description of Task
009	Cutting	3 minutes	Run 2 × 6 lumber through planer
009	Cutting	3 minutes	Run 2 × 10 lumber through planer
017	Cutting	2 minutes	Cut 2 × 6 lumber
017	Cutting	2 minutes	Cut 2 × 10 lumber
042	Drilling	4 minutes	Drill holes in 2 × 6 segments
048	Drilling	4 minutes	Drill holes in 2 × 12 segments
079	Sanding	18 minutes	Sand face and edge of lumber
093	Finishing	4 minutes	Spray one coat of paint on lumber segments
067	Packaging	5 minutes	Assemble bolts into plastic bag and bundle all components for shipping

VARIANCE COMPUTATIONS

A **total variance** is the difference between total actual cost incurred and total standard cost applied to the output produced during the period. This variance can be diagrammed as follows:

total variance

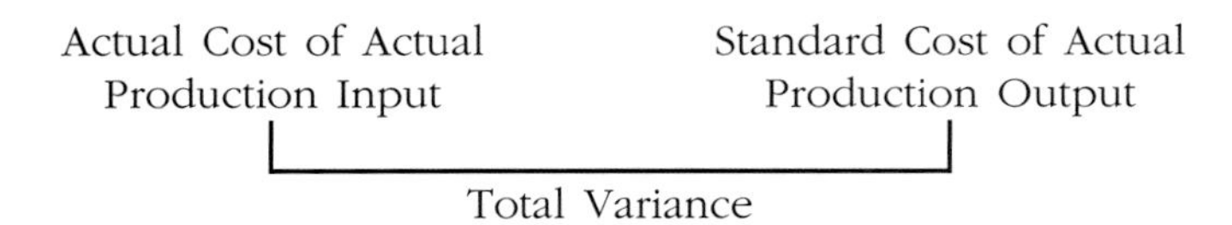

Total variances do not provide useful information for determining why cost differences occurred. To help managers in their control objectives, total variances are subdivided into price and usage components. The total variance diagram can be expanded to provide a general model indicating the two subvariances as follows:

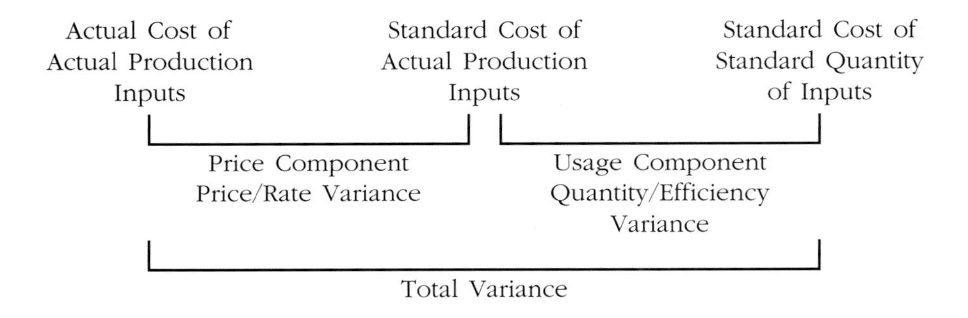

EXHIBIT 10–4

Parkside Products' Standard Cost Card for Picnic Table

Product: Picnic Table
Product # 017
Date Established: June 30, 2000

DIRECT MATERIAL			
ID#	**Unit Price**	**Total Quantity**	**Total Cost**
L-04	$4.00	2	$ 8.00
L-07	8.00	1	8.00
P-13	7.00	2	14.00
P-19	0.05	16	0.80
P-21	0.10	8	0.80
F-33	1.20	1	1.20
P-100	0.20	1	0.20
I-09	3.00	1	3.00
Total direct material cost			$36.00

DIRECT LABOR								
			DEPARTMENT					
ID#	**Avg. Wage Rate per Minute**	**Total Minutes**	**Cutting**	**Drilling**	**Sanding**	**Finishing**	**Packaging**	**Total Cost**
009	$0.40	3	$1.20					$ 1.20
009	0.40	3	1.20					1.20
017	0.40	2	0.80					0.80
017	0.40	2	0.80					0.80
042	0.30	4		$1.20				1.20
048	0.30	4		1.20				1.20
079	0.35	18			$6.30			6.30
093	0.45	4				$1.80		1.80
067	0.25	5					$1.25	1.25
Totals for direct labor			$4.00	$2.40	$6.30	$1.80	$1.25	$15.75

MANUFACTURING OVERHEAD	
Variable overhead ($24 per labor hour) (45 DL minutes)	$18.00
Fixed overhead ($15 per unit produced)*	15.00
Total overhead	$33.00

*Based on expected annual production of 6,000 units.

A price variance reflects the difference between what was paid for inputs and what should have been paid for inputs. A usage variance shows the cost difference between the quantity of actual input and the quantity of standard input allowed for the actual output of the period. The quantity difference is multiplied by a standard price to provide a monetary measure that can be recorded in the accounting records. Usage variances focus on the efficiency of results or the relationship of input to output.

The diagram moves from actual cost of actual input on the left to standard cost of standard input quantity on the right. The middle measure of input is a hybrid of actual quantity and standard price. The change from input to output reflects the fact that a specific quantity of production input will not necessarily produce the standard quantity of output. The far right column uses a measure of output known as the **standard quantity allowed**. This quantity measure translates the actual production output into the standard input quantity that should have been needed to achieve that output. The monetary amount shown in the right-hand column is computed as the standard quantity allowed times the standard price of the input.

standard quantity allowed

The price variance portion of the total variance is measured as the difference between the actual and standard prices multiplied by the the actual input quantity:

$$\text{Price Element} = (AP - SP)(AQ)$$

The usage variance portion of the total variance is measured as measuring the difference between actual and standard quantities multiplied by the standard price:

$$\text{Usage Element} = (AQ - SQ)(SP)$$

The following sections illustrate variance computations for each cost element.

MATERIAL AND LABOR VARIANCE COMPUTATIONS

The standard costs of production for January 2001 for producing 400 picnic tables (the actual number made) are shown in the top half of Exhibit 10–5 (page 390). The lower half of the exhibit shows actual quantity and cost data for January 2001. This standard and actual cost information is used to compute the monthly variances.

4

How are material, labor, and overhead variances calculated and recorded?

Material Variances

The model introduced earlier is used to compute price and quantity variances for materials. A price and quantity variance can be computed for each type of material. To illustrate the calculations, direct material item L-04 is used.

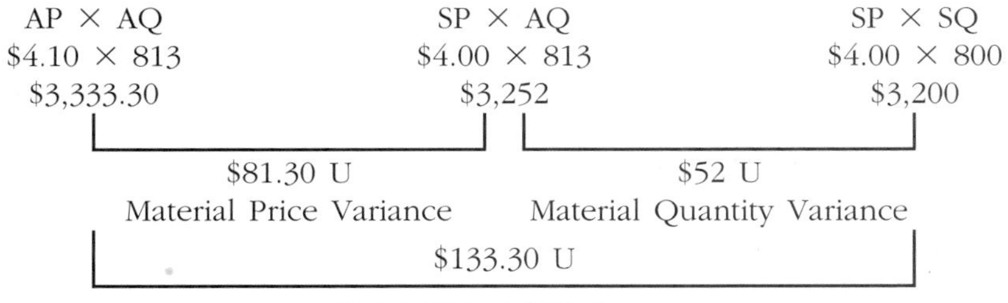

where: AP is actual price paid for the input
AQ is the actual quantity purchased and consumed
SP is the standard price of the input
SQ is the standard quantity of the input

If the actual price or quantity amounts are larger than the standard price or quantity amounts, the variance is unfavorable (U); if the standards are larger than the actuals, the variance is favorable (F).

The **material price variance** (MPV) indicates whether the amount paid for material was below or above the standard price. For item L-04, the price paid

material price variance

EXHIBIT 10-5

Standard and Actual Cost Data for Picnic Tables: January 2001

STANDARD COSTS FOR 400 PICNIC TABLES

Direct Material

Item	Quantity	Price	Total Cost
L-04	800	$4.00	$ 3,200
L-07	400	8.00	3,200
P-13	800	7.00	5,600
P-19	6,400	0.05	320
P-21	3,200	0.10	320
F-33	400	1.20	480
P-100	400	0.20	80
I-09	400	3.00	1,200
Total standard direct material cost			$14,400

Direct Labor

Department	Minutes	Rate	Total Cost
Cutting	4,000	$0.40	$ 1,600
Drilling	3,200	0.30	960
Sanding	7,200	0.35	2,520
Finishing	1,600	0.45	720
Packaging	2,000	0.25	500
Total standard direct labor cost			$ 6,300

Overhead

Variable (300 × $24)*	$ 7,200
Fixed (400 × $15)	6,000
Total standard overhead cost	$13,200

ACTUAL COSTS FOR 400 PICNIC TABLES

Direct Material

Item	Quantity	Price	Total Cost
L-04	813	$4.10	$ 3,333.30
L-07	400	7.75	3,100.00
P-13	810	7.05	5,710.50
P-19	6,700	0.06	402.00
P-21	3,300	0.12	396.00
F-33	411	1.30	534.30
P-100	425	0.18	76.50
I-09	413	2.80	1,156.40
Total actual direct material cost			$14,709.00

Direct Labor

Department	Minutes	Rate	Total Cost
Cutting	4,200	$0.45	$ 1,890.00
Drilling	3,300	0.32	1,056.00
Sanding	7,000	0.35	2,450.00
Finishing	1,800	0.46	828.00
Packaging	2,120	0.28	593.60
Totals	18,420		$ 6,817.60

Overhead

Variable	$ 7,061
Fixed	7,400
Total actual overhead cost	$14,461

*300 hours = (4,000 + 3,200 + 7,200 + 1,600 + 2,000) ÷ 60

was $4.10 per board, whereas the standard was $4.00. The unfavorable MPV of $81.30 can also be calculated as [($4.10 − $4.00)(813) = ($0.10)(813) = $81.30]. The variance is unfavorable because the actual price paid is greater than the standard allowed.

material quantity variance

The **material quantity variance** (MQV) indicates whether the actual quantity used was below or above the standard quantity allowed for the actual output. This difference is multiplied by the standard price per unit of material. Picnic table production used 13 more boards than the standard allowed, resulting in an unfavorable material quantity variance [(813 − 800)($4.00) = (13)($4.00) = $52]. The variance sign is positive because actual quantity is greater than standard.

The total material variance ($133.30 U) can be calculated by subtracting the total standard cost of input ($3,200) from the total actual cost of input ($3,333.30). The total variance also represents the summation of the individual variances: ($81.30 + $52.00) = $133.30 (an unfavorable variance).

To find the total direct material cost variances, the computation of the price and quantity variances is repeated for each direct material item. The price and quantity variances are then summed across items to obtain the total price and quantity variances.

Point of Purchase Material Variance Model

A total variance for a cost component is generally equal to the sum of the price and usage variances. An exception to this rule occurs when the quantity of material purchased is not the same as the quantity of material placed into production. Because the material price variance relates to the purchasing (not production) function, the point of purchase model calculates the material price variance using the quantity of materials purchased rather than the quantity of materials used. The general model can be altered slightly to isolate the variance as close to the source as possible and provide more rapid information for management control purposes.

As shown in Exhibit 10–5, Parkside Products used 813 boards to make 400 picnic tables in January 2001. However, rather than purchasing only 813 boards, assume the company purchased 850 at the price of $4.10. Using this information, the material price variance is calculated as

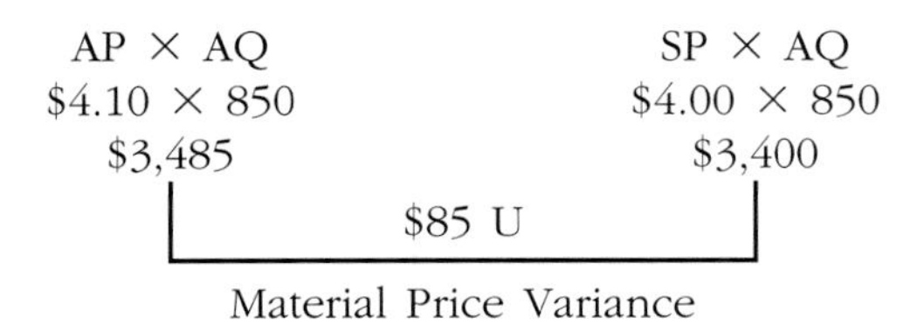

This change in the general model is shown below, using subscripts to indicate actual quantity purchased (p) and used (u).

$AP \times AQ_p$ $SP \times AQ_p$

Material Price Variance

$SP \times AQ_u$ $SP \times SQ_u$

Material Quantity Variance

The material quantity variance is still computed on the basis of the actual quantity used. Thus, the MQV remains at $52 U. Because the price and quantity variances have been computed using different bases, they should not be summed and no total material variance can be meaningfully determined.

Labor Variances

The labor variances for picnic table production in January 2001 would be computed on a departmental basis and then summed across departments. To illustrate the computations, the Cutting Department data are applied as follows:

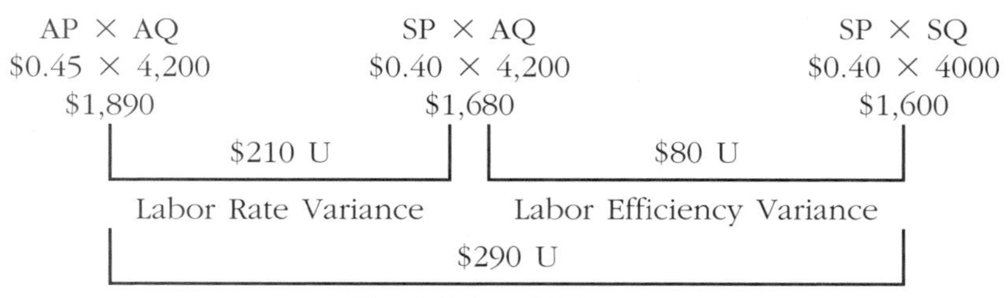

labor rate variance

labor efficiency variance

The **labor rate variance** (LRV) shows the difference between the actual wages paid to labor for the period and the standard wages for all hours worked. The LRV can also be computed as [($0.45 − $0.40)(4,200) = ($0.05)(4,200) = $210 U]. Multiplying the standard labor rate by the difference between the actual minutes worked and the standard minutes for the production achieved results in the **labor efficiency variance** (LEV): [(4,200 − 4,000)($0.40) = (200)($0.40) = $80].

OVERHEAD VARIANCES

In developing overhead application rates, a company must specify an operating level or capacity. Capacity refers to the level of activity. Alternative activity measures include theoretical, practical, normal, and expected capacity. Because total variable overhead changes in direct relationship with changes in activity and fixed overhead per unit changes inversely with changes in activity, a specific activity level must be chosen to determine budgeted overhead costs.

theoretical capacity

practical capacity

normal capacity

The estimated maximum potential activity for a specified time is the **theoretical capacity**. This measure assumes that all factors are operating in a technically and humanly perfect manner. Theoretical capacity disregards realities such as machinery breakdowns and reduced or stopped plant operations on holidays. Reducing theoretical capacity by ongoing, regular operating interruptions (such as holidays, downtime, and start-up time) provides the **practical capacity** that could be achieved during regular working hours. Consideration of historical and estimated future production levels and the cyclical fluctuations provides a **normal capacity** measure that encompasses the long-run (5 to 10 years) average activity of the firm. This measure represents a reasonably attainable level of activity, but will not provide costs that are most similar to actual historical costs. Thus, many firms use expected capacity as the selected measure of activity. Expected capacity is a short-run concept that represents the anticipated level of the firm for the upcoming annual period. If actual results are close to budgeted results (in both dollars and volume), this measure should result in product costs that most closely reflect actual costs. The News Note on page 393 discusses the challenges inherent in selecting a capacity measure.

http://www.howmet.com/home.nsf/facilitypages/whitehall+casting

flexible budget

A **flexible budget** is a planning document that presents expected overhead costs at different activity levels. In a flexible budget, all costs are treated as either variable or fixed; thus, mixed costs must be separated into their variable and fixed elements.

The activity levels shown on a flexible budget usually cover the contemplated range of activity for the upcoming period. If all activity levels are within the relevant

GENERAL BUSINESS NEWS NOTE

The Fixed Cost Challenge

Bring up the topic of standard costing and you're almost certain to touch off a lively debate. Cost accountants have varying opinions on how to set standards and how to interpret them.

Tim McDonald, information systems manager and assistant controller at Howmet's Whitehall (MI) casting facility, finds the biggest challenge he faces with standard costing is handling fixed and semi-fixed costs. Volume changes will result in different fixed costs per unit because, by definition, these costs do not change (in total) with different volumes (at least within a certain range of production). There's a danger management will mistakenly think its fixed costs have decreased due to higher volumes and underprice its parts, even when future volumes are lower.

To determine volume for standard fixed cost allocation, Whitehall's cost managers look at the various operations or capital equipment required, and use 80% of total capacity (to allow for normal downtime for maintenance and as a buffer for unforeseen breakdowns). Accounting textbooks might refer to this as "practical capacity." Using practical capacity in developing fixed cost allocation rates results in cost standards that include only the cost of capacity actually used in production. Whitehall partially tracks the cost of unused capacity through efficiency percentages.

SOURCE: Kip R. Krumwiede, "Tips from the Trenches on Standard Costing," *Cost Management Update* (April 2000), pp. 1–3.

range, costs at each successive level should equal the previous level plus a uniform monetary increment for each variable cost factor. The increment is equal to variable cost per unit of activity times the quantity of additional activity.

The predetermined variable and fixed overhead rates shown in Exhibit 10–4 were calculated for picnic table production using expected capacity of 6,000 units and 4,500 labor hours (3/4 hour each × 6,000). At this level of activity, expected annual variable overhead for picnic table production is $108,000 ($24 × 4,500) and expected fixed overhead is $90,000 ($15 × 6,000). Exhibit 10–6 provides a flexible budget for picnic table production at three alternative activity levels: 5,000, 6,000, and 7,000 units. The flexible budget indicates that the unit cost for overhead declines as volume increases. This results because the per-unit cost of fixed overhead moves inversely with volume changes. Managers of Parkside Products selected 6,000 units of production as a basis for determining rates of overhead application.

The use of separate variable and fixed overhead application rates and accounts allows separate price and usage variances to be computed for each type of overhead. Such a four-variance approach provides managers with the greatest detail and, thus, the greatest flexibility for control and performance evaluation.

EXHIBIT 10–6

Flexible Overhead Budget for Picnic Table Production

Units of Production	5,000	6,000	7,000
Labor hours	3,750	4,500	5,250
× hourly overhead rate	× $24	× $24	× $24
Total variable overhead	$ 90,000	$108,000	$126,000
Fixed overhead	90,000	90,000	90,000
Total overhead	$180,000	$198,000	$216,000
Total overhead cost per unit	$36.00	$33.00	$30.86

Variable Overhead

The general variance analysis model can be used to calculate the price and usage subvariances for variable overhead (VOH) as follows:

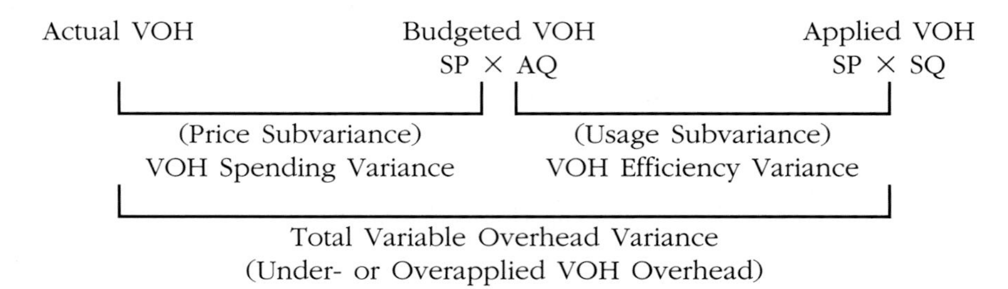

Actual VOH cost is debited to the Variable Manufacturing Overhead account; applied VOH reflects the standard overhead application rate multiplied by the standard quantity of activity for the actual output of the period. Applied VOH is debited to Work in Process Inventory and credited to Variable Manufacturing Overhead. The total VOH variance is the balance in the variable overhead account at year-end and equals the amount of underapplied or overapplied VOH.

Using the information in Exhibit 10–5, the variable overhead variances for picnic table production are calculated as follows:

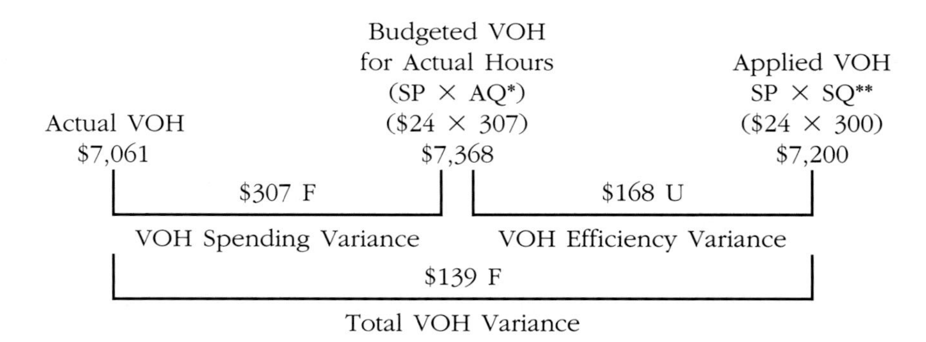

*Actual hours = 18,420 ÷ 60 = 307
**Standard hours = 400 × (45/60) = 300

variable overhead spending variance

The difference between actual VOH and budgeted VOH based on actual hours is the **variable overhead spending variance**. Variable overhead spending variances are often caused by price differences—paying higher or lower prices than the standard prices allowed. Such fluctuations may occur because, over time, changes in variable overhead prices have not been reflected in the standard rate. For example, average indirect labor wage rates or utility rates may have changed since the predetermined variable overhead rate was computed. Managers usually have little control over prices charged by external parties and should not be held accountable for variances arising because of such price changes. In these instances, the standard rates should be adjusted.

Another possible cause of the VOH spending variance is waste or shrinkage associated with production resources (such as indirect materials). For example, deterioration of materials during storage or from lack of proper handling may be recognized only after those materials are placed into production. Such occurrences usually have little relationship to the input activity basis used, but they do affect the VOH spending variance. If waste or spoilage is the cause of the VOH spending variance, managers should be held accountable and encouraged to implement more effective controls.

The difference between budgeted VOH for actual hours and standard VOH is the **variable overhead efficiency variance**. This variance quantifies the effect of using more or less actual input than the standard allowed for the production achieved. When actual input exceeds standard input allowed, production operations are considered to be inefficient. Excess input also indicates that a larger VOH budget is needed to support the additional input.

variable overhead efficiency variance

Fixed Overhead

The total fixed overhead (FOH) variance is divided into its price and usage subvariances by inserting budgeted fixed overhead as a middle column into the general model as follows:

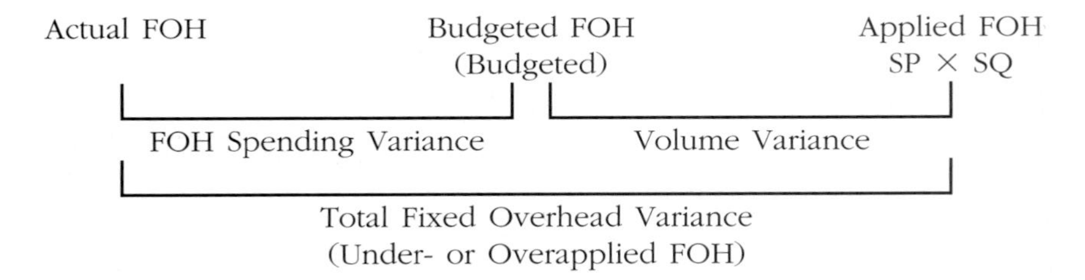

In the model, the left column is simply labeled "actual cost" and is not computed as a price times quantity measure because FOH is incurred in lump sums. Actual FOH cost is debited to Fixed Manufacturing Overhead. Budgeted FOH is a constant amount throughout the relevant range; thus, the middle column is a constant figure regardless of the actual quantity of input or the standard quantity of input allowed. This concept is a key element in computing FOH variances. The budgeted amount of fixed overhead can also be presented analytically as the result of multiplying the standard FOH application rate by the capacity measure that was used to compute that standard rate (5,000 units for Parkside Products' picnic tables).

The difference between actual and budgeted FOH is the **fixed overhead spending variance**. This amount normally represents a weighted average price variance of the multiple components of FOH, although it can also reflect mismanagement of resources. The individual FOH components are detailed in the flexible budget, and individual spending variances should be calculated for each component.

fixed overhead spending variance

As with variable overhead, applied FOH is related to the standard application rate and the standard hours allowed for the actual production level. In regard to fixed overhead, the standard input allowed for the achieved production level measures capacity utilization for the period. Applied fixed overhead is debited to Work in Process Inventory and credited to Fixed Manufacturing Overhead.

The fixed overhead **volume variance** is the difference between budgeted and applied fixed overhead. The volume variance is caused solely by producing at a level that differs from that used to compute the predetermined overhead rate. The volume variance occurs because, by using an application rate per unit of activity, FOH cost is treated as if it were variable even though it is not.

volume variance

Although capacity utilization is controllable to some degree, the volume variance is the variable over which managers have the least influence and control, especially in the short run. So volume variance is also called **noncontrollable variance**. This lack of influence is usually not too important. What is important is whether managers exercise their ability to adjust and control capacity utilization properly. The degree of capacity utilization should always be viewed in relationship to inventory and sales. Managers must understand that underutilization of capacity is not always an undesirable condition. It is significantly more appropriate

noncontrollable variance

for managers to regulate production than to produce goods that will end up in inventory stockpiles. Unneeded inventory production, although it serves to utilize capacity, generates substantially more costs for materials, labor, and overhead (including storage and handling costs). The positive impact that such unneeded production will have on the volume variance is insignificant because this variance is of little or no value for managerial control purposes.

The difference between actual FOH and applied FOH is the total fixed overhead variance and is equal to the amount of underapplied or overapplied fixed overhead.

Inserting the data from Exhibit 10–5 for picnic table production into the model gives the following:

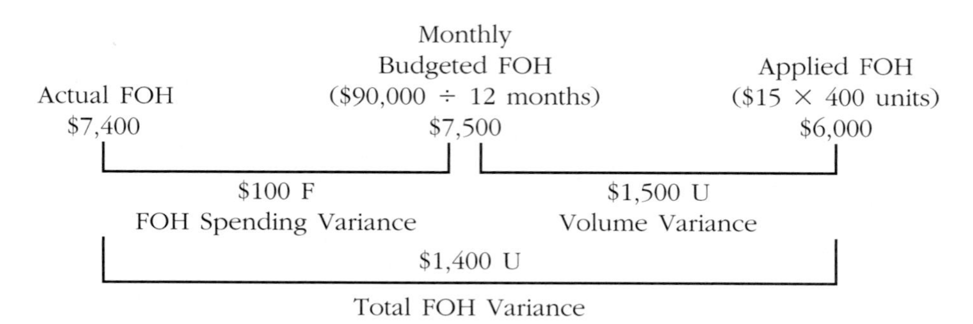

The reason the FOH application rate is $15 per unit is that a capacity level of 6,000 units for the year was chosen. Had any other capacity level been chosen, the rate would have differed, even though the total amount of budgeted monthly fixed overhead ($7,500) would have remained the same. If any level of capacity other than that used in determining the application rate is used to apply FOH, a volume variance will occur. For example, if the department had chosen 4,800 units as the denominator level of activity to set the predetermined FOH rate, there would be no volume variance for January 2001—expected volume would be equal to actual production volume.

Management is usually aware, as production occurs, of the physical level of capacity utilization even if a volume variance is not reported. The volume variance, however, translates the physical measurement of underutilization or overutilization into a dollar amount. An unfavorable volume variance indicates less-than-expected utilization of capacity. If available capacity is currently being utilized at a level below (or above) that which was anticipated, managers are expected to recognize that condition, investigate the reasons for it, and (if possible and desirable) initiate appropriate action. Managers can sometimes influence capacity utilization by modifying work schedules, taking measures to relieve any obstructions to or congestion of production activities, and carefully monitoring the movement of resources through the production process. Preferably, such actions should be taken before production rather than after it. Efforts made after production is completed may improve next period's operations, but will have no impact on past production.

Alternative Overhead Variance Approaches

total overhead variance

If the accounting system does not distinguish between variable and fixed costs, a four-variance approach is unworkable. Use of a combined (variable and fixed) overhead rate requires alternative overhead variance computations. A one-variance approach calculates only a **total overhead variance** as the difference between total actual overhead and total overhead applied to production. The amount of applied overhead is determined by multiplying the combined rate by the standard input activity allowed for the actual production achieved. The one-variance model is diagrammed as follows:

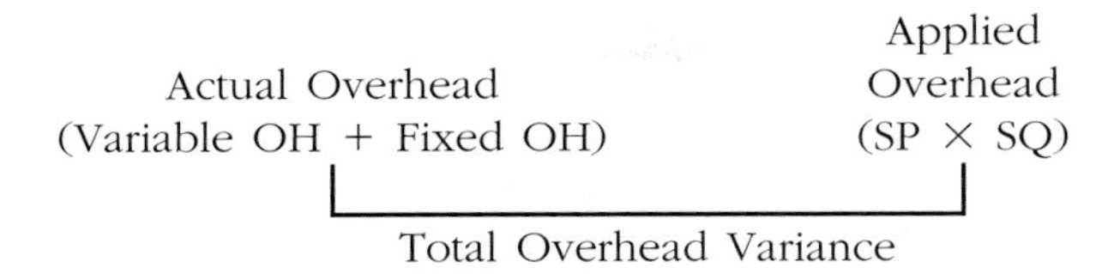

Like other total variances, the total overhead variance provides limited information to managers. Two-variance analysis is performed by inserting a middle column in the one-variance model as follows:

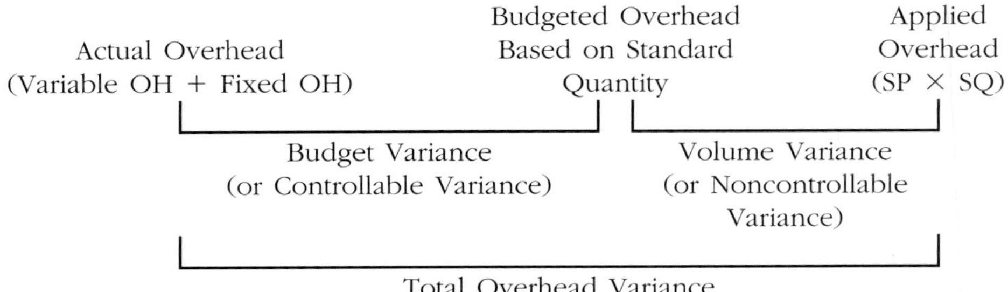

The middle column provides information on the expected total overhead cost based on the standard quantity. This amount represents total budgeted variable overhead at standard hours plus budgeted fixed overhead, which is constant across all activity levels in the relevant range.

budget variance

controllable variance

The **budget variance** equals total actual overhead minus budgeted overhead based on the standard quantity for this period's production. This variance is also referred to as the **controllable variance** because managers are somewhat able to control and influence this amount during the short run. The difference between total applied overhead and budgeted overhead based on the standard quantity is the volume variance.

A modification of the two-variance approach provides a three-variance analysis. Inserting another column between the left and middle columns of the two-variance model separates the budget variance into spending and efficiency variances. The new column represents the flexible budget based on the actual hours. The three-variance model is as follows:

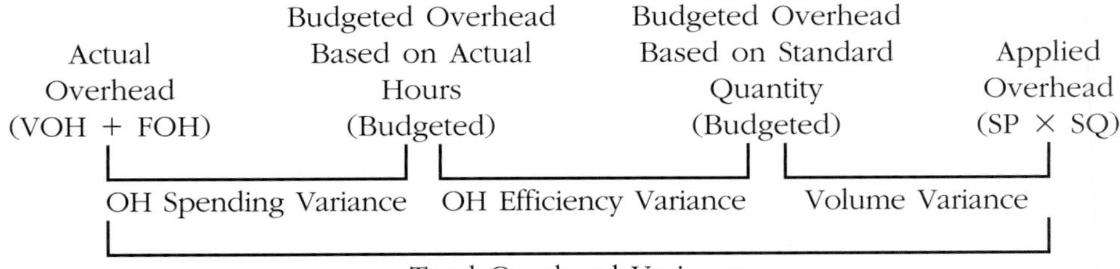

overhead spending variance

overhead efficiency variance

The spending variance shown in the three-variance approach is a total **overhead spending variance**. It is equal to total actual overhead minus total budgeted overhead at the actual activity level. The **overhead efficiency variance** is related solely to variable overhead and is the difference between total budgeted overhead at the actual activity level and total budgeted overhead at the standard activity level. This variance measures, at standard cost, the approximate amount of variable overhead caused by using more or fewer inputs than is standard for the actual production. The sum of the overhead spending and overhead efficiency variances of the three-variance analysis is equal to the budget variance of the two-variance analysis. The volume variance amount is the same as that calculated using the two-variance or the four-variance approach.

If variable and fixed overhead are applied using the same base, the one-, two-, and three-variance approaches will have the interrelationships shown in Exhibit 10–7. (The demonstration problem at the end of the chapter shows computations for each of the overhead variance approaches.) Managers should select the method that provides the most useful information and that conforms to the company's accounting system. As more companies begin to recognize the existence of multiple cost drivers for overhead and to use multiple bases for applying overhead to production, computation of the one-, two-, and three-variance approaches will diminish.

EXHIBIT 10–7

Interrelationships of Overhead Variances

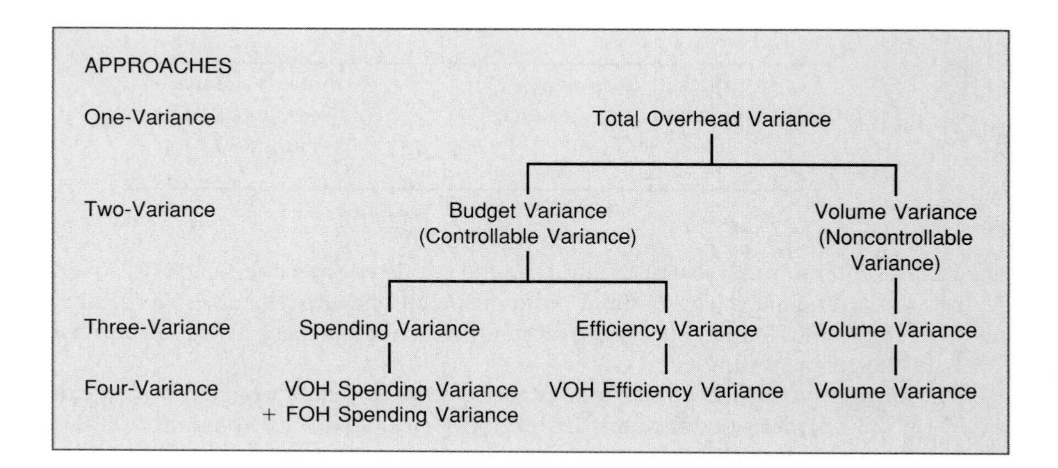

STANDARD COST SYSTEM JOURNAL ENTRIES

Journal entries using Parkside Products' picnic table production data for January 2001 are given in Exhibit 10–8. The following explanations apply to the numbered journal entries.

1. The debit to Raw Material Inventory is for the standard price of the actual quantity of materials purchased. The credit to Accounts Payable is for the actual price of the actual quantity of materials purchased. The debit to the variance account reflects the unfavorable material price variance. It is assumed that all materials purchased were used in production during the month.
2. The debit to Work in Process Inventory is for the standard price of the standard quantity of material, whereas the credit to Raw Material Inventory is for the standard price of the actual quantity of material used in production. The credit to the Material Quantity Variance account reflects the overuse of materials valued at the standard price.
3. The debit to Work in Process Inventory is for the standard hours allowed to produce 400 picnic tables multiplied by the standard wage rate. The Wages Payable credit is for the actual amount of direct labor wages paid during the period. The debit to the Labor Rate Variance account reflects the unfavorable rate differential. The Labor Efficiency Variance debit reflects the greater-than-standard hours allowed multiplied by the standard wage rate.

EXHIBIT 10-8

Journal Entries for Picnic Table Production: January 2001

(1)	Raw Material Inventory	14,604.20	
	Material Purchase Price Variance[1]	104.80	
	Accounts Payable		14,709.00
	To record the acquisition of material.		
(2)	Work in Process Inventory	14,400.00	
	Material Quantity Variance[2]	204.20	
	Raw Material Inventory		14,604.20
	To record actual material issuances.		
(3)	Work in Process Inventory	6,300.00	
	Labor Rate Variance[3]	160.00	
	Labor Efficiency Variance[4]	357.60	
	Wages Payable		6,817.60
	To record incurrence of direct labor costs in all departments.		
(4)	Variable Manufacturing Overhead	7,061.00	
	Fixed Manufacturing Overhead	7,400.00	
	Various accounts		14,461.00
	To record the incurrence of actual overhead costs.		
(5)	Work in Process Inventory	13,200.00	
	Variable Manufacturing Overhead		7,200.00
	Fixed Manufacturing Overhead		6,000.00
	To apply standard overhead cost to production.		
(6)	Variable Overhead Efficiency Variance	168.00	
	Variable Manufacturing Overhead	139.00	
	Variable Overhead Spending Variance		307.00
	To close the variable overhead account.		
(7)	Volume Variance	1,500.00	
	Fixed Manufacturing Overhead		1,400.00
	Fixed Overhead Spending Variance		100.00
	To close the fixed overhead account.		

[1]The price material variance by item is as follows:

L-04	$ 81.30 U
L-07	100.00 F
P-13	40.50 U
P-19	67.00 U
P-21	66.00 U
F-33	41.10 U
P-100	8.50 F
I-09	82.60 F
Total	$104.80 U

[2]The quantity material variance by item is as follows:

L-04	$ 52.00 U
L-07	0.00
P-13	70.00 U
P-19	15.00 U
P-21	10.00 U
F-33	13.20 U
P-100	5.00 U
I-09	39.00 U
Total	$204.20 U

[3]The labor rate variance by department is as follows:

Cutting	$210.00 U
Drilling	66.00 U
Sanding	0.00
Finishing	18.00 U
Packaging	63.60 U
Total	$357.60 U

[4]The labor rate variance by department is as follows:

Cutting	$ 80.00 U
Drilling	30.00 U
Sanding	70.00 F
Finishing	90.00 U
Packaging	30.00 U
Total	$160.00 U

4. During the period, actual costs incurred for the various variable and fixed overhead components are debited to the manufacturing overhead accounts. These costs are caused by a variety of transactions including indirect material and labor usage, depreciation, and utility costs.
5. Overhead is applied to production using the predetermined rates multiplied by the standard input allowed. Overhead application is recorded at completion of production or at the end of the period, whichever is earlier. The difference

between actual debits and applied credits in each overhead account represents the total variable and fixed overhead variances and is also the underapplied or overapplied overhead for the period.

6. & 7. These entries assume an end-of-month closing of the Variable Manufacturing Overhead and Fixed Manufacturing Overhead accounts. The balances in the accounts are reclassified to the appropriate variance accounts. This entry is provided for illustration only. This process would typically not be performed at month-end, but rather at year-end, because an annual period is used to calculate the overhead application rates.

Note that all unfavorable variances have debit balances and favorable variances have credit balances. Unfavorable variances represent excess production costs; favorable variances represent savings in production costs. Standard production costs are shown in inventory accounts (which have debit balances); therefore, excess costs are also debits.

Although standard costs are useful for internal reporting, they can only be used in financial statements when they produce figures substantially equivalent to those that would have resulted from using an actual cost system. If standards are realistically achievable and current, this equivalency should exist. Standard costs in financial statements should provide fairly conservative inventory valuations because effects of excess prices and/or inefficient operations are eliminated.

At year-end, adjusting entries must be made to eliminate standard cost variances. The entries depend on whether the variances are, in total, insignificant or significant. If the combined impact of the variances is immaterial, unfavorable variances are closed as debits to Cost of Goods Sold; favorable variances are credited to Cost of Goods Sold. Thus, unfavorable variances have a negative impact on operating income because of the higher-than-expected costs, whereas favorable variances have a positive effect on operating income because of the lower-than-expected costs. Although the year's entire production may not have been sold yet, this variance treatment is based on the immateriality of the amounts involved.

In contrast, large variances are prorated at year-end among ending inventories and Cost of Goods Sold. This proration disposes of the variances and presents the financial statements in a manner that approximates the use of actual costing. Proration is based on the relative size of the account balances. Disposition of significant variances is similar to the disposition of large amounts of underapplied or overapplied overhead shown in Chapter 3.

To illustrate the disposition of significant variances, assume that there is a $2,000 unfavorable (debit) year-end balance in the Material Purchase Price Variance account of Parkside Products. Other relevant year-end account balances are as follows:

Raw Material Inventory	$ 49,126
Work in Process Inventory	28,072
Finished Goods Inventory	70,180
Cost of Goods Sold	554,422
Total of affected accounts	$701,800

The theoretically correct allocation of the material purchase price variance would use actual material cost in each account at year-end. However, as was mentioned in Chapter 3 with regard to overhead, after the conversion process has begun, cost elements within account balances are commingled and tend to lose their identity. Thus, unless a significant misstatement would result, disposition of the variance can be based on the proportions of each account balance to the total, as shown below:

Account	Percent	Computation
Raw Material Inventory	7%	($ 49,126 ÷ $701,800)
Work in Process Inventory	4%	($ 28,072 ÷ $701,800)
Finished Goods Inventory	10%	($ 70,180 ÷ $701,800)
Cost of Goods Sold	79%	($554,422 ÷ $701,800)

Applying these percentages to the $2,000 material price variance gives the amounts shown in the following journal entry to assign to the affected accounts:

Raw Material Inventory ($2,000 × 0.07)	140	
Work in Process Inventory ($2,000 × 0.04)	80	
Finished Goods Inventory ($2,000 × 0.10)	200	
Cost of Goods Sold ($2,000 × 0.79)	1,580	
Material Purchase Price Variance		2,000
To dispose of the material price variance at year-end.		

All variances other than the material price variance occur as part of the conversion process. Raw material purchases are not part of conversion, but raw material used is. Therefore, the remaining variances are prorated only to Work in Process Inventory, Finished Goods Inventory, and Cost of Goods Sold. The preceding discussion about standard setting, variance computations, and year-end adjustments indicates that a substantial commitment of time and effort is required to implement and use a standard cost system. Companies are willing to make such a commitment for a variety of reasons.

WHY STANDARD COST SYSTEMS ARE USED

What are the benefits organizations derive from standard costing and variance analysis?

"A standard cost system has three basic functions: collecting the actual costs of a manufacturing operation, determining the achievement of that manufacturing operation, and evaluating performance through the reporting of variances from standard."[7] These basic functions result in six distinct benefits of standard cost systems.

Clerical Efficiency

A company using standard costs usually discovers that less clerical time and effort are required than in an actual cost system. In an actual cost system, the accountant must continuously recalculate changing actual unit costs. In a standard cost system, unit costs are held constant for some period. Costs can be assigned to inventory and cost of goods sold accounts at predetermined amounts per unit regardless of actual conditions.

Motivation

Standards are a way to communicate management's expectations to workers. When standards are achievable and when workers are informed of rewards for standards attainment, those workers are likely to be motivated to strive for accomplishment. The standards used must require a reasonable amount of effort on the workers' part.

Planning

Planning generally requires estimates about the future. Managers can use current standards to estimate future quantities and costs. These estimates should help in the determination of purchasing needs for material, staffing needs for labor, and capacity needs related to overhead that, in turn, will aid in planning for company cash flows. In addition, budget preparation is simplified because a standard is, in fact, a budget for one unit of product or service. Standards are also used to provide the cost basis needed to analyze relationships among costs, sales volume, and profit levels of the organization.

[7] Richard V. Calvasina and Eugene J. Calvasina, "Standard Costing Games That Managers Play," *Management Accounting* (March 1984), p. 49. Although the authors of the article only specified manufacturing operations, these same functions are equally applicable to service businesses.

Controlling

variance analysis

The control process begins with the establishment of standards that provide a basis against which actual costs can be measured and variances calculated. **Variance analysis** is the process of categorizing the nature (favorable or unfavorable) of the differences between actual and standard costs and seeking explanations for those differences. A well-designed variance analysis system captures variances as early as possible, subject to cost-benefit assessments. The system should help managers determine who or what is responsible for each variance and who is best able to explain it. An early measurement and reporting system allows managers to monitor operations, take corrective action if necessary, evaluate performance, and motivate workers to achieve standard production.

In implementing control, managers must recognize that they are faced with a specific scarce resource: their time. They must distinguish between situations that can be ignored and those that need attention. To make this distinction, managers establish upper and lower limits of acceptable deviations from standard. These limits are similar to tolerance limits used by engineers in the development of statistical process control charts. If variances are small and within an acceptable range, no managerial action is required. If an actual cost differs significantly from standard, the manager responsible for the cost is expected to determine the variance cause(s). If the cause(s) can be found and corrective action is possible, such action should be taken so that future operations will adhere more closely to established standards.

The setting of upper and lower tolerance limits for deviations allows managers to implement the management by exception concept, as illustrated in Exhibit 10–9. In the exhibit, the only significant deviation from standard occurred on Day 5, when the actual cost exceeded the upper limit of acceptable performance. An exception report should be generated on this date so that the manager can investigate the underlying variance causes.

Variances large enough to fall outside the acceptability ranges often indicate problems. However, a variance does not reveal the cause of the problem nor the person or group responsible. To determine variance causality, managers must investigate significant variances through observation, inspection, and inquiry. The

EXHIBIT 10–9

Illustration of Management by Exception Concept

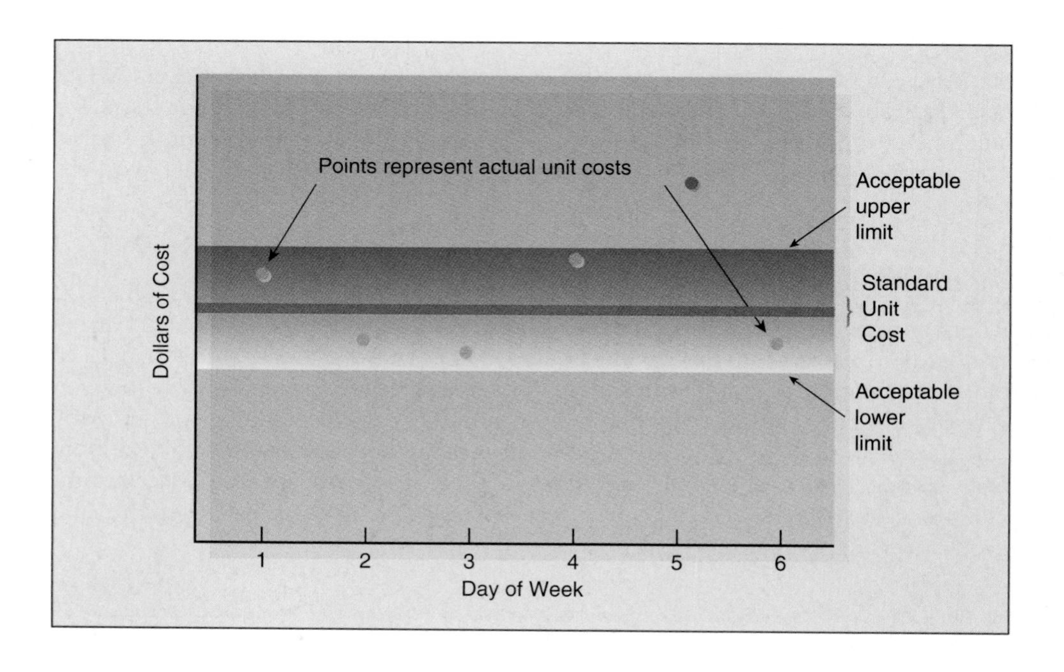

investigation will involve people at the operating level as well as accounting personnel. Operations personnel should be alert in spotting variances as they occur and record the reasons for the variances to the extent they are discernable. For example, operating personnel could readily detect and report causes such as machine downtime or material spoilage.

One important point about variances: An extremely favorable variance is not necessarily a good variance. Although people often want to equate the "favorable" designation with good, an extremely favorable variance could mean an error was made when the standard was set or that a related, offsetting unfavorable variance exists. For example, if low-grade material is purchased, a favorable price variance may exist, but additional quantities of the material might need to be used to overcome defective production. An unfavorable labor efficiency variance could also result because more time was required to complete a job as a result of using the inferior materials. Not only are the unfavorable variances incurred, but internal quality failure costs are also generated. Another common situation begins with labor rather than material. Using lower paid workers will result in a favorable rate variance, but may cause excessive use of raw materials. Managers must constantly be aware that relationships exist and, hence, that variances cannot be analyzed in isolation.

The time frame for which variance computations are made is being shortened. Monthly variance reporting is still common, but the movement toward shorter reporting periods is obvious. As more companies integrate various world-class concepts such as total quality management and just-in-time production into their operations, reporting of variances will become more frequent. Proper implementation of such concepts requires that managers be continuously aware of operating activities and recognize (and correct) problems as soon as they arise. As discussed in the accompanying News Note, control of product costs must begin well before the life-cycle stage where standard costing is appropriate. Most costs are committed by the time a product enters the manufacturing stage.

GENERAL BUSINESS NEWS NOTE

Controlling Costs by Design

Between 75% and 90% of a product's costs are predetermined when the product design is finished, according to experts. It follows that if such a large proportion of costs are immutable once design is complete, then to manage costs effectively management accountants must participate during the design of products, providing useful cost data and financial expertise.

At first glance, management accountants may recoil from this notion, fearing that they have little to contribute to the design or engineering of a product, but recent trends make it feasible for management accountants to be involved in product development without requiring that they be experts in product aesthetics or product engineering. At many firms, product design has evolved from a sequential process where the new product was thrown "over the wall" from one department to another. This process often involves a team effort with team members drawn from marketing, industrial design, product engineering, and manufacturing. The product design team integrates views of all key constituencies to make the tradeoffs necessary to ensure that the design meets the needs of all: Is it designed for manufacturability? Does it possess the features that will provide customers valuable benefits? Is it engineered to provide consistent quality?

The cross-functional product team provides the ideal opportunity for the management accountant to participate to ensure control of product costs. Through interactions among the management accountant and members of other functions, the team can ensure that the appropriate balance is maintained between cost and other important product characteristics such as quality, function, appearance, and manufacturability.

SOURCE: Julie H. Hertenstein and Marjorie B. Platt, "Why Product Development Teams Need Management Accountants," *Management Accounting* (April 1998), pp. 50–55.

Decision Making

Standard cost information facilitates decision making. For example, managers can compare a standard cost with a quoted price to determine whether an item should be manufactured in-house or instead be purchased. Use of actual cost information in such a decision could be inappropriate because the actual cost may fluctuate from period to period. Also, in making a decision on a special price offering to purchasers, managers can use standard product cost to determine the lower limit of the price to offer. In a similar manner, if a company is bidding on contracts, it must have some idea of estimated product costs. Bidding too low and receiving the contract could cause substantial operating income (and, possibly, cash flow) problems; bidding too high might be uncompetitive and cause the contract to be awarded to another company.

The accompanying News Note discusses an alternative standard costing systems that can improve information used for decision making.

Performance Evaluation

When top management receives summary variance reports highlighting the operating performance of subordinate managers, these reports are analyzed for both positive and negative information. Top management needs to know when costs

NEWS NOTE  GENERAL BUSINESS

Which Standard Costing System?

Anyone preparing to install or overhaul a costing system needs to think along three main dimensions: according to whether the cost is established before or after the event, i.e., standard or actual, respectively; according to whether indirect costs are included or not, i.e., absorption costing or variable costing, respectively; and according to the cost units which are the focal point, e.g., product, process, or customer.

On this basis, one can contrast product costing with process costing, standard costing with actual costing, or absorption costing with variable costing, but it is completely illogical to contrast standard costing with any form of absorption costing. The fact is that various combinations are feasible, e.g., standard variable product costs or actual absorption process costs.

Faced with the task of making decisions, those who are members of management teams are unlikely to be interested in the average costs produced by absorption systems. Rather, we are more likely to be interested in incremental costs, e.g., what do we think will be the increase in costs in response to an increase in volume arising from an investment in advertising? Do we think it would be cheaper to produce a given item in factory A or factory B, or to outsource it? What are we losing by shunning the next best alternative?

Only variable costing can embrace these concepts. Absorption costs are needed for various backward looking tasks, like computing the inventory figure for balance sheet purposes, but it is difficult to make a case for them in the context of any forward looking work, such as decision support.

Moreover, decision making being a totally forward-looking process, the management accounting system to support it is almost certain to call for costs to be established before the event, i.e., standard costing. Standard costing does not purport to calculate true costs since, assuming there are such things, they can only be identified after the event, by which time they are too late to be input to decisions.

Putting these two strands of thought together, it should not come as a surprise to find that the overwhelmingly popular choice, as regards management accounting systems in support of the making and monitoring of decisions, is standard variable costing.

SOURCE: David Allen, "Alive and Well," *Management Accounting (London)* (September 1999), p. 50.

were and were not controlled and by which managers. Such information allows top management to provide essential feedback to subordinates, investigate areas of concern, and make performance evaluations about who needs additional supervision, who should be replaced, and who should be promoted. For proper performance evaluations to be made, the responsibility for variances must be traced to specific managers.[8]

CONSIDERATIONS IN ESTABLISHING STANDARDS

When standards are established, appropriateness and attainability should be considered. Appropriateness, in relation to a standard, refers to the basis on which the standards are developed and how long they will be expected to last. Attainability refers to management's belief about the degree of difficulty or rigor that should be incurred in achieving the standard.

Appropriateness

Although standards are developed from past and current information, they should reflect relevant technical and environmental factors expected during the time in which the standards are to be applied. Consideration should be given to factors such as material quality, normal material ordering quantities, expected employee wage rates, degree of plant automation, facility layout, and mix of employee skills. Management should not think that, once standards are set, they will remain useful forever. Current operating performance is not comparable to out-of-date standards. Standards must evolve over the organization's life to reflect its changing methods and processes. Out-of-date standards produce variances that do not provide logical bases for planning, controlling, decision making, or evaluating performance.

Attainability

Standards provide a target level of performance and can be set at various levels of rigor. The level of rigor affects motivation, and one reason for using standards is to motivate employees. Standards can be classified as expected, practical, and ideal. Depending on the type of standard in effect, the acceptable ranges used to apply the management by exception principle will differ. This difference is especially notable on the unfavorable side.

expected standard

Expected standards are set at a level that reflects what is actually expected to occur. Such standards anticipate future waste and inefficiencies and allow for them. As such, expected standards are not of significant value for motivation, control, or performance evaluation. If a company uses expected standards, the ranges of acceptable variances should be extremely small (and, commonly, favorable) because the actual costs should conform closely to standards.

practical standard

Standards that can be reached or slightly exceeded approximately 60 to 70 percent of the time with reasonable effort are called **practical standards**. These standards allow for normal, unavoidable time problems or delays such as machine downtime and worker breaks. Practical standards represent an attainable challenge and traditionally have been thought to be the most effective at inducing the best worker performance and at determining the effectiveness and efficiency of workers at performing their tasks. Both favorable and unfavorable variances result from the use of such moderately rigorous standards.

[8] Cost control relative to variances is discussed in greater depth in Chapter 15. Performance evaluation is discussed in greater depth in Chapters 19, 20 and 21.

ideal standard

Standards that provide for no inefficiency of any type are called **ideal standards**. Ideal standards encompass the highest level of rigor and do not allow for normal operating delays or human limitations such as fatigue, boredom, or misunderstanding. Unless a plant is entirely automated (and then the possibility of human or power failure still exists), ideal standards are impossible to attain. Attempts to apply such standards have traditionally resulted in discouraged and resentful workers who, ultimately, ignored the standards. Variances from ideal standards will always be unfavorable and were commonly not considered useful for constructive cost control or performance evaluation. Such a perspective has, however, begun to change.

CHANGES IN STANDARDS USAGE

In using variances for control and performance evaluation, many accountants (and, often, businesspeople in general) believe that an incorrect measurement is being used. For example, material standards generally include a factor for waste, and labor standards are commonly set at the expected level of attainment even though this level compensates for downtime and human error. Usage of standards that are not aimed at the highest possible (ideal) level of attainment are now being questioned in a business environment concerned with world-class operations.

Use of Ideal Standards and Theoretical Capacity

Japanese influence on Western management philosophy and production techniques has been significant. Just-in-time (JIT) production systems and total quality management (TQM) both evolved as a result of an upsurge in Japanese productivity. These two concepts are inherently based on a notable exception to the traditional disbelief in the use of ideals in standards development and use. Rather than including waste and inefficiency in the standards and then accepting additional waste and spoilage deviations under a management by exception principle, JIT and TQM both begin from the premises of zero defects, zero inefficiency, and zero downtime. Under JIT and TQM, ideal standards become expected standards and there is no (or only a minimal allowable) level of acceptable deviation from standards.

When the standard permits a deviation from the ideal, managers are allowing for inefficient uses of resources. Setting standards at the tightest possible level results in the most useful information for managerial purposes as well as the highest quality products and services at the lowest possible cost. If no inefficiencies are built into or tolerated in the system, deviations from standard should be minimized and overall organizational performance improved. Workers may, at first, resent the introduction of standards set at a "perfection" level, but it is in their and management's best long-run interest to have such standards.

If theoretical standards are to be implemented, management must be prepared to go through a four-step "migration" process. First, teams should be established to determine current problems and the causes of those problems. Second, if the causes relate to equipment, the facility, or workers, management must be ready to invest in plant and equipment items, equipment rearrangements, or worker training so that the standards are amenable to the operations. (Training is essential if workers are to perform at the high levels of efficiency demanded by theoretical standards.) If problems are related to external sources (such as poor-quality materials), management must be willing to change suppliers and/or pay higher prices for higher grade input. Third, because the responsibility for quality has been assigned to workers, management must also empower those workers with the authority to react to problems. "The key to quality initiatives is for employees to move beyond their natural resistance-to-change mode to a highly focused, strategic, and empowered mind-set. This shift unlocks employees' energy and creativity, and leads them to ask 'How can I do my job even better today?'"[9] Fourth, requiring people to work at their maximum potential demands recognition and means that management must provide rewards for achievement.

A company that wants to be viewed as a world-class competitor may want to use theoretical capacity in setting fixed overhead rates. If a company were totally automated or if people consistently worked to their fullest potential, such a measure would provide a reasonable overhead application rate. Thus, any underapplied overhead resulting from a difference between theoretical and actual capacity would indicate capacity that should be either used or eliminated; it could also indicate human capabilities that have not been fully developed. If a company uses theoretical capacity as the defined capacity measure, any end-of-period underapplied overhead should be viewed as a period cost and closed to a loss account (such as "Loss from Inefficient Operations") on the income statement. Showing the capacity potential and the use of the differential in this manner should attract managerial attention to the inefficient and ineffective use of resources.

Whether setting standards at the ideal level and using theoretical capacity to determine FOH applications will become norms of non-Japanese companies cannot be determined at this time. However, we expect that attainability levels will move away from the expected or practical and closer to the ideal. This conclusion is based on the fact that a company whose competitor produces goods based on the highest possible standards must also use such standards to compete on quality and to meet cost (and, thus, profit margin) objectives. Higher standards for efficiency automatically mean lower costs because of the elimination of non-value-added activities such as waste, idle time, and rework.

Adjusting Standards

Standards have generally been set after comprehensive investigation of prices and quantities for the various cost elements. Traditionally, these standards were almost always retained for at least one year and, sometimes, for multiple years. Currently, the business environment (which includes suppliers, technology, competition, product design, and manufacturing methods) changes so rapidly that a standard may no longer be useful for management control purposes for an entire year.[10]

Company management must consider whether to incorporate changes in the environment into the standards during the year in which significant changes occur. Ignoring the changes is a simplistic approach that allows the same type of cost to be recorded at the same amount all year. Thus, for example, any material purchased during the year would be recorded at the same standard cost regardless of when the purchase was made. This approach, although making recordkeeping easy, eliminates any opportunity to adequately control costs or evaluate performance. Additionally, such an approach could create large differentials between standard and actual costs, making standard costs unacceptable for external reporting.

Changing the standards to reflect price or quantity changes would make some aspects of management control and performance evaluation more effective and others more difficult. For instance, budgets prepared using the original standards would need to be adjusted before appropriate actual comparisons could be made against them. Changing of standards also creates a problem for recordkeeping and inventory valuation. At what standard cost should products be valued—the standard

[9] Sara Moulton, Ed Oakley, and Chuck Kremer, "How to Assure Your Quality Initiative Really Pays Off," *Management Accounting* (January 1993), p. 26.

[10] According to a 1999 Institute of Management Accountants' survey, 54 percent of companies update their standards annually and another 20 percent update them on an as-needed basis. SOURCE: Kip R. Krumwiede, "Results of 1999 Cost Management Survey: The Use of Standard Costing and Other Costing Practices," *Cost Management Update* (December 1999/January 2000), pp. 1–4.

in effect when they were produced or the standard in effect when the financial statements are prepared? Although production-point standards would be more closely related to actual costs, many of the benefits discussed earlier in the chapter might be undermined.

If possible, management may consider combining these two choices in the accounting system. The original standards can be considered "frozen" for budget purposes and a revised budget can be prepared using the new current standards. The difference between these budgets would reflect variances related to business environment cost changes. These variances could be designated as uncontrollable (such as those related to changes in the market price of raw material) or internally initiated (such as changes in standard labor time resulting from employee training or equipment rearrangement). Comparing the budget based on current standards with actual costs would provide variances that would more adequately reflect internally controllable causes, such as excess material and/or labor time usage caused by inferior material purchases.

Price Variance Based on Purchases versus on Usage

The price variance computation has traditionally been based on purchases rather than on usage. This choice was made so as to calculate the variance as quickly as possible relative to the cost incurrence. Although calculating the price variance for material at the purchase point allows managers to see the impact of buying decisions more rapidly, such information may not be most relevant in a just-in-time environment. Buying materials in quantities that are not needed for current production requires that the materials be stored and moved, both of which are non-value-added activities. The trade-off in price savings would need to be measured against the additional costs to determine the cost-benefit relationship of such a purchase.

Additionally, computing a price variance on purchases, rather than on usage, may reduce the probability of recognizing a relationship between a favorable material price variance and an unfavorable material quantity variance. If the favorable price variance resulted from the purchase of low-grade material, the effects of that purchase will not be known until the material is actually used.

Decline in Direct Labor

As the proportion of product cost related to direct labor declines, the necessity for direct labor variance computations is minimized. Direct labor may simply become a part of a conversion cost category, as noted in Chapter 3. Alternatively, the increase in automation often relegates labor to an indirect category because workers become machine overseers rather than product producers.

CONVERSION COST AS AN ELEMENT IN STANDARD COSTING

6

How will standard costing be affected if a company uses a single conversion element rather than the traditional labor and overhead elements?

Conversion cost consists of direct labor and manufacturing overhead. The traditional view of separating product cost into three categories (direct material, direct labor, and overhead) is appropriate in a labor-intensive production setting. However, in more highly automated factories, direct labor cost generally represents only a small part of total product cost. In such circumstances, one worker might oversee a large number of machines and deal more with troubleshooting machine malfunctions than with converting raw material into finished products. These new conditions mean that workers' wages are more closely associated with indirect, rather than direct, labor.

Many companies have responded to the condition of large overhead costs and small direct labor costs by adapting their standard cost systems to provide for only two elements of product cost: direct material and conversion. In these situations, conversion costs are likely to be separated into their variable and fixed components. Conversion costs may also be separated into direct and indirect categories based on the ability to trace such costs to a machine rather than to a product. Overhead may be applied using a variety of cost drivers including machine hours, cost of material, number of production runs, number of machine setups, or throughput time.

Variance analysis for conversion cost in automated plants normally focuses on the following: (1) spending variances for overhead costs; (2) efficiency variances for machinery and production costs rather than labor costs; and (3) volume variance for production. These types of analyses are similar to the traditional three-variance overhead approach. In an automated system, managers are likely to be able to better control not only the spending and efficiency variances, but also the volume variance. The idea of planned output is essential in a just-in-time system. Variance analysis under a conversion cost approach is illustrated in Exhibit 10–10. Regardless of the method by which variances are computed, managers must analyze those variances and use them for cost control purposes to the extent that such control can be exercised.

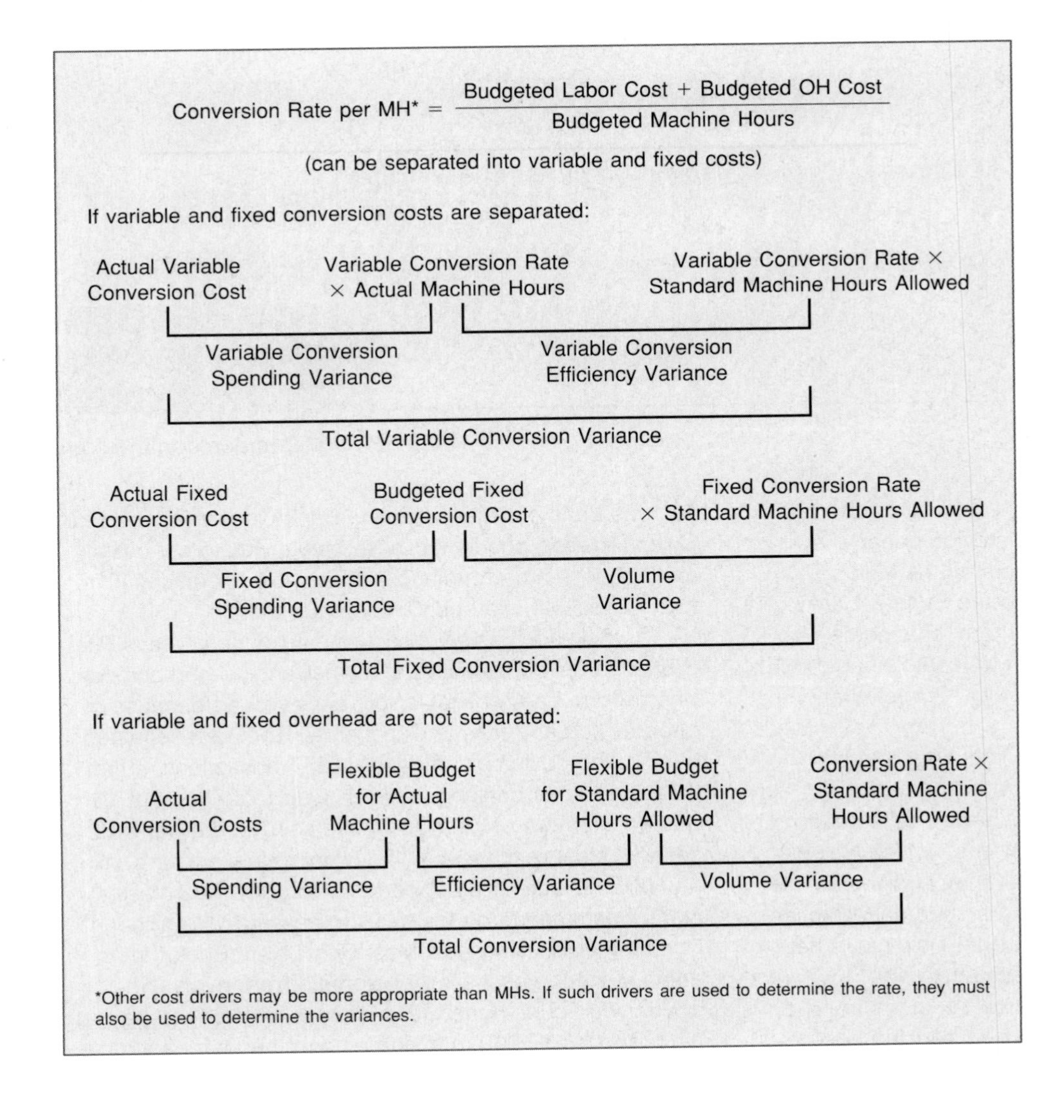

EXHIBIT 10–10

Variances under Conversion Approach

Assume that Parkside Products makes a wrought iron park bench in a process that is fully automated and direct labor is not needed; that is, all labor required for this product is considered indirect. Conversion cost information for this product for 2001 follows:

Expected production	12,000 units
Actual production	13,000 units
Budgeted machine hours	24,000
Actual machine hours	25,000
Budgeted variable conversion cost	$ 96,000
Budgeted fixed conversion cost	192,000
Actual variable conversion cost	97,500
Actual fixed conversion cost	201,000

Variable conversion rate: $96,000 ÷ 24,000 = $4 per MH
Fixed conversion rate: $192,000 ÷ 24,000 = $8 per MH
Standard machine hours = 13,000 × 2 = 26,000

The variance computations for conversion costs follow.

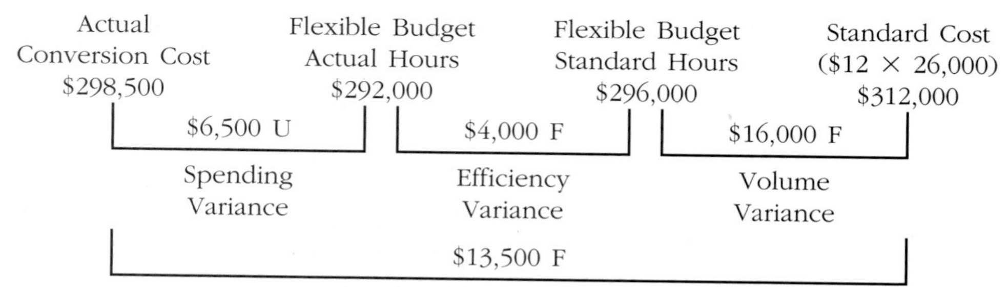

http://www.bankofamerica.com
http://www.bankone.com
http://www.firstunion.com

REVISITING

Commerce Bancorp

http://www.commerceonline.com

Commerce grew slowly at first, adding a few branches each year, and its service became a draw for the small-business customers on the lending side. By 1994, Commerce had pioneered Sunday banking, opening branches from 11 a.m. to 4 p.m. That same year, Mr. Hill took another page from the McDonald's handbook with the launch of Commerce University—modeled after Hamburger U. at McDonald's.

"We are different!" shouts John Manning, a training manager at the facility, before a room full of students. Classes cover everything from loan underwriting to counting cash. Today's course is called "Traditions," which includes basics such as answering the phone in a chirpy voice. One by one, students stand behind a screen and practice their greeting—"Hello! My name is Linda! How may I help you?!"—while the rest of the class rates the effort.

In 1994, the same year Commerce set up its training facility, legislators in Washington revised banking laws to allow interstate mergers, spurring the growth of behemoths such as Bank of America Corp., Bank One Corp. and First Union. The top priority for these banks was to cut costs and squeeze more profits out of merged operations. Often that started with staff cuts, which hurt morale.

"It makes for a very insecure environment," says Rita O'Brien, a retired executive at a small engineering company who used to bank at First Union, but switched because of poor service and fees to Commerce. "That gets reflected back to the customer." Indeed, U.S. Transactions, a firm that researches banking markets, found that 3 out of 10 retail customers of merged banks say the merger hurt service. Most of those say they want to leave their bank.

Mr. Hill, seeing an opportunity to grow much faster, started hammering on the service message. He billed Commerce as "America's Most Convenient Bank," in an effort to steal dissatisfied customers from rivals. He advertised hours, honed teller service, and began paying his branches $5,000 to divide among the staff each time a rival branch nearby closes its doors.

For Commerce, the challenge now is to maintain service while growing. The company spends $100,000 on marketing each new branch opening to create a hometown feeling, and the event is a flashback to another banking era. On a recent Saturday in the Philadelphia suburb of Flourtown, the neighborhood slowly turned out to pick up free Commerce cups and pens. A magician twisted balloons, while a disk jockey spun oldies. There was a raffle and free soft drinks and hot dogs. Wayne Gomes, a Philadelphia Phillies relief pitcher, signed photos for kids in Little League outfits.

With assets of $7 billion, Commerce is the largest bank headquartered in southern New Jersey. Its retail approach to banking uses chain concepts that feature standardized facilities, standardized hours, standardized service, and aggressive marketing. The consistent delivery and reinforcement of this strategy for over 26 years has built a brand that the consumer has accepted as truth.

SOURCES: Jathon Sapsford, "Local McBanker: A Small Chain Grows by Borrowing Ideas from Burger Joints—Jersey's Commerce Bancorp Stretches Hours, Cuts Fees to Build Volume—The Catch: Lower Interest," *The Wall Street Journal* (May 17, 2000), p. A1; Corporate Profile Web site, http://www.commerceonline.com (June 16, 2000).

CHAPTER SUMMARY

A standard cost is computed as a standard price multiplied by a standard quantity. In a true standard cost system, standards are derived for prices and quantities of each product component and for each product. A standard cost card provides information about a product's standards for components, processes, quantities, and costs. The material and labor sections of the standard cost card are derived from the bill of materials and the operations flow document, respectively.

A variance is any difference between an actual and a standard cost. A total variance is composed of a price and a usage subvariance. The material variances are the price and the quantity variances. The material price variance can be computed on either the quantity of material purchased or the quantity of material used in production. This variance is computed as the quantity measure multiplied by the difference between the actual and standard prices. The material quantity variance is the difference between the standard price of the actual quantity of material used and the standard price of the standard quantity of material allowed for the actual output.

The two labor variances are the rate and efficiency variances. The labor rate variance indicates the difference between the actual rate paid and the standard rate allowed for the actual hours worked during the period. The labor efficiency variance compares the number of hours actually worked against the standard number of hours allowed for the level of production achieved and multiplies this difference by the standard wage rate.

If separate variable and fixed overhead accounts are kept (or if this information can be generated from the records), two variances can be computed for both the variable and fixed overhead cost categories. The variances for variable overhead are the VOH spending and VOH efficiency variances. The VOH spending variance is the difference between actual variable overhead cost and budgeted variable overhead based on the actual level of input. The VOH efficiency variance is the difference between budgeted variable overhead at the actual activity level and variable overhead applied on the basis of standard input quantity allowed for the production achieved.

The fixed overhead variances are the FOH spending and volume variances. The fixed overhead spending variance is equal to actual fixed overhead minus budgeted fixed overhead. The volume variance compares budgeted fixed overhead to applied fixed overhead. Fixed overhead is applied based on a predetermined rate using a selected measure of capacity. Any output capacity utilization actually achieved (measured in standard input quantity allowed), other than the level selected to determine the standard rate, will cause a volume variance to occur.

Depending on the detail available in the accounting records, a variety of overhead variances may be computed. If a combined variable and fixed overhead rate is used, companies may use a one-, two-, or three-variance approach. The one-variance approach provides only a total overhead variance, which is the difference between actual and applied overhead. The two-variance approach provides information on a budget and a volume variance. The budget variance is calculated as total actual overhead minus total budgeted overhead at the standard input quantity allowed for the production achieved. The volume variance is calculated in the same manner as under the four-variance approach. The three-variance approach calculates an overhead spending variance, overhead efficiency variance, and a volume variance. The spending variance is the difference between total actual overhead and total budgeted overhead at the actual level of activity worked. The efficiency variance is the difference between total budgeted overhead at the actual activity level and total budgeted overhead at the standard input quantity allowed for the production achieved. The volume variance is computed in the same manner as it was using the four-variance approach.

Actual costs are required for external reporting, although standard costs may be used if they approximate actual costs. Adjusting entries are necessary at the end of the period to close the variance accounts. Standards provide a degree of clerical efficiency and assist management in its planning, controlling, decision making, and performance evaluation functions. Standards can also be used to motivate employees if the standards are seen as a goal of expected performance.

A standard cost system should allow management to identify significant variances as close to the time of occurrence as feasible and, if possible, to help determine the variance cause. Significant variances should be investigated to decide whether corrective action is possible and practical. Guidelines for investigation should be developed using the management by exception principle.

Standards should be updated periodically so that they reflect actual economic conditions. Additionally, they should be set at a level to encourage high-quality production, promote cost control, and motivate workers toward production objectives.

Automated manufacturing systems will have an impact on variance computations. One definite impact is the reduction in or elimination of direct labor hours or costs for overhead application. Machine hours, production runs, and number of machine setups are examples of more appropriate activity measures than direct labor hours in an automated factory. Companies may also design their standard cost systems to use only two elements of production cost: direct material and conversion. Variances for conversion under such a system focus on machine or production efficiency rather than on labor efficiency.

APPENDIX

How do multiple material and labor categories affect variances?

Mix and Yield Variances

Most companies use a combination of many materials and various classifications of direct labor to produce goods. In such settings, the material and labor variance computations presented in the chapter are insufficient.

When a company's product uses more than one material, a goal is to combine those materials in such a way as to produce the desired product quality in the most cost-beneficial manner. Sometimes, materials can be substituted for one another without affecting product quality. In other instances, only one specific material or type of material can be used. For example, a furniture manufacturer might use either oak or maple to build a couch frame and still have the same basic quality. A perfume manufacturer, however, may be able to use only a specific fragrance oil to achieve a desired scent.

Labor, like materials, can be combined in many different ways to make the same product. Some combinations will be less expensive than others; some will be more efficient than others. Again, all potential combinations may not be viable: Unskilled laborers would not be able to properly cut Baccarat or Waterford crystal.

Management desires to achieve the most efficient use of labor inputs. As with materials, some amount of interchangeability among labor categories is assumed. Skilled labor is more likely to be substituted for unskilled because interchanging unskilled labor for skilled labor is often not feasible. However, it may not be cost effective to use highly skilled, highly paid workers to do tasks that require little or no training. A rate variance for direct labor is calculated in addition to the mix and yield variances.

mix

Each possible combination of materials or labor is called a **mix**. Management's standards development team sets standards for materials and labor mix based on experience, judgment, and experimentation. Mix standards are used to calculate mix and yield variances for materials and labor. An underlying assumption in product mix situations is that the potential for substitution exists among the material and labor components. If this assumption is invalid, changing the mix cannot improve the yield and may even prove wasteful. In addition to mix and yield variances, price and rate variances are still computed for materials and labor. Consider the following example.

The Fish Place has begun packaging a frozen one-pound "Gumbo-combo" that contains processed crab, shrimp, and oysters. This new product is used to illustrate the computations of mix and yield variances. To some extent, one ingredient may be substituted for the other. In addition, it is assumed that the company uses two direct labor categories (A and B). There is a labor rate differential between these two categories. Exhibit 10–11 provides standard and actual information for the company for December 2000.

Material Price, Mix, and Yield Variances

material mix variance

A material price variance shows the dollar effect of paying prices that differ from the raw material standard. The **material mix variance** measures the effect of substituting a nonstandard mix of materials during the production process. The

EXHIBIT 10–11

Standard and Actual Information for December 2000

Material standards for one lot (200 1-pound packages):		
Crab:	60 pounds at $7.20 per pound	$ 432
Shrimp:	90 pounds at $4.50 per pound	405
Oysters:	50 pounds at $5.00 per pound	250
Total	200 pounds	$1,087

Labor standards for one lot (200 1-pound packages):		
Category A workers:	20 hours at $10.50 per hour	$210
Category B workers:	10 hours at $14.30 per hour	143
Total	30 hours	$353

Actual production and cost data for December:		
Production:	40 lots	
Material:		
Crab:	Purchased and used	2,285.7 pounds at $7.50 per pound
Shrimp:	Purchased and used	3,649.1 pounds at $4.40 per pound
Oysters:	Purchased and used	2,085.2 pounds at $4.95 per pound
Total		8,020.0 pounds
Labor:		
Category A	903 hours at $10.50 per hour ($9,481.50)	
Category B	387 hours at $14.35 per hour ($5,553.45)	
Total	1,290 hours	

material yield variance

material yield variance is the difference between the actual total quantity of input and the standard total quantity allowed based on output; this difference reflects standard mix and standard prices. The sum of the material mix and yield variances equals a material quantity variance similar to the one shown in the chapter; the difference between these two variances is that the sum of the mix and yield variances is attributable to multiple ingredients rather than to a single one. A company can have a mix variance without experiencing a yield variance.

yield

For Gumbo-combo, the standard mix of materials is 30 percent (60 pounds of 200 pounds per lot) crab, 45 percent shrimp, and 25 percent oysters. The **yield** of a process is the quantity of output resulting from a specified input. For Gumbo-combo, the yield from 60 pounds of crab, 90 pounds of shrimp, and 50 pounds of oysters is one lot of 200 one-pound packages. Computations for the price, mix, and yield variances are given below in a format similar to that used in the chapter:

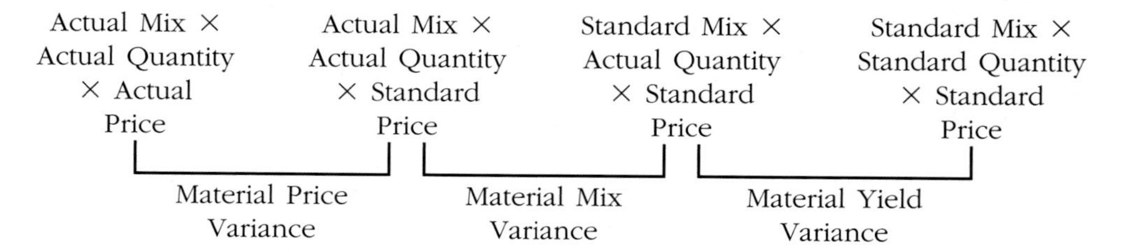

Assume The Fish Place used 8,020 total pounds of ingredients to make 40 lots of Gumbo-combo. The standard quantity necessary to produce this quantity of Gumbo-combo is 8,000 total pounds of ingredients. The actual mix of crab, shrimp, and oysters was 28.5, 45.5, and 26.0 percent, respectively:

Crab	(2,285.7 pounds out of 8,020)	= 28.5%
Shrimp	(3,649.1 pounds out of 8,020)	= 45.5%
Oysters	(2,085.2 pounds out of 8,020)	= 26.0%

Computations necessary for the material variances are shown in Exhibit 10–12. These amounts are then used to compute the variances.

EXHIBIT 10–12

Computations for Material Mix and Yield Variances

(1) Total actual data (mix, quantity, and prices):		
Crab—2,285.7 pounds at $7.50	$17,142.75	
Shrimp—3,649.1 pounds at $4.40	16,056.04	
Oysters—2,085.2 pounds at $4.95	10,321.74	$43,520.53
(2) Actual mix and quantity; standard prices:		
Crab—2,285.7 pounds at $7.20	$16,457.04	
Shrimp—3,649.1 pounds at $4.50	16,420.95	
Oysters—2,085.2 pounds at $5.00	10,426.00	$43,303.99
(3) Standard mix; actual quantity; standard prices:		
Crab—30% × 8,020 pounds × $7.20	$17,323.20	
Shrimp—45% × 8,020 pounds × $4.50	16,240.50	
Oysters—25% × 8,020 pounds × $5.00	10,025.00	$43,588.70
(4) Total standard data (mix, quantity, and prices):		
Crab—30% × 8,000 pounds × $7.20	$17,280.00	
Shrimp—45% × 8,000 pounds × $4.50	16,200.00	
Oysters—25% × 8,000 pounds × $5.00	10,000.00	$43,480.00

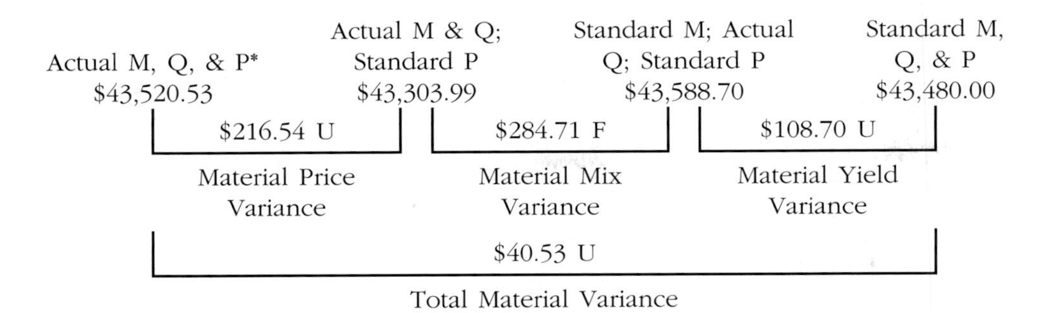

*Note: M = mix, Q = quantity, and P = price.

The above computations show a single price variance being calculated for materials. To be more useful to management, separate price variances can be calculated for each material used. For example, the material price variance for crab is $685.71 U ($17,142.75 − $16,457.04), for shrimp $364.91 F ($16,056.04 − $16,420.95), and for oysters $104.26 F ($10,321.74 − $10,426.00). The savings on the shrimp and oysters was less than the added cost for the crab, so the total price variance was unfavorable. Also, less than the standard proportion of the most expensive ingredient (crab) was used, so it is reasonable that there would be a favorable mix variance. The company also experienced an unfavorable yield because total pounds of material allowed for output (8,000) was less than actual total pounds of material used (8,020).

Labor Rate, Mix, and Yield Variances

The two labor categories used by The Fish Place are unskilled (A) and skilled (B). When preparing the labor standards, the development team establishes the labor categories required to perform the various tasks and the amount of time each task is expected to take. During production, variances will occur if workers are not paid the standard rate, do not work in the standard mix on tasks, or do not perform those tasks in the standard time.

labor mix variance

labor yield variance

The labor rate variance is a measure of the cost of paying workers at other than standard rates. The **labor mix variance** is the financial effect associated with changing the proportionate amount of higher or lower paid workers in production. The **labor yield variance** reflects the monetary impact of using more or fewer total hours than the standard allowed. The sum of the labor mix and yield variances equals the labor efficiency variance. The diagram for computing labor rate, mix, and yield variances is as follows:

Actual Mix × Actual Hours × Actual Rate	Actual Mix × Actual Hours × Standard Rate	Standard Mix × Actual Hours × Standard Rate	Standard Mix × Standard Hours × Standard Rate

Labor Rate Variance | Labor Mix Variance | Labor Yield Variance

Standard rates are used to make both the mix and yield computations. For Gumbo-combo, the standard mix of A and B labor shown in Exhibit 10–11 is two-thirds and one-third (20 and 10 hours), respectively. The actual mix is 70 percent (903 of 1,290) A and 30 percent (387 of 1,290) B. Exhibit 10–13 presents the labor computations for Gumbo-combo production. Because standard hours to produce one lot of Gumbo-combo were 20 and 10, respectively, for categories A and B labor, the standard hours allowed for the production of 40 lots are 1,200 (800 of A and 400 of B). Using the amounts from Exhibit 10–13, the labor variances for Gumbo-combo production in December are calculated in diagram form:

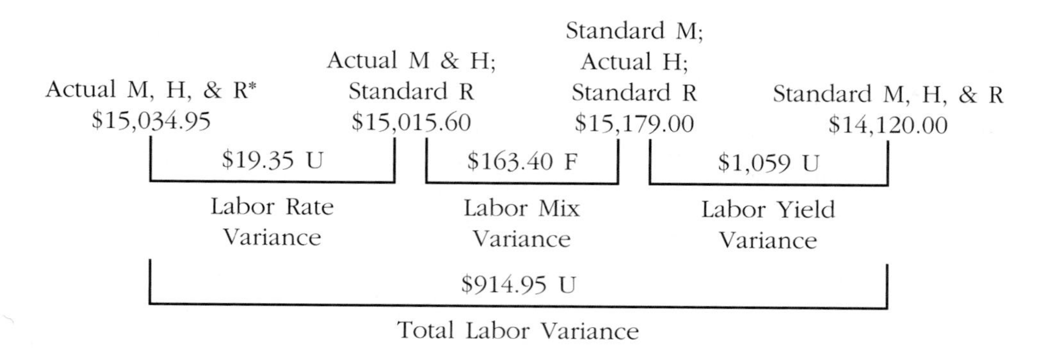

*Note: M = mix, H = hours, and R = rate.

As with material price variances, separate rate variances can be calculated for each class of labor. Because category A does not have a labor rate variance, the total rate variance relates to category B.

The company has saved $163.40 by using the actual mix of labor rather than the standard. A higher proportion of the less expensive class of labor (category A) than specified in the standard mix was used. One result of substituting a greater proportion of lower paid workers seems to be that an unfavorable yield occurred because total actual hours (1,290) were greater than standard (1,200).

Because there are trade-offs in mix and yield when component qualities and quantities are changed, management should observe the integrated nature of price, mix, and yield. The effects of changes of one element on the other two need to be considered for cost efficiency and output quality. If mix and yield can be increased by substituting less expensive resources while still maintaining quality, managers and product engineers should change the standards and the proportions of components. If costs are reduced but quality maintained, selling prices could also be reduced to gain a larger market share.

EXHIBIT 10-13

Computations for Labor Mix and Yield Variances

(1) Total actual data (mix, hours, and rates):		
Category A—903 hours at $10.50	$9,481.50	
Category B—387 hours at $14.35	5,553.45	$15,034.95
(2) Actual mix and hours; standard rates:		
Category A—903 hours at $10.50	$9,481.50	
Category B—387 hours at $14.30	5,534.10	$15,015.60
(3) Standard mix; actual hours; standard rates:		
Category A—2/3 × 1,290 × $10.50	$9,030.00	
Category B—1/3 × 1,290 × $14.30	6,149.00	$15,179.00
(4) Total standard data (mix, hours, and rates):		
Category A—2/3 × 1,200 × $10.50	$8,400.00	
Category B—1/3 × 1,200 × $14.30	5,720.00	$14,120.00

KEY TERMS

bill of material (p. 383)
budget variance (p. 397)
controllable variance (p. 397)
expected standard (p. 405)
fixed overhead spending variance (p. 395)
flexible budget (p. 392)

ideal standard (p. 406)
labor efficiency variance (p. 392)
labor mix variance (p. 415)
labor rate variance (p. 392)
labor yield variance (p. 415)
material price variance (p. 389)
material quantity variance (p. 391)
material mix variance (p. 413)
material yield variance (p. 414)
mix (p. 413)
noncontrollable variance (p. 395)
normal capacity (p. 392)
operations flow document (p. 385)
overhead efficiency variance (p. 397)
overhead spending variance (p. 397)
practical capacity (p. 392)
practical standard (p. 405)
standard cost (p. 382)
standard cost card (p. 386)
standard quantity allowed (p. 389)
theoretical capacity (p. 392)
total overhead variance (p. 396)
total variance (p. 387)
variable overhead efficiency variance (p. 395)
variable overhead spending variance (p. 394)
variance analysis (p. 402)
volume variance (p. 395)
yield (p. 414)

SOLUTION STRATEGIES

Actual Costs

Direct Material: Actual Price × Actual Quantity Purchased or Used
DM: AP × AQ = AC

Direct Labor: Actual Price (Rate) × Actual Quantity of Hours Worked
DL: AP × AQ = AC

Standard Costs

Direct Material: Standard Price × Standard Quantity Allowed
DM: SP × SQ = SC

Direct Labor: Standard Price (Rate) × Standard Quantity of Hours Allowed
DL: SP × SQ = SC

Standard Quantity Allowed: Standard Quantity of Input (SQ) × Actual Quantity of Output Achieved

Variances in Formula Format

The following abbreviations are used:

AFOH = actual fixed overhead
AM = actual mix
AP = actual price or rate
AQ = actual quantity or hours
AVOH = actual variable overhead
BFOH = budgeted fixed overhead (remains at constant amount regardless of activity level as long as within the relevant range)
SM = standard mix
SP = standard price
SQ = standard quantity
TAOH = total actual overhead

Material price variance = (AP × AQ) − (SP × AQ)
Material quantity variance = (SP × AQ) − (SP × SQ)
Labor rate variance = (AP × AQ) − (SP × AQ)
Labor efficiency variance = (SP × AQ) − (SP × SQ)

Four-variance approach:

Variable OH spending variance = AVOH − (VOH rate × AQ)
Variable OH efficiency variance = (VOH rate × AQ) − (VOH rate × SQ)
Fixed OH spending variance = AFOH − BFOH
Volume variance = BFOH − (FOH rate × SQ)

Three-variance approach:

Spending variance = TAOH − [(VOH rate × AQ) + BFOH]
Efficiency variance = [(VOH rate × AQ) + BFOH)] − [(VOH rate × SQ) + BFOH]
Volume variance = [(VOH rate × SQ) + BFOH] − [(VOH rate × SQ) + (FOH rate × SQ)] (This is equal to the volume variance of the four-variance approach.)

Two-variance approach:

Budget variance = TAOH − [(VOH rate × SQ) + BFOH]
Volume variance = [(VOH rate × SQ) + BFOH] − [(VOH rate × SQ) + (FOH rate × SQ)] (This is equal to the volume variance of the four-variance approach.)

One-variance approach:

Total OH variance = TAOH − (Combined OH rate × SQ)

MULTIPLE MATERIALS:

Material price variance = (AM × AQ × AP) − (AM × AQ × SP)
Materials mix variance = (AM × AQ × SP) − (SM × AQ × SP)
Materials yield variance = (SM × AQ × SP) − (SM × SQ × SP)

MULTIPLE LABOR CATEGORIES:

Labor rate variance = (AM × AQ × AP) − (AM × AQ × SP)
Labor mix variance = (AM × AQ × SP) − (SM × AQ × SP)
Labor yield variance = (SM × AQ × SP) − (SM × SQ × SP)

VARIANCES IN DIAGRAM FORMAT:

Direct Materials and Direct Labor

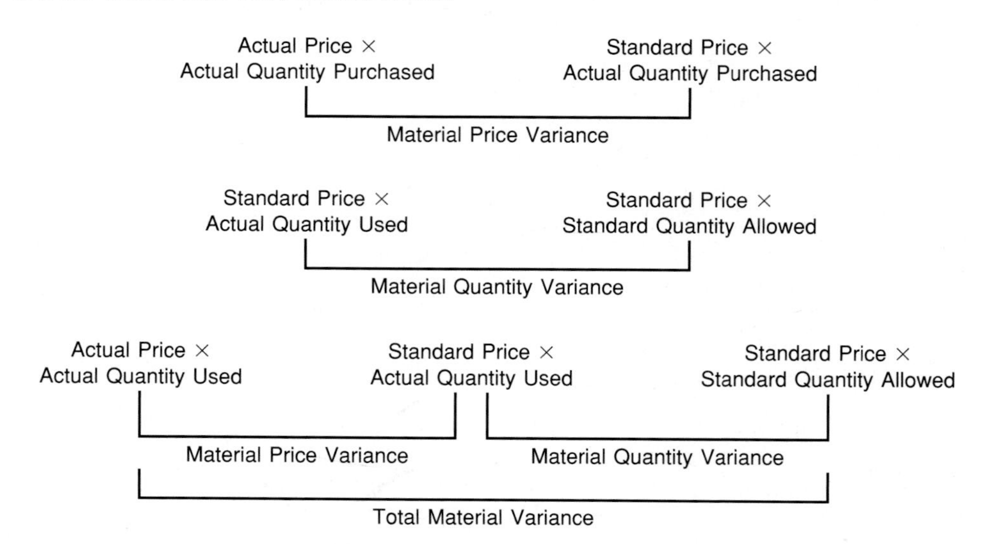

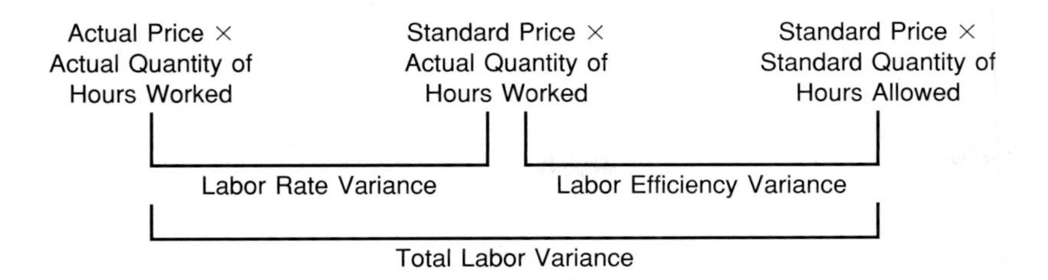

Overhead four-variance approach:

Variable Overhead

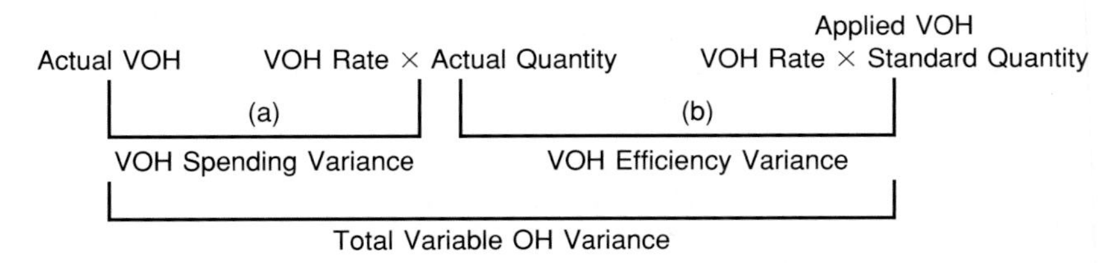

Fixed Overhead

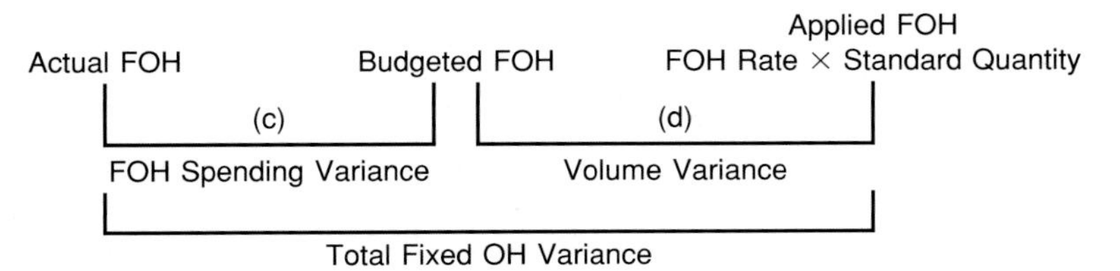

Overhead one-, two-, and three-variance approaches:

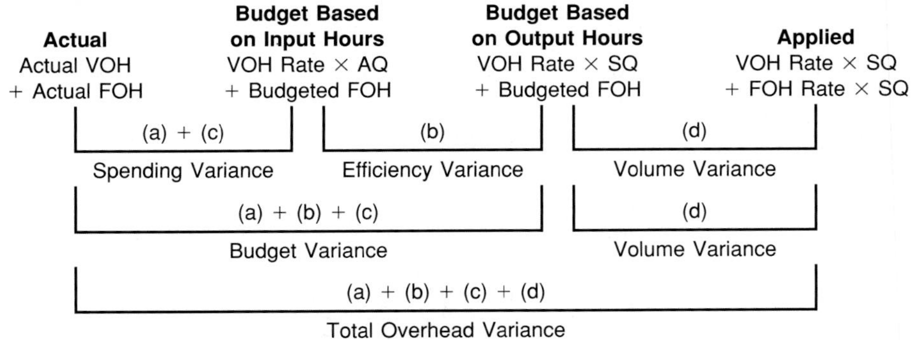

Mix and Yield Variances

MULTIPLE MATERIALS:

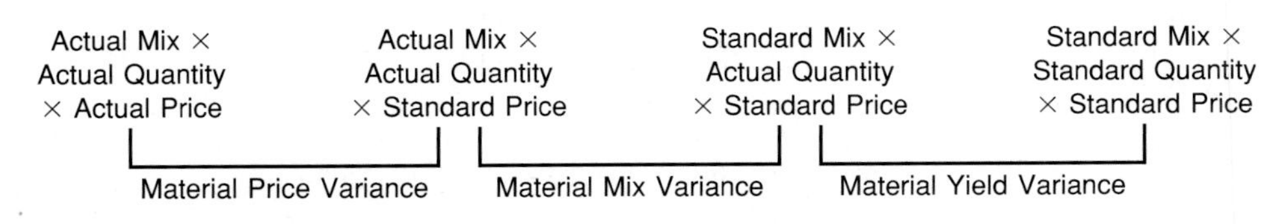

MULTIPLE LABOR CATEGORIES:

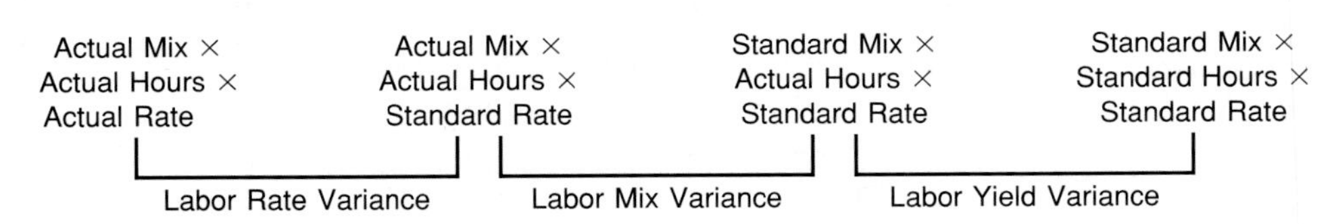

DEMONSTRATION PROBLEM

Poly Containers makes 300-gallon plastic water tanks for a variety of commercial uses. The standard per unit material, labor, and overhead costs are as follows:

Direct material: 80 pounds @ $2	$160
Direct labor: 1.25 hours @ $16 per hour	20
Variable overhead: 30 minutes of machine time @ $50.00 per hour	25
Fixed overhead: 30 minutes of machine time @ $40.00 per hour	20

The overhead application rates were developed using a practical capacity of 6,000 units per year. Production is assumed to occur evenly throughout the year.

During May 2001, the company produced 525 tanks. Actual data for May 2001 are as follows:

Direct material purchased: 46,000 pounds @ $1.92 per pound
Direct material used: 43,050 pounds (all from May's purchases)
Total labor cost: $10,988.25 for 682.5 hours
Variable overhead incurred: $13,770 for 270 hours of machine time
Fixed overhead incurred: $10,600 for 270 hours of machine time

Required:
Calculate the following:

a. Material price variance based on purchases
b. Material quantity variance
c. Labor rate variance
d. Labor efficiency variance
e. Variable overhead spending and efficiency variances
f. Fixed overhead spending and volume variances
g. Overhead variances using a three-variance approach
h. Overhead variances using a two-variance approach
i. Overhead variance using a one-variance approach

Solution to Demonstration Problem

a.

$AP \times AQ_p$		$SP \times AQ_p$
$1.92 × 46,000		$2.00 × 46,000
$88,320		$92,000
	$3,680 F	
	MPV	

b.

$$SQ = 525 \times 80 \text{ pounds} = 42{,}000 \text{ pounds}$$

$SP \times AQ_u$		$SP \times SQ$
$2 × 43,050		$2 × 42,000
$86,100		$84,000
	$2,100 U	
	MQV	

c. & d.

$$AR = \$10{,}988.25 \div 682.5 \text{ hours} = \$16.10 \text{ per hour}$$

$$SQ = 525 \times 1.25 \text{ hours} = 656.25 \text{ hours}$$

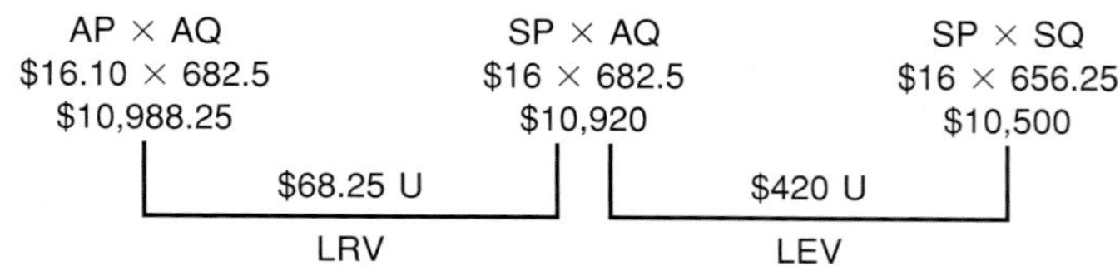

e. $SQ = 525 \times 0.5 = 262.5$ hours

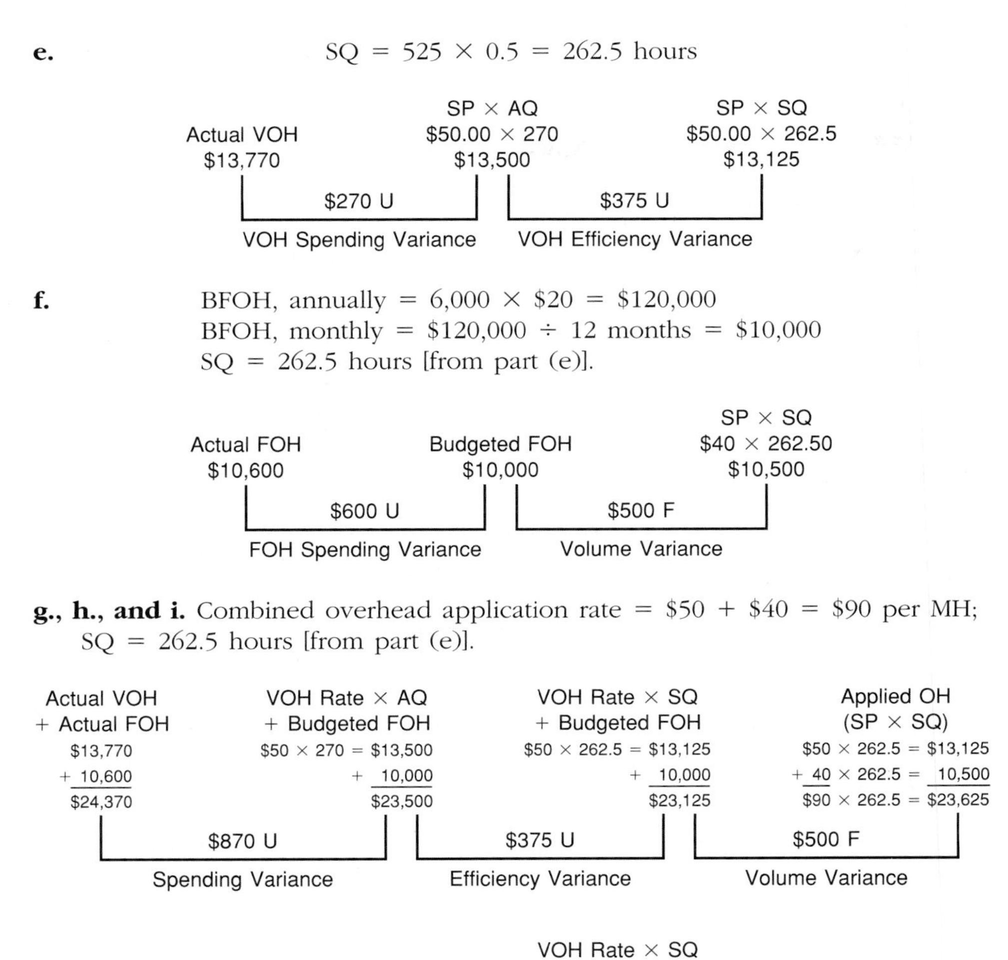

f. BFOH, annually = $6,000 \times \$20 = \$120,000$
BFOH, monthly = $\$120,000 \div 12$ months = $10,000
$SQ = 262.5$ hours [from part (e)].

g., h., and i. Combined overhead application rate = $50 + $40 = $90 per MH;
SQ = 262.5 hours [from part (e)].

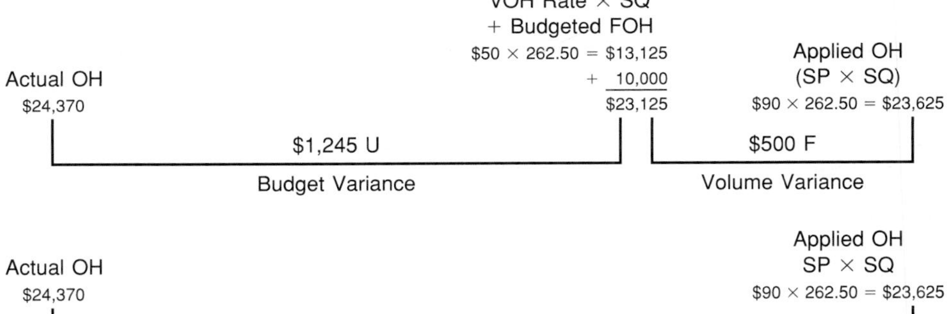

Actual OH
$24,370

Applied OH
SP × SQ
$90 × 262.50 = $23,625

$745 U

Total Overhead Variance
(Total Under/Overapplied Overhead)

QUESTIONS

1. What are the three primary uses of a standard cost system? In a business that routinely manufactures the same products or performs the same services, why would standards be helpful?
2. The standards development team should be composed of what experts? Why are these people included?
3. Discuss the development of standards for a material. How is the quality standard established for a material?

4. What is a standard cost card? What information is contained on it? How does it relate to a bill of materials and an operations flow document?
5. Why are the quantities shown in the bill of materials not always the same quantities shown in the standard cost card?
6. A total variance can be calculated for each cost component of a product. Into what variances can this total be separated and to what does each relate? (Discuss separately for material and labor.)
7. What is meant by the term *standard hours*? Does the term refer to inputs or outputs?
8. Why are the overhead spending and overhead efficiency variances said to be controllable? Is the volume variance controllable? Why or why not?
9. How are actual and standard costs recorded in a standard cost system?
10. "Unfavorable variances will always have debit balances, whereas favorable variances will always have credit balances." Is this statement true or false? Why?
11. How are immaterial variances closed at the end of an accounting period? How are significant variances closed at the end of an accounting period? Why is there a difference in treatment?
12. What is meant by the process of "management by exception"? How is a standard cost system helpful in such a process?
13. Discuss the three types of standards with regard to the level of rigor of attainment. Why are some companies currently adopting the most rigorous standard?
14. Why might traditional methods of setting standards lead to less than desirable material resource management and employee behavior?
15. Why do managers care about the utilization of capacity? Are they controlling costs when they control utilization?
16. How are variances used by managers in their efforts to control costs?
17. Fixed overhead costs are generally incurred in lump-sum amounts. What implications does this have for control of fixed overhead?
18. Can combined overhead rates be used for control purposes? Are such rates more or less appropriate than separate overhead rates? Discuss.
19. Which overhead variance approach (two-variance, three-variance, or four-variance) provides the most information for cost control purposes? Why?
20. Why are some companies replacing the two traditional cost categories of direct labor and manufacturing overhead with a "conversion cost" category?
21. How has automation affected standard costing? How has automation affected the computation of variances?
22. *(Appendix)* What variances can be computed for direct material and direct labor when some materials or labor inputs are substitutes for others? What information does each of these variances provide?

EXERCISES

23. *(Direct material variances)* Iron Eagle makes wrought iron table and chair sets. During April 2001, the purchasing agent bought 12,800 pounds of scrap iron at $0.89 per pound. Each set requires a standard quantity of 35 pounds at a standard cost of $0.85 per pound. During April, the company used 10,700 pounds and produced 300 sets.
    a. For April, compute the direct material price variance (based on the quantity purchased) and the direct material quantity variance.
    b. Identify the titles of individuals in the firm who would be responsible for each of the variances.
    c. Identify some potential explanations for the variances computed in part (a).

24. *(Direct material variances)* In August 2001, East Publishing Company's costs and quantities of paper consumed in manufacturing its 2002 Executive Planner and Calendar were as follow:

Actual unit purchase price	$0.16 per page
Standard quantity allowed for good production	195,800 pages
Actual quantity purchased during August	230,000 pages
Actual quantity used in August	200,000 pages
Standard unit price	$0.15 per page

a. Calculate the total cost of purchases for August.
b. Compute the material price variance (based on quantity purchased).
c. Calculate the material quantity variance.

25. *(Direct labor variances)* Nelson Prefabricated Walls builds standard prefabricated wooden frames for apartment walls. The standard quantity of direct labor is 5 hours for each frame at an average standard hourly wage of $22. During May 2001, the company produced 630 frames. The payroll records indicated that the carpenters worked 3,100 hours and earned $71,300.
a. What were the standard hours allowed for May construction?
b. Calculate the direct labor variances.

26. *(Direct labor variances)* In auditing the inventory account of a client, the accounting firm of Freeman and Associates set the following standard: 300 hours at an hourly rate of $45. The firm actually worked 270 hours auditing inventory. The total labor variance for the inventory audit was $0.
a. Compute the total actual payroll.
b. Compute the labor efficiency variance.
c. Compute the labor rate variance.
d. Offer a brief explanation that is consistent with the two variances.

27. *(Direct material and direct labor variances)* Lisa Scamponi Ltd. produces evening bags. In December 2001, Ms. Scamponi, president of the company, received the following information from Antonio Buffa, the new controller, in regard to November production:

Production during month	1,200 handbags
Actual cost of material purchased and used	$4,767.18
Standard material allowed	1/3 square yard per bag
Material quantity variance	$594 U
Actual hours worked	2,520
Standard labor time per handbag	2 hours
Labor rate variance	$630 F
Standard labor rate per hour	$7
Standard price per yard of material	$8

Ms. Scamponi asked Mr. Buffa to provide her with the following specific information:
a. The standard quantity of material allowed for November production
b. The standard direct labor hours allowed for November production
c. The material price variance
d. The labor efficiency variance
e. The standard prime (direct material and direct labor) cost to produce one bag
f. The actual cost to produce one bag in November
g. An explanation for the difference between standard and actual cost. Be sure the explanation is consistent with the pattern of the variances.

28. *(Missing information for materials and labor)* For each of the independent cases, fill in the missing figures.

	Case A	Case B	Case C	Case D
Units produced	800	?	240	1,500
Standard hours per unit	3	0.8	?	?
Standard hours allowed	?	600	480	?
Standard rate per hour	$7	?	$9.50	$6
Actual hours worked	2,330	675	?	4,875
Actual labor cost	?	?	$4,560	$26,812.50
Labor rate variance	$466F	$1,080F	$228U	?
Labor efficiency variance	?	$780U	?	$2,250U

29. *(Four-variance approach; journal entries)* For 2001, Blankly Manufacturing has set 60,000 direct labor hours as the annual capacity measure for computing its predetermined variable overhead rate. At that level, budgeted variable overhead costs are $270,000. The company has decided to apply fixed overhead on the basis of machine hours. Total budgeted annual machine hours are 3,300 and annual budgeted fixed overhead is $118,800. Both machine hours and fixed overhead costs are expected to be incurred evenly each month.

During March 2001, Blankly incurred 4,900 direct labor hours and 250 machine hours. Variable and fixed overhead were, respectively, $21,175 and $10,500. The standard times allowed for March production were 4,955 direct labor hours and 240 machine hours.

a. Using the four-variance approach, determine the overhead variances for March 2001.

b. Prepare all journal entries for Blankly Manufacturing for March 2001.

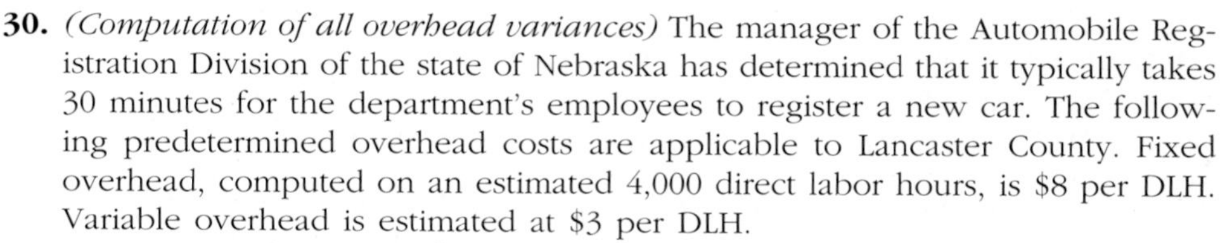

30. *(Computation of all overhead variances)* The manager of the Automobile Registration Division of the state of Nebraska has determined that it typically takes 30 minutes for the department's employees to register a new car. The following predetermined overhead costs are applicable to Lancaster County. Fixed overhead, computed on an estimated 4,000 direct labor hours, is $8 per DLH. Variable overhead is estimated at $3 per DLH.

During July 2001, 7,600 cars were registered in Lancaster County, taking 3,700 direct labor hours. For the month, variable overhead was $10,730 and fixed overhead was $29,950.

a. Compute overhead variances using a four-variance approach.

b. Compute overhead variances using a three-variance approach.

c. Compute overhead variances using a two-variance approach.

31. *(Missing data, three-variance approach)* The flexible budget formula for total overhead for the Windlass Corporation is $720,000 + $16 per direct labor hour. The combined overhead rate is $40 per direct labor hour. The following data have been recorded for the year:

Actual total overhead	$1,160,000
Total overhead spending variance	$ 32,000 U
Volume variance	$ 48,000 U

Use a three-variance approach to determine the following:

a. Number of standard hours allowed

b. Actual direct labor hours worked

32. *(Variances and cost control)* North Diamond Inc. applies overhead on a direct labor hour basis. Each unit of product requires 12 machine hours. Overhead is applied on a 30 percent variable and 70 percent fixed basis; the overhead application rate is $40 per hour. Standards are based on a normal monthly capacity of 24,000 machine hours.

During September 2001, North Diamond produced 2,300 units of product and incurred 25,000 machine hours. Actual overhead cost for the month was $1,000,000.

a. What were standard hours allowed for September?
b. What is total annual budgeted fixed overhead cost?
c. What is the controllable overhead variance?
d. What is the noncontrollable overhead variance?

33. *(Journal entries)* Miami Chemical had the following balances in its trial balance at year-end 2001:

	Debit	Credit
Direct Material Inventory	$ 36,600	
Work in Process Inventory	43,920	
Finished Goods Inventory	65,880	
Cost of Goods Sold	585,600	
Material Price Variance	7,250	
Material Quantity Variance		$10,925
Labor Rate Variance		1,200
Labor Efficiency Variance	4,390	
VOH Spending Variance		3,600
VOH Efficiency Variance	200	
FOH Spending Variance	650	
Volume Variance	1,375	

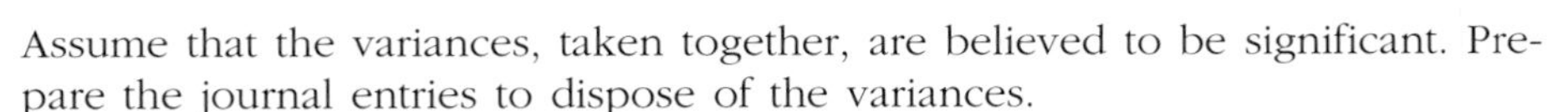

Assume that the variances, taken together, are believed to be significant. Prepare the journal entries to dispose of the variances.

34. *(Variances and conversion cost category)* Baltimore Brake makes brake rotors. Until recently, the company used a standard cost system and applied overhead to production based on direct labor hours. The company automated its facilities in March 2001 and revamped its accounting system so that there are only two cost categories: direct material and conversion. Estimated variable conversion costs for April 2001 were $170,000, and estimated fixed conversion costs were $76,000; machine hours were estimated at 10,000 for April. Expected output for April was 5,000 rotors. In April, the firm actually used 9,000 machine hours to make 4,800 rotors. The firm incurred conversion costs totaling $230,000; $150,000 of this amount was variable cost.

a. Using the four-variance approach, compute the variances for conversion costs in April.
b. Evaluate the effectiveness of the firm in controlling costs in April.

35. *(Appendix)* Genine Nut Company produces 12-ounce cans of mixed pecans and cashews. Standard and actual information follows.

Standard quantities and costs (12-oz. can):	
Pecans: 6 ounces at $3.00 per pound	$1.125
Cashews: 6 ounces at $4.00 per pound	1.500

Actual quantities and costs for February 2001 when production was 18,000, 12-oz. cans:

Pecans: 7,473 pounds at $2.90 per pound
Cashews: 6,617 pounds at $4.25 per pound

Determine the material price, mix, and yield variances.

36. *(Appendix)* Righting Moment Inc. is a mechanical engineering firm. The firm employs both engineers and draftspeople. The average hourly rates are $80 for engineers and $40 for draftspeople. For one project, the standard was set at 375 hours of engineer time and 625 hours of draftsperson time. Actual hours worked on this project were:

Engineers—500 hours at $85 per hour
Draftspeople—500 hours at $42.00 per hour

Determine the labor rate, mix, and yield variances for this project.

37. *(Developing standard cost card and discussion)* The Frozen Fruitcup Company is a small producer of fruit-flavored frozen desserts. For many years, Frozen Fruitcup products have had strong regional sales on the basis of brand recognition; however, other companies have begun marketing similar products in the area, and price competition has become increasingly important. Tanya Morse, the company's controller, is planning to implement a standard cost system for Frozen Fruitcup and has gathered considerable information from her coworkers on production and material requirements for the company's products. Morse believes that the use of standard costing will allow the firm to improve cost control and make better pricing decisions.

Frozen Fruitcup's most popular product is raspberry sherbet. The sherbet is produced in 10-gallon batches, and each batch requires 6 quarts of good raspberries. The fresh raspberries are sorted by hand before they enter the production process. Because of imperfections in the raspberries and normal spoilage, 1 quart of berries is discarded for every 4 quarts of acceptable berries. The standard direct labor time is 3 minutes for the sorting that is required to obtain 1 quart of acceptable raspberries. The acceptable raspberries are then blended with the other ingredients; blending requires 12 minutes of direct labor time per batch. During blending, there is some loss of material. After blending, the sherbet is packaged in quart containers. Morse has gathered the following cost information:

- Frozen Fruitcup purchases raspberries at a cost of $0.80 per quart.
- All other ingredients cost a total of $0.45 per gallon.
- Direct labor is paid at the rate of $9.00 per hour.
- The total cost of material and labor required to package the sherbet is $0.38 per quart.

a. Develop the standard cost for the direct cost components of a 10-gallon batch of raspberry sherbet. The standard cost should identify the standard quantity, the standard rate, and the standard cost per batch for each direct cost component of a batch of raspberry sherbet.

b. As part of the implementation of a standard cost system at the company, Morse plans to train those responsible for maintaining the standards on how to use variance analysis. She is particularly concerned with the causes of unfavorable variances.

1. Discuss the possible causes of unfavorable material price variances, and identify the individual(s) who should be held responsible for these variances.
2. Discuss the possible causes of unfavorable labor efficiency variances, and identify the individual(s) who should be held responsible for these variances. *(CMA adapted)*

38. *(Behavioral implications of standard costing)* Contact a local company that uses a standard cost system. Make an appointment with a manager at that company to interview him or her on the following issues:

- The characteristics that should be present in a standard cost system to encourage positive employee motivation
- How a standard cost system should be implemented to positively motivate employees
- What "management by exception" is and how variance analysis often results in the use of management by exception
- How employee behavior could be adversely affected when "actual to standard" comparisons are used as the basis for performance evaluation

Prepare a paper and an oral presentation based on your interview.

39. *(Flexible budget, variances, and cost control)* Overland Corp. planned to produce at the 8,000-unit level for its single type of product. Because of unexpected demand, the firm actually operated at the 8,800-unit level. The company's flexible budget appears as follows:

	6,000 units	8,000 units	10,000 units
Overhead costs:			
Variable	$24,000	$32,000	$40,000
Fixed	16,000	16,000	16,000
Total	$40,000	$48,000	$56,000

Actual costs incurred in producing the 8,800 units:

Variable	$34,320
Fixed	16,400
Total	$50,720

The production manager was upset because the company planned to incur $48,000 of costs and actual costs were $50,720. Prepare a memo to the production manager regarding the following questions.

a. Was it correct to compare the $50,720 to the $48,000 for cost control purposes?

b. Analyze the costs and explain where the company did well or poorly in controlling its costs.

40. *(Standard setting; team project)* As a four-person team, choose an activity that is commonly performed every day, such as taking a shower/bath, preparing a meal, or doing homework. Have each team member time himself/herself performing that activity for two days and then develop a standard time for the team. Now have the team members time themselves performing the same activity for the next five days.

a. Using an assumed hourly wage rate of $12, calculate the labor efficiency variance for your team.

b. Prepare a list of reasons for the variance.

c. How could some of the variance have been avoided?

41. *(Cost control evaluation)* The Arizona Concrete Company makes precast concrete steps for use with manufactured housing. The plant had the following 2001 budget based on expected production of 3,200 units:

	Standard Cost	Amount Budgeted
Direct material	$22.00	$ 70,400
Direct labor	12.00	38,400
Variable overhead:		
Indirect material	4.20	13,440
Indirect labor	1.75	5,600
Utilities	1.00	3,200
Fixed overhead:		
Supervisory salaries		40,000
Depreciation		15,000
Insurance		9,640
Total		$195,680

Cost per unit = $195,680 ÷ 3,200 = $61.15

Actual production for 2001 was 3,500 units, and actual costs for the year were as follows:

Direct material used	$ 80,500
Direct labor	42,300
Variable overhead:	
Indirect material	14,000
Indirect labor	6,650
Utilities	3,850
Fixed overhead:	
Supervisory salaries	41,000
Depreciation	15,000
Insurance	8,800
Total	$212,100

Cost per unit = $212,100 ÷ 3,500 = $60.60

The plant manager, John Wessly, whose annual bonus includes (among other factors) 20 percent of the net favorable cost variances, states that he saved the company $1,925 [($61.15 − $60.60) × 3,500]. He has instructed the plant cost accountant to prepare a detailed report to be sent to corporate headquarters comparing each component's actual per-unit cost with the per-unit amounts set forth above in the annual budget to prove the $1,925 cost savings.

a. Is the actual-to-budget comparison proposed by Wessly an appropriate one? If Wessly's comparison is not appropriate, prepare a more appropriate comparison.

b. How would you, as the plant cost accountant, react if Wessly insisted on his comparison? Suggest what alternatives are available to you.

42. *(Appendix)* Buffin Legal Services has three labor classes: secretaries, paralegals, and attorneys. The standard wage rates are shown in the standard cost system as follows: secretaries, $25 per hour; paralegals, $40 per hour; and attorneys, $85 per hour. The firm has established a standard of 0.5 hours of secretarial time and 2 hours of paralegal time for each hour of attorney time in probate cases. The actual direct labor hours worked on probate cases and the standard hours allowed for the work accomplished for one month in 2001 were as follows:

	Actual DLHS	Standard Hours for Output Achieved
Secretarial	500	500
Paralegal	1,800	2,000
Attorney	1,100	1,000

a. Calculate the amount of the direct labor efficiency variance for the month and decompose the total into the following components:

1. Direct labor mix variance

2. Direct labor yield variance

b. Prepare a memo addressing whether management used an efficient mix of labor. *(CMA adapted)*

PROBLEMS

43. *(Material and labor variances)* Mississippi Marine uses a standard cost system for materials and labor in producing fishing boats. Production requires three materials: fiberglass, paint, and a prepurchased trim package. The standard costs and quantities for materials and labor are as follows:

Standards for 1 Fishing Boat	
2,500 pounds of fiberglass @ $0.80 per pound	$2,000
6 quarts gel coat paint @ $60.00 per gallon	90
1 trim package	400
40 hours of labor @ $25.00 per hour	1,000
Prime standard cost	$3,490

During July 2001, the company recorded the following actual data related to the production of 300 boats:

Material Purchased:

Fiberglass—820,000 pounds @ $0.83 per pound
Paint—500 gallons @ $55.50 per gallon
Trim packages—320 @ $405 per package

Material Used:

Fiberglass—790,000 pounds
Paint—462 gallons
Trim packages—304

Direct Labor Used:

12,100 hours @ $23.50 per hour

Calculate the material and labor variances for Mississippi Marine for July 2001. Base the material price variance on the quantity of material purchased.

44. *(Variance calculation and journal entries)* Montreal Toy Co. makes small plastic toys. Standard quantities and standard costs follow for material and labor.

	Standard Quantity	Standard Cost
Material	1/2 pound	$4 per pound ($2.00 per unit of output)
Labor	12 minutes	$16 per hour ($3.20 per unit of output)

During October 2001, 50,000 toys were produced. The purchasing agent bought 29,000 pounds of material during the month at $4.13 per pound. October payroll for the factory revealed direct labor cost of $160,680 on 10,300 direct labor hours. During the month, 26,300 pounds of raw material were used in production.

a. Compute material and labor variances, basing the material price variance on the quantity of material purchased.

b. Assuming a perpetual inventory system, prepare general journal entries for the month.

45. *(Incomplete data)* Surgical Supply manufactures latex surgical gloves. It takes 0.85 square feet of latex to manufacture a pair of gloves. The standard price for material is $0.80 per square foot. Most processing is done by machine; the only labor required is for operators, who are paid $25 per hour. The machines can produce 400 pairs of gloves per hour.

During one week in May, Surgical produced 30,000 pairs of gloves and experienced a $1,500 unfavorable material quantity variance. The company had purchased 1,500 more square feet of material than it used in production that week, producing an unfavorable price variance of $570. Based on 77 total actual labor hours to produce the gloves, a $104 favorable total labor variance was generated. Determine the following amounts:

a. Standard quantity of material

b. Actual quantity of material used

(continued)

c. Actual quantity of material purchased
d. Actual price of material purchased
e. Standard hours allowed for production
f. Labor efficiency variance
g. Labor rate variance
h. Actual labor rate

46. *(Incomplete data)* Learning Products, Inc., makes wooden lap desks. A small fire on October 1 partially destroyed the books and records relating to September's production. The charred remains of the standard cost card appear below.

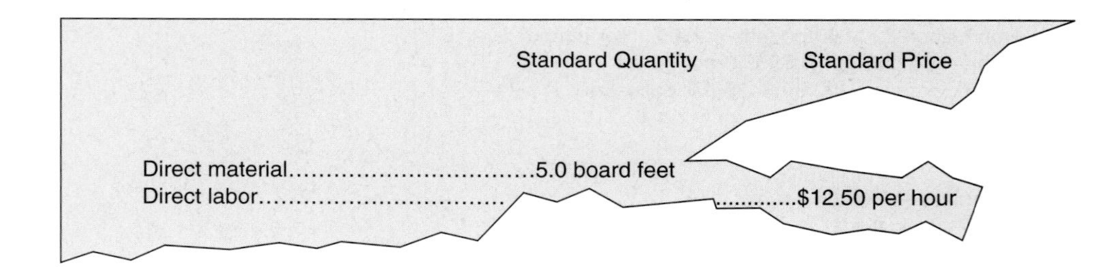

From other fragments of records and several discussions with employees, you learn the following:

1. The standard quantity of material used in September was 4,000 board feet.
2. The September payroll for direct labor was $19,220 based on 1,550 actual hours worked.
3. The production supervisor distinctly remembered being held accountable for 50 more hours of direct labor than should have been worked. She was upset because top management failed to consider that she saved several hundred board feet of material by creative efforts that required extra time.
4. The purchasing agent's files showed that 4,300 board feet had been purchased and used in September at $2.05 per board foot. She was proud of the fact that this price was $0.05 below standard cost per foot.

a. How many units were produced during September?
b. Calculate all variances for direct material and direct labor for September.
c. What is the standard number of hours allowed for the production of each unit?
d. Prepare general journal entries reflecting direct material and direct labor activity and variances for September, assuming a standard cost, perpetual inventory system.

47. *(Adjusting standards)* Maui Muumuus manufactures traditional Hawaiian dresses. The company was started early in 1995, and the following standards for materials and labor were developed at that time:

Material	3 yards at $6 per yard
Labor	1.5 hours at $10 per hour

In May 2001, Maui Muumuus hired a new cost accountant, Sally Rogers. At the end of May, Sally was reviewing the variances calculated for the month and was amazed to find that standards had never been revised since the company started. Actual data for May 2001 for material and labor are as follows:

Material	Purchased, 50,000 yards at $7.00 Used in production of 17,200 muumuus, 50,000 yards
Labor	17,800 hours at $13.50 per hour

Since 1995, material prices have risen 4 percent each year. However, the company can now buy at 94 percent of regular price due to the increased volume of purchases. Labor contracts have specified a 5 percent cost-of-living adjustment for each year, beginning in 1996. Because of revising the plant layout and purchasing more efficient machinery, the labor time per muumuu has decreased by one-third; also, direct material waste has been reduced from 1/4 yard to 1/8 yard per muumuu.

a. Determine the material and labor variances based on the standards originally designed for the company.

b. Determine the new standards against which Sally should measure the May 2001 results. (Round adjustments annually to the nearest penny.)

c. Compute the variances for material and labor using the revised standards.

48. *(Calculation of four variances)* Candy's Ceramics utilizes a standard cost system. Data for October are presented below:

	Standard Cost per Unit (1 Unit Takes 1 Labor Hour)
Direct material	$ 9.00
Direct labor	15.00
Variable overhead	8.00
Fixed overhead	16.00
Total	$48.00

The fixed overhead charge is based on an expected monthly capacity of 3,000 units, but due to a fire on the production floor, the company only produced 1,900 units. Actual variable overhead was $16,000 and actual fixed overhead was $44,000. The company recorded 2,000 direct labor hours for the month.

a. Compute and compare the actual overhead cost per unit with the expected overhead cost per unit.

b. Calculate overhead variances using the four-variance method.

49. *(Four-variance approach; journal entries)* Laramie Lumber produces picnic tables, swings, and benches and uses direct labor hours to apply overhead. Standard hours allowed for each product are as follows:

Picnic table:	10 standard direct labor hours
Swing:	3 standard direct labor hours
Bench:	12 standard direct labor hours

The standard variable overhead rate is $4 per direct labor hour; the standard fixed overhead application rate at expected annual capacity is $2 per direct labor hour. Expected capacity on a monthly basis is 3,000 direct labor hours.

Production for June 2001 was 100 picnic tables, 400 swings, and 60 benches. Actual direct labor hours incurred were 3,020. Actual variable overhead was $11,900, and actual fixed overhead was $6,100 for the month.

a. Prepare a variance analysis using the four-variance approach. (*Hint:* Convert the production of each type of product into standard hours allowed for all work accomplished for the month.)

b. Prepare journal entries for (1) incurring overhead costs, (2) applying overhead costs, and (3) closing the variance accounts (assume immaterial variances).

c. Evaluate the effectiveness of managers in controlling costs.

50. *(Variance analysis with unknowns)* ATTENTION Products manufactures a neon lamp sign with the following standard conversion costs:

Direct labor (4 hours @ $12 per hour)	$ 48
Factory overhead (10,000 DLH expected capacity)	
Variable (4 hours @ $16 per hour)	64
Fixed (4 hours @ $8 per hour)	32
Total unit conversion cost	$144

The following data are given for December, when 8,000 standard labor hours were used:

Labor rate variance	$ 4,500 U
Labor efficiency variance	12,000 U
Actual variable overhead	153,000
Actual fixed overhead	78,000

Calculate the answers for the following unknowns:

a. Total applied factory overhead
b. Volume variance
c. Variable overhead spending variance
d. Variable overhead efficiency variance
e. Total actual overhead
f. Number of units manufactured

51. *(Combined overhead rates)* Rocky Mountain Industries manufactures a down-filled sleeping bag with the following standard cost information for 2001:

- Each sleeping bag requires 1 hour of machine time to produce.
- Variable overhead: $9 per machine hour
- Fixed overhead: $12 per machine hour; calculated as total budgeted overhead divided by expected annual capacity of 30,000 machine hours

Production Statistics for 2001:	
Number of sleeping bags produced	31,000 units
Actual machine hours	33,300 hours
Variable overhead cost incurred	$266,400
Fixed overhead cost incurred	$353,500

a. Using a combined overhead rate, calculate variances according to the two-variance approach.
b. Using a combined overhead rate, calculate variances according to the three-variance approach.

52. *(Comprehensive)* Aluma Corporation manufactures metal screen doors for commercial buildings. The standard costs per screen door follow:

Direct Materials:		
Aluminum	4 sheets at $2	$ 8
Copper	3 sheets at $4	12
Direct labor	7 hours at $8	56
Variable overhead	5 machine hours at $3	15
Fixed overhead	5 machine hours at $2	10

Overhead rates were based on normal monthly capacity of 6,000 machine hours.

During November, 850 doors were produced. This was below normal levels due to the effects of a labor strike that occurred during union contract negotiations. Once the dispute was settled, the company scheduled overtime to try to catch up to regular production levels. The following costs were incurred in November:

Material:

Aluminum:	4,000 sheets purchased at $2; used 3,500 sheets
Copper:	3,000 sheets purchased at $4.20; used 2,600 sheets

Direct Labor:

Regular time:	5,200 hours at $8.00 (precontract settlement)
Regular time:	900 hours at $8.50 (postcontract settlement)

Variable Overhead:

$11,700 (based on 4,175 machine hours)

Fixed Overhead:

$9,300 (based on 4,175 machine hours)

Determine the following:

a. Total material price variance
b. Total material usage (quantity) variance
c. Labor rate variance
d. Labor efficiency variance
e. Variable overhead spending variance
f. Variable overhead efficiency variance
g. Fixed overhead spending variance
h. Volume variance
i. Budget variance

53. *(Comprehensive; all variances; all methods)* Rainbow Painting Services Inc. paints interiors of residences and commercial structures. The firm's management has established cost standards based on the amount of area to be painted.

Direct material ($18 per gallon of paint): $1.50 per 100 square feet
Direct labor: $2 per 100 square feet
Variable overhead: $0.60 per 100 square feet
Fixed overhead (based on 600,000 square feet per month): $1.25 per 100 square feet

Management has determined that 400 square feet can be painted by the average worker each hour. During May 2001, the company painted 600,000 square feet of wall and ceiling space. The following costs were incurred:

Direct material (450 gallons purchased and used)	$ 8,550.00
Direct labor (1,475 hours)	12,242.50
Variable overhead	3,420.00
Fixed overhead	7,740.00

a. Compute the direct material variances.
b. Compute the direct labor variances.
c. Use a four-variance approach to compute overhead variances.
d. Use a three-variance approach to compute overhead variances.
e. Use a two-variance approach to compute overhead variances.
f. Reconcile your answers for parts (c) through (e).
g. Discuss other cost drivers that could be used as a basis for measuring activity and computing variances for this company.

54. *(Variance disposition)* Ito Manufacturing had the following variances at year-end 2001:

Material price variance	$23,400 U
Material quantity variance	24,900 F
Labor rate variance	5,250 F
Labor efficiency variance	36,900 U
Variable overhead spending variance	3,000 U
Variable overhead efficiency variance	1,800 F
Fixed overhead spending variance	6,600 F
Volume variance	16,800 U

In addition, the inventory and cost of goods sold account balances were as follows at year-end 2001:

Raw Material Inventory	$ 338,793
Work in Process Inventory	914,277
Finished Goods Inventory	663,663
Cost of Goods Sold	2,724,267

a. Assuming that all variances are insignificant, prepare the journal entry at December 31 to dispose of them.
b. After posting your entry in part (a), what is the balance in Cost of Goods Sold?
c. Assuming that all variances are significant, prepare the necessary journal entries at December 31 to dispose of them.
d. What will be the balance in each of the inventory accounts and cost of goods sold account?

55. *(Conversion cost variances)* Sanchez Mfg. budgeted $1,080,000 of variable conversion costs and $360,000 of fixed conversion costs for May 2001. When the budget was developed, Sanchez estimated 72,000 machine hours would be required to make 24,000 units of product. During May, 76,000 machine hours were worked and the firm incurred $1,128,600 of variable conversion costs and $374,000 of fixed conversion costs. Twenty-five thousand units were produced in May.
a. Calculate the four conversion cost variances assuming separation of fixed and variable costs is maintained.
b. Calculate the three conversion cost variances assuming fixed and variable costs are combined.

56. *(Appendix)* Pablo's three-topping 18-inch frozen pizzas are produced by Quintella Food Industries in Los Angeles. The company uses a standard cost system. The three toppings (in addition to cheese) for each pizza are onions, olives, and mushrooms. To some extent, discretion may be used to determine the actual mix of these toppings. The company has two classes of labor, and discretion may be used to determine the mix of the labor inputs. The standard cost card for a pizza follows:

Onions: 3 ounces at $0.10 per ounce
Olives: 3 ounces at $0.35 per ounce
Mushrooms: 3 ounces at $0.50 per ounce
Labor category 1: 5 minutes at $12 per hour
Labor category 2: 6 minutes at $8 per hour

During May 2001, Quintella produced 12,000 pizzas and used the following inputs:

Onions:	2,000 pounds
Olives:	3,000 pounds
Mushrooms:	2,000 pounds
Labor category 1:	1,300 hours
Labor category 2:	1,000 hours

During the month there were no deviations from standards on material prices or labor rates.

a. Determine the material quantity, mix, and yield variances.
b. Determine the labor efficiency, mix, and yield variances.
c. Prepare the journal entries to record the above mix and yield variances.

57. *(Appendix)* Colson Products makes NOTAM, a new health food. For a 50-pound batch, the standard costs for materials and labor are as follows:

	Quantity	Unit Price	Total
Wheat	25 pounds	$0.20 per pound	$5.00
Barley	25 pounds	$0.10 per pound	2.50
Corn	10 pounds	$0.05 per pound	0.50
Skilled labor	0.8 hours	$12.00 per hour	9.60
Unskilled labor	0.2 hours	$ 8.00 per hour	1.60

During June, the following materials and labor were used in producing 600 batches of NOTAM:

Wheat	18,000 pounds at $0.22 per pound
Barley	14,000 pounds at $0.11 per pound
Corn	10,000 pounds at $0.04 per pound
Skilled labor	400 hours at $12.25 per hour
Unskilled labor	260 hours at $8.00 per hour

a. Calculate the material quantity, mix, and yield variances.
b. Calculate the labor efficiency, mix, and yield variances.

CASES

58. *(Standards revision)* Westlake Company produces a component for aircraft manufacturers. A standard cost system has been used for years with good results. Unfortunately, Westlake's original direct material source went out of business. The new source produces a similar but higher quality material. The price per pound from the original source averaged $7; the price from the new source is $7.77. The new material reduces scrap and, thus, reduces the use of direct material from 1.25 to 1.00 pounds per unit. In addition, direct labor is reduced from 24 to 22 minutes per unit because there is less scrap labor and machine setup time.

The direct material problem was occurring at the same time that labor negotiations resulted in an increase of over 14 percent in hourly direct labor costs. The average rate rose from $12.60 per hour to $14.40 per hour. Production of the main product requires a high level of labor skill. Because of a continuing shortage in that skill area, an interim wage agreement had to be signed.

Westlake started using the new direct material on April 1, the same date that the new labor agreement went into effect. However, the company is still using standards that were set at the beginning of the calendar year. The direct material and direct labor standards for the component are as follows:

Direct material	1.2 pounds at $6.80 per pound	$ 8.16
Direct labor	20 minutes at $12.30 per DLH	4.10
Standard cost per unit		$12.26

Howard Foster, cost accounting supervisor, had been examining the following April 30 performance report.

PERFORMANCE REPORT
STANDARD COST VARIANCE ANALYSIS FOR APRIL 2001

Standard		Price Variance		Quantity Variance		Actual
DM	$ 8.16	($0.97 × 1.0)	$0.97 U	($6.80 × 0.2)	$1.36 F	$ 7.77
DL	4.10	[$2.10 × (22/60)]	0.77 U	[$12.30 × (2/60)]	0.41 U	5.28
	$12.26					$13.05

COMPARISON OF 2001 ACTUAL COSTS

	Average 1st Quarter Costs	April Costs	% Increase (Decrease)
DM	$ 8.75	$ 7.77	(11.2)
DL	5.04	5.28	4.8
	$13.79	$13.05	(5.4)

Jane Keene, assistant controller, came into Foster's office and Foster said, "Jane, look at this performance report! Direct material price increased 11 percent and the labor rate increased over 14 percent during April. I expected greater variances, yet prime costs decreased over 5 percent from the $13.79 we experienced during the first quarter of this year. The proper message just isn't coming through."

"This has been an unusual period," said Keene. "With all the unforeseen changes, perhaps we should revise our standards based on current conditions and start over."

Foster replied, "I think we can retain the current standards but expand the variance analysis. We could calculate variances for the specific changes that have occurred to direct material and direct labor before we calculate the normal price and quantity variances. What I really think would be useful to management right now is to determine the impact the changes in direct material and direct labor had in reducing our prime costs per unit from $13.79 in the first quarter to $13.05 in April—a reduction of $0.74."

a. Discuss the advantages of (1) immediately revising the standards and (2) retaining the current standards and expanding the analysis of variances.

b. Prepare an analysis that reflects the impact of the new direct material and new labor contract on reducing Westlake's prime costs per unit from $13.79 to $13.05. The analysis should show the changes in direct material and direct labor costs per unit that are caused by (1) the use of new direct materials and (2) the new labor contract. This analysis should be in sufficient detail to identify the changes due to direct material price, direct labor rate, the effect of direct material quality on direct material usage, and the effect of direct material quality on direct labor usage. *(CMA adapted)*

59. *(Variances and variance responsibility)* Hobby Horse, Inc., began operations in 2000. In 2001, the company manufactured only one product, a handpainted toy horse. The 2001 standard cost per unit is as follows:

Material: one pound plastic at $2.00	$ 2.00
Direct labor: 1.6 hours at $4.00	6.40
Variable overhead cost	3.00
Fixed overhead cost	1.45
	$12.85

The overhead cost per unit was calculated from the following annual overhead cost budget for 60,000 units.

Variable Overhead Cost:		
Indirect labor—30,000 hours at $4.00	$120,000	
Supplies (oil)—60,000 gallons at $0.50	30,000	
Allocated variable service department costs	30,000	
Total variable overhead cost		$180,000
Fixed Overhead Cost:		
Supervision	$ 27,000	
Depreciation	45,000	
Other fixed costs	15,000	
Total fixed overhead cost		87,000
Total budgeted overhead cost at 60,000 units		$267,000

Following are the charges to the manufacturing department for November, when 5,000 units were produced:

Material (5,300 pounds at $2.00)	$10,600
Direct labor (8,200 hours at $4.10)	33,620
Indirect labor (2,400 hours at $4.10)	9,840
Supplies (oil) (6,000 gallons at $0.55)	3,300
Allocated variable service department costs	3,200
Supervision	2,475
Depreciation	3,750
Other fixed costs	1,250
Total	$68,035

The Purchasing Department normally buys about the same quantity as is used in production during a month. In November, 5,200 pounds of material were purchased at a price of $2.10 per pound.

a. Calculate the following variances from standard costs for the data given:
   1. Material purchase price
   2. Material quantity
   3. Direct labor rate
   4. Direct labor efficiency
   5. Overhead budget

b. The company has divided its responsibilities so that the Purchasing Department is responsible for the price at which materials and supplies are purchased. The Manufacturing Department is responsible for the quantities of materials used. Does this division of responsibilities solve the conflict between price and quantity variances? Explain your answer.

c. Prepare a report detailing the overhead budget variance. The report, which will be given to the Manufacturing Department manager, should show only that part of the variance that is her responsibility and should highlight the information in ways that would be useful to her in evaluating departmental performance and when considering corrective action.

d. Assume that the departmental manager performs the timekeeping function for this manufacturing department. From time to time, analyses of overhead and direct labor variances have shown that the manager has deliberately misclassified labor hours (i.e., listed direct labor hours as indirect labor hours and vice versa) so that only one of the two labor variances is unfavorable. It is not feasible economically to hire a separate timekeeper. What should the company do, if anything, to resolve this problem?

(CMA adapted)

REALITY CHECK

60. In the mid-1940s, a young man named Donald Roy was working on a Ph.D. at the University of Chicago. As part of his dissertation project, Mr. Roy posed (anonymously) for eleven months as a radial-drill operator at a steel-processing plant. Workers in this plant were paid on a piece-rate basis (with a minimum hourly base pay of 85 cents) for all of the jobs (parts) they worked on. Some of the most interesting behaviors that Mr. Roy observed involved games the employees played based on their perceptions of the fairness of piece rates. If the employees perceived that the piece rates were set too low (required too much output per hour to exceed the base rate) they would engage in work slowdowns. Thus, they would receive the base rate pay of 85 cents per hour rather than the piece-rate pay. The company's cost of components produced when employees engaged in slowdowns was consequently higher than the piece-rate cost. The slowdown was essentially a way to express discontentment with the piece rate and implied to management a need to revise the piece-rate pay. Communication among employees ensured that, with respect to a certain part, all employees participated in the slowdown. Other jobs were recognized by employees as "gravy jobs." On these jobs, the piece rates were sufficiently high to allow employees to easily exceed the base rate pay without exerting significant effort. On these jobs, employees carefully monitored each other so that no employee generated income substantially above the base rate of 85 cents per hour. The fear was that managers would revise the piece rate if employees generated too much hourly income from the piece rate pay.

SOURCE: Donald Roy, "Quota Restriction and Goldbricking in a Machine Shop," *American Journal of Sociology* (March 1952), pp. 427–442. Published by the University of Chicago Press. Reprinted with permission.

a. Why would it be difficult in the environment described by Donald Roy to develop credible standards of performance?
b. Was the behavior of the employees ethical?
c. Is it ethical for managers to revise piece-rate pay when it becomes obvious that standards can be easily met or beat?
d. How does honest communication between managers and workers help avoid the problems described by Donald Roy?

61. Tim Zeff is a plant manager who has done a good job of controlling some overhead costs during the current period and a poor job of controlling others. Tim's boss has asked him for a variance report for the period.
a. Discuss the ethics of using a two-variance approach to report the overhead variances rather than a three- or four-variance approach.
b. If Tim does not provide his boss with detailed information on the individual cost components and their related variances, can the boss judge Tim's performance during the period? Defend your answer.

62. *In 1993, when nearly 9 million people couldn't find jobs, other Americans were putting in the most overtime since the government started keeping records in the 1950s. With factory workers averaging 4.2 hours of overtime per week, the Bureau of Labor Statistics said more than a tenth of all work done in the nation's factories was performed on overtime.*

"If we could go back to the amount of overtime worked in 1982, we would create 3 million new jobs without increasing the federal deficit," said John Zalusky, an economist at the AFL-CIO. He said many workers are putting in extra hours against their wishes.

One reason employers were going the overtime route, economists said, was that overtime pay didn't cost much extra. Fringe benefits, representing as much as 40 percent of labor costs, were mostly covered by the first 40 hours worked.

And the overtime hours generally were worked by employers' most skilled and productive people. Beyond that, using overtime avoided the cost of hiring and training new workers, finding space for them and dealing with the added paperwork. Because of all those factors, Zalusky calculated that paying a skilled worker time-and-a-half actually cost employers only about 3 percent extra.

SOURCE: Mike Feinsliber, "Employers Paying Overtime Instead of Hiring," *(New Orleans) Times-Picayune* (March 18, 1993), p. C-2. © The Times-Picayune Publishing Corporation.

a. How does overtime pay affect direct labor cost? Variable overhead?
b. Obviously, paying overtime to already employed workers makes better financial business sense than does hiring additional workers. If, however, workers would prefer not to work overtime but do so to maintain their jobs, how does overtime affect the ethical contract between employers and employees?
c. What effects might overtime have on job efficiency? On job effectiveness (such as quality of production)?
d. Would you be in favor of limiting allowable hours of overtime to have more individuals employed? Discuss this question from the standpoint of the government, the employer, a currently employed worker, and an unemployed individual.

63. As of 1983, Medicare began reimbursing hospitals according to diagnostic related groups (DRGs). Each DRG has a specified standard length of stay. If a patient leaves the hospital early, the hospital is favorably financially impacted, but a patient staying longer than the specified time costs the hospital money.
a. From the hospital administrator's point of view, would you want favorable "length of stay" variances? How might you go about trying to obtain such variances?
b. From a patient's point of view, would you want favorable "length of stay" variances? Answer this question from the point of view of a patient who has had minor surgery and from the point of view of a patient who has had major surgery.
c. Would favorable "length of stay" variances necessarily equate to high-quality care?

64. *National standards for U.S. schools covering 13 subjects have been devised by educators in the arts, mathematics, history, English and the sciences. . . . Academic professional groups, meanwhile, have been so wary of offending minorities, and so protective of teachers' academic freedoms, that they have often come up with guidelines that are awash in generalities and impossible to codify into a curriculum.*

An analysis in 1995 by the American Federation of Teachers found that only 13 states had developed standards clear enough to be translated into actual classroom curriculum. The others had standards that "were too vague for teachers to use them, for parents to understand them," said AFT president Albert Shanker.

The report also found that only seven states planned to require students to meet the standards to graduate. "In most states, students wouldn't in any way be affected by whether or not they can meet the standards," the report said.

The AFT found that most states developed their standards without reviewing what high-achieving countries such as Japan, Germany and France require of students. According to the AFT, at least a quarter of all secondary-school students in Germany, France, England and Japan passed at least one advanced exam in mathematics, science or other subjects. In the U.S., only 5% of students passed one of the advanced-placement exams that could have given them college credit; but the exams weren't required, and there was no penalty for failure.

SOURCE: Gary Putka and Steve Stecklow, " 'A' for Effort: Educators Try to Set Standards—Again," *The Wall Street Journal* (March 26, 1996), p. B1. Reprinted by permission of *The Wall Street Journal*,

a. Research the education standards in your home state or country and prepare a report on them. Do you think these standards are measurable? Why or why not?

b. Why do standards, regardless of the purpose for which they are set, need to be tied to consequences?

c. Assume you have been elected state governor on an education reform platform. The state has in place some objective and measurable education standards. How would you tie these standards to consequences? What costs to the state's taxpayers would be associated with such consequences?

http://www.kimberly-clark.com/what/family

d. Consider the following: Scott Paper spent $400,000 screening 14,176 job applicants to hire 174. Of the 10,000 people who passed the initial screening, 4,000 failed a standardized English and high school algebra test. SOURCE: Raju Narisetti, "Manufacturers Decry a Shortage of Workers While Rejecting Many," *The Wall Street Journal* (September 8, 1995), p. A4. Scott was looking for employees to perform numerous tasks previously handled by managers, and the jobs had a starting salary of $29,000. Do you think that educational standards would help a company like Scott Paper find qualified employees? Explain.

PART 3

Planning and Controlling

CHAPTER

Absorption/Variable Costing and Cost-Volume-Profit Analysis

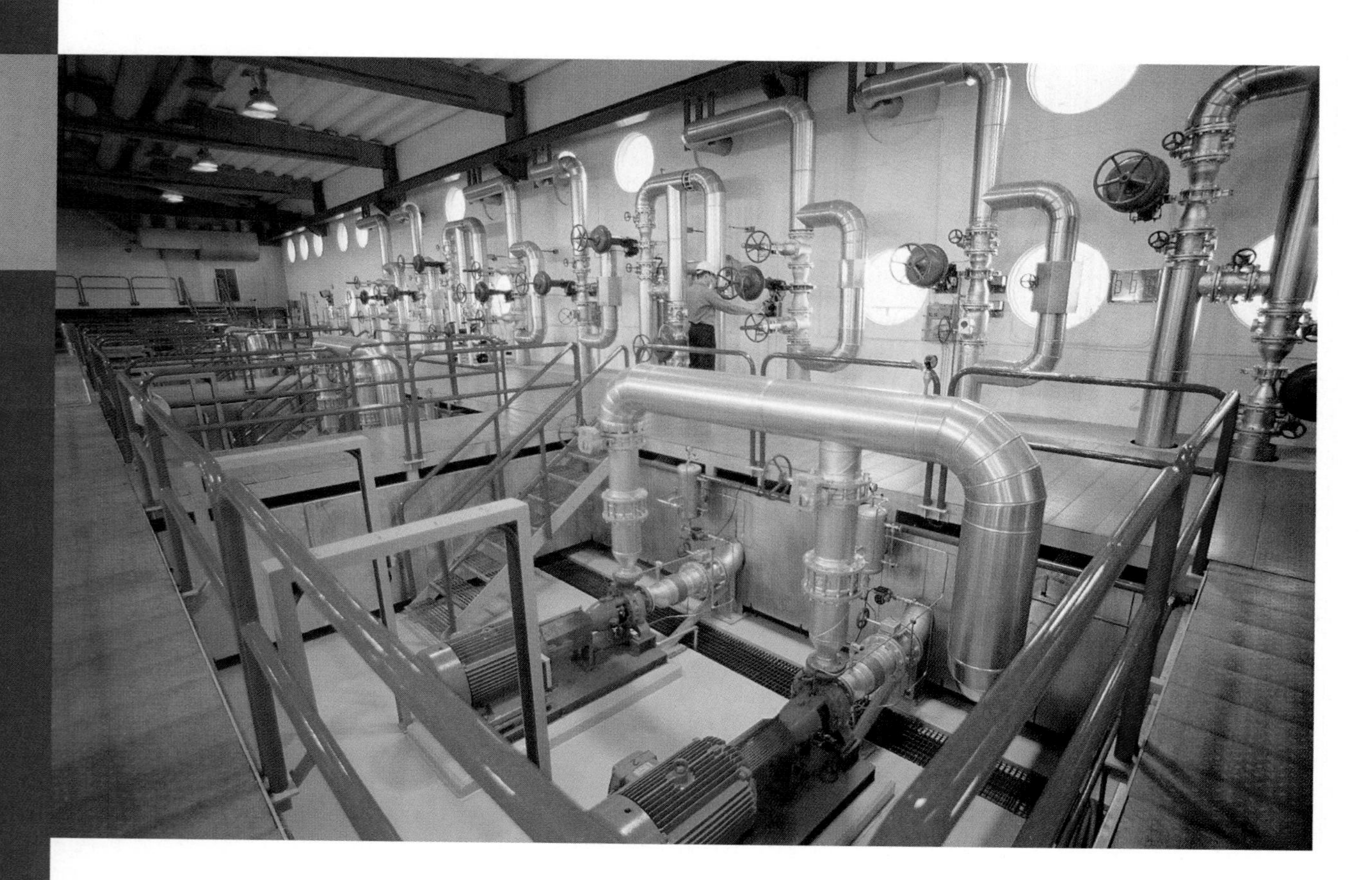

LEARNING OBJECTIVES

After completing this chapter, you should be able to answer the following questions:

1. What are the cost accumulation and cost presentation approaches to product costing?
2. What are the differences between absorption and variable costing?
3. How do changes in sales and/or production levels affect net income as computed under absorption and variable costing?
4. How can cost-volume-profit (CVP) analysis be used by a company?
5. How does CVP analysis differ between single-product and multiproduct firms?
6. How are margin of safety and operating leverage concepts used in business?
7. What are the underlying assumptions of CVP analysis?
8. (Appendix) How are break-even charts and profit-volume graphs constructed?

INTRODUCING Torrington Supply Co.

http://www.torringtonsupply.com

Torrington Supply Company is the largest Connecticut-based wholesale-distributor of residential, commercial, and industrial plumbing, heating and air conditioning equipment, pumps, and industrial piping supplies. The firm serves contractors, industry, and institutions throughout Connecticut. Torrington employs almost 100 employees and operates from four locations in the state.

Torrington has dedicated its resources to provide the best combination of hassle free service at the lowest price, and does everything it promises. Its goal is to eliminate non-value-added costs and pass the savings along to customers in the form of lower prices and increased services.

David Stein, a Lithuanian émigré who came to this country as a 17-year-old in 1905, established Torrington Supply Company in 1917. Lacking money or formal education, he learned the plumbing trade in New York City. Soon after, he moved to New Britain, Connecticut, and eventually opened a plumbing contracting business of his own in Waterbury. Almost immediately he developed a small but growing sideline, furnishing plumbing supplies to other local tradesmen. As that sideline grew, Stein realized that he preferred merchandising to contracting, and soon was in the wholesale business full-time: The Brass City Plumbing Supply Company.

Today, thanks to the inquisitive mind of chairman and CEO Joel Becker and CFO David Petitti, Torrington Supply Co. can run numbers that pinpoint to the dollar what percentage of gross margin on the average sale is profit—or loss—for any given customer. And they are able to use those numbers to improve profitability for both Torrington and the customer. These days, all Torrington salespeople can view customer information at a keystroke in a user-friendly format. With these numbers and the sales negotiating and pricing guidelines on the screen, the representative knows how large a commitment of services or how liberal a discount he can offer the customer on the phone.

SOURCES: Margie O'Conner, "A Full Measure of Customer Service," *Supply House Times* (December 1999) pp. 44ff; Torrington Supply Co. Web site, http://www.torringtonsupply.com (February 11, 2000).

This chapter discusses the cost accumulation and cost presentation approaches to product costing. The **cost accumulation** approach determines which manufacturing costs are recorded as part of product cost. Although one approach to cost accumulation may be appropriate for external reporting, that approach is not necessarily appropriate for internal decision making. The **cost presentation** approach focuses on how costs are shown on external financial statements or internal management reports. Accumulation and presentation procedures are accomplished using one of two methods: absorption costing or variable costing. Each method uses the same basic data, but structures and processes the data differently. Either method can be used in job order or process costing and with actual, normal, or standard costs.

cost accumulation

cost presentation

Absorption costing is the traditional approach to product costing. Variable costing facilitates the use of models for analyzing break-even point, cost-volume-profit relationships, margin of safety, and the degree of operating leverage. Use of these models is explained in this chapter after presentation of absorption costing and variable costing.

AN OVERVIEW OF ABSORPTION AND VARIABLE COSTING

1

What are the cost accumulation and cost presentation approaches to product costing?

Absorption costing treats the costs of all manufacturing components (direct material, direct labor, variable overhead, and fixed overhead) as inventoriable or product costs in accordance with generally accepted accounting principles (GAAP). Absorption costing is also known as **full costing**. This method has been used consistently in the previous chapters that dealt with product costing systems and valuation. In fact, the product cost definition given in Chapter 3 specifically fits the

absorption costing
full costing

absorption costing method. Under absorption costing, costs incurred in the non-manufacturing areas of the organization are considered period costs and are expensed in a manner that properly matches them with revenues. Exhibit 11–1 depicts the absorption costing model.

functional classification

Absorption costing presents expenses on an income statement according to their functional classifications. A **functional classification** is a group of costs that were all incurred for the same principal purpose. Functional classifications include categories such as cost of goods sold, selling expense, and administrative expense.[1]

variable costing

In contrast, **variable costing** is a cost accumulation method that includes only variable production costs (direct material, direct labor, and variable overhead) as product or inventoriable costs. Under this method, fixed manufacturing overhead is treated as a period cost. Like absorption costing, variable costing treats costs incurred in the organization's selling and administrative areas as period costs. Variable costing income statements typically present expenses according to cost behavior (variable and fixed), although they may also present expenses by functional classifications within the behavioral categories. Variable costing has also been known as **direct costing**. Exhibit 11–2 presents the variable costing model.

direct costing

EXHIBIT 11–1

Absorption Costing Model

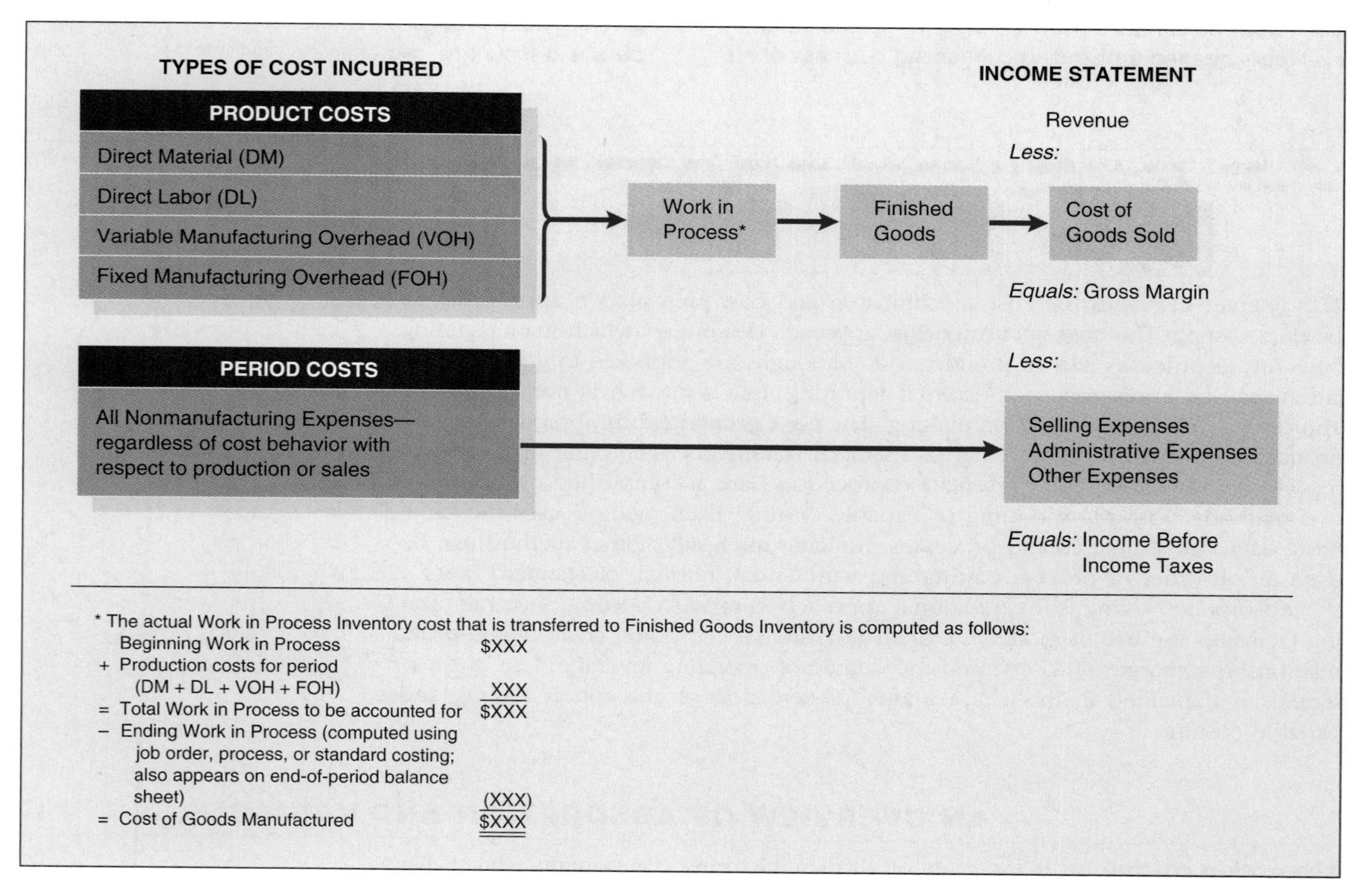

[1] Under FASB Statement 34, certain interest costs may be capitalized during a period of asset construction. If a company is capitalizing or has capitalized interest costs, these costs will not be shown on the income statement, but will become a part of fixed asset cost. The fixed asset cost is then depreciated as part of fixed overhead. Thus, although interest is typically considered a period cost, it may be included as fixed overhead and affect the overhead application rate.

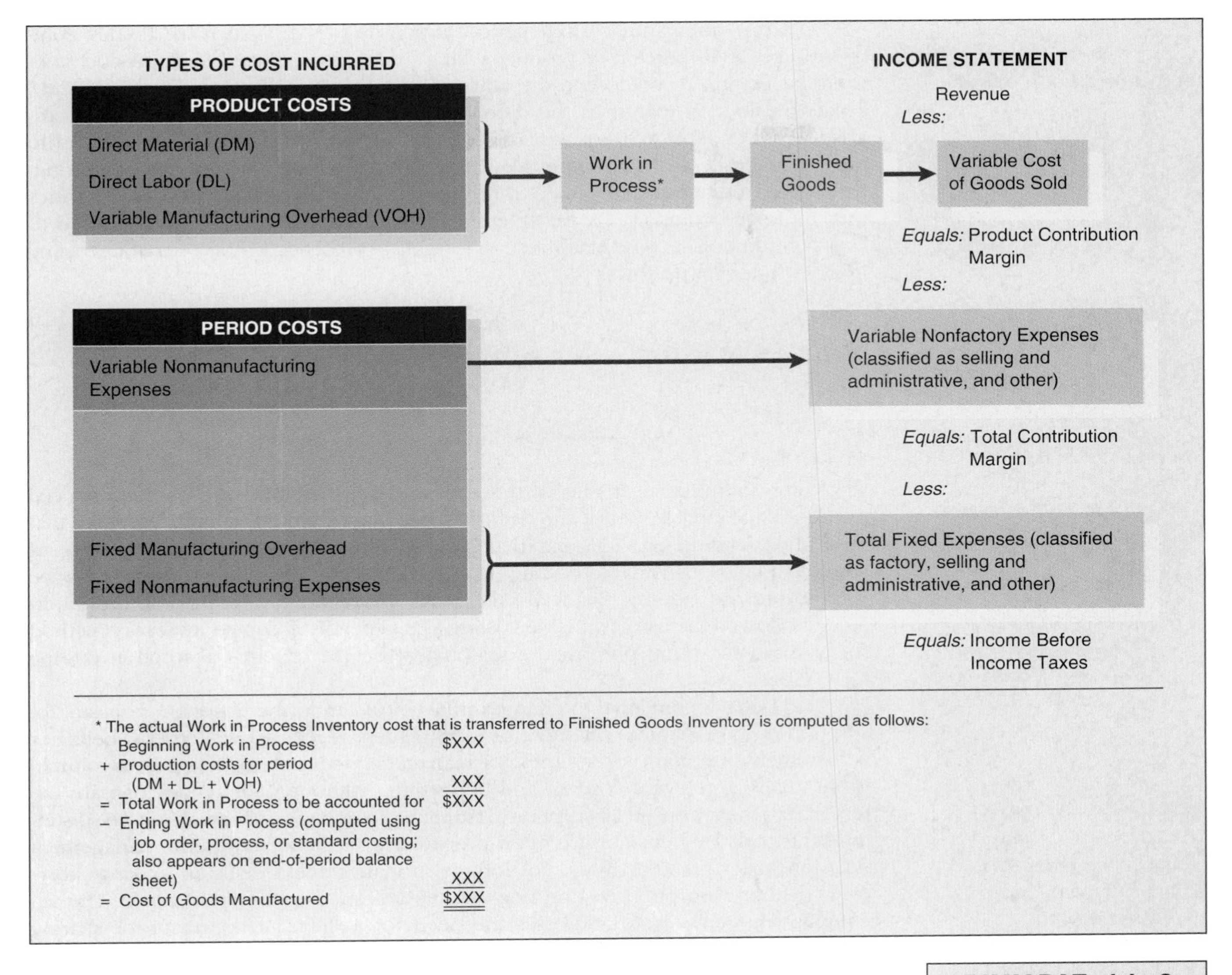

EXHIBIT 11-2

Variable Costing Model

Two basic differences can be seen between absorption and variable costing. The first difference is the way fixed overhead (FOH) is treated for product costing purposes. Under absorption costing, FOH is considered a product cost; under variable costing, it is considered a period cost. Absorption costing advocates contend that products cannot be made without the capacity provided by fixed manufacturing costs and so these costs are product costs. Variable costing advocates contend that the fixed manufacturing costs would be incurred whether or not production occurs and, therefore, cannot be product costs because they are not caused by production. The second difference is in the presentation of costs on the income statement. Absorption costing classifies expenses by function, whereas variable costing categorizes expenses first by behavior and then may further classify them by function.

Variable costing allows costs to be separated by cost behavior on the income statement or internal management reports. Cost of goods sold, under variable costing, is more appropriately called variable cost of goods sold (VCGS), because it is composed only of variable production costs. Sales (S) minus variable cost of goods sold is called **product contribution margin** (PCM) and indicates how much revenue is available to cover all period expenses and potentially to provide net income.

product contribution margin

total contribution margin

Variable, nonmanufacturing period expenses (VNME), such as a sales commission set at 10 percent of product selling price, are deducted from product contribution margin to determine the amount of **total contribution margin** (TCM). Total contribution margin is the difference between total revenues and total variable expenses. This amount indicates the dollar figure available to "contribute" to the coverage of all fixed expenses, both manufacturing and nonmanufacturing. After fixed expenses are covered, any remaining contribution margin provides income to the company. A variable costing income statement is also referred to as a contribution income statement. A formula representation of a variable costing income statement follows:

S − VCGS = PCM
PCM − VNME = TCM ⟶ Fixed Expenses
↳ Income Before Taxes

Major authoritative bodies of the accounting profession, such as the Financial Accounting Standards Board and Securities and Exchange Commission, believe that absorption costing provides external parties with a more informative picture of earnings than does variable costing. By specifying that absorption costing must be used to prepare external financial statements, the accounting profession has, in effect, disallowed the use of variable costing as a generally accepted inventory method for external reporting purposes. Additionally, the IRS requires absorption costing for tax purposes.[2]

Cost behavior (relative to changes in activity) cannot be observed from an absorption costing income statement or management report. However, cost behavior is extremely important for a variety of managerial activities including cost-volume-profit analysis, relevant costing, and budgeting.[3] Although companies prepare external statements on an absorption costing basis, internal financial reports distinguishing costs by behavior are often prepared to facilitate short-term management decision making and analysis. For long-term management decision making, however, neither absorption costing nor variable costing may be appropriate. The accompanying News Note addresses the need for a different approach for sharing long-term royalties in a technology licensing arrangement.

http://www.coke.com
http://www.gillette.com
http://abc.go.com
http://www.americanexpress.com
http://disney.go.com

The next section provides a detailed illustration using both absorption and variable costing.

ABSORPTION AND VARIABLE COSTING ILLUSTRATIONS

2

What are the differences between absorption and variable costing?

Comfort Valve Company makes a single product, the climate control valve. Comfort Valve Company is a 3-year-old firm operating out of the owner's home. Data for this product are used to compare absorption and variable costing procedures and presentations. The company employs standard costs for material, labor, and overhead. Exhibit 11–3 gives the standard production costs per unit, the annual budgeted nonmanufacturing costs, and other basic operating data for Comfort Valve Company. All standard and budgeted costs are assumed to remain constant over the three years 2000 through 2002 and, for simplicity, the company is assumed to

[2] The Tax Reform Act of 1986 requires all manufacturers and many wholesalers and retailers to include many previously expensed indirect costs in inventory. This method is referred to as "super-full absorption" or uniform capitalization. The uniform capitalization rules require manufacturers to assign to inventory all costs that directly benefit or are incurred because of production, including some administrative and other costs. Wholesalers and retailers, who previously did not need to include any indirect costs in inventory, now must inventory costs for items such as off-site warehousing, purchasing agents' salaries, and repackaging. However, the material in this chapter is not intended to reflect "super-full absorption."

[3] Cost-volume-profit analysis is discussed subsequently in this chapter. Relevant costing is covered in Chapter 12 and budgeting is discussed in Chapter 13.

GENERAL BUSINESS  NEWS NOTE

Using Goodwill as the Vital Income Determinant

Incremental profit is not the proper basis for sharing between a licensor and licensee involved in negotiations for a long-term royalty. Incremental profits are generally short-term in nature. Rarely can a successful company acquire, license or develop technology and have incremental profits that fairly represent long-term profitability. For the purposes of computing damages, however, incremental profits may be an appropriate basis, depending on the facts and the law.

Generally accepted accounting principles are not an adequate basis for determining full or partial absorption, or variable costing. Among other failures, conventional accounting statements do not recognize the true cost and benefit of goodwill, intellectual capital, distribution networks, brands and other intangibles. No less an investor than Warren Buffett finds GAAP a starting point, at best, for financial analysis. As he observes, goodwill according to GAAP often turns out to be "no-will." When Buffett analyzed the purchase of major interests in Coca-Cola Beverages Ltd., Gillette Co., ABC TV, American Express and Walt Disney Co., he found tangible assets to be almost irrelevant; rather, goodwill was the vital income and value determinant.

Goodwill increasingly represents intellectual capital in a global economy. That's why a number of large public companies are now making efforts to account for internally generated intellectual capital and other complementary assets—either directly in their financial statements or in the notes thereto. According to a recent Ernst & Young study, 75% of the assets held by Standard & Poor 500 companies are intangible. Ten years ago, the percentage stood at 40%.

In the context of determining a reasonable royalty rate (or damages in a related matter), the time frame, the product's nature and the complementary assets will dictate how best to consider intellectual capital and other intangibles.

SOURCE: Stephen R. Cole, A. Scott Davidson, and Alexander J. Stack, "Reasonable Royalty Rates," *CA Magazine* (May 1999), pp. 30ff. Reproduced with permission from *CA Magazine*, published by the Canadian Institute of Chartered Accountants, Toronto, Canada.

have no Work in Process Inventory at the end of a period.[4] Also, all actual costs are assumed to equal the budgeted and standard costs for the years presented. The bottom section of Exhibit 11–3 compares actual unit production with actual unit sales to determine the change in inventory for each of the three years.

The company determines its standard fixed manufacturing overhead application rate by dividing estimated annual FOH by expected annual capacity. Total estimated annual fixed manufacturing overhead for Comfort Valve is $16,020 and expected annual production is 30,000 units. These figures provide a standard FOH rate of $0.534 per unit. Fixed manufacturing overhead is typically under- or overapplied at year-end when a standard, predetermined fixed overhead rate is used rather than actual FOH cost.

Under- or overapplication is caused by two factors that can work independently or simultaneously. These two factors are cost differences and utilization differences. If actual FOH cost differs from expected FOH cost, a fixed manufacturing overhead spending variance is created. If actual capacity utilization differs from expected utilization, a volume variance arises.[5] The independent effects of these differences are as follows:

Actual FOH Cost > Expected FOH Cost = Underapplied FOH
Actual FOH Cost < Expected FOH Cost = Overapplied FOH
Actual Utilization > Expected Utilization = Overapplied FOH
Actual Utilization < Expected Utilization = Underapplied FOH

[4] Actual costs can also be used under either absorption or variable costing. Standard costing was chosen for these illustrations because it makes the differences between the two methods more obvious. If actual costs had been used, production costs would vary each year and such variations would obscure the distinct differences caused by the use of one method, rather than the other, over a period of time. Standard costs are also treated as constant over time to more clearly demonstrate the differences between absorption and variable costing and to reduce the complexity of the chapter explanations.

[5] These variances are covered in depth in Chapter 10.

EXHIBIT 11–3

Basic Data for 2000, 2001, and 2002

Sales price per unit	$ 6.00
Standard variable cost per unit:	
Direct material	$2.040
Direct labor	1.500
Variable manufacturing overhead	0.180
Total variable manufacturing cost per unit	$3.720

$$\text{Standard Fixed Factory Overhead Rate} = \frac{\text{Budgeted Annual Fixed Factory Overhead}}{\text{Budgeted Annual Capacity in Units}}$$

FOH rate = $16,020 ÷ 30,000 = $0.534

Total absorption cost per unit:	
Standard variable manufacturing cost	$3.720
Standard fixed manufacturing overhead (SFOH)	0.534
Total absorption cost per unit	$4.254
Budgeted nonproduction expenses:	
Variable selling expenses per unit	$0.24
Fixed selling and administrative expenses	$2,340

Total budgeted nonproductive expenses = ($0.24 per unit sold + $2,340)

	2000	2001	2002	Total
Actual units made	30,000	29,000	31,000	90,000
Actual unit sales	30,000	27,000	33,000	90,000
Change in FG inventory	0	+2,000	−2,000	0

In most cases, however, both costs and utilization differ from estimates. When this occurs, no generalizations can be made as to whether FOH will be under- or overapplied. Assume that Comfort Valve Company began operations in 2000. Production and sales information for the years 2000 through 2002 are shown in Exhibit 11–3.

Because the company began operations in 2000, that year has a zero balance for beginning Finished Goods Inventory. The next year, 2001, also has a zero beginning inventory because all units produced in 2000 were also sold in 2000. In 2001 and 2002, production and sales quantities differ, which is a common situation because production frequently "leads" sales so that inventory can be stockpiled for a later period. The illustration purposefully has no beginning inventory and equal cumulative units of production and sales for the 3 years to demonstrate that, regardless of whether absorption or variable costing is used, the cumulative income before taxes will be the same ($128,520 in Exhibit 11–4) under these conditions. Also, for any particular year in which there is no change in inventory levels from the beginning of the year to the end of the year, both methods will result in the same net income. An example of this occurs in 2000 as is demonstrated in Exhibit 11–4.

Because all actual production and operating costs are assumed to be equal to the standard and budgeted costs for the years 2000 through 2002, the only variances presented are the volume variances for 2001 and 2002. These volume variances are immaterial and are reflected as adjustments to the gross margins for 2001 and 2002 in Exhibit 11–4.

Volume variances under absorption costing are calculated as standard fixed overhead (SFOH) of $0.534 multiplied by the difference between expected capacity (30,000 valves) and actual production. For 2000, there is no volume variance because expected and actual production are equal. For 2001, the volume variance is $534 unfavorable, calculated as [$0.534 × (29,000 − 30,000)]. For 2002, it is $534

EXHIBIT 11–4

Absorption and Variable Costing Income Statements for 2000, 2001, and 2002

ABSORPTION COSTING PRESENTATION

	2000	2001	2002	Total
Sales ($6 per unit)	$180,000	$162,000	$198,000	$540,000
CGS ($4.254 per unit)	(127,620)	(114,858)	(140,382)	(382,860)
Standard Gross Margin	$ 52,380	$ 47,142	$ 57,618	$157,140
Volume Variance (U)	0	(534)	534	0
Adjusted Gross Margin	$ 52,380	$ 46,608	$ 58,152	$157,140
Operating Expenses				
Selling and administrative	(9,540)	(8,820)	(10,260)	(28,620)
Income before Tax	$ 42,840	$ 37,788	$ 47,892	$128,520

VARIABLE COSTING PRESENTATION

	2000	2001	2002	Total
Sales ($6 per unit)	$180,000	$162,000	$198,000	$540,000
Variable CGS ($3.72 per unit)	(111,600)	(100,440)	(122,760)	(334,800)
Product Contribution Margin	$ 68,400	$ 61,560	$ 75,240	$205,200
Variable Selling Expenses				
($0.24 × units sold)	(7,200)	(6,480)	(7,920)	(21,600)
Total Contribution Margin	$ 61,200	$ 55,080	$ 67,320	$183,600
Fixed Expenses				
Manufacturing	$ 16,020	$ 16,020	$ 16,020	$ 48,060
Selling and administrative	2,340	2,340	2,340	7,020
Total fixed expenses	$ (18,360)	$ (18,360)	$ (18,360)	$ (55,080)
Income before Tax	$ 42,840	$ 36,720	$ 48,960	$128,520
Differences in Income before Tax	$ 0	$ 1,068	$ (1,068)	$ 0

favorable, calculated as [$0.534 × (31,000 − 30,000)]. Variable costing does not have a volume variance because fixed manufacturing overhead is not applied to units produced but is written off in its entirety as a period expense.

In Exhibit 11–4, income before tax for 2001 for absorption costing exceeds that of variable costing by $1,068. This difference is caused by the positive change in inventory (2,000 shown in Exhibit 11–3) to which the absorption SFOH of $0.534 per unit has been assigned (2,000 × $0.534 = $1,068). This $1,068 is the fixed manufacturing overhead added to absorption costing inventory and therefore not expensed in 2001. Critics of absorption costing refer to this phenomenon as one that creates illusionary or phantom profits. **Phantom profits** are temporary absorption-costing profits caused by producing more inventory than is sold. When sales increase to eliminate the previously produced inventory, the phantom profits disappear. In contrast, all fixed manufacturing overhead, including the $1,068, is expensed in its entirety in variable costing.

phantom profit

Exhibit 11–3 shows that in 2002 inventory decreased by 2,000 valves. This decrease, multiplied by the SFOH ($0.534), explains the $1,068 by which 2002 absorption costing income falls short of variable costing income on Exhibit 11–4. This is because the fixed manufacturing overhead written off in absorption costing through the cost of goods sold at $0.534 per valve for all units sold in excess of production (33,000 − 31,000 = 2,000) results in the $1,068 by which absorption costing income is lower than variable costing income in 2002.

Variable costing income statements are more useful internally for short-term planning, controlling, and decision making than absorption costing statements. To carry out their functions, managers need to understand and be able to project how different costs will change in reaction to changes in activity levels. Variable costing, through its emphasis on cost behavior, provides that necessary information.

The income statements in Exhibit 11–4 show that absorption and variable costing tend to provide different income figures in some years. Comparing the two sets of statements illustrates that the difference in income arises solely from which production component costs are included in or excluded from product cost for each method.

If no beginning or ending inventories exist, cumulative total income under both methods will be identical. For the Comfort Valve Company over the three-year period, 90,000 valves are produced and 90,000 valves are sold. Thus, all the costs incurred (whether variable or fixed) are expensed in one year or another under either method. The income difference in each year is caused solely by the timing of the expensing of fixed manufacturing overhead.

COMPARISON OF THE TWO APPROACHES

3

How do changes in sales and/or production levels affect net income as computed under absorption and variable costing?

Whether absorption costing income is greater or less than variable costing income depends on the relationship of production to sales. In all cases, to determine the effects on income, it must be assumed that variances from standard are immaterial and that unit product costs are constant over time. Exhibit 11–5 shows the possible relationships between production and sales levels and the effects of these relationships on income. These relationships are as follows:

- If production is equal to sales, absorption costing income will equal variable costing income.
- If production is greater than sales, absorption costing income is greater than variable costing income. This result occurs because some fixed manufacturing overhead cost is deferred as part of inventory cost on the balance sheet under

EXHIBIT 11–5

*Production/Sales Relationships and Effects on Income Measurement and Inventory Assignments**

where P = Production and S = Sales
AC = Absorption Costing and VC = Variable Costing

	Absorption vs. Variable Income Statement Income before Taxes	Absorption vs. Variable Balance Sheet Ending Inventory
P = S	AC = VC No difference from beginning inventory $FOH_{EI} - FOH_{BI} = 0$	No additional difference $FOH_{EI} = FOH_{BI}$
P > S (Stockpiling inventory)	AC > VC By amount of fixed OH in ending inventory minus fixed OH in beginning inventory $FOH_{EI} - FOH_{BI} = +$ amount	Ending inventory increased (by fixed OH in additional units because P > S) $FOH_{EI} > FOH_{BI}$
P < S (Selling off beginning inventory)	AC < VC By amount of fixed OH released from balance sheet beginning inventory $FOH_{EI} - FOH_{BI} = -$ amount	Ending inventory difference reduced (by fixed OH from BI charged to cost of goods sold) $FOH_{EI} < FOH_{BI}$

*The effects of the relationships presented here are based on two qualifying assumptions:
(1) that unit costs are constant over time; and
(2) that any fixed cost variances from standard are written off when incurred rather than being prorated to inventory balances.

absorption costing, whereas the total amount of fixed manufacturing overhead cost is expensed as a period cost under variable costing.

- If production is less than sales, income under absorption costing is less than income under variable costing. In this case, absorption costing expenses all of the current period fixed manufacturing overhead cost and releases some fixed manufacturing overhead cost from the beginning inventory where it had been deferred from a prior period.

This process of deferring and releasing fixed overhead costs in and from inventory makes income manipulation possible under absorption costing, by adjusting production of inventory relative to sales. For this reason, some people believe that variable costing might be more useful for external purposes than absorption costing. For internal reporting, variable costing information provides managers with information about the behavior of the various product and period costs. This information can be used when computing the break-even point and analyzing a variety of cost-volume-profit relationships.

DEFINITION AND USES OF CVP ANALYSIS

Examining shifts in costs and volume and their resulting effects on profit is called **cost-volume-profit** (CVP) **analysis**. This analysis is applicable in all economic sectors, including manufacturing, wholesaling, retailing, and service industries. CVP can be used by managers to plan and control more effectively because it allows them to concentrate on the relationships among revenues, costs, volume changes, taxes, and profits. The CVP model can be expressed through a formula or graphically, as illustrated in the chapter Appendix. All costs, regardless of whether they are product, period, variable, or fixed, are considered in the CVP model. The analysis is usually performed on a companywide basis. The same basic CVP model and calculations can be applied to a single- or multiproduct business. CVP is a component of business intelligence (BI), which is gathered within the context of knowledge management (KM). The News Note (page 452) discusses this context.

cost-volume-profit analysis

CVP analysis has wide-range applicability. It can be used to determine a company's **break-even point** (BEP), which is that level of activity, in units or dollars, at which total revenues equal total costs. At breakeven, the company's revenues simply cover its costs; thus, the company incurs neither a profit nor a loss on operating activities. Companies, however, do not wish merely to "break even" on operations. The break-even point is calculated to establish a point of reference. Knowing BEP, managers are better able to set sales goals that should generate income from operations rather than produce losses. CVP analysis can also be used to calculate the sales volume necessary to achieve a desired target profit. Target profit objectives can be stated as either a fixed or variable amount on a before- or after-tax basis. Because profit cannot be achieved until the break-even point is reached, the starting point of CVP analysis is BEP. Over time, the break-even point for a firm or even an industry changes, as demonstrated in the News Note on page 453.

break-even point

http://www.pricewaterhousecoopers.com

THE BREAK-EVEN POINT

Finding the break-even point first requires an understanding of company revenues and costs. A short summary of revenue and cost assumptions is presented at this point to provide a foundation for CVP analysis. These assumptions, and some challenges to them, are discussed in more detail at the end of the chapter.

- *Relevant range:* A primary assumption is that the company is operating within the relevant range of activity specified in determining the revenue and cost information used in each of the following assumptions.[6]

[6] Relevant range is the range of activity over which a variable cost will remain constant per unit and a fixed cost will remain constant in total.

NEWS NOTE  GENERAL BUSINESS

Managing CVP Information

Information, like gold, is worthless if you can't find it. A few years ago the information wasn't there. Today's manufacturing managers are swamped.

The change, needless to say, is one outcome of the information technology revolution. Equally needless to say, the IT vendors who created the glut are now selling sieves—IBM said last year there were already 1,800 software products in the knowledge management (KM) arena alone.

The most pressing manufacturing need is to share information across the organization as well as up and down it. Manufacturers used to have no accurate idea of the true cost of making a product or whether it was profitable—a particular weak spot was the effect different product volumes had on profit margins. Today's tools remove any excuse for such ignorance.

Whichever [software] system provides the tools, BI lets senior management drill down into the business, identify the data that will provide good performance measures and manipulate it into a series of measures by which to steer the company.

By some definitions, true BI is a component of a data warehousing system; by others BI is a step towards data warehousing. Creating an effective data warehouse, one which is allied to the tools which will deliver information from the mere data it contains, is not straightforward. The choice of systems and tools has to be carefully made, and it should be based not just on current information needs but those that develop as the business develops.

Many BI systems are sold on the basis that they are powerful enough to overwhelm that last redoubt of technofear, the boardroom. But any company investigating BI would do well to avoid restricting access to BI tools to a small group of powerful individuals at the top. Some tools treat data exactly this way, as information there solely to be sucked from the bottom to the top of an organization. At the opposite extreme, other tools act as a single input and retrieval system for information, one that everyone has access to, and which can have thousands of users rather than these elect few. Still others treat BI as an information delivery system made up of a clutch of linked but distinct data management, access, analysis and presentation tools. The tools can be added or subtracted at will, as the user company chooses.

Ultimately, the data warehouse can reveal information not initially sought. With large amounts of data, stored in complex ways, it is becoming ever more difficult to make sense of the information either by eye or with analytical methods. Data mining can tell you what is important to a particular problem, and what to ignore.

Pattern detection is vital in gathering information from data. It can tie warranty problems to particular factories, machines, or even operators or purchasing staff. Whether you know what you're looking for or not, data mining can help you do the work better and quicker.

SOURCE: John Dwyer, "The Info-Filter," *Works Management* (July 1999), pp. 26ff.

- *Revenue:* Revenue per unit is assumed to remain constant; fluctuations in per-unit revenue for factors such as quantity discounts are ignored. Thus, total revenue fluctuates in direct proportion to level of activity or volume.
- *Variable costs:* On a per-unit basis, variable costs are assumed to remain constant. Therefore, total variable costs fluctuate in direct proportion to level of activity or volume. Note that assumed variable cost behavior is the same as assumed revenue behavior. Variable production costs include direct material, direct labor, and variable overhead; variable selling costs include charges for items such as commissions and shipping. Variable administrative costs may exist in areas such as purchasing.
- *Fixed costs:* Total fixed costs are assumed to remain constant and, as such, per-unit fixed cost decreases as volume increases. (Fixed cost per unit would increase as volume decreases.) Fixed costs include both fixed manufacturing overhead and fixed selling and administrative expenses.
- *Mixed costs:* Mixed costs must be separated into their variable and fixed elements before they can be used in CVP analysis. Any method (such as regression analysis) that validly separates these costs in relation to one or more predictors can be used. After being separated, the variable and fixed cost components of the mixed cost take on the assumed characteristics mentioned above.

GENERAL BUSINESS  NEWS NOTE

It Moves

The U.S. lodging industry's overall occupancy level is probably as high as it's going to be for the foreseeable future, and in many geographic markets and segments occupancy rates are declining. So, how can it be that the industry will still be turning a profit in future years?

The answer comes from a study by Bear Stearns and PricewaterhouseCoopers. As explained by Bjorn Hanson, chairman of the PricewaterhouseCoopers lodging and gaming group, the overall breakeven occupancy has declined from as high as 80 percent back in the 1980s, to 55.5 percent today.

"Three factors underlie the dramatic reduction in breakeven occupancy to 55.5 percent," noted Hanson. "They are: average daily room rates that have been increasing at greater than the rate of inflation; a redefined hotel revenue mix that emphasizes rooms revenue over revenue from low-margin food and beverage [F&B] operations; and lower debt and equity costs for the industry as a whole." Thus, even as occupancy declines, the industry's bid to control fixed costs has paid off.

By segment, upscale hotels (with their higher cost structure) are closest to breakeven, but the analysts say that upscale occupancy would have to drop 9.2 percent to hit breakeven. On the other hand, such segments as midscale without F&B, economy, and extended-stay (upper tier) are in a strong occupancy position and are operating far above breakeven.

SOURCE: Reprinted by permission of Elsevier Science from "U.S. Lodging Industry Breakeven Occupancy = 55.5%," by Glenn Withiam, *The Cornell Hotel and Restaurant Administration Quarterly* (August 1998), p. 10. Copyright 1998 by Cornell University.

contribution margin

An important amount in break-even and CVP analysis is **contribution margin** (CM), which can be defined on either a per-unit or total basis. Contribution margin per unit is the difference between the selling price per unit and the sum of variable production, selling, and administrative costs per unit. Unit contribution margin is constant because revenue and variable cost have been defined as remaining constant per unit. Total contribution margin is the difference between total revenues and total variable costs for all units sold. This amount fluctuates in direct proportion to sales volume. On either a per-unit or total basis, contribution margin indicates the amount of revenue remaining after all variable costs have been covered.[7] This amount contributes to the coverage of fixed costs and the generation of profits.

Data needed to compute the break-even point and perform CVP analysis are given in the income statement shown in Exhibit 11–6 for Comfort Valve Company.

EXHIBIT 11–6

Comfort Valve Company Income Statement for 2000

	Total		Per Unit	Percentage
Sales		$180,000	$ 6.00	100
Variable Costs:				
Production	$111,600		$ 3.72	62
Selling	7,200		0.24	4
Total Variable Cost		(118,800)	$(3.96)	(66)
Contribution Margin		$ 61,200	$ 2.04	34
Fixed Costs:				
Production	$ 16,020			
Selling and administrative	2,340			
Total Fixed Cost		(18,360)		
Income before Income Taxes		$ 42,840		

[7] Contribution margin refers to the total contribution margin discussed in the preceding section of the chapter rather than product contribution margin. Product contribution margin is the difference between revenues and total variable *production* costs for the cost of goods sold.

FORMULA APPROACH TO BREAKEVEN

The formula approach to break-even analysis uses an algebraic equation to calculate the exact break-even point. In this analysis, sales, rather than production activity, are the focus for the relevant range. The equation represents the variable costing income statement presented in the first section of the chapter and shows the relationships among revenue, fixed cost, variable cost, volume, and profit as follows:

$$R(X) - VC(X) - FC = P$$

where
R = revenue (selling price) per unit
X = volume (number of units)
$R(X)$ = total revenue
VC = variable cost per unit
$VC(X)$ = total variable cost
FC = total fixed cost
P = profit

Because the above equation is simply a formula representation of an income statement, P can be set equal to zero so that the formula indicates a break-even situation. At the point where P = \$0, total revenues are equal to total costs and break-even point (BEP) in units can be found by solving the equation for X.

$$R(X) - VC(X) - FC = \$0$$
$$R(X) - VC(X) = FC$$
$$(R - VC)(X) = FC$$
$$X = FC \div (R - VC)$$

Break-even point volume is equal to total fixed cost divided by (revenue per unit minus the variable cost per unit). Using the operating statistics shown in Exhibit 11–6 for Comfort Valve Company (\$6.00 selling price per valve, \$3.96 variable cost per valve, and \$18,360 of total fixed costs), break-even point for the company is calculated as

$$\$6.00(X) - \$3.96(X) - \$18{,}360 = \$0$$
$$\$6.00(X) - \$3.96(X) = \$18{,}360$$
$$(\$6.00 - \$3.96)(X) = \$18{,}360$$
$$X = \$18{,}360 \div (\$6.00 - \$3.96)$$
$$X = 9{,}000 \text{ valves}$$

Revenue minus variable cost is contribution margin. Thus, the formula can be shortened by using the contribution margin to find BEP.

$$(R - VC)(X) = FC$$
$$(CM)(X) = FC$$
$$X = FC \div CM$$

where CM = contribution margin per unit

Comfort Valve's contribution margin is \$2.04 per valve (\$6.00 − \$3.96). The calculation for BEP using the abbreviated formula is \$18,360 ÷ \$2.04 or 9,000 valves.

Break-even point can be expressed either in units or dollars of revenue. One way to convert a unit break-even point to dollars is to multiply units by the selling price per unit. For Comfort Valve, break-even point in sales dollars is \$54,000 (9,000 valves × \$6.00 per valve).

Another method of computing break-even point in sales dollars requires the computation of a **contribution margin** (CM) **ratio**. The CM ratio is calculated as contribution margin divided by revenue and indicates what proportion of revenue remains after variable costs have been covered. The contribution margin ratio represents that portion of the revenue dollar remaining to go toward covering fixed costs and increasing profits. The CM ratio can be calculated using either per-unit or total revenue minus variable cost information. Subtracting the CM ratio from 100 percent gives the **variable cost** (VC) **ratio**, which represents the variable cost proportion of each revenue dollar.

contribution margin ratio

variable cost ratio

The contribution margin ratio allows the break-even point to be determined even if unit selling price and unit variable cost are not known. Dividing total fixed cost by CM ratio gives the break-even point in sales dollars. The derivation of this formula is as follows:

$$\text{Sales} - [(\text{VC\%})(\text{Sales})] = \text{FC}$$

$$(1 - \text{VC\%})\text{Sales} = \text{FC}$$

$$\text{Sales} = \text{FC} \div (1 - \text{VC\%})$$

$$\text{because } (1 - \text{VC\%}) = \text{CM\%}$$

$$\text{Sales} = \text{FC} \div \text{CM\%}$$

where VC% = the % relationship of variable cost to sales
CM% = the % relationship of contribution margin to sales

Thus, the variable cost ratio plus the contribution margin ratio is equal to 100 percent.

The contribution margin ratio for Comfort Valve Company is given in Exhibit 11–6 as 34 percent (\$2.04 ÷ \$6.00). The company's computation of dollars of break-even sales is \$18,360 ÷ 0.34 or \$54,000. The BEP in units can be determined by dividing the BEP in sales dollars by the unit selling price or \$54,000 ÷ \$6.00 = 9,000 valves.

The break-even point provides a starting point for planning future operations. Managers want to earn operating profits rather than simply cover costs. Substituting an amount other than zero for the profit (P) term in the break-even formula converts break-even analysis to cost-volume-profit analysis.

USING COST-VOLUME-PROFIT ANALYSIS

4

How can cost-volume-profit (CVP) analysis be used by a company?

CVP analysis requires the substitution of known amounts in the formula to determine an unknown amount. The formula mirrors the income statement when known amounts are used for selling price per unit, variable cost per unit, volume of units, and fixed costs to find the amount of profit generated under given conditions. Because CVP analysis is concerned with relationships among the elements comprising continuing operations, in contrast with nonrecurring activities and events, profits, as used in this chapter, refer to operating profits before extraordinary and other nonoperating, nonrecurring items. The pervasive usefulness of the CVP model is expressed as follows:

Cost Volume Profit analysis (CVP) is one of the most hallowed, and yet one of the simplest, analytical tools in management accounting. [CVP provides a financial overview that] allows managers to examine the possible impacts of a wide range of strategic decisions. Those decisions can include such crucial areas as pricing policies, product mixes, market expansions or contractions, outsourcing contracts, idle plant usage, discretionary expense planning, and a variety of other important considerations in the planning process. Given the broad range of contexts in which CVP can be used, the basic simplicity of CVP is quite remarkable. Armed with just three inputs of data—sales price, variable cost per unit, and fixed costs—a managerial analyst can evaluate the effects of decisions that potentially alter the basic nature of a firm.[8]

An important application of CVP analysis is to set a desired target profit and focus on the relationships between it and other known income statement element amounts to find an unknown. A common unknown in such applications is volume because managers want to know what quantity of sales needs to be generated to produce a particular amount of profit.

Selling price is not assumed to be as common an unknown as volume because selling price is often market related and not a management decision variable. Additionally, because selling price and volume are often directly related, and certain costs are considered fixed, managers may use CVP to determine how high variable cost may be and still allow the company to produce a desired amount of profit. Variable cost may be affected by modifying product specifications or material quality or by being more efficient or effective in the production, service, and/or distribution processes. Profits may be stated as either a fixed or variable amount and on either a before- or after-tax basis. The following examples continue to use the Comfort Valve Company data using different amounts of target profit.

Fixed Amount of Profit

Because contribution margin represents the amount of sales dollars remaining after variable costs are covered, each dollar of CM generated by product sales goes first to cover fixed costs and then to produce profits. *After the break-even point is reached, each dollar of contribution margin is a dollar of profit.*

Theme parks have substantial fixed costs that must be covered before a profit can be earned. For parks that are closed part of the year, the contribution margin generated during the open season must be large enough to cover the fixed costs that continue even when revenues are not being generated.

[8] Flora Guidry, James O. Horrigan, and Cathy Craycraft, "CVP Analysis: A New Look," *Journal of Managerial Issues* (Spring 1998), pp. 74ff.

BEFORE TAX

Profits are treated in the break-even formula as additional costs to be covered. The inclusion of a target profit changes the formula from a break-even to a CVP equation.

$$R(X) - VC(X) - FC = PBT$$
$$R(X) - VC(X) = FC + PBT$$
$$X = (FC + PBT) \div (R - VC)$$
or
$$X = (FC + PBT) \div CM$$

where PBT = fixed amount of profit before taxes

Comfort Valve's management wants to produce a before-tax profit of $25,500. To do so, the company must sell 21,500 valves that will generate $129,000 of revenue. These calculations are shown in Exhibit 11–7.

AFTER TAX

Income tax represents a significant influence on business decision making. Managers need to be aware of the effects of income tax in choosing a target profit amount. A company desiring to have a particular amount of net income must first determine the amount of income that must be earned on a before-tax basis, given the applicable tax rate. The CVP formulas that designate a fixed after-tax net income amount are

$$PBT = PAT + [(TR)(PBT)] \text{ and}$$
$$R(X) - VC(X) - FC = PAT + [(TR)(PBT)]$$

where PBT = fixed amount of profit before tax
PAT = fixed amount of profit after tax
TR = tax rate

PAT is further defined so that it can be integrated into the original CVP formula:

$$PAT = PBT - [(TR)(PBT)]$$
or
$$PBT = PAT \div (1 - TR)$$

EXHIBIT 11–7

CVP Analysis—Fixed Amount of Profit before Tax

In units:

PBT desired = $25,500

$$R(X) - VC(X) = FC + PBT$$
$$CM(X) = FC + PBT$$
$$(\$6.00 - \$3.96)X = \$18,360 + \$25,500$$
$$\$2.04X = \$43,860$$
$$X = \$43,860 \div \$2.04 = 21,500 \text{ valves}$$

In sales dollars:

$$\text{Sales} = (FC + PBT) \div \text{CM ratio}$$
$$= \$43,860 \div 0.34 = \$129,000$$

Substituting into the formula,

$$R(X) - VC(X) = FC + PBT$$
$$(R - VC)(X) = FC + [PAT \div (1 - TR)]$$
$$CM(X) = FC + [PAT \div (1 - TR)]$$

Assume the managers at Comfort Valve Company want to earn $24,480 of profit after tax and the company's marginal tax rate is 20 percent. The number of valves and dollars of sales needed are calculated in Exhibit 11–8.

Variable Amount of Profit

Managers may wish to state profits as a variable amount so that, as units are sold or sales dollars increase, profits will increase at a constant rate. Variable amounts of profit may be stated on either a before- or after-tax basis. Profit on a variable basis can be stated either as a percentage of revenues or a per-unit profit. The CVP formula must be adjusted to recognize that profit (P) is related to volume of activity.

BEFORE TAX

This example assumes that the variable amount of profit is related to the number of units sold. The adjusted CVP formula for computing the necessary unit volume of sales to earn a specified variable amount of profit before tax per unit is

$$R(X) - VC(X) - FC = P_uBT(X)$$

where P_uBT = variable amount of profit per unit before tax

Moving all the Xs to the same side of the equation and solving for X (volume) gives the following:

$$R(X) - VC(X) - P_uBT(X) = FC$$
$$CM(X) - P_u\ BT(X) = FC$$
$$X = FC \div (CM - P_uBT)$$

EXHIBIT 11–8

CVP Analysis—Fixed Amount of Profit after Tax

In units:

PAT desired = $24,480; tax rate = 20%

PBT = PAT ÷ (1 − TR)
= $24,480 ÷ (1 − 0.20)
= $24,480 ÷ 0.80
= $30,600 necessary profit before tax

and

CM(X) = FC + PBT
$2.04X = $18,360 + $30,600
$2.04X = $48,960
X = $48,960 ÷ $2.04 = 24,000 valves

In sales dollars:

Sales = (FC + PBT) ÷ CM ratio
= ($18,360 + $30,600) ÷ 0.34
= $48,960 ÷ 0.34 = $144,000

The variable profit is treated in the CVP formula as if it were an additional variable cost to be covered. This treatment effectively "adjusts" the original contribution margin and contribution margin ratio. When setting the desired profit as a percentage of selling price, the profit percentage cannot exceed the contribution margin ratio. If it does, an infeasible problem is created because the "adjusted" contribution margin is negative. In such a case, the variable cost percentage plus the desired profit percentage would exceed 100 percent of the selling price, and such a condition cannot occur.

Assume that the president of Comfort Valve Company wants to know what level of sales (in valves and dollars) would be required to earn a 16 percent before-tax profit on sales. The calculations shown in Exhibit 11–9 provide the answers to these questions.

AFTER TAX

Adjustment to the CVP formula to determine variable profits on an after-tax basis involves stating profits in relation to both the volume and the tax rate. The algebraic manipulations are:

$$R(X) - VC(X) - FC = P_uAT(X) + \{(TR)[P_uBT(X)]\}$$

where P_uAT = variable amount of profit per unit after tax

P_uAT is further defined so that it can be integrated into the original CVP formula:

$$P_uAT(X) = P_uBT(X) - \{(TR)[P_uBT(X)]\}$$

$$= P_uBT(X)[(1 - TR)]$$

$$P_uBT(X) = [P_uAT \div (1 - TR)](X)$$

EXHIBIT 11–9

CVP Analysis—Variable Amount of Profit before Tax

In units:

P_uBT desired = 16% of sales revenues

$P_uBT = 0.16(\$6.00) = \$0.96$

$CM(X) - P_uBT(X) = FC$

$\$2.04X - \$0.96X = \$18,360$

$X = \$18,360 \div \$1.08$

$X = 17,000$ valves

In sales dollars, the following relationships exist:

	Per Valve	Percentage
Selling price	$ 6.00	100
Variable costs	(3.96)	(66)
Variable profit before tax	(0.96)	(16)
"Adjusted" contribution margin	$ 1.08	18

Sales = FC ÷ "Adjusted" CM ratio*

= $18,360 ÷ 0.18 = $102,000

*Note that it is not necessary to have per-unit data; all computations can be made with percentage information only.

Thus, the following relationship exists:

$$R(X) - VC(X) = FC + [P_uAT \div (1 - TR)](X)$$
$$= FC + P_uBT(X)$$
$$CM(X) = FC + P_uBT(X)$$
$$CM(X) - P_uBT(X) = FC$$
$$X = FC \div (CM - P_uBT)$$

Comfort Valve wishes to earn a profit after tax of 16 percent of revenue and has a 20 percent tax rate. The necessary sales in units and dollars are computed in Exhibit 11–10.

All of the preceding illustrations of CVP analysis were made using a variation of the formula approach. Solutions were not accompanied by mathematical proofs. The income statement model is an effective means of developing and presenting solutions and/or proofs for solutions to CVP applications.

THE INCOME STATEMENT APPROACH

The income statement approach to CVP analysis allows accountants to prepare pro forma (budgeted) statements using available information. Income statements can be used to prove the accuracy of computations made using the formula approach to CVP analysis, or the statements can be prepared merely to determine the impact of various sales levels on profit after tax (net income). Because the formula and income statement approaches are based on the same relationships, each should be able to prove the other.[9] Exhibit 11–11 proves each of the computations made in Exhibits 11–7 through 11–10 for Comfort Valve Company. The answers provided by break-even or cost-volume-profit analysis are valid only in relation to specific

EXHIBIT 11–10

CVP Analysis—Variable Amount of Profit after Tax

In units:

P_uAT desired = 16% of revenue = 0.16($6.00) = $0.96; tax rate = 20%

$P_uBT(X) = [\$0.96 \div (1 - 0.20)]X$

$P_uBT(X) = (\$0.96 \div 0.80)X = \$1.20X$

$CM(X) - P_uBT(X) = FC$

$\$2.04X - \$1.20X = \$18,360$

$\$0.84X = \$18,360$

$X = \$18,360 \div \$0.84 = 21,858$ valves (rounded)

	Per Valve	Percentage
Selling price	$6.00	100
Variable costs	(3.96)	(66)
Variable profit before tax	(1.20)	(20)
"Adjusted" contribution margin	$0.84	14

Sales = FC ÷ "Adjusted" CM ratio

= $18,360 ÷ 0.14 = $131,143 (rounded)

[9] The income statement approach can be readily adapted to computerized spreadsheets, which can be used to quickly obtain the results of many different combinations of the CVP factors.

EXHIBIT 11-11

Income Statement Approach to CVP—Proof of Computations

Previous computations:
Break-even point: 9,000 valves
Fixed profit ($25,500) before tax: 21,500 valves
Fixed profit ($24,480) after tax: 24,000 valves
Variable profit (16% on revenues) before tax: 17,000 valves
Variable profit (16% on revenues) after tax: 21,858 valves

R = $6.00 per valve; VC = $3.96 per valve; FC = $18,360;
tax rate = 20% for Exhibits 11-8 and 11-10

	Basic Data	Ex. 11-7	Ex. 11-8	Ex. 11-9	Ex. 11-10
Valves sold	**9,000**	**21,500**	**24,000**	**17,000**	**21,858**
Sales	$ 54,000	$129,000	$144,000	$102,000	$131,143
Total variable costs	(35,640)	(85,140)	(95,040)	(67,320)	(86,554)
Contribution margin	$ 18,360	$ 43,860	$ 48,960	$ 34,680	$ 44,589
Total fixed costs	(18,360)	(18,360)	(18,360)	(18,360)	(18,360)
Profit before tax	$ 0	$ 25,500	$ 30,600	$ 16,320*	$ 26,229
Taxes (20%)			(6,120)		(5,246)
Profit after tax (NI)			$ 24,480		$ 20,983**

*Desired profit before tax = 16% on revenue; 0.16 × $102,000 = $16,320
**Desired profit after tax = 16% on revenue; 0.16 × $131,143 = $20,983

selling prices and cost relationships. Changes that occur in the company's selling price or cost structure will cause a change in the break-even point or in the sales needed to obtain a desired profit figure. However, the effects of revenue and cost changes on a company's break-even point or sales volume can be determined through incremental analysis.

INCREMENTAL ANALYSIS FOR SHORT-RUN CHANGES

The break-even point may increase or decrease, depending on the particular changes that occur in the revenue and cost factors. Other things being equal, the break-even point will increase if there is an increase in the total fixed cost or a decrease in the unit (or percentage) contribution margin. A decrease in contribution margin could arise because of a reduction in selling price, an increase in variable cost per unit, or a combination of the two. The break-even point will decrease if there is a decrease in total fixed cost or an increase in unit (or percentage) contribution margin. A change in the break-even point will also cause a shift in total profits or losses at any level of activity.

incremental analysis

Incremental analysis is a process focusing only on factors that change from one course of action or decision to another. As related to CVP situations, incremental analysis is based on changes occurring in revenues, costs, and/or volume. Following are some examples of changes that may occur in a company and the incremental computations that can be used to determine the effects of those changes on the break-even point or profits. In most situations, incremental analysis is sufficient to determine the feasibility of contemplated changes, and a complete income statement need not be prepared.

We continue to use the basic facts presented for Comfort Valve Company in Exhibit 11-6. All of the following examples use before-tax information to simplify the computations. After-tax analysis would require the application of a (1 − tax rate) factor to all profit figures.

CASE 1

The company wishes to earn a before-tax profit of $10,200. How many valves does it need to sell? The incremental analysis relative to this question addresses the number of valves above the break-even point that must be sold. Because each dollar of contribution margin after BEP is a dollar of profit, the incremental analysis focuses only on the profit desired:

$$\$10{,}200 \div \$2.04 = 5{,}000 \text{ valves above BEP}$$

Because the BEP has already been computed as 9,000 valves, the company must sell a total of 14,000 valves.

CASE 2

Comfort Valve Company estimates that it can sell an additional 3,600 valves if it spends $1,530 more on advertising. Should the company incur this extra fixed cost? The contribution margin from the additional valves must first cover the additional fixed cost before profits can be generated.

Increase in contribution margin	
(3,600 valves × $2.04 CM per valve)	$7,344
− Increase in fixed cost	(1,530)
= Net incremental benefit	$5,814

Because the net incremental benefit is $5,814, the advertising campaign would result in an additional $5,814 in profits and, thus, should be undertaken.

An alternative computation is to divide $1,530 by the $2.04 contribution margin. The result indicates that 750 valves would be required to cover the additional cost. Because the company expects to sell 3,600 valves, the remaining 2,850 valves would produce a $2.04 profit per valve or $5,814.

CASE 3

The company estimates that, if the selling price of each valve is reduced to $5.40, an additional 2,000 valves per year can be sold. Should the company take advantage of this opportunity? Current sales volume, given in Exhibit 11–6, is 30,000 valves.

If the selling price is reduced, the contribution margin per unit will decrease to $1.44 per valve ($5.40 SP − $3.96 VC). Sales volume will increase to 32,000 valves (30,000 + 2,000).

Total new contribution margin	
(32,000 valves × $1.44 CM per valve)	$ 46,080
− Total fixed costs (unchanged)	(18,360)
= New profit before taxes	$ 27,720
− Current profit before taxes	
(from Exhibit 11–6)	(42,840)
= Net incremental loss	$(15,120)

Because the company will have a lower before-tax profit than is currently being generated, the company should not reduce its selling price based on this computation. Comfort Valve should investigate the possibility that the reduction in price might, in the long run, increase demand to more than the additional 2,000 valves per year and, thus, make the price reduction more profitable.

CASE 4

Comfort Valve Company has an opportunity to sell 10,000 valves to a contractor for $5.00 per valve. The valves will be packaged and sold using the contractor's own logo. Packaging costs will increase by $0.28 per valve, but no other variable selling costs will be incurred by the company. If the opportunity is accepted, a $1,000 commission will be paid to the salesperson calling on this contractor. This sale will not interfere with current sales and is within the company's relevant range of activity. Should Comfort Valve make this sale?

The new total variable cost per valve is $4.00 ($3.96 total current variable costs + $0.28 additional variable packaging cost − $0.24 current variable selling costs). The $5.00 selling price minus the $4.00 new total variable cost provides a contribution margin of $1.00 per valve sold to the contractor.

Total contribution margin provided by this sale (10,000 valves × $1.00 CM per valve)	$10,000
− Additional fixed cost (commission) related to this sale	(1,000)
= Net incremental benefit	$ 9,000

The total contribution margin generated by the sale is more than enough to cover the additional fixed cost. Thus, the sale produces a net incremental benefit to the firm in the form of increased profits and, therefore, should be made.

Similar to all proposals, this one should be evaluated on the basis of its long-range potential. Is the commission a one-time payment? Will sales to the contractor continue for several years? Will such sales not affect regular business in the future? Is such a sale within the boundaries of the law?[10] If all of these questions can be answered "yes," Comfort Valve should seriously consider this opportunity. In addition to the direct contractor sales potential, referral business might also arise to increase sales.

The contribution margin or incremental approach will often be sufficient to decide on the monetary merits of proposed or necessary changes. Joel Becker, CEO of Torrington Supply Company, provides an excellent example of combining cost behavior and activity-based costing techniques to understand and manage decisions about customer profitability in the accompanying News Note on page 464.

CVP ANALYSIS IN A MULTIPRODUCT ENVIRONMENT

5

How does CVP analysis differ between single-product and multiproduct firms?

Companies typically produce and sell a variety of products, some of which may be related (such as dolls and doll clothes or sheets, towels, and bedspreads). To perform CVP analysis in a multiproduct company, one must assume either a constant product sales mix or an average contribution margin ratio. The constant mix assumption can be referred to as the "bag" (or "basket") assumption. The analogy is that the sales mix represents a bag of products that are sold together. For example, whenever some of Product A is sold, a set amount of Products B and C is also sold. Use of an assumed constant mix allows the computation of a weighted average contribution margin ratio for the bag of products being sold. Without the assumption of a constant sales mix, break-even point cannot be calculated nor can CVP analysis be used effectively.[11]

In a multiproduct company, the CM ratio is weighted on the quantities of each product included in the "bag" of products. This weighting process means that the contribution margin ratio of the product making up the largest proportion of the bag has the greatest impact on the average contribution margin of the product mix.

The Comfort Valve Company example continues. Because of the success of the valves, company management has decided to produce regulators also. The vice president of marketing estimates that, for every three valves sold, the company will sell

[10] The Robinson-Patman Act addresses the legal ways in which companies can price their goods for sale to different purchasers.
[11] Once the constant percentage contribution margin in a multiproduct firm is determined, all situations regarding profit points can be treated in the same manner as they were earlier in the chapter. One must remember, however, that the answers reflect the "bag" assumption.

NEWS NOTE  GENERAL BUSINESS

Rationale for Activity-Based Costing Analysis

Most distributors' cost structure is such that they have high fixed costs and a very tight linkage between activities and variable costs. The key to any distributor's success is to minimize the variable cost component of his incremental margin once his fixed costs have been met. Sounds straightforward, but it is very hard to do. The first thing one has to do is decide which customers consume variable costs at a loss and eliminate those specialized services your fixed cost structure does not cover (i.e., special deliveries, special orders, special pricing, terms, etc.).

In order to do that we needed to know exactly which customers were asking us to perform activities that were not profitable. Thus, the activity-based costing analysis project was begun. It has obviously come a long way from there. Below I've outlined briefly how we come up with the costs and apply them.

We measure our operating costs to perform the following sales-related activities.

1. Cost to answer incoming sales calls and enter sales order header information (name, ship date, address, etc.)
2. Cost to enter each line item
3. Cost to pick a line item
4. Cost to pack an order
5. Cost to deliver an order
6. Cost to process an order (invoice, mail, collect, etc.)
7. Cost to make a field sales call
8. Cost to carry average receivable balance

We know the number of times we perform each activity company-wide each year. From this we calculate the average cost to do each activity. We test the data by calculating the median cost for each activity and have found each to be within pennies of the average. Once this is done we measure the number of times each of these activities is performed for each of our customers over the previous 52 weeks (we always use 52 weeks to eliminate large fluctuations week to week). The individual customer activity costs are subtracted from the customer's 52-week gross margin and a net ABC profit is calculated. We update our calculations every week and provide real-time displays at a single keystroke from most customer-related screens (i.e., sales entry and Accounts Receivable inquiries). We found that more important were the individualized service recommendations on how to respond to customer special pricing and service requests based on the customer's profitability profile.

The system works extremely well. Our goal is to service our unprofitable customers with fixed cost services only. This system has gone a long way to eliminate spending variable cost money on unprofitable customers.

SOURCE: Joel S. Becker, CEO, Torrington Supply Company, Inc., Waterbury, CT 06723-2838.

one regulator. Therefore, the "bag" of products has a 3:1 ratio. The company will incur an additional $4,680 in fixed costs related to plant assets (depreciation, insurance, and so forth) needed to support a higher relevant range of production. Exhibit 11–12 provides relevant company information and shows the break-even computations.

Any shift in the proportion of sales mix of products will change the weighted average contribution margin and the break-even point. If the sales mix shifts toward products with lower dollar contribution margins, the BEP will increase and profits decrease unless there is a corresponding increase in total revenues. A shift toward higher dollar margin products without a corresponding decrease in revenues will cause a lower break-even point and increased profits. As illustrated by the financial results shown in Exhibit 11–13 on page 466, a shift toward the product with the lower dollar contribution margin (regulators) causes a higher break-even point and lower profits (in this case, a loss). This exhibit assumes that Comfort Valve sells 3,200 "bags" of product, but the mix was not in the exact proportions assumed in Exhibit 11–12. Instead of a 3:1 ratio, the sales mix was 2.5:1.5 valves to regulators. A loss of $1,536 resulted because the company sold a higher proportion of the regulators, which have a lower contribution margin than the valves.

EXHIBIT 11-12

CVP Analysis—Multiple Products

	Valves		Regulators	
Product Cost Information				
Selling price	$6.00	100%	$2.00	100%
Total variable cost	(3.96)	(66)%	(0.92)	(46)%
Contribution margin	$2.04	34%	$1.08	54%

Total fixed costs = $18,360 previous + $4,680 new = $23,040

	Valves		Regulators		Total	Percentage
Number of products per bag		3		1		
Revenue per product	$6.00		$2.00			
Total revenue per "bag"		$18.00		$2.00	$20.00	100
Variable cost per product	(3.96)		(0.92)			
Total variable per "bag"		(11.88)		(0.92)	(12.80)	(64)
Contribution margin—product	$2.04		$1.08			
Contribution margin—"bag"		$ 6.12		$1.08	$ 7.20	36

BEP in units (where B = "bags" of products)

$$CM(B) = FC$$

$$\$7.20B = \$23,040$$

$$B = 3,200 \text{ bags}$$

Note: Each "bag" consists of 3 valves and 1 regulator; therefore, it will take 9,600 valves and 3,200 regulators to break even, assuming the constant 3:1 mix.
BEP in sales dollars (where CM ratio = weighted average CM per "bag"):

$$B = FC \div CM \text{ ratio}$$

$$B = \$23,040 \div 0.36$$

$$B = \$64,000$$

Note: The break-even sales dollars also represent the assumed constant sales mix of $18.00 of sales of valves to $2.00 of sales of regulators to represent a 90% to 10% ratio. Thus, the company must have $57,600 ($64,000 × 90%) in sales of valves and $6,400 in sales of regulators to break even.

Proof of the above computations using the income statement approach:

	Valves	Regulators	Total
Sales	$57,600	$6,400	$64,000
Variable costs	(38,016)	(2,944)	(40,960)
Contribution margin	$19,584	$3,456	$23,040
Fixed costs			(23,040)
Income before taxes			$ 0

MARGIN OF SAFETY

6

How are margin of safety and operating leverage concepts used in business?

margin of safety

When making decisions about various business opportunities and changes in sales mix, managers often consider the size of the company's **margin of safety** (MS). The margin of safety is the excess of a company's budgeted or actual sales over its break-even point. It is the amount that sales can drop before reaching the break-even point and, thus, it provides a measure of the amount of "cushion" from losses.

EXHIBIT 11–13

Effects of Product Mix Shift

	Valves		Regulators		Total	Percentage
Number of products per bag		2.5		1.5		
Revenue per product	$6.00		$2.00			
Total revenue per "bag"		$15.00		$3.00	$18.00	100.0
Variable cost per product	(3.96)		(0.92)			
Total variable per "bag"		(9.90)		(1.38)	(11.28)	(62.7)
Contribution margin—product	$2.04		$1.08			
Contribution margin—"bag"		$ 5.10		$1.62	$ 6.72	37.3

BEP in units (where B = "bags" of products)

CM(B) = FC

$6.72B = $23,040

B = 3,429 bags

Actual results: 3,200 "bags" with a sales mix ratio of 2.5 valves to 1.5 regulators; thus, the company sold 8,000 valves and 4,800 regulators.

	8,000 Valves	4,800 Regulators	Total
Sales	$48,000	$9,600	$57,600
Variable costs	(31,680)	(4,416)	(36,096)
Contribution margin	$16,320	$5,184	$21,504
Fixed costs			(23,040)
Net loss			$ (1,536)

The margin of safety can be expressed as units, dollars, or a percentage. The following formulas are applicable:

Margin of safety in units = Actual units − Break-even units

Margin of safety in $ = Actual sales in $ − Break-even sales in $

Margin of safety % = Margin of safety in units ÷ Actual unit sales

or

Margin of safety % = Margin of safety in $ ÷ Actual sales $

The break-even point for Comfort Valve (using the original, single-product data) is 9,000 units or $54,000 of sales. The income statement for the company presented in Exhibit 11–6 shows actual sales for 2000 or 30,000 kits or $180,000. The margin of safety for Comfort Valve is quite high, because it is operating far above its break-even point (see Exhibit 11–14).

EXHIBIT 11–14

Margin of Safety

In units: 30,000 actual − 9,000 BEP = 21,000 valves

In sales $: $180,000 actual − $54,000 BEP = $126,000

Percentage: 21,000 ÷ 30,000 = 70%

or

$126,000 ÷ $180,000 = 70%

The margin of safety calculation allows management to determine how close to a danger level the company is operating and, as such, provides an indication of risk. The lower the margin of safety, the more carefully management must watch sales figures and control costs so that a net loss will not be generated. At low margins of safety, managers are less likely to take advantage of opportunities that, if incorrectly analyzed or forecasted, could send the company into a loss position.

OPERATING LEVERAGE

Another measure that is closely related to the margin of safety and also provides useful management information is the company's degree of **operating leverage**. The relationship of a company's variable and fixed costs is reflected in its operating leverage. Typically, highly labor-intensive organizations, such as Pizza Hut and H & R Block, have high variable costs and low fixed costs and, thus, have low operating leverage. (An exception to this rule is a sports team, which is highly labor intensive, but the labor costs are fixed rather than variable.)

operating leverage

http://www.pizzahut.com
http://www.hrblock.com
http://www.ab.com

Conversely, organizations that are highly capital intensive (such as Lone Star Technologies, a Dallas producer of steel pipe used in oil wells) or automated (such as Allen-Bradley) have a cost structure that includes low variable and high fixed costs, providing high operating leverage. Because variable costs are low relative to selling prices, the contribution margin is high. However, the high level of fixed costs means that the break-even point also tends to be high. If the market predominantly sets selling prices, volume has the primary impact on profitability. As they become more automated, companies will face this type of cost structure and become more dependent on volume to add profits. Thus, a company's **cost structure**, or the relative composition of its fixed and variable costs, strongly influences the degree to which its profits respond to changes in volume.

cost structure

Companies with high operating leverage have high contribution margin ratios. Although such companies have to establish fairly high sales volumes to initially cover fixed costs, once those costs are covered, each unit sold after breakeven produces large profits. Thus, a small increase in sales can have a major impact on a company's profits. The accompanying News Note on page 468 illustrates some of the dynamics of operating leverage in the hotel industry.

The **degree of operating leverage** (DOL) measures how a percentage change in sales from the current level will affect company profits. In other words, it indicates how sensitive the company is to sales volume increases and decreases. The computation providing the degree of operating leverage factor is

degree of operating leverage

$$\text{Degree of Operating Leverage} = \text{Contribution Margin} \div \text{Profit before Tax}$$

This calculation assumes that fixed costs do not increase when sales increase.

Assume that Comfort Valve Company is currently selling 20,000 valves. Exhibit 11–15 on page 468 provides the income statement that reflects this sales level. At this level of activity, the company has an operating leverage factor of 1.818. If the company increases sales by 20 percent, the change in profits is equal to the degree of operating leverage multiplied by the percentage change in sales or 36.36 percent. If sales decrease by the same 20 percent, there is a negative 36.36 percent impact on profits. Exhibit 11–15 confirms these computations.

The degree of operating leverage decreases the farther a company moves from its break-even point. Thus, when the margin of safety is small, the degree of operating leverage is large. In fact, at breakeven, the degree of operating leverage is infinite because any increase from zero is an infinite percentage change. If a company is operating close to the break-even point, each percentage increase in sales can make a dramatic impact on net income. As the company moves away from break-even sales, the margin of safety increases, but the degree of operating leverage declines.

NEWS NOTE  GENERAL BUSINESS

Bucking the Hospitality Trend

In the highly cyclical lodging industry, profits and values vary according to changes in occupancy and room rate. For the most part, these changes depend on availability of financing and growth in new rooms supply.

A major risk in owning a hotel entails supply. In the last 40 years, investors who lost money in this industry suffered from overbuilding, not shrinking demand or poor management. During the building spree of the 1980s, some markets experienced supply gains of more than 100 percent. This rapid growth in new hotel rooms diluted areawide occupancies, eroded profits and forced many hotels into bankruptcy.

New hotel construction usually begins when a developer can build a hotel worth more when finished than its replacement cost.

As more hotels are built, occupancies and values fall. When it costs more to build new than to buy an existing hotel with the same utility, feasibility is negative, financing evaporates and new construction ceases. Construction loans on hotels lag feasibility, so when values rise, many lenders are slow to respond to new lending opportunities.

During 1997, hotel values in some parts of the U.S. rose by up to 70 percent. To someone not familiar with hotel operating leverage, this enormous rise was astonishing.

In 1991, the nadir of the hotel industry, 35 out of the 47 markets our firm tracks lost value. In 1997, the best year, only three markets sustained losses.

On the revenue side, hotels can continually adjust rates to take advantage of occupancy cycles. When a hotel is likely to reach capacity, management can aggressively raise rates, unlike conventional real estate.

As occupancies rise above breakeven, profitability and values rise significantly. But operating leverage works in reverse, causing profitability and values to crash as occupancies drop below the point where revenue can cover fixed expenses.

SOURCE: Stephen Rushmore, "Bucking the Hospitality Trend," *Lodging Hospitality* (July 1998), pp. 30ff.

EXHIBIT 11–15

Degree of Operating Leverage

	(20,000 valves) Current	(24,000 valves) 20% Increase	(16,000 valves) 20% Decrease
Sales	$120,000	$144,000	$96,000
Variable costs ($3.96 per valve)	(79,200)	(95,040)	(63,360)
Contribution margin	$ 40,800	$ 48,960	$32,640
Fixed costs	(18,360)	(18,360)	(18,360)
Profit before tax	$ 22,440	$ 30,600*	$14,280**
Degree of operating leverage:			
Contribution margin ÷ Profit before tax			
($40,800 ÷ $22,440)	1.818		
($48,960 ÷ $30,600)		1.600	
($32,640 ÷ $14,280)			2.286

*Profit increase = $30,600 − $22,440 = $8,160 (or 36.36% of the original profit)
**Profit decrease = $14,280 − $22,440 = $(8,160) (or −36.36% of the original profit)

The relationship between the margin of safety and degree of operating leverage is shown below:

Margin of Safety % = 1 ÷ Degree of Operating Leverage

Degree of Operating Leverage = 1 ÷ Margin of Safety %

This relationship is proved in Exhibit 11–16 using the 20,000-valve sales level information for Comfort Valve. Therefore, if one of the two measures is known, the other can be easily calculated.

EXHIBIT 11-16

Margin of Safety and Degree of Operating Leverage Relationship

Margin of Safety % = Margin of Safety in Units ÷ Actual Sales in Units

= [(20,000 − 9,000) ÷ 20,000] = 0.55 or 55%

Degree of Operating Leverage = Contribution Margin ÷ Profit before Tax

= $40,800 ÷ $22,440 = 1.818

Margin of Safety = (1 ÷ DOL) = (1 ÷ 1.818) = 0.55 or 55%

Degree of Operating Leverage = (1 ÷ MS %) = (1 ÷ 0.55) = 1.818

UNDERLYING ASSUMPTIONS OF CVP ANALYSIS

7

What are the underlying assumptions of CVP analysis?

CVP analysis is a short-run model that focuses on relationships among several items: selling price, variable costs, fixed costs, volume, and profits. This model is a useful planning tool that can provide information on the impact on profits when changes are made in the cost structure or in sales levels. However, the CVP model, like other human-made models, is an abstraction of reality and, as such, does not reveal all the forces at work. It reflects reality but does not duplicate it. Although limiting the accuracy of the results, several important but necessary assumptions are made in the CVP model. These assumptions follow.

1. All revenue and variable cost behavior patterns are constant per unit and linear within the relevant range.
2. Total contribution margin (total revenue − total variable costs) is linear within the relevant range and increases proportionally with output. This assumption follows directly from assumption 1.
3. Total fixed cost is a constant amount within the relevant range.
4. Mixed costs can be accurately separated into their fixed and variable elements. Although accuracy of separation may be questioned, reliable estimates can be developed from the use of regression analysis or the high-low method (discussed in Chapter 3).
5. Sales and production are equal; thus, there is no material fluctuation in inventory levels. This assumption is necessary because of the allocation of fixed costs to inventory at potentially different rates each year. This assumption requires that variable costing information be available. Because both CVP and variable costing focus on cost behavior, they are distinctly compatible with one another.
6. There will be no capacity additions during the period under consideration. If such additions were made, fixed (and, possibly, variable) costs would change. Any changes in fixed or variable costs would violate assumptions 1 through 3.
7. In a multiproduct firm, the sales mix will remain constant. If this assumption were not made, no weighted average contribution margin could be computed for the company.
8. There is either no inflation or, if it can be forecasted, it is incorporated into the CVP model. This eliminates the possibility of cost changes.
9. Labor productivity, production technology, and market conditions will not change. If any of these changes occur, costs would change correspondingly and selling prices might change. Such changes would invalidate assumptions 1 through 3.

These assumptions limit not only the volume of activity for which the calculations can be made, but also the time frame for the usefulness of the calculations to that period for which the specified revenue and cost amounts remain constant. Changes in either selling prices or costs will require that new computations be made for break-even and product opportunity analyses.

The nine assumptions listed above are the traditional ones associated with cost-volume-profit analysis. An additional assumption must be noted with regard to the distinction of variable and fixed costs. Accountants have generally assumed that cost behavior, once classified, remained constant over periods of time as long as operations remained within the relevant range. Thus, for example, once a cost was determined to be "fixed," it would be fixed next year, the year after, and 10 years from now.

It is more appropriate to regard fixed costs instead as long-term variable costs. Over the long run, through managerial decisions, companies can lay off supervisors and sell plant and equipment items. Fixed costs are not fixed forever. Generating cost information in a manner that yields a longer run perspective is presented in Chapter 4 on activity-based costing/management. Part of the traditional "misclassification" of fixed costs has been caused by improperly specifying the drivers of the costs. As companies become less focused on production and sales volumes as cost drivers, they will begin to recognize that "fixed costs" only exist under a short-term reporting period perspective.

Such a reclassification simply means that the cost drivers of the long-term variable costs will have to be specified in the break-even and CVP analyses. The formula will need to be expanded to include these additional drivers, and more information and a longer time frame will be needed to make the calculations. No longer will sales volume necessarily be the overriding nonmonetary force in the computations.

These adjustments to the CVP formula will force managers to take a long-run, rather than a short-run, view of product opportunities. Such a perspective could produce better organizational decisions. As the time frame is extended, both the time value of money and life-cycle costing become necessary considerations. Additionally, the traditional income statement becomes less useful for developing projects that will take several years to mature. A long-run perspective is important in a variety of circumstances, such as when variable or fixed costs arise only in the first year that a product or service is provided to customers.

QUALITY AND COSTS

One important long-run change that may create significant short-run costs is the implementation of a total quality management (TQM) program. A TQM program, as discussed in Chapter 8, generally causes prevention costs to increase. These costs probably will not be recouped in the short run by the decreases in appraisal and failure costs. However, in the long run, appraisal and failure costs should decline and the higher quality goods produced might command higher selling prices and sell better than the lower quality goods produced before the TQM program. Thus, the three primary factors in determining a company's profits (costs, price, and volume) are intimately related to a fourth factor: quality. Quality considerations are primarily concerned with improving or maintaining customer satisfaction. Keeping current customers satisfied costs far less than having to court new customers to replace former dissatisfied customers. Further, servicing long-term customers is less costly than servicing new customers.

It would seem that the costs of ensuring quality should, in the long run, outweigh the costs of having poor quality. Implementation of a TQM program could cause higher variable costs (in the form of higher quality materials) or fixed costs (for plant assets and training). Other costs (such as those attributable to rework, redesign, and product failure) should fall after a period of time. Higher variable costs will not necessarily result in a lower contribution margin because of the possibility of higher selling prices. Higher fixed costs may only be incurred for the short run, returning to lower levels after the implementation program is completed.

Recall that CVP behavior patterns were required to be stable for the model to produce valid results. If the CVP component elements are sensitive to continuous quality improvement efforts, they must be reevaluated frequently enough to compensate for changes that have occurred. Updating the CVP factors and their relationships for the impact of quality initiatives will help ensure the valid measurement of longer run results.

Although efforts to improve quality may take some time to produce noticeable results, it is widely believed that continuous quality improvement will increase sales volume and productivity, lower costs, and support management's ability to adjust product and service prices. As mentioned in the previous sections, when managers analyze break-even computations or product opportunities, managers should consider both quantitative and qualitative information. In addition, managers should consider the potential benefits generated by focusing their attention more on the long run and less on the short run.

REVISITING Torrington Supply Co.

http://www.torringtonsupply.com

Torrington has utilized the latest technology in every aspect of its business from the office operations of accounting, purchasing, sales management, and customer service, to all warehousing and shipping functions. The firm now is working with selected customers and vendors to eliminate duplicate processing costs. Torrington is using technology to implement programs to eliminate overlapping business functions such as order placement and stock replenishment and processing payables and receivables. The objective is to provide customers and suppliers hassle free, faster, and lower cost transactions.

Joel Becker [CEO] realized that kind of real-time information about a customer's net profitability would be very helpful to Torrington's inside-sales staff as they took orders. He and David Petitti [CFO] worked with Eclipse to develop a way to deliver the data with a single keystroke. But once they had it, they were shocked to discover that some of the company's "best" customers were also among its biggest profit drains.

Becker points to a sample report on one customer. This contractor was buying more than $200,000 in materials from Torrington every year and paying in less than 29 days. And Torrington was earning a gross profit of almost 20% on these orders. "Yet we were losing a fortune on him!" Becker says.

The problem was that Torrington was making less than $3 a line—$21 an order—on this customer. "There is a fixed cost associated with every single order," Becker says. "What matters is the gross profit per order, not the individual gross profit per line item. We actually make the lowest gross profit percent on our most profitable customers. The secret is the size of the order."

Becker decided that the best approach to take with such a delicate situation was the direct route. Armed with the profitability report, he called on the owner and the operations manager of the customer company. "I told them, 'You're a great customer,' " he recalls. " 'You've been doing business with us for a long time, and we love you. But we need you to do something if we're going to continue to do business. We need you to help us reduce our transaction costs.' And I specifically listed what I thought they could do."

The customers themselves were surprised. They realized that placing so many orders was undoubtedly costing them money, as well. They were happy to work with Torrington to reduce their shared business costs.

"They now place all their orders electronically," Becker says. "Most customers are surprised at the activity levels their business requires of us. It's a real win–win."

So far Becker has these conversations only with customers with significant opportunity for improvement. "I review the details of their activity with us over the last 52 weeks: how much business they've done; the gross profit we earned; the number of lines, invoices, returns, deliveries, counter pickups, direct shipments, everything. They forget about our costs for what they require of us. But when they see all this, they respond very well."

SOURCES: Margie O'Conner, "A Full Measure of Customer Service," *Supply House Times* (December 1999), pp. 44ff; Torrington Supply Co. Web site, http://www.torringtonsupply.com (February 11, 2000).

CHAPTER SUMMARY

Cost accumulation and cost presentation are two dimensions of product costing. Cost accumulation determines which costs are treated as product costs, whereas cost presentation focuses on how costs are shown on the financial statements or internal management reports.

Absorption and variable costing are two production-costing methods that differ in regard to product cost composition and income statement presentation. Under absorption costing, all manufacturing costs, both variable and fixed, are treated as product costs. The absorption costing method presents nonmanufacturing costs according to functional areas on the income statement, whereas the variable costing method presents both nonmanufacturing and manufacturing costs according to cost behavior on the income statement.

Variable costing computes product costs by including only the variable costs of production (direct material, direct labor, and variable manufacturing overhead). Fixed manufacturing overhead is viewed as a period expense in the period of occurrence by variable costing. Variable costing is not considered to be an acceptable method of inventory valuation for preparing external reports or filing tax returns.

Absorption costing income differs from variable costing income for any period in which production and sales volumes differ. This difference reflects the amount of fixed manufacturing overhead that is either attached to, or released from, inventory in absorption costing as opposed to being immediately expensed in variable costing.

Management planning includes planning for prices, volumes, fixed and variable costs, contribution margins, and break-even point. The interrelationships of these factors are studied when applying cost-volume-profit (CVP) analysis. Management should understand these interrelationships and combine them effectively and efficiently for company success.

The CVP model reflects linear relationships that can be used to calculate the level of sales volume necessary to achieve target profit objectives. CVP can also be used to compute break-even point (BEP), at which total contribution margin is equal to total fixed costs. Contribution margin equals sales minus all variable costs. BEP can be calculated using a cost-volume-profit formula that reflects basic income statement relationships. The BEP will change if the company's selling price(s) or costs change. Because most companies do not wish to operate at breakeven, CVP analysis extends the break-even point computation through the introduction of profit. The sales necessary to generate a desired amount of profit are computed by adding the desired profit to fixed costs and dividing that total by contribution margin. Profit can be stated as a fixed or a variable amount on a before- or after-tax basis. After fixed costs are covered, each dollar of contribution margin generated by company sales will produce a dollar of before-tax profit.

In a multiproduct firm, all break-even and cost-volume-profit analyses are performed using an assumed constant sales mix of products. This sales mix is referred to as the "bag" assumption. Use of the bag assumption requires the computation of a weighted average contribution margin (and, thus, contribution margin ratio) for the "bag" of products being sold by the company. Answers to break-even or CVP computations are in units or dollars of "bags" of products; these bag amounts can be converted to individual products by using the sales mix relationship.

The margin of safety (MS) of a firm indicates how far (in units, sales dollars, or a percentage) a company is operating from its break-even point. A company's degree of operating leverage (DOL) shows what percentage change in profit would occur given a specified percentage change in sales from the current level. The MS percentage is equal to (1 ÷ DOL) and the DOL is equal to (1 ÷ MS%).

CVP analysis enhances a manager's ability to beneficially influence current operations and to predict future operations, thereby reducing the risk of uncertainty. The model is, however, based on several assumptions that limit its ability to reflect reality. Managers may also wish to begin viewing the CVP relationships more on a long-range basis than the currently held short-range viewpoint.

APPENDIX

Graphic Approaches to Breakeven

(Appendix) How are break-even charts and profit-volume graphs constructed?

Solutions to break-even problems are determined in this chapter using an algebraic formula. Sometimes, however, the cost accountant may wish to present information to managers in a more visual format, such as graphs. Exhibit 11–17 graphically presents each income statement item for Comfort Valve Company's original data (see Exhibit 11–6), to provide visual representations of the behavior of revenue, costs, and contribution margin.

EXHIBIT 11–17

Graphical Presentation of Income Statement Items

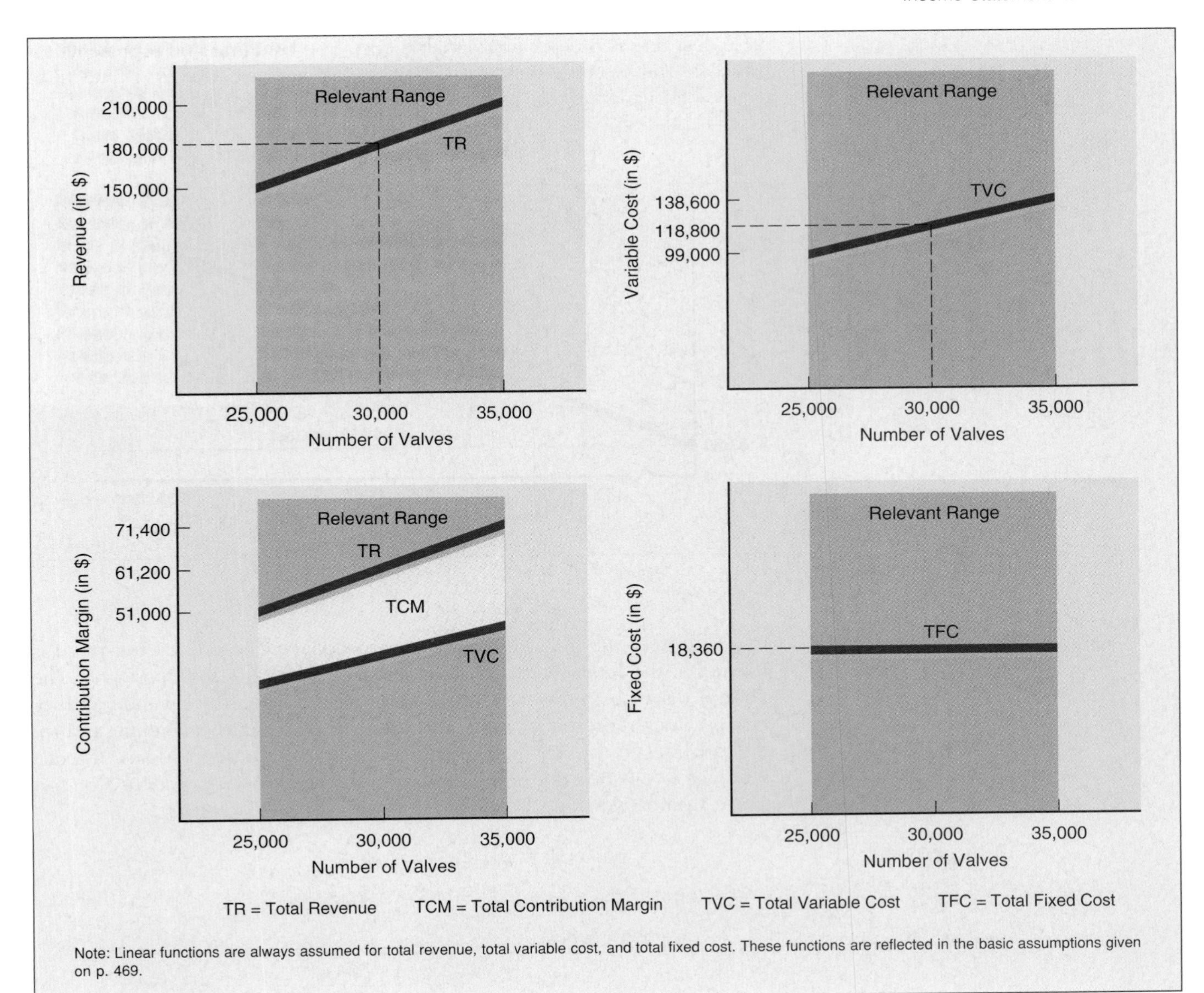

Note: Linear functions are always assumed for total revenue, total variable cost, and total fixed cost. These functions are reflected in the basic assumptions given on p. 469.

break-even chart

While illustrating individual behaviors, the graphs presented in Exhibit 11–17 are not very useful for determining the relationships among the various income statement categories. A **break-even chart** can be prepared to graph the relationships among revenue, volume, and the various costs. The break-even point on a break-even chart is located at the point where the total cost and total revenue lines cross.

Two approaches can be used to prepare break-even charts: the traditional approach and the contemporary approach. A third graphical presentation, the profit-volume graph, is closely related to the break-even chart.

Traditional Approach

The traditional approach to graphical break-even analysis focuses on the relationships among revenues, costs, and profits (losses). This approach does not show contribution margin. A traditional break-even chart for Comfort Valve Company is prepared as follows.

Step 1: Label each axis and graph the cost lines. The total fixed cost is drawn horizontal to the *x*-axis (volume). The variable cost line begins at the point where the total fixed cost line intersects the *y*-axis. The slope of the variable cost line is the per-unit variable cost. The resulting line represents total cost. The distance between the fixed cost and the total cost lines indicates total variable cost at each activity volume level.

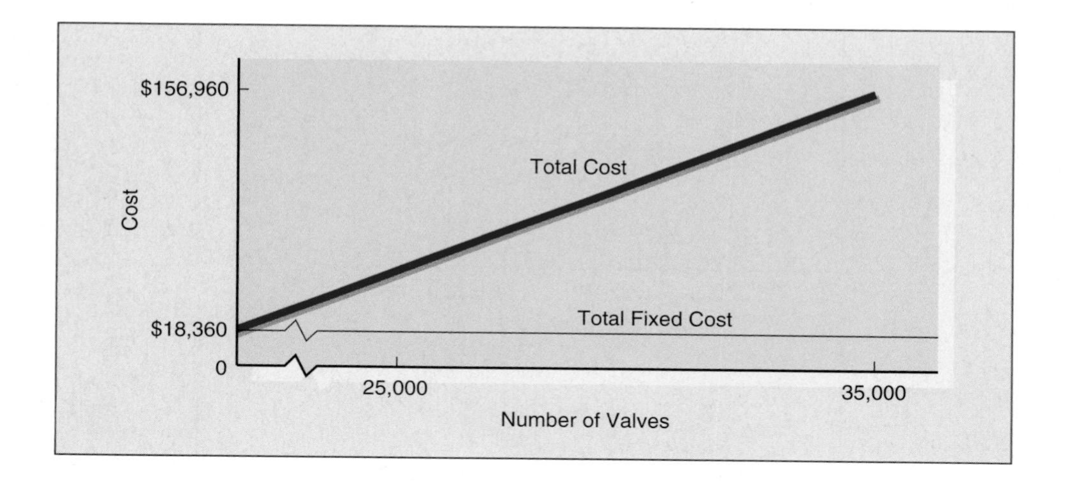

Step 2: Chart the revenue line, beginning at zero dollars. The break-even point is located at the intersection of the revenue line and the total cost line. The vertical distance to the right of the BEP and between the revenue and total cost lines represents profits; the distance between the revenue and total cost lines to the left of the break-even point represents losses. If exact readings could be taken on the graph, the break-even point for Comfort Valve Company would be $54,000 of sales or 9,000 valves.

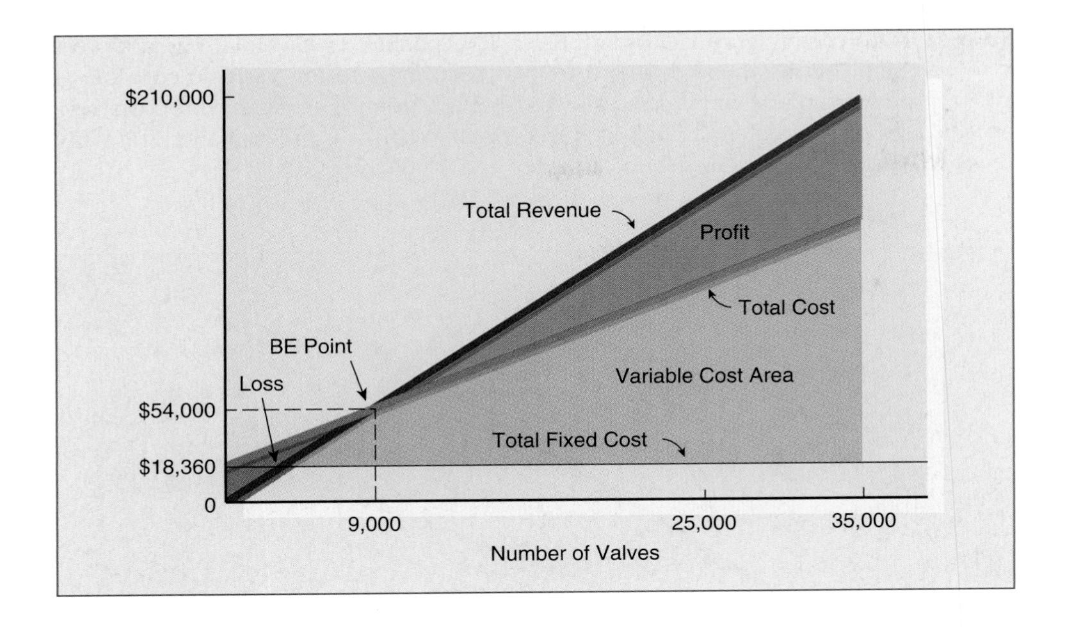

Contemporary Approach

The contribution margin provided by each level of sales volume is not apparent on the traditional break-even chart. Because contribution margin is so important in CVP analysis, another graphical approach can be used. The contemporary approach specifically presents CM in the break-even chart. The preparation of a contemporary break-even chart is detailed in the following steps.

Step 1: The contemporary break-even chart plots the variable cost first. The revenue line is plotted next and the contribution margin area is indicated.

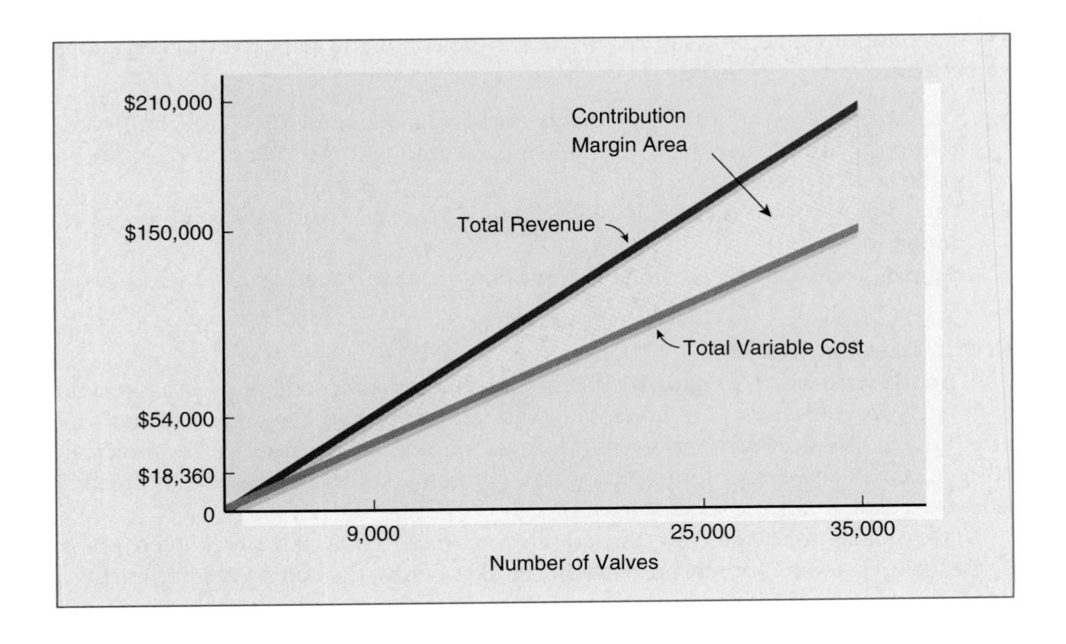

Step 2: Total cost is graphed by adding a line parallel to the total variable cost line. The distance between the total cost line and the variable cost line is the amount of fixed cost. The break-even point is located where the revenue and total cost lines intersect. Breakeven for Comfort Valve Company is again shown at $54,000 of sales and 9,000 valves.

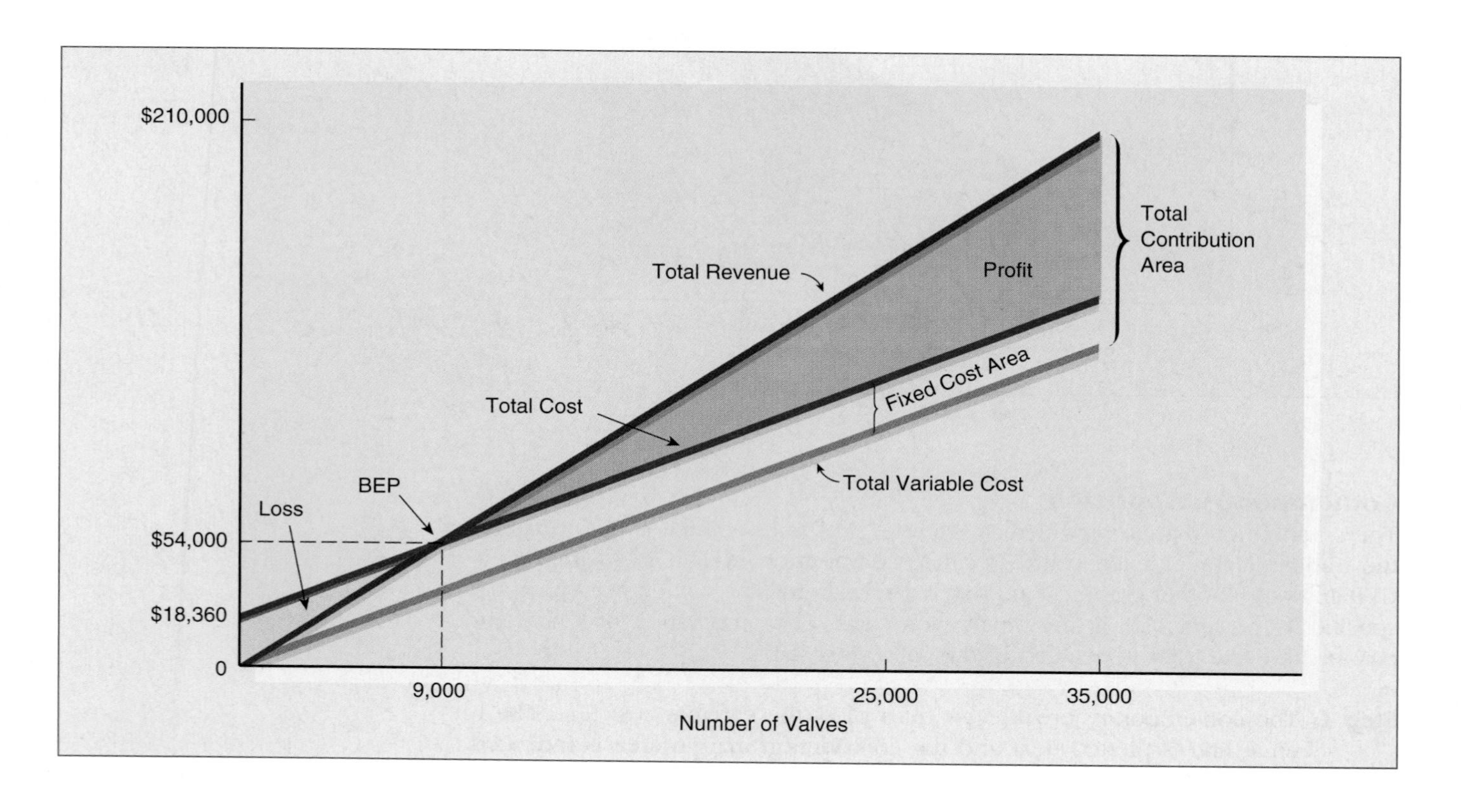

The contemporary graphic approach allows the following important observations to be made:

1. The excess of revenues over variable costs creates contribution margin. If variable costs are greater than revenues, no volume will ever allow a profit to be made.
2. Total contribution margin is always equal to total fixed cost plus profit or minus loss.
3. Before profits can be generated, contribution margin must exceed fixed costs.

Profit-Volume Graph

profit-volume graph

The **profit-volume** (PV) **graph** reflects the amount of profit or loss associated with each level of sales. The horizontal axis on the PV graph represents sales volume and the vertical axis represents dollars. Amounts shown above the horizontal axis are positive and represent profits; amounts shown below the horizontal axis are negative and represent losses.

Two points are located on the graph: total fixed costs and break-even point. Total fixed costs are shown on the vertical axis below the sales volume line as a negative amount. If no products were sold, fixed costs would still be incurred and a loss of the entire amount would result. The location of the break-even point may be determined algebraically or by using a break-even chart. Break-even point in units is shown on the horizontal axis because there is zero profit/loss at that point.

The last step in preparing the PV graph is to draw a profit line that passes between and extends through the two located points. Using this line, the amount of profit or loss for any sales volume can be read from the vertical axis. The profit line is really a contribution margin line and the slope of the line is determined by the unit contribution margin. The line shows that no profit is earned until the contribution margin covers the fixed costs.

The PV graph for Comfort Valve Company is shown in Exhibit 11–18. Total fixed costs are $18,360 and break-even point is 9,000 valves. The profit line reflects the original Exhibit 11–6 income statement data indicating a profit of $42,840 at a sales level of 30,000 valves.

The graphic approaches to breakeven provide detailed visual displays of break-even point. They do not, however, provide a precise solution because exact points cannot be determined on a graph. A definitive computation of break-even point can be found algebraically using the formula approach or a computer software application.

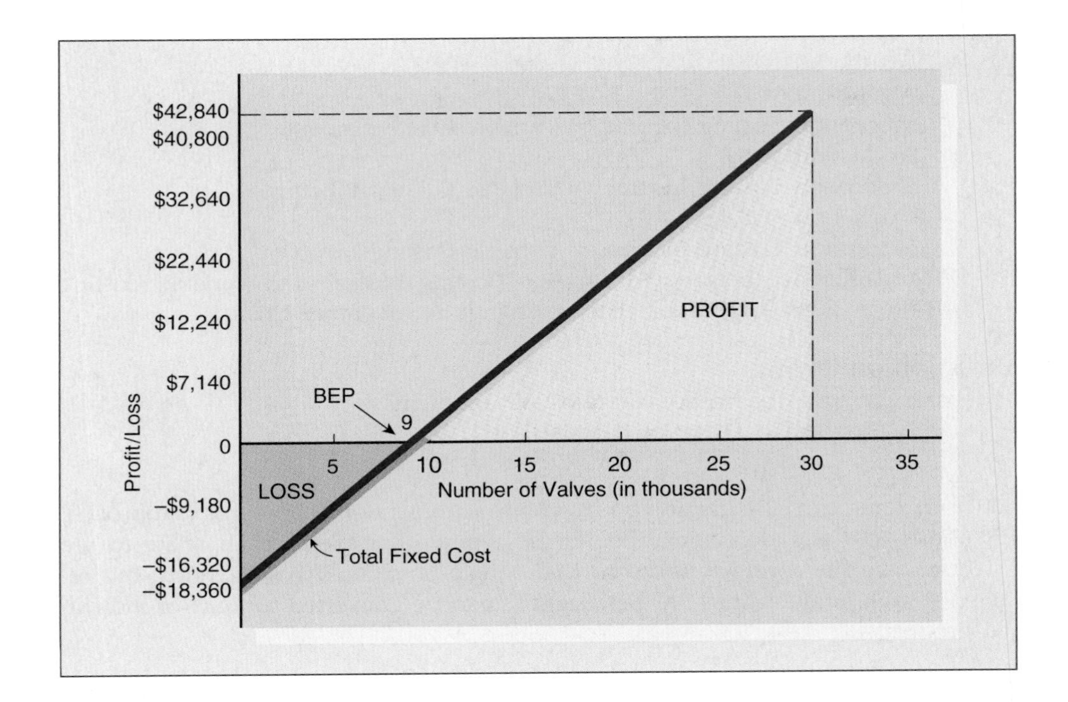

EXHIBIT 11–18

Profit-Volume Graph

KEY TERMS

absorption costing (p. 443)
break-even chart (p. 474)
break-even point (p. 451)
contribution margin (p. 453)
contribution margin ratio (p. 455)
cost accumulation (p. 443)
cost presentation (p. 443)
cost structure (p. 467)
cost-volume-profit analysis (p. 451)
degree of operating leverage (p. 467)
direct costing (p. 444)
full costing (p. 443)
functional classification (p. 444)
incremental analysis (p. 461)
margin of safety (p. 465)
operating leverage (p. 467)
phantom profit (p. 449)
product contribution margin (p. 445)
profit-volume graph (p. 476)
total contribution margin (p. 446)
variable cost ratio (p. 455)
variable costing (p. 444)

SOLUTION STRATEGIES

Absorption and Variable Costing

1. Which method is being used (absorption or variable)?
   a. If absorption:
      - What is the fixed manufacturing overhead application rate?
      - What denominator capacity is used in determining the fixed manufacturing overhead application rate?
      - Is production equal to the denominator capacity used in determining the fixed manufacturing overhead application rate? If not, there is a fixed overhead volume variance that must be properly assigned to cost of goods sold and, possibly, inventories.
      - What is the cost per unit of product? (DM + DL + VOH + FOH)
   b. If variable:
      - What is the cost per unit of product? (DM + DL + VOH)
      - What is total fixed manufacturing overhead? Assign to income statement in total as a period expense.
2. What is the relationship of production to sales?
   a. Production = Sales
      Absorption Costing Income = Variable Costing Income
   b. Production > Sales
      Absorption Costing Income > Variable Costing Income
   c. Production < Sales
      Absorption Costing Income < Variable Costing Income
3. Dollar Difference between Absorption Costing Income and Variable Costing Income = FOH Application Rate × Change in Inventory Units

Cost-Volume-Profit

The basic equation for break-even and CVP problems is

$$\text{Total Revenue} - \text{Total Cost} = \text{Profit}$$

CVP problems can also be solved by using a numerator/denominator approach. All numerators and denominators and the types of problems each relate to are listed below. The formulas relate to both single- and multiproduct firms, but results for multiproduct firms are per bag and can be converted to units of individual products.

Problem Situation	Numerator	Denominator
Simple BEP in units	FC	CM
Simple BEP in dollars	FC	CM%
CVP with fixed profit in units	FC + P	CM
CVP with fixed profit in dollars	FC + P	CM%
CVP with variable profit in units	FC	$CM - P_U$
CVP with variable profit in dollars	FC	$CM\% - P_U\%$

where FC = fixed cost

CM = contribution margin per unit

CM% = contribution margin percentage

P = total profit (on a before-tax basis)

P_U = profit per unit (on a before-tax basis)

$P_U\%$ = profit percentage per unit (on a before-tax basis)

To convert after-tax profit to before-tax profit, divide after-tax profit by (1 − tax rate).

Margin of Safety

Margin of Safety in Units = Actual units − Break-even units
Margin of Safety in Dollars = Actual sales $ − Break-even sales $
Margin of Safety % = (Margin of safety in units or $) ÷ (Actual sales in units or $)

Degree of Operating Leverage

Degree of Operating Leverage = Contribution margin ÷ Profit before tax

Predicted Profit = [1 + (DOL × Percent change in sales)] × Current profit

DEMONSTRATION PROBLEM

Andersen Company's management is interested in seeing the company's absorption costing income statements for 2000 and 2001 (the first two years of operation) recast using variable costing. The company incurred total fixed manufacturing overhead of $100,000 each year and produced 25,000 and 20,000 units, respectively, each year. The following absorption costing statements are based on standard costing using $3 variable production cost per unit and 25,000 units as the activity level on which to determine the standard fixed costs each year. Other than the volume variance occurring in 2001, there are no other variances.

	2000	2001
Net sales (a)	$300,000	$330,000
Cost of goods sold (b)	(140,000)	(154,000)
Volume variance (5,000 units @ $4)	0	(20,000)
Gross margin	$160,000	$156,000
Operating expenses (c)	(82,500)	(88,500)
Income before tax	$ 77,500	$ 67,500
(a) Net sales:		
20,000 units @ $15	$300,000	
22,000 units @ $15		$330,000
(b) Cost of goods sold:		
Beginning inventory	$ 0	$ 35,000
Cost of goods manufactured*	175,000	140,000
Goods available for sale	$175,000	$175,000
Ending inventory**	(35,000)	(21,000)
Cost of goods sold	$140,000	$154,000

	2000	2001
(c) Analysis of operating expenses:		
Variable	$ 50,000	$ 55,000
Fixed	32,500	33,500
Total	$ 82,500	$ 88,500
*CGM		
25,000 units @ $7.00 (of which $3 are variable)	$175,000	
20,000 units @ $7.00 (of which $3 are variable)		$140,000
**EI		
5,000 units @ $7.00	$ 35,000	
3,000 units @ $7.00		$ 21,000

Required:

a. Recast the 2000 and 2001 income statements on a variable costing basis.
b. Reconcile income for each year between absorption and variable costing.

Solution to Demonstration Problem

a.

	2000	2001
Net sales	$ 300,000	$ 330,000
Variable cost of goods sold	(60,000)	(66,000)
Product contribution margin	$ 240,000	$ 264,000
Variable operating expenses	(50,000)	(55,000)
Total contribution margin	$ 190,000	$ 209,000
Fixed costs		
Manufacturing	$ 100,000	$ 100,000
Operating	32,500	33,500
Total fixed costs	$(132,500)	$(133,500)
Income before tax	$ 57,500	$ 75,500

b.

Reconciliation 2000:	
Absorption costing income before tax	$77,500
− Fixed manufacturing overhead in ending inventory ($4.00 × 5,000)	(20,000)
Variable costing income before tax	$57,500
Reconciliation 2001:	
Absorption costing income before tax	$67,500
+ Fixed manufacturing overhead released from beginning inventory ($4.00 × 2,000)	8,000
Variable costing income before tax	$75,500

QUESTIONS

1. In what ways does absorption costing differ from variable costing?
2. What is the difference between absorption and variable costing in the treatment of fixed overhead?
3. What is meant by functionally classifying costs? What is meant by behaviorally classifying costs?
4. Which product costing alternative, variable or absorption, is generally required for external reporting? Why?
5. What do external users of financial reports emphasize that is different from internal users?
6. How do the income statement formats for variable and absorption costing differ?
7. Why do you think variable costing has also been called direct costing?
8. Why does the variable costing approach provide more useful information for making internal decisions?
9. On the Internet, find a discussion of a company that uses variable costing. State how the company uses variable costing and any advantages or disadvantages cited.
10. Why is income under absorption costing higher (lower) than under variable costing in years when production exceeds (is below) sales?
11. What is the break-even point? Why is calculating break-even point the starting point for cost-volume-profit analysis?
12. What is contribution margin and why does it fluctuate in direct proportion with sales volume?
13. Why is CVP analysis a short-run tool? Why is it inappropriate as a long-run model?
14. Why is the formula for a variable costing income statement the basis for break-even or cost-volume-profit analysis?

15. If a product's fixed costs increase and its selling price and variable costs remain constant, what will happen to (a) contribution margin and (b) break-even point?

16. How can contribution margin be used to calculate break-even point in both units and dollars?

17. What is the contribution margin ratio? How is it used to calculate the break-even point?

18. A company is in the 40 percent tax bracket. Why is desired profit after tax divided by 60 percent to determine the needed before-tax profit amount?

19. What is meant by the "bag" assumption and why is it necessary in a multiproduct firm? What additional assumption must be made in multiproduct CVP analysis that doesn't pertain to a single-product CVP situation?

20. How are BEP and margin of safety integrally related?

21. What is operating leverage? How does it pertain to CVP analysis? What is the margin of safety? How does it apply to CVP analysis?

22. *(Appendix)* What are the purposes of a break-even chart? What is the difference between the traditional approach and the contemporary approach to preparing a break-even chart? Between a break-even chart and a profit-volume graph?

EXERCISES

23. *(Ending inventory valuation; absorption vs. variable costing)* Harvard Hats Company produces baseball caps. In May 2000, the company manufactured 20,000 caps. May sales were 18,400 caps. The cost per unit for the 20,000 caps produced was

Direct material	$3.00
Direct labor	2.00
Variable overhead	1.00
Fixed overhead	1.50
Total	$7.50

There was no beginning inventory for May.

a. What is the value of ending inventory using absorption costing?

b. What is the value of ending inventory using variable costing?

c. Which accounting method, variable or absorption, would have produced the higher net income for May?

24. *(Absorption vs. variable costing)* The following data were taken from records of the Kitchen Juicer Company. The company uses variable costing. The data relate to the company's first year of operation.

Units produced:	40,000
Units sold:	37,500
Variable cost per unit:	
Direct material	$48
Direct labor	27
Variable overhead	14
Variable selling costs	12
Fixed costs:	
Selling and administrative	$750,000
Manufacturing	500,000

How much higher (or lower) would the company's first-year net income have been if the company had used absorption costing rather than variable costing? Show computations.

25. *(Production cost; absorption vs. variable costing)* Bright Smile Mouthwash began business in 1999. Production for the year was 100,000 bottles of mouthwash, and sales were 98,000 bottles. Costs incurred during the year were as follows:

Ingredients used	$28,000
Direct labor	13,000
Variable overhead	24,000
Fixed overhead	12,000
Variable selling expenses	5,000
Fixed selling and administrative expenses	14,000
Total actual costs	$96,000

a. What was the actual production cost per bottle under variable costing? Under absorption costing?
b. What was variable Cost of Goods Sold for 1999 under variable costing?
c. What was Cost of Goods Sold for 1999 under absorption costing?
d. What was the value of ending inventory under variable costing? Under absorption costing?
e. How much fixed overhead was charged to expense in 1999 under variable costing? Under absorption costing?

26. *(Net income; absorption vs. variable costing)* Skillful Scanners produces commercial scanners. Throughout 2000, unit variable cost remained constant and fixed overhead was applied at the rate of $5 per unit. Income before tax using the variable costing method was $90,000 for July 2000. Beginning and ending inventories for July were 17,000 and 15,000 units, respectively.
a. Calculate income before tax under absorption costing assuming no variances.
b. Assume instead that the company's July beginning and ending inventories were 15,000 and 18,000 units, respectively. Calculate income before tax under absorption costing.

27. *(Convert variable to absorption)* James Walton, vice president of marketing for Charming Curios, has just received the April 2000 income statement, shown below, which was prepared on a variable costing basis. The firm uses a variable costing system for internal reporting purposes.

CHARMING CURIOS
Income Statement
For the Month Ended April 30, 2000
($000 omitted)

Sales		$4,800
Variable standard cost of goods sold		(2,400)
Product contribution margin		$2,400
Fixed expenses		
Manufacturing (at budget)	$1,000	
Manufacturing spending variance	0	
Selling and administrative	800	(1,800)
Income before taxes		$ 600

The controller attached the following notes to the statements:
The unit sales price for April averaged $48.
The standard unit manufacturing costs for the month were:

Variable cost	$24
Fixed cost	10
Total cost	$34

→ look for volume variance

The unit rate for fixed manufacturing costs is a predetermined rate based on a normal monthly production of 100,000 units. Production for April was 5,000 units in excess of sales, and the April ending inventory consisted of 8,000 units.

a. The vice president of marketing is not comfortable with the variable cost basis and wonders what income before tax would have been under absorption costing.
   1. Present the April income statement on an absorption costing basis.
   2. Reconcile and explain the difference between the variable costing and the absorption costing income figures.

b. Explain the features associated with variable cost income measurement that should be attractive to the vice president of marketing. *(CMA adapted)*

28. *(Standard costing; variable and absorption costing)* Gramps' Remedy manufactures athletes' foot powder. The company uses a standard costing system. Following are data pertaining to the company's operations for 1999:

Production for the year	180,000 units
Sales for the year (sales price per unit, $1.25)	195,000 units
Beginning 1999 inventory	35,000 units

STANDARD COSTS TO PRODUCE 1 UNIT	
Direct material	$0.15
Direct labor	0.10
Variable overhead	0.05
Fixed overhead	0.15

SELLING AND ADMINISTRATIVE COSTS	
Variable (per unit sold)	$0.14
Fixed (per year)	$120,000

Fixed manufacturing overhead is assigned to units of production based on a predetermined rate using a normal production capacity of 200,000 units per year.

a. What is the estimated annual fixed manufacturing overhead?

b. If estimated fixed overhead is equal to actual fixed overhead, what is the amount of under- or overapplied overhead in 1999 under absorption costing? Under variable costing?

c. What is the product cost per unit under absorption costing? Under variable costing?

d. How much expense will be charged against revenues in 1999 under absorption costing? Under variable costing?

e. Will pretax income be higher under absorption or variable costing? By what amount?

29. *(Cost and revenue behavior)* The following financial data have been determined from analyzing the records of Jordan Appliances (a one-product firm):

Contribution margin per unit	$ 25
Variable costs per unit	21
Annual fixed costs	180,000

How do each of the following measures change when product volume goes up by one unit at Jordan Appliances?

a. Total revenue

b. Total costs

c. Income before taxes

30. *(Break-even point)* Thompson Company has the following revenue and cost functions:

Revenue = $60 per unit
Costs = $241,750 + $35 per unit

What is the break-even point in units? In dollars?

31. *(Incremental sales)* Brunswick Industries has annual sales of $2,500,000 with variable expenses of 60 percent of sales and fixed expenses per month of $40,000. By how much will annual sales have to increase for Brunswick Industries to have pretax income equal to 30 percent of sales?

32. *(CVP, taxes)* Joan Michaels has a small plant that makes playhouses. She sells them to local customers at $3,000 each. Her costs are as follows:

Costs	Per Unit	Total
Direct material	$1,200	
Direct labor	400	
Variable overhead	150	
Variable selling	50	
Fixed production overhead		$200,000
Fixed selling and administrative		80,420

Joan is in a 35 percent tax bracket.

a. How many playhouses must she sell to earn $247,507 after taxes?
b. What level of revenue is needed to yield an after-tax income equal to 20 percent of sales?

33. *(Operating leverage, margin of safety)* One of the products produced by Orlando Citrus is Citrus Delight. The selling price per half-gallon is $4.50, and variable cost of production is $2.70. Total fixed costs per year are $316,600. The company is currently selling 200,000 half-gallons per year.

a. What is the margin of safety in units?
b. What is the degree of operating leverage?
c. If the company can increase sales in units by 30 percent, what percentage increase will it experience in income? Prove your answer using the income statement approach.
d. If the company increases advertising by $41,200, sales in units will increase by 15 percent. What will be the new break-even point? The new degree of operating leverage?

34. *(Miscellaneous)* Compute the answers to each of the following independent situations.

a. SmallCo sells two products, M and N. The sales mix of these products is 2:4, respectively. M has a contribution margin of $10 per unit, and N has a contribution margin of $5 per unit. Fixed costs for the company are $90,000. What would be the total units of N sold at the break-even point?
b. Brooke Company has a break-even point of 2,000 units. At breakeven, variable costs are $3,200 and fixed costs are $800. If the company sells one unit over breakeven, what will be the pretax income of the company?
c. Cool Cologne sells its product for $5 per bottle. The fixed costs of the company are $108,000. Variable costs amount to 40 percent of selling price. What amount of sales (in units) would be necessary for Cool Cologne to earn a 25 percent pretax profit on sales?
d. Johnston Company has a break-even point of 1,400 units. The company is currently selling 1,600 units for $65 each. What is the margin of safety for the company in units, sales dollars, and percentage?

35. *(CVP, multiproduct)* Winnie Wholesalers sells baseball products. The Little League Division handles both bats and gloves. Historically, the firm has averaged three bats sold for each glove sold. Each bat has a $4 contribution margin and each glove has a $5 contribution margin. The fixed costs of operating the Little League Division are $200,000 per year. Each bat sells for $10 on average and each glove sells for $15 on average. The corporatewide tax rate for the company is 40 percent.

a. How much revenue is needed to break even? How many bats and gloves would this represent?

b. How much revenue is needed to earn a pretax profit of $90,000?

c. How much revenue is needed to earn an after-tax profit of $90,000?

d. If the Little League Division earns the revenue determined in part (b), but in doing so sells two bats for each glove, what would the pretax profit (or loss) be? Why is this amount not $90,000?

36. *(Appendix)* Tom & Jerry Inc. had the following income statement for 2000.

Sales (15,000 gallons @ $8)		$120,000
Variable Costs		
Production (20,000 gallons @ $3)	$60,000	
Selling (20,000 gallons @ $0.50)	10,000	(70,000)
Contribution Margin		$ 50,000
Fixed Costs		
Production	$22,000	
Selling and administrative	4,000	(26,000)
Income before Taxes		$ 24,000
Income Taxes (40%)		(9,600)
Net Income		$ 14,400

a. Prepare a CVP graph, in the traditional manner, to reflect the relations among costs, revenues, profit, and volume.

b. Prepare a CVP graph, in the contemporary manner, to reflect the relations among costs, revenues, profit, and volume.

c. Prepare a profit-volume graph.

d. Prepare a short explanation for company management about each of the graphs.

PROBLEMS

37. *(Convert variable to absorption)* George Massat started a new business in 1999 to produce portable, climate-controlled shelters. The shelters have many applications in special events and sporting activities. George's accountant prepared the variable costing income statement shown after part (d3) after the first year to help him in making decisions. During the year, the following variable production costs per unit were recorded: direct material, $800; direct labor, $300; and overhead, $200.

Mr. Massat was upset about the net loss because he had wanted to borrow funds to expand capacity. His friend who teaches accounting at a local university suggested that the use of absorption costing could change the picture.

a. Prepare an absorption costing pretax income statement.

b. Explain the source of the difference between the net income and the net loss figures under the two costing systems.

c. Would it be appropriate to present an absorption costing income statement to the local banker in light of Mr. Massat's knowledge of the net loss determined under variable costing? Explain.

(continued)

d. Assume that during the second year of operations, Mr. Massat's company produced 1,750 shelters, sold 1,850, and experienced the same total fixed costs. For the second year:
  1. Prepare a variable costing pretax income statement.
  2. Prepare an absorption costing pretax income statement.
  3. Explain the difference between the incomes for the second year under the two systems.

GEORGE MASSAT ENTERPRISES
Income Statement
For the Year Ended December 31, 1999

Sales (1,500 shelters @ $2,500)		$3,750,000
Variable cost of goods sold:		
Beginning inventory	$ 0	
Cost of goods manufactured (1,750 @ $1,300)	2,275,000	
Cost of goods available for sale	$2,275,000	
Less ending inventory (250 @ $1,300)	(325,000)	(1,950,000)
Product contribution margin		$1,800,000
Less variable selling and administrative expenses (1,500 @ $180)		(270,000)
Total contribution margin		$1,530,000
Less fixed expenses:		
Fixed factory overhead	$1,500,000	
Fixed selling and administrative expenses	190,000	(1,690,000)
Net loss		$ (160,000)

38. *(Income statements, variance)* Johnson Tools makes a unique workman's tool. The company produces and sells approximately 500,000 units per year. The projected unit cost data for 2001 follows; the company uses standard full absorption costing and writes off all variances to Cost of Goods Sold.

	Variable	Fixed
Direct material	$1.50	0
Direct labor	1.20	0
Variable overhead	0.40	0
Fixed overhead		$ 82,000
Selling and administrative	4.00	145,000

The fixed overhead application rate is $0.16 per unit.

a. Calculate the per-unit inventory cost for variable costing.
b. Calculate the per-unit inventory cost for absorption costing.
c. The projected income before tax from variable costing is $223,000 at production and sales of 500,000 units and 490,000 units, respectively. Projected beginning and ending finished goods inventories are 30,000 and 40,000 units, respectively. Calculate the projected income before tax using absorption costing.

39. *(Comprehensive)* Brookfield Fashions produces and sells cotton blouses. The firm uses variable costing for internal management purposes and absorption costing for external purposes. At the end of each year, financial information must be converted from variable costing to absorption costing to satisfy external requirements.

At the end of 1999, it was anticipated that sales would rise 20 percent from 1999 levels for 2000. Therefore, production was increased from 20,000 to 24,000 units to meet this expected demand. However, economic conditions kept the sales level at 20,000 for both years. The following data pertain to 1999 and 2000:

	1999	2000
Selling price per unit	$40	$40
Sales (units)	20,000	20,000
Beginning inventory (units)	2,000	2,000
Production (units)	20,000	24,000
Ending inventory (units)	2,000	?
Unfavorable labor, material, and variable overhead variances (total)	$5,000	$4,000

Standard variable costs per unit for 1999 and 2000 were

Material	$ 4.50
Labor	7.50
Overhead	3.00
Total	$15.00

Annual fixed costs for 1999 and 2000 (budgeted and actual) were

Production	$117,000
Selling and administrative	125,000
Total	$242,000

The overhead rate under absorption costing is based on practical capacity of 30,000 units per year. All variances and under- or overapplied overhead are taken to Cost of Goods Sold. All taxes are to be ignored.

a. Present the income statement based on variable costing for 2000.

b. Present the income statement based on absorption costing for 2000.

c. Explain the difference, if any, in the income figures. Assuming no Work in Process Inventory, give the entry necessary to adjust the book income amount to the financial statement income amount, if one is necessary.

d. The company finds it worthwhile to develop its internal financial data on a variable costing basis. What advantages and disadvantages are attributed to variable costing for internal purposes?

e. Many accountants believe that variable costing is appropriate for external reporting and many oppose its use for external reporting. What arguments for and against the use of variable costing can you think of in external reporting? *(CMA adapted)*

40. *(Income statements for 2 years, both methods)* Edison Digital manufactures palm-top computers. The following data from the company are available for 2000 and 2001:

	2000	2001
Selling price per unit	$170	$170
Number of units sold	20,000	24,000
Number of units produced	25,000	22,000
Beginning inventory (units)	15,000	20,000
Ending inventory (units)	20,000	?

Standard costs per unit for 2000 and 2001 were

Direct material	$20.00	
Direct labor	60.00	
Variable overhead	20.00	
Fixed overhead	30.00	(based on budget of $750,000 and normal capacity of 25,000 units)
Variable sales commission	20.00	

In addition, selling and administrative fixed costs were $190,000 for both years. All variances are charged or credited to Cost of Goods Sold.

Prepare income statements under absorption and variable costing for the years ended 2000 and 2001. Reconcile the differences in income between the methods. (Ignore taxes.)

41. *(CVP decision alternatives)* Norman Horn owns a small travel agency. His revenues are based on commissions earned as follows:

Airline bookings	8% commission
Rental car bookings	10% commission
Hotel bookings	20% commission

Monthly fixed costs include advertising ($1,100), rent ($900), utilities ($250), and other costs ($2,200). There are no variable costs.

During a normal month, Norman records the following items, which are subject to the above commission structure:

Airlines	$30,000
Cars	4,500
Hotels	7,000
Total	$41,500

Norman is concerned because he is experiencing a monthly loss.

a. What is Norman's normal monthly income?

b. Norman can increase his airline bookings by 40 percent with an increase in advertising of $600. Should he increase advertising?

c. Norman's friend Jeff has asked him for a job in the travel agency. Jeff has proposed that he be paid 50 percent of whatever additional commissions he can bring to the agency plus a salary of $300 per month. Norman has estimated Jeff can generate the following additional bookings per month:

Airlines	$10,000
Cars	1,500
Hotels	4,000
Total	$15,500

Hiring Jeff would also increase other fixed costs by $400 per month. Should Norman accept Jeff's offer?

d. Norman hired Jeff and in the first month Jeff generated an additional $8,000 of bookings for the agency. The bookings, however, were all airline tickets. Was the decision to hire Jeff a good one? Why or why not?

42. *(Retail merchant CVP)* Franklin Optical Shop has been in operation for several years. Analysis of the firm's recent financial statements and records reveals the following:

Average selling price per pair of glasses	$70
Variable expenses per pair:	
Lenses and frames	$28
Sales commission	12
Variable overhead	8
Annual fixed costs:	
Selling expenses	$18,000
Administrative expenses	48,000

The company's effective tax rate is 40 percent. Samantha Franklin, company president, has asked you to help her answer the following questions about the business.

a. What is the break-even point in pairs of glasses? In dollars?

b. How much revenue must be generated to produce $80,000 of pretax earnings? How many pairs of glasses would this level of revenue represent?

c. How much revenue must be generated to produce \$80,000 of after-tax earnings? How many pairs of glasses would this represent?

d. What amount of revenue would be necessary to yield an after-tax profit equal to 20 percent of revenue?

e. Franklin is considering adding a lens-grinding lab, which will save \$6 per pair of glasses in lens cost, but will raise annual fixed costs by \$8,000. She expects to sell 5,000 pairs of glasses. Should she make this investment?

f. A marketing consultant told Franklin that she could increase the number of glasses sold by 30 percent if she would lower the selling price by 10 percent and spend \$20,000 on advertising. She has been selling 3,000 pairs of glasses. Should she make these two related changes?

43. *(CVP single product—comprehensive)* Speedy Mouse Inc. makes a special mouse for computers. Each mouse sells for \$25 and annual production and sales are 120,000 units. Costs for each mouse are as follows:

Direct material	\$ 6.00
Direct labor	3.00
Variable overhead	0.80
Variable selling expenses	2.20
Total variable cost	\$12.00
Total fixed overhead	\$589,550

a. Calculate the unit contribution margin in dollars and the contribution margin ratio for the product.

b. Determine the break-even point in number of mice.

c. Calculate the dollar break-even point using the contribution margin ratio.

d. Determine Speedy Mouse Inc.'s margin of safety in units, in sales dollars, and as a percentage.

e. Compute Speedy Mouse Inc.'s degree of operating leverage. If sales increase by 25 percent, by what percentage would before-tax income increase?

f. How many mice must the company sell if it desires to earn \$996,450 in before-tax profits?

g. If Speedy Mouse Inc. wants to earn \$657,800 after tax and is subject to a 20 percent tax rate, how many units must be sold?

h. How many units would the company need to sell to break even if its fixed costs increased by \$7,865? (Use original data.)

i. Speedy Mouse Inc. has received an offer to provide a one-time sale of 4,000 mice to a network of computer superstores. This sale would not affect other sales or their costs, but the variable cost of the additional units will increase by \$0.60 for shipping and fixed costs will increase by \$18,000. The selling price for each unit in this order would be \$20. Based on quantitative measurement, should the company accept this offer? Show your calculations.

44. *(CVP, DOL, MS—two quarters, comprehensive)* Presented below is information pertaining to the first and second quarters of 2001 operations of the Oak Company:

	QUARTER	
	First	**Second**
Units:		
Production	35,000	30,000
Sales	30,000	35,000
Expected activity level	32,500	32,500
Unit selling price	\$75.00	\$75.00

(continued)

	QUARTER	
	First	Second
Unit variable costs:		
Direct material	$34.50	$34.50
Direct labor	16.50	16.50
Factory overhead	7.80	7.80
Operating expenses	5.70	5.70
Quarterly fixed costs:		
Factory overhead	$97,500.00	$97,500.00
Operating expenses	21,400.00	21,400.00

Additional information:

- There were no finished goods at January 1, 2001.
- Oak writes off any quarterly underapplied or overapplied overhead as an adjustment of Cost of Goods Sold.
- Oak's income tax rate is 35 percent.

a. Prepare an absorption costing income statement for each quarter.
b. Prepare a variable costing income statement for each quarter.
c. Calculate each of the following for 2001, if 130,000 units were produced and sold:
   1. Unit contribution margin
   2. Contribution margin ratio
   3. Total contribution margin
   4. Net income
   5. Degree of operating leverage
   6. Annual break-even unit sales volume
   7. Annual break-even dollar sales volume
   8. Annual margin of safety as a percentage

45. *(Multiproduct firm)* Elegant Books produces and sells two book products: an encyclopedia set and a dictionary set. The company sells these book sets in a ratio of three encyclopedia sets to five dictionary sets. Selling prices for the encyclopedia and dictionary sets are, respectively, $1,200 and $240; respective variable costs are $480 and $160. The company's fixed costs are $1,800,000 per year. Compute the volume of sales of each type of book set needed to
a. break even.
b. earn $800,000 of income before tax.
c. earn $800,000 of income after tax, assuming a 30 percent tax rate.
d. earn 12 percent on sales revenue in before-tax income.
e. earn 12 percent on sales revenue in after-tax income, assuming a 30 percent tax rate.

46. *(Comprehensive; multiproduct)* European Flooring makes three types of flooring products: tile, carpet, and parquet. Cost analysis reveals the following costs (expressed on a per-square-yard basis) are expected for 2000:

	Tile	Carpet	Parquet
Direct material	$5.20	$3.25	$8.80
Direct labor	1.80	0.40	6.40
Variable overhead	1.00	0.15	1.75
Variable selling expenses	0.50	0.25	2.00
Variable administrative expenses	0.20	0.10	0.30

Fixed overhead	$760,000
Fixed selling expenses	240,000
Fixed administrative expenses	200,000

Per-yard expected selling prices are as follows: tile, $16.40; carpet, $8.00; and parquet, $25.00. In 1999, sales were as follows and the mix is expected to continue in 2000:

	Tile	Carpet	Parquet
Square yards	18,000	144,000	12,000

Review of recent tax returns reveals an expected tax rate of 40 percent.

a. Calculate the break-even point for 2000.
b. How many square yards of each product are expected to be sold at the break-even point?
c. Assume that the company desires a pretax profit of $800,000. How many square yards of each type of product would need to be sold to generate this profit level? How much revenue would be required?
d. Assume that the company desires an after-tax profit of $680,000. Use the contribution margin percentage approach to determine the revenue needed.
e. If the company actually achieves the revenue determined in part (d), what is European Flooring's margin of safety in (1) dollars and (2) percentage?

47. *(Appendix)* The Hattiesburg Chamber of Commerce (HCC) has provided you with the following monthly cost and fee information: monthly membership fee per member, $25; variable cost per member per month, $12; fixed cost per month, $1,800. Costs are extremely low because almost all services and supplies are provided by volunteers.

a. Prepare a traditional break-even chart for HCC.
b. Prepare a contemporary break-even chart for the HCC.
c. Prepare a profit-volume graph for the HCC.
d. Indicate which of the above you would use in giving a speech to the membership to solicit volunteers to help with a fund-raising project. Assume at this time there are only 120 members belonging to the HCC.

CASES

48. *(Absorption costing versus variable costing)* Anderson Manufacturing builds engines for light airplane manufacturers. Company sales have increased yearly as the company gains a reputation for reliable and quality products. The company manufactures engines to customer specifications and it uses a job order cost system. Factory overhead is applied to the jobs based on direct labor hours, using the absorption costing method. Under- or overapplied overhead is treated as an adjustment to Cost of Goods Sold. The company's inventory balances and income statements for the last two years are presented below.

Inventory Balances	12/31/99	12/31/00	12/31/01
Raw material (direct)	$22,000	$30,000	$10,000
Work in process			
Costs	$40,000	$48,000	$64,000
Direct labor hours	1,335	1,600	2,100
Finished goods			
Costs	$25,000	$18,000	$14,000
Direct labor hours	1,450	1,050	820

2000–2001 COMPARATIVE INCOME STATEMENTS

	2000		2001	
Sales		$840,000		$1,015,000
Cost of goods sold				
Finished goods, 1/1	$ 25,000		$ 18,000	
Cost of goods manufactured	548,000		657,600	
Total available	$573,000		$675,600	
Finished goods, 12/31	(18,000)		(14,000)	
CGS before overhead adjustment	$555,000		$661,600	
Underapplied factory overhead	36,000		14,400	
CGS		(591,000)		(676,000)
Gross margin		$249,000		$ 339,000
Selling expenses	$ 82,000		$ 95,000	
Administrative expenses	70,000		75,000	
Total operating expenses		(152,000)		(170,000)
Operating income		$ 97,000		$ 169,000

The same predetermined overhead rate was used in applying overhead to production orders in both 2000 and 2001. The rate was based on the following estimates:

Fixed factory overhead	$25,000
Variable factory overhead	$155,000
Direct labor hours	25,000
Direct labor cost	$150,000

In 2000 and 2001, actual direct labor hours expended were 20,000 and 23,000, respectively. The cost of raw material put into production was $292,000 in 2000 and $370,000 in 2001. Actual fixed overhead was $37,400 for 2000 and $42,300 for 2001, and the planned direct labor rate was equal to the actual direct labor rate.

For both years, all of the reported administrative costs were fixed. The variable portion of the reported selling expenses results from a commission of 5 percent of sales revenue.

a. For the year ended December 31, 2001, prepare a revised income statement using the variable costing method.

b. Prepare a numerical reconciliation of the difference in operating income between the 2001 absorption and variable costing statements.

c. Describe both the advantages and disadvantages of using variable costing.

(CMA adapted)

49. *(Absorption costing versus variable costing)* Virginia Company, a wholly owned subsidiary of Bluebeard, Inc., produces and sells three main product lines. The company employs a standard cost accounting system for recordkeeping purposes. At the beginning of 1999, the president of Virginia Company presented the budget to the parent company and accepted a commitment to contribute $15,800 to Bluebeard's consolidated profit in 1999. The president has been confident that the year's profit would exceed the budget target, because the monthly sales reports that he has been receiving have shown that sales for the year will exceed budget by 10 percent. The president is both disturbed and confused when the controller presents an adjusted forecast as of November 30, 1999, indicating that profits will be 11 percent under budget. The two forecasts follow:

	1/1/99	11/30/99
Sales	$268,000	$294,800
Cost of sales at standard*	(212,000)	(233,200)
Gross margin at standard	$ 56,000	$ 61,600
(Under-) overapplied fixed overhead	0	(6,000)
Actual gross margin	$ 56,000	$ 55,600
Selling expenses	$ 13,400	$ 14,740
Administrative expenses	26,800	26,800
Total operating expenses	$ (40,200)	$ (41,540)
Earnings before tax	$ 15,800	$ 14,060

*Includes fixed manufacturing overhead of $30,000.

There have been no sales price changes or product mix shifts since the 1/1/99 forecast. The only cost variance on the income statement is the underapplied manufacturing overhead. This amount arose because the company produced only 16,000 standard machine hours (budgeted machine hours were 20,000) during 1999 as a result of a shortage of raw material while the company's principal supplier was closed because of a strike. Fortunately, Virginia Company's finished goods inventory was large enough to fill all sales orders received.

a. Analyze and explain why the profit has declined in spite of increased sales and effective control over costs.

b. What plan, if any, could Virginia Company adopt during December to improve its reported profit at year-end? Explain your answer.

c. Illustrate and explain how Virginia Company could adopt an alternative internal cost reporting procedure that would avoid the confusing effect of the present procedure.

d. Would the alternative procedure described in part (c) be acceptable to Bluebeard, Inc., for financial reporting purposes? Explain.

50. *(CVP analysis)* Susan Katz owns the Holiday Litter Box, a luxury hotel for dogs and cats. The capacity is 40 pets: 20 dogs and 20 cats. Each pet has an air-conditioned room with a window overlooking a garden. Soft music is played continuously. Pets are awakened at 7 a.m., served breakfast at 8 a.m., fed snacks at 3:30 p.m., and receive dinner at 5 p.m. Hotel services also include airport pickup, daily bathing and grooming, night lighting in each suite, carpeted floors, and daily play visits by pet "babysitters."

Pet owners are interviewed about their pets' health-care requirements, likes and dislikes, diet, and other needs. Reservations are essential and each pet's veterinarian must document health. The costs of operating the pet hotel are substantial. The hotel's original cost was $96,000. Depreciation is $8,000 per year. Other costs of operating the hotel include:

Labor costs	$16,000 per year plus $0.25 per animal per day
Utilities	$ 7,900 per year plus $0.05 per animal per day
Miscellaneous costs	$ 5,000 per year plus $0.30 per animal per day

In addition to these costs, costs are incurred for food and water for each pet. These costs are strictly variable and (on average) run $2.00 per day for dogs and $0.75 per day for cats.

a. Assuming that the hotel is able to maintain an average annual occupancy of 75 percent in both the cat and the dog units (based on a 360-day year), determine the minimum daily charge that must be assessed per animal day to generate $12,000 of income before taxes. *(continued)*

b. Assume that the price Susan charges cat owners is $10 per day and the price charged to dog owners is $12 per day. If the sales mix is 1 to 1 (one cat day of occupancy for each dog day of occupancy) compute the following:
   1. The break-even point in total occupancy days.
   2. Total occupancy days required to generate $20,000 of income before tax.
   3. Total occupancy days to generate $20,000 of after-tax income; Susan's personal tax rate is 35 percent.

c. Susan is considering adding an animal training service for guests to complement her other hotel services. Susan has estimated the costs of providing such a service would largely be fixed. Because all of the facilities already exist, Susan would merely need to hire a dog trainer. She estimates a dog trainer could be hired at a cost of $25,000 per year. If Susan decides to add this service, how much would her daily charges have to increase (assume equal dollar increases to cat and dog fees) to maintain the break-even level you computed in part (b)?

51. *(CVP analysis)* Reliable Airlines is a small local carrier in the Midwest. All seats are coach and the following data are available.

Number of seats per plane	120
Average load factor (percentage of seats filled)	75%
Average full passenger fare	$70
Average variable cost per passenger	$30
Fixed operating costs per month	$1,200,000

a. What is break-even point in passengers and revenues?

b. What is break-even point in number of flights?

c. If Reliable raises its average full passenger fare to $85, it is estimated that the load factor will decrease to 60 percent. What will be the break-even point in number of flights?

d. The cost of fuel is a significant variable cost to any airline. If fuel charges increase by $8 per barrel, it is estimated that variable cost per passenger will rise to $40. In this case, what would be the new break-even point in passengers and in number of flights? (Refer back to original data.)

e. Reliable has experienced an increase in variable cost per passenger to $35 and an increase in total fixed costs to $1,500,000. The company has decided to raise the average fare to $80. What number of passengers is needed to generate an after-tax profit of $400,000 if the tax rate is 40 percent?

f. (Use original data.) Reliable is considering offering a discounted fare of $50, which the company feels would increase the load factor to 80 percent. Only the additional seats would be sold at the discounted fare. Additional monthly advertising costs would be $80,000. How much pretax income would the discounted fare provide Reliable if the company has 40 flights per day, 30 days per month?

g. Reliable has an opportunity to obtain a new route. The company feels it can sell seats at $75 on the route, but the load factor would be only 60 percent. The company would fly the route 15 times per month. The increase in fixed costs for additional crew, additional planes, landing fees, maintenance, etc., would total $100,000 per month. Variable cost per passenger would remain at $30.
   1. Should the company obtain the route?
   2. How many flights would Reliable need to earn pretax income of $50,500 per month on this route?
   3. If the load factor could be increased to 75 percent, how many flights would be needed to earn pretax income of $50,500 per month on this route?
   4. What qualitative factors should be considered by Reliable in making its decision about acquiring this route?

REALITY CHECK

52. A group of prospective investors has asked your help in understanding the comparative advantages and disadvantages of building a company that is either labor intensive or, in contrast, one that uses significant cutting-edge technology and is therefore capital intensive. Prepare a report addressing the issues. Include discussions regarding cost structure, BEP, CVP, MS, DOL, risk, customer satisfaction, and the relationships among these constructs.

53. A colleague of yours alleged to your company's board of directors that CVP is a short-run-oriented model and is therefore of limited usefulness. Because you have used it many times in making presentations to the board, the CEO has asked you to evaluate the perspective voiced by your colleague and prepare a report addressing the contention for the board. In a second request, the CEO has asked you to prepare a separate report for internal management's use addressing how the CVP model could be adapted to become more useful for making long-run decisions. Prepare these two reports for the board and for management's use.

54. A significant difference between absorption costing and variable costing centers around the debate of whether fixed manufacturing overhead is justified as a product cost. Because your professor is scheduled to address a national professional meeting at the same time your class would ordinarily meet, the class has been divided into teams to confront selected issues. Your team's assignment is to prepare a report arguing both sides of the issue stated above. You are also expected as a team to draw your own conclusion and so state it in your report along with the basis for your conclusion.

55. Missouri Chemical Company's new president has learned that, for the past four years, the company has been dumping its industrial waste into the local river and falsifying reports to authorities about the levels of suspected cancer-causing materials in that waste. The plant manager says that there is no proof that the waste causes cancer and there are only a few fishing villages within a hundred miles downriver. If the company has to treat the substance to neutralize its potentially injurious effects and then transport it to a legal dump site, the company's variable and fixed costs would rise to a level that might make the firm uncompetitive. If the company loses its competitive advantage, 10,000 local employees could become unemployed and the town's economy could collapse.

a. What kinds of variable and fixed costs can you think of that would increase (or decrease) if the waste were treated rather than dumped? How would these costs affect product contribution margin?

b. What are the ethical conflicts the president faces?

c. What rationalizations can you detect that have been devised by plant employees?

d. What options and suggestions can you offer the president?

56. A significant trend in business today is increasing use of outsourcing. Go to the Internet and search Web sites with the objective of gaining an understanding for the vast array of outsourcing services that are available. Prepare a presentation in which you discuss the extensive use of outsourcing today and how outsourcing could be used as a tool to manage a firm's cost structure, and as a tool in CVP planning.

57. An article about the financial troubles of Air-India indicates that the airline plans to break even in 2000–2001:

http://www.airindia.com

http://indian-airlines.nic.in

Air-India has arrived at a difficult point in its history. Held back from modernization by government policy, it has no global alliance partners, an aging fleet and an enormous workforce. With no fuel for privatization, and an unwillingness to look at the carrier's synergies with Indian Airlines, will the management be able to steer it out of trouble? Air-India's financial position is precarious. Its net loss of $43 million in 1997 to 1998 is ample evidence of the fact. The airline is taking remedial action to reduce losses and aims to reach breakeven by 2000 to 2001. Losses in 1997 to 1998 were less than those for the previous year, when the carrier reported a loss of Rs2.97 billion, but the goal of breakeven in 2 years' time will be an uphill struggle. At the root of Air-India's difficulties are persistently low yields, on the one hand, and steadily rising costs on the other.

SOURCE: Dominic Jones, "Good Airline, Shame about Its Problems," *Airfinance Journal* (March 1999), p. 31.

In light of the discussion in the chapter that breakeven is a reference point rather than a goal of business, reconcile the comment in the article that Air-India has a goal of breaking even in two years.

CHAPTER

12

Relevant Costing

LEARNING OBJECTIVES

After completing this chapter, you should be able to answer the following questions:

1. What factors are relevant in making decisions and why?
2. How do opportunity costs affect decision making?
3. What are sunk costs and why are they not relevant in making decisions?
4. What are the relevant financial considerations in outsourcing?
5. How can management make the best use of a scarce resource?
6. How does sales mix pertain to relevant costing problems?
7. How are special prices set and when are they used?
8. How is segment margin used to determine whether a product line should be retained or eliminated?
9. (Appendix) How is a linear programming problem formulated?

INTRODUCING

Price-waterhouse-Coopers

http://www.pwcglobal.com

During the last decade, increasing competition has forced many companies to refocus their resources and to defend their core businesses against aggressors. In developing strategies to fight this war, managers have generally reached a consensus on two strategic criteria. First, to win a battle, the focus of organizations must be on delivering products and services in the manner most consistent with the desires of customers. Second, no company can do all things well.

The strategies managers devise in this intensive struggle evolve from internal evaluations in which the managers identify the functions they must do well to survive. These functions are regarded as core competencies and maintaining leadership in these areas is regarded as vital. All other functions, although important to the organization, are regarded as noncore functions.

By intensely focusing on core functions, managers try to maintain a competitive advantage. However, an undesirable consequence of focusing on only the core competencies is that the quality and capabilities of the noncore functions can deteriorate. This deterioration, in turn, can reduce a firm's ability to attract customers to its products and services.

Outsourcing the noncore functions to firms that have core competencies in those functions frequently solves the dilemma of maintaining a focus on core competencies while also maintaining excellence in noncore functions. A key player in outsourcing financial services is PricewaterhouseCoopers.

PricewaterhouseCoopers, PwC, serves its outsourcing clients by providing high-quality services including payroll, internal audit, tax compliance, accounts receivable collection and many other services. Clients hire PwC to provide financial services at a cost and quality level that cannot be achieved internally by the client. Outsourcing services has become a major revenue generator for PwC and other financial services firms.

In responding to the demand from its clients, PwC has created many innovative services. Today, PwC even provides some strategic services to its clients such as financial management, human resource management, supply chain management, and customer management processes.

SOURCE: PricewaterhouseCoopers Web site, http://www.pwcglobal.com (November 15, 1999).

Managers are charged with the responsibility of managing organizational resources effectively and efficiently relative to the organization's goals and objectives. Making decisions about the use of organizational resources is a key process in which managers fulfill this responsibility. Accounting and finance professionals contribute to the decision-making process by providing expertise and information.

Accounting information can improve, but not perfect, management's understanding of the consequences of decision alternatives. To the extent that accounting information can reduce management's uncertainty about economic facts, outcomes, and relationships involved in various courses of action, such information is valuable for decision-making purposes.

relevant costing

As discussed in Chapter 11, many decisions can be made using incremental analysis. This chapter continues that discussion by introducing the topic of **relevant costing,** which focuses managerial attention on a decision's relevant (or pertinent) facts. Relevant costing techniques are applied in virtually all business decisions in both short-term and long-term contexts. This chapter examines their application to several common types of business decisions: replacing an asset, outsourcing a product or part, allocating scarce resources, determining the appropriate sales/production mix, and accepting specially priced orders. The discussion of decision tools applied to some longer term decisions is deferred to Chapter 14. In general these decisions require a consideration of costs and benefits that are mismatched in time; that is, the cost is incurred currently but the benefit is derived in future periods.

In making a choice among the alternatives available, managers must consider all relevant costs and revenues associated with each alternative. One of the most important concepts discussed in this chapter is the relationship between time and relevance. As the decision time horizon becomes shorter, fewer costs and revenues are relevant because only a limited set of them are subject to change by short-term management actions. Over the long term, virtually all costs can be influenced by management actions. Regardless of whether the decision is short or long term, all decision making requires

> *relevant information at the point of decision; the knowledge of how to analyze that information at the point of decision; and enough time to do the analysis.*
>
> *In today's corporations, oceans of data drown most decision makers. Eliminating irrelevant information requires the knowledge of what is relevant, the knowledge of how to access and select appropriate data, and the knowledge of how best to prepare the data by sorting and summarizing it to facilitate analysis. This is the raw material of decision making.*[1]

THE CONCEPT OF RELEVANCE

1 What factors are relevant in making decisions and why?

For information to be relevant, it must possess three characteristics. It must (1) be associated with the decision under consideration, (2) be important to the decision maker, and (3) have a connection to or bearing on some future endeavor.

Association with Decision

incremental revenue
incremental cost
differential cost

Costs or revenues are relevant when they are logically related to a decision and vary from one decision alternative to another. Cost accountants can assist managers in determining which costs and revenues are relevant to decisions at hand. To be relevant, a cost or revenue item must be differential or incremental. An **incremental revenue** is the amount of revenue that differs across decision choices and **incremental cost (differential cost)** is the amount of cost that varies across the decision choices.

To the extent possible and practical, relevant costing compares the incremental revenues and incremental costs of alternative choices. Although incremental costs can be variable or fixed, a general guideline is that most variable costs are relevant and most fixed costs are not. The logic of this guideline is that as sales or production volume changes, within the relevant range, variable costs change, but fixed costs do not change. As with most generalizations, some exceptions can occur in the decision-making process.

The difference between the incremental revenue and the incremental cost of a particular alternative is the positive or negative incremental benefit (incremental profit) of that course of action. Management can compare the incremental benefits of alternatives to decide on the most profitable (or least costly) alternative or set of alternatives. Such a comparison may sound simple; it often is not. The concept of relevance is an inherently individual determination and the quantity of information available to make decisions is increasing. The challenge is to get information that identifies relevant costs and benefits:

> *If executives once imagined they could gather enough information to read the business environment like an open book, they have had to dim their hopes. The flow of information has swollen to such a flood that managers are in danger of drowning; extracting relevant data from the torrent is increasingly a daunting task.*[2]

Some relevant factors, such as sales commissions or prime costs of production, are easily identified and quantified because they are integral parts of the accounting system. Other factors may be relevant and quantifiable, but are not part of the

[1] Edward G. Mahler, "Perform as Smart as You Are," *Financial Executive* (July–August 1991), p. 18.
[2] Amitai Etzioni, "Humble Decision Making," *Harvard Business Review* (July–August 1989), p. 122.

College students have decided that the benefits of attending classes outweigh those of working full-time for four years. The opportunity costs to these students are the foregone wages and experience from jobs.

accounting system. Such factors cannot be overlooked simply because they may be more difficult to obtain or may require the use of estimates. For instance, **opportunity costs** represent the benefits foregone because one course of action is chosen over another. These costs are extremely important in decision making, but are not included in the accounting records.

opportunity cost

To illustrate the concept of an opportunity cost, assume that on August 1, Jane purchases a ticket for $50 to attend a play to be presented in November. In October, Jane is presented with an opportunity to sell her ticket to a friend who is very eager to attend the play. The friend has offered $100 for the ticket. The $100 price offered by Jane's friend is an opportunity cost—it is a benefit that Jane will sacrifice if she chooses to attend the play rather than sell the ticket.

Importance to Decision Maker

2

How do opportunity costs affect decision making?

The need for specific information depends on how important that information is relative to the objectives that a manager wants to achieve. Moreover, if all other factors are equal, more precise information is given greater weight in the decision-making process. However, if the information is extremely important, but less precise, the manager must weigh importance against precision. The News Note on the following page illustrates that in one of the most crucial industries, health care, accurate financial data are virtually nonexistent.

http://www.arthurandersen.com
http://www.idgresearch.com

Bearing on the Future

Information can be *based* on past or present data, but is relevant only if it pertains to a future decision choice. All managerial decisions are made to affect future events, so the information on which decisions are based should reflect future conditions. The future may be the short run (two hours from now or next month) or the long run (three years from now).

Future costs are the only costs that can be avoided, and a longer time horizon equates to more costs that are controllable, avoidable, and relevant. *Only information that has a bearing on future events is relevant in decision making.* But people too often forget this adage and try to make decisions using inapplicable data. One common error is trying to use a previously purchased asset's acquisition cost or book value in current decision making. This error reflects the misconception that sunk costs are relevant costs.

NEWS NOTE  GENERAL BUSINESS

Health Care Accounting Systems Are Seriously Sick

Managed care and an increased emphasis on cost management have created an urgent need among healthcare providers for relevant cost information, but organizations lack the necessary tools to gather the information. That was one of the key findings in a recent survey conducted by IDG Research. The respondents were 200 senior finance, operations, and information services executives from hospitals, integrated delivery networks, and clinics.

"The healthcare market has shifted from a revenue focus to a cost focus, but organizations haven't yet acquired the tools needed for success in this new environment," Doug Williams, a partner with Arthur Andersen's healthcare business consulting practice, explained. Here are other key findings:

Cost management is the dominant force in today's healthcare environment. It was cited by 95 percent of the respondents and ran far ahead of revenue generation, resource availability, and integration of multiple facilities.

There is a lack of actionable information for decision making. Eighty percent of the respondents want to measure costs over the entire episode of care, but only 33 percent are confident about the quality of their cost data, and only 26 percent said their data are timely for decision making. Fewer than a third thought they even had data they could use for decision making.

There is a dramatic lack of tools for bidding, administering, and evaluating managed care contracts. When respondents were asked about their ability to project revenue, costs, volume/utilization, and profit projections when bidding managed care contracts, 84 percent called the information necessary and valuable, yet only 48 percent were confident about their revenue projection abilities, 31 percent about costs, 26 percent about volume/utilization, and 20 percent about profit projection abilities.

SOURCE: Kathy Williams, "Cost Management Is Biggest Healthcare Issue," *Management Accounting* (May 1997), pp. 16–18. Copyright Institute of Management Accountants, Montvale, N.J.

SUNK COSTS

3

What are sunk costs and why are they not relevant in making decisions?

Costs incurred in the past for the acquisition of an asset or a resource are called sunk costs. They cannot be changed, no matter what future course of action is taken because past expenditures are not recoverable, regardless of current circumstances.

After an asset or resource is acquired, managers may find that it is no longer adequate for the intended purposes, does not perform to expectations, is technologically out of date, or is no longer marketable. A decision, typically involving two alternatives, must then be made: keep or dispose of the old asset. In making this decision, a current or future selling price may be obtained for the old asset, but such a price is the result of current or future conditions and does not "recoup" a historical cost. The historical cost is not relevant to the decision.

While asset-acquisition decisions are covered in depth in Chapter 14, these decisions provide an excellent introduction to the concept of relevant information. The following illustration makes some simplistic assumptions regarding asset acquisitions, but is used to demonstrate why sunk costs are not relevant costs.

Assume that Eastside Technologies purchases a statistical process control system for $2,000,000 on January 6, 2001. This system (the "original" system) is expected to have a useful life of five years and no salvage value. Five days later, on January 11, Trisha Black, vice president of production, notices an advertisement for a similar system for $1,800,000. This "new" system also has an estimated life of five years and no salvage value; its features will allow it to perform as well as the original system, and in addition, it has analysis tools that will save $50,000 per year in operating costs over the original system. On investigation, Ms. Black discovers that the original system can be sold for only $1,300,000. The data on the original and new statistical process control systems are shown in Exhibit 12–1.

Eastside Technologies has two options: (1) use the original system or (2) sell the original system and buy the new system. Exhibit 12–2 presents the costs Ms. Black should consider in making her asset replacement decision—that is, the *relevant*

EXHIBIT 12–1

Eastside Technologies: Statistical Process Control System Decision

	Original System (Purchased Jan. 6)	New System (Available Jan. 11)
Cost	$2,000,000	$1,800,000
Life in years	5	5
Salvage value	$0	$0
Current resale value	$1,300,000	Not applicable
Annual operating cost	$105,000	$55,000

costs. As shown in the computations in Exhibit 12–2, the $2,000,000 purchase price of the original system does not affect the decision process. This amount was "gone forever" when the company bought the system. However, if the company sells the original system, it will effectively reduce the net cash outlay for the new system to $500,000 because it will generate $1,300,000 from selling the old system. Using either system, Eastside Technologies will incur operating costs over the next five years, but it will spend $250,000 less using the new system ($50,000 savings per year × 5 years).

The common tendency is to include the $2,000,000 cost of the old system in the analysis. However, this cost is not differential between the decision alternatives. If Eastside Technologies keeps the original system, that $2,000,000 will be deducted as depreciation expense over the system's life. Alternatively, if the system is sold, the $2,000,000 will be charged against the revenue realized from the sale of the system. Thus, the $2,000,000 loss, or its equivalent in depreciation charges, is the same in magnitude whether the company retains the original or disposes of it and buys the new one. Since the amount is the same under both alternatives, it is not relevant to the decision process.

Ms. Black must condition herself to make decisions given her set of *future* alternatives. The relevant factors in deciding whether to purchase the new system are

1. cost of the new system ($1,800,000),
2. current resale value of the original system ($1,300,000), and
3. annual savings of the new system ($50,000) and the number of years (5) such savings would be enjoyed.[3]

EXHIBIT 12–2

Relevant Costs Related to Eastside Technologies' Alternatives

Alternative (1): Use original system		
Operating cost over life of original system ($105,000 × 5 years)		$ 525,000
Alternative (2): Sell original system and buy new		
Cost of new system	$1,800,000	
Resale value of original system	(1,300,000)	
Effective net outlay for new system	$ 500,000	
Operating cost over life of new system ($55,000 × 5 years)	275,000	
Total cost of new system		(775,000)
Benefit of keeping the old system		$(250,000)
The alternative, incremental calculation follows:		
Savings from operating the new system for 5 years		$ 250,000
Less: Effective incremental outlay for new system		(500,000)
Incremental advantage of keeping the old system		$(250,000)

[3] In addition, two other factors that were not discussed are also important: the potential tax effects of the transactions and the time value of money. The authors have chosen to defer consideration of these items to Chapter 14, which covers capital budgeting. Because of the time value of money, both systems were assumed to have zero salvage values at the end of their lives—a fairly unrealistic assumption.

This example demonstrates the difference between relevant and irrelevant costs, including sunk costs. The next section shows how the concepts of relevant costing, incremental revenues, and incremental costs are applied in making some common managerial decisions.

RELEVANT COSTS FOR SPECIFIC DECISIONS

Managers routinely choose a course of action from alternatives that have been identified as feasible solutions to problems. In so doing, managers weigh the costs and benefits of these alternatives and determine which course of action is best. Incremental revenues, costs, and benefits of all courses of action are measured against a baseline alternative. In making decisions, managers must provide for the inclusion of any inherently nonquantifiable considerations. Inclusion can be made by attempting to quantify those items or by simply making instinctive value judgments about nonmonetary benefits and costs.

In evaluating courses of action, managers should select the alternative that provides the highest incremental benefit to the company. One course of action that is often used as the baseline case is the "change nothing" option.

While other alternatives have certain incremental revenues and incremental costs associated with them, the "change nothing" alternative has a zero incremental benefit because it represents the current conditions. Some situations occur that involve specific government regulations or mandates in which a "change nothing" alternative does not exist. For example, if a company were polluting river water and a duly licensed governmental regulatory agency issued an injunction against it, the company (assuming it wishes to continue in business) would be forced to correct the pollution problem. The company could delay the installation of pollution control devices at the risk of fines or closure. Such fines would be incremental costs that would need to be considered; closure would create an opportunity cost amounting to the income that would have been generated had sales continued.

Rational decision-making behavior includes a comprehensive evaluation of the monetary effects of all alternative courses of action. The chosen course should be one that will make the business better off. Decision choices can be evaluated using relevant costing techniques.

OUTSOURCING DECISIONS

4

What are the relevant financial considerations in outsourcing?

A daily question faced by managers is whether the right components and services will be available at the right time to ensure that production can occur. Additionally, the inputs must be of the appropriate quality and obtainable at a reasonable price. Traditionally, companies ensured themselves of service and part availability and quality by controlling all functions internally. However, as discussed in the opening vignette, there is a growing trend toward "outsourcing" (buying) a greater percentage of required materials, components, and services.

outsourcing decision
make-or-buy decision

This **outsourcing decision (make-or-buy decision)** is made only after an analysis that compares internal production and opportunity costs with purchase cost and assesses the best uses of available facilities. Consideration of an insource (make) option implies that the company has available capacity for that purpose or has considered the cost of obtaining the necessary capacity. Relevant information for this type of decision includes both quantitative and qualitative factors. Exhibit 12–3 lists the top motivations for companies to pursue outsourcing.

Exhibit 12–4 presents factors that should be considered in the outsourcing decision. Several of the quantitative factors, such as incremental direct material and direct labor costs per unit, are known with a high degree of certainty. Other factors, such as the variable overhead per unit and the opportunity cost associated

EXHIBIT 12–3

Top Ten Reasons to Outsource

1. Reduce and control operating costs.
2. Improve company focus.
3. Gain access to world-class capabilities.
4. Free internal resources for other purposes.
5. Obtain resources not available internally.
6. Accelerate reengineering benefits.
7. Eliminate a function difficult to manage/out of control.
8. Make capital funds available.
9. Share risks.
10. Obtain cash infusion.

SOURCE: The Outsourcing Institute, *Survey of Current and Potential Outsourcing End-Users 1998,* http://www.outsourcing.com/howandwhy/research/surveyresults/main.htm (August 14, 1999).

EXHIBIT 12–4

Outsource Decision Considerations

Relevant Quantitative Factors:

Incremental production costs for each unit
Unit cost of purchasing from outside supplier (price less any discounts available plus shipping, etc.)
Number of available suppliers
Production capacity available to manufacture components
Opportunity costs of using facilities for production rather than for other purposes
  Amount of space available for storage
  Costs associated with carrying inventory
  Increase in throughput generated by buying components

Relevant Qualitative Factors:

Reliability of supply sources
Ability to control quality of inputs purchased from outside
Nature of the work to be subcontracted (such as the importance of the part to the whole)
Impact on customers and markets
Future bargaining position with supplier(s)
Perceptions regarding possible future price changes
Perceptions about current product prices (are the prices appropriate or, in some cases with international suppliers, is product dumping involved?)

with production facilities, must be estimated. The qualitative factors should be evaluated by more than one individual so personal biases do not cloud valid business judgment.

Although companies may gain the best knowledge, experience, and methodology available in a process through outsourcing, they also lose some degree of control. Thus, company management should carefully evaluate the activities to be outsourced. The pyramid shown in Exhibit 12–5 is one model for assessing outsourcing risk. Factors to consider include whether (1) a function is considered critical to the organization's long-term viability (such as product research and development); (2) the organization is pursuing a core competency relative to this function; or (3) issues such as product/service quality, time of delivery, flexibility of use, or reliability of supply cannot be resolved to the company's satisfaction.

Exhibit 12–6 provides information about cases for inkjet printers produced by Online Computers. The total cost to manufacture one case is $5.50. The company can purchase the case from a chemical products company for $4.30 per unit. Online Computers' cost accountant is preparing an analysis to determine if the company should continue making the cases or buy them from the outside supplier.

Production of each case requires a cost outlay of $4.10 per unit for materials, labor, and variable overhead. In addition, $0.50 of the fixed overhead is considered direct product cost because it specifically relates to the manufacture of cases.

EXHIBIT 12-5

Outsourcing Risk Pyramid

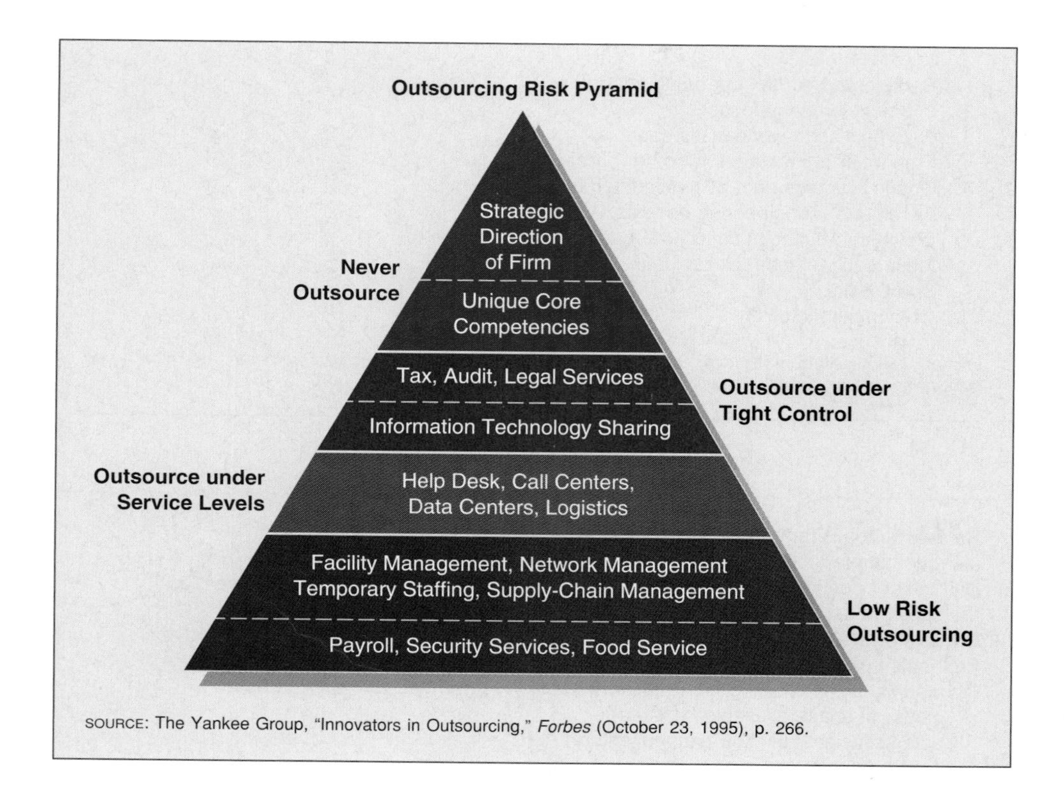

SOURCE: The Yankee Group, "Innovators in Outsourcing," *Forbes* (October 23, 1995), p. 266.

This $0.50 is an incremental cost since it could be avoided if cases were not produced. The remaining fixed overhead ($0.90) is not relevant to the outsourcing decision. This amount is a common cost incurred because of general production activity, unassociated with the cost object (cases). Therefore, because this portion of the fixed cost would continue under either alternative, it is not relevant.

The relevant cost for the insource alternative is $4.60—the cost that would be avoided if the product were not made. This amount should be compared to the $4.30 cost quoted by the supplier under the outsource alternative. Each amount is the incremental cost of making and buying, respectively. All else being equal, management should choose to purchase the cases rather than make them, because $0.30 will be saved on each case that is purchased rather than made. Relevant costs are those costs that are avoidable by choosing one decision alternative over another, regardless of whether they are variable or fixed. In an outsourcing decision, variable production costs are relevant. Fixed production costs are relevant if they can be avoided when production is discontinued.

EXHIBIT 12-6

Online Computers—Outsource Decision Cost Information

	Present Manufacturing Cost per Case		Relevant Cost of Manufacturing per Case
Direct material	$1.70		$1.70
Direct labor	2.00		2.00
Variable factory overhead	0.40		0.40
Fixed factory overhead*	1.40		0.50
Total unit cost	$5.50		$4.60
Quoted price from supplier		$4.30	

*Of the $1.40 fixed factory overhead, only $0.50 is actually caused by case production and could be avoided if the firm chooses not to produce cases. The remaining $0.90 of fixed factory overhead is allocated indirect (common) costs that would continue even if case production ceases.

The opportunity cost of the facilities being used by production is also relevant in this decision. If a company chooses to outsource a product component rather than to make it, an alternative purpose may exist for the facilities now being used for manufacturing. If a more profitable alternative is available, management should consider diverting the capacity to this use.

Assume that Online Computers has an opportunity to rent the physical space now used to produce printer cases for $90,000 per year. If the company produces 600,000 cases annually, there is an opportunity cost of $0.15 per unit ($90,000 ÷ 600,000 cases) from using, rather than renting, the production space. The existence of this cost makes the outsource alternative even more attractive.

The opportunity cost is added to the production cost since the company is foregoing this amount by choosing to make the cases. Sacrificing potential revenue is as much a relevant cost as is the incurrence of expenses. Exhibit 12–7 shows calculations relating to this decision on both a per-unit and a total cost basis. Under either format, the comparison indicates that there is a $0.45 per-unit advantage to outsourcing over insourcing.

Another opportunity cost associated with insourcing is the increased plant throughput that is sacrificed to make a component. Assume that case production uses a resource that has been determined to be a bottleneck in the manufacturing plant. Management calculates that plant throughput can be increased by 1 percent per year on all products if the cases are bought rather than made. Assume this increase in throughput would provide an estimated additional annual contribution margin (with no incremental fixed costs) of $210,000. Dividing this amount by the 600,000 cases currently being produced results in a $0.35 per-unit opportunity cost related to manufacturing. When added to the production costs of $4.60, the relevant cost of manufacturing cases becomes $4.95.

Based on the information in Exhibit 12–7 (even without the inclusion of the throughput opportunity cost), Online Computers' cost accountant should inform company management that it is more economical to outsource cases for $4.30 than to manufacture them. This analysis is the typical starting point of the decision process—determining which alternative is preferred based on the *quantitative* considerations. Managers then use judgment to assess the decision's qualitative aspects.

Assume that Online Computers' purchasing agent read in the newspaper that the supplier being considered was in poor financial condition and there was a high probability of a bankruptcy filing. In this case, management would likely decide to insource rather than outsource the cases from this supplier. In this instance,

EXHIBIT 12–7

Online Computers' Opportunity Costs and Outsource Decision

	Insource	Outsource
Per unit:		
Direct production costs	$4.60	
Opportunity cost (revenue)	0.15	
Purchase cost		$4.30
Cost per case	$4.75	$4.30

	Insource	Outsource	Difference in Favor of Outsourcing
In total:			
Revenue from renting capacity	$ 0	$ 90,000	$ 90,000
Cost for 600,000 cases	(2,760,000)	(2,580,000)	180,000
Net cost	$(2,760,000)	$(2,490,000)	$270,000*

*The $270,000 represents the net purchase benefit of $0.45 per unit multiplied by the 600,000 units to be purchased during the year.

quantitative analysis supports the purchase of the units, but qualitative considerations suggest this would not be a wise course of action because the stability of the supplying source is questionable.

This additional consideration also indicates that there are many potential long-run effects of a theoretically short-run decision. If Online Computers had stopped case production and rented its production facilities to another firm, and the supplier had then gone bankrupt, the company could be faced with high start-up costs to revitalize its case production process. This was essentially the situation faced by Stonyfield Farm, a New Hampshire-based yogurt company. Stonyfield Farm subcontracted its yogurt production, and one day found its supplier bankrupt—creating an inability to fill customer orders. It took Stonyfield two years to acquire the necessary production capacity and regain market strength.

http://www.stonyfield.com

This long-run view is also expressed in Chapter 3 where it is suggested that the term *fixed cost* is really a misnomer. These costs should be referred to as long-run variable costs because, while they do not vary with volume in the short run, they *do* vary in the long run. As such, they are relevant for long-run decision making.

For example, assume a part or product is manufactured (rather than outsourced) and the company expects demand for that item to increase in the next few years. At a future time, the company may be faced with a need to expand capacity and incur additional "fixed" capacity costs. These long-run costs would, in turn, theoretically cause product costs to increase because of the need to allocate the new overhead to production. To suggest that products made before capacity is added would cost less than those made afterward is a short-run view. The long-run viewpoint would consider both the current and "long-run" variable costs over the product life cycle. However, many firms expect prices charged by their suppliers to change over time and actively engage in cooperative efforts with their suppliers to control costs and reduce prices.

Outsourcing decisions are not confined to manufacturing entities. Many service organizations must also make these decisions. For example, accounting and law firms must decide whether to prepare and present in-house continuing education programs or to outsource such programs to external organizations or consultants. Private schools must determine whether to have their own buses or use independent contractors. Doctors investigate the differences in cost, quality of results, and convenience to patients between having blood samples drawn and tested in the office or in an independent lab facility. Outsourcing can include product and process design activities, accounting and legal services, utilities, engineering services, and employee health services.

Outsourcing decisions consider the opportunity costs of facilities. If capacity is occupied in one way, it cannot be used at the same time for another purpose. Limited capacity is only one type of scarce resource that managers need to consider when making decisions.

5

How can management make the best use of a scarce resource?

Scarce Resources Decisions

scarce resource

Managers are frequently confronted with the short-run problem of making the best use of scarce resources that are essential to production activity, but are available only in limited quantity. **Scarce resources** create constraints on producing goods or providing services and can include machine hours, skilled labor hours, raw materials, and production capacity and other inputs. Management may, in the long run, obtain a greater quantity of a scarce resource. For instance, additional machines could be purchased to increase availability of machine hours. However, in the short run, management must make the most efficient use of the scarce resources it has currently.

Determining the best use of a scarce resource requires managerial recognition of company objectives. If the objective is to maximize company profits, a scarce resource is best used to produce and sell the product having the highest contribution margin *per unit of the scarce resource.* This strategy assumes that the company is faced with only one scarce resource.

Exhibit 12–8 presents information on two products being manufactured by Online Computers. The company's scarce resource is a data chip that it purchases from a supplier. Each desktop computer requires one chip and each notebook computer requires three chips. Currently, the firm has access to only 5,100 chips per month to make either desktop or notebook computers or some combination of both. Demand is above 5,100 units per month for both products and there are no variable selling or administrative costs related to either product.

The desktop's $650 selling price less its $545 variable cost provides a contribution margin of $105 per unit. The notebook's contribution margin per unit is $180 ($900 selling price minus $720 variable cost). Fixed annual overhead related to these two product lines totals $6,570,000 and is allocated to products for purposes of inventory valuation. Fixed overhead, however, does not change with production levels within the relevant range and, accordingly, is not relevant in a short-run scarce resource decision.

Because fixed overhead per unit is not relevant in the short run, unit contribution margin rather than unit gross margin is the appropriate measure of profitability of the two products.[4] Unit contribution margin is divided by the input quantity of the scarce resource (in this case, data chips) to obtain the contribution margin per unit of scarce resource. The last line in Exhibit 12–8 shows the $105 contribution margin per chip for the desktop compared to $60 for the notebook. Thus, it is more profitable for Online Computers to produce desktop computers than notebooks.

At first glance, it would appear that the notebook would be, by a substantial margin, the more profitable of the two products because its contribution margin per unit ($180) is significantly higher than that of the desktop ($105). However, because the notebook requires three times as many chips as the desktop, a greater amount of contribution margin per chip is generated by the production of the desktops. If these were the only two products made by Online Computers and the company wanted to achieve the highest possible profit, it would dedicate all available data chips to the production of desktops. Such a strategy would provide a total contribution margin of $535,500 per month (5,100 × $105), if all units produced were sold.

When one limiting factor is involved, the outcome of a scarce resource decision will indicate that a single type of product should be manufactured and sold. Most situations, however, involve several limiting factors that compete with one another in the process of striving to attain business objectives. One method used to solve problems that have several limiting factors is linear programming, which is discussed in the Appendix to this chapter.

EXHIBIT 12–8

Online Computers—Desktop and Notebook Computer Information

	Desktop	Notebook
Selling price per unit (a)	$650	$900
Variable production cost per unit:		
Direct material	$345	$480
Direct labor	115	125
Variable overhead	85	115
Total variable cost (b)	$545	$720
Unit contribution margin [(c) = (a) − (b)]	$105	$180
Divided by chips required per unit (d)	1	3
Contribution margin per chip [(c) ÷ (d)]	$105	$ 60

[4] Gross margin (or gross profit) is unit selling price minus total production cost per unit. Total production cost includes allocated fixed overhead.

In addition to considering the monetary effects related to scarce resource decisions, managers must remember that all factors cannot be readily quantified and the qualitative aspects of the situation must be evaluated in addition to the quantitative ones. For example, before choosing to produce only desktops, Online Computers' managers would need to assess the potential damage to the firm's reputation and markets if the company limited its product line to a single item. Such a choice severely restricts its customer base and is especially important if the currently manufactured products are competitively related. For example, if Hewlett-Packard began making only ink jet printers, many printer buyers would not find that product appropriate for their needs. These buyers would purchase their printers from another company.

http://www.hp.com

Concentrating on a single product can also create market saturation or company stagnation. Some products, such as refrigerators and Rolex watches, are purchased by customers infrequently or in single units. Making such a product limits the company's opportunity for repeat business. And, if the company concentrates on the *wrong* single product (such as buggywhips or pet rocks), that exclusionary choice can be the beginning of the end for the company.

http://www.rolex.com

In some cases, the revenues and expenses of a group of products must be considered as a set of decisions in allocating scarce resources. It is possible that multiple products may be complementary or that one product is sold as part of a package with other products, cannot be used effectively without another product, or will be the key to revenue generation in future periods. To illustrate these possibilities, consider the following products: Cross's well-known ballpoint pen and mechanical pencil sets; dining room tables and dining room chairs produced by Drexel Heritage Furniture; and the Barbie "family" of products made by Mattel, Inc. Would it be reasonable for Cross to make only pens, Drexel Heritage to make only tables, or Mattel to make only Barbie dolls? In the case of Mattel, company management would probably choose to manufacture Barbie dolls even if they produced zero contribution so that profits could be earned on Barbie accessories.

http://www.cross.com
http://www.drexelheritage.com
http://www.mattel.com

Thus, company management may decide that production and sale of some number of less profitable products is necessary to maintain either customer satisfaction or sales of other products. Production mix translates on the revenue side into sales mix, which is addressed in the next section.

Sales Mix Decisions

6

How does sales mix pertain to relevant costing problems?

Managers continuously strive to achieve a variety of company objectives such as profit maximization, improvement of the company's relative market share, and generation of customer goodwill and loyalty. Selling products or performing services accomplishes these objectives. Regardless of whether the company is a retailer, manufacturer, or service organization, **sales mix** refers to "the relative quantities of the products that make up the total sales of a company."[5] Some important factors affecting the sales mix of a company are product selling prices, sales force compensation, and advertising expenditures. A change in one or all of these factors may cause a company's sales mix to shift. As indicated in the accompanying News Note, the management of sales mix requires a basic understanding of marketing.

sales mix

Information on Online Computers' ink jet printer line is presented in Exhibit 12–9 and is used to illustrate the effects of the three factors mentioned earlier on sales mix. The product line includes student, commercial, and professional printers, each having different features and being targeted at a different market segment.

[5] Institute of Management Accountants (formerly National Association of Accountants), *Statements of Management Accounting Number 2: Management Accounting Terminology* (Montvale, N.J.: NAA, June 1, 1983), p. 94.

GENERAL BUSINESS  NEWS NOTE

The A B Ps of Marketing

To understand clients and develop products and services, planners should consider the four P's of marketing: product, price, promotion, and position. Marketing is creating an environment conducive to sales. Unfortunately, with all that's going on in our business today, most of us don't spend any time reviewing our marketing mix. Taking the time to see how your marketing plan aligns with these classic Marketing 101 cornerstones will help you and your clients reach your goals.

In planning your four-P's strategy, it's a good idea to write a marketing plan that begins with the objectives you want to achieve in each area. One of the ways of defining objectives is to think of them as the intended results. Once you have identified your intended results, you can develop strategies for achieving those results.

Next determine your tactics, the specific actions you are going to use to achieve the intended results. Use the objective, strategy and tactic planning to map out each of the four P's. Make sure to assign responsibilities for each of the areas to either yourself or to key employees.

SOURCE: John J. Bowen, Jr., "Four P's of Marketing: Product, Price, Promotion and Position Are All Essential for Creating an Environment Conducive to Sales," *Financial Planning* (October 1, 1998), pp. 139–140.

EXHIBIT 12-9

Online Computers—Printer Product Information

		Student	Commercial	Professional
Unit selling price		$100	$250	$450
Unit costs:				
Variable costs:				
Direct material		$ 33	$ 95	$205
Direct labor		12	35	45
Variable factory overhead		15	25	30
Total variable production cost		$ 60	$155	$280
Product contribution margin		$ 40	$ 95	$170
Less variable selling expense*		(10)	(25)	(45)
Contribution margin per unit		$ 30	$ 70	$125
Total fixed costs:				
Production	$2,700,000			
Selling & administrative	1,300,000			
Total	$4,000,000			

*The only variable selling expense is for sales commissions, which are always set at 10% of the selling price per unit.

SALES PRICE CHANGES AND RELATIVE PROFITABILITY OF PRODUCTS

Managers must continuously monitor the relative selling prices of company products, both with respect to each other as well as to competitors' prices. This process may provide information that causes management to change one or more selling prices. Factors that might influence price changes include fluctuations in demand or production/distribution cost, economic conditions, and competition. Any shift in the selling price of one product in a multiproduct firm will normally cause a change in sales mix of that firm because of the economic law of demand elasticity with respect to price.[6]

[6] The law of demand elasticity indicates how closely price and demand are related. Product demand is highly elastic if a small price reduction generates a large demand increase. If demand is less elastic, large price reductions are needed to bring about moderate sales volume increases. In contrast, if demand is highly elastic, a small price increase results in a large drop in demand.

Online Computers' management has set profit maximization as the primary corporate objective. Such a strategy does not necessarily translate to maximizing unit sales of the product with the highest selling prices and minimizing unit sales of the product with the lowest selling price. The product with the highest selling price per unit does not necessarily yield the highest contribution margin per unit or per dollar of sales. In Online Computers' case, the printer with the highest selling price (the professional model) yields the highest unit contribution margin of the three products but the lowest contribution margin as a percent of sales. It is more profit-beneficial to sell a dollar's worth of the student printer than a dollar's worth of either the commercial or professional models. A dollar of sales of the student printer yields $0.30 of contribution margin; this compares to $0.28 for the commercial printer and $0.278 for the professional printer.

If profit maximization is a company's goal, management should consider the sales volume and unit contribution margin of each product. Total company contribution margin is the sum of the contribution margins provided by all of the products' sales. Exhibit 12–10 provides information on sales volumes and indicates the respective total contribution margins of the three types of printers. To maximize profits from this product line, company management must maximize total contribution margin rather than per-unit contribution margin.

A product's sales volume is almost always intricately related to its selling price. Generally, when the selling price of a product or service is increased and demand is elastic with respect to price, demand for that product decreases.[7] Thus, if Online Computers' management, in an attempt to increase profits, raises the price of the student printer to $120, there should be some decline in demand. Assume that consultation with the marketing research personnel indicates that such a price increase would cause demand for that product to drop from 42,000 to 31,000 printers per period. Exhibit 12–11 shows the effect of this pricing decision on the printer product line income of Online Computers.

EXHIBIT 12–10

Online Computers—Relationship Between Contribution Margin and Sales Volume

	Unit Contribution Margin (from Exhibit 12–9)	Current Sales Volume in Units	Income Statement Information
Student printers	$ 30	42,000	$ 1,260,000
Commercial printers	70	29,000	2,030,000
Professional printers	125	11,000	1,375,000
Total contribution margin of product sales mix			$ 4,665,000
Fixed expenses (from Exhibit 12–9)			(4,000,000)
Product line income at present volume and sales mix			$ 665,000

EXHIBIT 12–11

Online Computers—Relationship Between Selling Price and Demand

	Unit Contribution Margin	New Sales Volume in Units	Income Statement Information
Student printers	$ 48*	31,000	$ 1,488,000
Commercial printers	70	29,000	2,030,000
Professional printers	125	11,000	1,375,000
Total contribution margin of product sales mix			$ 4,893,000
Fixed expenses			(4,000,000)
Product line income at new volume of sales			$ 893,000

*New selling price of $120 minus [total variable production costs of $60 plus variable selling expense of $12 (10% of new selling price)].

[7] Such a decline in demand would generally not occur when the product in question has no close substitutes or is not a major expenditure in consumers' budgets.

Because the contribution margin per unit of the student printer increased, the total dollar contribution margin generated by sales of that product increased despite the decrease in sales volume. This example assumed that customers did not switch their purchases from student printers to other Online Computers products when the price of the student printer was raised. When prices of some products in a product line remain fixed while others are changed, customers will substitute the purchase of one product for another. Switching within the company was ignored in this instance and it should be recognized that some customers would likely purchase one of the more expensive printers after the price of the student printer is increased. For example, customers might believe that the difference in functionality between the student and commercial printer models is worth the price difference and make such a purchasing switch.

In making decisions to raise or lower prices, the relevant quantitative factors include (1) new contribution margin per unit of product; (2) both short-term and long-term changes in product demand and production volume because of the price change; and (3) best use of the company's scarce resources. Some relevant qualitative factors involved in pricing decisions are (1) impact of changes on customer goodwill toward the company; (2) customer loyalty toward company products; and (3) competitors' responses to the firm's new pricing structure.[8] Also, changes in the competitive environment create opportunities to produce new products. Exploiting such opportunities leads to changes in the sales mix.

When pricing proposed new products, a long-run view of the product's life cycle should be taken. This view would include assumptions about consumer behavior, competitor behavior, pace of technology changes, government posture, environmental concerns, size of the potential market, and demographic changes. These considerations would affect product price estimates at the various stages in the product's life cycle. Then, as discussed in Chapter 4, these estimates would be averaged to obtain the starting point in the process of target costing. Also, as discussed in the News Note on page 514, in pricing a service, prices should reflect consumer value, and should help signal the quality of the service provided.

COMPENSATION CHANGES

Many companies compensate their salespeople by paying a fixed rate of commission on gross sales dollars. This approach motivates salespeople to sell the highest priced product rather than the product providing the highest contribution margin to the company. If the company has a profit-maximization objective, a commission policy of a percentage of sales will not be effective in achieving that objective.

Assume Online Computers has a price structure for its printers as indicated in Exhibit 12–11: student, $120; commercial, $250; and professional, $450. The company has a current policy of paying sales commissions equal to 10 percent of selling price. This commission structure encourages sales of the professional printers, rather than the commercial or student printers. The company is considering a new compensation structure for its sales force. The new structure would provide for a base salary to all salespeople, which would total $875,000 per period.[9] In addition, the salespeople would be paid a 15 percent commission on product contribution margin (selling price minus total variable *production* costs). The per-unit product contribution margins of the printers are $60, $95, and $170, respectively, for student, commercial, and professional printers. The new compensation policy should motivate sales personnel to sell more of the products that produce the highest commission, which would correspondingly be the company's most profitable products.[10]

[8] With regard to actions of competitors, consider what occurs when one airline raises or lowers its fares between cities. It typically does not take very long for all the other airlines flying that route to adjust their fares accordingly. Thus, any competitive advantage is only for a short time span.

[9] The revised compensation structure should allow the sales personnel to achieve the same or higher income as before the change given a similar level of effort.

[10] This statement relies on the assumption that the salespersons' efforts are more highly correlated with unit sales than dollar sales. If the salespersons' efforts are more highly correlated with dollar sales, the commission structure should encourage sales of products with higher contribution margin ratios.

NEWS NOTE  QUALITY

Dental Practices Satisfy Patients or Get Flossed

There is a new game in the dental profession with new rules of competition. The new game has to do with creating patient value. With this game, good no longer is good enough.

Historically, a practice could be in one of three positions in the dental community. In the top 10 percent, you found the very successful practices, those with excellent profitability and the resources to stay on top. In the second position was the business-as-usual practice. Most diligent, hard-working practices filled this position in the competitive dental-practice environment. In the bottom 5–10 percent were the practices that were constantly struggling to make ends meet or were outright failing.

Today, there are only two positions in the competitive environment—a practice is either winning or losing. Indeed, good no longer is good enough. The business-as-usual group is quietly, but very rapidly, polarizing to the winner or loser ends of the spectrum. Here are the new rules of the game:

Rule 1 Cost and quality are enemies versus efficiency and excellence go hand in hand. The old rule was that to increase the quality in a practice you had to raise your cost. Although in some cases this can be true, in many instances this does not hold. The bottom line is dollars spent on increasing quality should raise the value to the patient and reduce the cost.

Rule 2 Suppliers must be price conscious versus value sensitive. The day when a practice thinks it should be out there alone fighting the battles is over. A practice's strategic alliances are critical.

Rule 3 Patients buy on price versus patients buy on value. How is it that Starbucks is able to charge more for a cup of coffee than the little coffee shop on the corner? It has to do with the value proposition offered. Do not market your practice as the best in town and then price it low. You sent a message and are wasting your marketing dollars.

Rule 4 Training is expensive versus training is a must. Training your team is one of the best investments practices you can adopt. You must keep your team members stimulated and at the top of their game.

SOURCE: Robert H. Maccario, "Patient Values: A New Game with New Rules," *Dental Economics* (August 1999), pp. 73–74.

Exhibit 12–12 compares Online Computers' total contribution margin using the original sales mix and commission with total contribution margin provided under a newly assumed sales mix and the new salesperson compensation structure. The new structure increases profits because sales are shifted from the lower contribution margin ratio printers toward the higher contribution margin ratio printers. The sales personnel also benefit from the new compensation structure because their combined incomes are significantly higher than under the original structure. Reflected in the sales mix change is the fact that student model printers can be sold with substantially less salesperson effort per unit than that required for the other models.

Fixed expenses would not be considered in setting compensation structures unless those expenses were incremental relative to the new policy or to changes in sales volumes. The new base salaries were an incremental cost of Online Computers' proposed compensation plan.

ADVERTISING BUDGET CHANGES

Either adjusting the advertising budgets respective to each company product or increasing the company's total advertising budget may also lead to shifts in the sales mix. This section continues using the data for Online Computers from Exhibit 12–11 and examines a proposed increase in the company's total advertising budget.

Online Computers' advertising manager, Harry Sells, has proposed increasing the advertising budget from $300,000 to $740,000 per year. Mr. Sells believes the

Old Policy—Commissions equal to 10% of selling price.

	Product Contribution Margin	–	Commission	=	Contribution Margin after Commission	×	Old Volume	=	Total Contribution Margin
Student	$ 60		(0.1 × $120), or $12		$ 48		31,000		$1,488,000
Commercial	95		(0.1 × $250), or $25		70		29,000		2,030,000
Professional	170		(0.1 × $450), or $45		125		11,000		1,375,000
Total contribution margin for product sales							71,000		$4,893,000

New Policy—Commissions equal to 15% of product contribution margin per unit and incremental base salaries of $875,000.

	Product Contribution Margin	–	Commission	=	Contribution Margin after Commission	×	Assumed New Volume	=	Total Contribution Margin
Student	$ 60		(0.15 × $60), or $9.00		$ 51.00		60,000		$3,060,000
Commercial	95		(0.15 × $95), or $14.25		80.75		25,000		2,018,750
Professional	170		(0.15 × $125), or $18.75		151.25		10,000		1,512,500
Total contribution margin for product sales							95,000		$6,591,250
Less sales force base salaries									(875,000)
Contribution margin adjusted for sales force base salaries									$5,716,250

EXHIBIT 12–12

Online Computers—Impact of Change in Commission Structure

increased advertising will result in the following additional unit sales during the coming year: student, 4,000; commercial, 1,500; and professional, 500.

The question to be answered is this: If the company spends the additional $440,000 for advertising, will the additional 6,000 units of sales produce larger profits than Online Computers is currently experiencing on this product line? The original fixed costs, as well as the contribution margin generated by the old sales level, are irrelevant to the decision. The relevant items are the increased sales revenue, increased variable costs, and increased fixed cost—the incremental effects of the advertising change. The difference between incremental revenues and incremental variable costs is the incremental contribution margin from which the incremental fixed cost is subtracted to provide the incremental benefit (or loss) of the decision.[11]

Exhibit 12–13 shows calculations of the expected increase in contribution margin if the increased advertising expenditure is made. The $359,500 of additional contribution margin is less than the $440,000 incremental cost for advertising, indicating company management should not increase its advertising by $440,000.

Increased advertising may cause changes in the sales mix or in the number of units sold. By targeting advertising efforts at specific products, either of these changes can be effected. Sales can also be influenced by opportunities that allow companies to obtain business at a sales price that differs from the normal price.

	Student	Commercial	Professional	Total
Increase in volume	4,000	1,500	500	6,000
Contribution margin per unit	× $48	× $70	× $125	
Incremental contribution margin	$192,000	$105,000	$62,500	$359,500
Incremental fixed cost of advertising				(440,000)
Incremental loss of increased advertising expenditure				$ (80,500)

EXHIBIT 12–13

Online Computers—Analysis of Increased Advertising Cost

[11] This same type of incremental analysis is shown in Chapter 11 in relation to CVP computations.

7

How are special prices set and when are they used?

special order decision

Special Order Decisions

A **special order decision** requires that management compute a reasonable sales price for production or service jobs outside the company's normal realm of operations. Special order situations include jobs that require a bid, are taken during slack periods, or are made to a particular buyer's specifications. Typically, the sales price quoted on a special order job should be high enough to cover the job's variable and incremental fixed costs and to generate a profit. Moreover, as discussed in Chapter 4, overhead costs tend to rise with increases in product variety and product complexity. The increases are typically experienced in receiving, inspection, order processing, and inventory carrying costs. Activity-based costing techniques allow managers to more accurately determine these incremental costs and, thereby, properly include them in analyzing special orders.

Sometimes companies will depart from their price-setting routine and "low-ball" bid jobs. A low-ball bid may cover only costs and produce no profit or may even be below cost. The rationale of low-ball bids is to obtain the job and have the opportunity to introduce company products or services to a particular market segment. Special pricing of this nature may provide work for a period of time, but it cannot be continued over the long run. To remain in business, a company must set selling prices to cover total costs and provide a reasonable profit margin.[12]

Another type of special pricing job is that of private-label orders in which the buyer's name (rather than the seller's) is attached to the product. Companies may accept these jobs during slack periods to more effectively use available capacity. Fixed costs are typically not allocated to special order, private-label products. Some variable costs (such as sales commissions) can be reduced or eliminated by the very nature of the private-label process. The prices on these special orders are typically set high enough to cover the actual variable costs and thereby contribute to overall profits.

Special prices may also be justified when orders are of an unusual nature (because of the quantity, method of delivery, or packaging) or because the products are being tailor-made to customer instructions. Last, special pricing may be used when goods are produced for a one-time job, such as an overseas order that will not affect domestic sales.

Assume that Online Computers has been given the opportunity to bid on a special order for 50,000 private-label printers for a major electronics retailer. Company management wants to obtain the order as long as the additional business will provide a satisfactory contribution to profit. Online Computers has available production capacity that is not currently being used and necessary components and raw material can be obtained from suppliers. Also, the company has no immediate opportunity to apply its currently unused capacity in another way, so there is no opportunity cost.

Exhibit 12–14 presents information that management has gathered to determine a price to bid on the printers. Direct material and components, direct labor, and *variable* factory overhead costs are relevant to setting the bid price because these costs will be incurred for each printer produced. Although all variable costs are normally relevant to a special pricing decision, the variable selling expense is irrelevant in this instance because no sales commission will be paid on this sale. Fixed manufacturing overhead and fixed selling and administrative expenses are not expected to increase because of this sale, so these expenses are not included in the pricing decision.

Using the available cost information, the relevant cost for determining the bid price for each printer is $120 (direct material and components, direct labor, and

[12] An exception to this general rule may occur when a company produces related or complementary products. For instance, an electronics company may sell a video game at or below cost and allow the ancillary software program sales to be the primary source of profit.

EXHIBIT 12-14

Online Computers—Printer Product Information

	Normal Costs	Relevant Costs
Per unit cost for 1 printer:		
Direct material and components	$ 87	$ 87
Direct labor	15	15
Variable overhead	18	18
Variable selling expense (commission)	6	0
Total variable cost	$126	$120
Fixed factory overhead (allocated)	30	
Fixed selling & administrative expense	9	
Total cost per printer	$165	

variable overhead). This cost is the *minimum* price at which the company should sell one printer. Any price higher than $120 will provide the company some profit on the sale.

Assume that Online Computers' printer line is currently experiencing a $2,420,000 net loss and that company managers want to set a bid price that would cover the net loss and create $400,000 of before-tax profit. In this case, Online Computers would spread the total $2,820,000 desired contribution margin over the 50,000 unit special order at $56.40 per printer. This decision would give a bid price of $176.40 per printer ($120 variable cost + $56.40). However, *any* price above the $120 variable cost will contribute toward reducing the $2,420,000 product line loss.

In setting the bid price, management must decide how much profit it would consider reasonable on the special order. Assume that Online Computers' usual selling price for this printer model is $190 and each sale provides a normal profit margin of $25 per printer or 15 percent (rounded) of the $165 total cost. Setting the bid price for the special order at $138 would cover the variable production costs of $120 and provide a normal 15 percent profit margin ($18) on the incremental unit cost. This computation illustrates a simplistic cost-plus approach to pricing, but ignores both product demand and market competition. Online Computers' bid price should also reflect these considerations. In addition, company management should consider the effect that the additional job will have on the activities engaged in by the company and whether these activities will create additional, unforeseen costs.

When setting a special order price, management must consider the qualitative issues as well as the quantitative ones. For instance, will setting a low bid price cause this customer (or others) to believe that a precedent has been established for future prices? Will the contribution margin on a bid, set low enough to acquire the job, earn a sufficient amount to justify the additional burdens placed on management and employees by this activity? Will the additional production activity require the use of bottleneck resources and reduce company throughput? How, if at all, will special order sales affect the company's normal sales? If the job is scheduled during a period of low business activity (off-season or recession), is management willing to take the business at a lower contribution or profit margin simply to keep a trained workforce employed?

Robinson-Patman Act

A final management consideration in special pricing decisions is the **Robinson-Patman Act**, which prohibits companies from pricing the same product at different levels when those amounts do not reflect related cost differences. Cost differences must result from actual variations in the cost to manufacture, sell, or distribute a product because of differing methods of production or quantities sold.

ad hoc discount

Companies may, however, give **ad hoc discounts**, which are price concessions that relate to real (or imagined) competitive pressures rather than to location of the merchandising chain or volume purchased. Such discounts are not usually subject to detailed justification, because they are based on a competitive market environment. While ad hoc discounts do not require intensive justification under the law, other types of discounts do because they may reflect some type of price discrimination. Prudent managers must understand the legalities of special pricing and the factors that allow for its implementation. For merchandise that is normally stocked, the only support for pricing differences is a difference in distribution costs.

In making pricing decisions, managers typically first analyze the market environment, including the degree of industry competition and competitor's prices. Then, managers normally consider full production cost in setting normal sales prices. Full production cost includes an allocated portion of fixed costs of the production process, which in a multiproduct environment could include common costs of production relating to more than one type of product. Allocations of common costs can distort the results of operations shown for individual products.

8

How is segment margin used to determine whether a product line should be retained or eliminated?

Product Line Decisions

Operating results of multiproduct environments are often presented in a disaggregated format that shows results for separate product lines within the organization or division. In reviewing these disaggregated statements, managers must distinguish relevant from irrelevant information regarding individual product lines. If all costs (variable *and* fixed) are allocated to product lines, a product line or segment may be perceived to be operating at a loss when actually it is not. The commingling of relevant and irrelevant information on the statements may cause such perceptions.

Exhibit 12–15 presents basic earnings information for the Printer Division of Online Computers, which manufactures three product lines: laser, ink jet, and dot matrix printers.

The format of the information given in the exhibit makes it appear that the dot matrix line is operating at a net loss of $165,000. Managers reviewing such results might reason that the firm would be $165,000 more profitable if dot matrix printers were eliminated. Such a conclusion may be premature because of the mixture of relevant and irrelevant information in the income statement presentation.

All fixed expenses have been allocated to the individual product lines in Exhibit 12–15. Such allocations are traditionally based on one or more measures of "presumed" equity, such as square footage of the manufacturing plant occupied by each product line, number of machine hours incurred for production of each product line, or number of employees directly associated with each product line. In all cases, however, allocations may force fixed expenses into specific product line operating results even though some of those expenses may not have actually been incurred for the benefit of the specific product line.

EXHIBIT 12–15

Printer Division of Online Computers Product Line Income Statements

	(In $000)			
	Laser	Ink Jet	Dot Matrix	Total
Sales	$8,000	$9,800	$3,000	$20,800
Total direct variable expenses	(5,400)	(5,700)	(2,200)	(13,300)
Total contribution margin	$2,600	$4,100	$ 800	$ 7,500
Total fixed expenses	(2,100)	(3,700)	(965)	(6,765)
Net income (loss)	$ 500	$ 400	$ (165)	$ 735
Fixed expenses are detailed below:				
(1) Avoidable fixed expenses	$1,200	$3,000	$ 450	$ 4,650
(2) Unavoidable fixed expenses	600	420	300	1,320
(3) Allocated common expenses	300	280	215	795
Total	$2,100	$3,700	$ 965	$ 6,765

In Exhibit 12–16, the fixed expenses of the Printer Division are segregated into three subcategories: (1) those that are avoidable if the particular product line is eliminated (these expenses can also be referred to as attributable expenses); (2) those that are directly associated with a particular product line but are unavoidable; and (3) those that are incurred for the benefit of the company as a whole (common expenses) and that are allocated to the individual product lines. The latter two subcategories are irrelevant to the question of whether to eliminate a product line. An unavoidable expense will merely be shifted to another product line if the product line with which it is associated is eliminated. Common expenses will be incurred regardless of which product lines are eliminated. An example of a common cost is the insurance premium on a manufacturing facility that houses all product lines.

If the dot matrix line is eliminated, total divisional profit will decline by $350,000. This amount represents the lost segment margin of the dot matrix product line. **Segment margin** represents the excess of revenues over direct variable expenses and avoidable fixed expenses. It is the amount remaining to cover unavoidable direct fixed expenses and common expenses, and to provide profits.[13] The segment margin figure is the appropriate one on which to base the continuation or elimination decision since it measures the segment's contribution to the coverage of indirect and unavoidable expenses. The decrease in total income that would result with only one product line can be shown in the following alternative computations. With only two product lines, laser and ink jet, the Printer Division would generate a total net income of only $385,000, computed as follows:

segment margin

	(In $000)
Current net income	$ 735
Decrease in income due to elimination of dot matrix (segment margin)	(350)
New net income	$ 385

This new net income can be proven by the following computation:

Total contribution margin of laser and ink jet lines	$6,700
Less avoidable fixed expenses of the laser and ink jet lines	(4,200)
Segment margin of laser and ink jet lines	$2,500
Less *all* remaining unavoidable and allocated expenses shown on Exhibit 12–16 ($1,320 + $795)	(2,115)
Remaining income with two product lines	$ 385

EXHIBIT 12–16

Printer Division of Online Computers Segment Margin Income Statements

	(In $000)			
	Laser	Ink Jet	Dot Matrix	Total
Sales	$8,000	$9,800	$3,000	$20,800
Total direct variable expenses	(5,400)	(5,700)	(2,200)	(13,300)
Total contribution margin	$2,600	$4,100	$ 800	$ 7,500
(1) Avoidable fixed expenses	(1,200)	(3,000)	(450)	(4,650)
Segment Margin	$1,400	$1,100	$ 350	$ 2,850
(2) Unavoidable fixed expenses	(600)	(420)	(300)	(1,320)
Product Line Result	$ 800	$ 680	$ 50	$ 1,530
(3) Allocated common expenses	(300)	(280)	(215)	(795)
Net income (loss)	$ 500	$ 400	$ (165)	$ 735

[13] All common expenses are assumed to be fixed; this is not always the case. Some common costs could be variable, such as expenses of processing purchase orders or computer time-sharing expenses for payroll or other corporate functions.

Based on the information shown in Exhibit 12–16, the Printer Division should not eliminate the dot matrix product line because it is generating a positive segment margin and, therefore, is generating enough revenue to cover its relevant expenses. If this product line were eliminated, total divisional profit would decrease by $350,000, the amount of the product line's segment margin.

In classifying product line costs, managers should be aware that some costs may appear to be avoidable but are actually not. For example, the salary of a supervisor working directly with a product line appears to be an avoidable fixed cost if the product line is eliminated. However, if this individual has significant experience, the supervisor is often retained and transferred to other areas of the company even if product lines are cut. Determinations such as these need to be made before costs can be appropriately classified in product line elimination decisions.

Depreciation on factory equipment used to manufacture a specific product is an irrelevant cost in product line decisions. But, if the equipment can be sold, the selling price is relevant to the decision because it would increase the marginal benefit of the decision to discontinue the product line. Even if the equipment will be kept in service and be used to produce other products, the depreciation expense is unavoidable and irrelevant to the decision.

Before making spontaneous decisions to discontinue a product line, management should carefully consider what it would take to "turn the product line around" and the long-term ramifications of the elimination decision. For example, elimination of a product line shrinks market assortment, which may cause some customers to seek other suppliers that maintain a broader market assortment. And, as in other relevant costing situations, a decision to eliminate a product line has qualitative as well as quantitative factors that must be analyzed. Also, as discussed in the accompanying News Note, in the same manner that product lines are scrutinized, unprofitable customers should also be identified and studied for ways to improve profitability.

Management's task is to effectively and efficiently allocate its finite stock of resources to accomplish its chosen set of objectives. A cost accountant needs to learn what uses will be made of the information requested by managers to make certain that the relevant information is provided in the appropriate form. Managers

NEWS NOTE

GENERAL BUSINESS

Firing Customers to Increase Profits

Managers across most industries are increasingly realizing the need for customer profitability information to run their businesses. The customer profitability information is required to focus expensive marketing, customer acquisition and customer retention programs on profitable customers. Constantly increasing competition means companies can no longer afford to subsidize non-profitable customers. Information is required to identify non-profitable customers and design actions to move them into profitability.

Good accounting and management practice dictates that only relevant costs should be considered in management decision making. That is, only costs that are incremental to the decision at hand are appropriate. Sunk costs and other costs that do not change based on the decision to be made are not relevant to the decision. This is often forgotten in the implementation of activity-based costing, often causing executives to throw away the hard work of the finance team by not using the information produced, or worse still, to make decisions which have a negative effect on the company.

A customer profitability analysis must provide flexible data which enables the relevant costs for specific decisions to be identified. Whether costs are predominantly fixed or variable is key to this type of analysis. While some managers like to see all of a company's costs allocated to products, it is vital that nonincremental costs are excluded from decision analysis.

SOURCE: Mark Pickering, "Customer Profitability: The Approach Counts," *Charter* (July 1998), pp. 32–35.

must have a reliable quantitative basis on which to analyze problems, compare viable solutions, and choose the best course of action. Because management is a social rather than a natural science, there are no fundamental "truths" and few problems are susceptible to black-or-white solutions. Relevant costing is a process of making human approximations of the costs of alternative decision results.

REVISITING

Price-waterhouse-Coopers

http://www.pwcglobal.com

Most organizations are now realizing that, to succeed, they must focus on a few core competencies, things they uniquely do very well. Most organizations have utilized outsourcing in the past, but the scope of outsourced activities is increasing in most firms.

PricewaterhouseCoopers, PwC, commissioned a study of outsourcing trends among 300 of the largest global companies, including 26 Canadian organizations. The research, conducted by an independent market research organization, highlighted some interesting issues and trends. Among the key findings were

1. Outsourcing is increasing in importance.
2. In general, the experience with outsourcing has been positive.
3. Outsourcing to date has been predominantly of lower risk, narrower activities. The outsourcing of broader, more important processes is increasing but is still in its early stages.
4. Organizations are starting to view outsourcing as a broad management strategy rather than just a cost reduction tool.

PwC sees the outsourcing market changing quite dramatically over the next few years towards a new relationship characterized by the following factors:

✓ a broadening of the scope of outsourcing relationships;

✓ a significant investment by the service provider, particularly in information technology and infrastructure to support service delivery; and

✓ sharing of risks and rewards associated with the outsourcing.

PwC has invested heavily in preparing for an increased role in the outsourcing market. As outsourcing activities increasingly encompass intangible inputs, i.e., knowledge, PwC's outsourcing services will be in greater demand. To meet this demand, the firm established its BPO (Business Process Outsourcing) group in 1996. The group is organized on a global basis, and operates as one cohesive network of professionals with centralized management, proprietary methodologies, and leading-edge technologies. These services provided by the BPO group center around the firm's core competencies which are ever-expanding.

Today, worldwide, PwC has more than 10,000 professionals dedicated to providing BPO services to more than 500 multinational and other large organizations.

SOURCE: PricewaterhouseCoopers Web site, http://www.pwcglobal.com (November 15, 1999).

CHAPTER SUMMARY

Relevant information is logically related and pertinent to a given decision. Relevant information may be both quantitative and qualitative. Variable costs are generally relevant to a decision; they are irrelevant only when they cannot be avoided under any possible alternative or when they do not differ across alternatives. Direct avoidable fixed costs are also relevant to decision making. Sometimes costs give the illusion of being relevant when they actually are not. Examples of such irrelevant costs include sunk costs, arbitrarily allocated common costs, and nonincremental fixed and variable costs.

Relevant costing compares the incremental revenues and/or costs associated with alternative decisions. Managers use relevant costing to determine the incremental benefits of decision alternatives. One decision is established as a base line against which the alternatives are compared. In many decisions the alternative of "change nothing" is the obvious base line case.

Common situations in which relevant costing techniques are applied include asset replacements, outsourcing decisions, scarce resource allocations, special price determinations, sales mix distributions, and retention or elimination of product lines. The following points are important to remember:

1. In an asset replacement decision, costs paid in the past are not relevant to decisions being made currently; these are sunk costs and should be ignored.
2. In an outsourcing decision, include the opportunity costs associated with the outsource alternative; nonproduction potentially allows management an opportunity to make plant assets and personnel available for other purposes.
3. In a decision involving a single scarce resource, if the objective is to maximize company contribution margin and profits, then production and sales should be focused toward the product with the highest contribution margin per unit of the scarce resource.
4. In a special order decision, the minimum selling price that a company should charge is the sum of all the incremental costs of production and sales on the order.
5. In a sales mix decision, changes in selling prices and advertising will normally affect sales volume and change the company's contribution margin ratio. Tying sales commissions to contribution margin will motivate salespeople to sell products that will most benefit the company's profits.
6. In a product line decision, product lines should be evaluated based on their segment margins rather than on net income. Segment margin captures the change in corporate net income that would occur if the segment were discontinued.

Quantitative analysis is generally short range in perspective. After analyzing the quantifiable factors associated with each alternative, a manager must assess the merits and potential risks of the qualitative factors involved to select the best possible course of action. Some of these qualitative factors (such as the community economic impact of closing a plant) may present long-range planning and policy implications. Other qualitative factors may be short range in nature, such as competitor reactions. Managers must decide the relevance of individual factors based on experience, judgment, knowledge of theory, and use of logic.

APPENDIX

How is a linear programming problem formulated?

Linear Programming

Factors exist that restrict the immediate attainment of almost any objective. For example, assume that the objective of the board of directors at Washington Hospital is to aid more sick people during the coming year. Factors restricting the attainment of that objective include number of beds in the hospital, size of the hospital staff, hours per week the staff is allowed to work, and number of charity patients the hospital can accept. Each factor reflects a limited or scarce resource and Washington Hospital must find a means of achieving its objective by efficiently and effectively allocating its limited resources.

Managers are always concerned with allocating scarce resources among competing uses. If a company has only one scarce resource, managers will schedule production or other measures of activity in a way that maximizes the use of the scarce resource. Most situations, however, involve several limiting factors that compete with one another during the process of striving to attain business objectives. Solving problems having several limiting factors requires the use of **mathematical programming**, which refers to a variety of techniques used to allocate limited resources among activities to achieve a specific goal or purpose. This appendix provides an introduction to linear programming, which is one form of mathematical programming.[14]

mathematical programming

Basics of Linear Programming

Linear programming (LP) is a method used to find the optimal allocation of scarce resources in a situation involving one objective and multiple limiting factors.[15] The objective and restrictions on achieving that objective must be expressible as linear equations.[16] The equation that specifies the objective is called the **objective function**; typically, the objective is to maximize or to minimize some measure of performance. For example, a company's objective could be to maximize contribution margin or to minimize product cost.

linear programming

objective function

A **constraint** is any type of restriction that hampers management's pursuit of the objective. Resource constraints involve limited availability of labor time, machine time, raw material, space, or production capacity. Demand or marketing constraints restrict the quantity of product that can be sold during a time period. Constraints can also be in the form of technical product requirements. For example, management may be constrained in the production requirements for frozen meals by caloric or vitamin content.

constraint

A final constraint in all LP problems is a **nonnegativity constraint**. This constraint specifies that negative values for physical quantities are not allowed. Constraints, like the objective function, are specified in mathematical equations and represent the limits imposed on optimizing the objective function.

nonnegativity constraint

Almost every allocation problem has multiple **feasible solutions** that do not violate any of the problem constraints. Different solutions generally give different values for the objective function, although in some cases, a problem may have several solutions that provide the same value for the objective function. Solutions can be generated that contain fractional values. If solutions for variables must be restricted to whole numbers, **integer programming** techniques must be used to add additional constraints to the problem. The **optimal solution** to a maximization or minimization goal is the one that provides the best answer to the allocation problem. Some LP problems may have more than one optimal solution.

feasible solution

integer programming
optimal solution

Formulating a LP Problem

Two common situations for applying linear programming techniques are scheduling production and combining ingredients. Management's goal in determining production mix in a multiproduct environment is to find the mix of products that, when sold, will maximize the company's contribution margin (the goal). The goal in determining the mix of ingredients for a specific product is to find that mix providing the specified level of quality at the minimum variable cost.

Each LP problem contains a dependent variable, two or more independent (or decision) variables, and one or more constraints. A **decision variable** is an unknown item for which the problem is being solved. The first and most important step in solving linear programming problems is setting up the information in mathematical equation form. The objective function and each of the constraints must be identified. The objective function is frequently stated such that the solution will

decision variable

[14] This chapter discusses basic linear programming concepts; it is not an all-inclusive presentation. Any standard management science text should be consulted for an in-depth presentation of the subject.
[15] Finding the best allocation of resources when multiple goals exist is called *goal programming*. This topic is not addressed in this text.
[16] If the objective and/or restrictions cannot be expressed in linear equations, the technique of nonlinear programming must be used. No general method has been developed that can solve all types of nonlinear programming problems.

either maximize contribution margin or minimize variable costs. Basic objective function formats for maximization and minimization problems are shown below:

Maximization problem

$$\text{Objective function: MAX CM} = CM_1X_1 + CM_2X_2$$

Minimization problem

$$\text{Objective function: MIN VC} = VC_1X_1 + VC_2X_2$$

where CM = contribution margin

CM_1 = contribution margin per unit of the first product

CM_2 = contribution margin per unit of the second product

X_1 = number of units of the first product

X_2 = number of units of the second product

VC = variable cost

VC_1 = variable cost per unit of the first product

VC_2 = variable cost per unit of the second product

Resource constraints are usually expressed as inequalities.[17] The following is the general formula for a less-than-or-equal-to resource constraint:

$$\text{Resource constraint(1): } A_1X_1 + A_2X_2 \leq \text{Resource 1}$$

where X_1 = number of units of the first product

X_2 = number of units of the second product

input–output coefficients

The coefficients (A_1 and A_2) are **input–output coefficients** that indicate the rate at which each decision variable uses up or depletes the scarce resource.

Machine time is an example of a resource constraint. Assume that Online Computers has only 10,000 machine hours available to produce disk drives and external modems. One-half machine hour is required to produce a disk drive unit and 0.25 hour is needed for one modem. The resource constraint is shown as:

$$0.5X_1 + 0.25X_2 \leq 10{,}000$$

where X_1 = number of disk drive units

X_2 = number of modem units

If Online Computers manufactured only one of the two types of products, it could produce 20,000 (10,000 ÷ 0.5) disk drives or 40,000 modems. In manufacturing both products, the company must recognize that producing one disk drive precludes manufacturing two modems. The mix of units to be produced will be determined by the contribution margin of each product and the other constraints under which the company operates.

All of the general concepts of formatting a linear programming problem are shown in the following maximization problem using data for the Office Storage Company. Office Storage sells two office storage products: file cabinets and storage shelves. Information on these products and the constraints that must be considered are provided in Exhibit 12–17. Office Storage managers want to know the mix

[17] It is also possible to have strict equality constraints. For example, in producing a ten-pound bag of dog food, ingredients could be combined in a variety of ways, but total weight is required to be ten pounds.

EXHIBIT 12-17

Office Storage Company Product Information and Constraints

FILE CABINET	
Contribution margin per unit	$25
Labor hours to manufacture one unit	3
Machine hours to assemble one unit	2
Cubic feet of warehouse space per unit	8
STORAGE SHELVES	
Contribution margin per unit	$9
Labor hours to manufacture one unit	2
Machine hours to assemble one unit	1
Cubic feet of warehouse space per unit	3
CONSTRAINTS	
Total labor time available each month	2,100 hours
Total machine time available each month	850 hours
Warehouse cubic feet available	4,000

of products to produce and sell that will generate the maximum contribution margin. The company is producing the items for future sale and must store them for the near term in its warehouse. For Office Storage Company, the problem is composed of the following factors: (1) the objective is to maximize contribution margin (CM); (2) the decision variables are the file cabinet (X_1) and storage shelves (X_2); and (3) the constraints are labor time, machine time, and warehouse storage space.

Equations used to express objective functions should indicate the purpose of the problem and how that purpose is to be realized. Office Storage Company's purpose (objective) is to maximize its contribution margin by producing and selling the combination of file cabinets and storage shelves that provide contribution margins of $25 and $9, respectively. The objective function is stated as

$$\text{MAX CM} = 25X_1 + 9X_2$$

The constraint inequalities indicate the demands made by each decision variable on scarce resource availability. Total labor time for producing the two products must be less than or equal to 2,100 hours per month. It is possible that all labor time will not be used each month. Each file cabinet and storage shelf produced takes 3 and 2 labor hours, respectively. The labor constraint is expressed as

$$3X_1 + 2X_2 \leq 2,100$$

Expressing the machine time constraint equation is similar to that of the labor time constraint. Each file cabinet requires 2 hours of machine time and each storage shelf requires 1 hour. Total machine time available per month is 850 hours. This resource constraint is

$$2X_1 + 1X_2 \leq 850$$

The file cabinets and storage shelves produced cannot exceed available warehouse storage space. Each file cabinet consumes substantially more space than each storage shelf. The production constraint is expressed as

$$8X_1 + 3X_2 \leq 4,000$$

Although not shown in Exhibit 12–17, nonnegativity constraints exist for this problem. The nonnegativity constraints simply state that production of either product cannot be less than zero units. Nonnegativity constraints are shown as

$$X_1 \geq 0$$
$$X_2 \geq 0$$

The mathematical formulas needed to solve the Office Storage Company LP production problem are shown in Exhibit 12–18. Next, a method for solving the problem must be chosen.

Solving a LP Problem

Linear programming problems can be solved by a graphical approach or by the simplex method. Graphs are simple to use and provide a visual representation of the problem. The computer-adaptable simplex method is a more efficient means to handle complex linear programming problems. Graphical methods of solving linear programming problems are useful only when there are two decision variables and few constraints or two constraints and few decision variables. Graphs also illustrate the process of solving a LP problem. Such illustrations are helpful in visualizing how the simplex method works.

The graphical method of solving a linear programming problem consists of five steps:

feasible region

vertex

1. State the problem in terms of a linear objective function and linear constraints.
2. Graph the constraints and determine the feasible region. The **feasible region** is the graphical space contained within and on all of the constraint lines.
3. Determine the coordinates of each corner (**vertex**) of the feasible region.
4. Calculate the value of the objective function at each vertex.
5. Select the optimal solution. The optimal solution for a maximization problem is the one with the highest objective function value. The optimal solution in a minimization problem has the lowest objective function value.

Exhibit 12–19 shows the labeled constraint lines and the corner values.

The feasible region is shaded and one can see that its corners are A–B–C. Only the machine hours constraint is binding; the other two constraints are redundant. The total contribution margin at each corner is calculated as follows:

	VALUES		
Corner	X_1	X_2	
A	0	0	CM = \$25(0) + \$9(0) = \$0
B	425	0	CM = \$25(425) + \$9(0) = \$10,625
C	0	850	CM = \$25(0) + \$9(850) = \$7,650

EXHIBIT 12–18

Office Storage Company LP Problem Statement

Objective Function: MAX CM = $25X_1 + 9X_2$

Constraints (Subject to):

$3X_1 + 2X_2 \leq 2{,}100$	(labor time in hours)
$2X_1 + 1X_2 \leq 850$	(machine time in hours)
$8X_1 + 3X_2 \leq 4{,}000$	(warehouse storage space)
$X_1 \geq 0$	(nonnegativity of file cabinets)
$X_2 \geq 0$	(nonnegativity of storage shelves)

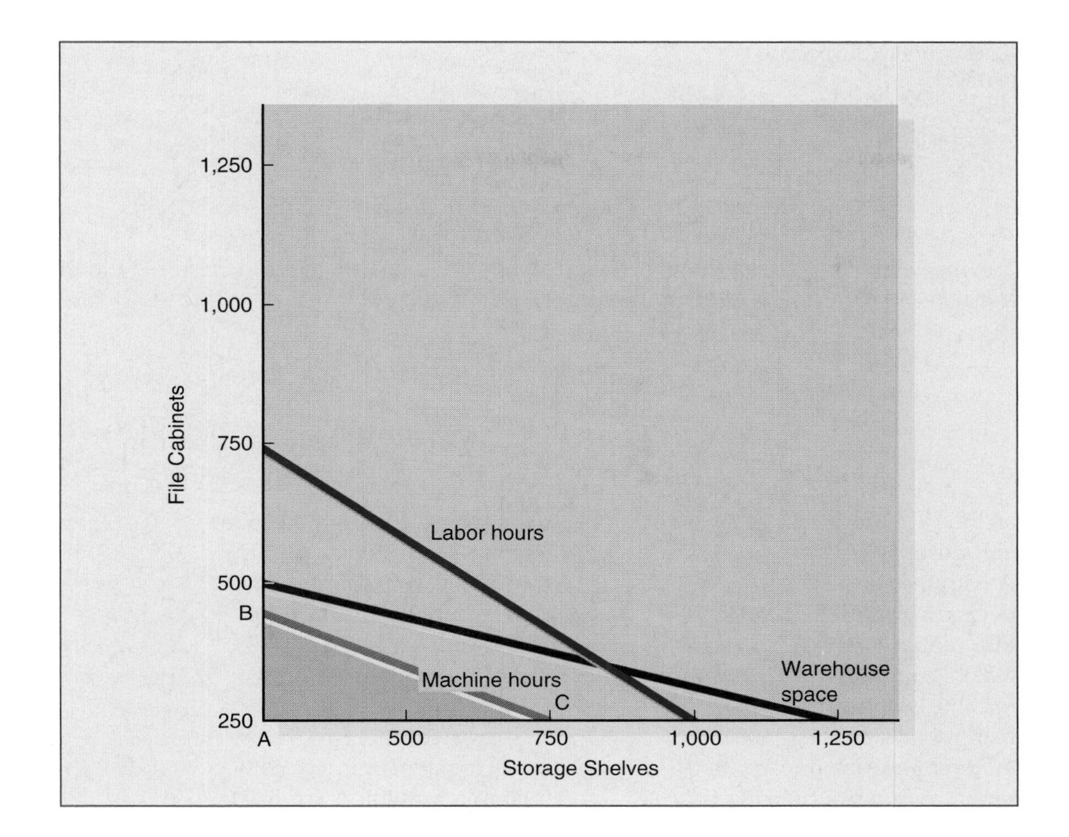

EXHIBIT 12-19

Office Storage Company Production Constraints

Inspection reveals that the contribution margin is at its highest ($10,625) at point B. The corners that are not part of the feasible region are not evaluated because they do not satisfy all of the constraints of the problem.

The **simplex method** is an iterative (sequential) algorithm that solves multivariable, multiconstraint linear programming problems. An **algorithm** is a logical step-by-step problem-solving technique (generally utilizing a computer) that continuously searches for an improved solution from the one previously computed. The simplex method does not check every feasible solution. It checks only those occurring at the corners of the feasible region. Because corners always represent the extremities of the feasible region, a corner is where the maximum or minimum value of the objective function is always located.

simplex method
algorithm

The simplex method begins with a mathematical statement of the objective function and constraints. The inequalities in the constraints must be expressed as equalities to solve the problems algebraically. Expressing inequalities as equalities is accomplished by introducing slack or surplus variables (S) into constraint equations. A **slack variable** represents the unused amount of a resource at any level of operation. The amount of the slack variable can range from zero to the total amount of the constrained resource. Slack variables are associated with "less than or equal to" (≤) constraints and are added to the left side of the constraint equation. A **surplus variable** represents overachievement of a minimum requirement and is associated with "greater than or equal to" (≥) constraints. Surplus variables are subtracted from the left side of a constraint equation. The formulas for Office Storage Company shown in Exhibit 12–18 are repeated below with the inclusion of slack variables (S_1, S_2, and S_3) for each constrained resource. There are no surplus variables for Office Storage Company because all constraints were "less than or equal to" constraints.

slack variable

surplus variable

$$\text{Objective Function: MAX CM} = 25X_1 + 9X_2$$

Constraints (Subject to):

$$3X_1 + 2X_2 + S_1 = 2{,}100 \text{ (labor time in hours)}$$
$$2X_1 + 1X_2 + S_2 = 850 \text{ (machine time in hours)}$$
$$8X_1 + 3X_2 + S_3 = 4{,}000 \text{ (warehouse storage in cubic feet)}$$

Solving a linear programming problem using the simplex method requires either the use of matrix algebra or a computer.

KEY TERMS

ad hoc discount (p. 517)
algorithm (p. 527)
constraint (p. 523)
decision variable (p. 523)
differential cost (p. 500)
feasible region (p. 526)
feasible solution (p. 523)
incremental cost (p. 500)
incremental revenue (p. 500)
input–output coefficients (p. 524)
integer programming (p. 523)
linear programming (p. 523)
make-or-buy decision (p. 504)
mathematical programming (p. 523)
nonnegativity constraint (p. 523)
objective function (p. 523)
opportunity cost (p. 501)
optimal solution (p. 523)
outsourcing decision (p. 504)
relevant costing (p. 499)
Robinson-Patman Act (p. 517)
sales mix (p. 510)
scarce resource (p. 508)
segment margin (p. 519)
simplex method (p. 527)
slack variable (p. 527)
special order decision (p. 516)
surplus variable (p. 527)
vertex (p. 526)

SOLUTION STRATEGIES

General rule of decision making: Choose the alternative that yields the greatest incremental benefit.

	Incremental (additional) revenues
−	Incremental (additional) costs
	Incremental benefit (positive or negative)

Relevant Costs

- Direct material
- Direct labor
- Variable production overhead
- Variable selling expenses related to *each* alternative (may be greater or less than under the "change nothing" alternative)
- Avoidable fixed production overhead
- Avoidable fixed selling/administrative costs (if any)
- Opportunity cost of choosing some other alternative (will either increase the cost of one alternative or reduce the cost of another alternative)

Relevant Cost Analysis in Specific Decisions

Single Scarce Resource

1. Determine the scarce resource.
2. Determine the production per unit of the scarce resource.
3. Determine the contribution margin per unit of the scarce resource.
4. Multiply production (step 2) times contribution margin (step 3) to obtain total contribution margin provided by the product per unit of the scarce resource. Production and sale of the product with the highest contribution margin per unit of scarce resource will maximize profits.

Product Lines Analysis

	Sales
−	Direct variable expenses
=	Product line contribution margin
−	Avoidable fixed expenses
=	Segment (product line) margin*
−	Unavoidable fixed expenses
=	Product line operating results

*Make decision to retain or eliminate based on this line item.

DEMONSTRATION PROBLEM

Green Thumb Industries produces a variety of equipment used by professional gardeners. The key machine in the company's product lineup is a riding lawnmower. Each lawnmower produced requires two hydraulic cylinders that allow the mower bed to be raised and lowered by the operator with the simple movement of a lever. The firm currently manufactures the cylinders and the costs incurred to make each cylinder unit are as follows:

Direct material	$24
Direct labor	16
Variable overhead	10
Fixed overhead	10

Of the per-unit fixed overhead, $4 could be avoided if the firm did not make the cylinders. Another company has offered to sell to Green Thumb an equivalent cylinder for $56. Green Thumb produces 20,000 cylinders annually.

Required: (Consider each requirement to be independent of the other requirements.)

a. Should Green Thumb outsource the component? Show calculations.

b. Green Thumb's vice president, Joe Weber, estimates that the company can rent out the facilities used to make the cylinders for $60,000 annually. What should the company do? Show calculations.

c. What are some of the qualitative factors that should be considered if Green Thumb is contemplating outsourcing the cylinder component?

Solution to Demonstration Problem

a. Relevant cost of making:

Direct material	$24
Direct labor	16
Variable overhead	10
Avoidable fixed overhead	4
Total	$54
Cost to outsource	$56

Therefore, Green Thumb should continue to make the cylinder.

b. \$60,000 rental income ÷ 20,000 components = \$3 opportunity cost per unit

Relevant cost to insource [part (a)]	\$54
Opportunity cost	3
Total	\$57

The cost to insource now exceeds the cost to outsource. Therefore, Green Thumb should purchase the item.

c. Some qualitative factors include the following:

- Future control by Green Thumb of quality, supply, cost, and price of the cylinder
- Supplier's long-run chances of being in business
- Existence and number of other suppliers
- Impact on customers and markets

QUESTIONS

1. Define a relevant cost. For a hospital considering the purchase of a new X-ray machine, what are examples of the relevant costs of the purchase decision? What would be one of the alternatives to purchasing the X-ray machine?

2. What are the characteristics of a relevant cost? Why are future costs not always relevant? Are all relevant costs found in accounting records? Explain.

3. What is an opportunity cost? In an outsourcing decision, what opportunity cost might be associated with the production facilities?

4. Which are more important in decision making: quantitative or qualitative factors? Why? How can qualitative factors be explicitly considered in making a decision?

5. Can a particular cost be relevant for one purpose, but not for other purposes? Give three examples in which this would be the case.

6. Are sunk costs ever relevant in decision making? If so, give one or more examples.

7. You are considering the sale of your old stereo system. According to your records, you paid \$500 for the stereo system. The current market value of the stereo is \$150. A new stereo of the same make and model could be purchased today for \$375. Which of these figures is relevant to your decision to sell or keep the stereo system? If any figures are not relevant, explain why.

8. Kelly O'Riley, owner of Juanita's Mexican Cafe, is trying to decide whether to make tortillas or buy them from a supplier, Ricardo's Super Mercado. Kelly has come to you for advice. What factors would you tell her to consider in making her choice?

9. What is a scarce resource? Why will the resource that is most scarce in an organization be likely to change from time to time?

10. Suggest possible alternatives to basing sales commissions on the sales revenue generated by each salesperson. What would be the benefits and drawbacks of your methods to the salesperson and to the company?

11. Why is the effect of a sales price change on volume partly determined by the elasticity of demand for the product?

12. What is the special order decision? What typical circumstances lead to the need to make this type of decision?

13. What are the differences among avoidable fixed costs, unavoidable direct fixed costs, and common fixed costs? Which are relevant and which are irrelevant in the decision to keep or eliminate a particular product line?

14. Lazlow Optical Mfg. produces a line of single-reflex cameras. Corporate records reveal that one of the midpriced cameras is producing a negative segment margin. Before discontinuing production of the camera, what factors should Lazlow's managers consider?

15. Are segment margin or product line operating results more important in product line decisions? Why?

16. (Appendix) Why is linear programming used in business organizations?

17. (Appendix) What are two typical objective function expressions that are stated in terms of accounting information?

18. (Appendix) What are nonnegativity constraints in the linear programming model? Why is it not necessary that they be specified for every linear programming problem?

19. (Appendix) What is the difference between a feasible solution and an optimal solution?

20. (Appendix) "Resource constraints are always inequalities." Is this statement true or false? Why?

21. (Appendix) What is the difference between a slack variable and a surplus variable? Can each exist in the same linear programming problem? If so, discuss how; if not, discuss why.

EXERCISES

22. *(Relevant costs)*

Businesses in Chattanooga, Tenn., will be asked to give up a bit of their independence to cut costs and help clean up the environment.

The Chattanooga Institute, a nonprofit advocate of environmentally friendly development, announced the next phase in the creation of a $70 million "eco-industrial park": a six-month feasibility study that would lay out the blueprint for a community in which businesses swap one another's waste and other by-products, from hot water to used paper. First envisioned in meetings two years ago with President Clinton's Council on Sustainable Development, planners said the park will be fully operational as early as 2001.

If successful, the city's blighted Southside community could become a magnet for companies willing to use one another's waste products as both raw materials and sources of energy.

"Everything [would be] reused or recycled to create something that is needed by someone else," says Woodley Murphy, Chattanooga Institute executive director.

http://www.csc2.org/index.htm

SOURCE: Adapted from Motoko Rich, "Urban Plan Taps Waste as a Resource," *The Wall Street Journal* (November 19, 1997) p. S1.

The preceding article discusses a way in which a company can take a more expansive view of its operations to define relevant costs. Discuss why firms of the future will increasingly find it necessary to look across the supply chain, rather than just internally, to identify relevant costs.

23. *(Time and relevant costs)* The following are costs associated with a product line of Johnson Safety Systems. The costs reflect capacity-level production of 45,000 units per year.

Variable production costs	$45
Fixed production costs	27
Variable selling costs	12
Fixed selling and administrative costs	16

Prepare a written presentation showing how time affects relevant costs for a product line. Determine which costs would be relevant at each of the following points in time:

a. The point in time at which the product and production facilities are in the planning stage.
b. The point in time just after acquisition of the production facilities but before actual production commences.
c. The point in time after production of products is complete but before the units are sold.

24. *(Relevant costs)* Assume that you are about to graduate from your university. You are trying to decide whether to apply for graduate school or enter the job market. To help make the decision you have gathered the following data:

Costs incurred for the bachelor's degree	$83,000
Out-of-pocket costs for the master's degree	$51,000
Estimated starting salary with B.A.	$38,300
Estimated starting salary with M.A.	$44,400
Estimated time to complete master's degree	2 years
Estimated time from the present to retirement	40 years

a. Which of these factors are relevant to your decision?
b. What is the opportunity cost associated with earning the master's degree? What is the out-of-pocket cost to obtain the master's degree?
c. What other factors should you consider before making a decision?

25. *(Relevant costs)* Because of a monumental error committed by its purchasing department, John's Super Grocery received 50,000 heads of lettuce rather than the 500 that were actually ordered. The company paid $0.50 per head for the lettuce. Although the management is confident that 1,000 units can be sold through its regular sales, the market is not large enough to absorb the other 49,000 heads. Management has identified two ways to dispose of the excess heads. First, a wholesaler has offered to purchase them for $0.25 each. Second, a restaurant chain has offered to purchase the heads if John's will agree to convert the heads into packaged lettuce salads. This option would require John's to incur additional costs of $11,000 for conversion and the heads could then be sold for $0.48 each.

a. Which costs are sunk in this decision?
b. There are actually three alternatives John's can consider. Describe the alternative that is not mentioned in the story.
c. What are the relevant costs of each decision alternative and what should the company do?

26. *(Relevant vs. sunk costs)* Your friend, Bill Hawkins, purchased a new, combination phone and answering machine just prior to the start of this school term. He paid $95 for the equipment. Shortly after the start of the semester, during a party at his apartment, Bill's answering machine was crushed by an errant "flying plant." Returning the equipment to his retailer, Bill was informed that the estimated cost of repairs was $45.

Bill, pondering the figures, was ready to conclude that repairs should be made; after all, he had recently paid $95 for the equipment. However, before making a decision, Bill decided to ask for your advice, knowing that you were enrolled in a cost accounting course this term.

a. Using concepts learned from this chapter, prepare a brief presentation which outlines factors Bill should consider in making his decision.
b. Continue the presentation in part (a) by discussing the options Bill should consider in making his decision. Start by defining a base case against which alternatives may be compared.

27. *(Relevant costs)*

An analysis of GM's labor costs at its parts plant in Dayton, Ohio, provided evidence of one source of the firm's competitive problems. Its UAW employees are provided fringe benefits that cost, on average, about $16 per labor hour. Fringe benefits provided include full health-care coverage (no deductibles or co-payments), vision care, dental care, full pension after 30 years, life insurance, disability benefits, legal services, and supplemental unemployment benefits. Add to the $16 cost per hour of fringe benefits about $18 per hour in base pay, plus an additional increment for profit sharing, and the total cost of the average laborer was about $43 an hour.

SOURCE: Adapted from Nichole M. Christian, "Rich Benefits Plan Gives GM Competitors Cost Edge," *The Wall Street Journal* (March 21, 1996), pp. B1, B4.

http://www.gm.com

Assume you have been hired as a cost analyst by GM management. Write a report offering specific suggestions as to actions GM could take to control its parts and components costs.

28. *(Asset replacement)* Certain production equipment used in Flatburg's Canadian plant has become obsolete relative to current technology. The company is considering whether it should keep its existing equipment or purchase new equipment. To aid in this decision, the company's controller gathered the following data:

	Old Equipment	New Equipment
Original cost	$72,000	$99,000
Remaining life	5 years	5 years
Accumulated depreciation	$39,500	$0
Annual cash operating costs	$17,000	$4,000
Current salvage value	$22,000	NA
Salvage value in 5 years	$0	$0

a. Identify any sunk costs listed in the data.
b. Identify any irrelevant (nondifferential) future costs.
c. Identify all relevant costs to the equipment replacement decision.
d. What are the opportunity costs associated with the alternative of keeping the old equipment?
e. What is the incremental cost to purchase the new equipment?
f. What qualitative considerations should be taken into account before making any decision?

29. *(Asset replacement)* Modern Products Co. purchased new computer scheduling software on April 1, 2001, for $120,000 to manage its production. On May 15, 2001, a representative of a computerized manufacturing technology company demonstrated new software that was clearly superior to that purchased by the firm earlier in the year. The price of this software is $210,000. Corporate managers estimate that the new software would save the company $18,000 annually in schedule-related costs compared to the recently installed software. Both software systems should last 10 years (the expected life of the computer hardware) and have no salvage value at that time. The company can sell its existing software for $60,000 if it chooses to purchase the new system. Should the company keep and use the software purchased earlier in the year or buy the new software?

30. *(Outsourcing)* Mountain Technologies manufactures fiberglass housings for portable generators. One of the parts required to manufacture a housing is a metal latch. Currently the company produces all of the metal latches that it requires (120,000 units annually). The company's management is considering purchasing the part from an external vendor, Austin Mechanical. The following data are available for making the decision:

COST PER UNIT TO MANUFACTURE	
Direct material	$0.40
Direct labor	0.34
Variable overhead	0.18
Fixed overhead—applied	0.28
Total cost	$1.20

COST PER UNIT TO BUY	
Purchase price	$0.98
Freight charges	0.02
Total cost	$1.00

a. Assuming all of Mountain Technologies' internal production costs are avoidable if it purchases rather than makes the latch, what would be the net annual cost advantage to Mountain Technologies of purchasing?

b. Assume that some of Mountain Technologies' fixed overhead costs could not be avoided if it purchases rather than makes the latches. How much of the fixed overhead must be avoidable for the company to be indifferent between making and buying the component?

31. *(Outsourcing)* Greenburg Automotive produces pickup truck bumpers that are sold on a wholesale basis to new car retailers. The average sales price of a bumper is $150. Normal annual sales volume is 100,000 units, which is maximum production capacity. At this capacity, the company's costs per unit are as follows:

Direct material	$ 56	(including mounting hardware @ $12 per unit)
Direct labor	16	
Overhead (2/3 is fixed)	36	
Total	$108	

A key component in the production of bumpers is the mounting hardware that is used to attach the bumpers to the vehicles. Pittsburgh Metal Stamping has offered to sell Greenburg as many mounting units as the company needs for its bumper production. The offering price is $16 per unit. If Greenburg accepts the offer, the released facilities (that are currently used to produce mounting hardware) could be used to produce an additional 4,800 bumpers. What alternative is more desirable and by what amount? (Assume the company is currently operating at its capacity of 100,000 units.)

32. *(Outsourcing)* The Air Ride Shoe Company manufactures various types of shoes for sports and recreational use. Several types of shoes require a built-in air pump. Presently, the company makes all of the air pumps it requires for production. However, management is presently evaluating an offer from Aire Supply Co. to provide air pumps at a cost of $3 each. Air Ride management has estimated that the variable production costs of the air pump are $2.50 per unit. The firm also estimates that it could avoid $20,000 per year in fixed costs if it purchased rather than produced the air pumps.

a. If Air Ride requires 20,000 pumps per year, should it make them or buy them from Aire Supply Co.?

b. If Air Ride requires 60,000 pumps per year, should it make them or buy them?

c. Assuming all other factors are equal, at what level of production would the company be indifferent between making and buying the pumps?

33. *(Allocation of scarce resources)* Because the employees of one of its plants are out on strike, Allentown Electronics has found itself operating at peak capacity. The firm makes two electronic products, beepers and cell phones. Presently, the company can sell as many of each product as it can make, but it takes twice as long in production labor time to make a cell phone as it does to make a beeper. The firm's production capacity is only 120,000 labor hours per month. Data on each product follow:

	Beepers	Cell Phones
Sales	$30	$56
Variable costs	(24)	(46)
Contribution margin	$ 6	$10
Labor hours required	2	4

Fixed costs are $140,000 per month.

a. How many of each product should the company make? Explain your answer.

b. What qualitative factors would you consider in making this product mix decision?

34. *(Allocation of scarce resources)* Jill Rose received her accounting degree in 1972. Since receiving her degree, Ms. Rose has obtained significant experience in a variety of job settings. Her skills include auditing, income and estate taxation, and business consulting. Ms. Rose currently has her own practice and her skills are in such demand that she limits her practice to taxation issues. Most of her engagements are one of three types: individual income taxation, estate taxation, or corporate taxation. Following are data pertaining to the revenues and costs of each tax area (per tax return):

	Individual	Estate	Corporate
Revenue	$350	$1,200	$750
Variable costs	$50	$200	$150
Hours per return required of Ms. Rose	2	8	5

Fixed costs of operating Ms. Rose's office are $40,000 per year. Ms. Rose has such significant demand for her work that she must ration her time. She desires to work no more than 2,500 hours in the coming year. She can allocate her time such that she works only on one type of tax return or on any combination of the three types.

a. How should Ms. Rose allocate her time in the coming year to maximize her income?

b. Based on the optimal allocation, what is Ms. Rose's projected pretax income for the coming year?

c. What other factors should Ms. Rose consider in allocating her time?

35. *(Special order)* Quality Fencing produces 18-gauge barbed wire that is retailed through farm supply companies. Presently, the company has the capacity to produce 42,000 tons of wire per year. The firm is operating at 85 percent of annual capacity, and at this level of operations the cost per ton of wire is as follows:

Direct material	$320
Direct labor	80
Variable overhead	50
Fixed overhead	160
Total	$610

The average sales price for the output produced by the firm is $800 per ton. The firm has been approached by an Australian company about supplying 400 tons of wire for a new game preserve. The company has offered Quality Fencing $480 per ton for the order (FOB Quality Fencing's plant). No production modifications would be necessary to fulfill the order from the Australian company.

a. What costs are relevant to the decision to accept this special order?

b. What would be the dollar effect on pretax income if this order were accepted?

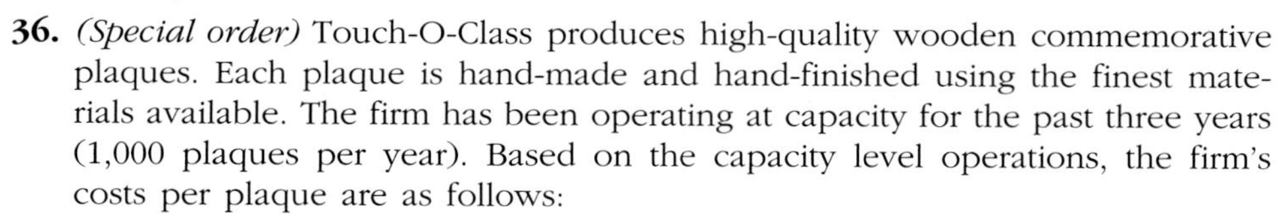

36. *(Special order)* Touch-O-Class produces high-quality wooden commemorative plaques. Each plaque is hand-made and hand-finished using the finest materials available. The firm has been operating at capacity for the past three years (1,000 plaques per year). Based on the capacity level operations, the firm's costs per plaque are as follows:

Material	$125
Direct labor	135
Variable overhead	35
Fixed overhead	60
Total cost	$355

All selling and administrative expenses incurred by the firm are fixed. The firm has generated an average selling price of $550 for its plaques.

Recently, a large corporation approached Connie Kwiken, the president of Touch-O-Class, about supplying the corporation with three special plaques commemorating the retirement of three high-level executives. These plaques would be approximately two times as large as the typical plaque the company now makes. Ms. Kwiken has estimated that the following per-unit costs would be incurred to make the three plaques:

Material	$425
Direct labor	465
Variable overhead	80
Total direct costs	$970

To accept the special order, the firm would have to sacrifice production of 25 regular units.

a. Identify all of the relevant costs that Ms. Kwiken should consider in deciding whether she will accept the special order.

b. Assume the large corporation offers a total of $3,400 for the three plaques. How would Touch-O-Class' pretax income be affected by the acceptance of this offer?

37. *(Sales mix)*

India's domestic airlines have battled antiquated airports, high fuel prices and government rules that force them to fly unprofitable routes.

In 1999, they were wounding one another with a price war.

Hints of the looming dogfight emerged even before the start of India's traditionally slack June-to-September travel season. Sahara Airlines, the smallest of three major domestic carriers, slashed rupee fares between 10% and 20% on some major routes in March.

At first, larger competitors Jet Airways and Indian Airlines were unruffled. But they followed suit in June, cutting fares and unveiling incentives to attract travelers, including hotel discounts and the chance to win trips abroad. Air India, the state-owned international carrier, joined the fray, with bargain fares on some domestic routes that made flying cheaper than taking the train.

http://www.saharaairline.com
http://www.indian-airlines.nic.in
http://www.airindia.com/
http://www.jetairways.com/homeie.htm

SOURCE: Adapted from Rasul Bailay, "Air-Fare War in India Lowers Sky-High Prices—Nation's Domestic Carriers Fight to Lure Travelers Away From Busy Trains," *The Wall Street Journal* (August 3, 1999), p. B11D.

a. Change in pricing is only one tool companies may wield to change the volume of their sales. Discuss why airlines tend to use this tool more so than other tools.

b. Why, in the airline industry as well as other industries, is it necessary to carefully consider the response of competitors before using price changes to stimulate demand for services?

c. How is the circumstance with the Indian air carriers similar to a special pricing decision?

38. *(Sales mix)* Wild Hound provides two types of services to dog owners: grooming and training. All company personnel can perform either service equally well. To expand sales and market share, the Wild Hound's manager, Jim Dachshund, relies heavily on radio and billboard advertising. For 2001, advertising funding is expected to be very limited. Information on projected operations for 2001 follows:

	Grooming	Training
Revenue per billable hour	$30	$50
Variable cost of labor	$10	$20
Material costs per billable hour	$2	$4
Allocated fixed costs per year	$200,000	$180,000
Projected billable hours for 2001	20,000	16,000

a. What is Wild Hound's projected pretax profit or (loss) for 2001?

b. If $1 spent on advertising could increase either grooming revenue by $20 or training revenue by $20, on which service should the advertising dollar be spent?

c. If $1 spent on advertising could increase grooming billable time by one hour or training billable time by one hour, on which service should the advertising dollar be spent?

39. *(Sales mix)* One of the products produced and sold by Industrial Supply Co. is a 90-quart cold drink cooler. The company's projections for this product for 2002 follow:

Sales price per unit	$36
Variable production costs	$21
Variable selling costs	$4
Fixed production costs	$225,000
Fixed selling & administration costs	$75,000
Projected volume	90,000 units

a. Compute the projected pretax profit to be earned on the cooler during 2002.

b. Corporate management estimates that unit volume could be increased by 20 percent if the sales price were decreased by 10 percent. How would such a change affect the profit level projected in part (a)?

c. Rather than cutting the sales price, management is considering holding the sales price at the projected level and increasing advertising by $200,000. Such a change would increase volume by 25 percent. How would the level of profit under this alternative compare to the profit projected in part (a)?

40. *(Product line)* Online Toy Co.'s operations are separated into two geographical divisions: United States and Mexico. The operating results of each division for 2001 are shown below:

	United States	Mexico	Total
Sales	$ 7,200,000	$ 3,600,000	$10,800,000
Variable costs	(4,740,000)	(2,088,000)	(6,828,000)
Contribution margin	$ 2,460,000	$ 1,512,000	$ 3,972,000
Fixed costs:			
Direct	(900,000)	(480,000)	(1,380,000)
Segment margin	$ 1,560,000	$ 1,032,000	$ 2,592,000
Fixed costs:			
Corporate	(1,800,000)	(900,000)	(2,700,000)
Operating income (loss)	$ (240,000)	$ 132,000	$ (108,000)

Corporate fixed costs are allocated to the divisions based on relative sales. Assume that all direct fixed costs of a division could be avoided if the division were eliminated. Because the U.S. Division is operating at a loss, the president is considering eliminating it.

a. If the U.S. Division had been eliminated at the beginning of the year, what would pretax income have been for Online Toy Co.?

b. Recast the income statements into a more meaningful format than the one given. Why would total corporate operating results go from a $108,000 loss to the results determined in part (a)?

41. *(Product line)* Johnson Metal Products produces three products: wire, tubing, and sheet metal. The company is currently contemplating the elimination of the tubing product line because it is showing a pretax loss. An annual income statement follows:

JOHNSON METAL PRODUCTS
Income Statement by Product Line
For the Year Ended July 31, 2001
(in thousands)

	Wire	Tubing	Sheet Metal	Total
Sales	$ 2,200	$ 1,600	$ 1,800	$ 5,600
Cost of sales	(1,400)	(1,000)	(1,080)	(3,480)
Gross margin	$ 800	$ 600	$ 720	$ 2,120
Avoidable fixed and variable costs	$ 630	$ 725	$ 520	$ 1,875
Allocated fixed costs	90	80	105	275
Total fixed costs	$ 720	$ 805	$ 625	$ 2,150
Operating profit	$ 80	$ (205)	$ 95	$ (30)

a. Should corporate management drop the tubing product line? Support your answer with appropriate schedules.

b. How would the pretax profit of the company be affected by the decision?

42. *(Appendix)* The contribution margins for three different products are $9.50, $5.00, and $1.50. State the objective function in equation form to maximize the contribution margin.

43. *(Appendix)* The variable costs for four different products are $0.65, $0.93, $1.39, and $0.72. State the objective function in equation form to minimize the variable costs.

44. *(Appendix)* Carolina Textiles makes three items: pants, shorts and shirts. The contribution margins are $3.25, $2.05, and $2.60 per unit, respectively. The manager must decide what mix of clothes to make. He has 800 labor hours and 4,000 yards of material available. Additional information for labor and material requirements is given here:

	Sewing Time	Fabric Needed
Pants	2.0 hours	3.0 yards
Shorts	1.5 hours	1.0 yards
Shirts	2.5 hours	1.5 yards

Write the objective function and constraints for the clothes manufacturer.

45. *(Appendix)* Janet Terwilliger is a college student and has set a budget of $120 per month for food. She wants to get a certain level of nutritional benefits from the food she has selected to buy. The following table lists the types of food she may buy, along with the nutritional information per serving of that food.

	Carbohydrates	Protein	Potassium	Calories	Cost
Pizza	38 g.	10 g.	-0-	500	$3.99
Tuna	1 g.	13 g.	-0-	60	1.29
Cereal	35 g.	7 g.	120 mg.	190	0.93
Macaroni & cheese	23 g.	3 g.	110 mg.	110	2.12
Spaghetti	42 g.	8 g.	100 mg.	210	3.42
Recommended daily allowance	50 g.	10 g.	100 mg.	2,000	

Write the objective function and constraints to minimize the cost and yet meet the recommended daily nutritional allowances.

PROBLEMS

46. *(Asset replacement)* The manager of the Plastics Fabrication Division of Gulf Chemical Corp., Kathy Johnson, has heard about a new extruding machine that could replace one of her existing machines. The manufacturer has suggested to Ms. Johnson that the new machine would save $90,000 per year in the costs of operations. Ms. Johnson's controller compiled additional information as follows:

OLD MACHINE	
Original cost	$375,000
Present book value	$250,000
Annual cash operating costs	$250,000
Market value now	$50,000
Market value in 5 years	$0
Remaining useful life	5 years

NEW MACHINE	
Cost	$450,000
Annual cash operating costs	$150,000
Market value in 5 years	$0
Useful life	5 years

a. Based on financial considerations alone, should Ms. Johnson purchase the new machine? Show computations to support your answer.

b. What qualitative factors should Ms. Johnson consider before making a decision about purchasing the new machine?

47. *(Asset replacement)* Sandhills Energy Company provides electrical services to several rural Nebraska counties. The company's efficiency has been greatly affected by changes in technology. Most recently, the company is considering replacement of its main steam turbine. The existing turbine was put in place in the 1970s but has become obsolete. While the system's operation is very reliable, it is much less efficient than newer turbines that are computer controlled. The company has gathered financial information pertaining to the new and old technologies. The following information was presented by the controller to corporate management:

	Old Turbine	New Turbine
Original cost	$3,000,000	$2,000,000
Market value now	$400,000	$2,000,000
Remaining life	8 years	8 years
Quarterly operating costs	$120,000	$45,000
Salvage value in 8 years	$0	$0
Accumulated depreciation	$1,000,000	—

a. Identify the costs that are relevant to the company's equipment replacement decision.
b. Determine which alternative is better from a financial perspective. Provide your own computations based on relevant costs only.
c. For this part only, assume that the cost of the new technology is unknown. What is the maximum amount that Sandhills could pay for the new technology and be no worse off financially?

48. *(Outsourcing)* Clothes Solutions Inc. manufactures vinyl-clad wire storage systems. Each system requires two to six standard fasteners to attach it to structural members of closets. Historically, the company has produced the fasteners. The costs to produce a fastener (based on capacity operation of 4,000,000 units per year) are:

Direct material	$0.06
Direct labor	0.03
Variable factory overhead	0.03
Fixed factory overhead	0.06
Total	$0.18

The fixed factory overhead includes $160,000 of depreciation on equipment for which there is no alternative use and no market value. The balance of the fixed factory overhead pertains to the salary of the production supervisor. While the supervisor of fastener production has a lifetime employment contract, she has skills that could be used to displace another manager (the supervisor of floor maintenance) who draws a salary of $30,000 per year but is due to retire from the company.

Modern Fastener Systems has recently approached Clothes Solutions Inc. with an offer to supply all required fasteners at a price of $0.13 per unit. Anticipated sales demand for the coming year will require 4,000,000 fasteners.
a. Identify the costs that are relevant in this outsourcing decision.
b. What is the total annual advantage or disadvantage (in dollars) of outsourcing the fasteners rather than making them?
c. What qualitative factors should be taken into account in this decision?

49. *(Outsourcing)* Omaha Building Systems manufactures steel buildings for agricultural and commercial applications. Currently, the company is trying to decide between two alternatives regarding a major overhead door assembly for the company's buildings. The alternatives are as follows:
#1: Purchase new equipment at a cost of $5,000,000. The equipment would have a five-year life and no salvage value. Omaha Building Systems uses straight-line depreciation and allocates that amount on a per unit of production basis.
#2: Purchase the door assemblies from an outside vendor who will sell them for $240 each under a five-year contract. Following is Omaha's present cost of producing the door assemblies. The costs are based on current and normal activity of 50,000 units per year.

Direct material	$139
Direct labor	66
Variable overhead	43
Fixed overhead*	36
Total	$284

*The fixed overhead includes $7 supervision cost, $9 depreciation, and $20 general company overhead.

The new equipment would be more efficient than the old and would reduce direct labor costs and variable overhead costs by 25 percent. Supervisory costs of $350,000 would be unaffected. The new equipment would have a capacity of 75,000 units per year. Omaha could lease the space occupied by subassembly production to another firm for $114,000 per year if the company decides to buy from the outside vendor.

a. Show an analysis, including relevant unit and total costs, for each alternative. Assume 50,000 subassemblies are needed each year.
b. How would your answer differ if 60,000 subassemblies were needed?
c. How would your answer differ if 75,000 subassemblies were needed?
d. In addition to quantitative factors, what qualitative factors should be considered?

50. *(Sales mix with scarce resources)* Hartford Furniture makes three unique wood products: desks, chairs, and footstools. These products are made wholly by hand; no electric or hydraulic machinery is used in production. All products are made by skilled craftspeople who have been trained to make all three products. Because it takes about a year to train each craftsperson, labor is a fixed production constraint over the short term. For 2002, the company expects to have available 34,000 labor hours. The average hourly labor rate is $25. Data regarding the current product line follow:

	Desks	Chairs	Footstools
Selling price	$900	$680	$240
Variable costs:			
Direct material	$220	$160	$ 60
Direct labor	300	275	75
Variable factory overhead	180	120	41
Variable selling	20	15	10
Fixed costs:			
Factory	$150,000		
Selling & administrative	75,000		

The company is in the 50 percent tax bracket.

a. If the company can sell an unlimited amount of any of the products, how many of each product should it make? What pretax income will the company earn given your answer?
b. How many of each product must the company make if it has a policy of devoting no more than 50 percent of its available skilled labor capacity to any one product and at least 20 percent to every product? What pretax income will the company earn given your answer?
c. Given the nature of the three products, is it reasonable to believe that there are market constraints on the mix of products that can be sold? Explain.
d. How does the company's tax rate enter into the calculation of the optimal labor allocation.

51. *(Sales mix)* Phoenix Fashions produces silk scarves and handkerchiefs, which sell for $40 and $10, respectively. The company currently sells 100,000 units of each type with the following operating results:

SCARVES		
Sales (100,000 × $40)		$ 4,000,000
Variable costs:		
Production (100,000 × $22)	$2,200,000	
Selling (100,000 × $6)	600,000	(2,800,000)
Contribution margin		$ 1,200,000
Fixed costs:		
Production	$ 400,000	
Selling & administrative	180,000	(580,000)
Income from Scarves		$ 620,000

HANDKERCHIEFS

Sales (100,000 × $10)		$1,000,000
Variable costs:		
Production (100,000 × $5)	$ 500,000	
Selling (100,000 × $1)	100,000	(600,000)
Contribution margin		$ 400,000
Fixed costs:		
Production	$ 100,000	
Selling & administrative	80,000	(180,000)
Income from Handkerchiefs		$ 220,000

Corporate management has expressed its disappointment with the income being generated from the sales of these two products. Managers have asked for your help to analyze alternative plans that have been formulated to improve operating results.

1. Change the sales commission to 11 percent of sales price less variable production costs for each product rather than the current 5 percent of selling price. The marketing manager believes that the sales of the scarves will decline by 5,000 units, but the sales of handkerchiefs will increase by 15,000 units.
2. Increase the advertising budget for scarves by $25,000. The marketing manager believes this will increase the sales of the scarves by 19,000 units but will decrease the sales of the handkerchiefs by 9,000 units.
3. Raise the price of the handkerchiefs by $3 per unit and the scarves by $5 per unit. The marketing manager believes this will cause a decrease in the sales of the scarves by 6,000 units and a decrease in the handkerchiefs by 10,000 units.

a. Determine the effects on income of each product line and the company in total if each of the alternative plans given is put into effect.
b. What is your recommendation to the management of Phoenix Fashions?

52. *(Product line)* Festival Packing Company sells two major lines of products, fish and chicken, to grocery chains and food wholesalers. Income statements showing revenues and costs of fiscal year 2000 for each product line follow:

	Fish	Chicken
Sales	$ 4,000,000	$ 1,800,000
Less: Cost of merchandise sold	(2,400,000)	(1,300,000)
Less: Commissions to salespeople	(400,000)	(150,000)
Less: Delivery costs	(600,000)	(120,000)
Less: Depreciation on equipment	(200,000)	(100,000)
Less: Salaries of division managers	(80,000)	(75,000)
Less: Allocated corporate costs	(100,000)	(100,000)
Net income (loss)	$ 220,000	$ (45,000)

Management is concerned about profitability of chicken sales and is considering the possibility of dropping the line. Management estimates that the equipment currently used to process chickens could be rented to a competitor for $85,000 annually. If the chicken product line is dropped, allocated corporate costs will decrease from a total of $200,000 to $185,000; and all employees, including the manager of the product line, would be dismissed. The depreciation would be unaffected by the decision, but $105,000 of the delivery costs charged to the chicken line could be eliminated if the chicken product line is dropped.

a. Recast the above income statements in a format that provides more information in making this decision regarding the chicken product line.
b. What is the net advantage or disadvantage (change in total company pretax profits) of continuing sales of chicken?

c. Should the company be concerned about losing sales of fish products if it drops the chicken line? Explain.
d. How would layoffs that would occur as a consequence of dropping the chicken line potentially adversely affect the whole company?

53. *(Product line)* You have been engaged to assist the management of Quality Chair Company in resolving certain decisions. Quality has its home office in Tennessee and leases facilities in Tennessee, Georgia, and Florida, which produce a high-quality bean bag chair designed for residential use. The management of Quality has provided you with a projection of operations for fiscal 2001, the forthcoming year, as follows:

	Total	Tennessee	Georgia	Florida
Sales	$ 8,800,000	$ 4,400,000	$ 2,800,000	$ 1,600,000
Fixed costs:				
Factory	$ 2,200,000	$ 1,120,000	$ 560,000	$ 520,000
Administration	700,000	420,000	220,000	60,000
Variable costs	2,900,000	1,330,000	850,000	720,000
Allocated home office costs	1,000,000	450,000	350,000	200,000
Total	$(6,800,000)	$(3,320,000)	$(1,980,000)	$(1,500,000)
Pretax profit from operations	$ 2,000,000	$ 1,080,000	$ 820,000	$ 100,000

The sales price per unit is $50.

Due to the marginal results of operations in Florida, Quality has decided to cease operations and sell that factory's machinery and equipment by the end of 2001. Managers expect proceeds from the sale of these assets will exceed the assets' book values by enough to cover termination costs.

However, Quality would like to continue serving its customers in that area if it is economically feasible and is considering one of the following three alternatives:

1. Expand the operations of the Georgia factory by using space that is currently idle. This move would result in the following changes in that factory's operations:

	Increase over Factory's Current Operations
Sales	50%
Fixed costs:	
Factory	20%
Administration	10%

Under this proposal, variable costs would be $16 per unit sold.

2. Enter into a long-term contract with a competitor who will serve that area's customers. This competitor would pay Quality a royalty of $8 per unit based on an estimate of 30,000 units being sold.

3. Close the Florida factory and not expand the operations of the Georgia factory.

To assist the management of Quality Chair Company in determining which alternative is more economically feasible, prepare a schedule computing Quality's estimated pretax profit from total operations that would result from each of the following methods:

a. Expansion of the Georgia factory.
b. Negotiation of a long-term contract on a royalty basis.
c. Shutdown the Florida operations with no expansion at other locations.

Note: Total home office costs of $500,000 will remain the same under each situation. *(AICPA adapted)*

54. *(Comprehensive)* Eastern Glass Products has processing plants in Ohio and New Jersey. Both plants use recycled glass to produce jars that are used in food canning by a variety of food processors. The jars sell for $10 per hundred units. Budgeted revenues and costs for the year ending December 31, 2001, are:

	(In $000)		
	Ohio	**New Jersey**	**Total**
Sales	$1,100	$2,000	$3,100
Variable production costs:			
Direct material	$ 275	$ 500	$ 775
Direct labor	330	500	830
Factory overhead	220	350	570
Fixed factory overhead	350	450	800
Fixed regional promotion costs	50	50	100
Allocated home office costs	55	100	155
Total costs	$1,280	$1,950	$3,230
Operating income (loss)	$ (180)	$ 50	$ (130)

Home office costs are fixed, and are allocated to manufacturing plants on the basis of relative sales levels. Fixed regional promotional costs are discretionary advertising costs needed to obtain budgeted sales levels.

Because of the budgeted operating loss, Eastern Glass is considering the possibility of ceasing operations at its Ohio plant. If Eastern Glass ceases operations at its Ohio plant, proceeds from the sale of plant assets will exceed asset book values and exactly cover all termination costs; fixed factory overhead costs of $25,000 would not be eliminated. Eastern Glass is considering the following three alternative plans:

PLAN A: Expand Ohio's operations from its budgeted 11,000,000 units to a budgeted 17,000,000 units. It is believed that this can be accomplished by increasing Ohio's fixed regional promotional expenditures by $120,000.

PLAN B: Close the Ohio plant and expand New Jersey's operations from the current budgeted 20,000,000 units to 31,000,000 units in order to fill Ohio's budgeted production of 11,000,000 units. The Ohio region would continue to incur promotional costs in order to sell the 11,000,000 units. All sales and costs would be budgeted through the New Jersey plant.

PLAN C: Close the Ohio plant and enter into a long-term contract with a competitor to serve the Ohio region's customers. This competitor would pay Eastern Glass a royalty of $1.25 per 100 units sold. Eastern Glass would continue to incur fixed regional promotional costs to maintain sales of 11,000,000 units in the Ohio region.

a. Without considering the effects of implementing Plans A, B, and C, compute the number of units that must be produced and sold by the Ohio plant to cover its fixed factory overhead costs and fixed regional promotional costs.

b. Prepare a schedule by plant, and in total, computing Eastern Glass's budgeted contribution margin and operating income resulting from the implementation of each of the following plans:

1. Plan A.
2. Plan B.
3. Plan C.

(AICPA adapted)

CASES

55. *(Sales and profit improvement)* Sixteen Candles is a retail organization that sells upscale clothing to girls and young women in the Northeast. Each year, store managers, in consultation with their supervisors, establish financial goals and then actual performance is captured by a monthly reporting system.

One sales district of the firm, District A, contains three stores. This district has historically been a very poor performer. Consequently, its supervisor has been searching for ways to improve the performance of her three stores. For the month of May, the district supervisor has set performance goals with the managers of Stores 1 and 2. The managers will receive bonuses if certain performance measures are exceeded. The manager of Store 3 decided not to participate in the bonus scheme. Since the district supervisor is unsure what type of bonus will encourage better performance, the manager of Store 1 will receive a bonus based on sales in excess of budgeted sales of $570,000, while the manager of Store 2 will receive a bonus based on net income in excess of budgeted net income. The company's net income goal for each store is 12 percent of sales. The budgeted sales for Store 2 are $530,000.

Other pertinent data for May follow:

- At Store 1, sales were 40 percent of total District A sales while sales at Store 2 were 35 percent of total District A sales. The cost of goods sold at both stores was 42 percent of sales.
- Variable selling expenses (sales commissions) were 6 percent of sales for all stores and districts.
- Variable administrative expenses were 2.5 percent of sales for all stores and districts.
- Maintenance cost includes janitorial and repair services and is a direct cost for each store. The store manager has complete control over this outlay; however, this cost should not be below 1 percent of sales.
- Advertising is considered a direct cost for each store and is completely under the control of the store manager. Store 1 spent two-thirds of District A's total outlay for advertising, which was ten times more than Store 2 spent on advertising.
- The rental expenses at Store 1 are 40 percent of District A's total, while Store 2 incurs 30 percent of District A's total.
- District A expenses are allocated to the stores based on sales.

a. Which store, Store 1 or Store 2, would appear to be generating the most profit under the new bonus scheme?

b. Which store, Store 1 or Store 2, would appear to be generating the most revenue under the new bonus scheme?

c. Why would Store 1 have an incentive to spend so much more on advertising than Store 2?

d. Which store manager has the most incentive to spend money on regular maintenance? Explain.

e. Which bonus scheme appears to offer the most incentive to improve the profit performance of the district in the short term? Long term?

(CMA adapted)

56. *(Special order)* Hastings Group is a multiproduct company with several manufacturing plants. The Cincinnati Plant manufactures and distributes two household cleaning and polishing compounds, regular and heavy-duty, under the HouseSafe label. The forecasted operating results for the first six months of 2001, when 100,000 cases of each compound are expected to be manufactured and sold, are presented in the following statement:

HOUSESAFE COMPOUNDS—CINCINNATI PLANT
Forecasted Results of Operations
For the Six-Month Period Ending June 30, 2001

	(In $000)		
	Regular	Heavy-Duty	Total
Sales	$ 2,000	$ 3,000	$ 5,000
Cost of sales	(1,600)	(1,900)	(3,500)
Gross profit	$ 400	$ 1,100	$ 1,500
Selling and administrative expenses			
Variable	$ 400	$ 700	$ 1,100
Fixed*	240	360	600
Total selling and administrative expenses	$ (640)	$(1,060)	$(1,700)
Income (loss) before taxes	$ (240)	$ 40	$ (200)

*The fixed selling and administrative expenses are allocated between the two products on the basis of dollar sales volume on the internal reports.

The regular compound sold for $20 a case and the heavy-duty sold for $30 a case during the first six months of 2001. The manufacturing costs by case of product are presented in the following schedule.

	COST PER CASE	
	Regular	Heavy-Duty
Raw material	$ 7.00	$ 8.00
Direct labor	4.00	4.00
Variable manufacturing overhead	1.00	2.00
Fixed manufacturing overhead*	4.00	5.00
Total manufacturing cost	$16.00	$19.00
Variable selling and administrative costs	$ 4.00	$ 7.00

*Depreciation charges are 50 percent of the fixed manufacturing overhead of each line.

Each product is manufactured on a separate production line. Annual normal manufacturing capacity is 200,000 cases of each product. However, the plant is capable of producing 250,000 cases of regular compound and 350,000 cases of heavy-duty compound annually.

The schedule below reflects the consensus of top management regarding the price/volume alternatives for the HouseSafe products for the last six months of 2001. These are essentially the same alternatives management had during the first six months of 2001.

REGULAR COMPOUND		HEAVY-DUTY COMPOUND	
Alternative Prices (per case)	Sales Volume (in cases)	Alternative Prices (per case)	Sales Volume (in cases)
$18	120,000	$25	175,000
20	100,000	27	140,000
21	90,000	30	100,000
22	80,000	32	55,000
23	50,000	35	35,000

Top management believes the loss for the first six months reflects a tight profit margin caused by intense competition. Management also believes that many companies will be forced out of this market by next year and profits should improve.

a. What unit selling price should Hastings Group select for each of the HouseSafe compounds for the remaining six months of 2001? Support your answer with appropriate calculations.

b. Without prejudice to your answer for requirement (a), assume the optimum price/volume alternatives for the last six months were a selling price of $23 and volume level of 50,000 cases for the regular compound and a selling price of $35 and volume of 35,000 cases for the heavy-duty compound.

1. Should Hastings Group consider closing down its operations until 2002 in order to minimize its losses? Support your answer with appropriate calculations.
2. Identify and discuss the qualitative factors that should be considered in deciding whether the Cincinnati plant should be closed down during the last six months of 2001. *(CMA adapted)*

57. *(Special order)* Hydraulic Engineering, located in Toronto, manufactures a variety of industrial valves and pipe fittings that are sold to customers in the United States. Currently, the company is operating at 70 percent of capacity and is earning a satisfactory return on investment.

Prince Industries Ltd. of Scotland has approached management with an offer to buy 120,000 units of a pressure valve. Prince Industries manufactures a valve that is almost identical to Hydraulic Engineering's pressure valve; however, a fire in Prince Industries' valve plant has shut down its manufacturing operations. Prince needs the 120,000 valves over the next four months to meet commitments to its regular customers; the company is prepared to pay $19 each for the valves, FOB shipping point.

Hydraulic Engineering's product cost, based on current attainable standards, for the pressure valve is

Direct material	$ 5
Direct labor	6
Manufacturing overhead	9
Total cost	$20

Manufacturing overhead is applied to production at the rate of $18 per standard direct labor hour. This overhead rate is made up of the following components:

Variable factory overhead	$ 6
Fixed factory overhead—direct	8
Fixed factory overhead—allocated	4
Applied manufacturing overhead rate	$18

Additional costs incurred in connection with sales of the pressure valve include sales commissions of 5 percent and freight expense of $1 per unit. However, the company does not pay sales commissions on special orders that come directly to management.

In determining selling prices, Hydraulic Engineering adds a 40 percent markup to product cost. This provides a $28 suggested selling price for the pressure valve. The marketing department, however, has set the current selling price at $27 to maintain market share.

Production management believes that it can handle the Prince Industries order without disrupting its scheduled production. The order would, however, require additional fixed factory overhead of $12,000 per month in the form of supervision and clerical costs.

If management accepts the order, 30,000 pressure valves will be manufactured and shipped to Prince Industries each month for the next four months. Shipments will be made in weekly consignments, FOB shipping point.

a. Determine how many additional direct labor hours would be required each month to fill the Prince Industries order.

b. Prepare an incremental analysis showing the impact of accepting the Prince Industries order.

c. Calculate the minimum unit price that Hydraulic Engineering's management could accept for the Prince Industries order without reducing net income.

d. Identify the factors, other than price, that Hydraulic Engineering should consider before accepting the Prince Industries order. *(CMA adapted)*

REALITY CHECK

58. *Some evidence suggests consumers are less than thrilled with what they are purchasing. American consumers are notoriously finicky, and pleasing them has always been difficult. But the latest results of the American Customer Satisfaction Index (ACSI) show consumers barely give companies a passing grade when it comes to satisfying their expectations of quality and service.*

The ACSI is based on a quarterly survey conducted by the National Quality Research Center at the University of Michigan Business School in partnership with Arthur Andersen consultants and the American Society for Quality. The overall index declined slightly in the second quarter (1999) to 72, out of a possible score of 100, from 72.1 in the first quarter. Since 1994, when the index made its debut, it has fallen 3.4%.

This is the downside of corporate America's cost cutting drive, says Claes Fornell, director of the research center and keeper of the index. Cost cutting has boosted earnings for many companies, but may hurt profits in the long term by undermining customer relationships. "If you cut too much on the cost side," says Mr. Fornell, "customer satisfaction goes down." And that, he contends could signal problems for the economy as a whole in years to come.

http://www.bus.umich.edu/research/nqrc/index.html
http://www.arthurandersen.com/
http://www.asq.org

SOURCE: Adapted from Darren McDermott, "Customer Satisfaction: Quality, Service Barely Pass Muster with Consumer—Satisfaction Index Fell Slightly During the Second Quarter: Cost Cutting Gets Blame," *The Wall Street Journal* (August 16, 1999), p. A2.

a. Does cost cutting automatically result in quality reductions? Defend your answer.

b. How can managers be confident that they are not harming long-term survival of their organizations as they strive to manage "relevant" costs?

59. In Japan, the decision to stop production of a product or to close down a plant has different cost consequences than in the United States. One principal difference is that Japanese managers are much less likely to fire workers who are displaced by an event such as a plant closing. Japanese managers would simply try to move the displaced workers to active plants. However, this concept of permanent or lifetime employment can be awkward to manage when economic times become difficult and prudent financial management suggests that activities, including employment, be scaled back to cut costs. One Japanese company found an interesting solution:

Nissan Motor Co., in a sign that its severe slump may be worsening, took the unusual step of loaning some of its idle factory workers to a rival automaker.

Nissan assigned 250 of its production employees to work for six months at factories run by Isuzu Motors Ltd., a 37% owned affiliate of General Motors Corp.

Nissan's spokesman, Koji Okuda, called the move an attempt to deal with the company's sharp drop in auto output in Japan. Nissan's Japanese auto production had fallen 26% from a year earlier. "Demand is low," Mr. Okuda said. "We have to adjust our operations."

http://www.nissan-usa.com
http://www.isuzu.com

SOURCE: Michael Williams, "Nissan Will Loan Workers to Rival Amid Low Demand," *The Wall Street Journal* (June 24, 1994), p. A4. Permission conveyed through the Copyright Clearance Center.

a. What specific types of costs might Nissan have considered relevant in its decision to loan employees to Isuzu?

b. Why would Isuzu be interested in hiring, on a temporary basis, workers of Nissan?

c. What are the likely impacts of this arrangement on quality of the output at Isuzu? The quality of output at Nissan?

60. Carter's Computers manufactures computers and all components. The purchasing agent informed the company owner, Abraham Carter, that another company has offered to supply keyboards for Carter's computers at prices below the variable costs at which Carter can make them. Incredulous, Mr. Carter hired an industrial consultant to explain how the supplier could offer the keyboards at less than Carter's variable costs. It seems that the competitor supplier is suspected by the consultant of using many illegal aliens to work in that plant. These people are poverty stricken and will take such work at substandard wages. The purchasing agent and the plant manager feel that Carter should buy the keyboards from the competitor supplier as "no one can blame us for his hiring practices and will not even be able to show that we knew of those practices."

a. What are the ethical issues involved in this case?

b. What are the advantages and disadvantages of buying from this competitor supplier?

c. What do you think Mr. Carter should do and why?

61. *In 1987 EEOC's [Equal Opportunity Employment Commission] local field office wrote me a letter saying they had reason to believe I didn't have enough women "food servers" and "busers." No woman had complained against me. So the EEOC advertised in the local paper to tell women whose job applications we had rejected—or even women who had just thought of applying—that they could be entitled to damages. Twenty-seven women became plaintiffs in a lawsuit against me. The EEOC interviewed me for hours to find out what kind of person I was. I told them in Sicily where I came from I learned to respect women. I supplied them with hundreds of pounds of paper. I had to hire someone full time for a year just to respond to EEOC demands. I finally settled. I agreed to pay $150,000 damages and as jobs open up, to hire the women on the EEOC's list. Even if they don't know what spaghetti looks like! I have to advertise twice a year even if I have no openings, just to add possible female employees to my files. I also had to hire an EEOC-approved person to teach my staff how not to discriminate. I employ 12 food servers in these two restaurants. Gross sales, around $2 million. How much did it all cost me? Cash outlay, about $400,000.*

What the government's done to me—devastating. I wouldn't wish it on my worst enemy.

Thomas Maggiore
Phoenix, Arizona

SOURCE: Brimelow, Peter and Leslie Spencer, "When Quotas Replace Merit, Everybody Suffers," *Fortune* (February 15, 1993), pp. 80–82, ff.

a. Do you think Mr. Maggiore's cash outlay of $400,000 includes all of the costs he incurred because of the EEOC regulation? Try breaking down the various costs that he may have incurred into three categories: direct costs, indirect costs, and opportunity costs.

b. Are hiring policies based on quotas ethical? How do quota systems affect the economic viability of American firms?

c. If EEOC regulations are intended to right past wrongs, should EEOC guidelines apply differently to immigrant Americans than to second-, third-, and fourth-generation Americans. (Consider, for example, that any immigrant that falls into a protected class qualifies for all U.S. quota programs just like an American whose great-great-great-grandfather was a slave.)

d. How can quota systems have an effect on the quality of American products?

CHAPTER

13

The Master Budget

LEARNING OBJECTIVES

After completing this chapter, you should be able to answer the following questions:

1
Why is budgeting important?

2
How is strategic planning related to budgeting?

3
What is the starting point of a master budget and why?

4
How are the various schedules in a master budget prepared and how do they relate to one another?

5
Why is the cash budget so important in the master budgeting process?

6
What benefits are provided by a budget?

7
(Appendix) How does a budget manual facilitate the budgeting process?

INTRODUCING

The HON Company

http://www.honcompany.com

The HON Company, a wholly-owned subsidiary of HON INDUSTRIES Inc. and a *Fortune 1000* company, is highly regarded in the office furniture manufacturing industry. The company is recognized as America's leader in value office furniture, and the largest domestic manufacturer of middle market office furniture, offering the industry's broadest lines of office furniture in both wood and steel. A nationwide distribution network and world-class manufacturing capabilities strategically located throughout the United States provide efficient product delivery.

The company was incorporated in 1944 under the leadership of founder C. Maxwell Stanley. He believed success in business would come to a company that anchored its activities in treating customers, suppliers, workforce, and neighbors with fairness and respect. Stanley invited Clement T. Hanson, a brother-in-law and successful advertising executive, and H. Wood Miller, an industrial designer, to join him in founding a company on these principles.

The three pooled their resources to incorporate "The Home-O-Nize Co." They planned to make a revolutionary design of steel kitchen cabinets, but a postwar shortage of steel delayed operations. The firm's first product was a small index card file box that sold for kitchen use.

They initially decided to provide manufacturing services to other companies, until the steel shortage abated. As small amounts of sheet steel became available, they made white metal storage cabinets. By painting them olive green, the cabinets were ideal for office use.

Eventually, the name "Home-O-Nize" evolved into "HON." Due to rapid growth in the 1960s and 1970s, a corporate identity was needed. Thus, the Home-O-Nize name was changed to HON INDUSTRIES. HON INDUSTRIES is the corporate entity of today under which the HON Company and other sister companies operate.

The HON Company has overcome obstacles of change through use of an effective budgeting system. Managers at the HON Company communicate and coordinate operating plans through a process called continuous quarterly budgeting. The typical quarterly budget process is done in five basic steps over a six-week period: (1) Develop the sales budget. (2) Convert the sales budget to a plant production and shipping schedule. (3) Prepare cost/expense budgets. (4) Consolidate budgets and compare with strategic plan. (5) Prepare a budget package for parent company and "sell it" to executive management.

Continuous budgeting is the vehicle for ensuring both understanding and ownership by frontline workers by communicating a corporate vision, empowering employees to act on the vision, and targeting and tracking short-term wins.

SOURCES: The HON INDUSTRIES Inc. Web site, http://www.honi.com, and the HON Company Web site, http://www.honcompany.com (March 3, 2000); Ralph Drtina, Steve Hoeger, and John Schaub, "Continuous Budgeting at the HON Company," *Management Accounting* (January 1996), p. 20.

In virtually any endeavor, intelligent behavior involves visualizing the future, imagining what results one wishes to occur, and determining the activities and resources required to achieve those results. If the process is complex, the means of obtaining results should be documented. Inscribing complex plans is necessary because of the human tendency to forget and the difficulty of mentally processing many facts and relationships at the same time.

Planning is the cornerstone of effective management, and effective planning requires that managers must predict, with reasonable precision, the key variables that affect company performance and conditions. These predictions provide management with a foundation for effective problem solving, control, and resource allocation. Planning (especially in financial terms) is important when future conditions are expected to be approximately the same as current ones, but it is *critical* when conditions are expected to change.

During the strategic planning process, managers attempt to agree on company goals and objectives and how to achieve them. Typically, goals are stated as desired abstract achievements (such as "to become a market leader for a particular product"). Objectives are desired quantifiable results for a specified time (such as "to manufacture 200,000 units of a particular product with fewer than 1 percent defects next year"). Achievement of a company's desired goals and objectives requires complex activities, uses diverse resources, and necessitates formalized planning.

A plan should include qualitative narratives of goals, objectives, and means of accomplishment. However, if plans were limited to qualitative narratives, comparing actual results to expectations would only allow generalizations, and no measurement of how well the organization met its specified objectives would be possible. The process of formalizing plans and translating qualitative narratives into a documented, quantitative format is called **budgeting**. The end result of this process is a **budget**, which expresses an organization's commitment to planned activities and resource acquisition and use. Such a commitment is based on predictions, protocols, and a collective promise to accomplish the agreed-on results.

budgeting
budget

This chapter covers the budgeting process and preparation of the master budget. Although budgeting is important for all organizations, the process becomes exceedingly complex in entities that have significant pools of funds and resources.

THE BUDGETING PROCESS

1

Why is budgeting important?

Budgeting is an important part of an organization's entire planning process. As with other planning activities, budgeting helps provide a focused direction or a path chosen from many alternatives. Management generally indicates the direction chosen through some accounting measure of financial performance, such as net income, earnings per share, or sales level expressed in dollars or units. Such accounting-based measures provide specific quantitative criteria against which future performance (also recorded in accounting terms) can be compared. Thus, a budget is a type of standard, allowing variances to be computed.

Budgets are the *financial* culmination of predictions and assumptions about achieving not only financial but also nonfinancial goals and objectives. Nonfinancial performance goals and objectives may include throughput, customer satisfaction, defect minimization, and on-time deliveries. Budgets can help identify potential problems in achieving specified organizational goals and objectives. By quantifying potential difficulties and making them visible, budgets can help stimulate managers to think of ways to overcome those difficulties before they are realized. Cross-functional teams are often used to balance the various agendas of functional management throughout the firm.

A well-prepared budget can also be an effective device to communicate objectives, constraints, and expectations to all organizational personnel. Such communication promotes understanding of what is to be accomplished, how those accomplishments are to be achieved, and the manner in which resources are to be allocated. Determination of resource allocations is made, in part, from a process of obtaining information, justifying requests, and negotiating compromises.

http://www.hackettbenchmarking.com
http://www.allstate.com
http://www.fujitsu.com
http://www.nationwidefinancial.com
http://www.owenscorning.com
http://www.sprint.com
http://www.texaco.com

Participation in the budgeting process helps to produce a spirit of cooperation, motivate employees, and instill a feeling of teamwork. Employee participation is needed to effectively integrate necessary information from various sources as well as to obtain individual managerial commitment to the resulting budget. At the same time, the greater the degree of participation by all personnel affected in the budgeting process, the greater the time and cost involved. Traditionally, to say that a company uses a large degree of participation has implied that budgets have been built from the bottom of the organization upward. As the accompanying News Note indicates, however, some larger companies are now using technology and top-down budgets to bring about significant advantages while preserving intense ongoing communications with employees at all levels.

The budget sets the resource constraints under which managers must operate for the upcoming budget period. Thus, the budget becomes the basis for controlling activities and resource usage. Most managers in U.S. companies make periodic

GENERAL BUSINESS  NEWS NOTE

Replacing a Whim and a Prayer with Relevant Data

A company cannot grow effectively without a well-conceived strategy and a supporting budget, yet many companies invest inordinate time, energy and financial resources to develop such plans only to change or even ignore them. Christine Gattenio, CPA and vice-president at Hackett Benchmarking Solutions, oversees corporate benchmarking surveys and says companies put an exhaustive amount of time into these exercises, "with very little return."

A few Fortune 1000 companies—including Allstate, Fujitsu, Nationwide Financial Services, Owens Corning, Sprint and Texaco—recognize they've been guilty of inadequate planning and budgeting. To improve those processes, they're trading their usual bottom-up planning and multi-iterative budgeting processes for top-down strategic plans budgeted by department managers. And they are compensating the managers for achieving measurable results.

The cost of such an overhaul is high, not only in time and effort but also in dollars. For large companies, the investment can run as much as $40 million. That price tag includes consulting fees, in-house staff time and the purchase and customizing of state-of-the-art software to link disparate corporate data across the enterprise—essential for effective planning and budgeting.

Planning and budgeting reengineering requires patience, intensive ongoing communication with employees, investment in new data-gathering software tools and, most important, the willingness of a company's finance group to evolve. Data collecting and disseminating—the traditional functions of a finance group—will be subsumed, with finance personnel morphing into analysts, strategists and advocates.

Consultants say the improved decision-making capabilities wrought by successful reengineering justify the high price tag. "Companies can double their initial return on investment within a few years, thanks to better decision making, reduced planning cycles, a more motivated, collaborative workforce and a sharper competitive edge," says Lawrence Serven, a principal at the Buttonwood Group, a Stamford, Connecticut, research and consulting firm. Serven believes that planning and budgeting reengineering is a trend that will build in momentum in the next 10 years. He estimates that a quarter of the Fortune 1000 are currently starting on such a course.

SOURCE: Russ Banham, "Better Budgets," *Journal of Accountancy* (February 2000), p. 37ff. Reprinted with permission from the *Journal of Accountancy*.

budget-to-actual comparisons that allow them to determine how well they are doing, assess variance causes, and implement rational and realistic changes that can, among other benefits, create greater budgetary conformity.

Although budgets are typically expressed in financial terms, they must begin with nonquantitative factors. The budgeting and planning processes are concerned with all organizational resources—raw material, inventory, supplies, personnel, and facilities—and can be viewed from a long-term or a short-term perspective.

2

How is strategic planning related to budgeting?

Managers who plan on a long-range basis (5 to 10 years) are engaged in strategic planning. Top-level management performs this process, often with the assistance of several key staff members. The result is a statement of long-range organizational goals and the strategies and policies that will help achieve those goals. Strategic planning is not concerned with day-to-day operations, although the strategic plan is the foundation on which short-term planning is based.

Managers engaging in strategic planning should identify key variables, believed to be the direct causes of the achievement or nonachievement of organizational goals and objectives. Key variables can be internal (under the control of management) or external (normally noncontrollable by management). Approximately 48 percent of planning time currently is spent analyzing external factors. In a study done by The Futures Group, the critical external factors as viewed by domestic respondents to the study are as follows:

- competitor actions,
- U.S. market conditions,

- political/regulatory climate (U.S.),
- emerging technology issues,
- consumer trends and attitudes,
- international market conditions,
- demographics, and
- political/regulatory climate (international).[1]

Effective strategic planning requires that managers build plans and budgets that blend and harmonize external considerations and influences with the firm's internal factors. Budgeting, in the context of Robert Kaplan's and David Norton's writings on the use of the balanced scorecard (BSC) in the accompanying News Note. (A BSC discussion is included in Chapter 20.)

After identifying key variables, management should gather information related to them. Much of this information is historical and qualitative and provides a useful starting point for tactical planning activities. Tactical planning determines the specific objectives and means by which strategic plans will be achieved. Some tactical

NEWS NOTE  GENERAL BUSINESS

The Balanced Scorecard and Drill-Down Software

Kaplan and Norton's balanced scorecard appeared to be a particular threat to the old style of budgeting and controlling. Kaplan and Norton's superb technique has taken the business world by storm. The idea is that companies should plan and monitor not just bottom-line profit or EPS figures, but the overall progress of the company in a balanced way. The company should, of course, measure financial performance, but also customer satisfaction, innovation and learning, and key performance indicators (KPIs) such as cycle time, yield, etc. Thus the company as a whole can get a favorable score when doing well on both short-term performance and indicators of future success. Prior to the balanced scorecard there was a belief that pressures to make short-term profits often obscured the need for continual internal improvement, new product development and the customer delight that would lead to repeat buys. Behavioral theorists certainly see merit in the balanced scorecard and Kaplan and others have developed the technique so that subsidiary objectives can be set down to operational level, helping employees understand how their contribution fits in with overall corporate strategy and success.

Software developed for the balanced scorecard includes Sapling's NetScore, where one can use the "Strategic Traceability Chain" to ensure that objectives with measurable targets or KPIs are set, made up of many subtargets. The control pyramid is thus strategic at the top and yet detailed or operational for supervisors or employees further down the organization. If supervisors and junior executives have appropriate targets and the information is fed correctly into the system the strategic performance can be easily monitored by senior management. Based on Kaplan's suggested image, the software's output resembles car or aircraft dials which show if the performance is empty/weak or all the way through to full/excellent. If one realizes that a measure such as customer satisfaction is below the halfway or target mark, one can click on the measure to drill-down and see what makes up the customer satisfaction score. It may be that there are four submeasures, of which one, say the company's percentage of sales returns, is the problem. Similarly, even if there are numerous levels to be drilled, the senior executive can get to the source of what the issue is, which if left unchecked could have had a strategic impact on the company's future.

The attraction of these types of systems to the CEO and senior executive is clear. Senior management can think lofty strategic thoughts while simply keeping an eye on the balanced scorecard dials; only getting involved in the exceptional issues which (with excellent graphics) "jump out" and call to him or her for action. Despite exaggerated hype the benefits of the balanced scorecard with its key performance indicators (KPI's) across various aspects of the business appears to be a winner.

Despite startling headings in some articles claiming that the budget was dead, a funeral would have been embarrassingly premature. Detailed reading of these cases indicate that where companies now had "no budget," they instead had a plan, a rolling forecast, or some other yardstick which could be called, er—well, a budget.

SOURCE: Paul Prendergast, "Budgets Hit Back," *Management Accounting* (January 2000), p. 15. Reprinted by permission of the Chartered Institute of Management Accountants, UK.

[1] Staff, "Extrovert or Introvert," *Public Utilities Fortnightly* (November 1, 1998), pp. 70ff.

plans, such as corporate policy statements, exist for the long term and address repetitive situations. Most tactical plans, however, are short term (1 to 18 months); they are considered "single-use" plans and have been developed to address a given set of circumstances or to cover a specific period of time.

The annual budget is an example of a single-use tactical plan. Although a budget is typically prepared for a one-year period, shorter period (quarterly and monthly) plans should also be included for the budget to work effectively. A well-prepared budget translates a company's strategic and tactical plans into usable guides for company activities. Exhibit 13–1 illustrates the relationships among strategic planning, tactical planning, and budgeting.

Both strategic and tactical planning require that the latest information regarding the economy, environment, technological developments, and available resources be incorporated into the setting of goals and objectives. This information is used to adjust the previously gathered historical information for any changes in the key variables for the planning period. The planning process also demands that, as activity takes place and plans are implemented, a monitoring system be in place to provide feedback so that the control function can be operationalized.

Management reviews the budget prior to approving and implementing it to determine whether the forecasted results are acceptable. The budget may indicate that results expected from the planned activities do not achieve the desired objectives. In this case, planned activities are reconsidered and revised so that they more effectively achieve the desired outcomes expressed during the tactical planning stage.

After a budget is accepted, it is implemented and considered a standard against which performance can be measured. Managers operating under budget guidelines should be provided copies of all appropriate budgets. These managers should also be informed that their performance will be evaluated by comparing actual results to budgeted amounts. Feedback should generally be made by budget category for specific times, such as one month.

EXHIBIT 13–1

Relationships Among Planning Processes

Who?	What?	How?	Why?
Top management	Strategic planning	Statement of organizational mission, goals, and strategies; long range (5–10 years)	Establish a long-range vision of the organization and provide a sense of unity of and commitment to specified purposes
Top management and mid-management	Tactical planning	Statement of organizational plans; short range (1–18 months)	Provide direction for achievement of strategic plans; state strategic plans in terms on which managers can act; furnish a basis against which results can be measured
Top management, mid-management, and operational management	Budgeting	Quantitative and monetary statements that coordinate company activities for a year or less	Allocate resources effectively and efficiently; indicate a commitment to objectives; provide a monetary control device

Once the budget is implemented, the control phase begins, which includes making actual-to-budget comparisons, determining variances, investigating variance causes, taking necessary corrective action, and providing feedback to operating managers. Feedback, both positive and negative, is essential to the control process, and, to be useful, must be provided in a timely manner.

The preceding discussion details a budgeting process, but like many other business practices, budgeting may be unique to individual countries. For example, the lengthy and highly specific budgeting process used by many U.S. companies differs dramatically from that used by many Japanese companies. Japanese companies view the budget more as a device to help focus on achieving group and firm-level targets than as a control device by which to gauge individual performance.

Regardless of the budgeting process, the result is what is known as a master budget. This budget is actually a comprehensive set of budgets, budgetary schedules, and pro forma organizational financial statements.

THE MASTER BUDGET

operating budget

financial budget

The master budget is composed of both operating and financial budgets as shown in Exhibit 13–2. An **operating budget** is expressed in both units and dollars. When an operating budget relates to revenues, the units presented are expected to be sold, and the dollars reflect selling prices. In contrast, when an operating budget relates to cost, the input units presented are expected to be either transformed into output units or consumed, and the dollars reflect costs.

Monetary details from the operating budgets are aggregated to prepare **financial budgets**, which indicate the funds to be generated or consumed during the budget period. Financial budgets include cash and capital budgets as well as projected or pro forma financial statements. These budgets are the ultimate focal points for top management.

The master budget is prepared for a specific period and is static in the sense that it is based on a single level of output demand.[2] Expressing the budget on a

EXHIBIT 13–2

Components of a Master Budget

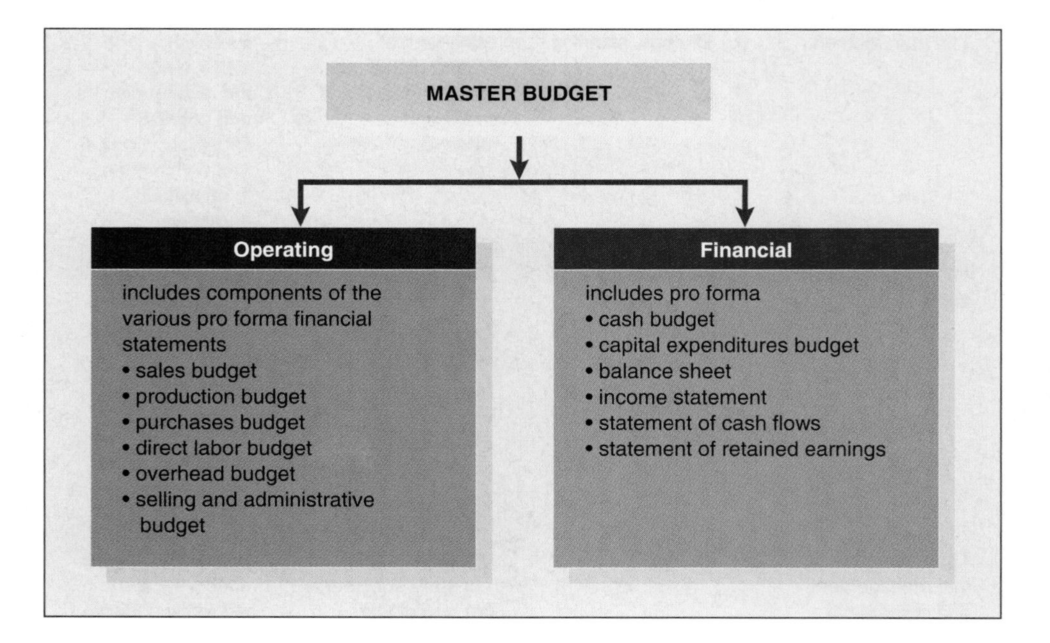

[2] Companies may engage in contingency planning, providing for multiple budgeting paths. For example, a company may construct three budgets, respectively, for a high level of activity, an expected level of activity, and a low level of activity. If actual activity turns out to be either higher or lower than expected, management has a budget ready.

single output level is necessary to facilitate the many time-consuming financial arrangements that must be made before beginning operations for the budget period. Such arrangements include making certain that an adequate number of personnel are hired, needed production and/or storage space is available, and suppliers, prices, delivery schedules, and quality of resources are confirmed.

3

What is the starting point of a master budget and why?

The sales demand level selected for use in the master budget preparation affects all other organizational components. Because of the budgetary interrelationships illustrated in Exhibit 13–3, all departmental components must interact in a coordinated manner. A budget developed by one department is often an essential ingredient in developing another department's budget.

The budgetary process shown in Exhibit 13–3 presents the interaction of the various functional areas of a manufacturing organization involved with preparing a master budget. The process begins with the Sales Department's estimates of the types, quantities, and timing of demand for the company's products. The budget is typically prepared for a year and then subdivided into quarterly and monthly periods.

A production manager combines sales estimates with additional information from Purchasing, Personnel, Operations, and Capital Facilities; the combined information allows the production manager to specify the types, quantities, and timing of products to be manufactured. The accounts receivable area uses sales estimates, in conjunction with estimated collection patterns, to determine the amounts and timing of cash receipts.

For the treasurer to manage the organization's flow of funds properly, cash receipts and cash disbursements information must be matched from all areas so that cash is available when needed and in the quantity needed.

EXHIBIT 13–3

The Budgetary Process in a Manufacturing Organization

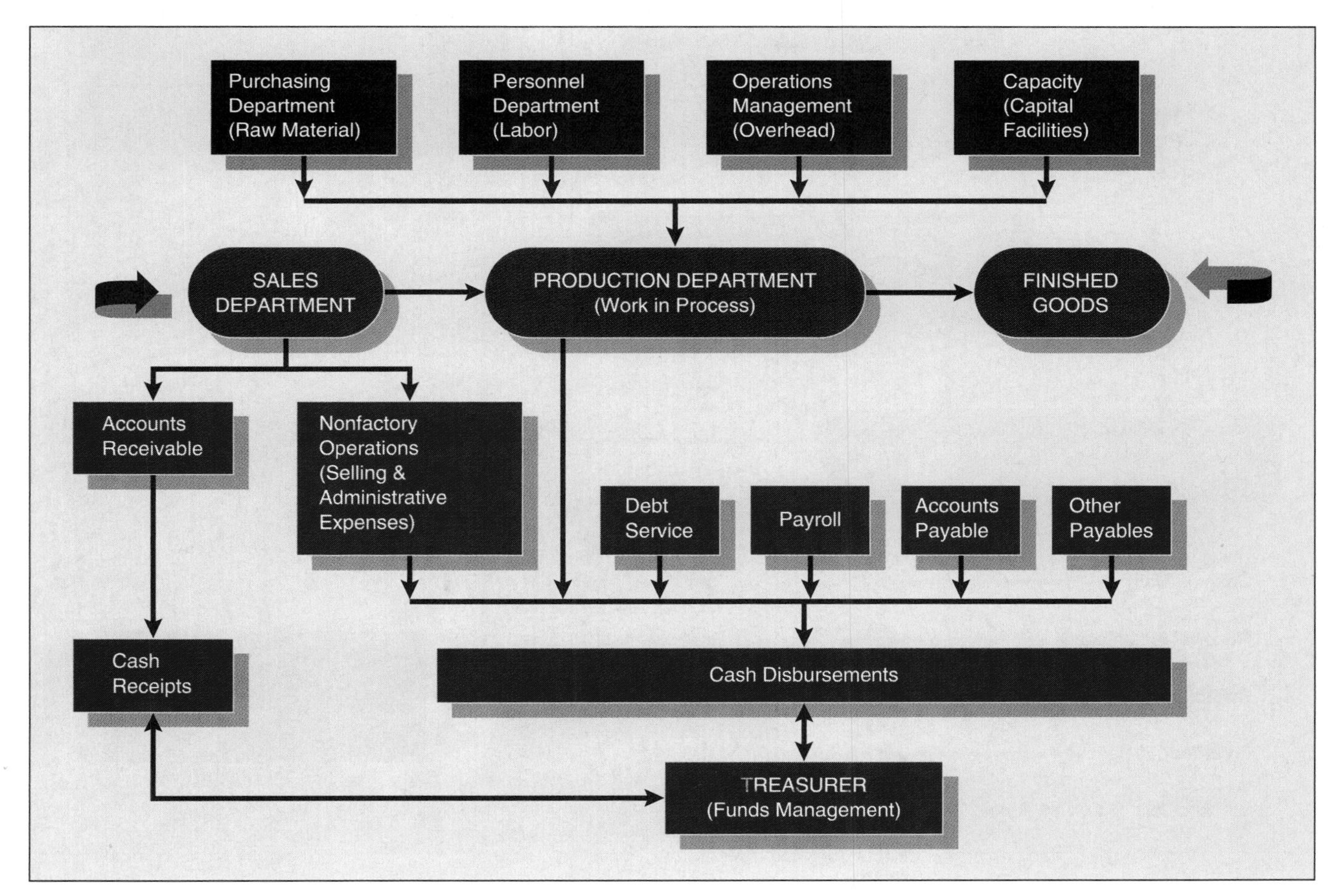

Note that some information must flow back into a department from which it began. For example, the Sales Department must receive finished goods information to know whether goods are in stock (or can be produced) before selling products. In addition, the treasurer must *receive* continual information on cash receipts and disbursements as well as *provide* information to various organizational units on funds availability so that proper funds management can be maintained.

If top management encourages participation by lower-level managers in the budgeting process, each department either prepares its own budget or provides information for inclusion in a budget. Exhibit 13–4 presents an overview of the component budget preparation sequence of the master budget, indicates which departments are responsible for which budget's preparation, and illustrates how the budgets interface with one another.

EXHIBIT 13-4

The Master Budget: An Overview

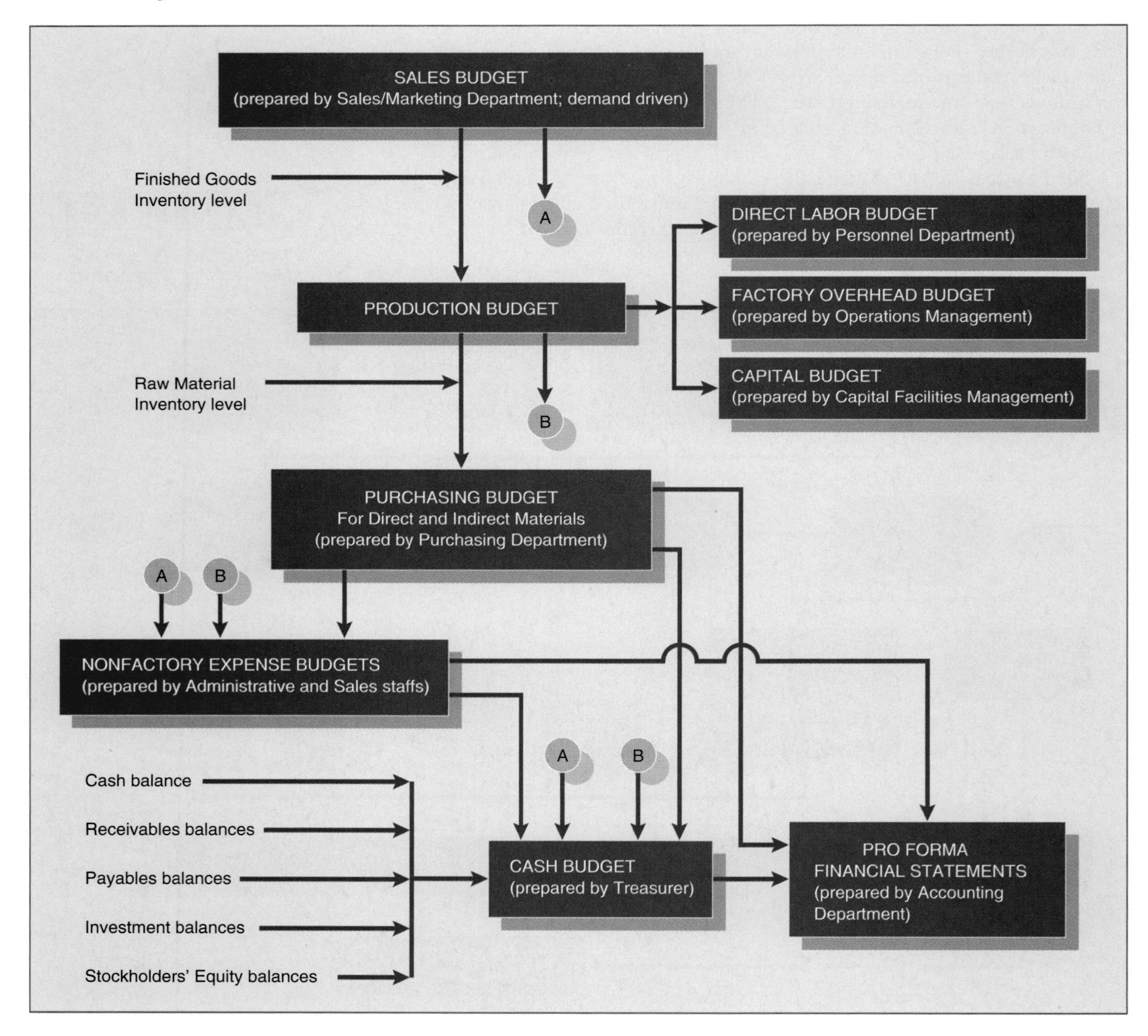

The master budget begins with a sales budget based on expected demand. Production and cash flows are planned using the chosen sales level, and ultimately pro forma financial statements are prepared. The information flow is visible from Exhibit 13–4, but the quantitative and monetary implications are not. Therefore, the next section of the chapter is devoted to the preparation of a master budget.

THE MASTER BUDGET ILLUSTRATED

4

How are the various schedules in a master budget prepared and how do they relate to one another?

This illustration uses information from Better Brackets, a small company that has been in business for several years. The company, which produces a bracket used to attach legs to tables and chairs, is preparing its 2001 budget and has estimated total annual sales at 900,000 brackets. Although annual sales would be detailed on a monthly basis, the Better Brackets illustration focuses only on the budgets for the first quarter of 2001. The process of developing the master budget is the same regardless of whether the time frame is one year or one quarter.

The December 31, 2000, balance sheet presented in Exhibit 13–5 provides account balances needed to begin preparation of the master budget. The December 31, 2000, balances are really estimates rather than actual figures because the budget process for 2001 must begin significantly before December 31, 2000. The company's budgetary time schedule depends on many factors, including its size and degree of forecasting sophistication. Assume that Better Brackets begins its budgeting process in November 2000, when the 2001 sales forecast is received by management or the budget committee.

Sales Budget

The sales budget is prepared in both units and sales dollars. The selling price set for 2001 is $0.50 per bracket, regardless of sales territory or customer. Monthly demand and its related revenue impact for the first four months of 2001 are shown in Exhibit 13–6. Dollar sales figures are computed by multiplying sales quantities by product selling prices. April information is presented because some elements of the March budget require the following month's information.

EXHIBIT 13-5

Balance Sheet—December 31, 2000

ASSETS			LIABILITIES AND STOCKHOLDERS' EQUITY		
Current Assets			Current Liabilities		
Cash		$ 6,000	Accounts Payable		$ 4,330
Accounts Receivable	$ 24,000		Dividends Payable (payment		
Less Allowance for Uncollectibles	(432)	23,568	scheduled for March 31)		25,000
			Total Current Liabilities		$ 29,330
Inventories					
Raw Material (31,800 ounces)	$ 636				
Finished Goods (4,000 units)	748	1,384			
Total Current Assets		$ 30,952			
Plant Assets			Stockholders' Equity		
Property, Plant, and Equipment	$370,000		Common Stock	$180,000	
Less Accumulated Depreciation	(90,000)	280,000	Retained Earnings	101,622	
			Total Stockholders' Equity		281,622
			Total Liabilities and		
Total Assets		$310,952	Stockholders' Equity		$310,952

EXHIBIT 13–6

Sales Budget for the Three Months and Quarter Ending March 31, 2001

	January	February	March	Total for Quarter	April*
Sales in units	80,000	70,000	75,000	225,000	64,000
Sales in dollars	$40,000	$35,000	$37,500	$112,500	$32,000

*Information for April is needed for subsequent computations.

Production Budget

The production budget follows from the sales budget and uses information regarding the type, quantity, and timing of units to be sold. Sales information is used in conjunction with beginning and ending inventory information so that managers can schedule necessary production. The following formula provides the computation for units to be produced:

Number of units to be sold (from sales budget)	XXX
+ Number of units desired in ending inventory	XXX
= Total units needed during period	XXX
− Number of units in beginning inventory	(XXX)
= Units to be produced	XXX

The number of units desired in ending inventory is determined and specified by company management. Desired ending inventory balance is generally a function of the quantity and timing of demand in the upcoming period as related to the firm's capacity and speed to produce particular units. Frequently, management stipulates that ending inventory be equal to a given percentage of the next period's projected sales. Other alternatives include a constant amount of inventory, a buildup of inventory for future high-demand periods, or near-zero inventory under a just-in-time system. The decision about ending inventory levels results from the consideration of whether a firm wants to have constant production with varying inventory levels or variable production with constant inventory levels.

Managers should consider the high costs of stockpiling inventory before making a decision about how much inventory to keep on hand. Demand for Better Brackets' products is relatively constant, but the company's most active sales season is in the fall. The company's ending finished inventory policy for December through March is that FG inventory equal 5 percent of the next month's sales. Considering this policy and using the sales information from Exhibit 13–6, the production budget shown in Exhibit 13–7 is prepared.

The January beginning inventory balance is 4,000 units that were on hand at December 31, 2000, which represents 5 percent of January's estimated sales of 80,000 units. Desired March ending inventory is 5 percent of April sales of 64,000 (given in Exhibit 13–6). Better Brackets does not have any work in process in-

EXHIBIT 13–7

Production Budget for the Three Months and Quarter Ending March 31, 2001

	January	February	March	Total
Sales in units (from Exhibit 13–6)	80,000	70,000	75,000	225,000
+ Desired ending inventory	3,500	3,750	3,200	3,200
= Total needed	83,500	73,750	78,200	228,200
− Beginning inventory	(4,000)	(3,500)	(3,750)	(4,000)
= Units to be produced	79,500	70,250	74,450	224,200

ventory because all units placed into production are assumed to be fully completed each period.[3]

Peter Pallans, director and production manager for Forbes, Inc., in New York, discusses developing a magazine production budget in the accompanying News Note.

Purchases Budget

Direct material is essential to production and must be purchased each period in sufficient quantities to meet production needs. In addition, the quantities of direct material purchased must be in conformity with the company's desired ending inventory policies.

Better Brackets' management ties its policy for ending inventories of direct material to its production needs for the following month. Because of occasional difficulty in obtaining the quality of materials needed, Better Brackets' ending inventories

GENERAL BUSINESS  NEWS NOTE

Primer on Production Budgets

What will it cost? How much will we spend? Can we do it cheaper? Production people are not accountants by trade, but a major part of their function is to understand and communicate the financial ramifications of producing a magazine. As publishers create new print products, advertising vehicles and promotions, production costs are becoming increasingly important for all magazine companies.

The production director's basic tool for providing financial data is the manufacturing budget. With a good working budget, the director can let management know what it will need to spend in a specified time frame. Because production represents such a large part of a magazine's overall budget, it's a major factor in how management makes fiscal decisions about the rest of the company's operations. Stay educated about suppliers' needs.

But a budget is really only a guess as to what will be spent. Annual manufacturing budgets are prepared long before suppliers announce any price increases. And departments such as ad sales and circulation must tell production what they plan to do (number of ad pages, special projects, distribution projections) in the year ahead, and keep production informed about any changes as the year progresses. Knowledge about future trends and past production spending is key. By staying educated about suppliers' market factors, internal needs and final costs, you can keep management abreast of how to spend wisely.

The manufacturing budget is based on three main components: printing and prepress, paper and distribution. Since printing cost increases are spelled out in the contract, you should be able to avoid getting hit with costs beyond your budget. These increases are frequently tied to statistics such as the consumer price index or the inflation rate, which are forecast fairly well.

Then you need accurate projections of what the sales and circulation departments want to produce. Now, I personally don't use all their proposed numbers exactly, because some projections may be inflated or deflated. Be sure to take a historical perspective. If a department gives me information that forecasts something different for a particular month, I know I should still budget for what we've produced in the past. But sales and circulation may not even know what they will end up needing. If sales sells 20 more ads than were budgeted for, the cost information originally communicated to management may be misleading. The only way to check accuracy is to compare the estimated to the actual costs on a regular basis, say monthly or quarterly.

SOURCE: Peter I. Pallans, "Primer on Production Budgets," *The Magazine for Magazine Management* (August 1999), pp. 62ff.

[3] Most manufacturing entities do not produce only whole units during the period. Normally, partially completed beginning and ending work in process inventories will exist. These inventories create the need to use equivalent units of production when computing the production budget.

of direct material from December through March equal 10 percent of the quantities needed for the following month's production.

Companies may have different policies for the direct material associated with different products or for different seasons of the year. For example, a company may maintain only a minimal ending inventory of a direct material that is consistently available in the quantity and quality desired. Alternatively, if a material is difficult to obtain at certain times of the year (such as certain components for spice preparation), a company may stockpile that material for use in future periods.

The purchases budget is first stated in whole units of finished products and then converted to direct material component requirements and dollar amounts. Production of a Better Brackets unit requires only one direct material: four ounces of metal. Material cost has been estimated by the purchasing agent as $0.02 per ounce of metal. Exhibit 13–8 shows Better Brackets' purchases cost for each month of the first quarter of 2001. Note that beginning and ending inventory quantities are expressed first in terms of brackets and then converted to the appropriate quantity measure (ounces of metal). The total budgeted cost of direct material purchases for the quarter is $17,816 ($6,286 + $5,654 + $5,876).

Personnel Budget

Given expected production, the Engineering and Personnel Departments can work together to determine the necessary labor requirements for the factory, sales force, and office staff. Labor requirements are stated in total number of people, specific number of types of people (skilled laborers, salespeople, clerical personnel, and so forth), and production hours needed for factory employees. Labor costs are computed from items such as union labor contracts, minimum wage laws, fringe benefit costs, payroll taxes, and bonus arrangements. The various personnel amounts will be shown, as appropriate, in either the direct labor budget, manufacturing overhead budget, or selling and administrative budget.

Direct Labor Budget

Better Brackets' management has reviewed the staffing requirements and has developed the direct labor cost estimates shown in Exhibit 13–9 for the first quarter

EXHIBIT 13–8

Purchases Budget for the Three Months and Quarter Ending March 31, 2001

	January	February	March	Quarter
Units to be produced (from Exhibit 13–7)	79,500	70,250	74,450	224,200
+ EI (10% of next month's production)*	7,025	7,445	6,450	6,450
= Total whole units needed	86,525	77,695	80,900	230,650
− Beginning inventory	(7,950)**	(7,025)	(7,445)	(7,950)
= Finished units for which purchases are required	78,575	70,670	73,455	222,700
METAL PURCHASES				
Finished units	78,575	70,670	73,455	222,700
× Ounces needed per unit	× 4	× 4	× 4	× 4
= Total ounces to be purchased	314,300	282,680	293,820	890,800
× Price per ounce	× $.02	× $.02	× $.02	× $.02
= Total cost of metal purchases	$ 6,286	$ 5,654	$ 5,876	$17,816

*April production is expected to be 64,500 units.
**BI of RM was 31,800; each unit requires 4 ounces, so there was enough RM for 7,950 units or 10% of the following month's production.

	January	February	March	Total
Units of production	79,500	70,250	74,450	224,200
× Standard hours allowed	.005	.005	.005	.005
= Total hours allowed	397.5	351.25	372.25	1,121
× Average wage rate (including fringe cost)	× $12	× $12	× $12	× $12
= Direct labor cost	$ 4,770	$ 4,215	$ 4,467	$ 13,452

EXHIBIT 13-9

Direct Labor Budget for the Three Months and Quarter Ending March 31, 2001

of 2001. Factory direct labor costs are based on the standard hours of labor needed to produce the number of units shown in the production budget. The average wage rate includes both the direct labor payroll rate and the payroll taxes and fringe benefits related to direct labor (because these items usually add between 25 and 30 percent to the base labor cost). All compensation is paid in the month in which it is incurred. Therefore, Better Brackets will have no accrued liability for direct labor cost at March 31, 2001.

Overhead Budget

Another production cost that management must estimate is overhead. Exhibit 13–10 presents Better Brackets' monthly cost of each overhead item for the first quarter of 2001. The company has determined that machine hours is the best predictor of overhead costs.

In estimating overhead, all fixed and variable costs must be specified and mixed costs must be separated into their fixed (a) and variable (b) components. Each overhead amount shown is calculated using the $y = a + bX$ formula discussed in Chapter 3. For example, March maintenance cost is the fixed amount of $175 plus ($0.30 times 1,240 estimated hours of machine time) or $175 + $372 = $547. Both total cost and cost net of depreciation are shown in the budget. The net of depreciation cost is expected to be paid in cash during the month and will affect the cash budget.

	Value of (fixed) *a*	Value of (variable) *b*	January	February	March	Total
Estimated machine hours (X) (assumed)			1,325	1,171	1,240	3,736
Overhead item:						
Depreciation	$ 600	$ —	$ 600	$ 600	$ 600	$ 1,800
Indirect material	—	0.20	265	234	248	747
Indirect labor	1,000	0.50	1,663	1,585	1,620	4,868
Utilities	100	0.20	365	334	348	1,047
Property tax	100	—	100	100	100	300
Insurance	50	—	50	50	50	150
Maintenance	175	0.30	573	526	547	1,646
Total cost (*y*)	$2,025	$1.20	$3,616	$3,429	$3,513	$10,558
Total cost net of depreciation			$3,016	$2,829	$2,913	$ 8,758

EXHIBIT 13-10

Overhead Budget for the Three Months and Quarter Ending March 31, 2001

Selling and Administrative Budget

Selling and administrative (S&A) expenses can be predicted in the same manner as overhead costs. Exhibit 13–11 presents the first quarter 2001 Better Brackets S&A budget. Sales figures, rather than production levels, are the activity measure used to prepare this budget. The company has two salespeople who receive $500 per month plus a 4 percent commission on sales. Administrative salaries total $2,000 per month.

Capital Budget

The budgets included in the master budget focus on the short-term or upcoming fiscal period. Managers, however, must also assess such long-term needs as plant and equipment purchases and budget for those expenditures in a process called capital budgeting. The capital budget is prepared separately from the master budget, but because expenditures are involved, capital budgeting does affect the master budgeting process.[4]

As shown in Exhibit 13–12, Better Brackets' managers have decided that a $23,000 piece of metal extruding machinery will be purchased and paid for in February. The machinery will be placed into service when installation is complete in April 2001 after installation and testing. Depreciation on the extruding machinery will not be included in the overhead calculation until installation is complete.

Cash Budget

5

Why is the cash budget so important in the master budgeting process?

After the preceding budgets have been developed, a cash budget can be constructed. The cash budget may be the most important schedule prepared during the budgeting process because, without cash, a company cannot survive.

EXHIBIT 13–11

Selling and Administrative Budget for the Three Months and Quarter Ending March 31, 2001

			January	February	March	Total
Predicted sales (from Exhibit 13–6)			$40,000	$35,000	$37,500	$112,500
	Value of (fixed) *a*	Value of (variable) *b*				
S&A Item:						
Supplies	$ —	$0.010	$ 400	$ 350	$ 375	$ 1,125
Depreciation	200	—	200	200	200	600
Miscellaneous	100	0.001	140	135	138	413
Compensation						
Salespeople	1,000	0.040	2,600	2,400	2,500	7,500
Administrative	2,000		2,000	2,000	2,000	6,000
Total cost (*y*)	$3,300	$0.051	$ 5,340	$ 5,085	$ 5,213	$ 15,638
Total cost (net of depreciation)			$ 5,140	$ 4,885	$ 5,013	$ 15,038

EXHIBIT 13–12

Capital Budget for the Three Months and Quarter Ending March 31, 2001

	January	February	March	Total
Acquisition—machinery	$0	$23,000	$0	$23,000
Cash payment for machinery	0	23,000	0	23,000

[4] Capital budgeting is discussed in depth in Chapter 14.

The following model can be used to summarize cash receipts and disbursements in a way that assists managers to devise appropriate financing measures to meet company needs.

Cash Budget Model

Beginning cash balance		XXX
+ Cash receipts (collections)		XXX
= Cash available for disbursements exclusive of financing		XXX
− Cash needed for disbursements (purchases, direct labor, overhead, S&A, taxes, bonuses, etc.)		(XXX)
= Cash excess or deficiency (*a*)		XXX
− Minimum desired cash balance		(XXX)
= Cash needed or available for investment or repayment		XXX
Financing methods:		
± Borrowing (repayments)	XXX	
± Issue (reacquire) capital stock	XXX	
± Sell (acquire) investments or plant assets	XXX	
± Receive (pay) interest or dividends	XXX	
Total impact (+ or −) of planned financing (*b*)		XXX
= Ending cash balance (*c*), where [(*c*) = (*a*) ± (*b*)]		XXX

CASH RECEIPTS AND ACCOUNTS RECEIVABLE

Once sales dollars have been determined, managers translate revenue information into cash receipts through the use of an expected collection pattern. This pattern considers the collection patterns experienced in the recent past and management's judgment about changes that could disturb current collection patterns. For example, changes that could weaken current collection patterns include recessionary conditions, increases in interest rates, less strict credit granting practices, or ineffective collection practices.

In specifying collection patterns, managers should recognize that different types of customers pay in different ways. Any sizable, unique category of clientele should be segregated. Better Brackets has two different types of customers: (1) cash customers who never receive a discount and (2) credit customers. Of the credit customers, manufacturers and wholesalers are allowed a 2 percent cash discount; retailers are not allowed the discount.

Although budgeting is not an exact science, neither is it random predictions about future events. Significant care must be taken with underlying assumptions and analysis of future economic conditions.

Better Brackets has determined from historical data that the collection pattern diagrammed in Exhibit 13–13 is applicable to its customers. Of each month's sales, 20 percent will be for cash and 80 percent will be on credit. The 40 percent of the credit customers who are allowed the discount pay in the month of the sale. Collections from the remaining credit customers are as follows: 20 percent in the month of sale; 50 percent in the month following the sale; and 29 percent in the second month following the sale. One percent of credit sales not taking a discount is uncollectible.

Using the sales budget, information on November and December 2000 sales, and the collection pattern, management can estimate cash receipts from sales during the first three months of 2001. Management must have November and December sales information because collections for credit sales extend over three months, meaning that collection of some of the previous year's sales occur early in the current year. Better Brackets' November and December sales were $44,000 and $46,000, respectively. Projected monthly collections in the first quarter of 2001 are shown in Exhibit 13–14. The individual calculations relate to the alternative collection patterns and the corresponding percentages that are presented in Exhibit 13–13. All amounts have been rounded to the nearest dollar.

The amounts for November and December collections can be reconciled to the December 31, 2000, balance sheet (Exhibit 13–5), which indicated an Accounts Receivable balance of $24,000. This amount appears in the collection schedule as follows:

December 31, 2000, Balance in Accounts Receivable:

January collections of November sales	$ 6,125
Estimated November bad debts	211
January collections of December sales	11,040
February collections of December sales	6,403
Estimated December bad debts	221
December 31, 2000, balance in Accounts Receivable	$24,000

EXHIBIT 13–13

Better Brackets' Collection Pattern for Sales

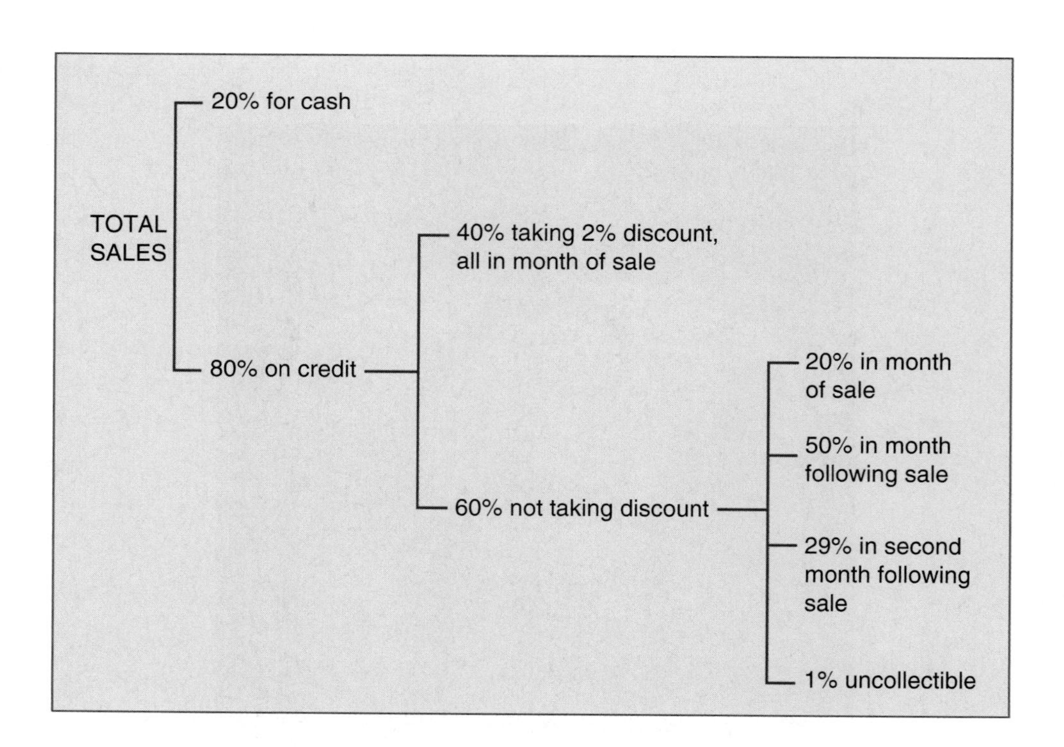

EXHIBIT 13–14

Cash Collections for the Three Months and Quarter Ending March 31, 2001

	January	February	March	Total	Disc.	Uncoll.
FROM:						
November 2000 sales:						
$44,000(0.8)(0.6)(0.29)	$ 6,125			$ 6,125		
$44,000(0.8)(0.6)(0.01)						$211
December 2000 sales:						
$46,000(0.8)(0.6)(0.5)	11,040			11,040		
$46,000(0.8)(0.6)(0.29)		$ 6,403		6,403		
$46,000(0.8)(0.6)(0.01)						221
January 2001 sales:						
$40,000(0.2)	8,000			8,000		
$40,000(0.8)(0.4)(0.98)	12,544N			12,544	$256	
$40,000(0.8)(0.6)(0.2)	3,840			3,840		
$40,000(0.8)(0.6)(0.5)		9,600		9,600		
$40,000(0.8)(0.6)(0.29)			$ 5,568	5,568		
$40,000(0.8)(0.6)(0.01)						192
February 2001 sales:						
$35,000(0.2)		7,000		7,000		
$35,000(0.8)(0.4)(0.98)		10,976N		10,976	224	
$35,000(0.8)(0.6)(0.2)		3,360		3,360		
$35,000(0.8)(0.6)(0.5)			8,400	8,400		
March 2001 sales:						
$37,500(0.2)			7,500	7,500		
$37,500(0.8)(0.4)(0.98)			11,760N	11,760	240	
$37,500(0.8)(0.6)(0.2)			3,600	3,600		
Totals	$41,549	$37,339	$36,828	$115,716	$720	$624

"N" stands for "Net of discount." To determine the gross amount, divide the net amount by 0.98 (i.e., 100% − 2%).

January 2001 sales of $40,000 are used to illustrate the collection calculations in Exhibit 13–14. The first line (for January) represents cash sales of 20 percent of total sales, or $8,000. The next two lines represent the 80 percent of the customers who buy on credit. The first of these lines represents the 40 percent of credit customers who take the discount, computed as follows:

Sales to credit customers (80% of $40,000)	$32,000
Sales to customers allowed discount (40% × $32,000)	$12,800
− Discount taken by customers (0.02 × $12,800)	(256)
= Net collections from customers allowed discount	$12,544

The second of these two lines relates to the remaining 20 percent of credit customers who paid in the month of sale but were not allowed the discount. The remaining amounts in Exhibit 13–14 are computed similarly.

Once the cash collections schedule is prepared, balances for Accounts Receivable, Allowance for Uncollectibles, and Sales Discounts can be projected. (These T-accounts for Better Brackets follow.) These amounts will be used to prepare pro forma quarter-end 2001 financial statements. All sales are initially recorded as Accounts Receivable. Immediate cash collections are then deducted from the Accounts Receivable balance.

Note that the estimated uncollectible accounts from November 2000 through March 2001 have not been written off as of the end of the first quarter of 2001.

Companies continue to make collection efforts for a substantial period before accounts are acknowledged as truly worthless. Thus, these receivables may remain on the books six months or more from the sale date. When accounts are written off, Accounts Receivable and the Allowance for Uncollectibles will both decrease; however, there will be no income statement impact relative to the write-off.

Accounts Receivable

12/31/00 Balance (Exhibit 13–5)	24,000	Collections in January from beginning A/R ($6,125 + $11,040)	17,165
January 2001 sales (Exhibit 13–6)	40,000	Cash sales in January (Exhibit 13–14)	8,000
		Credit collections subject to discount (cash received, $12,544)	12,800
		Credit collections not subject to discount	3,840
February 2001 sales (Exhibit 13–6)	35,000	Collections in February from beginning A/R	6,403
		Cash sales in February (Exhibit 13–14)	7,000
		Collections in February from January sales	9,600
		Credit collections subject to discount (cash received, $10,976)	11,200
		Credit collections not subject to discount	3,360
March 2001 sales (Exhibit 13–6)	37,500	Cash sales in March (Exhibit 13–14)	7,500
		Collections in March from January sales	5,568
		Collections in March from February sales	8,400
		Credit collections subject to discount (cash received, $11,760)	12,000
		Credit collections not subject to discount	3,600
3/31/01 Balance	20,064		

Allowance for Uncollectible Accounts

		12/31/00 Balance (Exhibit 13–5)	432
		January estimate (Exhibit 13–14)	192
		February estimate [$35,000(80%)(60%)(1%)]	168
		March estimate [$37,500(80%)(60%)(1%)]	180
		3/31/01 Balance	972

Sales Discounts

January discounts	256		
February discounts	224		
March discounts	240		
3/31/01 Balance	720		

CASH DISBURSEMENTS AND ACCOUNTS PAYABLE

Using the purchases information from Exhibit 13–8, management can prepare a cash disbursements schedule for Accounts Payable. Better Brackets makes all raw material purchases on account. The company pays for 40 percent of each month's purchases in the month of purchase. These purchases are from suppliers who allow Better Brackets a 2 percent discount for prompt payment. The remaining suppliers allow no discounts, but require payments be made within 30 days from the purchase date. Thus, the remaining 60 percent of each month's purchases are paid in the month following the month of purchase.

Exhibit 13–15 presents the first quarter 2001 cash disbursements information for purchases. The December 31, 2000, Accounts Payable balance of $4,330 (Exhibit 13–5) represents 60 percent of December purchases of $7,217. All amounts have been rounded to whole dollars.

Accounts payable activity is summarized in the following T-account. The March 31 balance represents 60 percent of March purchases that will be paid during April.

Accounts Payable

		12/31/00 Balance (Exhibit 13–5)	4,330
January payments for December purchases (Exhibit 13–15)	4,330	January purchases (Exhibit 13–8)	6,286
January payments for January purchases subject to discount (cash paid, $2,464)	2,514	February purchases (Exhibit 13–8)	5,654
February payments for January purchases (Exhibit 13–15)	3,772	March purchases (Exhibit 13–8)	5,876
February payments for February purchases subject to discount (cash paid, $2,216)	2,261		
March payments for February purchases (Exhibit 13–15)	3,393		
March payments for March purchases subject to discount (cash paid, $2,303)	2,350		
		3/31/01 Balance	3,526

Purchases Discounts

		January discounts	50
		February discounts	45
		March discounts	47
		3/31/01 Balance	142

Given the cash receipts and disbursements information for Better Brackets, the cash budget model is used to formulate the cash budget shown in Exhibit 13–16. The company has established $6,000 as its desired minimum cash balance. There are two primary reasons for having a desired minimum cash balance: one is internal; the other is external. The first reason reflects the uncertainty associated with the budgeting process. Because managers cannot budget with absolute precision, a "cushion" is maintained to protect the company from potential errors in forecasting

EXHIBIT 13-15

Cash Disbursements for Accounts Payable for the Three Months and Quarter Ending March 31, 2001

	January	February	March	Total	Discount
PAYMENT FOR PURCHASES OF:					
December 2000	$4,330			$ 4,330	
January 2001 (from Exhibit 13–8)					
$6,286(0.40)(0.98)	2,464N			2,464	$ 50
$6,286(0.60)		$3,772		3,772	
February 2001 (from Exhibit 13–8)					
$5,654(0.40)(0.98)		2,216N		2,216	45
$5,654(0.60)			$3,393	3,393	
March 2001 (from Exhibit 13–8)					
$5,876(0.40)(0.98)			2,303N	2,303	47
Total disbursements for A/P	$6,794	$5,988	$5,696	$18,478	$142

"N" stands for "Net of discount." The total amount of gross purchases being paid for in the month of purchase is the sum of the net of discount payment plus the amount shown on the same line in the Discount column.

EXHIBIT 13-16

Cash Budget for the Three Months and Quarter Ending March 31, 2001

	January	February	March	Total
Beginning cash balance	$ 6,000	$ 6,829	$ 6,461	$ 6,000
Cash collections (Exhibit 13–14)	41,549	37,339	36,828	115,716
Cash available exclusive of financing	$ 47,549	$ 44,168	$ 43,289	$121,716
DISBURSEMENTS:				
Accounts payable (for purchases, Ex. 13–15)	$ 6,794	$ 5,988	$ 5,696	$ 18,478
Direct labor (Ex. 13–9)	4,770	4,215	4,467	13,452
Overhead (Ex. 13–10)*	3,016	2,829	2,913	8,758
S&A expenses (Ex. 13–11)*	5,140	4,885	5,013	15,038
Total disbursements	$ 19,720	$ 17,917	$ 18,089	$ 55,726
Cash excess (inadequacy)	$ 27,829	$ 26,251	$ 25,200	$ 65,990
Minimum balance desired	(6,000)	(6,000)	(6,000)	(6,000)
Cash available (needed)	$ 21,829	$ 20,251	$ 19,200	$ 59,990
FINANCING:				
Borrowings (repayments)	$ 0	$ 0	$ 0	$ 0
Issue (reacquire) stock	0	0	0	0
Sell (acquire) investments	(21,000)	3,000	6,000	(12,000)***
Sell (acquire) plant assets	0	(23,000)	0	(23,000)
Receive (pay) interest**		210	180	390
Receive (pay) dividends			(25,000)	(25,000)
Total impact of planned financing	$(21,000)	$(19,790)	$(18,820)	$ (59,610)
Ending cash balance	$ 6,829	$ 6,461	$ 6,380	$ 6,380

*These amounts are the net of depreciation figures.
**Interest is calculated assuming a 12 percent annual rate (1 percent per month) and investments and disposals of investments are made at the end of the month in $1,000 increments.
***This is the net result of investments and disposals of investments.

collection and payment schedules. The second reason is the company's banks may require a minimum cash balance in relation to an open line of credit.

For simplicity, it is assumed that any investments or sales of investments are made in end-of-month $1,000 increments. Interest on company investments at 12 percent per annum or 1 percent per month is added to the company's bank account at month's end.

Exhibit 13–16 indicates that Better Brackets has a $27,829 excess of cash available over disbursements in January. Such an excess, however, does not consider the need for the $6,000 minimum balance. Thus, the company has $21,829 available. It used $21,000 of that amount to purchase temporary investments at the end of January.

In February, Better Brackets again will have enough cash to meet its desired minimum cash balance and, by liquidating $3,000 of its investments, pay for the machinery. In March, there is enough excess cash available, coupled with the liquidation of another $6,000 of investments, to pay the $25,000 dividend that is due in March.

Cash flow provides the short-run source of power in a business to negotiate and act. In addition to preparing and executing a sound cash budget, there are other measures a business can take. Exhibit 13–17 offers some suggestions in this regard for small businesses, although the same prescriptions are applicable to businesses of all sizes.

EXHIBIT 13–17

10 Ways to Improve Small Business Cash Flow

Cash flow is the lifeblood of any small business. A healthy stream is essential if a business is to succeed. In general, the key is to accelerate the flow of money coming in and delay what goes out. Having written credit and collection policies can also help. Here are 10 tips a business can use to improve cash flow.

1. **Establish sound credit practices.** Before dealing with a new customer, always get at least three trade references and a bank reference. Credit reports, available from Dun and Bradstreet and others, report on a company's general financial health as well as how quickly—or slowly—it pays its bills. Never give credit until you are comfortable with a customer's ability to pay.
2. **Expedite fulfillment and shipping.** Fill orders accurately and efficiently, and then use the quickest means available to deliver products and services to customers. Unnecessary delays can add days or weeks to customer payments.
3. **Bill promptly and accurately.** The faster you mail an invoice, the faster you will be paid. Where possible, send an invoice with the order. If deliveries do not automatically trigger an invoice, establish a set billing schedule, preferably weekly. Check invoices for accuracy before mailing them. All invoices should include a payment due date. An invoice without payment terms may fall to the bottom of a customer's pile of bills.
4. **Offer discounts for prompt payment.** Given an incentive, some customers will pay sooner rather than later. Trade discounts typically give 1% to 2% off the total amount due if customers pay in 10 days.
5. **Aggressively follow up on past due accounts.** As soon as a bill becomes overdue, call the customer and ask when you can expect payment. Keep a record of the conversation and the customer's response. Set a follow-up date in the event the promised payment is not received. Ask delinquent customers with genuine financial problems to try to pay at least a small amount every week. When necessary, don't hesitate to seek professional help from an attorney or collection agency.
6. **Deposit payments promptly.** Don't let checks sit in a drawer waiting to be deposited. The sooner you make a deposit, the sooner you can put the money to work for your business. If you are really serious about speeding up your cash flow, a post office box or bank lockbox can accelerate receipt of checks.
7. **Seek better payment terms from suppliers and banks.** Better payment terms from suppliers are the simplest way to slow down a company's cash outflow. While most suppliers provide terms of 30 days, 60 or 90 days are sometimes available, though it might mean changing suppliers. Better credit terms translate into borrowing money interest-free. Some banks also may be willing to restructure business loans to make them easier to repay.
8. **Keep a tight control on inventory.** Less cash tied up in inventory generally means better cash flow. While some suppliers offer deeper discounts on volume purchases, if inventory sits on the shelf too long, it ties up money that could be put to better use elsewhere.
9. **Review and reduce expenses.** Take a critical look at all expenses. If you're not sure an expense is necessary, hold back until you are confident it will have a favorable impact on the bottom line. Consider ways to decrease operating costs, such as switching from a weekly to a biweekly payroll to reduce payroll processing costs. Be careful not to cut costs that could hurt profits. For instance, rather than cutting the marketing budget, redirect the money to areas where it will have a more positive impact.
10. **Pay bills on time, but never before they are due.** The basic rule is to take as long as you are allowed to pay bills—without incurring late fees or interest charges. Make an exception to this rule only when you are offered a trade discount for early payment.

SOURCE: "10 Ways to Improve Small Business Cash Flow," New York State Society of CPAs, New York, http://www.nysscpa.org.

Budgeted Financial Statements

The final step in the budgeting process is the development of budgeted (pro forma) financial statements for the period. These financial statements reflect the results that will be achieved if the estimates and assumptions used for all previous budgets actually occur. Such statements allow management to determine whether the predicted results are acceptable. If they are not acceptable, management has the opportunity to change and adjust items before the period for which the budget is being prepared begins.

When expected net income is not considered reasonable, management may investigate the possibility of raising selling prices or finding ways to decrease costs. Any specific changes considered by management might have related effects that must be included in the revised projections. For example, raising selling prices may decrease volume. Alternatively, reductions in costs from using lower-grade material could increase spoilage during production or cause a decline in demand. With the availability of the computer, changes in budget assumptions and their resultant effects can be simulated quickly and easily.

COST OF GOODS MANUFACTURED SCHEDULE

Management must prepare a schedule of cost of goods manufactured before an income statement can be prepared. This schedule is necessary to determine cost of goods sold. Using information from previous budgets, the Better Brackets' budgeted cost of goods manufactured schedule is shown in Exhibit 13–18. Because there were no beginning or ending work in process inventories, the cost of goods manufactured equals the manufacturing costs of the period. Had work in process inventory existed, the computations would be more complex and would have involved the use of equivalent units of production.

INCOME STATEMENT

The projected income statement for Better Brackets for the first quarter of 2001 is presented in Exhibit 13–19. This statement uses much of the information previously developed in determining the revenues and expenses for the period.

EXHIBIT 13–18

Pro Forma Cost of Goods Manufactured Schedule for Quarter Ending March 31, 2001

Beginning work in process inventory		$ 0
Cost of raw material used:		
Beginning balance (Exhibit 13–5)	$ 636	
Net purchases (from Accounts Payable and Purchases Discounts, p. 569)	17,674	
Total raw material available	$18,310	
Ending balance of RM (Note A)	(516)	
Cost of raw material used	$17,794	
Direct labor (Exhibit 13–9)	13,452	
Factory overhead (Exhibit 13–10)	10,558	
Total costs to be accounted for		41,804
Ending work in process inventory		(0)
Cost of goods manufactured		$41,804

Note A:	METAL
Ending balance (Exhibit 13–8) required for FG	6,450
Ounces per unit	× 4
Total ounces of RM required	25,800
Price per ounce	× $0.02
Ending balance of RM	$ 516

EXHIBIT 13-19

Pro Forma Income Statement for Quarter Ending March 31, 2001

Sales (Exhibit 13–6)			$112,500
Less: Sales discounts (p. 568)			(720)
Net sales			$111,780
Cost of goods sold:			
Finished goods—12/31/00 (Exhibit 13–5)		$ 748	
Cost of goods manufactured (Exhibit 13–18)		41,804	
Cost of goods available for sale		$ 42,552	
Finished goods—3/31/01 (Note A)		(598)	(41,954)
Gross margin			$ 69,826
Expenses:			
Uncollectible accounts expense (Note B)		$ 540	
S&A expenses (Exhibit 13–11)		15,638	(16,178)
Income from operations			$ 53,648
Other revenue—interest earned (Exhibit 13–16)			390
Income before income taxes			$ 54,038
Income taxes (assumed rate of 40%)			(21,615)
Net income			$ 32,423

Note A:

Beginning finished goods units		4,000
Production (Exhibit 13–7)		224,200
Units available for sale		228,200
Sales (Exhibit 13–6)		(225,000)
Ending finished goods units		3,200
Cost per unit:		
Material	$0.080	
Conversion (assumed)	0.107	× $0.187
Cost of ending inventory		$ 598

Note B:

Total sales	$112,500
× % credit sales	× 0.80
= Credit sales	$ 90,000
× % not taking discount	× 0.60
= Potential bad debts	$ 54,000
× % estimated uncollectible	× 0.01
= Estimated bad debts	$ 540

BALANCE SHEET

On completion of the income statement, a March 31, 2001, balance sheet (Exhibit 13–20) can be prepared.

STATEMENT OF CASH FLOWS

The information found on the income statement, balance sheet, and cash budget is also used to prepare a Statement of Cash Flows (SCF). This statement can assist managers in judging the company's ability to handle fixed cash outflow commitments, adapt to adverse changes in business conditions, and undertake new commitments. Further, because the SCF identifies the relationship between net income and net cash flow from operations, it assists managers in judging the quality of the company's earnings.

Whereas the cash budget is essential to current cash management, the budgeted SCF gives managers a more global view of cash flows by rearranging them into three distinct major activities (operating, investing, and financing). Such a rearrangement permits management to judge whether the specific anticipated flows are consistent with the company's strategic plans.

In addition, the SCF would incorporate a schedule or narrative about significant noncash transactions if any have occurred, such as an exchange of stock for land, that are disregarded in the cash budget.

EXHIBIT 13-20

Pro Forma Balance Sheet, March 31, 2001

ASSETS		
Current Assets		
Cash (Exhibit 13–16)		$ 6,380
Accounts Receivable (p. 568)	$ 20,064	
Less Allowance for Uncollectibles (p. 568)	(972)	19,092
Inventory		
Raw Material (Exhibit 13–18, Note A)	$ 516	
Finished Goods (Exhibit 13–19, Note A)	598	1,114
Investments (Exhibit 13–16)		12,000
Total Current Assets		$ 38,586
Plant Assets		
Property, Plant, and Equipment (Note A)	$393,000	
Less Accumulated Depreciation (Note B)	(92,400)	300,600
Total Assets		$339,186
LIABILITIES AND STOCKHOLDERS' EQUITY		
Current Liabilities		
Accounts Payable (p. 569)		$ 3,526
Income Taxes Payable (Exhibit 13–19)		21,615
Total Current Liabilities		$ 25,141
Stockholders' Equity		
Common Stock	$180,000	
Retained Earnings (Note C)	134,045	314,045
Total Liabilities and Stockholders' Equity		$339,186

Note A:

Beginning balance (Exhibit 13–5)	$370,000
Purchased new computer	23,000
Ending balance	$393,000

Note B:

Beginning balance (Exhibit 13–5)	$ 90,000
Factory depreciation (Exhibit 13–10)	1,800
S&A depreciation (Exhibit 13–11)	600
Ending balance	$ 92,400

Note C:

Beginning balance (Exhibit 13–5)	$101,622
Net income (Exhibit 13–19)	32,423
Ending balance	$134,045

The operating section of the SCF prepared on either a direct or an indirect basis is acceptable for external reporting. The direct basis uses pure cash flow information (cash collections and cash disbursements) for operating activities. The operating section for a SCF prepared on an indirect basis begins with net income and makes reconciling adjustments to arrive at cash flow from operations. Exhibit 13–21 provides a Statement of Cash Flows for Better Brackets using the information from the cash budget in Exhibit 13–16; the second, indirect presentation of the operating section uses the information from the income statement in Exhibit 13–19 and the balance sheets in Exhibits 13–5 and 13–20.

Better Brackets generates both a large cash flow from operations ($60,380 from Exhibit 13–21) and a high net income per net sales dollar (29 percent). This strong showing by both measures suggests that Better Brackets has high-quality earnings.

EXHIBIT 13-21

Pro Forma Statement of Cash Flows for Quarter Ending March 31, 2001

Operating Activities:			
Cash collections from sales (Exhibit 13–16)		$115,716	
Interest earned (Exhibit 13–16)		390	
Total		$116,106	
Cash payments			
For inventory:			
Raw material (Exhibit 13–16)	$18,478		
Direct labor (Exhibit 13–16)	13,452		
Overhead (Exhibit 13–16)	8,758	(40,688)	
For nonfactory costs:			
Salaries and wages (Exhibit 13–11)	$13,500		
Supplies (Exhibit 13–11)	1,125		
Other S&A expenses (Exhibit 13–11)	413	(15,038)	
Net cash inflow from operating activities			$60,380
Investing Activities:			
Purchase of plant asset (Exhibit 13–12)		$ 23,000	
Short-term investment (Exhibit 13–16)		12,000	
Net cash outflow from investing activities			(35,000)
Financing Activities:			
Dividends (Exhibit 13–16)		$ 25,000	
Net cash outflow from financing activities			(25,000)
Net increase in cash			$ 380
Alternative (Indirect) Basis for Operating Activities:			
Net income			$32,423
+ Depreciation (Exhibit 13–10 and Exhibit 13–11)		$ 2,400	
+ Decrease in Accounts Receivable ($23,568 − $19,092)		4,476	
+ Decrease in total inventory ($1,384 − $1,114)		270	
+ Increase in Taxes Payable ($21,615 − $0)		21,615	
− Decrease in Accounts Payable ($4,330 − $3,526)		(804)	27,957
= Net cash inflow from operating activities			$60,380

Both cash flow from operations and net income are necessary for continued business success. Better Brackets' management is doing an effective job in pricing the company's product and an efficient job in controlling costs.

CONCLUDING COMMENTS

6

What benefits are provided by a budget?

A well-prepared budget provides the following benefits:

1. a guide to help managers align activities and resource allocations with organizational goals;
2. a vehicle to promote employee participation, cooperation, and departmental coordination;
3. a tool to enhance conduct of the managerial functions of planning, controlling, problem solving, and performance evaluating;
4. a basis on which to sharpen management's responsiveness to changes in both internal and external factors; and
5. a model that provides a rigorous view of future performance of a business in time to consider alternative measures.

Because of its fundamental nature in the budgeting process, demand must be predicted as accurately and with as many details as possible. Sales forecasts should indicate type and quantity of products to be sold, geographic locations of the sales, types of buyers, and when the sales are to be made. Such detail is necessary because different products require different production and distribution facilities, different customers have different credit terms and payment schedules, and different seasons or months may necessitate different shipping schedules or methods.

Estimated sales demand has a pervasive impact on the master budget. To arrive at a valid prediction, managers use as much information as is available and may combine several estimation approaches. Combining prediction methods provides managers with a means to confirm estimates and reduce uncertainty. Some ways of estimating future demand are (1) canvassing sales personnel for a subjective consensus, (2) making simple extrapolations of past trends, (3) using market research, and (4) employing statistical and other mathematical models.

Care should be taken to use realistic, rather than optimistic or pessimistic, forecasts of revenues and costs. Computer models can be developed that allow repetitive computer simulations to be run after changes are made to one or more factors. These simulations permit managers to review results that would be obtained under various circumstances.

continuous budgeting

The master budget is normally prepared for a year and detailed by quarters and months within those quarters. Some companies use a process of **continuous budgeting**. For companies using continuous budgeting, this generally means that an ongoing 12-month budget is presented by successively adding a new budget month (12 months into the future) as each current month expires. Such a process allows management to work, at any time, within the present 1-month component of a full 12-month annual budget. Continuous budgets make the planning process less sporadic. Rather than having managers "go into the budgeting period" at a specific time, they are continuously involved in planning and budgeting.

If actual results differ from plans, managers should find the causes of the differences and then consider budget revisions. Arrangements usually cannot be made rapidly enough to revise the current month's budget. However, under certain circumstances and if they so desire, managers may be able to revise future months' budgets. If actual performance is substantially worse than what was expected, the budget may or may not be adjusted, depending on the variance causes.

If the causes are beyond the organization's control and are cost related, management may decide to revise budget cost estimates upward to be more realistic. If the causes are internal (such as the sales staff not selling the product), management may leave the budget in its original form so that the lack of operational control is visible in the comparisons.

If actual performance is substantially better than expected, alterations may also be made to the budget, although management may decide not to alter the budget so that the positive performance is highlighted. Regardless of whether the budget is revised, managers should commend those individuals responsible for the positive performance and communicate the effects of such performance to other related departments. For example, if the sales force has sold significantly higher quantities of product than expected in the original budget, production and purchasing will need to be notified to increase the number of units manufactured and raw material purchased.

budget slack

participatory budget

imposed budget

When budgets are used for performance evaluations, management often encounters the problem of **budget slack**. Budget slack is the intentional underestimation of revenues and/or overestimation of expenses. Slack can be incorporated into the budget during the development process in a participatory budget. A **participatory budget** is developed through joint decision making by top management and operating personnel. However, slack is not often found in imposed budgets. **Imposed budgets** are prepared by top management with little or no input from operating personnel. After the budget is developed, operating personnel are informed of the budget goals and constraints.[5]

[5] The budgeting process can be represented by a continuum with imposed budgets on one end and participatory budgets on the other. It is probably rare that a budget is either purely imposed or purely participatory. The budget process in a particular company is usually defined by the degree to which the process is either imposed or participatory.

Having budget slack allows subordinate managers to achieve their objectives with less effort than would be necessary without the slack. Slack also creates problems because of the significant interaction of the budget factors. For example, if sales volumes are understated or overstated, problems can arise in the production, purchasing, and personnel areas.

Top management can try to reduce slack by tying actual performance to the budget through a bonus system. Operating managers are rewarded with large bonuses for budgeting relatively high performance levels and achieving those levels. If performance is set at a low or minimal level, achievement of that performance is either not rewarded or only minimally rewarded. Top management must be aware that budget slack has a tremendous negative impact on organizational effectiveness and efficiency.

Managers may want to consider expanding their budgeting process to recognize the concepts of activities and cost drivers in a manner consistent with activity-based management. An activity budget can be created by mapping the line items in the conventional budget to a list of activities. This type of budget can help management become more aware of the budgeted costs of proposed non-value-added activities and make managers question why such costs are being planned. Based on this enhanced awareness, managers can plan to reduce or eliminate some of these non-value-added activities.

REVISITING The HON Company

http://www.honcompany.com

In August 1999, HON INDUSTRIES Inc., which includes The HON Company and its companion companies, was selected by *Industry Week Magazine* as one of the world's 100 Best-Managed Companies.

Candidates for the *Industry Week Magazine* honor were culled from the magazine's 1000, a list of the world's largest publicly held manufacturing companies based on revenues. Each company was evaluated on measures that included financial performance, philanthropy, and safety.

"Industry Week's 100 Best-Managed Companies demonstrate superior, consistent financial performance," said John Brandt, editor-in-chief of IW. "We also honor these companies for investing heavily in such areas as research and development, new markets, employees, and society."

In The HON Company's aggressive but realistic budget philosophy, senior management expects each quarter's performance to exceed the previous one. New products and services drive company growth, and research to define and meet emerging customer demand is ongoing. Recognizing that service is critical, too, HON offers two- and three-week delivery for orders of any product size and combination. Competitors typically require four- to five-week lead-times for single product orders.

Budget targets must be supported by action plans that coordinate operational improvements throughout the organization. For example, when the strategic plan calls for a specified increase in productivity, all departments are expected to work together to bring about needed change. In manufacturing, production processes repeatedly are challenged and bottlenecks removed. Sales and marketing are expected to generate increased sales volume to make full use of capacity gained through manufacturing improvements. Distribution then must develop plans to handle increased deliveries while reducing the cost of delivery per sales dollar.

Does quarterly budget preparation consume a disproportionate amount of company time? Experience has shown that managers improve their budgeting skills over time and need no more time to do quarterly budgets than would be needed for one annual budget. Information technology advances also have shortened budget preparation time. A highly integrated computer budgeting system supplies each department manager with four-quarter histories and four-quarter projections of budget line items. Driver codes for revenue and cost targets are set by default, and, thus, managers need only change budgets for line items on an exception basis. The budget system speeds up information flows to higher levels, too, because proposed targets are rolled up to the next level immediately where they can be reviewed and revised quickly by senior management.

Most importantly, The HON Company's process of continuous quarterly budgeting unites senior-level strategy with a committed corporate culture. Corporate management best understands where energies need to be focused to enhance the firm's competitive edge, but attaining strategic goals depends on a workforce that can translate corporate strategies into a well coordinated action plan.

SOURCES: Ralph Drtina, Steve Hoeger, and John Schaub, "Continuous Budgeting at the HON Company," *Management Accounting* (January 1996), p. 20. The HON Company Web site, http://www.honcompany.com (March 3, 2000).

CHAPTER SUMMARY

Planning is the process of setting goals and objectives and translating them into activities and resources required for accomplishment within a specified time horizon. Budgeting is the quantifying of a company's financial plans and activities. Budgets facilitate communication, coordination, and teamwork.

A master budget is the comprehensive set of projections for a specific budget period, culminating in a set of pro forma financial statements. It is composed of operating and financial budgets and is usually detailed by quarters and months. Some companies prepare continuous budgets by successively adding a new budgetary month, 12 months into the future, as each current month expires.

Sales demand is the proper starting point for the master budget. Once sales demand is determined, the cost accountant forecasts revenues, production quantities and costs, and cash flows for the firm's activities for the upcoming period. These expectations reflect the firm's inflows and outflows of resources.

When preparing a budget, managers must remember that organizational departments interact with each other, and the budget for one department may form the basis of or have an effect on the budgets in other departments. Actual operating results can be compared to budget figures to measure how effectively and efficiently organizational goals were met. Significant unfavorable variances dictate that managers should either attempt to alter the behavior of personnel or alter the budget if it appears to be unrealistic; significant favorable variances most likely will not cause the budget to be adjusted, but rather will cause affected departments to be advised of on possible consequences (such as increased production needs indicated by a favorable difference in sales demand). Regardless of whether variances are unfavorable or favorable, feedback to operating personnel is an important part of the budgeting process.

APPENDIX

How does a budget manual facilitate the budgeting process?

budget manual

The Budget Manual

To be useful, a budget requires a substantial amount of time and effort from the persons who prepare it. This process can be improved by the availability of an organizational **budget manual**, which is a detailed set of information and guidelines about the budgetary process. The manual should include

1. statements of the budgetary purpose and its desired results;
2. a listing of specific budgetary activities to be performed;
3. a calendar of scheduled budgetary activities;
4. sample budgetary forms; and
5. original, revised, and approved budgets.

The statements of budgetary purpose and desired results communicate the reasons behind the process. These statements should flow from general to specific details. An example of a general statement of budgetary purpose is "The Cash Budget provides a basis for planning, reviewing, and controlling cash flows from and for various activities; this budget is essential to the preparation of a pro forma Statement of Cash Flows." Specific statements could include references to minimum desired cash balances and periods of intense cash needs.

Budgetary activities should be listed by position rather than person because the responsibility for actions should be assigned to the individual holding the designated position at the time the budget is being prepared. The manual's activities section should indicate who has the final authority for revising and approving the budget. Budget approval may be delegated to a budget committee or reserved by one or several members of top management.

The budget calendar helps coordinate the budgetary process; it should indicate a timetable for all budget activities and be keyed directly to the activities list. The timetable for the budget process is unique to each organization. The larger the organization, the more time that will be necessary to gather and coordinate information, identify weak points in the process or the budget itself, and take corrective action. The calendar should also indicate control points for the upcoming periods at which budget-to-actual comparisons are to be made and feedback provided to managers responsible for operations.

Sample forms are extremely useful because they provide for consistent presentations of budget information from all individuals, making summarization of information easier and quicker. The sample forms should be easy to understand and may include standardized worksheets that allow managers to update historical information to arrive at budgetary figures. This section of the budget manual may also provide standard cost tables for items on which the organization has specific guidelines or policies. For example, in estimating employee fringe benefit costs, the company rule of thumb may be 25 percent of base salary. Or, if company policy states that each salesperson's per diem meal allowance is $30, meal expenses would be budgeted as estimated travel days multiplied by $30.

The final section of the budget manual contains the budgets generated during the budgeting process. Numerous budgets probably will be submitted and revised prior to actual budget implementation. Understanding this revision process and why changes were made is helpful for future planning. The final approved master budget is included in the budget manual as a control document.[6]

KEY TERMS

budget (p. 552)
budget manual (p. 578)
budget slack (p. 576)
budgeting (p. 552)
continuous budgeting (p. 576)
financial budget (p. 556)
imposed budget (p. 576)
operating budget (p. 556)
participatory budget (p. 576)

SOLUTION STRATEGIES

Sales Budget

Units of sales
× Selling price per unit
= Dollars of sales

[6] In the event of changes in economic conditions or strategic plans, the "final" budget may be revised during the budget period.

Production Budget

Units of sales
+ Units desired in ending inventory
− Units in beginning inventory
= Units to be produced

Purchases Budget

Units to be produced
+ Units desired in ending inventory
− Units in beginning inventory
= Units to be purchased

Direct Labor Budget

Units of production*
× Standard time allowed per unit
= Standard labor time allowed
× Per hour direct labor cost
= Total direct labor cost

*Converted to direct material component requirements, if necessary

Overhead Budget

Predicted activity base
× Variable overhead rate per unit of activity
= Total variable OH cost
+ Fixed OH cost
= Total OH cost

Selling and Administrative Budget

Predicted sales dollars (or other variable measure)
× Variable S&A rate per dollar (or other variable measure)
= Total variable S&A cost
+ Fixed S&A cost
= Total S&A cost

Schedule of Cash Collections for Sales

Dollars of credit sales for month
× Percent collection for month of sale
= Credit to A/R for month's sales
− Allowed and taken sales discounts
= Receipts for current month's credit sales
+ Receipts from cash sales
+ Current month's cash receipts for prior months' credit sales
= Cash receipts for current month

Schedule of Cash Payments for Purchases

Units to be purchased
× Cost per unit
= Total cost of purchases
× Percent payment for current purchases
= Debit to A/P for month's purchases
− Purchase discounts taken
= Cash payments for current month's purchases
+ Cash purchases
+ Current month's payments for prior months' purchases
= Cash payments for A/P for current month

Cash Budget

Beginning cash balance
+ Cash receipts (collections)
= Cash available for disbursements
− Cash needed for disbursements:
  Cash payments for A/P for month
  Cost of compensation
  Total cost of overhead minus depreciation
  Total S&A cost minus depreciation
= Cash excess or deficiency
− Minimum desired cash balance
= Cash needed or available for investment or financing
+ or − various financing measures
= Ending cash balance

DEMONSTRATION PROBLEM

Bass Lighting Fixtures' July 31, 2001, balance sheet includes the following:

Cash	$30,000 debit
Accounts Receivable	92,000 debit
Allowance for Uncollectible Accounts	2,044 credit
Merchandise Inventory	12,266 debit

The firm's management has designated $30,000 as the firm's monthly minimum cash balance. Other information about Bass follows:

- Revenues of $200,000 and $240,000 are expected for August and September, respectively. All goods are sold on account.
- The collection pattern for Accounts Receivable is 55 percent in the month of sale, 44 percent in the month following the sale, and 1 percent uncollectible.
- Cost of goods sold approximates 60 percent of sales revenues.
- Management wants to end each month with 10 percent of that month's cost of sales in Merchandise Inventory.
- All Accounts Payable for inventory are paid in the month of purchase.
- Other monthly expenses are $26,000, which includes $4,000 of depreciation, but does not include uncollectible accounts expense.

Required:

a. Forecast the August cash collections.
b. Forecast the August and September cost of purchases.
c. Prepare the cash budget for August including the effects of financing (borrowing or investing).

Solution to Demonstration Problem

a.

August Collections	
From July ($92,000 − $2,044)	$ 89,956
From August ($200,000 × 0.55)	110,000
Total	$199,956

b.

	August	September
Sales	$200,000	$240,000
Cost of goods sold (60%)	$120,000	$144,000
Add desired ending balance	12,000	14,400
Total needed	$132,000	$158,400
Less beginning balance	(12,266)	(12,000)
Cost of purchases	$119,734	$146,400

c. August Cash Budget

Beginning cash balance		$ 30,000
August collections		199,956
Total cash available for disbursements		$229,956
Disbursements:		
Purchase of merchandise	$119,734	
Other monthly expenses ($26,000 − $4,000)	22,000	
Total disbursements		(141,734)
Cash excess or deficiency (*a*)		$ 88,222
Less minimum cash balance desired		(30,000)
Cash available or needed		$ 58,222
Financing:		
Acquire investment (*b*)		(58,222)
Ending cash balance (*c*); (*c* = *a* − *b*)		$ 30,000

QUESTIONS

1. Why do businesses formally document their plans?
2. Outline the basic budgeting process.
3. Why is a budget considered a communication device?
4. Discuss what is meant by the following comment: Budgeting is a process of translation.
5. What major factors are taken into account in formulating an organization's strategic plan?
6. Managers formulate strategic plans that have time horizons of 5 to 10 years. Why do managers also formulate shorter term plans?
7. A major management function is planning. How does budgeting facilitate management planning?
8. How does the process of budgeting assist managers in conducting the management control function?
9. How are budgets used as both planning and control tools?
10. The master budget contains both operational and financial budgets. What is the difference between an operating budget and a financial budget? How do they relate to each other?
11. It is said that the master budget is "demand driven." What does this mean?
12. Explain how managers estimate collections from sales. Why is this information important in the budgeting process?
13. How are the production budgets and material purchasing budgets similar? How are they different? When is each used?
14. In estimating the overhead budget, why is it necessary to separate overhead into its variable and fixed components?
15. Why is the cash budget so important to an organization? If the cash budget identifies a period in which a cash shortage is expected, what actions can the organization take?
16. Why would a company wish to maintain a minimum cash balance?

17. How does the cash budget interface with the sales budget and budgeted accounts receivable?

18. Although managers are not clairvoyant, budgeting may assist in viewing the future. How might this be so?

19. Why is it useful to complete the budgeting process with a presentation of pro forma financial statements?

20. How are the budgeted Statement of Cash Flows and the cash budget similar? How are they different?

21. What benefits should arise from a process of continuous budgeting?

22. What is budget slack? What induces managers to build slack into their budgets?

23. Why is employee participation in developing the budget important to an organization?

24. *(Appendix)* What are the various sections of the budget manual and why is each section necessary?

25. *(Appendix)* What does the budget manual provide for everyone involved in the budgeting process? What does it reflect about top management?

26. Go to the Internet to find a company that either uses an annual budget or claims it does not. What reasons does it give either for using an annual budget or for using some alternative?

EXERCISES

27. *(Production schedule)* The projected sales, in units, for Einstein Inc. by month for the first four months were

January	8,000
February	12,000
March	16,000
April	19,200

Inventory of finished goods on December 31 was 6,400 units. The company desires to have an ending inventory each month equal to one-half of next month's estimated sales.

Determine the company's production requirements for each month of the first quarter.

28. *(Production budget)* The sales budget for Leno Company shows the following sales projections (in units) for the quarters of the calendar year of 2000:

January–March	270,000
April–June	340,000
July–September	245,000
October–December	275,000
Total	1,130,000

Sales for the first quarter of 2001 are expected to be 295,000 units. Finished Goods Inventory at the end of each production period is scheduled to equal 30 percent of the next quarter's budgeted sales in units. The company is expected to be in compliance with this policy as of December 31, 1999. Develop a quarterly production budget for 2000. Include a column to show total expected production for 2000.

29. *(Material purchases budget)* Brennan Ski Company has projected sales of 21,480 ski boots in September. Each pair of boots requires 2.5 linear feet of leather. The beginning inventory of leather and boots, respectively, are 2,500 yards and 1,154 pairs. Brennan Ski wants to have 9,000 yards of leather and 3,800 pair of boots at the end of September due to high sales projections for the winter months. The leather comes in standard widths. Therefore, to convert linear feet to yards, divide by 3. If Brennan has no beginning or ending Work in Process Inventory, how many yards of leather must the company purchase in September?

30. *(Material purchases budget)* San Diego Culvert Company has budgeted sales of 190,000 feet of its concrete culvert products for June 2000. Each foot of product requires 12 pounds of concrete ($0.10 per pound) and 15 pounds of gravel ($0.03 per pound). Actual beginning inventories and projected ending inventories are shown below.

	June 1	June 30
Finished Goods Inventory (in feet)	24,500	20,000
Concrete (in pounds)	82,000	68,600
Gravel (in pounds)	65,300	92,500

a. How many pounds of concrete does San Diego Culvert plan to purchase in June? What will be the cost of those purchases?
b. How many pounds of gravel does San Diego Culvert plan to purchase in June? What will be the cost of those purchases?

31. *(Production and related schedules)* The Jansen Company manufactures and sells two products: plastic boxes and plastic trays. Estimated needs for a unit of each are

	Boxes	Trays
Material A	2 pounds	1 pound
Material B	4 pounds	4 pounds
Direct labor	2 hours	2 hours

Overhead is applied on the basis of $2 per direct labor hour.

The estimated sales by product for 2000 are:

	Boxes	Trays
Sales	42,000	24,000

The beginning inventories are expected to be as follows:

Material A	4,000 pounds
Material B	6,000 pounds
Boxes	1,000 units
Trays	500 units

The desired inventories are one month's production requirements, assuming constant sales throughout the year.

Prepare the following information:
a. Production schedule
b. Purchases budget in units
c. Direct labor budget in hours
d. Overhead to be charged to production

32. *(Cash collections)* Bentham Company is developing its first-quarter monthly cash budget for 2000 and is having difficulty determining its expected cash collections. On investigation, the following actual and expected sales information was revealed:

November	December	January	February	March
$41,500	$38,000	$29,500	$34,000	$39,500

Tracing of collections from prior-year monthly sales and discussions with the credit manager helped develop a profile of collection behavior patterns.

Of a given month's sales, 40 percent are typically collected in the month of sale. Because the company terms are 1 percent EOM (end of month), net 30, all collections within the month of sale are net of the 1 percent discount. Thirty percent of a given month's sales are collected in the month following the sale. The remaining 30 percent are collected in the second month following the month of the sale. Bad debts are negligible and should be ignored.

a. Prepare a schedule of cash collections for Bentham Company by month for January, February, and March.

b. Calculate the Accounts Receivable balance at March 31.

33. *(Cash budget)* The Accounts Receivable balance at October 1, 2000, for Skyscraper Architects was $606,900. Of that balance, $450,000 represents remaining Accounts Receivable from September billings. The normal collection pattern for the firm is 20 percent of billings in the month of service, 55 percent in the month after service, and 22 percent in the second month following service. The remaining billings are uncollectible. October billings are expected to be $700,000.

a. What were August billings for Skyscraper Architects?

b. What amount of September billings is expected to be uncollectible?

c. What are projected cash collections in October 2000 for the firm?

34. *(Cash collections, accounts receivable)* Atlanta Waterworks is developing a forecast of June 2001 cash receipts from sales. Total sales for June 2001 are expected to be $650,000. Of each month's sales, 75 percent is expected to be on credit. The Accounts Receivable balance at May 31 is $171,000 of which $135,000 represents the remainder of May credit sales. There are no receivables from months prior to April 2001. Atlanta Waterworks has an established collection pattern for credit sales of 60 percent in the month of sale, 25 percent in the month following the sale, and 15 percent in the second month following the sale. Atlanta Waterworks has no uncollectible accounts.

a. What were total sales for April 2001?

b. What were credit sales for May 2001?

c. What are projected cash collections for June 2001?

d. What will be the balance of Accounts Receivable at June 30, 2001?

35. *(Cash balance)* Jackson Fabrics has prepared a forecast for May 2000. Some of the projected information follows:

Income after tax	$260,000
Accrued Income Tax Expense	62,000
Increase in Accounts Receivable for month	41,000
Decrease in Accounts Payable for month	18,300
Depreciation Expense	71,200
Estimated Bad Debts Expense	13,100
Dividends declared	20,000

Using the above information, what is the company's projected increase in cash for May 2000?

36. *(Cash disbursements)* In trying to decide whether it was feasible for the company to acquire treasury stock during May 2000, Wyatt Jones, president of Dallas Leather, Inc., requested information on projected cash disbursements for that month. He received the following information from his new accountant:

Sales for May	$2,000,000
Gross profit on sales	40%
Wages expense for May	$412,500
Other cash expenses for May	$235,250
Decrease in Accounts Payable during May	$40,000
Decrease in Merchandise Inventory during May	$33,750

Not understanding how the above information could help him compute cash disbursements, Mr. Jones asked the accountant to show how cash disbursements can be computed from these figures. If all significant data are given, what are projected cash disbursements for May?

37. *(Cash budget)* The accountant for Georgia Pizza prepared the following cash budget for the third quarter of 2000. When the owner was reviewing it, he was eating a deep-dish pizza loaded with extra cheese. Some of the topping inadvertently spilled onto the page and smeared the figures. Complete the missing numbers on the cash budget, assuming that the accountant has projected a minimum cash balance at the start of each month of $2,500. All borrowings, repayments, and investments are made in even $500 amounts.

	July	August	September	Total
Beginning cash balance	$ 4,500	$?	$?	$?
Cash receipts	8,200	10,100	?	?
Total cash available	$?	$13,000	$19,500	$39,400
Cash disbursements:				
Payments on account	$?	$ 3,900	$ 5,700	$?
Wages expense	5,000	?	6,100	17,200
Overhead costs	4,000	4,600	?	13,000
Total disbursements	$10,300	$?	$16,200	$?
Cash excess (deficiency)	$?	$?	$?	$?
Minimum cash balance	(2,500)	(2,500)	?	?
Cash available (needed)	$?	$ (4,100)	$?	$ (4,200)
Financing:				
Borrowings (repayments)	$ 500	$?	$ (500)	$?
Acquire (sell) investments	0	0	?	?
Receive (pay) interest	0	0	?	(50)
Ending cash balance	$ 2,900	$?	$?	$ 2,750

38. *(Various budgets)* The following are four independent situations.

a. Tasty Frozen Foods is planning to produce two products: frozen dinners and frozen desserts. Sales of frozen dinners are expected to be 200,000 units at $4 per unit; projected sales for frozen desserts are 400,000 units at $3 per unit. Variable costs are 70 percent and 80 percent of sales for dinners and desserts, respectively. What are total fixed costs if Tasty expects net income to be $425,000?

b. Herringbone Suits is projecting sales of $20,000,000 and total fixed manufacturing costs of $4,000,000 for 2000. The company estimates that variable manufacturing costs will be 40 percent of sales. Assuming no change in inventory, what is the company's projected Cost of Goods Sold?

c. The Sizzle Company has projected the following information for October 2001:

Sales	$800,000
Gross profit (based on sales)	25%
Increase in Merchandise Inventory in October	$60,000
Decrease in Trade Accounts Payable for October	$24,000

What are expected cash disbursements for inventories for October 2001?

d. Sam's Calculators' preliminary forecast for its product in 2000 is as follows:

Selling price per unit	$20
Unit sales	200,000
Variable costs	$1,200,000
Fixed costs	$600,000

In preparing the above forecast, Sam included no advertising expenditures. Based on a market study conducted in December 1999, the firm estimated that it could increase the unit selling price by 15 percent and increase unit sales volume by 10 percent if $200,000 were spent on advertising. If Sam's Calculators adjusts its forecast by these amounts, what is the projected operating income for 2000? *(CPA adapted)*

39. *(Projected income statement)* Last year's income statement for Marano Company is presented below:

Sales (50,000 × $10)		$500,000
Cost of goods sold:		
Direct material	$200,000	
Direct labor	100,000	
Overhead	50,000	(350,000)
Gross profit		$150,000
Expenses		
Selling	$ 50,000	
Administrative	40,000	(90,000)
Income before taxes		$ 60,000

Sales are expected to decrease by 10 percent, and material and labor costs are expected to increase by 10 percent. Overhead is applied to production based on a percentage of direct labor costs. Ten thousand dollars of selling expenses are considered fixed. The balance varies with sales dollars. All administrative costs are fixed.

Management desires to earn 5 percent on sales this year and will adjust the unit selling price, if necessary. Develop a pro forma income statement for the year for Marano Company that incorporates the indicated changes.

40. *(Budgeted income, cash, accounts receivable)* In preparing its budget for July 2000, Expert Legal Services has the following accounts receivable information available:

Accounts Receivable at June 30	$500,000
Estimated credit sales for July	600,000
Estimated collections in July for credit sales in July and prior months	440,000
Estimated write-offs in July for uncollectible credit sales	32,000
Estimated provision for uncollectible accounts for credit sales in July	24,000

a. What is the projected balance of Accounts Receivable at July 31, 2000?
b. Which of the above amounts (if any) will affect the cash budget?
c. Which of the above amounts (if any) will affect the pro forma income statement for July? *(CPA adapted)*

41. *(Pro forma income statement)* Bennett Novelty Wholesale Store has prepared the following budget information for May 2001:

- Sales of $300,000. All sales are on account and a provision for bad debts is made monthly at 3 percent of sales.
- Inventory was $70,000 on April 30 and an increase of $10,000 is planned for May.
- All inventory is marked to sell at cost plus 50 percent.
- Estimated cash disbursements for selling and administrative expenses for the month are $40,000.
- Depreciation for May is projected at $5,000.

Prepare a pro forma income statement for Bennett Novelty Wholesale Store for May 2001. *(CPA adapted)*

42. *(Pro forma income)* Joan Wilson, president of Fresh Fashions, is considering buying a new piece of equipment for her plant. This piece of equipment will increase her fixed overhead by $300,000 per year, but reduce her variable expenses per unit of production by 35 percent. Budgeted sales of her only product, hand-painted scarves, for 2001 are 120,000 scarves at an average selling price of $25 each. Variable expenses are currently 75 percent of selling price and fixed costs total $400,000 per year. Assuming that Joan acquires the new piece of equipment, answer the following questions.

a. What is the projected variable cost per scarf?
b. What are the projected fixed costs per year?
c. What is the expected operating profit if actual sales are equal to budgeted sales?
d. Should Joan acquire the equipment?

PROBLEMS

43. *(Production and purchases budgets)* Aurora Products has prepared the following unit sales forecast for 2000:

	January–June	July–December	Total
Sales	380,000	420,000	800,000

Estimated ending finished goods inventories are 30,000 units at December 31, 1999; 76,000 units at June 30; and 90,000 units at December 31, 2000.

In manufacturing each unit of this product, Aurora Products uses five pounds of Material A and three gallons of Material B. The company carries no Work in Process Inventory. Direct material ending inventories are projected as follows:

	December 31, 1999	June 30, 2000	December 31, 2000
Material A (in pounds)	200,000	250,000	300,000
Material B (in gallons)	140,000	160,000	200,000

Prepare a production and purchases budget for each semiannual period of 2000.

44. *(Production, purchases, cash disbursements)* West Indies Tea Company has budgeted sales of 300,000 cans of iced tea mix during June 2000 and 375,000 cans during July. Production of the mix requires 14 ounces of tea and 2 ounces of sugar. Beginning inventories of tea and sugar are as follows:

Iced tea mix	4,300 cans of finished product
Tea	2,750 pounds
Sugar	600 pounds

West Indies Tea Company generally carries an inventory of 3 percent of the following month's needs for finished goods. Raw materials are stocked in relation to finished goods ending inventory. Assuming the desired ending inventory stock is achieved, answer the following questions.

a. How many cans of iced tea mix need to be produced in June?
b. How many pounds of tea need to be purchased in June? (There are 16 ounces in a pound.)
c. How many pounds of sugar need to be purchased in June?
d. If tea and sugar cost $4.50 and $0.30 per pound, respectively, what dollar amount of purchases is budgeted for June?
e. If West Indies Tea Company normally pays for 30 percent of its budgeted purchases during the month of purchase and takes a 2 percent discount, what are budgeted cash disbursements for June purchases during June?

45. *(Production, purchases, cash budgets)* Pop's Tops makes one style of men's hats. Sales and collections for the first three months of 2001 are expected to be

	January	February	March	Total
Sales quantity	3,200	2,600	3,700	9,500
Revenue	$57,600	$46,800	$66,600	$171,000
Collections	$58,080	$48,960	$62,640	$169,680

The December 31, 2000, balance sheet revealed the following selected balances: Cash, $18,760; Raw Material Inventory, $3,812.50; Finished Goods Inventory, $10,500; and Accounts Payable, $3,800. The Raw Material Inventory balance represents 457.50 yards of felt and 12,200 inches of ribbon. The Finished Goods Inventory consists of 800 hats.

During the first quarter of 2001, management expects that all work started within a month will be finished within that month, so no work in process is anticipated.

Management plans to have enough hats on hand at the end of each month to satisfy 25 percent of the subsequent month's sales. In this regard, the company predicts both production and sales of 3,600 hats in April.

Each hat requires 3/4 of a yard of felt and 20 inches of ribbon. Felt costs $7 per yard and ribbon costs $0.05 per inch. Ending inventory policy for raw materials is 20 percent of the next month's production.

The company normally pays for 80 percent of a month's purchases of raw materials in the month of purchase (on which it takes a 2 percent cash discount). The remaining 20 percent is paid in full in the month following the month of purchase.

The cost of direct labor is budgeted at $3 per hat produced and is paid in the month of production. Total out-of-pocket factory overhead can be predicted as $5,200 per month plus $2.25 per hat produced. Total nonfactory cash costs are equal to $2,800 per month plus 10 percent of sales revenue. All factory and nonfactory cash expenses are paid in the month of incurrence. In addition, the company plans to make an estimated quarterly tax payment of $5,000 and pay executive bonuses of $15,000 in January 2001.

The management of Pop's Tops wishes to have a minimum of $12,000 of cash at the end of each month. If the company has to borrow funds, it will do so in $1,000 multiples at the beginning of a month at a 12 percent annual interest rate. Loans are to be repaid at the end of a month in multiples of $1,000. Interest is paid only when a repayment is made.

a. Prepare a production budget by month and in total for the first quarter of 2001.

b. Prepare a raw material purchases budget by month and in total for the first quarter of 2001.

c. Prepare a schedule of cash payments for purchases by month and in total for the first quarter of 2001. The Accounts Payable balance on December 31, 2000, represents the unpaid 20 percent of December purchases.

d. Prepare a combined payments schedule for factory overhead and nonfactory cash costs for each month and in total for the first quarter of 2001.

e. Prepare a cash budget for each month and in total for the first quarter of 2001.

46. *(Cash budget)* The January 31, 1999, balance sheet of Sara's Plaques follows:

Assets		Liabilities and Stockholders' Equity		
Cash	$ 12,000	Accounts Payable		$ 70,200
Accounts Receivable (Net of Allowance for Uncollectibles of $1,440)	34,560			
Inventory	52,400	Common Stock	$90,000	
Plant Assets (Net of Accumulated Depreciation of $60,000)	36,000	Retained Earnings (Deficit)	(25,240)	64,760
Total Assets	$134,960	Total Liabilities and Stockholders' Equity		$134,960

Additional information about the company includes the following:

- Expected sales for February and March are $120,000 and $130,000, respectively.
- The collection pattern from the month of sale forward is 50 percent, 48 percent, and 2 percent uncollectible.
- Cost of goods sold is 75 percent of sales.
- Purchases each month are 55 percent of the current month's sales and 45 percent of the next month's projected sales. All purchases are paid for in full in the month following purchase.
- Other cash expenses each month are $21,500. The only noncash expense each month is $4,000 of depreciation.

a. What are budgeted cash collections for February 2000?
b. What will be the Inventory balance at February 29, 2000?
c. What will be the projected balance in Retained Earnings at February 29, 2000?
d. If the company wishes to maintain a minimum cash balance of $8,000, how much will be available for investment or need to be borrowed at the end of February 2000?

47. *(Cash budget)* Tim's Department Store typically makes 50 percent of its sales on credit. Sales are billed twice monthly, on the 10th of the month for the last half of the prior month's sales and on the 20th of the month for the first half of the current month's sales. All sales are made with terms of 2/10, n/30. Based on past experience, Accounts Receivable are collected as follows:

Within the discount period	80%
On the 30th day	18%
Uncollectible	2%

Sales for May 2000 were $600,000 and projected sales for the next four months are

June	$800,000
July	700,000
August	800,000
September	600,000

Tim's average profit margin on its products is 30 percent of selling price.

Tim's purchases merchandise for resale to meet the current month's sales demand and to maintain a desired monthly ending inventory of 25 percent of the next month's sales. All purchases are on account with terms of n/30. Tim's pays for one-half of a month's purchases in the month of purchase and the other half in the month following the purchase. All sales and purchases occur evenly throughout the month.

a. How much cash can Tim's plan to collect from Accounts Receivable during July 2000?
b. How much cash can Tim's plan to collect in September 2000 from sales made in August?
c. What will be the budgeted dollar value of Tim's inventory on August 31, 2000?
d. How much merchandise should Tim's plan to purchase during June 2000?
e. What are Tim's budgeted cash payments for merchandise during August 2000? *(CMA adapted)*

48. *(Cash budget)* Andrews Manufacturing has incurred substantial losses for several years and has decided to declare bankruptcy. The company petitioned the court for protection from creditors on March 31, 1999, and submitted the following balance sheet:

ANDREWS MANUFACTURING
Balance Sheet
March 31, 1999

	Book Value	Liquidation Value
Assets:		
Accounts Receivable	$100,000	$ 50,000
Inventories	90,000	40,000
Plant Assets (Net)	150,000	160,000
Totals	$340,000	$250,000

The liabilities and stockholders' equity of Andrews at this date are

Accounts Payable—General Creditors	$600,000
Common Stock	60,000
Retained Earnings Deficit	(320,000)
Total	$340,000

Andrews' management informed the court that the company has developed a new product and that a prospective customer is willing to sign a contract for the purchase of 10,000 units of this product during the year ending March 31, 2000, 12,000 units during the year ending March 31, 2001, and 15,000 units during the year ending March 31, 2002, at a price of $90 per unit. This product can be manufactured using Andrews' present facilities. Monthly production with immediate delivery is expected to be uniform within each year. Receivables are expected to be collected during the calendar month following sales. Unit production costs of the new product are estimated as follows:

Direct material	$20
Direct labor	30
Variable overhead	10

Fixed costs of $130,000 (excluding depreciation) are estimated per year. Purchases of direct material will be paid during the calendar month following purchase. Fixed costs, direct labor, and variable overhead will be paid as incurred. Inventory of direct material will be equal to 60 days' usage. After the first month of operations, 30 days' usage will be ordered each month.

The general creditors have agreed to reduce their total claims to 60% of their March 31, 1999, balances under the following conditions:

- Existing accounts receivable and inventories are to be liquidated immediately, with the proceeds turned over to the general creditors.
- The reduced balance of accounts payable is to be paid as cash is generated from future operations, but no later than March 31, 2001. No interest will be paid on these obligations.

Under this proposed plan, the general creditors would receive $110,000 more than the current liquidation value of Andrews' assets. The court has engaged you to determine the feasibility of this plan.

Ignoring any need to borrow and repay short-term funds for working capital purposes, prepare a cash budget for the years ending March 31, 2000 and 2001, showing the cash expected to be available to pay the claims of the general creditors, payments to general creditors, and the cash remaining after payment of claims. *(CPA adapted)*

49. *(Budgeted sales and S&A; other computations)* Grecian Urns has projected Cost of Goods Sold for June 2000 of $960,000. Of this amount, $60,000 represents fixed overhead costs. Total variable costs for the company each month average 70 percent of sales. The company's cost to retail (CGS to sales) percentage is

60 percent and the company normally shows a 15 percent rate of net income on sales. All purchases and expenses (except depreciation) are paid in cash: 55 percent in the month incurred and 45 percent in the following month. Depreciation is $30,000 per month.

a. What are Grecian Urns' expected sales for June?
b. What are Grecian Urns' expected variable selling and administrative costs for June?
c. What is Grecian Urns' normal contribution margin ratio?
d. What are Grecian Urns' total fixed costs?
e. Grecian Urns normally collects 45 percent of its sales in the month of sale and the rest in the next month. What are expected cash receipts and disbursements related only to June's transactions?

50. *(Pro forma results)* The James Company is attempting to set a new selling price for its single product, a metal file cabinet, for the upcoming year. The current variable production cost is $40 per unit and total fixed costs are $2,000,000. Fixed manufacturing costs are 80 percent of total fixed costs and are allocated to the product based on the number of units produced. There are no variable selling or administrative costs. Variable and fixed costs are expected to increase by 15 and 8 percent, respectively, next year. Estimated production and sales are 200,000 units. Selling price is normally set at full production cost plus 25 percent.

a. What is the expected full production cost per unit of James's file cabinets for next year?
b. What is the expected selling price of the product?
c. What is pro forma income before tax using the selling price computed in part (b)?
d. What would be the required selling price for the company to earn income before tax equal to 25 percent of sales?

51. *(Comprehensive)* Reliable Appliance Company produces and sells two kitchen appliances: mixers and doughmakers. In July 1999, Reliable's budget department gathered the following data to meet budget requirements for 2000.

2000 PROJECTED SALES

Product	Units	Price
Mixers	60,000	$ 50
Doughmakers	40,000	120

2000 INVENTORIES (UNITS)

Product	Expected 1/1/00	Desired 12/31/00
Mixers	15,000	20,000
Doughmakers	4,000	5,000

To produce one unit of each product, the following major internal components are used (in addition to the plastic housing for products, which is subcontracted in a subsequent operation):

Component	Mixer	Doughmaker
Motor	1	1
Beater	2	4
Fuse	2	3

Projected data for 2000 with respect to components are as follows:

Component	Anticipated Purchase Price	Expected Inventory 1/1/00	Desired Inventory 12/31/00
Motor	$15.00	2,000	3,600 units
Beater	1.25	21,000	24,000 units
Fuse	2.00	6,000	7,500 units

Projected direct labor requirements for 2000 and rates are as follows:

Product	Hours per Unit	Rate per Hour
Mixers	2	$7
Doughmakers	3	9

Overhead is applied at a rate of $5 per direct labor hour.

Based on the above projections and budget requirements for 2000 for mixers and doughmakers, prepare the following budgets for 2000:

a. Sales budget (in dollars).
b. Production budget (in units).
c. Internal components purchases budget (in units).
d. Internal components purchases budget (in dollars).
e. Direct labor budget (in dollars). *(CPA adapted)*

52. *(Master budget preparation)* Sopchoppy Company manufactures a red industrial dye. The company is preparing its 2000 master budget and has presented you with the following information.

1. The December 31, 1999, balance sheet for the company is shown below.

SOPCHOPPY COMPANY
Balance Sheet
December 31, 1999

Assets			Liabilities and Stockholders' Equity		
Cash		$ 5,080	Notes Payable		$ 25,000
Accounts Receivable		26,500	Accounts Payable		2,148
Raw Materials Inventory		800	Dividends Payable		10,000
Finished Goods Inventory		2,104	Total Liabilities		$ 37,148
Prepaid Insurance		1,200	Common Stock	$100,000	
Building	$300,000		Paid-in Capital	50,000	
Accumulated Depreciation	(20,000)	280,000	Retained Earnings	128,536	278,536
Total Assets		$315,684	Total Liabilities and Stockholders' Equity		$315,684

2. The Accounts Receivable balance at 12/31/99 represents the remaining balances of November and December credit sales. Sales were $70,000 and $65,000, respectively, in those two months.

3. Estimated sales in gallons of dye for January through May 2000 are shown below.

January	8,000
February	10,000
March	15,000
April	12,000
May	11,000

Each gallon of dye sells for $12.

4. The collection pattern for accounts receivable is as follows: 70 percent in the month of sale; 20 percent in the first month after the sale; 10 percent in the second month after the sale. Sopchoppy expects no bad debts and no customers are given cash discounts. *(continued)*

5. Each gallon of dye has the following standard quantities and costs for direct materials and direct labor:

1.2 gallons of direct material (some evaporation occurs during processing) @ $0.80 per gallon	$0.96
1/2 hour of direct labor @ $6 per hour	3.00

Variable overhead is applied to the product on a machine-hour basis. It takes 5 hours of machine time to process 1 gallon of dye. The variable overhead rate is $0.06 per machine hour; VOH consists entirely of utility costs. Total annual fixed overhead is $120,000; it is applied at $1.00 per gallon based on an expected annual capacity of 120,000 gallons. Fixed overhead per year is composed of the following costs:

Salaries	$78,000
Utilities	12,000
Insurance—factory	2,400
Depreciation—factory	27,600

Fixed overhead is incurred evenly throughout the year.

6. There is no beginning inventory of Work in Process. All work in process is completed in the period in which it is started. Raw Materials Inventory at the beginning of the year consists of 1,000 gallons of direct material at a standard cost of $0.80 per gallon. There are 400 gallons of dye in Finished Goods Inventory at the beginning of the year carried at a standard cost of $5.26 per gallon: Direct Material, $0.96; Direct Labor, $3.00; Variable Overhead, $0.30; and Fixed Overhead, $1.00.
7. Accounts Payable relates solely to raw material. Accounts Payable are paid 60 percent in the month of purchase and 40 percent in the month after purchase. No discounts are given for prompt payment.
8. The dividend will be paid in January 2000.
9. A new piece of equipment costing $9,000 will be purchased on March 1, 2000. Payment of 80 percent will be made in March and 20 percent in April. The equipment will have no salvage value and has a useful life of three years.
10. The note payable has a 12 percent interest rate; interest is paid at the end of each month. The principal of the note is paid off as cash is available to do so.
11. Sopchoppy's management has set a minimum cash balance at $5,000. Investments and borrowings are made in even $100 amounts. Investments will earn 9 percent per year.
12. The ending Finished Goods Inventory should be 5 percent of the next month's needs. This is not true at the beginning of 2000 due to a miscalculation in sales for December. The ending inventory of raw materials should be 5 percent of the next month's needs.
13. Selling and administrative costs per month are as follows: salaries, $18,000; rent, $7,000; and utilities, $800. These costs are paid in cash as they are incurred.

Prepare a master budget for each month of the first quarter of 2000 and pro forma financial statements as of the end of the first quarter of 2000.

CASES

53. *(Preparing and analyzing a budget)* Harvey & Company, a local accounting firm, has a formal budgeting system. The firm is comprised of five partners, two managers, four seniors, two secretaries, and two bookkeepers. The budgeting process has a bottom-line focus; that is, the budget and planning process continues to iterate and evolve until an acceptable budgeted net income is obtained. The determination of an acceptable level of net income is based on two factors: (1) the amount of salary the partners could generate if they were employed elsewhere and (2) a reasonable return on the partners' investment in the firm's net assets.

For 2001, after careful consideration of alternative employment opportunities, the partners agreed that the best alternative employment would generate the following salaries:

Partner 1	$150,000
Partner 2	225,000
Partner 3	110,000
Partner 4	90,000
Partner 5	125,000
Total	$700,000

The second input to determination of the desired net income level is more complex. This part of the desired net income is based on the value of the net assets owned by the accounting firm. The partners have identified two major categories of assets: tangible assets and intangible assets. The partners have agreed that the net tangible assets are worth $230,000. The intangible assets, consisting mostly of the accounting practice itself, are worth 1.1 times gross fees billed in 2000. In 2000, the firm's gross billings were $1,615,000. The partners have also agreed that a reasonable rate of return on the net assets of the accounting firm is 12 percent. Thus, the partners' desired net income from return on investment is as follows:

Tangible assets	$ 230,000
Intangible assets ($1,615,000 × 110%)	1,776,500
Total investment	$2,006,500
Times rate of return	× 0.12
Equals required dollar return	$ 240,780

The experience of the accounting firm indicates that other operating costs are incurred as follows:

Fixed Expenses (per year):	
Salaries (other than partners)	$300,000
Overhead	125,000

Variable Expenses:	
Overhead	15% of gross billings
Client service	5% of gross billings

SOURCE: Adapted from Jerry S. Huss, "Better Budgeting for CPA Firms," *Journal of Accountancy* (November 1977), pp. 65–72. Reprinted with permission from the *Journal of Accountancy*. Copyright © 2000 by American Institute of CPAs. Opinions of the authors are their own and do not necessarily reflect policies of the AICPA.

a. Determine the minimum level of gross billings that would allow the partners to realize their net income objective. Prepare a budget of costs and revenues at that level. *(continued)*

b. If the partners believe that the level of billings you have projected in part (a) is not feasible given the time constraints at the partner, manager, and senior levels, what changes can they make to the budget to preserve the desired level of net income?

54. *(Preparing a cash budget)* Collegiate Management Education (CME), Inc., is a nonprofit organization that sponsors a wide variety of management seminars throughout the Southwest. In addition, it is heavily involved in research into improved methods of teaching and motivating college administrators. The seminar activity is largely supported by fees, and the research program is supported by membership dues.

CME operates on a calendar-year basis and is finalizing the budget for 2000. The following information has been taken from approved plans, which are still tentative at this time:

SEMINAR PROGRAM

Revenue—The scheduled number of programs should produce $12,000,000 of revenue for the year. Each program is budgeted to produce the same amount of revenue. The revenue is collected during the month the program is offered. The programs are scheduled during the basic academic year and are not held during June, July, August, and December. Twelve percent of the revenue is generated in each of the first five months of the year and the remainder is distributed evenly during September, October, and November.

Direct expenses—The seminar expenses are made up of three types:

- Instructors' fees are paid at the rate of 70 percent of seminar revenue in the month following the seminar. The instructors are considered independent contractors and are not eligible for CME employee benefits.
- Facilities fees total $5,600,000 for the year. They are the same for each program and are paid in the month the program is given.
- Annual promotional costs of $1,000,000 are spent equally in all months except June and July when there is no promotional effort.

RESEARCH PROGRAM

Research grants—The research program has a large number of projects nearing completion. The main research activity this year includes feasibility studies for new projects to be started in 2001. As a result, the total grant expense of $3,000,000 for 2000 is expected to be paid out at the rate of $500,000 per month during the first six months of the year.

SALARIES AND OTHER CME EXPENSES

- Office lease—annual amount of $240,000 paid monthly at the beginning of each month.
- General administrative expenses—$1,500,000 annually or $125,000 per month. These are paid in cash as incurred.
- Depreciation expense—$240,000 per year.
- General CME promotion—annual cost of $600,000, paid monthly.
- Salaries and benefits are as follows:

Number of Employees	Monthly Cash Salary	Total Annual Salaries
1	$50,000	$ 50,000
3	40,000	120,000
4	30,000	120,000
15	25,000	375,000
5	15,000	75,000
22	10,000	220,000
50		$960,000

Employee benefits amount to $240,000 or 25 percent of annual salaries. Except for the pension contribution, the benefits are paid as salaries are paid. The annual pension payment of $24,000, based on 2.5 percent of total annual salaries, is due on April 15, 2000.

OTHER INFORMATION

- Membership income—CME has 100,000 members who each pay an annual fee of $100. The fee for the calendar year is invoiced in late June.
- The collection schedule is as follows: July, 60 percent; August, 30 percent; September, 5 percent; and October, 5 percent.
- Capital expenditures—The capital expenditures program calls for a total of $510,000 in cash payments to be spread evenly over the first five months of 2000.
- Cash and temporary investments at January 1, 2000, are estimated at $750,000.

a. Prepare a budget of the annual cash receipts and disbursements for 2000.
b. Prepare a cash budget for CME for January 2000.
c. Using the information developed in parts (a) and (b), identify two important operating problems of CME. *(CMA adapted)*

55. *(Revising and analyzing an operating budget)* The Mason Agency, a division of General Service Industries, offers consulting services to clients for a fee. The corporate management at General Service is pleased with the performance of the Mason Agency for the first nine months of the current year and has recommended that the division manager of the Mason Agency, Ramona Howell, submit a revised forecast for the remaining quarter, because the division has exceeded the annual year-to-date plan by 20 percent of operating income. An unexpected increase in billed hour volume over the original plan is the main reason for this gain in income. The original operating budget for the first three quarters for the Mason Agency is presented below.

2000 OPERATING BUDGET

	1st Quarter	2nd Quarter	3rd Quarter	Total 9 Months
Revenue:				
Consulting fees				
Management consulting	$ 315,000	$ 315,000	$ 315,000	$ 945,000
EDP consulting	421,875	421,875	421,875	1,265,625
Total	$ 736,875	$ 736,875	$ 736,875	$ 2,210,625
Other revenue	10,000	10,000	10,000	30,000
Total	$ 746,875	$ 746,875	$ 746,875	$ 2,240,625
Expenses:				
Consultant salaries	$(386,750)	$(386,750)	$(386,750)	$(1,160,250)
Travel and entertainment	(45,625)	(45,625)	(45,625)	(136,875)
Administrative	(100,000)	(100,000)	(100,000)	(300,000)
Depreciation	(40,000)	(40,000)	(40,000)	(120,000)
Corporate allocation	(50,000)	(50,000)	(50,000)	(150,000)
Total	$(622,375)	$(622,375)	$(622,375)	$(1,867,125)
Operating income	$ 124,500	$ 124,500	$ 124,500	$ 373,500

When comparing the actuals for the first three quarters to the original plan, Howell analyzed the variances and will reflect the following information in her revised forecast for the fourth quarter.

The division currently has 25 consultants on staff, 10 for management consulting and 15 for EDP consulting, and has hired 3 additional management consultants to start work at the beginning of the fourth quarter to meet the increased client demand.

The hourly billing rate for consulting revenues will remain at $90 per hour for each management consultant and $75 per hour for each EDP consultant. However, due to the favorable increase in billing hour volume when compared to the plan, the hours for each consultant will be increased by 50 hours per quarter. New employees are equally as capable as current employees and will be billed at the same rates.

The budgeted annual salaries and actual annual salaries, paid monthly, are the same at $50,000 for a management consultant and 8 percent less for an EDP consultant. Corporate management has approved a merit increase of 10 percent at the beginning of the fourth quarter for all 25 existing consultants, but the new consultants will be compensated at the planned rate.

The planned salary expense includes a provision for employee fringe benefits amounting to 30 percent of the annual salaries; however, the improvement of some corporatewide employee programs will increase the fringe benefit allocation to 40 percent.

The original plan assumes a fixed hourly rate for travel and other related expenses for each billing hour of consulting. These are expenses that are not reimbursed by the client, and the previously determined hourly rate has proven to be adequate to cover these costs.

Other revenues are derived from temporary rentals and interest income and remain unchanged for the fourth quarter.

Administrative expenses have been favorable at 7 percent below the plan; this 7 percent savings on fourth-quarter expenses will be reflected in the revised plan.

Depreciation for office equipment and computers will stay constant at the projected straight-line rate.

Due to the favorable experience for the first three quarters and the division's increased ability to absorb costs, the corporate management at General Service Industries has increased the corporate expense allocation by 50 percent.

a. Prepare a revised operating budget for the fourth quarter for the Mason Agency that Ramona Howell will present to General Service Industries. Be sure to furnish supporting calculations for all revised revenue and expense amounts.

b. Discuss the reasons why an organization would prepare a revised forecast.

c. Discuss your feelings about the 50 percent increase in corporate expense allocations. *(CMA adapted)*

REALITY CHECK

56. Many managers believe that, if all amounts in their budgets are not spent during a period, they will lose allocations in future periods and that little or no recognition will result from cost savings.

Discuss the behavioral and ethical issues involved in a spend-it-or-lose-it attitude. Include in your discussion the issue of negotiating budget allocation requests prior to the beginning of the period.

57. *(Key variables)* A consultant mentioned to Alpha Company's CEO that key variables are significant if the company is to control its destiny. The CEO has asked you to prepare a brief memo explaining what the consultant meant.

58. *(Continuous budgeting)* You own a small boat manufacturing company. At a recent manufacturers' association meeting, you overheard one of the other company owners saying how he liked using a continuous budgeting process. Discuss what you believe are the advantages and disadvantages of continuous budgeting for your company in a report to your top management group.

59. *(Planning versus control)* Your colleague, who loves riddles, has asked you the following question: "Is planning an extension of control or is control an extension of planning?" Prepare a reply.

60. Many companies prepare a simplified cash budget as follows: Beginning cash + Cash receipts − Cash disbursements = Ending cash. Discuss the advantages of the model presented in Exhibit 13–16 when compared with such a simplified cash budget.

61. Find the Web page for the International Red Cross. Review the variety of activities in which this organization is currently involved. What would be the greatest challenges in budgeting for such an organization? What actions has the organization taken to deal with its budgeting challenges?

62. *To evaluate different planning techniques used to develop strategic plans, The Futures Group recently interviewed senior corporate executives at more than 100 U.S. companies. According to 43% of the respondents, competitor actions are the top external factor impacting their business.*

SOURCE: Stephen H. Miller and Samuel Bentley, "Competitive Intelligence Increases Strategic Planning 'Comfort Level,'" *Competitive Intelligence Magazine* (January–March 1999), p. 5.

Discuss why you believe so many senior executives have indicated that competitor actions are the top external factor impacting their business.

CHAPTER

14

Capital Budgeting

LEARNING OBJECTIVES

After completing this chapter, you should be able to answer the following questions:

1
Why do most capital budgeting methods focus on cash flows?

2
What is measured by the payback period?

3
How are the net present value and profitability index of a project measured?

4
How is the internal rate of return on a project computed? What does it measure?

5
How do taxation and depreciation methods affect cash flows?

6
What are the underlying assumptions and limitations of each capital project evaluation method?

7
How do managers rank investment projects?

8
How is risk considered in capital budgeting analysis?

9
How and why should management conduct a postinvestment audit of a capital project?

10
(Appendix 1) How are present values calculated?

11
(Appendix 2) What are the advantages and disadvantages of the accounting rate of return method?

INTRODUCING Amazon.com

http://www.amazon.com

In a few short years, Amazon.com has evolved from an idea to the best-known firm on the Internet. The firm's president, Jeff Bezos, commands the attention of Wall Street and the financial press. On the morning of September 28, 1999, Amazon.com planned to make an "announcement significantly affecting the world of e-commerce." The following day, Mr. Bezos stepped up to a podium in the Sheraton Hotel in New York.

"Sixteen months ago Amazon.com was a place where you could find books," Bezos began, hands folded behind his back as he paced the stage. "Tomorrow Amazon.com will be a place where you can find anything." With that, he introduced the latest installment of the Amazon potboiler: the serialization story of one company's ambitious plan to take over the world—the e-commerce world that is.

Throughout 1999, Amazon.com has been on the move. On average it has announced a major initiative every six weeks. In February it bought 46% of Drugstore.com. In March it launched online auctions—two days after rival eBay announced a secondary stock offering. In May the company took a 35% piece of HomeGrocer.com. In June, 54% of Pets.com. In July, 49% of Gear.com. That same month Amazon opened two new online shops: toys and electronics. October's announcement was Z-shops (an online mall) and All Product Search (a product browser).

Forget about Amazon.com as the Wal-Mart of the Web. Bezos is aiming for something even bigger. So big, in fact, that it hasn't been invented yet. "I get asked a lot, Are you trying to be the Wal-Mart of the Web?" says Bezos. "The truth is, we're not trying to be the Anything of the Web. We're genetically pioneers. Everybody here wants to do something completely new. I wake up every morning trying to make sure I can confound journalists and pundits who try to encapsulate us in an eight-second sound bite."

In Bezos' vision, Amazon.com will be the center of the e-commerce universe. Books, pet food, tennis shoes, banjos; whatever e-shoppers want, they can buy it, or locate it, on Amazon.com. Picture Amazon as an octopus, its tentacles reaching out all over the Web. The potential payoff is huge. Investors certainly think so. After Amazon announced Z-shops and All Product Search, its stock rose 23%, to $80 a share. "This is so big, so important, that you have to be invested in it," says Morris Mark, a portfolio manager who added to his Amazon stake after the announcement.

SOURCE: Katrina Brooker, "Amazon vs. Everybody," *Fortune* (November 8, 1999), pp. 120–128. © 1999 Time Inc. Reprinted by permission.

Amazon.com's future will be determined by the success of the investments it is making today. Although the risks may be large, the potential payoff is proportionate. Choosing the assets in which an organization will invest is one of the most important business decisions of managers. In almost every organization, investments must be made in some short-term working capital assets, such as merchandise inventory, supplies, and raw material. Organizations must also invest in **capital assets** that are used to generate future revenues; cost savings; or distribution, service, or production capabilities. A capital asset can be a tangible fixed asset (such as a piece of machinery or a building) or an intangible asset (such as a capital lease or a patent).

capital asset

The acquisition of capital assets is often part of the solution to many of the issues discussed in this text. For example, the improvement of quality may depend on the acquisition of new technology and investment in training programs. Reengineering of business processes often involves investment in higher technology; and mergers and acquisitions involve decisions to invest in other companies. These examples illustrate capital asset decisions.

Financial managers, assisted by cost accountants, are responsible for capital budgeting. **Capital budgeting** is "a process for evaluating proposed long-range projects or courses of future activity for the purpose of allocating limited resources."[1]

capital budgeting

[1] Institute of Management Accountants (formerly National Association of Accountants), *Statements on Management Accounting Number 2: Management Accounting Terminology* (Montvale, N.J.: NAA, June 1, 1983), p. 14.

The process includes planning for and preparing the capital budget as well as reviewing past investments to assess and enhance the effectiveness of the process. The capital budget presents planned annual expenditures for capital projects for the near term (tomorrow to 5 years from now) and summary information for the long term (6 to 10 years). The capital budget is a key instrument in implementing organizational strategies.

Capital budgeting involves comparing and evaluating alternative projects within a budgetary framework. A variety of criteria are applied by managers and accountants to evaluate the feasibility of alternative projects. Although financial criteria are used to assess virtually all projects, today more firms are also using nonfinancial criteria. The nonfinancial criteria are critical to the assessment of activities that have financial benefits that are difficult to quantify. For example, high-technology investments and investments in research and development (R&D) are often difficult to evaluate using only financial criteria. One firm in the biotechnology industry uses nine criteria to evaluate the feasibility of R&D projects. These criteria are presented in Exhibit 14–1.

By evaluating potential capital projects using a portfolio of criteria, managers can be confident that all possible costs and contributions of projects have been considered. Additionally, the multiple criteria allow for a balanced evaluation of short- and long-term benefits, the fit with existing technology, and the roles of projects in both marketing and cost management. For this biotechnology company, the use of multiple criteria ensures that projects will be considered from the perspectives of strategy, marketing, cost management, quality, and technical feasibility.

Note that one of the criteria in Exhibit 14–1 is financial rate of return on investment. Providing information about the financial returns of potential capital projects is one of the important tasks of cost accountants. This chapter discusses a variety of techniques that are used in businesses to evaluate the potential financial costs and contributions of proposed capital projects. Several of these techniques are based on an analysis of the amounts and timing of project cash flows.

USE OF CASH FLOWS IN CAPITAL BUDGETING

Why do most capital budgeting methods focus on cash flows?

cash flow

Capital budgeting investment decisions can be made using a variety of techniques including payback period, net present value, profitability index, internal rate of return, and accounting rate of return. All but the last of these methods focus on the amounts and timing of **cash flows** (receipts or disbursements of cash). Cash receipts include the revenues from a capital project that have been earned and collected, savings generated by the project's reductions in existing operating costs, and any cash inflow from selling the asset at the end of its useful life. Cash dis-

EXHIBIT 14–1

Project Evaluation Criteria—R&D Projects

1. Potential for proprietary position.
2. Balance between short-term and long-term projects and payoffs.
3. Potential for collaborations and outside funding.
4. Financial rate of return on investment.
5. Need to establish competency in an area.
6. Potential for spin-off projects.
7. Strategic fit with the corporation's planned and existing technology, manufacturing capabilities, marketing and distribution systems.
8. Impact on long-term corporate positioning.
9. Probability of technical success.

SOURCE: Suresh Kalahnanam and Suzanne K. Schmidt, "Analyzing Capital Investments in New Products," *Management Accounting* (January 1996), pp. 31–36. Reprinted from *Management Accounting.* Copyright by Institute of Management Accountants, Montvale, N.J.

bursements include asset acquisition expenditures, additional working capital investments, and costs for project-related direct materials, direct labor, and overhead.

Any investment made by an organization is expected to earn some type of return, such as interest, cash dividends, or operating income. Because interest and dividends are received in cash, accrual-based operating income must be converted to a cash basis for comparison purposes. Remember that accrual accounting recognizes revenues when earned, not when cash is received, and recognizes expenses when incurred regardless of whether a liability is created or cash is paid. Converting accounting income to cash flow information puts all investment returns on an equivalent basis.

Interest cost is a cash outflow associated with debt financing and is not part of the project selection process. The funding of projects is a financing, not an investment, decision. A **financing decision** is a judgment regarding the method of raising capital to fund an investment. Financing is based on the entity's ability to issue and service debt and equity securities. On the other hand, an **investment decision** is a judgment about which assets to acquire to achieve an entity's stated objectives. Cash flows generated by the two types of decisions should not be combined. Company management must justify the acquisition and use of an asset prior to justifying the method of financing that asset.

financing decision

investment decision

Including receipts and disbursements caused by financing with other project cash flows conceals a project's true profitability because financing costs relate to the total entity. The assignment of financing costs to a specific project is often arbitrary, which causes problems in comparing projects that are to be acquired with different financing sources. In addition, including financing effects in an investment decision creates a problem in assigning responsibility. Investment decisions are typically made by divisional managers, or by top management after receiving input from divisional managers. Financing decisions are typically made by an organization's treasurer in conjunction with top management.

Cash flows from a capital project are received and paid at different points in time over the project's life. Some cash flows occur at the beginning of a period, some during the period, and some at the end. To simplify capital budgeting analysis, most analysts assume that all cash flows occur at a specific, single point in time—either at the beginning or end of the time period in which they actually occur. The following example illustrates how cash flows are treated in capital budgeting situations.

CASH FLOWS ILLUSTRATED

Assume that a variety of capital projects are being considered by eRAGs, a small company selling electronic versions of books and magazines on the Internet. One investment being considered by eRAGs is the acquisition of an Internet company, Com.com, that markets electronic advertising to other firms selling Internet products and services.

eRAGs' expected acquisition costs and expected cash income and expenses associated with the acquisition appear in Exhibit 14–2. This detailed information can be simplified to a net cash flow for each year. For eRAGs, the project generates a net negative flow in the first year and net positive cash flows thereafter. This cash flow information for eRAGs can be illustrated through the use of a time line.

Time Lines

A **time line** visually illustrates the points in time when cash flows are expected to be received or paid, making it a helpful tool for analyzing cash flows of a capital investment proposal. Cash inflows are shown as positive amounts on a time line and cash outflows are shown as negative amounts.

time line

EXHIBIT 14–2

e-RAGs' Com.com Acquisition Decision Information

CASH OUTFLOWS (000s)

Due diligence costs:	$ 500	(to be incurred immediately)
Acquisition cost:	8,200	(to be incurred immediately)
Cost to reorganize	700	(to be incurred in year 1)

CASH INFLOWS (000s)

Cash sales less cash operating costs:	
Year 1	$1,900
Year 2	2,500
Year 3	3,400
Year 4	2,900
Year 5	1,800
Year 6	1,500
Year 7	900

Note: After year 7, it is expected that competitive services will render the investment in Com.com worthless.

The following time line represents the cash flows from eRAGs' potential investment in Com.com.

End of period	0	1	2	3	4	5	6	7
Inflows	$ 0	+$1,900	+$2,500	+$3,400	+$2,900	+$1,800	+$1,500	+$ 900
Outflows	− 8,700	− 700	− 0	− 0	− 0	− 0	− 0	− 0
Net cash flow	−$8,700	+$1,200	+$2,500	+$3,400	+$2,900	+$1,800	+$1,500	+$ 900

On a time line, the date of initial investment represents time point 0 because this investment is made immediately. Each year after, the initial investment is represented as a full time period, and periods serve only to separate the timing of cash flows. Nothing is presumed to happen during a period. Thus, for example, cash inflows each year from royalties earned are shown as occurring at the end of, rather than during, the time period. A less conservative assumption would show the cash flows occurring at the beginning of the period.

2

What is measured by the payback period?

payback period

Payback Period

The information on timing of net cash flows is an input to a simple and often-used capital budgeting technique called **payback period**. This method measures the time required for a project's cash inflows to equal the original investment. At the end of the payback period, a company has recouped its investment.

In one sense, payback period measures a dimension of project risk by focusing on the timing of cash flows. The assumption is that the longer it takes to recover the initial investment, the greater is the project's risk because cash flows in the more distant future are more uncertain than relatively current cash flows. Another reason for concern about long payback periods relates to capital reinvestment. The faster that capital is returned from an investment, the more rapidly it can be invested in other projects.

Payback period for a project having unequal cash inflows is determined by accumulating cash flows until the original investment is recovered. Thus, using the information shown in Exhibit 14–2 and the time line presented earlier, the Com.com investment payback period must be calculated using a yearly cumulative total of inflows as follows:

Year	Annual Amount	Cumulative Total
0	−$8,700	−$8,700
1	+ 1,200	− 7,500
2	+ 2,500	− 5,000
3	+ 3,400	− 1,600
4	+ 2,900	+ 1,300
5	+ 1,900	+ 3,200
6	+ 2,500	+ 5,700
7	+ 900	+ 6,600

At the end of the third year, all but $1,600 of the initial investment of $8,700 has been recovered. The $2,900 inflow in the fourth year is assumed to occur evenly throughout the year. Therefore, it should take approximately 0.55 ($1,600 ÷ $2,900) of the fourth year to cover the rest of the original investment, giving a payback period for this project of 3.55 years (or slightly less than 3 years and 7 months).

When the cash flows from a project are equal each period (an **annuity**), the payback period is determined as follows:

annuity

$$\text{Payback Period} = \text{Investment} \div \text{Annuity}$$

Assume for a moment that an investment being considered by eRAGs requires an initial investment of $10,000 and is expected to generate equal annual cash flows of $4,000 in each of the next 5 years. In this case, the payback period would be equal to the $10,000 net investment cost divided by $4,000 or 2.5 years (2 years and 6 months).

Company management typically sets a maximum acceptable payback period as one of the financial evaluation criteria for capital projects. If eRAGs has set four years as the longest acceptable payback period, this project would be acceptable under that criterion. As indicated in the accompanying News Note, companies have a bias of investing in projects with a quick payoff. The News Note also highlights the government's role in funding longer term investments.

GENERAL BUSINESS NEWS NOTE

Dear Uncle Sam: Please Send Money

It may sound strange to hear a Silicon Valley executive credit the birth of such industries as the Internet and local-area networks to the prescience of the U.S. government. But in many cases it is the government that has provided the seeds, and industry that has provided the water and light, to cultivate the technological innovations that are improving the nation's economy and quality of life. Unfortunately, from 1987 to 1995, federal investment in basic research sank by 2.6% per year. As a fraction of gross domestic product, the federal investment in research and development is about half of what it was 30 years ago.

Meanwhile, the information technology sector alone has more than doubled its annual R&D investment over the last 10 years to a current level of $30 billion. In this searing-hot competitive environment, however, most of these expenditures must be allocated to short-term product development. It isn't feasible for the private sector to assume responsibility for long-term, high-risk research when shareholders require solid quarterly returns on investment.

A newly released study by the Council on Competitiveness confirms these findings and highlights both the long-term returns from, and the dangers of being complacent about, the U.S. investment in R&D. For every dollar spent on basic research, we can expect a 50 cents per year increase in national output.

SOURCE: Adapted from Eric A. Benhamou, "R&D Needs Washington's Support," *The Wall Street Journal* (June 17, 1999), p. A26.

Most companies use payback period as only one way of financially judging an investment project. After being found acceptable in terms of payback period, a project is subjected to evaluation by other financial capital budgeting techniques. A second evaluation is usually performed because the payback period method ignores three things: inflows occurring after the payback period has been reached, the company's desired rate of return, and the time value of money. These issues are incorporated into the decision process using discounted future cash flows.

DISCOUNTING FUTURE CASH FLOWS

Money has a time value associated with it; this value is created because interest is paid or received on money.[2] For example, the receipt of $1 today has greater value than the same sum received one year from today because money held today can be invested to generate a return that will cause it to accumulate to more than $1 over time. This phenomenon encourages the use of discounted cash flow techniques in most capital budgeting situations to account for the time value of money.

discounting

Discounting future cash flows means reducing them to present value amounts by removing the portion of the future values representing interest. This "imputed" amount of interest is based on two considerations: the length of time until the cash flow is received or paid and the rate of interest assumed. After discounting, all future values associated with a project are stated in a common base of current dollars, also known as their **present values**. Cash receipts and disbursements occurring at the beginning of a project (time 0) are already stated in their present values and are not discounted.

present value

Information on capital projects involves the use of estimates; therefore, having the best possible estimates of all cash flows (such as initial project investment) is extremely important. Care should be taken also to include all potential future inflows and outflows. To appropriately discount cash flows, managers must estimate the rate of return on capital required by the company in addition to the project's cost and cash flow estimates. This rate of return is called the **discount rate** and is used to determine the imputed interest portion of future cash receipts and expenditures. The discount rate should equal or exceed the company's **cost of capital** (COC), which is the weighted average cost of the various sources of funds (debt and stock) that comprise a firm's financial structure.[3] For example, if a company has a COC of 10 percent, it costs an average of 10 percent of each capital dollar annually to finance investment projects. To determine whether a capital project is a worthwhile investment, this company should generally use a minimum rate of 10 percent to discount its projects' future cash flows.

discount rate

cost of capital

A distinction must be made between cash flows representing a return *of* capital and those representing a return *on* capital. A **return of capital** is the recovery of the original investment or the return of principal, whereas a **return on capital** is income and equals the discount rate multiplied by the investment amount. For example, $1 invested in a project that yields a 10 percent rate of return will grow to a sum of $1.10 in one year. Of the $1.10, $1 represents the return of capital and $0.10 represents the return on capital. The return on capital is computed for each period of the investment life. For a company to be better off by making an investment, a project must produce cash inflows that exceed the investment made and the cost of capital. To determine whether a project meets a company's desired rate of return, one of several discounted cash flow methods can be used.

return of capital
return on capital

[2] The time value of money and present value computations are covered in Appendix 1 of this chapter. These concepts are essential to understanding the rest of this chapter; be certain they are clear before continuing.

[3] All examples in this chapter use an assumed discount rate or cost of capital. The computations required to find a company's cost of capital rate are discussed in any principles of finance text.

DISCOUNTED CASH FLOW METHODS

Three discounted cash flow techniques are the net present value method, the profitability index, and the internal rate of return. Each of these methods is defined and illustrated in the following subsections.

3

How are the net present value and profitability index of a project measured?

Net Present Value Method

The **net present value method** determines whether the rate of return on a project is equal to, higher than, or lower than the desired rate of return. Each cash flow from the project is discounted to its present value using the rate specified by the company as the desired rate of return. The total present value of all cash outflows of an investment project subtracted from the total present value of all cash inflows yields the **net present value** (NPV) of the project. Exhibit 14–3 presents net present value calculations, assuming the use of a 12 percent discount rate. The cash flow data are taken from Exhibit 14–2.

net present value method

net present value

The factors used to compute the net present value are obtained from the present value tables provided in Appendix A at the end of the text. Each period's cash flow is multiplied by a factor obtained from Table 1 (PV of $1) for 12 percent and the appropriate number of periods designated for the cash flow. Table 2 in Appendix A is used to discount annuities rather than single cash flows and its use is demonstrated in later problems.

The net present value of the Com.com investment is $815,000. The NPV represents the net cash benefit or net cash cost to a company acquiring and using the proposed asset. If the NPV is zero, the actual rate of return on the project is equal to the required rate of return. If the NPV is positive, the actual rate is greater than the required rate. If the NPV is negative, the actual rate is less than the required rate of return. Note that the exact rate of return is not indicated under the NPV method, but its relationship to the desired rate can be determined. If all estimates about the investment are correct, the Com.com investment being considered by eRAGs will provide a rate of return greater than 12 percent.

Had eRAGs chosen any rate other than 12 percent and used that rate in conjunction with the same facts, a different net present value would have resulted. For example, if eRAGs set 15 percent as the discount rate, a NPV of $8,000 would have resulted for the project (see Exhibit 14–4). Net present values at other selected discount rates are given in Exhibit 14–4. The computations for these values are made in a manner similar to those at 12 and 15 percent. (To indicate your understanding of the NPV method, you may want to prove these computations.)

EXHIBIT 14–3

Net Present Value Calculation for Com.com Investment

		DISCOUNT RATE = 12%				
		a	×	b	=	c
Cash Flow	Time	Amount		Discount Factor		Present Value
Initial investment	t_0	$(8,700)		1.0000		$(8,700)
Year 1 net cash flow	t_1	1,200		0.8929		1,071
Year 2 net cash flow	t_2	2,500		0.7972		1,993
Year 3 net cash flow	t_3	3,400		0.7118		2,420
Year 4 net cash flow	t_4	2,900		0.6355		1,843
Year 5 net cash flow	t_5	1,800		0.5674		1,021
Year 6 net cash flow	t_6	1,500		0.5066		760
Year 7 net cash flow	t_7	900		0.4524		407
Net Present Value						$ 815

EXHIBIT 14–4

Net Present Value Calculation for Com.com Investment

		DISCOUNT RATE = 15%		
		a ×	b =	c
Cash Flow	Time	Amount	Discount Factor	Present Value
Initial investment	t_0	$(8,700)	1.0000	$(8,700)
Year 1 net cash flow	t_1	1,200	0.8696	1,044
Year 2 net cash flow	t_2	2,500	0.7561	1,890
Year 3 net cash flow	t_3	3,400	0.6575	2,235
Year 4 net cash flow	t_4	2,900	0.5718	1,658
Year 5 net cash flow	t_5	1,800	0.4972	895
Year 6 net cash flow	t_6	1,500	0.4323	648
Year 7 net cash flow	t_7	900	0.3759	338
Net Present Value				$ 8

Net present value with 5% discount rate: $3,202
Net present value with 10% discount rate: $1,419
Net present value with 20% discount rate: $(1,121)

The table in Exhibit 14–4 indicates that the NPV is not a single, unique amount, but is a function of several factors. First, changing the discount rate while holding the amounts and timing of cash flows constant affects the NPV. Increasing the discount rate causes the NPV to decrease; decreasing the discount rate causes NPV to increase. Second, changes in estimated amounts and/or timing of cash inflows and outflows affect the net present value of a project. Effects of cash flow changes on the NPV depend on the changes themselves. For example, decreasing the estimate of cash outflows causes NPV to increase; reducing the stream of cash inflows causes NPV to decrease. When amounts and timing of cash flows change in conjunction with one another, the effects of the changes are determinable only by calculation.

The net present value method, although not providing the actual rate of return on a project, provides information on how that rate compares with the desired rate. This information allows managers to eliminate from consideration any project producing a negative NPV because it would have an unacceptable rate of return. The NPV method can also be used to select the best project when choosing among investments that can perform the same task or achieve the same objective.

The net present value method should not, however, be used to compare independent projects requiring different levels of initial investment. Such a comparison favors projects having higher net present values over those with lower net present values without regard to the capital invested in the project. As a simple example of this fact, assume that eRAGs could spend $200,000 on Investment A or $40,000 on Investment B. Investment A's and B's net present values are $4,000 and $2,000, respectively. If only NPVs were compared, the company would conclude that Investment A was a "better" investment because it has a larger NPV. However, Investment A provides an NPV of only 2 percent ($4,000 ÷ $200,000) on the investment, whereas Investment B provides a 5 percent ($2,000 ÷ $40,000) NPV. Logically, organizations should invest in projects that produce the highest return per investment dollar. Comparisons of projects requiring different levels of investment are made using a variation of the NPV method known as the profitability index.

Profitability Index

profitability index

The **profitability index** (PI) is a ratio comparing the present value of a project's net cash inflows to the project's net investment. The PI is calculated as

$$PI = \text{Present Value of Net Cash Flows} \div \text{Net Investment}$$

The present value of net cash flows equals the PV of future cash inflows minus the PV of future cash outflows. The PV of net cash inflows represents an output measure of the project's worth, whereas the net investment represents an input measure of the project's cost. By relating these two measures, the profitability index gauges the efficiency of the firm's use of capital. The higher the index, the more efficient is the capital investment.

The following information illustrates the calculation and use of a profitability index. eRAGs is considering two investments: a training program for employees costing $720,000 and a series of Internet servers costing $425,000. Corporate managers have computed the present values of the investments by discounting all future expected cash flows at a rate of 12 percent. Present values of the expected net cash inflows are $900,000 for the training program and $580,000 for the servers. Dividing the PV of the net cash inflows by initial cost gives the profitability index for each investment. Subtracting asset cost from the present value of the net cash inflows provides the NPV. Results of these computations are shown below.

	PV of Inflows	Cost	Profitability Index	NPV
Training program	$900,000	$720,000	1.25	$180,000
Server package	580,000	425,000	1.36	155,000

Although the training program's net present value is higher, the profitability index indicates that the server package is a more efficient use of corporate capital.[4] The higher PI reflects a higher rate of return on the server package than on the training program. The higher a project's PI, the more profitable is that project per investment dollar.

If a capital project investment is made to provide a return on capital, the profitability index should be equal to or greater than 1.00, the equivalent of an NPV equal to or greater than 0. Like the net present value method, the profitability index does not indicate the project's expected rate of return. However, another discounted cash flow method, the internal rate of return, provides the expected rate of return to be earned on an investment.

Internal Rate of Return

4

How is the internal rate of return on a project computed? What does it measure?

internal rate of return

A project's **internal rate of return** (IRR) is the discount rate that causes the present value of the net cash inflows to equal the present value of the net cash outflows. It is the project's expected rate of return. If the IRR is used to determine the NPV of a project, the NPV is zero. By examining Exhibits 14–3 and 14–4, it is apparent that eRAGs investment in Com.com would generate an IRR very close to 15 percent because a discount rate of 15 percent resulted in an NPV very close to $0.

The following formula can be used to determine net present value:

NPV = −Investment + PV of Cash Inflows − PV of Cash Outflows other than the investment
= −Investment + Cash Inflows (PV Factor) − Cash Outflows (PV Factor)

Capital project information should include the amounts of the investment, cash inflows, and cash outflows. Thus, the only missing data in the preceding formula are the present value factors. These factors can be calculated and then be found in the present value tables. The interest rate with which the factors are associated is

[4] Two conditions must exist for the profitability index to provide better information than the net present value method. First, the decision to accept one project must require that the other project be rejected. The second condition is that availability of funds for capital acquisitions is limited.

the internal rate of return. The internal rate of return is most easily computed for projects having equal annual net cash flows. When an annuity exists, the NPV formula can be restated as follows:

$$\begin{aligned} \text{NPV} &= -\text{Net Investment} + \text{PV of Annuity Amount} \\ &= -\text{Net Investment} + (\text{Cash Flow Annuity Amount} \times \text{PV Factor}) \end{aligned}$$

The investment and annual cash flow amounts are known from the expected data and net present value is known to be zero at the IRR. The IRR and its present value factor are unknown. To determine the internal rate of return, substitute known amounts into the formula, rearrange terms, and solve for the unknown (the PV factor):

$$\begin{aligned} \text{NPV} &= -\text{Net Investment} + (\text{Annuity} \times \text{PV Factor}) \\ 0 &= -\text{Net Investment} + (\text{Annuity} \times \text{PV Factor}) \\ \text{Net Investment} &= (\text{Annuity} \times \text{PV Factor}) \\ \text{Net Investment} \div \text{Annuity} &= \text{PV Factor} \end{aligned}$$

The solution yields a present value factor for the number of annuity periods corresponding to the project's life at an interest rate equal to the internal rate of return. Finding this factor in the PV of an annuity table and reading the interest rate at the top of the column in which the factor is found provides the internal rate of return.

To illustrate an IRR computation for a project with a simple annuity, information in Exhibit 14–5 pertaining to eRAGs' potential investment in a quality control system is used. The quality control system would be installed immediately and would generate cost savings over the five-year life of the system. The system has no expected salvage value.

The NPV equation is solved for the present value factor.

$$\begin{aligned} \text{NPV} &= -\text{Net Investment} + (\text{Annuity} \times \text{PV Factor}) \\ \$0 &= -\$99{,}560 + (\$29{,}000 \times \text{PV Factor}) \\ \$99{,}560 &= (\$29{,}000 \times \text{PV Factor}) \\ \$99{,}560 \div \$29{,}000 &= \text{PV Factor} \\ 3.43 &= \text{PV Factor} \end{aligned}$$

The PV of an ordinary annuity table (Table 2, Appendix A) is examined to find the internal rate of return. A present value factor is a function of time and the discount rate. In the table, find the row representing the project's life (in this case, five periods). Look across the table in that row for the PV factor found upon solving the equation. In row 5, a factor of 3.4331 appears under the column headed 14 percent. Thus, the internal rate of return for this machine is very near 14 percent. Using interpolation, a computer program, or a programmable calculator the exact

EXHIBIT 14–5

Information Pertaining to Quality Control System

	Cash Flow
Cost of software and hardware (t_0)	−\$85,000
Installation cost (t_0)	− 14,560
Operating savings (t_1–t_5)	+ 29,000

IRR can be found.[5] A computer program indicates the IRR of the quality control system is 13.9997 percent.

Exhibit 14–6 plots the net present values that result from discounting the quality control system cash flows at various rates of return. For example, the NPV at 4 percent is $28,407 and the NPV at 15 percent is −$2,041. (These computations are not provided here, but can be performed by discounting the $29,000 annual cash flows and subtracting $99,560 of investment cost.)

The internal rate of return is located on the graph's horizontal axis at the point where the NPV equals zero (13.9997 percent). Note that the graph reflects an inverse relationship between rates of return and NPVs. Higher rates yield lower present values because, at the higher rates, fewer dollars need to be currently invested to obtain the same future value.

Manually finding the IRR of a project that produces unequal annual cash flows is more complex and requires an iterative trial-and-error process. An initial estimate is made of a rate believed to be close to the IRR and the NPV is computed. If the resulting NPV is negative, a lower rate is estimated (because of the inverse relationship mentioned above) and the NPV is computed again. If the NPV is positive, a higher rate is tried. This process is continued until the net present value equals zero, at which time the internal rate of return has been found.

The project's internal rate of return is then compared with management's preestablished **hurdle rate**, which is the rate of return specified as the lowest acceptable return on investment. Like the discount rate mentioned earlier, this rate should generally be at least equal to the cost of capital. In fact, the hurdle rate is commonly the discount rate used in computing net present value amounts. If a project's IRR is equal to or greater than the hurdle rate, the project is considered viable from a financial perspective. As indicated in the following passage, hurdle rates are no longer simply an American concept.

hurdle rate

Faced with higher capital costs, Japanese managers are beginning to embrace such previously little-known Western concepts as "hurdle rates" and "required rates of return." That's a big switch for executives who once concerned themselves only with market share. Said Tsunehiko Ishibashi, general manager of finance for Mitsubishi Kasei, a major petrochemical company: "As a result of the higher cost of capital, the profitability standards for new investments must be raised."[6]

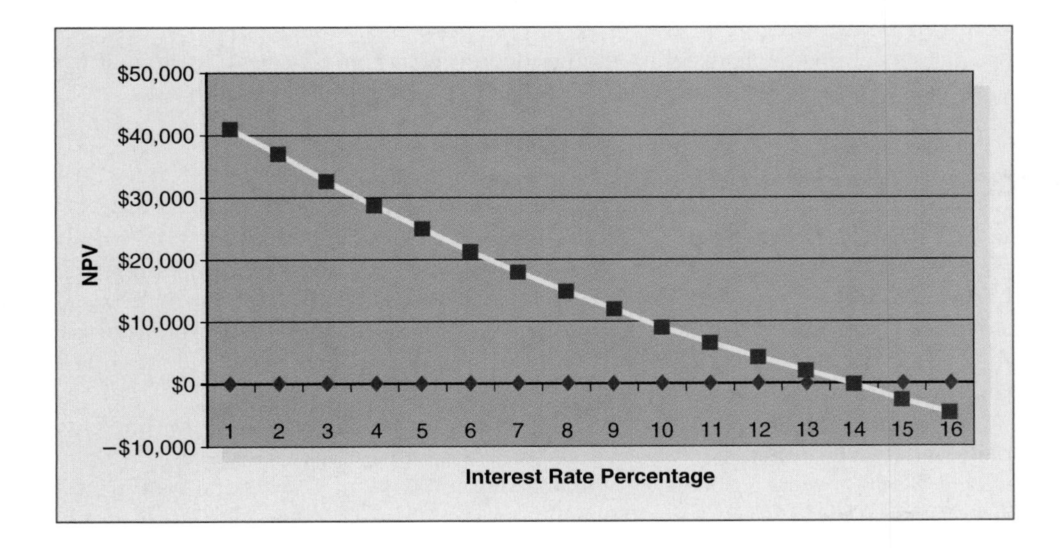

EXHIBIT 14–6

NPV by Various Discount Rates

[5] Interpolation is the process of finding a term between two other terms in a series.
[6] John J. Curran, "Japan Tries to Cool Money Mania," *Fortune* (January 28, 1991), p. 66.

The internal rate of return on an investment must clear the company's designated hurdle rate. That hurdle rate will be raised as the company's cost of debt and equity capital increases.

The higher the internal rate of return, the more financially attractive is the investment proposal. In choosing among alternative investments, however, managers cannot look solely at the internal rates of return on projects. The rates do not reflect the dollars involved. An investor would normally rather have a 10 percent return on $1,000 than a 100 percent return on $10!

Using the internal rate of return has three drawbacks. First, when uneven cash flows exist, the iterative process is inconvenient. Second, unless present value tables are available that provide factors for fractional interest rates, finding the precise IRR on a project is difficult. These two problems can be eliminated with the use of a computer or a programmable calculator. The last problem is that it is possible to find several rates of return that will make the net present value of the cash flows equal zero. This phenomenon usually occurs when there are net cash inflows in some years and net cash outflows in other years of the investment project's life (other than time 0).

In performing discounted cash flow analyses, accrual-based accounting information sometimes needs to be converted to cash flow data. One accrual that deserves special attention is depreciation. Although depreciation is not a cash flow item, it has cash flow implications because of its deductibility for income tax purposes.

THE EFFECT OF DEPRECIATION ON AFTER-TAX CASH FLOWS

How do taxation and depreciation methods affect cash flows?

Income taxes are an integral part of the business environment and decision-making process in our society. Tax planning is a central part of management planning and has a large impact on overall business profitability. Managers typically make decisions only after examining how company taxes will be affected by those decisions. In evaluating capital projects, managers should use after-tax cash flows to determine project acceptability.

tax shield
tax benefit

Note that depreciation expense is not a cash flow item. Although no funds are paid or received for it, depreciation on capital assets, similar to interest on debt, affects cash flows by reducing a company's tax obligation. Thus, depreciation provides a **tax shield** against the payment of taxes. The tax shield produces a **tax benefit** equal to the amount of taxes saved (the depreciation amount multiplied by the tax rate). The concepts of tax shield and tax benefit are shown on the following income statements. The tax rate is assumed to be 40 percent.

No Depreciation Deduction Income Statement		Depreciation Deduction Income Statement	
Sales	$250,000	Sales	$250,000
Cost of goods sold	(175,000)	Cost of goods sold	(175,000)
Gross margin	$ 75,000	Gross margin	$ 75,000
Expenses other than depreciation	(37,500)	Expenses other than depreciation	(37,500)
Depreciation expense	0	Depreciation expense	(37,500)
Income before taxes	$ 37,500	Income before tax	$ 0
Tax expense (40%)	(15,000)	Tax expense (40%)	0
Net income	$ 22,500	Net income	$ 0

The tax shield is the depreciation expense amount of $37,500. The tax benefit is the difference between $15,000 of tax expense on the first income statement and $0 of tax expense on the second income statement. The tax benefit is also equal to the 40 percent tax rate multiplied by the depreciation tax shield of $37,500, or $15,000. Because taxes are reduced by $15,000, the pattern of cash flows is improved.

It is the depreciation for purposes of computing income taxes rather than the amount used for financial accounting purposes that is relevant in discounted cash flow analysis. Income tax laws regarding depreciation deductions are subject to revision. In making their analyses of capital investments, managers should use the most current tax regulations for depreciation. Different depreciation methods may have significant impacts on after-tax cash flows. For a continuously profitable business, an accelerated method of depreciation, such as the modified accelerated cost recovery system (MACRS), allowed for U.S. tax computations, will produce higher tax benefits in the early years of asset life than will the straight-line method. These higher tax benefits will translate into a higher net present value over the life of the investment project.

Changes in the availability of depreciation methods or in the length of an asset's depreciable life may dramatically affect projected after-tax cash flows and also affect the net present value, profitability index, and internal rate of return expected from the capital investment. Because capital projects are analyzed and evaluated before investments are made, managers should be aware of the inherent risk of tax law changes. Original assumptions made about the depreciation method or asset life may not be valid by the time an investment is actually made and an asset is placed into service. However, once purchased and placed into service, an asset can generally be depreciated using the method and tax life allowed when the asset was placed into service regardless of the tax law changes occurring after that time.

Changes may also occur in the tax rate structure. Rate changes may be relatively unpredictable. For example, the maximum federal corporate tax rate for many years was 46 percent; the Tax Reform Act of 1986 lowered this rate to 34 percent, and the present top marginal U.S. tax rate is 35 percent.[7] A tax rate reduction lowers the tax benefit provided by depreciation because the impact on cash flow is lessened. Tax law changes (such as asset tax-life changes) can cause the expected outcomes of the capital investment analysis to vary from the project's actual outcomes.[8]

To illustrate such variations, assume that eRAGs is considering investing in a new Internet site. The site will require an investment of $540,000 in computer hardware and software. Assume these assets have a 10-year economic life and would produce expected net annual cash income of $110,000. Assume the company's after-tax cost of capital is 11 percent. Further assume that corporate assets are depreciated on a straight-line basis for tax purposes.[9]

[7] Surtaxes that apply to corporations may drive the top marginal rate above 35 percent for certain income brackets.

[8] Additionally, managers should be careful to consider effects of both applicable foreign and state tax laws.

[9] To simplify the presentation, the authors have elected to ignore a tax rule requirement called the half-year (or mid-quarter) convention that applies to personal assets and a mid-month convention that applies to most real estate improvements. Under tax law, only a partial year's depreciation may be taken in the year an asset is placed into service. The slight difference that such a tax limitation would make on the amounts presented is immaterial for purposes of illustrating these capital budgeting concepts.

In late 2000, prior to making the Internet site investment, eRAGs' cost accountant, Jill Flowers, calculated the project's net present value. The results of her calculations are shown in Exhibit 14–7 under Situation A. Note that depreciation is added to income after tax to obtain the amount of after-tax cash flow. Even though depreciation is deductible for tax purposes, it is still a noncash expense. The present value amounts are obtained by multiplying the after-tax cash flows by the appropriate PV of an annuity factor from Table 2 in Appendix A at the end of the text.

The NPV evaluation technique indicated the acceptability of the capital investment. At the time of Ms. Flowers' analysis, eRAGs' tax rate was 30 percent and the tax laws allowed a 10-year depreciable life on this property.

EXHIBIT 14–7

Internet Site Investment Analyses

ASSUMED FACTS

Initial investment	$540,000
Expected annual before-tax cash flows	110,000
Straight-line depreciation (10 years)	54,000
Expected economic life	10 years

Situation A: Tax rate of 30% (actual rate in effect)
Situation B: Tax rate of 25%
Situation C: Tax rate of 40%

	SITUATIONS		
	A	B	C
YEARS 1–10			
Before-tax cash flow	$110,000	$110,000	$110,000
Depreciation	(54,000)	(54,000)	(54,000)
Income before tax	$ 56,000	$ 56,000	$ 56,000
Tax	(16,800)	(14,000)	(22,400)
Net income	$ 39,200	$ 42,000	$ 33,600
Depreciation	54,000	54,000	54,000
Cash flow after tax	$ 93,200	$ 96,000	$ 87,600

SITUATION A—NPV CALCULATIONS ASSUMING AN 11% DISCOUNT RATE

Cash Flow	Time	Amount	Discount Factor	Present Value
Investment	t_0	$(540,000)	1.0000	$(540,000)
Annual inflows	t_1–t_{10}	93,200	5.8892	548,873
Net Present Value				$ 8,873

SITUATION B—NPV CALCULATIONS ASSUMING AN 11% DISCOUNT RATE

Cash Flow	Time	Amount	Discount Factor	Present Value
Investment	t_0	$(540,000)	1.0000	$(540,000)
Annual inflows	t_1–t_{10}	96,000	5.8892	565,363
Net Present Value				$ 25,363

SITUATION C—NPV CALCULATIONS ASSUMING AN 11% DISCOUNT RATE

Cash Flow	Time	Amount	Discount Factor	Present Value
Investment	t_0	$(540,000)	1.0000	$(540,000)
Annual inflows	t_1–t_{10}	87,800	5.8892	517,072
Net Present Value				$ (22,928)

Because Ms. Flowers was concerned about proposed changes in the U.S. tax rate, she also analyzed the project assuming that tax rates changed. Exhibit 14–7 shows the different after-tax cash flows and net present values that result if the same project is subjected to either a 25 percent (Situation B) or 40 percent (Situation C) tax rate.

This example demonstrates the expected NPV change when a different tax rate is used. If the tax rate changes to either 25 or 40 percent, the NPV changes. A decrease in the tax rate makes the Internet site a more acceptable investment, based on its net present value, and an increase in the tax rate has the opposite effect.

Understanding how depreciation and taxes affect the various capital budgeting techniques will allow managers to make the most informed decisions about capital investments.[10] Well-informed managers are more likely to have confidence in capital investments made by the company if they can justify the substantial resource commitment required. That justification is partially achieved by considering whether a capital project fits into strategic plans. To be confident of their conclusions, managers must also comprehend the assumptions and limitations of each capital budgeting method.

ASSUMPTIONS AND LIMITATIONS OF METHODS

What are the underlying assumptions and limitations of each capital project evaluation method?

As summarized in Exhibit 14–8, each financial capital budget evaluation method has its own underlying assumptions and limitations. To maximize benefits of the capital budgeting process, managers should understand the similarities and differences of the various methods and use several techniques to evaluate a project.

All of the methods have two similar limitations. First, except to the extent that payback indicates the promptness of the investment recovery, none of the methods provides a mechanism to include management preferences with regard to the timing of cash flows. This limitation can be partially overcome by discounting cash flows occurring further in the future at higher rates than those in earlier years, assuming that early cash flows are preferred. Second, all the methods use single, deterministic measures of cash flow amounts rather than probabilities. This limitation can be minimized through the use of probability estimates of cash flows. Such estimates can be input into a computer program to determine a distribution of answers for each method under various conditions of uncertainty.

THE INVESTMENT DECISION

Management must identify the best asset(s) for the firm to acquire to fulfill the company's goals and objectives. Making such an identification requires answers to the following four subhead questions.

Is the Activity Worthy of an Investment?

A company acquires assets when they have value in relation to specific activities in which the company is engaged. For example, Amazon.com invests heavily in product and service development because that is the primary path to new revenues (the activity). Before making decisions to acquire assets, company management must be certain that the activity for which the assets will be needed is worthy of an investment.

[10] These examples have all considered the investment project as a purchase. If a leasing option exists, the classification of the lease as operating or capital will affect the amounts deductible for tax purposes. A good illustration of this is provided in "The Lease vs. Purchase Decision," by Ralph L. Benke, Jr., and Charles P. Baril in *Management Accounting* (March 1990), pp. 42–46.

ASSUMPTIONS	LIMITATIONS
Payback Method	
■ Speed of investment recovery is the key consideration. ■ Timing and size of cash flows are accurately predicted. ■ Risk (uncertainty) is lower for a shorter payback project.	■ Cash flows after payback are ignored. ■ Cash flows and project life in basic method are treated as deterministic without explicit consideration of probabilities. ■ Time value of money is ignored. ■ Cash flow pattern preferences are not explicitly recognized.
Net Present Value	
■ Discount rate used is valid. ■ Timing and size of cash flows are accurately predicted. ■ Life of project is accurately predicted. ■ If the shorter lived of two projects is selected, the proceeds of that project will continue to earn the discount rate of return through the theoretical completion of the longer lived project.	■ Cash flows and project life in basic method are treated as deterministic without explicit consideration of probabilities. ■ Alternative project rates of return are not known. ■ Cash flow pattern preferences are not explicitly recognized. ■ IRR on project is not reflected.
Profitability Index	
■ Same as NPV. ■ Size of PV of net inflows relative to size of present value of investment measures efficient use of capital.	■ Same as NPV. ■ A relative answer is given but dollars of NPV are not reflected.
Internal Rate of Return	
■ Hurdle rate used is valid. ■ Timing and size of cash flows are accurately predicted. ■ Life of project is accurately predicted. ■ If the shorter lived of two projects is selected, the proceeds of that project will continue to earn the IRR through the theoretical completion of the longer lived project.	■ The IRR rather than dollar size is used to rank projects for funding. ■ Dollars of NPV are not reflected. ■ Cash flows and project life in basic method are treated as deterministic without explicit consideration of probabilities. ■ Cash flow pattern preferences are not explicitly recognized. ■ Multiple rates of return can be calculated on the same project.
Accounting Rate of Return (Presented in Appendix 2 of this chapter)	
■ Effect on company accounting earnings relative to average investment is key consideration. ■ Size and timing of increase in company earnings, investment cost, project life, and salvage value can be accurately predicted.	■ Cash flows are not considered. ■ Time value of money is not considered. ■ Earnings, investment, and project life are treated as deterministic without explicit consideration of probabilities.

EXHIBIT 14-8

Assumptions and Limitations of Capital Budgeting Methods

An activity's worth is measured by cost-benefit analysis. For most capital budgeting decisions, costs and benefits can be measured in monetary terms. If the dollars of benefits exceed the dollars of costs, then the activity is potentially worthwhile. In some cases, though, benefits provided by capital projects are difficult to quantify. However, difficulty in quantification is no reason to exclude benefits from capital budgeting analyses. In most instances, surrogate quantifiable measures can be obtained for qualitative benefits. For example, benefits from investments in day care centers for employees' children may be estimable based on the reduction in employee time off and turnover. At a minimum, managers should attempt to subjectively include such benefits in the analytical process.

In other circumstances, management may know in advance that the monetary benefits of the capital project will not exceed the costs, but the project is essential for other reasons. For example, a company may consider renovating the employee workplace with new carpet, furniture, paint, and artwork. The renovation would not make employee work any easier or safer, but would make it more comfortable. Such a project may be deemed "worthy" regardless of the results of a cost-benefit analysis. Companies may also invest in unprofitable products to maintain market share of a product group, and, therefore, protect the market position of profitable products. One of the most difficult investments to evaluate is technology, which is addressed in the accompanying News Note.

Which Assets Can Be Used for the Activity?

The determination of available and suitable assets to conduct the intended activity is closely related to the evaluation of the activity's worth. Management must have an idea of how much the needed assets will cost to determine whether the activity should be pursued. As shown in Exhibit 14–9, management should gather the following specific monetary and nonmonetary information for each asset to make this determination: initial cost, estimated life and salvage value, raw material and labor requirements, operating costs (both fixed and variable), output capability, service availability and costs, maintenance expectations, and revenues to be generated (if any). As mentioned in the previous section, information used in a capital project analysis may include surrogate, indirect measures. Management must have both quantitative and qualitative information on each asset and recognize that some projects are simply more crucial to the firm's future than others. This point is illustrated in the News Note below.

Of the Available Assets for Each Activity, Which Is the Best Investment?

Using all available information, management should select the best asset from the candidates and exclude all others from consideration. In most instances, a company has a standing committee to discuss, evaluate, and approve capital projects. In judging capital project acceptability, this committee should recognize that two types of capital budgeting decisions must be made: screening and preference decisions.

GENERAL BUSINESS NEWS NOTE

Technology: What's It Worth?

Remember the promises of expert systems, the paperless office, and other hype that technology created? Is technology all sizzle and no substance, or can technology re-gain its credibility? One of the ways of re-establishing confidence is by managing technology investments and by having realistic measurements that are meaningful to your business.

Evaluating the benefits of technology is not easy for two reasons. We know that information itself is useless unless it assists in making better decisions that could not have been made without the use of that information. What makes investment in technology difficult to measure is that having all the information available before making a decision guarantees only information overload, not the right decision. As well, the value of technology depends on what the business goals are that it is supporting, and to what degree technology is instrumental in achieving these goals.

You can't measure the value of information by examining the size of the disk storage, the number of PCs in the organization, the boxes of reports printed, or on-line queries processed, because none of these items is valuable until they are used in the business. More money spent on technology does not guarantee more value to the business: it is how technology is used that matters, not how much it costs. Expensive technology that only automates the existing manual processes will not add value to the business unless it provides additional benefits that do not exist in the manual environment.

SOURCE: Reprinted from an article, "Managing Technology Investments," appearing in *CMA Management Magazine* (formerly *CMA Magazine*) by Catherine A. Bovie, July/August 1998 (pp. 15–18), with permission of CMA Canada.

EXHIBIT 14-9

Capital Investment Information

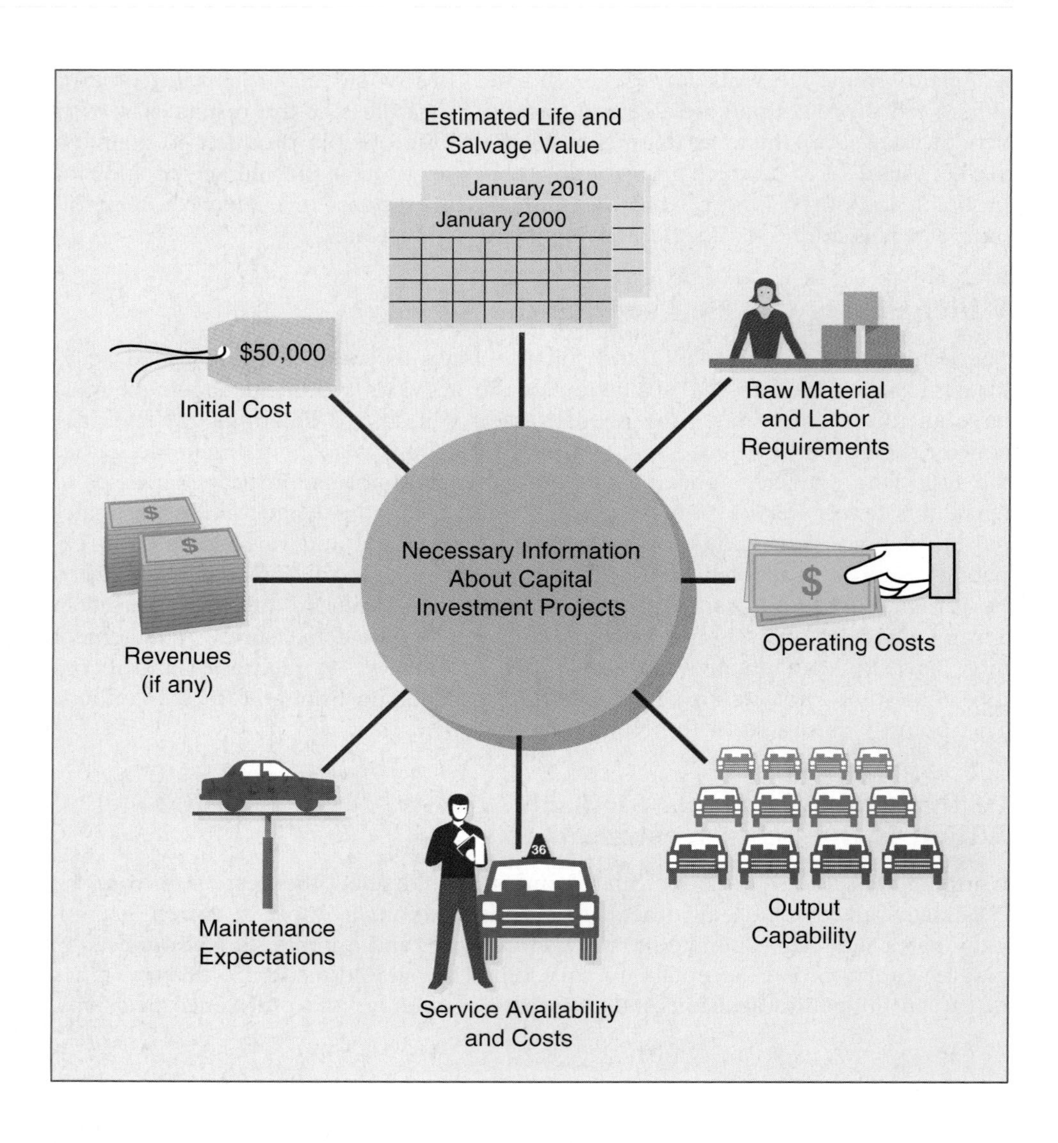

screening decision

preference decision

A **screening decision** determines whether a capital project is desirable based on some previously established minimum criterion or criteria. If the project does not meet the minimum standard(s), it is excluded from further consideration. The second decision is a **preference decision** in which projects are ranked according to their impact on the achievement of company objectives.

Deciding which asset is the best investment requires the use of one or several of the evaluation techniques discussed previously. Some techniques may be used to screen the projects as to acceptability; other techniques may be used to rank the projects in order of preferability. Although different companies use different techniques for screening and ranking purposes, payback period is commonly used only for screening decisions. The reasons for this choice are that payback focuses only on the short run and does not consider the time value of money. The remaining techniques may be used to screen or rank capital projects.

Of the "Best Investments" for All Worthwhile Activities, in Which Ones Should the Company Invest?

Although many worthwhile investment activities exist, each company has limited resources available and must allocate them in the most profitable manner. Therefore, after choosing the best asset for each activity, management must decide which activities and assets to fund. Investment activities may be classified as mutually exclusive, independent, or mutually inclusive.

mutually exclusive project

Mutually exclusive projects fulfill the same function. One project will be chosen from such a group, causing all others to be excluded from further consideration because they would provide unneeded or redundant capability. A proposal under consideration may be to replace a current asset with one that provides the same basic capabilities. If the company keeps the old asset, it will not buy the new one; if the new one is purchased, the old asset will be sold. Thus, the two assets are mutually exclusive. For example, if a bakery decided to buy a new delivery truck, it would no longer need its existing truck. The existing truck would be sold to help finance the new truck.

independent project

Other investments may be **independent projects** because they have no specific bearing on one another. For example, the acquisition of an office microcomputer system is not related to the purchase of a factory machine. These project decisions are analyzed and accepted or rejected independently of one another. Although limited resources may preclude the acquisition of all acceptable projects, the projects themselves are not mutually exclusive.

mutually inclusive project

Management may be considering certain investments that are all related to a primary project, or **mutually inclusive projects**. In a mutually inclusive situation, if the primary project is chosen, all related projects are also selected. Alternatively, rejection of the primary project will dictate rejection of the others. For example, when a firm chooses to invest in new technology, investing in an employee training program for the new technology may also be necessary.

Exhibit 14–10 shows a typical investment decision process in which a company is determining the best way to provide transportation for its sales force. Answers to the four questions asked in the subheadings to this section are provided for the transportation decision.

To ensure that capital funds are invested in the best projects available, managers must carefully evaluate all projects and decide which ones represent the most effective and efficient use of resources—a difficult determination. The evaluation

EXHIBIT 14–10

Typical Investment Decision Process

Activity—Provide transportation for a sales force of 10 people.

1. Is the activity worthy of an investment?
   Yes; this decision is based on an analysis of the cost of providing transportation in relationship to the dollars of gross margin to be generated by the sales force.
2. Which assets can be used for the activity?
   Available: Bus passes, bicycles, motorcycles, automobiles (purchased), automobiles (leased), automobiles (currently owned), small airplanes.
   Infeasible: Bus passes, bicycles, and motorcycles are rejected as infeasible because of inconvenience and inability to carry a reasonable quantity of merchandise; airplanes are rejected as infeasible because of inconvenience and lack of proximity of landing sites to customers.
   Feasible: Various types of automobiles to be purchased (assume asset options A through G); various types of leasing arrangements (assume availability of leases 1 through 5); current fleet.
   Gather all relevant quantitative and qualitative information on all feasible assets (assets A–G; leases 1–5; current fleet).
3. Which asset is the best investment?
   Compare all relevant information and choose the best asset candidate from the purchase group (assume Asset D) and the lease group (assume Lease 2).
4. Which investment should the company make?
   Compare the best asset candidate from the purchase group (Asset D) and the lease group (Lease 2); this represents a mutually exclusive, multiple-candidate project decision. The best candidate is found to be type D assets. Compare the type D assets to current fleet; this is a mutually exclusive, replacement project. The best investment is to sell the old fleet and purchase a new fleet of 10 type D automobiles.

process should consider activity priorities, cash flows, and risk of all projects. Projects should then be ranked in order of their acceptability. Ranking may be required for both independent projects and mutually exclusive projects. Ranking mutually exclusive projects is required to select the best project from the set of alternatives. Ranking independent projects is required to efficiently allocate scarce capital to competing uses.

RANKING MULTIPLE CAPITAL PROJECTS

How do managers rank investment projects?

When managers are faced with an accept/reject decision for a single asset, all time-value-of-money evaluation techniques will normally point to the same decision alternative. A project is acceptable under the NPV method when it has a nonnegative net present value. Acceptability of a capital asset is also indicated by a profitability index (PI) of 1.00 or more. Because the PI is an adaptation of the NPV method, these two evaluation techniques will always provide the same accept/reject decision.

To be acceptable using the IRR model, a capital acquisition must have an internal rate of return equal to or greater than the specified hurdle rate. The IRR method gives the same accept/reject decision as the NPV and PI methods if the hurdle rate and the discount rate used are the same.

More often, however, managers are faced with choosing among multiple projects. Multiple project decisions require that a selection ranking be made. This section of the chapter considers the use of the net present value, profitability index, and internal rate of return techniques for ranking mutually exclusive projects. Payback period also can be used to rank multiple projects. However, it does not provide as much useful information as NPV, PI, and IRR, because cash flows beyond the payback period are ignored.

Managers can use results from the evaluation techniques to rank projects in descending order of acceptability. For the NPV and PI methods, rankings are based, respectively, on magnitude of NPV and PI index. Although based on the same figures, the NPV and PI methods will not always provide the same order of ranking because the former is a dollar measure and the latter is a percentage. When the internal rate of return is used, rankings of multiple projects are based on expected rate of return. Rankings provided by the IRR method will not always be in the same order as those given by the NPV or PI methods.

reinvestment assumption

Conflicting results arise because of differing underlying **reinvestment assumptions** of the three methods. The reinvestment assumption presumes cash flows released during a project's life are reinvested until the end of the project's life. The NPV and PI techniques assume that released cash flows are reinvested at the discount rate which, at minimum, should be the cost of capital (COC). The IRR method assumes reinvestment of released cash flows can be made at the expected internal rate of return, which may be substantially higher than the COC. If it is, the IRR method may provide a misleading indication of project success because additional projects may not be found that have such a high return.

Three situations are discussed in the following subsections to illustrate conflicting rankings of multiple projects. In each situation the weighted average cost of capital is the discount rate used to compute NPV as well as the hurdle rate against which to measure IRR.

Multiple Projects—Equal Lives, Constant Cash Flows, Unequal Investments

eRAGs has gathered the following information pertaining to two potential projects. One project under consideration is the purchase of software that would improve the efficiency of processing customer orders. The other investment being contemplated is a customer service training program for the sales staff. Data on these projects are as follows:

	Software	Training Program
Investment	$390,000	$80,000
Annual after-tax cash flows	$ 64,000	$14,000
Asset life	10 years	10 years
Cost of capital	9%	9%

Note that in this example an assumed COC of 9 percent is used as the discount rate. The time lines, NPV, and PI computations appear in Exhibit 14–11 for both projects. The amounts on the time lines are shown in thousands of dollars. The IRR is approximated from the present value of an annuity table (Table 2, Appendix A), and the actual rate can be found using a computer or programmable calculator.

The net present value model indicates that the better investment for eRAGs is the software with a NPV of $11,843. However, in applying the profitability index or internal rate of return models, the training program would be selected because it has a higher PI and a higher IRR. Because these projects do not serve the same purpose, company management would most likely evaluate the selection based on priority needs rather than results of specific capital project evaluations. In the absence of a need to ration capital, eRAGs may invest in both projects.

EXHIBIT 14–11

Multiple Projects; Conflicting Rankings

SOFTWARE (000s)

End of period	0	1	2	3	4	5	6	7	8	9	10
Inflows		+64	+64	+64	+64	+64	+64	+64	+64	+64	+64
Outflows	(390)										

Cash Flow	Time	Amount	Discount Factor	Present Value
Investment	t_0	$(400,000)	1.0000	$(390,000)
Annual inflows	t_1–t_{10}	64,000	6.2788	401,843
Net Present Value				$ 11,843

PI = $401,843 ÷ $390,000 = 1.03

IRR factor = $390,000 ÷ $64,000 = 6.0938 (annuity for 10 periods)

The IRR is approximately 10.19%; calculator computations verify this finding.

TRAINING PROGRAM (000s)

End of period	0	1	2	3	4	5	6	7	8	9	10
Inflows		+14	+14	+14	+14	+14	+14	+14	+14	+14	+14
Outflows	(80)										

Cash Flow	Time	Amount	Discount Factor	Present Value
Investment	t_0	$(80,000)	1.0000	$(80,000)
Annual inflows	t_1–t_{10}	14,000	6.2788	87,903
Net Present Value				$ 7,903

PI = $87,903 ÷ $80,000 = 1.099

IRR factor = $80,000 ÷ $14,000 = 5.7143 (annuity for 10 periods)

The IRR is approximately 11.73%; calculator computations verify this finding.

Multiple Projects—Unequal Lives, Constant but Unequal Cash Flows, Unequal Investments

The second illustration of conflicting rankings again compares the software and training programs but with a new set of assumptions. The cost of capital is still assumed to be 9 percent. The facts now reflect different lives and different investment and annual cash flows.

	Software	Training Program
Investment	$800,000	$591,500
Annual after-tax cash flows	210,000	110,000
Asset life	5 years	8 years

The time lines for the two investments are as follows:

Software (000s)

End of period	0	1	2	3	4	5
Inflows		+210	+210	+210	+210	+210
Outflow	(800)					

Training Program (000s)

End of period	0	1	2	3	4	5	6	7	8
Inflows		+110	+110	+110	+110	+110	+110	+110	+110
Outflow	(591.5)								

The net present value, profitability index, and internal rate of return are calculated for each investment, and the calculated results are shown in Exhibit 14–12. If the net present value or profitability index method is used, the training program would be selected by eRAGs. If the internal rate of return method is used to choose between the two projects, the software appears to be the better investment.

EXHIBIT 14-12

Multiple Projects; Conflicting Rankings

SOFTWARE

Cash Flow	Time	Amount	Discount Factor	Present Value
Investment	t_0	$(800,000)	1.0000	$(800,000)
Annual inflows	t_1–t_5	210,000	3.8897	816,837
Net Present Value				$ 16,837

PI = $816,837 ÷ $800,000 = 1.02

IRR factor = $800,000 ÷ $210,000 = 3.8095 (annuity for 5 periods)

The IRR is approximately 9.81%; calculator computations verify this finding.

TRAINING PROGRAM

Cash Flow	Time	Amount	Discount Factor	Present Value
Investment	t_0	$(591,500)	1.0000	$(591,500)
Annual inflows	t_1–t_8	110,000	5.5348	608,828
Net Present Value				$ 17,328

PI = $608,828 ÷ $591,500 = 1.03

IRR factor = $591,500 ÷ $110,000 = 5.3773 (annuity for 5 periods)

The IRR is approximately 9.78%; calculator computations verify this finding.

Rankings using the internal rate of return are misleading because of the reinvestment assumption. The IRR method assumes that the cash inflows of $210,000 each year from the software investment will be reinvested at a rate of 9.81 percent; the $110,000 of cash flows from the training program are assumed to be reinvested at 9.78 percent. The NPV method, however, assumes reinvestment of the cash flows at the cost of capital of 9 percent, which is a more reasonable rate of return. The NPV computations show the training program to be the better investment.

A formal method is available for choosing the better investment. For eRAGs' management to select the better investment, the difference in the annual cash flows between the software and training program investments must first be determined. The cash flow differences are then evaluated as if they resulted from a separate investment opportunity. Because the software package requires a higher investment than the training program, the software package is used as the comparison base. The investment opportunity resulting from the cash flow differences is referred to here as *project difference*. If project difference provides a positive net present value, the software investment is ranked higher than the training program. This higher ranking is assigned because the additional investment required for the software is more than compensated for by the additional cash flows. If project difference shows a negative net present value, the training program is the better investment. The NPV of project difference is negative as shown in Exhibit 14–13 using present value factors from Table 2, Appendix A.

Multiple Projects—Equal Lives, Equal Investments, Unequal Cash Flows

eRAGs' management is interested in two additional projects: a joint venture to develop a new Web site that would market classic comic books and a marketing research study for a large traditional retailer. The research study is somewhat unique in that no payment would be received from the large retailer until the completion of the project. The company's cost of capital and discount rate are 9 percent. This

EXHIBIT 14–13

Net Present Value of Project Difference

NET CASH FLOWS

End of Period	Software	Training Program	Project Difference
0	$(800,000)	$(591,500)	$(208,500)
1	210,000	110,000	+100,000
2	210,000	110,000	+100,000
3	210,000	110,000	+100,000
4	210,000	110,000	+100,000
5	210,000	110,000	+100,000
6	0	110,000	(110,000)
7	0	110,000	(110,000)
8	0	110,000	(110,000)

NET PRESENT VALUE CALCULATION—PROJECT DIFFERENCE

Cash Flow	Time	Amount	Discount Factor	Present Value
Investment	t_0	$(208,500)	1.0000	$(208,500)
Annual inflows	$t_1–t_5$	100,000	3.8897	388,970
Annual inflow	t_6	(110,000)	0.5963	(65,593)
Annual inflow	t_7	(110,000)	0.5470	(60,170)
Annual inflow	t_8	(110,000)	0.5019	(55,209)
Net Present Value				$ (502)

set of projects illustrates another conflicting ranking situation; the relevant project data follow:

	Joint Venture	Research Study
Investment	$1,000,000	$1,000,000
Life	5 years	5 years
Net cash inflows		
Year 1	$ 360,000	$ 0
Year 2	360,000	0
Year 3	360,000	0
Year 4	360,000	0
Year 5	360,000	2,400,000

Using the same approach as presented in Exhibit 14–13, the following schedule computes a net present value for a project difference between the projects:

Period	Joint Venture	Research Study	Project Difference
0	$(1,000,000)	$(1,000,000)	$ 0
1	360,000	0	360,000
2	360,000	0	360,000
3	360,000	0	360,000
4	360,000	0	360,000
5	360,000	2,400,000	(2,040,000)

NET PRESENT VALUE CALCULATION—PROJECT DIFFERENCE

Cash Flow	Time	Amount	Discount Factor	Present Value
Investment	t_0	$ 0	1.0000	$ 0
Annual inflows	t_1–t_4	360,000	3.2397	1,166,292
Annual outflow	t_5	(2,040,000)	0.6499	(1,325,796)
Net Present Value				$ (159,504)

Fisher rate

Because the NPV of project difference is negative, the research study is the preferred investment.

Exhibit 14–14 presents the net present value, profitability index, and internal rate of return computations for these projects. The investment in the joint venture has the higher IRR, but the research study has a higher NPV and PI. The best selection depends on assumptions made about the future reinvestment rate applied to each of the $360,000 cash flows from the joint venture.

The point of indifference between the two projects occurs when the $360,000 annuity can be discounted at a certain rate (the **Fisher rate**) to equal $2,400,000 discounted for five years at that same rate. That rate is 14.43 percent and is calculated by solving for a discount rate that causes the net present values of the two projects to be equal. If worked manually, repeated trials are used; however, a computer or programmable calculator can be used to find this rate quickly.

For reinvestment rates above 14.43 percent, the joint venture generates a higher net present value. For reinvestment rates below 14.43 percent, the research study is the superior investment.

The preceding situations demonstrate that different capital budgeting evaluation methods often provide different rankings of projects. Because of this possibility, managers should select one primary evaluation method for capital projects. The critical question is whether higher cash flows or a higher rate of return is preferable. The answer is that higher present cash flows are always preferable to higher rates of return.

The net present value method is considered theoretically superior to the internal rate of return in evaluating capital projects for two reasons. First, the reinvestment assumption of the IRR method is less realistic than that of the NPV method. Second, when a project has both positive and negative net annual cash flows

EXHIBIT 14-14

Comparison of Investment Projects

JOINT VENTURE
DISCOUNT RATE = 9%

Cash Flow	Time	Amount	Discount Factor	Present Value
Investment	t_0	$(1,000,000)	1.0000	$(1,000,000)
Annual inflows	t_1–t_5	360,000	3.8897	1,400,292
Net Present Value				$ 400,292

PI = $1,400,292 ÷ $1,000,000 = 1.40

IRR factor = $1,000,000 ÷ $360,000 = 2.7778 (annuity for 5 periods)

The IRR is approximately 23.44%; calculator computations verify this finding.

RESEARCH STUDY
DISCOUNT RATE = 9%

Cash Flow	Time	Amount	Discount Factor	Present Value
Investment	t_0	$(1,000,000)	1.0000	$(1,000,000)
Annual inflows	t_1–t_8	2,400,000	0.6499	1,599,760
Net Present Value				$ 599,760

PI = $1,599,760 ÷ $1,000,000 = 1.60

The IRR is approximately 19.14%; calculator computations verify this finding.

during its life, there is the arithmetic possibility that projects will have multiple internal rates of return.

In addition, the net present value technique measures project results in dollars rather than rates, and dollar results are the objective of investment. To illustrate the problem that could occur by relying solely on the internal rate of return method, consider the following question: As discussed earlier, would a manager rather receive a 100 percent return on a $1 investment or a 10 percent return on a $100 investment? The answer indicates the fallacy of focusing only on rates of return.

Although useful as a measure of evaluation under some circumstances, the profitability index is subject to the same concern as presented in the previous paragraph. Because monetary results are the objective of investments and the PI is expressed as a rate rather than as dollars, it can, if used by itself, lead to incorrect decisions. Taken together with other tools, however, the profitability index is a measure of capital efficiency and can assist decision makers in their financial investment analyses.

RANKING PROJECTS UNDER CAPITAL RATIONING

Managers rank capital projects to select those projects providing the greatest return on company investment. A company often finds that it has the opportunity to invest in more acceptable projects than it has money. In fact, most companies operate under some measure of **capital rationing**, which means that there is an upper dollar constraint on the amount of capital available to commit to capital asset acquisition.[11] When capital rationing exists, the selection of investment projects must fall

capital rationing

[11] Many publicly traded companies have the luxury of being able to obtain additional capital through new issuances of debt or stock. This possibility may limit the degree to which they are subject to capital rationing but does not eliminate it. Nonpublicly traded companies operate under much more strict rationing of capital resources.

within the capital budget limit. In these circumstances, the NPV model may not produce rankings that maximize the value added to the firm, because it does not consider differences in investment amount.

Capital rationing is illustrated by the following situation. Assume that eRAGs has a capital budget of $7,500,000 and is considering the various investment projects listed in Exhibit 14–15. By all quantitative measures except NPV, Project 1 should be eliminated if the firm has only $7,500,000 available in the capital budget. Its NPV is larger than only Project 2, but deletion of Project 2 will not permit inclusion of any other project. The firm would need $8.1 million to complete all six projects and only $7.5 million is available. Because it does not help to eliminate Project 2, the project that would otherwise produce the smallest company NPV and return based on either the PI or IRR technique (Project 1) should be eliminated. Relatively speaking, Project 2 is of much less interest than Projects 3, 4, 5, and 6. Project 2 does meet minimum quantitative standards though.

Based on PIs, the attractiveness of the projects, in descending order, is 6, 4, 2, 5, and 3. Based on IRRs, the preferences would be 5, 3, 6, 4, and 2. Based on NPVs, the ranking would be 6, 5, 4, 3, and 2.

Although managers should select one primary evaluation technique, the eRAGs example shows that capital project evaluation should not be performed using only one method. Each evaluation tool should be used in conjunction with others, not to the exclusion of others. Each method provides valuable information. Even the nondiscounting technique of payback period can be helpful to management by indicating the quickness of return of investment.

In making their preference decisions, many company managers set ranking categories for projects such as those shown in Exhibit 14–16. Projects are first screened and placed into an appropriate category. Monetary resources are allocated to projects in a top-to-bottom fashion. Within each category, projects are usually ranked using net present value and profitability index techniques. Management's goal should be to select those projects that, within budget constraints, will maximize net present value to the firm. Selecting projects based solely on their internal rate of return rankings without consideration of the net present values may be incorrect.[12]

Regardless of the capital budgeting evaluation techniques used, managers must remember that the results provided are based on estimates of future events. The fact that estimates are involved indicates that a risk is associated with the decision. All project estimates should be carefully understood and analyzed using sound judgment. Capital project proposals are being "sold" by their sponsors using different reasons under different conditions.

EXHIBIT 14–15

Potential Investment Projects

Project	Project Cost	PI	IRR	NPV
1. Product research	$1,000,000	1.15	12%	$ 145,712
2. Computer upgrades	100,000	1.43	17	43,214
3. Employee training	1,200,000	1.41	24	495,888
4. Safety enhancements	1,800,000	1.45	20	801,365
5. Service automation	2,000,000	1.42	24	839,481
6. Purchase patents	2,000,000	1.62	20	1,233,902
Total cost of projects	$8,100,000			

[12] If the set of projects is very large, the selection of projects may require the use of integer programming techniques, which are outside the scope of this text.

EXHIBIT 14-16

Ranking Categories for Capital Projects

CATEGORY 1—REQUIRED BY LEGISLATION

This category would include such items as pollution control equipment that has been mandated by law. Most companies can ill afford the fines or penalties that can be assessed for lack of installation; however, these capital acquisitions may not meet the company's minimum established economic criteria.

CATEGORY 2—ESSENTIAL TO OPERATIONS

This category would include capital assets without which the primary functions of the organization could not continue. This category could include new purchases of capital assets or replacements of broken or no longer usable assets. For example, the purchase of a kiln for a ceramics manufacturer would fall into this category.

CATEGORY 3—NONESSENTIAL BUT INCOME GENERATING

This category would include capital assets that would improve operations of the organization by providing cost savings or supplements to revenue. Robots in an automobile manufacturer would be included in this group.

CATEGORY 4—OPTIONAL IMPROVEMENTS

Items in this category would be those that do not provide any cost savings or revenue increases but would make operations run more smoothly or improve working conditions. The purchase of computer hardware or software that is faster than that currently being used and the installation of a microwave oven in the employees' lounge would be included here.

CATEGORY 5—MISCELLANEOUS

This category exists for "pet projects" that might be requested. Such acquisitions may be more for the benefit of a single individual and not the organization as a whole. Such projects may not even be related to organizational objectives. The installation of new carpeting in a manager's office could be an example of this group of investments. Items in this category will normally be chosen only when the organization has substantial, unencumbered resources at its disposal.

COMPENSATING FOR RISK IN CAPITAL PROJECT EVALUATION

8

How is risk considered in capital budgeting analysis?

When choosing among multiple projects, managers must consider the **risk** or uncertainty associated with each project. In accounting, risk reflects uncertainty about differences between the expected and actual future returns from an investment. For example, the purchase of a $100,000, 10 percent treasury note would provide a virtually risk-free return of $10,000 annually because treasury notes are backed by the full faith and credit of the U.S. government. If the same $100,000 were used to purchase stock, the returns could range from −100 percent (losing the entire investment) to an abnormally high return. The potential for extreme variability makes the stock purchase a much more risky investment than the treasury note.

risk

For Internet companies, one of the key variables to success is getting on-line shoppers to access the companies' sites. One of the important variables influencing shopper traffic is advertising. For Internet companies, advertising is a capital investment—and a risky one. This is illustrated in the News Note on page 628.

http://www.yr.com
http://www.covad.com

Managers considering a capital investment should understand and compensate for the degree of risk involved in that investment. A manager may use three approaches to compensate for risk: the judgmental method, the risk-adjusted discount rate method, and sensitivity analysis. These methods do not eliminate risk, but they do help managers understand and evaluate risk in the decision-making process.

NEWS NOTE  GENERAL BUSINESS

Advertising—How Much Is Enough?

Dustin Grosse is sitting on the edge of his seat in a conference room at the ad agency Young & Rubicam in San Francisco. Grosse is the brand manager for Covad, a Silicon Valley company that sells high-speed access to the Internet, and he is about to review Y&R's final cuts of two television commercials. They will be the centerpiece of a $40 million, yearlong, coast-to-coast marketing campaign designed to trumpet little-known Covad as a broadband leader. A lot is at stake, especially when you consider that Covad's sales for the past 12 months totaled just over $20 million, or half its marketing budget.

Most net firms have wielded wacky, even dark humor to set themselves apart. Outpost.com showed gerbils shooting out from a cannon, while one Beyond.com ad features a buck-naked man working at home via the Net. Covad flirted with off-the-wall stuff, but Bob Roblin, Covad's executive vice president, believes milder comedy will appeal more to a mainstream audience.

If Roblin is right, the upside for Covad could be enormous. Beyond reaching consumers and businesses, Covad's campaign must make a big splash with Internet service providers. Covad is a wholesaler, with no direct retail relationship with its customers. If the campaign stimulates a groundswell of demand for Covad DSL, more ISPs will be driven to seek a partnership with the access provider which will boost the top line, thus achieving the ultimate, measurable goal of all the advertising.

SOURCE: Edward Robinson, "The $20 Million Company . . . and Its $40 Million Ad Campaign," *Fortune* (November 8, 1999), pp. 315–316.

Judgmental Method

judgmental method

The **judgmental method** of risk adjustment allows the decision makers to use logic and reasoning to decide whether a project provides an acceptable rate of return in relation to its risk. The decision maker is presented with all available information for each project, including the payback period, NPV, PI, and IRR. After reviewing the information, the decision maker chooses from among acceptable projects based on personal judgment of the risk-to-return relationship. The judgmental approach provides no formal process for adjusting data for the risk element.

Risk-Adjusted Discount Rate Method

risk-adjusted discount rate method

A more formal method of taking risk into account requires making adjustments to the discount or hurdle rate. Under the **risk-adjusted discount rate method**, the decision maker increases (decreases) the rate used for discounting future cash inflows (outflows) to compensate for increased risk. As the discount rate is increased (decreased), the present values of the cash flows are reduced (increased). Therefore, larger cash inflows are required to "cover" the investment and provide an acceptable rate of return. Changes in the discount rate should be reflective of the degree of cash flow variability and timing, other investment opportunities, and corporate objectives. If the internal rate of return is being used for project evaluation, the risk-adjusted discount rate method would increase the hurdle rate against which the IRR is compared for higher risk projects.

Assume that the management of eRAGs is considering developing a new Internet service. The company would operate the service for 10 years and then sell it at the end of those 10 years. Estimates of the development cost and annual cash flows for the service are as follows:

Initial development cost	$1,500,000
After-tax net cash flows	
Years 1–5	200,000
Years 6–10	300,000
Year 10 (sale)	600,000

eRAGs management uses its 9 percent cost of capital as the discount rate in evaluating capital projects under the NPV method. However, Pierre Stellar, a board member, feels that above-normal risk is created in this endeavor by two factors. First, revenues realized through service fees may differ from those planned. Second, the market value of the service in 10 years may vary substantially from the estimate of $600,000.

Mr. Stellar wants to compensate for these risk factors by using a 15 percent discount rate rather than the 9 percent cost of capital rate. Determination of the amount of adjustment to make to the discount rate (from 9 to 15 percent, for example) is most commonly an arbitrary one. Thus, even though a formal process is used to compensate for risk, the process still involves a degree of judgment on the part of the project evaluators. Exhibit 14–17 presents the NPV computations using both discount rates. When the discount rate is adjusted upward, the NPV of the project is lowered and, in this case, shows the project to be unacceptable.

The same type of risk adjustment can be used for payback period or accounting rate of return (Appendix 2). If the payback method is being used, managers may choose to shorten the maximum allowable payback period to compensate for increased risk. This adjustment assumes that cash flows occurring in the more distant future are more risky than those occurring in the near future. If the accounting rate of return (ARR) method is used, managers may increase the preestablished acceptable rate against which the ARR is compared to compensate for risk. Another way in which risk can be included in the decision process is through the use of sensitivity analysis.

Sensitivity Analysis

sensitivity analysis

Sensitivity analysis is a process of determining the amount of change that must occur in a variable before a different decision would be made. In a capital budgeting situation, the variable under consideration could be the discount rate, annual net cash flows, or project life. Sensitivity analysis looks at this question: What if a variable is different from that originally expected?

Except for the initial purchase price, all information used in capital budgeting is estimated. Use of estimates creates the possibility of introduction of errors, and sensitivity analysis identifies an "error range" for the various estimated values over

EXHIBIT 14–17

Product Development Evaluation

NPV USING 9% DISCOUNT RATE

Cash Flow	Time	Amount	Discount Factor	Present Value
Investment	t_0	$(1,500,000)	1.0000	$(1,500,000)
Annual inflows	t_1–t_5	200,000	3.8897	777,940
Annual inflows	t_1–t_6	300,000	2.5280	758,400
Final inflow	t_6	600,000	0.4224	253,440
Net Present Value				$ 289,780

NPV USING 15% DISCOUNT RATE

Cash Flow	Time	Amount	Discount Factor	Present Value
Investment	t_0	$(1,500,000)	1.0000	$(1,500,000)
Annual inflows	t_1–t_5	200,000	3.3522	670,440
Annual inflows	t_1–t_6	300,000	1.6666	499,980
Final inflow	t_6	600,000	0.2472	148,320
Net Present Value				$ (181,260)

which the project will still be acceptable. The following sections consider how sensitivity analysis relates to the discount rate, cash flows, and life of the asset.

RANGE OF THE DISCOUNT RATE

A capital project providing a rate of return equal to or greater than the discount or hurdle rate is considered an acceptable investment. But returns from a project are not certain because, for instance, the cost of capital may increase due to increases in interest rates on new issues of debt. Sensitivity analysis allows a company to determine what increases may occur in the estimated cost of capital before a project becomes unacceptable. The upper limit of increase in the discount rate is the project's internal rate of return. At the IRR, a project's net present value is zero; therefore, the present value of the cash inflows equals the present value of cash outflows. As long as the IRR for a project is equal to or above the cost of capital, the project will be acceptable.

To illustrate use of sensitivity analysis, eRAGs's Internet site investment project (Situation A), analyzed earlier in Exhibit 14–7 using an 11 percent discount rate, is reconsidered:

After-tax cash flows for 10 years discounted at 11% (93,200 × 5.8892)	$548,873
Initial investment	(540,000)
NPV	$ 8,873

The project provides a positive net present value and is considered an acceptable investment candidate.

The eRAGs management team wants to know how high the discount rate can rise before the project would become unacceptable. To find the upper limit of the discount rate, the present value factor for an annuity of 10 periods at the unknown interest rate is computed as follows:

$$\text{Cash flow} \times \text{PV factor} = \text{Investment}$$

$$\$93{,}200 \times \text{PV factor} = \$540{,}000$$

$$\text{PV factor} = 5.7940$$

Using the PV factor, the IRR is found to be 11.39 percent. As long as eRAGs' cost of capital is less than or equal to 11.39 percent, this project will be acceptable. As the discount rate is increased toward the project's IRR, the project becomes less desirable. These calculations assume that the cash flows and project life have been properly estimated.

RANGE OF THE CASH FLOWS

Another factor sensitive to changes in estimation is the investment's projected cash flows. eRAGs' data for the Internet site investment project from Exhibit 14–7 (Situation A) are also used to illustrate how to determine the range of acceptable cash flows. Company management wants to know how small the net cash inflows can be and still have the project remain desirable. This determination requires that the present value of the cash flows for 10 periods, discounted at 11 percent, be equal to or greater than the investment cost. The PV factor for 10 periods at 11 percent is 5.8892. The equation from the preceding section can be used to find the lowest acceptable annuity:

$$\text{Cash flow} \times \text{PV factor} = \text{Investment}$$

$$\text{Cash flow} \times 5.8892 = \$540{,}000$$

$$\text{Cash flow} = \$540{,}000 \div 5.8892$$

$$\text{Cash flow} = \$91{,}693$$

As long as the net annual cash flow equals or exceeds $91,693, the Internet site project will be financially acceptable.

RANGE OF THE LIFE OF THE ASSET

Asset life is related to many factors, some of which, like the quantity and timing of maintenance on equipment, are controllable. Other factors, such as technological advances and actions of competitors, are noncontrollable. An error in the estimated life will change the number of periods from which cash flows are to be derived. These changes could affect the accept/reject decision for a project. The eRAGs Internet site example is used to demonstrate how to find the minimum length of time the cash flows must be received from the project for it to be acceptable. The solution requires setting the present value of the cash flows discounted at 11 percent equal to the investment. This computation yields the PV factor for an unknown number of periods:

$$\text{Cash flow} \times \text{PV factor} = \text{Investment}$$

$$\$93{,}200 \times \text{PV factor} = \$540{,}000$$

$$\text{PV factor} = 5.7940$$

Review the present value of an annuity table in Appendix A under the 11 percent interest column to find the 5.7940 factor. The project life is approximately 9 years and 9 months.[13] If the project cash flows were to stop at any point before 9 years and 9 months, the project would be unacceptable.

Sensitivity analysis does not reduce the uncertainty surrounding the estimate of each variable. It does, however, provide management with a sense of the tolerance for estimation errors by providing upper and lower ranges for selected variables. The above presentation simplistically focuses on single changes in each of the variables. If all factors change simultaneously, the above type of sensitivity analysis is useless. More advanced treatments of sensitivity analysis, which allow for simultaneous ranging of all variables, can be found under the topic of simulation in an advanced mathematical modeling text.

POSTINVESTMENT AUDIT

How and why should management conduct a postinvestment audit of a capital project?

postinvestment audit

In a **postinvestment audit** of a capital project, information on actual project results is gathered and compared to expected results. This process provides a feedback or control feature to both the persons who submitted and those who approved the original project information. Comparisons should be made using the same technique or techniques used originally to determine project acceptance. Actual data should be extrapolated to future periods where such information would be appropriate. In cases where significant learning or training is necessary, start-up costs of the first year may not be appropriate indicators of future costs. Such projects should be given a chance to stabilize before making the project audit.

As the size of the capital expenditure increases, a postinvestment audit becomes more crucial. Although an audit cannot change a past investment decision, it can pinpoint areas of project operations that are out of line with expectations so that problems can be corrected before they get out of hand.

Secondarily, an audit can provide feedback on the accuracy of the original estimates for project cash flows. Sometimes, project sponsors may be biased in favor of their own projects and provide overly optimistic forecasts of future revenues or cost savings. Individuals providing unrealistic estimates should be required to explain all major variances. Knowing that postinvestment audits will be made may cause project sponsors to provide realistic cash flow forecasts in their capital requests.

[13] This solution was found by interpolating.

Performing a postinvestment audit is not an easy task. The actual information may not be in the same form as were the original estimates, and some project benefits may be difficult to quantify. Project returns fluctuate considerably over time, so results gathered at a single point may not be representative of the project. But, regardless of the difficulties involved, postinvestment audits provide management with information that can help to make better capital investment decisions in the future.

REVISITING Amazon.com

http://www.amazon.com

Amazon.com is the bellwether of the big Internet retailers. Many Internet investors are looking at Amazon.com to see the future of the battle between traditional retail sales and Internet retailing.

There is a tremendous amount of wealth at stake along with Amazon's future. Although its sales are meager compared to any of the nation's major retailers, its market value eclipses nearly all of them. For example, in 1999 its market cap was twice as big as that of Sears, five times bigger than Kmart's, 17 times bigger than Barnes & Nobles.

How will the Amazon story end? Will it win the race? Conquer the world? Bezos himself isn't sure. "I don't want to give the impression that our future success is assured. I believe the opposite. I believe our future success is not assured," he says, adding with a grin, "If you look at the history of pioneers, it's not good." He even seems fascinated by his own cliffhanger. Everywhere he goes, Bezos carries a small digital camera. "I try to take at least one picture a day so that I'll have some hope 50 years from now of reconstructing my life."

Right now, there seem to be two possible conclusions to the Amazon story. Ending No. 1 goes like this: In ten years Amazon becomes so huge, so omnipresent, that it will be hard to imagine that it started out as a tiny bookseller way back in 1995. Ending No. 2, equally believable: Amazon is undone by its own ambitions and winds up as a footnote in the history of business. In the meantime, Amazon watchers await the next big move.

SOURCE: Katrina Brooker, "Amazon vs. Everybody," *Fortune* (November 8, 1999), pp. 120–128.

CHAPTER SUMMARY

Capital budgeting is concerned with evaluating long-range projects involving the acquisition, operation, and disposition of one or more capital assets. Various criteria are employed to evaluate potential projects. Among the financial criteria used are payback period, net present value (NPV), profitability index (PI), and internal rate of return (IRR).

The payback period is the length of time needed for a firm to recoup its investment from the cash inflows of a project. If a project's payback period is less than a preestablished maximum, the project is acceptable. This method ignores the time value of money and all cash flows beyond the payback period.

Net present value, profitability index, and internal rate of return are discounted cash flow methods. As such, these methods require management to discount a project's cash inflows and outflows using a desired rate of return. The minimum rate at which the discount rate should be set is the cost of capital. Managers may compensate for a project's above-normal risk by using a discount rate that is higher than the cost of capital.

Under the NPV method, the total present value of future cash flows is reduced by the current investment to derive the net present value. If the NPV is equal to or greater than zero, the project provides a rate of return equal to or greater than the discount rate. A nonnegative NPV makes the project acceptable for investment.

The profitability index equals the present value of the net cash flows divided by the investment cost. The profitability index is considered an indicator of the company's efficiency in its use of capital. Revenue-producing projects should have a PI of 1.00 or more.

The internal rate of return method computes the rate of return expected on the investment project. The IRR is equal to the discount rate at which the net present value of all cash flows equals zero. If the internal rate of return of a project exceeds management's desired hurdle rate, the project is acceptable.

Each capital project evaluation technique is based on certain assumptions and, therefore, has certain limitations. To compensate for these limitations, managers subject capital projects to more than one evaluation technique.

Depreciation expense and changes in tax rates affect after-tax cash flows. The tax rates and allowable depreciation methods estimated when the investment is analyzed may not be the same as when the project is implemented. Such changes can cause a significant difference in the actual net present value and internal rate of return amounts from those originally estimated on the project.

Management should select investment projects that will help to achieve the organization's objectives and provide the maximum return on capital resources utilized. The company must determine whether the activities in which it wishes to engage are worthy of an investment and which assets can be used for those activities. Then, decisions must be made about the best investment to accept from those available. These decisions require that investment projects be ranked as to their desirability in relationship to one another.

Often the NPV, PI, and IRR computations will produce the same rankings of multiple investment projects. In some situations, however, the NPV, PI, and IRR methods produce different project rankings. The primary reason for differences is the underlying assumption of each method regarding the reinvestment rate of cash flows released during the life of the project. The NPV and PI methods assume reinvestment at the discount rate, whereas the IRR method assumes reinvestment at the internal rate of return provided by the project. The assumption of the NPV and PI methods is more likely to be realized than that of the IRR method.

Capital rationing indicates that management has imposed a spending limit in the capital budget. When capital rationing exists, the NPV model may provide the best first-cut ranking of projects in which the returns to the firm will be maximized. Projects can also be listed in descending order of their PI and IRR rates of return. Only projects having an IRR in excess of the weighted average cost of capital should be considered and then only to the extent of the budget. In addition, managers need to consider legal requirements as well as the goals and objectives of the firm when ranking projects. Categorization of projects is a useful way to rank investments.

Different risks can be associated with each capital project. Risk is defined as uncertainty about the expected returns from an asset. Project risk can be assessed and included in decision making judgmentally, or more formally, by calculating a risk-adjusted discount/hurdle rate. Sensitivity analysis can also be employed to compensate for risk by calculating a range for each of the variables (discount rate, cash flows, and life of project) in a capital budgeting problem. Sensitivity analysis assists management in determining the effect on project outcome of a change in the estimate of one or more of the critical variables in deriving the accept/reject conclusion about the project.

After a capital project is accepted and implemented, a postinvestment audit should be undertaken to compare actual results with expected results. The audit will help managers identify and correct any problems that may exist, evaluate the accuracy of estimates used for the original investment decision, and help improve the forecasts of future investment projects.

APPENDIX 1

How are present values calculated?

Time Value of Money

future value

The time value of money can be discussed in relationship to either its future or its present value. **Future value** (FV) refers to the amount to which a sum of money invested at a specified interest rate will grow over a specified number of time periods. Present value (PV) is the amount that future cash flows are worth currently, given a specified rate of interest.[14] Thus, future and present values depend on three things: (1) amount of the cash flow, (2) rate of interest, and (3) timing of the cash flow. Only present values are discussed in this appendix because they are most relevant to the types of management decisions discussed in this text.

Future and present values are related. A present value is a future value discounted back the same number of periods at the same rate of interest. The rate of return used in present value computations is called the discount rate.

simple interest
compound interest
compounding period

In computing future and present values, simple or compound interest may be used. **Simple interest** means that interest is earned only on the original investment or principal amount. **Compound interest** means that interest earned in prior periods is added to the original investment so that, in each successive period, interest is earned on both principal and interest. The time between each interest computation is called the **compounding period**. The more often interest is compounded, the higher is the actual rate of interest being received relative to the stated rate. The following discussion is based on use of compound interest, because most transactions use this method.

Interest rates are typically stated in annual terms. To compensate for more frequent compounding periods, the number of years is multiplied by the number of compounding periods per year and the annual interest rate is divided by the number of compounding periods per year.

Present Value of a Single Cash Flow

Assume that Charlotte Moore's bank pays interest at 10 percent per year. Charlotte wants to accumulate $30,000 in five years to attend graduate school and wants to know what amount to invest now to achieve that goal. The formula to solve for the present value is

$$PV = \frac{FV}{(1 + i)^n}$$

where
PV = present value of a future amount
FV = future value of a current investment
i = interest rate per compounding period
n = number of compounding periods

Substituting known values into the formula gives the following:

$$PV = \frac{\$30{,}000}{(1 + 0.10)^5}$$

$$PV = \frac{\$30{,}000}{1.61}$$

$$PV = \$18{,}634$$

[14] Interest can be earned or owed, received or paid. To simplify the discussion for definitional purposes, the topic of interest is viewed only from the inflow standpoint.

In capital budgeting analyses, many future value amounts need to be converted to present values. Rather than using the formula $[1 \div (1 + i)^n]$ to find PVs, a table of factors for the present value of $1 (Table 1) for a variety of "i" and "n" values is provided in Appendix A at the end of the text for ease of computation. Such factors are also available in programmable calculators, making the use of tables unnecessary.

Present Value of an Annuity

An annuity is a cash flow (either positive or negative) that is repeated over consecutive periods. For an **ordinary annuity**, the first cash flow occurs at the end of each period. In contrast, the cash flows for an **annuity due** occur at the beginning of each period.

ordinary annuity
annuity due

To illustrate the computation of the present value of an annuity, consider the following situation. Judy and Jerry Jamison are planning for their daughter's college education. Their daughter, Janice, will need $20,000 per year for the next four years. The Jamison's want to know how much to invest currently at 8 percent so that Janice can withdraw $20,000 per year. The following diagram presents the situation:

Time period	t_0	t_1	t_2	t_3	t_4
Future value		$20,000	$20,000	$20,000	$20,000
Present value	?				

The present value of each single cash flow can be found using 8 percent factors in Table 1 as follows:

PV of first receipt: $20,000 × 0.9259	$18,518
PV of second receipt: $20,000 × 0.8573	17,146
PV of third receipt: $20,000 × 0.7938	15,876
PV of fourth receipt: $20,000 × 0.7350	14,700
Total present value of future cash flows	$66,240

The present value factor for an ordinary annuity can also be determined by adding the present value factors for all periods having a future cash flow. Table 2 in Appendix A provides present value of ordinary annuity factors for various interest rates and time periods. From this table, the factor of 3.3121 can be obtained and multiplied by $20,000 to yield $66,242, or approximately the same result as above. (The difference is caused by decimal-fraction rounding.)

APPENDIX 2

Accounting Rate of Return

11

What are the advantages and disadvantages of the accounting rate of return method?

The **accounting rate of return** (ARR) measures the rate of earnings obtained on the average capital investment over a project's life. This evaluation method is consistent with the accounting model and uses profits shown on accrual-based financial statements. It is the one evaluation technique that is not based on cash flows. The formula to compute the accounting rate of return is

accounting rate of return

ARR = Average Annual Profits from Project ÷ Average Investment in Project

Investment refers to project cost as well as any other costs needed for working capital items (such as inventory) for project support. Investment cost, salvage value, and working capital released at the end of the project's life are summed and divided by 2 to obtain the average investment over the life of the project.[15] The cost and working capital needed represent the initial investment and the salvage value and working capital released represent the ending investment.

The following information pertains to a new service line being considered by eRAGs. The information is used to illustrate after-tax calculation of the ARR.

Beginning investment:	
Initial cost of equipment and software	$80,000
Additional working capital needed for the service line	40,000
Return over life of project:	
Average increase in profits after taxes	20,000
Return at end of project:	
Salvage value of equipment and software in 10 years (end of life of project)	8,000
Working capital released at the end of 10 years	40,000

Solving the formula for the accounting rate of return gives

$$\begin{aligned} \text{ARR} &= \$20{,}000 \div [(\$120{,}000 + \$48{,}000) \div 2] \\ &= \$20{,}000 \div \$84{,}000 \\ &= \underline{\underline{23.81\%}} \end{aligned}$$

The 23.81 percent ARR on this project can be compared with a preestablished hurdle rate set by management. This hurdle rate may not be the same as the desired discount rate because the data used in calculating the accounting rate of return do not represent cash flow information. The ARR hurdle rate may be set higher than the discount rate because the discount rate automatically compensates for the time value of money. In addition, the 23.81 percent ARR for this project should be compared with ARRs on other projects under investment consideration by the RAGs to see which projects have the higher accounting rates of return.

KEY TERMS

accounting rate of return (p. 635)
annuity (p. 605)
annuity due (p. 635)
capital asset (p. 601)
capital budgeting (p. 601)
capital rationing (p. 625)
cash flow (p. 602)
compound interest (p. 634)
compounding period (p. 634)
cost of capital (p. 606)
discount rate (p. 606)
discounting (p. 606)
financing decision (p. 603)
Fisher rate (p. 624)
future value (p. 634)
hurdle rate (p. 611)
independent project (p. 619)
internal rate of return (p. 609)
investment decision (p. 603)
judgmental method (of risk adjustment) (p. 628)
mutually exclusive project (p. 619)
mutually inclusive project (p. 619)
net present value (p. 607)
net present value method (p. 607)
ordinary annuity (p. 635)
payback period (p. 604)
postinvestment audit (p. 631)
preference decision (p. 618)
present value (p. 606)
profitability index (p. 608)
reinvestment assumption (p. 620)
return of capital (p. 606)
return on capital (p. 606)
risk (p. 627)
risk-adjusted discount rate method (p. 628)
screening decision (p. 618)

[15] Sometimes ARR is computed using initial cost rather than average investment as the denominator. Such a computation ignores the return of funds at the end of the project life and is less appropriate than the computation shown.

sensitivity analysis (p. 629)
simple interest (p. 634)
tax benefit (of depreciation) (p. 612)
tax shield (of depreciation) (p. 612)
time line (p. 603)

SOLUTION STRATEGIES

Prepare a time line to illustrate all moments in time when cash flows are expected. The discount rate used should be the cost of capital.

Payback Period

1. For projects with an equal annual cash flow:

Payback Period = Investment ÷ Annuity

2. For projects with unequal annual cash flows:

Sum the annual cash flows until investment is reached to find payback period.

If payback period is equal to or less than a preestablished maximum number of years, the project is acceptable.

Net Present Value

− Investment made currently (always valued at a factor of 1.000)
+ PV of future cash inflows or cost savings
− PV of future cash outflows
= NPV

If NPV is equal to or greater than zero, the project is expected to return a rate equal to or greater than the discount rate and the project is acceptable.

Profitability Index

+ PV of future cash inflows or cost savings
− PV of future cash outflows
= PV of net cash flows

$$PI = \frac{\text{PV of Net Cash Flows}}{\text{PV of Net Investment}}$$

If PI is 1.00 or greater, the project is expected to return a rate equal to or greater than the discount rate and the project is acceptable.

Internal Rate of Return

1. *For projects with equal annual cash flows:*

$$\text{PV Factor} = \frac{\text{Net Investment}}{\text{Annuity}}$$

Find the PV factor (or the one closest to it) in the table on the row for the number of periods of the cash flows. The percentage at the top of the column where this factor is found will approximate the IRR. (*Note:* For projects with equal annual cash flows, this factor is also equal to the payback period.)

2. *For projects with unequal annual cash flows:* Make an estimate of rate provided by project; compute NPV. If NPV is positive (negative), try a higher (lower) rate until the NPV is zero.

Compare IRR to the discount or preestablished hurdle rate. If the IRR equals or is greater than the hurdle rate, the project is acceptable.

Tax Benefit of Depreciation = Depreciation Amount × Tax Rate

Accounting Rate of Return

ARR = Average Annual Profits from Project ÷ Average Investment in Project

Average Investment = (Beginning Investment + Recovery of Investment at End of Project Life) ÷ 2

Compare calculated ARR to hurdle ARR. If the calculated ARR is equal to or greater than the hurdle ARR, the project is acceptable.

Basic Concepts of Capital Budgeting Techniques

	Payback	NPV	PI	IRR	ARR
Uses time value of money?	No	Yes	Yes	Yes	No
Specifies a rate of return?	No	No	No	Yes	Yes
Uses cash flows?	Yes	Yes	Yes	Yes	No
Considers returns during life of project?	No	Yes	Yes	Yes	Yes
Uses discount rate in calculation?	No	Yes	Yes	No*	No*

*Discount rate is not used in the calculation, but it may be used as the hurdle rate.

DEMONSTRATION PROBLEM

Chesapeake Chandlery is considering the development of on-line sales of its boating products. The necessary inventory and distribution capabilities are already in place; however, the company would invest $800,000 to develop the necessary on-line storefront. The investment would have an expected economic life of six years with an expected salvage value of $25,000 at the end of its life.

At the end of the fourth year, the firm anticipates it would spend $80,000 for on-line advertising and updating of its Web site. This amount would be fully deductible for tax purposes in the year incurred. Management requires that investments of this type be recouped in four years or less. The pretax increase in income is expected to be $175,000 in each of the first four years and $132,000 in each of the next two years. The company's discount rate is 10 percent; its tax rate is 30 percent; and the investment would be depreciated for tax purposes using the straight-line method with no consideration of salvage value over a period of five years.

Required:

a. Prepare a time line for displaying cash flows. Be certain to consider the effects of taxes.
b. Calculate the after-tax payback period.
c. Calculate the after-tax net present value on the project.
d. Discuss the appropriateness of making such an investment.

Solution to Demonstration Problem

a.

End of period	0	1	2	3	4	5	6
Investment	−$800,000						
Operating inflows[1]		$122,500	$122,500	$122,500	$122,500	$92,400	$92,400
Depreciation[2]		48,000	48,000	48,000	48,000	48,000	
Operating outflows[3]					−56,000		
Salvage value[4]							17,500

[1]$175,000 × (1 − 0.30) = $122,500
$132,000 × (1 − 0.30) = $92,400
[2]($800,000 ÷ 5) × 0.30 = $48,000
[3]$80,000 × (1 − 0.30) = $56,000
[4]$25,000 × (1 − 0.30) = $17,500
Note that all proceeds received from the sale of the equipment are taxable because the entire cost of the equipment was depreciated. Expected salvage value is ignored in computing depreciation deductions for tax purposes.

b.

Year	Annual Flow	Cumulative Flow
0	$(800,000)	$(800,000)
1	170,500	(629,500)
2	170,500	(459,000)
3	170,500	(288,500)
4	114,500	(174,000)
5	140,400	(33,600)
6	109,900	76,300

The payback is complete in 5.31 years or in April in the last year. The portion of the sixth year (0.31) required to complete the payback is equal to $33,600 ÷ $109,900.

c.

Cash Flow	Time	Amount	Discount Factor	Present Value
Investment	t_0	$(800,000)	1.0000	$(800,000)
Annual flow	t_1–t_3	170,500	2.4869	424,016
Annual flow	t_4	114,500	0.6830	78,204
Annual flow	t_5	140,400	0.6209	87,174
Annual flow	t_6	109,900	0.5645	62,039
Net present value				$ 148,567

d. The project is unacceptable based on the payback period and fails to qualify based on the NPV criterion as well. Accordingly, from strictly a financial perspective, the project is not acceptable. However, nonquantitative factors must be considered. These factors may include effects on competitive position and ability to adopt future technological advances.

QUESTIONS

1. What is a capital asset? How is it distinguished from other assets?
2. Why do firms use multiple criteria when evaluating potential capital investments?
3. Why do capital budgeting evaluation methods use cash flows rather than accounting income?
4. Why are cash flows related to financing not included in evaluating a capital project?
5. Why are time lines helpful in evaluating capital projects?
6. What does the payback method measure? What are its major weaknesses?
7. Why is the time value of money important in capital budgeting? Which evaluation methods use this concept? Which do not?
8. Differentiate between a return *of* capital and a return *on* capital.

9. What is measured by the net present value of a potential project? If the net present value of a project equals zero, is it an acceptable project? Explain.

10. Will the NPV amount determined in the capital budgeting process be the same amount as that which actually occurs after a project is undertaken? Why or why not?

11. How is the profitability index related to the NPV method? What does the PI measure?

12. Under what circumstance will the PI exceed 1? Discuss the rationale for your answer.

13. What is measured by the internal rate of return? When is a project considered acceptable using this method?

14. What is the relationship between NPV and IRR? Why does this relationship hold true?

15. Depreciation does not represent a cash flow. Why, then, is it important in capital budgeting evaluation techniques that use discounted cash flows?

16. What is the difference between the tax shield of depreciation and the tax benefit of depreciation?

17. What are four questions that managers should ask when choosing the investment proposals to be funded?

18. How would managers rank projects using each of the following methods: net present value, profitability index, internal rate of return, payback period, and accounting rate of return?

19. Why should managers use several techniques to rank capital projects? Which technique should be used as the primary evaluator and why?

20. Why does capital rationing exist, and how do managers consider it when ranking capital projects?

21. How is risk defined in capital budgeting analysis? List several aspects of a project in which risk is involved and how risk can affect the net present value of a project.

22. How is sensitivity analysis used in capital budgeting?

23. Why are postinvestment audits performed? When should they be performed?

24. *(Appendix 1)* What is meant by the term *time value of money?* Why is a present value always less than the future value to which it relates?

25. *(Appendix 1)* How does an annuity differ from a single cash flow?

26. *(Appendix 2)* How is the accounting rate of return computed? How does this rate differ from the discount rate and the internal rate of return?

EXERCISES

27. *(Terminology)* Match the numbered item on the right with the lettered item on the left.

a. Annuity
b. Cost of capital
c. Financing decision
d. Investment decision
e. Judgmental method
f. Mutually exclusive projects
g. Mutually inclusive projects
h. Net present value
i. Payback period
j. Present value

1. A measure of the time that will elapse until an initial investment is recouped.
2. A decision regarding what type of capital will be used to fund an investment.
3. A cash flow that is repeated in consecutive periods.
4. Present value of cash inflows less present value of cash outflows.
5. A method of evaluating risk.
6. A decision in which accepting one project requires acceptance of another.

7. A future amount that has been discounted to the present.
8. A decision in which the acceptance of one project implies the rejection of others.
9. A decision about which assets a firm will acquire.
10. The discount rate often used in investment analysis.

28. *(Terminology)* Match the numbered item on the right with the lettered item on the left.

a. Capital asset
b. Compound interest
c. Discount rate
d. Future value
e. Hurdle rate
f. Internal rate of return
g. Profitability index
h. Return of capital
i. Return on capital
j. Risk

1. Effect of uncertainty.
2. Recapture of the original investment.
3. Sum plus its accumulated interest.
4. Interest earned on interest.
5. Discount rate that causes the NPV to equal $0.
6. Benchmark for evaluating the internal rate of return on a project.
7. Rate used to find the present value of a future amount.
8. Interest.
9. Long-lived asset.
10. Derivation of NPV used to compare projects of unequal size.

29. *(Payback period)* Cimarron Manufacturing is considering the purchase of new production technology. The new technology would require an initial investment of $750,000 and have an expected life of 10 years. At the end of its life, the equipment would have no value. By installing the new equipment, the firm's annual labor and quality costs would decline by $150,000.

a. Compute the payback period for this investment (ignore tax).
b. Assume, now, that the annual cost savings would vary according to the following schedule:

	Annual Cost Savings
Years 1–5	$ 75,000
Years 6–10	100,000

Compute the payback period under the revised circumstances (ignore tax).

30. *(Payback)* John's Clothing Store is considering a new product line: umbrellas and rain gear. The new product line would require an investment of $20,000 in equipment and fixtures and $40,000 in working capital. Store managers expect the following pattern of net cash inflows from the new product line over the life of the investment.

Year	Amount
1	$ 5,000
2	9,000
3	16,000
4	18,000
5	15,000
6	14,000
7	12,000

a. Compute the payback period for the proposed new product line. If John's requires a four-year pretax payback on its investments, should the company invest in the new product line? Explain. *(continued)*

b. Should John's use any other capital project evaluation methods before making an investment decision? Explain.

31. *(NPV)* Seattle Fish Processing Company is considering the installation of an automated product handling system. The initial cost of such a system would be $400,000. This system would generate labor cost savings over its 10-year life as follows:

Years	Annual Labor Cost Savings
1–2	$70,000
3–5	85,000
6–8	86,400
9–10	62,000

The system will have no salvage at the end of its 10-year life, and the company uses a discount rate of 12 percent. What is the pretax net present value of this potential investment?

32. *(NPV)* Atlanta Industrial has been approached by one of its customers about producing 400,000 special-purpose parts for a new farm implement product. The parts would be required at a rate of 50,000 per year for eight years. To provide these parts, Atlanta Industrial would need to acquire several new production machines. These machines would cost $500,000 in total. The customer has offered to pay Atlanta Industrial $50 per unit for the parts. Managers at Atlanta Industrial have estimated that, in addition to the new machines, the company would incur the following costs to produce each part:

Direct labor	$ 8
Direct material	10
Variable overhead	4
Total	$22

In addition, annual fixed out-of-pocket costs would be $40,000. The new machinery would have no salvage value at the end of its eight-year life. The company uses a discount rate of 8 percent to evaluate capital projects.

a. Compute the net present value of the machine investment (ignore tax).

b. Based on the NPV computed in part (a), is the machine a worthwhile investment? Explain.

c. Aside from the NPV, what other factors should Atlanta Industrial's managers consider when making the investment decision?

33. *(PI)* Texas Flooring is interested in purchasing a computer and software that would allow its salespeople to demonstrate to customers how a finished carpet installation would appear. Managers have estimated the cost of the computer, software, and peripheral equipment to be $30,000. Based on this cost, the managers have determined that the net present value of the investment is $5,000. Compute the profitability index of the investment (ignore tax).

34. *(PI)* The Omaha Transit Authority (OTA) is considering adding a new bus route. To add the route, OTA would be required to purchase a new bus, which would have a life of 10 years and cost $250,000. If the new bus is purchased, OTA managers expect that net cash inflows from bus ridership would rise by $44,000 per year for the life of the bus. The OTA uses an 8 percent required rate of return for evaluating capital projects. No salvage value is expected from the bus at the end of its life.

a. Compute the profitability index of the bus investment (ignore tax).

b. Should the OTA buy the new bus?

c. What is the minimum acceptable value for the profitability index for an investment to be acceptable?

35. *(IRR)* Island Paradise is considering adding a new dock to its marina facilities to accommodate larger yachts. The facilities would cost $140,000 and would generate $18,200 annually in new cash inflows. The expected life of the facilities would be eight years, and there would be no expected salvage value. The firm's cost of capital and discount rate are 10 percent.

a. Calculate the internal rate of return for the proposed improvement (round to the nearest whole percent; ignore tax).

b. Based on your answer to part (a), should the company build the dock?

c. How much annual cash inflow would be required for the project to be minimally acceptable?

36. *(Multiple methods)* Indiana Furniture Mart is considering buying a delivery truck at a cost of $52,000. Presently, the store relies on a delivery service to deliver its products to area customers. The truck is expected to last six years and have a $7,500 salvage value. Annual operating savings (in delivery costs) are expected to be $14,000 for each of the first two years, $11,000 for each of the next two years, and $9,000 for the last two years. The company's cost of capital is 10 percent and this rate was set as the discount rate.

a. Calculate the payback period (ignore tax).

b. Calculate the net present value (ignore tax).

c. Calculate the profitability index (ignore tax).

37. *(Multiple methods)* Toys for Big Boys is considering purchasing a robot to apply shrink wrap packaging to some of its products. The robot will cost $2,300,000 and will produce annual labor and quality cost savings of $300,000. The robot is expected to last 11 years and have no salvage value. For this project answer the following questions.

a. What is the payback period (ignore tax)?

b. If Toys for Big Boys' discount rate is 10 percent, what is the net present value (ignore tax)?

c. Using a 10 percent discount rate, what is the profitability index (ignore tax)?

d. What is the internal rate of return (to the nearest percent) (ignore tax)?

38. *(Depreciation)* Kansas System Solutions operates consulting offices in three Midwest locations. The firm is presently considering an investment in a new mainframe computer and communication software. The computer would cost $1,000,000 and have an expected life of eight years. For tax purposes, the computer can be depreciated using the straight-line method over five years. No salvage value is recognized in computing depreciation expense and no salvage is expected at the end of the life of the equipment. The company's cost of capital is 10 percent and its tax rate is 35 percent.

a. Compute the present value of the depreciation tax benefit if the company uses the straight-line depreciation method.

b. Compute the present value of the depreciation tax benefit assuming the company uses the double declining balance method of depreciation with a five-year life.

c. Why is the depreciation tax benefit computed in part (b) larger than that computed in part (a)?

39. *(Alternative depreciation methods; NPV)* Chicago Hydraulic is considering an investment in computer-based production technology as part of a business reengineering process. The necessary equipment, installation, and training will cost $40,000,000, have a life of eight years, and generate annual net before-tax cash flows from operations of $8,400,000. The technology will have no value at the end of its eight-year estimated life. The company's tax rate is 30 percent, and its cost of capital is 8 percent.

a. If Chicago Hydraulic uses straight-line depreciation for tax purposes, is the project acceptable using the net present value method?

(continued)

b. Assume the tax law allows the company to take accelerated annual depreciation on this asset in the following manner:

Years 1–2	23 percent of cost
Years 3–8	9 percent of cost

What is the net present value of the project? Is it acceptable?

c. Recompute parts (a) and (b), assuming the tax rate is increased to 50 percent.

40. *(Tax effects of asset sale)* Delta Mechanical Systems purchased a material conveyor system three years ago. Now, the company is going to sell the system and acquire more advanced technology. Data relating to this equipment follow:

Market value now	$15,000
Original cost	24,000
Book value now, for tax purposes	8,000
Book value now, for financial accounting purposes	15,000
Corporate tax rate	40%

a. How much depreciation has been claimed on the conveyor system for tax purposes? For financial accounting purposes?

b. What will be the after-tax cash flow from the sale of this asset?

c. What will be the after-tax cash flow from the sale of the asset if its market value is only $6,000?

41. *(Project ranking)* Two independent potential capital projects are under evaluation by Bird & Company. Project 1 costs $400,000, will last 10 years, and will provide an annual annuity of after-tax cash flows of $85,000. Project 2 will cost $600,000, last 10 years, and provide an annual annuity of $110,000 in annual after-tax cash flows.

a. At what discount rate would management be indifferent between these two projects?

b. What is this indifference rate called?

c. If the firm's cost of capital is 10 percent, which project would be ranked higher?

42. *(Uncertain annual cash flow)* Jones and Associates, CPAs, is considering the installation of a new system for electronically filing tax returns. The initial cost of the system would be $25,000. The expected life of the technology is five years.

a. Given that the company's cost of capital is 12 percent, how much annual increase in cash flows is necessary to minimally justify the investment?

b. Based on your answer to part (a), what would be the payback period for this investment?

43. *(Uncertain project life)* Jake's Exercise Products Inc. is evaluating a potential investment project that would have an initial cost of $400,000 and will return $150,000 annually for six years. The company's cost of capital is 9 percent. Assume that the company is fairly certain regarding the initial cost and the annual return of $150,000, but uncertain as to how many years the $150,000 cash flows will be realized. How many years must the project generate cash flows of $150,000 to be minimally acceptable (ignore tax)?

44. *(Uncertain cash flow; uncertain discount rate)* Quixote Wind Systems manufactures wind-powered electricity generators. The company is considering investing in new technology to allow storage of wind-generated power in batteries. Initial cost of the technology is expected to be $1,200,000. The investment is expected to increase after-tax cash flows by $204,000 for 12 years. The company uses its 9 percent cost of capital rate to discount cash flows for purposes of capital budgeting.

a. What is the lowest acceptable annual cash flow that would allow this project to be considered acceptable (ignore tax)?

b. Assume the company is uncertain as to its actual cost of capital. What is the maximum the company's cost of capital could be (rounded to the nearest whole percent) and still allow this project to be considered acceptable (ignore tax)?

45. *(Appendix 1)* You have just invested $13,000 in a bank account that guarantees to pay you 12 percent interest, compounded annually. At the end of five years, how much money will have accumulated in your investment account (ignore tax)?

46. *(Appendix 1)* You have just purchased a new car. Assume you made a down payment of $8,000 and financed the balance of the purchase cost on an installment credit plan. According to the credit agreement, you agreed to pay $1,200 per month for a period of 36 months. If the credit agreement was based on a monthly interest rate of 1 percent, what was the cost of the car?

47. *(Appendix 1)* Use the tables in Appendix A to determine the answers to the following questions.

a. Elijah Santos wishes to have $50,000 in six years. He can make an investment today that will earn 8 percent each year, compounded annually. What amount of investment should he make to achieve his goal (ignore tax)?

b. Frederick Frazier is going to receive $200,000 on his 50th birthday, 15 years from today. Frederick has the opportunity to invest money today in a government-backed security paying 8 percent, compounded semiannually. How much would he be willing to receive today instead of the $200,000 in 15 years (ignore tax)?

c. Marshall Dillon has $60,000 today that he intends to use as a down payment on a house. How much money did Marshall invest 10 years ago to have $60,000 now, if his investment earned 11 percent compounded annually (ignore tax)?

d. Pat Sawhack is the host of a television game show that gives away thousands of dollars each day. One prize on the show is an annuity, paid to the winner, in equal installments of $210,000 at the end of each year for the next five years. If the winner has an investment opportunity to earn 8 percent, semiannually, what present amount would the winner take in exchange for the annuity (ignore tax)?

e. Ginger is going to be paid modeling fees for the next 10 years as follows: year 1, $30,000; year 2, $50,000; year 3, $60,000; years 4–8, $100,000; year 9, $70,000; and year 10, $45,000. Ginger can invest her money at 8 percent, compounded annually. What is the present value of her future modeling fees (ignore tax)?

f. Your friend has just won the lottery. The lottery will pay her $200,000 per year for the next five years. If this is the only asset owned by your friend, is she a millionaire (one who has a net worth of $1,000,000 or more)? Explain (ignore tax).

48. *(Appendix 2)* Allison Aftercare operates a rehabilitation center for individuals with physical disabilities. The company is considering the purchase of a new piece of equipment that costs $750,000, has a life of five years, and has no salvage value. The company depreciates its assets on a straight-line basis. The expected annual cash flow on a before-tax basis for this piece of equipment is $250,000. Allison requires that an investment be recouped in less than five years and have an accounting rate of return (pretax) of at least 18 percent.

a. Compute the payback period and the accounting rate of return for this piece of equipment (ignore taxes).

b. Is the equipment an acceptable investment for Allison? Explain.

49. *(Appendix 2; comprehensive)* Kopy Korner is evaluating the purchase of a state-of-the-art desktop publishing system that costs $50,000. The company's controller has estimated that the system will generate $16,000 of annual cash receipts for six years. At the end of that time, the system will have no salvage value. The controller also has estimated that cash operating costs will be $2,000 annually. The company's tax rate is expected to be 35 percent during the life of the asset, and the company uses straight-line depreciation.

a. Determine the annual after-tax cash flows from the project.
b. Determine the after-tax payback period for the project.
c. Determine the after-tax accounting rate of return for the project. (Assume tax and financial accounting depreciation are equal.)

50. *(Comprehensive)* Hollywood Games operates a video arcade in the Lincoln Mall. The owner of Hollywood Games, Joe Lynch, is considering acquiring a new "centerpiece" video machine. The cost of the new equipment would be $60,000. The equipment would have an expected life of five years and no salvage value. Straight-line depreciation would be used for both financial and tax purposes.

Mr. Lynch expects the new machine to generate an additional $25,000 per year in net, pretax cash flows. The cost of capital and tax rate for Mr. Lynch are 10 and 28 percent, respectively.

a. Determine the after-tax cash flows from the new machine.
b. Determine the net present value of the machine.
c. Determine the accounting income of the machine.
d. Determine the accounting rate of return and the payback period on an after-tax basis.

http://www.gm.com

51. *(Technology acquisition)* In 1996 General Motors announced that it was preparing to invest $850 million to update its metal-stamping operations. The new metal-stamping operations would be more flexible and less labor intensive than current equipment. GM's Metal Fabricating Division expected to reduce employment of hourly workers by 30,000 and salaried workers by 4,000.

Much of the new investment would be spent on modern transfer presses. Unlike some of GM's older presses, such units accept different dies, or forms for shaping sheet metal. As Japanese automakers proved, such flexible machinery is much more efficient, because it allows an auto maker to alter its production mix to match what's selling and to compensate for breakdowns.

SOURCE: Adapted from Rebecca Blumenstein, "GM to Spend $850 Million to Update Its Sheet-Metal Stamping Operations," *The Wall Street Journal* (May 21, 1996), p. A12.

a. Assume that the only justification for upgrading the metal-stamping machinery is the labor costs to be saved; also, assume the average pay of the 34,000 workers to be displaced by the upgraded machinery is $25,000. Compute the payback period for the upgrade project (ignore tax).
b. The two major financial dimensions of the upgrade project mentioned in the news article were the initial cost of $850 million and the labor cost savings. Prepare a brief oral report in which you identify other cost savings and other costs of the upgrade project.

52. *(Change in investment assumption)* Lenin's Linen provides laundered items to various commercial and service establishments in a large metropolitan city. Lenin's is scheduled to acquire new cleaning equipment in mid-2001 that should provide some operating efficiencies. The new equipment would enable Lenin's to increase the volume of laundry it handles without any increase in labor costs. In addition, the estimated maintenance costs in terms of pounds of laundry would be reduced slightly with the new equipment.

The new equipment was justified on the basis not only of reduced cost but also of expected increase in demand starting in late 2001. However, since the original forecast was prepared, several potential new customers have either delayed or discontinued their own expansion plans in the market area that is serviced by Lenin's. The most recent forecast indicates that no great increase in demand can be expected until late 2002 or early 2003.

Identify and explain the factors that Lenin's should consider in deciding whether to delay the investment in the new cleaning equipment. In the presentation of your response, distinguish between those factors that tend to indicate that the investment should be made as scheduled versus those that tend to indicate that the investment should be delayed. *(CMA adapted)*

53. *(Links between short- and long-term operations)* Drug companies rely on their research activities as the primary source of future revenues and profits. The capital budget is the principal tool used to allocate resources to research activities.

In 1996 Merck & Co., a giant in the drug industry, unveiled a list of its products in early development stages. The products included drugs to treat major maladies such as arthritis and cancer. Analysts who were present at the unveiling were unimpressed. Some of the analysts commented that it was not Merck's long-term prospects that were in question; rather, "its short-term pipeline contains no clear breakthroughs. That poses potential problems for the bottom line, because the company's core products—cardiovascular drugs—face increasing competition, and several new drugs have fallen short of expectations."

http://www.merck.com

SOURCE: Adapted from Robert Langreth, "Drug Pipeline at Merck Gets Weak Review," *The Wall Street Journal* (May 22, 1996), p. B6.

Prepare a written report in which you explain how short-term operations and plans are linked to long-term operations and plans. This report should be directed at an audience that is expected to have little knowledge of formal business planning systems. The major point to be explained in your report is why stock analysts would meet Merck's announcement of an aggressive R&D program with apathy because success of current operations is marginal.

54. *(Capital budget)* Find the home page of the Institute of Management Accountants (IMA). From the home page, locate articles addressing the processes of budgeting. Among these materials is a discussion of the master budget and its component budgets including the capital budget. Read these materials and write a summary of how the capital budget affects, and is affected by, the other budgets that comprise the master budget.

55. *(Application of discounting methods)* Several of the capital budgeting techniques presented in this chapter depend on discounted cash flow concepts. These concepts are applied in business in a variety of settings. Select a business that relies on discounted cash flow analysis, such as a bond investor, and prepare an oral report on how the firm applies discounting methods to manage the business.

56. *(Application of discounting methods)* In the opening and closing vignettes, the point is made that Amazon.com has a huge market value relative to its actual cash flows. Using the concept of net present value, discuss what investors must be expecting about the future of Amazon.com to rationalize the extraordinary relationship between current market value of the company and current cash flows.

57. *(Application of discounting methods)* In recent years, the stock price averages, e.g., Dow Jones Industrial average, have shown sensitivity to changes in interest rates. Based on your understanding of the factors that determine stock price, and how future cash flows are discounted, prepare a brief oral report in which you explain why stock prices should be sensitive to changes in interest rates.

58. *(Product life-cycle applications)* Different accounting and finance tools can be used to control costs as the product life cycle advances through its stages. With this thought in mind, discuss whether capital budgeting as a cost control tool would be relatively more important to an established firm or a .com firm.

PROBLEMS

59. *(Time line; payback; NPV)* Black Hills Souvenir Show is considering expanding its building so it can stock additional merchandise for travelers and tourists. Store manager Allison Crowe anticipates that building expansion costs would be $90,000. Although Ms. Crowe would need to invest in additional inventory, her suppliers are willing to provide inventory on a consignment basis. Annual incremental fixed cash costs for the store expansion are expected to be as follows:

Year	Amount
1	$ 5,550
2	7,200
3	7,200
4	7,200
5	7,950
6	9,450
7	9,750
8	11,250

Ms. Crowe estimates that annual cash inflows could be increased by $120,000 from the additional merchandise sales. The firm's contribution margin is typically 20 percent of sales. Because of uncertainty about the future, Ms. Crowe does not want to consider any cash flows after eight years. The firm uses a 10 percent discount rate.

a. Construct a time line for the investment.
b. Determine the payback period (ignore tax).
c. Calculate the net present value of the project (ignore tax).

60. *(Time line; payback; NPV)* Fred's Freightline is considering the purchase of a new van to replace an existing truck. The van would cost $35,000 and would have a life of seven years with no salvage value at that time. The truck could be sold currently for $4,000; alternatively, if it is kept, it will have a remaining life of seven years with no salvage value. By purchasing the van, Fred's would anticipate operating cost savings as follows:

Year	Amount
1	$6,300
2	7,100
3	7,200
4	7,000
5	7,000
6	7,100
7	7,200

Fred's cost of capital and capital project evaluation rate is 12 percent.

a. Construct a time line for the purchase of the van.
b. Determine the payback period (ignore tax).
c. Calculate the net present value of the van (ignore tax).

61. *(Payback; IRR)* Ted's Bookkeeping Service prepares tax returns for individuals and small businesses. The firm employs four professional people in the tax practice. Currently, all tax returns are prepared on a manual basis. The firm's owner, Ted Moore, is considering purchasing a computer system that would allow the firm to service all its existing clients with only three employees. To evaluate the feasibility of the computerized system, Ted has gathered the following information:

Initial cost of the hardware and software	$32,000
Expected salvage value in 4 years	$0
Annual depreciation	$8,000
Annual operating costs	$4,500
Annual labor savings	$25,000
Expected life of the computer system	4 years

Ted has determined that he will invest in the computer system if its pretax payback period is less than 3.5 years and its pretax IRR exceeds 12 percent.

a. Compute the payback period for this investment. Does the payback meet Ted's criterion? Explain.

b. Compute the IRR for this project to the nearest percent. Based on the computed IRR, is this project acceptable to Ted?

62. *(NPV; PI)* Houston Storage provides warehousing services for industrial firms. Usual items stored include records, inventory, and waste items. The company is evaluating more efficient methods of moving inventory items into and out of storage areas. One vendor has proposed to sell Houston Storage a conveyor system that would offer high-speed routing of inventory items. The required equipment would have an initial cost of $2,500,000 including installation. The vendor has indicated that the machinery would have an expected life of seven years, with an estimated salvage value of $200,000. Below are estimates of the annual labor savings as well as the additional costs associated with the operation of the new equipment:

Annual labor cost savings (14 workers)	$465,000
Annual maintenance costs	20,000
Annual property taxes	14,000
Annual insurance costs	22,000

a. Assuming the company's cost of capital is 9 percent, compute the NPV of the investment in the conveyor equipment (ignore tax).

b. Based on the NPV, should the company invest in the new machinery?

c. Compute the profitability index for this potential investment (ignore tax).

d. What other factors should the company consider in evaluating this investment?

63. *(NPV; PI; payback; IRR)* Custom Driveways provides custom paving of sidewalks and driveways for residential and commercial customers. One of the most labor-intensive aspects of the paving operation is the preparation and mixing of materials. Joe Click, corporate engineer, has learned of a new computerized technology to mix (and monitor mixing of) materials. According to information received by Mr. Click, the cost of the required equipment would be $280,000, and the equipment would have an expected life of seven years. If purchased, the new equipment would replace manually operated equipment. Data relating to the old and new mixing equipment follow:

	OLD TECHNOLOGY
Original cost	$25,000
Present book value	$15,000
Annual cash operating costs	$75,000
Current market value	$6,000
Market value in 7 years	$0
Remaining useful life	7 years

	NEW TECHNOLOGY
Cost	$280,000
Annual cash operating costs	$15,000
Market value in 7 years	$0
Useful life	7 years

a. Assume that the cost of capital in this company is 12 percent, which is the rate to be used in a discounted cash flow analysis. Compute the net present value and profitability index of investing in the new machine. Ignore taxes. Should the machine be purchased? Why or why not?
b. Compute the payback period for the investment in the new machine. Ignore taxes.
c. Rounding to the nearest whole percentage, compute the internal rate of return for the machine investment.

64. *(NPV; taxes)* The manager of Crain Street Cold Storage is considering the installation of a new refrigerated storage room. She has learned that the installation would require an initial cash outlay of $780,000. The installation would have an expected life of 20 years with no salvage value. The installation would increase annual labor and maintenance costs by $75,000. The firm's cost of capital is estimated to be 11 percent, and its tax rate is 30 percent. The storage room is expected to generate net annual cash revenues (before tax, labor, and maintenance costs) of $172,000.
a. Using straight-line depreciation, calculate the after-tax net present value of the storage room.
b. Based on your answer to part (a), is this investment financially acceptable? Explain.
c. What is the minimum amount by which net annual cash revenues must increase to make this an acceptable investment?

65. *(After-tax cash flows; payback; NPV; PI; IRR)* Forrester Fashions is considering the purchase of computerized clothes designing software. The software is expected to cost $160,000, have a useful life of five years, and have a zero salvage value at the end of its useful life. Assume tax regulations permit the following depreciation patterns for this asset:

Year	Percent Deductible
1	20
2	32
3	19
4	15
5	14

The company's tax rate is 30 percent, and its cost of capital is 8 percent. The software is expected to generate the following cash savings and cash expenses:

Year	Cash Savings	Cash Expenses
1	$60,000	$ 9,000
2	67,000	7,000
3	72,000	13,000
4	60,000	8,000
5	49,000	5,000

a. Prepare a time line presenting the after-tax operating cash flows.
b. Determine the following on an after-tax basis: payback period, net present value, profitability index, and internal rate of return.

66. *(NPV; project ranking; risk)* Florida Financial Consultants is expanding operations, and the firm's president, Ms. Hillary Rose, is trying to make a decision about new office space. The following are Ms. Rose's options:

Maple Commercial Plaza	5,000 square feet; cost, $800,000; useful life, 10 years; salvage, $400,000
High Tower	20,000 square feet; cost, $3,400,000; useful life, 10 years; salvage, $1,500,000

If the Maple Commercial Plaza is purchased, the company will occupy all of the space. If High Tower is purchased, the extra space will be rented for $620,000 per year. If purchased, either building will be depreciated on a straight-line basis. For tax purposes, the buildings would be depreciated assuming a 25-year life. By purchasing either building, the company will save $210,000 annually in rental payments. All other costs of the two purchases (such as land cost) are expected to be the same. The firm's tax rate is 40 percent.

a. Determine the before-tax net cash flows from each project for each year.
b. Determine the after-tax cash flows from each project for each year.
c. Determine the net present value for each project if the cost of capital for Florida Financial Consultants is 11 percent. Which purchase is the better investment based on the NPV method?
d. Ms. Rose is concerned about the ability to rent the excess space in High Tower for the 10-year period. To compute the NPV for that portion of the project's cash flows, she has decided to use a discount rate of 20 percent to compensate for risk. Compute the NPV and determine which investment is more acceptable.

67. *(NPV; PI; IRR; Fisher rate)* Scrooge Investments, which has a cost of capital of 12 percent, is evaluating two mutually exclusive projects (A and B), which have the following projections:

	Project A	Project B
Investment	$96,000	$160,000
After-tax cash flows	$25,600	$30,400
Asset life	6 years	10 years

a. Determine the net present value, profitability index, and internal rate of return for Projects A and B.
b. Using the answers to part (a), which is the more acceptable project? Why?
c. What is the Fisher rate for the two projects?

68. *(Capital rationing)* Following are the capital projects being considered by the management of UpTown Productions:

Project	Cost	Annual After-Tax Cash Flows	Number of Years
Film studios	$18,000,000	$2,800,000	15
Cameras and equipment	3,200,000	800,000	8
Land improvement	5,000,000	1,180,000	10
Motion picture #1	17,800,000	4,970,000	5
Motion picture #2	11,400,000	3,920,000	4
Motion picture #3	7,800,000	2,100,000	7
Corporate aircraft	2,400,000	770,000	5

Assume that all projects have no salvage value and that the firm uses a discount rate of 10 percent. Company management has decided that only $25,000,000 can be spent in the current year for capital projects.

a. Determine the net present value, profitability index, and internal rate of return for each of the seven projects.
b. Rank the seven projects according to each method used in part (a).
c. Indicate how you would suggest to the management of Uptown Production that the money be spent. What would be the total net present value of your selected investments?

69. *(Sensitivity analysis)* A 50-room motel is for sale in Houston and is being considered by the Lone Star Motel Chain as an investment. The current owners indicate that the occupancy of the motel averages 80 percent each day of the year that the motel is open. The motel is open 300 days per year. Each room

rents for \$75 per day, and variable cash operating costs are \$10 per day that the room is occupied. Fixed annual cash operating costs are \$100,000.

An acquisition price of \$2,000,000 is being offered by Lone Star. The chain plans on keeping the motel for 14 years and then disposing of it. Because the market for motels is so difficult to predict, Lone Star estimates the salvage value to be zero at the time of disposal. Depreciation will be taken on a straight-line basis for tax purposes. In making the following computations, assume that there will be no tax consequences of the sale in 14 years. The chain's tax rate is estimated at 35 percent for all years.

a. Determine the after-tax net present value of the motel to Lone Star, assuming a cost of capital rate of 13 percent.

b. What is the highest level that the discount rate can be and still allow this project to be considered acceptable by Lone Star? If this discount rate exceeds the highest rate shown in the table (20 percent), simply state this fact and provide supporting computations and reasons.

c. How small can the net after-tax cash flows be and still allow the project to be considered acceptable by Lone Star, assuming a cost of capital rate of 13 percent?

d. What is the shortest number of years for which the net after-tax cash flows can be received and still have the project be considered acceptable?

e. Assume that the answer to part (c) is \$217,425. If all costs remain as they are currently stated and the motel continues to stay open 300 days per year, approximately how many rooms would have to be rented each night to achieve this level of cash flows?

70. *(Postinvestment audit)* Ten years ago, based on a before-tax NPV analysis, Johnson Wholesaling decided to add a new product line. The data used in the analysis were as follows:

Discount rate	12%
Life of product line	10 years
Annual sales increase:	
Years 1–4	\$125,000
Years 5–8	\$175,000
Years 9–10	\$100,000
Annual fixed cash costs	\$20,000
Contribution margin ratio	40%
Cost of production equipment	\$125,000
Investment in working capital	\$10,000
Salvage value	\$0

Because the product line was discontinued this year, corporate managers decided to conduct a postinvestment audit to assess the accuracy of their planning process. Accordingly, the actual cash flows generated from the product line were estimated to be as follows:

Actual Investment	
Production equipment	\$120,000
Working capital	17,500
Total	\$137,500
Actual Revenues	
Years 1–4	\$110,000
Years 5–8	\$200,000
Years 9–10	\$105,000
Actual Fixed Cash Costs	
Years 1–4	\$15,000
Years 5–8	\$17,500
Years 9–10	\$25,000
Actual contribution margin ratio	35%
Actual salvage value	\$5,000
Actual cost of capital	12%

a. Determine the projected NPV on the product line investment.
b. Determine the NPV of the project based on the postinvestment audit.
c. Identify the factors that are most responsible for the differences between the projected NPV and the postinvestment audit NPV.

71. *(Appendix 2; payback; NPV)* Caldwell Department Stores is a growing business that is presently considering adding a new product line. The firm would be required by the manufacturer to incur setup costs of $1,600,000 to handle the new product line. Caldwell has estimated that the product line would have an expected life of eight years. Following is a schedule of revenues and annual fixed operating expenses (including $200,000 of annual depreciation on the investment) associated with the new product line. Variable costs are estimated to average 65 percent of revenues. All revenues are collected as earned. All expenses shown, except for the included amount of straight-line depreciation, are paid in cash when incurred.

Year	Revenues	Expenses
1	$ 720,000	$360,000
2	800,000	320,000
3	960,000	320,000
4	1,280,000	360,000
5	1,600,000	320,000
6	1,600,000	320,000
7	1,120,000	320,000
8	680,000	280,000

The company has a cost of capital of 13 percent. Management uses this rate in discounting cash flows for evaluating capital projects.
a. Calculate the accounting rate of return (ignore tax).
b. Calculate the payback period (ignore tax).
c. Calculate the net present value (ignore tax).

72. *(Comprehensive; Appendix 2)* The management of Custom Metalworks is evaluating a proposal to purchase a new turning lathe as a replacement for a less efficient piece of similar equipment that would then be sold. The cost of the new lathe including delivery and installation is $700,000. If the equipment is purchased, Custom Metalworks will incur $20,000 of costs in removing the present equipment and revamping service facilities. The present equipment has a book value of $400,000 and a remaining useful life of 10 years. Due to new technical improvements that have made the equipment outmoded, it presently has a resale value of only $160,000.

Management has provided you with the following comparative manufacturing cost tabulation:

	Present Equipment	New Equipment
Annual production in units	400,000	500,000
Cash revenue from each unit	$1.20	$1.20
Annual costs:		
Labor	$120,000	$100,000
Depreciation (10% of asset book value or cost)	40,000	70,000
Other cash operating costs	192,000	80,000

Management believes that if the equipment is not replaced now, the company must wait seven years before replacement is justified. The company uses a 12 percent discount or hurdle rate in evaluating capital projects and expects all capital project investments to recoup their costs within five years.

Both pieces of equipment are expected to have a negligible salvage value at the end of 10 years.

a. Determine the net present value of the new equipment (ignore tax).
b. Determine the internal rate of return on the new equipment (ignore tax).
c. Determine the payback period for the new equipment (ignore tax).
d. Determine the accounting rate of return for the new equipment (ignore tax).
e. Determine whether the company should keep the present equipment or purchase the new lathe.

CASES

73. *(Investment financing)* HMG Corporation is a for-profit health-care provider that operates three hospitals. One of these hospitals, Metrohealth, plans to acquire new X-ray equipment. Management has already decided the equipment will be cost beneficial and will enhance the technology available in the outpatient diagnostic laboratory. Before Metrohealth prepares the requisition to corporate headquarters for the purchase, Paul Monden, Metrohealth's controller, has to prepare an analysis to compare financing alternatives.

The equipment is a Supraimage X-ray 400 machine priced at $1,000,000, including shipping and installation; it would be delivered January 2, 2001. Under the tax regulations, this machine qualifies as "qualified technological equipment" with a five-year recovery period. It will be depreciated over five years for tax purposes using the double-declining balance method, with a switch to the straight-line method at a point in time to maximize the depreciation deduction. The machine will have no salvage value at the end of five years. The three financing alternatives Metrohealth is considering are described next.

1. *Finance Internally:* HMG Corporation would provide Metrohealth with the funds to purchase the equipment. The supplier would be paid on the day of delivery.
2. *Finance with a Bank Loan:* Metrohealth could obtain a bank loan to finance 90 percent of the equipment cost at 10 percent annual interest, with five annual payments of $237,420 each due at the end of each year, with the first payment due on December 31, 2001. The loan amortization schedule is presented next.

   Metrohealth would provide the remaining $100,000, which would be paid on delivery.

Year	Beginning Balance	Payment	Interest	Principal Reduction
1	$900,000	$237,420	$90,000	$147,420
2	752,580	237,420	75,258	162,162
3	590,418	237,420	59,042	178,378
4	412,040	237,420	41,204	196,216
5	215,824	237,420	21,596	215,824

3. *Lease from a Lessor:* The equipment could be leased from MedLeasing, with an initial payment of $50,000 due on equipment delivery and five annual payments of $220,000 each, commencing on December 31, 2001. At the option of the lessee, the equipment can be purchased at the fair market value at lease termination (the lessor is currently estimating a 30 percent salvage value).

   The lease satisfies the requirements to be an operating lease for both FASB and income tax purposes. This means that all lease payments are deductible for tax purposes each year. Because of expected technological changes in medical equipment, Metrohealth would not plan to purchase the X-ray equipment at the end of the lease commitment.

Both HMG Corporation and Metrohealth have an effective income tax rate of 40 percent, an incremental borrowing rate of 10 percent, and an after-tax corporate hurdle rate of 12 percent. Income taxes are paid at the end of the year.

a. Prepare a present value analysis as of January 1, 2001, of the expected after-tax cash flows for each of the three financing alternatives available to Metrohealth to acquire the new X-ray equipment. As part of your present value analysis, (1) justify the discount rates you used and (2) identify the financing alternative most advantageous to Metrohealth.

b. Discuss the qualitative factors Paul Monden should include for management consideration before a final decision is made regarding the financing of this new equipment. *(CMA adapted)*

74. *(NPV)* Michigan Motor Company is considering a proposal to acquire new manufacturing equipment. The new equipment has the same capacity as the current equipment but will provide operating efficiencies in direct and indirect labor, direct material usage, indirect supplies, and power. Consequently, the savings in operating costs are estimated to be $150,000 annually.

The new equipment will cost $300,000 and will be purchased at the beginning of the year when the project is started. The equipment dealer is certain that the equipment will be operational during the second quarter of the year it is installed. Therefore, 60 percent of the estimated annual savings can be obtained in the first year. Michigan Motor will incur a one-time expense of $30,000 to transfer the production activities from the old equipment to the new equipment. No loss of sales will occur, however, because the plant is large enough to install the new equipment without disrupting operations of the current equipment. The equipment dealer states that most companies use a 4-year life when depreciating this equipment.

The current equipment has been fully depreciated and is carried in the accounts at zero book value. Management has reviewed the condition of the current equipment and has concluded that it can be used an additional four years. Michigan Motor would receive $5,000 net of removal costs if it elected to buy the new equipment and dispose of its current equipment at this time.

Michigan Motor currently leases its manufacturing plant. The annual lease payments are $60,000. The lease, which will have four years remaining when the equipment installation would begin, is not renewable. Michigan Motor would be required to remove any equipment in the plant at the end of the lease. The cost of equipment removal is expected to equal the salvage value of either the old or the new equipment at the time of removal.

The company uses the sum-of-the-years'-digits depreciation method for tax purposes. A full-year's depreciation is taken in the first year an asset is put into use.

The company is subject to a 40 percent income tax rate and requires an after-tax return of at least 12 percent on an investment.

a. Calculate the annual incremental after-tax cash flows for Michigan Motor Company's proposal to acquire the new manufacturing equipment.

b. Calculate the net present value of Michigan Motor's proposal to acquire the new manufacturing equipment using the cash flows calculated in part (a) and indicate what action Michigan Motor's management should take. Assume all recurring cash flows occur at the end of the year. *(CMA adapted)*

75. *(Postinvestment audit)* Smyth Brothers Inc. has formal policies and procedures to screen and approve capital projects. Proposed capital projects are classified as one of the following types:

1. Expansion requiring new plant and equipment
2. Expansion by replacement of present equipment with more productive equipment
3. Replacement of old equipment with new equipment of similar quality

All expansion projects and replacement projects that will cost more than $50,000 must be submitted to the top management capital investment committee for approval. The investment committee evaluates proposed projects considering the costs and benefits outlined in the supporting proposal and the long-range effects on the company.

The projected revenue and/or expense effects of the projects, once operational, are included in the proposal. Once a project is accepted, the committee approves an expenditure budget for the project from its inception until it becomes operational. The expenditures required each year for the expansions or replacements are also incorporated into Smyth Brothers' annual budget procedure. The budgeted revenue and/or cost effects of the projects, for the periods in which they become operational, are incorporated into the five-year forecast.

Smyth Brothers Inc. does not have a procedure for evaluating projects once they have been implemented and become operational. The vice president of finance has recommended that Smyth Brothers establish a postcompletion audit program to evaluate its capital expenditure projects.

a. Discuss the benefits a company could derive from a postcompletion audit program for capital expenditure projects.

b. Discuss the practical difficulties in collecting and accumulating information that would be used to evaluate a capital project once it becomes operational. *(CMA adapted)*

REALITY CHECK

76. *Traditionally, capital budgeting in health care has tended to focus on projected financial returns from investments. To justify the commitment of capital resources, a proposed investment must be shown to provide sufficient benefits in the form of additional revenues or reduced expenses. A hospital, for example, might invest in an automated drug-dispensing system if forecasted savings from reduced labor and supplies are greater than the initial outlay for the equipment. Present-value calculations are used to weigh immediate costs against eventual benefits over the life of an investment.*

This approach, however, discourages strategic investments in areas where long-term benefits are difficult to measure in financial terms, such as investing in healthcare technologies to improve quality of care or patient satisfaction. Upgrading diagnostic equipment, for example, may be seen as a way to enhance revenues over the long term based on the rationale that patients and physicians are drawn to healthcare organizations that demonstrate a commitment to providing high-quality care. The problem with such an investment from a traditional capital-budgeting perspective is that it is difficult to predict when this benefit will occur or how large it will be. Similarly, capital investments whose objectives are to attract physicians or boost an organization's market share eventually may increase revenues or reduce costs, but are hard to justify solely in terms of short-term financial benefits.

SOURCE: Catherine E. Kleinmuntz and Don N. Kleinmuntz, "A Strategic Approach to Allocating Capital in Healthcare Organizations," *Healthcare Financial Management* (April 1999), p. 52.

a. Assume, as the article states, that health-care entities tend to not invest in *strategic investments in areas where long-term benefits are difficult to measure in financial terms.* Should these firms invest in certain assets even if they cannot measure the outcomes financially? Explain.

b. As an accountant, how could you contribute to the quality of investment analysis of a health-care provider?

77. In February 1996, the German firm, Jos. L. Meyer GmbH was negotiating for the right to build ships in the United States. The family-owned German shipbuilder, which specializes in cruise ships, gas tankers and other complex, labor-intensive vessels would employ as many as 2,000 workers at the U.S. shipyard where wages and benefit rates would be significantly lower than in Germany.

Under the plan being negotiated, Meyer Werft (as the company is known) would invest $60 million in the Philadelphia yard and seek additional private and public funding of about $300 million. The money would be used to enclose one of the yard's huge drydocks and to fund worker retraining and facility improvements.

SOURCE: Adapted from Daniel Machalaba, "Germany's Meyer Werft Seeks to Build Ships at Philadelphia's Naval Yard," *The Wall Street Journal* (February 16, 1996), p. A4.

a. For labor-intensive operations, such as shipbuilding, how would labor quality considerations affect capital budgeting (and location) decisions of firms with global operations?

b. In addition to labor rates, what other factors might be considered in global firms' location decisions for new capital investment?

78. In the United States, companies generally respond to economic downturns by reducing spending on capital projects. A frequently observed strategy is to delay investment in new capital projects and products and to cut spending on research and development activities, advertising, and customer-service activities.

a. In economic downturns how can companies cut costs and activities without affecting quality or service?

b. What are the likely effects of short-term cost-cutting strategies such as those outlined above on long-term profitability and quality control?

79. *Dial Corp., a one-time bus company that in 1996 sold everything from soap to nuts, said it would separate into consumer products and services concerns, splitting a company with about $3 billion in current stock market value.*

http://www.dialcorp.com

The Phoenix-based company's consumer businesses, with revenue in 1995 of about $1.3 billion, would continue to operate under the Dial name. Its diverse airline-catering, convention, travel and money-order businesses, among others, would operate as a separate, as-yet-unnamed unit that in 1995 had revenue of about $2.2 billion.

Dial joined a host of U.S. companies that decided that the sum of the parts is worth more than the whole. Companies that announced or completed spin-offs include AT&T Corp., ITT Corp., Minnesota Mining & Manufacturing Co., Dun & Bradstreet Corp., and Melville Corp. The stocks of companies that announce spin-offs outperform the overall stock market, according to a J.P. Morgan & Co. study.

http://www.att.com
http://www.mmm.com
http://www.dnb.com
http://www.jpmorgan.com

SOURCE: Adapted from Steven Lipin, "Dial to Split into Two Companies," *The Wall Street Journal* (February 16, 1996), p. A3.

a. The conglomerate form of business is perhaps the most difficult to manage in terms of directing new capital investments. Spin-offs can be likened to "undoing" a prior capital investment in a business. What ethical obligation do managers of conglomerates have to stockholders in the event that a higher stock price could be obtained if a business was spun off rather than held?

b. What obligation do managers have to employees who are affected by spin-offs?

80. Although they should be considered independently, often the investing and financing decisions are considered together.

It's easy to understand the allure of auto leasing: Consumers make lower monthly payments; dealers gain volume, move expensive inventory—and keep customers. So it's not surprising to find that one of every three new cars on the road today is leased.

The truth is, dealers have profited more from leasing than from selling. An Atlanta-based leasing expert says, "On a sale a dealer makes about $1,200 to $1,500 in profit. On a lease, it might be $2,500 or $3,000." That's fine, he notes, "unless it's done deceptively."

SOURCE: Deanna Oxender Burgess, "Buy or Lease: The Eternal Question," *Journal of Accountancy* (April 1999), p. 25. Reprinted with permission from the *Journal of Accountancy*.

Complex lease contracts combined with hidden costs complicate the decision to lease or buy. Only recently have key lease terms such as the cost of the car been disclosed to consumers. Laws in a handful of states, as well as Federal Reserve Board Regulation M, which became effective in October 1997, and leasing data available on the Internet are prompting dealers to make increased disclosures. Unfortunately, some fees, including the interest rate the dealer uses to calculate the lease payment, known in the industry as the money factor, still remain unknown to the consumer.

a. Discuss why some consumers might find leasing a car to be more appealing than purchasing one.

b. Even if not required by law, is the practice of not disclosing lease information ethical? Discuss.

c. As an accountant, how could you aid a client in a car-buying situation?

CHAPTER 15

Financial Management

LEARNING OBJECTIVES

After completing this chapter, you should be able to answer the following questions:

1 Why is cost consciousness important to all members of an organization?

2 How are costs determined to be committed or discretionary?

3 How are the benefits of expenditures for discretionary costs measured?

4 When are standards applicable to discretionary costs?

5 How does a budget help control discretionary costs?

6 What is an activity-based budget and how does it differ from traditional budgets?

7 What are the objectives managers strive to achieve in managing cash?

8 (Appendix) How is program budgeting used in not-for-profit entities?

9 (Appendix) Why is zero-base budgeting useful in cost control?

INTRODUCING Lucent Technologies

http://www.lucent.com

Lucent Technologies, formerly known as Western Electric and then AT&T Network Systems, became a stand-alone company on October 1, 1996, when AT&T separated into three companies. (The other two are the new AT&T and NCR.) Lucent, supported by Bell Laboratories, designs, develops, manufactures, and markets communications systems and technologies ranging from microchips to whole networks.

Throughout 1994 and 1995, Lucent's CFO (financial services) operation, while still embedded in various divisions and subsidiaries of AT&T, became involved in a benchmarking initiative that compared its costs with those of "best-in-class" companies. Company representatives worked with an outside consultant who manages a database containing current data on financial processes for more than 1,100 companies. They compared Lucent's financial processes to those of 22 other large companies in various industries with revenues ranging from $5 billion to $90 billion and with financial staffs of up to 15,000 employees.

The benchmarking data revealed that the cost of Lucent's CFO organization was significantly greater than that of several best-in-class companies. Inefficiencies fell primarily into the areas of staffing and systems (related costs included salaries, benefits, overtime, outside services such as for temps and contractors, system development, processing, storage, and printing). Benchmarking also revealed that the most efficient CFO organizations were operating at or below 1% of revenue. Lucent would have to make some significant changes to its systems and processes before it could operate that efficiently.

Lucent's change initiative began in early 1996 when it started the process toward becoming stand-alone. At that time, the CFO organization's mission was clear: Revamp systems and processes to meet its goal of costing the corporation no more than 1% of revenue, one of the benchmarks associated with the existing best-in-class companies.

SOURCE: Thomas A. Francesconi, "Transforming Lucent's CFO," *Management Accounting* (July 1998), p. 22. Copyright Institute of Management Accountants, Montvale, NJ.

This chapter focuses on several major topics related to cost control. First, discussion is provided on **cost control systems**, which are the formal and/or informal activities designed to analyze and evaluate how well costs are managed during a period. The second topic is control over costs (such as advertising) that management sets each period at specified levels. Because the benefits of these costs are often hard to measure, they may be more difficult to control than costs that relate either to the long-term asset investments or to "permanent" organizational personnel. Third, methods of using budgets to help in cost control are discussed. Next, a new approach to budgeting, activity-based budgeting, is introduced. Finally, costs associated with cash management are presented. The chapter appendix considers two alternative budgeting methods: program budgeting, which is often used in governmental and not-for-profit entities, and zero-base budgeting, which can be effective in some cost control programs.

cost control system

http://www.att.com
http://www.ncr.com

COST CONTROL SYSTEMS

The cost control system is an integral part of the overall organizational decision support system. The cost control system focuses on intraorganizational information and contains the detector, assessor, effector, and network components discussed in Chapter 2. Relative to the cost management system, the cost control system provides information for planning and for determining the efficiency of activities while they are being planned and after they are performed, as indicated in Exhibit 15–1.

EXHIBIT 15–1

Functions of an Effective Cost Control System

Control Point	Reason	Cost Control Method
Before an event	Preventive; reflects planning	Budgets; standards; policies concerning approval for deviations; expressions of quantitative and qualitative objectives
During an event	Corrective; ensures that the event is being pursued according to plans; allows management to correct problems as they occur	Periodic monitoring of ongoing activities; comparison of activities and costs against budgets and standards; avoidance of excessive expenditures
After an event	Diagnostic; guides future actions	Feedback; variance analysis; responsibility reports (discussed in Chapter 18)

Managers alone cannot control costs. An organization is composed of many individuals whose attitudes and efforts should help determine how an organization's costs can be controlled. Cost control is a continual process that requires the support of all employees at all times.

Exhibit 15–2 provides a general planning and control model. As shown in this exhibit, control is part of a management cycle that begins with planning. Without first preparing plans for the organization (such as those discussed in Chapter 13), control cannot be achieved because no operational targets and objectives have been established. The planning phase establishes performance targets that become the inputs to the control phase.

EXHIBIT 15–2

General Planning and Control Model

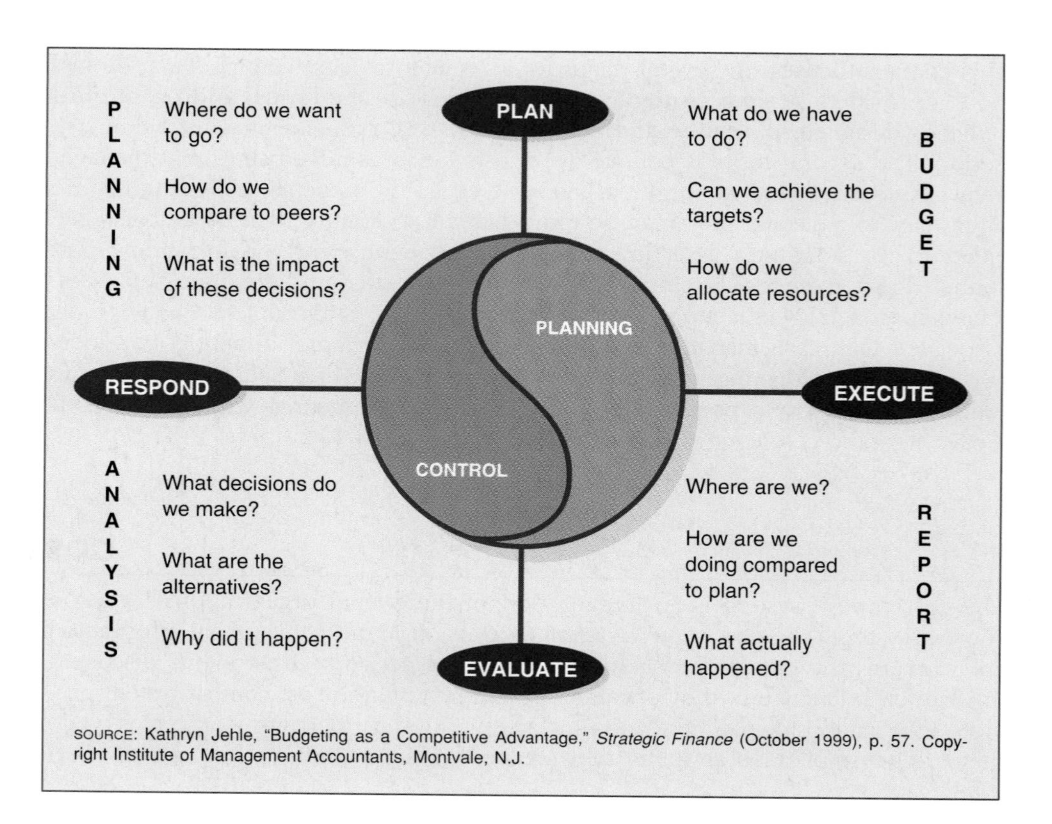

SOURCE: Kathryn Jehle, "Budgeting as a Competitive Advantage," *Strategic Finance* (October 1999), p. 57. Copyright Institute of Management Accountants, Montvale, N.J.

Exhibit 15–3 depicts a more specific model for controlling costs. A good control system encompasses not only the functions shown in Exhibit 15–1, but also the ideas about cost consciousness shown in Exhibit 15–3. **Cost consciousness** refers to a companywide employee attitude toward the topics of cost understanding, cost containment, cost avoidance, and cost reduction. Each of these topics is important at a different stage of control.

1

Why is cost consciousness important to all members of an organization?

cost consciousness

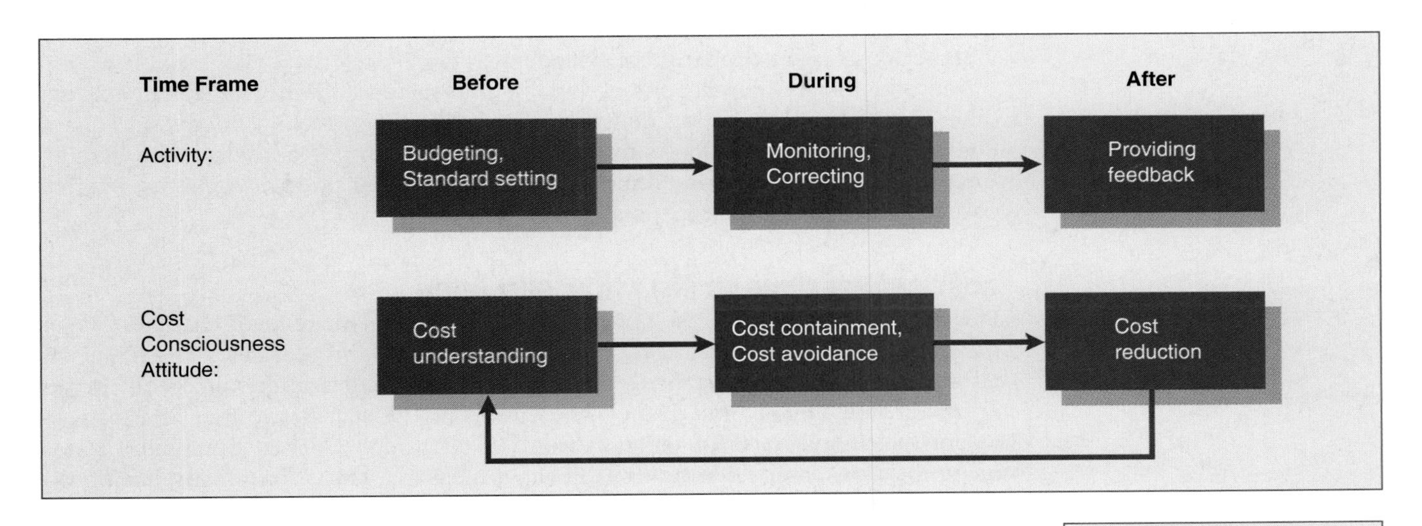

EXHIBIT 15–3

Cost Control System

Cost Understanding

Control requires that a set of expectations exist. Thus, cost control is first exercised when the budget is prepared. However, budgets cannot be prepared without an understanding of the reasons underlying period cost changes, and cost control cannot be achieved without understanding why costs may differ from the budgeted amounts. The opening vignette and the accompanying News Note show the increased use of shared services is one way companies are converting cost understanding into lower costs and higher profits.

http://www.fordvehicles.com
http://www.ge.com

GENERAL BUSINESS NEWS NOTE

Finding Value in Sharing

A dozen years ago, pioneering companies began consolidating finance functions into "shared services" centers. They reasoned that handling all transactions in one place would save millions of dollars. They were right. Now these companies are moving beyond their original aims and are bringing in other functions like human resources and legal. They're also linking their centers into regional and global networks and leveraging their capabilities. The centers create values that expand beyond administration to benefit the entire company and drive the growth of revenue and share value. Advisers can base recommendations on information that's standardized worldwide, and managers can use "apples to apples" comparisons to make better strategic decisions. Sixteen of the top 20 Fortune 500 companies use shared service centers. For example:

> Ford reduced its worldwide finance headcount from more than 14,000 to about 3,000. The center supports 300,000 Ford employees and $125 billion in sales. General Electric cut its staff to one-fourth its original size. The smaller staff provides analytical insights as well as low-cost administrative work.

SOURCE: Bob Cecil, "Shared Services: Moving Beyond Success," *Strategic Finance* (April 2000), pp. 67, 68. Copyright Institute of Management Accountants, Montvale, N.J.

COST CHANGES DUE TO COST BEHAVIOR

Costs may change from previous periods or differ from budget expectations for many reasons. Some costs change because of their underlying behavior. Total variable or mixed cost increases or decreases with, respectively, increases or decreases in activity. If the current period's actual activity differs from a prior period's or the budgeted activity level, total actual variable or mixed cost will differ from that of the prior period or of the budget. A flexible budget can compensate for such differences by providing expected costs at any activity level. By using a flexible budget, managers can then make valid budget-to-actual cost comparisons to determine whether costs were properly controlled.

In addition to the reactions of variable and mixed costs to changes in activity, other factors such as inflation/deflation, supply/supplier cost adjustments, and quantity purchased can cause costs to differ from those of prior periods or the budget. In considering these factors, remember that an external price becomes an internal cost when a good or service is acquired.

COST CHANGES DUE TO INFLATION/DEFLATION

Fluctuations in the value of money are called general price-level changes. When the general price level changes, the prices of goods and services also change. If all other factors are constant, general price-level changes affect almost all prices approximately equally and in the same direction. The statistics in Exhibit 15–4 represent the annual rates of inflation from 1970 through 1997 in the United States using the Consumer Price Index (CPI) as a measure. Thus, a company having office supplies expense of $10,000 in 1970 would expect to have approximately $41,300 of office supplies expense in 1997, for the same basic "package" of supplies. Inflation indexes by industry or commodity can be examined to obtain more accurate information about inflation effects on prices of particular inputs, e.g., paper products.

Some companies include price-escalation clauses in sales contracts to cover the inflation occurring from order to delivery. Such escalators are especially prevalent in industries having production activities that require substantial time. For instance, Congress passed the Debt Collection Improvement Act of 1996, which contained a provision to adjust the Environmental Protection Agency's fines for inflation on a periodic basis. The law allows EPA's penalties to keep pace with inflation and thereby maintain the deterrent effect Congress intended when it originally specified penalties. The first adjustments to penalties were made in 1997.[1]

EXHIBIT 15–4

Cumulative Rate of Inflation (1970–1997)

Year	Index	Year	Index	Year	Index	Year	Index
1970	1.00	1977	1.29	1984	1.68	1991	3.09
1971	1.03	1978	1.34	1985	1.85	1992	3.43
1972	1.05	1979	1.39	1986	2.10	1993	3.65
1973	1.09	1980	1.42	1987	2.34	1994	3.76
1974	1.12	1981	1.47	1988	2.52	1995	3.93
1975	1.17	1982	1.53	1989	2.68	1996	4.04
1976	1.23	1983	1.58	1990	2.83	1997	4.13

Note: For 1998 and thereafter the manner in which the Bureau of Labor Statistics computes the Consumer Price Index changed. Thus, it is difficult to compare data after 1997 to prior data.

SOURCE: Bureau of Labor Statistics, **http://146.142.4.24/cgi-bin/surveymost** (July 8, 2000).

[1] http://www.epa.gov/docs/fedrgstr/EPA-GENERAL/1996/Dece.../pr-23925.htm (July 9, 2000).

COST CHANGES DUE TO SUPPLY/SUPPLIER COST ADJUSTMENTS

The relationship between the availability of a good or service and the demand for that item affects its selling price. If supply is low but demand is high, the selling price of the item increases. The higher price often stimulates greater production, which, in turn, increases supply. In contrast, if demand falls but supply remains constant, the price falls. This reduced price should motivate lower production, which lowers supply. Therefore, price is consistently and circularly influenced by the relationship of supply and demand. Price changes resulting from independent causes are specific price-level changes, and these may move in the same or opposite direction as a general price-level change.

To illustrate, gasoline prices soared in the spring of 1996 because of two supply-related factors. The first factor was a harsh winter that caused refineries to reduce gasoline production so as to increase heating oil production. Second, several refineries had problems that caused shutdowns, which also reduced supply in the third week of April from 7.5 million barrels a day to 7.29 million barrels a day.[2] Specific price-level changes may also be caused by advances in technology. As a general rule, as suppliers advance the technology of producing a good or performing a service, its cost to producing firms declines. Assuming competitive market conditions, such cost declines are often passed along to consumers of that product or service in the form of lower selling prices. Consider the following: "You receive one of those little greeting cards that plays 'Happy Birthday' when you open it. Casually toss it into the trash, and you've just discarded more computer processing power than existed in the entire world before 1950."[3] This is a simple example of the interaction of increasing technology and decreasing selling prices and costs. The News Note on page 666 describes how Alcoa is leveraging existing technology to develop new production methods that squeeze out costs.

http://www.alcoa.com
http://www.toyota.com

Alternatively, when suppliers incur additional production or performance costs, they typically pass such increases on to their customers as part of specific price-level changes. Such costs may be within or outside the control of the supplier. For example, an increase in fuel prices in the first half of 2000 caused the prices of many products and services to rise—especially those having a high freight or energy content.

The quantity of suppliers of a product or service can also affect selling prices. As the number of suppliers increases in a competitive environment, price tends to fall. Likewise, a reduction in the number of suppliers will, all else remaining equal, cause prices to increase. A change in the number of suppliers is not the same as a change in the quantity of supply. If the supply of an item is large, one normally expects a low price; however, if there is only one supplier, the price can remain high because of supplier control. Consider that combating illnesses commonly requires the use of various medications. When drugs are first introduced under patent, the supply may be readily available, but the selling price is high because there is only a single source. As patents expire and generic drugs become available, selling prices decline because more suppliers can produce the item. For example, when the patents on Syntex Corporation's antiarthritis drugs Naprosyn and Anaprox expired in December 1993, two-thirds of the prescriptions filled within a month were filled with generic versions and the price plummeted more than 80 percent.[4]

http://www.syntexcorp.com

Sometimes, cost increases are caused by increases in taxes or regulatory requirements. For example, paper manufacturers are continually faced with more stringent clean air, clean water, and safety legislation. Complying with these regulations increases costs for paper companies. The companies can (1) pass along the costs as price increases to maintain the same income level, (2) decrease other

[2] "They're Back: High Gas Costs Fuel Carpools," *(New Orleans) Times-Picayune* (April 26, 1996), p. C3.
[3] John Huey, "Waking Up to the New Economy," *Fortune* (June 27, 1994), p. 37.
[4] Elyse Tanouye, "Price Wars, Patent Expirations Promise Cheaper Drugs," *The Wall Street Journal* (March 24, 1994), p. B1.

NEWS NOTE  GENERAL BUSINESS

Real Time . . . Real Money

In 1999, Alcoa reduced inventories by more than a quarter of a billion dollars while increasing sales by just under $1 billion. Credit goes to the Alcoa Business System, an adaptation of Toyota's production methods that will take more than $1.1 billion out of the aluminum maker's cost base. A big piece of it: getting Alcoa, as much as possible, to operate in real time.

Managing in real time—making decisions now, on the basis of accurate, live information; eliminating filters and emptying catch basins of information and resources; producing to actual demand rather than to forecast or budget—is changing how business works.

Alcoa, already the aluminum industry's cost leader, began rolling out its new manufacturing methods in 1998, aiming to cut costs and improve responsiveness. "We were ill prepared to meet customers' needs," says executive vice president P. Keith Turnbull, who leads the effort. "We'd ship out a pile of dead 'inventory,' and if we didn't have what the customer wanted, we'd make the pile bigger." Inventories are a hedge against inefficiency: your own or that of your supplier or customer. Alcoa CEO Alain Belda calls them "monuments to incompetence."

Managing in real time is central to Alcoa's process. First, it's how Alcoa fixes plants: As at Toyota, any worker who has any problem—a machine out of kilter, a product defect—or has an idea pulls a cord summoning a leader, with the aim of fixing the problem or implementing the idea then and there. One problem, one cause, one time, at once—that's how the plant gets better, rather than by batching tasks off to engineers. Second, inside the plants, real demand dictates production as much as possible; that is, a worker upstream responds to live "pull" signals from workers downstream—ideally workers he can actually see. Says Turnbull, "Workers need to have the authority to buy and sell. Joe says to Marie, 'I need three extrusions by such and such a time'; Marie says yes or no; then she in turn buys what she needs."

The results show up all over the company. A plant in Sorocaba, Brazil, turns its inventory 60 times a year. A Hernando, Miss., extrusion plant, a money loser when it was acquired in 1998, delivers custom orders in two days (versus three weeks previously) and makes money. In Portland, Australia, producing molten metal to real-time demand from an adjacent ingot mill raised asset utilization so much that the plant eliminated ten of 24 vacuum crucibles, saving about $60 million a year. All this—$832 million so far, toward the $1.1 billion target—has taken just over two years. Real time flies.

SOURCE: Thomas A. Stewart, "How Cisco and Alcoa Make Real Time Work," *Fortune* (May 29, 2000), pp. 284–286.

costs to maintain the same income level, or (3) experience a decline in net income. The News Note on page 667 illustrates the cost of regulation in the case of pharmaceutical companies.

COST CHANGES DUE TO QUANTITY PURCHASED

Firms are normally given quantity discounts, up to some maximum level, when they make purchases in bulk. Therefore, a cost per unit may change because quantities are purchased in lot sizes differing from those of previous periods or those projected. Involvement in group purchasing arrangements can make quantity discounts easier to obtain.

The preceding reasons indicate why costs change. Next, the discussion addresses actions firms can take to control costs.

Cost Containment

cost containment

To the extent possible, period-by-period increases in per-unit variable and total fixed costs should be minimized through a process of **cost containment**. Cost containment is not possible for inflation adjustments, tax and regulatory changes, and supply and demand adjustments because these forces occur outside the organization. Additionally, in most Western companies, adjustments to prices resulting from factors within the supply chain are not controlled by managers.

GENERAL BUSINESS  NEWS NOTE

Who Regulates the Cost of Regulation?

U.S. drug companies discover almost half the new drugs in the world. Americans now lead longer, more productive lives, due in part to the new drugs. New heart medicines have contributed greatly to the 74% drop in cardiac deaths over the past 40 years. AIDS deaths have dropped 70% because of new drug cocktails. Even deaths from cancer are beginning to decline.

Yet today, thanks in large part to FDA requirements, the average cost of developing a new drug is about $650 million. American drug companies invest $24 billion annually in research and development. It takes 12 to 15 years to discover and develop a new medicine. Only one in 5,000 chemicals looked at in the laboratory ever gets to market. Once approved by the FDA, only three in 10 return more than the development costs. This is a prohibitively costly process, and only some of the costs are justified.

Since the 1960s, the FDA has promoted the standard that a drug must be "safe and effective" to enter the U.S. market. Pre-approval safety studies cost less than $50 million per drug. The remaining $600 million in development costs for a new drug is spent on clinical human efficacy trials. Most of this money goes to research institutes. The trials create a four-to-eight year delay, and produce conflicting data. The conclusion often drawn is that more studies are necessary—in other words, please send us more grant money. This process simply transfers wealth from drug companies to research institutes, bypassing the sick.

The market does a better job of screening, rejecting 70% of drugs as not effective. This shouldn't be surprising. The market is where real patients—many on numerous medications—use a new drug, and it's also where ordinary doctors, unrestricted by protocols, observe a new drug in action.

SOURCE: William K. Summers and James Driscoll, "To Cut Drug Prices, Reform the FDA," *The Wall Street Journal* (June 21, 2000), p. A26. Permission conveyed through the Copyright Clearance Center.

Japanese companies may not have the same view of supply-chain cost containment techniques. In some circumstances, a significant exchange of information occurs among members of the supply chain, and members of one organization may actually be involved in activities designed to reduce costs of another organization. For example, Citizen Watch Company has long set target cost reductions for external suppliers. If suppliers could not meet the target, they would be assisted by Citizen engineers in efforts to meet the target the following year.[5]

http://www.citizenwatch.com

In the United States, some interorganizational arrangements of this kind do exist. For instance, an agreement between Baxter International (a hospital supply company) and BJC Health System allowed Baxter access to BJC's hospital computer information database. The information obtained was used by Baxter "to measure more precisely the types of procedures conducted and the exact amount of supplies needed."[6]

http://www.baxter.com
http://www.bjc.org

However, costs that rise because of reduced supplier competition, seasonality, and quantities purchased are subject to cost containment activities. A company should look for ways to cap the upward changes in these costs. For example, purchasing agents should be aware of new suppliers for needed goods and services and determine which, if any, of those suppliers can provide needed items in the quantity, quality, and time desired. Comparing costs and finding new sources of supply can increase buying power and reduce costs.

If bids are used to select suppliers, the purchasing agent should remember that a bid is merely the first step in negotiating. Although a low bid may eliminate some competition from consideration, additional negotiations between the purchasing agent and the remaining suppliers may reveal a purchase cost even lower than the bid amount, or concessions (such as faster and more reliable delivery) might be

[5] Robin Cooper, *Citizen Watch Company, Ltd.* (Boston: Harvard Business School Case No. 194-033).
[6] Thomas M. Burton, "Baxter Reaches Novel Supply Pact with Duke Hospital," *The Wall Street Journal* (July 15, 1994), p. B2.

obtained. However, purchasing agents must remember that the supplier offering the lowest bid is not necessarily the best supplier to choose. Other factors such as quality, service, and reliability are important.

http://www.ochsner.org/ofh.htm

Reduced costs can often be obtained when long-term or single-source contracts are signed. For example, Ochsner Hospital in New Orleans has several limited (between one and three) source relationships for office and pharmaceutical supplies, food, and sutures. Most of these suppliers also provide just-in-time delivery. For instance, operating room (OR) supplies are ordered based on the next day's OR schedule. Two hours later, individual OR trays containing specified supplies for each operation are delivered by the vendor. By engaging in supplier relationships of this kind, Ochsner has not only introduced volume purchasing discounts but also effected timely delivery with total quality control.[7]

A company may circumvent seasonal cost changes by postponing or advancing purchases of goods and services. However, such purchasing changes should not mean buying irresponsibly or incurring excessive carrying costs. Economic order quantities, safety stock levels, and materials requirements planning as well as the just-in-time philosophy should be considered when making purchases. These concepts are discussed in the next chapter.

As to services, employees could repair rather than replace items that have seasonal cost changes. For example, maintenance workers might find that a broken heat pump can be repaired and used for the spring months so that it would not have to be replaced until summer when the purchase cost is lower.

Cost Avoidance and Reduction

cost avoidance

Cost containment can prove very effective if it can be implemented. In some instances, although cost containment may not be possible, cost avoidance might be. **Cost avoidance** means finding acceptable alternatives to high-cost items and/or not spending money for unnecessary goods or services. Avoiding one cost may require that an alternative, lower cost be incurred. For example, some companies have decided to self-insure for many workers' compensation claims rather than pay high insurance premiums. Gillette avoids substantial costs by warehousing and shipping Oral-B toothbrushes, Braun coffeemakers, Right Guard deodorant, and Paper Mate ballpoint pens together because all of these products share common distribution channels.[8]

http://www.gillette.com

cost reduction

Closely related to cost avoidance, **cost reduction** refers to lowering current costs. Benchmarking is especially important in this area so that companies can become aware of costs that are in excess of what is necessary. The News Note on page 669 discusses benchmarks for the financial services function—the area in which Lucent Technologies is striving to cut costs and improve quality.

As discussed in Chapter 1 relative to core competencies, companies may also reduce costs by outsourcing rather than maintaining internal departments. Data processing and the financial and legal functions are prime targets for outsourcing in many companies. Distribution is also becoming a highly viable candidate for outsourcing, because "for many products, distribution costs can be as much as 30% to 40% of a product's cost."[9]

http://www.arthurandersen.com

Sometimes money must be spent to generate cost savings. Accountants may opt to use videotaped rather than live presentations to reduce the cost of continuing education programs. Some of the larger firms (such as Arthur Andersen) have their own in-house studios and staffs. Although the cost of producing a tape is high, the firms feel the cost is justified because many copies can be made and used in multiple presentations over time by all the offices. Other firms bring in specialists

[7] Interview with Graham Cowie, Ochsner Medical Institutions, 1994.
[8] Pablo Galarza, "Nicked and Cut," *Financial World* (April 8, 1996), p. 38.
[9] Rita Koselka, "Distribution Revolution," *Forbes* (May 25, 1992), p. 58.

GENERAL BUSINESS **NEWS NOTE**

Accounting for the Accounting Function

Finance is an expensive function. It costs the typical company 1.4 percent of its annual revenues to provide financial services. This cost includes processing basic transactions such as payables, payroll and receivables, as well as management reporting, budgeting and activities like tax, treasury and financial analysis. Three components make up the cost: fully loaded labor (wages, salaries and benefits), outsourcing systems (run time and maintenance for finance systems only) and "other" (such as facilities, suppliers and corporate allocations).

While finance costs remain high, they've been dropping quickly, as companies make a concerted effort to eliminate their unnecessary activities, streamline their organizations and leverage technology. The benchmark shows that costs have declined 36 percent since 1988, when they were 2.2 percent of revenue. Given this trend, we anticipate that the average cost of finance will drop to less than 1 percent of revenue within the next several years.

Leading the pack in our most recent analysis of the database is a multibillion-dollar global manufacturer that has finance costs of 0.36 percent of revenue—and incorporates a high degree of best practices into the function while providing exceptional levels of service. Yet even this stellar performer acknowledges that it still has room and plans for improvement. A point that's important to note: The best keep getting better, elevating the standard for all competitors.

While, on average, finance costs a company 1.4 percent of revenue, the range between the lowest and the highest costs is large. The top 25 percent of companies in the database have costs of less than 1 percent of revenue, and fourth quartile companies have costs that are greater than 2.2 percent.

SOURCE: Greg Hackett, "But Are My Finance Costs Typical?" *Financial Executive* (July/August 1998), pp. 44–45. Copyright 1998 Financial Executives Institute, Morristown, N.J. Reprinted with permission.

or use satellite or two-way interactive television to provide continuing education to their employees.

Some companies are also beginning to look outside for information about how and where to cut costs. Consulting firms, such as Fields & Associates in Burlingame, California, review files for duplicate payments and tax overpayments. Fields "recovered about $1 million for Intel Corp. in two years, in exchange for part of the savings."[10]

http://www.intel.com

Although many companies believe that eliminating jobs and labor are effective ways to reduce costs, the following quote provides a more appropriate viewpoint:

> *Cutting staffs to cut costs is putting the cart before the horse. The only way to bring costs down is to restructure the work. This will then result in reducing the number of people needed to do the job, and far more drastically than even the most radical staff cutbacks could possibly do. Indeed, a cost crunch should always be used as an opportunity to re-think and to re-design operations.*[11]

In fact, sometimes cutting costs by cutting people merely creates other problems. The people who are cut may have been performing a value-added activity; and by eliminating such people, a company may reduce its ability to do necessary and important tasks as well as reduce organizational learning and memory.

On-the-job training is an important component in instilling cost consciousness within an organization's quest for continuous improvement. Giving training to personnel throughout the firm is an effective investment in human resources because workers can apply the concepts and skills they are learning directly to the jobs they are doing.

[10] Jeffrey A. Tannenbaum, "Entrepreneurs Thrive by Helping Big Firms Slash Costs," *The Wall Street Journal* (November 10, 1993), p. B2.

[11] Peter Drucker, "Permanent Cost Cutting," *The Wall Street Journal* (January 11, 1991), p. A8. Permission conveyed by the Copyright Clearance Center.

Managers may adopt the five-step method of implementing a cost control system shown in Exhibit 15–5. First, the type of costs incurred by an organization must be understood. Are the costs under consideration fixed or variable, product or period? What cost drivers affect those costs? Does management view the costs as committed or discretionary? Second, the need for cost consciousness must be communicated to all employees for the control process to be effective. Employees must be aware of which costs need to be better controlled and why cost control is important to both the company and the employees themselves. Third, employees must be educated in cost control techniques, encouraged to provide ideas on how to control costs, and motivated by incentives to embrace the concepts. The incentives may range from simple verbal recognition to monetary rewards to time off with pay. Managers must also be flexible enough to allow for changes from the current method of operation. Fourth, reports must be generated indicating actual results, budget-to-actual comparisons, and variances. These reports must be evaluated by management to determine why costs were or were not controlled in the past. Such analysis may provide insightful information about cost drivers so that the activities causing costs to be incurred may be better controlled in the future. Last, the cost control system should be viewed as a long-run process, not a short-run solution. "To be successful, organizations must avoid the illusion of short-term, highly simplified cost-cutting procedures. Instead, they must carefully evaluate proposed solutions to ensure that these are practical, workable, and measure changes based on realities, not illusions."[12]

EXHIBIT 15–5

Implementing a Cost Control System

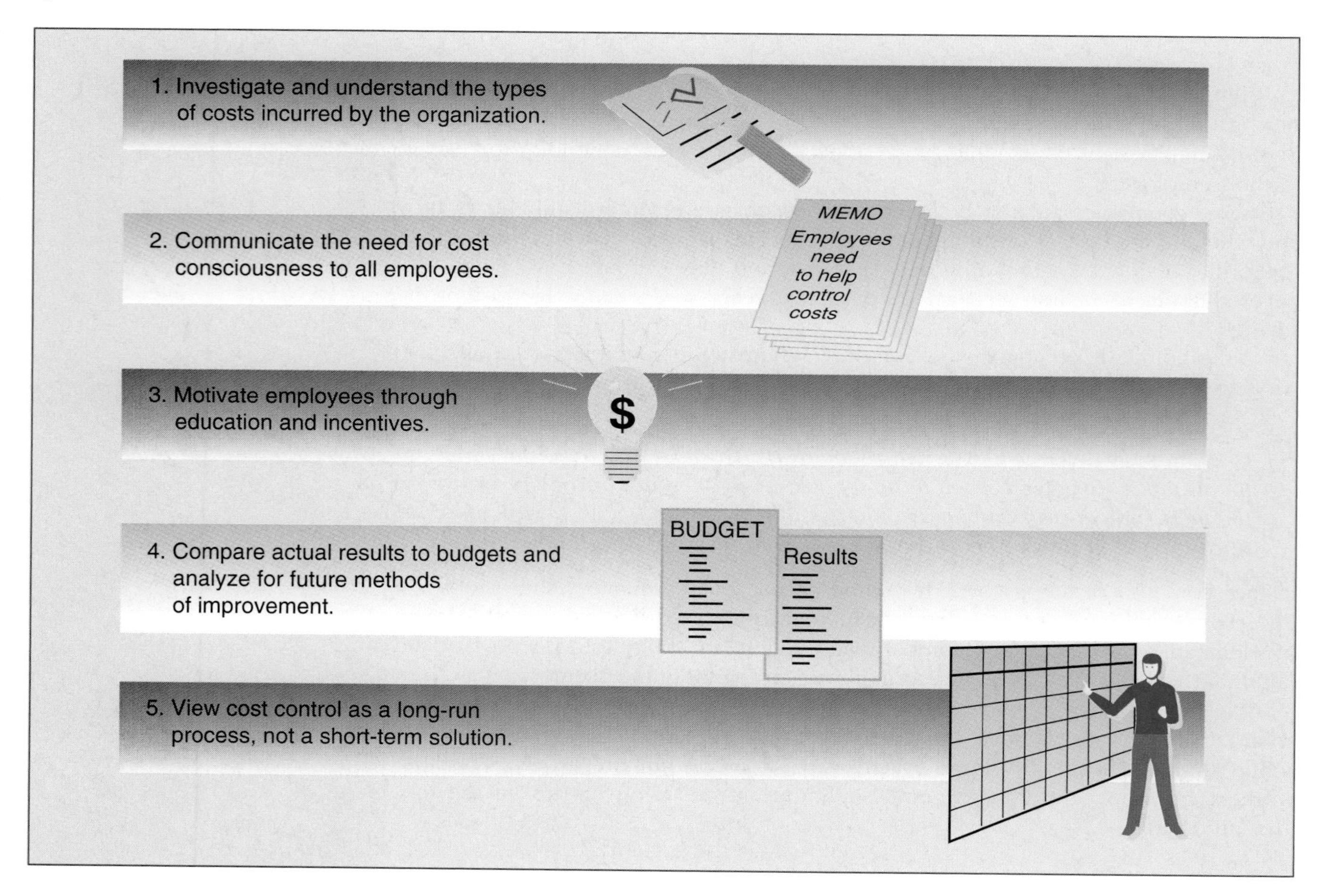

[12] Mark D. Lutchen, "Cost Cutting Illusions," *Today's CPA* (May/June 1989), p. 46.

Following these five steps will provide an atmosphere conducive to controlling costs to the fullest extent possible as well as deriving the most benefit from the costs that are incurred. Costs to be incurred should have been compared to the benefits expected to be achieved before cost incurrence took place. The costs should also have been incorporated into the budgeting system because costs cannot be controlled after they have been incurred. Future costs, on the other hand, may be controlled based on information learned about past costs. Cost control should not cease at the end of a fiscal period or because costs were reduced or controlled during the current period. However, distinct differences exist in the cost control system between committed and discretionary costs.

COMMITTED FIXED COSTS

2

How are costs determined to be committed or discretionary?

Managers are charged with planning and controlling the types and amounts of costs necessary to conduct business activities. Many activities required to achieve business objectives involve fixed costs. All fixed costs (and the activities that create them) can be categorized as either committed or discretionary. The difference between the two categories is primarily the time period for which management binds itself to the activity and the cost.

committed cost

The costs associated with basic plant assets or with the personnel structure that an organization must have to operate are known as **committed costs**. The amount of committed costs is normally dictated by long-run management decisions involving the desired level of operations. Committed costs include depreciation, lease rentals, and property taxes. Such costs cannot be reduced easily even during temporarily diminished activity.

One method of controlling committed costs involves comparing the expected benefits of having plant assets (or human resources) with the expected costs of such investments. Managers must decide what activities are needed to attain company objectives and what (and how many) assets are needed to support those activities. Once the assets are acquired, managers are committed to both the activities and their related costs for the long run. However, regardless of how good an asset investment appears to be on the surface, managers must understand how committed fixed costs could affect income in the event of changes in operations.

Assume the managers at Ace Engineered Products are considering an investment of $1,000,000 in design technology. The technology will be depreciated at the rate of $100,000 per year. The company's cost relationships indicate that variable costs are 45 percent of revenues, giving a contribution margin of 55 percent. Exhibit 15–6 (p. 672) shows the potential effects on net income of this long-term commitment under three conditions: maintenance of current revenues, a 20 percent increase in revenues, and a 20 percent decrease in revenues.

Note that the $100,000 increase in depreciation expense affects the income statement more significantly when sales decline than when sales increase. This effect is caused by the operating leverage factor discussed in Chapter 11. Companies that have fairly high contribution margins can withstand large increases in fixed costs as long as revenues increase. However, these same companies feel greater effects of decreases in revenue because the margin available to cover fixed costs erodes so rapidly. As the magnitude of committed fixed costs increases, so does the risk of incurring an operating loss in the event of a downturn in demand. Therefore, managers must be extremely careful about the level of fixed costs to which the organization is committed.

A second method of controlling committed costs involves comparing actual and expected results from plant asset investments. During this process, managers are able to see and evaluate the accuracy of their cost and revenue predictions relative to the investment. This comparison is called a postinvestment audit and is discussed in Chapter 14.

EXHIBIT 15-6

Risk Related to Committed Costs

	Current Level of Operations	(a) Current Level of Revenues and Increase in Depreciation	(b) Increase in Revenues of 20% and Increase in Depreciation	(c) Decrease in Revenues of 20% and Increase in Depreciation
Revenues	$2,500,000	$2,500,000	$3,000,000	$2,000,000
Variable costs	(1,125,000)	(1,125,000)	(1,350,000)	(900,000)
Contribution margin	$1,375,000	$1,375,000	$1,650,000	$1,100,000
Fixed costs	(1,200,000)	(1,300,000)	(1,300,000)	(1,300,000)
Net income	$ 175,000	$ 75,000	$ 350,000	$ (200,000)

Each change from the original income level to the new income level is explained as the change in the contribution margin minus the increase in fixed costs:

Change to (a) = Increase in CM − Increase in FC = $0 − $100,000 = $(100,000)
Change to (b) = Increase in CM − Increase in FC = $275,000 − $100,000 = $175,000
Change to (c) = Decrease in CM − Increase in FC = $(275,000) − $100,000 = $(375,000)

An organization cannot operate without some basic levels of plant and human assets. Considerable control can be exercised over the process of determining how management wishes to define "basic" and what funds will be committed to those assets. The benefits from committed costs can generally be predicted and are commonly compared with actual results in the future.

DISCRETIONARY COSTS

discretionary cost

In contrast to a committed cost, a **discretionary cost** is one "that a decision maker must periodically review to determine if it continues to be in accord with ongoing policies."[13] A discretionary fixed cost is one that reflects a management decision to fund a particular activity at a specified amount for a specified period of time. Discretionary costs relate to company activities that are important but are viewed as optional. Discretionary cost activities are usually service oriented and include employee travel, repairs and maintenance, advertising, research and development, and employee training and development. There is no "correct" amount at which to set funding for discretionary costs, and there are no specific activities whose costs are always considered discretionary (or discretionary fixed) in all organizations. In the event of cash flow shortages or forecasted operating losses, discretionary fixed costs may be more easily reduced than committed fixed costs.

http://www.mcdonalds.com

Discretionary costs, then, are generated by unstructured activities that vary in type and magnitude from day to day and whose benefits are often not measurable in monetary terms. For example, in 1996, McDonald's decided to spend more than $200 million to promote its quarter-pound Arch Deluxe hamburger and several other adult entrees.[14] How could McDonald's know whether this advertising campaign actually created a demand for these products? Expenditures of this magnitude require that management have some idea of the benefits that are expected, but measuring results is often difficult. Management can employ market research in an effort to gain knowledge of the effectiveness of advertising and other promotional tools.

Just as discretionary cost activities vary, the quality of performance may also vary according to the tasks involved and the skill levels of the persons performing

[13] Institute of Management Accountants (formerly National Association of Accountants), *Statements on Management Accounting Number 2: Management Accounting Terminology* (Montvale, N.J.: June 1, 1983), p. 35.
[14] Bruce Horovitz and Dottie Enrico, "Chain Hoping Grown-Up Chow Boosts Sales," *USA Today* (May 9, 1996), p. 1A.

them. Because of these two factors—varying activities and varying quality levels—discretionary costs are not usually susceptible to the precise measures available to plan and control variable production costs or the cost-benefit evaluation techniques available to control committed fixed costs. Because the benefits of discretionary cost activities cannot be assessed definitively, these activities are often among the first to be cut when profits are lagging. Thus, proper planning for discretionary activities and costs may be more important than subsequent control measures. Control after the planning stage is often restricted to monitoring expenditures to ensure conformity with budget classifications and preventing managers from overspending their budgeted amounts.

Budgeting Discretionary Costs

Budgets, described in Chapter 13 as both planning and controlling devices, serve to officially communicate a manager's authority to spend up to a predetermined amount (**appropriation**) or rate for each budget item. Budget appropriations serve as a basis for comparison with actual costs. Accumulated expenditures in each budgetary category are periodically compared with appropriated amounts to determine whether funds have been under- or overexpended.

appropriation

Before top management can address the issue of discretionary costs, company goals must be translated into specific objectives and policies that management believes will contribute to organizational success. Then, management must budget the types and funding levels of discretionary activities that will accomplish those objectives. Funding levels should be set only after discretionary cost activities have been prioritized and cash flow and income expectations for the coming period have been reviewed. Management tends to be more generous about making discretionary cost appropriations during periods of strong economic outlook for the organization than in periods of weak economic outlook.

Discretionary costs are generally budgeted on the basis of three factors: (1) the related activity's perceived significance to the achievement of objectives and goals, (2) the upcoming period's expected level of operations, and (3) managerial negotiations in the budgetary process. For some discretionary costs, managers are expected to spend the full amount of their appropriations within the specified time frame. For other discretionary cost activities, the "less is better" adage is appropriate.

As an example of "less is *not* better," consider the cost of preventive maintenance. This cost can be viewed as discretionary, but reducing it could result in diminished quality, production breakdowns, or machine inefficiency. Although the benefits of maintenance expenditures cannot be precisely quantified, most managers believe that incurring less maintenance cost than budgeted is not a positive type of cost control. In fact, spending (with supervisory approval) more than originally appropriated might be necessary or even commendable—assuming that positive results (such as a decline in quality defects) are obtained. Such a perspective illustrates the perception mentioned earlier that cost control should be a long-run process rather than a short-run concern.

Alternatively, spending less than budgeted on travel and entertainment (while achieving the desired results) would probably be considered positive performance, but requesting travel and entertainment funds in excess of budget appropriations might be considered irresponsible.

Managers may view discretionary activities and costs as though they were committed. A discretionary expenditure may be budgeted on an annual basis as a function of planned volume of company sales. Once this appropriation has been justified, management's intention may be that it is not to be reduced within that year regardless of whether actual sales are less than planned sales. A manager who states that a particular activity's cost will not be reduced during a period has chosen to view that activity and cost as committed. This viewpoint does not change the underlying discretionary nature of the item. In such circumstances, top management must have a high degree of faith in the ability of lower-level management to perform the specified tasks in an efficient manner.

However, if revenues, profits, or cash flows are reduced, funding for discretionary expenditures should be evaluated not simply in reference to reduced operations, but relative to activity priorities. Eliminating the funding for one or more discretionary activities altogether may be possible while maintaining other funding levels at the previously determined amounts. For instance, if a company experiences a downturn in demand for its product, the discretionary cost budget for advertising is often reduced—a potentially illogical reaction. Instead, increasing the advertising budget and reducing the corporate executives' travel budget might be more appropriate.

Discretionary cost activities involve services that vary significantly in type and magnitude from day to day. The output quality of discretionary cost activities may also vary according to the tasks and skill levels of the persons performing the activities. Because of varying service levels and quality, discretionary costs are generally not susceptible to the precise planning and control measurements that are available for variable production costs or to the cost-benefit evaluation techniques available for committed fixed costs.

Part of the difference in management attitude between committed and discretionary costs has to do with the ability to measure the benefits provided by those costs. Whereas benefits of committed fixed costs can be measured on a before-and-after basis (through the capital budgeting and postinvestment audit processes), the benefits from discretionary fixed costs are often not distinctly measurable in terms of money.

How are the benefits of expenditures for discretionary costs measured?

Measuring Benefits from Discretionary Costs

Because benefits from some activities traditionally classified as discretionary cannot be adequately measured, companies often assume that the benefits—and, thus, the activities—are unimportant. But many of the activities previously described as discretionary (repairs, maintenance, R&D, and employee training) are critical to a company's position in a world-class environment. These activities, in the long run, produce quality products and services; therefore, before reducing or eliminating expenditures in these areas, managers should attempt to more appropriately recognize and measure the benefits of these activities.

Research and development is often considered a discretionary cost activity. Companies in industries such as pharmaceuticals and food, however, might consider some level of R&D cost as committed. In comparing actual and budgeted R&D costs in such companies, would "less" be "better?"

The value of discretionary costs should be estimated using nonmonetary, surrogate measures. Devising such measures often requires substantial time and creativity. Exhibit 15–7 presents some useful surrogate measures for determining the effectiveness of various types of discretionary costs. Some of these measures are verifiable and can be gathered quickly and easily; others are abstract and require a longer time horizon before they can be obtained.

Discretionary Cost Activity	Surrogate Measure of Results
Preventive maintenance	• Reduction in number of equipment failures • Reduction in unplanned downtime • Reduction in frequency of production interruptions caused by preventable maintenance activities
Advertising	• Increase in unit sales in the two weeks after an advertising effort relative to the sales two weeks prior to the effort • Number of customers referring to the ad • Number of coupons clipped from the ad and redeemed
University admissions recruiting trip	• Number of students met who requested an application • Number of students from area visited who requested to have ACT/SAT scores sent to the university • Number of admissions that year from that area
Prevention and appraisal quality activities	• Reduction in number of customer complaints • Reduction in number of warranty claims • Reduction in number of product defects discovered by customers
Staffing law school indigent clinic	• Number of clients served • Number of cases effectively resolved • Number of cases won
Executive retreat	• Proportion of participants still there at end of retreat • Number of useful suggestions made • Values tabulated from an exit survey

EXHIBIT 15–7

Nonmonetary Measures of Output from Discretionary Costs

The amounts spent on discretionary activities reflect resources that are consumed by an activity and should provide some desired monetary or surrogate output. Comparing input costs and output results can help to determine whether a reasonable cost-benefit relationship exists between the two. Managers can judge this cost-benefit relationship by how efficiently inputs (represented by costs) were used and how effectively those resources (again represented by costs) achieved their purposes. These relationships can be seen in the following model:

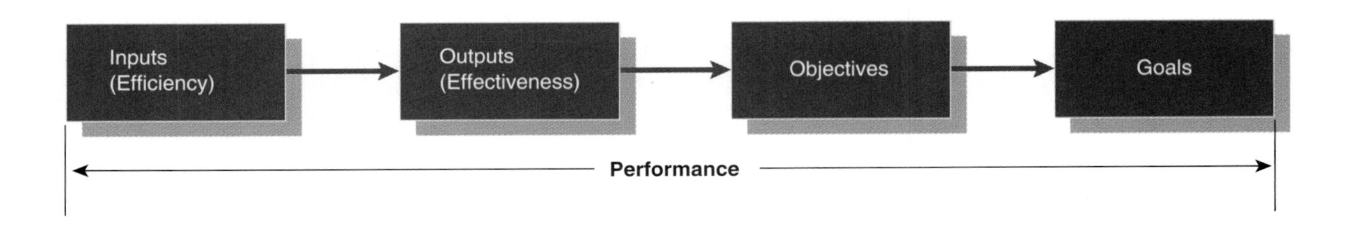

The degree to which a satisfactory relationship occurs when comparing outputs to inputs reflects the efficiency of the activity. Thus, efficiency is a yield concept and is usually measured by a ratio of output to input. For instance, one measure of automobile efficiency is miles driven per gallon of fuel consumed. The higher the number of miles per gallon, the greater the fuel efficiency of the car.

Comparing actual output results to desired results indicates the effectiveness of an activity or how well the objectives of the activity were achieved. When a valid output measure is available, efficiency and effectiveness can be determined as follows:

$$\text{Actual Result} \longrightarrow \text{compared to} \longrightarrow \text{Desired Result}$$

$$\text{Efficiency} = \frac{\text{Actual Output}}{\text{Actual Input}} \longrightarrow \frac{\text{Planned Output}}{\text{Planned Input}}$$

or, alternatively

$$\text{Efficiency} = \frac{\text{Actual Input}}{\text{Actual Output}} \longrightarrow \frac{\text{Planned Input}}{\text{Planned Output}}$$

$$\text{Effectiveness} = \frac{\text{Actual Output}}{\text{Planned Output}} \longrightarrow \text{Preestablished Standard}$$

A reasonable measure of efficiency can exist only when inputs and outputs can be matched in the same period and when a credible causal relationship exists between them. These two requirements make measuring the efficiency of discretionary costs very difficult. First, several years may pass before output occurs from some discretionary cost expenditures. Consider, for example, the length of time between making expenditures for research and development or a drug rehabilitation program and the time at which results of these types of expenditures are visible. Second, there is frequently a dubious cause-and-effect relationship between discretionary inputs and resulting outputs. For instance, assume that you clip and use a cents-off coupon for Crest toothpaste from the Sunday paper. Can Procter & Gamble be certain that it was the advertising coupon that caused you to buy the product, or might you have purchased the toothpaste anyway?

http://www.crest.com
http://www.pg.com

Effectiveness, on the other hand, is determined for a particular period by comparing the results achieved with the results desired. Determination of an activity's effectiveness is unaffected by whether the designated output measure is stated in monetary or nonmonetary terms. But management can only subjectively attribute some or all of the effectiveness of the cost incurrence to the results. Subjectivity is required because the comparison of actual output to planned output is not indicative of a perfect causal relationship between activities and output results. Measurement of effectiveness does not require the consideration of inputs, but measurement of efficiency does.

Assume that last month Ace Engineered Products increased its quality control training expenditures and, during that period, defective output dropped by 12 percent. The planned decrease in defects was 15 percent. Although management was 80 percent effective ($0.12 \div 0.15$) in achieving its goal of decreased defects, that result was not necessarily related to the quality control training expenditures. The decline in defects may have been caused partially or entirely by such factors as use of higher grade raw materials, more skilled production employees, or more properly maintained production equipment. Management, therefore, does not know for certain whether the quality control training program was the most effective way in which to decrease production defects.

The relationship between discretionary costs and desired results is inconclusive at best, and the effectiveness of such costs can only be inferred from the relationship of actual to desired output. Because many discretionary costs result in benefits that must be measured on a nondefinitive and nonmonetary basis, exercising control of these costs during activities or after they have begun is difficult. Therefore, planning for discretionary costs may be more important than subsequent control measures. Control after the planning stage is often relegated to monitoring discretionary expenditures to ensure conformity with budget classifications and preventing managers from overspending their budgeted amounts.

CONTROLLING DISCRETIONARY COSTS

Control of discretionary costs is often limited to a monitoring function. Management compares actual discretionary expenditures with standards or budgeted amounts to determine variances in attempting to understand the cause-and-effect relationships of discretionary activities.

4

When are standards applicable to discretionary costs?

Control Using Engineered Costs

Some discretionary activities are repetitive enough to allow the development of standards similar to those for manufacturing costs. Such activities result in **engineered costs**, which are costs that have been found to bear observable and known relationships to a quantifiable activity base. Such costs can be treated as either variable or fixed. Discretionary cost activities that can fit into the engineered cost category are usually geared to a performance measure related to work accomplished. Budget appropriations for engineered costs are based on the static master budget level. However, control can be exerted through the use of flexible budgets if the expected level of activity is not achieved.

engineered cost

To illustrate the use of engineered costs, assume that Ace Engineered Products has found that quality control can be treated as an engineered cost. Taken as a whole, quality control inspections are similar enough to allow management to develop a standard inspection time. Company management, in a cost reduction effort, is willing to contract with part-time qualified quality control inspectors who will be paid on an hourly basis. Ace managers have found that inspection of each product averages slightly less than four minutes. Thus, each inspector should be able to perform approximately 15 inspections per hour. From this information, the company can obtain a fairly valid estimate of what inspection costs should be based on a particular activity level and can compare actual cost against the standard cost each period. The activity base of this engineered cost is the number of inspections performed.

In April, Ace management predicts that 26,250 inspections will be performed and, thus, 1,750 inspection hours should be provided. If the standard average hourly pay rate for inspectors is $10, the April budget is $17,500. In April, 25,575 inspections are made at a cost of $17,034 for 1,670 actual hours. Using the generalized cost analysis model for variance analysis presented in Chapter 10, the following calculations can be made:

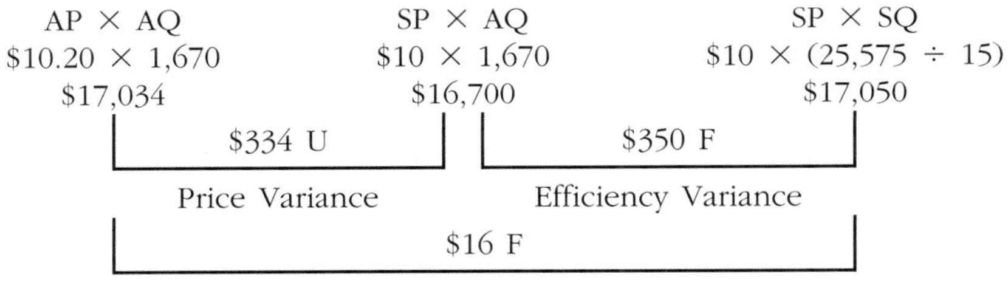

The price variance shows that, on average, Ace Engineered Products paid $0.20 more per hour for inspectors during April than was planned. The favorable efficiency variance results from using fewer hours than standard; however, recall that the standard requires only 15 inspections per hour even though the average inspection is expected to take "slightly less" than four minutes. Thus, a favorable variance is not surprising. A "generous" standard was set by Ace Engineered Products to reinforce the importance of making high-quality inspections regardless of the time taken.

The preceding analysis is predicated on the company being willing and able to hire the exact number of inspection hours needed. If Ace Engineered Products has to employ only full-time employees on a salary basis, analyzing inspection costs in the above manner is not very useful. In this instance, quality inspection cost becomes a discretionary fixed cost and Ace Engineered Products may prefer the following type of fixed overhead variance analysis:

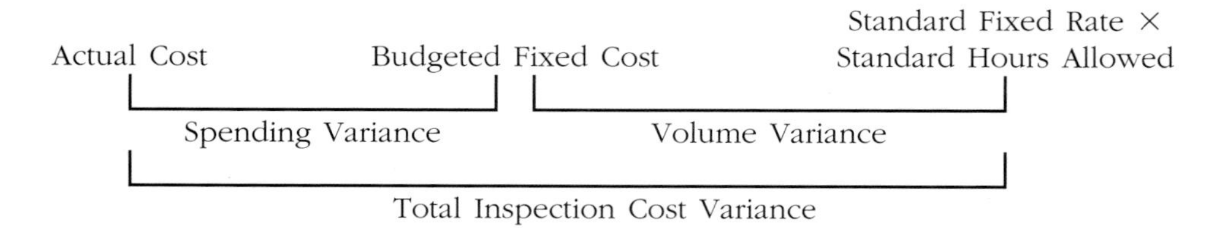

In a third type of analysis, it is assumed that part-time help will be needed in addition to the full-time staffing, and the flexible budget is used as the center column measure in the following diagram. Assume the following facts: (1) There are three full-time inspectors, each earning $1,600 per month and working 160 hours per month; (2) the standard hourly rate for part-time help is $10; (3) the standard quantity of work is 15 inspections per hour; (4) 25,575 inspections were made during the month; and (5) actual payroll for 1,670 total hours was $4,800 for full-time inspectors and $12,269 for part-time inspectors who worked 1,190 hours. Ace Engineered Products prepares a flexible budget for its fixed inspection cost at $4,800 (3 × $1,600) based on a normal processing volume of 7,200 inspections and $10 per hour for part-time workers. The following variances can be computed:

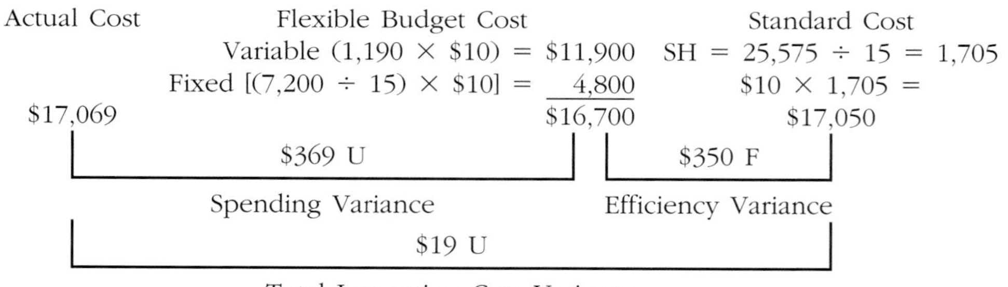

The unfavorable spending variance was incurred because part-time employees had to be hired at approximately $0.31 more per hour than standard [($12,269 ÷ 1,190) − $10]. The favorable efficiency variance reflects above-normal productivity (1,705 standard hours allowed − 1,670 actual hours). To determine the implications of these figures, Ace Engineered Products management would need to know which employees did and did not perform 15 inspections per hour. Management can evaluate an individual's productivity to ascertain whether it is within preestablished control limits. If productivity is outside those limits, management should seek the causes and work with the employee to improve performance.

The method of variance analysis and, thus, cost control must be appropriate to the cost category and management information needs. Regardless of the variance levels or the explanations provided, managers should always consider whether the activity itself and, therefore, the cost incurrence was sufficiently justified. For example, assume that $76,000 is spent on the salary of an additional systems analyst in the Systems Department. During the year, systems activities take place, but there is no measurable output such as systems modifications or a new system. Before determining that the discretionary cost expenditure was justified, top management should review the systems manager's activity reports for the analysts in the department. The discretionary expenditure would not be considered effective if the new analyst spent a significant portion of the period doing menial tasks. In other words, postincurrence audits of discretionary costs are important in determining the value of the expenditure.

Control Using the Budget

5

How does a budget help control discretionary costs?

Once discretionary cost budget appropriations have been made, monetary control is effected through the use of budget-to-actual comparisons in the same manner as for other costs in the budget. Actual results are compared to expected results and explanations should be provided for variances. Explanations for variances can often be found by recognizing cost consciousness attitudes. The following illustration involving two discretionary cost activities provides a budget-to-actual comparison that demonstrates employee cost consciousness.

Ace Engineered Products and several other companies outsource their payroll processing activities to Quality Financial Services. That company has prepared the condensed budget shown in Exhibit 15–8 for the first quarter of 2001. Ms. Toya Brown, the controller for Quality Financial Services, estimates 900,000 paychecks will be processed during that period; the company charges its clients $0.85 per check processed.

In pursuing a strategy of total quality and continuous improvement, Quality Financial Service's management has chosen to fund employee training to improve employee and customer satisfaction. Maintenance is also considered a discretionary cost and is budgeted at $1.00 per 30 checks processed. Office costs include utilities, phone service, supplies, and delivery. These costs are variable and are budgeted at $70 for each hour that the firm operates. Quality Financial Services expects to operate 600 hours in the budget quarter. Wages are for the 10 employees who are paid $31 per hour. Salaries and fringe benefits are for management level personnel and, like depreciation, are fixed amounts.

Ms. Brown collected the revenue and expense data shown in Exhibit 15–9 during the first quarter of 2001. Because of computer downtime during the quarter, Quality Financial Services stayed open 3 extra hours on 10 different workdays. Additional contracts were responsible for the majority of the increase in checks processed.

EXHIBIT 15-8

Budget—First Quarter 2001

Revenues:		
Processing fees (900,000 × $0.85)		$765,000
Expenses:		
Employee training	$ 40,000	
Maintenance	30,000	
Office	42,000	
Wages and fringe benefits	186,000	
Salaries and fringe benefits	114,000	
Depreciation	65,000	(477,000)
Operating Income before Tax		$288,000

EXHIBIT 15–9

Actual Results—First Quarter 2001

Revenues:		
Processing fees (960,000 × $0.85)		$816,000
Expenses:		
Employee training	$ 52,000	
Maintenance	30,720	
Office	44,730	
Wages and fringe benefits	199,080	
Salaries and fringe benefits	117,400	
Depreciation	74,000	(517,930)
Operating Income before Tax		$298,070

After reviewing the actual results, the company's board of directors requested a budget-to-actual comparison from Ms. Brown and explanations for the cost variances. Because every cost was higher than budgeted, the board was of the opinion that costs had not been properly controlled. Ms. Brown prepared the comparison presented in Exhibit 15–10 and provided the following explanations for the variances. Each explanation is preceded by the related budget item number.

1. The discretionary cost for employee training was increased because the company took advantage of an unforeseen opportunity to obtain training on the company's new enterprise resource software. Additionally, employees received training on a new electronic data interchange (EDI) system that Quality Financial Services installed. *Comment: These explanations reflect an understanding of long-term variable cost behavior and of the long-run quality considerations of having well-trained employees.*
2. Maintenance cost decreased because managers obtained a favorable price on maintenance supplies obtained from a new Internet vendor. *Comment: This explanation reflects an understanding of how costs can be reduced without adversely affecting quality. The company has found a way to reduce costs without decreasing levels of maintenance or the quality of service delivered to clients. Costs have been reduced by obtaining the maintenance inputs at a lower unit cost.*
3. Office expenses were influenced by two factors: the additional 30 hours of operation and an increase in local utility rates, which caused Quality Financial Service's costs to rise $1 per operating hour. *Comment: The first part of the explanation reflects an understanding of the nature of variable costs: additional hours worked caused additional costs to be incurred. The second part of*

EXHIBIT 15–10

Budget-to-Actual Comparison for First Quarter 2001

	Budget Item #	Original Budget	Budget for Actual Results	Actual	Variances
Revenues:					
Processing fees		$765,000	$816,000	$816,000	$ 0
Expenses:					
Training	(1)	$ 40,000	$ 40,000	$ 52,000	(12,000)
Maintenance	(2)	30,000	32,000	30,720	1,280
Office	(3)	42,000	44,730*	44,730	0
Wages and fringe benefits	(4)	186,000	195,300	199,080	(3,780)
Salaries and fringe benefits	(5)	114,000	114,000	117,400	(3,400)
Depreciation	(6)	65,000	65,000	74,000	(9,000)
Total expenses		$477,000	$491,030	$517,930	$(26,900)
Operating Income before Tax		$288,000	$324,970	$298,070	

*This amount is based on the assumption that the higher hourly rate was attributable to an unforeseen utility rate increase: 630 hours × $71 = $44,730.

the explanation reflects an understanding of the nature of specific price-level adjustments. The increase in utility rates could possibly have been caused by inflation, an increase in demand with no corresponding increase in supply, or additional utility regulatory costs being passed along to the utility's customers.

4. The increase in wages was caused by two factors: 30 additional operating hours, and an increase in the hourly cost of fringe benefits because of an increase in health insurance premiums.

10 employees × 630 hours × $31 per hour	$195,300
Increase in cost of fringe benefits (10 × 630 × $0.60)	3,780
Total wages cost	$199,080

Comment: These cost changes reflect the nature of variable costs and an unavoidable increase caused by a vendor cost adjustment.

5. A new purchasing agent, hired at the beginning of the quarter, is being paid $13,600 more per year than the previous agent. *Comment: Increases in salaries are typically caused either by inflation or supply-and-demand relationships for professional staff. In this case, the new manager is trained in EDI transactions, which should result in substantial cost savings to the company in future periods.*
6. The depreciation increase was related to the purchase and installation of the new EDI system. The purchase was made with board approval when a competitor went bankrupt during the quarter and had a distress liquidation sale. The purchase of this technology had been included in the capital budget for the end of 2001, not during the first quarter. *Comment: Acquiring the EDI technology is a good example of the cost containment concept. Quality Financial Services wanted to buy the software and equipment and had an opportunity to buy it at a substantial savings, but earlier than anticipated. This purchase created an unfavorable cost variance for depreciation in the first quarter, but it shows an instance of planning, foresight, and flexibility. The long-run benefits of this purchase are twofold. First, a favorable variance will be shown in the capital budget when the cost of this equipment is compared to the expected cost. Second, in future periods, the budgeted committed cost for depreciation will be less than it would have been had the purchase not been made at this time.*

Note that the variance computations in Exhibit 15–10 are based on comparisons between a revised budget that uses actual checks processed as the cost driver and the actual revenues and costs incurred. When comparing budgeted and actual expenditures, managers must be careful to analyze variances using an equitable basis of comparison. These variance computations illustrate the use of flexible budgeting. Comparisons between the original budget and actual results for the variable cost items would not have been useful for control purposes because variable costs automatically rise with increases in cost driver activity.

Suppose Quality Financial Services's board also wanted a better understanding of why the original budget indicated an operating income before tax of $288,000, but the actual results showed $298,070—an increase of $10,070. A set of comparisons of each cost line of the original budget with its counterpart actual cost indicates an increase in expenses of $40,930. Revenue can be analyzed in the following manner:

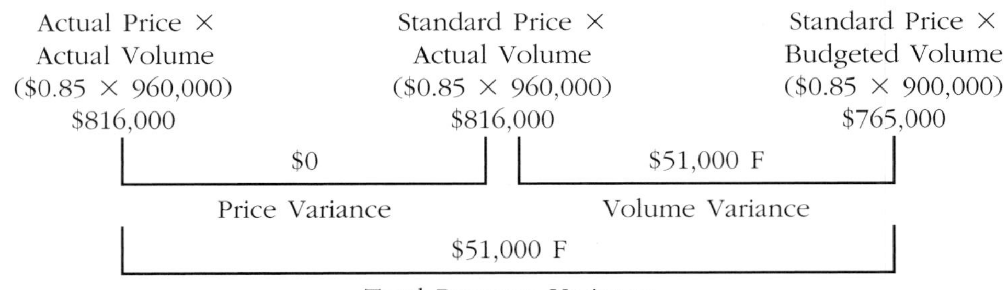

The $51,000 favorable variance for revenue is assigned completely to the 60,000 unit increase in checks processed over budget because there was no change in the per-check price. Thus, the increase in income from the original budget is ($51,000 − $40,930) or $10,070. The standard costing models presented in Chapter 10 can be adapted if further analysis of expenses is desired. For the immediate purpose of explaining the increase in operating income before tax, the report shown in Exhibit 15–10 coupled with the previous explanations should suffice.

Quality Financial Services was more profitable by $10,070 than originally planned. With the explanations presented to the board of directors, it does appear that costs were relatively well controlled. The larger variances were based on rational management decisions to incur greater-than-planned costs and uncontrollable cost increases.

Another approach to evaluating cost management and control is activity-based budgeting. This tool is used in the planning stage of the operating cycle.

ACTIVITY-BASED BUDGETING

6

What is an activity-based budget and how does it differ from traditional budgets?

Chapter 4 illustrates the benefits of activity-based management (ABM) and activity-based costing (ABC) in controlling costs. Specifically, it shows that reducing or eliminating non-value-added activities will cause the associated costs to be reduced or eliminated. This section introduces activity-based budgeting as an extension of activity-based management focused on the planning stage of the operating cycle.

Most companies rely on an annual budget as a key planning and control tool. Traditionally, budgetary expense categories are organized to align with subsequent reporting categories. For example, expense categories typically include cost of goods sold, marketing expenses, and administrative expenses. These categories are commonly found in both planning and reporting documents. However, when budgets are prepared using these categories, little insight is gained about how costs in these categories can be reduced—and if they were reduced, what consequences would result.

activity-based budgeting

Activity-based budgeting (ABB) is a planning approach applying activity drivers to estimate the levels and costs of activities necessary to provide the budgeted quantity and quality of production. ABB can be applied to nearly any activity and is useful for managing product and period costs. ABB is typically used in the course of an annual budgeting process that begins with the preparation of a sales budget followed by a production budget (as discussed in Chapter 13). These budgets establish expected output targets for sales, distribution, and manufacturing. Using these documents as basic inputs, the subsequent steps of ABB are given in Exhibit 15–11.

The distinction between ABB and traditional budgeting is illustrated in Exhibit 15–12 for the accounting department in a small manufacturing firm. On the left side of the exhibit is a traditional budget; on the right side is the activity-based budget. Both budgets provide for the same overall level of spending. The traditional budget provides an excellent delineation of the expected costs of various resources for the

EXHIBIT 15–11

Activity-Based Budgeting Steps

1. Select a function for which costs are to be estimated, i.e., distribution, marketing, finance, accounting.
2. Identify all activities necessary to execute the selected function.
3. Identify the activity driver for each activity.
4. Estimate the necessary volume of each activity driver to meet output objectives, i.e., sales and production levels specified in the master budget.
5. Identify the resources consumed by each activity.
6. Estimate the cost of providing each resource.

Traditional Budget		Activity Description	Unit Cost	Activity Level	Activity Cost
Salaries	$800,000	Compliance reporting	$500	450	$225,000
Occupancy	80,000	Answering phone calls	$10	12,000	120,000
Supplies	28,000	Preparing mgmt reports	$1,200	250	300,000
Depreciation	22,000	Gathering transaction data	$2	55,000	110,000
Utilities	12,000	Transaction analysis	$5	37,000	185,000
Travel	38,000	Training & mentoring	$800	50	40,000
Total	$980,000				$980,000

SOURCE: Adapted from James A. Brimson and John Antos, *Driving Activity Value Using Activity-Based Budgeting* (New York: John Wiley & Sons, 1999), p. 11.

EXHIBIT 15–12

Traditional versus Activity-Based Budgeting

period. However, it leaves the reader with no understanding of how those resources specifically support the activities necessary for the firm to meet its objectives; and it leads to no strategies about how costs might be reduced without harming the achievement of the objectives. For example, managers could mandate a cut in travel cost for the accounting department with the hope that such a cut would increase profits. However, it is unlikely that managers understand how travel costs relate to achievement of corporate goals.

Alternatively, the activity-based budget provides a listing of costs associated with specific activities executed in the accounting department. With ABB data, costs can be managed by changing the level of specific activities and the impact on the objective function will be more easily understood. Also, the activity-based budget leads to more interesting questions about cost incurrence and cost management opportunities. For example, why are we processing 55,000 transactions per year? Can we recontract with our vendors under long-term supply agreements to reduce the number of transactions? Why does it cost us $5 each to analyze transactions? Why are we analyzing 37,000 transactions per year? Why does it cost us $10 to answer a phone call? Can we automate phone answering services to reduce the cost of handling phone calls? Can we outsource our compliance reporting to reduce expenses?

Once the budgeted level of activities is set for the period, the expected cost of each activity is determined. Then, the activity-based budget can be converted into a resource budget like the traditional budget shown in Exhibit 15–12 by relating the activity costs to specific resources.

If activity-based budgeting is effectively implemented, the result should be an increase in profits and cash flows. However, other tools are available that can be used with ABB to improve efficiency and increase available cash.

CASH MANAGEMENT ISSUES

7

What are the objectives managers strive to achieve in managing cash?

Of all organizational resources, cash is one of the most important and challenging to manage. Two key cash management tools were introduced in Chapter 13: the cash budget and cash flow statement. This section provides an overview of cash management objectives and tools.

An organization's liquidity depends on having enough cash available to retire debts and other obligations as they come due. However, holding too much cash reduces a firm's profitability because the return on idle cash is below the return that can be earned on other productive assets.

Firms hold cash to liquidate transactions, to cover unexpected events, and for speculation. The objectives in managing cash are similar to objectives in managing inventories. Cash levels should be sufficient to cover all needs (i.e., avoid stockouts), but be low enough to constrain opportunity costs associated with alternative uses of the cash (carrying costs). Models useful in managing inventory are also useful for managing cash levels. Optimal cash management requires answers to three questions.

What Variables Influence the Optimal Level of Cash?

The cash budget and pro forma cash flow statement provide managers with information about amounts and timing of cash flows. These data are the primary inputs to the determination of the "inventory" of cash that should be available at a specific point in the budget year. However, the actual level of cash maintained may differ from that necessary to meet the cash flow requirements in the cash budget.

The level of confidence managers have in the cash budget is a subjective factor that influences the desired cash balance. For example, the less certain managers are of either the amount or the timing of cash inflows or outflows, the more cash managers will hold. If actual cash flows fail to match the budgetary amounts, more cash may be required to satisfy all transactions. Similarly, the greater the variability in cash requirements throughout the year, the more conservative managers must be in managing cash. To avoid liquidity problems, managers of firms with higher variability in the operating cycle must hold more cash than managers of firms with very stable, predictable operating cycles. Firms that would have difficulty arranging for short-term credit to cover unexpected cash shortages are forced to carry an extra amount of cash to cover contingencies.

Also, securities ratings, particularly bond ratings, may induce firms to hold larger cash balances than justified based on all other considerations. A favorable bond rating is contingent on the organization having an ability to pay interest and principal. Security rating agencies encourage organizations to demonstrate conservative practices in managing cash. Related to bond ratings, firms with debt may be obligated by loan covenants to maintain minimum levels of cash.

What Are the Sources of Cash?

There are three usual sources for cash. Cash is generated by the sale of equity or debt securities and other shorter term instruments. Assets no longer necessary or productive are liquidated to provide cash. Last, cash is generated in the normal production/sales cycle assuming goods are sold above their costs of production. The capital budget is the key control tool for the first two sources of cash (Chapter 14).

working capital

Management of cash consumed by and derived from the operating cycle is integral to the management of working capital. **Working capital** is total current assets minus current liabilities. In the operating cycle, cash is first invested in material and conversion costs, then finished goods inventory, followed by marketing and administrative activities, and finally accounts receivable. The cycle is completed when the accounts receivable are collected. Exhibit 15–13 illustrates the cash collection cycle.

Effective management of the cash collection cycle can both reduce the demand for cash and increase its supply. For example, if the amount of cash invested in the operating cycle (i.e., invested in inventories and receivables) can be reduced by speeding up the cycle, the cash balance will increase. In the utopian case, material would be instantly obtained when a customer placed an order. The material would then be instantly converted into a product and the finished product would instantly be converted to cash. Even without achieving the utopian ideal, any reduction in the length of the operating cycle will serve to reduce balances in inventory and accounts receivable and increase the cash balance.

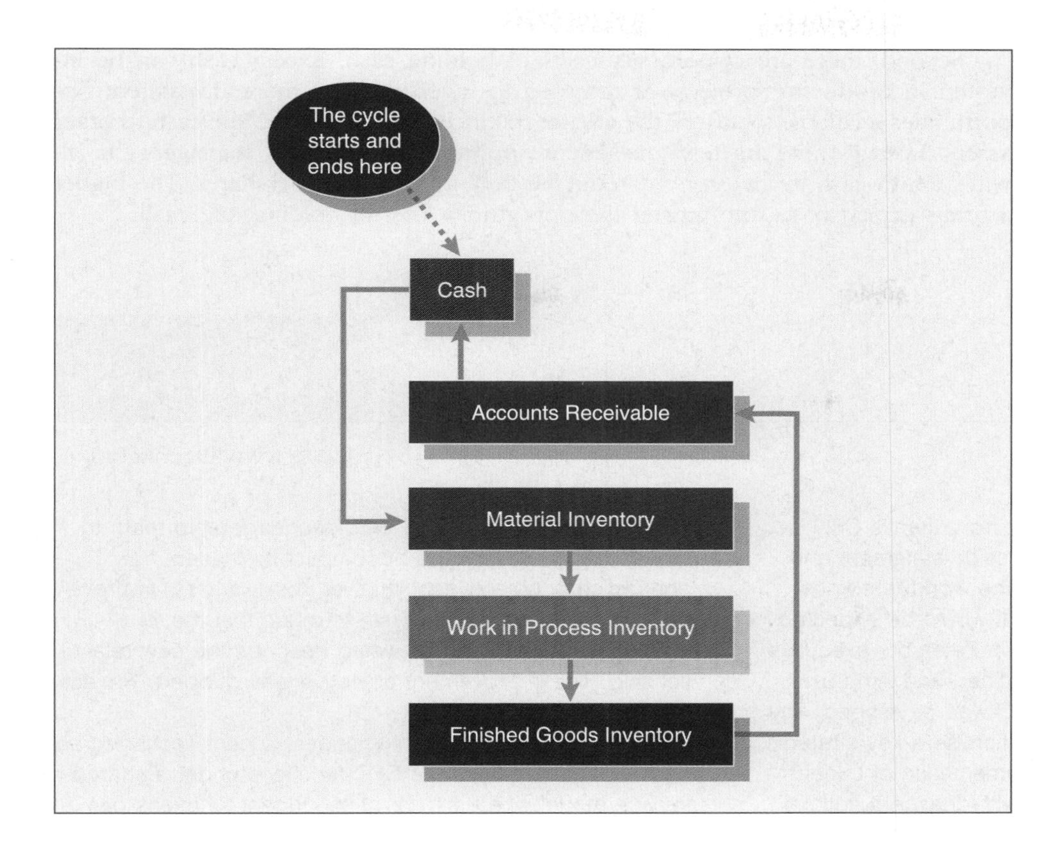

EXHIBIT 15-13

The Cash Collection Cycle—Balance Sheet: Current Assets

Managers can take explicit measures to accelerate cash collections. Inventory levels can be reduced if products can be produced more quickly after customer orders are received. Just-in-time and other inventory management practices that serve this objective are discussed in Chapter 16.

In addition to reducing inventory levels, cash collections can be accelerated to increase cash levels. The turnover of accounts receivable can be directly influenced by terms given on credit sales, policies governing credit approval, discounts given for early payment, and use of the services of financial intermediaries that specialize in purchasing or factoring accounts receivable. Other practices can be developed to accelerate customer payments including using electronic payments, customer debit cards, lock boxes, and bank courier services. Centralizing cash collection functions will also allow accounts receivable to be converted to cash more quickly.

Alternatively, the cash balance can be increased by slowing down payments for inputs. Managers can search among alternative vendors for the most desirable credit terms and policies. Credit cards rather than cash can be used to purchase inputs. Rather than paying factory employees weekly, a bi-monthly or monthly pay plan can be instituted. Also, decentralizing cash disbursement functions will increase the interval from when a check is issued until it clears.

What Variables Influence the Cost of Carrying Cash?

The cost of carrying cash varies over time. There are two classes of costs to manage. One is the cost of borrowing and cost of issuing equity capital. For example, short-term borrowing costs will rise and fall with changes in inflation rates, credit worthiness of the borrower, and availability of funds for lending. The higher these costs, the greater the incentive to minimize idle cash balances.

Second, there are opportunity costs of holding cash. Excess cash can be invested in productive projects or returned to investors. The more investment opportunities available to a firm, the greater the incentive to convert idle cash to other assets. Even if there are few investment opportunities available, managers can always return cash to investors by reducing debt or repurchasing shares. The higher a firm's capital costs, the greater the opportunity cost of holding idle cash.

REVISITING Lucent Technologies

http://www.lucent.com

An important step in redesigning Lucent's CFO function was to design a mission statement and develop a program that would let the workforce know exactly what was going on and what would be expected of them. Under the leadership of Don Peterson, executive vice president and chief financial officer, and Jim Lusk, controller, the concept of Team CFO was developed. The goal was to have the CFO organization be a key strategic partner in the formulation and implementation of Lucent strategies. It would furnish Lucent with finance functions that would allow its internal business partners to provide more competitive services to their customers. Then the people in the CFO organization would be seen as positive contributors to corporate results. The group adopted a souped-up race car as its symbol (Team CFO . . . Engine of Excellence . . . Powering Lucent) and began "racing to the future together."

Most of Lucent CFO's transaction-intensive operations are located in Alpharetta, Ga., where more than 800 Lucent colleagues perform various accounting, inventory, invoicing, accounts receivable, collections, analysis, payroll, and accounts payable functions for the corporation. (Lucent has about 130,000 employees overall.) In March 1996, the director of Lucent Financial Services' (LFS) Financial Process in Alpharretta met the challenge of reducing costs and becoming more efficient head-on. He called a meeting with his Financial Services leadership team to devise a plan that would accomplish two seemingly contradictory objectives: (1) lower costs, and (2) improve service to internal customers—so much that the term *strategic business partner* would describe the new relationship. The improvement objective was dubbed "Project Quantum Leap."

Among other significant changes, Lucent Technologies decided to reorganize the CFO functions under a shared service model where similar or redundant functions performed within individual business units and the corporate controller's organization were combined. Many financial functions previously performed within the business units have been transferred to LFS and to LFS financial hubs located in Mexico, Argentina, Brazil, Singapore, China, Ireland, and the Netherlands.

LFS Financial Process, under the leadership of Danny Lanier, had cut operating costs by about 40% by 1998 from their 1996 levels. Over the same period, service levels improved and stress levels of CFO colleagues declined. When asked what key ingredients made Project Quantum Leap successful, Danny Lanier commented, "The commitment and sacrifices made by all LFS colleagues, top-down measurable commitments, a willingness to learn from others, and the project-by-project approach to continuous process improvement."

SOURCE: Thomas A. Francesconi, "Transforming Lucent's CFO," *Management Accounting* (July 1998), pp. 22, 30. Copyright Institute of Management Accountants, Montvale, NJ.

CHAPTER SUMMARY

Cost control over expenditures is essential to an organization's long-run success. An effective cost control system encompasses efforts before, during, and after a cost is incurred. Regardless of the type of cost involved, managers and employees must exercise attitudes of cost consciousness to provide the best means of cost control. Cost consciousness reflects cost understanding, cost containment, cost avoidance, and cost reduction.

Fixed costs can be classified as either committed or discretionary. Committed fixed costs relate to long-run investments in plant assets or personnel. Discretionary costs are annually appropriated for the conduct of activities that could be temporarily reduced without impairing the firm's capacity to function.

Costs are incurred to provide results, but measuring the outputs generated by cost inputs is not always easy. Comparing inputs to actual outputs reflects efficiency, whereas comparing actual outputs to desired results reflects effectiveness. Efficiency plus effectiveness indicates performance.

Budgeting is a primary tool in planning and controlling discretionary costs. Budget appropriations provide authorization for spending and the bases against which actual costs are compared. Managers should clearly state and adhere to an overall management philosophy so that expenditures for discretionary items can be budgeted to achieve results that fit within this philosophy. Managers must avoid making expenditures for discretionary activities that may be conducted efficiently, but for which the results are of dubious effectiveness. To obtain effective cost control, care must be taken to use appropriate levels of activity for budget-to-actual comparisons.

Difficulty is often encountered with discretionary fixed costs because many of these costs are incurred to provide service-type activities that are often considered optional in the short run. Additionally, the outputs of discretionary cost activities often are not measurable in dollars. Surrogate measures of the outputs provided by discretionary costs can be developed; however, even when surrogate measures are used, ascribing a cause-and-effect relationship between the result and the current amounts of input costs may be questionable.

Some discretionary costs, such as quality control costs, may be conducive to treatment as engineered costs. Engineered costs are those that are routine and structured enough to allow for the computation of standards. One aspect of control over engineered costs can be provided by performing variance analysis similar to that used for variable manufacturing overhead.

Activity-based budgeting is a new planning tool. This approach reassigns costs in traditional resource budgets to the activities that must be executed to achieve organizational objectives. The activity-based budget is an effective mechanism to understand how resource consumption is tied to organizational objectives.

The cash budget and the pro forma cash flow statement are effective tools for managing cash. However, before these tools can be wielded, managers must understand the objectives that are to be achieved in cash management. There are costs associated with having too much cash on hand just as there are costs associated with cash shortages. Effective cash management requires a proper evaluation of both classes of costs.

APPENDIX

Program and Zero-Base Budgeting

In addition to the traditional master, flexible, and activity based budgets, two other types of budgets (program and zero-base) are useful for cost control in certain types of organizations. Program budgeting focuses on the relationship of benefits to cost expenditures; zero-base budgeting requires that all budgeted amounts be justified.

Program Budgeting

8

How is program budgeting used in not-for-profit entities?

The problems of controlling discretionary costs are particularly acute in governmental and other not-for-profit entities. These organizations' activities produce results that are often difficult to measure in monetary terms or that may take several

program budgeting

years to be measured (although the related activities must continue to be funded annually). Thus, relating outputs to inputs is often extremely difficult. **Program budgeting** is an approach that relates resource inputs to service outputs.[15]

Program budgeting generally starts by defining objectives in terms of output results rather than in terms of quantity of input activities. For instance, an input measure of an executive development program would be the number of courses each person must complete by year-end. An output measure would state the objective in terms of expected improvement rates on executive annual performance evaluations. Once output results have been defined in some measurable terms, effectiveness can be measured.

The process of program budgeting requires a thorough analysis of the alternative activities that may achieve an organization's objectives. Such an analysis includes projecting both quantitative and qualitative costs and benefits for each alternative. Then, those alternatives are selected that, in the judgment of top management, yield a satisfactory result at a reasonable cost. These choices are translated into budget appropriations to be acted on by the manager(s) responsible for the related programs.

Program budgeting requires the use of detailed surrogate measures of output and necessitates answers to the following questions.

1. When should results be measured? Because many not-for-profit programs are effective only after some period of time, multiple measurements are necessary to determine effectiveness. When should these measures begin to be made and how often should they be made thereafter?
2. What results should be chosen as output measures? Many not-for-profit programs have multiple results. For example, the institution of reading programs for illiterate adults can reduce unemployment rates, overall crime statistics, welfare dollars provided, and so forth. Should a determination be made of which results are more important than others or should all results be given equal weight?
3. What program actually caused the result? There are questions about the legitimacy of cause-and-effect relationships when measuring the results of not-for-profit programs. For example, did an adult literacy program reduce the unemployment statistics or was that reduction more appropriately deemed a result of money spent for job placement programs?
4. Did the program actually affect the target population? An adult literacy program may be aimed at the unemployed. If the majority of persons who attended the program already had jobs, the program had no impact on the target group. However, the program could still be considered effective if the participants increased their job skills and employment levels.

Program budgeting is useful in government and not-for-profit organizations as well as for service activities in for-profit businesses. This process can help managers evaluate and control discretionary costs, avoid excessive cost expenditures, and make certain that expenditures are used for programs and activities that generate the most beneficial results.

9

Why is zero-base budgeting useful in cost control?

Zero-Base Budgeting

Traditional budgeting is often limited in its usefulness as a cost control tool because poor budgeting techniques are used. For instance, many managers prepare budgets

[15] *Program* and *performance* budgeting have often been used as interchangeable terms. The Municipal Finance Officers Association has suggested that the term *program budgeting* be used when dealing with one function regardless of the number of organizational units involved and *performance budgeting* be used when dealing with the inputs and outputs of a single organizational unit.

by beginning with the prior year's funding levels and treat these appropriations as given and essential to operations. Decisions are then made about whether, and by what percentage, to raise existing appropriations. Such an approach has often resulted in what is known as the "creeping commitment syndrome" in which activities are funded without systematic annual regard for priorities or alternative means for accomplishing objectives.

zero-base budgeting

Zero-base budgeting (ZBB) is a comprehensive budgeting process that systematically considers the priorities and alternatives for current and proposed activities in relation to organizational objectives. Annual justification of programs and activities is required to have managers rethink priorities within the context of agreed-on objectives. ZBB does not necessarily mean that each operation is specified from a zero-cost base, because this would be unrealistic and extreme. However, ZBB requires that managers reevaluate all activities at the start of the budgeting process to make decisions about which activities should be continued, eliminated, or funded at a lower level. Some basic differences between traditional budgeting and zero-base budgeting are shown in Exhibit 15–14.

ZBB is difficult to implement because of the significant effort needed to investigate the causes of prior costs and justify the purposes of budgeted costs. To be workable, it also requires a wholehearted commitment by the organization's personnel. Without the necessary time, effort, and commitment, ZBB should not be attempted. With these ingredients, an organization can be more effective in planning and controlling costs.

EXHIBIT 15–14

Differences between Traditional Budgeting and Zero-Base Budgeting

Traditional Budgeting	Zero-Base Budgeting
Starts with last year's funding appropriation	Starts with a minimal (or zero) figure for funding
Focuses on money	Focuses on goals and objectives
Does not systematically consider alternatives to current operations	Directly examines alternative approaches to achieve similar results
Produces a single level of appropriation for an activity	Produces alternative levels of funding based on fund availability and desired results

KEY TERMS

activity-based budgeting (p. 682)
appropriation (p. 673)
committed cost (p. 671)
cost avoidance (p. 668)
cost consciousness (p. 663)
cost containment (p. 666)
cost control system (p. 661)
cost reduction (p. 668)
discretionary cost (p. 672)
engineered cost (p. 677)
program budgeting (p. 688)
working capital (p. 684)
zero-base budgeting (p. 689)

SOLUTION STRATEGIES

Efficiency: Relationship of input and output

Actual Yield Ratio = Actual Output ÷ Actual Input
or
Actual Input ÷ Actual Output

Desired Yield Ratio = Planned Output ÷ Planned Input
or
Planned Input ÷ Planned Output

Effectiveness: Relationship of actual output and desired output

Efficiency + Effectiveness = Performance

Cost Variances

Comparison of actual costs with budgeted costs: allows management to compare discrepancies from the original plan

Comparison of actual costs with budgeted costs at actual activity level: allows management to determine how well costs were controlled; uses a flexible budget

Variance analysis using standards for discretionary costs: allows management to compute variances for routine, structured discretionary costs

For discretionary costs susceptible to engineered cost treatment:

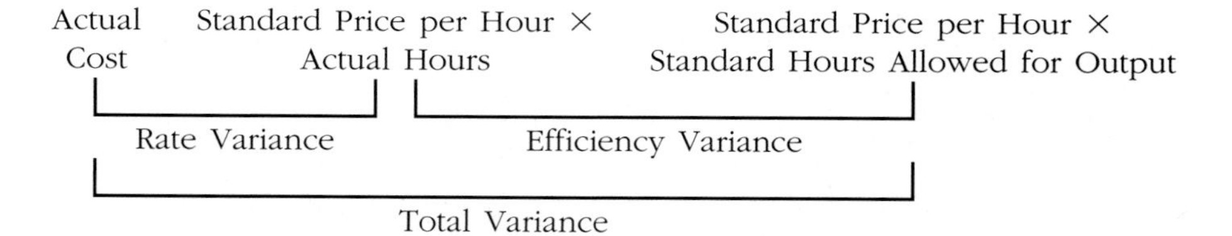

For discretionary costs that are managed as lump-sum fixed costs:

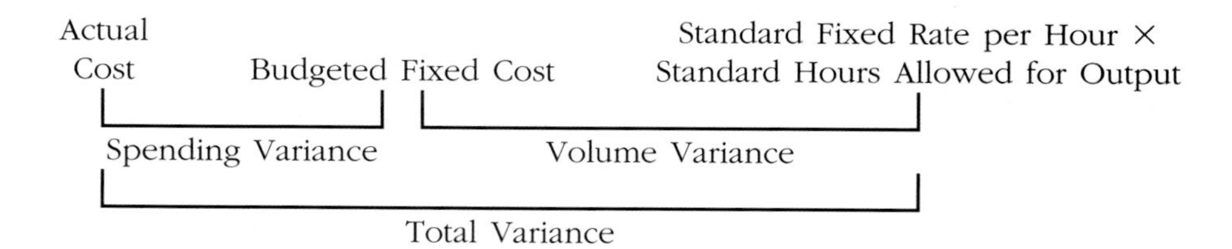

For discretionary costs involving both fixed and variable elements:

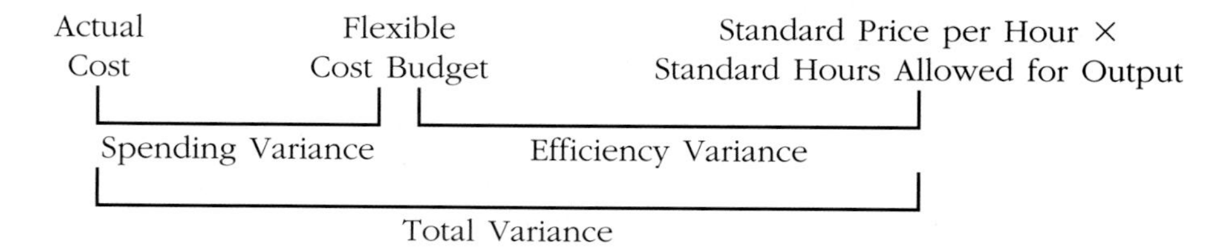

Activity-Based Budgeting Steps

1. Select a function for which costs are to be estimated; i.e., distribution, marketing, finance, accounting.
2. Identify all activities necessary to execute the selected function.
3. Identify the activity driver for each activity.
4. Estimate the volume for each activity driver necessary to meet output objectives, i.e., sales and production levels specified in the master budget.
5. Identify the resources consumed by each activity.
6. Estimate the cost of providing each resource.

DEMONSTRATION PROBLEM

Cantrell Manufacturing just purchased an evolutionary metal stamping machine. It operated for 130 hours during the first month. Management wants to know the efficiency and effectiveness of the machine. The production supervisor has provided you with the following statistics:

Planned output:	80 product components per hour
Power usage planned:	600 kWh per running hour
Actual output:	10,800 product components
Actual power used:	80,000 kWh

Required:

a. Calculate the planned output for 130 operating hours.
b. Calculate the degree of effectiveness of the machine in its first week.
c. Calculate planned efficiency for the machine.
d. Calculate the actual efficiency of the machine in its first week.
e. Comment on the machine's performance.

Solution to Demonstration Problem

a. Planned output: 130 hours × 80 units = 10,400 components
b. Degree of effectiveness: Actual output ÷ Planned output = 10,800 components ÷ 10,400 components = 104 percent
c. Planned efficiency: Planned input ÷ Planned output = 600 kWh ÷ 80 units = 7.5 kWh per unit
d. Actual efficiency: Actual input ÷ Actual output = 80,000 kWh ÷ 10,800 units = 7.41 kWh per unit
e. The performance of the machine is better than expected. The machine exceeded both effectiveness and efficiency expectations.

QUESTIONS

1. How does the cost control system interact with the overall cost management system?
2. The general control model begins with planning activities. Why?
3. When is cost control for any specific organizational activity exercised? Why are these points of cost control important?
4. What factors can cause costs to change? Which of these are subject to cost containment and which are not? What creates the difference in controllability?

5. Compare and contrast general and specific price-level changes.
6. How might members of the supply chain be helpful in an organization's quest for cost containment activities?
7. "A company will always experience reduced costs if long-term or single-source contracts are signed." Is this statement true or false? Discuss the rationale for your answer.
8. How are cost avoidance and cost reduction related? How do they differ?
9. What are some reasons supporting the use of temporaries in what used to be full-time labor positions? What are some reasons against such usage?
10. Differentiate between committed and discretionary costs. Could a cost be considered discretionary by one firm and committed by another? If so, discuss and give an example. If not, discuss why not.
11. Are all discretionary costs fixed? If yes, justify your answer. If no, provide an example to prove your point.
12. Is an investment in expensive, automated technology wise in an industry characterized by wide variations in demand? What if that industry were highly competitive? Provide underlying reasons for your answers.
13. What issues does management need to consider when setting the budget appropriations for discretionary costs?
14. Why are income levels generally more important considerations for budget decisions about discretionary costs than for committed costs?
15. Why is it difficult to measure the output of activities funded by discretionary costs?
16. What are surrogate measures of output and how are they used in conjunction with discretionary costs?
17. Define efficiency and effectiveness and distinguish one from the other. Why is measuring the efficiency of discretionary costs often difficult? Explain how effectiveness of discretionary cost activities can be measured.
18. Why does performance encompass the spectrum from organizational goals to inputs to outputs?
19. What is an engineered cost? How can engineered costs be used in controlling some discretionary costs?
20. What types of discretionary costs are subject to control as engineered costs? Provide several examples.
21. How can variance analysis be used to investigate the control of engineered costs?
22. Is a budget-to-actual comparison essential in the control of discretionary costs? Provide reasoning for your answer.
23. Why is the budget used for planning purposes not necessarily the best budget to use for evaluating cost control?
24. How is activity-based budgeting an improvement over traditional financial budgeting?
25. For what purposes do firms hold cash balances? Why do some firms require larger cash balances than other firms?
26. *(Appendix)* Compare and contrast a programmed budget, a zero-base budget, and a traditional budget.
27. *(Appendix)* What problems are encountered in using program budgeting? Why might such problems arise?
28. *(Appendix)* What problems are encountered in using zero-base budgeting? Why might such problems arise?

EXERCISES

29. *(Matching)* Match the following lettered terms on the left with the appropriate numbered description on the right.

a. Appropriation
b. Committed cost
c. Cost avoidance
d. Cost consciousness
e. Cost containment
f. Discretionary cost
g. Effectiveness
h. Efficiency
i. Engineered cost

1. An attitude regarding cost understanding, cost containment, cost avoidance, and cost reduction
2. A cost incurred to provide physical or organizational capacity
3. A measure of input–output yield
4. Any cost that bears an observable and known relationship to an activity base
5. A process of finding acceptable alternatives for high-priced items and not buying unnecessary goods or services
6. A maximum allowable expenditure
7. An assessment of how well a firm's goals and objectives were achieved
8. A fixed cost incurred to fund an activity for a specified period of time
9. A process by which unit variable costs and total fixed costs are not allowed to increase from prior periods

30. *(Cost control activities)* The firm of Kanton Associates, CPAs, hires full- and part-time clerical employees. Full-time clerical staff can be hired for $27,500 per year; fringe benefit costs for each full-time employee amount to 20 percent of base salary. Kanton Associates pays part-time clerical employees $20 per hour, but does not provide any fringe benefits. If, however, a part-time employee has worked for the firm for over 1,600 hours by year-end, he or she receives a $2,000 bonus.

a. Does the firm's policy of hiring part-time clerical staff represent an example of cost containment, cost avoidance, or cost reduction? Explain.
b. For a given clerical position, at what level of annual hours worked should the firm consider hiring full-time clerical staff rather than part-time?

31. *(Cost control activities)* Kendra Smith has just been appointed the new director of Youth Hot-Line, a not-for-profit organization that operates a phone bank for individuals experiencing emotional difficulties. The phones are staffed by qualified social workers and psychologists who are paid on an hourly basis. Ms. Smith took the following actions in the first week at Youth Hot-Line. Indicate whether the actions represent cost understanding, cost containment, cost avoidance, or cost reduction. Some actions may have more than one implication; if they do, indicate the reason.

a. Increased the budget appropriation for advertising of the Hot-Line.
b. Exchanged the more expensive pushbutton, cream-colored designer telephones for regular, pushbutton desk telephones.
c. Eliminated the call-forwarding feature installed on all telephones because Youth Hot-Line will now be staffed 24 hours a day.
d. Eliminated two paid clerical positions and replaced these individuals with volunteers.
e. Ordered blank notepads for the counselors to keep by their phones; the old notepads (stock now depleted) had the Youth Hot-Line logo and address printed on them.

(continued)

f. Negotiated a new contract with the telephone company; Youth Hot-Line will now pay a flat rate of $100 per month, regardless of the number of telephones installed by the Hot-Line. The previous contract charged the organization $10 for every telephone. At the time that contract was signed, Youth Hot-Line only had ten telephones. With the increased staff, Ms. Smith plans to install at least five additional telephones.

32. *(Committed versus discretionary costs)* A list of committed and discretionary costs follows:

Annual audit fees	Internal audit salaries
Annual report preparation and printing	Marketing research
Building flood insurance	Preventive maintenance
Charitable contributions	Property taxes
Corporate advertising	Quality control inspection
Employee continuing education	Research and development salaries
Equipment depreciation	Research and development supplies
Interest on bonds payable	Secretarial pool salaries

a. Classify each of the above costs as normally being either committed (C) or discretionary (D).

b. Which of the above costs may be either committed or discretionary based on management philosophy?

c. For the expenses marked discretionary in part (a), provide a monetary or nonmonetary surrogate output measure. For each output measure, briefly discuss any objections that may be raised to it.

33. *(Committed versus discretionary costs)* Choose letter C (for committed cost) or D (for discretionary cost) to indicate which type of cost each of the sentences below best relates. Explain the rationale for your choice.

a. Control is first provided during the capital budgeting process.

b. Examples include advertising, research and development, and employee training.

c. This type of cost cannot be easily reduced even during temporary slowdowns in activity.

d. There is usually no "correct" amount at which to set funding levels.

e. Examples include depreciation, lease rentals, and property taxes.

f. This type of cost often provides benefits that are not monetarily measurable.

g. Temporary reductions can usually be made without impairing the firm's long-range capacity or profitability.

h. This cost is primarily affected by long-run decisions regarding desired capacity levels.

i. It is often difficult to ascribe outcomes as being closely correlated with this type of cost.

j. This cost usually relates to service-type activities.

34. *(Effectiveness measures)* Lakeside Wellness Center has used funds during 2001 for the following purposes. Provide nonmonetary, surrogate measures that would help evaluate the effectiveness of the monies spent.

a. Sent two cost accounting staff members to seminars on activity-based costing.

b. Installed a kidney dialysis machine.

c. Built an attached parking garage for the hospital.

d. Redecorated the main lobby.

e. Placed a full-page advertisement in the local Yellow Pages.

f. Acquired new software to track patient charges and prepare itemized billings.

35. *(Surrogate measures of output)* The Coast Casino and Hotel has established performance objectives for each major operational area for the budget year. Some of the major objectives that were established for the budget year 2001 follow. For each objective, identify a surrogate measure of performance.

a. Increase volume of customer traffic at the gaming tables.
b. Decrease the labor cost per beverage served to customers.
c. Increase the length of stay per hotel guest.
d. Attract more out-of-state visitors and reduce the number of in-state visitors.
e. Increase convention business.
f. Increase the quality of room-cleaning services.
g. Increase the relative amount of gaming revenue generated by the slot machines.

36. *(Effectiveness and efficiency measures)* The president at Midland State University has formed a new department to recruit top out-of-state students. The department's funding for 2001 is $400,000 and the department was given a goal of recruiting 300 new nonresident students. By year-end 2001, the department had been credited with recruiting 325 new students. The department actually consumed $460,000 in its recruiting efforts.

a. How effective was the newly formed department? Show calculations.
b. How efficient was the department? Show calculations.

37. *(Engineered cost variances)* Candyland Courier employs three drivers who are paid an average of $16 per hour for regular time and $24 for overtime. A pickup and delivery requires, on average, one hour of driver time. Drivers are paid for a 40-hour week because they must be on call all day. One driver stands by for after-hour deliveries.

Analyze the labor costs for one week in which the company made 105 daytime deliveries and 12 after-hour deliveries. The payroll for drivers for that week was $2,280. The employees worked 120 hours of regular time and 15 hours of overtime.

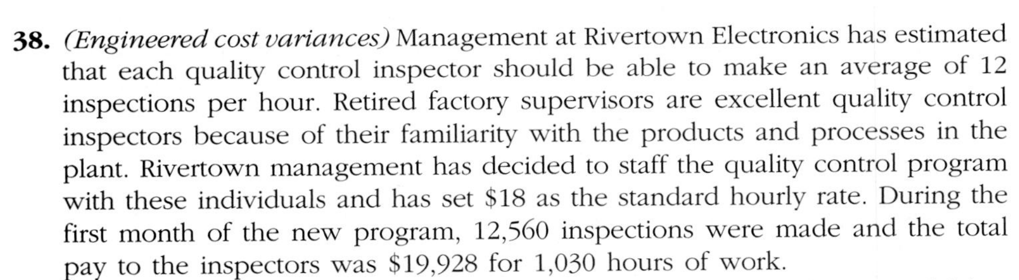

38. *(Engineered cost variances)* Management at Rivertown Electronics has estimated that each quality control inspector should be able to make an average of 12 inspections per hour. Retired factory supervisors are excellent quality control inspectors because of their familiarity with the products and processes in the plant. Rivertown management has decided to staff the quality control program with these individuals and has set $18 as the standard hourly rate. During the first month of the new program, 12,560 inspections were made and the total pay to the inspectors was $19,928 for 1,030 hours of work.

a. Perform a variance analysis for management on the quality control labor cost.
b. Assume that management could hire four full-time inspectors for a monthly salary of $5,000 each and hire part-timers for the overflow. Each full-time inspector would work 170 hours per month. How would total cost of this alternative compare to the cost of a 1,030-hour month at the standard rate of $18?

39. *(Revenue variances)* The manager of a lumber mill has been asked to explain to the company president why sales of scrap firewood were above budget by $4,200. He requests your help. On examination of budget documents, you discover that budgeted revenue from firewood was $75,000 based on expected sales of 1,875 cords of wood at $40 per cord. Further investigation reveals that 1,800 cords were actually sold at an average price of $44. Prepare an analysis of firewood sales and explain what happened.

40. *(Revenue variances)* "Tot Toons" is a videotape series that is marketed to day care centers and parents. The series has been found to make babies who watch it extremely content and quiet. In 2001, Angels Ltd., maker of the tapes, sold 400 of the series for $60 per package. In preparing the 2002 budget, company management estimated a 15 percent increase in sales volume because the price was to be reduced by 10 percent. At the end of 2002, company management is disappointed that actual revenue is only $24,440 although 470 packages of the series were sold.

a. What was the expected revenue for 2002?

b. Calculate the price and volume variances for Angels Ltd.

41. *(Budgeting concepts; includes appendix)* Select the letter of the budget category from the list below that best corresponds to items a through j.

T = traditional budgeting
Z = zero-base budgeting
P = program budgeting
B = both zero-base and program budgeting

a. Requires annual justification of programs and activities.

b. Is concerned with alternative approaches to achieve similar results.

c. Begins by defining objectives in terms of output results rather than quantity of input activities.

d. Requires development and assessment of decision packages.

e. Treats prior year's funding levels as given and essential to operations.

f. Is particularly well suited to budgeting for discretionary cost expenditures.

g. Produces alternative levels of funding based on fund availability and desired results.

h. Requires the use of detailed surrogate measures of output.

i. Focuses more on monetary levels of appropriations rather than on goals, objectives, and outputs.

j. Results in the "creeping commitment syndrome."

42. *(Cost changes)* Alyssa Enterprises has been in existence since 1996. The company board of directors is interested in how well certain office costs have been controlled from 1996 to 2001. Following are several cost categories and the related 1996 and 2001 expenditures:

Cost Category	1996 Cost	2001 Cost
Wages and fringe benefits	$160,000	$125,000
Supplies	50,000	85,000
Equipment depreciation	36,000	58,000
Utilities	4,800	6,600

Over this five-year period, Alyssa Enterprises has downsized from eight office staff to five and made substantial investments in computer hardware and software.

a. Use the above information and information in Exhibit 15–4 to prepare an alternative comparison for the board of directors relative to the office costs in these two years.

b. Write a detailed memo to provide explanations of the cost changes.

43. *(Variance analysis)* Cost control in the Personnel Office of Minnesota Wholesale is evaluated based on engineered cost concepts. The office incurs both variable and fixed costs. The variable costs are largely driven by the amount of employee turnover. For 2000, budgeted costs in the Personnel Office were:

Fixed	$200,000
Variable	400,000 (based on projected turnover of 1,000 employees)

For 2000, actual costs in the Personnel Office were:

Fixed	$210,000
Variable	450,000 (actual turnover of 1,050 employees)

Using traditional variance analysis, evaluate the control of fixed and variable costs in the Personnel Office of Minnesota Wholesale. Does this method of evaluation encourage the Personnel Office managers to hire low-quality workers? Explain.

44. *(Cost consciousness; team activity)* All organizations seek to be aware of and control costs. In a team of three or four, choose one of the following industries and do research to identify methods that have been used to control costs. Prepare a written presentation that discusses the various methods of cost control, dollars of costs saved (if available), and your perceptions of the positive and negative implications of each of the cost control methodologies. You may choose a particular company within the industry should you so desire.

a. Internet e-tailers
b. Automobile manufacturers
c. Hospitals
d. Software companies
e. Government entities

45. *(Cost control)* The California State University system once placed a purchase order (PO) for a book published by a small New Canaan, Conn., company, The Information Economics Press. The following is a copy of the letter the Press sent back to the California procurement officer:

We have your eight page PO#940809 for one copy of our book "The Politics of Information Management." We are unable to fill your $49 order for the following reasons:

- *In the Purchase Order Terms and Conditions you wish us to waive any infringement of our copyrighted materials by officers, agents and employees of the California State University. We cannot agree to make available a valuable Copyright for the price of a book.*
- *You will withhold all payments or make a 38% withholding in order to file a year-end 1099 form. We are unable to handle the paperwork of a separate 1099 for every book we sell. That would double our paperwork.*
- *You are requiring us to file a Vendor Data Record (form 204) which is largely identical with your Vendor Information form. Filing both forms takes excessive amounts of time.*
- *We are a small business, and therefore you require that we submit a copy of the OSMB Small Business Certification. We do not have an OSMB Certification and we do not know where to get one.*
- *Your attachment to form 204 specifies that I obtain a determination with regard to my being classified either as resident or non-resident subject to California tax withholdings, to be reclaimed by filing at year-end California tax returns. We do not plan to make any tax filings in California.*
- *Your contract rider contains a Privacy Statement on unspecified disclosures that makes us liable for penalties of up to $20,000.*
- *As a condition of our filling out the order you are asking us to post statements notifying all employees of compliance with Code Section 8355 and certifying as to our adopting a four point Drug-Free Awareness program that complies with California law. Deviations are punishable as perjury under the laws of the State of California. Please note our firm has only two employees, who do not take even an aspirin.*
- *Your Minority/Women Business Enterprise Self Certification Form 962 requires detailed statistics on ethnic characteristics of our firm, defining each ethnic group according to their stated geographic origins. To assist in making such*

distinctions you provide a check-list of ethnic identity of the owners of this firm, leaving us by default with only one open choice, Caucasian, which you do not define. My husband and I do not know of any ancestors who may have ever been in the proximity of the Caucasian mountains, and therefore we are unable to comply with your requirement to identify our ethnic origin according to your geographic rules.

We therefore suggest that you purchase our book at a bookstore.

Mona Frankel
Publisher

SOURCE: Mona Frankel, "Just Go to the Bookstore and Buy One," *The Wall Street Journal* (October 18, 1994), p. A20.

a. What cost control strategy was the author of the preceding letter employing in her decision to reject the book order? Explain.

b. What appears to be the source of most of the complexity associated with the purchase order? Explain.

c. What does the letter suggest about the opportunity for improved cost control in the California State University purchasing system? Explain.

46. *(Cost control and financial records)* Robotic Solutions is a medium-sized manufacturing plant in a capital-intensive industry. The corporation's profitability is very low at the moment. As a result, investment funds are limited and hiring is restricted. These consequences of the corporation's problems have placed a strain on the plant's repair and maintenance program. The result has been a reduction in work efficiency and cost control effectiveness in the repair and maintenance area.

The assistant controller proposes the installation of a maintenance work order system to overcome these problems. This system would require a work order to be prepared for each repair request and for each regular maintenance activity. The maintenance superintendent would record the estimated time to complete a job and send one copy of the work order to the department in which the work was to be done. The work order would also serve as a cost sheet for a job. The actual cost of the parts and supplies used on the job as well as the actual labor costs incurred in completing the job would be recorded directly on the work order. A copy of the completed work order would be the basis of the charge to the department in which the repair or maintenance activity occurred.

The maintenance superintendent opposes the program on the grounds that the added paperwork will be costly and nonproductive. The superintendent states that the departmental clerk who now schedules repairs and maintenance activities is doing a good job without all the extra forms the new system would require. The real problem, in the superintendent's opinion, is that the department is understaffed.

a. Discuss how such a maintenance work order system would aid in cost control.

b. Explain how a maintenance work order system might assist the maintenance superintendent in getting authorization to hire more mechanics.

(CMA adapted)

47. *(Activity-based budgeting)* As a newly hired staff person in the accounting department of Midwest Technical Products, you have been invited to help the controller and her staff prepare for a meeting with the CFO and CEO to discuss ways to improve the profitability of the Medical Products Division. Profitability in the division has leveled off in the past three years and the division is now mediocre relative to the rest of the industry in the return it generates on invested assets. Discuss how you could apply activity-based budgeting concepts to explore ways to improve profitability in the Medical Products Division.

48. *(Cash management)* Data extracted from a recent balance sheet of Huntington Tire Company follow. The firm manufactures tires that are sold both to car manufacturers and tire wholesalers.

Current assets (in millions)	
Cash	$ 10
Accounts receivable	140
Finished goods inventory	25
Work in process inventory	170
Materials	90
Current liabilities	
Accounts payable	$ 22
Other	7

Discuss recommendations that could be made to Huntington Tire Company managers to improve its cash position. Focus your discussion on the operating cycle rather than on other means of raising cash.

PROBLEMS

49. *(Cost consciousness)* Tony and Keri Calihan are preparing their household financial budget for December. They have started with their November budget and are adjusting it to reflect the difference between November and December in planned activities. The Calihans are expecting out-of-town guests for two weeks over the holiday season. The following list describes the budgetary changes from November to December that are contemplated by the Calihan family:

a. Increase the grocery budget by $135.
b. Decrease the commuter transportation budget by $50 to reflect the days off from work.
c. Change food budget to reflect serving pizza rather than steak and lobster each weekend.
d. Budget an extra $70 for utilities.
e. Reduce household maintenance budget by $60 to reflect the fact that outside maid services will not be needed over the holiday period.
f. Buy generic breakfast cereal rather than name brand due to the quantity the guests will consume.
g. Buy paper plates rather than run the dishwasher.
h. Buy the institutional-size packages of paper plates rather than smaller size packages.
i. Budget the long-distance phone bill at $50 less because there will be no need to call the relatives who will be visiting.
j. Budget movie rentals for $3 per tape rather than spend $7 per person to go to the movies.
k. Postpone purchasing needed work clothes until January.
l. Budget funds to repair the car. Keri plans to use part of her vacation time to make the repairs herself rather than take the car to a garage in January.

Indicate whether each of the above items is indicative of cost understanding (CU), cost containment (CC), cost avoidance (CA), or cost reduction (CR). Some items may have more than one answer.

50. *(Use of temporaries)* Temporary or part-time employees may be used rather than full-time employees in each of the following situations:

a. To teach undergraduate accounting courses at a university.
b. To serve as security guards.
c. To staff a health clinic in a rural area.
d. To write articles for a monthly technical magazine.

(continued)

e. To clean the house when the regular maid is ill.
f. To answer questions on a tax help-line during tax season.
g. To work in department stores during the Christmas rush.
h. To do legal research in a law firm.
i. To perform quality control work in a car manufacturing plant.
j. To do seamstress work in a custom dress shop.
k. To work as a clerk/cashier in a small retail store. The store is a mom-and-pop operation and the clerk is the only employee in the store when he or she works.

Indicate the potential advantages and disadvantages of the use of temporaries in each of the above situations. These advantages and disadvantages can be viewed from the standpoint of the employer or the user of the employer's products or services.

51. *(Efficiency standards)* Tory Kline has been asked to monitor the efficiency and effectiveness of a newly installed machine. The specialized machine has been guaranteed by the manufacturer to package 7,800 engine gaskets per kilowatt-hour (kWh). The rate of defects on production is estimated at 1.5 percent. The machine is equipped with a device to measure the number of kWhs used. During the first month of use, the machine packaged 1,390,000 gaskets, of which 17,900 were flawed, and it used 175 kWhs.

a. What is the efficiency standard for flawless output?
b. Calculate the achieved efficiency for the first month and briefly comment on it.
c. Determine the achieved effectiveness and briefly comment on it.
d. Assume that the company was charged $3.20 per kWh during the first month this machine was in service. Estimate the company's savings or loss in power costs because of the machine's efficiency level in the first month of operations.
e. If you were a customer buying this company's gaskets for use in automobile production, what amount of quality control would you want the company to have and why?

52. *(Effectiveness/efficiency)* Top management of RX Hospital Administrators observed that the budget for the EDP department had been growing far beyond what was anticipated for the past several years. Each year, the EDP manager would demonstrate that increased usage by the company's non-EDP departments would justify the enlarged appropriations. The administrative vice president commented that she was not surprised because user departments were not charged for the EDP department services and EDP department personnel were creative and eager to continue expanding services.

A review of the current year's statistics of the EDP department revealed the following:

Budgetary appropriation	$500,000, based on 2,000 hours of run time; $400,000 of this appropriation is related to fixed costs
Actual department expenses	Variable, $87,750 (incurred for 1,950 hours of run time) Fixed, $402,000

a. Did the EDP manager stay within his appropriation? Show calculations.
b. Was the EDP department effective? Show calculations. Comment.
c. Was the EDP department efficient? Show calculations. (*Hint:* Treat variable and fixed expenses separately.)
d. Using the formulas for analyzing variable and fixed costs, calculate the variances incurred by the EDP department.
e. Propose a rate per hour to charge user departments for EDP services. Do you think charging users will affect the demand for services by user departments? Why or why not?

53. *(Efficiency versus effectiveness)* The health-care industry has recently found itself in a new era that is characterized by cost competition. As a result of the new emphasis on cost management, many existing practices are being revised or dropped. A list follows of changes that have been made by specific health-care providers. For each change mentioned, indicate whether the change is intended to control cost through increased efficiency or increased effectiveness. Also indicate whether the change represents cost understanding, cost containment, cost avoidance, or cost reduction. Discuss your justification for each answer.

a. Before entering the hospital for chemotherapy, a patient's health-care provider required her to drink more than two quarts of water at home. By doing so, a day's stay in the hospital for hydration was avoided.

b. By administering an antibiotic within two hours of each operation, a hospital reduced the postoperative infection rate from 1.8 percent of patients to 0.4 percent of patients.

c. Some surgeons have started removing the drainage tubes from heart-bypass patients 24 hours after the operation rather than 48 hours after the operation. The change reduces the length of the typical hospital stay.

d. Doctors at a major hospital tightened scheduling requirements for blood analysis so that results were obtained on the same day that the blood was drawn. The change allowed many patients to be dismissed immediately.

e. A hospital began a practice of paying about $130 per average dose of a new antinausea drug to be administered to chemotherapy patients. The drug allowed vomiting to be controlled much faster and the patient to be more comfortable and dismissed a day earlier.

SOURCE: Facts based on Ron Winslow, "Health-Care Providers Try Industrial Tactics to Reduce Their Costs," *The Wall Street Journal* (November 3, 1993), pp. A1, A5.

54. *(Budget-to-actual comparison)* Lighting Systems, Inc., evaluates performance in part through the use of flexible budgets. Selling expense budgets at three activity levels within the relevant range are shown below.

ACTIVITY MEASURES			
Unit sales volume	15,000	17,500	20,000
Dollar sales volume	$15,000,000	$17,500,000	$20,000,000
Number of orders processed	1,500	1,750	2,000
Number of salespersons	100	100	100
MONTHLY EXPENSES			
Advertising and promotion	$ 1,500,000	$ 1,500,000	$ 1,500,000
Administrative salaries	75,000	75,000	75,000
Sales salaries	90,000	90,000	90,000
Sales commissions	450,000	525,000	600,000
Salesperson travel	200,000	225,000	250,000
Sales office expense	445,000	452,500	460,000
Shipping expense	650,000	675,000	700,000
Total	$ 3,410,000	$ 3,542,500	$ 3,675,000

The following assumptions were used to develop the selling expense flexible budgets:

- The average size of the company's sales force during the year was planned to be 100 people.
- Salespersons are paid a monthly salary plus commission on gross dollar sales.
- The travel costs have both a fixed and a variable element. The fixed portion is related to the number of salespersons, whereas the variable portion tends to fluctuate with gross dollars of sales.

- Sales office expense is a mixed cost with the variable portion related to the number of orders processed.
- Shipping expense is a mixed cost with the variable portion related to the number of units sold. (An order consists of 10 units.)

A sales force of 90 persons generated a total of 1,600 orders, resulting in a sales volume of 16,000 units during November. The gross dollar sales amounted to $14.9 million. The selling expenses incurred for November were as follows:

Advertising and promotion	$1,450,000
Administrative salaries	80,000
Sales salaries	92,000
Sales commissions	460,000
Salesperson travel	185,000
Sales office expense	500,000
Shipping expense	640,000
Total	$3,407,000

a. Explain why the selling expense flexible budget would not be appropriate for evaluating the company's November selling expense, and indicate how the flexible budget would have to be revised.

b. Determine the budgeted variable cost per salesperson and variable cost per sales order for the company.

c. Prepare a selling expense report for November that the company can use to evaluate its control over selling expenses. The report should have a line for each selling expense item showing the appropriate budgeted amount, the actual selling expense, and the monthly dollar variation.

d. Determine the actual variable cost per salesperson and variable cost per sales order processed for the company.

e. Comment on the effectiveness and efficiency of the salespersons during November. *(CMA adapted)*

55. *(Appendix)* Joe Cannon is the controller of Winston Labs, a manufacturer and distributor of generic prescription pharmaceuticals. He is currently preparing the annual budget and reviewing the current business plan. The business unit managers of Winston Labs prepare and assemble the detailed operating budgets, with technical assistance from the corporate accounting staff. The final budgets are then presented by the business unit managers to the corporate executive committee for approval. The corporate accounting staff reviews the budgets for adherence to corporate accounting policies, but not for reasonableness of the line items within the budget.

Cannon is aware that the upcoming year for Winston may be a difficult one due to the expiration of a major patent and the loss of a licensing agreement for another product line. He also knows that during the budgeting process, budget slack is created in varying degrees throughout the organization. He believes this slack has a negative effect on the overall business objectives of Winston Labs and should be eliminated where possible.

a. Define budget slack.

b. Explain the advantages and disadvantages of budget slack for (1) the business unit manager who must achieve the budget and (2) corporate management.

c. Mr. Cannon is considering implementing zero-base budgeting at Winston Labs. (1) Define zero-base budgeting. (2) Describe how zero-base budgeting could be advantageous to Winston Labs in controlling budget slack. (3) Discuss the disadvantages Winston Labs might encounter from using zero-base budgeting. *(CMA adapted)*

56. *(Activity-based budgeting)* Several years ago, Kingsley Electronic Systems adopted activity-based management and activity-based costing. This year the firm also prepared an activity-based budget for all of its major functions. An illustrative budget is presented below for the receiving department.

Signing receipts for shipments received	$ 3,000
Opening shipping containers	80,000
Verifying count and content of container	63,000
Inspecting goods	120,000
Writing receiving reports	48,000
Supervising	68,000
Delivering goods to inventory warehouses	56,000
Total	$438,000

While managers are enthused with the potential of the activity-based budgets, they are concerned about how the activity-based budgets relate to resource consumption. Write a memo to management discussing how the activity-based budget can be converted to a resource budget.

57. *(Cash management)* As the economy enters the new millennium, Internet companies are competing head-to-head in many markets with established, traditional retailers for the consumer's dollar. In comparing the financial statements of "e-tailers" relative to traditional retailing firms such as Wal-mart, one interesting difference is the comparatively large amount of cash held by the Internet firms. Using concepts presented in this chapter, discuss the most plausible explanations for the Internet companies holding such large sums of cash.

CASES

58. *(Cost control)* The following graph indicates where each part of the dollar that a student pays for a new college textbook goes.

SOURCE: Association of American Publishers and National Association of College Stores, "Where Does the Textbook Dollar Go?," *The Chronicle of Higher Education* (September 22, 1995), p. A51.

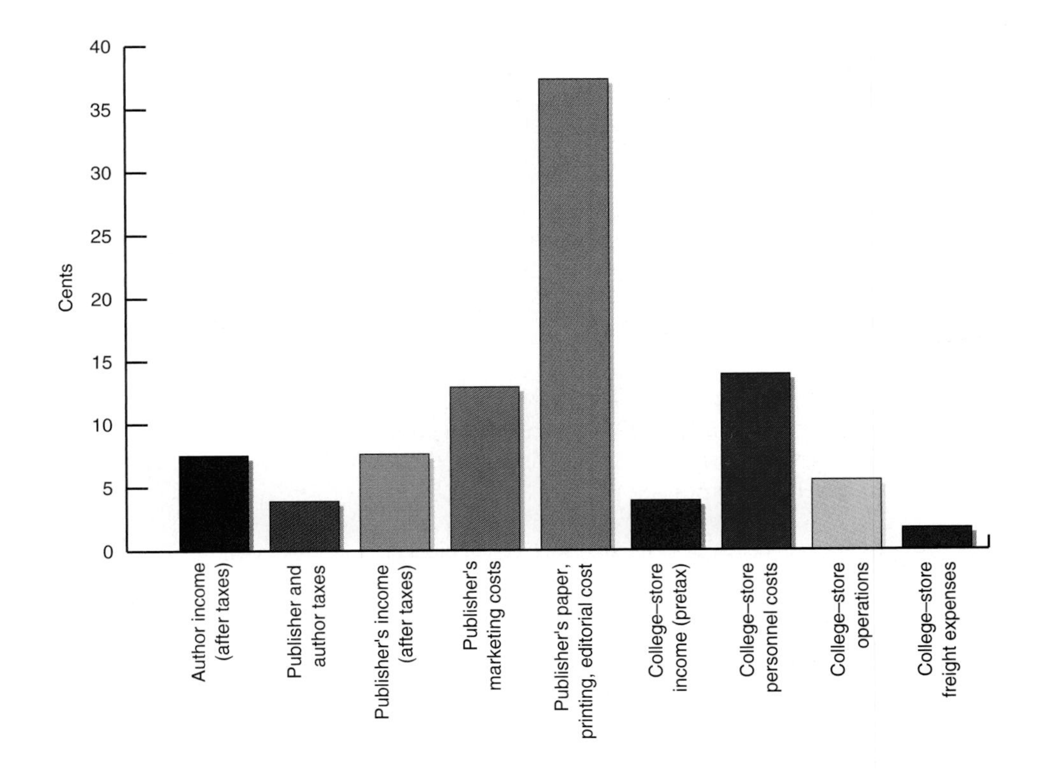

Students are frustrated with the cost of their textbooks, but most publishers would say that the selling prices have merely kept pace with inflation. Buying used books is an option, but publishers say that used books simply drive up the cost of future texts: If the publisher cannot sell as many of the new edition as are printed, the price is raised "to compensate for decreased sales volume, and the cycle starts again." Publishers also must cover the costs of many nonsalable supplements that are requested by faculty such as instructor's manuals, solutions manuals, transparency acetates, videos, and test banks (hard copy and electronic). Additionally, as the books become "fancier" with multiple colors, photographs, and periodical cites, costs also increase. Write a paper that does the following:

a. Provides suggestions for ways the college/university bookstore could control costs.

b. Provides suggestions for ways the publisher could control costs.

c. Provides suggestions for ways students can legally control textbook expenditures (i.e., substantial reproduction of the text is illegal).

d. Discusses why college textbooks today are so different from college textbooks of 20 years ago. Are these differences cost beneficial from your perspective?

59. *(Analyzing cost control)* The financial results for the Continuing Education Department of BusEd Corporation for November 2001 are presented in the schedule at the end of the case. Mary Ross, president of BusEd, is pleased with the final results but has observed that the revenue and most of the costs and expenses of this department exceeded the budgeted amounts. Barry Stein, vice president of the Continuing Education Department, has been requested to provide an explanation of any amount that exceeded the budget by 5 percent or more.

Stein has accumulated the following facts to assist in his analysis of the November results:

- The budget for calendar year 2001 was finalized in December 2000, and at that time, a full program of continuing education courses was scheduled to be held in Chicago during the first week of November 2001. The courses were scheduled so that eight courses would be run on each of the five days during the week. The budget assumed that there would be 425 participants in the program and 1,000 participant days for the week.
- BusEd charges a flat fee of $150 per day of course instruction, so the fee for a three-day course would be $450. BusEd grants a 10 percent discount to persons who subscribe to its publications. The 10 percent discount is also granted to second and subsequent registrants for the same course from the same organization. However, only one discount per registration is allowed. Historically, 70 percent of the participant day registrations are at the full fee of $150 per day, and 30 percent of the participant day registrations receive the discounted fee of $135 per day. These percentages were used in developing the November 2001 budgeted revenue.
- The following estimates were used to develop the budgeted figures for course-related expenses.

Food charges per participant day (lunch/coffee breaks)	$27
Course materials per participant	$8
Instructor fee per day	$1,000

- A total of 530 individuals participated in the Chicago courses in November 2001, accounting for 1,280 participant days. This number included 20 persons who took a new, two-day course on pension accounting that was not on the original schedule; thus, on two of the days, nine courses were offered, and an additional instructor was hired to cover the new course. The breakdown of the course registrations were as follows:

Full fee registrations	704
Discounted fees	
Current periodical subscribers	128
New periodical subscribers	128
Second registrations from the same organization	320
Total participant day registrations	1,280

- A combined promotional mailing was used to advertise the Chicago program and a program in Cincinnati that was scheduled for December 2001. The incremental costs of the combined promotional price were $5,000, but none of the promotional expenses ($20,000) budgeted for the Cincinnati program in December will have to be incurred. This earlier-than-normal promotion for the Cincinnati program has resulted in early registration fees collected in November as follows (in terms of participant days):

Full fee registrations	140
Discounted registrations	60
Total participant day registrations	200

- BusEd continually updates and adds new courses, and includes $2,000 in each monthly budget for this purpose. The additional amount spent on course development during November was for an unscheduled course that will be offered in February for the first time.

Barry Stein has prepared the following quantitative analysis of the November 2001 variances:

BUSED CORPORATION
Statement of Operations
Continuing Education Department
For the Month Ended November 30, 2001

	Budget	Actual	Favorable (Unfavorable) Dollars	Favorable (Unfavorable) Percent
Revenue				
Course fees	$145,500	$212,460	$ 66,960	46.0
Expenses				
Food charges	$ 27,000	$ 32,000	$ (5,000)	(18.5)
Course materials	3,400	4,770	(1,370)	(40.3)
Instructor fees	40,000	42,000	(2,000)	(5.0)
Instructor travel	9,600	9,885	(285)	(3.0)
Staff salaries and benefits	12,000	12,250	(250)	(2.1)
Staff travel	2,500	2,400	100	4.0
Promotion	20,000	25,000	(5,000)	(25.0)
Course development	2,000	5,000	(3,000)	(150.0)
Total expenses	$116,500	$133,305	$(16,805)	(14.4)
Revenue over expenses	$ 29,000	$ 79,155	$ 50,155	172.9

(continued)

BUSED CORPORATION
Analysis of November 2001 Variances

Budgeted revenue		$145,500
Variances:		
Quantity variance [(1,280 − 1,000) × $145.50]	$40,740 F	
Mix variance [($143.25 − $145.50) × 1,280]	2,880 U	
Timing difference ($145.50 × 200)	29,100 F	66,960 F
Actual revenue		$212,460
Budgeted expenses		$116,500
Quantity variances		
Food charges [(1,000 − 1,280) × $27]	$ 7,560 U	
Course materials [(425 − 530) × $8]	840 U	
Instructor fees (2 × $1,000)	2,000 U	10,400 U
Price variances		
Food charges [($27 − $25) × 1,280]	$ 2,560 F	
Course materials [($8 − $9) × 530]	530 U	2,030 F
Timing differences		
Promotion	$ 5,000 U	
Course development	3,000 U	8,000 U
Variances not analyzed (5% or less)		
Instructor travel	$ 285 U	
Staff salaries and benefits	250 U	
Staff travel	100 F	435 U
Actual expenses		$133,305

After reviewing Barry Stein's quantitative analysis of the November variances, prepare a memorandum addressed to Mary Ross explaining the following: (See chapter 18 for more discussion of revenue variances.)

a. The cause of the revenue mix variance
b. The implication of the revenue mix variance
c. The cause of the revenue timing difference
d. The significance of the revenue timing difference
e. The primary cause of the unfavorable total expense variance
f. How the favorable food price variance was determined
g. The impact of the promotion timing difference on future revenues and expenses
h. Whether or not the course development variance has an unfavorable impact on the company *(CMA adapted)*

REALITY CHECK

60. *Ferdows and De Meyer argue that long-term cost improvement is the result of having first achieved improvement in quality, then dependability, and finally speed. There is a cumulative effect by which prior gains influence current gains, a process that can be illustrated as a pile of sand with four layers: quality at the bottom and cost at the top (see figure). [The sand represents management effort and resources.] Increases in quality help increase dependability; then gains in both quality and dependability spur gains in speed. Finally, the cumulative effects of these prior gains result in cost efficiency gains.*

Ferdows and De Meyer also point out that, due to the shape of the pile of sand, achieving a small gain in cost requires successively larger gains for the other aspects of performance (e.g., a 10 percent cost gain may require a 15 percent gain in speed, a 25 percent gain in dependability, and a 40 percent gain in quality). The implication is that long-term successful cost reduction is achieved indirectly—through gains made in other strategically important ar-

eas. Thus, the cost reduction strategy should be deeply embedded in the firm's competitive strategy.

SOURCE: Michael D. Shields and S. Mark Young, "Effective Long-Term Cost Reduction: A Strategic Perspective," *Journal of Cost Management* (Spring 1992), pp. 20–21. © 1992 Warren Gorham & Lamont. Reprinted with permission of RIA.

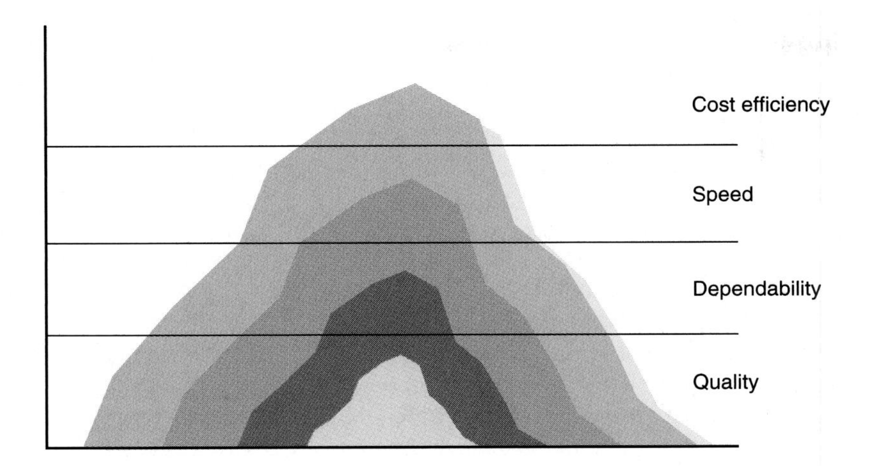

SOURCE: Reprinted from "Lasting Improvements in Manufacturing Performance: In Search of a New Theory," *Journal of Operations Management* (April 1990), p. 175, by Karsa Ferdows and Arnoud De Meyer, with permission of Elsevier Science.

a. How does the depiction of cost control in the figure relate to the concept of activity-based management?

b. If the relation between cost and quality is as depicted in the figure, how does the quality level of the production process serve as a constraint on organizational profitability?

c. What does the figure suggest about the prospects of competing via a strategy of offering low-cost/low-quality products?

61. *The cost of "people" constitutes 75 percent to 80 percent of the total costs of operating a public accounting firm. In periods of economic contractions (such as the late 1980s and early 1990s), accounting firms have to look to cut labor costs to keep costs in line with decreasing revenues. Many firms have resorted to the restricted use of part-time employees who can be laid off during the slack periods in the year. Part-timers include college interns, and parents with young children who only want to work during the busy season. Firms have also resorted to the use of paraprofessionals, individuals with two-year degrees in business.*

SOURCE: Don Istvan, "Cost Cutting: A Survival Plan," *Accounting Today* (November 11, 1991), p. 26. © 2000 Thomson Financial. Reprinted with permission.

a. Discuss the use of part-timers and paraprofessionals from the perspective of controlling costs.

b. How could the use of part-timers and paraprofessionals impair the quality of work performed by public accounting firms?

c. How could the use of part-timers and paraprofessionals affect the effectiveness and efficiency with which work is performed in public accounting firms?

62. *For Caesar O'Neal, a nausea-free day is priceless. But for the hospital treating the 6-foot-8-inch University of Florida football player for liver cancer, the price of delivering that relief is becoming troublesome.*

Mr. O'Neal has been getting massive chemotherapy, including a round last fall that left him vomiting so much that he nearly quit treatment. After that crisis, doctors gave him Zofran, a powerful anti-nausea drug. Now chemotherapy isn't so frightening, Mr. O'Neal says as he sits on his bed sipping Gatorade. Instead of suffering anguish after each treatment, he can enjoy small pleasures such as video games, big meals or chats with relatives.

But Zofran is one of the most expensive drugs around—and a hot issue as hospitals and drug makers clash over the cost of medications. A standard 32-milligram dose of Zofran—less than a single teardrop—costs hospitals $143. Factor in expenses for stocking it and having nurses administer it intravenously, and each use of Zofran can turn into a $300 patient charge. By weight, gem-quality diamonds are cheaper.

Many doctors and nurses, however, think they can slash Zofran costs without making patients feel worse. "We may be overusing the drug," says Robert Benjamin, an oncologist who treats Mr. O'Neal at the University of Texas M.D. Anderson Cancer Center in Houston. He and other doctors around the U.S. think Glaxo's official package inserts, though approved by the Food and Drug Administration, overstate the Zofran dose that many patients need.

M.D. Anderson is seeking to trim its spending on costly anti-nausea drugs such as Zofran by 10% this year. Other teaching hospitals, in Boston, New York and Chicago, are looking for cuts of 25% to 50%—mostly by drafting new treatment standards that lean on doctors to shrink dosages or try less costly substitutes.

SOURCE: George Anders, "Costly Medicine Meets Its Match: Hospitals Just Use Lower Doses," *The Wall Street Journal* (August 1, 1994), pp. A1, A6. Reprinted by permission of *The Wall Street Journal*,

a. What cost control strategy are health administrators attempting to employ for Zofran?

b. What are the ethical considerations in cutting drug costs by cutting doses and switching to less costly substitutes?

c. What is the ethical responsibility of the pharmaceutical manufacturer in setting the prescribed doses for medicines it develops?

63. *Kirsh Guilory pumped out Cajun music, vendors hawked Creole crafts, but the crawfish delicacies dished out along food row at the New Orleans Jazz and Heritage Festival were not from the bayous and backwaters of Louisiana. The Chinese have taken over the crawfish pies, etouffee, file gumbo and most other crawfish dishes served at the festival. Captured, cooked, peeled and processed with low-cost labor in China, the crawfish from overseas are too cheap to pass up, say the merchants who sell food at the fest.*

"I had to go to the Chinese tails," said Clark Hoffpauer, whose festival specialty is crawfish etouffee. "They're at least $2 a pound cheaper, and when you talk 1,700 pounds, that's quite a bit of change. I'd rather use Louisiana crawfish. After all, this is about Louisiana heritage, but business is business."

SOURCE: Mary Foster, "China Syndrome," *(New Orleans) Times-Picayune* (May 3, 1996), p. C1.

a. Is "business is business" a true statement? Discuss the concept of this statement relative to costs, to employment, and to tradition.

b. Provide some examples in which you would believe that the quality of a product and/or the ethics of a company would be enhanced if management considered all of the stakeholders in an organization in addition to costs when making a "business is business" decision.

PART

4

Decision Making

CHAPTER 16

Innovative Inventory and Production Management Techniques

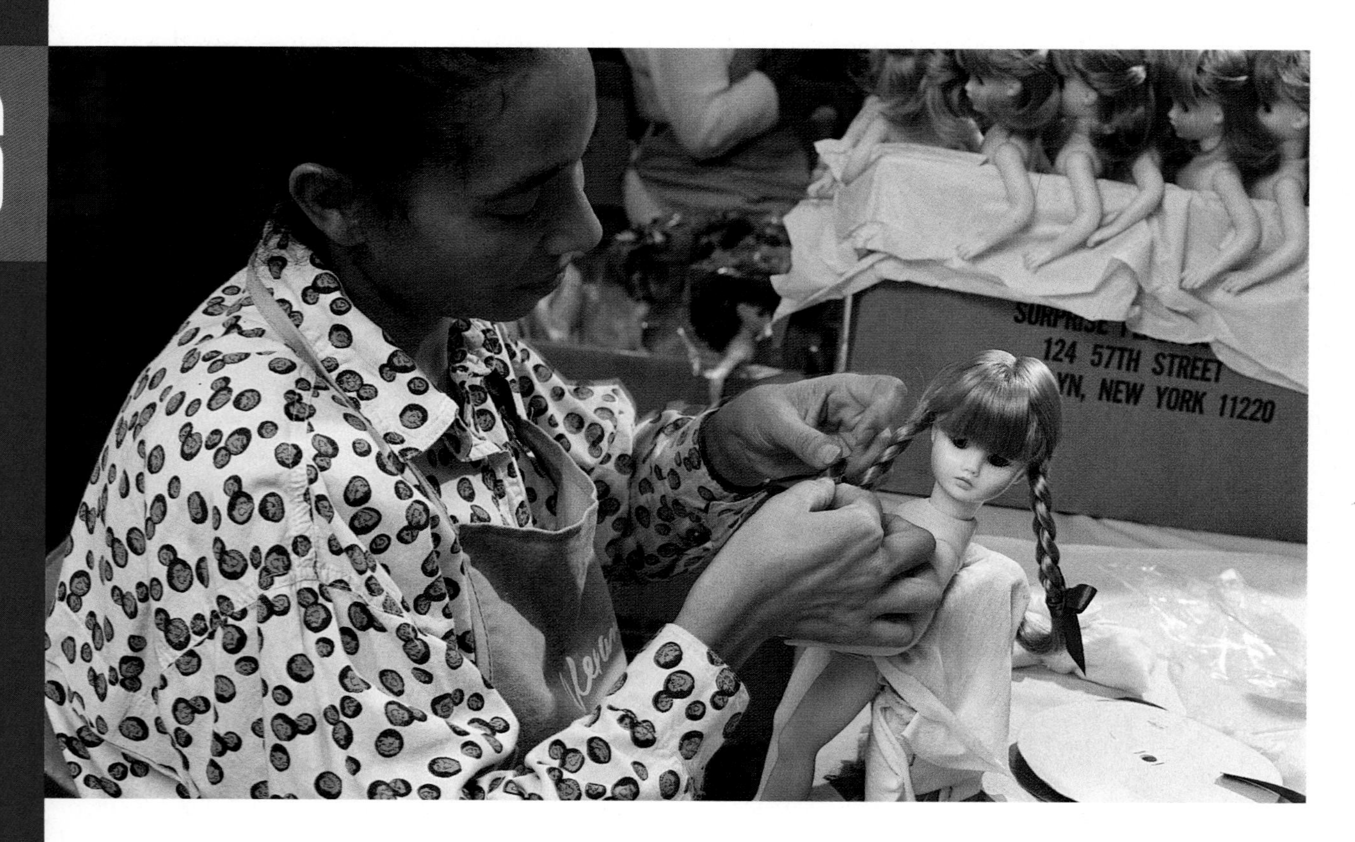

LEARNING OBJECTIVES

After completing this chapter, you should be able to answer the following questions:

1
What are the most important relationships in the value chain, and how can these relationships be managed to benefit the company?

2
Why are inventory management and inventory costs so significant to the firm?

3
How do push and pull systems of production control work?

4
How do product life cycles affect product costing and profitability?

5
How does target costing influence production cost management?

6
What is the just-in-time philosophy and how does it affect production and accounting?

7
What are flexible manufacturing systems and how do they relate to computer-integrated manufacturing?

8
How can the theory of constraints help in determining production flow?

9
(Appendix) How are economic order quantity, reorder point, and safety stock determined and used?

INTRODUCING Alexander Doll Co.

http://www.onlinedolls.com/ma/index.htm

In the three-quarters of a century since "Madame" Beatrice Alexander founded the Alexander Doll Co. in 1923, little girls have been unwrapping Madame Alexander dolls at Christmastime. These charming collectibles with hand-painted faces and decorative costumes are modeled either after the fictional Cinderella or the real Elizabeth Taylor, and cost from $40 to $600.

During the 1950s through the 1980s the Alexander Doll Co. prospered under the direction of its founder, but under new management in 1995, the company was struggling so much financially that it filed bankruptcy. However, the company was purchased by the Kaizen Breakthrough Partnership, L.P. (KBP) an investment partnership formed by Gefinor Group, an international merchant bank, in partnership with TBM Consulting Group, Inc., which specializes in helping clients implement *kaizen.* KBP saw an opportunity to use the *kaizen* process to turn Alexander Doll Co. around.

Beginning with the company's small production line for dolls, TBM set up a cross-functional team of 10 Alexander employees to evaluate problems with the production line. The team observed 25 operations and measured each with a stopwatch.

Operations had been spread out over three floors, causing extra handling that wasted time and damaged the dolls. The batch process that had been used caused hundreds of dolls in various stages of completion to collect at each operation.

"We physically moved the operation [within the building] and combined everything in one location," says William Schwartz, director of Alexander Doll and a vice president of TBM. The distance each doll traveled from the beginning to the end of the process was reduced from 630 feet to 40 feet. The time that was required to complete a doll went from 90 days to 90 minutes. The number of unfinished doll pieces was reduced from 29,000 to 34. The square footage used for the line was reduced from 2,010 to 980. And productivity increased from eight dolls per person per day to 25.

SOURCES: Robert Maynard, "A Company Is Turned Around Through Japanese Principles," *Nation's Business* (February 1996), p. 9; and Alex Taylor III, "It Worked for Toyota. Can It Work for Toys?" *Fortune* (January 11, 1999), p. 36.

http://www.tbmcg.com

In recent years, some people have questioned whether some segments of American industry are as productive and efficient as their counterparts in Japan, Germany, or other parts of the world. Many U.S. companies are concentrating on ways to improve productivity and utilization of available technology. These efforts are often directed toward reducing the costs of producing and carrying inventory. Consider the following comments regarding the role of information technology in creating economic value for American business:

> *Federal Reserve Chairman Alan Greenspan gave unexpected support to "New Economy" theorists in a speech at the Gerald R. Ford Foundation in Grand Rapids [September 8, 1999]. Information technology, he said, "has begun to alter, fundamentally, the manner in which we do business and create economic value." By enabling businesses to remove "large swaths of unnecessary inventory, real-time information is accelerating productivity growth and raising living standards. This has contributed to the greatest prosperity the world has ever witnessed."*[1]

The amount spent on inventory may be the largest investment, other than plant assets, made by a company. Investment in inventory, though, provides no return until that inventory is sold. This chapter deals with ways for companies to minimize

[1] George Melloan, "Global View: America's 'New Economy' Is Technology," *The Wall Street Journal Interactive Journal* (September 21, 1999), p. 1. Permission conveyed through the Copyright Clearance Center.

their monetary commitments to inventory. These techniques include the just-in-time (JIT) inventory philosophy and its accounting implications, flexible manufacturing systems (FMS), and computer-integrated manufacturing (CIM). The appendix to this chapter covers the concepts of economic order quantity (EOQ), order point, safety stock, and Pareto inventory analysis.

IMPORTANT SETS OF RELATIONSHIPS IN THE VALUE CHAIN

1

What are the most important relationships in the value chain, and how can these relationships be managed to benefit the company?

Every company has a set of upstream suppliers and a set of downstream customers. In a one-on-one context, these parties can be depicted by the following model:

It is at the interfaces of these relationships where real opportunities for improvements exist. By building improved cooperation, communication, and integration, the entities within the value chain can treat each other as extensions of themselves. In so doing, they can enjoy gains in quality, throughput, and cost efficiency. Non-value-added activities can be reduced or eliminated and performance of value-added activities can be enhanced. Shared expertise and problem solving can be very beneficial. Products and services can be provided faster and with fewer defects, and activities can be performed more effectively and reliably with fewer deficiencies and less redundancy. Consider the following opportunities for improvement between entities:

- improved communication of requirements and specifications,
- greater clarity in requests for products or services,
- improved feedback regarding unsatisfactory products or services,
- improvements in planning, controlling, and problem solving, and
- shared managerial and technical expertise, supervision, and training.

All of these opportunities are also available to individuals and groups within an organization. Within the company, each employee or group of employees has both an upstream supplier and a downstream customer that form the context of an intraorganizational value chain. When employees see their internal suppliers and customers as extensions of themselves and work to exploit the opportunities for improvement, teamwork will be significantly enhanced. Improved teamwork helps companies in their implementation of pull systems, which are part of a just-in-time work environment. Greater productivity benefits all company stakeholders. The impact of greater productivity is addressed in the following quote:

> *[From 1994 to 1999], productivity growth [in the U.S.] averaged about 2% a year, up from the 1% average annual rate during the 20 years ending in 1993. The faster productivity rises, the more employers can afford to raise wages and benefits without raising prices or squeezing profits.*[2]

[2] Alejandro Bodipo-Memba, "Productivity Grew at Slower, 3.5% Rate in First Quarter Than First Estimated," *The Wall Street Journal* (June 9, 1999), p. A2.

BUYING OR PRODUCING AND CARRYING INVENTORY

2

Why are inventory management and inventory costs so significant to the firm?

In manufacturing organizations, one basic cost is for raw material. Although possibly not the largest production cost, raw material purchases cause a continuous cash outflow each period. Similarly, retailers invest a significant proportion of their assets in merchandise purchased for sale to others. Profit margins in both types of organizations can benefit from reducing or minimizing inventory investments, assuming that demand for products could still be met. The term *inventory* is used in this chapter to refer to any of the following: raw material, work in process, finished goods, indirect material (supplies), or merchandise inventory.

Good inventory management relies largely on cost-minimization strategies. As indicated in Exhibit 16–1, the basic costs associated with inventory are (1) purchasing/production, (2) ordering/setup, and (3) carrying/not carrying goods in stock. The **purchasing cost** for inventory is the quoted purchase price minus any discounts allowed, plus shipping charges.

purchasing cost

For a manufacturer, *production cost* refers to the costs associated with purchasing direct material, paying for direct labor, incurring traceable overhead, and absorbing allocated fixed manufacturing overhead. Of these production costs, fixed manufacturing overhead is the least susceptible to cost minimization in the short run.

EXHIBIT 16–1

Categories of Inventory Costs

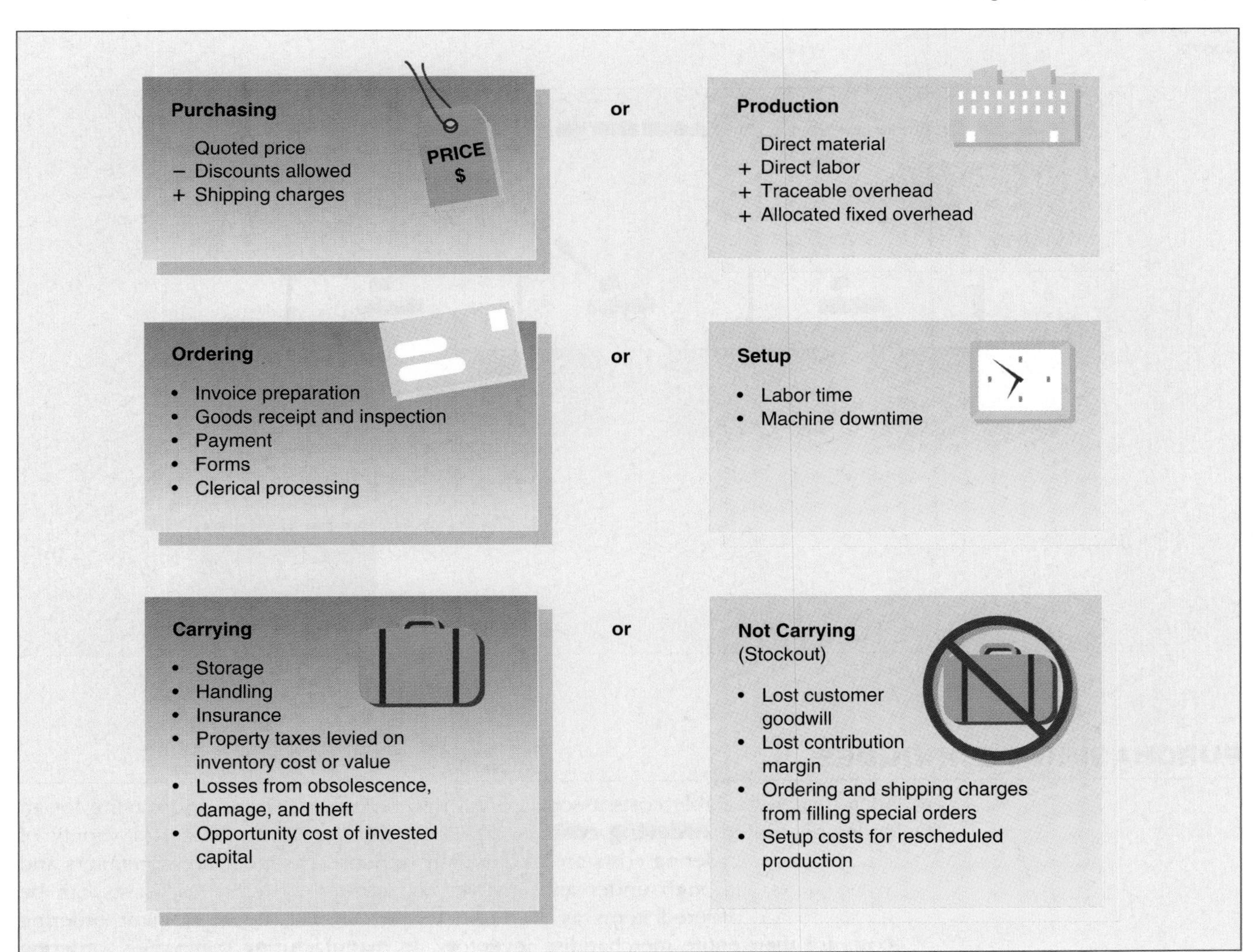

An exception is that management is able to somewhat control the fixed component of unit product cost through capacity utilization measures within the context of product demand in the short run. Most efforts to minimize fixed manufacturing overhead costs involve long-run measures.

Purchasing/production cost is the amount to be recorded in the appropriate inventory account (Raw Material Inventory, Work in Process Inventory, Finished Goods Inventory, or Merchandise Inventory).

3

How do push and pull systems of production control work?

push system

pull system

The two fundamental approaches to producing inventory are push systems and pull systems. In a traditional approach, production is conducted in anticipation of customer orders. In this approach, known as a **push system** (illustrated in Exhibit 16–2), work centers may buy or produce inventory not currently needed because of lead time or economic order or production quantity requirements. This excess inventory is stored until it is needed by other work centers.

To reduce the cost of carrying inventory until needed at some point in the future, many companies have begun to implement **pull systems** of production control (depicted in Exhibit 16–3). In these systems, parts are delivered or produced only as they are needed by the work center for which they are intended. Although some minimal storage must exist by necessity, work centers do not produce to compensate for lead times or to meet some economic production run model.

Discussion of matters such as managing inventory levels and optimum order size is presented in the Appendix to this chapter.

EXHIBIT 16–2

Push System of Production Control

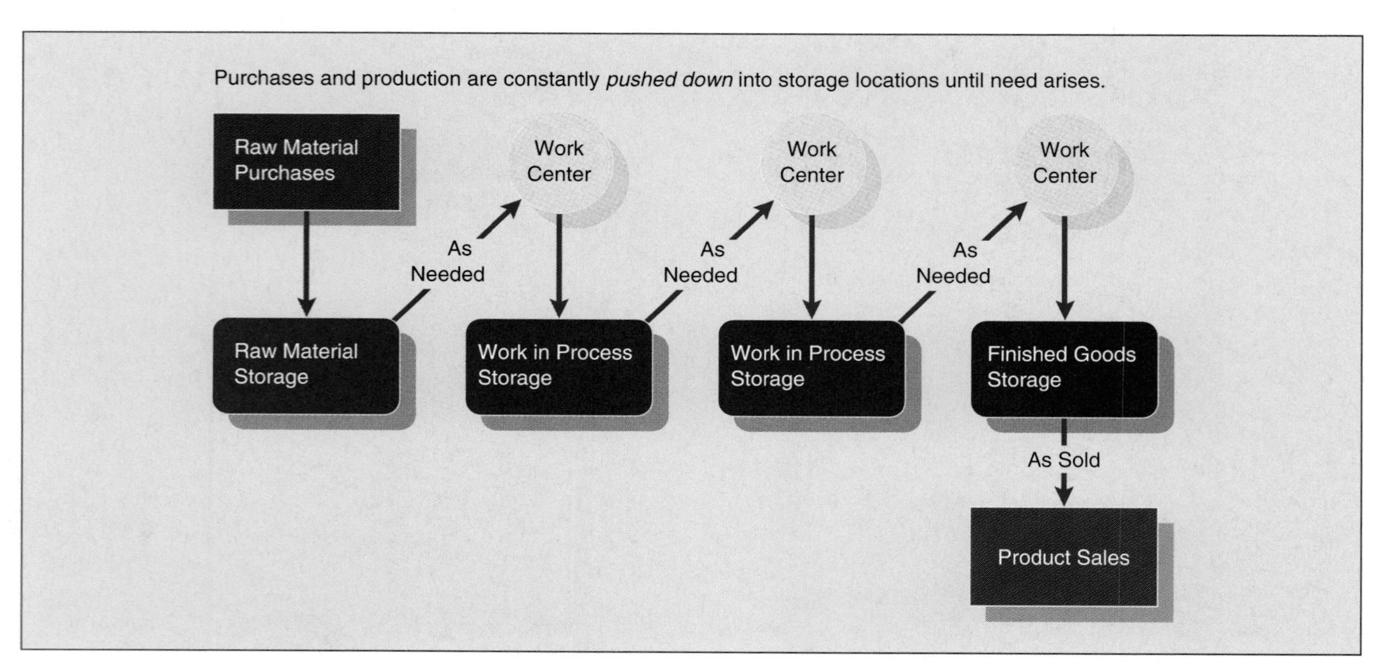

PURCHASING TECHNIQUES

ordering cost

Incremental, variable costs associated with preparing, receiving, and paying for an order are called **ordering costs** and include the cost of forms and a variety of clerical costs. Ordering costs are traditionally expensed as incurred by retailers and wholesalers, although under an activity-based costing system these costs can be traced to the ordered items as an additional direct cost. Retailers incur ordering costs for their entire merchandise inventory. In manufacturing companies, ordering costs are incurred for raw material purchases. If the company intends to produce

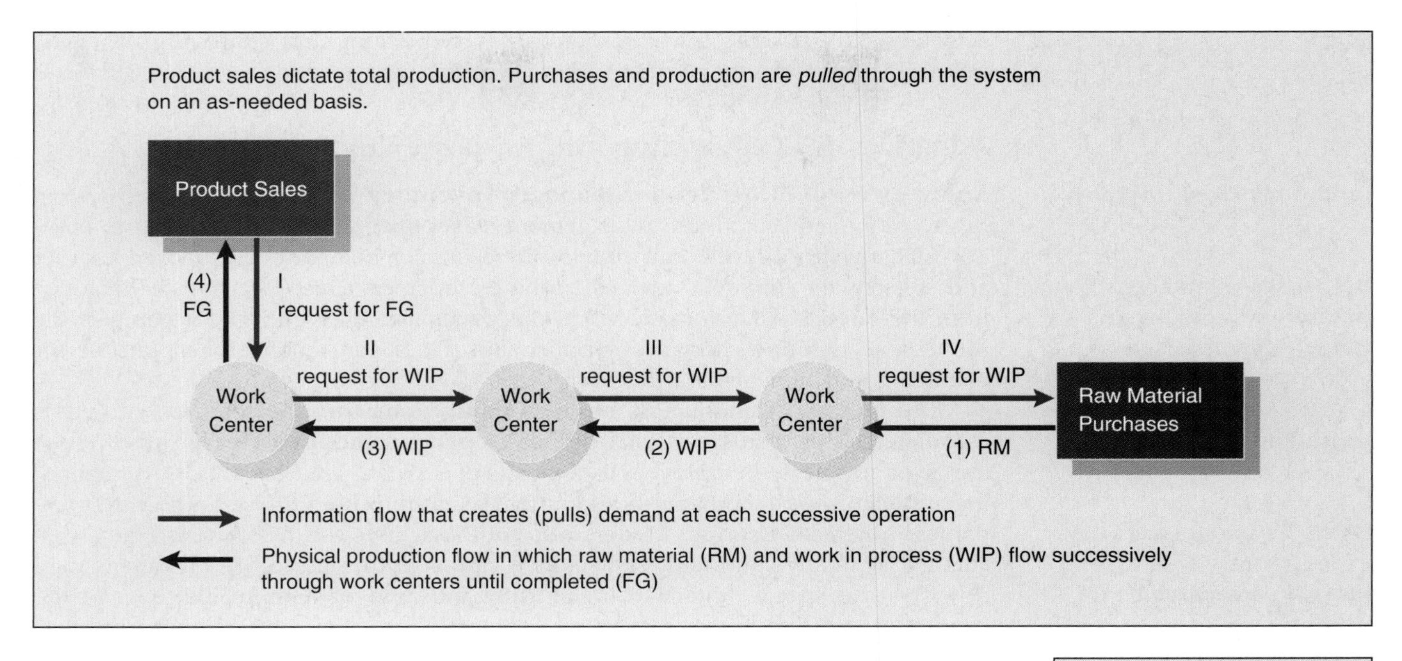

EXHIBIT 16-3

Pull System of Production Control

rather than order a part, direct and indirect **setup costs** (instead of ordering costs) are created as equipment is readied for each new production run. Setup necessitates costs for changing dies or drill heads, recalibrating machinery, and resetting tolerance limits for quality control equipment. For decision analysis purposes, only the direct or incremental setup costs are relevant.

setup cost

Information Technology and Purchasing

Advances in information technology have greatly improved the efficiency and effectiveness of purchasing. Bar coding and electronic data interchange (EDI) are expected to reduce procurement costs from "an average $9.50 per transaction to $1.87."[3]

bar code

Bar codes are groups of lines and spaces arranged in a special machine-readable pattern by which a scanner measures the intensity of the light reflections of the white spaces between the lines and converts the signal back into the original data.[4] The bar code can be used as a simple identifier of a record of a product in a database where a large amount of information is stored, or the bar code itself may contain a vast amount of information about the product.

Manufacturers can use bar codes to gain information about raw material receipts and issuances, products as they move through an assembly area, and quality problems. Bar codes have reduced clerical costs, paperwork, and inventory, and simultaneously made processing faster, less expensive, and more reliable.

electronic data interchange

http://www.ansi.org/

Because the need for prompt and accurate communication between company and supplier is essential in a pull system, many companies are eliminating paper and telephone communication processes and relying instead on **electronic data interchange** (EDI). EDI refers to the computer-to-computer transfer of information in virtual real time using standardized formats developed by the American National Standards Institute. In addition to the cost savings obtained from reduced paperwork and data entry errors, EDI users experience more rapid transaction processing and response time than can occur using traditional communication channels. Workers and teams of workers can also reduce the time required to perform

[3] Joseph McKendrick, "Procurement: The Next Frontier in E-Businesss," *Midrange Systems* (Spring House: July 19, 1999), pp. 27ff.
[4] Mark Rowh, "The Basics of Bar Coding," *Office Systems* (April 1999), pp. 44ff.

activities and consume fewer resources by cooperating and conferring on cross-functional interface activities as discussed in the next section.

Advances in Authorizing and Empowering Purchases

vendor-managed inventory

http://www.kraft.com
http://www.motts.com
http://www.walmart.com

An extension of EDI is **vendor-managed inventory** (VMI), a streamlined system of inventory acquisition and management. A supplier can be empowered to monitor EDI inventory levels and provide its customer company a proposed e-order and subsequent shipment after electronic acceptance. Electronic transfer of funds from the buyer's bank is made when the goods are received.[5] The accompanying News Note describes how the supplier, not the buying entity, is responsible for managing and replenishing inventory.

procurement card

http://www.americanexpress.com
http://www.mastercard.com
http://www.visa.com

The process of conducting business transactions over the Internet, known as e-commerce, has made possible the use of **procurement cards** (p-cards). These are given to selected employees as a means of securing greater control over spending and eliminating the paper-based purchase authorization process. The card companies, American Express, MasterCard, and Visa, increase the buying entity's assurance by tightly controlling how each p-card is used, states Ellen Messmer, "right down to the specific merchant dealt with, the kind of item purchased and the amount spent." She further says, "One of the main reasons corporate bean-counters love p-cards is that American Express, MasterCard and Visa promise to deliver detailed transaction information—sometimes directly into companies' back-end enterprise resource planning systems—on every purchase."[6]

open purchase ordering

Companies are also currently decreasing their order costs significantly by using **open purchase ordering**. A single purchase order—sometimes known as a blanket purchase order—that expires at a set or determinable future date is prepared to authorize a supplier to provide a large quantity of one or more specified items. The goods will then be requisitioned in smaller quantities as needed by the buyer over the extended future period.

NEWS NOTE  GENERAL BUSINESS

Vendor-Managed Inventory

Throughout the supply chain, vendor-managed inventory (VMI) is a way to cut costs and keep inventory levels low. Its practitioners range from food manufacturers like Kraft Inc. in New York and Mott's USA in Stamford, Conn., to chain-store wizard Wal-Mart Stores, Inc., in Bentonville, Ark.

VMI lets companies reduce overhead by shifting responsibility for managing and replenishing inventory to vendors. "If you're smart enough to transfer the ownership of inventory to your vendors, your raw materials and work-in-process inventory comes off your balance sheets. Your assets go down, and you need less working capital to run your business," says Ron Barris, global leader of supply-chain management for the high-tech industry at Ernst & Young LLP.

In VMI, the vendor tracks the number of products shipped to distributors and retail outlets. Tracking tells the vendor whether or not the distributor needs more supplies. Products are automatically replenished when supplies run low, and goods aren't sent unless they're needed, consequently lowering inventory at the distribution center or retail store. Suppliers and buyers use written contracts to determine payment terms, frequency of replenishment, and other terms of the agreement.

SOURCE: Jacqueline Emigh, "Vendor-Managed Inventory," *Computerworld* (August 23, 1999), pp. 52ff. Reprinted with permission.

[5] Jacqueline Emigh, "Vendor-Managed Inventory," *Computerworld* (August 23, 1999), pp. 52ff.
[6] Ellen Messmer, "The Good, the Bad, and the Ugly of P-Cards," *Network World* (August 23, 1999), pp. 42ff.

A variation of the annual blanket purchase order is a long-term open purchasing arrangement in which goods are provided at fixed or determinable prices according to specified requirements. These arrangements may or may not involve electronic procurement cards.

Inventory Carrying Costs

carrying cost

Inventory **carrying costs** are the variable costs of carrying one inventory unit in stock for one year. Carrying costs are incurred for storage, handling, insurance, property taxes based on inventory cost or value, and possible losses from obsolescence or damage. In addition, carrying costs should include an amount for opportunity cost. When a firm's capital is invested in inventory, that capital is unable to earn interest or dividends from alternative investments. Inventory is one of the many investments made by an organization and should be expected to earn a satisfactory rate of return.

Some Japanese managers have referred to inventory as a liability. One can readily understand that perspective considering that carrying costs, which can be estimated using information from various budgets, special studies, or other analytical techniques, "can easily add 20 percent to 25 percent per year to the initial cost of inventory."[7]

stockout

Although carrying inventory in excess of need generates costs, a fully depleted inventory can also generate costs. A **stockout** occurs when a company does not have inventory available when requested internally or by an external customer. The cost of having a stockout is not easily determinable, but some of the costs involved might include lost customer goodwill, lost contribution margin from not being able to make a sale, additional ordering and shipping charges incurred from special orders, and possibly lost customers.

For a manufacturer, another important stockout cost is incurred for production adjustments arising from not having inventory available. If a necessary raw material is not on hand, the production process must be rescheduled or stopped, which in turn may cause additional setup costs before production resumes.

UNDERSTANDING AND MANAGING PRODUCTION ACTIVITIES AND COSTS

Managing production activities and costs requires an understanding of product life cycles and the various management and accounting models and approaches to effectively and efficiently engage in production planning, controlling, decision making, and performance evaluation.

Product Life Cycles

4

How do product life cycles affect product costing and profitability?

Product profit margins are typically judged on a period-by-period basis without consideration of the product life cycle. However, products, like people, go through a series of sequential life-cycle stages. As mentioned in Chapter 1, the product life cycle is a model depicting the stages through which a product class (not necessarily each product) passes from the time that an idea is conceived until production is discontinued. Those stages are development (which includes design), introduction, growth, maturity, and decline. A sales trend line through each stage is illustrated in Exhibit 16–4. Companies must be aware of where their products are in their life cycles, because in addition to the sales effects, the life-cycle stage may have a tremendous impact on costs and profits. The life-cycle impact on each of these items is shown in Exhibit 16–5.

[7] Bill Moseley, "Boosting Profits and Efficiency: The Opportunities Are There," *(Grant Thornton) Tax & Business Adviser* (May–June 1992), p. 6.

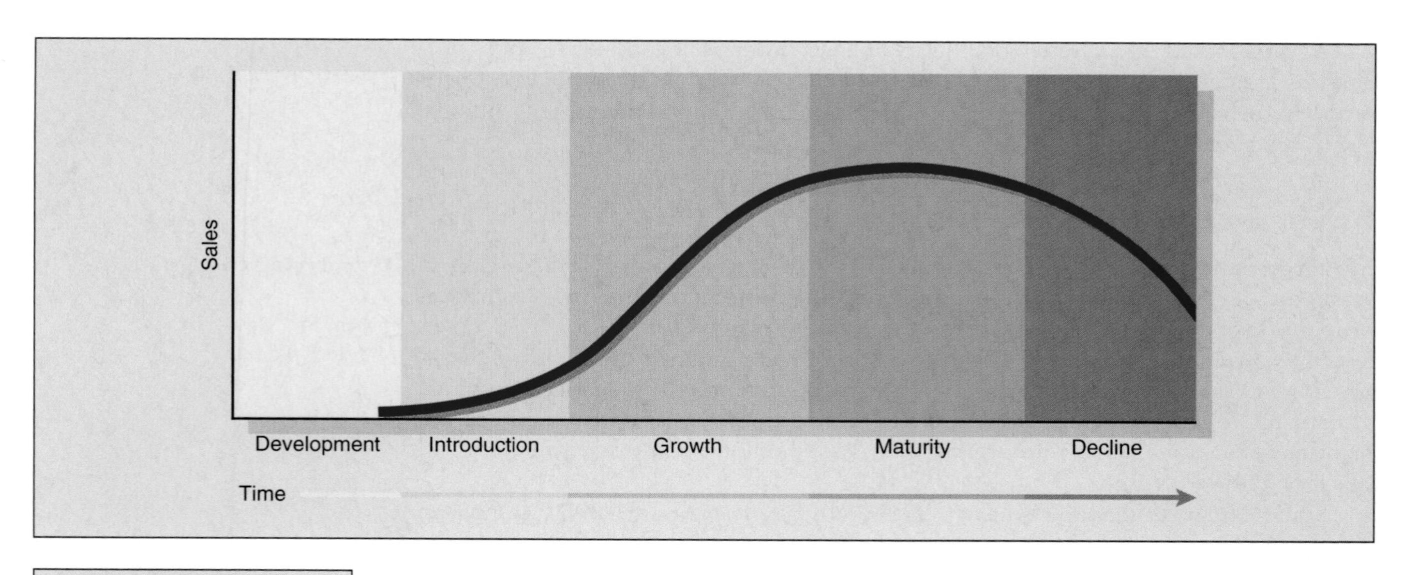

EXHIBIT 16-4

Product Life Cycle

LIFE CYCLE AND TARGET COSTING

From a cost standpoint, the development stage is an important one that is almost ignored by the traditional financial accounting model. Financial accounting requires that development costs be expensed as incurred—even though most studies indicate that decisions made during this stage determine approximately 80 to 90 percent of a product's total life-cycle costs. That is, the materials and the manufacturing process specifications made during development generally affect production costs for the rest of the product's life.

EXHIBIT 16-5

Effects of Product Life Cycles on Costs, Sales, and Profits

Stage	Costs	Approach to Costing	Sales	Profits
Development	No production costs, but R&D costs very high	Target costing (explained later in this section)	None	None; large loss on product due to expensing of R&D costs
Introduction	Production cost per unit; probably engineering change costs; high advertising cost	Kaizen costing (explained in next section of this chapter)	Very low unit sales; selling price may be high (for early profits) or low (for gaining market share)	Typically losses are incurred partially due to expensing of advertising
Growth	Production cost per unit decreases (due to learning curve and spreading fixed overhead over many units)	Kaizen costing	Rising unit sales; selling price is adjusted to meet competition	High
Maturity	Production cost per unit stable; costs of increasing product mix begin to rise	Standard costing (explained in Ch. 10)	Peak unit sales; reduced selling price	Falling
Decline	Production cost per unit increases (due to fixed overhead being spread over a lower volume)	Standard costing	Falling unit sales; selling price may be increased in an attempt to raise profits or lowered in an attempt to raise volume	May return to losses

Although technology and competition have tremendously shortened the time required in the development stage, effective development efforts are critical to a product's profitability over its entire life cycle. Time spent in the planning and development process often results "in lower production costs, reduced time from the design to manufacture stage, higher quality, greater flexibility, and lower product life cycle cost."[8] All manufacturers are acutely aware of the need to focus attention on the product development stage, and the performance measure of "time-to-market" is becoming more critical.

Once a product or service idea has been formulated, the market is typically researched to determine the features customers desire. Sometimes, however, such product research is forgone for innovative new products, and companies occasionally ignore the market and simply develop and introduce products. For example:

> *[E]very season Seiko "throws" into the market several hundred new models of its watches. Those that the customers buy, it makes more of; the others it drops. Capitalizing on the design-for-response strategy, Seiko has a highly flexible design and production process that lets it quickly and inexpensively introduce new products. [The company's] fast, flexible product design process has slashed the cost of failure.*[9]

http://seikousa.com

Because many products can now be built to specifications, companies can further develop the product to meet customer tastes once it is in the market. Alternatively, flexible manufacturing systems allow rapid changeovers to other designs.

After a product is designed, manufacturers have traditionally determined product costs and set a selling price based, to some extent, on costs. If the market will not bear the resulting selling price (possibly because competitors' prices are lower), the firm either makes less profit than hoped or attempts to lower production costs.

5

How does target costing influence production cost management?

target costing

In contrast, since the early 1970s, a technique called target costing has been used by some companies (especially Japanese ones) to view the costing process differently. **Target costing** develops an "allowable" product cost by analyzing market research to estimate what the market will pay for a product with specific characteristics. This is expressed in the following formula:

$$TC = ESP - APM$$

where TC = target cost
ESP = estimated selling price
APM = acceptable profit margin

Subtracting an acceptable profit margin from the estimated selling price leaves an implied maximum per-unit target product cost, which is compared to an expected product cost. Exhibit 16–6 compares target costing with traditional Western costing.

cost table

If the expected cost is greater than the target cost, the company has several alternatives. First, the product design and/or production process can be changed to reduce costs. Preparation of cost tables helps determine how such adjustments can be made. **Cost tables** are databases that provide information about the impact on product costs of using different input resources, manufacturing processes, and design specifications. Second, a less-than-desired profit margin can be accepted. Third, the company can decide that it does not want to enter this particular product market at the current time because it cannot make the profit margin it desires. If, for example, the target costing system at Olympus (the Japanese camera company) indicates that life-cycle costs of a product are insufficient to make profitability

[8] James A. Brimson, "How Advanced Manufacturing Technologies Are Reshaping Cost Management," *Management Accounting* (March 1986), p. 26.

[9] Williard I. Zangwill, "When Customer Research Is a Lousy Idea," *The Wall Street Journal* (March 8, 1993), p. A10. Permission conveyed through the Copyright Clearance Center.

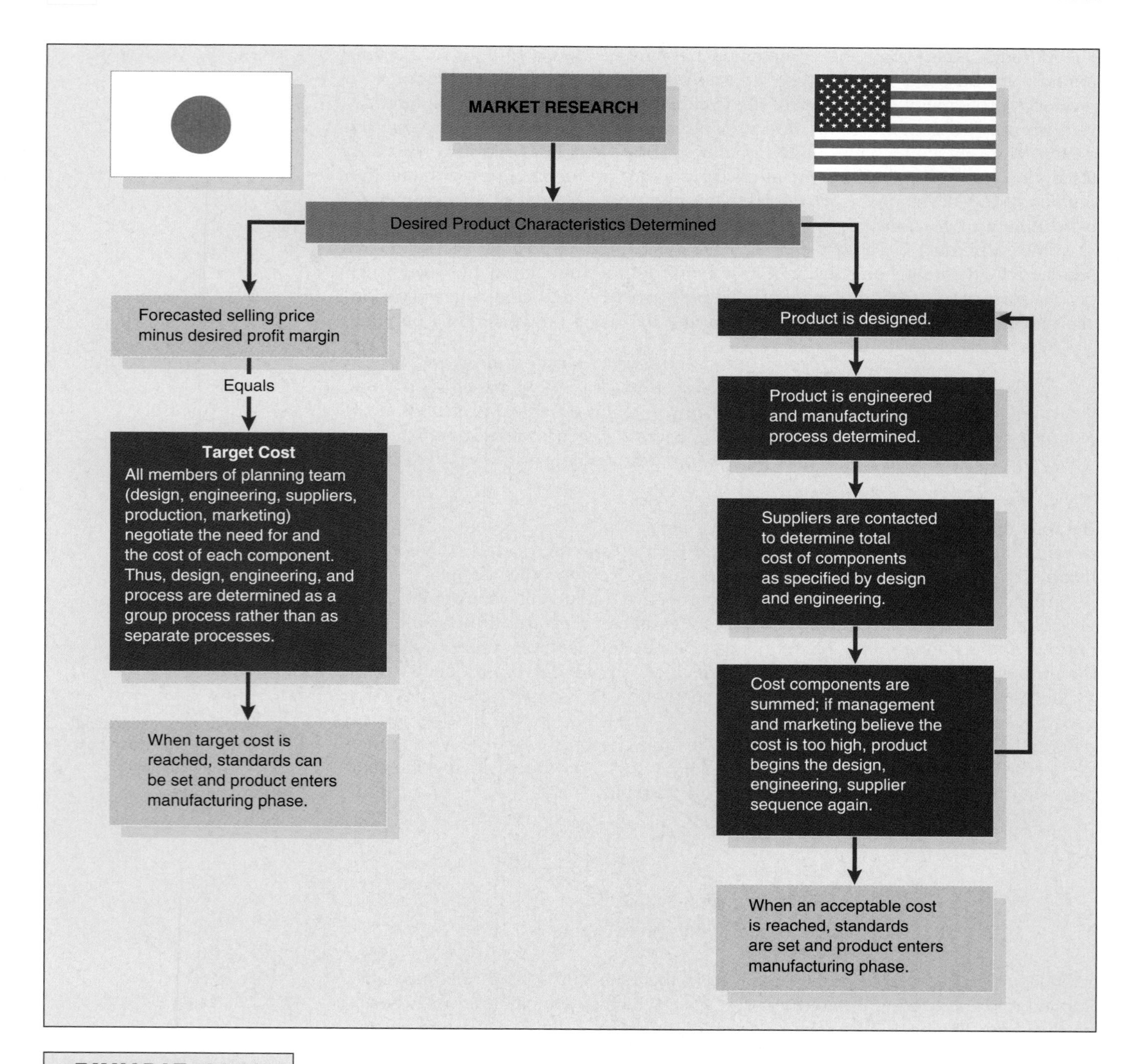

EXHIBIT 16-6

Developing Product Costs

acceptable, "the product is abandoned unless there is a strategic reason, such as maintaining a full product line or creating a 'flagship' product, for keeping the product."[10]

value engineering

Value engineering is an important step in successful product development. It involves a disciplined search for various feasible combinations of resources and methods that will increase product functionality and reduce costs. Multidisciplinary teams using various problem-solving tools such as brainstorming, Pareto analysis, and engineering tools seek an improved product cost-performance ratio considering such factors as reliability, conformance, and durability. Cost reduction is considered the major focus of value engineering.[11]

[10] Robin Cooper, *When Lean Enterprises Collide* (Boston: Harvard Business School Press, 1995), p. 159.
[11] Eric Meng, "The Project Manager's Toolbox," *PM Network* (1999), pp. 52ff.

Target costing can be applied to services if they are sufficiently uniform to justify the modeling effort required. Assume that a print shop wants to offer its customers the opportunity to buy personalized picture calendars and other similar personalized documents with photographs. A market survey indicates that the metropolitan area could sustain an annual 500-order volume and that customers believe $18 is a reasonable fee per service. The print shop manager believes that a reasonable profit for this service is $8 per customer order. Thus, the shop has an allowable target cost of $10 per order. The manager will invest in the equipment necessary to provide the new service if he or she believes the indicated volume suggested by market research is sufficient to support the effort.

If a company decides to enter a market, the target cost computed at the beginning of the product life cycle does not remain the final focus. Over the product's life, the target cost is continuously reduced in an effort to spur a process of continuous improvement in actual production cost. **Kaizen costing** involves ongoing efforts for continuous improvement to reduce product costs, increase product quality, and/or improve the production process after manufacturing activities have begun. These cost reductions are designed to keep the profit margin relatively stable as the product price is reduced over the product life cycle. Exhibit 16–7 compares target and kaizen costing.

kaizen costing

In designing a product to meet an allowable cost, engineers strive to eliminate all nonessential activities from the production process. Such reductions in activities will, in turn, reduce costs. The production process and types of components to be used should be discussed among appropriate parties (including engineering,

EXHIBIT 16–7

Differences between Target and Kaizen Costing

	Target Costing	Kaizen Costing
What?	A procedural approach to determining a maximum allowable cost for an identifiable, proposed product assuming a given target profit margin	A mandate to reduce costs, increase product quality, and/or improve production processes through continuous improvement efforts
Used for?	New products	Existing products
When?	Development stage (includes design)	Primary production stages (introduction and growth; possibly, but not probably, maturity)
How?	Works best through aiming at a specified cost reduction objective; used to set original production standards	Works best through aiming at a specified cost reduction objective; reductions are integrated into original production standards to sustain improvements and provide new challenges
Why?	Extremely large potential for cost reduction because 80% to 90% of a product's lifelong costs are embedded in the product during the design and development stages	Limited potential for reducing cost of existing products, but may provide useful information for future target costing efforts
Focus?	All product inputs (material, labor, and overhead elements) as well as production processes and supplier components	Depends on where efforts will be most effective in reducing production costs; generally begins with the most costly component and (in the more mature companies) ends with overhead components

management, accounting, and marketing) in recognition of the product quality and cost desired. Suppliers also may participate in the design phase by making suggestions for modifications that would allow regularly stocked components to be used rather than more costly special-order items.

Properly designed products should require only minimal engineering changes after being released to production. Each time an engineering change is made, one or more of the following problems can occur and create additional costs: production documents must be reprinted; workers must relearn tasks; machine setups must be changed; and parts in stock or currently ordered may be made obsolete. If costs are to be affected significantly, any design changes must be made early in the process—preferably before production begins.

Using target costing requires a shift in the way managers think about the relationships among cost, selling price, and profitability. The traditional attitude has been that a product is developed, production cost is identified and measured, a selling price is set (or a market price is met), and profits or losses result. In target costing, a product is developed, a selling price and desired profit amount are determined, and maximum allowable costs are calculated. When costs rely on selling prices, all costs must be justified. Unnecessary costs should be eliminated without reducing quality.

substitute good

During the product introduction stage, costs can be substantial and are typically related to engineering changes, market research, advertising, and promotion. Sales are usually low and prices are often set in relationship to the market price of similar or **substitute goods** if such goods are available.

The growth stage begins when the product has been accepted by the market and begins to show increased sales. Product quality also may improve during this life-cycle stage, especially if competitors have improved on original production designs. Prices are fairly stable during the growth stage because many substitutes exist or because consumers have become "attached" to the product and are willing to pay a particular price for it rather than buy a substitute.

In the maturity stage, sales begin to stabilize or slowly decline and firms often compete on the basis of selling price. Costs may be at their lowest level during this period, so profits may be high. Some products remain at this stage for a very long time.

The decline stage reflects waning sales. Prices may be cut dramatically to stimulate business. Production cost per unit generally increases during this stage because fixed overhead is spread over a smaller production volume.

LIFE-CYCLE COSTING

Customers are concerned with obtaining a quality product or service for a perceived "reasonable" price. In making such a determination, the consumer views the product from a life-cycle perspective. When purchasing a car, one would investigate not only the original purchase price but also the cost of operation, cost of maintenance, length of warranty period, frequency and cost of repairs not covered by warranty, and projected obsolescence period.

From a manufacturing standpoint, because product selling prices and sales volumes change over a product's life cycle, target costing requires that profitability be viewed on a long-range rather than a period-by-period basis. Thus, producers of goods and providers of services should be concerned about planning to maximize profits over a product or service's life cycle. Therefore, revenues must be generated in excess of total (not just the current period) costs for a product to be profitable.

For financial statement purposes, costs incurred during the development stage must be expensed in the period. However, the research and development (R&D) costs that result in marketable products represent a life-cycle investment rather than a period expense. Capitalization and product allocation of such costs for managerial purposes would provide better long-range profitability information and a means by which to determine the cost impact of engineering changes on product design and manufacturing process. Thus, companies desiring to focus on life-cycle costs and profitability will need to change their internal accounting treatments of costs.

life-cycle costing

Life-cycle costing is the "accumulation of costs for activities that occur over the entire life cycle of a product, from inception to abandonment by the manufacturer and consumer."[12] Manufacturers would base life-cycle costing expense allocations on an expected number of units to be sold over the product's life. Each period's internal income statement using life-cycle costing would show revenues on a life-to-date basis. This revenue amount would be reduced by total cost of goods sold, total R&D project costs, and total distribution and other marketing costs. If life-cycle costing were to be used externally, only annual sales and cost of goods sold would be presented in periodic financial statements. But all preproduction costs would be capitalized, and a risk reserve could be established "to measure the probability that these deferred product costs will be recovered through related product sales."[13] The risk reserve is a contra asset offsetting the capitalized preproduction costs. This contra asset represents the estimated portion of the preproduction costs expected to be unrecoverable through future related product sales.

Life-cycle costing is especially important in industries that face rapid technological or style changes. If substantial money is spent on development, but technology improves faster or customer demand diminishes more rapidly than that money can be recouped from total product sales, was the development investment worthwhile? Periodic external financial statements may make a product appear to be worthwhile because its development costs were initially expensed. But, in total, the company may not even have recovered its original investment. Thus, over the product or service life cycle, companies need to be aware of and attempt to control the total costs of making a product or providing a service. One way of creating awareness is to evaluate all activities related to a product or service as value-added or non-value-added at relatively frequent intervals.

Just-in-Time Systems

6

What is the just-in-time philosophy and how does it affect production and accounting?

just-in-time

Just-in-time (JIT) is a philosophy about when to do something. The "when" is as needed and the "something" is a production, purchasing, or delivery activity. The JIT philosophy is applicable in all departments of all types of organizations. JIT's three primary goals are as follows:

1. elimination of any production process or operation that does not add value to the product/service,
2. continuous improvement in production/performance efficiency, and
3. reduction in the total cost of production/performance while increasing quality.

These goals are totally consistent with and supportive of the total quality management program discussed in Chapter 8. The elements of the JIT philosophy are outlined on the next page in Exhibit 16–8.

kanban
just-in-time manufacturing system

Because JIT is most commonly discussed with regard to manufacturing or production activities, this is a logical starting point. Just-in-time manufacturing originated in Japan where a card, or **kanban** (pronounced "kahn-bahn"), was used to indicate a work center's need for additional components. A **just-in-time manufacturing system** attempts to acquire components and produce inventory units only as they are needed, minimize product defects, and reduce cycle/setup times for acquisition and production.

[12] Callie Berliner and James A. Brimson (eds.), *Cost Management for Today's Advanced Manufacturing* (Boston: Harvard Business School Press, 1988), p. 241.
[13] Dennis E. Peavy, "It's Time for a Change," *Management Accounting* (February 1990), p. 34.

EXHIBIT 16–8

Elements of a JIT Philosophy

- Quality is essential at all times; work to eliminate defects and scrap.
- Employees often have the best knowledge of ways to improve operations; listen to them.
- Employees generally have more talents than are being used; train them to be multiskilled and increase their productivity.
- Ways to improve operations are always available; constantly look for them, being certain to make fundamental changes rather than superficial ones.
- Creative thinking doesn't cost anything; use it to find ways to reduce costs before making expenditures for additional resources.
- Suppliers are essential to operations; establish and cultivate good relationships with suppliers and use, if possible, long-term contracts.
- Inventory is an asset that generates no revenue while it is held in stock. Thus, it can be viewed as a "liability"; eliminate it to the extent possible.
- Storage space is directly related to inventories; eliminate it in response to the elimination of inventories.
- Long cycle times cause inventory buildup; keep cycle times as short as possible by using frequent deliveries.

Production has traditionally been dictated by the need to smooth operating activities over a period of time. Although allowing a company to maintain a steady workforce and continuous machine utilization, smooth production often creates products that must be stored until future sales arise. In addition, although smooth production works well with the economic order quantity (EOQ) concept (see the Appendix to this chapter for a discussion of EOQ), managers recognize that EOQ is based on estimates and therefore a stock of parts is maintained until they are needed. Traditionally, companies filled warehouses with products that were not currently in demand, while often failing to meet promised customer delivery dates. One cause of this dysfunctional behavior was management preoccupation with spreading overhead over a maximum number of products being produced. This obsession unwittingly resulted in much unwanted inventory, huge inventory carrying costs, and other operations problems to be discussed subsequently.

Thus, raw material and work in process inventories historically were maintained at levels considered sufficient to cover up inefficiencies in acquisition and/or production. Exhibit 16–9 depicts these inefficiencies or problems as "rocks" in a stream of "water" that represents inventory. The traditional philosophy is that the water level should be kept high enough for the rocks to be so deeply submerged that there will be "smooth sailing" in production activity. This technique is intended to avoid the original problems, but in fact, it creates a new one. By covering up the problems, the excess "water" adds to the difficulty of making corrections. The JIT manufacturing philosophy is to lower the water level, expose the rocks, and eliminate them to the extent possible. The shallower stream will then flow more smoothly and rapidly than the deep river.

CHANGES NEEDED TO IMPLEMENT JIT MANUFACTURING

Implementation of a just-in-time system in a manufacturing firm does not occur overnight. It took Toyota over 20 years to develop the system and realize significant benefits from it. But JIT techniques are becoming better known and more easily implemented and it is now possible for a company to have a system in place and be recognizing benefits in a fairly short time.

In a world where managers work diligently to produce improvements of a percentage point or two, some numbers just do not look real. One success story among many involves Johnson Control's Automotive Systems Group, which successfully adopted just-in-time manufacturing, with its Lexington, Tennessee, plant achieving 100 percent on-time delivery for three years, during which sales rose 55 percent.

http://www.toyota.com
http://www.johnson controls.com

> *The key to Johnson Controls JIT program is process standardization. John Rog, purchasing manager of supplier manufacturing development at JCI, says*

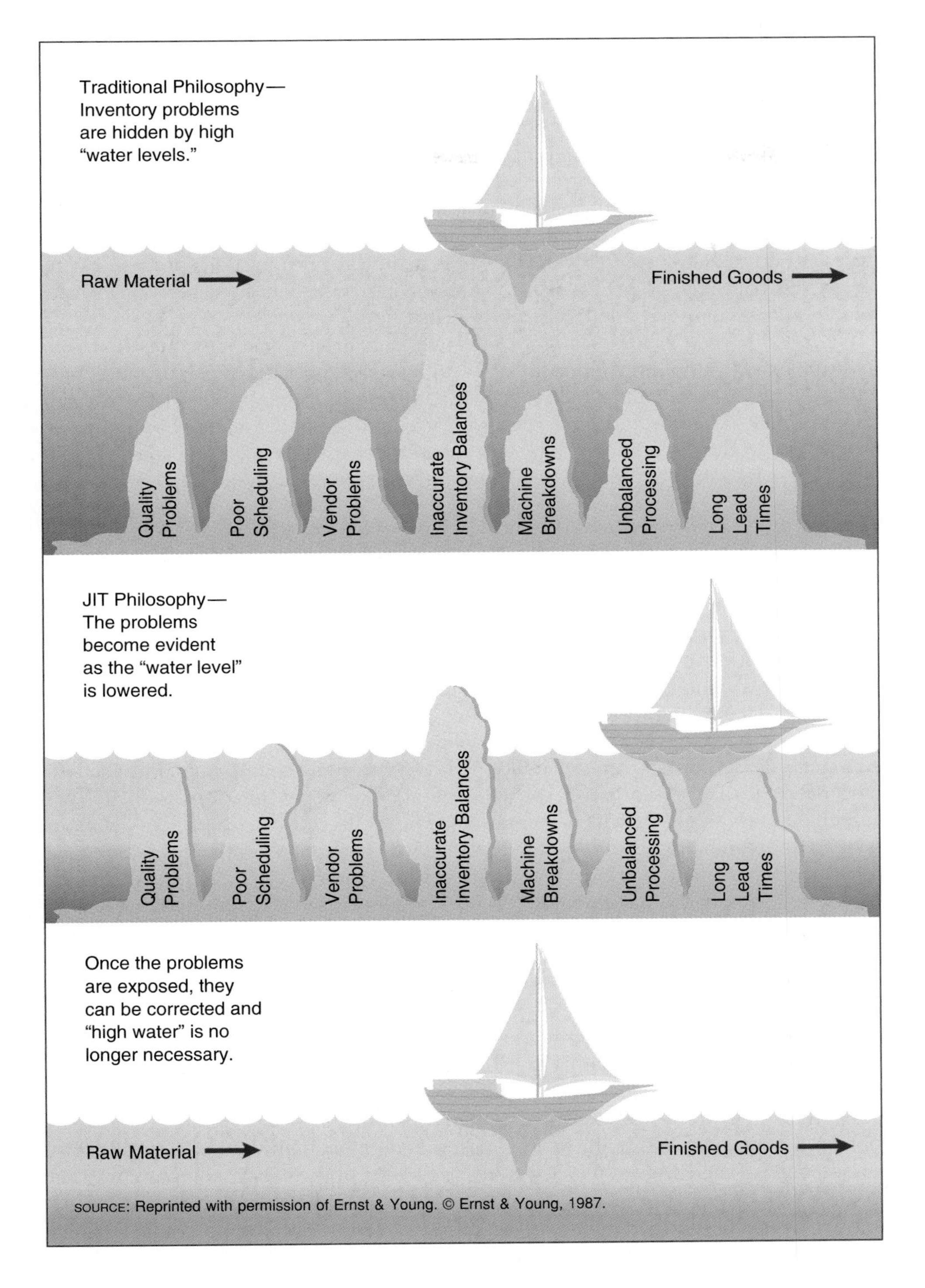

SOURCE: Reprinted with permission of Ernst & Young. © Ernst & Young, 1987.

EXHIBIT 16–9

Depiction of Traditional and JIT Production Philosophies

that all their plants rely heavily on such Toyota-inspired strategies as visual management, kanban, and poka-yoke. JCI has also adopted the Japanese idea of the "five S's," namely, sort, stability, shine, standardize, and sustain, which intend to bring order and uniformity to the plant floor. Finally, JCI has created a training program to help its supply base enforce JIT, kaizen, lean manufacturing, and other manufacturing strategies.[14]

[14] Tim Minahan, "JIT Moves Up the Supply Chain," *Purchasing* (September 1, 1998), pp. 46ff.

The most impressive benefits from JIT, though, are normally reached only after the system has been operational for 5 to 10 years. JIT is not easy and takes time and perseverance. Further, JIT must have strong backing and resource commitment from top management. Without these ingredients, considerable retraining, and support from all levels of company personnel, implementation of JIT will not succeed.

JIT and activity-based management (ABM) are similar because they are both aimed at reducing operating and producing costs and the time, space, and energy necessary for effective and efficient operations and production. Both processes center on the planning, control, and problem solving of activities. Also, both include quality and continuous improvement as prime considerations.

For just-in-time production to be effective, certain modifications must be made in purchasing, supplier relationships, distribution, product design, product processing, and plant layout. JIT depends on employees and suppliers being able to compress the time, distance, resources, and activities, and to enhance interactions needed to produce a company's products and services. The methods currently being used successfully by many companies are discussed next.

Purchasing Considerations When applying JIT to purchasing, managers must first recognize that the lowest quoted purchase price is not necessarily the lowest cost. Suppliers should be screened to systematically consider other factors. If other costs such as the failure costs of poor quality (machine downtime, labor idle time, rework, and scrap) are considered, the lowest price could become the most expensive. Additionally, the vendor willing to quote the lowest price may not be willing to make frequent small-quantity deliveries, sign a long-term contract, or form a strategic alliance with the JIT firm.

Long-term contracts are negotiated with suppliers, and continuance of those contracts is based on delivery reliability. Vendors missing a certain number of scheduled deliveries by more than a specified number of hours are dismissed. Vendor agreements are made in which components are delivered "ready for use" without packaging, eliminating the need for the JIT manufacturer to unpack components; other agreements may specify that goods will be received from suppliers in modular form, so that less subassembly work is required in the assembly plant.

Suppliers may be requested to bar code raw material sent to a JIT company so that inventory management techniques are improved. Bar coding allows raw material inventory records to be updated more quickly, raw material received to be processed more precisely, work in process to be tracked more closely, and finished goods shipments to be quickly made—all with incredible accuracy.

http://www.ab.com

Although bar codes on purchased goods will improve recordkeeping and inventory management, even that would not be necessary if the ideal JIT purchase quantity of one unit could be implemented. Such a quantity is typically not a feasible ordering level, although Allen-Bradley and other highly automated, flexible manufacturers can produce in such a lot size. Thus, the closer a company can get to a lot size of one, the more effective the JIT system is. This reduction in ordering levels means more frequent orders and deliveries. Some automobile companies, for example, have some deliveries made every two hours! Thus, vendors chosen by the company should be located close to the company to minimize both shipping costs and delivery time. The ability to obtain suppliers close to the plant is easy in a country the size of Japan. Such an objective is not as readily accomplished in the United States where a plant can be located in New Jersey and a critical parts vendor in California. However, air express companies help to make just-in-time more practical.

Vendor Certification The optimal JIT situation would be to have only one vendor for any given item. Such an ideal, however, creates the risk of not having alternative sources (especially for critical parts) in the event of vendor business failure, production strikes, unfair pricing, or shipment delays. Thus, it is often more feasible and realistic to limit the number of vendors to a few that are selected and company certified as to quality and reliability. The company then enters into long-term relationships with these suppliers, who become "partners" in the process. Vendor certification is becoming more and more popular. For example, Allen-Bradley, a world-class electronics manufacturer, has been named the preferred automation controls supplier to Ford's Automotive Components Group network of more than 30 manufacturing plants worldwide.

http://www.fordvehicles.com

Vendor certification requires substantial efforts on the purchasing company's part, such as obtaining information on the supplier's operating philosophy, costs, product quality, and service. People from various areas must decide on the factors by which the vendor will be rated; these factors are then weighted as to relative importance. Rapid feedback should be given to potential suppliers so that they can, if necessary, make changes prior to the start of the relationship or, alternatively, to understand why the relationship will not occur.

Factors commonly considered include supplier reliability and responsiveness, delivery performance, ability to service, ability of vendor personnel, research and development strength of supplier, and production capacity of supplier. Evaluations of new and infrequent vendors are more difficult because of the lack of experience by which the purchasing company vendor analysis team can make informed judgments.

Forming partnerships with fewer vendors on a long-term basis provides the opportunity to continuously improve quality and substantially reduce costs. Such partnerships are formal agreements in which both the vendor and the buying organization commit to specific responsibilities to each other for their mutual benefit. These agreements usually involve long-term purchasing arrangements according to specified terms and may provide for the mutual sharing of expertise and information. Such partnerships permit members of the supply chain to eliminate redundancies in warehousing, packaging, labeling, transportation, and inventories.

Product Design Products need to be designed to use the fewest number of parts, and parts should be standardized to the greatest extent possible. For example, at Harley-Davidson, engines and their components were traditionally designed without regard for manufacturing efficiency. Harley was making two similar crankpins, one with an oil hole drilled at a 45-degree angle, and the other at a 48-degree angle. (A crankpin is a cylindrical bar that attaches a connecting rod to a crank in an engine.) Repositioning the machines to make these different crankpins required about two hours. Engineers designed a common angle on both parts and common tools for drilling the holes, which cut changeover time for that process to three minutes.[15]

http://www.harley-davidson.com/home.asp

Another company discovered that it used 29 different types of screws to manufacture a single product. Downtime was excessive because screwdrivers were continuously being passed among workers. Changing to all of the same type screws significantly reduced production time.

Parts standardization does not have to result in identical finished products. Many companies (such as Ford Motor Company) are finding that they can produce a great number of variations in finished products from just a few basic models. Many of the variations can be made toward the end of the production process so that the vast proportion of parts and tasks are standardized and are added before the latter stages of production when the variations take place. Such differentiation can be substantially aided by flexible manufacturing systems and computer-integrated manufacturing, as discussed later in this chapter.

Products should be designed for the quality desired and should require only a minimal number of engineering changes after the design is released for production. Approximately 80 to 90 percent of all product costs are established when the

[15] John Van, "Leaks No Longer Stain Harley-Davidson Name," *Chicago Tribune* (November 4, 1991), Sec. 1, p. 6.

product design reached by the production team is only 25 to 50 percent complete. An effective arrangement for a vendor–purchaser partnership is to have the vendor's engineers participate in the design phase of the purchasing company's product; an alternative is to provide product specifications and allow the vendor company to draft the design for approval.

If costs are to be significantly affected, any design changes must be made early in the process. When an engineering change is made, one or more of the following activities occurs, creating additional costs: The operations flow document must be prepared again; workers must learn new tasks; machine dies or setups must be altered; and parts currently ordered or in stock may be made obsolete. Regardless of whether a company embraces JIT, time that is spent doing work that adds no value to the production process should be viewed as wasted. Effective activity analysis eliminates such non-value-added work and its unnecessary cost.

From another point of view, good product design should address all concerns of the intended consumers, even the degree of recyclability of the product. For example, an automobile plant may be equipped to receive and take apart used-up models, remanufacture various parts, and then send them back into the marketplace. Thus, companies are considering remanufacturing as part of their design and processing capabilities.

Product Processing In the production processing stage, one primary JIT consideration is reduction of machine setup time. Reduction of setup time allows processing to shift between products more often and at a lower cost. The costs of reducing setup time are more than recovered by the savings derived from reducing downtime, WIP inventory, and material handling as well as increasing safety, flexibility, and ease of operation.

Most companies implementing rapid tool-setting procedures have been able to obtain setup times of 10 minutes or less. Such companies use a large number of low-cost setups rather than the traditional processing approach of a small number of more expensive setups. Under JIT, setup cost is considered almost purely variable rather than fixed, as it was in the traditional manufacturing environment. One way to reduce machine setup time is to have workers perform as many setup tasks as possible while the machine is on line and running. All unnecessary movements by workers or of material should be eliminated. Teams similar to pit-stop crews at auto races can be used to perform setup operations, with each team member handling a specialized task. Based on past results, it appears that with planning and education, setup times can be reduced by 50 percent or more.

Another essential part of product processing is the institution of high-quality standards because JIT has the goal of zero defects. Under just-in-time systems, quality is determined on a continual basis rather than at quality control checkpoints. Continuous quality is achieved by first ensuring vendor quality at point of purchase. Workers and machines (such as optical scanners or chutes for size dimensions) are used to monitor quality while production is in process. Controlling quality on an ongoing basis can significantly reduce the costs of obtaining good quality. The JIT philosophy recognizes that it is less costly not to make mistakes than to correct them after they are made. Unfortunately, as mentioned in Chapters 8 and 10, quality control costs and costs of scrap are frequently buried in the standard cost of production, making such costs hard to ascertain.

Standardizing work is an important aspect of any process. This means that every worker conducts work according to standard procedures, without variation, on time, every time. Such standard procedures are devised to produce the most efficient way to conduct the tasks to which they relate. Planning, supervising, and training are more efficiently and effectively conducted when work has been standardized. Standard work also provides the ability to improve processes. As Dr. W. Edwards Deming so aptly demonstrated during his many courses on TQM, it is nearly impossible to improve an unstable process because there is too much variation in it to ascribe cause and effect to modifications that might be made.

Plant Layout Traditionally, manufacturing plants were designed in conformity with functional areas, and machines of like type and workers of specialized skills were placed together. For a JIT system to work effectively, the physical plant must be conducive to the flow of goods and organization of workers and to increasing the value added per square foot of plant space. Manufacturing plants should be designed to minimize material handling time, lead time, and movement of goods from raw material input to completion of the finished product.

This goal often means establishing S-shaped or U-shaped production groupings of workers or machines, commonly referred to as **manufacturing cells**, arranged to address the efficient and effective production processes to make a particular product type. A manufacturing cell is depicted in Exhibit 16–10. This streamlined design allows for more visual controls to be instituted for problems such as excess inventory, production defects, equipment malfunctions, and out-of-place tools. It also allows for greater teamwork and quicker exchange of vital information.

manufacturing cell

The informational arrows show how production is "pulled" through a system as successive downstream work centers issue their kanbans to acquire goods or services needed from their upstream suppliers in order to produce the goods or services demanded by their downstream "customers." Many pull systems today use electronic means such as computer networks to send requests for goods or services to upstream workstations.

Exhibit 16–11 illustrates the flow of three products through a factory before and after the redesign of factory floor space. In the "before" diagram, processes were grouped together by function and products flowed through the plant depending on the type of processing needed to be performed. If the company uses JIT and a cellular design, substantial storage is eliminated because goods should only be ordered as needed. Products also flow through the plant more rapidly. Product 2 can use the same flow as Product 1, but skip the cell's grinding process.

When plant layout is redesigned to incorporate manufacturing cells, an opportunity arises for workers to broaden their skills and deepen their involvement

EXHIBIT 16–10

Depiction of a Manufacturing Cell

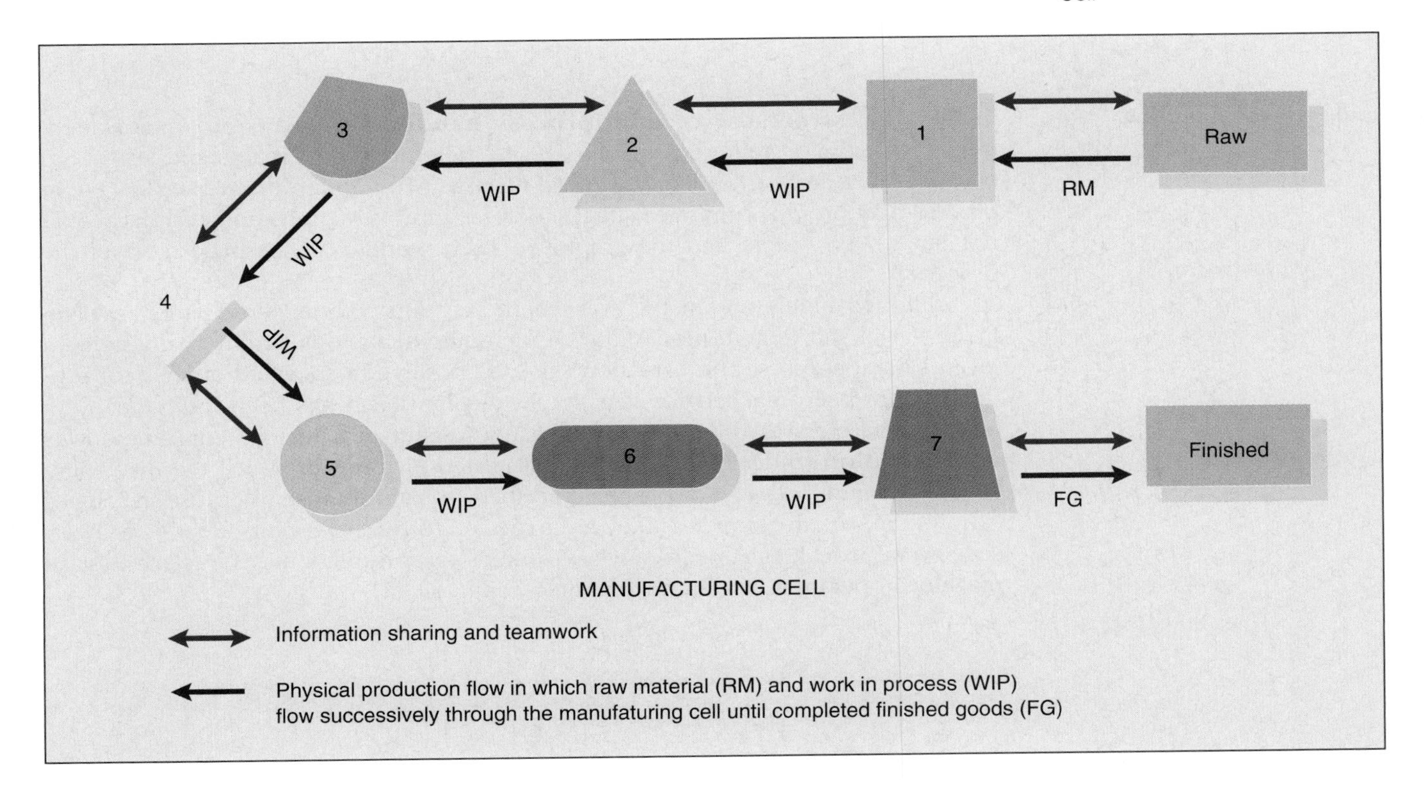

EXHIBIT 16–11

Factory Floor Space Redesign

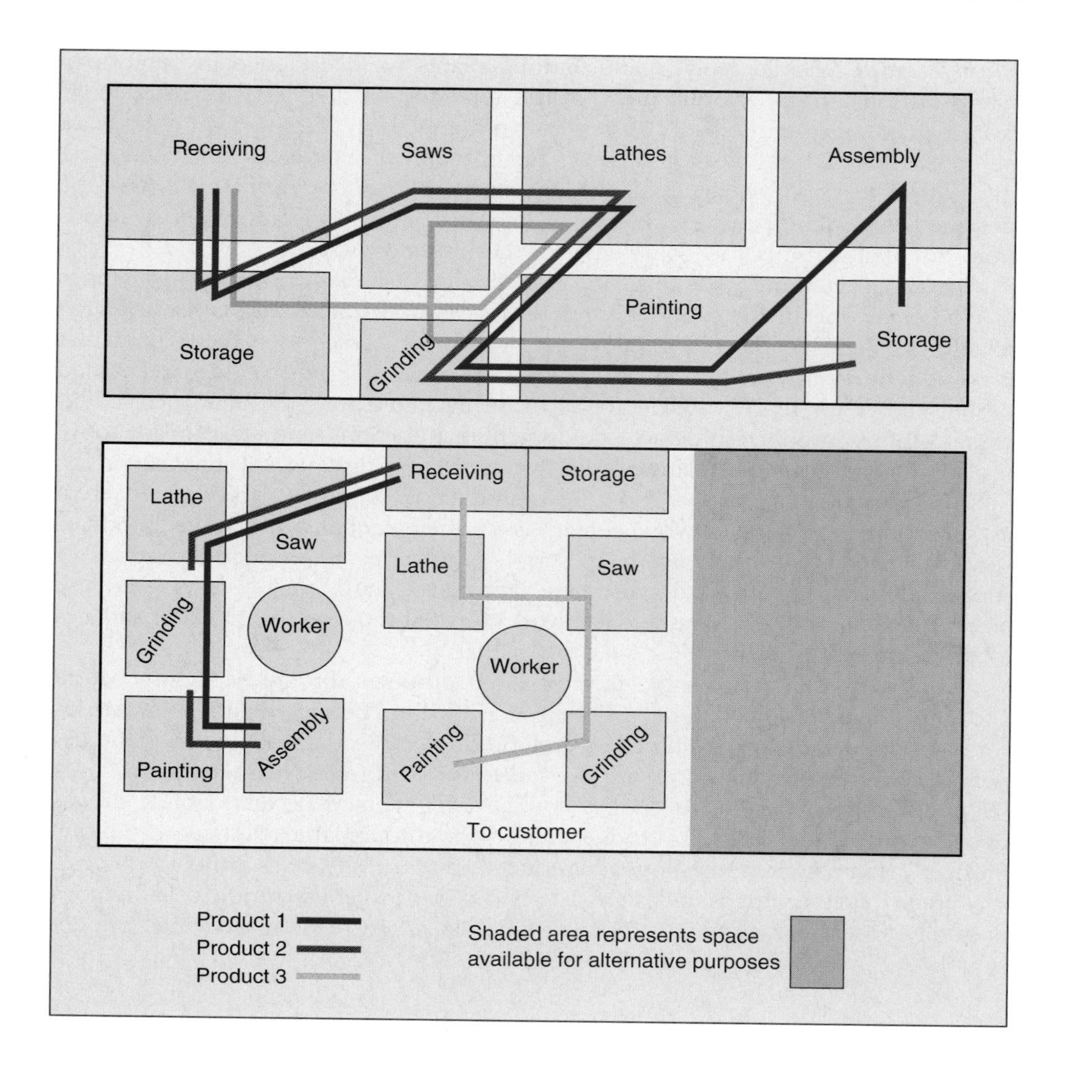

multiprocess handling

in the process because of **multiprocess handling**. Workers are multiskilled, trained to monitor numerous machines, and therefore more flexible and less bored because they are performing a variety of tasks. The ability to oversee an entire process may prompt employee suggestions on improvement techniques that would not have been visible had the employee been working on a single facet of the process.[16]

Although highly automated equipment may run without direct labor involvement, it will still require monitoring. Some equipment stops automatically when a given situation arises. The "situation" may be positive (a specified quantity of production has been reached) or negative (a quality defect has been indicated).

autonomation

Toyota refers to the usage of such equipment in a factory environment as **autonomation** to distinguish it from automated factories in which the machinery is not programmed to stop when specified situations arise. Because machines "know" the certain conditions they are expected to sense, workers are able to oversee several machines concurrently. A worker's responsibility may be to monitor all machines operating in a single manufacturing cell.

[16] The average American company receives about one suggestion per year from every six eligible employees. On the other hand, Japanese companies receive an average of 32 suggestions. [John Tschohl, "Be Bad: Employee Suggestion Program Cuts Costs, Increases Profit," *The Canadian Manager* (Winter 1998), pp. 23–24.]

THE LOGISTICS OF THE JIT ENVIRONMENT

A certain degree of logistical assistance is developing in the JIT environment in the areas of information technology (IT), new support services, and new value-chain relationships. Such advancements can enhance the effectiveness and efficiency of companies employing JIT. These can be viewed in overriding support systems, in the preproduction stage, during production, and after production.

Overriding Support Systems JIT can be employed within the context of more comprehensive management models such as the TQM (discussed in Chapter 8) and six-sigma method. The **six-sigma method** is a high-performance, data-driven approach to analyzing and solving the root causes of business problems. Four steps for a successful application of the six-sigma method follow: first, an initial team determines what the organization knows about its customers and competitors; second, an executive action planning workshop is conducted to develop a vision of how six sigma can assist the organization to achieve its business goals; third, improvement workshops are held to familiarize personnel with methods and strategy and how they will be combined into the unit's business plan to push improved performance; and fourth, team-leader training is conducted for application of just-in-time.[17]

six-sigma method

The **Internet business model** has become the new orthodoxy, and it is transforming cost and service equations across the corporate landscape. It involves (1) few physical assets, (2) little management hierarchy, and (3) a direct pipeline to customers. In this environment, electronic commerce is transforming supply-chain integration and delivering cost savings.[18]

Internet business model

Christopher Gopal, national director of Ernst and Young's supply-chain and operations consulting says:

http://www.ey.com

> *Web-based technology allows the sharing of information, not just one-to-one—but one-to-many—and even many-to-many. . . . It is not simply a case of providing access to a Web site, but creating "extranets" where key customers and suppliers have access to "virtual private networks" that enable collaborative planning, forecasting, and replenishment. It is like traditional one-to-one customer/supplier scheduling, but now it has gone to one-to-many—and the supplier can turn around and do the same thing with all of its suppliers. It is basically linking the entire supply chain.*[19]

Supply-chain management is the cooperative strategic planning, controlling, and problem solving by a company and its vendors and customers to conduct efficient and effective transfers of goods and services within the supply chain. A recent report on supply-chain management by ARM Research Inc., Boston, notes three levels of business-to-business relationships in e-commerce: transactional, information-sharing, and collaboration. The report discusses these as follows:

supply-chain management

> *Transactional relationships include the use of EDI to automate such things as purchase orders and invoices. At the information-sharing level, firms might exchange production schedules or details on the status or orders. At the highest level—collaboration—information is not just exchanged and transmitted, but the buyer and seller also jointly develop it. Generally this information deals with future product plans and needs. . . . However, unlike an information-sharing relationship, information is not shared on an FYI-basis, since either trading partner may change it until both parties agree.*[20]

[17] Jerome A. Blakeslee, Jr., "Implementing the Six Sigma Solution," *Quality Progress* (July 1999), pp. 77ff.
[18] Nuala Moran, "E-Commerce Based Procurement Solutions for the Chemical Industry Eliminating Paper Trail," *Chemical Week* (August 18, 1999), pp. S9ff.
[19] John H. Sheridan, "Pushing Production to New Heights," *Industry Week* (September 21, 1998), pp. 43ff. Reprinted with permission from *Industry Week*. Copyright Penton Media, Inc., Cleveland, Ohio.
[20] Ibid.

Logistical Support in the Preproduction Stage In addition to the IT improvements in product design for manufacturability that will be discussed subsequently, simulation software is available to develop production systems that can enhance financial performance. The benefits of improving processes based on such simulations include greater throughput, reduced inventory levels, and further cost savings from reduced run time and setup time. Analyzing the important interaction and dependence that exist in production systems through software simulation can help answer questions such as these: (1) How many items can the system produce? (2) What will result if the equipment is rearranged? (3) Can delivery dates be met?[21]

A new standard for Open Buying on the Internet (OBI) is being developed by the on-line industry to establish guidelines for information flow between customers and suppliers, methods of communications and security procedures, and the format and content of on-line purchase orders, invoices, and other purchasing documents. The standard is intended to help a manufacturer communicate with all its suppliers in a more uniform and efficient way.[22]

Transportation analysis and arrangements can be enhanced to make the acquisition of materials and parts a more efficient and effective process. This involves the use of computer software and working more closely with material and logistics suppliers to gather essential information to guide decisions to improve transportation.[23]

Logistical Support during Production Companies are replacing the batch processing systems that supported traditional labor-intensive assembly-line production runs with on-line, real-time systems that can monitor and control production. These systems permit computer-controlled robots to move material and perform assembly and other manufacturing tasks.

just-in-time training

Although industry is moving toward automation, humans will not soon be entirely replaced. **Just-in-time training** systems map the skill sets employees need and deliver the training they need just as they need it.[24]

In the near future, workers unfamiliar with some tasks may be able to get just-in-time training whenever and wherever needed. The accompanying News Note describes this worker support.

focused factory arrangement

Focused factory arrangements are often adopted to connect a vendor more closely to a JIT manufacturer's operations. Such an arrangement means that a vendor agrees to provide a limited number of products according to specifications or to perform a limited number of unique services for the JIT company. The supplier may be an internal division of the same organization or an external party. Focused factory arrangements may also involve relocation or plant modernization by the vendor, and financial assistance from the JIT manufacturer may be available to recoup such investments. In addition, the vendor benefits from long-term supply contracts.

Major reliance on a single customer can be difficult, especially for small vendors. A decline in the business of the primary customer or demands for lower prices can be disastrous for the focused factory. To maintain customers, some companies are submitting to vendor certification processes.

Postproduction Logistical Support Real-time information processing software for inventory management of finished goods can better serve the customer, minimize errors, and yield savings in labor, transportation, capital, and carrying costs.[25]

[21] Mike C. Patterson, "A Simulation Analysis of Production Process Improvement," *Journal of Business Education* (November 1998), pp. 87ff.
[22] Mike Bielen, "Commerce on the Information Highway," *Chemical Market Reporter* (July 21, 1997), pp. 16ff.
[23] Peter Bradley, "A New Strategy for Managing Transportation," *Purchasing* (July 13, 1995), pp. 76ff.
[24] Anonymous, "Movement toward JIT Training," *Industry Week* (May 4, 1998), p. 13.
[25] Anonymous, "Improving Productivity and Customer Service: Real Time Intelligent Information Processing Reaps Gains from Warehouse Inventory Management," *Plant* (October 23, 1995), pp. 16–17.

GENERAL BUSINESS

NEWS NOTE

Wearable Computer Gives Workers Just-in-Time Help

Georgia Tech Research Institute (GTRI) researchers have developed a prototype system that integrates job performance support software with wireless communication to create a wearable computer. The hands-free system, called Factory Automation Support Technology (FAST), is designed to support mobile employees while they perform their job functions.

Researchers' challenge in developing the system was to create a lightweight interactive system that is comfortable and does not interfere with vision or hearing. In addition, they had to include a large enough battery to provide the processing power for supporting robust voice recognition. On the software side, noise-canceling microphones and a limited vocabulary for giving commands were used to overcome the high ambient noise in factories.

The development team created both an information database for each application and a prototype delivery system in the form of a wearable computer. The basic FAST hardware comprises:

- a credit card-sized computer worn on a belt that transmits data in real time to other computer systems;
- a visor that is worn like safety glasses that displays information via a miniaturized CRT;
- earphones for listening to auditory information provided by the computer;
- a microphone that enables voice-activated operation of the computer;
- flexible eight-hour battery packs worn on the belt.

The system, which is in its fourth generation, will have increased processing power and a flexible battery belt, which will let an operator work an entire shift without recharging.

SOURCE: Staff, "Wearable Computer Gives Workers Just-in-Time Help," *R&D* (August 1999), p. S-21.

Third-party logistics services involve moving and warehousing finished goods between manufacturer and merchant and sometimes, as in automobile leasing, back to the manufacturer. Outsourcing of these functions to logistics specialists can save the manufacturer time and money.[26]

third-party logistics

ACCOUNTING IMPLICATIONS OF JIT

Companies adopting a just-in-time inventory and/or flexible manufacturing system must be aware of the significant accounting implications such a system creates. A primary accounting impact occurs in variance analysis. Because a traditional standard cost accounting system is primarily historical in nature, its main goal is variance reporting. The reports allow the variances to be analyzed for cause-and-effect relationships to eliminate future similar problems.

Variances under JIT Variance reporting and analysis in JIT systems essentially disappear. Because most variances first appear in a physical (rather than financial) fashion, JIT mandates that variances be recognized on the spot so that causes can be ascertained and, if possible, promptly removed. JIT workers are trained and expected to monitor quality and efficiency continually while production occurs rather than just at the end of production. Furthermore, if the firm is using statistical process controls, workers can predict the impending occurrence of production defects and take measures to prevent them from ever actually occurring. Therefore, the number and monetary significance of end-of-period variances being reported for managerial control should be limited.

[26] Chris Isidore, "Outbound Logistic Expertise Needed," *Journal of Commerce* (October 23, 1995), p. 6A.

Under a JIT system, long-term price agreements have been made with vendors, so material price variances should be minimal. The JIT accounting system should be designed so that purchase orders cannot be cut for an amount greater than the designated price without manager approval.[27] In this way, the variance amount and its cause are known in advance, providing an opportunity to eliminate the excess expenditure before it occurs. Calls can be made to the vendor to negotiate the price, or other vendors can be contacted for quotes.

The ongoing use of specified vendors also provides the ability to control material quality. It is becoming relatively common around the world for companies to require that their vendors maintain quality standards and submit to quality assurance audits. Because better control of raw material quality is expected, little or no material quantity variances should be caused by substandard material. If usage standards are accurate based on established machine-paced efficiency, there should be virtually no favorable usage variance of material during production. Unfavorable use of material should be promptly detected because of ongoing machine and/or human observation of processing. When an unfavorable variance occurs, the manufacturing process is stopped and the error causing the unfavorable material usage is corrected to minimize material quantity variances.

One type of quantity variance is not caused by errors but by engineering changes (ENCs) made to the product specifications. A JIT system has two comparison standards: an annual standard and a current standard. Design modifications would change the current standard, but not the annual one. The annual standard is one of the bases for preparation and execution of the company's master budget and is ordinarily kept intact because all of the financial plans and arrangements for the year covered by the master budget are predicated on the standards and plans used to prepare the master budget.

Such a procedure allows comparisons to be made that indicate the cost effects of engineering changes implemented after a product has begun to be manufactured. A material quantity variance caused by an ENC is illustrated in Exhibit 16–12. In the illustration, the portion of the total quantity variance caused by the engineering change ($10,800 U) is shown separately from that caused by efficiency ($2,160 F). Labor, overhead, and/or conversion can also have ENC variances.

Labor variances in an automated just-in-time system should be minimal if standard rates and times have been set appropriately. Labor time standards should be carefully evaluated after the implementation of a JIT production system. If the plant is not entirely automated, redesigning the physical layout and minimizing any non-value-added labor activities should decrease the direct labor time component.

An accounting alternative that may occur in a JIT system is the use of a "conversion cost" category for purposes of cost control rather than use of separate labor and overhead categories. This category becomes more useful as factories reduce the direct labor cost component through continuous improvements and automation. A standard departmental or manufacturing cell conversion cost per unit of product (or per hour of production time per manufacturing cell) may be calculated rather than individual standards for labor and overhead. Denominators in each case would be practical or theoretical capacity in an appropriate activity.[28] If time were used as the base, the conversion cost for a day's production would be equal to the number of units produced multiplied by the standard number of production hours multiplied by the standard cost per hour. Variances would be determined by comparing actual cost to the designated standard. However, direct labor is a very small part of production in such an environment. Use of efficiency variances to evaluate workers can cause excess inventory because these workers are trying

[27] This same procedure can be implemented under a traditional standard cost system as well as under a JIT system. However, it is less commonly found in a traditional system, but it is a requirement under JIT.

[28] Practical or theoretical capacity is the appropriate measure because the goal of JIT is virtually continuous processing. In a highly automated plant, these capacities more closely reflect world-class status than does expected annual capacity.

Annual standard:	8 feet of material M @ $6.10	$48.80	
	5 feet of material N @ $6.70	33.50	
		$82.30	
Current standard:	7 feet of material M @ $6.10	$42.70	
	6 feet of material N @ $6.70	40.20	
		$82.90	
Production during month:	18,000 units		
Usage during month:	129,600 feet of material M @ $6.10		$ 790,560
	104,400 feet of material N @ $6.70		699,480
	Total cost of material used		$1,490,040

Material quantity variance:	
18,000 × 7 × $6.10	$ 768,600
18,000 × 6 × $6.70	723,600
Material cost at current standard	$1,492,200
Actual material cost	1,490,040
Material quantity variance	$ 2,160F
Engineering change variance for material:	
18,000 × 8 × $6.10	$ 878,400
18,000 × 5 × $6.70	603,000
Material cost at annual standard	$1,481,400
Material cost at current standard	1,492,200
ENC variance	$ 10,800U

EXHIBIT 16–12

Material Variances under a JIT System

to "keep busy" to minimize this variance. Therefore, direct labor efficiency variances in this setting may be counterproductive.

In addition to minimizing and adjusting the variance calculations, a JIT system can have a major impact on inventory accounting. Companies employing JIT production processes would no longer require a separate raw material inventory classification because material would be acquired only when and as production occurs. Instead, JIT companies could use a Raw and In Process (RIP) Inventory account.

Backflush Costing The focus of accounting in a JIT system is on the plant's output to the customer.[29] Because each sequential activity in a production process is dependent on the previous activity, any problems will quickly cause the system to stop the production process. Individual daily accounting for the costs of production will no longer be necessary because all costs should be at standard, and variations will be observed and corrected almost immediately.

Additionally, fewer costs need to be allocated to products because more costs can be traced directly to their related output in a JIT system. Costs are incurred in specified cells on a per-hour or per-unit basis. Energy is a direct production cost in a comprehensive JIT system because there should be a minimum of downtime by machines or unplanned idle time for workers. Virtually the only costs still being allocated are costs associated with the structure (building depreciation, rent, taxes, and insurance) and machinery depreciation. The reduction of allocations provides more useful measures of cost control and performance evaluation than have been traditionally available.

[29] A company may wish to measure output of each manufacturing cell or work center rather than plant output. Such measurements may indicate problems in a given area, but do not correlate with the JIT philosophy of the team approach, plantwide attitude, and total cost picture.

Robotic equipment, such as this welder, can perform tasks much more rapidly and with higher quality than humans often can. This equipment also allows for more rapid changeover time so that multiple products can be produced on the same line.

backflush costing

Backflush costing is a streamlined cost accounting method that speeds up, simplifies, and minimizes accounting effort in an environment that minimizes inventory balances, requires few allocations, uses standard costs, and has minimal variances from standard. During the period, this costing method records purchases of raw material and accumulates actual conversion costs. Then, at a predetermined trigger point such as (1) at completion of production or (2) on the sale of goods, an entry is made to allocate the total costs incurred to Cost of Goods Sold and to Finished Goods Inventory using standard production costs.

Molly Memories is a company that makes dolls and is used to illustrate just-in-time system backflush entries. The entries related to one of Molly Memories' products are presented in Exhibit 16–13 to establish a foundation set of transactions from which to illustrate subsequent alternative recordings in a backflush costing system. The product's standard production cost is $130.50. The company has a long-term contract with its direct material supplier for raw material at $38.50 per unit, so there is no material price variance on purchase. Beginning inventories for July are assumed to be zero. Standard conversion cost per unit is $92.00.

The following selected T-accounts summarize the activity presented in Exhibit 16–13.

Raw and In Process Inventory

	Debit		Credit
(1)	785,000	(4)	2,610,000
(3)	1,840,000		
Bal.	15,000		

Conversion Costs

	Debit		Credit
(2)	1,843,500	(3)	1,840,000

Finished Goods Inventory

	Debit		Credit
(4)	2,610,000	(5)	2,583,900
Bal.	26,100		

Cost of Goods Sold

	Debit		Credit
(5)	2,583,900		

Accounts Receivable

	Debit		Credit
(5)	4,455,000		

Sales

	Debit		Credit
		(5)	4,455,000

EXHIBIT 16–13

Basic Entries Used to Illustrate Backflush Costing

Molly Memories standard production cost per unit:

Direct material	$ 38.50
Conversion	92.00
Total cost	$130.50

No beginning inventories exist.

	Debit	Credit
(1) Purchased $765,000 of direct material in July:		
Raw and In Process Inventory	785,000	
Accounts Payable		785,000
Purchased material at standard cost under a long-term agreement with supplier.		
(2) Incurred $1,843,500 of conversion costs in July:		
Conversion Costs	1,843,500	
Various accounts		1,843,500
Recorded conversion costs; various accounts include Wages Payable for direct and indirect labor, Accumulated Depreciation, Supplies, etc.		
(3) Applied conversion costs to RIP for 20,000 units completed:		
Raw and In Process Inventory (20,000 × $92.00)	1,840,000	
Conversion Costs		1,840,000
(4) Transferred 20,000 units of production in July:		
Finished Goods Inventory (20,000 × $130.50)	2,610,000	
Raw and In Process Inventory		2,610,000
(5) Sold 19,800 units on account in July for $225 each:		
Accounts Receivable (19,800 × $225)	4,455,000	
Sales		4,455,000
Cost of Goods Sold (19,800 × $130.50)	2,583,900	
Finished Goods Inventory		2,583,900

Ending Inventories:

Raw and In Process Inventory ($2,625,000 − $2,610,000)	$15,000
Finished Goods Inventory ($2,610,000 − $2,583,900)	$26,100

In addition, there are underapplied conversion costs of $3,500 ($1,843,500 − $1,840,000).

Four alternatives are given below to the entries presented in Exhibit 16–13. First, if production time were extremely short, Molly Memories might not journalize raw material purchases until completion of production. In that case, the entry [in addition to recording entries (2) and (5) in Exhibit 16–13] to replace entries (1), (3), and (4) follows. Completion of the finished goods is the trigger point for this entry.

	Debit	Credit
Raw and In Process Inventory	15,000	
Finished Goods Inventory (20,000 × $130.50)	2,610,000	
Accounts Payable		785,000
Conversion Costs (20,000 × $92.00)		1,840,000

If goods were shipped immediately to customers on completion, Molly Memories could use a second alternative in which the entries to complete and sell would be combined. It would replace entries (3), (4), and the first element in (5) in Exhibit 16–13. Entries (1), (2), and the second element in (5) in Exhibit 16–13 would still be needed. Sale of the products is the trigger point for this entry.

	Debit	Credit
Finished Goods Inventory (200 × $130.50)	26,100	
Cost of Goods Sold (19,800 × $130.50)	2,583,900	
Raw and In Process Inventory (20,000 × $38.50)		770,000
Conversion Costs (20,000 × $92.00)		1,840,000

The third alternative reflects the ultimate JIT system, in which only one entry [other than recording entry (2) in Exhibit 16–13] is made. Sale of the products is the trigger point for this entry. For Molly Memories, this entry would be

Raw and In Process Inventory (minimal overpurchases)	15,000	
Finished Goods Inventory (minimal overproduction)	26,100	
Cost of Goods Sold	2,583,900	
Accounts Payable		785,000
Conversion Costs		1,840,000

A fourth alternative charges all costs to the Cost of Goods Sold account, with a subsequent backflush of costs to the Raw and In Process Inventory and the Finished Goods Inventory accounts at the end of the period. The following entries replace entries (1), (3), (4), and (5) shown in Exhibit 16–13. Entry (2) in Exhibit 16–13 would still be made.

Cost of Goods Sold	2,625,000	
Accounts Payable		785,000
Conversion Costs		1,840,000

Sale of the products is the trigger point for the following entry.

Raw and In Process Inventory	15,000	
Finished Goods Inventory	26,100	
Cost of Goods Sold		41,100

Implementation of the just-in-time philosophy can cause significant cost reductions and productivity improvements. But, even within a single company, all inventory situations do not necessarily have to be on a just-in-time system. The costs and benefits of any inventory control system must be evaluated before management should consider installing the system. The use of JIT, however, does allow workers as well as managers to concentrate on providing quality service to customers.

JIT IN NONMANUFACTURING SITUATIONS

Although a JIT manufacturing system can be adopted only by a company actually producing a product, nonmanufacturers can employ other just-in-time systems. An all-encompassing view of JIT covers a variety of policies and programs that are implemented to continuously improve the use of company human and mechanical resources. Thus, just-in-time is a type of management control system having a distinct underlying philosophy of which inventory minimization is only one element. In addition to being used by manufacturers, the JIT philosophy can be adopted within the purchasing and delivery departments of any organization involved with inventory, such as retailers, wholesalers, and distributors.

Many of the just-in-time techniques do not require a significant investment in new equipment but depend, instead, on the attitude of company management and the involvement of the organization's people and their willingness to work together and trust one another. People working under a JIT system must be open to change and question established routines and procedures. The company should use all of its employees' talents by empowering its total workforce. Employee empowerment gives the employee authority, resources, support and encouragement to be proactively involved and to continuously seek improvements in the workplace. Creative abilities have sometimes been overlooked or neglected.

JIT emphasizes that there is always room for workplace improvement, whether in floor space design, training and education, equipment and technology, vendor relationships, or any one of many other items. Managers and employees should be continuously alert to the possibilities for lowering costs while increasing quality and service. But JIT is more than a cost-cutting endeavor or a matter of reducing personnel; it requires good human resources management. It involves assessing the company's products and processes not only by internal measures but also by continuously comparing them with changing customer needs and requirements and by performance of competitors and organizations identified as "best-in-class." In many respects, JIT really requires management to act with common sense.

DESIGN FOR MANUFACTURABILITY

Design for manufacturability (DFM) is a process that is part of the project management of a new product. DFM is concerned with finding optimal solutions to minimizing product failures and other adversities in the delivery of a new product to customers. Objectives of DFM include optimizing customer satisfaction, cost to the customer of owning and using the product over its life for the customer, and cost, time, effort, and ease of producing and delivering the product to customers.

design for manufacturability

Cross-functional teams seeking advice from customers and assistance from suppliers gather and manipulate information to determine the material, methods, processes and their trade-offs that will best meet their objectives. This process involves activity analysis to minimize the presence of non-value-added activities and to streamline the performance of value-added activities.

Flexible Manufacturing Systems and Computer-Integrated Manufacturing

7

What are flexible manufacturing systems and how do they relate to computer-integrated manufacturing?

Many manufacturers have changed their basic manufacturing philosophy in the past few decades. Causes of change include: (1) automated equipment and a cellular plant layout, (2) computer hardware and software technology, and (3) new manufacturing systems and philosophies such as JIT and activity-based management.

Traditionally, most manufacturing firms employed long production runs to make thousands of identical models of the same products; this process was encouraged by the idea of economies of scale. After each run, the machines would be stopped and a slow and expensive setup would be made for the next massive production run to begin. Now, an entirely new generation of manufacturing known as **flexible manufacturing systems** (FMSs) is being developed.

flexible manufacturing system

An FMS involves a network of robots and material conveyance devices monitored and controlled by computers that allows for rapid production and responsiveness to changes in production needs. Two or more FMSs connected via a host computer and an information networking system are generally referred to as **computer-integrated manufacturing** (CIM). Exhibit 16–14 contrasts the dimensions of a traditional manufacturing system with an FMS. Although an FMS is typically associated with short-volume production runs, many companies (such as Werthan Packaging, Allen-Bradley, and Cummins Engine) have also begun to use CIM for high-volume lines.

computer-integrated manufacturing

http://www.werthan.com
http://www.cummins.com

EXHIBIT 16–14

Comparison of Traditional Manufacturing and FMS

Factor	Traditional Manufacturing	FMS
Product variety	Few	Extensive
Response time to market needs	Slow	Rapid
Worker tasks	Specialized	Diverse
Production runs	Long	Short
Lot sizes	Massive	Small
Performance rewards basis	Individual	Team
Setups	Slow and expensive	Fast and inexpensive
Product life-cycle expectations	Long	Short
Work area control	Centralized	Decentralized
Technology	Labor intensive	Technology intensive
Information requirements	Batch based	On line, real time
Worker knowledge of technology	Low to medium	High

FMSs are used in modular factories and are able to customize output on request for customers. Customization can be accomplished because of the ability to introduce new products quickly, produce in small lot sizes, make rapid machine and tool setups, and communicate and process large amounts of information. Information is transferred through an electronic network to the computers that control the robots performing most of the production activities. The system functions with on-line, real-time production flow control, using fiber optics and local-area networks.

Companies are able to quickly and inexpensively stop producing one item and start producing another. This ability to make quick and inexpensive production changes and to operate at great speed permits a company to build a large assortment of products and thereby offer its customers a wide variety of high-quality products while minimizing product costs. In effect, machines are able to make other machines and can do so with little human intervention. The system can operate in a "lights-out" environment and never tire.

The need for direct labor is diminished in such a technology-intensive environment. The workers in a company employing an FMS must be more highly trained than those working in traditional manufacturing environments. These workers find themselves handling a greater variety of tasks than the narrowly specialized workers of earlier manufacturing eras. Persons with greater authority and responsibility manage the manufacturing cells. This increase in control occurs because production and production scheduling changes happen so rapidly on the shop floor that an FMS relies on immediate decisions by persons who "live there" and have a grasp of the underlying facts and conditions.

http://www.nissan-usa.com/menu_nf.html

The FMS works so fast that moving products along and out of the way of other products is sometimes a problem. Japan's Nissan Motor Company's FMS facility on Kyushu Island replaced the time-honored conveyor belt with a convoy of little yellow intelligent motor-driven dollies that "tote cars at variable speeds down the assembly line sending out a stream of computer-controlled signals to coach both robots and workers along the way."[30]

THEORY OF CONSTRAINTS

8

How can the theory of constraints help in determining production flow?

theory of constraints

constraint

The **theory of constraints** (TOC) can help management reduce cycle time. The theory of constraints indicates that the flow of goods through a production process cannot be at a faster rate than the slowest bottleneck in the process.[31]

Production limitations in a manufacturing environment are caused by human, material, and machine constraints. A **constraint** is anything that confines or limits a person or machine's ability to perform a project or function. Some constraints are not related to speed—they relate to absolute production limits such as availability materials or machine hours. Other constraints are related to speed.

Human constraints can be caused by an inability to understand, react, or perform at some particular rate of speed. These constraints cannot be totally overcome (because humans will never be able to work at the speed of an automated machine), but can be reduced through proper hiring and training. Because the labor content contained in products is declining rapidly as automation increases, constraints caused by machines are often of more concern than human constraints in reducing cycle time.

bottleneck

Machine constraints, also called **bottlenecks**, are points at which the processing levels are sufficiently slow to cause the other processing mechanisms in the network to experience idle time. Bottlenecks cause the processing of an activity

[30] Clay Chandler and Joseph B. White, "It's Hello Dollies at Nissan's New 'Dream Factory'," *The Wall Street Journal* (July 6, 1992), p. 1.

[31] The theory of constraints was introduced to business environments by Eliyahu Goldratt and Jeff Cox in the book *The Goal* (New Haven, Conn.: North River Press, Inc./Spectrum Publishing Company, Inc., 1986).

to be impeded. Even a totally automated, "lights-out" process will have some constraints, because all machines do not operate at the same speed or handle the same capacity. Therefore, the constraints must be identified and worked around.

Exhibit 16–15 provides a simplified illustration of a constraint in a production process. Although Machine 1 can process 90,000 pounds of raw material in an hour, Machine 2 can handle only 40,000 pounds. Of an input of 70,000 pounds, 30,000 pounds of processed material must wait at the constraining machine after an hour of processing. The constraint's effect on production is obvious, but the implications are not quite as clear. Managers have a tendency to want to see machines working, not sitting idle. Consider what this tendency would mean if the desired output were 450,000 pounds rather than 70,000. If Machine 1 were kept in continual use, all 450,000 pounds would be processed through Machine 1 in five hours. However, a backlog of 250,000 pounds [450,000 − 5(40,000)] of processed material would now be waiting in front of Machine 2! All of this material would require storage space and create an additional cost of a non-value-added activity.

Machine constraints also impact quality control. Managers normally choose quality control points to follow the completion of some particular process. When constraint points are known, quality control points should be placed in front of them.

> *Make sure the bottleneck works only on good parts by weeding out the ones that are defective. If you scrap a part before it reaches the bottleneck, all you have lost is a scrapped part. But if you scrap the part after it's passed through the bottleneck, you have lost time that cannot be recovered.*[32]

Once constraints are known, the best use of the time or productive capacity they provide should be made. Subsequently, "after having made the best use of the existing constraints, the next step is to reduce their limitations on the system's performance."[33] Options to reduce limitations, such as adding more machines to perform the constrained activity or processing material through other machines, should be investigated.

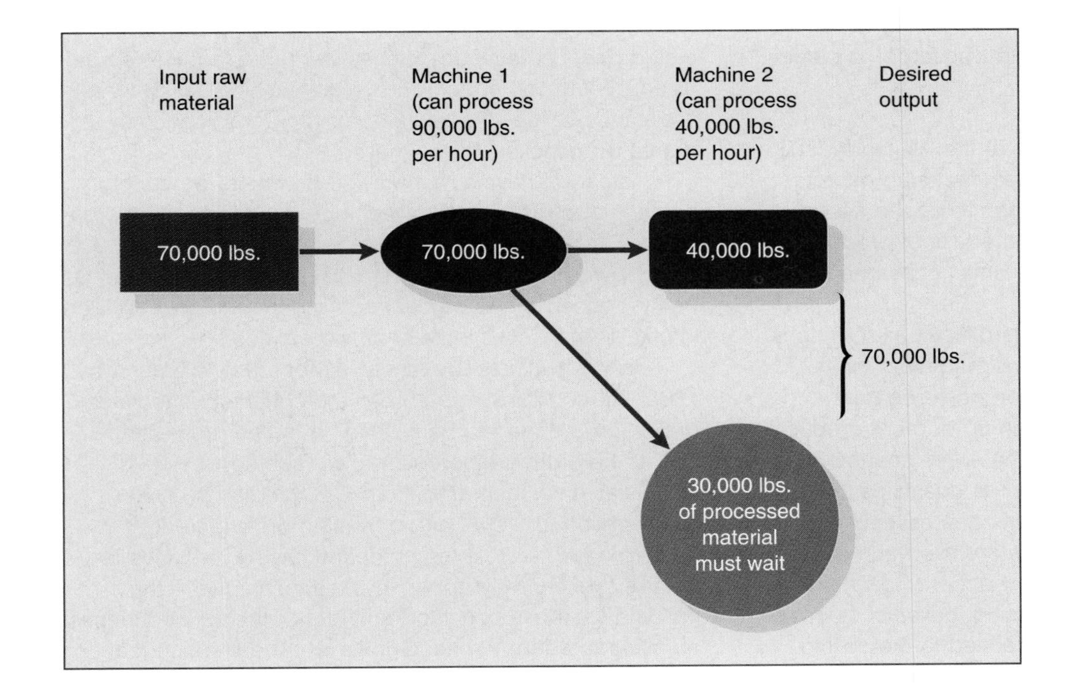

EXHIBIT 16–15

Production Constraint

[32] Ibid., p. 156.
[33] Robert E. Fox, "The Constraint Theory," in *Cost Accounting for the '90s Responding to Technological Change Proceedings* (Montvale, N.J.: National Association of Accountants, 1988), p. 51.

Managing constraints is a process of continuous improvement. After the constraint(s) in the system is (are) identified, and managers have decided how to "exploit" the constraint to avoid wasting constrained resources, better solutions are continually sought. When a constraint becomes difficult to improve, Goldratt suggests the use of what he refers to as the "evaporating clouds" method.[34] Eric Noreen *et al* describe an important step in this process, that involves identifying and challenging assumptions about a constraint, as follows:

http://www.blackanddecker.com
http://www.jj.com
http://www.bain.com

> *The key is to identify the assumptions that lead us to* believe *that a clean solution is not possible. The specific technique used to identify the assumptions underlying the apparent conflict and to break the deadlock is called an "Evaporating Cloud."*[35]

[34] Eliyahu M. Goldratt, *Theory of Constraints* (Great Barrington, Mass.: The North River Press, 1990), pp. 36–38.
[35] Eric Noreen, Debra Smith, and James T. Mackey, *The Theory of Constraints and Its Implications for Management Accounting* (Great Barrington, Mass.: The North River Press, 1995), p. 50.

REVISITING Alexander Doll Co.

http://www.onlinedolls.com/ma/index.htm

A company that's a good candidate for *kaizen,* says William Schartz, TBM vice president, usually displays two key characteristics:

- Long lead times, usually accompanied by a lot of work-in-process inventory; and
- A dedicated and knowledgeable workforce, to participate in problem solving.

This profile reflected conditions at the Alexander Doll Co. before that unusual group of manufacturing experts translated their experience from streamlining the assemblies of fenders and crankshafts to the task of producing wigs, shoes, and all the many other small components that comprise a doll.

Although making a doll is not as difficult as making a Lexus, the endeavor is more rigorous than most might imagine. The costumes contain 20 or more separate items, which may have to go through 30 or more production steps. Because 75 percent of the styles change annually and doll fabric is bought in small quantities that cannot be reordered, accurate planning is essential.

Before TBM arrived, the doll factory used archaic methods: Because it was organized according to old-fashioned principles of batch processing, boxes of costume material and vinyl doll parts were stacked to the ceiling. Since nothing was built to order, more than 90,000 dolls were stored in partly finished condition, and customers waited up to 16 weeks for delivery.

In 1996 when the new CEO, Herbert Brown, a manufacturing expert who had previously run operations for Black & Decker and Johnson & Johnson, tried to fill a customer order for 300 dolls, only 117 could be completed because so many pieces were missing. He reorganized the factory, and in true Toyota fashion, sought the assistance of the 470 workers, mostly Dominican immigrants who spoke limited English.

Instead of having the individual workers producing batches of parts, seven- or eight-person teams were organized. Each team is responsible for completing about 300 dolls or wardrobe assemblies a day. Work in progress has been reduced by 96 percent and orders can now be filled in one or two weeks instead of two months.

Having successfully turned the operations around by 1998, the company was able to switch its focus to sales growth, and engaged Bain & Co., a top-tier consulting firm, to help devise the best growth strategies.

Sales have increased from $23.8 million in 1995 to $31.6 million for 1998, and operating profit increased by $4 million. Workers at the company have an obvious incentive to effectively apply Toyota's techniques—the building itself is a constant reminder of the consequences of failing to adapt to changing times. The first occupant of the building was Studebaker.

SOURCE: Alex Taylor III, "It Worked for Toyota. Can It Work for Toys?" *Fortune* (January 11, 1999), p. 36; and Robert Maynard, "A Company Is Turned Around Through Japanese Principles," *Nation's Business* (February 1996), p. 9.

CHAPTER SUMMARY

Costs associated with inventory can be significant for any company and sound business practices seek to limit the amount of those costs. Inventory costs include the costs of purchasing, ordering, carrying, and not carrying inventory.

A push system of production control is dictated by lead times and order-size requirements preestablished by company personnel. Work centers may buy or produce inventory not currently needed because of these requirements. This excess inventory is stored until it is needed by other work centers. In contrast, a pull system of production control (such as just-in-time manufacturing) involves the purchase and/or production of inventory only as the need arises. Storage is eliminated except for a minimal level of safety stock.

Target costing can be combined with life-cycle costing to determine an allowable product cost based on an estimated selling price and a desired profit margin. Because sales volume, costs, and profits fluctuate over a product's life cycle, these items would need to be estimated over the entire life rather than on a periodic basis to determine a target cost.

The goals of a just-in-time system are to eliminate non-value-added processes, continuously improve efficiency, and reduce costs while increasing quality. The JIT philosophy can be applied to some extent to any company having inventories. JIT requires that purchases be made in small quantities and deliveries be frequent. Production lot sizes are minimized so that many different products can be made on a daily basis. Products are designed for quality and component parts are standardized to the extent possible. Machine setup time is reduced so that production runs can be easily shifted between products. Plant layout emphasizes manufacturing cells, and the operating capabilities of all factory equipment are considered to eliminate the need for or buildup of buffer inventories between operations.

The institution of a JIT system has accounting implications. Variances should be negligible, but their occurrence should be recognized earlier in the process so that causes are found and corrective action taken quickly. Because few raw materials would be stocked (because they are only acquired as needed in production) and work in process time should be short, JIT companies may use a merged raw material and work in process inventory classification. The traditional categories of direct labor and overhead may be combined and accounted for under the single category of conversion cost, and a greater number of costs will be directly traceable to production under a JIT system. Backflush accounting techniques can be used that reduce the number of journal entries currently needed to trace production costs through the process.

Design for manufacturability is a process to help management minimize product failures and other problems in delivering a new product to customers. Information is sought from customers and suppliers to determine the methods, materials, and processes that best meet management objectives.

A special type of just-in-time company is one that engages in flexible manufacturing. Flexible manufacturing systems are so fast and versatile that products can be tailored to customer requests with only an insignificant delay in production time in most instances.

Flexible manufacturing systems involve a network of robots and material conveyance devices monitored and controlled by computers that allows for rapid production and responsiveness to changes in production needs. Two or more FMSs connected by a host computer and an information networking system are referred to as computer-integrated manufacturing.

The theory of constraints indicates that the flow of goods through a production process cannot be at a faster rate than the slowest constraint in the process. Managing constraints is a process of continuous improvement. After a constraint in the system is identified, and managers have decided how to "exploit" the constraint to avoid wasting constraint resources, better solutions are continually sought.

APPENDIX

How are economic order quantity, reorder point, and safety stock determined and used?

economic order quantity

EOQ and Related Issues

Economic Order Quantity

Companies making purchasing (rather than production) decisions often compute the **economic order quantity** (EOQ), which represents the least costly number of units to order. The EOQ indicates the optimal balance between ordering and carrying costs by mathematically equating total ordering costs to total carrying costs. The EOQ is a tool that is used in conjunction with traditional "push" production and inventory management systems. Because EOQ implies acquiring and holding inventory before it is needed, it is incompatible with "pull" systems such as JIT.

Purchasing managers should first determine which supplier could offer the appropriate quality of goods at the best price in the most reliable manner. After the supplier is selected, the most economical inventory quantity to order—at a single time—is determined. The EOQ formula is

$$EOQ = \sqrt{\frac{(2QO)}{C}}$$

where EOQ = economic order quantity in units

Q = estimated annual quantity used in units (can be found in the annual purchases budget)

O = estimated cost of placing one order

C = estimated cost to carry one unit in stock for one year

Note that unit purchase cost is not included in the EOQ formula. Purchase cost relates to the question of from whom to buy, which is considered separately from the question of how many to buy at a single time. Inventory unit purchase cost does not affect the other EOQ formula costs except to the extent that opportunity cost is calculated on the basis of investment.

All inventory-related costs must be evaluated when purchasing or production decisions are made. The costs of ordering and carrying inventory offset each other when estimating the economic order quantity.

Molly Memories uses 80,000 pounds of a particular plastic in producing the Molly Memories' dolls. The cost associated with placing each order is \$12.25. The carrying cost of 1 pound of the plastic is \$1.00 per period. Therefore, Molly Memories' EOQ for this plastic is calculated as follows:

$$EOQ = \sqrt{(2 \times 80{,}000 \times \$12.25) \div \$1.00}$$
$$= 1{,}400 \text{ pounds}$$

Economic Production Run

economic production run

In a manufacturing company, managers are concerned with how many units to produce in a batch in addition to how many units (of raw material) to buy. The EOQ formula can be modified to calculate the appropriate number of units to manufacture in an **economic production run** (EPR). This estimate reflects the production quantity that minimizes the total costs of setting up a production run and carrying a unit in stock for one year. The only change in the EOQ formula is that the terms of the equation are redefined as manufacturing, rather than purchasing, costs. The formula is

$$EPR = \sqrt{\frac{(2QS)}{C}}$$

where EPR = economic production run quantity

Q = estimated annual quantity to be produced in units (can be found in annual production budget)

S = estimated cost of setting up a production run

C = estimated cost to carry one unit in stock for one year

Another product manufactured by Molly Memories is a doll crib. A total of 162,000 units of this product are made each year. The setup cost for a doll crib production run is $40 and the annual carrying cost for each doll crib is $4. The economic production run quantity of 1,800 doll cribs is determined as

$$EPR = \sqrt{(2 \times 162{,}000 \times \$40) \div \$4}$$

The cost differences among various run sizes around the EPR may not be significant. If such costs were insignificant, management would have a range of acceptable, economical production run quantities.

The critical element in using either an EOQ or EPR model is to properly identify costs. Identifying all the relevant inventory costs (especially carrying costs) is very difficult, and some costs (such as those for facilities, operations, administration, and accounting) traditionally viewed as irrelevant fixed costs may, in actuality, be long-term relevant variable costs. The EOQ model also does not provide any direction for managers attempting to control all of the separate costs that collectively comprise purchasing and carrying costs. By only considering the trade-off between ordering and carrying costs, the EOQ model does not lead managers to consider inventory management alternatives that may simultaneously reduce both categories of costs.

Additionally, as companies significantly reduce the necessary setup time (and thus cost) for operations and move toward a "stockless" inventory policy, a more comprehensive cost perspective will indicate a substantially smaller cost per setup and a substantially larger annual carrying cost. If the setup and carrying cost information given for Molly Memories were reversed, the EPR would be only 180 units. Using either a new perspective of variable cost or minimizing setup cost will provide much lower economic order or production run quantities than indicated in the past.

Order Point and Safety Stock

The economic order quantity or production run model indicates how many units to order or produce. But managers are also concerned with the **order point**. This quantity reflects the level of inventory that triggers the placement of an order for additional units. Determination of the order point is based on three factors: usage, lead time, and safety stock. **Usage** refers to the quantity of inventory used or sold each day. The **lead time** for an order is the time in days it takes from the placement of an order to when the goods arrive or are produced. Many times companies can project a constant, average figure for both usage and lead time. The quantity of inventory kept on hand by a company in the event of fluctuating usage or unusual delays in lead time is called **safety stock**.

order point

usage

lead time

safety stock

If usage is entirely constant and lead time is known with certainty, the order point is equal to daily usage multiplied by lead time:

$$\text{Order point} = \text{Daily usage} \times \text{Lead time}$$

As an example, assume that Molly Memories produces rhinestone tiaras for sale to chain department stores. Molly Memories uses 400 rhinestones per day, and the supplier can have the stones to Molly Memories in four days. When the stock of rhinestones reaches 1,600 units, Molly Memories should reorder.

The order point formula minimizes the dollars a company has invested in its inventory. Orders would arrive at precisely the time the inventory reached zero. This formula, however, does not take into consideration unusual events such as variations in production schedules, defective products being provided by suppliers, erratic shipping schedules of the supplier, or late arrival of units shipped. To provide for these kinds of events, managers carry a "buffer" safety stock of inventory to protect the company from stockouts. When a safety stock is maintained, the order point formula becomes:

$$\text{Order point} = (\text{Daily usage} \times \text{Lead time}) + \text{Safety stock}$$

Safety stock size should be determined based on how crucial the item is to production or to the retail business, the item's purchase cost, and the amount of uncertainty related to both usage and lead time.

One way to estimate the quantity of safety stock is to allow one factor to vary from the norm. For example, either excess usage during normal lead time or normal usage during an excess lead time can be considered in the safety stock calculation. Assume that Molly Memories never uses more than 500 rhinestones in one day. One estimate of the necessary safety stock is 400 stones, computed as follows:

Maximum daily usage	500	stones
Normal daily usage	(400)	stones
Excess usage	100	stones
Lead time	× 4	days
Safety stock	400	stones

Using this estimate of safety stock, Molly Memories would reorder rhinestones when 2,000 stones (1,600 original order point + 400 safety stock) were on hand.

Pareto Inventory Analysis

Unit cost commonly affects the degree of control that should be maintained over an inventory item. As unit cost increases, internal controls (such as inventory access) are typically tightened and a perpetual inventory system is more often used. Recognition of cost-benefit relationships may result in a **Pareto inventory analysis**, which separates inventory into three groups based on annual cost-to-volume usage.

Pareto inventory analysis

Items having the highest value are referred to as A items; C items represent the lowest dollar volume usage. All other inventory items are designated as B items. Exhibit 16–16 provides the results of a typical Pareto inventory analysis—20 percent of the inventory items (A items) accounts for 80 percent of the cost; an additional 30 percent of the items (B items), taken together with the first 20 percent (the A items), accounts for 90 percent of the cost; and the remaining 50 percent of the items (C items) accounts for the remaining 10 percent of the cost.

Once inventory is categorized as A, B, or C, management can determine the best inventory control method for items in each category. A-type inventory should require a perpetual inventory system and would be a likely candidate for just-in-time purchasing techniques that minimize the funds tied up in inventory investment. The highest control procedures would be assigned to these items. Such a treatment reflects the financial accounting concept of materiality.

Items falling into the C category may need only periodic inventory procedures and may use a two-bin or red-line system. Under a **two-bin system**, one container (or stack) of inventory is available for production needs. When production

two-bin system

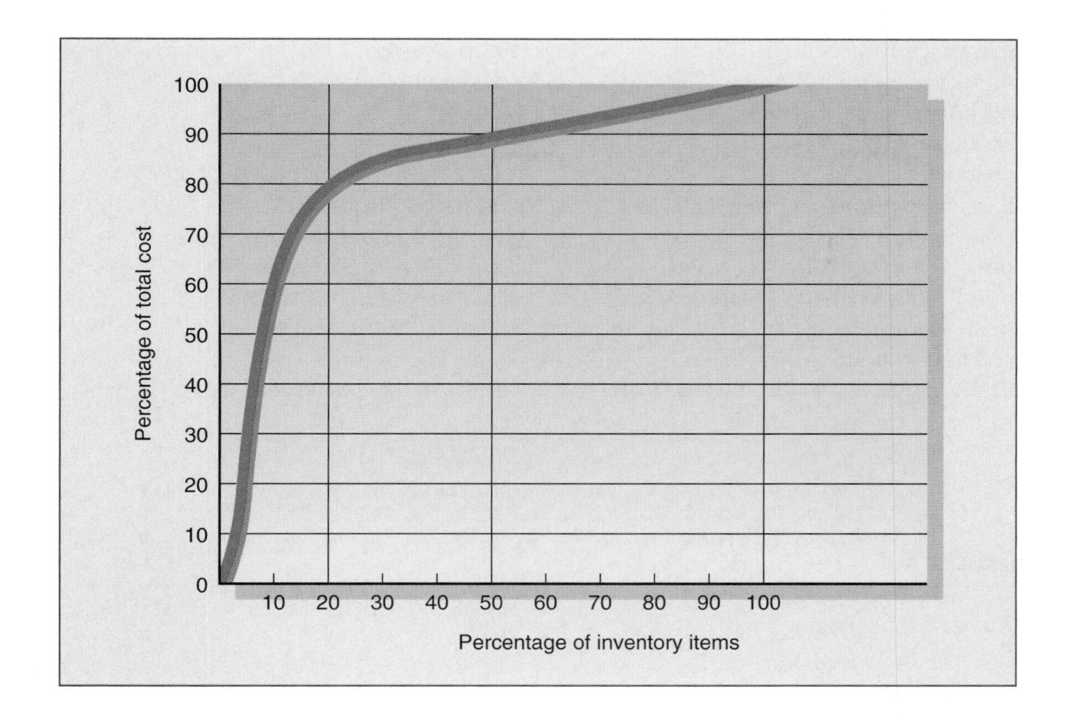

EXHIBIT 16–16

Pareto Inventory Analysis

begins to use materials in the second bin, a purchase order is placed to refill the first bin. In a **red-line system**, a red line is painted on the inventory container at the point at which to reorder. Both systems require that production needs and estimates of receipt time from suppliers be fairly accurate.

red-line system

Having the additional container or stack of inventory on hand is considered to be reasonable based on the insignificant dollar amount of investment involved with C category items. The degree of control placed on C items will probably be minimal because of the lack of materiality of the inventory cost. The type of inventory system (perpetual or periodic) and level of internal controls associated with items in the B category will depend on management's judgment. Such judgment will be based on significance of the item to the production process, quickness of response time of suppliers, and estimates of benefits to be gained by increased accounting or access controls. Computers and bar coding have made additional controls over inventory easier and more cost beneficial.

KEY TERMS

autonomation (p. 730)
backflush costing (p. 736)
bar code (p. 715)
bottleneck (p. 740)
carrying cost (p. 717)
computer-integrated manufacturing (p. 739)
constraint (p. 740)
cost table (p. 719)
design for manufacturability (p. 739)
economic order quantity (p. 744)
economic production run (p. 744)
electronic data interchange (p. 715)
flexible manufacturing system (p. 739)
focused factory arrangement (p. 732)
Internet business model (p. 731)
just-in-time (p. 723)
just-in-time manufacturing system (p. 723)
just-in-time training (p. 732)
kaizen costing (p. 721)
kanban (p. 723)
lead time (p. 745)
life-cycle costing (p. 723)

manufacturing cell (p. 729)
multiprocess handling (p. 730)
open purchase ordering (p. 716)
order point (p. 745)
ordering cost (p. 714)
Pareto inventory analysis (p. 746)
procurement card (p. 716)
pull system (p. 714)
purchasing cost (p. 713)
push system (p. 714)
red-line system (p. 747)
safety stock (p. 745)
setup cost (p. 715)
six-sigma method (p. 731)
stockout (p. 717)
substitute good (p. 722)
supply-chain management (p. 731)
target costing (p. 719)
theory of constraints (p. 740)
third-party logistics (p. 733)
two-bin system (p. 746)
usage (p. 745)
value engineering (p. 720)
vendor-managed inventory (p. 716)

SOLUTION STRATEGIES

Target Costing

Target cost = Expected long-range selling price − Desired profit

Compare predicted total life-cycle cost to target cost; if life-cycle cost is higher, determine ways to reduce life-cycle cost.

Material and Labor Variances under JIT

Two standards may exist:

1. an annual standard (set and held constant for the year) or
2. a current standard (based on design modifications or engineering changes).

Generally firms will have minimal, if any, material price variances because prices are set by long-term contracts. A labor rate variance may exist and would be calculated in the traditional manner.

Material Quantity Variance

  Actual material cost
− Material cost at current standard
  Material quantity variance

Engineering Change Variance for Material

  Material cost at annual standard
− Material cost at current standard
  ENC variance

Labor Efficiency Variance

  (Actual labor hours × current standard rate)
− (Standard labor hours × current standard rate)
  Labor efficiency variance

Engineering Change Variance for Labor

(Would exist only if a change occurred in the mix of labor used to manufacture the product or through the automation of processes.)

  (Standard labor hours × annual standard rate)
− (Standard labor hours × current standard rate)
  ENC variance

Economic Order Quantity

$$EOQ = \sqrt{(2QO) \div C}$$

where EOQ = economic order quantity in units
Q = estimated annual quantity to be used in units
O = estimated cost of placing one order
C = estimated cost to carry one unit in stock for one year

Economic Production Run

$$EPR = \sqrt{(2QS) \div C}$$

where EPR = economic production run quantity
Q = estimated annual quantity to be produced in units
S = estimated cost of setting up a production run
C = estimated cost to carry one unit in stock for one year

Order Point

Order point = (Daily usage × Lead time) + Safety stock

DEMONSTRATION PROBLEM

Free Enterprise Manufacturing Company (FEM) has designed a new doll that is expected to have a five-year life cycle. Based on its market research, management at FEM has determined that the new doll could sell for $175 in the first three years and $100 during the last two years. Unit sales are expected as follows:

Year 1	3,000 units
Year 2	4,500 units
Year 3	4,800 units
Year 4	5,000 units
Year 5	1,500 units

Variable selling costs are expected to be $15 per doll throughout the product's life. Annual fixed selling and administrative costs of $200,000 are expected. FEM desires a 25 percent profit margin on selling price.

Required:

a. Compute the life-cycle target cost to manufacture the product. (Round to the nearest penny.)

b. If FEM anticipates the doll to cost $52 to manufacture in the first year, what is the maximum that manufacturing cost can be in the following four years? (Round to the nearest penny.)

c. Suppose that engineers at FEM determine that expected manufacturing cost per doll is $50. What actions might the company take to reduce this cost?

Solution to the Demonstration Problem

a. Step 1—Determine total product life revenue:

Year 1	3,000 × $175 =	$ 525,000
Year 2	4,500 × $175 =	787,500
Year 3	4,800 × $175 =	840,000
Year 4	5,000 × $100 =	500,000
Year 5	1,500 × $100 =	150,000
Total Revenue		$2,802,500

Step 2—Determine average product life revenue (AR):

$$\begin{aligned}AR &= \text{Total revenue} \div \text{Total product life units}\\ &= \$2{,}802{,}500 \div 18{,}800 \text{ units}\\ &= \underline{\underline{\$149.07}}\end{aligned}$$

Step 3—Determine average total fixed selling and administrative cost (ATFS&A):

$$\begin{aligned}\text{ATFS\&A} &= (5 \text{ years} \times \$200{,}000) \div 18{,}800 \text{ units}\\ &= \underline{\underline{\$53.19}}\end{aligned}$$

Step 4—Determine unit selling and administrative cost (US&AC):

$$\begin{aligned}\text{US\&AC} &= \text{ATFS\&A} + \text{Variable selling cost}\\ &= \$53.19 + \$15\\ &= \underline{\underline{\$68.19}}\end{aligned}$$

Step 5—Calculate target cost (TC):

$$\begin{aligned}TC &= AR - 0.25(AR) - \text{US\&AC}\\ &= \$149.07 - \$37.27 - \$68.19\\ &= \underline{\underline{\$43.61}}\end{aligned}$$

b. Step 1—Determine total allowable cost over product life:

$$18{,}800 \text{ units} \times \$43.61 = \$819{,}868$$

Step 2—Determine expected cost in first year equals unit cost × unit sales:

$$\begin{aligned}&= \$52 \times 3{,}000 \text{ units}\\ &= \underline{\underline{\$156{,}000}}\end{aligned}$$

Step 3—Determine allowable unit cost in last 4 years:

$$(\$819{,}868 - \$156{,}000) \div 15{,}800 \text{ units} = \underline{\underline{\$42.02}}$$

c. The following actions are potential options for the company:

- Product design and/or production processes can be changed to reduce costs. Cost tables may be used that provide information on the impact of using different input resources, processes, or design specifications.
- The 25 percent acceptable profit margin can be reduced.
- FEM can suspend consideration of the project at the present time.

QUESTIONS

1. What are the important relationships in a value chain and how can they be beneficially exploited?

2. What are the three basic costs associated with inventory? Explain each and give examples.
3. What are the differences between push and pull systems of production?
4. What is the relationship between ordering costs and setup costs?
5. How have advances in information technology affected the purchasing function? Give four examples and briefly describe each.
6. What is a stockout? What costs are associated with a stockout?
7. Does the product life-cycle stage have a bearing on production cost management? Explain.
8. What are the five stages in the product life cycle and why is each important?
9. Why do costs, sales, and profits change over the product life cycle?
10. What is target costing and how is it useful in assessing a product's total life-cycle costs?
11. Does target costing require that profitability be viewed on a period-by-period basis or on a long-term basis? Explain.
12. From a marketing standpoint, why can some companies (such as Seiko) introduce products with little or no product research while other companies cannot?
13. Why would a cost table be a valuable tool in designing a new product or service?
14. What is kaizen costing and how does it differ from target costing?
15. Discuss the concept of substitute goods and why these would affect pricing.
16. How would focusing on total life-cycle costs call for a different treatment of research and development costs than is made for financial accounting?
17. What are the primary goals of a JIT philosophy and how does JIT attempt to achieve these goals?
18. What kinds of changes need to occur in a production environment to effectively implement JIT? Why are these changes necessary? Is JIT a push or a pull system?
19. "JIT cannot be implemented as effectively in the United States as it can be in Japan." Discuss the rationale behind this statement.
20. How can the JIT philosophy be used by nonmanufacturers?
21. Describe the production system found in a "lights-out" environment.
22. How would switching from a traditional manufacturing system to a flexible manufacturing system affect a firm's inventory and production control systems?
23. In what areas of accounting can a company implementing a JIT manufacturing system expect changes? Why will such changes arise? Why is backflush costing used in JIT environments?
24. What is meant by the theory of constraints? How is this concept appropriate for manufacturing and service companies?
25. Why should quality control inspection points be placed in front of bottleneck operations?
26. *(Appendix)* How do ordering costs and carrying costs relate to one another?
27. *(Appendix)* How are economic order quantity and order point related?
28. *(Appendix)* What is safety stock and why is it necessary?
29. *(Appendix)* What is Pareto inventory analysis? Why do A items and C items warrant different inventory control methods? What are some methods that can be employed to control C items?
30. *(Appendix)* How and why is the cost of capital used in economic order quantity computations?
31. *(Appendix)* You own a manufacturing company and your friend Joe owns a retail appliance store. Joe is concerned about how many VCRs to order at a time. You proceed to tell him about using economic production runs at your company. How do EPRs relate to Joe's concerns? What adjustments must he make to the formula you use?

EXERCISES

32. *(Terminology)* Match the lettered terms on the left with the numbered descriptions on the right. A letter may be used more than once.

a. Autonomation
b. Electronic data interchange
c. Flexible manufacturing system
d. Just-in-time
e. Multiprocess handling
f. Order point
g. Pull system
h. Push system
i. Safety stock
j. Stockout
k. Target cost
l. Backflush

1. Expected selling price less desired profit
2. A system in which inventory is produced before it is needed and placed in storage until needed
3. Streamlined accounting system
4. The situation of not having a product or component available when it is needed
5. A manufacturing environment in which machinery is programmed to stop work when specified situations arise
6. The use of machines and robots to perform the production process
7. The broadening of worker involvement to include monitoring all machines in a manufacturing cell
8. Computer-to-computer transfer of information in virtual real time using standardized formats developed by the American National Standards Institute.
9. A buffer supply of inventory that minimizes the possibility of running out of a product or component
10. A system in which purchases and production are made only on an as-needed basis
11. A philosophy that focuses on value-added activities
12. The inventory level at which a purchase order is to be issued

33. *(Cost classification)* For each of the following costs, indicate whether it would be considered an ordering cost (O), a carrying cost (C), or a cost of not carrying (N) inventory. For any costs that do not fit these categories, indicate N/A for "not applicable."

1. Telephone call to supplier
2. Stationery and purchase order forms
3. Purchasing agent's salary
4. Purchase price of product
5. Goodwill of customer lost due to unavailability of product
6. Postage on purchase order
7. Freight-in cost on product
8. Insurance for products on hand
9. Wages of receiving clerks
10. Preparing and issuing checks to suppliers
11. Contribution margin lost due to unavailability of product
12. Storage costs for products on hand
13. Quantity discounts on products ordered

14. Opportunity cost of funds invested in inventory
15. Property taxes on warehouses
16. Handling costs for products on hand
17. Excess ordering and shipping charges for rush orders of standard product lines
18. Spoilage of products awaiting use

34. *(Carrying costs)* Determine the carrying costs for an item costing $4.30, given the following per-unit cost information:

Storage cost	$0.04
Handling cost	0.03
Production labor cost	0.80
Insurance cost	0.02
Opportunity cost	10% of investment

35. *(Target costing)* Millennium Attire has developed a new material that has significant potential in the manufacture of sports caps. The firm has conducted significant market research and estimated the following pattern for sales of the new caps:

Year	Expected Volume	Expected Price per Unit
1	16,000 units	$7
2	40,000 units	8
3	70,000 units	6
4	30,000 units	5

If the firm desires to net $1.50 per unit in profit, what is the target cost to produce the new caps?

36. *(Target costing)* The marketing department at Walters Production Company has an idea for a new product that is expected to have a life cycle of five years. After conducting market research, the company has determined that the product could sell for $250 per unit in the first three years of life and $175 per unit for the last two years. Unit sales are expected as follows:

Year 1	3,000 units
Year 2	4,600 units
Year 3	4,700 units
Year 4	5,000 units
Year 5	1,500 units

Per-unit variable selling costs are estimated at $30 throughout the product's life; annual fixed selling and administrative costs are expected to be $1,750,000. Walters Production Company desires a profit margin of 20 percent of selling price per unit.

a. Compute the life-cycle target cost to manufacture the product. (Round to the nearest penny.)
b. If the company expects the product to cost $65 to manufacture in the first year, what is the maximum that manufacturing cost can be in the following four years? (Round to the nearest penny.)
c. Assume Walters Production Company engineers indicate that the expected manufacturing cost per unit is $70. What actions might the company take to reduce this cost?

37. *(Target costing)* Pickles Corporation is in the process of developing an outdoor power source for various electronic devices used by campers. Market research has indicated that potential purchasers would be willing to pay $175 per unit for this product. Company engineers have estimated first-year production costs would amount to $180 per unit. On this type of product, Pickles would normally expect to earn $10 per unit in profits. Using the concept of target costing, write a memo that (1) analyzes the prospects for this product and (2) discusses possible organizational strategies.

38. *(JIT variances)* James Company uses a JIT system. The following standards are related to Materials A and B, which are used to make one unit of the company's final product:

Annual Material Standards	
6 pounds of material A @ $2.25	$13.50
8 pounds of material B @ $3.40	27.20
	$40.70

Current Material Standards	
7 pounds of material A @ $2.25	$15.75
7 pounds of material B @ $3.40	23.80
	$39.55

The current material standards differ from the original because of an engineering change made near the end of June. During July, the company produced 3,000 units of its final product and used 22,000 pounds of Material A and 20,500 pounds of Material B. All material is acquired at the standard cost per pound.

a. Calculate the material variance and the ENC material variance.
b. Explain the effect of the engineering change on product cost.

39. *(JIT variances)* Erica Tommasen uses a JIT system in her manufacturing firm, which makes "Mew" for cats. Erica provides you with the following standards for a can of Mew:

Annual Material Standards	
5 ounces of component X @ $0.10	$0.50
1 ounce of component Y @ $0.25	0.25
	$0.75

Current Material Standards	
4 ounces of component X @ $0.10	$0.40
2 ounces of component Y @ $0.25	0.50
	$0.90

The standards were changed because of a nutritional (engineering) adjustment. Production during March was 60,000 cans of Mew. Usage of raw material (all purchased at standard costs) was 250,000 ounces of Component X and 108,000 ounces of Component Y.

a. Calculate the material quantity variance for each component.
b. Calculate the engineering change variance for each component.
c. Why would a company implement an engineering change that increases the standard production cost by 20 percent?

40. *(Backflush costing)* Kuchen Manufacturing uses backflush costing to account for an electronic meter it makes. During August 2001, the firm produced 16,000 meters, of which it sold 15,800. The standard cost for each meter is

Direct material	$20
Conversion costs	44
Total cost	$64

Assume that the firm had no inventory on August 1. The following events took place in August:

1. Purchased $320,000 of direct material.
2. Incurred $708,000 of conversion costs.
3. Applied $704,000 of conversion costs to Raw and In Process Inventory.
4. Finished 16,000 meters.
5. Sold 15,800 meters for $100 each.

a. Prepare journal entries using backflush costing with a minimum number of entries.
b. Post the amounts in part (a) to T-accounts.
c. Explain any inventory account balances.

41. *(Production constraints)* Office Superstore produces commercial calendars in a two-department operation: Department 1 is labor intensive and Department 2 is automated. The average output of Department 1 is 45 units per hour. The units are then transferred to Department 2 where they are finished by a robot. The robot can finish a maximum of 45 units per hour. Office Superstore needs to complete 180 units this afternoon for an order that has been backlogged for four months. The production manager has informed the people in Department 1 that they are to work on nothing else except this order from 1 p.m. until 5 p.m. The supervisor in Department 2 has scheduled the same times for the robot to work on the order. Department 1's activity for each hour of the afternoon follows:

Time	1:00–2:00	2:00–3:00	3:00–4:00	4:00–4:58
Production	44 units	40 units	49 units	47 units

Assume that each unit moves directly from Department 1 to Department 2 with no lag time. Did Office Superstore complete the 180 units by 5:00 p.m.? If not, explain and provide detailed computations.

42. *(Carrying cost)* Feline Delights manufactures a variety of pet food products from dried seafood "pellets." The firm has determined that its EOQ is 20,000 pounds of pellets. Based on the EOQ, the firm's annual ordering costs for pellets is $12,700. Given this information, what is the firm's annual carrying cost of pellets? Explain.

43. *(Appendix: Multiproduct EOQs)* A drugstore carries three types of face cream: Wonder Cream, Skin-so-Bright, and Fresh & Sweet. Determine the economic order quantity for each, given the following information:

Product	Order Cost	Carrying Cost	Demand
Wonder Cream	$4.30	$1.90	1,200 units
Skin-so-Bright	6.25	1.45	1,000 units
Fresh & Sweet	3.70	1.25	900 units

44. *(Appendix: Product demand)* Compute the annual estimated demand if the economic order quantity for a product is 78 units; carrying cost is $0.65 per unit; and ordering cost is $3.04 per order.

45. *(Appendix: EPR)* Lars Gonzalez has taken a new job as production superintendent in a plant that makes briefcases. He is trying to determine how many cases to produce on each production run. Discussions reveal that last year the plant made 2,500 such cases, and this level of demand is expected for the coming year. The setup cost of each run is $200, and the cost of carrying a case in inventory for a year is estimated at $5.

a. Calculate the economic production run (EPR) and the total cost associated with it.
b. Recalculate the EPR and total cost if the annual cost of carrying a case in inventory is $10 and the setup cost is $20.

46. *(Appendix: EPR)* Johns Company manufactures parts to be sold to other companies. Part No. 48 has the following data related to its production:

Annual quantity produced in units	3,200
Cost of setting up a production run	$200
Cost of carrying one unit in stock for a year	$2

Calculate the economic production run for Part No. 48.

47. *(Appendix: EPR)* Mohawk Manufacturing requires 10,000 castings a year for use in assembling lawn and garden tractors. The foundry can produce 30,000 castings a year. The cost associated with setting up the production line is $25, and the carrying cost per unit is $2 annually. Lead time is 60 days.

a. Find the production quantity that minimizes cost.

b. Calculate the total annual cost of setting up for and carrying inventory, based on the answer to part (a) for a year.

48. *(Appendix: EOQ, number of orders)* Jonathan Jingles is a wholesale distributor of videotapes. He sells approximately 9,000 tapes every year. He estimates that it costs $0.25 per tape to carry inventory for 12 months and it costs $15 each time he orders tapes from the factory.

a. How many tapes should he order to minimize costs?

b. Based on the order size computed in part (a), how many orders will he need to place each year?

c. Based on your answer to part (b), at what time interval will Jonathan be placing orders for videotapes?

PROBLEMS

49. *(Identification of carrying, ordering costs)* Catalina Metal Works has been evaluating its policies with respect to control of costs of metal tubing, one of the firm's major component materials. The firm's controller has gathered the following financial data, which may be pertinent to controlling costs associated with the metal tubing:

Ordering Costs	
Annual salary of purchasing department manager	$41,500
Depreciation of equipment in purchasing department	$22,300
Cost per order for purchasing department supplies	$0.30
Typical phone expense per order placed	$30.20
Monthly expense for heat and light in purchasing department	$400
Carrying Costs	
Annual depreciation on materials storage building	$15,000
Annual inventory insurance premium (per dollar of inventory value)	$0.05
Annual property tax on materials storage building	$2,500
Obsolescence cost per dollar of average annual inventory	$0.07
Annual salary of security officer assigned to the materials storage building	$18,000

a. Which of the ordering costs would Catalina's controller take into account in performing short-run decision analysis? Explain.

b. Which of the carrying costs would Catalina's controller take into account in performing short-run decision analysis? Explain.

50. *(Life-cycle costing)* The Products Development Division of Lite & Fine Cuisine has just completed its work on a new microwave entrée. The marketing group has decided on an original price for the entrée, but the selling price will be reduced as competitors appear. Market studies indicate that the following quantities of the product can be sold at the following prices over its life cycle:

Year	Quantity	Selling Price	Year	Quantity	Selling Price
1	100,000	$2.50	5	600,000	$2.00
2	250,000	2.40	6	450,000	2.00
3	350,000	2.30	7	200,000	1.90
4	500,000	2.10	8	130,000	1.90

Development costs plus other startup costs for this product will total $600,000. Engineering estimates of direct material and direct labor costs are $0.85 and $0.20, respectively, per unit. These costs can be held constant for approximately four years and in year 5 will each increase by 10 percent. Variable overhead per unit is expected to be $0.25, and fixed overhead is expected to be $100,000 per year. Lite & Fine Cuisine management likes to earn a 20 percent gross margin on products of this type.

a. Prepare an income statement for each year of the product's life, assuming all product costs are inventoried and using eight-year amortization of the development and startup costs. What is the cost per unit each year? What rate of gross margin will the product generate each year?

b. Determine the total gross margin to be generated by this product over its life. What rate of gross margin is this?

c. Discuss the differences in the information provided by the analyses in parts (a) and (b).

51. *(Just-in-time features)* Given the features below concerning just-in-time systems, indicate by letter which of the three categories apply to the following items. If more than one category applies, indicate with an additional letter.

D = desired intermediate result of using JIT
U = ultimate goal of JIT
T = technique associated with JIT

a. Reducing setup time
b. Reducing total cost of producing and carrying inventory
c. Using focused factory arrangements
d. Designing products to minimize design changes after production starts
e. Monitoring quality on a continuous basis
f. Using manufacturing cells
g. Minimizing inventory stored
h. Measuring variances caused by engineering changes
i. Using autonomation processes
j. Pulling purchases and production through the system based on sales demand

52. *(JIT journal entries)* Brandt Production Company has implemented a just-in-time inventory system for the production of its insulated wire. Inventories of raw material and work in process are so small that Brandt uses a Raw and In Process account. In addition, almost all labor operations are automated and Brandt has chosen to cost products using standards for direct material and conversion. The following production standards are applicable at the beginning of 2000 for one roll of insulated wire:

Direct material (100 yards @ $2.00)	$200
Conversion (4 machine hours @ $35)	140
Total cost	$340

The conversion cost of $35 per machine hour was estimated on the basis of 500,000 machine hours for the year and $17,500,000 of conversion costs. The following activities took place during 2000:

1. Raw material purchased and placed into production totaled 12,452,000 yards. All except 8,000 yards were purchased at the standard price of $2 per yard. The other 8,000 yards were purchased at a cost of $2.06 per yard due to the placement of a rush order. The order was approved in advance by management. All purchases are on account.

2. From January 1 to February 28, Brandt manufactured 20,800 rolls of insulated wire. Conversion costs incurred to date totaled $3,000,000. Of this amount, $600,000 was for depreciation, $2,200,000 was paid in cash, and $200,000 was on account.
3. Conversion costs are applied to the Raw and In Process account from January 1 to February 28 on the basis of the annual standard.
4. The Engineering Department issued a change in the operations flow document effective March 1, 2000. The change decreased the machine time to manufacture one roll of wire by 5 minutes per roll. However, the standard raises the quantity of direct material to 100.4 yards per roll. The Accounting Department requires that the annual standard be continued for costing the Raw and In Process Inventory for the remainder of 2000. The effects of the engineering changes should be shown in two accounts: Material Quantity Engineering Change Variance and Machine Hours Engineering Change Variance.
5. Total production for the remainder of 2000 was 103,200 rolls of wire. Total conversion costs for the remaining 10 months of 2000 were $14,442,000. Of this amount, $4,000,000 was depreciation, $9,325,000 was paid in cash, and $1,117,000 was on account.
6. The standard amount of conversion cost is applied to the Raw and In Process Inventory for the remainder of the year.

Note: Some of the journal entries for the following items are not explicitly covered in the chapter. This problem challenges students regarding the accounting effects of the implementation of a JIT system.

a. Prepare entries for items 1, 2, 3, 5, and 6 above.
b. Determine the increase in material cost due to the engineering change related to direct material.
c. Prepare a journal entry to adjust the Raw and In Process Inventory account for the engineering change cost found in part (b).
d. Determine the reduction in conversion cost due to the engineering change related to machine time.
e. Prepare a journal entry to reclassify the actual conversion costs by the savings found in part (d).
f. Making the entry in part (e) raises conversion costs to what they would have been if the engineering change related to machine time had not been made. Are conversion costs under- or overapplied and by what amount?
g. Assume the reduction in machine time could not have been made without the corresponding increase in material usage. Is the net effect of these engineering changes cost beneficial? Why?

53. *(Appendix: EOQ)* Andrew Jackson operates a health food bakery that uses a special type of ground flour in its products. The bakery operates 365 days a year. Andrew finds that he seems to order either too much or too little flour and asks for your help. After some discussion, you find he does not have any idea of when or how much to order. An examination of his records and Andrew's answers to further questions reveal the following information:

Annual usage of flour	14,000 pounds
Average number of days delay between initiating and receiving an order	12
Estimated cost per order	$8.00
Estimated annual cost of carrying a pound of flour in inventory	$0.25

a. Calculate the economic order quantity for flour.
b. Assume that Andrew desires a safety stock cushion of seven days' usage. Calculate the appropriate order point.

54. *(Appendix: EPR)* The Town and Country Nursery grows and sells a variety of household and outdoor plants. The firm also grows and sells garden vegetables. One of the more popular vegetables grown by the firm is a red onion. The company sells approximately 30,000 pounds of red onions per year. Two of the major inputs in the growing of onions are seeds and fertilizer. Due to the poor germination rate, two seeds must be purchased for each onion plant grown (a mature onion plant provides 0.5 pound of onion). Also, 0.25 pound of fertilizer is required for each pound of onion produced. The following information summarizes costs pertaining to onions, seeds, and fertilizer. Carrying costs for onions are expressed per pound of onion; carrying costs for seeds are expressed per seed; and for fertilizer, carrying costs are expressed per pound of fertilizer. To plant onions, the company incurs a cost of $50 to set up the planter and the fertilizing equipment.

	Onions	Seeds	Fertilizer
Carrying cost	$0.25	$0.01	$0.05
Ordering cost	—	$4.25	$8.80
Setup cost	$50.00	—	—

a. What is the economic production run for onions?
b. How many production runs will Town and Country make for onions annually?
c. What are the economic order quantities for seeds and fertilizer?
d. How many orders will be placed for seeds? For fertilizer?
e. What is the total annual cost of ordering, carrying, and setting up for onion production?
f. How is the planting of onions similar to and different from a typical factory production run?
g. Are there any inconsistencies in your answers to parts (a) through (c) that need to be addressed? Explain.

CASE

55. *(Using EOQ for cash/securities management)* Chemcon Corporation sells various industrial supplies used for general-purpose cleaning. Approximately 85 percent of its sales are to not-for-profit and governmental institutions. These sales are on a contract basis with an average contract length of two years. Al Stanly, Chemcon's treasurer, wants to initiate a system that will maximize the amount of time Chemcon holds its cash in the form of marketable securities. Chemcon currently has $9 million of securities that have an expected annual earnings rate of 8 percent. Chemcon is expecting a cash drain over the next 12-month period. Monthly cash outflows are expected to be $2,650,000, but inflows are only expected to be $2,500,000. The cost of either buying or selling securities is $125 per transaction. Stanly has heard that the EOQ inventory model can be applied to cash management. Therefore, he has decided to employ this model to determine the optimal value of marketable securities to be sold to replenish Chemcon's cash balance.

a. Use the EOQ model in the chapter to
(1) explain the costs Al Stanly is attempting to balance in this situation, and
(2) calculate the optimal dollar amount of marketable securities Stanly should sell when Chemcon needs to replenish its cash balance.

(continued)

b. Without prejudice to your solution in part a(2), assume that the optimal dollar amount of marketable securities to be sold is $60,000.

(1) Calculate the average cash balance in Chemcon's checking account that will be on hand during the course of the year.

(2) Determine the number of times during the year that Stanly will have to sell securities.

c. Describe two different economic circumstances applicable to Chemcon that would render its use of the EOQ inventory model inappropriate as a cash management model. *(CMA adapted)*

REALITY CHECK

56. The Smith Company manufactures various electronic assemblies that it sells primarily to computer manufacturers. Smith's reputation has been built on quality, timely delivery, and products that are consistently on the cutting edge of technology. Smith's business is fast paced. The typical product has a short life; the product is in development for about a year and in the growth stage, with sometimes spectacular growth, for about a year. Each product then experiences a rapid decline in sales as new products become available.

Smith's competitive strategy requires a reliable stream of new products to be developed each year. This is the only way that the company can overcome the threat of product obsolescence. Although the products go through the first half of the product life cycle like products in other industries, they do not go through the second half of the product life cycle in a similar manner. Smith's products never reach the mature product or declining product stage. Toward the end of the growth stage, products just die as new ones are introduced.

a. In the competitive market facing Smith Company, what would be key considerations in production and inventory control?

b. How would the threat of immediate product obsolescence affect Smith's practices in purchasing product components and materials?

c. How would the threat of product obsolescence affect the EPR for a typical product produced by Smith Company? *(CMA adapted)*

57. The director of supply management at Benson Tool & Die has contracted for $1 million of spare parts that are currently unneeded. His rationale for the contract was that the parts were available for purchase at a significantly reduced price. The company just hired a new president who, on learning about the contracts, stated that the parts contracts should be canceled because the parts would not be needed for at least a year. The supply director informed the president that the penalties for canceling the contracts would cost more than letting the orders go through. How would you respond to this situation from the standpoint of the president? From the standpoint of the supply director?

58. A plant manager and her controller were discussing the plant's inventory control policies one day. The controller suggested to the plant manager that the ordering policies needed to be reviewed because of new technology that had been put in place in the plant's purchasing department. Among the changes that had been implemented in the plant were installation of (1) computerized inventory tracking, (2) electronic data interchange capabilities with the plant's major suppliers, and (3) in-house facilities for electronic fund transfers.

a. As technology changes, why should managers update ordering policies for inventory?

b. Write a memo to the plant manager describing the likely impact of the changes made in this plant on the EOQ of material input.

59. Johnson Manufacturing Company began implementing a just-in-time inventory system several months ago. The production and purchasing managers, however, have not seen any dramatic improvements in throughput. They have decided that the problems are related to their suppliers. The suppliers (there are three) seem to send the wrong materials at the wrong times. Prepare a discussion of the problems that might exist in this situation. Be certain to address the following items: internal and external communications; possible engineering changes and their impacts; number, quality, and location of suppliers; and length of system implementation.

60. According to Barry Bayus, a marketing professor, the perception that product life cycles are getting shorter is a mistaken one. Bayus identified three reasons for the appearance of shortened product life cycles:

1. New knowledge is being applied faster. The time between an invention and its first application is decreasing, from 90 years during the 1700s to 20 years from 1901 to 1950.

2. More new products are being introduced. In 1986, for example, the number of new-product introductions was just under 13,000. By 1991, the number had increased to more than 15,000.

3. The time between innovations is decreasing.

SOURCE: Glenn Rifkin, "The Myth of Short Life Cycles," *Harvard Business Review* (July–August 1994), p. 11.

a. As a team, investigate the reality or myth of shortened product life cycles. Use all resources (library, Internet, personal) at your disposal.

b. Prepare a report on your findings.

61. Choose a fast-food restaurant and prepare a report showing how JIT can be used to improve operations.

62. Everyone in your company seems excited about the suggestion that the firm implement a JIT system. Being a cautious person, your company president has asked you to write a report describing situations in which JIT will not work. Prepare such a report.

63. General Motors Corp. is now spending about $1 billion a year to implement "an integrated portfolio of computer math-based tools" to streamline its product design and development processes by eliminating the need for physical models "making it possible to solve manufacturing problems in 'virtual' factories rather than real ones."

http://www.gm.com

SOURCE: Adapted from Robert L. Simison, "GM Turns to Computers to Cut Development Costs," *The Wall Street Journal* (October 12, 1998), p. B4.

Discuss the advantages of spending so much money on this sort of technology.

64. Research the topic of manufacturing cells on the Internet and write a brief report on company experiences using them.

65. Research the topic of value engineering on the Internet and write a brief report on a company or an organization's experiences using this technique.

CHAPTER

17

Emerging Management Practices

LEARNING OBJECTIVES

After reading this chapter, you should be able to answer the following questions:

1
Why does business process reengineering cause radical changes in how firms execute processes?

2
What competitive forces are driving decisions to downsize and restructure operations?

3
Why are the operations of many firms becoming more diverse and how does the increasing diversity affect the roles of the firms' accounting systems?

4
What benefits do firms hope to attain by adopting enterprise resource planning systems?

5
Why are firms increasing their use of strategic alliances?

6
What is open-book management and why does its adoption require changes in accounting methods and practices?

7
What are the three generic approaches firms can take in controlling environmental costs?

INTRODUCING CarPoint

http://www.carpoint.msn.com

Ford Motor Co. and Microsoft Corp., in a move that could transform the auto factory, are creating a strategic alliance to develop an online build-to-order system that will let consumers customize their cars and order them on the Internet.

The two companies announced a joint venture in which Ford will take a significant minority interest in CarPoint, Microsoft's car-buying site. Financial details weren't disclosed. The popular Web site is being made independent of Microsoft but won't be spun off from the software company. While other automakers are being offered stakes in the new site, Ford will be the lead partner, and Microsoft will retain a majority interest in CarPoint. Lindsay Sparks, general manager of CarPoint, will be the chief executive officer of the new entity.

"This isn't just a communication tool," Jacques Nasser, chief executive of Ford, based in Dearborn, Mich., said at a press conference. "It's a different way of running our business." Mr. Nasser expects that coupling the virtual world to the physical world will cut costs and time out of what is still an inefficient manufacturing and distribution system.

Until recently, most automakers and car-buying sites used the Internet to put buyers in touch with dealers or to let consumers research cars before they buy. Now, the alliance takes the Internet into the factory as well. "Until now, there's been no deep coupling with consumers and the back end (upstream side of the supply chain)," Steve Ballmer, president of Microsoft, Redmond, Wash., said.

SOURCE: Adapted from Fara Warner, "Ford and Microsoft Forge Alliance to Create Online Car-Sales System," *The Wall Street Journal Online* (September 21, 1999).

http://www.fordvehicles.com
http://www.microsoft.com

CarPoint illustrates a strategic joint venture between a technology company and a car manufacturer. The concept of CarPoint as a business model would have been inconceivable a few years ago. It is only because of the advancements in Internet and e-commerce technologies that this idea could be implemented. Ford views CarPoint not so much as a novelty as a necessity. Ford must have a strong capability to deliver its products through the marketing medium many predict will become dominant in the United States and other developed countries—the Internet.

For Ford and Microsoft to launch CarPoint as a viable competitor in the Internet marketing of autos, managers of the two companies had to consider several factors: how to combine the two firms' resources, how to manage the new entity, who would be responsible for the new entity's operations, and how the fruits of the effort would be shared. Making such decisions is now a common activity for general managers and functional experts of many firms, and using joint ventures to structure new enterprises is a common business event. The pressures of global competition cause managers to be ever vigilant in identifying ways to become more effective and efficient in serving customers. As a result, a proliferation of business practices have emerged in the past decade or so.

The "age of change" is an apt description for the current environment in which managers and finance professionals must function. Some changes have been driven by the fast pace of evolution in management practices and techniques. However, many of the changes have been driven by the even faster evolution of technology. For example, some technologies directly impacting the lives of public accountants are listed in Exhibit 17–1. This chapter introduces management practices that are emerging and maturing in firms around the globe. An emphasis is placed on the impact and roles of the financial professional in these new management methods. The discussion begins with dramatic structural changes occurring in the workplace that are affecting many employers and employees.

EXHIBIT 17-1

Top Ten Technologies Affecting CPAs in 1999–2000

1. *Net-enabled applications:* Internet/intranet/extranet—these applications run the gamut from e-mail to sophisticated supply chain communications
2. *Messaging applications:* e-mail, voicemail, and universal inbox
3. *Document management:* electronic storage and retrieval of documents
4. *Business process reengineering:* major changes in how a company operates
5. *Telecommuting applications:* applications allowing work outside the office
6. *Electronic commerce:* business conducted over the Internet
7. *Electronic document submission:* IRS and SEC filings
8. *Videoconferencing:* real-time meetings in the virtual office
9. *Self-service applications:* technology that lets you do it yourself
10. *Collaborative computing applications:* different applications working together and sharing information

SOURCE: Anonymous, "Top 10 Technologies: The Applications," *Journal of Accountancy* 187, No. 3 (March 1999), pp. 12–13. Reprinted with permission from the *Journal of Accountancy*. Copyright (2000) by American Institute of CPAs. Opinions of the authors are their own and do not necessarily reflect policies of the AICPA.

THE CHANGING WORKPLACE

The forces of global competition and technological advancements have caused profound changes in business organizations. To survive, managers must develop mechanisms to achieve needed competitive changes in their organizations. In general, change can be achieved in two ways: immediately or gradually. Managers seek both types of change.

Exhibit 17–2 provides some overriding change implementation principles that managers should follow when implementing changes. Note that principles 5 through 8 involve major roles for financial professionals within the firm. These roles will be explained further as the chapter unfolds.

When major operational improvements are mandated, managers completely revise the way activities are executed. Business process reengineering is a tool to achieve large, quick gains in effectiveness or efficiency through redesigning the execution of specific business functions.

Business Process Reengineering

1

Why does business process reengineering cause radical changes in how firms execute processes?

business process reengineering

Business process reengineering (BPR) is a method of examining processes to identify, and then eliminate, reduce, or replace functions and processes that add little customer value to products or services. The focus of BPR is on discrete initiatives to improve specific processes. Examples of processes include handling or storing purchased materials and components, issuing checks to pay labor and other production expenses, wrapping finished products for shipment to customers, recording journal entries, and developing an organizational strategic plan.

BPR is designed to bring radical changes to an organization's operations; BPR is often associated with employee layoffs, outsourcing initiatives, and technology acquisition. Three major business trends are promoting the increased use of BPR in the 21st century.

The first trend is the advancement of technology. Neither the electronic remittance of accounts payable nor the use of robotic equipment to move and assemble components in a manufacturing facility were possible 50 years ago. Both of these are commonly done today, even in small companies, because of technological advancements. Because BPR focuses on alternative ways to execute required organizational functions, it is useful in automating processes that cannot be eliminated. Advancements in technology have improved efficiencies throughout the supply chain. The feasibility of automating processes is constantly changing because technology is constantly evolving.

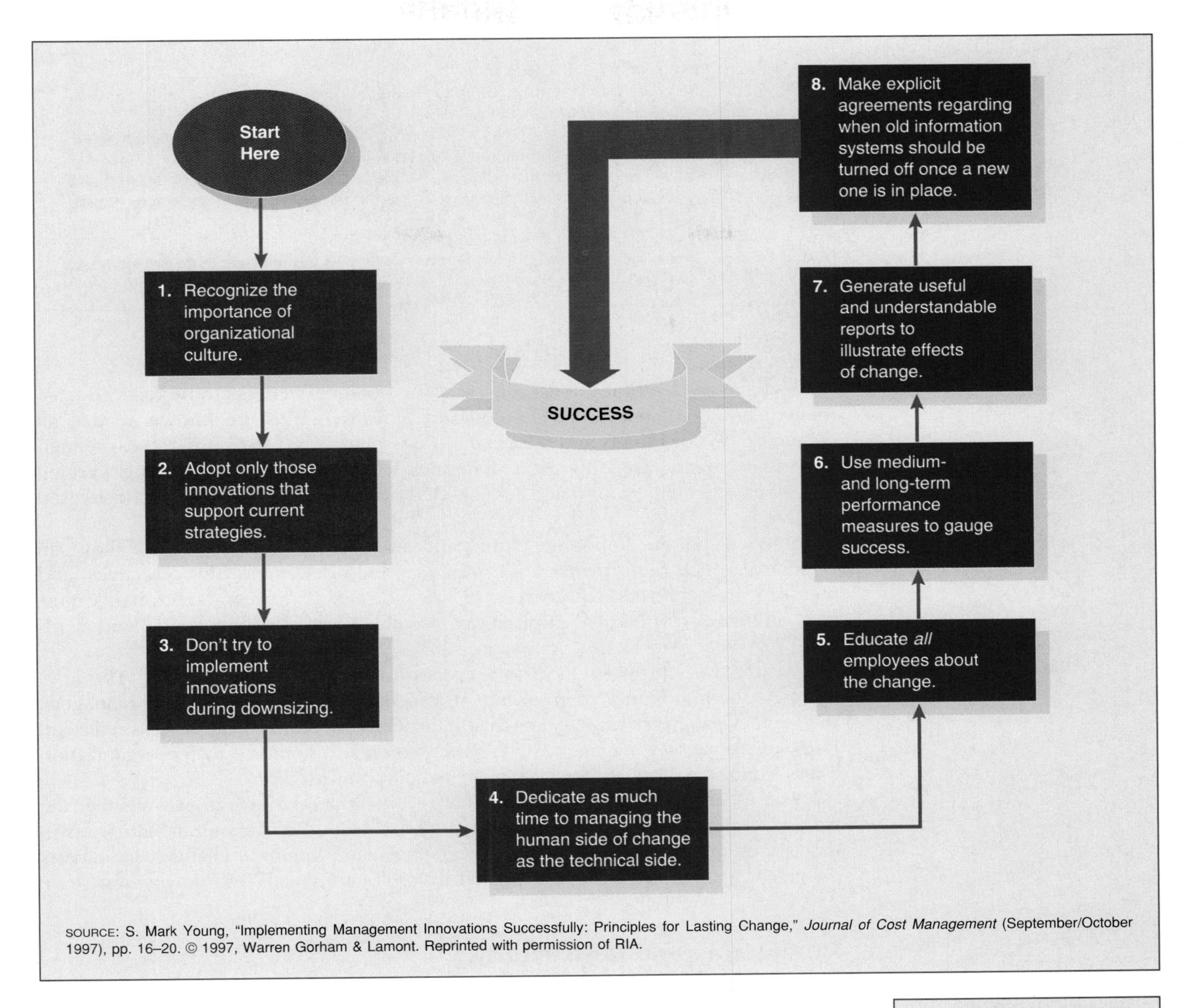

SOURCE: S. Mark Young, "Implementing Management Innovations Successfully: Principles for Lasting Change," *Journal of Cost Management* (September/October 1997), pp. 16–20. © 1997, Warren Gorham & Lamont. Reprinted with permission of RIA.

EXHIBIT 17–2

Managerial Principles for Successfully Managing Change

The second trend leading toward increased use of BPR is the pursuit of increased quality. As discussed in Chapter 8, global competition allows consumers to purchase products and services from the highest quality providers in the world. In many product and service markets, quality has become one of the most important criteria applied by consumers in purchasing decisions. BPR is a useful tool for increasing quality because it focuses attention on processes associated with poor quality and indicates ways in which quality can be improved by replacing, changing, or eliminating those processes.

The third trend resulting in increased BPR usage is the increase in price competition caused by globalization. To successfully compete on the basis of price, firms must identify ways to become more efficient and, thus, reduce costs. BPR can be used to improve efficiency, particularly when a process needs a major overhaul or a new generation of technology is needed.

Because BPR is a methodical way to revolutionize business practices, formal steps can be defined; however, creativity is an important element of the method. Exhibit 17–3 provides the steps for implementing BPR.

EXHIBIT 17–3

Steps to Business Process Reengineering

1. Define the objectives of the BPR project.
2. Identify the processes that are to be reengineered.
3. Determine a baseline for measuring the success of the BPR project.
4. Identify the technology levers. These are the potential sources of innovation, increased quality, increased output, and decreased costs.
5. Develop initial prototypes of the reengineered processes and then, through subsequent iterations, develop incremental improvements to the prototypes until satisfactory results are achieved.

SOURCE: Adapted from Yogesh Malhotra, "Business Process Redesign: An Overview," http://www.brint.com/papers/bpr.htm (1996).

Objectives of a BPR project represent the potential benefits to be realized from reengineering. All relevant technological innovations must be known so that all technological constraints and opportunities are considered. Because process reengineering is much more involved than merely automating or upgrading existing processes, creativity and vision are needed to design a prototype of the revised process.

Accountants are important participants in the BPR process because they can provide baseline performance measurements, help determine BPR objectives, and measure the achieved performance of the redesigned process. Accountants must also be aware of potential applications for newly developed software and hardware that may lead to BPR innovations.

Exhibit 17–4 provides keys to a successful implementation of BPR. The keys highlight the importance of involving customers, suppliers, and top-level managers. Involvement of customers ensures that their perspective drives the process redesign. Involvement of top managers signals the project's importance to the organization and secures the resources necessary to execute the project.

The focus of BPR is on improvement of organizational operations. Whether the issue is quality, cost, or customer value, BPR can help effect organizational improvements and change. Because BPR is designed to achieve radical changes, its impacts on organizational employees are potentially profound: layoffs and downsizing.

Downsizing and Restructuring

2

What competitive forces are driving decisions to downsize and restructure operations?

Global competition is a fact of life in many industries and survival requires firms to continually improve product quality while maintaining competitive prices. Not all firms are able to adapt and survive under the pressures of global competition.

EXHIBIT 17–4

Keys to Successful Use of Process Reengineering

- *Set aggressive objectives for reengineering projects.* Objectives can be expressed in dollars, quality measurements, or other dimensions of performance.
- *Commit support of top executives to the project.* A significant time commitment ensures that the high-level support and involvement necessary to execute a successful project are available.
- *Involve customers and suppliers.* Customer and supplier considerations should drive reengineering efforts.
- *Make someone accountable for implementing reengineering efforts.* The reengineering project is more likely to be successful if a specific person oversees the implementation and is responsible for the outcome.
- *Conduct a pilot project before fully implementing the new design.* The pilot will identify problems and issues that can be resolved before full implementation is attempted.

SOURCE: Adapted from Gene Hall, Jim Rosenthal, and Judy Wade, "How to Make Reengineering Really Work," *Harvard Business Review* (November–December 1993), pp. 119–131.

Just as global competition has driven firms to higher and higher levels of quality and efficiency, competitive pressures drive some businesses out of competition altogether. Firms are now forced to evaluate which businesses they want to defend and which they are willing to sacrifice to the competition.

Many methods discussed in this chapter, including using automated technologies to replace manual ones, have proven useful in improving efficiency, effectiveness, and quality. However, as firms realize improvements they also realize additional problems. Foremost among these problems is the handling of excess personnel. Both the businesses that are striving to remain viable and those that are retreating from the competition are forced into restructuring operations and reducing the workforce.

One of the grim realities of ever-improving efficiency is that ever fewer workers are required to achieve a given level of output. Using business practices such as business process reengineering, firms are constantly restructuring operations to maintain or gain competitive advantages. Each successful restructuring leverages the work of employees into more output. At higher levels of efficiency, fewer workers are needed and a reduction in workforce is required.

downsizing

Downsizing is any management action that reduces employment upon restructuring operations in response to competitive pressures. The accompanying News Note describes a typical downsizing and restructuring decision.

http://www.packardbell.com

The events at Packard Bell NEC Inc. are typical of downsizing: reduction of the workforce, restructuring of jobs and processes, and reduction or elimination of noncore businesses. One study estimates that downsizing has eliminated over 3 million jobs in the United States alone since 1990.[1] Additionally, the recent Laborforce 2000 survey of more than 400 American-based businesses provides insight into how downsizing relates to competitive pressures facing businesses. When asked

GENERAL BUSINESS NEWS NOTE

In the High-Tech Market, It's Eat or Be Eaten

At a Lake Tahoe retreat last fall, Alain Couder, Packard Bell NEC Inc.'s chairman, president and chief executive officer, lectured his staff on the need to eat or be eaten in the cutthroat personal-computer industry.

In recent years, Packard Bell has found itself on the being-eaten side of the business as its share of the world's PC market has shrunk under an onslaught of competition. The PC maker has lost nearly $1 billion over the past two years and underwent a management upheaval last summer as Mr. Couder was brought in by Japan's NEC Corp., the parent company, to attempt a turnaround.

His moves have been draconian. Each department was ordered to slash annual costs by 50%. The cutbacks have ranged from laying off nearly 40% of the company's workforce to eliminating the company suite at an arena where basketball's Sacramento Kings play. And top officials now have to pay their own medical insurance premiums like everybody else.

With PC revenue relatively stagnant despite unit-sales gains, hardware profits have roughly fallen in half over the past two years. The situation is especially grim at the retail level, where manufacturers are saddled with store costs not borne by direct and online vendors.

"People are discounting the hell out of everything and there is no going back," says Seymour Merrin, an industry consultant in Sante Fe, N.M.

The 53-year-old Mr. Couder instituted a cost-cutting campaign almost immediately upon arriving from his Paris home. "You must lead by example," he says. Seeking to achieve the 50% cost cuts, Mr. Couden reduced headcount and consolidated facilities.

SOURCE: Jim Carlton, "Computers: At Packard Bell, Survival Mode Means Big Cuts," *The Wall Street Journal* (June 3, 1999), p. B1. Permission conveyed through the Copyright Clearance Center.

[1] Tomasz Mroczkowski and Masao Hanaoka, "Effective Rightsizing Strategies in Japan and America: Is There a Convergence of Employment Practices?" *Academy of Management Executive* (May 1997), pp. 57–67.

what strategic issues were of greatest concern to their companies, managers indicated the following three areas[2]:

- global competitiveness,
- economic concerns such as a need to cut costs and improve profitability, and
- quality, productivity, and customer service.

The most common response to these strategic issues has been downsizing. Of the survey respondents, 64 percent downsized plants and facilities and slightly over 50 percent sold off some business units. The primary reason cited for downsizing was the need to reduce costs and improve profits. Seventy-five percent of the firms surveyed also made substantial investments in advanced technology in conjunction with downsizing.

Downsizing as a response to competitive pressures can result in many risks and dangers. First, firms may find that, through rounds of layoffs, the in-house talent pool has been depleted. The collective workforce knowledge or organizational memory may have been reduced to the point that the ability to solve problems creatively and generate innovative ideas for growth is greatly diminished. Also, after downsizing, many firms have found that positions that once served as feeder pools for future top management talent have been eliminated.

Second, to survive in the presence of global competition, trust and effective communication must exist between workers and managers. Successive rounds of layoffs diminish worker morale, cause worker trust in managers to wane, and lead to lessened communication between workers and managers. Workers fear that sharing information may provide managerial insights about how to further increase productivity and reduce costs by eliminating more of the workforce. Many of the management methods discussed in this chapter depend heavily on cooperation among all employees of a firm. As indicated in Exhibit 17–2, firms that are downsizing should not concurrently attempt to implement other innovative practices.

Third, downsizing can destroy a corporate culture in which lifetime employment has been a key factor in attracting new employees. Downsizing can also obliterate a corporate culture that was perceived as "nurturing" by employees. Significant negative change in an organization's culture is likely to have an impact on employee morale and trust.

Downsizing is an accounting issue because of its implications for financial reporting and its role in cost management. The financial consequences of downsizing can be significant. When restructuring and downsizing occur in the same year, the firm often reports, in that year, large, one-time losses caused by sales of unprofitable assets and severance costs connected with employee layoffs. From a cost management perspective, accountants must understand the full consequences, both monetary and nonmonetary, of downsizing. Before recommending downsizing to improve organizational efficiency, accountants should examine the likely impacts on customer service, employee morale and loyalty, and future growth opportunities.

Exhibit 17–5 provides a framework for analyzing downsizing decisions. The exhibit demonstrates that strategic decisions affect the manner in which inputs, such as labor, technology, purchased material, and services, are converted into outputs for customers. Downsizing involves a change in the mix of inputs used to produce outputs. Downsizing increases the emphasis on technologically based conversion processes and reduces the emphasis on manual conversion processes and, thus, the labor requirement. The two-directional arrow shows increased outsourcing from suppliers and increased dependence on technology as substitutes for labor.

The financial analysis of the downsizing decision is complex. The decision relies on comparing cost savings from reduced labor costs to be generated in the future to the current outlay for restructuring and acquiring additional technology. The

[2] Philip H. Mirvis, "Human Resource Management: Leaders, Laggards, and Followers," *Academy of Management Executive* (May 1997), pp. 43–56.

EXHIBIT 17-5

The Value Chain and Cost Management

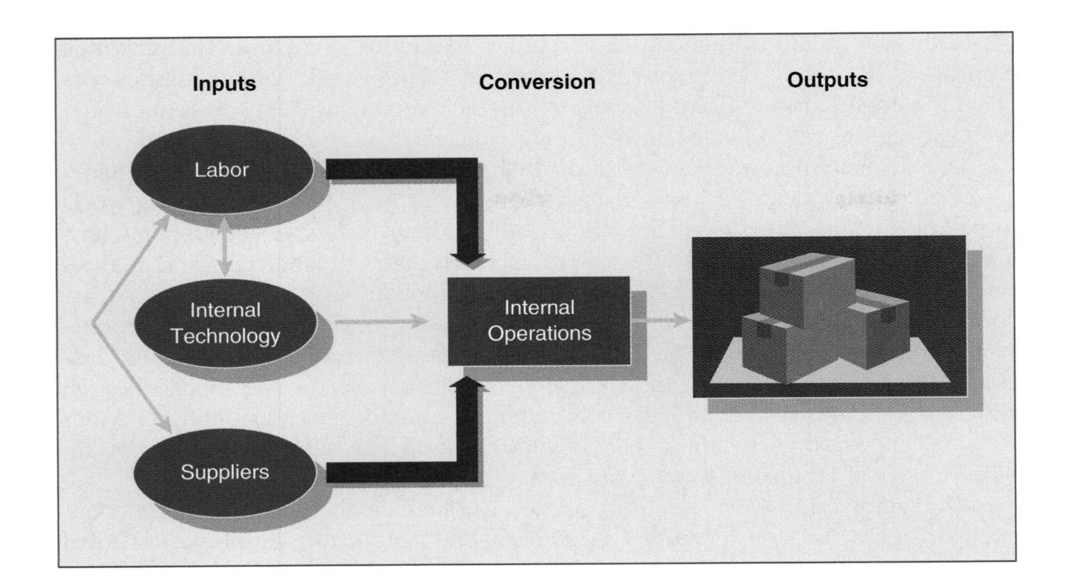

capital budgeting methods discussed in Chapter 14 should be applied to this decision. If downsizing involves asset sales, the financial analysis must compare the cash to be realized from the sale to the annual net revenues or net cash flows that will not be realized in the future because of the asset reduction. Capital budgeting tools provide managers with information about how downsizing is likely to affect profitability and the return on invested capital.

Workforce Diversity

Why are the operations of many firms becoming more diverse and how does the increasing diversity affect the roles of the firms' accounting systems?

Under the pressure of global competition, many firms have expanded operations geographically. By sourcing and marketing worldwide, firms are able to develop new markets, reduce input costs, and manage the effects of peaks and valleys in local economies. The globalization of operations presents managers with new opportunities and challenges.

Diversity policies in an organization help recruit and retain top talent. The issue is so important in business that there's even a Web site devoted to it: www.DiversityInc.com.

With widespread manufacturing and other operations, companies find that their employees have very divergent religions, races, values, work habits, cultures, political ideologies, and education levels. As the accompanying News Note indicates, such differences are reflected in business practices.

The diversity across countries is evident within companies that operate globally. Corporate policies and information systems must adapt to the changing workforce and greater diversity of operations, which often results in accounting's having a larger role in managing operations. Although different languages and cultures can impede unambiguous communication within globally dispersed operations, accounting information can be a powerful coordinating mechanism. The interpretation of accounting information need not be dependent on local culture or language. Accounting concepts, tools, and measurements can be the media through which people of diverse languages and cultures communicate. Accounting provides an ideal international technical language because it is a basic application of another universal language—mathematics.

Managing a global business, as opposed to one that operates in a single country, involves many considerations in addition to coordinating employees. Global businesses must consider country differences in currency values, labor practices, political risks, tax rates, commercial laws, and infrastructure such as ports, airports, and highways. These considerations require development of new systems and controls to manage risks and exploit opportunities.

http://www.veba.de
http://www.viag-interkom.de

NEWS NOTE  ETHICS

Is It Just a Little White Lie?

FRANKFURT—Veba AG and Viag AG announced plans on Monday to merge in a 13.4 billion euros deal that would create Germany's largest utility company. But can we really take their word for it? These are, after all, the same companies that repeatedly denied throughout the dog days of August 1999 that they were in merger talks. Consider two categorical assertions:

"There are no merger negotiations with Viag," a Veba spokeswoman told journalists who phoned the company's Duesseldorf headquarters on August 19, three days after German antitrust watchdogs confirmed that Veba and Viag officials had paid them a joint visit.

"Everyone is talking to everyone," a Viag spokeswoman echoed that day. "The talks don't have the character of negotiations."

While Viag didn't respond to repeated requests to comment on the apparent fib, Veba is far from apologetic. "A denial basically means we don't want to say anything," explains Veba spokeswoman Marie-Luise Wolff. "In Germany, a 'no comment' amounts to a confirmation of talks. The resulting rumors send the stock price up like crazy and it's a really bad situation."

"If a company falsely denies its takeover plans, we see that as misleading investors," says David Sirignano, associate director for the international division of corporation finance at the U.S. Securities and Exchange Commission. "And that applies to all companies that trade in the U.S. When a company's securities are trading in the public market, people make trading decisions based on the available information about the company," he says. "Normally, information about a merger is considered very material."

In the U.K., rules are equally stringent. If a company's stock price starts to move considerably on market speculation, the London Stock Exchange will order the company to say something promptly if the rumors are true. If they're not, the company doesn't have to deny them. "Reasonable things we'll tolerate," a spokesman says, "but not ducking."

In Italy, the stock market regulator Consob asks companies to make a statement under the same circumstances, first informally, and if it doesn't respond in an hour, via a formal request. But the rules give companies a lot of room for ambiguity. "It can often be a lot of smoke," says one Consob official.

SOURCE: Dagmar Aalun and Vanessa Fuhrmans, "When Firms Talk About Mergers, Truth Is 1st Casualty," *The Wall Street Journal Online* (September 28, 1999). Permission conveyed through the Copyright Clearance Center.

Within the United States, there is a trend to increase workplace diversity. The trend is partly driven by legal requirements and business initiatives to increase opportunities for minorities and is partly driven by organizational self-interest. Exhibit 17–6 provides reasons, other than legal requirements, that firms may seek a more diverse workforce. Unfortunately, this trend can be problematic in light of other business practices discussed in this chapter. Business process reengineering and downsizing diminish the opportunity to diversify and become more responsive to the marketplace.

A diverse workplace is one significant change in the social structure of business. Technology plays a major role in the communication among employees that is necessary to harmonize their actions to serve customers. The integration of information systems is accomplished with enterprise systems.

ENTERPRISE RESOURCE PLANNING SYSTEMS (ERP)

4

What benefits do firms hope to attain by adopting enterprise resource planning systems?

As the capabilities of personal computers (PCs) and minicomputers have increased, their use has proliferated within firms. Firms now commonly use networked PCs to handle the information management requirements of specific functions, such as finance, marketing, and manufacturing. The PC allows maximum user flexibility in accessing and manipulating data in real time. However, with the increased use of PCs and local-area networks has come the decentralization of information.

As data management and storage have become more decentralized, firms have lost both the ability to integrate information across functions and to quickly access information that spans multiple functions. Exhibit 17–7 shows how internal processes and functions are distributed across the supply chain and the lack of information integration.

enterprise resource planning (ERP) system

Enterprise resource planning (ERP) systems are packaged software programs that allow companies to (1) automate and integrate the majority of their business processes, (2) share common data and practices across the entire enterprise, and (3) produce and access information in a real-time environment.[3]

Exhibit 17–8 demonstrates a solution to the problem of nonintegrated, noncentralized information. Implementing an ERP system should help a company to provide customers with the highest quality products and best possible service. In theory, the ERP system should link the customer end of the supply chain with all functional areas responsible for the production and delivery of a product or service all the way upstream to suppliers. Increasingly, the front end of the business (the area that deals directly with customers) will allow customers to access all necessary data about their orders through the Internet. The following quote describes

EXHIBIT 17–6

Why Self-Interested Firms Seek a Diverse Group of Employees

1. *Increase market share.* A more diverse workforce connects to a more diverse market.
2. *Decrease costs.* Increased diversity leads to lower employee turnover.
3. *Increase productivity.* A heterogeneous group is more creative than a homogeneous group.
4. *Improve management quality.* A more diverse employee pool yields more management talent.
5. *Improve recruiting efforts.* Fewer worker/talent shortages affect firms that recruit from the broadest possible future employee pools.

SOURCE: Ann Morrison, *The New Leaders: Guidelines on Leadership Diversity in America* (San Francisco: Jossey-Bass, 1992), pp. 20–27. Copyright 1992. Reprinted by permission of Jossey-Bass, Inc., a subsidiary of John Wiley & Sons, Inc.

[3] Win G. Jordan and Kip R. Krumwiede, "ERP Implementers Beware!" *Cost Management Update* (March 1999), p. 1.

EXHIBIT 17-7

Internal Supply Chain and Traditional Information Management

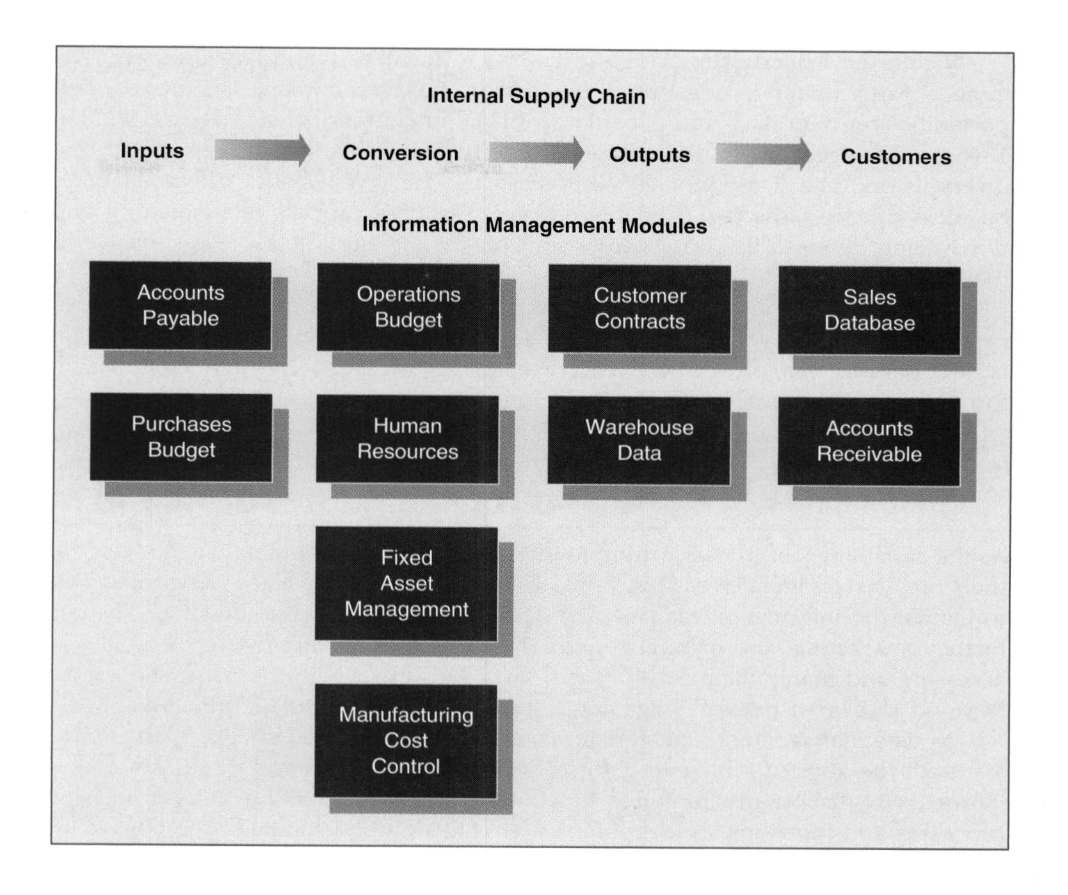

EXHIBIT 17-8

Enterprise Resource Planning Information Management

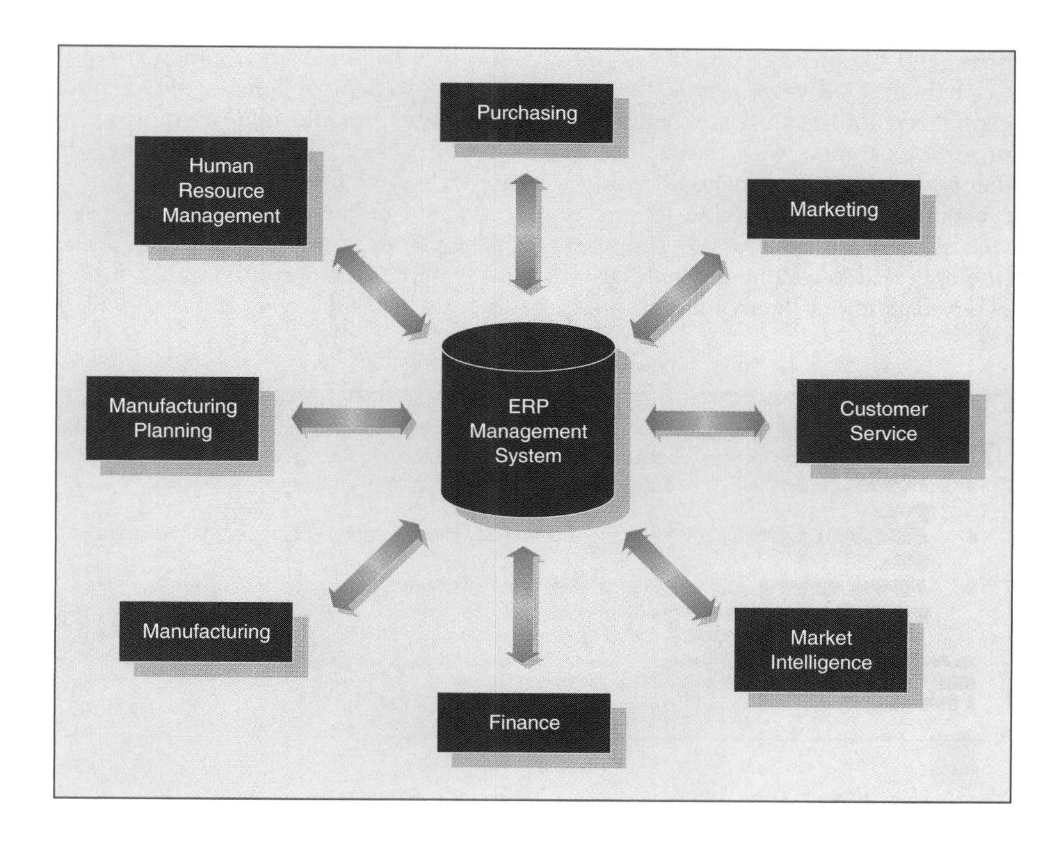

the benefits from ERP implementation for the whole business, its marketing function, and its customers[4]:

> *The benefits of an ERP package to a business are in reduced overheads, improved customer service and better quality, and more timely management information. Reduced overheads should be achieved through the elimination of duplication of effort in duplicate keying and reconciliation of independent systems. Better management information becomes available when all company information is held in one database which can be queried to provide quality reports on margins broken down by customer, product, rep, area, etc. E-commerce has the potential to offer a quantum leap in customer service by giving the customer direct access to your systems.*

ERP's key concept is a central depository for all organizational data so that they are accessible in real time by and in an appropriate format for a decision maker. Data are entered into the central depository through a series of modules. Usually 30 or more modules are required to complete an ERP installation.[5] Exhibit 17–9 provides a list of typical modules included in an ERP system.

EXHIBIT 17-9

Typical Modules in an ERP Installation

Finance Function (bookkeeping, paying bills, collecting cash)

General ledger: Keeps centralized charts of accounts and corporate financial balances.

Accounts receivable: Tracks payments due the company.

Accounts payable: Schedules bill payments.

Fixed assets: Manages costs related to property, plant, and equipment.

Treasury management: Monitors and manages cash holdings and investment risks.

Cost control: Analyzes costs related to overhead, products, and customers.

Human Resources Management (personnel-related tasks)

Human resources administration: Automates processes such as recruitment, business travel management, and vacation allotments.

Payroll: Handles accounting and preparation of checks to employees for salary and bonuses.

Self-service HR: Lets workers select benefits and manage their personal information.

Manufacturing and Logistics

Production planning: Performs capacity planning and creates a daily production schedule.

Materials management: Controls purchasing of materials and manages inventory.

Order entry and processing: Automates entry of customer orders and tracks their status.

Warehouse management: Maintains records of stored goods and follows their movement through warehouses.

Transportation management: Arranges, schedules, and monitors delivery of products to customers.

Project management: Monitors costs and work schedules on a project-by-project basis.

Plant maintenance: Sets plans and oversees upkeep of facilities.

Customer service management: Administers service agreements and checks contracts and warranties when customers contact them.

SOURCE: Computerworld (www.computerworld.com) September 14, 1998. Reprinted with permission.

[4] Paddy White, "ERP: The Big Company Solution for Small Companies," *Accountancy Ireland* (August 1999), p.4.

[5] Ibid.

The ERP system is an extension of earlier software packages. Manufacturing resource planning (MRP and MRP II) programs were designed to control and coordinate the production process. MRP systems generated master production schedules, coordinated ordering of materials necessary to meet the schedule, and projected labor inputs necessary to complete conversion.

By having organizational data in a common depository, new insights can be gained from data analysis. For example:

> *[A] music chain learned that people older than 65 bought many rap and alternative music CDs. These buyers had not changed their tastes for music: they were buying Christmas presents for their grandchildren. A target marketing program to this group increased sales by 37%.*
>
> *[Additionally,] a 600-store office supply company was able to substantially improve its return on personal computer sales. [The system] allowed management to calculate gross margin by store and product type. This showed that some stores carried too much slow-moving stock. To eliminate unnecessary inventory and future write downs, the company reduced its PC assortment from 22 products to 12.*[6]

http://www.SAP.com/
http://www.peoplesoft.com/
http://www.baan.com
http://www.bridgestone-firestone.com
http://www.toyota.com

Installation of an ERP system impacts the finance function in three significant ways. First, finance and system specialists will bear the responsibility of selecting and installing the software. ERP software includes brand names such as SAP, R/3, PeopleSoft, and Baan. Installing an ERP system in a large company involves thousands of hours of labor and millions of dollars of capital. The accompanying News Note provides a flavor of the complexity in information technology decisions.

NEWS NOTE  GENERAL BUSINESS

E-Biz and ERP

Tire-maker Bridgestone/Firestone may not be selling radials over the Web, but that does not mean that electronic business is not shaking up its industry.

"As competition heats up any business, one of the key things you can do is not only provide what the customer wants, but when [the customer] wants it and faster than you could before," Gary Larson, a senior computer engineer, says above the whirring sounds of Bridgestone/Firestone's tire plant in Aiken, S.C. "That's what we're driving for."

IT executives in the manufacturing industry, many of whom have an opportunity to look up from years of enterprise resource planning (ERP) implementation, are discovering the new rigors of the fast-paced, customer-driven Internet age. As a result, manufacturers are optimizing operations via better integrated IT and production systems and are extending these systems down the supply chain and to their customers.

"E-business has raised the bar for speed for all of us," says Andy Chatam, president of ARC Advisory Group, a manufacturing industry consultancy in Dedham, Mass. "Customers have come to expect much better service than in the past."

For further evidence of the need for speed in manufacturing, consider industry-leader Toyota, which revealed in August 1999 new, sophisticated manufacturing computer systems that allow the company to produce a car within five days of a customer's order.

But plowing millions of dollars and thousands of work-years into new systems to address business imperatives, such as instantly giving customers a ship date on an order, is unthinkable to shell-shocked IT groups—and a tough sell to CEOs. Instead, manufacturers are leveraging massive ERP investments to increase efficiency and flexibility.

SOURCE: LaMonica Martin, "Life after ERP: E-Business Shakes up the Manufacturing Industry with a Push for Optimization and Supply-Chain Integration," *InfoWorld* (August 16, 1999), p. 24.

[6] Ibid.

Second, finance specialists will bear the responsibility of analyzing the data repository to support management decisions. Data analysis often involves "drilling down" from aggregate data (such as total sales for the firm) to detailed data (such as sales by store) to identify market opportunities and to better manage costs. For example, this type of analysis may explain why a certain product moves well at some stores but not at others.

Analysis may also involve **data mining,** which uses statistical techniques to uncover answers to important questions about business operations.[7] Data mining is useful to uncover quality problems, study customer retention, determine which promotions generate the greatest sales impact, and identify cost drivers.

data mining

ERP installation places a burden on finance specialists to maintain the integrity of the data depository. Fulfilling this obligation requires accountants and other specialists to monitor the ERP modules and to be confident that the system successfully converts raw data into the standardized format required for the main depository. Also, the finance specialists are accountable for integrating externally purchased data (such as industry sales data and other external intelligence) with internally generated data.

ERP systems represent a generational leap in the gathering, processing, and analysis of information. As ERP systems are increasingly integrated into Internet-based technology, customers will have ease of access to a worldwide marketplace. In turn, customer-driven competition will cause firms to continually seek innovative ways to attract potential customers. These innovations are often obtained through strategic efforts that combine the talents and capabilities of two or more firms.

STRATEGIC ALLIANCES

5

Why are firms increasing their use of strategic alliances?

In the usual supply chain structure, there are clear distinctions between supplier and customer firms—there are no fuzzy boundaries where one firm ends its contribution to the supply chain and another begins its contribution. However, in some instances, companies have incentives to develop interorganizational agreements that go beyond normal supplier/customer arrangements. Generically, these agreements are called strategic alliances. CarPoint is an illustration of a **strategic alliance**—an agreement, involving two or more firms with complementary core competencies, to jointly contribute to the supply chain.

strategic alliance

Strategic alliances can take many forms including joint ventures, equity investments, licensing, joint R&D arrangements, technology swaps, and exclusive buyer/seller agreements.[8] A strategic alliance differs from the usual interactions among independent firms in that the output is joint and the rewards of the joint effort are split among the allied firms.

The News Note on page 776 describes an alliance between a giant telecommunications firm in Europe and AT&T in the United States. The alliance is typical of many others: It involves the exploitation of technology, has partners with access to different markets, and allows sharing of risks and rewards. The use of strategic alliances to exploit or create business opportunities is pervasive. The quote that follows portrays the economic significance of alliances and the challenges in measuring the frequency of their use[9]:

http://www.att.com

> *In Silicon Valley and Hollywood, alliances are old hat: in a sense, almost every movie is an ad-hoc alliance, as is the development of every new computer chip. But, as in so much else, these two fashionable places are proving models for older industries. The most obvious change is in the sheer number of alliances.*

[7] Ibid.

[8] T. K. Das and Bing-Sheng Teng, "Resource and Risk Management in the Strategic Alliance Making Process," *Journal of Management* (January–February 1998), p. 21.

[9] Anonymous, "Mergers and Alliances," *The Economist* (May 15, 1999), p. 73.

http://www.bah.com

Mergers, like marriages, can be legally defined and therefore readily counted. Alliances are more like love affairs: they take many forms, may be transient or lasting, and live beyond the easy reach of statisticians. But one recent book by John Harbison and Peter Pekar of Booz-Allen & Hamilton, a consultancy, estimated that more than 20,000 alliances were formed worldwide in 1996–1998. And they account for a rising share of corporate revenue: doubling since the early 1990s to 21% of the revenues of America's 1,000 largest firms in 1997, according to Mr. Harbison. In Europe, he reckons, the figure is in "the high 20s."

In a typical strategic alliance a new entity is created, and in the process important decisions are made. In structuring the new entity, the contributions required of the parent organizations must be determined. Beyond simply contributing cash, many new ventures will require inputs of human capital, technology, access to distribution channels, patents, and supply contracts.

Further, a governing board or set of directors must be established and agreement must be reached as to how many directors can be appointed by each parent. The composition of the governing board will determine which of the parent entities is more influential in directing the management of the new entity.

Simultaneous agreements must be executed to stipulate the rights of the parents in sharing gains and specify obligations for bearing losses. Such agreements will have significant implications for the risks borne by the parent organizations.

http://www.bt.com
http://www.vodafone.co.uk
http://www.airtouch.com
http://www.hutchison-whampoa.com

An overriding concern in designing a strategic alliance is aligning the interests of the parent organizations with the new entity. The alliance is likely to work only if both parent organizations perceive they are receiving adequate value for their contributions. This caveat is especially true today when many strategic alliances involve agreements between competitors.

NEWS NOTE  INTERNATIONAL

Cell Phone Competition Rings Up a New Strategy

British Telecommunications PLC and AT&T Corp. formed an alliance to sell mobile-phone service around the world, intensifying the competitive battle with the newly merged Vodafone-AirTouch team.

The move falls far short of a merger of the two telecommunication companies' mobile operations, which serve about 41 million customers in 17 countries, including their share of customers from minority interests. But BT and AT&T expect the arrangement will help them attract more roaming fees, save on cost of buying equipment and make it easier to offer one-stop shopping for roving corporate customers.

The agreement signals the gradual transformation of local wireless wars into international face-offs. Partly because they want to better serve multinational customers, wireless companies are increasingly trying to extend their reach. Leading the pack is Vodafone Group PLC, which acquired AirTouch Communications Inc. of the U.S. and created a giant company with operations in the U.S. and much of Europe. Now BT and AT&T are moving in the same direction. And there is Hutchison Whampoa Ltd. of Hong Kong, which owns direct or indirect stakes in wireless companies in Asia, Australia, Britain, continental Europe and the United States.

The BT–AT&T arrangement is aimed at everyday customers who want to use their phones everywhere. One of the frustrations for roving U.S. subscribers is that they can't use their mobile phones when traveling in Europe, and vice versa. That is because the wireless networks of the two continents use different technologies and are incompatible.

BT of London and New York's AT&T hope to get around this problem by offering a two-phone package to users early next year. One device will work in the home market; the other can be carried across the Atlantic and will work using the original phone number and voice-mail system. The next step—a single device that works on AT&T's and BT's network—won't be available for 12 to 18 months, according to BT.

SOURCE: Adapted from Gautam Naik and Rebecca Blumenstein, "BT, AT&T Plan a Global Mobile-Phone Service," *The Wall Street Journal* (September 17, 1999), p. B2.

Establishing strategic alliances involves a series of complex decisions that are based on inputs from many functional specialists. For example, the financial professional must assess risk and develop strategies for its management. These experts must also design a financial structure, develop management control systems, and install accounting and other information systems. The execution of a strategic alliance is as involved as the establishment of any new business. Virtually every tool and concept discussed in this text applies to some facet of managing an alliance; these include cost management systems, product costing systems, cost allocation, inventory management, decision making, and performance evaluation.

The theme evident throughout this chapter of the technology evolution on management practices and the activities of the finance professional is followed in the next section with a discussion of how technological and other organizational changes are affecting nonprofessional workers and of how finance professionals have been pressured to develop ways to convey information to those without technical finance and accounting expertise.

OPEN-BOOK MANAGEMENT

6

What is open-book management and why does its adoption require changes in accounting methods and practices?

open-book management

Open-book management is a philosophy about increasing a firm's performance by involving all workers and by ensuring that all workers have access to operational and financial information necessary to achieve performance improvements. Although no specific definition of open-book management exists, it has some defined principles. Firms practicing open-book management typically disclose detailed financial information to all employees, train them to interpret and use the information, empower them to make decisions, and tie a portion of their pay to the company's bottom line.[10] The application of this philosophy is appropriate in decentralized organizations that have empowered employees to make decisions. Proponents of open-book management argue that the approach helps employees understand how their work activities affect the costs and revenues of the firm. With this understanding, employees can adopt or change work practices to either increase revenues or decrease costs.

However, merely opening the financial records to a firm's employees will neither necessarily solve any problems nor improve anyone's performance. Most employees, particularly nonmanagerial workers, neither have developed skills in interpreting business financial information nor understand accounting concepts and methods. Even many highly educated functional specialists have little knowledge of how profits are generated and performance is measured in financial terms. The key to understanding is training. Springfield Remanufacturing, a recession-era spin-off of General Motors, first introduced the concept of open-book management. Gary Brown, human resources director at Springfield Remanufacturing, has written about the learning curve for nonfinancial workers to become financially literate[11]:

http://www.gm.com

> *Brown estimates that it generally takes two years for people to become financially literate (two iterations of the planning cycle). However, formal financial education and training is not the major expense, nor does training consume the most time, according to Brown. He emphasizes that the most valuable learning takes place in the "huddles" and when employees study the figures by themselves. An exceptionally motivated employee who does a great deal of self-study may become financially literate in six months.*

If financial information is to be the basis of employee decision making, the information must be structured with the level of sophistication of the decision maker

[10] Edward J. Stendardi and Thomas Tyson, "Maverick Thinking in Open-Book Firms: The Challenge for Financial Executives," *Business Horizons* (September–October 1997), p. 35.

[11] Tim Davis, "Open Book Management: Its Promises and Pitfalls," *Organizational Dynamics* (Winter 1997), p. 13.

in mind. Providing such information requires accountants to become much more creative in the methods used to compile and present financial data. Some common principles of open-book management are provided in Exhibit 17–10.

Effective open-book management requires sharing accounting and financial information with employees who have little knowledge of accounting concepts. Games can be used to teach these concepts to financially unsophisticated employees.

Games People Play

Games make learning both fun and competitive while allowing for complex financial practices to be simplified. To illustrate how games can be used in open-book management, assume that Northside Building Systems, a manufacturer of steel doors and frames, has decided to implement open-book management concepts. One of its key departments is Assembly.

Assembly is responsible for combining components of various models of doors and frames into finished products. Most of the components that are required for assembly are manufactured in other departments of the company.

Assembly employees consist of one manager and 10 workers. All workers are highly skilled in the technical aspects of assembling door and frame components; however, none of the workers knows anything about financial management or accounting techniques. For these workers, the game must begin with very simple accounting principles. The outcomes of the game, as determined by financial and nonfinancial performance measurements, must be easy to comprehend and must be easily related to the motivation for establishing the game—for example, to maximize firm profit, maximize customer satisfaction, and maximize shareholder value.

The data in Exhibit 17–11 pertain to one product, an economy garage door, that passes through Assembly. These data have been provided by the controller of Northside and have been gathered from production and accounting records for the most recent month.

In designing a system to provide information to the Assembly Department employees, the starting point is to determine the objectives of the system. Reasonable initial design objectives include

- causing Assembly Department employees to understand how their work affects achievement of corporate objectives;
- making Assembly Department workers understand how their work affects upstream and downstream departments; and
- generating demand from the employees for information and training that leads to improvements in performance in the Assembly Department.

EXHIBIT 17–10

Ten Common Principles of Open-Book Management

1. Turn the management of a business into a game that employees can win.
2. Open the books and share financial and operating information with employees.
3. Teach the employees to understand the company's financial statements.
4. Show employees how their work influences financial results.
5. Link nonfinancial measures to financial results.
6. Target priority areas and empower employees to make improvements.
7. Review results together and keep employees accountable. Regularly hold performance review meetings.
8. Post results and celebrate successes.
9. Distribute bonus awards based on employee contributions to financial outcomes.
10. Share the ownership of the company with employees. Employee stock ownership plans (ESOPs) are routinely established in firms that practice open-book management.

SOURCE: Tim Davis, "Open-Book Management: Its Promises and Pitfalls," *Organizational Dynamics* (Winter 1997), pp. 6–20. Copyright (1997), with permission from Elsevier Science.

EXHIBIT 17-11

Economy Garage Door Assembly Department Cost Data

Item	Quantity	Unit Cost	Total Cost
Door panels	6	$ 5.00	$ 30.00
Door frame			
Top	1	7.00	7.00
Bottom	1	8.00	8.00
Sides	2	4.00	8.00
Panel connectors	24	2.00	48.00
Bolts	96	0.10	9.60
Nylon bushings	96	0.03	2.88
Total direct material			$113.48
Direct labor	2 hours	12.00	24.00
Total direct costs			$137.48

Because overhead is a more difficult cost to comprehend, relative to direct material and direct labor, information on overhead costs may be excluded from the initial system that is developed for assembly employees. Direct material and direct labor will be the information focus. Further, because employees can exert no control over the price of materials purchased or the labor rate paid per hour, these data might be presented at budgeted or standard, rather than actual, cost. If presented at actual cost, variations in purchase prices occurring throughout the year might disguise other more important information from the financially unsophisticated workers (e.g., quantities of materials consumed). If desirable, a more sophisticated system can be developed once the workers fully understand the initial system.

One of the motivations for providing information to the assembly workers is to cause the workers to understand how their actions affect achievement of the overall corporate objectives. To initiate this understanding, management can establish a sales price for the output of the Assembly Department. Assume the initial price for the assembled economy door is set at $150; it is not necessary for the established sales price to represent actual market value. It is important that a sales price be established so that a measure of the department's contribution to corporate profits can be established. For the assembly workers, the per-unit profit calculation is as follows:

Sales price	$150.00
Direct costs (from Exhibit 17-11)	(137.48)
Profit contribution	$ 12.52

Total profits equal per-unit profit multiplied by the number of units produced. Workers will soon realize as they analyze this simple profit calculation that they can increase profits by decreasing costs or by increasing the number of units made. However, because the information contains no quality effects, some elementary quality information could be added. For example, quality defect costs could be charged to the Assembly Department. An income statement for the Assembly Department for a period would then appear as follows:

Sales	$XXXXXX
Direct costs	(XXXXXX)
Rework and defects	(XXXX)
Profit contribution	$ XXXX

With this profit calculation, workers will comprehend that profit maximization requires maximization of output, minimization of direct costs, and minimization of quality defects.

One Japanese company, Higashimaru Shoyu, a maker of soy sauce, has gone so far as to create its own internal bank and currency.[12] Each department purchases its required inputs from other departments using the currency and established transfer prices. In turn, each department is paid in currency for its outputs. The flow of currency reinforces the profit calculations applying to each department.

To exploit the financial information they are given, workers should be educated about ways to improve profits. The "game" of trying to increase profits serves as motivation for workers to learn about cost and operational management methods. By relating the training to the game, its relevance is immediately obvious to the workers and they will seek training to help them both understand how to read and comprehend a simple income statement, and to identify approaches that can be used to improve results.

Motivating Employees

It cannot be assumed that the assembly workers are internally motivated to play the game well. Instead, the game should be promoted by upper management. The obvious way to motivate workers to use the information that they receive to improve profits is to link their compensation to profits. Workers in the Assembly Department could be paid bonuses if profits are above a target level. Alternatively, the workers could be paid a bonus that is a percentage of profits. In either case, the linkage of compensation to profits is a necessary step to motivate workers to have an interest in the game and to improve their performance. The positive effects of a good bonus program are described in the following quotation[13]:

> *Open-book management works only if it is accompanied by adequate incentives. "People start to back away if they don't have some sort of reward. In effect, you are asking people to take on ownership behaviors, but not treating them like owners. That's like getting to smell lunch, but not being allowed to taste it," says [Corey] Rosen of the National Center for Employee Ownership. "If people don't have a stake in the company, why should they care?"*
>
> *Some companies offer performance-based bonuses and others lean toward employee stock ownership plans (ESOPs). For short-term bonuses, at AmeriSteel, for example, employees can earn up to one-fifth of their total compensation based on performance measures specific to their operation. Mill-employee incentives are tied to tons of finished steel produced, while marketing-personnel incentives are tied to sales volume. In addition, employees are awarded six options for every share of AmeriSteel they purchase.*[13]

http://www.ameristeel.com

Pay and performance links can be based on more specific data also. For example, measures can be devised for on-time delivery rates (to the next downstream department), defect rates, output per labor hour, and other performance areas to make workers aware of how their inputs and outputs affect other departments and financial outcomes. All critical dimensions of performance including costs, quality, and investment management can be captured in performance measurements. And, as illustrated in the accompanying News Note, games can be devised to encourage learning by workers.

http://www.foldcraft.com

Once the workers have become accustomed to receiving financial and other information to manage their departments, more elaborate information systems can be developed as the sophistication of the information consumers (workers) evolves. For example, once the direct labor, direct material, and quality costs are understood, workers in the Assembly Department can learn to evaluate overhead cost information.

[12] Robin Cooper, *When Lean Enterprises Collide (Competing Through Confrontation)* (Boston: Harvard Business School Press, 1995).
[13] Julie Carrick Dalton, "Between the Lines," CFO: The Magazine for Senior Financial Executives (Vol. 15, No. 3, March 1999), p. 61. © 1999 CFO Publishing Corporation. Reprinted with permission.

GENERAL BUSINESS  NEWS NOTE

Learning by Earning

The open-book management style of Foldcraft Co. is evident at the company's monthly employee meetings. Dubbed "ESOP Huddles," the one-hour meetings consist of a financial review, followed by a question-and-answer period which includes contests.

In the first half hour, managers essentially "build the financial statement," including sales, expenses and profits. This financial reporting segment of the meeting covers results for the month completed and projects those of the next month.

The Q&A period in the second half-hour takes a more playful approach. First, any non-manager employee who asks a question receives $1 and a ribbon.

Next, there is a drawing of employee questionnaires which were distributed at the outset of the meeting. The first employee whose questionnaire is drawn and found to have answered correctly three questions about the company receives $50. The drawing gives managers a chance "to revisit the questions" and make sure that all employees hear the correct answers in a context that is more compelling.

The final game at the meeting is called "Pass or Play." Employees' names are drawn randomly. These employees then are asked another question—almost always financially oriented—about the company. They then have the opportunity to "pass" on the question if they don't know the answer, or "play" if they think they do. If they play and get the right answer, they receive $100. Other than potential embarrassment, there is no penalty for a wrong answer or a "pass."

SOURCE: Staff, "Information-Sharing, Games Motivate Employee Owners," *PR News* (April 22, 1996), not paged.

Implementation Challenges

Open-book management can be difficult to implement. Characteristics of firms that are best suited to a successful implementation include small size, decentralized management, a history of employee empowerment, and the presence of trust between employees and managers. In small firms, employees can more easily understand how their contributions influence the bottom-line performance of the organization. Firms with decentralized structures and empowered employees have workers who are accustomed to making decisions. Trust among employees and managers is necessary for games to be devised that result in higher pay and greater job satisfaction for all employees.

Accountants face unique challenges in implementing open-book management in even the most favorable environments. The challenges are present in both the obstacles to be overcome and the innovations in reporting to be designed and implemented.

One significant obstacle to overcome in most organizations is a history of carefully guarding financial information. Even in publicly owned organizations that are required to release certain financial information to the general public, top mangers have historically limited access of employees to financial data that the top managers regard as sensitive. Accountants have historically viewed themselves as the custodians of this sensitive information rather than the conveyors. To successfully implement open-book management, accountants must develop an attitude about information sharing that is as fervent as traditional attitudes of information guarding.

Accountants have been grounded in higher education courses and other training to expertly compile information according to prescribed rules of financial accounting, and they have generally operated under the assumption that users of financial information have an adequate understanding of the rules used to compile financial data. However, open-book management requires dissemination of accounting data to users who have little understanding of accounting conventions and rules. Thus, accountants must develop methods of conveying accounting information such that it will be understood by unsophisticated users. Further, because a sophisticated user of financial data is better able to use information in decision making than an unsophisticated user, accountants must assume roles as teachers as well as information disseminators. By teaching users to become more sophisticated consumers of financial information, accountants facilitate better organizational decision making.

Accountants must also be innovative to implement open-book management. One significant requirement is the development of information systems that are capable of generating information for an organizational segment in a format that can be understood by employees of that segment. Thus, the information system must be designed to be sensitive to the financial sophistication of the user.

Similarly, performance measures must be devised that can be understood by employees. The measures must capture the actual performance relative to the objectives of organizational segments and the organization as a whole. The objectives may be stated in terms of performance of competitors or industry norms. For example, an objective of a firm may be to surpass the average product quality level of the industry. Measurement of actual achievement relative to this objective requires accountants to develop information systems that are focused on gathering nontraditional types of information—in this instance, quality level of output in the industry.

Finally, because principles of open-book management include involving all employees and measuring and rewarding their performance, measures must be devised that can be integrated across segments and functional areas. For example, if one of a firm's major objectives is to increase profitability, performance measures must be devised for engineers, accountants, production workers, administrators, janitors, etc., that cause all of these functional groups to work toward a common end: increased profits.

An emerging area of concern for managers, in nearly all operating environments, is the impact of their operations on the environment. The concerns have arisen as a result of a greater consciousness of environmental issues and new governmental regulations enacted to protect the environment.

ENVIRONMENTAL MANAGEMENT SYSTEMS

7

What are the three generic approaches firms can take in controlling environmental costs?

The impact of organizations on the environment is of increasing concern to governments, citizens, investors, and businesses. Accountants are increasingly concerned with both measuring business performance with regard to environmental issues and management of environmental costs. In the future, investors are likely to evaluate a company's environmental track record along with its financial record when making investment decisions.

Management of environmental costs requires that environmental issues be considered in every aspect of operations. For example, environmental effects are related to the amount of scrap and by-products produced in manufacturing operations, the materials selected for product components (recyclable or not), the actions of suppliers who produce necessary inputs, and habits of customers in consuming and disposing of products and packaging. In short, environmental issues span the entire value chain.

There are three generic strategies for dealing with environmental effects of operations; each strategy has unique financial implications. First, end-of-pipe strategies may be employed. With this approach, managers "produce the waste, or pollutant, and then find a way to clean it up."[14] Common tools used in this approach are wastewater cleaning systems and smokestack scrubbers.

A second strategy involves process improvements. Process improvements involve changes to "recycle wastes internally, reduce the production of wastes, or adopt production processes that generate no waste."[15]

A third strategy is pollution prevention. This approach involves "complete avoidance of pollution by not producing any pollutants in the first place."[16]

Although minimizing the impact of operations on the environment may be a reasonable goal, it must be remembered that some impact on the environment is unavoidable. For example, energy must be consumed to manufacture products; similarly, materials must be consumed as goods are produced. Without energy and material consumption, no goods can be manufactured.[17]

In the management of environmental costs, accountants must analyze environmental dimensions of investment decisions.

> *In the capital investment area, accountants can help managers by including quality and environmental benefits in the analysis. If a proposed project is more energy efficient or produces less pollution than an alternative, those factors should be included in the analysis. The financial data should include any cost savings from lower energy usage. If the company must control pollution, the financial impact should be recognized.*[18]

Other topical managerial concerns discussed in this text and chapter embedded in the management of environmental costs include managing quality, managing research and development, and managing technology acquisition. Although the relationship between quality costs and environmental costs is not fully understood, many cases can be cited suggesting that quality and environmental costs are highly related. For example, the reduction in scrap and waste production (quality improvements) serves to reduce environmental costs and concerns (waste disposal).

Through research and development, new products and new production processes are identified, and new materials are developed. The design of new products influences (1) the types and quantities of materials to be produced, (2) the types and quantities of waste, scrap, and by-products to be produced, (3) the amount of energy to be consumed in the production process, and (4) the potential for gathering and recycling the products when they reach obsolescence.

Technology acquisition also has many impacts on the environment. For instance, technology affects energy consumption and conservation; environmental emissions; the quantity, types, and characteristics (for instance, whether the equipment is made of materials that can be recycled) of future obsolete equipment; the rate of defective output produced; the quantities of scrap, waste, and by-products produced; and the nature and extent of support activities necessary to keep the technology operating.

Exhibit 17–12 provides a checklist of considerations for the financial professional to evaluate whether a firm's information systems provide relevant information for managing environmental costs. An analysis of the checklist will show that the financial professional must effectively gather both quantitative and nonquantitative data from both within and outside of the firm.

[14] German Böer, Margaret Curtin, and Louis Hoyt, "Environmental Cost Management," *Management Accounting* (September 1998), pp. 28–30, 32, 34, 36, 38.
[15] Ibid.
[16] Ibid.
[17] For more information on this concept, see Frances Cairncross, *Costing the Earth* (Boston: Harvard Business School Press, 1992), p. 26.
[18] Harold P. Roth and Carl E. Keller, Jr., "Quality, Profits, and the Environment: Diverse Goals or Common Objectives?" *Management Accounting* (July 1997), pp. 50–55.

EXHIBIT 17-12

Checklist for Environmental Cost Control

Cost Management Systems

- ➢ How much does each of our divisions spend on environmental management?
- ➢ Do we have consistent and reliable systems in place to measure environmental costs?
- ➢ How does our cost management system support good environmental management decisions?
- ➢ How do we track compliance costs?
- ➢ How do we connect line management decisions to the environmental costs they create?
- ➢ Which divisions manage environmental costs the best?
- ➢ How do we compare with competitors in managing environmental costs?
- ➢ What kinds of waste do we produce?
- ➢ What are the proposed regulations that will affect our company?

Cost Reporting Systems

- ➢ Who receives reports on environmental costs in our company?
- ➢ Does our bonus plan explicitly consider environmental costs?
- ➢ How do we charge internal environmental costs to managers?
- ➢ How does the financial system capture environmental cost data?
- ➢ Do our managers have all necessary tools to measure total costs of the wastes generated?
- ➢ Do our systems identify environmental cost reduction opportunities?

SOURCE: German Böer, Margaret Curtin, and Louis Hoyt, "Environmental Cost Management," *Management Accounting* (September 1998) p. 32. Copyright by Institute of Management Accountants, Montvale, N.J.

REVISITING CarPoint

http://www.carpoint.msn.com

Ford's interest in CarPoint is to find a better way to connect its production operations to consumer needs. Almost all the big global automakers are scrambling to refashion their Web sites and their factories to be flexible enough to let consumers configure a car to their specific needs.

That is virtually opposite of how cars are made and sold now. Traditionally, automakers have built millions of cars with options packages based on consumer research. The problem: The research isn't perfect, leaving dealers carrying inventories of unpopular products that need profit-draining incentives to sell them.

Ford is hoping to make that system a memory with its build-to-order system that should be up and running in its earliest stages by early 2000. Toyota Motor Corp. already is working on its own build-to-order system, and General Motors Corp. has created a new unit to oversee all of its Internet strategies, including online custom ordering.

In its earliest stages, Ford's build-to-order system will simply let consumers find the kind of car they want that has already been built and is somewhere between the factory and the dealer. Within two years, Mr. Nasser said, custom orders, which now can take as long as eight weeks, will take less time and be more flexible with paint and interior options being changed on the factory floor.

In addition to build to order, the new CarPoint site gives Ford access to three million people who go visit the CarPoint site every month. Ford's Internet strategy is to be everywhere in cyberspace, executives said, including its own Web sites, electronic communities such as iVillage.com, as well as in-car technology such as satellite navigation systems.

SOURCE: Adapted from Fara Warner, "Ford and Microsoft Forge Alliance to Create Online Car-Sales System," *The Wall Street Journal Online* (September 21, 1999).

CHAPTER SUMMARY

The global economy has raised the consumer to the position of ultimate arbiter of success in the marketplace. To maintain market share, find new growth opportunities, and operate profitably, firms must be innovative in satisfying customer wants. Many emerging management practices are built around the goal of increasing organizational performance by increasing customer satisfaction.

Business process reengineering (BPR) targets specific business processes for improvement. A key idea of BPR is to bring about evolutionary or generational changes in processes rather than incremental changes. Three forces that create a demand for BPR are advancement of technology, pursuit of increased quality, and increasing price-based competition.

Accountants have an important role in BPR. The success of BPR projects is assessed based on performance measures. Accountants are responsible for developing baseline measures, and comparing the baseline level measures to performance levels achieved after the reengineering is completed.

Restructuring and downsizing are irreversible actions that are monumental events in the life of an organization. These actions shake the foundations of firms and bring about cultural changes and new responsibilities for employees. Also, the role of the accounting function is affected.

To compete in a global marketplace, many firms have pursued strategies leading to global operations—operations distributed in many countries. With global operations, firms expect to gain cost and market advantages over rival firms. However, the potential cost advantage and market opportunities notwithstanding, the global enterprise creates many management challenges.

In globalizing operations, managers take on the challenges of dealing with customers, suppliers, and employees who have different languages, cultures, work practices, legal statutes, currencies, and infrastructures. Globalizing operations leads to new challenges and roles for the accounting function. Accountants play a pivotal role in coordinating the efforts of diverse employees. Accounting information can have a common meaning to employees who are geographically dispersed and who otherwise have limited, common means of communicating. Thus, accounting is the common "language" in the organization that communicates information about roles, performance expectations, achieved performance, cost management, coordination of operations, and other operational dimensions.

Enterprise resource planning (ERP) is a technological approach to tighten the connection of a firm to its suppliers and customers. Some ERP software programs allow companies to (1) automate and integrate the majority of their business processes, (2) share common data and practices across the entire enterprise, and (3) produce and access information in a real-time environment. The drive to adopt ERP is partially driven by the advancing Internet technology that allows consumers a new ease-of-entry into the front door of businesses.

Cooperative interorganizational agreements are common in the global market and take many forms in addition to those of the traditional vendor/customer. Some common examples include strategic alliances and joint ventures. These cooperative efforts often involve the creation of a new entity to which two or more existing entities contribute resources and technical knowledge. It is through the combining of complementary core competencies that the main partners in such a transaction hope to realize synergies leading to new products and exploitation of new markets. Selecting strategic partners, monitoring and measuring performance of joint ventures, and determining when to unwind cooperative ventures all create new demands on the accounting function in organizations.

Open-book management philosophy is built on the notion that all employees are responsible for achieving an organization's goals. And, to deliver a high level of performance, each employee must understand how his or her job affects organizational performance. The burden of providing performance information belongs largely to accountants. Adding to the burden is the knowledge that some employees have greater abilities than other employees to understand and interpret accounting data. Accordingly, accountants must be prepared to issue simplified reports, identify new performance measurements, and train employees to understand financial information. Over time, and with practice, employees increase their abilities to apply financial information to enhance their contribution to organizational performance.

The operations of organizations impact the environment. Managers can act in three ways to manage effects on the environment: (1) Produce the waste, or pollutant, and then find a way to clean it up, (2) reduce the production of wastes or adopt production processes that generate no waste, or (3) avoid pollution by not producing any pollutants in the first place. Managers use all three approaches, and accountants play the important role of designing and maintaining the cost management and cost reporting systems that provide managers information necessary to make effective environmental decisions.

KEY TERMS

business process reengineering (BPR) (p. 764)
data mining (p. 775)
downsizing (p. 767)
enterprise resource planning (ERP) system (p. 771)
open-book management (p. 777)
strategic alliance (p. 775)

QUESTIONS

1. What are the forces causing managers to develop innovative business practices?
2. What is business process reengineering (BPR)? Does BPR lead to radical or modest changes in business practices? Discuss.
3. How can business process reengineering be used as a tool to improve the quality of manufacturing operations?
4. In designing a business process reengineering project, why is it wise to include customer input?
5. Business process reengineering and downsizing often occur together. Why?
6. Describe "downsizing." What are the causes of downsizing?
7. What are the major risks of downsizing?
8. In what ways does downsizing create issues for the accounting function in a business?
9. Why does the management and analysis of a downsizing decision require analysis using capital budgeting techniques?
10. How has the globalization of firms affected the diversity of their employees? Why has increased diversity put an additional burden on accounting systems?
11. Besides increasing globalization, what trends within the United States are causing firms to seek more diversified workforces?
12. What is an enterprise resource planning (ERP) system? How do ERP systems improve upon prior generations of information systems?
13. How do ERP systems integrate the flow of information throughout the supply chain?
14. How are modules used as building blocks in the expansion of an ERP system?
15. How is an ERP system built around the concept of a central repository for information?

16. How does the adoption of an ERP system affect the finance function in a business?
17. What is data mining? Why does an ERP system facilitate data mining?
18. New strategic alliances are formed every day. What are strategic alliances and why are they increasingly used today?
19. What are some of the typical ways in which strategic alliances are structured?
20. Discuss the issues that management must address in structuring a typical strategic alliance.
21. Open-book management is a relatively new philosophy about the use of information in organizations. Describe open-book management and how, philosophically, it differs from the traditional view of how information should be managed in an organization.
22. How does the implementation of open-book management require the accountants in the organization to change their traditional practices?
23. How can games be used as a tool in implementing open-book management concepts?
24. In providing information to less financially sophisticated managers, how can accountants adapt accounting data to make it more easily understood?
25. Why is it necessary to tie incentives to financial measures to successfully implement open-book management?
26. Not all firms are well suited to implementing open-book management. Discuss the characteristics that a firm should possess for a successful implementation.
27. Why has the management of the environmental impacts of company operations become a major concern for businesses?
28. There are three generic strategies for dealing with the environmental effects of operations. Describe these strategies. Is one of the strategies always preferred to the others? Discuss.

EXERCISES

29. *(Technology acquisition)* The acquisition of new technology is often a perilous event for firms. The successful acquisition and implementation of new systems require much more than merely purchasing hardware and software. For example, expenditures for a typical installation of a new financial system are split as follows:

Presales consultancy and advice	11.74%
Software	37.64%
Implementation	28.27%
Training	14.12%
Other services	14.24%

SOURCE: Anonymous, "An Overview of Accounting Software Packages," *Management Accounting* (London; March 1999), pp. 50–53.

a. Why is it necessary that training be included as a cost of the technology acquisition?

b. How can the finance function of a business improve the internal process of technology acquistion?

30. *(Technological change)* Financial professionals are at the forefront in adopting new technologies. Many of these technologies are at the core of business strategies. Discuss how the increasing reliance of business on technology, coupled with the responsibility of the finance professional to manage technology, has changed the skills required of corporate accountants.

31. *(Business process reengineering)* Business process reengineering can be an effective tool to achieve breakthroughs in quality improvement and cost management. Total quality management, or TQM, is another philosophy about achieving organizational change. Conduct a library or Internet search to identify articles that discuss TQM and write a report in which you compare and contrast TQM and BPR.

32. *(Business process reengineering)* Process mapping and value analysis are tools often used in business process reengineering. A process map is a flowchart of the set of activities that comprise a process. Value (or activity) analysis examines each of the activities identified in the flowchart and determines to what extent it provides "value" to the customer. Those activities that add no value are targets to be designed out of the process.

Select a process at your college or university such as admissions or enrollment, prepare a process map, and conduct value analysis of the process map. Then, develop a plan (using Exhibit 17–3 as a guide) to design out of the process those activities that add no value to the customer (the student).

33. *(Downsizing)* In the past decade, the economy of Japan has fallen from the lofty levels reached in the 1980s. As a consequence many Japanese companies have been forced to downsize. In most companies, one of two strategies can be pursued in downsizing. First, a company can lay off employees. Second, a company can cut employment through natural attrition and by reducing future hiring.

Conduct a library or Internet search of "Japanese management culture" to identify attitudes of Japanese managers about employees. Then, prepare a report in which you explain why Japanese companies might prefer one of these downsizing strategies to the other.

34. *(Downsizing)*

http://www.sgi.com

In 1999 Silicon Graphics Inc. (SGI) said it would lay off up to 17% of its workforce and sell or spin off several divisions, including its Cray supercomputer unit, as the computer maker faces an increasingly difficult market.

http://www.hewlett-packard.com

http://www.sun.com

Yesterday's announcements, made before an analysts' meeting scheduled for New York, were a setback for Richard E. Belluzzo, brought in 1998 from Hewlett-Packard Co. to turn around SGI. While SGI had a sterling reputation for its graphics-based workstations, used to create special effects for many movies, it had been badly outmaneuvered in the high end of the market by such competitors as Sun Microsystems Inc., and was losing sales in the low end to generic PCs.

SOURCE: Lee Gomes, "Silicon Graphics to Lay Off Up to 1,500, Sell or Spin Off Units, Including Cray," *The Wall Street Journal* (August 11, 1999), p. A3. Permission conveyed through the Copyright Clearance Center.

a. How do the layoffs in this situation suggest that SGI's strategy has failed?
b. As a market analyst, would you interpret these layoffs to be good news or bad news?

35. *(Diversity)* Is diversity an organizational asset or liability? This question has been hotly debated in the past. Some argue that Japan has an inherent advantage in competing with the United States because of its homogeneous workforce. The benefits of a homogeneous workforce arise from a common language, religion, work ethic, etc. Prepare a two-minute oral report in which you take a position and persuasively present an argument on whether diversity aids or hinders an organization.

http://www.boeing.com

36. *(Diversity and discrimination)* Recently, Boeing Co. settled a lawsuit for $15 million brought by its own African-American workers claiming discrimination in promotions. On the heels of that decision, a group of Asian workers, also claiming discrimination in promotions, filed suit against Boeing. Similar stories make headlines in the financial press nearly every day.

Discuss the contributions that can be made by the accounting and finance professionals in an organization to actively promote diversification of the workforce while managing real and perceived discrimination in promotion of workers and managers.

37. *(Open-book management)* The *Monopoly* game by Parker Brothers has been a popular board game for many years. Assume that you have just been hired by a company in the steel industry. The company manufactures a variety of products from stock steel components. The management of your new employer is examining the potential use of open-book management techniques. Prepare a written report for the top managers in your company discussing your recommendations for implementing open-book management. In your report, discuss how you would use *Monopoly* as a training tool for workers who have little knowledge of accounting concepts.

http://www.monopoly.com

38. *(Enterprise resource planning)* With an ERP system, a company can develop a "storefront" on the Internet. Through the storefront connection with customers, much information can be gathered about the market and the demand for specific products.

Assume that you are employed by an automaker. How could you use the Internet storefront and data mining to learn more about the purchasers of your vehicles for the purpose of improving the market share of your future generations of autos?

39. *(Enterprise resource planning)* ERP software programs are allowing tighter linkages within a supply chain than were possible with earlier generations of software. Consider the possibility of a tighter link between the marketing and engineering functions within a firm that makes consumer electronics. Discuss how the tighter link between these two functions could improve

a. customer satisfaction,
b. time to bring new products to market, and
c. cost management.

40. *(Enterprise resource planning; Internet)* ERP software can facilitate the sharing of information throughout the supply chain. For example, an Internet storefront can be used to interact (downstream) with the final customer. The sales data gathered from the storefront can then be used as a basis for determining the quantity and mix of products to be produced. From this information a production schedule can be compiled. Discuss how posting the production schedule on the Internet could result in improved coordination with the upstream side of the supply chain.

41. *(Strategic alliances)* In their annual reports, companies provide brief descriptions of their most important contracts. These descriptions include strategic alliances. Select a large publicly traded company and obtain a copy of its most recent annual report. Review the portions of the annual report that discuss strategic alliances. Based on your review, prepare an oral report in which you discuss the following points:

a. motivations for establishing strategic alliances,
b. the extent to which strategic alliances are used to conduct business, and
c. the relative financial success of the strategic alliances.

42. *(Strategic alliances)* Assume you are employed by a technology company that is considering entering into a strategic alliance with a communications company to provide certain innovative services delivered via the Internet.

As a financial professional, how could you contribute to the organization and management of the strategic alliance?

43. *(Open-book management)* You have been hired as a consultant by a company that manufactures toys from plastic stocks and resins.

The company management is presently wrestling with ways to improve the quality of its products. Evidence of quality problems is everywhere: high rates of product defects, many customer returns, poor rate of customer retention, and high warranty costs. Top management has traced virtually all quality-related problems to the production department.

Production workers in the company are paid based on a flat hourly rate. No bonuses are paid based on corporate profits or departmental performance measures. As the outside consultant, prepare an oral report to present to the top management of your client discussing how open-book management could be applied to address the quality problems. At a minimum, include in your report the following: how quality information would be conveyed to workers, how workers would be trained to understand the information, and how incentives would be established for improved quality performance.

44. *(Environmental costs)* Following are descriptions of environmental waste situations. Identify the environmental strategy you would select to deal with each situation and discuss your logic.

a. A relatively small amount of low toxicity waste is produced. This waste is not easily recycled, nor is technology available to avoid its production. Disposal costs are relatively modest.

b. This waste is highly toxic and is associated with several lethal diseases in humans. The cost of disposal is extraordinarily high.

c. A moderate amount of this waste is produced. The waste is nearly identical to a chemical purchased and used in an etching operation. The waste differs from the purchased chemical only because of a small amount of contaminants introduced in the production process.

45. *(Environmental costs)* Galveston Chemical produces a variety of chemicals that are used in an array of commercial applications. One popular product, a chemical solvent, has among its required materials two very caustic acids, A and B. These acids are a very serious environmental hazard if not disposed of properly. For every ton of chemical produced, 500 pounds of acid A are required as well as 300 pounds of acid B. Because of inefficiencies in the present production process, 40 pounds of acid A and 20 pounds of acid B remain as waste with each ton of chemical manufactured. Because of impurities in the waste acids, they cannot be used in the production of future batches of product. The company incurs a cost of $2 per pound to dispose of the waste acid produced.

Recently, the company has become aware of new technology that reduces the quantity of waste acids produced. This technology would generate only 1 pound of acid A and 5 pounds of acid B as waste from each ton of chemical manufactured. Corporate management has estimated the new technology could be acquired and installed at a cost of $500,000. The technology would have a life expectancy of six years. The new technology would not otherwise affect the cost of producing the chemical solvent.

a. Which environmental cost management strategy is Galveston Chemical considering in this example?

b. Why would the application of discounted cash flow methods be appropriate to evaluate the new technology?

46. *(Environmental cost management)* The increasing awareness by firms of their impacts on the environment has led to the development of firms that specialize in all aspects of managing the environmental effects of operations. Search the Internet using the term "environmental cost management." Review the Web pages of the vendors of environmental services identified by the search. Write a brief report in which you describe the types of services that can be purchased to manage environmental costs.

CASES

47. *(Downsizing and restructuring)*

With pioneering feats like the discovery of the hepatitis C virus, Chiron became one of the nation's largest biotech companies. Then some of its academic-style research and gambles on technology didn't pan out commercially, and growth stalled. In 1998, the proud scientists running Chiron reluctantly turned it over to a no-nonsense manager from the pharmaceutical industry.

Chiron now is seeking a comeback by taking fewer research risks and squeezing more profit from its assets—acting, that is, more like a traditional pharmaceutical company.

Recently, chairman and chief executive, Sean Lance, unveiled the first significant research cuts ever at Chiron. The retrenchment, announced only to employees, is part of a plan to cap its bulging R&D budget at $290 million, and could result in layoffs of as many as 90 scientists, or 20% of its research staff.

The cuts, mainly in gene-therapy and vaccine programs, are designed to help sustain earnings growth, a priority for Mr. Lance. In the first nine months of 1999, earnings from continuing operations, at $102.5 million, leapt 66% over the year-earlier period.

SOURCE: Ralph King, "New Therapy for Chiron: Fiscal Austerity," *The Wall Street Journal* (November 2, 1999) p. B1. Permission conveyed through the Copyright Clearance Center.

http://www.chiron.com

a. Assume you are a market analyst for the biotech industry. Discuss how you would evaluate the news (as good or bad) about Chiron making deep cuts in R&D spending.

b. As a finance professional at Chiron, how could you help Mr. Lance identify opportunities for reducing costs and improving profitability?

48. *(Downsizing)*

In 1997 the current employment market for top talent was the tightest in 25 years. The number of searches for senior-level executives was at an all-time high, nearly 15% ahead of last year's record clip. Among some of the hottest searches under way: chief executives for Unisys Corp., Delta Air Lines, Quaker Oats Co. and a president and chief operating officer for St. Jude Medical Inc.

Why is the labor market so thin for the "performance elite"—the top 4% or so of executives and senior managers? The long-term impact of corporate downsizing is a principal reason. The cutbacks in the ranks of middle managers during the past two decades have meant a loss of career-development patterns for employees. Because there are fewer rungs on the career ladder, "45-year-olds are basically doing the same thing they were at 30," says Roger I. Sekara, an Alexandria, Va., vice president of A.T. Kearney Executive Search.

SOURCE: Timothy D. Schellhardt, "Star Search: Talent Pool Is Shallow as Corporations Seek Executives for Top Jobs," *The Wall Street Journal* (June 26, 1997) p. A1. Permission conveyed through the Copyright Clearance Center.

http://www.unisys.com
http://www.delta-air.com
http://www.quakeroats.com
http://www.sjm.com

http://www.executivesearch.atkearney.com

In light of the scarcity of qualified leaders, what can the accounting function in an organization do to help identify potential top management talent from internal operations?

49. *(Open-book management)* Jennifer Gale, Technical Instruments Division manager of Wetherford Technologies Corporation, attended a 30-minute seminar on open-book management recently. As a result of the seminar, Ms. Gale decided to implement some open-book management practices in her division. She began the process of implementation today upon receipt of the latest quarterly results for her division.

Laslow Wallace, the production supervisor of the finishing department in Ms. Gale's division, was surprised to receive the following note in his afternoon mail.

Dear Wally:

I have just finished reviewing the financial results for the last quarter. I have included some data from the financial reports below. Because our firm must identify ways to become more cost competitive, I intend to share data from the financial reports with you each quarter. I want you to use the information as the basis for making your department more efficient. By early in the coming year, I intend to put in place an incentive pay system that will replace your current salary. Accordingly, your income in the future will depend on your ability to manage costs of your department.

To begin reducing costs, I suggest you concentrate on the cost items which I have circled below. Please give me a call if you have any questions.

Regards,

JG

FINISHING DEPARTMENT COST ANALYSIS

	This Quarter	This Quarter Last Year	Last Quarter
Direct material	$ 95,000	$ 75,000	$ 90,000
Direct labor	925,000	840,000	940,000
Material-based overhead	27,000	22,000	23,000
Labor-based overhead	(413,000)	382,700	396,500
Machine-based overhead	(657,000)	589,000	617,000

As corporate controller of Wetherford Technology Corporation, you are surprised when Mr. Wallace calls your office and asks to meet with your staff to discuss the financial report and to discuss the meaning of "overhead." As you consider how to deal with Mr. Wallace, you begin to contemplate the memo which you are going to write to Ms. Gale. Before any decisions are implemented, you realize that Ms. Gale can use your expertise to design and implement open-book management practices. As you write the memo, you know that your suggestions must be specific, positive, and informative.

50. *(Various)* Peter Wyndale, president of Mallory Industrial, sat dejected in his chair after reviewing the 2001 first-quarter financial reports on one of the company's core products: a standard, five-speed transmission (product number 2122) used in the heavy equipment industry in the manufacture of earth-moving equipment. Some of the information in the report follows.

MARKET REPORT, PRODUCT NUMBER 2122, QUARTER 1, 2001

Sales Data	
Total sales (dollars), Quarter 1, 2001	$4,657,500
Total sales (units), Quarter 1, 2001	3,450
Total sales (dollars), Quarter 1, 2000	$6,405,000
Total sales (units), Quarter 1, 2000	4,200
Market Data	
Industry unit sales, Quarter 1, 2001	40,000
Industry unit sales, Quarter 1, 2000	32,000
Industry average sales price, Quarter 1, 2001	$1,310
Industry average sales price, Quarter 1, 2000	$1,640

MARKET REPORT, PRODUCT NUMBER 2122, QUARTER 1, 2001

Profit Data	
Mallory average gross profit per unit, Quarter 1, 2001	$ 45
Mallory average gross profit per unit, Quarter 1, 2000	$160
Industry average gross profit per unit, Quarter 1, 2001	$ 75
Industry average gross profit per unit, Quarter 1, 2000	$140

Mallory's strategy for this transmission is to compete on the basis of price. Mallory's transmission offers no features that allow it to be differentiated from those of major competitors and Mallory's level of quality is similar to the average of the industry.

Also on Mr. Wyndale's desk was a report from his business intelligence unit. Mr. Wyndale underlined some key pieces of information from the report. The underlined items follow.

- Commodity transmission components (nuts, bolts, etc.), which all major transmission producers acquire from specialty vendors, decreased in price by approximately 5% from January 2000 to January 2001.
- Two major competitors moved their main assembly operations to China from the United States in early 2000. These competitors are believed to have the lowest unit production cost in the industry.
- A third major competitor ceased manufacture of major gear components and began outsourcing these parts from a Mexican firm in mid-2000. This firm increased its market share in 2000 from 10 to 14 percent following a major decrease in sales price.
- Mallory's production operations did not change in any material respect from 2000 to 2001.
- Mallory manufactures approximately 83 percent of the components used in the heavy industrial transmission. The industry norm is to make 57 percent of the components.
- For the balance of 2001, industry experts agree that quarterly demand for the heavy industrial transmission will be even higher than the levels posted for the first quarter of 2001.

a. Examine the information Mr. Wyndale has gathered. Analyze the data that are given to identify as specifically as possible the problems that have led to Mallory's loss of profit and market share in the heavy industrial transmission market.

b. Based on your analysis in part (a), and the information given to Mr. Wyndale, suggest specific alternatives that Mr. Wyndale should consider to make his firm more competitive in the heavy industrial transmission market. Use concepts presented in the chapter as the basis of your recommendations.

51. *(Enterprise resource management)* Barnes & Noble and Amazon.com are competitors in vending books and other consumer items. The two are differentiated to an extent by their marketing strategies. Although Amazon.com relies exclusively on Internet marketing, Barnes & Noble operates both retail stores and an Internet outlet.

http://www.barnesandnoble.com
http://www.amazon.com

Assume that you work for a financial services firm that specializes in ERP installations. Your personal specialty involves ERP solutions that link the marketing function to the "back end" of businesses.

Write a report in which you discuss the benefits that could be realized by Barnes & Noble and Amazon.com from purchasing ERP software from you. In your report discuss how the ERP solution that you would design for Barnes & Noble would differ from the solution you design for Amazon.com.

52. *(Environmental cost management)* ABX Plastics has experienced serious problems as a result of attempts to manage its impacts on the environment. To illustrate the problems, consider the following events, which occurred during the past five years:

- ABX was assessed $75 million in fines and penalties for toxic emissions. These amounts related to several separate regulatory investigations.
- ABX received reprimands from several regulatory bodies for failing to maintain required records regarding hazardous waste.
- ABX is currently facing a class-action lawsuit filed by former employees of a subsidiary in Mexico alleging management failed to disclose information to employees about the toxicity of certain materials—and as a consequence the health of the former employees has been permanently harmed.
- ABX must submit bids to obtain most of its business. Managers have casually observed that the company is successful more frequently when it bids on jobs that require handling the most toxic chemicals.
- ABX has a very basic accounting system that tracks costs on a job order basis, but is not sensitive to quality or environmental costs.

Assume that you are an employee of a consulting firm that has been hired by ABX to improve management of all environmental effects. As the finance expert on the consulting team, you are expected to make recommendations as to how the information systems should be modified to reduce environmental costs. Prepare a report discussing your recommendations for ABX.

REALITY CHECK

53. *Slightly more than half of working Americans question their bosses' integrity; when they do, they're more likely to leave their jobs over it, according to a study by the Hudson Institute and Walker Information.*

The firms surveyed more than 2,000 full and part-time workers from the public and private sectors in 48 states. Fewer than half of them, 42%, believe their company deserves their loyalty. And slightly more than half of the surveyed employees would recommend their place of employment to another.

Employees also fear retaliation for reporting inappropriate behavior like drug use, sexual harassment, record falsification, and unfair treatment of employees, representatives of the research firms said. They also worry complaints won't be kept confidential.

SOURCE: Scott Scholten, "Boss Lacks Integrity, Say 50% of Workers, Study Shows," *The Wall Street Journal Interactive* (October 27, 1999). Permission conveyed through the Copyright Clearance Center.

a. In your opinion, does the achievement of high-quality operations mandate that a firm treat its employees ethically? Discuss.

b. Assume a firm has adopted open-book management. Discuss how the survey respondents' perceptions of their employers mesh with the open-book management requirement to have honest exchanges of information between employees and managers.

http://www.pwcglobal.com

54. Strategic alliances and joint ventures are being used with increasing frequency to exploit market opportunities. For example, according to Coopers and Lybrand (now PricewaterhouseCoopers), over half of the nation's fastest growing companies are involved in an average of three alliances.

a. From the perspective of controlling the quality of production, discuss how a strategic alliance is significantly different from a typical vendor/customer relationship.

b. How can the accounting function contribute to the management of quality for strategic alliances?

55. Automakers provide an interesting study in cost management strategies. General Motors often provides a contrast to the other U.S. manufacturers. For example, while Chrysler and Ford have opted to outsource many product components, GM continues to manufacture a much higher percentage of the parts needed to produce its cars. One of the variables driving GM's strategy is its high level of unionization. The unions have resisted attempts made by General Motors to restructure operations and outsource more components.

a. From the perspective of price-based competition, why would GM want the flexibility to outsource more of its parts and components?

b. From the perspective of managing quality, how could outsourcing positively or negatively affect GM's ability to manage quality relative to its competitors?

c. What ethical responsibility does GM bear to the union in seeking to restructure and outsource more of its parts manufacturing?

56. Andy Vickers was reprimanded by the home office for recommending a pollution abatement project because the project did not meet the standard financial criterion of a 10 percent rate of return. However, Andy had concluded that the $60,000 piece of equipment was necessary to prevent small amounts of arsenic from seeping into the city's water system. No EPA warnings had been issued to the company.

a. Discuss the company requirement of a 10 percent rate of return on all projects.

b. What might be the ultimate consequence to Vickers' company if it fails to prevent arsenic seepage into the groundwater system?

c. How should (or can) Vickers justify the purchase of the equipment to the home office?

57. This chapter discusses three approaches to managing environmental costs. Some strategies deal with hazardous waste only after it has been produced.

a. Do firms have any ethical obligations not to produce hazardous waste regardless of how successfully the company deals with the waste?

b. Assume you are a key financial adviser in a firm that produces a large amount of toxic waste. Further assume that the firm faces severe financial pressures and risks bankruptcy. By improperly disposing of certain waste materials your company could save many millions of dollars, avoid bankruptcy, and preserve 10,000 local jobs. What action would you recommend your company take?

CHAPTER 18

Responsibility Accounting and Transfer Pricing in Decentralized Organizations

LEARNING OBJECTIVES

After completing this chapter, you should be able to answer the following questions:

1. Why is decentralization appropriate for some companies but not for others?
2. How are responsibility accounting and decentralization related?
3. What are the differences among the four basic types of responsibility centers?
4. Why and how are service department costs allocated to producing departments?
5. Why are transfer prices used in organizations?
6. What are the advantages and disadvantages of service transfer prices?
7. How can multinational companies use transfer prices?

INTRODUCING

Abbott Laboratories

http://www.abbott.com

More than a century ago, 30-year-old Wallace C. Abbott, M.D., began making a new form of medicine. Using the active part of medicinal plants, he formed tiny pills, called "dosimetric granules," which provided a precisely measured amount of drug. Within two years, the demand for these granules far exceeded the needs of his own medical practice.

From a small operation based in Dr. Abbott's Chicago apartment, Abbott Laboratories has evolved into one of the world's leading health care companies with 57,000 employees around the globe. Today, you can find Abbott products in more than 130 countries on five continents. Abbott is involved in five broad business arenas:

- Nutritional Products—medical and nutritional help for adults and children.
- Pharmaceutical Products—including anti-infective, cardiovascular, neuroscience, hormonal, anti-ulcer drugs, and new non-invasive drug therapy for enhancing health.
- Diagnostic Products—*in vitro* diagnostics, and diagnostics for HIV infection, hepatitis, and blood glucose self-testing for people with diabetes.
- Hospital Products—a full line of anesthetics, injectable drugs, infection-control products, diagnostic imaging agents, intravenous solutions, advanced drug-delivery systems and other medical specialty products for hospitals, clinical labs and alternate health care sites.
- Chemical and Agricultural Products—environmentally compatible insecticides and plant growth regulators, animal health products and efficient bulk drug development and manufacturing for internal and external customers.

The company has four decentralized business divisions: pharmaceuticals, hospital products, nutritional, and diagnostics. These divisions require the use of responsibility accounting and transfer pricing for internal purchases and sales.

SOURCE: "Abbott Laboratories Online," Abbott Laboratories Web site, http://www.abbott.com (March 29, 2000).

An organization's structure evolves as its goals, technology, and employees change, and the progression is typically from highly centralized to highly decentralized. When top management retains the major portion of authority, centralization exists. Decentralization refers to top management's downward delegation of decision-making authority to subunit managers. Abbott Laboratories recognizes the need for decentralization in its corporate structure because the company's global operations demand that the managers on location in any particular region be able to most effectively use corporate resources.

This chapter describes the degree to which top managers delegate authority to subordinate managers and the accounting methods—responsibility accounting and transfer pricing—that are appropriate in decentralized organizations.

DECENTRALIZATION

1

Why is decentralization appropriate for some companies but not for others?

The degree of centralization can be viewed as a continuum. It reflects a chain of command, authority and responsibility relationships, and decision-making capabilities. In a completely centralized firm, a single individual (usually the company owner or president) performs all major decision making and retains full authority and responsibility for that organization's activities.

Alternatively, a purely decentralized organization would have virtually no central authority, and each subunit would act as a totally independent entity. Either extreme of the centralization–decentralization continuum represents a clearly undesirable arrangement.

In the totally centralized company, the single individual may have neither the expertise nor sufficient and timely information to make effective decisions in all areas. In the totally decentralized firm, subunits may act in ways that are inconsistent with the organization's goals.

http://www.jj.com

Johnson & Johnson recognized each of these possibilities in the management of its 160 almost wholly autonomous businesses operating in 50 countries. Decentralization gives Johnson & Johnson managers a sense of ownership and control and the ability to act on information more quickly. However, Johnson & Johnson's chairman, Ralph Larsen, also stated that "The glue that binds this company together" is an ethical code of conduct—which Johnson & Johnson dubs its "credo"—that is literally set in stone at the company's headquarters.[1]

Each organization tends to structure itself in light of the pure centralization versus pure decentralization factors presented in Exhibit 18–1. Most businesses are, to some extent, somewhere in the middle part of the continuum because of practical necessity. The combination of managers' personal characteristics, the nature of decisions required for organizational growth, and the nature of organizational activities lead a company to find the appropriate degree of decentralization. For example, to be more responsive to market needs, Hewlett-Packard decentralized, as discussed below:

http://www.hewlett-packard.com

> *[Lew Platt, taking over leadership as CEO in November 1992] started running the company like a conglomerate of little ventures, each responsible for its own success. He changed the focus of H-P from technology to people. [The company is] asking customers what problems they have, then saying H-P has the talent to create technology to solve those problems. Reacting to customers keeps H-P growing and changing, grafting different pieces of itself together, spitting out new products.*[2] *[Platt retired December 31, 1999.]*

Decentralization does not necessarily mean that a unit manager has the authority to make all decisions concerning that unit. Top management selectively determines the types of authority to delegate and the types to withhold. For example,

EXHIBIT 18–1

Degree of Decentralization in an Organizational Structure

FACTOR	CONTINUUM		
	Pure Centralization	→	**Pure Decentralization**
Age of firm	Young	→	Mature
Size of firm	Small	→	Large
Stage of product development	Stable	→	Growth
Growth rate of firm	Slow	→	Rapid
Expected impact on profits of incorrect decisions	High	→	Low
Top management's confidence in subordinates	Low	→	High
Historical degree of control in firm	Tight	→	Moderate or loose

[1] Staff "Dusting the Opposition," *The Economist* (April 29, 1995), p. 71.

[2] Kevin Maney, "Giant Goes from Stodgy to Nimble," *USA Today* (May 18, 1994), pp. 1B–2B. Copyright 1994, *USA Today*. Also, Eric Nee, "Lew Platt: Why I Dismembered HP," *Fortune* (March 29, 1999), pp. 167ff.

after Alcoa implemented a major decentralization program in 1991, Chairman Paul H. O'Neill still viewed safety, environmental matters, quality, insurance, and information strategy to be "central resource" issues such as cash management, evaluation of division profitability, and capital project approval. He thought that centralization was the most sensible and cost-effective method of handling those specific functions.[3]

http://www.alcoa.com

As with any management technique, decentralization has advantages and disadvantages. These pros and cons are discussed in the following sections and are summarized in Exhibit 18–2.

Advantages of Decentralization

Decentralization has many personnel advantages. Decentralized units provide excellent settings for training personnel and for screening aspiring managers for promotion. Managers in decentralized units have the need and occasion to develop their leadership qualities, creative problem-solving abilities, and decision-making skills. Managers can be comparatively judged on their job performance and on the results of their units relative to those headed by other managers; such comparisons can encourage a healthy level of organizational competition. Decentralization also often leads to greater job satisfaction for managers because it provides for job enrichment and gives a feeling of increased importance to the organization.[4] Employees are given more challenging and responsible work, providing greater opportunities for advancement.

In addition to the personnel benefits, decentralization is generally more effective than centralization in accomplishing organizational goals and objectives. The decentralized unit manager has more knowledge of the local operating environment, which means (1) a reduction of decision-making time, (2) a minimization of difficulties that may result from attempting to communicate problems and instructions through an organizational chain of command, and (3) quicker perceptions of environmental changes than is possible for top management. Thus, the manager of a decentralized unit is both in closest contact with daily operations and charged with making decisions about those operations.

A decentralized structure also allows the management by exception principle to be implemented. Top management, when reviewing divisional reports, can address issues that are out of the ordinary rather than dealing with operations that are proceeding according to plans.

EXHIBIT 18–2

Advantages and Disadvantages of Decentralization

ADVANTAGES

- Helps top management recognize and develop managerial talent
- Allows managerial performance to be comparatively evaluated
- Can often lead to greater job satisfaction
- Makes the accomplishment of organizational goals and objectives easier
- Allows the use of management by exception

DISADVANTAGES

- May result in a lack of goal congruence or suboptimization
- Requires more effective communication abilities
- May create personnel difficulties upon introduction
- Can be extremely expensive

[3] Paul H. O'Neill, Remarks at Alcoa organizational meeting (Pittsburgh Hilton Hotel, August 9, 1991), p. 5.
[4] Job enrichment refers to expanding a job to provide for personal achievement and recognition.

Disadvantages of Decentralization

Not all aspects of decentralization are positive. For instance, the authority and responsibility for making decisions may be divided among too many individuals. This division of authority and responsibility may result in a lack of goal congruence among the organizational units. **Goal congruence** exists when the personal goals of the decision maker, the goals of the decision maker's unit, and the goals of the broader organization are mutually supportive and consistent.

goal congruence

In a decentralized company, unit managers are essentially competing with each other because results of unit activities are compared. Because of this competition, unit managers may make decisions that positively affect their own units, but are detrimental to other organizational units or to the company. This process results in suboptimization.

suboptimization

Suboptimization is a situation in which individual managers pursue goals and objectives that are in their own and/or their segments' particular interests rather than in the company's best interests. Because of their greater degree of flexibility in financial decisions, managers of profit and investment centers (to be discussed later in the chapter) must remember that their operations are integral parts of the entire corporate structure. Therefore, all actions taken should be in the best long-run interest of both the responsibility center and the organization. Unit managers should be aware of and accept the need for goal congruence throughout the entity. To assume awareness of such goal congruence, management may keep certain organizational functions at "headquarters" or recentralize some functions if they have been delegated to unit managers.

A decentralized organization requires that more effective methods of communicating plans, activities, and achievements be established because decision making is removed from the central office. Top management has delegated the authority to make decisions to unit managers, but top management retains the responsibility for the ultimate effects of those decisions. Thus, to determine whether those operations are progressing toward established goals, top management must maintain an awareness of operations at lower levels.

In attempts to introduce decentralization policies, some top managers may have difficulty relinquishing the control they previously held over the segments or may be unwilling or unable to delegate effectively. Reasons for this unwillingness or inability include the belief of managers that they can do the job better than anyone else, a lack of confidence in the lower-level managers' abilities, and a lack of ability to communicate directions and assignments to subordinates.

A final disadvantage of decentralization is that it may be extremely costly. In a large company, all subordinate managers are unlikely to have equally good decision-making skills. Thus, companies must often incur a cost to train lower-level managers to make better decisions. Another potential cost is that of poor decisions, because decentralization requires managerial tolerance if and when subordinates make mistakes. The potentially adverse consequences of poor decisions by subordinates cause some top managers to resist a high degree of decentralization.

Decentralization also requires that a company develop and maintain a sophisticated planning and reporting system. With more organizations like Abbott Laboratories having decentralized units worldwide, integrated ways to transfer information are extremely important. A manager at an Abbott Laboratories office in Europe may need to work with an Abbott Laboratories manager in South America on a report for the home office in Chicago. For companies having operations spanning the globe, modems, fax machines, interactive computer networks, management information systems, and videoconferencing are no longer on capital budgeting "wish lists"; they have become capital investment necessities. Frito Lay, for example, installed a network that linked all senior staff and field managers at all levels nationwide and allowed decisions to be made quickly from a well-informed perspective. The company referred to the system (shown in Exhibit 18–3) as "directed decentralization."

http://www.fritolay.com

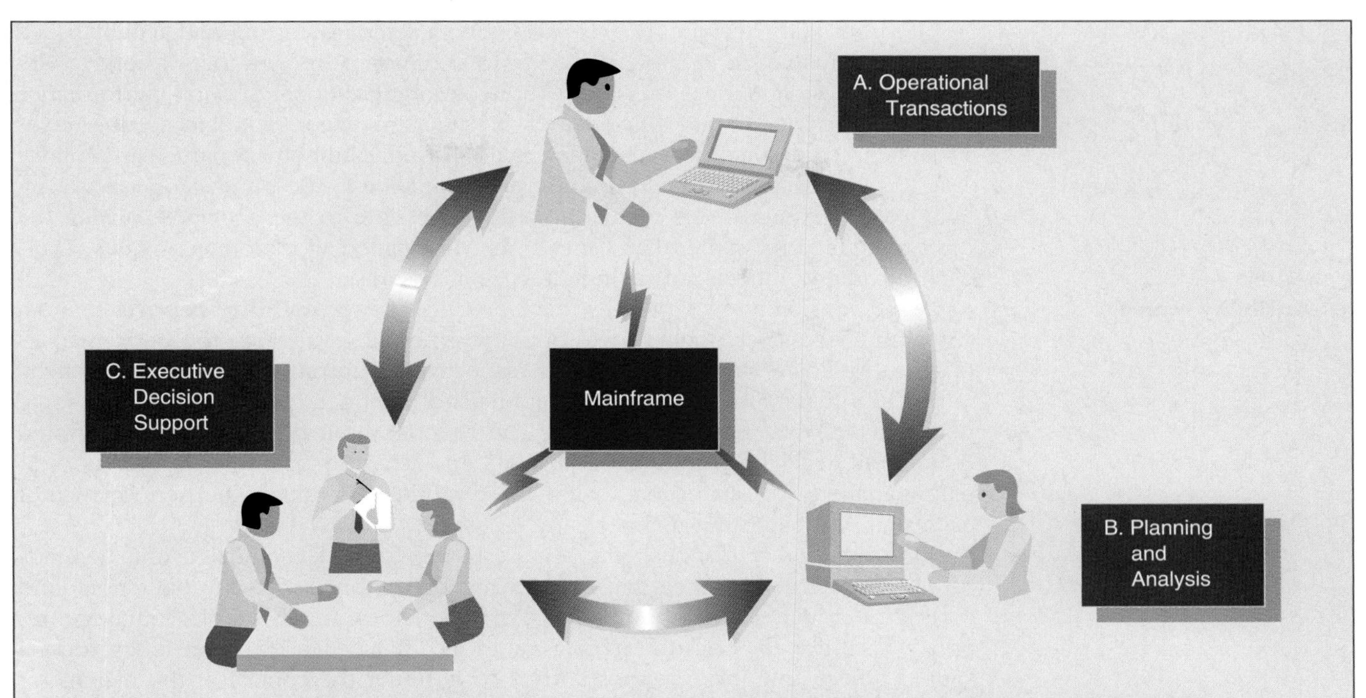

Frito Lay's system is built on a relational database. Any information entered into the system is immediately accessible to all users.

A. A salesperson processes an order on his or her [laptop] computer. The purchasing, manufacturing, and logistics facilities are notified immediately and begin processing the order. Each successive transaction is entered as it occurs; that is, the company can track where the order is in manufacturing, when it left the plant, and when it will be delivered.

B. At the same time, this information is available to the planning and analysis system. This allows the brand manager, the channel manager, and the area manager to spot trends in consumption. Competitive information from supermarket scanners is also fed into the mix, enabling managers to see their markets in wider perspective and to develop appropriate strategies to respond to market needs.

C. This information, broader and more general in scope, becomes instantly available to top management. This allows managers to understand what is going on throughout the company, where the firm is losing market share, and why. This in turn allows the executive process to enter the picture sooner and with greater impact.

SOURCE: Charles S. Field, "Directed Decentralization: The Frito Lay Story," *Financial Executive* (November/December 1990), p. 25. Reprinted with permission from *Financial Executive*, copyright 1990 by Financial Executives Institute, 10 Madison Avenue, P.O. Box 1938, Morristown, N.J. 07962.

EXHIBIT 18–3

Frito Lay's Directed Decentralization System

In a decentralized organization, top management delegates decision-making authority but retains ultimate responsibility for decision outcomes. Thus, a reporting system must be implemented to provide top management with information about, as well as the ability to measure, the overall accountability of the subunits. This accounting and information reporting system is known as a responsibility accounting system.

RESPONSIBILITY ACCOUNTING SYSTEMS

2

How are responsibility accounting and decentralization related?

A responsibility accounting system is an important tool in making decentralization work effectively by providing information to top management about the performance of organizational subunits. As companies became more decentralized, responsibility accounting systems evolved from the increased need to communicate operating results through the managerial hierarchy. Responsibility accounting implies subordinate managers' acceptance of communicated authority from top management.

Responsibility accounting is consistent with standard costing and activity-based costing because each is implemented for a common purpose—that of control. Responsibility accounting focuses attention on organizational subunit performance and the effectiveness and efficiency of that unit's manager. Standard costing traces variances to the person (or machine) having responsibility for a particular variance (such as tracing the material purchase price variance to the purchasing agent). Activity-based costing traces as many costs as possible to the activities causing the costs to be incurred rather than using highly aggregated allocation techniques. Thus, each technique reflects cause-and-effect relationships.

responsibility report

A responsibility accounting system produces **responsibility reports** that assist each successively higher level of management in evaluating the performances of its subordinate managers and their respective organizational units. Much of the information communicated in these reports is of a monetary nature, although some nonmonetary data may be included. The reports about unit performance should be tailored to fit the planning, controlling, and decision-making needs of subordinate managers. Top managers review these reports to evaluate the performance of each unit and each unit manager.

The number of responsibility reports issued for a decentralized unit depends on the degree of influence that unit's manager has on day-to-day operations and costs. If a manager strongly influences all operations and costs of a unit, one report will suffice for both the manager and the unit because responsibility reports should reflect only the revenues and/or costs under the control of the manager.

Normally, though, some costs of an organizational unit are not controlled (or are only partially or indirectly controlled) by the unit manager. In such instances, the responsibility accounting report takes one of two forms. First, a single report can be issued showing all costs incurred in the unit, separately classified as either controllable or noncontrollable by the manager. Alternatively, separate reports can be prepared for the organizational unit and the unit manager. The unit's report would include all costs; the manager's would include only costs under his or her control.

Responsibility accounting systems help to establish control procedures at the point of cost incidence rather than allocating such costs in a potentially arbitrary manner to all units, managers, and/or products. Managers implement control procedures for three reasons. First, managers attempt to cause actual operating results to conform to planned results; this conformity is known as *effectiveness*. Second, managers attempt to cause the standard output to be achieved with minimum possible input costs; this conformity is known as *efficiency*. Third, managers need to ensure reasonable plant and equipment utilization, which is primarily affected by product or service demand. At higher volumes of activity or utilization, fixed capacity costs can be spread over more units, resulting in a lower unit cost. Reasonable utilization must be tied to demand and thus does not mean producing simply for the sake of lowering fixed cost per unit if sales demand cannot support production.

A responsibility accounting system helps organizational unit managers to conduct the five basic control functions shown in Exhibit 18–4. A budget is prepared and used to officially communicate output expectations (e.g., sales and production) and delegate authority to spend. Ideally, subunit managers negotiate budgets and standards for their units with top management for the coming year. The responsibility accounting system should be designed so that actual data are captured in conformity with budgetary accounts. Thus, during the year, the system can be used to record and summarize data for each organizational unit.

Operating reports comparing actual account balances with budgeted or standard amounts are prepared periodically and issued to unit and top managers for their review. However, because of day-to-day contact with operations, unit managers should have been aware of any significant variances before they were reported, identified the variance causes, and attempted to correct the causes of the problems.

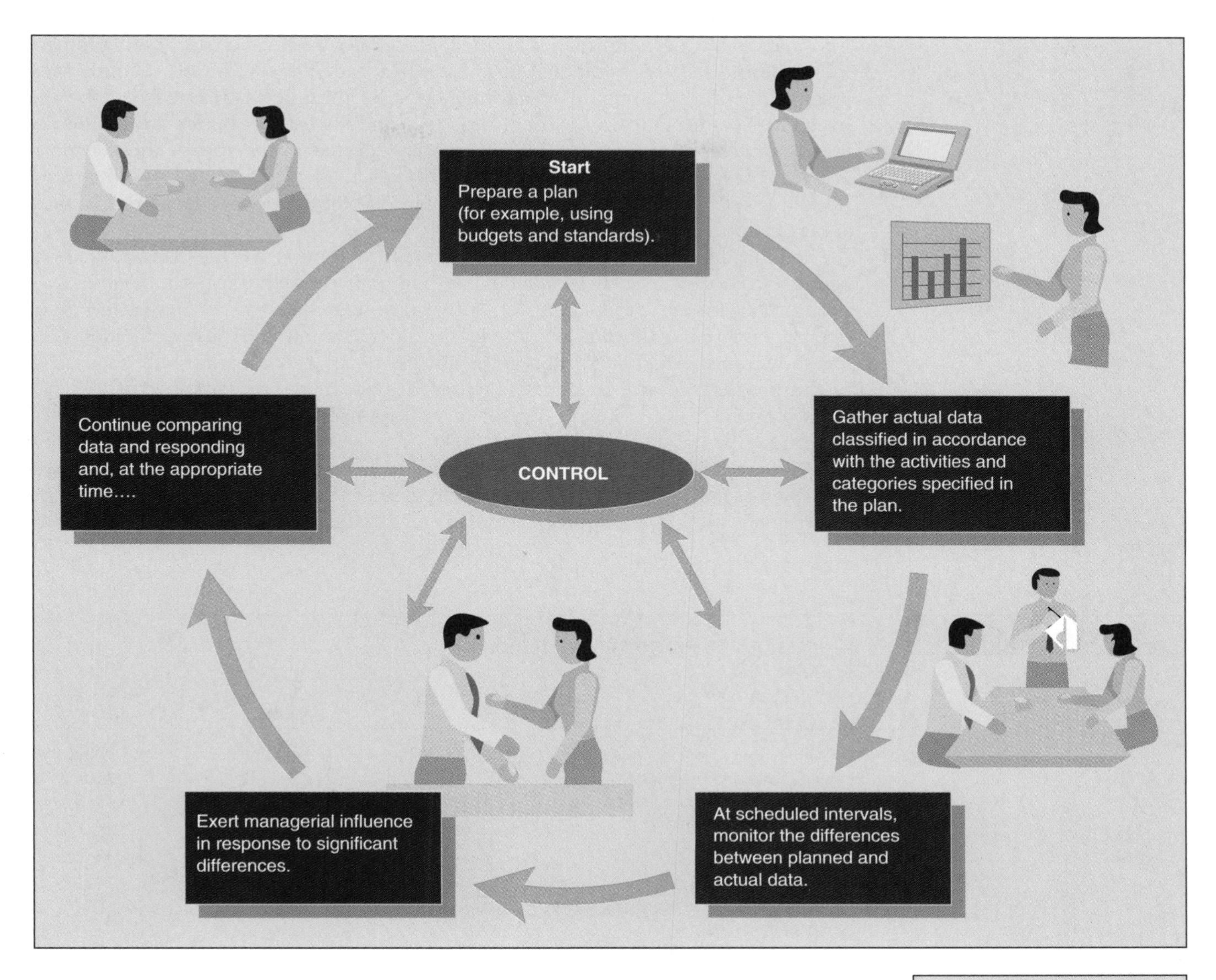

EXHIBIT 18-4

Basic Steps in a Control Process

Top management, on the other hand, may not know about operational variances until responsibility reports are received. By the time top management receives the reports, the problems causing the variances should have been corrected, or subordinate managers should have explanations as to why the problems were not or could not have been resolved.

Responsibility reports for subordinate managers and their immediate supervisors normally compare actual results with flexible budget figures. These comparisons are more useful for control purposes because both operating results and flexible budget figures are based on achieved levels of activity. In contrast, top management may receive responsibility reports comparing actual performance to the master budget. Such a budget-to-actual comparison yields an overall performance evaluation, because the master budget reflects management's expectations about volume, mix, costs, and prices. This type of comparison is especially useful when accompanied by a supporting detailed variance analysis identifying the effect of sales volume differences on segment performance.

Regardless of the type of comparison provided, responsibility reports reflect the upward flow of information from operational units to company top management and illustrate the broadening scope of responsibility. Managers receive detailed information on the performance of their immediate areas of control and summary information on all organizational units for which they are responsible. Summarizing results causes a pyramiding of information. Like the information received by the executives in the Frito Lay exhibit, reports at the lowest level units are highly detailed, whereas more general information is reported at the top of the organization. Upper-level managers desiring more detail than is provided in summary reports can obtain it by reviewing the responsibility reports prepared for their subordinates.

Exhibit 18–5 illustrates a set of performance reports for the Sanger Pharmaceutical Company. The division's flexible budget is presented for comparative purposes. Data for the production department are aggregated with data of the other departments under the production vice president's control. (These combined data are shown in the middle section of Exhibit 18–5.) In a like manner, the total costs of the production vice president's area of responsibility are combined with other costs for which the company president is responsible and are shown in the top section of Exhibit 18–5.

Variances are the responsibility of the manager under whose direct supervision they occur. Variances are individually itemized in performance reports at the lower levels so that the appropriate manager has the necessary details to take any

EXHIBIT 18-5

Sanger Pharmaceutical Company Performance Reports for Costs Incurred

PRESIDENT'S PERFORMANCE REPORT
JUNE 2000

	Budget	Actual	Variance Fav. (Unfav.)
Administrative office—president	$ 298,000	$ 299,200	$(1,200)
Financial vice president	236,000	234,100	1,900
Production vice president	737,996	744,400	(6,404)
Sales vice president	275,000	276,400	(1,400)
Totals	$1,546,996	$1,554,100	$(7,104)

PRODUCTION VICE PRESIDENT'S PERFORMANCE
REPORT JUNE 2000

	Budget	Actual	Variance Fav. (Unfav.)
Administrative office—VP	$180,000	$182,200	$(2,200)
Distribution and storage	124,700	126,000	(1,300)
Production department	433,296	436,200	(2,904)
Totals	$737,996	$744,400	$(6,404)

DISTRIBUTION AND STORAGE MANAGER'S PERFORMANCE
REPORT JUNE 2000

	Budget	Actual	Variance Fav. (Unfav.)
Direct material	$ 36,000	$ 35,400	$ 600
Direct labor	54,500	55,300	(800)
Supplies	4,700	5,300	(600)
Indirect labor	12,400	12,900	(500)
Power	11,200	10,900	300
Repairs and maintenance	3,500	3,700	(200)
Other	2,400	2,500	(100)
Totals	$124,700	$126,000	$(1,300)

(continued)

EXHIBIT 18–5

(Concluded)

PRODUCTION DEPARTMENT MANAGER'S PERFORMANCE REPORT JUNE 2000

	Budget	Actual	Variance Fav. (Unfav.)
Direct material	$119,300	$122,500	$(3,200)
Direct labor	190,880	188,027	2,853
Supplies	17,656	18,500	(844)
Indirect labor	46,288	47,020	(732)
Depreciation	38,653	38,653	0
Repairs and maintenance	12,407	12,900	(493)
Other	8,112	8,600	(488)
Totals	$433,296	$436,200	$(2,904)

required corrective action related to significant variances.[5] Under the management by exception principle, major deviations from expectations are highlighted under the subordinate manager's reporting section to assist upper-level managers in making decisions about when to become involved in subordinates' operations. If no significant deviations exist, top management is free to devote its attention to other matters. In addition, such detailed variance analyses alert operating managers to items that may need to be explained to superiors. For example, the items of direct material and direct labor in Exhibit 18–5 on the production department manager's section of the report would probably be considered significant and require explanations to the production vice president.

In addition to the monetary information shown in Exhibit 18–5, many responsibility accounting systems are now providing information on critical nonmonetary measures of the period's activity. Some examples of these types of information are shown in Exhibit 18–6. Many of these measures are equally useful for manufacturing and service organizations and can be used along with financial measurements to judge performance.

The performance reports of each management layer are reviewed and evaluated by each successively higher management layer. Managers are likely to be more careful and alert in controlling operations if they know that the reports generated

EXHIBIT 18–6

Nonmonetary Information for Responsibility Reports

- Departmental/divisional throughput
- Number of defects (by product, product line, supplier)
- Number of orders backlogged (by date, quantity, cost, and selling price)
- Number of customer complaints (by type and product); method of complaint resolution
- Percentage of orders delivered on time
- Manufacturing (or service) cycle efficiency
- Percentage of reduction of non-value-added time from previous reporting period (broken down by idle time, storage time, move time, and quality control time)
- Number and percentage of employee suggestions considered significant and practical
- Number and percentage of employee suggestions implemented
- Number of unplanned production interruptions
- Number of schedule changes
- Number of engineering change orders; percentage change from previous period
- Number of safety violations; percentage change from previous period
- Number of days of employee absences; percentage change from previous period

[5] In practice, the variances presented in Exhibit 18–5 would be further separated into the portions representing price and quantity effects as is shown in Chapter 10 on standard costing.

by the responsibility accounting system will reveal financial accomplishments and problems. Thus, in addition to providing a means for control, responsibility reports can motivate managers to influence operations in ways that will reflect positive performance.

responsibility center

The focus of responsibility accounting is on the manager who is responsible for a particular cost object. In a decentralized company, the cost object is an organizational unit such as a division, department, or geographical region. The cost object under the control of a manager is called a **responsibility center**.

BASIC TYPES OF RESPONSIBILITY CENTERS

3

What are the differences among the four basic types of responsibility centers?

Responsibility accounting systems identify, measure, and report on the performance of people controlling the activities of responsibility centers. Responsibility centers are classified according to their manager's scope of authority and type of financial responsibility. Companies may define their organizational units in various ways based on management accountability for one or more income-producing factors—costs, revenues, profits, and/or asset base. The four basic types of responsibility centers are illustrated in Exhibit 18–7 and discussed in the following sections.

Cost Centers

cost center

In a **cost center**, the manager has the authority only to incur costs and is specifically evaluated on the basis of how well costs are controlled. Theoretically, revenues cannot exist in a cost center because the unit does not engage in revenue-producing activity. Cost centers commonly include service and administrative departments. For example, the equipment maintenance center in a hospital may be a cost center because it does not charge for its services, but it does incur costs.

In other instances, revenues do exist for a cost center, but they are either not under the manager's control or are not effectively measurable. The first type of situation exists in a community library that is provided a specific proration of

EXHIBIT 18–7

Types of Responsibility Centers

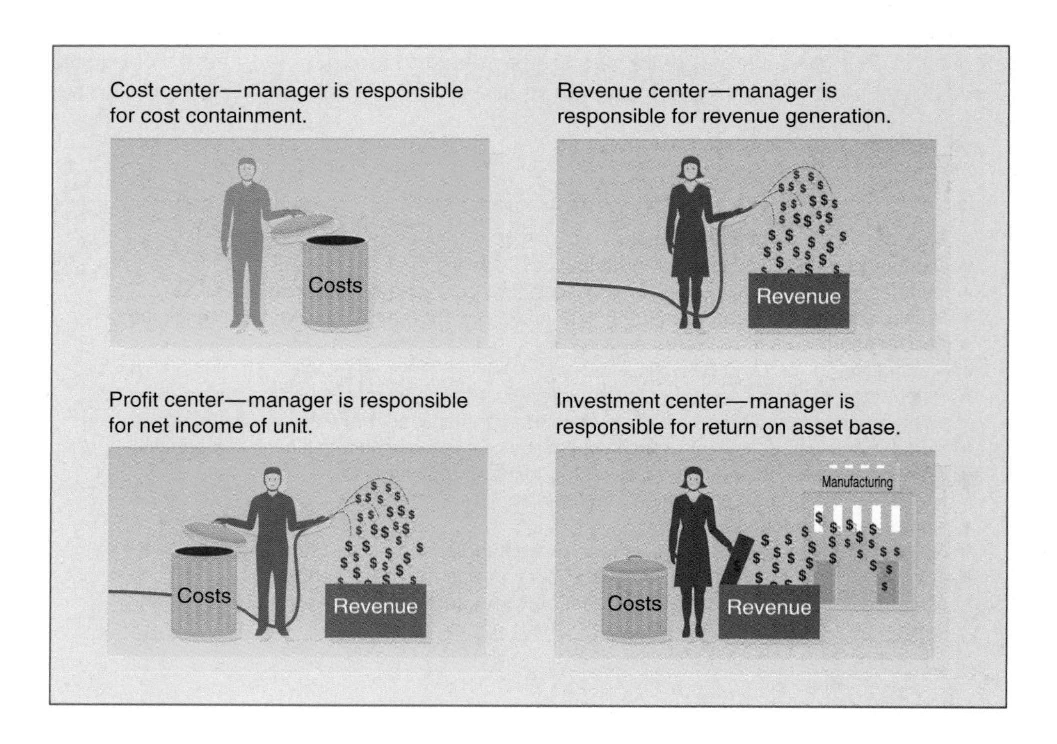

property tax dollars, but has no authority to levy or collect the related taxes. The second situation could exist in discretionary cost centers, such as a research and development center, in which the outputs (revenues or benefits generated from the cost inputs) are not easily measured.[6] In these two types of situations, the revenues should not be included in the manager's responsibility accounting report.

In the traditional manufacturing environment, a standard costing system is generally used and variances are reported and analyzed. In such an environment, the highest priority in a cost center is normally the minimization of unfavorable cost variances. Top management often concentrates only on the unfavorable variances occurring in a cost center and ignores the efficient performance indicated by favorable variances. To illustrate this possibility, the June 2000 operating results for a production department are shown in Exhibit 18–8.

Sandra Parrish is the manager of the production department of Exhibit 18–8. During June, the department made 477,200 units of product at a unit cost of \$0.914 (\$436,200 ÷ 477,200); standard unit production cost for these units is \$0.908. Top management's analysis of the responsibility report issued for the production department for June might focus on the large unfavorable direct material variance rather than on the large favorable variance for the direct labor. Ms. Parrish's job is to control costs and she did so relatively well when both favorable and unfavorable variances are considered together.

Significant favorable variances should not be disregarded if the management by exception principle is applied appropriately. Using this principle, top management should investigate all variances (both favorable and unfavorable) that fall outside the range of acceptable deviations.

The unfavorable direct material variance in the production department should be investigated further to find its cause. For example, a substandard grade of material may have been purchased and caused excessive usage. If this is the case,

EXHIBIT 18-8

Production Department Costs June 2000

Units of product made: 477,200

Standard cost per unit of production:		
Direct material		\$0.250
Direct labor		0.400
Overhead		
Supplies	\$0.037	
Indirect labor	0.097	
Depreciation (units of production method)	0.081	
Repairs and maintenance	0.026	
Other	0.017	0.258
Total		\$0.908

	Standard Cost	Actual Cost	Variance Fav. (Unfav.)
Direct material	\$119,300	\$122,500	\$(3,200)
Direct labor	190,880	188,027	2,853
Supplies	17,656	18,500	(844)
Indirect labor	46,288	47,020	(732)
Depreciation	38,653	38,653	0
Repairs and maintenance	12,407	12,900	(493)
Other	8,112	8,600	(488)
Total	\$433,296	\$436,200	\$(2,904)

[6] Discretionary costs are discussed in Chapter 15.

the purchasing agent, not Ms. Parrish, should be assigned the responsibility for the variance. Other possible causes for the unfavorable direct material variance include increased material prices, excess waste, or some combination of all causes. Only additional inquiry will determine whether Ms. Parrish could have controlled the variance.

The favorable direct labor variance should also be analyzed for causes. Ms. Parrish might have used inexperienced personnel who were being paid lower rates. This could explain the favorable direct labor variance and, to some extent, the unfavorable direct material variance (because a lack of employee skill could result in overuse of material). Alternatively, the production department workers could have been very efficient in June or the labor standard was inappropriate.

Revenue Centers

revenue center

A **revenue center** is strictly defined as an organizational unit for which a manager is accountable only for the generation of revenues and has no control over setting selling prices or budgeting costs. In many retail stores, the individual sales departments are considered independent units, and managers are evaluated based on the total revenues generated by their departments. Departmental managers, however, may not be given the authority to change selling prices to affect volume, and often they do not participate in the budgeting process. Thus, the departmental managers might have no impact on costs.

In most instances, however, pure revenue centers do not exist. Managers of revenue centers are typically not only responsible for revenues, but also are involved in the planning and control over some (but not necessarily all) costs incurred in the center. A more appropriate term for this organizational unit is a *revenue and limited cost center.*

For example, Vincent Rey is the district sales manager for the Commercial Sales Division of the Sanger Pharmaceutical Company and is responsible for the sales revenues generated in his territory. In addition, he is accountable for controlling the mileage and other travel-related expenses of his sales staff. Vincent is not, however, able to influence the types of cars his sales staff obtains because cars are acquired on a fleetwide basis by top management.

Salaries, if directly traceable to the center, are often a cost responsibility of the "revenue center" manager. This situation reflects the traditional retail environment in which sales clerks are assigned to a specific department and are only allowed to finalize sales for customers wanting to purchase that particular department's merchandise. Most stores, however, have found such an arrangement to be detrimental to business because customers are forced to wait for the appropriate clerk. Clerks in many stores are now allowed to assist all customers with all types of merchandise. Such a change in policy converts what was a traceable departmental cost into an indirect cost. Those stores carrying high-cost, high-selling-price merchandise normally retain the traditional system. Managers of such departments are thus able to trace sales salaries as a direct departmental cost.

The effects of price, sales mix, and volume variances from budget are illustrated in the following revenue variance model:

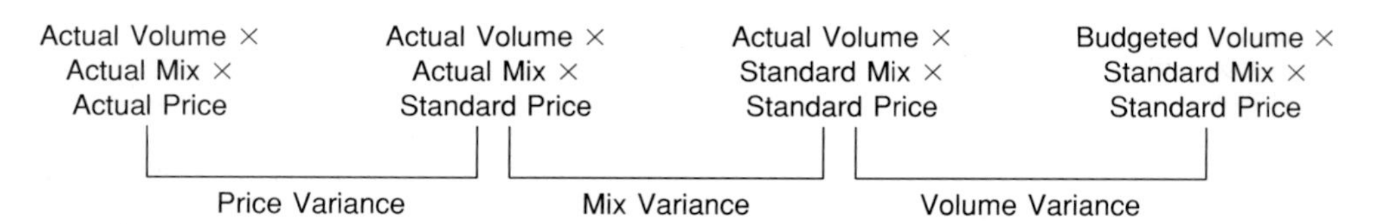

The following revenue statistics are presented for the three products of the Consumer Products Division of the Sanger Pharmaceutical Company for June 2000:

Budget	Units	Unit Price	Revenue	Standard Mix
Flarin [F]	1,000	$1.80	$1,800	1,000 ÷ 2,700 = 37.0%
Sucrain [S]	500	0.80	400	500 ÷ 2,700 = 18.5%
Wassine [W]	1,200	1.00	1,200	1,200 ÷ 2,700 = 44.5%
Totals	2,700		$3,400	100.0%
Actual				
Flarin	1,100	$2.00	$2,200	
Sucrain	540	0.70	378	
Wassine	1,180	1.10	1,298	
Totals	2,820		$3,876	

Using the revenue variance model and the information presented for the Consumer Products Division of Sanger Pharmaceutical, variances can be determined as follows:

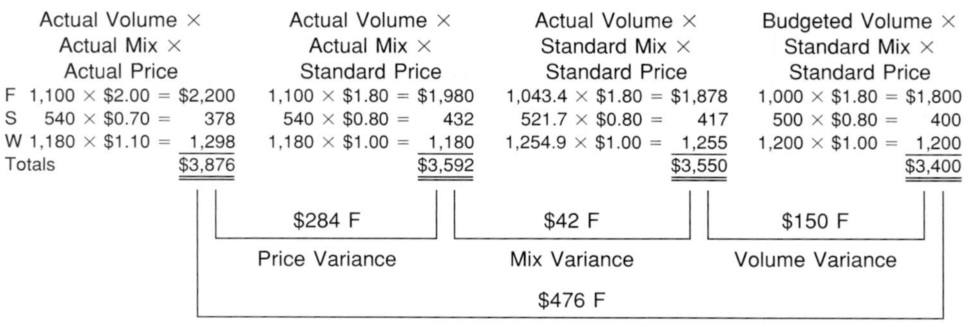

	Actual Volume × Actual Mix × Actual Price	Actual Volume × Actual Mix × Standard Price	Actual Volume × Standard Mix × Standard Price	Budgeted Volume × Standard Mix × Standard Price
F	1,100 × $2.00 = $2,200	1,100 × $1.80 = $1,980	1,043.4 × $1.80 = $1,878	1,000 × $1.80 = $1,800
S	540 × $0.70 = 378	540 × $0.80 = 432	521.7 × $0.80 = 417	500 × $0.80 = 400
W	1,180 × $1.10 = 1,298	1,180 × $1.00 = 1,180	1,254.9 × $1.00 = 1,255	1,200 × $1.00 = 1,200
Totals	$3,876	$3,592	$3,550	$3,400

Inspection of the results reveals that (1) prices increased (except for Sucrain), causing an overall favorable price variance; (2) the actual mix included more of the highest priced product (Flarin) than the standard mix, causing an overall favorable mix variance; and (3) the total actual units (2,820) sold was greater than the budgeted total units (2,700), causing a favorable volume variance. The Consumer Products Division's manager should be commended for a good performance.

Profit Centers

profit center

In a **profit center**, the manager is responsible for generating revenues and planning and controlling expenses related to current activity. (Expenses not under a profit center manager's control are those related to long-term investments in plant assets; such a situation creates a definitive need for separate evaluations of the subunit and the subunit's manager.) A profit center manager's goal is to maximize the center's net income.

Profit centers should be independent organizational units whose managers have the ability to obtain resources at the most economical prices and to sell products at prices that will maximize revenue. If managers do not have complete authority to buy and sell at objectively determined costs and prices, a meaningful evaluation of the profit center is difficult to make.

Profit centers are not always manufacturing divisions or branches of retail stores. Banks may view each department (checking and savings accounts, loans, and credit cards) as a profit center; trucking companies may view each 18-wheeler as a profit center; and a university may view certain educational divisions as profit centers (undergraduate education, non-degree-seeking night school, and graduate programs).

To illustrate the computations for a profit center, assume that Thompson Wholesale Company uses 18-wheelers to deliver products in the United States and each truck is considered a profit center. The segment margin income statement budgeted

Grocery stores may designate their deli areas as profit centers. Deli managers would then be responsible for determining how much to charge for prepared foods, how best to control costs, and whether a seating area is cost-beneficial.

and actual results of the "Colorado," a truck for which Randolph Green is responsible, are shown in Exhibit 18–9. These comparisons can be used to explain to top management why the budgeted income was not reached. The profit center should be judged on the $34,400 of profit center income, but Randolph Green should be judged on the controllable margin of $63,900. Because actual volume was greater than budgeted, the comparison in Exhibit 18–9 shows unfavorable variances for all of the variable costs. A comparison of actual results to a flexible budget at the actual activity level would provide better information for assessing cost control in the profit center.

Investment Centers

investment center

An **investment center** is an organizational unit in which the manager is responsible for generating revenues and planning and controlling expenses. In addition, the center's manager has the authority to acquire, use, and dispose of plant assets in a manner that seeks to earn the highest feasible rate of return on the center's asset base. Many investment centers are independent, freestanding divisions or

EXHIBIT 18–9

Profit Center Comparisons for "Colorado" for the Month Ended June 30, 2000

	Budget	Actual	Variance
Fees	$120,000	$124,000	$4,000 F
Cost of services rendered			
Direct labor	$ 3,000	$ 3,200	$ 200 U
Gas and oil	25,200	26,300	1,100 U
Variable overhead	5,200	5,800	600 U
Total	$ 33,400	$ 35,300	$1,900 U
Contribution margin	$ 86,600	$ 88,700	$2,100 F
Fixed overhead—controllable	(24,600)	(24,800)	200 U
Controllable segment margin	$ 62,000	$ 63,900	$1,900 F
Fixed overhead—not controllable by profit center manager	(28,000)	(29,500)	1,500 U
Profit center income	$ 34,000	$ 34,400	$ 400 F

subsidiaries of a firm. This independence gives investment center managers the opportunity to make decisions about all matters affecting their organizational units and to be judged on the outcomes of those decisions.

Assume that the Drug Store Sales Division of Thompson Wholesale Company is an investment center headed by Angela Timmons. The 2000 income statement for the plant is as follows:

Sales	$1,720,000
Variable expenses	(900,000)
Contribution margin	$ 820,000
Fixed expenses	(690,000)
Income before tax	$ 130,000

Ms. Timmons has the authority to set selling prices, incur costs, and acquire and dispose of plant assets. The plant has an asset base of $1,480,000 and thus the rate of return on assets for the year was approximately 8.8 percent ($130,000 ÷ $1,480,000). This rate of return would be compared with the rates desired by Thompson Wholesale Company management and would also be compared with other investment centers in the company. Rate of return and other performance measures for responsibility centers are treated in greater depth in Chapters 19 and 20.

Because of their closeness to daily divisional activities, responsibility center managers should have more current and detailed knowledge about sales prices, costs, and other market information than top management does. If responsibility centers are designated as profit or investment centers, managers are encouraged, to the extent possible, to operate those subunits as separate economic entities that exist for the same organizational goals.

Regardless of the size, type of ownership, or product or service being sold, one goal for any business is to generate profits. For other organizations, such as a charity or governmental entity, the ultimate financial goal is to break even. The ultimate goal will be achieved through the satisfaction of organizational critical success factors—those items that are so important that, without them, the organization would cease to exist. Five critical success factors organizations frequently embrace are quality, customer service, speed, cost control, and responsiveness to change. If all of these factors are managed properly, the organization should be financially successful; if they are not, sooner or later the organization will fail. All members of the organization—especially those in management—should work toward the same basic objectives if the critical success factors are to be satisfied. Losing sight of the organizational goal while working to achieve an independent responsibility center's conflicting goal results in suboptimization.

PSEUDO AND REAL MICROPROFIT CENTERS

Every person, workstation, or responsibility center has upstream suppliers and downstream customers. These can be internal or external suppliers and customers. Each set of three organizational units (supplier, responsibility center, and customer) forms a miniature value chain, the relationships of which can be exploited for the good of all units in the set and that of the larger organization. Traditionally, however, for the responsibility center and its customers that are viewed as internal in a given company, the responsibility center has most often been treated as either a cost or a revenue center from a managerial accounting perspective.

Converting a cost or revenue center to a microprofit center requires that each responsibility center manager of a microprofit center be responsible for both revenue and costs. His or her unit can then be treated as a mini-business, the performance of which is subject to evaluation, recognition, and reward.

The purpose of establishing microprofit centers is behavioral. By creating an entity reflecting many small operational units for which profits are measured, more individuals are empowered as more complete managers. They are thus motivated to embrace ownership responsibilities, use their best managerial skills, and engage in creative continuous improvement engendered by an entrepreneurial spirit.

real microprofit center

pseudo microprofit center

A microprofit center must have measurable output that can be expressed either as market value based or as artificial revenue. A center is designated as a **real microprofit center** if its output has a market value. A microprofit center for which a surrogate of market value must be used to measure output revenue is known as a **pseudo microprofit center**.[7]

SERVICE DEPARTMENT COST ALLOCATION

Organizations incur two types of overhead (OH) costs: manufacturing-related OH costs and non-manufacturing-related OH costs. Typically, as the number of product lines or service types increases, so does the need for additional support activities.

service department

administrative department

An organization's support areas consist of both service and administrative departments. A **service department** is an organizational unit (such as central purchasing, personnel, maintenance, engineering, security, or warehousing) that provides one or more specific functional tasks for other internal units. **Administrative departments** perform management activities that benefit the entire organization and include the personnel, legal, payroll, and insurance departments, and organization headquarters. Costs of service and administrative departments are referred to collectively as "service department costs," because corporate administration services the rest of the company.

4

Why and how are service department costs allocated to producing departments?

Reasons for Service Department Cost Allocations

All service department costs are incurred, in the long run, to support production or service-rendering activities. An organization producing no goods or performing no services has no need to exist; thus, it also would have no need for service departments. Conversely, as long as operating activities occur, there is a need for service department activity. The conclusion can therefore be drawn that service department costs are merely another form of overhead that must be allocated to revenue-generating departments and, finally, to units of product or service.

The three objectives of cost allocation are full cost computation, managerial motivation, and managerial decision making. Each of these objectives can be met if service department costs are assigned to revenue-producing departments in a reasonable manner. Exhibit 18–10 presents the reasons for and against allocating service department costs in relationship to each allocation objective; some of the positive points follow.

The full cost of a cost object includes all costs that contribute to its existence. Thus, full cost includes all traceable material, labor, and overhead costs incurred by the cost object plus a fair share of allocated costs that support the cost object. If the cost object is defined as a revenue-producing department, the full cost of its operations includes all traceable departmental costs plus an allocated amount of service department costs.[8]

[7] Robin Cooper and Regine Slagmulder, "Micro-Profit Centers," *Strategic Finance* (June 1998), pp. 16ff.

[8] This concept of full cost for revenue-producing departments is recognized to an extent by the Financial Accounting Standards Board in Statement of Financial Accounting Standards No. 14 (*Financial Reporting for Segments of a Business Enterprise*). Based on this statement, certain indirect costs must be allocated to reportable segments on a benefits-received basis. The statement does not, however, allow corporate administrative costs to be allocated to segments. In several pronouncements, the Cost Accounting Standards Board also provides guidance on how to include service and administrative costs in full product cost when attempting to determine a "fair" price to charge under government contracts. For example, CAS 403 (*Allocation of Home Office Expenses to Segment*) indicates acceptable allocation bases using benefits-provided or causal relationships; CAS 410 (*Allocation of Business Unit General and Administrative Expenses to Final Cost Objectives*) also discusses allocation principles.

EXHIBIT 18-10

Allocating Service Department Costs: Pros and Cons

OBJECTIVE: TO COMPUTE FULL COST

Reasons for:

1. Provides for cost recovery.
2. Instills a consideration of support costs in production managers.
3. Reflects production's "fair share" of costs.
4. Meets regulations in some pricing instances.

Reasons against:

1. Provides costs that are beyond production manager's control.
2. Provides arbitrary costs that are not useful in decision making.
3. Confuses the issues of pricing and costing. Prices should be set high enough for each product to provide a profit margin that should cover all nonproduction costs.

OBJECTIVE: TO MOTIVATE MANAGERS

Reasons for:

1. Instills a consideration of support costs in production managers.
2. Relates individual production unit's profits to total company profits.
3. Reflects usage of services on a fair and equitable basis.
4. Encourages production managers to help service departments control costs.
5. Encourages the usage of certain services.

Reasons against:

1. Distorts production divisions' profit figures because allocations are subjective.
2. Includes costs that are beyond production managers' control.
3. Will not materially affect production divisions' profits.
4. Creates interdivisional ill will when there is lack of agreement about allocation base or method.
5. Is not cost beneficial.

OBJECTIVE: TO COMPARE ALTERNATIVE COURSES OF ACTION

Reasons for:

1. Provides relevant information in determining corporatewide profits generated by alternative actions.
2. Provides best available estimate of expected changes in costs due to alternative actions.

Reasons against:

1. Is unnecessary if alternative actions will not cause costs to change.
2. Presents distorted cash flows or profits from alternative actions since allocations are arbitrary.

SOURCE: Adapted from copyright by Institute of Management Accountants (formerly National Association of Accountants), Montvale, N.J., *Statements on Management Accounting Number 4B: Allocation of Service and Administrative Costs* (June 13, 1985), pp. 9–10.

Managers of revenue-producing areas may be made more aware of and sensitive to the support provided by the service areas when full costs are used. This increased sensitivity should motivate operations managers to use support areas in the most cost-beneficial manner and to provide recommendations on service department cost control. In addition, assigning service department costs to revenue-producing divisions and segments allows managers to more effectively compare the performance of their units to independent companies that must incur such costs directly.[9]

[9] The use of a full cost that includes allocated service department costs should be restricted to performance comparisons with entities outside the company. This type of full cost should not be used for internal performance evaluations by top management because the division or segment manager has no direct control over the allocated costs.

The third objective of cost allocation is to help provide a basis for comparing alternative courses of action. Including service department costs with the traceable costs of revenue-producing departments gives an indication of the future differential costs involved in an activity. (A **differential cost** is one that differs in amount among the alternatives being considered.) This comparison is especially useful in and relevant to making decisions about capacity utilization.

differential cost

Meeting one allocation objective may, however, preclude the achievement of another. For example, assignment of full cost to a cost object may not, in some situations, motivate the manager of that cost object. These potential conflicts of objectives may create disagreement as to the propriety of such allocations. If service department costs are to be assigned to revenue-producing areas, a rational and systematic means by which to make the assignment must be developed. Numerous types of allocation bases are available.

Allocation Bases

A rational and systematic allocation base for service department costs should reflect consideration of four criteria. The first criterion is the benefit received by the revenue-producing department from the service department, such as the number of computer reports prepared for each revenue-producing department by the computer department. The second criterion is a causal relationship between factors in the revenue-producing department and costs incurred in the service department; the need for the accounting department to produce paychecks for revenue-department employees illustrates this type of relationship. The third criterion is the fairness or equity of the allocations between or among revenue-producing departments; the assignment of fire and casualty premiums to the revenue-producing departments on the basis of relative fair market values of assets illustrates this type of allocation. The fourth criterion is the ability of revenue-producing departments to bear the allocated costs; this criterion is used, for example, when the operating costs of the public relations department are assigned to revenue-producing departments on the basis of relative revenue dollars.

The benefit received and causal relationship criteria are used most often to select allocation bases, because they are reasonably objective and will produce rational allocations. Fairness is a valid theoretical basis for allocation, but its use may cause dissension because everyone does not have the same perception of what is fair or equitable. The ability-to-bear criterion often results in unrealistic or profit-detrimental actions: managers might manipulate operating data related to the allocation base to minimize service department allocations. For example, the manager of a revenue-producing department that is charged a standard maintenance fee per delivery truck mile might manipulate the mileage logs depending on how well the department is otherwise doing.

Applying the two primary criteria (benefits and causes) to the allocation of service department costs can help to specify some acceptable allocation bases. The allocation base selected should be a valid one because an improper base will yield improper information regardless of how complex or mathematically precise the allocation process appears to be. Exhibit 18–11 lists appropriate bases to assign various types of service department assets.

Methods of Allocating Service Department Costs

The allocation process for service department costs is, like that of revenue-producing areas, a process of pooling, allocating, repooling, and reallocating costs. When service departments are considered in the pooling process, the primary pools are composed of all costs of both the revenue-producing and service departments. These costs can be gathered and specified by cost behavior (variable and fixed) or in total.

EXHIBIT 18–11

Appropriate Service/Administrative Cost Allocation Bases

Type of Cost	Acceptable Allocation Bases
Research and development	Estimated time or usage, sales, assets employed, new products developed
Personnel functions	Number of employees, payroll, number of new hires
Accounting functions	Estimated time or usage, sales, assets employed, employment data
Public relations and corporate promotion	Sales
Purchasing function	Dollar value of purchase orders, number of purchase orders, estimated time of usage, percentage of material cost of purchases
Corporate executives' salaries	Sales, assets employed, pretax operating income
Treasurer's functions	Sales, estimated time or usage, assets or liabilities employed
Legal and governmental affairs	Estimated time or usage, sales, assets employed
Tax department	Estimated time or usage, sales, assets employed
Income taxes	Pretax operating income*
Property taxes	Square feet, real estate valuation

*The source lists "net income" as the base of allocation. The authors believe that pretax operating income is more realistic because net income has taxes already deducted.

SOURCE: Adapted from copyright by Institute of Management Accountants (formerly National Association of Accountants), Montvale, N.J., *Statements on Management Accounting Number 4B: Allocation of Service and Administration Costs* (June 13, 1985), p. 8.

Intermediate pools are then developed in the allocation process. There may be one or more layers of intermediate pools; however, the last layer will consist of only revenue-producing departments. The number of layers and the costs shown in the intermediate pools depend on the type of allocation method selected. The costs of the intermediate pools are then distributed to final cost objects (such as products, services, programs, or functional areas) using specified, rational cost driver allocation bases (such as machine hours, direct labor hours, machine throughput time, or number of machine setups).

The pooled service department costs to revenue-producing departments can be allocated in three ways: by the direct, step, or algebraic methods. These methods are listed in order of ease of application, not necessarily in order of soundness of results. The **direct method** assigns service department costs to revenue-producing areas with only one set of intermediate cost pools or allocations. Cost assignment under the direct method is made using one specific cost driver to the intermediate pool; for example, personnel department costs are assigned to production departments (the intermediate-level pools) based on the number of people in each production department.

direct method

The **step method** of cost allocation considers the interrelationships of the service departments before assigning indirect costs to cost objects. Although a specific base is also used in this method, the step method employs a ranking for the

step method

"benefits-provided" ranking

quantity of services provided by each service department to other areas. This **"benefits-provided" ranking** lists service departments in an order that begins with the one providing the most service to all other corporate areas (both non-revenue-producing and revenue-producing areas); the ranking ends with the service department providing the least service to all but the revenue-producing areas. After the ranking is developed, service department costs are sequentially allocated down the list until all costs have been assigned to the revenue-producing areas. This ranking sequence allows the step method to partially recognize reciprocal relationships among the service departments. For example, because the personnel department provides services for all company areas, it might be the first department listed in the ranking, and all other areas would receive a proportionate allocation of the personnel department's costs.

algebraic method

The **algebraic method** of allocating service department costs considers all departmental interrelationships and reflects these relationships in simultaneous equations. These equations provide for reciprocal allocation of service costs among the service departments as well as to the revenue-producing departments. Thus, no benefits-provided ranking is needed and the sequential step approach is not used. The algebraic method is the most complex of all the allocation techniques, but it is also the most theoretically correct and, if relationships are properly formulated, will provide the best allocations.

SERVICE DEPARTMENT COST ALLOCATION ILLUSTRATION

Data for Katz Pharmaceuticals are used to illustrate the three methods of allocating budgeted service department costs. Katz has two revenue-producing divisions: Cincinnati Division (dermatological products) and St. Paul Division (internal medicines). The company's service departments are corporate administration, personnel, and maintenance. Budgeted costs of each service department are assigned to each revenue-producing area and are then added to the budgeted overhead costs of those areas to determine an appropriate divisional overhead application rate.

Exhibit 18–12 presents an abbreviated 2000 budget of the direct and indirect costs for each department and division of Katz Pharmaceuticals. These costs were budgeted using historical information adjusted for expected changes in factors affecting costs such as increases or decreases in volume and personnel from prior periods. Budgeted 2000 revenues are $2,250,000 for the Cincinnati Division and $1,500,000 for the St. Paul Division.

Exhibit 18–13 shows the bases that Katz Pharmaceuticals has chosen for allocating its service department costs. The service departments are listed in a benefits-provided ranking. Katz Pharmaceuticals' management believes that Administration

EXHIBIT 18–12

Budgeted Departmental and Divisional Costs

	Administration	Personnel	Maintenance	Cincinnati	St. Paul	Total
Initial Departmental Costs						
Direct costs:						
Material	$ 0	$ 0	$ 0	$ 425,200	$223,200	$ 648,400
Labor	450,000	50,000	120,000	245,400	288,000	1,153,400
Total	$ 450,000	$50,000	$120,000	$ 670,600	$511,200	$1,801,800
Departmental overhead*	550,400	23,250	79,400	559,000	89,200	1,301,250
Total initial departmental costs	$1,000,400	$73,250	$199,400	$1,229,600	$600,400	$3,103,050

*Would be specified by type and cost behavior in actual budgeting process.

EXHIBIT 18–13

Service Department Allocation Bases

Administration costs—allocated on dollars of assets employed
Personnel costs—allocated on number of employees
Maintenance costs—allocated on machine hours used

	Dollars of Assets Employed	Number of Employees	Machine Hours Used
Administration	$ 4,000,000	8	0
Personnel	1,200,000	2	0
Maintenance	2,000,000	6	0
Cincinnati Division	10,000,000	25	86,000
St. Paul Division	8,000,000	7	21,500

provides the most service to all other areas of the company; Personnel provides the majority of its services to Maintenance and the revenue-producing areas; and Maintenance provides its services only to the Cincinnati and St. Paul Divisions (equipment used in other areas is under a lease maintenance arrangement and is not serviced by Katz's Maintenance Department).

Direct Method Allocation

In the direct method of allocation, service department costs are assigned using the specified bases only to the revenue-producing areas. The direct method cost allocation for Katz Pharmaceuticals is shown in Exhibit 18–14. (All percentages have been rounded to the nearest whole number.)

Use of the direct method of service department allocation produces the total budgeted costs for Cincinnati Division and St. Paul Division shown on page 818 in Exhibit 18–15. If budgeted revenues and costs equal actual revenues and costs, Cincinnati Division would show a 2000 profit of $243,521 or 11 percent on revenues, and St. Paul Division would show a profit of $403,429 or 27 percent.

EXHIBIT 18–14

Direct Allocation of Service Department Costs

	Base	Proportion of Total Base	Amount to Allocate	Amount Allocated
Administration costs ($s of assets employed)				
Cincinnati Division	$10,000,000	10* ÷ 18* = 56%	$1,000,400	$ 560,224
St. Paul Division	8,000,000	8* ÷ 18* = 44%	$1,000,400	440,176
Total	$18,000,000			$1,000,400
Personnel costs (# of employees)				
Cincinnati Division	25	25 ÷ 32 = 78%	$ 73,250	$ 57,135
St. Paul Division	7	7 ÷ 32 = 22%	$ 73,250	16,115
Total	32			$ 73,250
Maintenance costs (# of machine hours used)				
Cincinnati Division	86,000	86,000 ÷ 107,500 = 80%	$ 199,400	$ 159,520
St. Paul Division	21,500	21,500 ÷ 107,500 = 20%	$ 199,400	39,880
Total	107,500			$ 199,400

*In millions

	Cincinnati	St. Paul	Total
Total budgeted revenues (a)	$2,250,000	$1,500,000	$3,750,000
Allocated overhead			
From Administration	$ 560,224	$ 440,176	$1,000,400
From Personnel	57,135	16,115	73,250
From Maintenance	159,520	39,880	199,400
Subtotal	$ 776,879	$ 496,171	$1,273,050
Departmental overhead	559,000	89,200	648,200
Total overhead (for OH application rate determination)	$1,335,879	$ 585,371	$1,921,250
Direct costs	670,600	511,200	1,181,800
Total budgeted costs (b)	$2,006,479	$1,096,571	$3,103,050
Total budgeted pretax profits (a − b)	$ 243,521	$ 403,429	$ 646,950

VERIFICATION OF ALLOCATION

To:		Administration	Personnel	Maintenance	Cincinnati	St. Paul	Total
Initial costs		$1,000,400	$73,250	$199,400			$1,273,050
From:	Administration	(1,000,400)			$560,224	$440,176	
	Personnel		(73,250)		57,135	16,115	
	Maintenance			(199,400)	159,520	39,880	
Totals		$ 0	$ 0	$ 0	$776,879	$496,171	$1,273,050

EXHIBIT 18–15

Direct Method Allocation to Revenue-Producing Areas

Step Method Allocation

To apply the step method of allocation, a benefits-provided ranking must be specified. This ranking for Katz Pharmaceuticals was given in Exhibit 18–13. Costs are assigned using an appropriate, specified allocation base to the departments receiving service. Once costs have been assigned from a department, no costs are charged back to that department. Step allocation of Katz Pharmaceuticals service costs is shown in Exhibit 18–16.

In this case, the amount of service department costs assigned to each revenue-producing area differs only slightly between the step and direct methods. However, in many situations, the difference can be substantial. If budgeted revenues and costs equal actual revenues and costs, the step method allocation process will cause Cincinnati Division and St. Paul Division to show profits of $213,643 and $433,307, respectively, as follows:

	Cincinnati Division	St. Paul Division
Revenues	$2,250,000	$1,500,000
Direct costs	(670,600)	(511,200)
Indirect departmental costs	(559,000)	(89,200)
Allocated service department costs	(806,757)	(466,293)
Profit	$ 213,643	$ 433,307

These profit figures reflect rates of return on revenues of 9 percent and 29 percent, respectively.

The step method is a hybrid allocation method between the direct and algebraic methods. This method is more realistic than the direct method in that it partially recognizes relationships among service departments, but it does not recognize the two-way exchange of services between service departments that may exist. A service department is eliminated from the allocation sequence in the step method

	Base	Proportion of Total Base	Amount to Allocate	Amount Allocated
Administration costs ($s of assets employed; 000s omitted)				
Personnel	$ 1,200	1,200 ÷ 21,200 = 6%	$1,000,400	$ 60,024
Maintenance	2,000	2,000 ÷ 21,200 = 9%	$1,000,400	90,036
Cincinnati	10,000	10,000 ÷ 21,200 = 47%	$1,000,400	470,188
St. Paul	8,000	8,000 ÷ 21,200 = 38%	$1,000,400	380,152
Total	$21,200			$1,000,400
Personnel costs (# of employees)				
Maintenance	6	6 ÷ 38 = 16%	$133,274*	$ 21,324
Cincinnati	25	25 ÷ 38 = 66%	$133,274	87,961
St. Paul	7	7 ÷ 38 = 18%	$133,274	23,989
Total	38			$ 133,274
Maintenance (# of machine hours used)				
Cincinnati	86,000	86,000 ÷ 107,500 = 80%	$310,760**	$ 248,608
St. Paul	21,500	21,500 ÷ 107,500 = 20%	$310,760	62,152
Total	107,500			$ 310,760

*Personnel costs = Original cost + Allocated from Administration = $73,250 + $60,024 = $133,274
**Maintenance costs = Original cost + Allocated from Administration + Allocated from Personnel = $199,400 + $90,036 + $21,324 = $310,760

VERIFICATION OF ALLOCATION

To:	Administration	Personnel	Maintenance	Cincinnati	St. Paul	Total
Initial costs	$1,000,400	$ 73,250	$199,400			$1,273,050
From:						
Administration	(1,000,400)	60,024	90,036	$470,188	$380,152	0
Personnel		(133,274)	21,324	87,961	23,989	0
Maintenance			(310,760)	248,608	62,152	0
Totals	$ 0	$ 0	$ 0	$806,757	$466,293	$1,273,050

EXHIBIT 18-16

Step Allocation of Service Department Costs

once its costs have been assigned outward. If a service department further down the ranking sequence provides services to departments that have already been eliminated, these benefits are not recognized by the step method cost allocation process.

Algebraic Method Allocation

The algebraic method of allocation eliminates the two disadvantages of the step method in that all interrelationships among departments are recognized and no decision must be made about a ranking order of service departments. The algebraic method involves formulating a set of equations that reflect reciprocal relationships among departments. Solving these equations simultaneously recognizes the fact that costs flow both into and out of each department.

The starting point for the algebraic method is a review of the bases used for allocation (shown in Exhibit 18–13) and the respective amounts of those bases for each department. A schedule is created that shows the proportionate usage by each department of the other departments' services. These proportions are then used to develop equations that, when solved simultaneously, will give cost allocations that fully recognize the reciprocal services provided.

The allocation proportions for all departments of Katz Pharmaceuticals are shown in Exhibit 18–17. Allocation for the Personnel Department is discussed to illustrate how these proportions were derived. The allocation basis for personnel cost is number of employees; there are 46 employees in the organization exclusive of those in the Personnel Department. Personnel employees are ignored because costs are being removed from that department and assigned to other areas. Because the Maintenance Department has six employees, the proportionate amount of Personnel services used by Maintenance is 6 ÷ 46 or 13 percent.

Using the calculated percentages, algebraic equations representing the interdepartmental usage of services can be formulated. The departments are labeled A, P, and M in the equations for Administration, Personnel, and Maintenance, respectively. The initial costs of each service department are shown first in the formulas:

$$A = \$1{,}000{,}400 + 0.18P + 0.00M$$

$$P = \$\quad 73{,}250 + 0.06A + 0.00M$$

$$M = \$\quad 199{,}400 + 0.09A + 0.13P$$

These equations are solved simultaneously by substituting one equation into the others, gathering like-terms, and reducing the unknowns until only one unknown exists. The value for this unknown is then computed and substituted into the remaining equations. This process is continued until all unknowns have been eliminated.

1. Substituting the equation for A into the equation for P gives the following:

$$P = \$73{,}250 + 0.06(\$1{,}000{,}400 + 0.18P)$$

Multiplying and combining terms produces the following results:

$$P = \$\ 73{,}250 + \$60{,}024 + 0.01P$$

$$P = \$133{,}274 + 0.01P$$

$$P - 0.01P = \$133{,}274$$

$$0.99P = \$133{,}274$$

$$P = \$134{,}620$$

EXHIBIT 18–17

Interdepartmental Proportional Relationships

	ADMINISTRATION ($S OF ASSETS EMPLOYED*)		PERSONNEL (# OF EMPLOYEES)		MAINTENANCE (# OF MACHINE HOURS USED)	
	Base	Percent**	Base	Percent**	Base	Percent**
Administration	n/a	n/a	8	18	0	0
Personnel	1,200	6	n/a	n/a	0	0
Maintenance	2,000	9	6	13	n/a	n/a
Cincinnati	10,000	47	25	54	86,000	80
St. Paul	8,000	38	7	15	21,500	20
Total	21,200	100	46	100	107,500	100

*000s omitted
**Percentages rounded to total 100 percent.

2. The value for P is now substituted in the formula for Administration:

$$A = \$1,000,400 + 0.18(\$134,620)$$
$$A = \$1,000,400 + \$24,232$$
$$A = \$1,024,632$$

3. Substituting the values for A and P into the equation for M gives the following:

$$M = \$199,400 + 0.09(\$1,024,632) + 0.13(\$134,620)$$
$$M = \$199,400 + \$92,217 + \$17,501$$
$$M = \$309,118$$

The amounts provided by these equations are used to reallocate costs among all the departments; costs will then be assigned only to the revenue-producing areas. These allocations are shown in Exhibit 18–18.

The $1,024,632 of administration costs are used to illustrate the development of the amounts in Exhibit 18–18. Administration costs are assigned to the other areas based on dollars of assets employed. Exhibit 18–18 indicates that Personnel has 6 percent of the dollars of assets of Katz Pharmaceuticals; thus, costs equal to $61,478 (0.06 × $1,024,632) are assigned to that area. This same process of proration is used for the other departments. Allocations from Exhibit 18–18 are used in Exhibit 18–19 to determine the reallocated costs and finalize the total budgeted overhead of the Cincinnati and St. Paul Divisions.

By allocating costs in this manner, total costs shown for each service department have increased over the amounts originally given. For example, Administration now shows total costs of $1,024,632 rather than the original amount of $1,000,400. These added "costs" are double-counted in that they arise from the process of service reciprocity. As shown on the line labeled "Less reallocated costs" in Exhibit 18–19, these additional double-counted costs are not recognized in the revenue-producing areas for purposes of developing an overhead application rate.

When the company has few departmental interrelationships, the algebraic method can be solved by hand. If a large number of variables are present, this method must be performed by a computer. Because computer usage is now prevalent in all but the smallest organizations, the results obtained from the algebraic method are easy to generate and provide the most rational and appropriate means of allocating service department costs.

EXHIBIT 18–18

Algebraic Solution of Service Department Costs

Costs are allocated based on percentages computed in Exhibit 18–17.

	ADMINISTRATION		PERSONNEL		MAINTENANCE	
	Percent	**Amount**	**Percent**	**Amount**	**Percent**	**Amount**
Administration	n/a	n/a	18	$ 24,231	0	$ 0
Personnel	6	$ 61,478	n/a	n/a	0	0
Maintenance	9	92,217	13	17,501	n/a	n/a
Cincinnati	47	481,577	54	72,695	80	247,294
St. Paul	38	389,360	15	20,193	20	61,824
Total*	100	$1,024,632	100	$134,620	100	$309,118

*Total costs are the solution results of the set of algebraic equations.

	Total Service Department Cost (from equations)	Administration	Personnel	Maintenance	Cincinnati	St. Paul
Administration	$1,024,632	$ 0	$61,478	$ 92,217	$ 481,577	$389,360
Personnel	134,620	24,231	0	17,501	72,695	20,193
Maintenance	309,118	0	0	0	247,294	61,824
Total costs	$1,468,370	$24,231	$61,478	$109,718	$ 801,566	$471,377
Less reallocated costs	(195,427)	(24,231)	(61,478)	(109,718)		
Budgeted costs	$1,272,943*	$ 0	$ 0	$ 0		
Departmental overhead costs of revenue-producing areas					559,000	89,200
Total budgeted cost for OH application rate determination					$1,360,566	$560,577

*Off due to rounding.

EXHIBIT 18–19

Final Determination of Revenue-Producing Department Overhead Costs

Regardless of the method used to allocate service department costs, the final step is to determine the overhead application rates for the revenue-producing areas. Once service department costs have been assigned to production, they are included as part of production overhead and allocated to products or jobs through normal overhead assignment procedures.

The final figures shown in Exhibit 18–19, costs of $1,360,566 and $560,577 for Cincinnati Division and St. Paul Division, respectively, are divided by an appropriate allocation base to assign both manufacturing and nonmanufacturing overhead to products. For example, assume that Katz Pharmaceuticals has chosen total ounces of internal medicine products as the overhead allocation base for St. Paul Division. If the division expects to produce 750,000 ounces of internal medicine products in 2000, the overhead cost assigned to each ounce would be $0.75 or ($560,577 ÷ 750,000).

For simplicity, cost behavior in all departments has been ignored. A more appropriate allocation process would specify different bases in each department for the variable and fixed costs. Such differentiation would not change the allocation process, but would change the results of the three methods (direct, step, or algebraic). Separation of variable and fixed costs would provide better allocation; use of the computer makes this process more practical than otherwise.

Before any type of allocation is made, management should be certain that the allocation base is reasonable. Allocations are often based on the easiest available measure, such as number of people or number of documents processed. Use of such measures can distort the allocation process.

When service department cost allocations have been made to revenue-producing areas, income figures derived from the use of these amounts should not be used for manager performance evaluations. Any attempt to evaluate the financial performance of a manager of a revenue-producing department should use an incremental, rather than a full allocation, approach. Although full allocation should not be used for performance evaluations, allocating service department costs to revenue-producing areas does make managers more aware of and responsible for controlling service usage.

The next section of Chapter 18 discusses the concept of setting transfer prices for the provision of services between two organizational units. To properly evaluate segments and their managers, useful information about performance must be available. When the various segments of a firm exchange goods or services among themselves, a "price" for those goods or services must be set so that the "selling" segment can measure its revenue and the "buying" segment can measure its costs. Such an internal price is known as a transfer price.

TRANSFER PRICING

5

Why are transfer prices used in organizations?

transfer price

Transfer prices (or prices in a chargeback system) are internal charges established for the exchange of goods or services between responsibility centers of the same company. Although a variety of transfer prices may be used for internal reporting purposes, intracompany inventory transfers should be presented on an external balance sheet at the producing segment's actual cost. Internal transfers would be eliminated for external income statement purposes altogether. Thus, if transfers are "sold" at an amount other than cost, any intersegment profit in inventory, expense, and/or revenue accounts must be eliminated.

Transfer prices may be established to promote goal congruence, make performance evaluation among segments more comparable, and/or "transform" a cost center into a profit center. The appropriate transfer price should ensure optimal resource allocation and promote operating efficiency. A number of different approaches are used to establish a transfer price for goods or services. The basic caveat is that intracompany transfers should be made only if they are in the best interest of the total organization. Within this context, the general rules for choosing a transfer price follow.[10]

- The maximum price should be no greater than the lowest market price at which the buying segment can acquire the goods or services externally.
- The minimum price should be no less than the sum of the selling segment's incremental costs associated with the goods or services plus the opportunity cost of the facilities used.

From the company's perspective, any transfer price set between these two limits is generally considered appropriate. To illustrate the use of these rules, assume that a product is available from external suppliers at a price below the lower limit (selling division's incremental costs plus opportunity cost). The immediate short-run decision might be that the selling division is to stop production and allow the purchasing division to buy the product from the external suppliers. This decision may be reasonable because, compared with the external suppliers, the selling division does not appear to be cost efficient in its production activities. Stopping production would release the facilities for other, more profitable purposes. A longer run solution may be to have the selling division improve its efficiency and reduce the internal cost of making the product. This solution could be implemented without stopping internal production, but internal production might need to be reduced by making some external purchases until costs are under control.

After the transfer price range limits have been established, one criterion used to select a particular price in the range is the ease by which that price can be determined. Managers should be able to understand the computation of a transfer price and to evaluate the impact of that transfer price on their responsibility centers' profits. The more complex the method used to set a transfer price, the less comfortable managers will be with both the method and the resulting price. In addition, from a cost standpoint, it takes more time and effort to administer and account for a complicated transfer pricing system than a simple one.

The difference between the upper and lower transfer price limits is the corporate "profit" (or savings) generated by producing internally rather than buying externally. The transfer price chosen acts to "divide the corporate profit" between the buying and selling segments. For external statements, it is irrelevant which segment shows the profits from transfers because such internal profit allocations are

[10] These rules are more difficult to implement when the selling division is in a "captive" relationship, in that it is not able to transfer its products to customers outside the corporate entity. Captive relationships often exist when the selling division was acquired or established in a company's move toward vertical integration. In such situations, opportunity cost must be estimated to provide the selling division an incentive to transfer products.

eliminated in preparing these statements. For internal reporting, though, this division of profits may be extremely important. Use of transfer prices affects the responsibility reports that are prepared, and top management may have established a subunit performance measurement system that is affected by such "profit" allocations.

Segment managers in a decentralized company often have competing vested interests if managerial performance is evaluated on a competitive basis. Such internal competition could lead to suboptimization because both buying and selling segment managers want to maximize their financial results in the responsibility accounting reports. The supplier-segment manager attempts to obtain the highest transfer (selling) price, whereas the buying-segment manager attempts to acquire the goods or services at the lowest transfer (purchase) price. Thus, transfer prices should be agreed on by the company's selling and buying segments.

Many top managers believe in giving subunit managers a considerable amount of autonomy to negotiate divisional transfer prices. Division managers are expected to make choices that will maximize the effectiveness and efficiency of their divisions as well as contribute to overall company performance.

Three traditional methods are used for determining transfer prices: cost-based prices, market-based prices, and negotiated prices. A discussion follows of each method and its advantages and disadvantages. This discussion will use information on the Scott Company, an Australian subsidiary of Thompson Wholesale Company. Scott Company is composed of two investment centers: a marine biochemical producing division (managed by Lynn Hume) and an evergreen chemicals plant (managed by Tom Forsyth). The managers are attempting to establish a reasonable transfer price for a particular unit of chemical product from evergreen trees. The Evergreen Division data (shown in Exhibit 18–20 in Australian dollars) are used to illustrate various transfer pricing approaches. Note that the Evergreen Division is capable of supplying all external and internal production needs.

Cost-Based Transfer Prices

A cost-based transfer price is, on the surface, an easily understood concept until one realizes the variations that can exist in the definition of the term *cost.* Different companies use different definitions of cost in conjunction with transfer pricing. These definitions range from variable production cost to absorption cost plus additional amounts for selling and administrative costs (and, possibly, opportunity cost) of the selling unit. Another consideration in a cost-based transfer price is

EXHIBIT 18–20

Scott Company Evergreen Division

Standard unit production cost:		
Direct material	A$0.20	
Direct labor	0.06	
Variable overhead	0.10	
Variable selling and administrative	0.04	
Total variable costs		A$0.40
Fixed overhead*	A$0.09	
Fixed selling and administrative*	0.03	
Total fixed cost		0.12
Total cost		A$0.52
Normal markup on variable cost (50%)		0.20
List selling price		A$0.72

Estimated annual production: 700,000 units
Estimated sales to outside entities: 400,000 units
Estimated intracompany transfers: 300,000 units

*Fixed costs are allocated to all units produced based on estimated annual production.

whether actual or standard cost is used. Actual costs may vary according to the season, production volume, and other factors, whereas standard costs can be specified in advance and are stable measures of efficient production costs. For these two reasons, standard costs provide a superior basis for transfer pricing. When standard costs are used, any variances from standard are borne by the selling segment because otherwise the selling division's efficiencies or inefficiencies are passed on to the buying division.

COST ALTERNATIVE—VARIABLE COST

Using the data provided in Exhibit 18–20, a variable cost transfer price for a unit of evergreen chemicals can be either A$0.36 (production variable costs only) or A$0.40 (total variable costs). The difference depends on whether variable cost is defined as variable production cost or total variable cost. Even using A$0.40 as the transfer price provides little incentive to Mr. Forsyth to sell to the Marine Biochemical Division. Fixed costs of the Evergreen Division are not reduced by selling internally, and no contribution margin is being generated by the transfers to help cover fixed costs. The low transfer prices could result in a poor financial showing for the Evergreen Division that, in turn, could detrimentally affect Mr. Forsyth's performance evaluation.

Considering the total standard cost per unit of A$0.52 in Mr. Forsyth's division, a loss of A$0.12 will result on each evergreen chemical unit sold internally at a transfer price of A$0.40. If all sales and transfers occur as expected and there are no variances from standard costs, Mr. Forsyth's responsibility report will appear as follows:

Sales		
External (400,000 × A$0.72)	A$288,000	
Internal (300,000 × A$0.40)	120,000	A$408,000
Costs:		
Total variable and fixed costs (700,000 × A$0.52)		(364,000)
Income before tax		A$ 44,000

Had the Evergreen Division been able to sell all of its production externally, it would have shown a net income for the period of A$140,000:

Sales (700,000 × A$0.72)	A$504,000
Costs (shown previously)	(364,000)
Income before tax	A$140,000

This A$96,000 difference can be reconciled as the 300,000 units multiplied by the A$0.32 per unit (A$0.72 − A$0.40) "lost" revenue from making internal sales.

Assume, on the other hand, that the 400,000 units represented the total number of units that could be sold externally and the Evergreen Division has no other opportunity to use the facilities. In this instance, the opportunity cost of the facilities used is zero and the division is no worse off by transferring the 300,000 evergreen units internally than by sitting with idle capacity. Relating this situation to the general transfer pricing rules, the transfer price of A$0.40 is at its lower limit.

COST ALTERNATIVE—ABSORPTION COST

Transfer prices based on absorption cost (direct material, direct labor, and variable and fixed overhead) at least provide a contribution toward covering the selling division's fixed production overhead. Such a transfer price does not produce the same amount of income that would be generated if the transferring division sold the goods externally, but it does provide for coverage of all production costs. Absorption cost for an evergreen chemical unit is A$0.45 (A$0.20 DM + A$0.06 DL + A$0.10 VOH + A$0.09 FOH). The Evergreen Division's income statement would appear as follows using absorption cost as the transfer price:

Sales:		
External (400,000 × A$0.72)	A$288,000	
Internal (300,000 × A$0.45)	135,000	A$423,000
Costs (shown previously)		364,000
Income before tax		A$ 59,000

Although the absorption cost transfer price provides a reasonable coverage of costs to the selling segment, that same cost could create a suboptimization problem because of the effects on the buying segment.

Suppose the Marine Biochemical Division of Scott Company can purchase evergreen units externally from United Evergreen for A$0.44 and that the externally purchased evergreen units are of the same quality and specifications as those produced internally. If the transfer price is set at the absorption cost of A$0.45, the Marine Biochemical Division may decide to purchase the evergreen units from United Evergreen for A$0.44. Purchasing at the lower price would give the buying unit's manager more favorable financial results than would making the acquisition internally. In such an instance, Scott Company is paying A$0.44 for a product its Evergreen Division can make for a variable cost of A$0.40. Thus, although the buying segment manager appears to "save" A$0.01 per evergreen unit, the company would be better off by A$12,000 if the evergreen units were purchased internally rather than externally:

Unit cost to Marine Biochemical Division to purchase externally	A$0.44
Unit cost to produce in Evergreen Division (out-of-pocket costs)	0.40
Net advantage of company to produce per unit	A$0.04
Multiplied by number of units transferred	× 300,000
Total savings to produce internally	A$ 12,000

These facts assume that the Evergreen Division does not have an opportunity cost of more than A$0.04 per evergreen unit for the use of the facilities devoted to the 300,000 units. If, however, the Evergreen Division can sell all the units it produces at list price, the division should do so. The Marine Biochemical Division could then purchase its evergreen units from United Evergreen, and Scott Company would be optimizing its resources. Computations to arrive at this conclusion are as follows:

Evergreen Division's additional contribution margin from outside sales (300,000 × A$0.32)	A$96,000
Additional cost caused by Marine Biochemical Division's purchase from outside source (300,000 × A$0.04)	(12,000)
Net incremental income to company before tax	A$84,000

The company is better off by A$84,000 because the A$0.32 contribution margin (A$0.72 − A$0.40) realized on each additional unit sale to outsiders is greater than the A$0.04 difference between the A$0.44 external purchase price paid by the Marine Biochemical Division and the A$0.40 incremental cost of the Evergreen Division to produce the units.

Under the above circumstances, the general transfer pricing rules also would have yielded the decision not to make the internal transfer. The sum of the A$0.40 incremental cost to produce and the A$0.32 opportunity cost of additional contribution on external sales is A$0.72, which exceeds the upper limit of the A$0.44 market price. Scott Company should not make the transfer as long as the Marine Biochemical Division can purchase the units externally for a price less than A$0.72.

COST ALTERNATIVE—MODIFICATIONS TO VARIABLE AND/OR ABSORPTION COST

Modifications can be made to minimize the definitional and motivational problems associated with cost-based transfer prices. When variable cost is used as a base, an additional amount can be added to cover some fixed costs and provide a measure of profit to the selling division. This adjustment is an example of a *cost-plus* arrangement. Some company managers think cost-plus arrangements are acceptable substitutes for market-based transfer prices, especially when market prices for comparable substitute products are unavailable.

Absorption cost can be modified by adding an amount equal to an average of the nonproduction costs associated with the product and/or an amount for profit to the selling division. In contrast, a transfer price could be set at less than absorption cost on the theory that there might be no other use for the idle capacity, and the selling division should receive some benefit from partial coverage of its fixed factory overhead. Alternatively, absorption cost can be reduced by the estimated savings in production costs on internally transferred goods. For example, packaging may not be necessary or as expensive if the inventory is sold intracompany rather than externally.

Market-Based Transfer Prices

To eliminate the problems of defining "cost," some companies simply use a market price approach to setting transfer prices. Market price is believed to be an objective, arm's-length measure of value that simulates the selling price that would be offered and paid if the subunits were independent, autonomous companies. If a selling division is operating efficiently relative to its competition, it should be able to show a profit when transferring products or services at market prices. Similarly, an efficiently operating buying division should not be troubled by a market-based transfer price because that is what it would have to pay for the goods or services if the alternative of buying internally did not exist. Using such a system, the Evergreen Division would transfer all evergreen units to the Marine Biochemical Division at the A$0.72 price charged to external purchasers.

Although this approach appears logical, several problems may exist with the use of market prices for intracompany transfers. First, transfers can involve products having no exact counterpart in the external market. Second, market price is not entirely appropriate because of cost savings on internal sales arising from reductions in bad debts and/or in packaging, advertising, or delivery expenditures. Third, difficulties can arise in setting a transfer price when the external market is depressed because of a temporary reduction in demand for the product. Should the current depressed price be used as the transfer price or should the expected long-run market price be used? Fourth, different prices are quoted and different discounts and credit terms are allowed to different buyers. Which market price is the "right" one to use?

Negotiated Transfer Prices

negotiated transfer price

Because of the problems associated with both cost- and market-based prices, **negotiated transfer prices** are often set through a process of bargaining between the selling and purchasing unit managers. Such prices are typically below the normal market purchase price of the buying unit, but above the sum of the selling unit's incremental and opportunity costs. A negotiated price meeting these specifications falls within the range limits of the transfer pricing rules.

A negotiated transfer price for the Scott Company would be bounded on the top side by the Marine Biochemical Division's external buying price and on the bottom side by the A$0.40 incremental variable costs of the Evergreen Division. If some of the variable selling costs could be eliminated, the incremental cost would be less. If the Evergreen Division could not sell any additional evergreen units externally or downsize its facilities, no opportunity cost would be involved. Otherwise, the amount of the opportunity cost would need to be determined, and it could be as much as the A$0.32 contribution margin (if all units could be sold externally).

Ability to negotiate a transfer price implies that segment managers have the autonomy to sell or buy products externally if internal negotiations fail. Because such extensive autonomy may lead to dysfunctional behavior and suboptimization, top management may provide a means of arbitrating a price in the event that the units cannot agree. This arbitration arrangement must be specified and agreed on in advance and be skillfully handled or the segment managers may perceive that their autonomy is being usurped by upper-level management.

To encourage cooperation between the transferring divisions, top management may consider joint divisional profits as one performance measurement for both the selling and buying unit managers. Another way to reduce difficulties in establishing a transfer price is simply to use a dual pricing approach.

Dual Pricing

dual pricing arrangement

Because a transfer price is used to satisfy internal managerial objectives, a **dual pricing arrangement** can be used to provide for different transfer prices for the selling and buying segments. Such an arrangement lets the selling division record the transfer of goods or services at a market or negotiated market price and the buying division to record the transfer at a cost-based amount.[11] Use of dual prices would provide a profit margin on the goods transferred and thus reflects a "profit" for the selling division. The arrangement would also provide a minimal cost to the buying division. Dual pricing eliminates the problem of having to divide the profits artificially between the selling and buying segments and allows managers to have the most relevant information for both decision making and performance evaluation.

When dual pricing is used, the sum of the individual segment performances will not equal the companywide performance. The selling segment's recorded sales price is not equal to the buying segment's recorded purchase price for the same transaction. The difference is assigned to an internal reconciliation account used to adjust revenues and costs when company financial statements are prepared. Such reconciliation is the same as would exist in preparing consolidated statements when sales are made between the consolidated entities at an amount other than cost.

Several benefits can result from the use of dual transfer pricing. These are expressed in the accompanying News Note about dual pricing arrangements in which the writer advocates market price for the selling segment and variable cost for the buying segment.

In contrast, while reducing disagreements, dual pricing might also eliminate some of the benefits of managerial competition. These include the understanding and cooperation resulting from negotiation and the opportunity for creative solutions to mutual problems.

Using the information for the Evergreen and Marine Biochemical Divisions of Scott Company, journal entries to record transfers under various transfer pricing systems are shown in Exhibit 18–21.

Selecting a Transfer Pricing System

Setting a reasonable transfer price is not an easy task. Everyone involved in the process must be aware of the positive and negative aspects of each type of transfer price and be responsive to suggestions of change if needed. The determination of the type of transfer pricing system to use should reflect the organizational units' characteristics as well as corporate goals. No single method of setting a transfer price is best in all instances. Also, transfer prices are not intended to be permanent; they are frequently revised in relation to changes in costs, supply, demand, competitive forces, and other factors. Flexibility by the selling segment to increase

[11] Typically, the cost-based amount used by the buying division reflects only the variable costs of the selling division.

GENERAL BUSINESS  NEWS NOTE

Dual Pricing

Transfer pricing, or the pricing of products or services supplied by one division to another division, should accomplish three things:

1. It must always result in goal congruence, or guide division managers to take actions not just in their own interests but for the good of the entire organization.
2. It should ease the fundamental tension between decision making and control.
3. It should provide essential information so that managers can make suitable, short-run decisions.

For most domestic transfers of products with a fairly developed intermediate market in which the buyer can seek out alternative suppliers, a modified dual transfer pricing method would enable the organization's divisions to make optimal, short-run decisions and to work toward common goals. The dual transfer price method recognizes that the interests of selling and buying divisions are always opposed. Under the dual price method, the selling division is credited with the market price and the buying division pays the variable cost of the product. The resulting difference is then debited to a reconciliation or adjustment account at the head office. This method helps resolve conflicts between buyer and seller, and gives both divisions adequate incentive to transact internally in the interests of the corporation.

SOURCE: Manmohan Rai Kapoor, "Dueling Divisions: A New Dual Transfer Pricing Method," *CMA Management* (March 1998), p. 23.

EXHIBIT 18-21

Journal Entries for Transfer Prices

Assume that 1,000 units of product are transferred from the Evergreen Division to the Marine Biochemical Division:
Variable production cost (1,000 × A\$0.36) = A\$360
Full production cost (1,000 × A\$0.45) = A\$450
External selling price (1,000 × A\$0.72) = A\$720

SITUATION	EVERGREEN (E)			MARINE BIOCHEMICAL (MB)		
Transfer at variable production cost	A/R—Division MB	360		Inventory	360	
	Intracompany Sales		360	A/P—Division E		360
	Intracompany CGS	450				
	Finished Goods		450			
Transfer at full production cost	A/R—Division MB	450		Inventory	450	
	Intracompany Sales		450	A/P—Division E		450
	Intracompany CGS	450				
	Finished Goods		450			
Transfer at external selling price	A/R—Division MB	720		Inventory	720	
	Intracompany Sales		720	A/P—Division E		720
	Intracompany CGS	450				
	Finished Goods		450			
Transfer at dual price of external selling price for selling division and full production cost for buying division	A/R—Division MB	450		Inventory	450	
	Intracompany Sales in Excess of Assigned Costs	270		A/P—Division E		450
	Intracompany Sales		720			
	Intracompany CGS	450				
	Finished Goods		450			

NOTE: Entries for negotiated transfer prices would be similar to those at full production cost, except that the negotiated transfer price would be shown for the first entry for the selling division and the purchase entry for the buying division.

a transfer price when reduced productive capacity is present and to increase a transfer price when excess productive capacity exists is a strong management lever. Regardless of what method is used, a thoughtfully set transfer price will provide

- an appropriate basis for the calculation and evaluation of segment performance,
- the rational acquisition or use of goods and services between corporate divisions,
- the flexibility to respond to changes in demand or market conditions, and
- a means of motivation to encourage and reward goal congruence by managers in decentralized operations.

TRANSFER PRICES FOR SERVICE DEPARTMENTS

The practice of setting prices for products transferred between one organizational segment and another is well established. Instituting transfer prices for services is a less common but effective technique for some types of service departments.

Setting Service Transfer Prices

Setting transfer prices for services requires that practical internal guidelines be developed to provide meaningful information for both the user and provider departments. For an organization to be profitable, revenue-producing areas must cover service department costs. These costs can be allocated internally to user departments based on the methods shown in an earlier section of this chapter, or services can be "sold" to user departments using transfer prices. In either case, service department costs are included in the costs of revenue-producing departments so that those departments' sales can cover the service departments' costs. The decision as to the most useful information is at the discretion of top management.

Transfer prices for services can take the same forms as those for products: cost based, market based, negotiated, or dual. Traditionally, these transfer prices are most often negotiated between buyer and seller. This is especially true for services because the value is often qualitative—expertise, reliability, convenience, and responsiveness—and can only be assessed judgmentally from the perspective of the parties involved. The type of transfer price to use should depend on the cost and volume level of the service as well as whether comparable substitutes are available. Examples include the following:

- Market-based transfer prices are effective for common, standardized services that are high-cost, high-volume services such as storage and transportation.
- Negotiated transfer prices are useful for customized services that are high-cost, high-volume services such as risk management and specialized executive training.
- Cost-based or dual transfer prices are generally chosen for services that are low-cost, low-volume services such as temporary maintenance and temporary office staff assistance.

6

What are the advantages and disadvantages of service transfer prices?

A company should weigh the advantages and disadvantages of service transfer prices before instituting such a transfer policy. Transfer prices are useful when service departments provide distinct, measurable benefits to other areas or provide services having a specific cause-and-effect relationship.

Advantages of Service Transfer Prices

Transfer prices in these circumstances are useful and can provide certain organizational advantages in both the revenue-producing and service departments. These advantages (listed in Exhibit 18–22) are as follows. First, transfer prices can encourage more involvement between service departments and their users. Service

EXHIBIT 18–22

Advantages of Transfer Prices for Services

	Revenue Departments	Service Departments
User Involvement	Encourages ways to improve services to benefit users	Promotes development of services more beneficial to users
Cost Consciousness	Relates to services used; restricts usage to those necessary and cost beneficial	Relates to cost of services provided; must justify transfer price established
Performance Evaluations	Includes costs for making performance evaluations if control exists over amount of services used	Promotes making a service department a profit center rather than a cost center and thus provides more performance evaluation measures

departments are more likely to interact with users to determine the specific services that are needed and to eliminate or reduce services that are not cost beneficial. If charged a transfer price, users may be more likely to suggest ways the service department could reduce costs and improve its performance, and thereby lower the transfer prices charged.

Second, using transfer prices for services should cause service department and user department managers to be more cost conscious and eliminate wasteful usage. If service departments incur excessive costs, a reasonable transfer price may not cover those costs or a high transfer price may not be justifiable to users. If user departments are charged for all services they receive, they might decide their service demands have been excessive. For example, if the Management Information Department charged other departments for the number of reports received, managers would be less likely to request reports simply to be "on the receiving list," as sometimes occurs.

Last, transfer prices result in useful information for performance evaluations. Responsibility reports show a controllable service department cost relative to the actual services used by individual managers instead of noncontrollable allocated expense amounts. The use of transfer prices can also allow service departments to become profit rather than cost centers. Although transfer prices are effective responsibility accounting tools, there are disadvantages to their use.

Disadvantages of Service Transfer Prices

Transfer prices for services do have certain disadvantages, including the following:

- There can be (and most often is) disagreement among organizational unit managers as to how the transfer price should be set.
- Implementing transfer prices in the accounting system requires additional organizational costs and employee time.
- Transfer prices do not work equally well for all departments or divisions. For example, service departments that do not provide measurable benefits or cannot show a distinct cause-and-effect relationship between cost behavior and service use by other departments should not attempt to use transfer prices.
- The transfer price may cause dysfunctional behavior among organizational units or may induce certain services to be under- or overutilized.

- U.S. tax regulations regarding transfer prices in multinational companies are quite complicated.

These same disadvantages are associated with transfer prices for products.

TRANSFER PRICES IN MULTINATIONAL SETTINGS

7

How can multinational companies use transfer prices?

Because of the differences in tax systems, customs duties, freight and insurance costs, import/export regulations, and foreign-exchange controls, setting transfer prices for products and services becomes extremely difficult when the company is engaged in multinational operations. In addition, as shown in Exhibit 18–23, the internal and external objectives of transfer pricing policies differ in multinational enterprises (MNEs).

Because of these differences, the determination of transfer prices in MNEs has no simple resolution. Multinational companies may use one transfer price when a product is sent to or received from one country and a totally different transfer price for the same product when it is sent to or received from another.

However, some guidelines on transfer pricing policies should be set by the company and be followed on a consistent basis. For example, a company should not price certain parent company services to foreign subsidiaries in a manner that would send the majority of those costs to the subsidiary in the country with the highest tax rate unless that method of pricing were reasonable and equitable to all subsidiaries. The general test of reasonableness is that transfer prices should reflect an arm's-length transaction.

Tax authorities in both the home and host countries carefully scrutinize multinational transfer prices because such prices determine which country taxes the income from the transfer. The U.S. Congress is concerned about both U.S. multinationals operating in low-tax-rate countries and foreign companies operating in the United States. In both situations, Congress believes that companies could avoid paying U.S. corporate income taxes because of misleading or inaccurate transfer pricing. Thus, the Internal Revenue Service (IRS) may be quick to investigate U.S. subsidiaries that operate in low-tax areas and suddenly have unusually high profits.

If foreign companies charge their U.S. subsidiaries higher prices than what they would charge subsidiaries in their home country, U.S. taxable income and thus the

EXHIBIT 18–23

Multinational Company Transfer Pricing Objectives

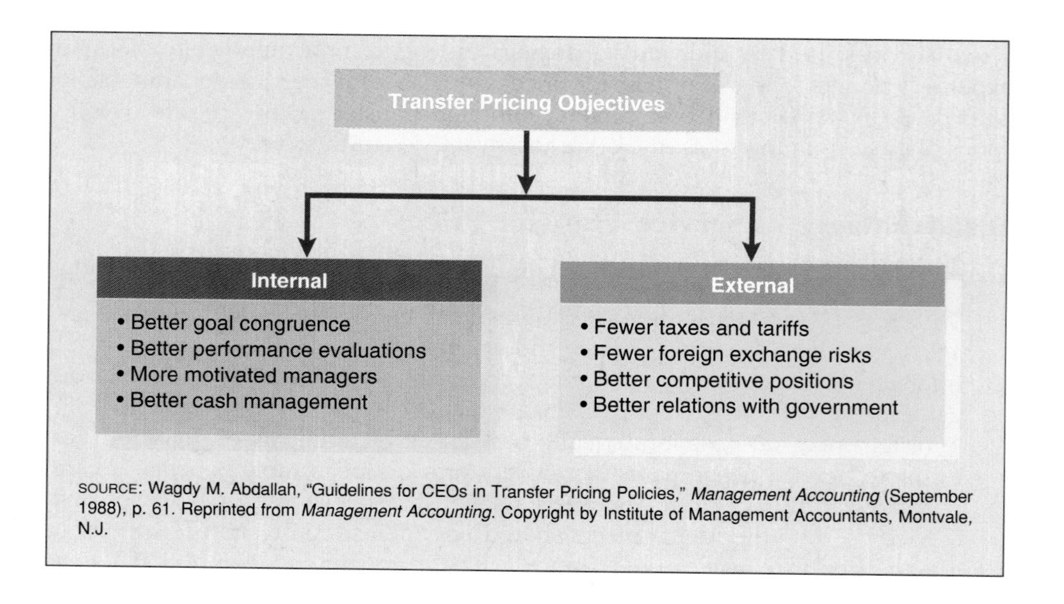

SOURCE: Wagdy M. Abdallah, "Guidelines for CEOs in Transfer Pricing Policies," *Management Accounting* (September 1988), p. 61. Reprinted from *Management Accounting*. Copyright by Institute of Management Accountants, Montvale, N.J.

tax base will decline—which can also provoke an IRS review. The accompanying News Note discusses the IRS's Advanced Pricing Agreement Program.

Transfers among nations are becoming easier through the institution of trade integration arrangements such as the European Union and the North American Free Trade Agreement. These arrangements should help reduce the significance of transfer price manipulations through (among other features) the harmonization of tax structures and the reduction in import/export fees, tariffs, and capital movement restrictions.

To determine the effectiveness of their transfer pricing policies, multinational company managers should consider the following two questions:

1. Does the system achieve economic decisions that affect MNE performance positively, including international capital investment decisions, output level decisions for both intermediate and final products, and product pricing decisions for external customers?
2. Do subsidiary managers feel that they are being fairly evaluated and rewarded for their divisional contributions to the MNE as a whole?[12]

If the answers to both of these questions are yes, then the company appears to have a transfer pricing system that appropriately coordinates the underlying considerations, minimizes the internal and external goal conflicts, and balances the short- and long-range perspectives of the multinational company.

INTERNATIONAL  **NEWS NOTE**

Get The Transfer Price Right!

First, let's define "transfer price." This term refers to the price at which an enterprise transfers goods or intangible property or provides services to a related enterprise, such as a parent company to a subsidiary. The Internal Revenue Service is concerned that companies could use these transfer prices to shift profits between related entities through cost of goods sold. Thus, transfer pricing manipulation could be used by taxpayers to shift income from high tax jurisdictions like the U.S. to low tax jurisdictions.

The right price from the IRS's perspective is the market value price. Because it's difficult to prove that the transfer price was equal to the market price, companies often find themselves in disputes with the IRS. But now there's help. The IRS's Advanced Pricing Agreement (APA) Program provides companies an opportunity to avoid costly audits and litigation by allowing them to negotiate a prospective agreement with the IRS regarding the facts, the transfer pricing methodology, and an acceptable range of results. The program is aimed at multinational corporations interested in avoiding penalties, managing risk, and determining their tax liability with certainty.

In the APA Program, you as a financial professional and representative of your company would work proactively with the IRS in a cooperative negotiating environment rather than in an adversarial examination or litigation environment. The APA Program's goal? To agree upon the best method to calculate market-driven prices, which allows you to determine your transfer price and, ultimately, your tax liability with certainty. An APA results in no surprises for the taxpayer. Because the IRS has agreed prospectively, you won't find yourself involved in transfer pricing disputes later as long as you comply with the agreement, which can cover as many as five years and can also be applied to prior years.

SOURCE: Steven C. Wrappe, Ken Milani, and Julie Joy, "The Transfer Price Is Right . . . Or Is It?" *Strategic Finance* (July 1999), pp. 38ff. Copyright by Institute of Management Accountants, Montvale, N.J.

[12] Wagdy M. Abdallah, "Guidelines for CEOs in Transfer Pricing Policies," *Management Accounting* (September 1988), p. 61. Reprinted from *Management Accounting*. Copyright by Institute of Management Accountants, Montvale, N.J.

REVISITING Abbott Laboratories

http://www.abbott.com

Abbott's mission is to improve lives. The company does this by developing technologies that build, protect and improve people's health. With one of the most diverse product lines in the industry and unique expertise in many of the most common and important medical conditions, Abbott touches the lives of millions of people around the world every year.

Above all, Abbott is a science company. More than 5,000 Abbott scientists around the world are committed to developing new health care technologies to improve lives. To support Abbott's commitment to advancing medical science, the company devotes more than $1 billion every year toward the research and development of innovative health care solutions.

While the demand for health is boundless, the willingness to pay for its benefits is limited—sometimes sharply. Abbott has operated in a cost-constrained environment for many years—bounded by government controls around the world and payer pressures in the United States.

What the market will reward is innovation—new medical technologies that advance care cost effectively. New products that deliver unique benefits will always find a market. Abbott delivers products that provide meaningful, distinctive advantages to users and closely manages costs to ensure that the company stays as efficient as its markets.

Another major force shaping Abbott's environment is the continually accelerating pace of change. The demand for new health care products creates a parallel need to rapidly advance the state of scientific knowledge. To achieve this, companies in the industry have been combining at a previously unparalleled rate to create companies of unparalleled size.

Abbott's diversified product base, its size, and its presence around the globe require that it empower managers who can respond quickly and appropriately to local changes and conditions anywhere the company conducts business. At the same time, these managers must also maintain the high standards of the worldwide company. Therefore, Abbott maintains an appropriate degree of decentralization. Responsibility accounting reports provide for the needed two-way flow of information. Transfer pricing with international considerations is employed.

Is it any wonder that *Industry Week* in its "Best-Managed Companies" (published in the April 19, 1999, issue) ranked Abbott as one of the 100 best-managed companies in the world, for the fourth year in a row? In 1998, Abbott paid its 300th consecutive quarterly dividend.

SOURCE: "Abbott Laboratories Online," Abbott Laboratories Web site, http://www.abbott.com (March 29, 2000).

CHAPTER SUMMARY

A decentralized organization is composed of operational units led by managers who have some degree of decision-making autonomy. The degree to which a company is decentralized depends on top management philosophy and on the ability of unit managers to perform independently. Decentralization provides managers the opportunity to develop leadership qualities, creative problem-solving abilities, and decision-making skills. It also lets the individual closest to the operational unit make decisions for that unit, thereby reducing the time spent in communicating and making decisions.

One disadvantage of decentralization is that responsibility may be spread too thinly throughout the organization. Competition can also result among the managers of decentralized units, which could lessen the organizational goal congruence. Some disruption may occur during a transition to decentralization because top managers resist delegating a portion of their authority to subordinates. Last, the costs of incorrect decisions made by the decentralized unit managers could be high.

Responsibility accounting systems are used to provide information on the revenues and/or costs under the control of unit managers. Responsibility reports reflect the upward flow of information from each decentralized unit to top management. Managers receive information regarding the activities under their immediate control as well as the control of their direct subordinates. The information is successively aggregated, and the reports allow the application of the management by exception principle.

Responsibility centers are classified as cost, revenue, profit, or investment centers. Managers of cost and revenue centers have control primarily over, respectively, costs and revenues. Profit center managers are responsible for maximizing their segments' incomes. Investment center managers must generate revenues and control costs to produce a satisfactory return on the asset base under their influence. All responsibility center managers should perform their functions within the framework of organizational goal congruence, although there is a possibility of suboptimization of resources.

Converting a cost or revenue center to a microprofit center requires that each of these responsibility center managers be responsible for both revenue and costs. Then the responsibility center can be treated as a mini-business, the performance of which is subject to evaluation, recognition, and reward.

Management may want to allocate service department costs to revenue-producing areas using one of the following three methods: the direct method, step method, or algebraic method. The direct method assigns service department costs only to revenue-producing departments and does not consider services that may be provided by one service department to another.

The step method uses a benefits-provided ranking that lists service departments from the one providing the most service to other departments to the one servicing primarily the revenue-producing areas. Costs are assigned from each department in order of the ranking. Once costs have been assigned from an area, they cannot flow back into that area.

The algebraic method recognizes the interrelationships among all departments through the use of simultaneous equations. This method provides the best allocation information and is readily adaptable to computer computations.

A transfer price is an intracompany charge for goods or services bought and sold between segments of a decentralized company. A transfer price for products is typically cost based, market based, or negotiated. The upper limit of a transfer price is the lowest market price at which the product can be acquired externally. The lower limit is the incremental cost of production plus the opportunity cost of the facilities used. A dual pricing system may also be used that assigns different transfer prices to the selling and buying units. Top management should promote a transfer pricing system that enhances goal congruence, provides segment autonomy, motivates managers to strive for segment effectiveness and efficiency, is practical, and is credible in measuring segment performance.

Setting transfer prices in multinational enterprises is a complex process because of the differences existing in tax structures, import/export regulations, customs duties, and other factors of the international subsidiaries and divisions. A valid transfer price for a multinational company achieves economic benefit for the entire company and support from the domestic and international managers using the system.

KEY TERMS

administrative department (p. 812)
algebraic method (p. 816)
"benefits-provided" ranking (p. 816)
cost center (p. 806)
differential cost (p. 814)
direct method (p. 815)
dual pricing arrangement (p. 828)
goal congruence (p. 800)
investment center (p. 810)
negotiated transfer price (p. 827)
profit center (p. 809)
pseudo microprofit center (p. 812)
real microprofit center (p. 812)
responsibility center (p. 806)
responsibility report (p. 802)
revenue center (p. 808)
service department (p. 812)
step method (p. 815)
suboptimization (p. 800)
transfer price (p. 823)

SOLUTION STRATEGIES

Transfer Prices (Cost-Based, Market-Based, Negotiated, Dual)

Upper Limit: Lowest price available from external suppliers

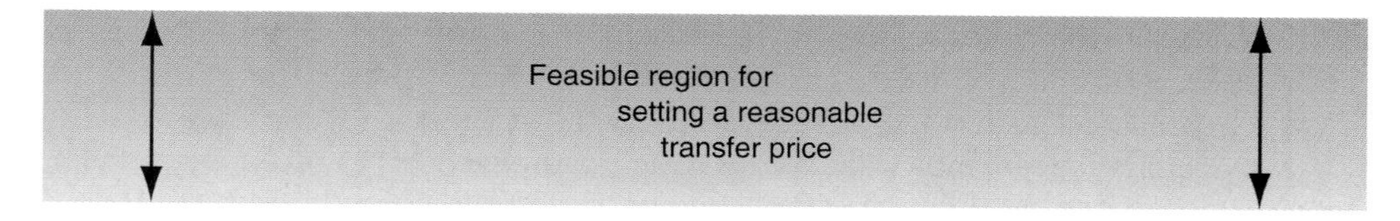

Lower Limit: Incremental costs of producing and selling the transferred goods or services plus the opportunity cost for the facilities used

Service Department Cost Allocation

Direct Method

1. Determine rational and systematic allocation bases for each service department.
2. Assign costs from each service department directly to revenue-producing areas using specified allocation bases.

Step Method

1. Determine rational and systematic allocation bases for each service department.
2. List service departments in sequence (benefits-provided ranking) from the one that provides the most service to all other areas (both revenue- and non-revenue-producing areas) to the one that provides service to only revenue-producing areas.
3. Beginning with the first service department listed, allocate the costs from that department to all remaining departments; repeat the process until only revenue-producing departments remain.

Algebraic Method

1. Determine rational and systematic allocation bases for each department.
2. Develop algebraic equations representing the services provided by each department to other service departments and to revenue-producing departments using the allocation bases.
3. Solve the simultaneous equations for the service departments through an iterative process or by computer until all values are known.
4. Allocate costs using allocation bases developed in step 2. Eliminate "reallocated" costs from consideration.

DEMONSTRATION PROBLEM

Kala Marina Inc. is a diversified company of which one segment makes spear guns and another produces air tanks. Costs for a tank produced by the Tank Division are as follows:

Direct material	$12	
Direct labor	5	
Variable overhead	3	
Variable S&A (both for external and internal sales)	1	
Total variable cost		$21
Fixed overhead*	$ 3	
Fixed S&A	2	
Total fixed cost		5
Total cost per tank		$26
Markup on total variable cost (33 1/3%)		7
List price to external customers		$33

*Fixed costs are allocated to all units produced based on estimated annual production.

- Estimated annual production: 400,000 tanks
- Estimated sales to outside entities: 300,000 tanks
- Estimated sales by the Tank Division to the Spear Gun Division: 100,000 tanks

The managers of the two divisions are currently negotiating a transfer price.

Required:

a. Determine a transfer price based on variable product cost.
b. Determine a transfer price based on total variable cost plus markup.
c. Determine a transfer price based on full production cost.
d. Determine a transfer price based on total cost per tank.
e. Assume that the Tank Division has no alternative use for the facilities that make the tanks for internal transfer. Also assume that the Spear Gun Division can buy equivalent tanks externally for $25. Calculate the upper and lower limits for which the transfer price should be set.
f. Compute a transfer price that divides the "profit" between the two divisions equally.
g. In contrast to the assumption in part (e), assume that the Tank Division can rent the facilities in which the 100,000 tanks are produced for $100,000. Determine the lower limit of the transfer price.

Solution to Demonstration Problem

a.

Direct material	$12
Direct labor	5
Variable overhead	3
Transfer price	$20

b.

Total variable cost	$21
Markup	7
Transfer price	$28

c.

Variable production cost	$20
Fixed production cost	3
Transfer price	$23

d.

Total variable cost	$21
Total fixed cost	5
Transfer price	$26

e. Upper limit: Spear Gun Division's external purchase price = $25
Lower limit: Total variable cost of Tank Division = $21

f. (Lower limit + Upper limit) ÷ 2 = ($21 + $25) ÷ 2 = $23

g. $100,000 ÷ 100,000 tanks = $1 opportunity cost per tank
Lower limit: Incremental cost of Tank Division + Opportunity cost = $21 + $1 = $22

QUESTIONS

1. What is the distinction between a centralized organizational structure and a decentralized organizational structure? In what types of companies is decentralization appropriate and why?
2. "A company's operations are either centralized or decentralized." Discuss this statement.
3. Bill Barnes is the president and chief operating officer of Barnes Electronics. Bill founded the company and has led it to its prominent place in the electronics field. He has manufacturing plants and outlets in 40 states. Bill, however, is finding that he cannot "keep track" of things the way he did in the past. Discuss the advantages and disadvantages of decentralizing the firm's decision-making activities among the various local and regional managers.
4. Even in a decentralized company, some functions may be best performed centrally. List several of these functions and the reasons you have for suggesting them.
5. Why is it suggested that decentralization has many costs associated with it? Describe some of the significant costs associated with decentralization.
6. How does decentralization affect accounting?
7. Why are responsibility reports prepared?
8. Is it appropriate for a single responsibility report to be prepared for a division of a major company? Why or why not?
9. Discuss the way in which a performance report consolidates information at each successively higher level of management.
10. Why might firms use both monetary and nonmonetary measures to evaluate the performance of subunit managers?
11. Discuss the differences among the various types of responsibility centers.
12. Why might salaries be included in the responsibility report of a revenue center manager?
13. What is suboptimization and what factors contribute to suboptimization in a decentralized firm?
14. Define and give four examples of a service department. How do service departments differ from operating departments?
15. Why are service department costs often allocated to revenue-producing departments? Is such a process of allocation always useful from a decision-making standpoint?
16. How might service department cost allocation create a feeling of cost responsibility among managers of revenue-producing departments?
17. "The four criteria for selecting an allocation base for service department costs should be applied equally." Discuss the merits of this statement.
18. How do the direct, step, and algebraic methods of allocating service department costs differ? In what ways are these methods similar?
19. What are the advantages and disadvantages of the direct, step, and algebraic methods of allocating service department costs?
20. Why is a benefits-provided ranking necessary in the step method of allocation but not in the algebraic method?
21. When the algebraic method of allocating service department costs is used, total costs for each service department increase from what they were prior to the allocation. Why does this occur and how are the additional costs treated?
22. How has the evolution of computer technology enhanced the feasibility of using the algebraic method of service department cost allocation?
23. What are transfer prices and why are they used by companies?
24. Would transfer prices be used in each of the following responsibility centers: cost, revenue, profit, and investment? If so, how would they be used?

25. How could the use of transfer prices improve goal congruence? Impair goal congruence?

26. What are the high and low limits of transfer prices and why do these limits exist?

27. A company is considering the use of a cost-based transfer price. What arguments favor the use of standard rather than actual cost?

28. What problems might be encountered when attempting to implement a cost-based transfer pricing system?

29. What practical problems could impede the use of a market-based transfer price?

30. Why would the element of negotiation be "potentially both the most positive and the most negative aspect of negotiated transfer prices"?

31. What is dual pricing? What is the intended effect of dual pricing on the performance of each division affected by the dual price?

32. How can service departments use transfer prices and what advantages do transfer prices have over cost allocation methods?

33. What are some of the major disadvantages of using transfer prices?

34. Explain why the determination of transfer prices may be more complex in a multinational setting than in a domestic setting.

35. Use the Internet to identify a multinational company encountering tax problems related to transfer pricing between its organizational units in different countries. Prepare a brief discussion of the issues and the actual or potential consequences.

EXERCISES

36. *(Terminology)* Match the following lettered terms on the left with the appropriate numbered description on the right.

a. Centralized organization
b. Cost center
c. Decentralized organization
d. Dual pricing arrangement
e. Goal congruence
f. Investment center
g. Profit center
h. Revenue center
i. Suboptimization
j. Transfer price

1. Situation in which buying division is charged a price that differs from that credited to the selling division
2. Structure in which most decisions are made by segment managers
3. Situations in which decisions are made that are sometimes not in the best interest of whole firm
4. Segment whose manager is responsible primarily for costs
5. Segment whose manager is responsible primarily for revenues, expenses, and assets
6. Segment whose manager is responsible for both revenues and expenses
7. Segment whose manager is primarily responsible for revenues
8. Structure in which most decisions are made by top management
9. An internal exchange price
10. Situation in which mutual support exists among goals of individual managers and the organization

37. *(Decentralization advantages and disadvantages)* Indicate which of the following is a potential advantage (A), disadvantage (D), or neither (N) of decentralization.

a. Promotion of goal congruence
b. Support of training in decision making
c. Development of leadership qualities
d. Complication of communication process
e. Cost of developing the planning and reporting system
f. Placement of decision maker closer to time and place of problem
g. Speed of decisions
h. Use of management by exception principle by top management
i. Provision of greater job satisfaction
j. Delegation of ultimate responsibility

38. *(Centralization versus decentralization)* For each situation below, indicate whether the firm would tend to be more centralized (C) or more decentralized (D), or if the tendency is indefinite (I).
a. The firm's growth rate is rapid.
b. The firm is small.
c. The firm is in a growth stage of product development.
d. Top management expects that incorrect subordinate management decisions could have a disastrous impact on company profits.
e. The company was founded two years ago.
f. Top management has a high level of confidence in subordinates' judgment and skills.
g. Top management is proud of its record of tight control.
h. Both d and f.
i. Both c and g.
j. Both a and b.

39. *(Revenue variances)* The Sales Department of Porcelain Works is responsible for sales of two figurines. One is called "Elegant Maiden" and the other is called "Summer Memories." For April 2001, the Sales Department's actual and budgeted sales were as follows:

	ELEGANT MAIDEN		SUMMER MEMORIES	
	Dollars	Units	Dollars	Units
Budgeted sales	$10,000	1,000	$15,000	3,000
Actual sales	9,000	750	15,750	3,500

For April 2001, compute each of the following for the Sales Department of Porcelain Works:
a. Price variance
b. Mix variance
c. Volume variance

40. *(Revenue variances)* Athletes' Friend, Inc., manufactures two products: baseball bats and gloves. For 2001, the firm budgeted the following:

	Bats	Gloves
Sales	$400,000	$600,000
Unit sales price	40	30

At the end of 2001, managers were informed that total actual sales amounted to 35,000 units and totaled $1,225,000. Glove sales for the year amounted to 20,000 units at an average price of $35.
a. Compute the total revenue variance for 2001.
b. Compute the price variance for 2001.
c. Compute the mix variance for 2001.
d. Compute the volume variance for 2001.

41. *(Direct method)* Chance Corporation allocates its service department costs to its production departments using the direct method. Information for June 2001 follows:

	Personnel	Maintenance
Service department costs	$68,000	$50,000
Services provided to other departments		
Personnel		10%
Maintenance	15%	
Fabricating	45%	60%
Finishing	40%	30%

a. What amount of personnel and maintenance costs should be assigned to Fabricating for June?

b. What amount of personnel and maintenance costs should be assigned to Finishing for June?

42. *(Direct method)* Palisade Bank has three revenue-generating areas: checking accounts, savings accounts, and loans. The bank also has three service areas: administration, personnel, and accounting. The direct costs per month and the interdepartmental service structure are shown below in a benefits-provided ranking.

		PERCENTAGE OF SERVICE USED BY					
Department	Direct Costs	Admin.	Personnel	Accounting	Checking	Savings	Loan
Administration	$ 90,000		10	10	30	40	10
Personnel	60,000	10		10	30	20	30
Accounting	90,000	10	10		40	20	20
Checking	90,000						
Savings	75,000						
Loans	150,000						

Compute the total cost for each revenue-generating area using the direct method.

43. *(Step method)* Using the step method and the information in Exercise 42, compute the total cost for each revenue-generating area.

44. *(Step method)* Cognevich Company is organized in three service departments (Personnel, Administration, and Maintenance) and two revenue-generating departments (Stamping and Assembly). The company uses the step method to allocate service department costs to operating departments. In October 2000, Personnel incurred $60,000 of costs, Administration incurred $90,000, and Maintenance incurred $40,000. Proportions of services provided to other departments for October 2000 follow:

	Personnel	Administration	Maintenance
Personnel		10%	5%
Administration	15%		10%
Maintenance	10%	15%	
Stamping	45%	50%	50%
Assembly	30%	25%	35%

a. Assuming that the departments are listed in a benefits-provided ranking, what amount of Personnel cost should be assigned to each of the other departments for October? Administration costs? Maintenance costs?

b. What is the total service department cost that was assigned to Stamping in October? To Assembly?

c. Explain why the cost allocation is affected by the order in which costs are assigned.

45. *(Algebraic method)* Use the information for Palisade Bank in Exercise 42 to compute the total cost for each revenue-generating area using the algebraic method.

46. *(Algebraic method)* Colleague Press has two revenue-producing divisions (College Textbooks and Professional Publications) and two service departments (Administration and Personnel). Direct costs and allocation bases for each of these areas are presented below:

		ALLOCATION BASES	
Department	**Direct Costs**	**Number of Employees**	**Dollars of Assets Employed**
Administration	$ 225,000	10	$310,000
Personnel	175,000	5	75,000
College Textbooks	1,125,000	50	600,000
Professional Publications	475,000	30	525,000

Company management has decided to allocate administration and personnel costs on the basis of dollars of assets employed and number of employees, respectively. Use the algebraic method to allocate the service department costs and determine the final costs of operating the College Textbooks and Professional Publications Departments.

47. *(Transfer pricing)* Motchip Division, a decentralized plant of Pazazz Motor Company, is considering what transfer price to charge the Engine Division for transfers of computer chips to that division. The following data on production cost per computer chip have been gathered:

Direct material	$1.50
Direct labor	4.00
Variable overhead	1.70
Fixed overhead	2.40
Total	$9.60

The Motchip Division sells the computer chips to external buyers for $21.75. Managers of the Engine Division have received external offers to provide the division comparable chips, ranging from $15 at one company to $23 at another.

a. Determine the upper and lower limits for the transfer price between the Motchip Division and the Engine Division.

b. If the Motchip Division is presently selling all the chips it can produce to external buyers, what is the minimum price it should set for transfers to the Engine Division?

48. *(Transfer pricing)* Keeler Enterprises is decentrally organized. One of its divisions, Trustypad Division, manufactures truck and trailer brake pads for sale to other company divisions as well as to outside entities. Corporate management treats Trustypad Division as a profit center. The normal selling price for a pair of Trustypad's brake pads is $12; costs for each pair are:

Direct material	$2.00
Direct labor	1.40
Variable overhead	0.80
Fixed overhead (based on production of 700,000 pairs)	2.75
Variable selling expense	0.50

Another division of Keeler, the Trailer Division, wants to purchase 25,000 pairs of brake pads from Trustypad Division during next year. No selling costs are incurred on internal sales.

a. If Trustypad's manager can sell all the brake pads it produces externally, what should the minimum transfer price be? Explain.

b. Assume that Trustypad Division is experiencing a slight slowdown in external demand and will be able to sell only 600,000 pairs of brake pads to outsiders next year at the $12 selling price. What should be the minimum selling price to the Trailer Division under these conditions? Explain.

c. Assume that Mr. Leon, the manager of Trailer Division, offers to pay Trustypad Division's production costs plus 25 percent for each pair of brake pads. He receives an invoice for $217,187.50, and he was planning on a cost of $131,250. How were these amounts determined? What created the confusion? Explain.

49. *(Transfer pricing)* Two investment centers of Jones Products Company are the Electronics Division and the Appliance Division. The Electronics Division manufactures an electronic computer chip that can be sold externally and is also used by the Appliance Division in making motors for its appliances. The following information is available about the computer chip:

Total production annually: 200,000 units; internal requirements: 150,000 units; all others are sold externally
List selling price: $25.60
Variable production costs: $12
Fixed overhead: $300,000; allocated on the basis of units of production
Variable selling costs: $3; includes $1 per unit in advertising cost
Fixed selling costs: $400,000

Determine the transfer price under each of the following methods:

a. Total variable cost
b. Full production cost
c. Total variable production cost plus necessary selling costs
d. Market price

50. *(Transfer pricing and management motivation)* Franklin Food Stores operates 12 large supermarkets in New England. Each store is evaluated as a profit center, and store managers have complete control over purchases and their inventory policy. The policy is that if a store runs short of an item and a sister store has a sufficient supply, a transfer will be made between stores. Company policy requires that all such transfers be made at cost.

During a recent period of rapid increases in food prices, company management officials have noted that transfers between stores have decreased sharply. Store managers have indicated that if they ran short of a particular item, they could not locate a sister store with sufficient inventory to make the transfer.

Company management officials have observed several recent cases in which a store manager inquired about the availability of a particular item and was told that the sister store did not have sufficient inventory to make a transfer. Further checking indicated that the sister store had more than sufficient inventory to make the transfer.

a. Why were the store managers reluctant to make the transfers?
b. How could the transfer pricing policy be changed to avoid this situation?

51. *(Transfer pricing in service departments)* Indicate whether each of the following statements constitutes a potential advantage (A), disadvantage (D), or neither (N) of using transfer prices for service department costs.

a. Can make a service department into a profit center
b. Can reduce goal congruence
c. Can make users and providers more cost conscious
d. Can increase resource waste
e. Can increase disagreements among departments
f. Can put all service departments on an equal footing
g. Can cause certain services to be under- or overutilized
h. Can improve ability to evaluate performance
i. Can increase communication about what additional services are needed and which may be reduced or eliminated
j. Can require additional organizational data and employee time

52. *(Transfer pricing for services)* Reliable Insurance Company's computer department is developing a transfer price for its services. Capacity is defined as minutes of computer time. Expected capacity for 2001 is 350,000 minutes and full capacity is 450,000 minutes. Costs of the computer area for 2001 are expected to total $280,000.

a. What is the transfer price based on expected capacity?

b. What is the transfer price based on full capacity?

c. Assume the actual cost of operating the computer area in 2001 is $297,500. What is the total variance from budget of that department? What are some possible causes of that variance?

PROBLEMS

53. *(Profit center performance)* Jane Booth, head of the accounting department at Pacific State University, has felt increasing pressure to raise external funds to compensate for dwindling state financial support. Accordingly, in early January 2001, she conceived the idea of offering a three-day accounting workshop on income taxation for local CPAs. She asked Jim Cost, a tenured tax professor, to supervise the planning process for the seminar, which was to be held in late February 2001. In mid January, Professor Cost presented Ms. Booth with the following budget plan:

Revenues ($400 per participant)		$40,000
Expenses		
Speakers ($500 each)	$ 5,000	
Rent on facilities	3,600	
Advertising	2,100	
Meals and lodging	18,000	
Departmental overhead allocation	3,500	(32,200)
Profit		$ 7,800

Explanations of budget items: The facilities rent of $3,600 is a fixed rental, which is to be paid to a local hotel for use of its meeting rooms. The advertising is also a fixed budgeted cost. Meal expense is budgeted at $5 per person per meal (a total of nine meals are to be provided for each participant); lodging is budgeted at the rate of $45 per participant per night. The departmental overhead includes a specific charge for supplies costing $10 for each participant as well as a general allocation of $2,500 for use of departmental secretarial resources. After reviewing the budget, Ms. Booth gave Professor Cost approval to proceed with the seminar.

a. Recast the above income statement in a segment margin income statement format.

b. Assume the actual financial results of the seminar were as follows:

Revenues (120 participants)		$38,500
Expenses		
Speakers ($750 each)	$ 7,500	
Rent on facilities	4,200	
Advertising	2,900	
Meals and lodging	21,600	
Departmental overhead allocation	3,700	(39,900)
Loss		$ (1,400)

Explanation of actual results: Because sign-ups were running below expectations, the seminar fee was reduced from $400 to $300 for late enrollees and advertising expense was increased. In budgeting for the speakers, Professor Cost neglected to include airfare, which averaged $250 per speaker. After the fees were reduced and advertising increased, the number of participants grew and was larger than expected; therefore, a larger meeting room had to be rented from the local hotel. Recast the actual results in a segment margin income format.

c. Compute variances between the budgeted segment margin income statement and the actual segment income statement. Identify and discuss the factors that are primarily responsible for the difference between the budgeted profit and the actual loss on the tax seminar.

54. *(Responsibility accounting reports)* Hartz Mountain Inc. manufactures small industrial tools and has an annual sales volume of approximately $3.5 million. Sales growth has been steady during the year and there is no evidence of cyclical demand. The company's market has expanded only in response to product innovation; therefore, R&D is very important to the company.

Janice Bennett, controller, has designed and implemented a new budget system. An annual budget has been prepared and divided into 12 equal segments to use for monthly performance evaluations. The vice president of operations was upset upon receiving the following responsibility report for the Machining Department for October 2000:

MACHINING DEPARTMENT—RESPONSIBILITY REPORT
FOR THE MONTH ENDED OCTOBER 31, 2000

	Budget	Actual	Variance
Volume in units	3,000	3,185	185F
Variable manufacturing costs:			
Direct material	$24,000	$ 24,843	$ 843U
Direct labor	27,750	29,302	1,552U
Variable factory overhead	33,300	35,035	1,735U
Total	$85,050	$ 89,180	$4,130U
Fixed manufacturing costs:			
Indirect labor	$ 3,300	$ 3,334	$ 34U
Depreciation	1,500	1,500	0
Tax	300	300	0
Insurance	240	240	0
Other	930	1,027	97U
Total	$ 6,270	$ 6,401	$ 131U
Corporate costs:			
Research and development	$ 2,400	$ 3,728	$1,328U
Selling and administration	3,600	4,075	475U
Total	$ 6,000	$ 7,803	$1,803U
Total costs	$97,320	$103,384	$6,064U

a. Identify the weaknesses in the responsibility report for the Machining Department.

b. Prepare a revised responsibility report for the Machining Department that reduces or eliminates the weaknesses indicated in part (a).

c. Deviations in excess of 5 percent of budget are considered material and worthy of investigation. Should any of the variances of the Machining Department be investigated? Regardless of materiality, is there any area that the vice president of operations might wish to discuss with the manager of the Machining Department? *(CMA adapted)*

55. *(Revenue center performance)* Juan Louis manages the sales department at the Boulder Lighting Company. Juan is evaluated based on his ability to meet budgeted revenues. For June 2001, Juan's revenue budget was as follows:

	Price per Unit	Unit Sales
Floor lamps	$120	1,600
Hanging lamps	65	2,150
Ceiling fixtures	80	4,200

The actual sales generated by Mr. Louis's sales department in June were as follows:

	Price per Unit	Total Sales in Dollars
Floor lamps	$115	$195,500
Hanging lamps	70	141,400
Ceiling fixtures	75	311,250

a. Compute the revenue price variance.
b. Compute the revenue mix variance.
c. Compute the revenue volume variance.
d. Based on your answers to parts (a) through (c), evaluate the performance of Mr. Louis.
e. If Mr. Louis is to be held accountable for meeting the revenue budget, why might it be advisable to also give him the authority to set the salesperson salary and commission structure?

56. *(Direct method)* The management of Santa Fe Community Hospital (SFCH) has decided to allocate the budgeted costs of its three service departments (Administration, Public Relations, and Maintenance) to its three revenue-producing programs (Surgery, In-Patient Care, and Out-Patient Services). Budgeted information for 2000 follows:

Budgeted costs:	
Administration	$2,000,000
Public Relations	700,000
Maintenance	500,000
Allocation bases:	
Administration	Dollars of assets employed
Public Relations	Number of employees
Maintenance	Hours of equipment operation

	EXPECTED UTILIZATIONS		
	Dollars of Assets Employed	Number of Employees	Hours of Equipment Operation
Administration	$ 740,090	4	1,020
Public Relations	450,100	7	470
Maintenance	825,680	5	1,530
Surgery	1,974,250	10	12,425
In-Patient Care	1,229,250	18	8,875
Out-Patient Services	521,500	22	14,200

Using the direct method, allocate the expected service department costs to the revenue-producing areas.

57. *(Step method)* McDougle Real Estate classifies its operations into three departments: Commercial Sales, Residential Sales, and Property Management. The owner, William McDougle, wants to know the full cost of operating each department. Direct costs of each department, along with several allocation bases associated with each, are as follows:

	AVAILABLE ALLOCATION BASES			
	Direct Costs	Number Employees/ Salespersons	Dollars of Assets Employed	Dollars of Revenue
Administration	$ 750,000	10	$1,240,000	n/a
Accounting	495,000	5	682,000	n/a
Promotion	360,000	6	360,000	n/a
Commercial Sales	5,245,000	21	500,000	$4,500,000
Residential Sales	4,589,510	101	725,000	9,500,000
Property Management	199,200	13	175,000	500,000

The service departments are shown in a benefits-provided ranking. McDougle has also selected the following allocation bases: number of employees/salespersons for Administration; dollars of assets employed for Accounting; and dollars of revenue for Promotion.

a. Using the step method, allocate the service department costs to the revenue-generating departments.

b. Which department is apparently the most profitable?

58. *(Transfer prices)* In each of the following cases, the Speaker Division can sell all of its production of audio speakers to outside customers or it can sell some of it to the Sound System Division and the remainder to outside customers. Speaker Division's speaker production capacity is 200,000 units annually. The data related to each independent case are as follows:

	SPEAKER DIVISION	
	Case 1	Case 2
Production costs per unit:		
Direct material	$30	$20
Direct labor	10	8
Variable overhead	3	2
Fixed overhead (based on capacity)	1	1
Other variable selling and delivery costs per unit*	6	4
Selling price to outside customers	75	60

*In either case, $1 of the selling expenses will not be incurred on intracompany transfers.

	SOUND SYSTEM DIVISION	
Number of speakers needed annually	40,000	40,000
Current unit price being paid to outside supplier	$65	$52

a. For each case, determine the upper and lower limits for a transfer price for speakers.

b. For each case, determine a transfer price for the Speaker Division that will provide a $10 contribution margin per unit.

c. Using the information developed for part (b), determine a dual transfer price for Case 1 assuming that Sound System will be able to acquire the speakers from the Speaker Division at $10 below Sound System's purchase price from outside suppliers.

59. *(Transfer price)* Two of the divisions of Construction Equipment Company are the Engine Division and the Mobile Systems Division. The Engine Division produces engines used by both the Mobile Systems Division and a variety of external industrial customers.

For external sales, sales orders are generally produced in 50-unit lots. Using this typical lot size, the cost per engine is as follows:

Variable production cost	$1,050
Fixed manufacturing overhead	450
Variable selling expense	150
Fixed selling expense	210
Fixed administrative expense	320
Total unit cost	$2,180

The Engine Division normally earns a profit margin of 20 percent by setting the external selling price at $2,616. Because a significant number of sales are being made internally, Engine Division managers have decided that $2,616 is the appropriate price to use for all transfers to the Mobile Systems Division.

When the managers in the Mobile Systems Division heard of this change in the transfer price, they became very upset because the change would have a major negative impact on Mobile Systems' net income figures. Because of competition, Mobile Systems has asked the Engine Division to lower its transfer price; by reducing the transfer price, Engine's profit margin will be 15 percent. Mobile Systems' managers have asked Construction Equipment top management whether the Division can buy engines externally. Bud Dawkins, Construction Equipment's president, has gathered the following price information to help the two divisional managers negotiate an equitable transfer price:

Current external sales price	$2,616
Total variable production cost plus a 20% profit margin ($1,050 × 1.2)	1,260
Total production cost plus a 20% profit margin ($1,500 × 1.2)	1,800
Bid price from external supplier (if motors are purchased in 50-unit lots)	2,320

a. Discuss advantages and disadvantages of each of the above transfer prices to both the selling and buying divisions and to Construction Equipment.
b. If the Engine Division could sell all of its production externally at $2,616, what is the appropriate transfer price and why?

60. *(Journal entries)* Athlete's Companion Division makes top-of-the-line sports travel bags that are sold to external buyers and are also being used by the Travel America Division. During the month just ended, Travel America acquired 2,000 bags from Athlete's Companion Division. Athlete's Companion's standard unit costs are

Direct material	$10
Direct labor	3
Variable factory overhead	4
Fixed factory overhead	6
Variable selling expense	2
Fixed selling and administrative expense	3

Travel America can acquire comparable bags externally for $40 each. Give the entries for each division for the past month if the transfer is to be recorded
a. at Travel America's external purchase price.
b. at a negotiated price of variable cost plus 15 percent of production cost.
c. by Athlete's Companion at Travel America's external price and by Travel America at Athlete's Companion's variable production cost.
d. at Athlete's Companion's absorption cost.

61. *(Internal versus external sale)* Providence Products Inc. consists of three decentralized divisions: Park Division, Quayside Division, and Ridgetop Division. The president of Providence Products has given the managers of the three divisions the authority to decide whether to sell internally at a transfer price determined by the division managers, or externally. Market conditions are such that sales made internally or externally will not affect market or transfer prices. Intermediate markets will always be available for Park, Quayside, and Ridgetop to purchase their manufacturing needs or sell their product. Division managers attempt to maximize their contribution margin at the current level of operating assets for the division.

The Quayside Division manager is considering the following two alternative orders.

The Ridgetop Division needs 3,000 units of a motor that can be supplied by the Quayside Division. To manufacture these motors, Quayside would purchase components from the Park Division at a transfer price of $600 per unit; Park's variable cost for these components is $300 per unit. Quayside Division would further process these components at a variable cost of $500 per unit.

If the Ridgetop Division cannot obtain the motors from the Quayside Division, the motors will be purchased from Essex Company for $1,500 per unit. Essex Company would also purchase 3,000 components from Park at a price of $400 for each of these motors; Park's variable cost for these components is $200 per unit.

The Saxon Company wants to buy 3,500 similar motors from the Quayside Division for $1,250 per unit. Quayside would again purchase components from the Park Division at a transfer price of $500 per unit; Park's variable cost for these components is $250 per unit. Quayside Division would further process these components at a variable cost of $400 per unit.

The Quayside Division's plant capacity is limited and, as such, the company can accept either the Saxon contract or the Ridgetop order, but not both. The president of Providence Products and the manager of Quayside Division agree that it would not be beneficial in the short or long run to increase capacity.

a. If the Quayside Division manager wants to maximize short-run contribution margin, determine whether the Quayside Division should (1) sell motors to the Ridgetop Division at the prevailing market price or (2) accept the Saxon Company contract. Support your answer with appropriate calculations.

b. Without prejudice to your answer to part (a), assume that the Quayside Division decides to accept the Saxon Company contract. Determine whether this decision is in the best interest of Providence Products Inc. Support your answer with appropriate calculations. *(CMA adapted)*

62. *(Transfer prices)* Robert Brown, CPA, has three revenue departments: Auditing and Accounting (A&A), Tax (T), and Consulting (C). In addition, the company has two support departments: Administration and EDP. Administration costs are allocated to the three revenue departments on the basis of number of employees. The EDP Department's fixed costs are allocated to revenue departments on the basis of peak hours of monthly service expected to be used by each revenue department. EDP's variable costs are assigned to the revenue departments at a transfer price of $40 per hour of actual service. Following are the direct costs and the allocation bases associated with each of the departments:

			ALLOCATION BASES	
	Direct Costs (Before Transfer Costs)	Number of Employees	Peak Hours	EDP Hours Used
Administration	$450,000	4	30	290
EDP—Fixed	300,000	2	n/a	n/a
EDP—Variable	90,000	2	n/a	n/a
A&A	200,000	10	80	1,220
T	255,000	5	240	650
C	340,000	3	25	190

a. Was the variable EDP transfer price of $40 adequate? Explain.
b. Allocate the other service department costs to A&A, T, and C using the direct method.
c. What are the total costs of the revenue-producing departments after the allocation in part (b)?

CASES

63. *(Interdivisional transfers; deciding on alternatives)* Carolyn Williams, a management accountant, has recently been employed as controller in the Fashions Division of Deluxe Products, Inc. The company is organized on a divisional basis with considerable vertical integration.

Fashions Division makes several luggage products, including a slim leather portfolio. Sales of the portfolio have been steady, and the marketing department expects continued strong demand. Carolyn is looking for ways the Fashions Division can contain its costs and thus boost its earnings from future sales. She discovered that the Fashions Division has always purchased its supply of high-quality tanned leather from another division of Deluxe Products, the LeatherWorks Division. LeatherWorks Division has been providing the three square feet of tanned leather needed for each portfolio for $9 per square foot.

Carolyn wondered whether it might be possible to purchase Fashions' leather needs from a supplier other than LeatherWorks at a lower price for comparable quality. Top management at Deluxe Products reluctantly agreed to allow the Fashions Division to consider purchasing outside the company.

The Fashions Division will need leather for 100,000 portfolios during the coming year. Fashions management has requested bids from several leather suppliers. The two best bids are $8 and $7 per square foot from Koenig and Thompson, respectively. Carolyn has been informed that another subsidiary of Deluxe Products, Ridley Chemical, supplies Thompson with chemicals that have been an essential ingredient of the tanning process for Thompson. Ridley Chemical charges Thompson $2 for enough chemicals to prepare three square feet of leather. Ridley's profit margin is 30 percent.

The LeatherWorks Division wants to continue supplying Fashions' leather needs at the same price per square foot as in the past. Tom Reed, LeatherWorks' controller, has made it clear that he believes Fashions should continue to purchase all its needs from LeatherWorks to preserve LeatherWorks' healthy profit margin of 40 percent of sales.

You, as Deluxe Products' vice president of finance, have called a meeting of the controllers of Fashions and LeatherWorks. Carolyn is eager to accept Thompson's bid of $7. She points out that Fashions' earnings will show a significant increase if the division can buy from Thompson.

Tom Reed, however, wants Deluxe Products to keep the business within the company and suggests that you require Fashions to purchase its needs from LeatherWorks. He emphasizes that LeatherWorks' profit margin should not be lost to the company.

From whom should the Fashions Division buy the leather? Consider both Fashions' desire to minimize its costs and Deluxe Products' corporate goal of maximizing profit on a companywide basis. *(IMA adapted)*

64. *(Transfer prices; discussion)* Southeast Products Inc. is a decentralized company. Each division has its own sales force and production facilities and is operated as an investment center. Top management uses return on investment

(ROI) for performance evaluation. The Hazlett Division has just been awarded a contract for a product that uses a component manufactured by the Andalusia Division as well as by outside suppliers. Hazlett used a cost figure of $3.80 for the component when the bid was prepared for the new product. Andalusia supplied this cost figure in response to Hazlett's request for the average variable cost of the component.

Andalusia has an active sales force that is continually soliciting new customers. Andalusia's regular selling price for the component Hazlett needs for the new product is $6.50. Sales of the component are expected to increase. Andalusia management has the following costs associated with the component:

Standard variable manufacturing cost	$3.20
Standard variable selling and distribution cost	0.60
Standard fixed manufacturing cost	1.20
Total	$5.00

The two divisions have been unable to agree on a transfer price for the component. Corporate management has never established a transfer price because interdivisional transactions have never occurred. The following suggestions have been made for the transfer price:

- regular selling price,
- regular selling price less variable selling and distribution expenses,
- standard manufacturing cost plus 15 percent, or
- standard variable manufacturing cost plus 20 percent.

a. Compute each of the suggested transfer prices.
b. Discuss the effect each of the transfer prices might have on the Andalusia Division management's attitude toward intracompany business.
c. Is the negotiation of a price between the Hazlett and Andalusia Divisions a satisfactory method to solve the transfer price problem? Explain your answer.
d. Should the corporate management of Southeast Products Inc. become involved in this transfer controversy? Explain your answer.

(CMA adapted)

65. *(Effect of service department allocations on reporting and evaluation)* Shiell Corporation is a diversified manufacturing company with corporate headquarters in Tampa, Florida. The three operating divisions are the Kennedy Division, the Plastic Products Division, and the Outerspace Products Division. Much of the manufacturing activity of the Kennedy Division is related to work performed for the government space program under negotiated contracts.

Shiell Corporation headquarters provides general administrative support and computer services to each of the three operating divisions. The computer services are provided through a computer time-sharing arrangement. The central processing unit (CPU) is located in Tampa, and the divisions have remote terminals that are connected to the CPU by telephone lines. One standard from the Cost Accounting Standards Board provides that the cost of general administration may be allocated to negotiated defense contracts. Further, the standards provide that, in situations in which computer services are provided by corporate headquarters, the actual costs (fixed and variable) of operating the computer department may be allocated to the defense division based on a reasonable measure of computer usage.

The general managers of the three divisions are evaluated based on the before-tax performance of each division. The November 2000 performance evaluation reports (in millions of dollars) for each division are presented below:

	Kennedy Division	Plastics Products Division	Outerspace Products Division
Sales	$23	$15	$55
Cost of goods sold	(13)	(7)	(38)
Gross profit	$10	$ 8	$17
Selling and administrative:			
Division selling and administration costs	$ 5	$ 5	$ 8
Corporate general administration costs	1	—	—
Corporate computing	1	—	—
Total	$ 7	$ 5	$ 8
Profit before taxes	$ 3	$ 3	$ 9

Without a charge for computing services, the operating divisions may not make the most cost-effective use of the Computer Systems Department's resources. Outline and discuss a method for charging the operating divisions for use of computer services that would promote cost consciousness by the operating divisions and operating efficiency by the Computer Systems Department.

(CMA adapted)

REALITY CHECK

66. *(Selection of type of transfer pricing)* A multiple-division company is considering the effectiveness of its transfer pricing policies. One of the items under consideration is whether the transfer price should be based on variable production cost, absorption production cost, or external market price. Describe the circumstances in which each of these transfer prices would be most appropriate.

67. *(Transfer pricing and performance measurement)* Appleby Industries consists of eight divisions that are evaluated as profit centers. All transfers between divisions are made at market price. Precision Regulator is a division of Appleby that sells approximately 20 percent of its output externally. The remaining 80 percent of the output from Precision Regulator is transferred to other divisions within Appleby. No other division of Appleby Industries transfers internally more than 10 percent of its output.

Based on any profit-based measure of performance, Precision Regulator is the leading division within Appleby Industries. Other divisional managers within Appleby always find that their performance is compared to that of Precision Regulator. These managers argue that the transfer pricing situation gives Precision Regulator a competitive advantage.

a. What factors may contribute to any advantage that the Precision Regulator Division might have over the other divisions?

b. What alternative transfer price or performance measure might be more appropriate in this situation?

68. *(Multinational company transfers)* The Arizona Instruments Company (AIC) is considering establishing a division in Ireland to manufacture integrated circuits. Some of the circuits will be shipped to the United States and incorporated into the firm's line of computers. The remaining output from the Ireland division will be sold in the European Union. AIC plans to operate the Ireland division as a profit center. Compose a report describing some of the problems related to transfer pricing that AIC must consider in establishing the Ireland division.

69. A large American corporation participates in a highly competitive industry. To meet the competition and achieve profit goals, the company has chosen the decentralized form of organization. Each manager of a decentralized center is measured on the basis of profit contribution, market penetration, and return on investment. Failure to meet the objectives established by corporate management for these measures is not accepted and usually results in demotion or dismissal of a center manager.

An anonymous survey of managers in the company revealed that the managers felt pressure to compromise their personal ethical standards to achieve the corporate objectives. For example, certain plant locations felt pressure to reduce quality control to a level that could not ensure that all unsafe products would be rejected. Also, sales personnel were encouraged to use questionable sales tactics to obtain orders, including offering gifts and other incentives to purchasing agents.

The chief executive officer is disturbed by the survey findings. In her opinion, the company cannot condone such behavior. She concludes that the company should do something about this problem.

a. Discuss what might be the causes for the ethical problems described.

b. Outline a program that could be instituted by the company to help reduce the pressures on managers to compromise personal ethical standards in their work. *(CMA adapted)*

70. Search the Internet to identify three decentralized companies. Based on the information you find on each, either determine directly or infer from the information given the types of responsibility centers used by these companies. Further, determine or speculate about whether the companies use transfer prices or allocation of costs for intracompany transfers of services. Prepare a report on your findings and inferences. In cases for which you had to infer, explain what information or reasoning led you to that inference.

PART 5

Evaluating Performance

CHAPTER

19

Measuring Short-Run Organizational Performance

LEARNING OBJECTIVES

After completing this chapter, you should be able to answer the following questions:

1
How are performance measures tied to organizational missions and strategies?

2
What roles do performance measurement serve in organizations?

3
What guidelines or criteria apply to the design of performance measures?

4
What are traditional short-term financial performance measures of profit and investment centers?

5
How might the Statement of Cash Flows be useful for performance measurement?

6
How are return on investment and residual income similar? How do they differ?

7
How is economic value added used to measure performance?

8
Why might the use of ROI create suboptimization in investment decisions?

INTRODUCING Wachovia

http://www.wachovia.com

The environment in which banks will compete in the next decade may force them to perform much more like retailers than like the financial institutions our parents knew. This means that whether bank managers and employees are in the service or sales arena, operations, product management, or channel management, they will need the skills and behavior of the "best in class" retailers. Banks must harness the power of information to create a banking experience that is customized to their target customers. Successful banking in this new millennium will require focusing on the customer.

Wachovia is a $68.8-billion-asset bank that believes it has found the formula for success in the new banking environment. At Wachovia, information drives the development and retention of profitable relationships. With dual headquarters in Winston-Salem and Atlanta, the bank serves customers in five states: Florida, Georgia, North Carolina, South Carolina, and Virginia. Overall, the bank operates 700 "stores" that are complemented by a robust ATM network.

Wachovia has developed a process called continuous relationship management (CRM) as a crucial tool in differentiating its services from those of competitors. CRM is built around the idea that the bank must maintain the very best intelligence information about its customers. By wielding this information effectively, Wachovia's managers believe they can deliver superior service to their customers and generate higher profits than their competitors.

The ability to attract the right new customer is the next horizon in revenue and earnings growth for banks. Wachovia has recognized that the key to achieving high profits is serving the right mix of products to the right customers. Accordingly, the company has also developed sophisticated information systems to evaluate customer profitability, which, in turn, have led to the development of systems to profile and target new customers.

Raw information provides no advantage. The way financial service companies distinguish themselves is to competently process, distribute, and use information to serve customers. At Wachovia, the goal of employees is to know and understand customers and their cares and concerns better than any other financial institution.

SOURCES: Wachovia 1998 Annual Report; Beverly B. Wells, "At Wachovia, Customer Focus Means Information-Driven Continuous Relationship Management," *Journal of Retail Banking Services* (Summer 1999), pp. 33–36.

The information systems of Wachovia demonstrate the latest generation of tools for managing information and feedback. The two characteristics that differentiate this generation from preceding generations of systems are the focus on the customer rather than the bottom line, and the integration of information feeder systems.

The switch in focus from profitability to the customer is somewhat illusory. Managers of today are no less concerned with profits than managers of other eras; however, to achieve profitability in the face of global competition, managers recognize that the single most important variable is to attract and satisfy customers. Hence, there is high correlation between achieving profitability and effectively serving the marketplace.

Exhibit 19–1 provides the links between customer types and profitability effects. Common reasons why some customers are unprofitable are given and the exhibit demonstrates why customer targeting and screening are so essential to profitably operating businesses.

The ability to integrate information from a set of information systems allows managers to gain new insights about the value chains in which they are participants. Like Wachovia, firms are striving to integrate all available information to identify innovative ways of serving existing customers and attracting new customers. The overriding goal is to find ways to serve customers that generate acceptable profits for the investors.

EXHIBIT 19-1

Common Causes of Unprofitable Customers

Common Cause	Examples
1. Large customers demanding low prices and high levels of service	Customer negotiates low price, purchases lower margin goods and causes high selling, administration, and delivery costs.
2. Undifferentiated service with low-sales-value customers receiving the same high-cost service as large, high-volume customers	Customer is serviced through costly weekly sales visits and deliveries. Such customers will never generate sufficient net margins to cover these costs.
3. Providing high service levels as a competitive advantage	Management considers its ability to deliver goods overnight to be a competitive advantage. Unfortunately the high cost of delivery makes every order unprofitable.
4. Overall high-cost sales, administration, and delivery processes	A company's sales process is relying on costly sales visits for all transactions and customers. There is no use of lower cost channels, such as call centers or EDI.
5. Providing highly customized products/services	Highly customized products are produced for a small number of small customers.
6. High customer turnover	The cost of obtaining and setting up customers is high and/or customers profitability increases over time, e.g., insurance and telecommunications.

SOURCE: Mark Pickering, "Using Customer Profitability Information to Drive the Bottom Line," *Charter* (March 1999), pp. 32–34.

One type of information system that is crucial to effectively compete today is the performance measurement system. This chapter and the next two cover general concepts of performance measurement. The focus of this chapter is traditional, shorter term performance measures; Chapter 20 covers performance measurement over the longer term and nonfinancial performance measures. Chapter 21 discusses how and why managerial rewards are linked to organizational performance measures. The discussion in the following section explains how performance measures are used in organizations.

ORGANIZATIONAL ROLES OF PERFORMANCE MEASURES

1

How are performance measures tied to organizational missions and strategies?

Organizations have reasons or missions for which they exist. In fulfilling organizational missions, managers design and implement strategies that apply organizational resources to activities. The activities are intended to execute management's strategies. Management talent and time are dedicated to planning, decision making, controlling, and evaluating performance with respect to these activities. The intent in these managerial processes is for management to take actions that maximize the efficiency and effectiveness of resources used. For an organization to be successful in its missions, managers must devise appropriate information systems to track resource applications.

Gauging effective and efficient management of resources is possible only if (1) the terms *effective* and *efficient* can be defined, and (2) measures that are consistent with the definitions can be formulated. Definitions of *effective* and *efficient* could be relative to historical performance, competitors, or expectations. Once defined, effectiveness and efficiency of performance can be assessed by comparing measures of actual performance with defined performance goals.

Ultimately, performance is assessed to be effective and efficient if shareholders receive an adequate return on their investment. This places pressure on top management to achieve returns that are attractive to shareholders. Failing to satisfy shareholders has severe consequences financially and for the reputations of management teams[1]:

> *Those companies that are not taking good care of the precious capital they manage are finding themselves coming under tremendous pressure from powerful institutional investors. If they don't find a way to generate appropriate returns for investors, they are often forced to sell out to someone that may do a better job. . . . As we all know investors will cease to provide capital to management teams that destroy value.*

Thus, the need for managers to generate a satisfactory return to shareholders is the key driver of performance measurement[2]:

> *Nobody ever said it was easy to track down shareholder value. . . . [but] shareholder return [is] the single most important measure. . . . the measure most relevant to the shareholders and most relevant to managers trying to manage for shareholder value.*

2

What roles do performance measurement serve in organizations?

Performance measurement provides a foundation for[3]

- judging organizational performance,
- relating organizational missions and goals to managerial performance,
- fostering the growth of subordinate managers,
- stimulating managerial motivation,
- enhancing organizational communication,
- making judgments about promotion, and
- implementing organizational control.

By linking performance measures to managerial rewards, managers are given incentives to concentrate on improving specific performance areas. As the measured dimensions of performance are improved, managerial rewards are increased. The linking of management rewards to organizational performance measures creates the incentive that drives managers to take desired actions.

Performance measures should be devised for all critical resources consumed by operations. Additionally, the performance measurements should lead to insights about how to improve resource use and how to achieve organizational changes that allow firms to remain competitive. The following subsections provide details of performance measurement information in areas that are critical to survival in the global market.

Information for Evaluating Capital Market Performance

A traditional area of performance measurement relates to the effective and efficient use of capital resources. This area is the domain of financial accounting. Generally accepted accounting principles (GAAP) are formulated for providing information that is comparable across firms to capital markets and other external users. This comparability facilitates investor/creditor judgments about which firms are worthy of capital investments. On the other side of the capital equation, to obtain needed capital at competitive rates, managers must demonstrate to investors that the managers' firms offer excellent returns relative to the risks assumed. Absent an ability to acquire capital at reasonable rates, a firm will stagnate for want of funds to capitalize on growth opportunities.

[1] Vincent J. Calabrese, "Economic Value Added: Finance 101 on Steroids," *The Journal of Bank Cost & Management Accounting* (1999), pp. 3–34.
[2] C. Frederic Wiegold, "Quest for Shareholder Value, Ranking America's Best & Worst Companies," *The Wall Street Journal* (February 26, 1998), p. R1.
[3] Adapted from Harry Levinson, "Management by Whose Objectives?" *Harvard Business Review* (July–August 1970), pp. 125–134.

Another consideration that makes managers focus on capital management is stockholder influence. Stockholders, acting through their boards of directors, have the right to determine who will manage their businesses. Naturally, stockholders are interested in hiring a management team that will maximize the return on the stockholders' investment in the firm. Managers are in constant competition to obtain and maintain their positions. Only if managers satisfy the demands of shareholders will these managers be allowed to maintain their positions, be promoted, and enhance their personal human capital.

Stockholders achieve returns on their investments through dividends and appreciation in stock prices. Both types of returns depend on the ability of the firm to generate future earnings. Accordingly, stockholders and other capital providers are most intensely interested in measures of performance that indicate the ability of the firm to generate profits[4]:

> *Part of the battle is fought by trying to prove whose metric best correlates with changes in stock prices. . . . What matters most is that companies are focusing on creating shareholder value by rationalizing their businesses, setting financial hurdles that have to be met before investing in new ventures and attempting to drive the incentives deep into their organizations.*

Information for Evaluating Organizational Learning and Change

The emerging global market has created a pronounced trend in designing performance measures. The quality and quantity of firms competing in markets have placed the consumer at the center of attention, and success in a market depends on the ability of a firm to satisfy some segment of the market better than can any rival firm. In recent years, managers, like those at Wachovia, have focused more attention on assessment of their firms' performance in serving customers.

Exhibit 19–2 provides an outline of Wachovia's profitable relationship optimization system. This is one of the key systems used to exploit customer data in targeting and delivering services to customers. Steps five and six measure the results of sales efforts and provide feedback to the participants in the process.

Although the level of profit achieved may be the arbiter's ultimate measure of success in serving customers, profit is a very aggregated measure. Other measures can be developed that give indications of relative success in specific areas of market performance.

For example, under the forces of global competition, markets are always evolving as firms constantly search for ways to be innovative in providing customers with more value at less cost. To compete in this environment, a firm must develop an organizational culture that fosters learning and innovation. Measures can be used to track a firm's performance against customer expectations. Other measures can be designed to identify waste and assess relative efficiency in resource consumption.

With appropriate measures in place, the focus of managers and workers is on the success of the firm in serving its customers. As the organization strives to improve its performance, a climate embracing change and organizational evolution is created. Such a culture is necessary for a firm to be opportunistic and aggressive as it confronts world-class competition. The measures may also provide the incentive that is necessary to foster cooperation across functional specialties in an organization. The accompanying News Note describes how Sears has developed performance measures that managers use to control the company.

http://www.sears.com

Managers develop products and organizational structures to support strategies that have been devised to serve a firm's customers. Once these strategies are deployed, measures must be developed to assess the performance of the products and organizational structure.

[4] Vincent J. Calabrese, "Economic Value Added: Finance 101 on Steroids," *The Journal of Bank Cost & Management Accounting* (1999), pp. 3–34.

EXHIBIT 19–2

Wachovia's Profitable Relationship Optimization (PRO) System

1. PRO begins with Robust Customer Information.

2. Customer information is analyzed.

3. Targeted customer leads distributed and customers contacted for relationship-based dialogue.

4. Human, network and brand resources aligned for relationship-based selling.

5. Results of customer contacts and market impacts analyzed.

6. Feedback loop enriches customer file; facilitates learning.

SOURCE: Beverly B. Wells, "At Wachovia, Customer Focus Means Information-Driven Continuous Relationship Management," *Journal of Retail Banking Services* (Summer 1999), pp. 33–36.

GENERAL BUSINESS **NEWS NOTE**

The Bottom Side of Sears

In many businesses, it is difficult to measure even relatively hard behaviors like customer retention, and the inevitable result is that many companies are unwilling to expend the time, energy, and resources to do it effectively. Not surprisingly, many companies do not have a realistic grasp of what their customers and employees actually think and do.

Sears does. By means of an ongoing process of data collection, analysis, modeling, and experimentation, we have developed and continue to refine what we call our Total Performance Indicators, or TPI—a set of measures that shows us how well we are doing with customers, employees, and investors. We understand the several layers of factors that drive employee attitudes, and we know how employee attitudes affect employee retention, how employee retention affects the drivers of customer satisfaction, how customer satisfaction affects financials, and a great deal more. We have also calculated the lag time between a change in any of those metrics and a corresponding change in financial performance, so that when we see a shift in, say, employee attitudes, we know not only how but also when it will affect results. Our TPI makes the employee–customer–profit chain operational because we manage the company on the basis of these indicators, with remarkably positive results.

SOURCE: Anthony J. Rucci, Steven P. Kirn, and Richard T. Quinn, "The Employee–Customer–Profit Chain at Sears," *Harvard Business Review* (January–February 1998), p. 84.

Information for Evaluating Product/Subunit Performance

A company may place its products in a market to compete on the dimensions of price, quality, and/or functionality (or product features).[5] Superior performance in any of these three areas can provide the competitive advantage needed for a firm to be successful. By developing specific performance measures for each competitive dimension, alternative ways can be identified to leverage the firm's competencies.

The organizational structure reflects the manner in which a firm assigns and coordinates its people in deploying strategies. By subdividing the overall firm, subunits can be created and charged with making specific contributions to the business. Managers of each subunit can then concentrate on developing the skills and competencies necessary to satisfy their organizational roles. The extent to which each subunit succeeds in its mission can be assessed using carefully designed performance measures. Such measures must be tailored to capture the important performance dimensions of each subunit.

DESIGNING A SYSTEM OF PERFORMANCE MEASUREMENT

3

What guidelines or criteria apply to the design of performance measures?

Through the linking of performance measures to a reward structure, managers are given an incentive to improve their segment's performance. Once this incentive is created, it will work to advance the organization toward its established missions, or it will cause managers to act in manners contrary to the missions. The outcome depends largely on how well performance measures have been designed to capture the performance dimensions that are critical to accomplishing the organization's missions. Exhibit 19–3 identifies warning signs of performance measures that are flawed.

Each manager in a firm is expected to make a particular contribution to the organization. This concept was introduced in Chapter 18 in discussions of responsibility centers and responsibility accounting. The performance measurements selected must be appropriate for the type of responsibility assigned and the type of behavior desired. The point that performance measures are created to cause managers to act cannot be overemphasized. The critical question to address in evaluating a performance evaluation measure is: What managerial actions will this performance measure encourage? This section discusses important issues to be considered in designing a system of performance measurement.

Selecting Performance Measures

To evaluate performance benchmarks must be established against which accomplishments can be measured. A benchmark can be a monetary one (such as a standard cost or a budget appropriation) or a nonmonetary one (such as zero defects

EXHIBIT 19–3

Seven Warning Signs of Problems with Performance Measures

- Performance is acceptable in all dimensions except profit.
- Customers don't buy even when prices are competitive.
- No one notices when performance measurement reports aren't produced.
- Managers spend significant time debating the meaning of the measures.
- Share price is lethargic despite solid financial performance.
- You haven't changed your measures in a long time.
- You've recently changed your corporate strategy.

SOURCE: Michael R. Vitale and Sarah C. Mavrinac, "How Effective Is Your Performance Measurement System?" *Management Accounting* (August 1995), pp. 43–47. Reprinted from *Management Accounting*. Copyright by Institute of Management Accountants, Montvale, N.J.

[5] For more details, see Robin Cooper, *When Lean Enterprises Collide* (Boston: Harvard Business School Press, 1995).

or the market share of another organization). Regardless of the specific measures used (whether monetary or nonmonetary), four general criteria should be considered in designing a performance measurement system:

1. The measures should be established to assess progress toward organizational goals and objectives.
2. The persons being evaluated should be aware of the measurements to be used and have had some input in developing them.
3. The persons being evaluated should have the appropriate skills, equipment, information, and authority to be successful under the measurement system.
4. Feedback of accomplishment should be provided in a timely and useful manner.

One key to designing an effective system of performance measurement is to recognize that no single performance measure is capable of capturing all of the important dimensions of performance.

Multiple Performance Measures

The first criterion establishes the reason for using multiple performance measures rather than a single measure or measures of only a single type. Organizations have a variety of operational objectives. A primary objective is to be financially viable. If the organization is a profit-oriented one, this objective is satisfied by generating a net income considered by the owners to be satisfactory relative to the assets invested. That level of "satisfactory" earnings may change over time or differ based on the type of business or subunit mission. Therefore, financial performance measures must be relevant for the type of company or organizational subunit being evaluated. Also, any financial measures chosen must reflect an understanding of accounting information and its potential for manipulation.

In addition to financial success, many companies are now establishing operational targets of total customer satisfaction, zero defects, minimal lead time to market, and social responsibility for the environment. These goals cannot be defined directly using traditional, financial terms. Even though poor or excellent performance in these areas will eventually be reflected in financial measures, alternative short-term performance measures are needed to capture the nonfinancial dimensions of performance. Nonfinancial performance measures can be developed that indicate progress—or lack thereof—toward the achievement of these important critical success factors of a world-class company.

balanced scorecard

The current trend is to apply the concept of the balanced scorecard to performance measurement.[6] A **balanced scorecard** is an approach to performance measurement that weighs performance measures from four perspectives. The first is the traditional perspective: financial performance. The other three include an internal business perspective, a customer perspective, and innovation and learning. Managers choosing to apply the balanced scorecard are demonstrating a belief that traditional financial performance measures alone are insufficient to assess how the firm is doing and what specific actions must be taken to improve performance. A balanced scorecard is illustrated in Exhibit 19–4 for a company in the semiconductor business.

http://www.att.com

As discussed in the News Note on page 865, the keys to successfully implementing a balanced scorecard in a technology company are to know what to measure and to not measure everything.

Awareness of and Participation in Performance Measures

Regardless of the number or types of measures chosen, top management must set high performance standards and communicate them to lower-level managers and

[6] The balanced scorecard was created by Robert Kaplan, Harvard University, and David Norton, Renaissance Strategy Group.

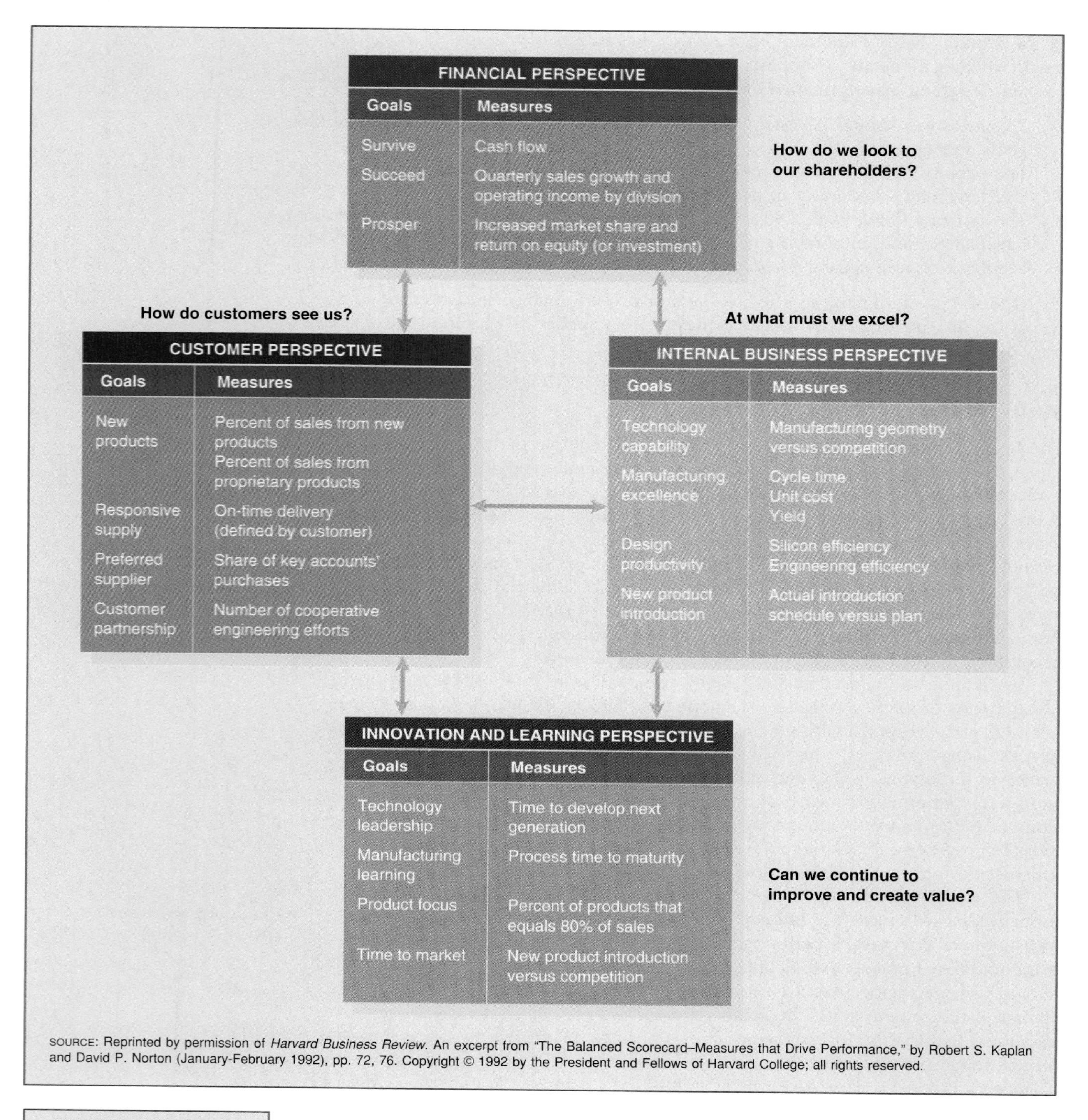

SOURCE: Reprinted by permission of *Harvard Business Review*. An excerpt from "The Balanced Scorecard–Measures that Drive Performance," by Robert S. Kaplan and David P. Norton (January-February 1992), pp. 72, 76. Copyright © 1992 by the President and Fellows of Harvard College; all rights reserved.

EXHIBIT 19-4

The Balanced Scorecard for a Semiconductor Firm

employees. Additionally, the measures should promote harmonious operations among organizational units. This factor is important to minimize the effects of suboptimization (as discussed in Chapter 18) that might occur in a decentralized company.

People will normally act specifically in accordance with how they are to be measured. Thus, the individuals must know of and understand the performance measures used, so that managers can make decisions in light of the effects of alternative decisions on the performance measures. Withholding information about

GENERAL BUSINESS **NEWS NOTE**

Putting Balance into the Scorecard

The balanced scorecard divides business strategy into four perspectives: Financial, Customer, Internal and Learning. Each perspective breaks down into tactics and measures, although you must take care to link tactics and measure across all four perspectives. The result is a simple set of metrics describing how well information technology (IT) accomplishments are supporting the business strategy.

Clearly, some effort is necessary to create, fine-tune and execute a balanced scorecard. It is especially important to avoid the impulse to measure everything. Only a small number of metrics is necessary. Informing your business managers isn't the only benefit of using a balanced scorecard. For example, according to John Hendrick, industry benchmarking director for AT&T, the company's $5 billion IT organization uses about 50 distinct metrics, only five of which are regularly reviewed at the executive level. More important, all AT&T business units use the same five top-level metrics, making easier comparisons of how each unit, including IT, is contributing to the business.

SOURCE: Phillip Gordon, "What Is the Balanced Scorecard?" *InformationWeek* (October 18, 1999), p. 76.

measures will not allow employees to perform at their highest level, which is frustrating for them and does not foster feelings of mutual respect and cooperation.

To illustrate, assume your teacher said, "Turn in the answer to Problem 7 and it will be graded." You work the problem and turn in only the answer, as requested. Your homework is returned and you receive two points out of a possible ten because the teacher's grading key assigned points to supporting computations of the final answer. Do you believe your performance has been properly measured? Had you known that supporting computations were to be counted, and you chose not to turn them in, would your performance have been properly measured? Thus, proper measurement is influenced by proper information about what is expected.

If actual-to-standard or actual-to-budget comparisons are to be used as performance measures, people are more likely to be committed to the process if they participated in setting the standards or the budget. Participation captures the interest and attention of those persons involved and results in a "social contract" between participants and evaluators. This allows individuals to demonstrate a mutual respect for each other's ability to contribute effectively to the development process. The participants who will be evaluated understand and accept the reasonableness of the standards or budget and generally attempt to achieve the results to affirm that the plans were well founded. Employee involvement in a performance measurement system is so important that "management attempts to bolster productivity will plateau without employee support, which is the key to achieving maximum productivity."[7]

Appropriate Tools for Performance

Anyone who has accepted a job understands that there will be a performance measurement and evaluation process. For performance measures to be fair, placement personnel must first put the right individuals in the available jobs. If candidates placed in jobs do not have the appropriate skills, they are usually destined to fail. Thus, the organization is responsible for making certain that either job skills exist or can be obtained through available training.

[7] Dan J. Seidner and Glenn Kieckhaefer, "Using Performance Measurement Systems to Create Gainsharing Programs," *(Grant Thornton) Manufacturing Issues* (Summer 1990), p. 8.

Given job competence, people must then be given the necessary tools (equipment, information, and authority) to perform their jobs in a manner consistent with the measurement process. No matter where an employee is in the organizational hierarchy, each job has certain requirements. A carpenter must have a saw and a drawing or idea of the product to be made; an accountant must have transaction information and/or source documents and a manual or electronic means by which to capture monetary changes; the company president must have the authority to obtain the needed resources to accomplish organizational objectives. Competent individuals having the necessary job "tools" can be held responsible for their performance. If the appropriate tools are unavailable, people cannot be presumed to be able to accomplish their tasks.

In decentralized firms, upper-level managers have little opportunity to observe the actions of subordinates. These managers are able to observe the outcomes as captured by performance measures. This fact makes it imperative that the performance measures selected be (1) highly correlated with the subunit mission, (2) fair and complete reflections of the subunit manager's performance, and (3) measuring performance that is under the subunit manager's control.

Need for Feedback

Managerial performance should be monitored (though not evaluated) on a continuous basis, and feedback should be provided to the appropriate individuals. Thus, performance monitoring and feedback should be ongoing activities, whereas performance evaluation should be scheduled for specified points in time. Positive feedback serves to motivate employees to future success by encouraging continuation of favorable behaviors. Employees receiving negative feedback are made aware of problems and can attempt to change behaviors. Waiting to provide feedback on performance until some "measurement date" is reached allows employees no opportunity for early adjustment. As indicated by the survey data presented in Exhibit 19–5, some employees do not believe that the feedback they are receiving is of the highest quality.

Performance measurement has typically relied on information generated from the cost management system during the management control process. Exhibit 19–6 provides a diagram of the basic management control process and indicates the point at which performance has traditionally been evaluated. Although this type of measurement system was easy to implement, it often focused on performance traits that were not the most conducive to sound, competitive positions. Because of this, traditional performance measures are being supplemented with additional ones.

TRADITIONAL SHORT-TERM FINANCIAL PERFORMANCE MEASURES

4

What are traditional short-term financial performance measures of profit and investment centers?

The traditional focus of performance evaluation at the managerial level is on the financial aspects of operations and concentrates on monetary measures such as divisional profits, achievement of budget objectives, individual and total variances from budget or standard, and cash flow. Each of these measures provides different information that can be used to analyze the effectiveness and efficiency of managerial performances.

The type of responsibility center being evaluated affects the performance measure(s) used because managers should be evaluated using only performance measures relating to their authority and responsibility. In a cost center, the primary financial performance measure is the materiality of the variances from budgeted or standard costs. Performance in a pure revenue center can be primarily judged by comparing budgeted revenues with actual revenues. These two responsibility centers are accountable for only one type of monetary object: costs and revenues, respectively. When a manager is responsible for only one monetary item, the financial

EXHIBIT 19–5

Feedback and Performance Measurement

Regular feedback is the ultimate tool for shaping workers' performance, yet few employees feel their managers give it. Nor do workers really believe that performance leads to promotion, according to a survey of more than 1,000 employees in 15 small, midwestern companies. None of the following statements managed to earn a full "agree" rating–a dismal comment on the quality of employee feedback. (The shaded area represents the average response.)

Strongly disagree	Disagree	Agree	Strongly agree

- I receive adequate feedback on my performance.
- Promotions are based on employee performance.
- Performance is evaluated regularly.
- Managers communicate openly and honestly.
- Performance reviews are fair.
- My supervisor provides feedback on performance.
- The feedback I receive is balanced — negative and positive.
- Negative feedback expressed in our organization addresses the problem, not the person.

SOURCE: Ross Culbert Lavery and Russman Inc. (New York), compiled from company organizational audits, Perz Inc., Maumee, Ohio, 1992; presented in *Inc.* (September 1992), p. 32. Reprinted with permission of *Inc.* magazine. © 1992 by Goldhirsh Group, Inc.

EXHIBIT 19–6

Diagram of Management Control Process

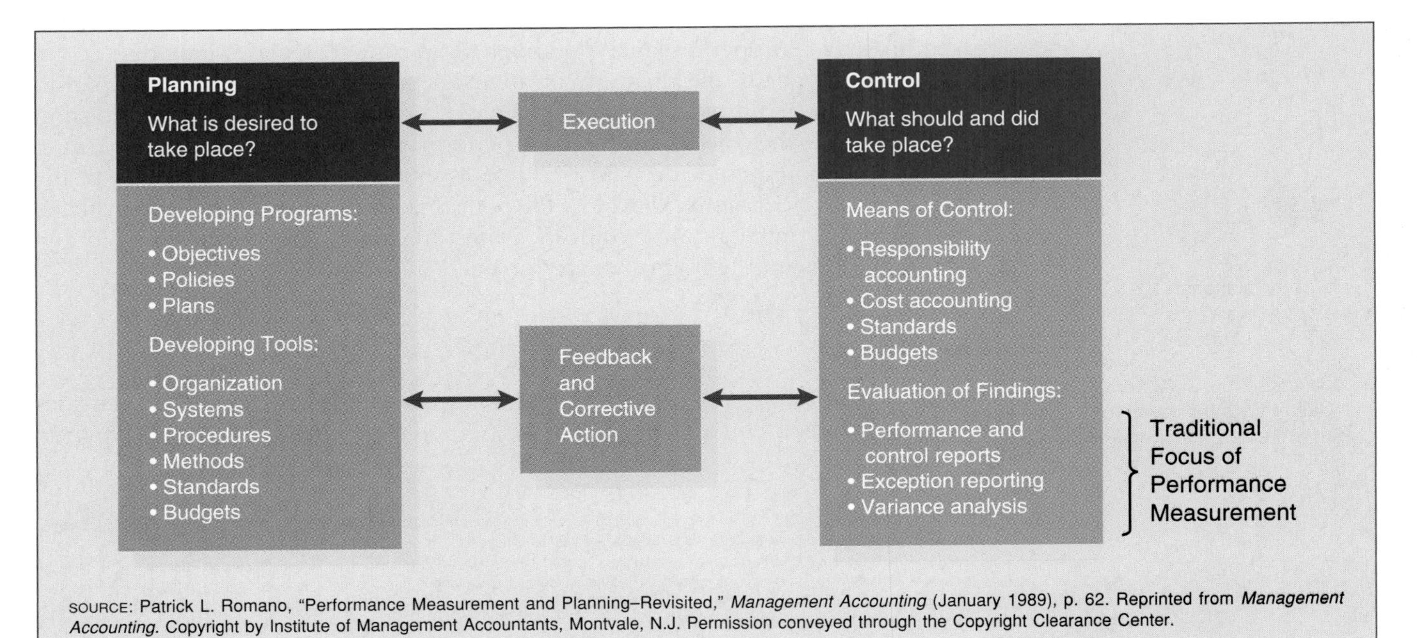

SOURCE: Patrick L. Romano, "Performance Measurement and Planning–Revisited," *Management Accounting* (January 1989), p. 62. Reprinted from *Management Accounting*. Copyright by Institute of Management Accountants, Montvale, N.J. Permission conveyed through the Copyright Clearance Center.

measurements appropriate for performance evaluations are limited to those relevant to that single monetary item. However, nonmonetary performance measures are now being coupled with monetary measures in balanced scorecards to provide multidimensional views of responsibility center performance.

Profit and investment center managers are responsible for both the revenues and expenses of those centers. Given this greater accountability, more financial performance measures can be used for these responsibility centers than the rather simplistic ones used by cost and revenue centers.

Divisional Profits

The segment margin of a profit or investment center is a frequently used measure of divisional performance.[8] This amount is compared with the center's budgeted income objective, and variances are computed to determine where objectives were exceeded or were not achieved.

One problem with the use of segment margin for measuring performance is that the individual components used to derive it (like any other accounting income-based amount) are subject to manipulation. Segment margin manipulation can take many forms, for example:

- If the center is using a cost flow method other than FIFO, inventory purchases can be accelerated or deferred at the end of the period to change the Cost of Goods Sold amount for the period.
- Replacement of workers who have resigned or been terminated can be deferred to minimize salary expense for the period.
- Routine maintenance can be delayed or eliminated to reduce expenses.
- If actual overhead is being allocated to inventory, production can be increased so that cost per unit declines.
- Sales recognition can be shifted between periods.
- Advertising expenses or other discretionary costs can be delayed or accelerated.
- Depreciation methods may be changed.

These tactics can be used to "cause" reported segment margin to conform to budget expectations, but such manipulations are normally not in the center's long-run best interest.

Divisional segment margin (or profit) represents a short-term, rather than a long-term, objective. Most reward systems (promotions, pay raises, bonuses) are based on short-term performance. Although short-run efficiency is important, companies should not use the quarterly or annual segment margin as the only performance measure of a profit or investment center's manager. A year is often too short a time over which to judge managerial performance. The performance measurement period should coincide with the time it takes to evaluate the quality of the center manager's decisions.[9] Similarly, the performance measures should be matched to the subunit's mission. Short-term measures are more appropriate for hold and harvest missions and less appropriate for build missions.

5

How might the Statement of Cash Flows be useful for performance measurement?

Cash Flow

Managers who have authority over operating, investing, and financing activities know that for their entities to succeed, two requirements must be met: (1) long-run

[8] The term *segment margin* is defined in Chapter 12 as segment sales minus (direct variable expenses and avoidable fixed expenses). Thus, the margin would not include allocated common costs.

[9] Quality and financial benefits to the organization should be measured concurrently. The accounting system should be designed to capture both types of information (qualitative and quantitative) that can be used as valid predictors of long-term profitability. See Sue Y. Whitt and Jerry D. Whitt, "What Professional Services Firms Can Learn from Manufacturing," *Management Accounting* (November 1988), pp. 39–42.

profitability and (2) continuous liquidity. Because external financial statements use accrual-based figures, management's attention can become diverted from the size and direction of cash inflows and outflows. The Statement of Cash Flows (SCF) helps to correct this situation by providing information about the cash impacts of the three major categories of business activities (operating, investing, and financing). The SCF explains the change in the cash balance by reflecting the entity's sources and uses of cash. Such knowledge can assist in judging the entity's ability to meet current fixed cash outflow commitments, to adapt to adverse changes in business conditions, and to undertake new commitments. Further, because the cash flow statement identifies the relationships between segment margin (or net income) and net cash flow from operations, the SCF assists managers in judging the quality of the entity's earnings.

Although the cash budget presented in Chapter 13 is essential to current cash management, the budgeted SCF gives managers a more global view of cash flows by arranging them by major activity. Such an arrangement permits management to judge whether the anticipated flows are consistent with the entity's strategic plans and, thus, provides an opportunity to evaluate performance. In addition, the cash budget disregards significant noncash transactions that are incorporated into a schedule or narrative on a Statement of Cash Flows. Because most noncash transactions will ultimately result in cash flows, disclosure of noncash transactions provides a more complete picture of future operations and their potential effect on cash availability. Analysis of the SCF in conjunction with budgets and other financial reports provides information on cost reductions, collection policies, dividend payout, impact of capital projects on total cash flows, and liquidity position.

Like segment margins and income, cash flow can be manipulated and relates to the short run rather than the long run. As a measure of performance, cash flow suffers from some of the same problems as divisional profits because managers can defer purchases of inventory and equipment or misassign collections to a period to enhance the appearance of cash flow. But adequate cash flow is a necessity for conducting business activities. Inadequate cash flow may reflect poor judgment and decision making on the part of the profit or investment center manager. Many useful financial ratios (such as the current ratio, quick ratio, and number of days' collections in accounts receivable) involve cash flow available to assist managers in the effective conduct of their functions. Three other financial measures often used to evaluate divisional performance in an investment center are return on investment, residual income, and economic value added.

Return on Investment

6

How are return on investment and residual income similar? How do they differ?

The difference between a profit center and an investment center is that the investment center manager also has responsibility for assets under the center's control. Giving the manager responsibility for acquisition, use, and disposal of assets increases the number of financial performance measures available because another dimension of accountability is added. **Return on investment** (ROI) is a ratio relating income generated by the investment center to the resources (or the asset base) used to produce that income. The return on investment formula is

return on investment

$$\text{ROI} = \text{Income} \div \text{Assets Invested}$$

Before ROI can be used effectively, both terms in the formula must be specifically defined. To do this, Exhibit 19–7 asks and answers several definitional questions about this ratio. Once definitions have been assigned to the terms, ROI can be used to evaluate individual investment centers as well as to make intracompany, intercompany, and multinational comparisons. However, managers making these comparisons must consider differences in the entities' characteristics and accounting methods.

EXHIBIT 19–7

ROI Definitional Questions and Answers

Question	Preferable Answer
Is income defined as segment or operating income?	Segment income
Is income on a before- or after-tax basis?	Before-tax
Should assets be defined as ■ total assets utilized; ■ total assets available for use; or ■ net assets (equity)?	Total assets available for use
Should plant assets be included at ■ original cost; ■ depreciated book value; or ■ current value?	Current value
Should beginning, ending, or average assets be used?	Average assets

Using segment margin rather than operating income is preferred in the ROI calculation because the investment center manager does not have control in the short run over unavoidable fixed expenses and allocated corporate costs. Therefore, unavoidable fixed expenses and allocated corporate costs should not be a part of the performance evaluation criteria.[10] The same logic applies to the exclusion of taxes (or corporate interest) in determining investment center income. Company tax rates are determined based on total company income. Investment centers might pay higher or lower rates if they were separate taxable entities.

Investment center managers may have a substantial number of assets that are not being used. Eliminating these assets from the ROI denominator provides no encouragement for the manager to dispose of duplicate or unnecessary assets. Thus, total assets available for use is preferable to total assets utilized. Disposition of idle assets will provide the manager with additional cash flow that could be used for alternative projects. In contrast, if the objective is to measure how well the segment is performing, given the funds stockholders have provided for that segment, then net assets should be used to measure return on equity funds.

Use of the original cost of plant assets is more appropriate than net book value when determining the amount of assets invested. As assets age and net book value declines, an investment center earning the same income each year would show a continuously increasing return on investment solely because of the diminishing asset base. Such false impressions of increasing returns could cause erroneous assessments of a manager's performance. The use of current plant asset values is, however, preferable to original costs. Current values measure the opportunity cost of using the assets. Such values, though, are more difficult to obtain and may be determined only by very subjective methods.

Regardless of which plant asset base is chosen for the ROI denominator, that value should be a periodic average. Because income is earned over a period rather than at a specific point in time, the averaging period for the denominator should be the same as that used to determine the ROI numerator.

Data for Southwest Real Estate (Exhibit 19–8) are used to illustrate return on investment computations. The company has divisions in Dallas, Houston, and San Antonio. All are operated as separate investment centers. All three divisions operate in the same industry and offer the same types of services to their customers.

[10] When assets and costs cannot be directly traced and must be allocated to an investment center, ROI calculations may not carry the same credibility as when allocations are not necessary. ROI calculations for an entire company or its autonomous, free-standing divisions are easier to make and are more meaningful than ROI calculations for units requiring such allocations. Criticism of ROI comparisons may also arise when such comparisons are made among divisions of very unequal sizes or at different stages of growth and product development.

EXHIBIT 19-8

Data for Southwest Real Estate

	IN THOUSANDS			
	Dallas	**Houston**	**San Antonio**	**Total**
Revenues	$1,600,000	$ 337,500	$215,000	$2,152,500
Direct costs:				
Variable	(560,000)	(155,250)	(86,000)	(801,250)
Fixed (avoidable)	(275,000)	(58,750)	(30,000)	(363,750)
Segment margin	$ 765,000	$ 123,500	$ 99,000	$ 987,500
Unavoidable fixed and allocated costs	(186,000)	(39,000)	(25,000)	(250,000)
Operating income	$ 579,000	$ 84,500	$ 74,000	$ 737,500
Taxes (34%)	(196,860)	(28,730)	(25,160)	(250,750)
Net income	$ 382,140	$ 55,770	$ 48,840	$ 486,750
Current assets	$ 24,250	$ 16,560	$ 10,000	
Fixed assets	3,089,500	2,305,000	450,000	
Total asset cost	$3,113,750	$2,321,560	$460,000	
Accumulated depreciation	(616,250)	(635,000)	(31,250)	
Asset book value	$2,497,500	$1,686,560	$428,750	
Liabilities	(1,065,000)	(300,000)	(81,250)	
Net assets	$1,432,500	$1,386,560	$347,500	
Proportion of total assets utilized	100%	93%	85%	
Current value of fixed assets	$2,750,000	$1,200,000	$390,000	

NOTE: A summarized corporate balance sheet would not balance with the investment center balance sheets because of the existence of general corporate assets and liabilities.

Also, each division is charged with a hold mission. The similarity in mission and business line allows comparisons to be made among the three investment centers.

Return on investment computations (using a variety of bases) for Southwest Real Estate divisions are shown in Exhibit 19–9. This exhibit illustrates that ROI figures differ dramatically depending on the definitions used for the formula terms. Therefore, how the numerator and denominator in the ROI computation are to be determined must be precisely specified before making computations or comparisons.

The ROI formula can be restated to provide useful information about individual factors that compose the rate of return. This restatement indicates that ROI is affected by both profit margin and asset turnover. **Profit margin** is the ratio of income to sales and indicates what proportion of each sales dollar is not used for expenses and, thus, becomes profit. **Asset turnover** measures asset productivity and shows the number of sales dollars generated by each dollar of assets. The restatement of the ROI formula is referred to as the **Du Pont model** and is

profit margin

asset turnover

Du Pont model

$$\begin{aligned} \text{ROI} &= \text{Profit Margin} \times \text{Asset Turnover} \\ &= (\text{Income} \div \text{Sales}) \times (\text{Sales} \div \text{Assets}) \end{aligned}$$

As with the original ROI formula, terms in the restated formula must be specifically defined before the formula is usable for comparative or evaluative purposes. The Du Pont model provides refined information about an investment center's opportunities for improvement. Profit margin can be used to judge the center's operating leverage by indicating management's efficiency with regard to the relationship between sales and expenses. Asset turnover can be used to

EXHIBIT 19–9

ROI Computations

	Dallas	Houston	San Antonio
Operating Income	$579,000	$84,500	$74,000
Assets Utilized	$2,497,500	$1,568,501	$364,438
ROI	23.2%	5.4%	20.3%
Operating Income	$579,000	$84,500	$74,000
Asset Current Value	$2,750,000	$1,200,000	$390,000
ROI	21.1%	7.0%	19.0%
Segment Margin	$765,000	$123,500	$99,000
Total Asset Cost	$3,113,750	$2,321,560	$460,000
ROI	24.6%	5.3%	21.5%
Segment Margin	$765,000	$123,500	$99,000
Asset Book Value	$2,497,500	$1,686,560	$428,750
ROI	30.6%	7.3%	23.1%
Segment Margin	$765,000	$123,500	$99,000
Asset Current Value	$2,750,000	$1,200,000	$390,000
ROI	27.8%	10.3%	25.4%
Segment Margin	$765,000	$123,500	$99,000
Net Assets	$1,432,500	$1,386,560	$347,500
ROI	53.4%	8.9%	28.5%

judge marketing leverage with regard to the effectiveness of asset use relative to revenue production.

Calculations showing the ROI components using the Southwest Real Estate information are given in Exhibit 19–10 and use segment margin and total historical cost asset valuation as the income and asset base definitions. Thus, these computations provide the same answers as those given in the third calculation of Exhibit 19–9.

The calculations indicate that the Houston investment center is performing very poorly relative to the other two divisions. Its performance trails for both profit margin and asset turnover measures. Based on the amount of accumulated depreciation, the Houston investment center appears to be the oldest, which may be related to its

EXHIBIT 19–10

ROI Components

Dallas Investment Center:

ROI = (Income ÷ Sales) × (Sales ÷ Assets)

= ($765,000 ÷ $1,600,000) × ($1,600,000 ÷ $3,113,750)

= 0.478 × 0.514 = 24.6%

Houston Investment Center:

ROI = (Income ÷ Sales) × (Sales ÷ Assets)

= ($123,500 ÷ $337,500) × ($337,500 ÷ $2,321,560)

= 0.366 × 0.145 = 5.3%

San Antonio Investment Center:

ROI = (Income ÷ Sales) × (Sales ÷ Assets)

= ($99,000 ÷ $215,000) × ($215,000 ÷ $460,000)

= 0.460 × 0.467 = 21.5%

NOTE: For purposes of these computations, income is defined as segment margin and assets are defined as total asset cost.

poor performance. For age-related reasons or others that cannot be identified from the data shown, the Houston investment center is generating too little revenue relative to both the expenses it is incurring and the assets it is employing. Houston's manager might consider purchasing more modern facilities to generate more sales dollars and greater profits. Such an investment could, however, cause ROI to decline, because the asset base would be increased. Rate of return computations can encourage managers to retain and use old plant assets (especially when accumulated depreciation is excluded from the asset base) to keep ROIs high as long as those assets are effective in keeping revenues up and expenses down.

Dallas enjoys both the highest profit margin and the highest turnover. It appears that Dallas may be benefiting from economies of scale relative to the other divisions, which could partially account for its superior performance. Additionally, Dallas is better leveraging its assets because they are 100 percent utilized.

The San Antonio investment center appears to be the youngest of the three. It has a lower level of accumulated depreciation relative to its investment, and it has a lower level of asset utilization. Even so, it is generating an ROI that is close to that generated by Dallas. With greater utilization of its assets, the San Antonio investment center should be able to generate a higher asset turnover and raise its ROI.

ROI is affected by decisions involving sales prices, volume and mix of products sold, expenses, and capital asset acquisitions and dispositions. Return on investment can be increased through various management actions including (1) improving profit margins by raising sales prices if doing so will not impair demand, (2) decreasing expenses, and (3) decreasing dollars invested in assets, especially if those assets are no longer productive. Action should be taken only after considering all the interrelationships that determine ROI. A change in one of the component elements can affect others. For instance, an increase in price could reduce sales volume if demand is elastic with respect to price.

Assessments about whether profit margin, asset turnover, and return on investment are favorable or unfavorable can be made only by comparing actual results for each component with some valid benchmark. Bases of comparison include expected results, prior results, or results of other similar entities. Many companies establish target rates of return either for the company or, alternatively, for the division based on the industry or market in which that division operates. Favorable results should generate rewards for investment center managers.

When managers are responsible for their asset investment base, ROI is often used as a financial measure of performance. But, because of its reliance on income, this metric can be manipulated and may not be comparable across divisions.

Unfavorable rates of return should be viewed as managerial opportunities for improvement. Factors used in the computation should be analyzed for more detailed information. For example, if asset turnover is low, additional calculations can be made for inventory turnover, accounts receivable turnover, machine capacity level experienced, and other rate-of-utilization measures. This investigation should help to indicate to the manager the direction of any problem(s) involved, so that causes can be determined and adjustments made.

Residual Income

residual income

An investment center's **residual income** (RI) is the profit earned that exceeds an amount "charged" for funds committed to the center. The amount charged for funds is equal to a specified rate of return multiplied by the asset base. Top management establishes a target minimum rate of return against which the investment center's ROI can be judged.[11] This target rate is comparable to an imputed rate of interest on the assets used by the division. The rate can be changed from period to period consistent with market rate fluctuations or to compensate for risk. The residual income computation is as follows:

$$\text{Residual Income} = \text{Income} - (\text{Target Rate} \times \text{Asset Base})$$

The advantage of residual income over return on investment is that residual income yields a dollar figure rather than a percentage. It would always be to a company's advantage to obtain new assets if they would earn a dollar amount of return greater than the dollar amount charged for the additional investment. Expansion (or additional investments in assets) could occur in an investment center as long as positive residual income is expected on the additional investment.

Continuing the Southwest Real Estate example, residual income is calculated for each investment center. Southwest has established 15 percent as the target rate of return on total assets and has defined income as segment margin. The calculations are shown in Exhibit 19–11. The Dallas and San Antonio investment centers show positive residual income, which means that these responsibility centers are earning above what top management considers a reasonable charge for funds. The residual income computation for the Houston investment center indicates that income is being significantly underproduced relative to the asset investment. The division manager should be apprised of the situation so that he or she can take steps to discover the cause of and correct this unsatisfactory result.

EXHIBIT 19–11

Southwest Real Estate Residual Income Calculations

Residual Income = Income − (Target Rate × Asset Base)

Dallas:
$765,000 − (0.15 × $3,113,750) = $765,000 − $467,062 = $297,938

Houston:
$123,500 − (0.15 × $2,321,560) = $123,500 − $348,234 = $(224,734)

San Antonio:
$99,000 − (0.15 × $460,000) = $99,000 − $69,000 = $30,000

NOTE: For purposes of these computations, income is defined as segment margin and assets are defined as total asset cost.

[11] The target rate established for measuring residual income is similar to the discount rate used in capital budgeting (discussed in Chapter 14). For management to invest in a capital project, that project must earn at least a minimum specified rate of return. In the same manner, ROI of an investment center must be equal or higher than the target rate used to compute residual income.

Top management must interpret the performance measures in light of the organizational mission of each investment center. In the case of Southwest, all divisions have the same organizational mission and products that facilitate direct comparisons.

Economic Value Added

Perhaps the most popular trend in performance measurement is the development of measures intended to more directly align the interests of common shareholders and managers. Leading this trend is corporate adoption of the measure **economic value added** (EVA).[12] Conceptually similar to RI, EVA is a measure of the profit produced above the cost of capital. The major distinction between RI and EVA is that the target rate of return for EVA is applied to the capital invested in the division or firm as opposed to the market value or book value of booked assets, which is the measure used for RI. Furthermore, because only after-tax profits are available to stockholders, EVA is calculated based on after-tax profits:

economic value added

7

How is economic value added used to measure performance?

$$EVA = \text{After-Tax Profits} - (\text{Capital Invested} \times \text{Cost of Capital } \%)$$

Capital invested is defined as the market value of total equity and interest-bearing debt. The market value of invested capital can differ considerably from the book or market value of recorded assets. As this difference increases, so do the relative benefits of using EVA rather than RI as a performance measure. It is not uncommon today for the market value of a firm to be as high as five or six times the book value of the firm. Accordingly, RI, which is based on a target rate of return applied to the book value of assets, is likely to indicate much better performance than EVA. This point is illustrated in Exhibit 19–12. The exhibit builds on data taken from Exhibit 19–8 pertaining to Southwest Real Estate.

The data in Exhibit 19–12 show substantial differences between the market and book values of all investment centers. The differences are positive for the Dallas center and negative for the other two. Calculations of EVA for each investment center are given in Exhibit 19–13. The after-tax cost of capital is assumed to be 13 percent.

The results given in Exhibit 19–13 show a completely different portrayal of performance than the results of the ROI and RI calculations. The ROI and RI calculations failed to capture the extraordinarily large difference between the market and book values of the Dallas investment center. Accordingly, the ROI and RI measures overstate by a large margin the performance of the Dallas investment center. The Houston investment center still appears to be performing poorly, although

EXHIBIT 19–12

Data for Southwest Real Estate's Economic Value Added Calculations

	(IN THOUSANDS)			
	Dallas	Houston	San Antonio	Total
Operating income	$ 579,000	$ 84,500	$ 74,000	$737,500
Taxes (34%)	(196,860)	(28,730)	(25,160)	(250,750)
Net income	$ 382,140	$ 55,770	$ 48,840	$486,750
Current assets	$ 24,250	$ 16,560	$ 10,000	
Fixed assets	3,089,500	2,305,000	450,000	
Total asset cost	$3,113,750	$2,321,560	$460,000	
Total market value	$9,125,000	$1,200,000	$250,000	

[12] EVA is a registered trademark of Stern Stewart & Co. It was first discussed by Alfred Marshall, an English economist in about 1890.

EXHIBIT 19-13

Southwest Real Estate's Economic Value Added Calculations

EVA = After-Tax Profits − (Market Value of Capital Invested × Cost of Capital %)

Dallas:
$382,140 − ($9,125,000 × 0.13) = $382,140 − $1,186,250 = $(804,110)

Houston:
$55,750 − ($1,200,000 × 0.13) = $55,750 − $156,000 = $(100,250)

San Antonio:
$48,480 − ($250,000 × 0.13) = $48,480 − $32,500 = $15,980

better than the Dallas center. The San Antonio center is shown to be the stellar performer.

Despite the growing popularity of the EVA measure, it cannot measure all dimensions of performance and it is a short-term measure of performance. Accordingly, the EVA measure can discourage investment in long-term projects because such investments drive up the amount of invested capital immediately but increase after-tax profits only at some point in the future. The result is a near-term decrease in EVA. Thus, EVA should be supplemented with longer term financial performance measures (especially for growth-oriented organizational subunits) and with nonfinancial performance measures.

When used to measure investment center performance, each of the financial measures of performance discussed has certain limitations. For example, the limitations of divisional profit and cash flow are their potential for income and cash flow manipulation.

Limitations of Return on Investment, Residual Income and Economic Value Added

ROI, RI, and EVA have three primary limitations. The first limitation is a triple dimension problem related to income. Income can be manipulated on a short-run basis. Income also depends on the methods selected to account for items such as inventory cost flow or depreciation. Secondly, for perfectly valid comparisons to be made among investment centers, all centers must use the same accounting methods. Finally, income is based on accrual accounting, which does not consider the pattern of cash flows or the time value of money and, therefore, may not always provide the best basis for evaluating investment center performance. This problem is illustrated in the accompanying News Note.

The second limitation is also a triple dimension problem related to the asset investment base on which ROI, R1, and EVA measures rely. Asset investment is difficult to properly measure and assign to center managers. Some expenditures have residual values beyond the accounting period, but are not capitalized (for example, research and development costs) and, therefore, create an understated asset base.[13] Also, assets included in the asset base might be the result of decisions made by previous investment center managers. Thus, current managers can potentially be judged on investment decisions over which they had no control. Third, "[w]hen fixed assets and inventory are not restated for [rising] price level changes after acquisition, net income is overstated and investment is understated. Thus managers who retain older, mostly depreciated assets [often] report much

[13] Life-cycle accounting can help to eliminate this problem.

GENERAL BUSINESS  **NEWS NOTE**

But, If the Bird's Not in the Hand . . .

While EVA may be the best single-period measure of performance currently known, it is not the universal answer to the search for the perfect performance measure, according to Michael C. Jensen of the Harvard Business School and William H. Meckling of the University of Rochester. Like all flow measures, EVA fails to solve what they call the "capital value" problem.

This problem arises for projects where early years' EVA is negative, but the future annual EVA of a project is sufficiently large to justify an investment. Perfect measures of capitalized value will never be found, the authors conclude, because value cannot be known with certainty until after a project has run its course to completion and shutdown.

SOURCE: Anonymous, "EVA Bandwagon," *Journal of Commerce* (October 21, 1999), p. 7. Reprinted with permission from the Journal of Commerce.

higher ROIs than managers who invest in new assets."[14] This is much less of a problem for the EVA measure, at least for measurement of assets. It is no less of a problem for EVA's income measure.

The third limitation of these measures is a single, potentially critical problem. Each of these measures focuses attention on how well an investment center performs in isolation, rather than how well that center performs relative to companywide objectives. Such a focus can result in suboptimization of resources, meaning that the firm is not maximizing its operational effectiveness and efficiency.

7

Why might the use of ROI create suboptimization in investment decisions?

The San Antonio Division of Southwest Real Estate is used to illustrate the effects of suboptimization. As indicated in Exhibit 19–8, the San Antonio investment center has revenues of $215,000, direct costs of $116,000, and an asset base of $460,000. ROI for the center is 21.5 percent ($99,000 ÷ $460,000). Assume that the San Antonio center has an opportunity to increase income by $20,000 by installing a new computer network. This venture requires an additional capital investment of $100,000. Considered separately, this venture would result in a return on investment of 20 percent ($20,000 ÷ $100,000). If the San Antonio manager accepts this opportunity, the center's return on investment will fall:

$$
\begin{aligned}
\text{ROI} &= (\text{Original Income} + \text{New Income}) \div (\text{Original Assets} + \text{New Assets}) \\
&= (\$99{,}000 + \$20{,}000) \div (\$460{,}000 + \$100{,}000) \\
&= \$119{,}000 \div \$560{,}000 \\
&= \underline{\underline{21.25\%}}
\end{aligned}
$$

If Southwest Real Estate evaluates investment center managers based only on ROI, the San Antonio center manager will not accept this investment opportunity because it would cause the center's ROI to drop.

Assume, however, that Southwest Real Estate has established a target rate of return of 16 percent on investment dollars. The decision by the San Antonio manager to reject the new opportunity suboptimizes the companywide returns. This venture should be accepted because it provides a return higher than the firm's target rate. Top management should be informed of such opportunities, made aware of the effects acceptance will have on divisional performance measurements, and be willing to reward such acceptance based on the impact on company performance.

[14] Robert S. Kaplan, "Yesterday's Accounting Undermines Production," *Harvard Business Review* (July–August 1984), p. 99.

REVISITING Wachovia

http://www.wachovia.com

Wachovia's managers are fundamental believers in the idea that technology is changing the world and changing the way firms compete to attract consumers. As captured by this passage from their annual report, Wachovia's managers also believe that information has allowed consumers to become much more savvy consumers.

> *In history, major changes in products, processes and technology have evolved through gradual periods of development. For decades, computers and communication systems processed information for select audiences. Information was controlled by large entities such as governments, universities and large corporations. Now, useful technology and inexpensive information are available to everyone. Information is diffused throughout society and across the globe. For almost every purpose, large and small organizations and individuals have economical access to vast storehouses of knowledge. The lower cost and greater availability of information make it a trump card for innovators and, in the future, this incredible capability will destroy artificial, inefficient structures at all levels of society. This revolution threatens the existence of traditional distribution systems.*

Wachovia perceives both threats and opportunities in this age of technology and information diffusion. Threats come from an endless onslaught of products and services from large and small firms including those that have developed new technology-based strategies.

Wachovia's opportunities arise from the endless ways that technology and information can be used to better serve its markets and to manage risks. Wachovia has invested heavily to develop the information systems and technology necessary to monitor and measure performance including customer scoring. The results of these investments are encouraging. For example, in 1997 21 percent of loan applications were converted to loans. In 1998, 32 percent of applications resulted in loans.

One of Wachovia's latest investments is Prime Capture and Archive. This system economically creates, indexes, stores, and retrieves every paid or deposited check and all related paper documents Wachovia receives. Speedy retrieval of these images keeps a tight rein on Wachovia's costs and offers customers easy access to essential information as they collect returns, monitor credit, field inquiries, and reduce document storage expense.

Wachovia's basic equation for success is simple—attract the right customers, sell them multiple services important to their lives, do the right things to keep their business, deliver as efficiently as possible, and let them know that they have a friend to trust.

SOURCES: Wachovia 1998 annual report; Beverly B. Wells, "At Wachovia, Customer Focus Means Information-Driven Continuous Relationship Management," *Journal of Retail Banking Services* (Summer 1999), pp. 33–36.

CHAPTER SUMMARY

Organizations exist to achieve specific missions. In fulfilling an organizational mission, managers design and implement strategies that apply organizational resources to activities. If the organization is to be successful, managers must apply resources with the objective of maximizing effectiveness and efficiency. Only if a properly designed performance measurement system exists can managers gauge their success. Performance measures should be designed for all critical resources consumed by operations. Also, the measurement system should lead to insights about how resource usage can be improved and create a climate for desired organizational changes to be implemented. By linking performance measures to rewards, managers are provided incentives to concentrate on improving specific performance areas. Some of the most critical performance areas for businesses today include capital market performance, organizational learning, and product and subunit evaluation.

Standard design considerations are used when developing performance measurement systems. Performance measures must be appropriate for the type of responsibility center under review and can be either financial or nonfinancial. The measures selected should be sensitive to the strategies and missions of the organizations and their subunits. These measures should assess progress toward goals and objectives and should be accepted by persons being evaluated. Persons to be evaluated should have the appropriate skills, equipment, information, and authority for meeting their organizational responsibilities. Moreover, feedback on accomplishment should be provided in a timely and useful manner. Using multiple measures regarding the firm's critical success factors is more effective than using single measures. Those persons to be evaluated should participate in the development of the measures by which their performance will be evaluated. The performance measurements should lead to insights about how to improve resource use and how to achieve organizational changes that allow firms to remain competitive.

Of the short-term financial performance measures, divisional profits and cash flow are frequently used performance measures. Care must be taken that these measures are not manipulated. Two additional major financial measures of performance for investment centers are return on investment and residual income. Return on investment is income divided by assets. Residual income is the amount of income in excess of income calculated by using an imputed interest charge on the asset base.

Two of the most popular, evolving performance measure tools are the balanced scorecard (BSC) and economic value added (EVA). A BSC links multiple perspectives of performance. EVA is the difference between after-tax profits for a period and the cost of invested capital for that period. EVA is superior to other short-term performance measures in its close linkage to stockholders' interests.

Although financial measures provide important information about the efficiency and effectiveness of managers, they should not be used alone or used without recognizing the limitations inherent in each measure. Financial measures should be coupled with nonfinancial measures to provide a more complete and useful picture of performance, and long-term measures should be coupled with short-term measures.

KEY TERMS

asset turnover (p. 871)
balanced scorecard (p. 863)
Du Pont model (p. 871)
economic value added (p. 875)
profit margin (p. 871)
residual income (p. 874)
return on investment (p. 869)

SOLUTION STRATEGIES

Performance Measures for Responsibility Centers

- **Cost Center**
  Budgeted costs
  − Actual costs
  Variances (consider materiality)

- **Revenue Center**
  Budgeted revenues
  − Actual revenues
  Variances (consider materiality)

- **Profit Center**

    Budgeted profits
  − Actual divisional profits
    Variances (consider materiality)

    Cash inflows
  − Cash outflows
    Net cash flow (adequate to operations?)

- **Investment Center**

    Budgeted profits
  − Actual profits
    Variances (consider materiality)

    Cash inflows
  − Cash outflows
    Net cash flow (adequate to operations?)

Return on Investment = Income ÷ Assets (high enough rate?)

Du Pont Model = Profit Margin × Asset Turnover
= (Income ÷ Sales) × (Sales ÷ Assets)(high enough rate?)

Residual Income = Income − (Target Rate × Asset Base)(positive or negative? amount?)

Economic Value Added = Income − (Market Value of Capital Invested × Cost of Capital %) (positive or negative? amount?)

DEMONSTRATION PROBLEM

L.A. Solutions, a division of Global Office Technologies, manufactures and installs modular office components. For the most recent year, the division had the following performance targets:

Asset turnover	2.2
Profit margin	7%
Target rate of return on investments for RI	13%
Cost of capital	10%
Income tax rate	30%

Actual information concerning the company's performance for last year follows:

Total assets at beginning of year	$ 7,200,000
Total assets at end of year	10,600,000
Total invested capital (annual average)	16,000,000
Sales	18,000,000
Variable operating costs	7,300,000
Direct fixed costs	9,540,000
Allocated fixed costs	1,350,000

Required:

a. For L.A. Solutions, compute the segment margin and average assets for the year.
b. Based on segment margin and average assets, compute the profit margin, asset turnover, and ROI.
c. Evaluate the ROI performance of L.A. Solutions.
d. Using your answers from part (b), compute L.A. Solutions' residual income.
e. Compute the EVA of L.A. Solutions. Why are the EVA and RI levels different?
f. Based on the data given in the problem, discuss why ROI, EVA, and RI may be inappropriate measures of performance for L.A. Solutions.

Solution to Demonstration Problem

a.

Sales	$18,000,000
Variable costs	(7,300,000)
Direct fixed costs	(9,540,000)
Segment margin	$ 1,160,000

Average assets = ($7,200,000 + $10,600,000) ÷ 2
= $8,900,000

b. Profit margin = $ 1,160,000 ÷ $18,000,000 = 6%

Asset turnover = $18,000,000 ÷ $8,900,000 = 2.02

ROI = 6% × 2.02 = 12.12%

c. The target ROI for the division was 7% × 2.2 = 15.4%. The division generated a ROI of only 12.12%. Thus, the division did not achieve its target rate of return. The poor performance resulted from the division's failure to achieve the target profit margin. The asset turnover target was not met, but the ROI fell short of the target level primarily because the profit margin was below its target level.

d. RI = $1,160,000 − (0.13 × $8,900,000)
= $1,160,000 − $1,157,000 = $3,000

e. After-Tax Profits = Pretax Income − Taxes
= $1,160,000 − ($1,160,000 × 0.30) = $812,000

EVA = $812,000 − ($16,000,000 × 0.10) = $(788,000)

EVA and RI differ for three reasons. First, RI is based on pretax, rather than after-tax, income; RI is based on the book value of investment, whereas EVA is based on the market value of investment; and the target rates of return differ between the methods.

f. ROI, RI, and EVA are measures of short-term performance. These measures may be particularly inappropriate for divisions that have long-term missions (such as high growth). In this case, the relatively large growth in assets of L.A. Solutions from the beginning to the end of the period may indicate that this division is oriented to growth. If so, the ROI, RI, and EVA measures will provide an incentive contrary to the growth mission.

QUESTIONS

1. Why is performance measurement important to the success of businesses today?
2. How are organizational missions and strategies related to performance measures?
3. Why is it necessary to establish benchmarks for performance measurements to be meaningful?
4. What roles does performance measurement serve in the management of an organization?
5. Why do firms need to track measures regarding capital market performance?
6. In today's environment of world-class competition, why do organizations need to develop a culture that is accepting of change?
7. How do managers use information regarding performance of specific product groups and specific subunits?
8. In designing a performance measurement system, why should managerial rewards be linked to the performance measures?

9. How should one decide on a basis for measuring the performance of a responsibility center?
10. Should performance measures be qualitative, quantitative, or both? Justify your answer.
11. Can the same quantitative measures of performance be used for all types of responsibility centers? If so, why? If not, why not?
12. What is the balanced scorecard? What perspectives are considered in selecting performance measures for the balanced scorecard?
13. What benefits can be gained by allowing a manager to participate in developing the performance measures that will be used to assess that manager's performance?
14. How can feedback, both positive and negative, be used to improve managerial performance?
15. What is the traditional financial performance measure for a cost center? A revenue center?
16. Why is managerial manipulation of reported results an important concern when designing performance evaluation measures? Are internal or external measures more susceptible to manipulation? Explain.
17. How can cash flow be used as a performance measure? In what ways is cash flow a relatively stronger or weaker performance measure than accrual measures such as segment income?
18. Do the Statement of Cash Flows and the cash budget provide identical information on performance? Explain.
19. The president of Toys for Boys evaluates the performance of Annie and Andy, the divisional managers, on the basis of a variety of net income measures. Drew, the controller, informs the president that such measures could be misleading. What are the major concerns in defining the "income" measures?
20. What is the major difference between a profit center and an investment center? How does this difference create the need for a different financial performance measure in an investment center relative to a profit center?
21. What is the Du Pont model? What are its component ratios?
22. The senior managers of Jambino's Bakery Inc. were gathering for their monthly breakfast meeting when Mr. Jambino came in. Norm Henry, the cost accountant, was overheard to say, ". . . turnover looks good." Mr. Jambino, in a rather unpleasant mood that morning, turned to Norm and hollered, "Of course, the turnovers are good, but what does that have to do with the return this company should be making on its investment?" Norm calmly explained that he was discussing ROI. What kind of turnover was Norm discussing and how does it relate to ROI?
23. What is residual income and how is it used to measure divisional performance? How is it similar to, and different from, the return on investment measure? How is residual income similar to, and different from, economic value added?
24. Identify and discuss the major weaknesses associated with the use of ROI and RI as performance measures.
25. How is economic value added superior to residual income as a performance measure?
26. Describe the circumstances in which use of ROI would be likely to create a suboptimization problem. Under what circumstances would use of this measure be less likely to create a suboptimization problem?

EXERCISES

27. *(ROI)* Lansing Industries has three autonomous divisions. Data for each division for the year 2000 follow:

	Division 1	Division 2	Division 3
Segment income	$ 25,000	$ 75,000	$ 200,000
Asset investment	100,000	500,000	2,000,000

Compute the return on investment for each division.

28. *(ROI)* Wisconsin Industrial has asked you to help its managers determine the ROI for the year just ended. You gather the following information: average assets invested, $3,600,000; revenues, $13,200,000; and expenses, $12,300,000.

a. Calculate return on investment.
b. Calculate profit margin.
c. Calculate asset turnover.
d. Using parts (b) and (c), prove your answer to part (a).

29. *(ROI)* Your cost accounting class has been assigned a case, but the teacher provides only partial information. You have been told that a division of California Plastics has an ROI of 20 percent, average total assets of $8,000,000, and total direct expenses of $7,200,000. You have been asked to

a. determine segment income.
b. determine revenues.
c. determine asset turnover.
d. determine profit margin.
e. prove that ROI is 20 percent from the amounts calculated in parts (a) to (d).

30. *(ROI)* Carol Janicek, a division manager of Southwood Corp., provides you with the following information regarding her division:

Beginning of the year assets	$150,000
End of the year assets	$194,000
Revenues for year	$150,500
Expenses for year	$122,500

Variable expenses, 30 percent of total revenues; remaining expenses, fixed.

a. Compute the profit margin for the year.
b. Compute average assets for the year.
c. Compute asset turnover for the year.
d. Compute return on investment for the year.
e. If Ms. Janicek could increase revenues next year by 25 percent with an increase in advertising of $15,000 and no changes in asset investment, what would be her new rate of return?

31. *(ROI)* For the most recent fiscal year, the Nebraska Division of Sandhill Wholesaling generated an asset turnover ratio of 3 and a profit margin (as measured by the segment margin) ratio of 8 percent on sales of $1,200,000.

a. Compute the average assets employed.
b. Compute the segment margin.
c. Compute the ROI.

32. *(RI)* The French Division of Weston Electrical accepted a 15 percent target ROI for 2000. The following data have been gathered for the division's operations for 2000: average total assets, $11,200,000; revenues, $30,000,000; and expenses, $28,000,000. What is the division's residual income? Did the division successfully meet the target ROI?

33. *(RI)* Cal Engineering has two divisions that are operated as investment centers. Information about these divisions is shown below.

	Division 1	Division 2
Sales	$600,000	$1,050,000
Total variable costs	150,000	717,500
Total fixed costs	350,000	125,000
Average assets invested	550,000	1,525,000

a. What is the residual income of each division if the "charge" on invested assets is 10 percent? Which division is doing a better job?
b. If the only change expected for next year is a sales increase of 15 percent, what will be the residual income of each division? Which division will be doing a better job financially?
c. Why did the answers to the second questions in parts (a) and (b) differ?

34. *(ROI, RI)* Jersey Environmental Services has a target rate of return of 14 percent for its Residential Division. For 2001, the Residential Division generated gross fees of $10,000,000 on average assets of $5,000,000. The Residential Division's variable costs were 35 percent of sales, and fixed costs were $3,750,000. For 2001, compute the following for the Residential Division:
a. ROI
b. Residual income
c. Profit margin
d. Asset turnover

35. *(EVA)* Dallas Catapult Systems relies on the EVA measure to evaluate the performance of segment managers. The cost of capital is 16 percent. One subsidiary, Hydraulic Systems, generated after-tax income of $900,000 for the year just ended. For the same period, the invested capital in the subsidiary was $6,000,000. Compute the subsidiary's EVA.

36. *(EVA)* Alabama Technology has a cost of capital of 12 percent on invested capital. The firm's chip division generated an EVA of $2,000,000 last year. The value of capital invested in the chip division was $19,000,000 last year.
a. How much after-tax income was generated by the chip division last year?
b. As the controller of Alabama Technology, how could you determine the level of capital investment for a particular division?

37. *(Missing data)* Phil Banderas is preparing a case for his cost accounting class for which he has only partial information. He knows that a company has an ROI of 25 percent, average total assets of $8,000,000, and total expenses of $10,000,000. He needs to know the income, revenues, asset turnover, and profit margin.
a. Find each of the amounts needed by Phil.
b. Prove that ROI is 25 percent from the amounts computed in part (a).

38. *(Missing data)* Green Manufacturing relies on residual income measure to evaluate the performance of certain segment managers. The target rate of return for all segments is 14 percent. One segment, Lawn Furniture, generated net income of $800,000 for the year just ended. For the same period, the segment's residual income was $240,000.
a. Compute the amount of average assets employed by the Lawn Furniture segment.
b. Compute the ROI for the Lawn Furniture segment.

39. *(Investment acquisition)* ABC Corporation has a target rate of return of 12 percent. C Division is analyzing a new investment that promises to generate an ROI of 20 percent, and a residual income of $40,000.
a. What is the acquisition cost of the investment C Division is considering?
b. What is the estimated net income from the new project?

40. *(Performance measures and suboptimization)* Sarah Birch is a division manager of Georgia Pine Inc. She is presently evaluating a potential revenue-generating investment that has an initial cost of $8,000,000 and the following characteristics:

Net annual increase in divisional income before consideration of depreciation:

Year 1	$ 800,000
Year 2	1,200,000
Year 3	1,520,000
Year 4	6,400,000
Year 5	6,400,000

The project would have a 5-year life with no salvage value. All assets are depreciated according to the straight-line method. Sarah is evaluated and compensated based on the amount of pretax profit her division generates. More precisely, she receives an annual salary of $150,000 plus a bonus equal to 8 percent of divisional segment income. Before consideration of the above project, Sarah anticipates that her division will generate $9,200,000 in pretax profit.

a. Compute the effect of the new investment on the level of divisional pretax profits for years 1 through 5.

b. Determine the effect of the new project on Sarah's compensation for each of the five years.

c. Based on your computations in part (b), will Sarah be hesitant to invest in the new project? Explain.

d. Would upper management likely view the new investment favorably? Explain.

41. *(Internet exercise)* Many governmental units, such as the City of Grand Prairie, Alberta, have revised the methods they use to evaluate the performance of employees and managers. Search the Internet for discussions of performance evaluation in government and read articles discussing recent revisions made to systems of performance evaluation. Then, write an article that discusses the changes that have been made and the change in operational results that is expected because of the changes.

42. *(Internet exercise)* Search the Internet using the term *economic value added.* Read articles you find that discuss how firms, such as Quaker Oats Company, are using the economic value added concept to measure performance. Write a summary of your findings.

43. *(Selecting performance measures)* Houston Property Management provides management services for a variety of commercial real estate development projects. The firm has recently created a new division to market video game services to the company's existing clients. The new division will purchase and maintain the video equipment that is placed in client buildings. Clients will be paid 20 percent of gross video equipment revenues.

Assume that you have been hired as a management consultant by Houston Property Management. You have been charged with the task of preparing a written report recommending performance measures to be used to monitor and evaluate the success of the new division and its manager. Begin your report with a discussion of your perception of the strategic mission of the new division.

44. *(Choosing performance standards)* Oklahoma Pipeline Services (OPS) is a division of Ardmore Petroleum. Prior to the current year, the manager of OPS and corporate managers agreed to a target ROI for OPS of 13 percent. Subsequently, an incentive pay contract was executed between Gerome Green, the manager of OPS, and corporate management. The contract stipulated that in the event OPS achieved an ROI of 13 percent, certain bonus payments would be made to Mr. Green. Any achieved ROI below 13 percent would result in no bonus payments. At year-end, the measured ROI of OPS was 5 percent.

Mr. Green has approached corporate management with the following information as the basis of arguing that he deserves a bonus payment for the year, despite the fact that his division failed to meet the stipulated 13 percent ROI.

ROI of top competitor for the year	2.7%
Average ROI in the industry for the year	−2.9%

You have been selected to be an arbitrator between Mr. Green and Ardmore Petroleum's top managers. Prepare a brief oral report in which you interpret the meaning of the additional information provided by Mr. Green.

45. *(Comparing performance of divisions)* Training Services Ltd. has two divisions operating in the management training field. One division, Domestic, operates strictly in the United States; the other division, Foreign, operates exclusively in the Pacific Rim countries. Both divisions are evaluated, in part, based on a measure of ROI. For the most recent year, Domestic's ROI was 14 percent and Foreign's ROI was 8 percent. One of the tasks of upper management is to evaluate the relative performance of the divisions so that an appropriate performance pay bonus can be determined for each manager. In evaluating relative performance, provide arguments as to why the determination of relative performance should

a. include a comparison of the ROI measures of the two divisions.
b. not include a comparison of ROI measures of the two divisions.

46. *(Performance measurement manipulation)* A number of transactions follow that affect a specific division within a multiple-division company. For each transaction described, indicate whether the transaction would increase (IN), decrease (D), have no effect (N), or have an indeterminate (I) effect on the following measures: asset turnover, profit margin, ROI, and RI for the present fiscal year. Each transaction is independent.

a. The division writes down an inventory of obsolete finished goods. The journal entry is

Cost of Goods Sold	80,000	
Finished Goods Inventory		80,000

b. A special overseas order is accepted. The sales price for this order is well below the sales price on normal business but is sufficient to cover all costs traceable to this order.
c. A piece of equipment is sold for $150,000. The equipment's original cost was $900,000. At the time of sale, the book value of the equipment is $180,000. The sale of the equipment has no effect on product sales.
d. The division fires its R&D manager. The manager will not be replaced during the current fiscal year.
e. The company raises its target rate of return for this division from 10 to 12 percent.
f. At midyear, the divisional manager decides to increase scheduled annual production by 1,000 units. This decision has no effect on scheduled sales.
g. During the year, the division manager spends an additional $250,000 on advertising. Sales immediately increase thereafter.
h. The divisional manager replaces a labor-intensive operation with machine technology. This action has no effect on sales, but total annual expenses of the operation are expected to decline by 10 percent.

47. *(Selecting performance criteria)* The Chicago Trading and Production Company is a large, divisionalized manufacturing company. Each division is viewed as an investment center and has virtually complete autonomy for product development, marketing, and production.

Performance of division managers is evaluated periodically by senior management. Divisional economic value added (EVA) is the sole criterion used in performance evaluation under current corporate policy. Corporate management believes EVA is an adequate measure because it incorporates quantitative information from the divisional income statement and balance sheet in the analysis.

Some division managers complained that a single criterion for performance evaluation is insufficient and ineffective. These managers have compiled a list of criteria that they believe should be used in evaluating a division manager's performance. The criteria include profitability, market position, productivity, product leadership, personnel development, employee attitudes, public responsibility, and balance between short-range and long-range goals.

a. Discuss the shortcomings or possible inconsistencies of using economic value added as the sole criterion to evaluate divisional management performance.

b. Discuss the advantages of using multiple criteria such as a balanced scorecard versus a single criterion to evaluate divisional management performance.

c. Discuss some ways in which each of the multiple criteria listed by the managers could be evaluated.

d. Describe the problems or disadvantages that can be associated with the implementation of the multiple performance criteria measurement system suggested to the Chicago Trading and Production Company by its division managers. *(CMA adapted)*

PROBLEMS

48. *(Divisional profit)* The Management Consulting Division (MCD) of Total Financial Services is evaluated by corporate management based on the profits it generates. Budgeted pretax income is the benchmark performance measure. For 2001, the budgeted income statement for MCD was as follows:

Sales	$6,000,000
Variable costs	(4,200,000)
Contribution margin	$1,800,000
Fixed costs	(1,200,000)
Pretax income	$ 600,000

At the end of 2001, the actual results for MCD were determined. Those results follow:

Sales	$6,500,000
Variable costs	(4,875,000)
Contribution margin	$1,625,000
Fixed costs	(1,205,000)
Pretax income	$ 420,000

a. Based on the preceding information, evaluate the performance of MCD. What was the principal reason for the poor profit performance?

b. Why do complete income statements provide a more complete basis for evaluating the profit performance of a manager than mere comparisons of the bottom lines of the budgeted and actual income statements?

49. *(Cash flow)* Lois Harvak, the controller of California Mining Co., has become increasingly disillusioned with the company's system of evaluating the performance of profit centers and their managers. The present system focuses on a comparison of budgeted to actual income from operations. Ms. Harvak's major concern with the current system is the ease with which the measure "income from operations" can be manipulated by profit center managers. Most corporate sales are made on credit and most purchases are made on account. The profit centers are organized according to product line. Below is a typical quarterly income statement for a profit center, Mine #107, that appears in the responsibility report for the profit center:

Sales	$11,000,000
Cost of goods sold	(9,000,000)
Gross profit	$ 2,000,000
Selling and administrative expenses	(1,500,000)
Income from operations	$ 500,000

Ms. Harvak has suggested to top management that the company replace the accrual income evaluation measure, "income from operations," with a measure called "cash flow from operations." Ms. Harvak suggests that this measure will be less susceptible to manipulation by profit center managers. To defend her position, she compiles a cash flow income statement for the same profit center:

Cash receipts from customers	$8,800,000
Cash payments for production labor, materials, and overhead	(7,200,000)
Cash payments for selling and administrative activities	(1,400,000)
Cash flow from operations	$ 200,000

a. If Ms. Harvak is correct about profit center managers manipulating the income measure, where are manipulations likely taking place?
b. Is the proposed cash flow measure less subject to manipulation than the income measure?
c. Could manipulation be reduced if both the cash flow and income measures were utilized? Explain.
d. Do the cash and income measures reveal different information about profit center performance?
e. Could the existing income statement be used more effectively in evaluating performance? Explain.

50. *(Statement of Cash Flows)* Mechanical System's controller prepared the following Statements of Cash Flows (in thousands of dollars) for the past two years, the current year and the upcoming year (2001):

				BUDGET
	1998	**1999**	**2000**	**2001**
Net cash flows from operating activities				
Net income	$41,700	$39,200	$43,700	$45,100
Add net reconciling items	2,200	4,300	3,000	4,000
Total	$43,900	$43,500	$46,700	$49,100
Net cash flows from investing activities				
Purchase of plant and equipment	$(18,700)		$(12,200)	$ (4,600)
Sale (purchase) of investments	8,700	$ (3,600)	(12,600)	(15,800)
Other investing inflows	1,200	800	600	2,400
Total	$ (8,800)	$ (2,800)	$(24,200)	$(18,000)
Net cash flows from financing activities				
Payment of notes payable	$(12,000)	$(24,000)	$(15,000)	$ (7,000)
Payment of dividends	(20,000)	(7,000)	(13,300)	(20,000)
Total	$(32,000)	$(31,000)	$(28,300)	$(27,000)
Net change in cash	$ 3,100	$ 9,700	$ (5,800)	$ 4,100

After preparation of the above budgeted SCF for 2001, Leslie Nelson, the company president, asked you to recompile it based on a separate set of facts. She is evaluating a proposal to purchase a local-area network (LAN) computer system for the company at a total cost of $50,000. The proposal has been deemed to provide a satisfactory rate of return. However, she does not want to issue additional stock and she would prefer not to borrow any more money to finance the project.

Projecting the market value of the accumulated investments for the previous three years ($3,600 and $12,600) reveals an estimate that these investments could be liquidated for $18,400. Ms. Nelson said the investments scheduled for 2001 did not need to be purchased and that dividends could be reduced to 40 percent of the budgeted amount. These are the only changes that can be made to the original forecast.

a. Evaluate the cash trends for the company during the 1998–2000 period.

b. Giving effect to the preceding changes, prepare a revised 2001 budgeted Statement of Cash Flows and present the original and revised in a comparative format.

c. Based on the revised budgeted SCF, can the LAN computer system be purchased if Ms. Nelson desires an increase in cash of at least $1,000?

d. Comment on the usefulness of the report prepared in part (b) to Leslie Nelson.

51. *(ROI)* Hearne Hardware operates a chain of lumber and hardware stores. For 2001, corporate management examined industry-level data and determined the following performance targets for lumber retail stores:

Asset turnover	2.7
Profit margin	7%

The actual 2001 results for the lumber retail stores are summarized below:

Total assets at beginning of year	$10,200,000
Total assets at end of year	12,300,000
Sales	26,250,000
Operating expenses	23,885,000

a. For 2001, how did the lumber retail stores perform relative to their industry norms?

b. Where, as indicated by the performance measures, are the most likely areas to improve performance in the retail lumber stores?

c. What are the advantages and disadvantages of setting a performance target at the start of the year compared with one that is determined at the end of the year based on actual industry performance?

52. *(Adjusting income for ROI purposes)* Daunita White manages a division of Miami Chemical. She is evaluated on the basis of return on investment and residual income. Near the end of November 2001, Ms. White was at home reviewing the division's financial information as well as some activities projected for the remainder of the year. The information she was reviewing is given below.

1. Sales for the year are projected at 100,000 units. Each unit has a selling price of $30. Ms. White has received a purchase order from a new customer for 5,000 units. The purchase order states that the units should be shipped on January 3, 2002, for arrival on January 5.

2. The division had a beginning inventory for the year of 500 units, each costing $10. Purchases of 99,500 units have been made steadily throughout the year, and the cost per unit has been constant at $10. Ms. White intends to make a purchase of 5,200 units before year-end. This purchase will leave her with a 200-unit balance in inventory after she makes the shipment to the new customer. Carrying costs for the units are quite high, but ordering costs are extremely low. The division uses a LIFO cost flow assumption for inventory.

3. Ms. White has just received a notice from her primary supplier that he is going out of business and is selling his remaining stock of 15,000 units for $9.00 each. Ms. White makes a note to herself to place her final order for the year from this supplier.

4. Shipping expenses are $0.50 per unit sold.

5. Advertising is $5,000 per month. The advertising for the division is in newspapers and television spots. No advertising has been discussed for December; Ms. White intends to have the sales manager call the paper and TV station early next week.

6. Salaries are projected through the end of the year at $700,000. This assumes that the position to be vacated by Ms. White's personnel manager is filled on December 1. The personnel manager's job pays $66,000 per year. Ms. White has an interview on Monday with an individual who appears to be a good candidate for the position.
7. Other general and administrative costs for the full year are estimated to total $590,000.
8. As Ms. White is preparing her pro forma income statement for the year, she receives a telephone call from the maintenance supervisor at the office. He informs Ms. White that electrical repairs to the office heating system are necessary, which will cost $10,000. She asks if the repairs are essential, to which the supervisor replies, "No, the office won't burn down if you don't make them, but they are advisable for energy efficiency and long-term operation of the system." Ms. White tells the supervisor to see her on Monday at 8:00 a.m.

Ms. White was fairly pleased with her pro forma results. Although the results did provide the 13 percent rate of return on investment desired by corporate management, the results did not reach the 16 percent rate needed for Ms. White to receive a bonus. Ms. White has an asset investment base of $4,500,000.

a. Prepare a pro forma income statement for Ms. White's division. Determine the amount of residual income for the division.

b. Ms. White's less-than-scrupulous friend, Ms. Green, walked into the house at this time. When she heard that Ms. White was not going to receive a bonus, Ms. Green said, "Here, let me take care of this for you." She proceeded to recompute the pro forma income statement and showed Ms. White that, based on her computation of $723,000 in income, she would be receiving her bonus. Prepare Ms. Green's pro forma income statement.

c. What future difficulties might arise if Ms. White acts in a manner that will make Ms. Green's pro forma income statement figures a reality?

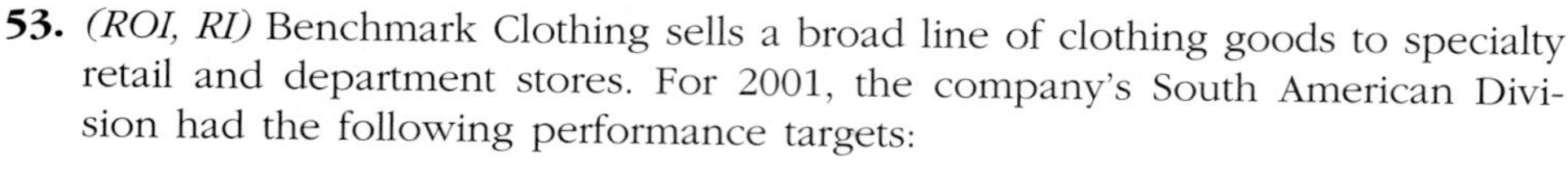

53. *(ROI, RI)* Benchmark Clothing sells a broad line of clothing goods to specialty retail and department stores. For 2001, the company's South American Division had the following performance targets:

Asset turnover	1.8
Profit margin	8%

Actual information concerning the performance of the South American Division in 2001 follows:

Total assets at beginning of year	$ 4,700,000
Total assets at end of year	7,300,000
Sales	12,000,000
Operating expenses	11,280,000

a. For 2001, did the South American Division achieve its target objectives for ROI, asset turnover, and profit margin?

b. Where, as indicated by the performance measures, are the most likely areas to improve performance?

c. If the company has an overall target return of 13 percent, what was the South American Division's residual income for 2001?

54. *(Decisions based on ROI, RI)* Groverton Marine evaluates the performance of its two division managers using an ROI formula. For the forthcoming period, divisional estimates of relevant measures are

	Power Boats	Sailboats	Total Company
Sales	$12,000,000	$48,000,000	$60,000,000
Expenses	10,800,000	42,000,000	52,800,000
Divisional assets	10,000,000	30,000,000	40,000,000

The managers of both operating divisions have the autonomy to make decisions regarding new investments. The manager of the Power Boats division is contemplating an investment in an additional asset that would generate an ROI of 14 percent, and the manager of the Sailboats division is considering an investment in an additional asset that would generate an ROI of 18 percent.

a. Compute the projected ROI for each division disregarding the contemplated new investments.

b. Based on your answer in part (a), which of the managers is likely to actually invest in the additional assets under consideration?

c. Are the outcomes of the investment decisions in part (b) likely to be consistent with overall corporate goals? Explain.

d. If the company evaluated the division managers' performances using a residual income measure with a target return of 17 percent, would the outcomes of the investment decisions be different from those described in part (b)? Explain.

55. *(EVA)* You are the division manager of Flotex Engineering. Your performance as a division manager is evaluated primarily on one measure: after-tax divisional segment income less the cost of capital invested in divisional assets. For existing operations in your division, projections for 2001 follow:

Sales	$20,000,000
Expenses	(17,500,000)
Segment income	$ 2,500,000
Taxes	(750,000)
After-tax segment income	$ 1,750,000

The value of invested capital of the division is $12,500,000, the required return on capital is 12 percent, and the tax rate is 30 percent.

At this moment, you are evaluating an investment in a new product line that would, according to projections, increase 2001 pretax segment income by $200,000. The cost of the investment has not yet been determined.

a. Ignoring the new investment, what is your projected EVA for 2001?

b. In light of your answer in part (a), what is the maximum amount that you would be willing to invest in the new product line?

c. Assuming the new product line would require an investment of $1,100,000, what would be the revised projected EVA for your division in 2001 if the investment were made?

CASES

56. *(ROI, RI)* Raddington Industries produces tool and die machinery for manufacturers. The company expanded vertically in 1993 by acquiring one of its suppliers of alloy steel plates, Reigis Steel Company. To manage the two separate businesses, the operations of Reigis are reported separately as an investment center.

Raddington monitors its divisions on the basis of both unit contribution and return on average investment (ROI), with investment defined as average operating assets employed. Management bonuses are determined based on

ROI. All investments in operating assets are expected to earn a minimum return of 11 percent before income taxes.

Reigis's cost of goods sold is considered to be entirely variable, whereas the division's administrative expenses are not dependent on volume. Selling expenses are a mixed cost with 40 percent attributed to sales volume. Reigis's ROI has ranged from 11.8 percent to 14.7 percent since 1993. During the fiscal year ended November 30, 2000, Reigis contemplated a capital acquisition with an estimated ROI of 11.5 percent; however, division management decided that the investment would decrease Reigis's overall ROI.

The 2000 income statement for Reigis follows. The division's operating assets employed were $15,750,000 at November 30, 2000, a 5 percent increase over the 1999 year-end balance.

REIGIS STEEL DIVISION
Income Statement
For the Year Ended November 30, 2000
($000 Omitted)

Sales revenue		$25,000
Less expenses:		
Cost of goods sold	$16,500	
Administrative expenses	3,955	
Selling expenses	2,700	(23,155)
Income from operations before income taxes		$ 1,845

a. Calculate the segment contribution for Reigis Steel Division if 1,484,000 units were produced and sold during the year ended November 30, 2000.

b. Calculate the following performance measures for 2000 for the Reigis Steel Division:

  1. pretax return on average investment in operating assets employed (ROI), and

  2. residual income calculated on the basis of average operating assets employed.

c. Explain why the management of the Reigis Steel Division would have been more likely to accept the contemplated capital acquisition if residual income rather than ROI were used as a performance measure.

d. The Reigis Steel Division is a separate investment center within Raddington Industries. Identify several items that Reigis should control if it is to be evaluated fairly by either the ROI or residual income performance measures.

(CMA adapted)

57. *(ROI and management incentives)* The Notewon Corporation is a highly diversified company that grants its divisional executives a significant amount of authority in operating the divisions. Each division is responsible for its own sales, pricing, production, costs of operations, and the management of accounts receivable, inventories, accounts payable, and use of existing facilities. Cash is managed by corporate headquarters; all cash in excess of normal operating needs of the divisions is transferred periodically to corporate headquarters for redistribution or investment.

The divisional executives are responsible for presenting requests to corporate management for investment projects. The proposals are analyzed and documented at corporate headquarters. The final decision to commit funds to acquire equipment, to expand existing facilities, or for other investment purposes rests with corporate management.

The corporation evaluates the performance of division executives by the return on investment (ROI) measure. The asset base is composed of fixed assets employed plus working capital exclusive of cash.

The ROI performance of a divisional executive is the most important appraisal factor for salary changes. In addition, the annual performance bonus is based on the ROI results with increases in ROI having a significant impact on the amount of the bonus.

The Notewon Corporation adopted the ROI performance measure and related compensation structure about 10 years ago. The corporation did so to increase the awareness of divisional management of the importance of the profit/asset relationship and to provide additional incentive to the divisional executives to seek investment opportunities.

The corporation seems to have benefited from the program. The ROI for the corporation as a whole increased during the first years of the program. Although ROI has continued to grow in each division, the corporate ROI has declined in recent years. The corporation has accumulated a large amount of cash and short-term marketable securities in the past three years.

Corporate management is concerned about the increase in the short-term marketable securities. A recent article in a financial publication suggested that the use of ROI was overemphasized by some companies with results similar to those experienced by Notewon.

a. Describe the specific actions division managers might have taken to cause the ROI to grow in each division but decline for the corporation. Illustrate your explanations with appropriate examples.

b. Explain, using the concepts of goal congruence and motivation of divisional executives, how Notewon Corporation's overemphasis on the ROI measure might result in the recent decline in the corporation's return on investment and the increase in cash and short-term marketable securities.

c. Discuss how divisional statements of cash flows might provide some additional useful information to divisional executives and corporate management.

d. What changes could be made in Notewon Corporation's compensation policy to avoid the current problems? Explain your answer. *(CMA adapted)*

58. *(Providing feedback on performance)* Terry Travers is the manufacturing supervisor of the Aurora Manufacturing Company, which produces a variety of plastic products. Some of these products are standard items that are listed in the company's catalog, whereas others are made to customer specifications. Each month, Travers receives a performance report displaying the budget for the month, the actual activity for the period, and the variance between budget and actual. Part of Travers' annual performance evaluation is based on his department's performance against budget. Aurora's purchasing manager, Bob Christensen, also receives monthly performance reports and is evaluated in part on the basis of these reports.

The most recent monthly reports had just been distributed, on the 21st of the month, when Travers met Christensen in the hallway outside their offices. Scowling, Travers began the conversation, "I see we have another set of monthly performance reports hand-delivered by that not very nice junior employee in the budget office. He seemed pleased to tell me that I was in trouble with my performance again."

Christensen: "I got the same treatment. All I ever hear about are the things I haven't done right. Now, I'll have to spend a lot of time reviewing the report and preparing explanations. The worst part is that the information is almost a month old, and we spend all this time on history."

Travers: "My biggest gripe is that our production activity varies a lot from month to month, but we're given an annual budget that's written in stone. Last month, we were shut down for three days when a strike delayed delivery of the basic ingredient used in our plastic formulation, and we had already exhausted our inventory. You know that, of course, since we had asked you to call all over the country to find an alternate source of supply. When we got what we needed on a rush basis, we had to pay more than we normally do."

Christensen: "I expect problems like that to pop up from time to time—that's part of my job—but now we'll both have to take a careful look at the report to see where charges are reflected for that rush order. Every month, I spend more time making sure I should be charged for each item reported than I do making plans for my department's daily work. It's really frustrating to see charges for things I have no control over."

Travers: "The way we get information doesn't help, either. I don't get copies of the reports you get, yet a lot of what I do is affected by your department, and by most of the other departments we have. Why do the budget and accounting people assume that I should be told only about my operations even though the president regularly gives us pep talks about how we all need to work together as a team?"

Christensen: "I seem to get more reports than I need, and I am never getting asked to comment until top management calls me on the carpet about my department's shortcomings. Do you ever hear comments when your department shines?"

Travers: "I guess they don't have time to review the good news. One of my problems is that all the reports are in dollars and cents. I work with people, machines, and materials. I need information to help me solve this month's problems—not another report of the dollars expended last month or the month before."

a. Based on the conversation between Terry Travers and Bob Christensen, describe the likely motivation and behavior of these two employees resulting from the Aurora Manufacturing Company's performance reporting system.

b. When properly implemented, both employees and companies should benefit from performance reporting systems.

  1. Describe the benefits that can be realized from using a performance reporting system.

  2. Based on the situation presented above, recommend ways for Aurora Manufacturing Company to improve its performance system so as to increase employee motivation. *(CMA adapted)*

59. *(ROI and suboptimization)* Northstar Offroad Company (NOC), a subsidiary of Allston Automotive, manufactures go-carts and other recreational vehicles. Family recreational centers that feature go-cart tracks, miniature golf, batting cages, and arcade games have increased in popularity. As a result, NOC has been receiving some pressure from Allston Automotive top management to diversify into some of these other recreational areas. Recreational Leasing Inc. (RLI), one of the largest firms that leases arcade games to family recreation centers, is looking for a friendly buyer. Allston Automotive management believes that RLI's assets could be acquired for an investment of $3.2 million and has strongly urged Bill Grieco, division manager of NOC, to consider acquiring RLI.

Grieco has reviewed RLI's financial statements with his controller, Marie Donnelly, and they believe that the acquisition may not be in the best interest of NOC. "If we decide not to do this, the Allston Automotive people are not going to be happy," said Grieco. "If we could convince them to base our bonuses on something other than return on investment, maybe this acquisition would look more attractive. How would we do if the bonuses were based on residual income using the company's 15 percent cost of capital?"

Allston Automotive has traditionally evaluated all of its divisions on the basis of return on investment, which is defined as the ratio of operating income to total assets; the desired rate of return for each division is 20 percent. The management team of any division reporting an annual increase in the return on investment is automatically eligible for a bonus. The management of divisions reporting a decline in the return on investment must provide convincing explanations for the decline to be eligible for a bonus, and this bonus is limited to 50 percent of the bonus paid to divisions reporting an increase.

Following are condensed financial statements for both NOC and RLI for the fiscal year ended May 31, 2000.

	NOC	RLI
Sales revenue	$10,500,000	
Leasing revenue		$2,800,000
Variable expenses	(7,000,000)	(1,000,000)
Fixed expenses	(1,500,000)	(1,200,000)
Operating income	$ 2,000,000	$ 600,000
Current assets	$ 2,300,000	$1,900,000
Long-term assets	5,700,000	1,100,000
Total assets	$ 8,000,000	$3,000,000
Current liabilities	$ 1,400,000	$ 850,000
Long-term liabilities	3,800,000	1,200,000
Shareholders' equity	2,800,000	950,000
Total liabilities and shareholders' equity	$ 8,000,000	$3,000,000

a. Under the present bonus system, how would the acquisition of RLI affect Mr. Grieco's bonus expectations?

b. If Mr. Grieco's suggestion to use residual income as the evaluation criterion is accepted, how would acquisition of RLI affect Mr. Grieco's bonus expectations?

c. Given the present bonus arrangement, is it fair for Allston Automotive management to expect Mr. Grieco to acquire RLI? Explain.

d. Is the present bonus system consistent with Allston Automotive's goal of expansion of NOC into new recreational products? Why or why not?

(CMA adapted)

60. *(Balanced scorecard)* International Glass manufactures a variety of glass products having both commercial and household applications. One of its newest divisions, Fiber Optic, manufactures fiber optic cable and other high-tech products. Recent annual operating results (in millions) for Fiber Optic and two older divisions follow:

	Fiber Optic	Industrial Glass	Flatware
Sales	$250	$900	$750
Segment income	25	92	85

International Glass uses economic value added (EVA) as its only segment performance measure. Jim Wilson, CEO of International Glass, posed some serious questions in a memo to his controller, Janie Ware, after studying the operating results.

> *Dear Janie:*
> *I'm concerned about Fiber Optic. Fiber Optic's key competitor's sales and market share are growing at about twice the pace of Fiber Optic. I am not comforted by the fact that Fiber Optic is generating substantially more profits than the competitor. The mission we have established for Fiber Optic is high growth. Do you think we should use EVA to measure the division's performance and as a basis to compensate Fiber Optic's divisional management? Do we need to change our performance criteria?*
> *Jim Wilson*

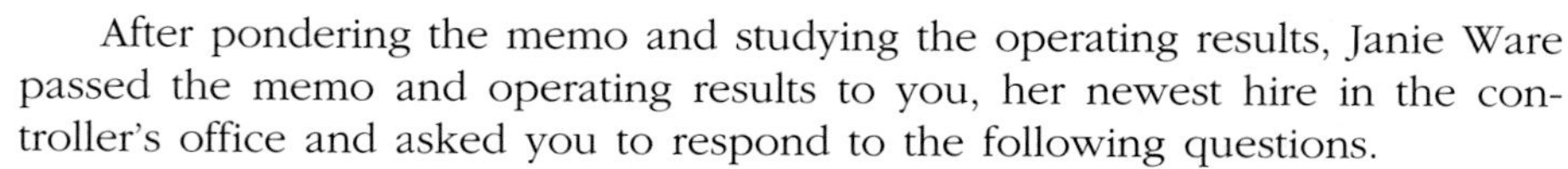

After pondering the memo and studying the operating results, Janie Ware passed the memo and operating results to you, her newest hire in the controller's office and asked you to respond to the following questions.

a. Why would the use of EVA discourage a high-growth strategy?

b. Could the concept of the balanced scorecard be used to encourage a higher rate of growth in Fiber Optics? Explain.

REALITY CHECK

61. *Could any philosophy or cast-of-mind be seen as more vile these days than that of being "antibusiness"? It is like being "soft-on-communism" back when there were communists to be soft on.*

And according to prominent corporate executives, an antibusiness view, disgraceful and opprobrious though it may be, has permeated an unlikely home—the Financial Accounting Standards Board. This seemingly banal organization, which sets the rules governing corporate accounting, reflects "an implicit antibusiness bias." It fails to recognize "business reality" and is unresponsive to business's "valid concerns."

This broadside has been leveled by the Financial Executives Institute, a 14,000-member corporate executives group, and it is only the latest in a series of attacks on FASB from business. . . . But what gives rise to the "antibusiness" rhetoric and the overall virulence of the FEI attack? P. Norman Roy, its president, said his members think FASB has become an accounting "policeman" (a role he would prefer to see played by individual auditors). FASB's thick encyclicals, he added, are too "prescriptive." Naturally, executives want flexibility over how they report earnings.

http://www.fasb.org

SOURCE: Robert Lowenstein, "Can FASB Be Considered Antibusiness?" *The Wall Street Journal* (March 21, 1996), p. C1. Reprinted by permission of *The Wall Street Journal*, © 1996 Dow Jones & Company, Inc. All Rights Reserved Worldwide. Permission conveyed through the Copyright Clearance Center.

a. Why would corporate executives desire more flexibility in how they report earnings?

b. How would more managerial flexibility in the reporting of accounting data affect the quality of accounting information?

c. What are the ethical obligations of the FASB in setting rules for reporting financial information?

62. Bailey Manufacturing has just initiated a formula bonus plan whereby plant managers are rewarded for various achievements. One of the current criteria for bonuses is the improvement of asset turnover. The plant manager of the Carson City Plant told Horace Appleby, his young assistant, to meet him Saturday when the plant is closed. Without explanation, the plant manager specified that certain raw materials were to be loaded on one of the plant's dump trucks. When the truck was loaded, the plant manager and Horace drove to a secluded mountain road where, to Horace's astonishment, the plant manager flipped a switch and the truck dumped the raw materials down a steep ravine. The plant manager grinned and said that these were obsolete raw materials and the company would run more smoothly without them. For the next several weekends, Horace observed the plant manager do the same thing. The following month, the plant manager was officially congratulated for improving asset turnover.

a. How did the dumping improve asset turnover?

b. What are the ethical problems in this case?

c. What are Horace's options? Which should he choose and why?

63. Manhattan Electronics Corporation produces a variety of computer products. Recently the firm has revealed plans to expand into new office automation products. To realize the expansion plans, the firm will need to go to the stock market for additional capital in October of this year. Present plans call for raising $200,000,000 in new common equity.

Historically, the firm's small notebook computer has been a significant contributor to corporate profits. However, a competitor has recently introduced a notebook model that has rendered Manhattan Electronic's notebook computer obsolete. At some point, the controller has informed the president, the inventory of notebooks needs to be "written down" to realizable value. Because Manhattan Electronics has a large inventory of the notebooks on hand, the write-down will have a very detrimental effect on both the balance sheet and income statement.

The president, whose compensation is determined in part by corporate profits and in part by stock price, has suggested that the write-downs be deferred until the next fiscal year (next January). He argues that, by deferring the write-down, existing shareholders will realize more value from the shares to be sold in October because the stock market will not be informed of the pending write-downs.

a. What effects are the performance evaluation measures of the president likely to have on his decision to defer the write-down of the obsolete inventory?

b. Is the president's decision to defer the write-down of the inventory an ethical treatment of existing shareholders? Of potential new shareholders?

c. If you were the controller of Manhattan Electronics, how would you respond to the president's decision to defer the write-down until after issuance of the new stock?

64. *A typical executive is in his mid-40's, frequently travels on business, says he values "self-respect," and is very likely to commit financial fraud.*

That, anyway, is the conclusion of four business school professors, whose study on fraud was published in the February issue of the Journal of Business Ethics.

After getting nearly 400 people (more than 85% of them men) over the past seven years to play the role of a fictional executive named Todd Folger, the professors found that 47% of the top executives, 41% of the controllers and 76% of the graduate-level business students they surveyed were willing to commit fraud by understating write-offs that cut into their companies' profits.

SOURCE: Dawn Blalock, "Study Shows Many Execs Are Quick to Write Off Ethics," *The Wall Street Journal* (March 16, 1996), pp. C1, C13.

a. What creates the incentive for managers to understate write-offs?

b. How does the use of accounting as a performance measurement system of managers affect the objectivity of accounting information?

c. What are the ethical obligations of accountants in dealing with managers who desire to manipulate accounting information for their personal benefit?

CHAPTER 20

Measuring Long-Run and Nonfinancial Organizational Performance

LEARNING OBJECTIVES

After completing this chapter, you should be able to answer the following questions:

1. Why should company management focus on long-run performance?
2. Why is a vision statement so important to a firm?
3. How do long-run objectives differ from short-run objectives?
4. Of what value are nonfinancial performance measures to managers?
5. What should managers consider when selecting nonfinancial performance measures?
6. Why is it important for managers to develop bases for comparison for performance measures?
7. How can activity-based management be used in long-run performance evaluation?
8. What difficulties are encountered in trying to measure performance for multinational firms?
9. How can a balanced scorecard be used to measure performance?
10. (Appendix 1) What steps need to be taken to implement a new performance measurement system?
11. (Appendix 2) What are some major areas of a manufacturing company for which performance measures and their cost drivers have been delineated?

INTRODUCING **WMC Limited**

http://www.wmc.com.au

WMC (Western Mining Company) Limited of Australia was incorporated in 1933 as a gold exploration, mining, and management company. It has diversified and expanded to become one of the world's largest resources companies. WMC is comprised of five competitive and world-class core businesses: copper/uranium, alumina, nickel, fertilizers, and gold.

The company has stated its vision as being "a minerals company determined to be BEST." BEST has been defined as the aims of (1) Bottom-line performance; (2) Environmental responsibility; (3) Safety and well-being of our people; and (4) Teamwork. To promote this vision, WMC has established underlying objectives for these aims, some of which are short term but many of which are long term.

Specified strategies and measurable targets have been set for each commodity. For example, the 1997 annual report indicated a strategy for the gold business as being "to achieve economies of scale by developing large, low-cost operations, and acquiring and exploring for gold in the most favorably endowed locations." Targets for gold operations for the period July 1, 1997, to December 31, 1998, were to:

- Reduce the unit total cost of sales by more than 10%.
- Have combined lost time and medically treated injury frequency rate below 30 per million hours worked.
- Reduce the number of environmental noncompliances.

SOURCE: WMC Limited, *1997 Annual Report to Shareholders* and http://www.wmc.com.au (October 28, 1999).

1

Why should company management focus on long-run performance?

Historically, managers focused on short-run performance measures almost exclusively while ignoring the long-run implications of short-run outlooks and most performance measures that were nonfinancial in nature. In part, such tunnel vision was caused because managers were commonly judged on a short-term basis and because long-run and nonfinancial performance data were often not captured in the accounting system and, thus, were unavailable for managerial purposes. With increased global competition, world-class companies such as WMC Limited have begun to recognize the virtues of using long-run and nonfinancial performance measures.

Although short-run financial performance measures cannot and should not be eliminated, the benefits of long-run and nonfinancial performance measurements are being highlighted by both professional literature and corporate success stories. Enlightened chief executive officers such as Hugh Morgan at WMC are well aware that there must be a balance between short-run and long-run activities and their measurements for a company to thrive in today's global economy.

Management must conduct company affairs in such a way that both the firm's short-term and long-term needs are met. Short-term needs are associated with current period operating, financing, and investing activities. These needs and their measurements, discussed in Chapter 19, tend to be primarily financial. This chapter addresses the long-range and nonfinancial performance of a firm. What seems efficient in the short run may not be in the company's long-run best interests.

VISION AND MISSION STATEMENTS

Why is a vision statement so important to a firm?

vision statement

Developing a company vision statement is a necessary step in the chain of management endeavors to perform well in the future. To be useful, a **vision statement** should provide a conceptual view of the organization's future that is better than its present. The statement should provide a unifying focus on which all company personnel can base their decisions and behaviors. Thus, all employees will be working for the same long-run results. The accompanying News Note discusses the importance of vision statements.

NEWS NOTE  GENERAL BUSINESS

What a Vision Statement Does

A unifying, clarifying vision is [extremely] important to the interdependent organization, in which the leaders expect their people to participate in the process of delivering (and, in the best of cases, helping to create) the vision. In my opinion, we need vision for a number of critical reasons:

To guide us. Like the stars that have guided sailors to their destinations and safe harbors for millennia, an articulated vision leads us from point to point on our organizational journey. It also aligns our various priorities and goals and keeps us from fragmenting.

To remind us. The same organization that can remember one of its mistakes for years can forget what it represents and wants to become in a matter of months. Like the Declaration of Independence, a vision should be something we can reflect on during the coming years to remember the important "whys."

To inspire us. People, at least the sane ones who have a life, are not inspired by work in and of itself. Rather, they are inspired by the purpose of work, the result of work and the transcendent priorities and goals it encompasses.

To control us. When we get the "crazies" and start wandering into unrelated businesses or core incompetencies, our vision statement can snap us back to reality.

To free us. It's hard to have a forward-looking, high-performance organization when we don't know who we are or what we want to become. The events of our past push us along with their inertia, to a chorus of "this is the way we've always done it" in the past. A living vision pulls us loose from that mire and opens the door to a fresh future.

SOURCE: James R. Lucas, "Anatomy of a Vision Statement," *Management Review* (February 1998), pp. 22–26. http://www.amanet.org.

Collis P. Huntington, founder of the Newport News Shipbuilding and Dry Dock Company created a model vision statement in 1886. It reads:

We shall build good ships here.
At a profit—if we can.
At a loss—if we must.
But always good ships.[1]

Notice that the statement is short, to the point, and gives greater importance to ship quality than to profits. Mr. Huntington was a frontrunner in recognizing that customer satisfaction will, in most cases, lead in the long run to profitability.

mission statement

A **mission statement** expresses the organization's purposes and should identify how the organization will meets its targeted customers' needs through its products or services. The mission statement must support the firm's vision statement. WMC's statement of purpose follows:

Our business is to maximize shareholder value by finding, acquiring, developing and operating mineral resource projects throughout the world. We will maintain a diversified portfolio of commodities and exercise prudent financial management. To achieve our purpose, we will develop and retain top quality people, management, skills and technology.[2]

values statement

In addition, a **values statement** can be generated that reflects the organization's culture by identifying fundamental beliefs about what is important to the organization. These values may be objective (such as profitability and increased market share) or subjective (such as ethical behavior and respect for individuals). WMC's values statement details a commitment to

- the safety, health, and well-being of all people affected by its activities,
- ethical behavior and compliance with its Code of Conduct,

[1] Richard C. Whitely, *The Customer Driven Company* (Reading, Mass.: Addison-Wesley, 1991), p. 21.
[2] WMC Limited, *1997 Annual Report*, p. 1.

- responsible management of the environment,
- mutual understanding and respect for indigenous and local communities, and
- success in its business.[3]

Note that both WMC's mission and values statements include identification of multiple classes of internal and external stakeholders. Additionally, the values statement, considered in order of presentation, could be taken to indicate that the company believes that business success will follow from a concern about people, ethics, and the environment.

Mission, vision, and (if provided) values statements are the underlying bases for setting organizational goals (abstract targets to be achieved) and objectives (more concrete targets with quantifiable performance measures and expected completion dates). Goals and objectives may be short term or long term, but they are inexorably linked: Without achieving at least some short-run success, there will never be a long run; without engaging in long-run planning, short-run success will probably fade rapidly.

DIFFERENCES IN PERSPECTIVES

3

How do long-run objectives differ from short-run objectives?

Traditionally, managers have measured performance based almost solely on financial results. But concentrating on financial results alone is analogous to a baseball player, in hopes of playing well, focusing solely on the scoreboard. Both the game score and financial measures reflect the *results of past decisions.* Achieving success when playing baseball and when managing a business requires that considerable attention be placed on actionable steps for effectively competing in the stadium, whether it is the baseball stadium or the global marketplace. The baseball player must focus on hitting, fielding, and pitching; the company must focus on performing well in activities such as customer service, product development, manufacturing, marketing, and delivery. Performance measurement for improving the conduct of these activities requires tracking of statistical data about the actionable steps that the activities involve.[4]

Managing for the long run has commonly been viewed as managing a series of short runs. Theory held that if a firm performed well in each of its short runs, then its future was secure. Although this approach has some appeal, it fails when the firm has not kept pace with long-range technical and competitive improvement trends. An organization needs time to improve its technology, human resources, and modes of operations. If managers think solely in terms of short-run performance and ignore the time required to make long-term improvements, the firm may be doomed in the global competitive environment. Some problems with traditional short-term financial performance measurements are listed in Exhibit 20–1.

EXHIBIT 20–1

Shortcomings of Traditional Performance Measures

- Unrelated to strategic goals
- Irrelevant to managerial decision making
- Add little or no value to business or customer
- Too late
- Clog the information systems
- Send false positive signals
- Create barriers to improvements
- Send wrong messages

SOURCE: Lakshmi U. Tatikonda and Rao J. Tatikonda, "We Need Dynamic Performance Measures," *Management Accounting* (September 1998), p. 50. Copyright by Institute of Management Accountants, Montvale, N.J.

[3] Ibid.
[4] Joseph Fisher, "Use of Nonfinancial Performance Measures," *Journal of Cost Management* (Spring 1992), p. 31.

In a sense, the long run never arrives: Future periods become the short run as soon as they become current and other periods replace them as the future. Even so, managers must focus on continuous improvements for the long run so that when the future becomes "now," the company will be strategically able to survive and prosper. For example, in the 1950s, Japan's automobile manufacturing companies were poorly financed and struggling to survive. Product quality was extremely low. Managers in these firms were motivated to adopt approaches such as kaizen, total quality management, and just-in-time processes to efficiently raise quality and lower costs. Such methods normally require years of dedication and commitment before implementation is truly effective and substantial benefits can be realized. This strategy was based on a belief that profitability and liquidity, both short-run measures, would result as the long run became the present. By making this commitment to the long run, these companies gained significant market share. Managing the long run requires building long-term relationships, proactively making investments in people and technology, and exerting effort according to a plan confidently believed to yield beneficial results in the future.

Short-run objectives generally reflect a focus on the effective and efficient management of current operating, financing, and investing activities. Although these objectives are predominantly financial, they may also be concerned with immediate customer satisfaction issues such as quality, delivery, cost, and service. In contrast, a firm's long-term objectives involve resource investments and proactive efforts made to enhance the firm's competitive position. Unfortunately, competitive position results from the interaction of a variety of factors. This situation requires that the firm be able to identify what factors are the most important contributors to the achievement of a particular long-run objective. Thus, as discussed in Chapter 4 relative to costs, the firm needs to determine the underlying *drivers* of competitive position, not just the predictors. For example, predictors of increased market share might include increased spending on employee training or capital improvements. But the true drivers of increased market share are likely to be an organization's product and service quality, speed of delivery, and reputation relative to those similar attributes of its competitors.

During each short-run period, the organization is striving not only for short-run success, but also toward achieving its long-run objectives. Although achievement will not be known until the future has become the present, the organization should establish its performance measurement system to ascertain long-run progress. The measurements used may need to be nonfinancial ones rather than the financial ones typically used to determine short-run success. One way to classify these nonfinancial measures is into the following four categories[5]:

- operational measures (including administration, customer service, and human resources),
- customer measures (including product development, order processing, and inventory),
- soft measures (including shortages frequency, late shipments, and delivery errors), and
- employee measures (including staff turnover and staff morale).

Such nonfinancial metrics are appropriate in the performance measurement system under the following circumstances: if they can be clearly articulated and defined; if they are relevant to the objective; if responsibility can be ascertained; if valid data can be gathered; if targets can be set; and if internal and/or external benchmarks can be established. Under these conditions, such measurements are appropriate for the managerial purposes of planning, controlling, decision making, and evaluating performance.

[5] Andrew Campbell, "Performance Measurement—Keeping the Engine Humming," *Business Quarterly* (Summer 1997), pp. 40–47.

NONFINANCIAL PERFORMANCE MEASURES

Performance can be evaluated using both qualitative and quantitative measures. Qualitative measures are often subjective; for example, a manager may be evaluated using simple low-to-high rankings on job skills, such as knowledge, quality of work, and need for supervision. The rankings can be given for an individual on a stand-alone basis, in relationship to other managers, or on a group or team basis. Such a system is discussed in the accompanying News Note. Although such measures provide useful information, at some point and in some way, performance should also be compared to a quantifiable—but not necessarily financial—standard.

4

Of what value are nonfinancial performance measures to managers?

http://www.ford.com

Selection of Nonfinancial Measures

5

What should managers consider when selecting nonfinancial performance measures?

Individuals are generally more comfortable with and respond better to quantitative measures of performance because such measures provide a defined target at which to aim. Quantifiable performance measures are of two types: financial and nonfinancial. Nonfinancial performance measures (NFPMs) "rely on data outside of a conventional financial or cost system, such as on-time delivery, manufacturing cycle time, set-up time, productivity for the total work force and various measures of quality."[6] According to the Institute of Management Accountants' *Statement on Management Accounting Number 4D,* NFPMs have two distinct advantages over financial performance measures:

1. Nonfinancial indicators directly measure an entity's performance in the activities that create shareholder wealth, such as manufacturing and delivering quality goods and services and providing service for the customer.
2. Because they measure productive activity directly, nonfinancial measures may better predict the direction of future cash flows. For example, the long-term financial viability of some industries rests largely on their ability to keep promises of improved product quality at a competitive price.[7]

Additional advantages are listed in Exhibit 20–2.

GENERAL BUSINESS **NEWS NOTE**

What Grade Did I Make?

A new Ford Motor Co. evaluation policy could leave some of its top 20,000 executives in the sort of cold sweat they haven't experienced since college. Ford is instituting a global performance-review system for 2000 that's similar to the college practice of grading on the curve: Ten percent of the executives will get A's, 80 percent will get B's, and 10 percent will get C's. Those getting C's will see their raises, bonuses and stock options go to the folks who get the A's and B's. And if someone gets a C two years in a row, he or she may be demoted or fired, according to an internal company memo.

"This program is designed to improve the interaction and coaching between employees and their managers," said Ford spokesman Ed Miller. "We want a lot of feedback—from the people being rated as well as from the managers." The program will be revisited at the end of 2000.

SOURCE: Knight Ridder Newspapers, "Ford Execs Must Now Make Grade," *(New Orleans) Times-Picayune* (December 24, 1999), pp. C1–2. Reprinted with permission of Knight Ridder/Tribune Information Services.

[6] Peter R. Santori, "Manufacturing Performance in the 1990s: Measuring for Excellence," *Journal of Accountancy* (November 1987), p. 146.

[7] Institute of Management Accountants (formerly National Association of Accountants), *Statements on Management Accounting Number 4D: Measuring Entity Performance* (Montvale, N.J.: NAA, January 3, 1986), p. 12.

EXHIBIT 20–2

Advantages of Nonfinancial over Financial Performance Measures

Nonfinancial performance measures
- are more relevant to nonmanagement employees because they are generally more familiar with nonfinancial items (such as times and quantities) rather than financial items (such as costs or profits);
- are more apt to indicate where problems lie or where benefits can be obtained because nonfinancial data are more timely than historical financial data;
- are less likely to cause dysfunctional behavior or suboptimization because nonfinancial measures tend to promote long-term success rather than the short-term success promoted by financial measures;
- can be more easily structured to measure organizational effectiveness because nonfinancial measures can be designed to focus on processes rather than simply outputs;
- can be more easily structured to measure teamwork because nonfinancial measures can be designed to focus on outputs that result from organizational effort (such as quality) rather than inputs (such as costs);
- are more likely to be crossfunctional than financial measures, which are generally "silo" related;
- are more likely to indicate organizational success because nonfinancial measures (such as on-time delivery) can be more easily benchmarked externally than financial measures (which can be dramatically affected by differences in accounting methods); and
- can be more easily tied to the reward system because nonfinancial measures are more likely to be under the control of lower-level employees than are financial measures.

An organization must determine which areas are key to long-term success and develop specific metrics for these areas. The accompanying News Note indicates some activities that are critical to most organizations. At WMC Limited, safety and health, the environment, and indigenous peoples are also considered critical success factors. Policies have been established for each of these areas that point to a dedicated commitment to integrate long-run ramifications into short-term decisions, as indicated in the following quote about environmental performance and shareholder value:

> *Poor environmental performance poses a potential risk against meeting the Company goals, and a risk to the financial well-being of the Company. That makes environmental protection a core business for WMC. . . .*
>
> *Good environmental performance contributes to company reputation which is a positive for shareholder value. The challenge is to demonstrate the linkage between the two. I believe that financial institutions and investors are increasingly looking to management indicators, additional to financial metrics, such as environmental performance, to assess a company's capabilities to manage all aspects of business risk.*[8]

For each success factor chosen, management should select some short-run and long-run attribute measures to properly steer the company's activities toward both immediate and long-range success. For example, a short-range success measure for quality is the number of customer complaints in the current period and a long-range success measure for quality is the number of patents obtained for quality improvements of the company's products. It is up to the organization to decide how and how often to measure performance in these areas. There is likely to be considerable interdependence among some of the measures. For instance, increased product service should increase customer satisfaction.

Choosing appropriate performance measures can significantly help a company focus on the activities that cause its costs to be incurred and, thereby, attempt to control those costs and improve processes. These measures may be frequently related to the activity cost drivers discussed in Chapter 4 on activity-based management. Control the activity and the cost resulting from that activity is controlled.

[8] Don Morley, *WMC Limited Environment Progress Report 1998,* p. 23.

GENERAL BUSINESS  NEWS NOTE

Measure What You Want to Manage

Faced with global competition, the reengineering fallout of the 1980s merger wave, and increasingly active institutional investors, corporations are focusing more than ever on new performance measures. [A Conference Board's study group] indicated that a growing number of major companies are developing performance measures characterized as "non-traditional" or "non-financial." The study group concluded that these measures should be labeled "key"—to be converted through a company's process of strategic achievement into more recognizable financial outputs such as sales, profits, and rate of return on investment. Typical key measures, which are meant to capture not only the value of existing assets, but also the potential for future performance, include:

- Quality of output
- Customer satisfaction/retention
- Employee training
- Research and development investment and productivity
- New product development
- Market growth/success
- Environmental competitiveness

Key measures are intended not to replace, but to augment, more traditional historical and financial performance measures. Only those activities that are actionable and will lead to enhanced performance should be measured. By tying key measures to the strategic vision of the company, there is assurance that as the vision changes so do the measures.

SOURCE: Deloitte & Touche LLP, "Challenging Traditional Measures of Performance," *Deloitte & Touche Review* (August 7, 1995), pp. 1–2.

The nonfinancial performance measures that could be used are limited only by the imagination. Notwithstanding this, using a very large number of NFPMs is counterproductive and wasteful. Management should strive to identify the firm's critical success factors (CSFs) and to choose a few qualitative attributes of each CSF to monitor for continuous long-run improvement. Critical success factors are those believed to be the direct causes of achievement or nonachievement of organizational goals and objectives.

Establishment of Comparison Bases

6

Why is it important for managers to develop bases for comparison for performance measures?

Once the NFPMs are selected, managers should establish acceptable performance levels to provide bases of comparison against which actual statistical data can be compared. These benchmark comparison bases can be developed internally (such as from another world-class division) or determined from external sources (such as competitors, regardless of whether they are in the company's industry). Unless a manager analyzing data has a basis for comparison, usually little meaning can be assigned to actual results. An appropriate basis for comparison allows the manager to assess meaning from the actual data.

Managers need to agree to assign specific responsibility for performance and to be evaluated in each area in which a performance measurement is to be made. In this regard, a system of monitoring and reporting comparative performance levels should be established at appropriate intervals. Exhibit 20–3 on page 906, reflects a responsibility hierarchy of performance standards, with the broader issues addressed by higher levels of management and the more immediately actionable issues addressed by the lower management levels. It represents a good blend of short-run and long-run performance measurements. Note also that the lower-level activities are monitored more frequently (continuously, daily, or weekly), whereas the upper-level measures are investigated less frequently (monthly, quarterly, and annually). Those measures used by middle management (in Exhibit 20–3, the Plant Manager) are intermediate links between the lower- and upper-level performance measures and require monitoring at intermediate points (weekly, monthly, and annually). The annual measurements can be plotted to reveal long-run trends and progress toward long-run objectives.

A general model for measuring the relative success of an activity compares a numerator representing number of successes with a logical and valid denominator representing total activity volume. For example, delivery success could be measured for the period as follows (with assumed statistics provided):

$$\text{Delivery Success Rate} = \text{\# of On-time Deliveries} \div \text{Total Deliveries}$$
$$= 822 \div 1{,}000 = 82.2\%$$

If a competitive benchmark for on-time delivery success had been previously set at 85 percent, success would be evaluated at close to, but slightly below, the mark.

EXHIBIT 20-3

Performance Measurement Factors and Timetables

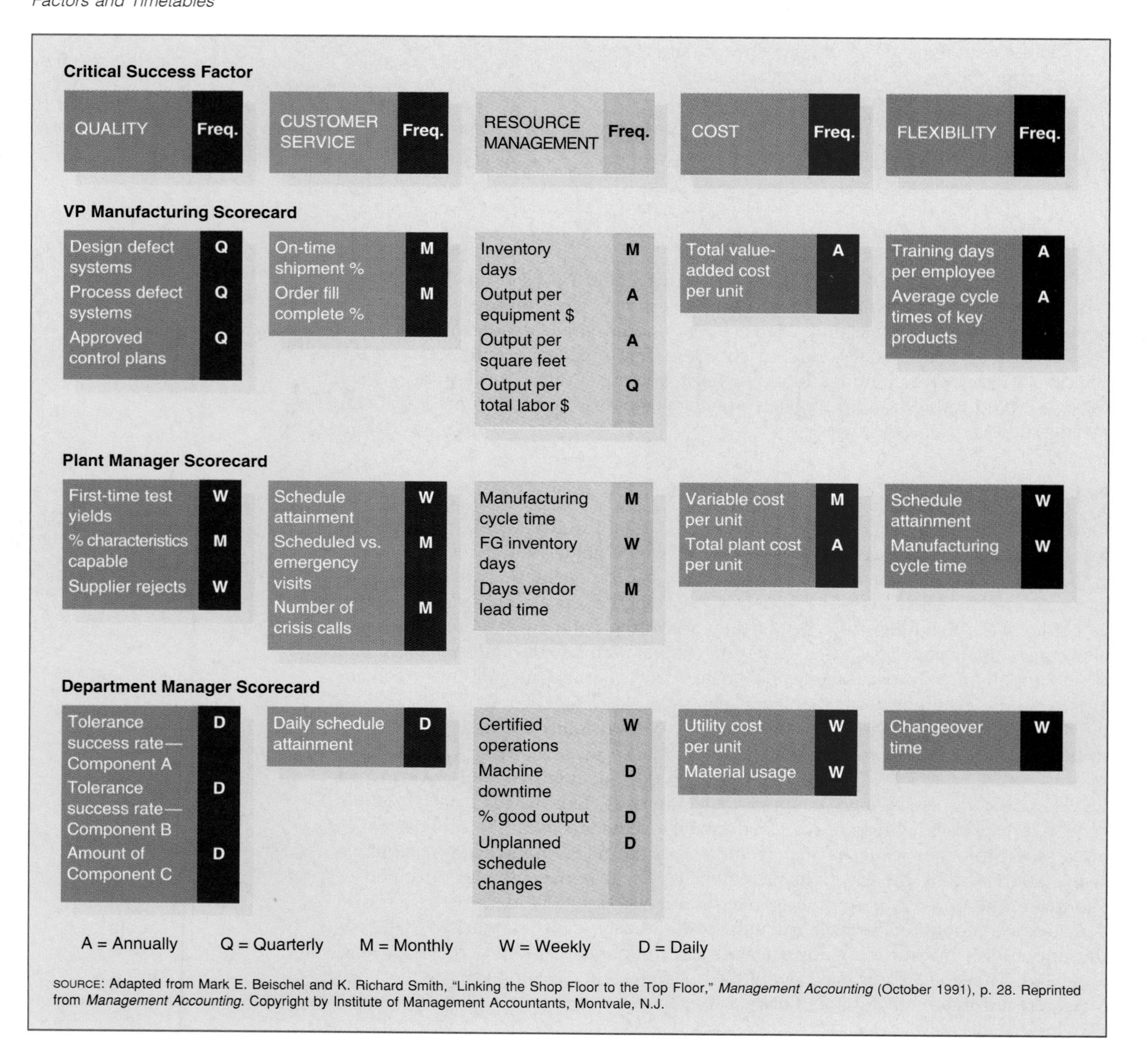

SOURCE: Adapted from Mark E. Beischel and K. Richard Smith, "Linking the Shop Floor to the Top Floor," *Management Accounting* (October 1991), p. 28. Reprinted from *Management Accounting*. Copyright by Institute of Management Accountants, Montvale, N.J.

In contrast, management may prefer that a failure rate be measured. If near perfect to perfect performance is expected, using a failure rate would indicate the degree to which perfect performance did not occur. If success were defined as total quality, the benchmark would be 100 percent on-time deliveries. The delivery measurement can be adapted to reflect nonperformance and, using the same information as above, would be as follows:

$$\text{Delivery Failure Rate} = \text{\# of Late Deliveries} \div \text{Total Deliveries}$$
$$= 178 \div 1{,}000 = 17.8\%$$

In this case, the benchmark is implied as zero errors, and the company was unsuccessful at achieving its performance goal. If, however, this failure rate were less than the prior period's, the conclusion can be drawn that improvement is occurring. Analysis of the types and causes of the 178 late deliveries should allow management to consider actions to eliminate these causes in the process of continuous long-term improvement.

Appendix 2 to this chapter presents numerous nonfinancial performance measures that can also be viewed as cost drivers in an activity-based costing system. Care must be taken, though, to evaluate all selected measures relative to one another and make certain that any competing or inhibiting measures are eliminated. Additionally, the number of performance measurements used for any given area must be limited. Top management should choose several measures on which to concentrate during a period; those measures should be the ones most reflective of the company's objectives for that time frame.

Use of Multiple Measures

A progressively designed performance measurement system should encompass various types of measures, especially those that track factors considered necessary for world-class status. The "performance pyramid" (Exhibit 20–4, page 908) summarizes the types of measures needed at different organizational levels and for different purposes. Within the pyramid are measures that consider both long-term and short-term organizational objectives. These measures can be financial and nonfinancial.

Although internal measures of performance are used, the true measure of performance is judged by a company's customers. Good performance is typically defined as providing a product or service that equals or exceeds a customer's quality, price, and delivery expectations. Such a definition of good performance is totally unrelated to internal measurements such as standard cost variances or capacity utilization. Thus, nonfinancial measures that detect the degree to which customer desires are being met are becoming more important. Companies that cannot meet quality, price, and delivery expectations will find themselves without customers and without any need for financial measures of performance.

Knowing that performance is to be judged using external criteria of success should cause companies to implement concepts such as just-in-time inventory management, total quality management, and continuous improvement. Two common themes of these concepts are to make the organization, its products, and its processes (production and customer responsiveness) better, and to provide better value through lower costs.

Exhibit 20–5 (page 909) provides ideas for judging managerial performance in four areas. Some of these measures should be monitored for both short-run and long-run implications. For example, a short-run measure of market improvement is the growth rate of sales transactions. A long-run measure is the growth rate of the repeat customer pool constituting the customer base. Forming employee groups to "brainstorm" about the identification of both short-run and long-run measures can be an effective approach to identifying what measures to use. A particular set

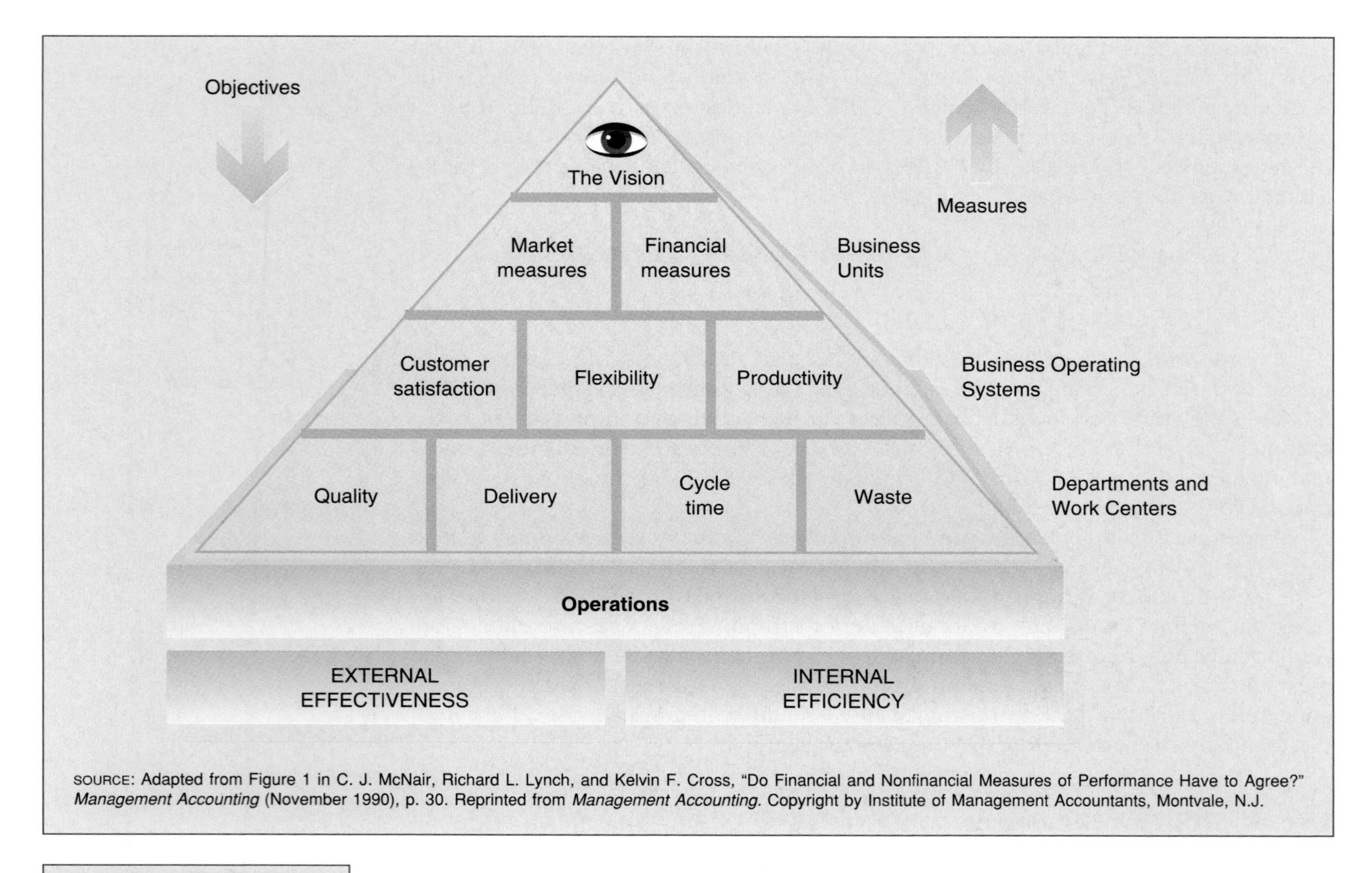

SOURCE: Adapted from Figure 1 in C. J. McNair, Richard L. Lynch, and Kelvin F. Cross, "Do Financial and Nonfinancial Measures of Performance Have to Agree?" *Management Accounting* (November 1990), p. 30. Reprinted from *Management Accounting.* Copyright by Institute of Management Accountants, Montvale, N.J.

EXHIBIT 20-4

The Performance Pyramid

of performance measures reflects a company management's expectations and philosophies. If management's philosophy changes, many of the performance measures will also change, as indicated in the following passage:

> *Performance measurements are the emblems of a management philosophy because people measure what they consider important. When the philosophy of management changes, the measurement systems change—or should change. However, changing measurement systems is more difficult than reworking a machine. Performance measurement is the basis of every system in a company: cost systems, planning systems, capital budgeting systems, personnel assignments, promotions, reorganizations, budget allocations—the mechanisms, built up over years, by which everything runs.*
>
> *Major overhauls bring out the same emotions as if the perpetrators were to hold a rock concert in a cemetery. Performance measurement changes are only possible with strong leadership at the top of the company—and those leaders have to be careful if their performance is judged by a horde of impatient investors.*[9]

THROUGHPUT AS A NONFINANCIAL PERFORMANCE MEASURE

throughput

One nonfinancial performance indicator that is becoming widely accepted is **throughput**, which refers to the number of good units or quantity of services that are produced and sold by an organization within a specified time. An important aspect of this definition is that the company must sell the units and not simply

[9] Robert W. Hall, *Attaining Manufacturing Excellence* (Homewood, Ill.: Dow Jones-Irwin, 1987), pp. 43–44.

	QUALITATIVE	QUANTITATIVE	
		Nonfinancial	Financial
PERSONNEL	Acceptance of additional responsibility Increased job skills Need for supervision Interaction with upper- and lower-level employees	Proportion of direct to indirect labor (low or high depending on degree of automation) Diversity of ethnic background in hiring and promotion Hours of continuing professional education Scores on standardized examinations	Comparability of personnel pay levels with those of competitors Savings from using part-time personnel
MARKET	Addition of new product features Increased product durability Improved efficiency of product Improved effectiveness of product	Number of sales transactions Number of repeat customers Generation of new ideas Number of customer complaints Number of days to deliver an order Proportion of repeat business Number of new patents obtained Number of new (lost) customers	Increase in revenue from previous period Percent of total market revenue Revenue generated per advertising dollar (by product or product line)
COSTS	Better traceability of costs Increased cost consciousness Better employee suggestions for cost reductions Increased usage of automated equipment for routine tasks	Time to design new products Number of engineering change orders issued for new (old) products Proportion of product defects Number of different product parts Number of days of inventory in stock Length of process time Proportion of material generated as scrap/waste Reduction in setup time since prior period	Reduction in production cost since prior period—individually for material, labor, and overhead, and collectively Reduction in distribution and scrap/waste cost since prior period Cost of engineering changes Variances from standard
RETURNS (PROFITABILITY)	Customer satisfaction Product brand loyalty	Proportion of on-time deliveries Degree of accuracy in sales forecasts of demand Frequency of customer willingness to accept an exchange rather than a refund	Increase in market price per share Return on investment Increase in net income Increase in cash flow

EXHIBIT 20-5

Examples of Performance Measurements

produce them for inventory. Because a primary goal of a profit-oriented organization is to make money, inventory must be sold for that goal to be achieved.

Management should strive to increase throughput both in terms of time and quality. Some benefits of improved throughput are increasing the ability to respond better to customer needs and demands, to reduce production costs, and to reduce inventory levels and, therefore, the non-value added costs of moving and storing goods.

Throughput can be analyzed as a set of component elements (in a manner similar to which the Du Pont model, presented in Chapter 19, includes components of return on investment). Components of throughput include manufacturing cycle efficiency, process productivity, and process quality yield.[10] Throughput can be measured as follows:

$$\text{Manufacturing cycle efficiency} \times \text{Process productivity} \times \text{Process quality yield} = \text{Throughput}$$

$$\frac{\text{Value-added processing time}}{\text{Total time}} \times \frac{\text{Total units}}{\text{Value-added processing time}} \times \frac{\text{Good units}}{\text{Total units}} = \frac{\text{Good units}}{\text{Total time}}$$

Manufacturing cycle efficiency (as defined in Chapter 4) is the proportion of value-added processing time to total processing time. Value-added processing time reflects activities that increase the product's worth to the customer. For example, assume that Melbourne Manufacturing worked a total of 20,000 hours in May 2001 producing 25,000 tons of fertilizer. Of these hours, only 5,000 were considered value added; thus, the company had a manufacturing cycle efficiency of 25 percent.

process productivity

Total units started during the period divided by the value-added processing time determines **process productivity**. Melbourne Manufacturing produced 25,000 tons in May's 5,000 hours of value-added processing time and all units were sold. Thus, the company had a productivity rate of 5 (meaning that 5 tons could be produced in each value-added processing hour).

process quality yield

Production activities may produce both good and defective units. The proportion of good units resulting from activities is the **process quality yield**. Only 22,000 of the 25,000 tons produced by Melbourne Manufacturing in May were good tons; the defect was caused by an ingredients mixing problem. Thus, the company had an 88 percent process quality yield for the period.

The total product throughput of Melbourne Manufacturing in May was 1.1 ($0.25 \times 5 \times 0.88$); that is, the company produced and sold only 1.1 good tons for every hour of actual processing time. This result is significantly different from the 5 tons indicated as process productivity.

A company can increase throughput by decreasing non-value-added activities, increasing total unit production and sales, decreasing the per-unit processing time, or increasing the process quality yield. Throughput has been increased significantly in some companies through the use of flexible manufacturing systems. Computer technologies such as bar coding, computer-integrated manufacturing, and electronic data interchange have also enhanced throughput at many firms. Merely reorganizing the assembly operations can sometimes yield greater throughput.

ACTIVITY-BASED MANAGEMENT AND PERFORMANCE EVALUATION

7

How can activity-based management be used in long-run performance evaluation?

Traditional accounting performance measurements often use factors that contribute to non-value-added activities. Materials standards are developed that include waste allowances, and labor standards are developed that include idle time allowances. Predetermined overhead rates are set using expected annual capacity rather than full capacity. Inventories are produced to meet budget expectations rather than sales demand. There are detailed methods for accounting for spoiled and defective units (under the presumption that these will be incurred). Exhibit 20–6 provides some traditional performance indicators and potential suboptimizing results they may create.

[10] These terms and formulas are based on the following article: Carole Cheatham, "Measuring and Improving Throughput," *Journal of Accountancy* (March 1990), pp. 89–91. One assumption that must be made with regard to this model is that the quantity labeled "throughput" is sold. Another assumption is that the units started are always completed before the end of the measurement period.

EXHIBIT 20-6

Traditional Performance Measurements and Suboptimized Results

Measurement	Action	Result
Purchase price variance	Purchasing agent buys more than needed to get lower price or buys lower quality or ignores delivery speed and accuracy	Excess inventory; increased carrying cost; use of suppliers who may not have the best quality and/or delivery options
Machine utilization percentage or use of an overhead rate based on expected capacity	Supervisor produces more than needed to increase the utilization rate	Excess inventory; increased carrying cost; wrong inventory; lack of time for machine maintenance or worker training
Waste/idle time built into standard cost	Supervisor takes no action if the lax standard for material or labor is met	Inflated standard cost (thus, possibly, inflated selling price or misinformation about product profitability); acceptance and encouragement of less-than-the-best efforts
Cost center reporting	Managers focus on costs instead of activities	Cost reduction opportunities may be missed if costs are within budget; may not be able to determine if the cost center is operating efficiently

To adapt the traditional perspective, some companies are implementing activity-based management (ABM) and activity-based costing (ABC) techniques. ABM is concerned with increasing throughput by reducing non-value-added activities; ABC is concerned with long-run, rather than short-run, cost measurement. ABM and ABC can provide information on the overhead impact created by reengineered processes to streamline activities and minimize nonquality work. As quality improves, management's threshold of "acceptable" performance becomes more demanding and performance is evaluated against progressively more rigorous benchmarks.

World-class companies have begun to adopt ABM so as to remove any implied acceptance of non-value-added (NVA) activities from performance measurements or, if that is impossible, to design performance measurements that highlight those activities. The adages "you get what you measure" and "measure what you want to get" are appropriate. Activity-based management paired with a good pay-for-performance system encourages workers to develop new skills, accept greater responsibilities, and make suggestions for improvements in plant layout, product design, and worker utilization. Such improvements will reduce non-value-added time and cost. In addition, by focusing on activities and costs, ABM is better able to provide more appropriate measures of performance than are found in most traditional systems.

Performance measurements should concentrate on things that create customer value. Measures can be quantitative or qualitative, nonfinancial or financial. Measurement selection should be related to the performance that management wishes to either encourage or discourage. Probably the two most important performance measures of U.S. businesses at this time are quality and service.

Companies that are concerned about the cost of quality (COQ) and the non-value-added activities associated with lack of quality should develop COQ measurements such as those presented in Exhibit 20–7. For example, if a performance measurement is the cost of defective units produced during a period, the expectation is that defects will occur and management will accept some stated or understood

EXHIBIT 20-7

Cost of Quality Measurements

Element of COQ	Operational Cost Drivers	Measure	VA or NVA
Prevention	Investment in reducing overall COQ operations	Prevention Cost* / Total COQ	VA
Appraisal	Setup frequency Tight tolerance operations Complex design	Number of inspections	NVA
Internal failure	Machine reliability Tooling age or condition Design error Operator error	Number of pieces rejected	NVA
External failure	Order entry errors Incorrect assembly instructions Product failure Operator error	Number of customer complaints	NVA

*Ideally, the formula should equal 1. Prevention costs are, by definition, all value-added costs. As non-value-added costs included in the denominator are eliminated, total COQ is composed of only value-added costs. Therefore, the formula ideally ends up equaling 1 (value-added costs ÷ value-added costs), which is the target measurement.

SOURCE: Michael R. Ostrenga, "Return on Investment Through the Cost of Quality," *Journal of Cost Management* (Summer 1991), p. 43. © 1991 Warren Gorham & Lamont. Reprinted with permission of RIA.

defect cost. If, instead, the performance measurement is zero defects, the expectation is that no defects will occur. This second measurement would create an atmosphere more conducive to eliminating defects than would the first one.

A commitment to quality requires that a company make major adjustments in the way it designs products, trains and develops its workforce, makes decisions on asset acquisition and utilization, and interacts with suppliers and customers. Products should be designed to provide the maximum quality possible for the forecasted selling price. Spoilage and defects should not be built into product or service costs. ABM, with its focus on value-added and non-value-added activities, helps to eliminate building such costs into a product.

One nonfinancial measure of service is how quickly customers receive their goods or lead time. Measuring lead time should cause products to be available to customers more rapidly. In addition, using fewer parts, interchangeable parts, and parts that require few or no engineering changes after the start of production will shorten lead time. Lead time measurement could also provide an incentive to revise a building layout so that work flow is quicker, to increase workforce productivity, and to reduce defects and reworks. Last, lead time measurement should cause managers to observe and correct any non-value-added activities or constraints that are creating production, performance, or processing delays.

Some performance measurements, such as zero defects and lead time, are important regardless of where a company or division is located. However, foreign operations may require some additional considerations in performance measurement and evaluation than do domestic operations.

PERFORMANCE EVALUATION IN MULTINATIONAL SETTINGS

Many large, decentralized companies have overseas operations whose performance must be measured and evaluated. Unfortunately, regardless of the location of these subunits, management often uses income as the overriding performance criterion.

Such a singular focus is usually not appropriate for domestic responsibility centers; it is even less appropriate for multinational segments. This conclusion is valid regardless of whether the organization is Dell Computer Corporation headquarters in Austin, Texas, with manufacturing operations in Ireland and Malaysia or WMC domiciled in Australia with operations in Singapore, Rotterdam, Kazakhstan, Canada, and the United States.

8

What difficulties are encountered in trying to measure performance for multinational firms?

http://www.dell.com

Differences among cultures and economies are as important as differences in accounting standards and reporting practices when attempting comparisons of multinational organizational units. In Japan, for instance, a company president views shareholders as basically inconsequential. When the head of a large Japanese conglomerate was asked "whether stock-market movements would ever affect his business decisions, he answered in a single word: 'Never!' "[11] This type of attitude has allowed Japanese companies to focus on both long-run and short-run business decisions. Such a concept is relatively unheard of in the United States where top management is often removed by stockholders for making decisions that appear not to maximize current shareholder value.

The investment cost necessary to create the same type of organizational unit in different countries may differ substantially. For example, because of the exchange rate and legal costs, it is significantly more expensive for a U.S. company to open a Japanese subsidiary than an Indonesian one. If performance were measured using residual income calculated with the same target rate of return, the Japanese unit would be placed at a distinct disadvantage because of its larger investment base. However, the company may have believed that the possibility of future joint ventures with the Japanese was a primary corporate goal that justified the larger investment. One method of handling such a discrepancy in investment bases is to assign a lower target rate to compute residual income for the Japanese subsidiary than for the Indonesian one. This type of differential would also be considered appropriate because of the lower political, financial, and economic risks.

Income comparisons between multinational units may be invalid because of important differences in trade tariffs, income tax rates, currency fluctuations, and the possibility of restrictions on the transfer of goods or currency from a country. Income earned by a multinational unit may also be affected by conditions totally outside its control, such as protectionism of local companies, government aid, or varying wage rates caused by differing standards of living, level of industrial development, and/or the quantity of socialized services. If the multinational subunit adopts the local country's accounting practices, differences in international standards can make income comparisons among units difficult and inconvenient even after the statements are translated to a single currency basis.

The diverse economic, legal/political, and tax structures of countries have affected the development and practice of accounting. Although the International Accounting Standards Committee is working to achieve harmonization of accounting standards, many of this organization's standards reflect compromise positions, allow for a significant number of alternatives, and are accepted only through voluntary compliance. In addition, within the constraints of legal, moral, and social responsibility, managers may be able to transfer goods between segments at prices that minimize profits or tariffs in locations where taxes are high by shifting profits or cost values to more advantageous climates.

U.S. firms that have multinational profit or investment centers (or subsidiaries) need to establish flexible systems of measuring profit performance for those units. Such systems should recognize that differences in sales volumes, accounting standards, economic conditions, and risk might be outside the control of an international subunit's manager. In such cases, qualitative performance measures may become significantly more useful. Performance evaluations can include factors such as market share increases, quality improvements (defect reductions), improvement

[11] Alan S. Blinder, "Doing It Their Way," *Business Edge* (October 1992), p. 27.

When piloting a plane, information from multiple instruments is necessary for flight safety. In the same manner, the balanced scorecard provides information about a variety of organizational activities that are crucial to business operations and success.

of inventory management with the related reduction in working capital, and new product development. Use of measures that limit suboptimization of resources is vital to the proper management of both domestic and multinational responsibility centers.

USING A BALANCED SCORECARD FOR MEASURING PERFORMANCE

How can a balanced scorecard be used to measure performance?

As mentioned in Chapter 19, an organization seeking an effective, integrated performance measurement system might choose to adopt a balanced scorecard approach. A balanced scorecard was originally developed to provide top managers with a set of measures that give

> *a fast but comprehensive view of the business. The balanced scorecard includes financial measures that tell the results of actions already taken. And it complements the financial measures with operational measures on customer satisfaction, internal processes, and the organization's innovation and improvement activities—operational measures that are the drivers of future financial performance.*[12]

Since Kaplan and Norton first introduced the scorecard in the early 1990s, its use in some organizations is now at multiple levels: top management, subunit, and even individual employees. Additionally, as indicated in the News Note (page 916), the scorecard can be used by not-for-profit organizations as well. Regardless of the level of use, the scorecard approach directly links its measurements to the organization's strategies and values. Exhibit 20–8 provides an alternative balanced scorecard to the one presented in Chapter 19. Both scorecards, however, allow measurement data to be disaggregated into four segments that reflect past performance and provide indicators of investments in future performance. "Taken together, the measures provide a holistic view of what is happening both inside and outside the

[12] Robert S. Kaplan and David P. Norton, "The Balanced Scorecard-Measures That Drive Performance," *Harvard Business Review* (January–February 1992), p. 71.

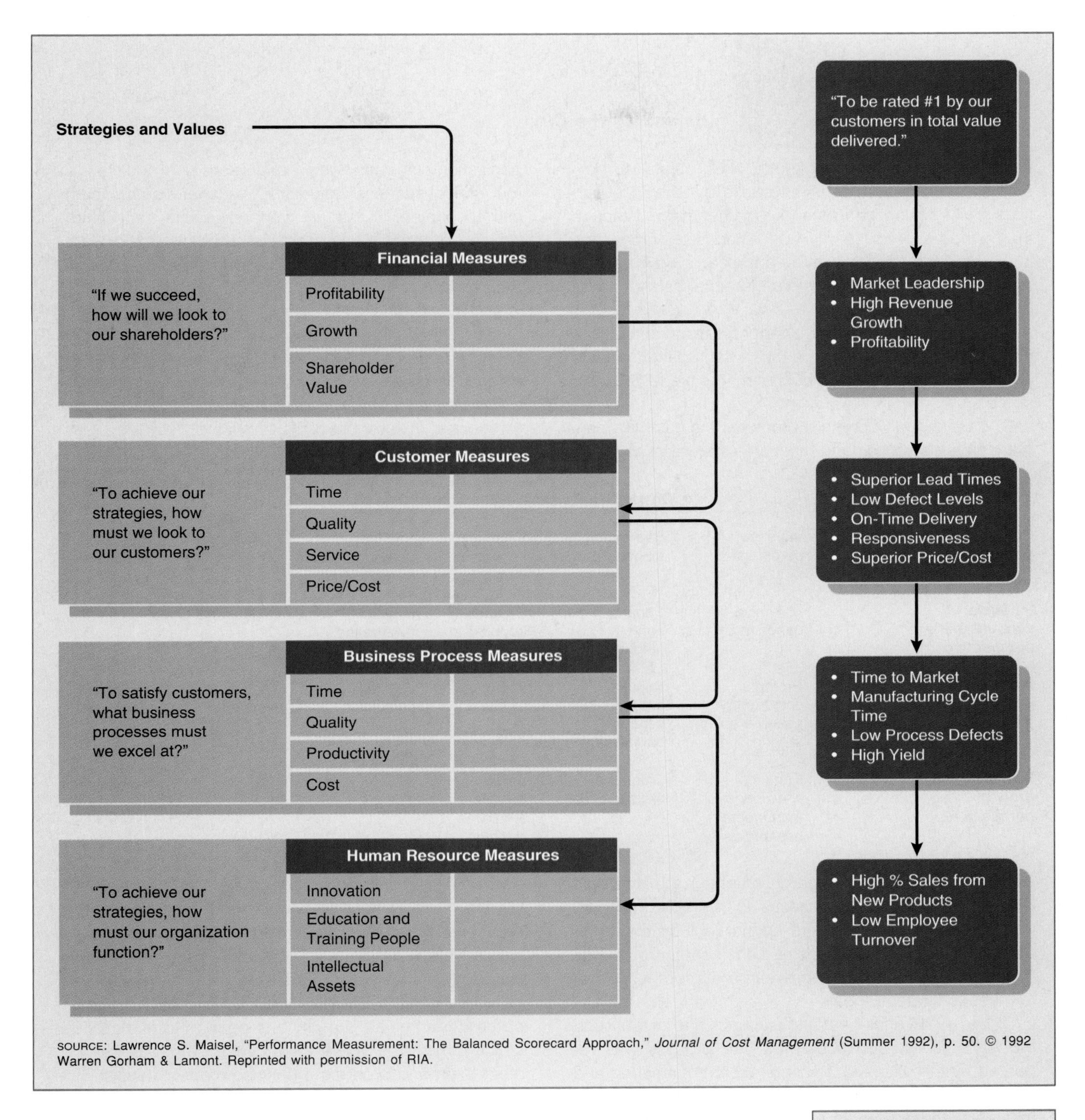

SOURCE: Lawrence S. Maisel, "Performance Measurement: The Balanced Scorecard Approach," *Journal of Cost Management* (Summer 1992), p. 50. © 1992 Warren Gorham & Lamont. Reprinted with permission of RIA.

EXHIBIT 20-8

Performance Measurement Balanced Scorecard

organization or level, thus allowing all constituents of the organization to see how their activities contribute to attainment of the organization's overall mission."[13]

The financial measures of the balanced scorecard should be designed to reflect shareholder-relevant issues of profitability and organizational growth. Such measures can include subunit operating income, bottom-line net income, cash flow, change in market share, and return on assets. Although these measures indicate

[13] Chee W. Chow *et al.*, "The Balanced Scorecard: A Potent Tool for Energizing and Focusing Healthcare Organization Management," *Journal of Healthcare Management* (May–June 1998), pp. 263–280.

NEWS NOTE  GENERAL BUSINESS

Balancing the City

For more than 25 years, Charlotte, N.C., measured government efficiency and effectiveness by setting objectives and tracking performance against them. Although the method served the city well, it focused primarily on the past. Therefore, the city began searching for a performance measurement system that emphasized strategic planning for the future.

In the early '90s the city manager researched the "Balanced Scorecard," [and] Charlotte adapted the model to apply to the public sector, becoming the first U.S. city to do so.

The Balanced Scorecard promotes the establishment of tangible objectives and measures that relate to an organization's mission, vision and strategy. It focuses on four critical success indicators: customer service, financial accountability, internal work efficiencies, and learning and growth. Priorities are set within the major categories, first at the corporate level and then at division, department, team and even individual levels.

In 1990, Charlotte City Council chose five areas, community safety, transportation, economic development, neighborhoods and restructuring government, on which to focus its strategic plan. Those priorities were later modeled (as shown in the following table), representing the "corporate" level of the city's scorecard.

Charlotte's Corporate Scorecard

Customer perspective	Reduce crime	Increase perception of safety	Strengthen neighborhoods	Improve service quality	Provide safe, convenient transportation	Maintain competitive tax rates	Promote economic opportunity
Financial accountability perspective		Maximize benefit/cost	Expand non-city funding	Grow the tax base	Maintain AAA rating		
Internal process perspective	Increase positive contacts	Promote community-based problem solving	Secure funding/service partners	Improve productivity	Streamline customer interactions	Increase infrastructure capacity	Promote business mix
Learning and growth perspective		Enhance knowledge management capabilities	Close the skills gap	Achieve positive employee climate			

The Balanced Scorecard emphasizes strategic processes over routine processes. In Charlotte, the council's scorecard does not and cannot include every important service delivered. Instead, the scorecard reflects the processes that must improve in order for the council to meet its strategic goals.

In late 1996, after Charlotte's council had established the city's "corporate" scorecard, the process was repeated by the planning, transportation, engineering and property management, and police departments. Department-level objectives were matched with council-level objectives to ensure that the city would achieve its highest priorities.

By 1998, all of the city's departments had scorecards, but the measurement system will not become a routine part of the city's business until 2001. The concept of having only a few performance indicators has been troublesome since previously there were unlimited measures. However, with the council's support and the participation of the departments, the city has been able to clarify its critical objectives, identify the processes necessary to meet them and produce a concise model to assist officials in tracking the city's progress.

SOURCE: Pamela Syfert, Nancy Elliott, and Lisa Schumacher, "Charlotte Adapts the 'Balanced Scorecard,'" *The American City & County* (October 1998), p. 32ff.

past performance, "the hard truth is that if improved performance fails to be reflected in the bottom line, executives should reexamine the basic assumptions of their strategy and mission."[14]

[14] Kaplan and Norton, "The Balanced Scorecard," p. 77.

Balanced scorecard measures of the customer perspective should indicate how the organization is faring relative to customer issues of speed (lead time), quality, service, and price (both purchase and after-purchase). These measures can be internal or external and should help an organization assess its future success in the eyes of its customers.

Business process measures should focus on the internal things that the organization needs to do to make certain that it is meeting customers needs and expectations. For example, for customers to judge an organization's products or services as "high quality," that organization must have internal processes that have high process yields by not producing or providing defective goods or services. Other measures in this area include manufacturing or service cycle efficiency, time-to-market on new products, on-time delivery, and cost variances (assuming that the costing system has been designed to determine the most realistic costs).

The final category of the scorecard should indicate those measures that the organization can use to help judge continuous improvement and predict longevity. These measures focus on using the organization's intellectual capital to adapt to changing customer needs or influence new customer needs and expectations through product or service innovations. Measures such as number of patents or copyrights applied for, percentage of research and development projects resulting in patentable products, average time of R&D project from conception to commercialization, and percentage of capital investments on "high-tech" projects can help an organization ascertain its ability to learn, grow, improve—and, thus, survive.

Regardless of whether organizational management decides to use a balanced scorecard approach to performance measurement, some method of assessing performance must be developed. A variety of decisions must be integrated into a **performance management system** (depicted in Exhibit 20–9). This system reflects the entire package of decisions regarding performance measurement and evaluation.

performance management system

EXHIBIT 20–9

Performance Management System

IDENTIFY

Perform strategic planning

Goals

MOTIVATE

Create employee motivation system

Improvement objectives

PERFORM

Focus productivity improvement

Improvement results

MEASURE

Monitor and reward

Corporate results

EVALUATE

Reevaluate performance measures to corporate goals

Modifications

Prescription for profitability

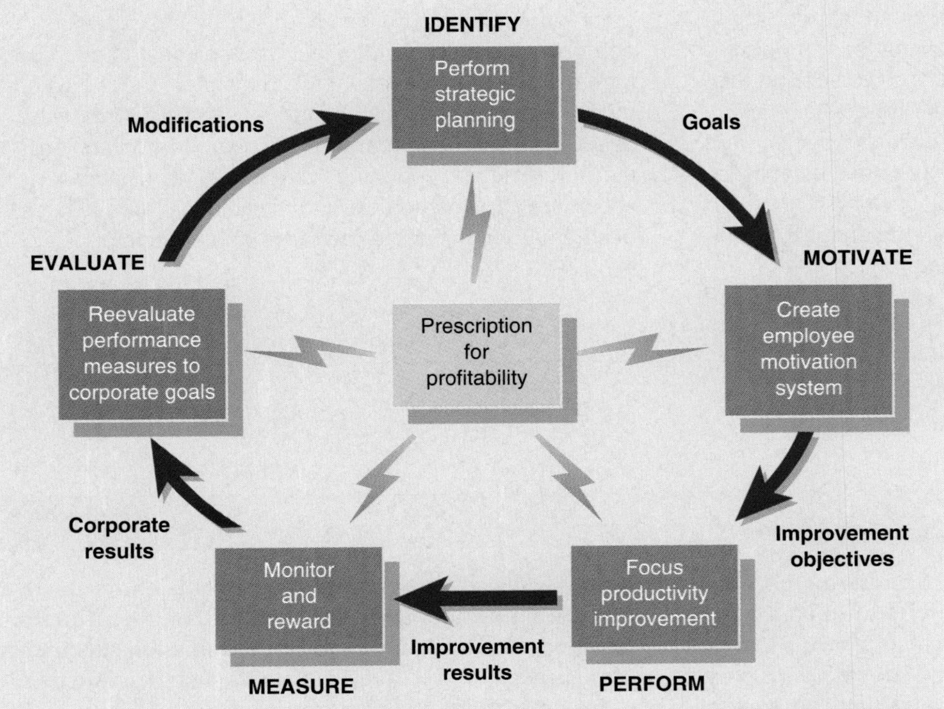

SOURCE: Dan J. Seidner and Glenn Kieckhaefer, "Using Performance Measurement Systems to Create Gainsharing Programs," *(Grant Thorton) Manufacturing Issues* (Summer 1990), p. 9. Reprinted by permission from Grant Thorton's *Manufacturing Issues*. Copyright 1990.

The cycle of maintaining this system should be a continuous process. When employees meet performance objectives, rewards follow, and organizational results such as growth in market share, faster throughput, and higher profits can be expected. Reevaluating the performance measurement links to the satisfaction of organizational goals completes the cycle so that it may start anew.

No single system is appropriate for all organizations or, possibly, even all responsibility centers within the same company. The measurement of performance is the measurement of people. Because people are unique and have multiple facets, the performance management system must reflect those characteristics.

REVISITING WMC Limited

http://www.wmc.com.au

Because of the importance that WMC Limited has placed on the environment, the company has separate vision and mission statements for this factor. The vision statement is "Employee pride and community respect for our environmental performance in managing resources for the future." The 1998 mission statement was: "Within five years develop a WMC employee and contractor culture that ensures continual improvement in environmental performance, manages the environmental risks and improves shareholder value while considering customer and community expectations."

The company's environmental plan links environmental management with business planning, so that environmental considerations are seen as a usual part of doing business and making business decisions. To support this, the company has established eight environmental plan objectives related to systems, eight related to people, and six related to performance. Targets have been established for and are measured against the objectives.

But, more importantly, WMC Limited management understands that these measurements are critical to the company's long-run success. Thus, WMC issues an environmental performance report in conjunction with its annual financial report. These reports include nonfinancial measurements of eco-efficiency, management environmental performance, and noncompliance incidents. All stakeholders can review this pertinent nonfinancial information about the achievement of or progress toward environmental targets and commitments. Financial information about capital and operating expenditures related to environmental control and protection is also included.

To an Australian minerals company, sound environmental performance is essential to being welcome to operate in foreign countries in the process of exploration and development. To indicate its commitment to such performance, WMC believes that its measurement of environmental accomplishments should not just be for internal use. Given the breadth and depth of its environmental measurement and reporting activities, WMC Limited should be considered as world-class in this area and be used as a benchmark for activities of other companies.

SOURCE: WMC Limited, *Environmental Progress Report 1998.*

CHAPTER SUMMARY

A firm's long-term objectives are always associated with investments and proactive efforts to enhance the company's long-run competitive position. Long-term performance measures should be designed within the firm's vision and mission statements and should assess progress toward goals and objectives. Managers should assure themselves that the persons being evaluated have the appropriate skills, equipment, information, and authority for accomplishment. Moreover, feedback on progress toward accomplishment should be provided in a timely and useful manner. Using multiple measures regarding the firm's critical success factors is more effective than using a single measure.

One useful nonfinancial measure of performance is throughput. Throughput refers to the goods or services started, completed, and sold by an organization. When throughput is increased, the company goal of making money is enhanced. Activity-based management also provides an excellent base from which to identify long-term performance measurements.

Performance measures of multinational units may be more difficult to establish than those of domestic units because of differences in taxes, tariffs, currency exchange rates, and transfer restrictions. Top management may wish to consider extending the use of qualitative performance measures because of such differences.

A balanced scorecard can help an organization assess its performance through the use of financial and nonfinancial as well as internal and external measurements. The four areas of the scorecard (financial, customer, business processes, and human resource or innovation and growth) reflect the dissimilar activities in which an organization must engage to prosper and survive.

APPENDIX 1

Developing Comprehensive Performance Indicators

10

(Appendix 1) What steps need to be taken to implement a new performance measurement system?

The following discussion is from Management Accounting Guideline 31, published by The Society of Management Accountants of Canada.[15] It provides a framework for developing a comprehensive performance measurement or indicator system.

Firms need a performance indicator system that focuses externally on the business environment and its changing demands and on market/customers and competitors as well as internally on key nonfinancial indicators (such as market penetration, customer satisfaction, quality, delivery, flexibility, and value). These measures should be used in addition to the more traditional financial measures of sales growth, profits, return on investment, and cash flows.

Performance indicators should have five dimensions: output or results information, input information, process information, quality assessment, and efficiency or productivity information. Although these indicators will vary based on the firm's needs, they are likely to include environmental, market/customer, competitor, internal business processes, human resource, and financial measures.

The following steps are necessary to effectively implement new performance indicators:

1. Recognize the need for enhanced performance indicators by identifying new critical success factors (such as changes in customer behavior patterns).
2. Ensure top management support and commitment by underlining the need for change and by involving top management in steering committees to oversee the new system's development and refinement.
3. Create an implementation team to develop a common understanding of the firm's strategies, goals, and objectives; identify obstacles to implementation; and structure the approach. Input from all functions and levels of the firm as well as customers is helpful.
4. Develop a business performance model that can put the goals, strategies, objectives, critical success factors, and performance indicators into context by viewing the firm as one stage in a value chain of suppliers, the firm, markets, and customers.

[15] Society of Management Accountants of Canada, "Management Accounting Guideline 31: Developing Comprehensive Performance Indicators," *CMA Magazine* (March 1997), p. 39. Reprinted from an article appearing in *CMA Management* (formerly *CMA Magazine*) from Management Accounting Guideline 31, with permission of CMA Canada.

5. Understand the firm's goals and strategies by subdividing them into environment, markets and customers, products and lines, technology, operations, finance, and organization/management issues.
6. Define the firm's critical success factors.
7. Assess the current performance measurement system relative to current needs, the business model, and the firm's goals, strategies, and critical success factors.
8. Determine which current measures should be eliminated: those that are redundant or overlapping and those that do not support the critical success factors.
9. Develop the performance indicator structure by consulting with different levels of management to determine what information should be tracked, how it should be tracked, how often it should be tracked, and how it will be used.
10. Establish the underlying technology (software, hardware, and telecommunications) necessary for the performance indicator system. Consider the information that is to be provided, its degree of detail, its frequency, its source, and the amount of data manipulation to occur.
11. Reevaluate the performance evaluation and reward systems to ensure that they are consistent with the new measurement system.
12. Ensure continual improvement by updating the system to reflect changes in the firm and in its external environment.

The challenge is to implement new performance measures that will contribute to the firm's success in an ever-changing business environment. Included among these challenges are:

- developing an awareness of a need for modifications;
- obtaining top management support and commitment as well as cross-functional support;
- obtaining the necessary resources to design and develop the performance indicator system;
- assuring accurate, timely, and useful data;
- linking new indicators to long-term economic value; and
- assessing the effects of the new system.

APPENDIX 2

11

(Appendix 2) What are some major areas of a manufacturing company for which performance measures and their cost drivers have been delineated?

http://www.pwcglobal.com

Performance Measurement Areas and Cost Drivers

Exhibit 20–10 is from a joint study by the Institute of Management Accountants (formerly the National Association of Accountants) and the international public accounting firm of Coopers & Lybrand LLP (now PricewaterhouseCoopers LLP). The exhibit indicates some activity cost drivers that need to be measured to determine performance in the six specified areas.

KEY TERMS

mission statement (p. 900)
performance management system (p. 917)
process productivity (p. 910)
process quality yield (p. 910)
throughput (p. 908)
values statement (p. 900)
vision statement (p. 899)

EXHIBIT 20–10

Performance Measures

PERFORMANCE MEASUREMENT AREA: DESIGN FOR MANUFACTURABILITY

Key Characteristics	Cost Drivers/Measures
Quantity and quality of engineering changes	Number of engineering changes
	Severity of engineering changes
Test results	First pass reject rate
	Materials used versus design specification
	Manufacturing skills required
Parts standardization	Number of products
	Percent common parts per product
Engineering cycle time	Lead time to engineer (design) a finished product
	Startup time from design to production
Product complexity	Number of components per finished product
	Number of manufacturing operations per finished product
	Number of tools required per finished product

PERFORMANCE MEASUREMENT AREA: ZERO DEFECTS

Key Characteristics	Cost Drivers/Measure
Product specification	Tolerances of critical components
	Historical capability of process versus current performance
Parts quality	First pass reject rate versus test results
	Units scrapped by cell
	Cell downtime due to quality problems
	Yield of finished product per raw material batch
	Units reworked by cell
Quality control checkpoints	Sampling requirements for incoming materials
	Time required for sample/test procedures
	Production time loss due to quality control procedures/queues
	Number of checkpoints
	Effectiveness—number of returned units

PERFORMANCE MEASUREMENT AREA: MINIMIZE RAW AND IN PROCESS INVENTORY

Key Characteristics	Cost Drivers/Measures
Supplier performance	Number and location of vendors
	Number/frequency of deliveries
	Lead time from order initiation to delivery
	Flexibility in order quantity, delivery and variety
Components standardization	Complexity of components
	Number of components to support total production
Market characteristics	Demand variation
	Forecast accuracy
	Availability/accuracy of information

PERFORMANCE MEASUREMENT AREA: ZERO LEAD TIME

Key Characteristics	Cost Drivers/Measures
Velocity of units through cell	Actual production time
	Queue time between operations
	Move, setup, and inspection times
	Manufacturing cycle efficiency = value-added time ÷ total time
Quality of components	Scrap percent
	Rework percent
	Yield percent
Customer service levels	Late deliveries
	On-time deliveries
	Back orders
	Cancelled orders
Complexity of flow	Mix of products
	New product introductions
	Routing required per product

(continued)

EXHIBIT 20-10

(Concluded)

PERFORMANCE MEASUREMENT AREA: MINIMIZE PROCESS TIME

Key Characteristics	Cost Drivers/Measures
Product design	Number of components
■ Complexity	Number of manufacturing procedures/steps
■ Tolerance	Required tolerance versus matching optimum
■ Materials	Maximum tolerance range per component
■ Producibility	Packaging of component versus use configuration
	Quality of components
	Availability/ease of use
	Skills necessary to meet engineering requirements
Process capabilities and limitations	Information system capabilities
	Plant layout: optimum versus current
	Work rules: percent changed

PERFORMANCE MEASUREMENT AREA: OPTIMIZE PRODUCTION

Key Characteristics	Cost Drivers/Measures
Resource limitations	Bottleneck capacity level
	Setup time
	Lot size constraints
	Labor availability, qualifications, flexibility
	Material resources (e.g., availability, lead time, quality, proximity)
	Number of distribution centers
	Number of storerooms
Demand fluctuation	Volume variations (total units produced)
	Mix changes (number and magnitude)
	Schedule changes (number and magnitude)
Configuration of plant	Plant layout (e.g., move time, move distance, number of total moves)
Information processing constraints	Information accuracy and availability
	Data accuracy in planning (routing, bills, standards)

SOURCE: C. J. McNair, William Mosconi and Thomas Norris, *Meeting the Technology Challenge: Cost Accounting in a JIT Environment* (Montvale, N.J.: National Association of Accountants, now Institute of Management Accountants, 1988), pp. 199–210. Copyright by Institute of Management Accountants (formerly National Association of Accountants), Montvale, N.J.

SOLUTION STRATEGIES

Measuring Throughput

$$\text{Manufacturing cycle efficiency} \times \text{Process productivity} \times \text{Process quality yield} = \text{Throughput}$$

$$\frac{\text{Value-added processing time}}{\text{Total time}} \times \frac{\text{Total units}}{\text{Value-added processing time}} \times \frac{\text{Good units}}{\text{Total units}} = \frac{\text{Good units}}{\text{Total time}}$$

DEMONSTRATION PROBLEM

Andrew Brown Company makes computer chips. During November 2001, managers compiled the following data:

Total chips processed	741,000
Good chips	703,950
Total hours	7,600
Value-added processing hours	2,660

Required:

a. Calculate the manufacturing cycle efficiency.
b. Calculate the process productivity.
c. Calculate the process quality yield.
d. Calculate the throughput using one ratio.
e. Confirm your answer to part (d) using the results of parts (a), (b), and (c).

Solution to Demonstration Problem

a. $$\frac{\text{Value-added processing time}}{\text{Total time}} = \frac{2{,}660}{7{,}600} = 0.35$$

b. $$\frac{\text{Total chips produced}}{\text{Value-added processing time}} = \frac{741{,}000}{2{,}660} = 279 \text{ (rounded)}$$

c. $$\frac{\text{Good chips}}{\text{Total chips produced}} = \frac{703{,}950}{741{,}000} = 0.95$$

d. $$\frac{\text{Good chips}}{\text{Total time}} = \frac{703{,}950}{7{,}600} = 93 \text{ (rounded)}$$

e. $(0.35 \times 279 \times 0.93) = 91$ chips per hour (rounded)

QUESTIONS

1. What are the benefits of a vision and a values statement to the firm?
2. How does a mission statement differ from a vision statement?
3. How do long-run objectives differ from short-run objectives?
4. Why does management need to focus on long-run performance?
5. In what four categories can nonfinancial performance measures be classified? Why is each of these categories important?
6. Why are qualitative measures sometimes difficult to use in evaluating performance?
7. According to the NAA's (now IMA's) *Statement Number 4D,* what are the two distinct advantages of using nonfinancial performance measures?
8. What advantages do nonfinancial performance measures have over financial performance measures?
9. How does development of bases for comparison of performance measures assist managers?
10. Once effectively designed, should a performance measurement system remain constant? Why or why not?
11. Why is throughput defined on the basis of goods sold rather than goods produced?
12. How can activity-based management concepts be used to design performance measures?
13. What organizational changes might be implemented if lead time to customers is established as a high-priority performance measure?
14. What difficulties are encountered in trying to measure performance for multinational firms?
15. What is a balanced scorecard and what makes it balanced?

16. "Because of its inclusion of a financial perspective, a balanced scorecard can only be used for profit-oriented companies." Is this statement true or false? Explain your answer.

17. *(Appendix 1)* Summarize the important points in the Society of Management Accountants of Canada's framework for developing a comprehensive performance measurement system.

EXERCISES

18. *(Terminology)* Match the following lettered terms on the left with the appropriate numbered descriptions on the right.

a. Balanced scorecard
b. Mission statement
c. Performance management system
d. Process productivity
e. Process quality yield
f. Throughput
g. Values statement
h. Vision statement
i. None of the above

1. An expression of how a firm's products or services meet customers' needs
2. The package of decisions regarding performance measurement and evaluation
3. An expression of a future state that is better than present
4. An expression of organizational culture
5. Relationship between total units and value-added time
6. Number of good units produced and sold within a specified time period
7. An integrated business performance measurement model
8. All endeavors helping a firm to achieve its goals
9. Good units produced and sold relative to total units

19. *(Vision statement)* The board of directors of your company has asked you to explain what a vision statement is and to devise several criteria that might be used in preparing a good vision statement. Write a brief report complying with the board's request. In your report, also explain how a well-prepared vision statement will benefit the firm.

20. *(Organizational statements)* On the Internet, find an annual report for a company having vision, mission, and values statements. How do these three statements flow from one another? How do these three statements differ?

21. *(Time perspective)* Choose a company that has either gone out of business or is currently in very poor financial condition. Research that company to investigate its history. Prepare a report on your finding, concentrating on indicators that might have provided a perspective of failure. Describe these indicators as short term or long term.

22. *(Qualitative measures)* Prepare a discussion of how you would react to and behave if you were one of Ford's top managers who was being graded on the curve. (See the chapter News Note.) Provide three perspectives, assuming you fell into each of the grade categories.

23. *(Nonfinancial performance measures)* One of the "old time" accountants in your company says that nonfinancial performance measures are not accounting and should be left for others to accumulate and evaluate. How would you respond?

24. *(Throughput)* Ben's Barn's makes pre-fab buildings and is examining its throughput. Analysis of May production revealed the following:

Good units produced and sold	12,000
Total units produced	16,000
Total processing time	288,000 hours
Value-added time	96,000 hours

a. Determine the manufacturing cycle efficiency.
b. Determine the process productivity.
c. Determine the process quality yield.
d. Determine the throughput.

25. *(Throughput)* Ishmal Cannery packs dates for worldwide shipment. The owner has asked you to analyze the cannery's throughput. You find that in June, the cannery generated the following:

Cans packed and shipped	30,000
Total cans (some defective)	37,500
Value-added processing time	12,500 hours
Total processing time	48,000 hours

a. Calculate the manufacturing cycle efficiency.
b. Calculate the process productivity.
c. Calculate the process quality yield.
d. Calculate the throughput using only good units and total time.
e. Verify your answer to part (d) by using your answers to parts (a), (b), and (c).

26. *(Quality performance measures)* Birmingham Metalworks manufactures iron railings for ornamental fences. Recently, the company has become much more concerned about reducing the number of flaws in its completed products. Identify some performance measures that the company could use to monitor the effectiveness of its efforts to improve product quality.

27. *(ABM and long-run performance measurement)* A consultant has just recommended that activity-based management would help the company generate much of the information necessary for long-run performance measurements. Prepare a brief report for the CEO explaining some of the ways ABM would help in long-run measurement.

PROBLEMS

28. *(Organizational statements)* You and three friends have just started a company called "Hot Stuf" that produces hot sauce. You intend to sell your product through grocery stores and on the Internet. Before you begin hiring employees, you believe that the company needs mission, vision, and values statements. Prepare these statements for the company and provide the logic behind the statements.

29. *(Long-run performance)* As the new controller of your company, you have been asked by the company president to comment on any deficiencies of the firm. After saying you believe that the firm needs long-run performance measurements, the president says that the long run is really just a series of short runs. He says that if you do a good job of evaluating these short-run performances, that the long run will take care of itself. He sees that you are unconvinced and agrees to keep an open mind if you can make a good case for measuring and evaluating long-run performance. He suggests that you prepare a report stating your case.

30. *(Performance measures)* An article entitled "New Metrics for a New Age," in the April 7, 1997 issue of *Forbes ASAP,* provided a wide variety of measurements that might help indicate corporate success.

a. Assume that you are the CEO of a company and provide basic information about this company (type of company, product, customer base, market, etc.).

b. Using the *Forbes ASAP* article as a base, select the 15 indicators that you believe would provide the best information to judge your company's performance. Explain why you selected these particular indicators.

31. *(Throughput)* Historically, Kaleidoscope Corp. has evaluated divisional performance on financial measures. Top managers are now seeking alternative measures that more accurately assess success in the activities that generate customer value. One promising measure is throughput. Management has gathered the following information on one of its larger operating divisions:

Units started and completed	60,000
Total good units completed	39,000
Total value-added hours of processing time	24,000
Total hours of divisional time	36,000

a. What is the division's manufacturing cycle efficiency?
b. What is the division's process productivity?
c. What is the division's process quality yield?
d. What is the total hourly throughput?
e. What can Kaleidoscope Corp.'s management do to raise hourly throughput?

32. *(Throughput)* Maria Rocco is concerned about the quantity of goods being produced by the Latin American Division of AutoWorld. The following production data are available for April 2001:

Total units completed	60,000
Total good units completed	47,500
Total value-added hours of processing time	15,000
Total hours of division time	56,000

Determine each of the following for this division for April.

a. What is the manufacturing cycle efficiency?
b. What is the process productivity?
c. What is the process quality yield?
d. What is the total throughput per hour?
e. If only 22,500 of the units produced in April had been sold, would your answers to any of the above questions differ? If so, how? If not, why not?
f. If Rocco can eliminate 20 percent of the non-value-added time, how would throughput per hour for these data differ?
g. If Rocco can increase quality output to a yield of 94 percent and eliminate 20 percent of the non-value-added time, how would throughput per hour for these data differ?
h. How would Rocco determine how the non-value-added time was being spent in the division? What suggestions do you have to decrease non-value-added time and increase yield?

33. *(Balanced scorecard)* You have been elected president of your university's newly chartered accounting honor society. The society is a chapter of a national organization that has the following mission: "To promote the profession of accountancy as a career and to imbue members with high ethical standards."

a. Determine the balanced scorecard categories that you believe would be appropriate for the honor society.
b. Under each category, determine between four and six important performance measures.
c. How would you choose benchmarks against which to compare your chapters to others of the national organization?

REALITY CHECK

34. An article by Alan Owen, entitled "A Measure of Their Worth," appeared in the July–August 1997 issue of *CMA Magazine*. This article discussed how BC Rail's managers tied performance measures to the company's strategic goals. Review this article and discuss the company's performance for the years since this process was implemented.

35. *(Performance measures)* As the cost of health care continues to increase, hospital and clinic managers need to be able to evaluate the performance of their organizations. Numerous articles have been written on performance measurements in health care organizations. Obtain some of these articles and prepare a report on what you believe to be the best balanced scorecard set of measures for such an organization.

36. The following is a quote from Mindy Fried at the Center for Work and Family: "The research is pretty clear that as people work over a certain number of hours, productivity goes down, stress goes up, and work isn't as good." You have taken this quote to heart and want to establish some performance measures in your accounting firm to help indicate that there is a balance by employees between work and leisure. Use all resources available to research this topic and prepare your list of performance measures. How will you benchmark these measures? How will you react to employees who are "workaholics?"

37. *A few New Orleans hoteliers reneged on promises to set aside hotel rooms for the National Football League's Super Bowl XXXI, a senior NFL executive and New Orleans tourism executives said. Tourism officials said they feared the conflict created ill will with the football league, which could make future Super Bowls more difficult to land.*

. . . According to Jim Steeg, director of special events for the NFL, several hoteliers decided to ignore the promise and sell about 400 [of approximately 15,000] rooms reserved for the NFL.

SOURCE: Stewart Yerton, "Some Hotels Stiff NFL for Rooms," *(New Orleans) Times-Picayune* (September 4, 1996), p. C1. Permission granted by The Time-Picayune Publishing Corporation.

a. Discuss the strategy of the hotels reneging on their promise to the NFL. Do you think that these hotels are considering the long-run implications of their actions?
b. Is it possible for a few hotels to hurt the larger community in which they operate? How or why?
c. Suggest an alternative strategy to the managers of these hotels.

38. Many companies are now preparing environmental, health, and safety reports for public review. Use the Internet to obtain one of these companies' reports for two consecutive periods (or more, if available).
a. What measures are being used to evaluate performance?
b. What targets have been set as comparison bases?
c. How well is the company performing?
d. Given the trend data available, do you think the company has set "stretch" targets or easily achievable targets? Discuss the rationale for your answer.

CHAPTER

21

Rewarding Performance

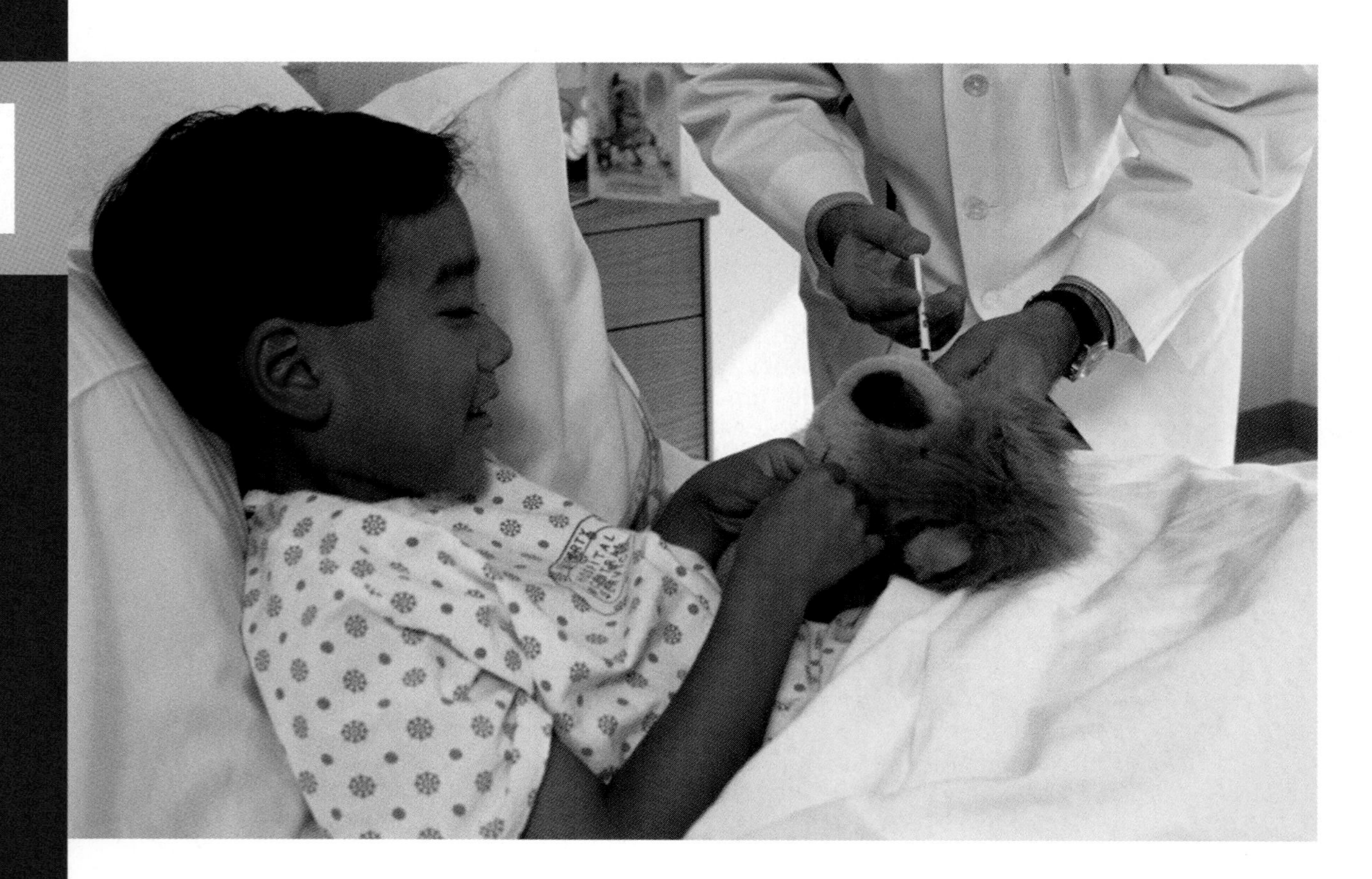

LEARNING OBJECTIVES

After completing this chapter, you should be able to answer the following questions:

1. How are employee compensation and maximization of stockholder wealth related?
2. What are the alternative means of rewarding performance?
3. Why is there a movement toward rewarding group, as well as individual, performance?
4. What are the potential positive and negative consequences of incentive pay programs?
5. Why do many financial incentive programs involve shares of, or options for, common stock?
6. Of what importance are nonmonetary rewards in motivating managers?
7. How do taxes affect the design of compensation plans?
8. Why should ethics be considered in designing a compensation package?
9. What concerns need to be addressed in developing compensation packages for expatriates?

INTRODUCING

Meridia Health System

http://www.meridia.com

Healthcare organizations that are trying to increase the productivity of their employed physicians often find that the physicians lack sufficient financial incentives and managerial skills to meet desired productivity levels. One health system in the Cleveland, Ohio, area, however, has rejuvenated the performance of its physician network by overhauling its physician compensation program and introducing effective incentives.

Since its formation through the merger of four independent hospitals in the 1980s, Meridia Health System has enjoyed a strong market position in Cleveland's eastern suburbs. Competition in the Cleveland healthcare market, however, has gradually intensified as a result of hospital consolidations, the acquisition of independent hospitals by for-profit systems, and the development of integrated delivery systems (IDS) that incorporate health plans, physician practices, and ancillary services into hospital-owned networks.

In 1992, Meridia decided that to remain competitive it had to develop a primary care physician network to form the core of an IDS. By 1995, through practice acquisitions and expansions, Meridia was operating four primary care practices employing about 40 primary care physicians. An independent company was engaged to provide billing and management services for the network.

All physicians received two- or three-year guaranteed salary and benefit packages. Salaries were based on a review of each physician's existing salary level and years of experience, as well as industry compensation surveys. Benefit packages mirrored those of Meridia's senior executives, though some were modified to fit individual circumstances. Bonuses were available for physicians who met productivity targets. Most of these targets were based on a combination of the historical production level of each individual physician and industry averages.

Meridia executives had assumed that their physician practices would continue to function as they had before they were acquired. This assumption proved faulty for several reasons. First, physician productivity declined. Second, the transition to using contracted billing and management services caused disruptions to routine practice operations. Third, new physicians recruited into the groups placed increased demands on practice resources and absorbed existing and new patient volume. Fourth, as practice sites were expanded or consolidated into new facilities, practice operations were disrupted. Patient volumes dropped in part due to practice location changes. Losses from primary care network operations were in excess of $100,000 per physician, per year.

SOURCE: Alexsandra Davis and C. Thompson Hardy, "New Compensation Model Improves Physician Productivity," *Journal of the Healthcare Financial Management Association* (July 1999), pp. 46–49.

In analyzing its problems and searching for solutions, Meridia Health Systems focused intense scrutiny on its model for evaluating physician compensation. The company determined that revisions in the compensation model were necessary to make physicians' pay more sensitive to the fortunes of the company and its patients. A performance-based pay plan was devised that resulted in some physicians receiving less pay, but that resulted in greater organizational efficiency and more sensitivity of the physicians to productivity and higher quality patient care.

The performance evaluation and reward systems in an organization are the key tools to align the incentives of workers, managers, and owners. When workers help to control costs and the bottom line increases, stockholders benefit through increased dividends and/or stock market prices. Throughout American business management literature, the expressed primary function of managers is to maximize stockholder value or stockholder wealth.

Stockholders are granted this special attention because they (acting through the board of directors) have the unique power to hire, fire, and set compensation for top managers who, in turn, can hire, fire, and set compensation for workers.[1] Alternatively, workers and managers are self-interested and would prefer to maximize their own wealth rather than that of the stockholders. Consequently, the burden of motivating employees to maximize stockholder wealth is borne by stockholders through specification of managerial pay and other performance rewards and by managers in design of the employee performance measurement and reward system.

Accounting frequently plays a primary role in defining expected performance, monitoring and measuring actual performance, and determining the quantity and quality of appropriate employee rewards. In the two preceding chapters, a variety of techniques to measure employee performance were discussed. This chapter explores the relationship of organizational plans, strategies, and performance to employee rewards as well as the tax and ethical implications of various compensation systems.

COMPENSATION STRATEGY

1 How are employee compensation and maximization of stockholder wealth related?

As noted in previous chapters, many changes (technological advances, globalization, customer and quality orientation) have occurred in business in the recent past. These changes have created problems and opportunities in establishing responsibility and rewarding individuals for organizational performance. Each organization has a unique compensation plan. A rational compensation plan will tie its component elements (organizational goals and strategies, performance measurements, and employee rewards) together into a cohesive package. The relations and interactions among these elements are shown in Exhibit 21–1. In this model, the organizational strategic goals are determined by the board of directors (the governing body representing stockholder interests) and top management. From these strategic goals, the organization's critical success factors are identified and operational performance targets are defined. Operational targets, for example, could include specified annual net income, unit sales of specific products, quality measures, customer service measures, or costs.

compensation strategy

The board of directors and top management must also decide on a **compensation strategy** for the organization. This strategy provides a foundation for the compensation plan by addressing the role compensation should play in the organization. This strategy should be made known to everyone, from the board of directors to the lowest-level worker. Many companies establish a **compensation committee** comprised mainly of members of the board of directors. The compensation committee has the responsibility of establishing compensation packages for top management and setting general compensation policies and guidelines. As the accompanying News Note indicates, shareholders may perceive a conflict of interest if the CEO serves on this committee.

compensation committee

http://www.aflcio.org
http://www.nike.com
http://www.amd.com

financial incentive

The traditional American compensation strategy differentiates among three employee groups that are compensated differently. Top managers' compensation contains a salary element and significant **financial incentives** that are provided for performance above targeted objectives. Usually these targeted objectives are specified in some financial accounting measure such as companywide net income or earnings per share. Middle managers are given salaries with the opportunity for future raises based on some—again, usually accounting-related—measure of performance such as segment income or divisional return on investment. Workers are paid wages (usually specified by union contract or tied to the minimum wage law) for the number of hours worked or production level achieved; current or year-end bonuses may arise when performance is above some specified quantitative mea-

[1] The authors use the term *employees* to refer to all of the personnel of an organization. The terms *workers* and *managers* are used to identify mutually exclusive groups of employees.

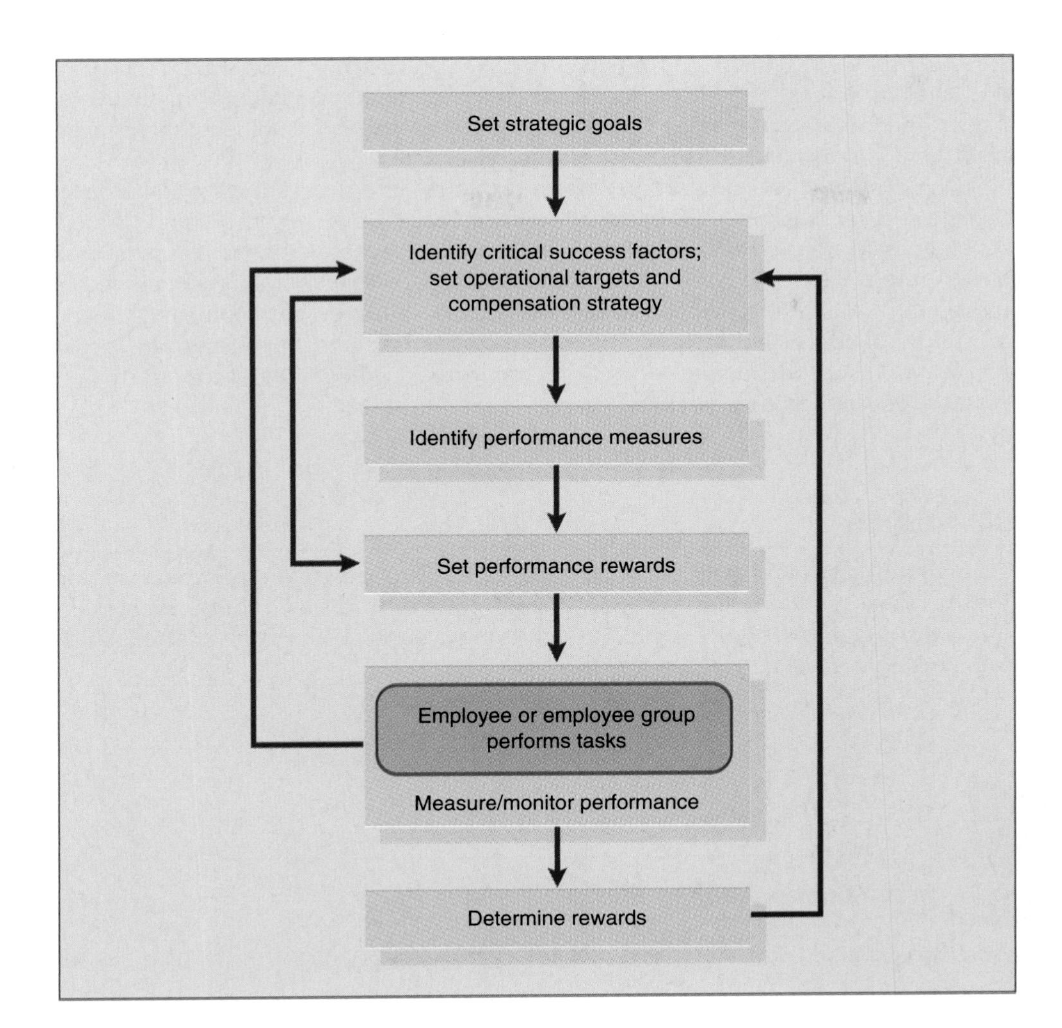

EXHIBIT 21-1

Plan–Performance–Reward Model

ETHICS NEWS NOTE

Should CEOs Help Set Their Own Pay?

At a surprising number of companies, the chief executive officer ignores an obvious conflict of interest by serving on the board's compensation committee.

The practice angers activist investors, who have long clamored for truly independent compensation committees. "This is the most egregious expression of runaway executive pay," says William Patterson, director of the AFL-CIO's Office of Investment, which advises union pension funds. "These [corporate chiefs] have no shame."

In early 1999, Mr. Patterson wrote 21 CEOs who still served on their company's pay panel, demanding that they give up their seats by the company's next annual meeting. Otherwise, "we will begin communicating with other institutional investors about appropriate next steps to restore integrity and independence to the corporate governance process." These steps might include filing a shareholder resolution or raising a ruckus at the annual meeting. Mr. Patterson received responses from a dozen chief executives, most of whom said they were leaving the pay panel or no longer served on it.

Union-backed proposals sought independent compensation committees at seven companies in 1998; they won support that ranged from 15.4% of stockholder votes at Nike Inc. to 30.9% at Advanced Micro Devices Inc., the IRRC reports.

Business chiefs with seats on pay panels scoff at such criticism, saying they simply avoid voting on their own compensation.

SOURCE: John S. Lubin, "In Whose Interest? Compensation Committees Are Supposed to be Independent; That May be Tough When the CEO Is a Member," *The Wall Street Journal* (April 8, 1999), p. R4. Permission conveyed through the Copyright Clearance Center.

sure. If provided, worker performance bonuses are usually fairly small relative to the level of wages. Significant incentive pay is generally limited to top management (and possibly the sales force)—regardless of the levels of employees who may have contributed to increased profits.

The traditional compensation system provides little motivation for lower-level managers to improve organizational performance. However, the trend in pay schemes is to tie pay to performance by providing incentive-based compensation to all employees, regardless of organizational level or function. A recent survey of more than 1,800 employers found that 51 percent said they give nonmanagement, nonsales employees compensation tied to individual or group performance.[2] As indicated in the accompanying News Note, the increasing use of pay-for-performance plans is not limited to U.S. firms.

http://www.towers.com

PAY-FOR-PERFORMANCE PLANS

2

What are the alternative means of rewarding performance?

Compensation plans should encourage higher levels of employee performance and loyalty, while concurrently lowering overall costs and raising profits. Such plans must encourage behavior essential to achieving organizational goals and maximizing stockholder value.

NEWS NOTE  INTERNATIONAL

New Fashion Trend in Europe: Variable Pay

Pay-for-performance plans are at the forefront of a trend that is sweeping across Europe according to a study by Towers Perrin, a human-resources consulting firm.

In findings from a survey of 460 companies in 13 countries, performance-based pay now dominates throughout Europe, with 58% of survey participants now giving wholly merit-based pay increases to senior executives and only a quarter still using "across-the-board" pay increases for all staffers.

"The U.S. pay-for-performance model, which was first introduced in the U.K., is now becoming common throughout Continental Europe," says the study's author, Duncan Brown, a principal of Towers Perrin in London.

The study found that European employers have been steadily increasing their use of variable pay since Tower Perrin's last survey in 1996. Then, for example, senior executives of the companies surveyed received 20% of their total compensation in variable pay, such as bonuses and stock options. In 1999, variable pay rose to 25% of total compensation among senior executives. By 2002, it is expected to climb to 31%.

Bonus plans, profit sharing, and stock-option programs are all forms of variable pay. They are being embraced by European companies as a way of linking business goals—such as a higher stock price or profit—with pay. By making a larger percentage of its total employee compensation variable pay, companies can protect themselves in the event of a business downturn and reward employees when the business is performing well.

That explains why the use of variable pay is seeping down to the ranks of ordinary workers. Based on its study, Tower Perrin forecasts that variable pay will account for more than 10% of the pay of nonmanagement employees in Europe by 2002, double the 5% of 1999.

More changes are coming: Almost a third of the study participants say they are considering removing base-pay increases altogether in favor of wholly variable systems of paying employees.

SOURCE: Julia Flynn, "Use of Performance-Based Pay Spreads Across Continental Europe, Survey Says," *The Wall Street Journal* (November 17, 1999), p. D1. Permission conveyed through the Copyright Clearance Center.

[2] Albert R. Karr, "A Special News Report about Life on the Job—and Trends Taking Shape There," *The Wall Street Journal* (April 6, 1999), p. A1.

These sweat shop workers are being paid for "performance" in that they receive pay for each unit worked on. However, given the paltry sums received, their compensation system is both unfair and unethical.

Correlation with Organizational Goals

In a pay-for-performance plan, the defined performance measures must be highly correlated with the organization's operational targets. Otherwise, suboptimization may occur and workers could earn incentive pay even though the broader organizational objectives are not achieved. More than any other goal or objective, maximization of shareholder wealth drives the design of reward systems.

Appropriate Time Horizon

A second important consideration when designing a performance-based system involves the time horizon. One recent criticism leveled at American businesses is that the measures (such as annual net income) used to monitor performance are too focused on the short run. The primary objective of American business, maximization of shareholder wealth, is inherently a long-run consideration. The message of this criticism is that short-run measures are not necessarily viable proxies for long-run wealth maximization. In particular, short-term profits may be garnered at the expense of long-term growth.

Pay-for-performance criteria should encourage workers to adopt a long-run perspective. Many financial incentives now involve shares of corporate common stock or stock options. When employees become stockholders in their employer company, they tend to develop the same perspective as other stockholders: long-run wealth maximization. Exhibit 21–2 (page 934) provides a breakdown of compensation received by some of the highest paid executives in the United States as determined in a recent survey. For many companies, a large portion of the compensation is paid in the form of stock and stock options to link the executive's incentives to those of shareholders.

Subunit Mission

Each organizational subunit has a unique mission and must possess unique competencies. Both the performance measurement system and the reward structure should be crafted with the mission of the subunit in mind. What is measured and

EXHIBIT 21–2

How America's Top Executives Are Paid

Name	Salary	Bonus	Stock-Based Compensation
Stephen M. Case America Online	$ 427,000	$ 750,000	$158,057,000
Charles Heimbold, Jr. Bristol-Myers Squibb	1,250,000	1,944,000	30,372,000
Walter V. Shipley Chase Manhattan	1,031,000	5,198,000	3,666,000
Michael S. Dell Dell Computer	788,000	2,000,000	0
Kenneth L. Lay Enron	1,267,000	3,150,000	13,095,000
Jacques Nasser Ford Motor	1,050,000	5,000,000	0
Louis V. Gerstner, Jr. IBM	1,875,000	7,500,000	32,802,000
Floyd Hall K-mart	1,300,000	690,000	0
William H. Gates Microsoft	369,000	173,000	0
Philip J. Purcell Morgan Stanley Dean Witter	775,000	8,113,000	40,051,000
William C. Steere, Jr. Pfizer	1,380,000	2,579,000	21,006,000
Timothy Koogle Yahoo!	195,000	0	7,318,000

SOURCE: "Nifty Fifty U.S. (CEO's Pay at Some of the Most Powerful Firms in the U.S.)," *Forbes* (May 17, 1999), http://www.forbes.com/forbesglobal/99/0517/0210059table.htm. Reprinted by permission of Forbes Global Business & Finance Magazine. © Forbes Global Inc., 1999.

rewarded affects the focus of the subunit employees, and the focus of the employees should be specifically on factors that determine the success of each subunit's operations. Exhibit 21–3 indicates how the form of reward is influenced by the subunit mission.

EXHIBIT 21–3

Different Strategic Missions: Implications for Incentive Compensation

	Build	Hold	Harvest
Percent of compensation as bonus	Relatively high	⟶	Relatively low
Bonus criteria	Emphasis on nonfinancial criteria	⟶	Emphasis on financial criteria
Bonus determination approach	More subjective	⟶	More formula-based
Frequency of bonus payment	Less frequent	⟶	More frequent

SOURCE: Vijay Govindarajan and John K. Shank, "Strategic Cost Management: Tailoring Controls to Strategies," *Journal of Cost Management* (Fall 1992), pp. 14–24. © 1992 Warren Gorham & Lamont. Reprinted with permission of RIA.

Consideration of Employee Age

Employee age is another important factor in designing employee incentive plans. Younger employees, for natural reasons, may have a longer term perspective than older employees who expect to retire from the firm within a few years. In designing employee incentives, this difference in perspective between younger and older employees should be given due regard.

To illustrate how age can affect decision processes, consider the case of Connie Taylor, a division manager evaluating two new projects. Each project would require an initial investment of $250,000. The projects promise to generate the following annual net returns:

Year	Project 1	Project 2
1	$(125,000)	$150,000
2	(75,000)	100,000
3	0	0
4	150,000	(50,000)
5	300,000	(150,000)
6	250,000	(20,000)
Total	$ 500,000	$ 30,000

Assume that, based on the net present value criterion, Project 1 is acceptable and Project 2 is unacceptable. Based on other criteria, however, both projects are acceptable. Further, assume that Connie is evaluated, in part, based on the return on investment (ROI) generated by her division. If Connie is two years from retirement, she would be reluctant to invest in Project 1 because she would never realize the positive ROI effects of this project. The positive benefits from Project 1 (or the negative effects of Project 2) would be realized by her successor. Connie would be more enthusiastic about investing in Project 2, because in the two years prior to her retirement, her division's ROI would be enhanced. A younger manager with a longer term time perspective is more likely to find Project 1 acceptable and Project 2 unacceptable.

Balance Group and Individual Benefits

3

Why is there a movement toward rewarding group, as well as individual, performance?

Another consideration in designing worker incentives is balancing the incentives provided for both groups (or teams) and individuals. In automated production systems, workers devote more time to indirectly monitoring and controlling machinery and are, therefore, less directly involved in hands-on production. At the same time, many organizational and managerial philosophies stress group performance and the performance of work in teams.

Incentives for small groups and individuals are often virtual substitutes. As the group grows larger, incentives must be in place for both the group and the individual. Group incentives are necessary to encourage cooperation among workers. On the other hand, if only group incentives are offered, the incentive compensation system may be ineffective because the reward for individual effort goes to the group. The larger the group size, the smaller the individual's share of the group reward becomes. Eventually, individual workers will be encouraged to shirk or take a "free ride" on the group. **Shirking** occurs when individuals perceive their proportional shares of the group reward as insufficient to compensate for their efforts. Managing the balance between individual and group rewards requires skill and a careful consideration of incentives.

shirking

Management Ownership

A final consideration in designing a performance reward system for upper management is to increase the extent of management ownership. Unlike many small firms, managers of large firms are often not owners. When the managers and owners are different groups, a new set of organizational performance issues emerges. The two groups do not automatically have compatible interests with respect to using organizational resources. Consequently, incentive systems must be designed to align the interests of the two groups.

Many companies are now mandating that top management own common stock. However, many companies do not have a similar requirement for their outside directors. As the accompanying News Note indicates, some companies are rethinking this policy.

CONSIDERATIONS IN SETTING PERFORMANCE MEASURES

4

What are the potential positive and negative consequences of incentive pay programs?

Once the target objectives and compensation strategy are known, performance measures for individual employees or employee groups can be determined based on their required contributions to the operational plan. Performance measures should, directly or indirectly, link individual actions with the basic business strategies. As discussed in the previous two chapters, employee performance is typically measured relative to some designated set of financial and nonfinancial performance standards.

Degree of Control over Performance Output

As companies shift from evaluating workers through observing their inputs to evaluating workers based on their outputs, new problems for the pay and performance relationship are created. Earlier chapters stressed the importance of evaluating managers and workers only on the basis of controllable factors. Most performance measures tend to capture results that are a function of both controllable and noncontrollable factors.

NEWS NOTE

GENERAL BUSINESS

Paying the Board of Directors

The use of stock, stock options and other incentives is commonplace to attract and retain top performers in an organization. Despite this push to keep top employees loyal and content, many companies continue to throw large amounts of cash compensation at their outside directors.

These individuals, who make the decisions that drive the organization's direction and focus, often do not have to worry about the effect their decisions will have on the company's performance. Recently, however, many companies have turned to making the compensation of outside directors dependent upon the performance of the company.

Traditionally, a director's compensation package includes cash payment for retainers and meeting fees. A stock component typically is included in the compensation package as an additional incentive, and benefit packages often are offered to those on the board.

A recent study by Pearl Meyer & Partners Inc., an executive compensation consulting firm, revealed that stock payments to outside directors in the 200 largest firms in the United States has grown three-fold from 1995 through 1999, with stock-based pay representing 60 percent of an outside director's pay.

The survey also showed that in 1999, 95 percent of companies paid at least some portion of director compensation in stock. Stock options were used by 63 percent of corporations utilizing equity pay, while "full value shares," in the form of restricted and unrestricted stock and deferred stock, were used by 78 percent of companies.

Rhoda Edelman, managing director of Pearl Meyer & Partners, said full value shares, as opposed to option grants, are the way to go in paying outside directors. This puts the directors immediately in an ownership position, while further emphasizing their responsibility to the success of the company.

SOURCE: Jeremy Handel, "Cash No Longer King," *ACA News* (February 2000), pp. 32–33.

Actual performance is a function of worker effort, worker skill, and random effects. The random effects include performance measurement error, problems or inefficiencies created by coworkers or adjacent workstations, illness, and weather-related production problems. After the actual performance is measured, determining the contributions of the controllable and noncontrollable factors to the achieved performance is impossible in many instances. Consequently, workers bear the risk of outcome effects of both types of factors. Thus, using performance-based pay systems causes workers to bear more risk than when less comprehensive input–output measurements are used to determine compensation. Efforts should be made to identify performance measures that minimize the risk borne by workers.

At the worker level, performance measures should be specific and typically have a short-run focus—usually on cost and/or quality control. Each higher level in the organizational hierarchy should include increasingly more elements related to the critical success factors under an individual's control and responsibility. Performance measures should, by necessity, become less specific, focus on a longer time horizon, and be more concerned with organizational longevity rather than short-run cost control or income.

Once the operational targets, compensation strategy, and performance measurements are determined, appropriate target rewards can be specified. These rewards should motivate individual employees to contribute in a manner congruent with the operational objectives, and employees must be able to relate their performance to the reward structure.

Incentives Relative to Organizational Level

As with performance measures, an employee's organizational level and current compensation should affect the types of rewards chosen. Individuals at different organizational levels typically view monetary rewards differently because of the relationship of pay to standard of living. Relative pay scales are essential to recognizing the value of monetary rewards to different employees. At lower employee levels, more incentives should be monetary and short term; at higher levels, more incentives should be nonmonetary and long term. The system should, though, include some nonmonetary and long-term incentives for lower-level employees and some monetary and short-term incentives for top management. Such a two-faceted compensation system provides lower-paid people with tangible rewards (more money) that directly enhance their lifestyles, but also provides rewards (such as stock options) that cause them to take a long-run "ownership" view of the organization. In turn, top managers, who are well paid by most standards, should receive more rewards (such as stock and stock options) that cause them to be more concerned about the organization's long-term well-being rather than short-term personal gains.

Performance Plans and Feedback

As employees perform their required tasks, performance related to the measurement standards is monitored. The two feedback loops in the model shown in Exhibit 21–1 exist so that any problems identified in one period can be corrected in future periods. The first feedback loop relates to the monitoring and measurement of performance, which must be considered in setting targets for the following periods. The second feedback loop relates to the rewards given and the compensation strategy's effectiveness. Both loops are essential in the managerial planning process.

Just as there are numerous ways to tie organizational performance to employee rewards, there is also a wide variety of reward plans available to organizations. The major types of compensatory arrangements in use for workers and managers are discussed next.

Worker Compensation

In addition to the recent changes in competitive focus, organizational culture, local laws, union affiliation, and political considerations will affect the choice of pay plan. For example, although the piece rate pay plan may work effectively for some U.S. businesses, such a compensation plan may not work at all in a Japanese plant. The Japanese workforce is more attuned to the group and organization than to the individual. A plan that determines worker compensation based on individual performance would clash with the Japanese culture. Also, installing a performance-based pay plan in any firm can be difficult if the plan's objectives are not clearly specified or if the organizational culture is not suited to such a plan. Even differences in labor laws among countries can affect pay plans. Exhibit 21–4 indicates how stock-based plans would have been received in various countries several years ago. As indicated in the News Note on page 932, however, the same reactions may no longer occur.

periodic compensation

The most basic of all reward plans consists of hourly, weekly, monthly, or other **periodic compensation**, which is based on time spent at work rather than on tasks accomplished. Different workers command different periodic pay rates/amounts because of seniority, skill, or education level. However, this type of compensation provides no immediate link between performance and reward. The only motivational aspects of periodic compensation are the prospects for advancement to a higher periodic pay rate/amount, demotion to a lower pay rate/amount, or dismissal. Because this pay plan provides little incentive to achieve, worker performance is monitored by superiors rather than tracked by financial records. Organizational performance is ensured through monitoring and instruction instead of the motivation of the performance/reward relationship.

Worker Pay and Performance Links

The competitive environment in many industries has undergone substantial changes that have, among other effects, led to companies using greater automation and fewer labor-intensive technologies. Also, evolving management philosophies are

EXHIBIT 21–4

Thinking about a Stock-Based Compensation Plan in that Foreign Sub?

Below are predicted reactions to the installation of a stock-based compensation plan in various parts of the world as of 1995:

Belgium Problematic. Some stock plans conflict with a government-imposed wage freeze.

Brazil Impossible. Foreign-exchange controls prohibit out-of-country stock investment, phantom stock plans are a headache.

Britain Easy. But sometimes labor unions can get in the way.

Eastern Europe Forget it. Even if you get government permission, chances are you've talked to the wrong bureaucrat.

Germany Can I get that in deutsche marks? U.S. plans suffer when the dollar is weak.

Israel Difficult. Exchange controls forced National Semiconductor to a third-party system, but plan has only scant participation.

Luxembourg Tax haven. Great place to set up a trust to administer stock plans.

Mexico May regret it. Labor laws can force a one-time stock grant into an annual event.

Netherlands No thanks. Employees may like the stock options, but they won't appreciate a hefty tax bill upfront.

Philippines Time-consuming. Requires government approval and lots of worker education.

SOURCE: Tara Parker-Pope, "Culture Clash: Do U.S.-Style Stock Compensation Plans Make Sense in Other Countries?" *The Wall Street Journal* (April 13, 1995), p. R7. Reprinted by permission of *The Wall Street Journal*,

now emphasizing the need for workers to perform in teams and groups. An interesting paradox has been created by these changes. Workers are more detached from the production function and more involved with higher technology tasks, so it is more difficult to control workers through direct oversight and supervision. These changes require firms to rely more on results-based evaluations even though identifying appropriate performance evaluation criteria is now more difficult because of the more indirect worker/production relationship. Nevertheless, the trend is to rely more on performance-based evaluation and less on direct supervision to control worker behavior. This trend is consistent with the movement to empower workers and decrease levels of supervision and layers of management.

merit pay

One common performance-based pay plan is **merit pay**, in which a pay increment is earned after achieving a specific performance level. Although merit pay typically represents a raise in the base pay that continues throughout the worker's tenure with the firm, some merit pay may expire at a future date or be made contingent on a continuing high level of performance.

contingent pay

A variety of other performance-based pay plans exists. For some workers, the basic wage may be partly replaced with a contingent pay plan. **Contingent pay** is not guaranteed like the basic wage, but is dependent on the achievement of some performance objective. The contingent pay plan adds a pay-for-performance dimension to the compensation package. The contingent pay can be a fixed amount or may vary with, for example, the level of achieved sales or profit. It can be paid in cash, stock, or another form. Also, the plan can be structured to apply to group or individual performance.

piece rate pay

At the extreme end of the performance-based pay incentive plans are **piece rate** payment arrangements wherein workers are paid a flat rate for each unit of work accomplished. Some alternatives may combine the piece rate with a basic hourly rate to guarantee workers a minimal return on their time and effort. Such combination-type piece rate plans serve to protect workers from poor judgments or errors in setting piece rates.

Promoting Overall Success

5

Why do many financial incentive programs involve shares of, or options for, common stock?

A significant problem with piece rate payment plans is their failure to provide incentives for workers to consider overall organizational success. Alternative performance-based plans exist for this purpose, many of which have the expressed goal of getting common stock into the hands of employees. One popular arrangement is profit sharing, which provides incentive payments to employees. These current and/or deferred incentive payments are contingent on organizational performance and may be in the form of cash or stock. Allocation of the total profit-sharing payment among individual employees is made on the basis of personal performance measurements, seniority, team performance, managerial judgment, or specified formulas.

stock option

stock appreciation right

In addition to profit-sharing arrangements, some firms pay employees a portion of their compensation in stock options or stock appreciation rights. **Stock options** allow the holder to purchase shares of company common stock at specified terms. These terms usually relate to price and designate the future time frame during which the stock may be purchased. **Stock appreciation rights** allow employees to receive cash, stock, or a combination of cash and stock based on the difference between a specified amount per share of stock and the quoted market price per share at some future date. In each situation, the amount of compensation cannot be determined with certainty at the date the incentive reward is received; instead, the options or rights will become more valuable if the price of the common stock rises.

Employee Stock Ownership Plan (ESOP)

Another popular profit-sharing compensation program is the **Employee Stock Ownership Plan (ESOP)**, in which investments are made in the securities of the employer. An ESOP must conform to rules in the *Internal Revenue Code,* but offers both tax and incentive advantages. Under an ESOP arrangement, the employer makes tax-deductible payments of cash or stock to a trust fund. If cash is contributed, it is used by the trust to purchase shares of the employing company's stock. The trust beneficiaries are the employees, and their wealth grows with both the employer contributions and advances in the price of the stock.

Nonfinancial Incentives

Besides various forms of monetary compensation, workers may also be motivated by nonfinancial factors. Although all employees value and require money to satisfy basic human needs, other human needs cannot necessarily be fulfilled with monetary wealth. Employees desire some compensation that satisfies their higher order social needs. For example, workers and managers will typically be more productive in environments in which they think their efforts are appreciated. Simple gestures such as compliments and small awards can be used by superiors to formally recognize contributions of subordinates. Allowing subordinates to participate in decisions affecting their own welfare and the welfare of the firm also contributes to making employment socially fulfilling. Such efforts provide assurance to employees that they are serving productive roles in the firm and that superiors are attentive to, and appreciative of, employee contributions.

MANAGERIAL COMPENSATION

6

Of what importance are nonmonetary rewards in motivating managers?

Managers are primary decision makers in organizations and are subject to less direct supervision than workers. They are more likely than workers to be evaluated and compensated based on the results achieved and the contributions made toward achieving the organization's strategic objectives. Frequently, top-level managerial compensation is directly linked to company stock price and/or to corporate earnings performance. Bonuses based on organizational performance comprise a significant portion of the income of chief executive officers in most U.S. industries.

Prior chapters discuss various incentive-compatible ways to evaluate managerial performance. For example, Chapter 19 indicates that residual income, economic value added, and return on investment are three useful financial performance measures for managers of decentralized operations. Other chapters discuss the roles of standard costing, variance analysis, and budget-to-actual comparisons in performance evaluation. Chapter 20 discusses a variety of nonfinancial indicators used as bases to assess the efficiency and effectiveness of managerial efforts. Managers will find improving these performance measures to be much more important when the reward structure is directly linked to them. "When many things are measured but only financial results are rewarded, it is obvious which measures will be regarded as most important."[3] Thus, the rewards to be provided in a performance-based compensation plan should be based on both monetary and nonmonetary, short-term and long-term measures. The mixture of monetary and long-term/short-term measures should be related to the organizational subunit's mission.

perks

In addition to the monetary benefits, managers frequently are offered a variety of perquisites, or perks, for short. **Perks** are fringe benefits provided by the employer and include items such as vacations, free child care, free parking, personal assistants or private secretaries, health care, recreational club memberships, an office with a view, or flexible work hours. Exhibit 21–5 shows a mix of CEO compensation components from a sample of countries for a typical $250 million industrial firm. Perks can be offered as an incidental benefit of the position or they can be offered as compensation for specific performance. Exhibit 21–6 indicates some popular perks that are offered to those same surveyed executives.

[3] Robert G. Eccles and Philip J. Pyburn, "Creating a Comprehensive System to Measure Performance," *Management Accounting* (October 1992), p. 44.

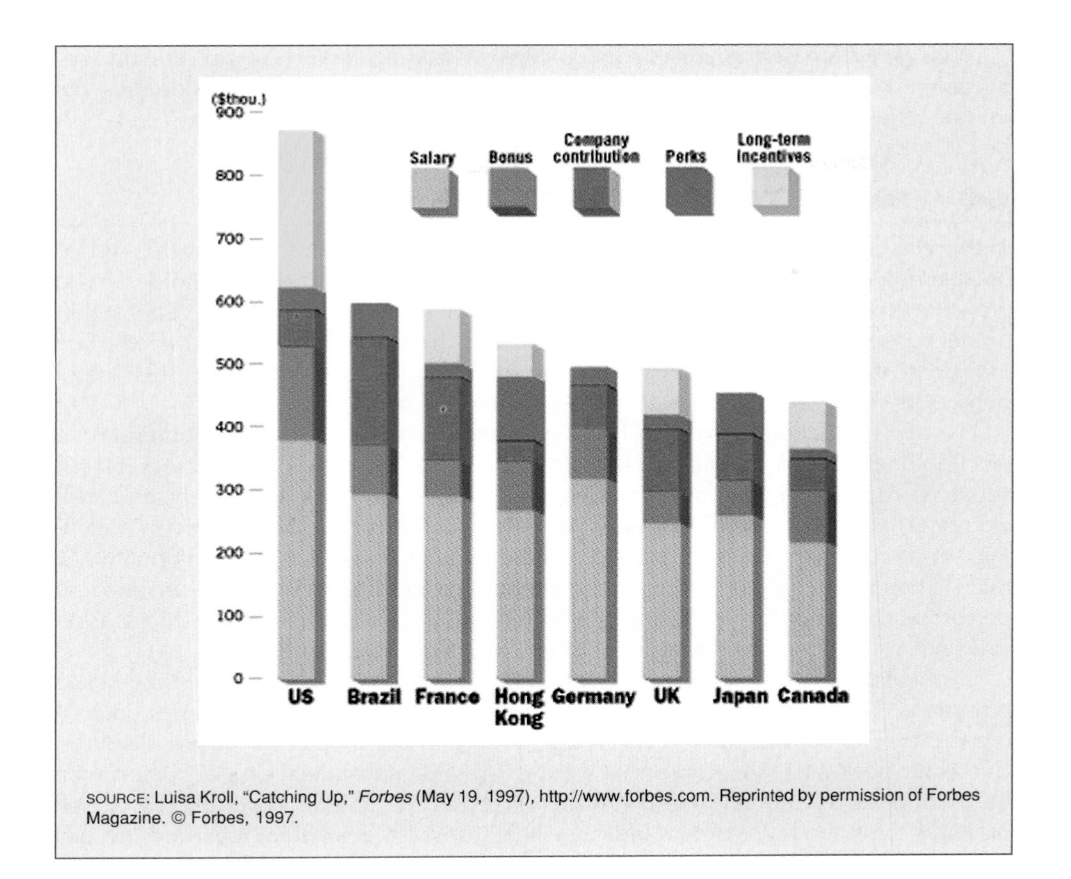

SOURCE: Luisa Kroll, "Catching Up," *Forbes* (May 19, 1997), http://www.forbes.com. Reprinted by permission of Forbes Magazine. © Forbes, 1997.

EXHIBIT 21-5

CEO Compensation Mix from around the Globe for $250 Million Industrial Firm

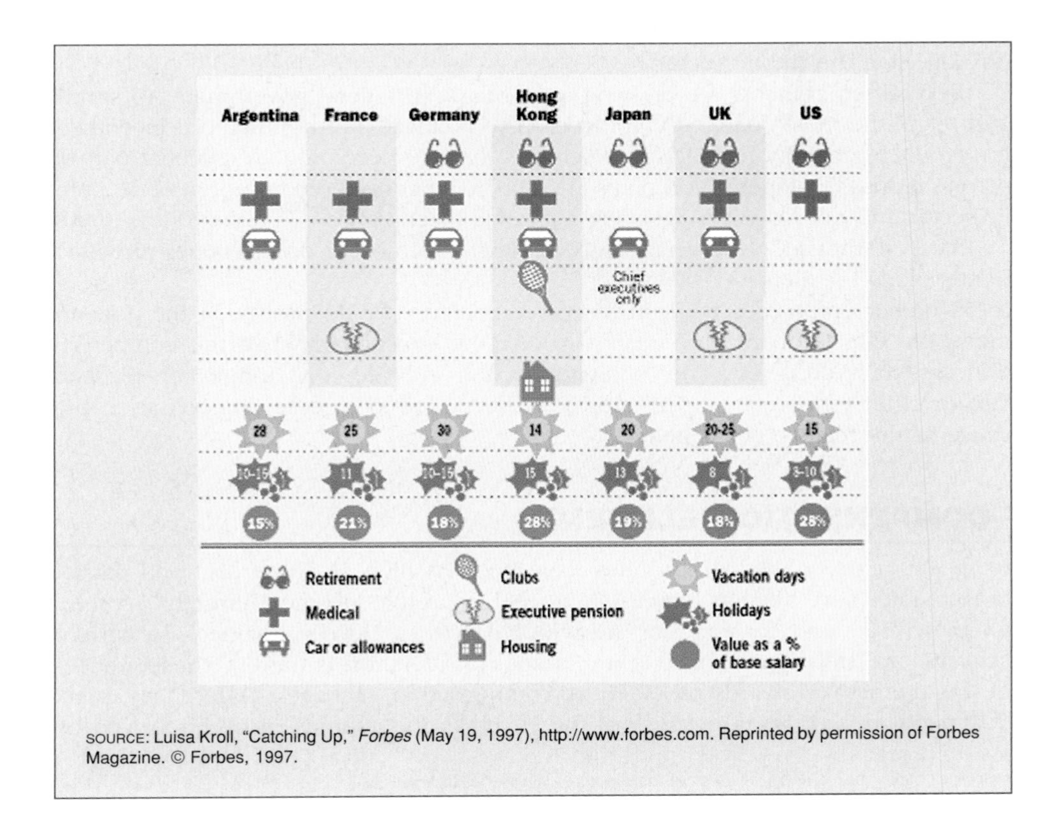

SOURCE: Luisa Kroll, "Catching Up," *Forbes* (May 19, 1997), http://www.forbes.com. Reprinted by permission of Forbes Magazine. © Forbes, 1997.

EXHIBIT 21-6

Perks and Benefits from around the Globe

The pay and performance relationships discussed earlier are not equally applicable to all types of organizations. The discussion that follows addresses the unique aspects of not-for-profit and governmental organizations.

NOT-FOR-PROFIT AND GOVERNMENTAL COMPENSATION

The preceding discussion assumed that employee performance and rewards would be determined under the oversight of a self-interested group of stockholders who are concerned about the effectiveness and efficiency of operations. The stockholders assume this oversight role because they are the residual claimants who are entitled to be paid only after all other involved parties have received their compensation—be it wages, salaries, perks, or interest payments.

Not-for-profit and governmental organizations have no direct counterpart to stockholders. No single self-interest group has the financial incentive to seek assurances that employees and managers perform their work effectively and efficiently. This one distinct factor may partially account for the horror stories, detailing out-of-control purchasing practices in the Pentagon or other governmental units, that occasionally appear in the press. Although some link exists between pay and performance in not-for-profit and governmental agencies, this relationship is typically not as direct or as strong as that existing in private companies.

The historical norm for public and not-for-profit organizations is time-based pay plans. The use of such plans has several nonperformance advantages, including the ease of predicting and budgeting costs and the avoidance of pay disputes. But as far back as 1988, employees were expressing substantial dissatisfaction with the performance evaluation and reward system in the federal government. "A poll of some 4,000 federal workers indicated that 70% of the workers regarded the pay as unfair, 74% felt that the bonus and merit pay systems were unfair, and a whopping 90% supported innovation in pay plans that would more closely link pay and performance."[4] Such complaints are not unusual in many governmental and not-for-profit entities. The trend in these organizations has been to try to tighten the linkage between pay and performance so that the best and brightest employees do not leave the public sector.

Several experiments are ongoing, particularly in federal government, to attract and retain the most qualified employees. The financial and nonfinancial incentives for producing quality products and services that are becoming an essential part of private industry compensation plans are also being considered for adoption in public-sector and not-for-profit agencies. However, according to a survey in the 1990s by PricewaterhouseCoopers, LLP, only 20 percent of not-for-profit entities provided bonus plans for their top executives.[5]

Whether employees work in the private sector, not-for-profits, or the government, the effects of income taxation should be considered when the compensation system is designed. The following section indicates that fringe benefits and certain other forms of compensation may be preferred to cash compensation because of the relative tax benefits.

TAX IMPLICATIONS OF COMPENSATION ELEMENTS

7

How do taxes affect the design of compensation plans?

In recent years, individual tax rates have been as high as 50 percent and corporate tax rates have been as high as 46 percent of taxable income. Currently, tax rates for individuals and corporations are well below these levels. But because current tax rates are still significant, one important consideration is the tax consequences of the alternative rewards provided by compensation packages. Differences in tax treatments are important because of the effect on the after-tax income received by

[4] Albert C. Hyde, "The New Environment for Compensation and Performance Evaluation in the Public Sector," *Public Personnel Management* (Winter 1988), pp. 351–358.

[5] From the no longer existing Coopers & Lybrand home page, Web site.

the employee and the after-tax cost of the pay plan to the employer. There are three different tax treatments for employee compensation: full and immediate taxation, deferral of taxation, and exemption from taxation.[6] **Tax deferral** indicates that taxation occurs at a future, rather than current, date. **Tax exemption** is the most desirable form of tax treatment because the amount is never subject to income taxation. Tax rates vary greatly around the world among cities, states, and countries. Exhibit 21–7 illustrates tax rates and the amount of after-tax compensation realized by an executive earning $650,000 in various cities in the late 1990s.

tax deferral
tax exemption

In the United States, most forms of compensation are fully and currently taxable to the employee and fully and currently deductible by the employer. For instance, wages represent income that is taxable to the employee when earned and tax deductible to the employer when incurred. The special, favorable tax treatments of deferral and exemption are provided under the tax code to encourage certain socially desirable behavior on the part of employers and employees.

For two reasons, the discussion of the tax aspects of compensation must center on the federal income tax and its effect on the employer and employee. First, although other taxes (such as payroll taxes, state income taxes, and unemployment taxes) may be affected differently by choices in reward structures, the impact of such taxes is rather minimal relative to the corporate and individual federal income taxes. Second, the impact of state income tax will vary from state to state and, thus, is beyond the scope of this text.

Fringe Benefits

When analyzing the compensation plan, employers and employees must consider the entire package—not simply one element of the package. For the employer, compensation above wages and salaries will create additional costs; for employees, such compensation creates additional benefits. Fringe benefits may include employee health insurance, child care, physical fitness facilities, and pension plans. However, different types of fringe benefits have different tax consequences.

Certain employee fringe benefits are not treated as taxable income to the employee, but are fully and currently deductible by the employer. One important type of these fringe benefits is employer-provided accident and health insurance plans. Premiums on such plans can be deducted for tax purposes when paid by the

EXHIBIT 21–7

Compensation and Global Taxation

City	Effective Tax Rate	After-Tax Amount Realized from $650,000 Pretax Income
Dubai	0%	$650,000
Hong Kong	11.24%	576,937
Singapore	22.26%	505,306
Sao Paulo	22.90%	501,163
Bombay	26.02%	480,852
Mexico City	26.28%	479,169
Seattle	32.21%	440,624
Moscow	33.94%	429,382
Zurich	37.06%	409,118
London	38.13%	402,168
New York	38.77%	397,982
Milan	40.20%	388,693
Tokyo	45.94%	351,380
Brussels	48.32%	335,889

SOURCE: Alexandra Kirkman, "A Taxing Question," *Forbes* (May 18, 1998), http://www.forbes.com. Reprinted by permission of Forbes Global Business & Finance Magazine. © Forbes Global Inc., 1998.

[6] Myron S. Scholes and Mark A. Wolfson, *Taxes and Business Strategy: A Planning Approach* (Englewood Cliffs, N.J.: Prentice Hall, 1992), p. 33.

employer, but the premium is not treated as taxable income to the employee. If each employee purchased the insurance individually, there might also be certain tax benefits. However, the tax treatment available when employees spend after-tax earnings for the services is not as preferable as the full exemption from taxation that occurs in an employer-provided plan.

cafeteria plan

The importance of various fringe benefits is directly related to an individual employee's needs and wants, which is why some companies have instituted flexible fringe benefit programs called **cafeteria plans**. These plans contain a "menu" of fringe benefit options including cash compensation and nontaxable benefits alternatives. If the employee elects to receive cash in lieu of nontaxable fringe benefits, the cash is fully taxable. However, employees who elect fringe benefits such as health care, group term life insurance, or child care receive these benefits free of tax. Flexibility is the greatest benefit of cafeteria plans because employees, based on their perceptions of the benefits' values, choose which benefits to receive.

Deferred Compensation

deferred compensation

Various forms of deferred compensation were identified earlier in this discussion. **Deferred compensation** represents pay related to current performance that will be received at a later point in time, typically after retirement. Among the diverse types of deferred compensation plans are profit-sharing arrangements, pensions, and various stock-based plans (including the ESOP). Many of these plans receive substantially identical treatment under the tax rules. The employer is allowed a current deduction for payments made to the plan, but the employee is not taxed until distributions are received from the plan. This treatment creates two significant tax benefits. First, no immediate taxable income is created for the employee by the employer's contribution. Second, no taxation of earnings on the plan occurs between the year of contribution and the year of distribution. In short, the employer's contributions and the earnings on the contributions are accorded tax-deferred treatment. When the employee reaches retirement and receives payments from the plan, all receipts are wholly taxable. However, the employee is frequently in a lower tax bracket at that time and will have enjoyed tax-free growth in the contributions over his or her working career.

Although the tax treatment to the employee of the various types of deferred compensation may not be significantly different, substantial differences exist in incentive effects. For example, the growth in the value of a pension plan may be largely unrelated to the employing corporation's stock performance. However, reward plans involving the employing company's stock have both a compensatory and an incentive element. Growth in the value of the deferred compensation depends on both the current contribution amounts and the change in the stock's value. Hence, employees are motivated to be concerned with stock performance—which is partly determined by corporate earnings. Exhibit 21–8 provides a summary of the pay elements and their relationships to the various concepts discussed in the chapter.

Because the self-serving motives of managers, workers, and stockholders frequently diverge, a proper reward structure needs to balance the interests of the three groups. Each group is entitled to an adequate return for the risks it bears and contributions it makes to the organization's success. Inevitably, ethical dilemmas will be encountered when opportunities arise for one of the three groups to gain advantage over one or both of the other groups.

ETHICAL CONSIDERATIONS OF COMPENSATION

8

Why should ethics be considered in designing a compensation package?

A phenomenon that has accompanied corporate growth is the emergence of professional managers and the dispersion of organizational ownership. In the largest corporations, no individual or group may own a large enough portion of common stock to directly influence the efforts and decisions of professional managers. This

	Link to Performance	Tied to Company Objectives	Promotes Quality	Level of Motivation	Time Focus	Taxable to Employee*	Deductible by Employer*
Hourly Wages/ Monthly Salary	Little	No	No	Low	Short term	Currently	Currently
Merit Pay	Some	Possibly	Possibly	Medium	Short term	Currently	Currently
Contingent Pay	High	Possibly	Possibly	Medium	Short term	Currently	Currently
Piece Rate	High	Possibly	No	High	Short term	Currently	Currently
Profit Sharing	Some	Yes	Yes	Medium	Depends	Depends	Currently
Stock Options/ Appreciation Rights	High	Yes	Yes	Medium	Long term	Deferred	Depends
ESOPs	High	Yes	Yes	Medium	Long term	Deferred	Currently
Perks	Some	Possibly	Possibly	Medium	Short term	Depends	Currently
Health Insurance	Little	No	No	Low	Short term	Exempt	Currently
Cafeteria Plan	Little	Possibly	Possibly	Medium	Depends	Depends	Currently
Pensions	Some	Possibly	Possibly	Medium	Depends	Deferred	Currently

*Subject to proper compliance and to potential regulatory changes.

EXHIBIT 21-8

Summary of Pay Plans

circumstance gives top managers greater discretion in operating the business and may also allow them to feel insulated from stockholders and their desires. Some observers argue that this atmosphere of discretion and insulation may be used to the managers' benefit rather than to the stockholders'. A number of ethical issues need to be resolved in this new millennium with regard to organizational governance and compensation of workers and managers.

Organizational Governance

Some argue that laws protecting the rights of stockholders failed to evolve with the dispersion of corporate ownership in the United States. Further, stockholder interests have become more diverse as institutional traders (such as pension funds) have moved into the capital markets along with individuals and industrial firms. Institutions have historically been passive investors and have not been diligent in voting their shares or monitoring managerial performance. Thus, professional managers have become less sensitive to stockholder concerns and have occasionally forgotten a manager's primary duty is to act in good faith for the organization.

Role of Capital Markets

Under these circumstances, the capital markets have assumed an important role in ensuring that management teams are disciplined in their use of corporate resources.

For example, partly as a response to ineffective, entrenched management groups, the 1970s and 1980s were witness to many attempted and successful hostile takeovers. In a **takeover**, an outside or inside investor acquires managerial control of a corporation by acquiring enough common stock and stockholder votes to control the board of directors, and thereby control management. The adjective *hostile* (as opposed to *friendly*) indicates that the takeover is not welcomed by management and frequently indicates that one objective of the takeover is to replace management.

takeover

Raider is a pejorative term used to describe a firm or individual who specializes in hostile takeovers. Raiders commonly identify firms as takeover targets when those firms are believed to be undervalued because managers are not acting in the stockholders' best interests. For example, managers of some conglomerates could increase stockholder value by selling pieces of the conglomerate that are not synergistic with other pieces.

raider

Takeovers can have either positive or negative effects on existing shareholders and employees, depending on the acquiring firm's objectives and the actions taken by the management of the target firm. A takeover can represent an attempt to steal value from the existing managers and workers; alternatively, it can represent an effective mechanism to revitalize an organization plagued by ineffective management. In either case, managers have often been permitted to include certain elements in their compensation packages that allow a retention of power in the face of a hostile takeover.

One compensation device that has helped discourage takeover attempts and protect managers is the **golden parachute**, which is a benefits package payable to incumbent managers if those managers are terminated following a successful hostile takeover (or in some cases a friendly merger). Both the ethical and incentive effects of golden parachutes are difficult to assess. Some proponents argue that golden parachutes serve stockholder interests because "top managers are free to devote their attention to serving the interests of existing stockholders in the face of a takeover threat."[7] These parachutes are viewed as providing managers with financial protection that will keep them unbiased in their actions, regardless of the outcome.

golden parachute

However, critics view the golden parachute as a means for entrenched managers to protect themselves in the event they are ousted. Proponents of this perspective are offended by the notion that managers who mismanage and create the conditions that originally attracted a takeover effort should profit by a takeover designed to remove those same managers for inept performance.

Golden parachutes also have taxation issues. When these devices were first introduced, corporations were allowed to deduct the payments as normal business expenses. Such deductibility was affected significantly by the 1984 Deficit Reduction Act, which added a 20 percent excise tax on amounts received by an executive that are in excess of three times a five-year average salary. Although many companies have agreed to pay this tax as part of a manager's severance package, a corporate deduction is disallowed for the excess payment.

Compensation Differentials

A major issue of discussion and contention involves perceptions of disparity between the pay of ordinary workers and top managers. Plato argued that no one should earn more than five times the income earned by the lowest-paid worker. In the early 1900s, however, J. P. Morgan stated that the differential should be no more than 20 times. Today, there are numerous examples of CEOs earning many times the pay of the average worker. The accompanying News Note provides more information on the contrast between upper-management earnings and the pay realized by lower-level workers.

http://www.dismal.com
http://www.continental.com

[7] Bob L. Sellers, "Bankers Discover the Golden Parachute," *Bankers Monthly* (June 1988), p. 54.

ETHICS  NEWS NOTE

What Would Plato Think?

Everyone knows that Internet entrepreneurs and Wall Street wizards have seen their salaries zoom during the current economic expansion. But what about everybody else?

The answer isn't very encouraging. According to data prepared by Dismal Sciences, an economic consulting firm in West Chester, Penn., workers in many occupations have seen wage and salary gains so small since the economic expansion began in 1991 that they just barely kept up with inflation.

Out of 129 common occupations tracked by Dismal Sciences, which uses data provided by the Labor Department, 24 saw wage declines after adjusting for inflation. Dismal Sciences figures that inflation, as measured by the consumer price index, rose 22.3% between 1991 and 1999. So workers whose salaries rose less than that amount lost ground.

But the story isn't as simple as widely assumed. Yes, wages for low-skilled workers in service industries, including cashiers and restaurant workers, languished. Average wages for hotel desk clerks were $15,520 in 1999, down about 3.6% from $16,100 in 1991 before adjusting for inflation.

But some high-skilled workers lost out, too. Consider airline pilots. Their salaries remain high relative to other professional workers, but average wages for the group declined to $78,880 in 1999 from $79,900 in 1991. "We've been playing catch-up ever since" corporate restructurings in the 1980s and early 1990s drove pilots' wages down 38%, says James Moody, a spokesman for the Independent Association of Continental Pilots, a union for Continental Airline's pilots. More recently "we've caught up," he adds, noting pilots recently agreed to a contract that significantly boosted salaries.

The boom hasn't been particularly kind to government employees, who until recently have been held back by fiscally conservative state and local governments. Law-enforcement professionals' wages grew at about the rate of inflation, 22.5%, to $37,540, and firefighters were barely better, notching a 22.8% increase to $36,980.

SOURCE: Adapted from Patrick Barta, "The Longest Boom/The American Worker: Rises in Many Salaries Barely Keep Pace with Inflation—Data Show Some Wages Have Even Fallen Despite Economic Boom," *The Wall Street Journal* (February 1, 2000), p. A2.

A new, major conflict between workers and managers surfaced in the 1990s. As more bonus plans of upper managers were revised to make them more sensitive to stockholder issues, top managers became more aggressive in controlling costs to generate profits. Simultaneously, technological advantages allowed firms to increase their productivity; that is, generate more output using fewer workers. These two forces combined to create an historically rare circumstance: firms reporting record levels of profits while they concurrently fired hundreds or thousands of workers. Thus, as top executives were receiving record levels of pay, many average workers were losing their jobs. The salary differentials between workers and CEOs are often created by a type of self-fulfilling prophecy caused by the board of directors. Although it is the job of the board of directors to protect the interests of stockholders, the composition of boards is usually split between outsiders and insiders. Insider directors may be officers of the corporation and naturally identify more with the management group than the owners. Accordingly, these directors are sympathetic with the manager's position in stockholder/manager conflicts.

Oftentimes, a company's board of directors will survey a group of similar organizations to determine the "average" compensation for an executive. If the company's executive appears to be underpaid, the board will increase his or her compensation. Therefore, the next time the survey is performed, the average will have been increased—regardless of managerial performance. Such indiscreet consumption of organizational resources can cause common stock prices to decline and can undermine the stockholder value maximization goal.

Thus, the greatest ethical dilemmas involve circumstances that pit the welfare of employees against those of stockholders or the welfare of managers against the welfare of workers. Only if there is a perception of equity across the contributions and entitlements of labor, management, and capital will the organization be capable of achieving the efficiency to compete in global markets.

GLOBAL COMPENSATION

What concerns need to be addressed in developing compensation packages for expatriates?

expatriate

As more companies engage in multinational operations, compensation systems must be developed that compensate expatriate employees and managers on a fair and equitable basis. **Expatriates** are parent-company and third-country nationals assigned to a foreign subsidiary or foreign nationals assigned to the parent company. Relocating individuals in foreign countries requires consideration of compensation. A fair and reasonable compensation package in one locale may not be fair and reasonable in another. An early 1990s survey of 45 multinationals indicated that every respondent considered differing pay levels, benefits, and perks as one of the biggest problems in developing an international workforce.[8]

The compensation package paid to expatriates must reflect labor market factors, cost-of-living considerations, and currency fluctuations as well as give recognition to tax consequences. Typically, an expatriate's base salary and fringe benefits should reflect what he or she would have been paid domestically. This base should then be adjusted for reasonable cost-of-living factors. These factors could be quite apparent (such as obtaining housing, education, and security needs similar to those that would have been obtained in the home country or compensating for a spouse's loss of employment) or they could be less obvious (such as a need to hire someone in the home country to care for an elderly relative or to handle real estate investments).

Because expatriates have a variety of monetary needs, these individuals may be paid in the currency of the country in which they reside or in their home currency or a combination of both. Frequently, price-level adjustment clauses will be built into the compensation system to counteract any local currency inflation or deflation. But, regardless of the currency makeup of the pay package, the fringe benefits related to retirement must be related to the home country and should be paid in that currency.

Exhibit 21–9 provides a recent summary of flexible benefits provided by European companies to their expatriates. These data were obtained from a survey of more than 270 of Europe's leading business organizations.

Income taxes are important in the compensation package of expatriates because they may pay taxes in the local country, home country, or both. Some countries (such as the United States and Great Britain) exempt expatriates from taxation on a specified amount of income earned in a foreign country. If a tax treaty exists and local taxes are paid on the balance of the nonexempt income of expatriates, such taxes may be credited against the expatriate's home nation income taxes. Regardless of how the package is ultimately determined, an ethical company will make certain that the system is as fair as possible to all employees involved and that it is cost beneficial and not an administrative nightmare.

Tying compensation to performance is essential because everyone in business recognizes that what gets measured and rewarded is what gets accomplished. Businesses must focus their reward structures to motivate employees to succeed at all activities that will create shareholder and personal value. In this highly competitive age, the new paradigm of success is to provide quality products and services at a reasonable price while generating a reasonable profit margin. Top management compensation has traditionally been tied to financial measures of performance; more and more companies are beginning to tie compensation to nonfinancial performance measures.

[8] Organizational Resources Counselors Inc., "Global Headaches," cited in *The Wall Street Journal* (April 21, 1993), p. R5.

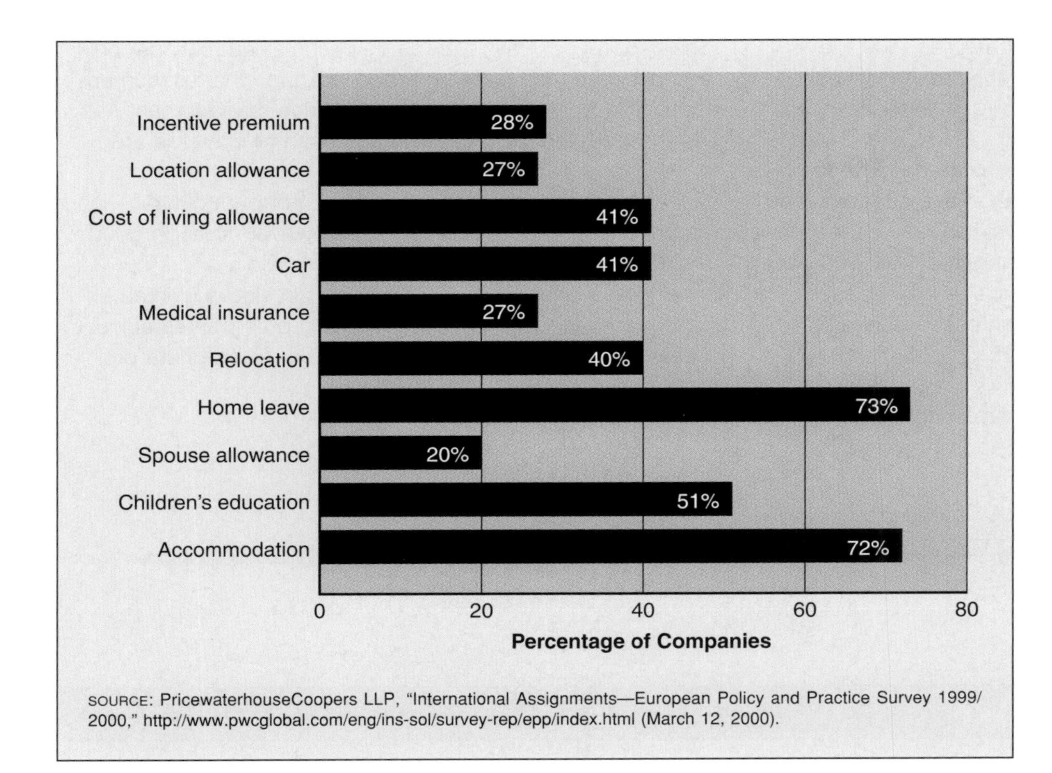

SOURCE: PricewaterhouseCoopers LLP, "International Assignments—European Policy and Practice Survey 1999/2000," http://www.pwcglobal.com/eng/ins-sol/survey-rep/epp/index.html (March 12, 2000).

EXHIBIT 21-9

Benefits Provided by European Companies to Their Expatriates

REVISITING Meridia Health System

http://www.meridia.com

Meridia implemented many changes to end its operating losses and achieve profitability. For example, the company placed a moratorium on physician recruitment and practice acquisitions. A practice management and billing system was acquired and implemented internally. In addition, the practice administrative staff was restructured and augmented, with the hospital system's human resource and accounting departments assuming expanded responsibilities for network operations. But, the biggest changes were made to the compensation model for physicians. The system established a budget reduction target for physician compensation of approximately $500,000, roughly 14 percent of current compensation levels.

The system began by formally establishing a physician compensation task force composed of all its physician group presidents, additional physician representatives, and representatives from Meridia's practice management, human resource, and finance and accounting staffs.

[It was agreed that] compensation would vary from physician to physician and that receipt of historical compensation levels could not be guaranteed. Multilevel incentives were needed to demonstrate to the physicians that, as employees, they are accountable not only for their individual activities but also for the effect of those activities on group and network results.

To determine physician compensation, the network reviews each physician's productivity during the most current 12-month period and determines the calculated [cash] collections he or she generated. From this amount, overhead is deducted to arrive at the physician's total budgeted salary. The physician then is paid 100 percent of this amount for the next six months. If, at the end of six months, the physician has fallen below his or her targeted productivity level, the physician's salary is adjusted downward to a maximum 35 percent reduction. If the physician's productivity level has been above the target, he or she receives a bonus. The bonus is put into escrow, if the physician wishes, to use to supplement his or her income should the physician's earnings decrease in the future.

Following approval of the plan, all physicians began to receive monthly reports that showed their current production and what their compensation would be under the new plan compared with their current salary. The group presidents were responsible for helping the physicians interpret the results and develop strategies to achieve their compensation goals. Administration committed to providing accurate reports of practice results within three working days of the end of the month.

Results of the new compensation plan have been positive. In the first year, 25 physicians were compensated under the new plan: 13 of these physicians exceeded the budget target for their practices, generating $400,000 over budget in revenues. Increases in practice productivity ranged from 10 to 25 percent. Patient encounters also increased by 6,000 visits among the 25 physicians on the plan.

Actual network overhead costs are shrinking, and the relationship between the physicians and administration has improved. Physician participation in educational programs on topics such as billing, coding, chart documentation, clinical protocols, and utilization management has improved, and most importantly, practice patterns are changing for the better.

Meridia's compensation plan is not perfectly fair—no compensation plan ever will be. However, through good faith negotiations and compromise, Meridia and its primary care physicians were able to develop a workable compensation system that is helping both parties achieve their mutual goals of high-quality care, appropriate productivity, and operating efficiency.

SOURCE: Alexsandra Davis and C. Thompson Hardy, "New Compensation Model Improves Physician Productivity," *Journal of the Healthcare Financial Management Association* (July 1999), pp. 46–49.

CHAPTER SUMMARY

In American industry, corporate stockholders play a unique role. Stockholders do not receive benefit from their investments until all other parties have been paid for their contributions. For bearing this risk, stockholders have the right to establish the contributions to be made and rewards to be received by the corporation's employees.

Although maximizing stockholder value is the maintained objective of profit-oriented corporations, employees are not naturally concerned with stockholder welfare. Thus, incentives must be provided to employees to motivate them to maximize their own wealth while concurrently maximizing that of the stockholders.

In the past, compensation was often based solely on individual performance and short-run, financial results. Because of operational changes and shifts in managerial philosophies, performance measurements and their related rewards now encompass group success, nonfinancial performance attributes, and long-run considerations. Some of the rewards provide short-run satisfaction (merit pay and bonuses), whereas others provide long-run satisfaction (common stock ownership).

Pay plans are available that involve current compensation, deferred compensation, and perks. Three important dimensions of pay plans are incentive effects, tax effects, and ethical considerations. Incentive effects vary from plan to plan. The periodic pay plan is the least effective in directly motivating employees to perform and provides the weakest link between performance and reward. At the other extreme, the piece rate pay plan provides a direct link between the work accomplished and the employee reward, as long as it promotes quality and group cooperation.

Not-for-profit and governmental entity employees have historically been dissatisfied with their compensation plans. Some of these organizations are now attempting to strengthen the association between compensation and performance to encourage retention of high-quality employees in public-sector careers.

Tax benefits vary among reward structure types. For the employee, rewards may be fully and currently taxable, tax deferred, or tax exempt. Although regular pay is generally fully and currently taxable, certain employer-provided fringe benefits are tax exempt to employees while providing current deductions for employers. Additionally, some elements of incentive compensation plans can be structured to defer taxation.

In designing reward structures, consideration should be given to ethical questions. Three changes that have influenced the power structure in the corporate world are the rise of professional managers, dispersion of stock ownership, and extensive involvement of institutional investors in capital markets. Additionally, some top managers' compensation grossly exceeds pay to ordinary workers. Such excesses can be counterproductive, causing a demoralizing effect within the firm and, ultimately, the failure to succeed in maximizing long-term stockholder wealth. Additional stress between management and workers is being created by employee layoffs that are driven by management's pursuit of higher profits. These situations create ethical issues that should be considered when establishing a compensation strategy that will ensure fairness, effectiveness, and efficiency in an organization.

KEY TERMS

cafeteria plan (p. 944)
compensation committee (p. 930)
compensation strategy (p. 930)
contingent pay (p. 939)
deferred compensation (p. 944)
Employee Stock Ownership Plan (ESOP) (p. 939)
expatriate (p. 948)
financial incentive (p. 930)
golden parachute (p. 946)
merit pay (p. 939)
periodic compensation (p. 938)
perks (p. 940)
piece rate pay (p. 939)
raider (p. 946)
shirking (p. 935)
stock appreciation right (p. 939)
stock option (p. 939)
takeover (p. 946)
tax deferral (p. 943)
tax exemption (p. 943)

SOLUTION STRATEGIES

The design of an effective reward structure depends heavily on each organization's unique characteristics. It is impossible to design a generic incentive model that would be effective in a variety of firms. However, affirmative answers to the following questions provide guidance as to the applicability of a proposed incentive and reward plan for a particular organization.

1. Will the organizational objectives be achieved if the proposed compensation structure is implemented?
2. Is the proposed structure consistent with organizational design and culture, and management philosophy?
3. Are there reasonable and objective performance measures that are good surrogates for the organizational objectives and subunit missions?
4. Are factors beyond employee/group control minimized under the performance measures of the proposed compensation structure?
5. Is there minimal ability of employees to manipulate the performance measurements tied to the proposed compensation structure?
6. In the light of the interests of managers, workers, and stockholders, is the proposed reward structure fair and does it encourage and promote ethical behavior?
7. Is the proposed reward structure arranged to take advantage of potential employee/employer tax benefits?
8. Does the proposed reward structure promote harmony among employee groups?
9. Is there an adequate balance between group and individual incentives?

QUESTIONS

1. How are organizational strategies linked to managerial reward structures?
2. Why would an effective compensation strategy treat top managers, middle managers, and other workers differently?
3. The trend in American business is away from automatic pay increases and toward increased use of incentive compensation plans. Why has this trend developed?
4. If worker performance measures used in a pay-for-performance plan are not highly correlated with corporate goals, what is the likely result for the organization? For the workers?
5. How does the time perspective of a performance-based plan affect the selection of performance measures?
6. Why should different missions for two subunits result in different performance reward structures for the managers of the two subunits?
7. Why should worker age be taken into account when designing performance-based pay systems?
8. If a firm offers substantial group-level performance incentives, but no individual performance incentives, how might workers respond?
9. Why are performance-based worker evaluations riskier for workers than evaluations based on direct observation by superiors?
10. Why are additional performance measurement and reward issues created when managers are not shareholders in the firms they manage?
11. How do performance-based rewards create risk for the managers and employees who are so evaluated?
12. How is feedback used in a performance-based reward system?
13. Identify the more important differences between periodic compensation and contingent compensation. Why do you believe these to be important?
14. Why is piece rate pay the extreme form of a performance-based pay system?
15. Many pay structures involve both cash compensation and stock-based compensation. Why do firms want employees to be holders of the firm's common stock?
16. How is the mix of financial and nonfinancial, and short-term and long-term, rewards affected by the mission of an organizational subunit?
17. What are perks? What are the advantages associated with the use of perks in rewarding performance?
18. Why must reward structures in not-for-profit and governmental organizations be structured differently than those for profit-oriented firms?
19. Why must income taxation be taken into account in designing a reward system? What are the alternative tax treatments of the various compensation alternatives?
20. Why is flexibility the distinguishing characteristic of cafeteria plans? Why is flexibility important?
21. What are raiders? What positive and negative roles are served by raiders in capital markets?
22. What is a golden parachute? What are the alternative explanations for the existence of such plans?
23. What are some of the important equity issues in designing reward structures? Why is the achievement of equity in the reward structure important?
24. For global enterprises, what are the additional concerns in designing a reward system, relative to single-country operations?

EXERCISES

25. *(Terminoloy)* Match the following lettered terms on the left with the appropriate numbered descriptions on the right.

a. Cafeteria plan
b. Compensation committee
c. Deferred compensation
d. Expatriate
e. Piece rate pay
f. Shirking
g. Stock appreciation right
h. Stock option
i. Tax deferral
j. Tax-exempt income

1. A right for the holder to purchase common shares
2. A menu of fringe benefit options
3. Income that is taxed later rather than currently
4. Compensation contingent on increases in stock price
5. Free-riding
6. Income that is not subject to tax
7. Group that sets pay for CEO
8. Pay for current performance to be received in the future
9. A specific type of contingent pay plan
10. A foreign national assigned to the parent company

26. *(Characteristics of alternative pay plans)* For each of the following pay plan alternatives, indicate whether it provides a high (H) or low (L) level of motivation; whether the time focus is short term (S) or long term (LT); and whether there is a strong (ST), weak (W), or moderate (M) link with employee performance.

a. Periodic pay plan
b. Cafeteria plan
c. Pension
d. ESOP
e. Profit sharing
f. Merit pay
g. Contingent pay
h. Piece rate pay
i. Stock option
j. Perks

27. *(Pay plan and suboptimization)* Larry Smith is a division manager of Carroll Manufacturing Inc. Mr. Smith is presently evaluating a potential revenue-generating investment that has the following characteristics: An initial cost of $1,000,000 and net annual increase in divisional income before consideration of depreciation:

Year 1	$100,000
Year 2	150,000
Year 3	190,000
Year 4	800,000
Year 5	800,000

The project would have a five-year life with no salvage value. All assets are depreciated according to the straight-line method. Mr. Smith is evaluated and compensated based on the amount of pretax profit his division generates. More precisely, he receives an annual salary of $300,000 plus a bonus equal to 2 percent of divisional pretax profit. Before consideration of the above project, Mr. Smith anticipates that his division will generate $2,000,000 in pretax profit.

a. Compute the effect of the new investment on the level of divisional pretax profits for years 1 through 5.
b. Determine the effect of the new project on Mr. Smith's compensation for each of the five years.

(continued)

c. Based on your computations in part (b), will Mr. Smith be hesitant to invest in the new project? Explain.

d. Would upper management likely view the new investment favorably? Explain.

28. *(Internet exercise)* Executive Alliance is a firm that specializes in designing executive compensation services. Find the home page of this company and review the services it offers. Assume that you are on the board of directors of a midsize manufacturing company. Discuss how you might use the services of a firm such as Executive Alliance to develop your firm's compensation strategy.

29. *(Internet exercise)* National Center for Employee Ownership is a nonprofit organization that distributes information regarding employee ownership of businesses. Review the materials provided on the home page of this organization. Assume that you work for a company that is about to introduce an incentive stock option plan for its employees. Prepare a report in which you present to your company's top executives a strategy as to how materials from this organization could be used to introduce the idea of stock ownership to your employees.

30. *(Internet exercise)* Find the home page of Columbia/HCA Healthcare Corporation. This company is one of the United States' largest healthcare providers. Review the information provided by the company on its home page. Assume that you are a top executive of Columbia and that you have been charged with designing a compensation system for the doctors and nurses employed by the firm. Describe the major concerns that you would have in designing the compensation system and the major features you would incorporate in the compensation system.

31. *(Incentives and rewards)*

Why would anybody who runs a hot Internet start-up firm that's about to go public choose to get a fat salary, and not just wait for the usual stock windfall after the offering?

Why not, when you can get both?

To the consternation of many venture capitalists, potential investors and executive recruiters, that's exactly what has happened at Digital Entertainment Network Inc.

http://www.den.net

The company, one of the first pure-entertainment Internet start-ups that has filed for an initial public stock offering, has the Internet world buzzing about the huge, Hollywood-style salaries the company is paying to its top executives, alongside stock and options grants.

SOURCE: Peter Gumbel, "Deals & Deal Makers: Start-Up's High Salaries Raise Eyebrows—Internet Firm DEN's Pay Doesn't Follow Equity Path," *The Wall Street Journal* (Nov. 5, 1999), p. C1. Permission conveyed through the Copyright Clearance Center.

a. As an investor in this start-up enterprise, how would you interpret the payment of a large salary in addition to stock and options to the top executives?

b. What changes in compensation structure would you make in this firm if you were given the opportunity?

32. *(Pay plan, age, and suboptimization)* Big Green Inc. has operations in 13 states. Big Green is in the business of growing soybeans and processing the beans into two products: soybean oil and soybean meal. These products are then sold for various commercial uses. Operations in each state are under the control of an autonomous state manager whose performance is evaluated (in large part) based on the magnitude of annual profit. State managers typically receive an annual bonus equal to 1 percent of net state profits. The manager of North Carolina operations is Beano DuMars. Beano has just turned 63 years old and has been with Big Green for 39 years. He would like to sell his existing bean crusher and purchase a new, technologically superior one. To evaluate the feasibility of such a move, Beano's controller prepared the information presented below. This information has created a tremendous dilemma for Beano.

Incremental cost of the new crusher	$1,000,000
Expected remaining life of the old crusher	5 years
Expected life of the new crusher	5 years
Expected effect of the new crusher on net profit for the next 5 years:	
Year 1: Decrease in operating costs	$ 300,000
Loss on disposal of old crusher	(750,000)
Net decrease in profit	$ (450,000)
Year 2: Net increase in profit	200,000
Year 3: Net increase in profit	200,000
Year 4: Net increase in profit	255,000
Year 5: Net increase in profit	300,000

a. Assume Beano expects to retire when he reaches age 65. Compute the effect of purchasing the new crusher on Beano's divisional profit and his compensation over his remaining career with Big Green.

b. If Beano had just turned 60 rather than 63, what would be the effect of purchasing the new crusher on Beano's compensation over his remaining career?

c. Is Beano's age likely to be an important factor in his decision regarding the purchase of the new crusher?

d. Would Beano's superiors prefer that he purchase the new crusher? Explain.

33. *(Performance measurement)* You have just reviewed a proposal issued by the College of Business at your university. The proposal is about the methods to be used for evaluating the performance of, and rewarding of, professors. The principal provision of the proposal is to change the measures for evaluating performance of professors to emphasize achievements in research and professional service and to deemphasize teaching achievements. Another important provision is to more tightly link merit pay raises and promotion to the performance measurements.

Assume you have been nominated to provide the student perspective in responding to this proposal. Prepare a report that will be presented to the college dean that summarizes your response.

34. *(Suboptimization)* Compensation consultant Craig Schneier describes an experience by one of his clients who decided to pay the purchasing department employees bonuses if they kept the cost of purchases down:

The problem was, to make that happen they were relying on second-tier sources and accepting poor-quality materials. The company was in the middle of a very big order, and the fasteners were lousy and ended up costing millions of dollars, while the [purchasing] department walked away with big bonuses.

SOURCE: Adapted from Amanda Bennett, "Paying Workers to Meet Goals Spreads, But Gauging Performance Proves Tough," *The Wall Street Journal* (September 10, 1991), pp. B1, B4. Reprinted by permission of *The Wall Street Journal*, © 1991 Dow Jones & Company, Inc. All rights reserved worldwide.

a. Using the plan–performance–reward model in Exhibit 21–1, identify where the company described above went awry in structuring the performance-based pay plan.

b. How can the company use the feedback received regarding the purchasing department's performance to improve the design of the pay plan?

c. How could the purchasing department's behavior be changed by combining the purchasing department with the production department for group-level performance evaluation purposes?

35. *(Variable pay and incentives)*

Salaries for CFOs of multi-billion dollar U.S. corporations rose 7% in 1999 to about $466,000, but that figure was only 20% of their average overall compensation of $2.37 million. The other 80% represented variable components—stock options (47%), annual incentives (17%), and long-term incentives (16%).

"CFOs hold a solid position among the ranks of executives rewarded more like owners than employees. The only other executives with a higher level of compensation at risk were CEOs, whose variable portion of pay amounted to 88%," said Steven E. Hall, managing director of Pearl Meyer & Partners, executive compensation consultants.

SOURCE: Kathy Williams, "CFO, Controller Pay Is Up—With More at Risk," *Strategic Finance* (February 2000), p. 23.

a. What does the high portion of variable CFO pay indicate about the importance of CFOs to their organizations?

b. Discuss any concerns investors might have about such a high percentage of CFO pay being variable.

36. *(Pay and incentives)* Global Oil Company is a multinational firm that markets a variety of chemicals for industrial uses. One of the many autonomous divisions is the North America Petro-Chemical Division (NAPCD). The manager of NAPCD, Carol Black, was recently overheard discussing a vexing problem with her controller, William Michaels. The topic of discussion was whether the division should replace its existing chemical-handling equipment with newer technology that is safer, more efficient, and cheaper to operate.

According to an analysis by Mr. Michaels, the cost savings over the life of the new technology would pay for the initial cost of the technology several times over. However, Ms. Black remained reluctant to invest. Her most fundamental concern involved the disposition of the old processing equipment. Because the existing equipment has been in use for only two years, it has a very high book value relative to its current market value. To illustrate, Ms. Black noted that if the new technology is not purchased, the division will earn a net income of $8,000,000 for the year. However, if the new technology is purchased, the old equipment will have to be sold, and Ms. Black noted that the division can probably sell the equipment for $2.4 million. This equipment has an original cost of $16 million and $3.0 million in depreciation has been recorded. Thus a book loss of $10.6 million ($13m − $2.4m) would be recorded on the sale.

Ms. Black's boss, Jim Heitz, is the president of the Western Chemical Group, and his compensation is based almost exclusively on the amount of ROI generated by his group, which includes NAPCD.

After thoroughly analyzing the facts, Ms. Black concluded, "The people in the Western Chemical Group will swallow their dentures if we book a $10.6 million loss."

a. Why is Ms. Black concerned about the book loss on disposal of the old technology in her division?

b. What are the weaknesses in the performance pay plan in place for Western Chemical Group that are apparently causing Ms. Black to avoid an investment that meets all of the normal criteria to be an acceptable investment (ignoring the ROI effect)?

37. *(Incentive compensation)*

http://www.gm.com

General Motors Corp. earned record profit in 1995—but because results fell short of aggressive targets set by the board, bonus payouts to top GM executives were cut.

For John F. Smith Jr., GM's chairman and chief executive officer, that meant a 9.2% reduction in salary and bonus to $5.6 million from his 1994 total of $6.1 *million. The cut in compensation continues efforts by the GM board to hold management accountable for meeting financial-performance goals. Corporate governance experts observe that much of corporate America has been criticized for not tying executive compensation directly to company performance.*

Unlike GM, Ford Motor Co. and Chrysler Corp. both reported earnings declines for 1995. They both cut executive bonuses accordingly.

SOURCE: Adapted from Rebecca Blumenstein, "GM Cuts Bonuses of Top Executives, Citing Unmet Goals Despite '95 Profit," *The Wall Street Journal* (April 10, 1996), p. A3.

http://www.fordvehicles.com
http://www.chryslercorp.com

Assume you are an advocate of John Smith Jr. Prepare a brief oral argument suggesting a reason or reasons why Mr. Smith should have been awarded a larger bonus.

38. *(Performance measurement)* In the mid-1990s:

Boston Scientific was giving Baxter International Inc. a run for its money.

Boston Scientific, a small but growing maker of medical devices, didn't compete directly with health-care giant Baxter. But Baxter's top executives were keenly watching the performance of their new rival. Their compensation, in part, was based on it.

Baxter's payout of stock to its senior managers was linked to how the company's shares perform compared with the Standard & Poor's Medical Products and Supplies Index, which included the two companies plus seven others.

It was the latest twist in executive pay: awarding stock benefits according to how well a corporation stacked up against its rivals. Many comparisons, like Baxter's, are based on total shareholder return, though some used other measures such as return on assets. Whatever they used, the purpose was the same: to ensure that managers keep a gimlet eye on other companies competing for the same customer and investor dollars.

SOURCE: Adapted from Lauren Young, "Compare and Contrast: More Pay Plans Are Linked to How Well a Corporation Fares Against Its Rivals. The Problem: Finding an Appropriate Rival," *The Wall Street Journal* (April 11, 1996), p. R8.

http://www.bsci.com
http://www.baxter.com

Write a report in which you discuss the benefits and risks of evaluating and rewarding performance based on comparisons with competitors.

CASES

39. In the arena of worker compensation, there is no topic as hotly debated as the minimum wage law. In March 2000, the United States approved a $1 an hour increase in the minimum wage, which would be phased in over two years. By 2002, the minimum wage would be $6.15 per hour.

Two arguments advanced in favor of increasing the minimum wage were (1) that "the minimum wage has fallen sharply in real (inflation-adjusted) terms since 1991," and (2) "that raising the minimum wage actually reduced unemployment." However, virtually no facts exist to support the second argument and virtually all evidence suggests increases in the minimum wage cause loss of employment.

SOURCE: Bruce Bartlett, "Minimum Wage Hikes Help Politicians, Not the Poor," *The Wall Street Journal* (May 27, 1999), p. A26.

Using concepts from this chapter prepare a report in which you explain why increases in the minimum wage are not desirable and how alternative mechanisms could be used to increase the compensation of lower-paid workers.

40. *(Pay plans and goal congruence)* In 2000, the lead story in your college newspaper reports the details of the hiring of the new football coach. The old football coach was fired for failing to win games and attract fans. In his last season his record was 1 win and 11 losses. The news story states that the new coach's contract provides for a base salary of $200,000 per year plus an annual bonus computed as follows:

Win less than 5 games	$ 0
Win 5 to 7 games	25,000
Win 8 games or more	75,000
Win 8 games and conference championship	95,000
Win 8 games, win conference, get a bowl bid	150,000

The coach's contract has essentially no other features or clauses.

The first year after the new coach is hired, the football team wins 3 games and loses 8. The second year the team wins 6 games and loses 5. The third year the team wins 9 games, wins the conference championship, and is invited to a prestigious bowl. Shortly after the bowl game, articles appear on the front page of several national sports publications announcing your college's football program has been cited by the National Collegiate Athletic Association (NCAA) for nine major rule violations including cash payoffs to players, playing academically ineligible players, illegal recruiting tactics, illegal involvement of alumni in recruiting, etc. All the national news publications agree that your college's football program will be disbanded by the NCAA. One article also mentioned that during the past three years only 13 percent of senior football players managed to graduate on time. Additional speculation suggests the responsible parties including the coaching staff, athletic director, and college president will be dismissed by the board of trustees.

a. Compute the amount of compensation paid to the new coach in each of his first three years.

b. Did the performance measures in the coach's contract foster goal congruence? Explain.

c. Would the coach's actions have been different if other performance measures were added to the compensation contract? Explain.

d. What performance measures should be considered for the next coach's contract, assuming the football program is kept alive?

http://www.coca-cola.com

41. *Coca-Cola's new chairman and chief executive officer, Douglas Daft, said he will tie his compensation to diversity goals and create an executive position to develop strategies for promoting minorities.*

The moves come as Coke faces a lawsuit by current and former African-American employees accusing the soft-drink company of racial bias.

In a memo e-mailed in March 2000 to employees worldwide, Mr. Daft said Coke will establish "a series of goals, objectives and targets" for achieving diversity throughout the company "over the next few months," and that "everyone in the organization, including the CEO, will be held accountable for meeting them." He added that his "success and compensation" will be tied to meeting the diversity goals, "and the same will be true throughout the management ranks."

SOURCE: Betsy McKay, "Coke CEO to Tie Pay to Diversity Goals, Create Post on Promotion of Minorities," *The Wall Street Journal* (March 10, 2000), p. A3. Permission conveyed through the Copyright Clearance Center.

a. Assume the stock market reacted negatively to the news article. Discuss why the market might react this way.

b. Assume the stock market reacted positively to the news article. Discuss why the market might react this way.

c. Discuss any problems you perceive in tying diversity objectives to managerial rewards.

d. Is tying managerial rewards to diversity an ethical way to change managerial behaviors regarding hiring minorities?

REALITY CHECK

42. United for a Fair Economy is a group that believes the disparity in pay in the United States between top executives and ordinary workers has grown too large. The group offers research data to support their position. Find the group's Internet site and read the article entitled "A Decade of Executive Excess: The 1990s." Read the article and write a report that summarizes the article and expresses your views of the group's arguments.

43. In a survey, 649 managers responded to a questionnaire and provided their opinions from an ethical perspective as to the acceptability of manipulating accounting earnings to achieve higher managerial compensation. One of the questions dealt with the acceptability of changing a sales practice to pull some of next year's sales into the current year so that reported current earnings could be pushed up. The results of the survey indicated that about 43 percent of the respondents felt this practice was ethically acceptable, 44 percent felt the practice was ethically questionable, and 13 percent felt the practice was ethically unacceptable.

Other results of the survey indicate the managers felt large manipulations were more unethical than small manipulations, and income-increasing manipulations were more ethically unacceptable than income-decreasing manipulations.

SOURCE: Adapted from William J. Bruns and Kenneth A. Merchant, "The Dangerous Morality of Managing Earnings," *Management Accounting* (August 1990), pp. 22–25. Reprinted from *Management Accounting*. Copyright by Institute of Management Accountants, Montvale, N.J.

a. If managers are able to manipulate earnings to effect a change in their pay, is this a signal of a weakness in the pay-for-performance plan? Explain.
b. In your view, does the materiality of a manipulation partly determine the extent to which the manipulation is ethically acceptable?
c. Describe any circumstances in which you believe manipulations would be ethically acceptable.

44. Recall from your academic career the various ways in which your academic performance has been measured and rewarded. Have the ways that your class grades been determined always provided the best indications of performance? Provide at least two positive and two negative examples. What would you have done to change the measurement system in the negative examples?

45. When David P. Gardner, president of the University of California, announced his retirement unexpectedly in April 1992, he received a severance package worth $1 million—in a year in which the university's budget was cut by $255 million. The university also announced that student fees would rise for the third straight year—for a three-year total increase of 85 percent.

Mr. Gardner, who retired early at age 58, earned an official salary of $243,500—double that of California's governor. But his actual compensation was more than $400,000. And although his official pension would be $126,000 a year, he received an additional $933,000 when he departed.

In addition to Mr. Gardner's base salary, the regents found ways to pay him an additional $160,000 annually. Deferred income, severance pay, and a special supplemental retirement program made the difference. In fact, a secret deferred-income plan was established by the regents in 1988 for about a dozen top UC executives, after a private study concluded that their compensation lagged behind that of top administrators in a nationwide comparison group of universities. (The conclusions of the study were challenged by the California Postsecondary Education Commission, an independent state agency.)

SOURCE: Adapted from Jon Wiener, "Lavish Compensation Is Not Appropriate for Top Executives at Public Universities," *Chronicle of Higher Education* (November 25, 1992), p. B3.

a. Assume you were one of the students in the UC system. Discuss your perceptions about Mr. Gardner's compensation package.

b. How ethical do you think it was for Mr. Gardner to accept such a compensation package? Consider both the information in the comparative study and the budget problems that California was experiencing.

c. Could this simply be a case of trying to retain the "best and the brightest" in a not-for-profit institution? Discuss the rationale for your answer.

Appendix A

Present Value Tables

TABLE 1 *Present Value of $1*

Period	1.00%	2.00%	3.00%	4.00%	5.00%	6.00%	7.00%	8.00%	9.00%	9.50%	10.00%	10.50%	11.00%
1	0.9901	0.9804	0.9709	0.9615	0.9524	0.9434	0.9346	0.9259	0.9174	0.9132	0.9091	0.9050	0.9009
2	0.9803	0.9612	0.9426	0.9246	0.9070	0.8900	0.8734	0.8573	0.8417	0.8340	0.8265	0.8190	0.8116
3	0.9706	0.9423	0.9151	0.8890	0.8638	0.8396	0.8163	0.7938	0.7722	0.7617	0.7513	0.7412	0.7312
4	0.9610	0.9239	0.8885	0.8548	0.8227	0.7921	0.7629	0.7350	0.7084	0.6956	0.6830	0.6707	0.6587
5	0.9515	0.9057	0.8626	0.8219	0.7835	0.7473	0.7130	0.6806	0.6499	0.6352	0.6209	0.6070	0.5935
6	0.9421	0.8880	0.8375	0.7903	0.7462	0.7050	0.6663	0.6302	0.5963	0.5801	0.5645	0.5493	0.5346
7	0.9327	0.8706	0.8131	0.7599	0.7107	0.6651	0.6228	0.5835	0.5470	0.5298	0.5132	0.4971	0.4817
8	0.9235	0.8535	0.7894	0.7307	0.6768	0.6274	0.5820	0.5403	0.5019	0.4838	0.4665	0.4499	0.4339
9	0.9143	0.8368	0.7664	0.7026	0.6446	0.5919	0.5439	0.5003	0.4604	0.4419	0.4241	0.4071	0.3909
10	0.9053	0.8204	0.7441	0.6756	0.6139	0.5584	0.5084	0.4632	0.4224	0.4035	0.3855	0.3685	0.3522
11	0.8963	0.8043	0.7224	0.6496	0.5847	0.5268	0.4751	0.4289	0.3875	0.3685	0.3505	0.3334	0.3173
12	0.8875	0.7885	0.7014	0.6246	0.5568	0.4970	0.4440	0.3971	0.3555	0.3365	0.3186	0.3018	0.2858
13	0.8787	0.7730	0.6810	0.6006	0.5303	0.4688	0.4150	0.3677	0.3262	0.3073	0.2897	0.2731	0.2575
14	0.8700	0.7579	0.6611	0.5775	0.5051	0.4423	0.3878	0.3405	0.2993	0.2807	0.2633	0.2471	0.2320
15	0.8614	0.7430	0.6419	0.5553	0.4810	0.4173	0.3625	0.3152	0.2745	0.2563	0.2394	0.2237	0.2090
16	0.8528	0.7285	0.6232	0.5339	0.4581	0.3937	0.3387	0.2919	0.2519	0.2341	0.2176	0.2024	0.1883
17	0.8444	0.7142	0.6050	0.5134	0.4363	0.3714	0.3166	0.2703	0.2311	0.2138	0.1978	0.1832	0.1696
18	0.8360	0.7002	0.5874	0.4936	0.4155	0.3503	0.2959	0.2503	0.2120	0.1952	0.1799	0.1658	0.1528
19	0.8277	0.6864	0.5703	0.4746	0.3957	0.3305	0.2765	0.2317	0.1945	0.1783	0.1635	0.1500	0.1377
20	0.8195	0.6730	0.5537	0.4564	0.3769	0.3118	0.2584	0.2146	0.1784	0.1628	0.1486	0.1358	0.1240
21	0.8114	0.6598	0.5376	0.4388	0.3589	0.2942	0.2415	0.1987	0.1637	0.1487	0.1351	0.1229	0.1117
22	0.8034	0.6468	0.5219	0.4220	0.3419	0.2775	0.2257	0.1839	0.1502	0.1358	0.1229	0.1112	0.1007
23	0.7954	0.6342	0.5067	0.4057	0.3256	0.2618	0.2110	0.1703	0.1378	0.1240	0.1117	0.1006	0.0907
24	0.7876	0.6217	0.4919	0.3901	0.3101	0.2470	0.1972	0.1577	0.1264	0.1133	0.1015	0.0911	0.0817
25	0.7798	0.6095	0.4776	0.3751	0.2953	0.2330	0.1843	0.1460	0.1160	0.1034	0.0923	0.0824	0.0736
26	0.7721	0.5976	0.4637	0.3607	0.2812	0.2198	0.1722	0.1352	0.1064	0.0945	0.0839	0.0746	0.0663
27	0.7644	0.5859	0.4502	0.3468	0.2679	0.2074	0.1609	0.1252	0.0976	0.0863	0.0763	0.0675	0.0597
28	0.7568	0.5744	0.4371	0.3335	0.2551	0.1956	0.1504	0.1159	0.0896	0.0788	0.0693	0.0611	0.0538
29	0.7493	0.5631	0.4244	0.3207	0.2430	0.1846	0.1406	0.1073	0.0822	0.0719	0.0630	0.0553	0.0485
30	0.7419	0.5521	0.4120	0.3083	0.2314	0.1741	0.1314	0.0994	0.0754	0.0657	0.0573	0.0500	0.0437
31	0.7346	0.5413	0.4000	0.2965	0.2204	0.1643	0.1228	0.0920	0.0692	0.0600	0.0521	0.0453	0.0394
32	0.7273	0.5306	0.3883	0.2851	0.2099	0.1550	0.1147	0.0852	0.0634	0.0058	0.0474	0.0410	0.0355
33	0.7201	0.5202	0.3770	0.2741	0.1999	0.1462	0.1072	0.0789	0.0582	0.0500	0.0431	0.0371	0.0319
34	0.7130	0.5100	0.3660	0.2636	0.1904	0.1379	0.1002	0.0731	0.0534	0.0457	0.0391	0.0336	0.0288
35	0.7059	0.5000	0.3554	0.2534	0.1813	0.1301	0.0937	0.0676	0.0490	0.0417	0.0356	0.0304	0.0259
36	0.6989	0.4902	0.3450	0.2437	0.1727	0.1227	0.0875	0.0626	0.0449	0.0381	0.0324	0.0275	0.0234
37	0.6920	0.4806	0.3350	0.2343	0.1644	0.1158	0.0818	0.0580	0.0412	0.0348	0.0294	0.0249	0.0210
38	0.6852	0.4712	0.3252	0.2253	0.1566	0.1092	0.0765	0.0537	0.0378	0.0318	0.0267	0.0225	0.0190
39	0.6784	0.4620	0.3158	0.2166	0.1492	0.1031	0.0715	0.0497	0.0347	0.0290	0.0243	0.0204	0.0171
40	0.6717	0.4529	0.3066	0.2083	0.1421	0.0972	0.0668	0.0460	0.0318	0.0265	0.0221	0.0184	0.0154
41	0.6650	0.4440	0.2976	0.2003	0.1353	0.0917	0.0624	0.0426	0.0292	0.0242	0.0201	0.0167	0.0139
42	0.6584	0.4353	0.2890	0.1926	0.1288	0.0865	0.0583	0.0395	0.0268	0.0221	0.0183	0.0151	0.0125
43	0.6519	0.4268	0.2805	0.1852	0.1227	0.0816	0.0545	0.0365	0.0246	0.0202	0.0166	0.0137	0.0113
44	0.6455	0.4184	0.2724	0.1781	0.1169	0.0770	0.0510	0.0338	0.0226	0.0184	0.0151	0.0124	0.0101
45	0.6391	0.4102	0.2644	0.1712	0.1113	0.0727	0.0476	0.0313	0.0207	0.0168	0.0137	0.0112	0.0091
46	0.6327	0.4022	0.2567	0.1646	0.1060	0.0685	0.0445	0.0290	0.0190	0.0154	0.0125	0.0101	0.0082
47	0.6265	0.3943	0.2493	0.1583	0.1010	0.0647	0.0416	0.0269	0.0174	0.0141	0.0113	0.0092	0.0074
48	0.6203	0.3865	0.2420	0.1522	0.0961	0.0610	0.0389	0.0249	0.0160	0.0128	0.0103	0.0083	0.0067
49	0.6141	0.3790	0.2350	0.1463	0.0916	0.0576	0.0363	0.0230	0.0147	0.0117	0.0094	0.0075	0.0060
50	0.6080	0.3715	0.2281	0.1407	0.0872	0.0543	0.0340	0.0213	0.0135	0.0107	0.0085	0.0068	0.0054

11.50%	12.00%	12.50%	13.00%	13.50%	14.00%	14.50%	15.00%	15.50%	16.00%	17.00%	18.00%	19.00%	20.00%
0.8969	0.8929	0.8889	0.8850	0.8811	0.8772	0.8734	0.8696	0.8658	0.8621	0.8547	0.8475	0.8403	0.8333
0.8044	0.7972	0.7901	0.7832	0.7763	0.7695	0.7628	0.7561	0.7496	0.7432	0.7305	0.7182	0.7062	0.6944
0.7214	0.7118	0.7023	0.6931	0.6839	0.6750	0.6662	0.6575	0.6490	0.6407	0.6244	0.6086	0.5934	0.5787
0.6470	0.6355	0.6243	0.6133	0.6026	0.5921	0.5818	0.5718	0.5619	0.5523	0.5337	0.5158	0.4987	0.4823
0.5803	0.5674	0.5549	0.5428	0.5309	0.5194	0.5081	0.4972	0.4865	0.4761	0.4561	0.4371	0.4191	0.4019
0.5204	0.5066	0.4933	0.4803	0.4678	0.4556	0.4438	0.4323	0.4212	0.4104	0.3898	0.3704	0.3521	0.3349
0.4667	0.4524	0.4385	0.4251	0.4121	0.3996	0.3876	0.3759	0.3647	0.3538	0.3332	0.3139	0.2959	0.2791
0.4186	0.4039	0.3897	0.3762	0.3631	0.3506	0.3385	0.3269	0.3158	0.3050	0.2848	0.2660	0.2487	0.2326
0.3754	0.3606	0.3464	0.3329	0.3199	0.3075	0.2956	0.2843	0.2734	0.2630	0.2434	0.2255	0.2090	0.1938
0.3367	0.3220	0.3080	0.2946	0.2819	0.2697	0.2582	0.2472	0.2367	0.2267	0.2080	0.1911	0.1756	0.1615
0.3020	0.2875	0.2737	0.2607	0.2483	0.2366	0.2255	0.2149	0.2049	0.1954	0.1778	0.1619	0.1476	0.1346
0.2708	0.2567	0.2433	0.2307	0.2188	0.2076	0.1969	0.1869	0.1774	0.1685	0.1520	0.1372	0.1240	0.1122
0.2429	0.2292	0.2163	0.2042	0.1928	0.1821	0.1720	0.1625	0.1536	0.1452	0.1299	0.1163	0.1042	0.0935
0.2179	0.2046	0.1923	0.1807	0.1699	0.1597	0.1502	0.1413	0.1330	0.1252	0.1110	0.0986	0.0876	0.0779
0.1954	0.1827	0.1709	0.1599	0.1496	0.1401	0.1312	0.1229	0.1152	0.1079	0.0949	0.0835	0.0736	0.0649
0.1752	0.1631	0.1519	0.1415	0.1319	0.1229	0.1146	0.1069	0.0997	0.0930	0.0811	0.0708	0.0618	0.0541
0.1572	0.1456	0.1350	0.1252	0.1162	0.1078	0.1001	0.0929	0.0863	0.0802	0.0693	0.0600	0.0520	0.0451
0.1410	0.1300	0.1200	0.1108	0.1024	0.0946	0.0874	0.0808	0.0747	0.0691	0.0593	0.0508	0.0437	0.0376
0.1264	0.1161	0.1067	0.0981	0.0902	0.0830	0.0763	0.0703	0.0647	0.0596	0.0506	0.0431	0.0367	0.0313
0.1134	0.1037	0.0948	0.0868	0.0795	0.0728	0.0667	0.0611	0.0560	0.0514	0.0433	0.0365	0.0308	0.0261
0.1017	0.0926	0.0843	0.0768	0.0700	0.0638	0.0582	0.0531	0.0485	0.0443	0.0370	0.0309	0.0259	0.0217
0.0912	0.0826	0.0749	0.0680	0.0617	0.0560	0.0509	0.0462	0.0420	0.0382	0.0316	0.0262	0.0218	0.0181
0.0818	0.0738	0.0666	0.0601	0.0543	0.0491	0.0444	0.0402	0.0364	0.0329	0.0270	0.0222	0.0183	0.0151
0.0734	0.0659	0.0592	0.0532	0.0479	0.0431	0.0388	0.0349	0.0315	0.0284	0.0231	0.0188	0.0154	0.0126
0.0658	0.0588	0.0526	0.0471	0.0422	0.0378	0.0339	0.0304	0.0273	0.0245	0.0197	0.0160	0.0129	0.0105
0.0590	0.0525	0.0468	0.0417	0.0372	0.0332	0.0296	0.0264	0.0236	0.0211	0.0169	0.0135	0.0109	0.0087
0.0529	0.0469	0.0416	0.0369	0.0327	0.0291	0.0258	0.0230	0.0204	0.0182	0.0144	0.0115	0.0091	0.0073
0.0475	0.0419	0.0370	0.0326	0.0289	0.0255	0.0226	0.0200	0.0177	0.0157	0.0123	0.0097	0.0077	0.0061
0.0426	0.0374	0.0329	0.0289	0.0254	0.0224	0.0197	0.0174	0.0153	0.0135	0.0105	0.0082	0.0064	0.0051
0.0382	0.0334	0.0292	0.0256	0.0224	0.0196	0.0172	0.0151	0.0133	0.0117	0.0090	0.0070	0.0054	0.0042
0.0342	0.0298	0.0260	0.0226	0.0197	0.0172	0.0150	0.0131	0.0115	0.0100	0.0077	0.0059	0.0046	0.0035
0.0307	0.0266	0.0231	0.0200	0.0174	0.0151	0.0131	0.0114	0.0099	0.0087	0.0066	0.0050	0.0038	0.0029
0.0275	0.0238	0.0205	0.0177	0.0153	0.0133	0.0115	0.0099	0.0086	0.0075	0.0056	0.0043	0.0032	0.0024
0.0247	0.0212	0.0182	0.0157	0.0135	0.0116	0.0100	0.0088	0.0075	0.0064	0.0048	0.0036	0.0027	0.0020
0.0222	0.0189	0.0162	0.0139	0.0119	0.0102	0.0088	0.0075	0.0065	0.0056	0.0041	0.0031	0.0023	0.0017
0.0199	0.0169	0.0144	0.0123	0.0105	0.0089	0.0076	0.0065	0.0056	0.0048	0.0035	0.0026	0.0019	0.0014
0.0178	0.0151	0.0128	0.0109	0.0092	0.0078	0.0067	0.0057	0.0048	0.0041	0.0030	0.0022	0.0016	0.0012
0.0160	0.0135	0.0114	0.0096	0.0081	0.0069	0.0058	0.0049	0.0042	0.0036	0.0026	0.0019	0.0014	0.0010
0.0143	0.0120	0.0101	0.0085	0.0072	0.0060	0.0051	0.0043	0.0036	0.0031	0.0022	0.0016	0.0011	0.0008
0.0129	0.0108	0.0090	0.0075	0.0063	0.0053	0.0044	0.0037	0.0031	0.0026	0.0019	0.0013	0.0010	0.0007
0.0115	0.0096	0.0080	0.0067	0.0056	0.0046	0.0039	0.0033	0.0027	0.0023	0.0016	0.0011	0.0008	0.0006
0.0103	0.0086	0.0077	0.0059	0.0049	0.0041	0.0034	0.0028	0.0024	0.0020	0.0014	0.0010	0.0007	0.0005
0.0093	0.0077	0.0063	0.0052	0.0043	0.0036	0.0030	0.0025	0.0020	0.0017	0.0012	0.0008	0.0006	0.0004
0.0083	0.0068	0.0056	0.0046	0.0038	0.0031	0.0026	0.0021	0.0018	0.0015	0.0010	0.0007	0.0005	0.0003
0.0075	0.0061	0.0050	0.0041	0.0034	0.0028	0.0023	0.0019	0.0015	0.0013	0.0009	0.0006	0.0004	0.0003
0.0067	0.0054	0.0044	0.0036	0.0030	0.0024	0.0020	0.0016	0.0013	0.0011	0.0007	0.0005	0.0003	0.0002
0.0060	0.0049	0.0039	0.0032	0.0026	0.0021	0.0017	0.0014	0.0011	0.0009	0.0006	0.0004	0.0003	0.0002
0.0054	0.0043	0.0035	0.0028	0.0023	0.0019	0.0015	0.0012	0.0010	0.0008	0.0005	0.0004	0.0002	0.0002
0.0048	0.0039	0.0031	0.0025	0.0020	0.0016	0.0013	0.0011	0.0009	0.0007	0.0005	0.0003	0.0002	0.0001
0.0043	0.0035	0.0028	0.0022	0.0018	0.0014	0.0012	0.0009	0.0007	0.0006	0.0004	0.0003	0.0002	0.0001

TABLE 2 *Present Value of an Ordinary Annuity of $1*

Period	1.00%	2.00%	3.00%	4.00%	5.00%	6.00%	7.00%	8.00%	9.00%	9.50%	10.00%	10.50%	11.00%
1	0.9901	0.9804	0.9709	0.9615	0.0524	0.9434	0.9346	0.9259	0.9174	0.9132	0.9091	0.9050	0.9009
2	1.9704	1.9416	1.9135	1.8861	1.8594	1.8334	1.8080	1.7833	1.7591	1.7473	1.7355	1.7240	1.7125
3	2.9410	2.8839	2.8286	2.7751	2.7233	2.6730	2.6243	2.5771	2.5313	2.5089	2.4869	2.4651	2.4437
4	3.9020	3.8077	3.7171	3.6299	3.5460	3.4651	3.3872	3.3121	3.2397	3.2045	3.1699	3.1359	3.1025
5	4.8534	4.7135	4.5797	4.4518	4.3295	4.2124	4.1002	3.9927	3.8897	3.8397	3.7908	3.7429	3.6959
6	5.7955	5.6014	5.4172	5.2421	5.0757	4.9173	4.7665	4.6229	4.4859	4.4198	4.3553	4.2922	4.2305
7	6.7282	6.4720	6.2303	6.0021	5.7864	5.5824	5.3893	5.2064	5.0330	4.9496	4.8684	4.7893	4.7122
8	7.6517	7.3255	7.0197	6.7327	6.4632	6.2098	5.9713	5.7466	5.5348	5.4334	5.3349	5.2392	5.1461
9	8.5660	8.1622	7.7861	7.4353	7.1078	6.8017	6.5152	6.2469	5.9953	5.8753	5.7590	5.6463	5.5371
10	9.4713	8.9826	8.5302	8.1109	7.7217	7.3601	7.0236	6.7101	6.4177	6.2788	6.1446	6.0148	5.8892
11	10.3676	9.7869	9.2526	8.7605	8.3064	7.8869	7.4987	7.1390	6.8052	6.6473	6.4951	6.3482	6.2065
12	11.2551	10.5753	9.9540	9.3851	8.8633	8.3838	7.9427	7.5361	7.1607	6.9838	6.8137	6.6500	6.4924
13	12.1337	11.3484	10.6350	9.9857	9.3936	8.8527	8.3577	7.9038	7.4869	7.2912	7.1034	6.9230	6.7499
14	13.0037	12.1063	11.2961	10.5631	9.8986	9.2950	8.7455	8.2442	7.7862	7.5719	7.3667	7.1702	6.9819
15	13.8651	12.8493	11.9379	11.1184	10.3797	9.7123	9.1079	8.5595	8.0607	7.8282	7.6061	7.3938	7.1909
16	14.7179	13.5777	12.5611	11.6523	10.8378	10.1059	9.4467	8.8514	8.3126	8.0623	7.8237	7.5962	7.3792
17	15.5623	14.2919	13.1661	12.1657	11.2741	10.4773	9.7632	9.1216	8.5436	8.2760	8.0216	7.7794	7.5488
18	16.3983	14.9920	13.7535	12.6593	11.6896	10.8276	10.0591	9.3719	8.7556	8.4713	8.2014	7.9452	7.7016
19	17.2260	15.6785	14.3238	13.1339	12.0853	11.1581	10.3356	9.6036	8.9501	8.6496	8.3649	8.0952	7.8393
20	18.0456	16.3514	14.8775	13.5903	12.4622	11.4699	10.5940	9.8182	9.1286	8.8124	8.5136	8.2309	7.9633
21	18.8570	17.0112	15.4150	14.0292	12.8212	11.7641	10.8355	10.0168	9.2922	8.9611	8.6487	8.3538	8.0751
22	19.6604	17.6581	15.9369	14.4511	13.1630	12.0416	11.0612	10.2007	9.4424	9.0969	8.7715	8.4649	8.1757
23	20.4558	18.2922	16.4436	14.8568	13.4886	12.3034	11.2722	10.3711	9.5802	9.2209	8.8832	8.5656	8.2664
24	21.2434	18.9139	16.9355	15.2470	13.7986	12.5504	11.4693	10.5288	9.7066	9.3342	8.9847	8.6566	8.3481
25	22.0232	19.5235	17.4132	15.6221	14.0939	12.7834	11.6536	10.6748	9.8226	9.4376	9.0770	8.7390	8.4217
26	22.7952	20.1210	17.8768	15.9828	14.3752	13.0032	11.8258	10.8100	9.9290	9.5320	9.1610	8.8136	8.4881
27	23.5596	20.7069	18.3270	16.3296	14.6430	13.2105	11.9867	10.9352	10.0266	9.6183	9.2372	8.8811	8.5478
28	24.3164	21.2813	18.7641	16.6631	14.8981	13.4062	12.1371	11.0511	10.1161	9.6971	9.3066	8.9422	8.6016
29	25.0658	21.8444	19.1885	16.9837	15.1411	13.5907	12.2777	11.1584	10.1983	9.7690	9.3696	8.9974	8.6501
30	25.8077	22.3965	19.6004	17.2920	15.3725	13.7648	12.4090	11.2578	10.2737	9.8347	9.4269	9.0474	8.6938
31	26.5423	22.9377	20.0004	17.5885	15.5928	13.9291	12.5318	11.3498	10.3428	9.8947	9.4790	9.0927	8.7332
32	27.2696	23.4683	20.3888	17.8736	15.8027	14.0840	12.6466	11.4350	10.4062	9.9495	9.5264	9.1337	8.7686
33	27.9897	23.9886	20.7658	18.1477	16.0026	14.2302	12.7538	11.5139	10.4664	9.9996	9.5694	9.1707	8.8005
34	28.7027	24.4986	21.1318	18.4112	16.1929	14.3681	12.8540	11.5869	10.5178	10.0453	9.6086	9.2043	8.8293
35	29.4086	24.9986	21.4872	18.6646	16.3742	14.4983	12.9477	11.6546	10.5668	10.0870	9.6442	9.2347	8.8552
36	30.1075	25.4888	21.8323	18.9083	16.5469	14.6210	13.0352	11.7172	10.6118	10.1251	9.6765	9.2621	8.8786
37	30.7995	25.9695	22.1672	19.1426	16.7113	14.7368	13.1170	11.7752	10.6530	10.1599	9.7059	9.2870	8.8996
38	31.4847	26.4406	22.4925	19.3679	16.8679	14.8460	13.1935	11.8289	10.6908	10.1917	9.7327	9.3095	8.9186
39	32.1630	26.9026	22.8082	19.5845	17.0170	14.9491	13.2649	11.8786	10.7255	10.2207	9.7570	9.3299	8.9357
40	32.8347	27.3555	23.1148	19.7928	17.1591	15.0463	13.3317	11.9246	10.7574	10.2473	9.7791	9.3483	8.9511
41	33.4997	27.7995	23.4124	19.9931	17.2944	15.1380	13.3941	11.9672	10.7866	10.2715	9.7991	9.3650	8.9649
42	34.1581	28.2348	23.7014	20.1856	17.4232	15.2245	13.4525	12.0067	10.8134	10.2936	9.8174	9.3801	8.9774
43	34.8100	28.6616	23.9819	20.3708	17.5459	15.3062	13.5070	12.0432	10.8380	10.3138	9.8340	9.3937	8.9887
44	35.4555	29.0800	24.2543	20.5488	17.6628	15.3832	13.5579	12.0771	10.8605	10.3322	9.8491	9.4061	8.9988
45	36.0945	29.4902	24.5187	20.7200	17.7741	15.4558	13.6055	12.1084	10.8812	10.3490	9.8628	9.4163	9.0079
46	36.7272	29.8923	24.7755	20.8847	17.8801	15.5244	13.6500	12.1374	10.9002	10.3644	9.8753	9.4274	9.0161
47	37.3537	30.2866	25.0247	21.0429	17.9810	15.5890	13.6916	12.1643	10.9176	10.3785	9.8866	9.4366	9.0236
48	37.9740	30.6731	25.2667	21.1951	18.0772	15.6500	13.7305	12.1891	10.9336	10.3913	9.8969	9.4449	9.0302
49	38.5881	31.0521	25.5017	21.3415	18.1687	15.7076	13.7668	12.2122	10.9482	10.4030	9.9063	9.4524	9.0362
50	39.1961	31.4236	25.7298	21.4822	18.2559	15.7619	13.8008	12.2335	10.9617	10.4137	9.9148	9.4591	9.0417

11.50%	12.00%	12.50%	13.00%	13.50%	14.00%	14.50%	15.00%	15.50%	16.00%	17.00%	18.00%	19.00%	20.00%
0.8969	0.8929	0.8889	0.8850	0.8811	0.8772	0.8734	0.8696	0.8658	0.8621	0.8547	0.8475	0.8403	0.8333
1.7012	1.6901	1.6790	1.6681	1.6573	1.6467	1.6361	1.6257	1.6154	1.6052	1.5852	1.5656	1.5465	1.5278
2.4226	2.4018	2.3813	2.3612	2.3413	2.3216	2.3023	2.2832	2.2644	2.2459	2.2096	2.1743	2.1399	2.1065
3.0696	3.0374	3.0056	2.9745	2.9438	2.9137	2.8841	2.8850	2.8263	2.7982	2.7432	2.6901	2.6386	2.5887
3.6499	3.6048	3.5606	3.5172	3.4747	3.4331	3.3922	3.3522	3.3129	3.2743	3.1994	3.1272	3.0576	2.9906
4.1703	4.1114	4.0538	3.9976	3.9425	3.8887	3.8360	3.7845	3.7341	3.6847	3.5892	3.4976	3.4098	3.3255
4.6370	4.5638	4.4923	4.4226	4.3546	4.2883	4.2236	4.1604	4.0988	4.0386	3.9224	3.8115	3.7057	3.6046
5.0556	4.9676	4.8821	4.7988	4.7177	4.6389	4.5621	4.4873	4.4145	4.3436	4.2072	4.0776	3.9544	3.8372
5.4311	5.3283	5.2285	5.1317	5.0377	4.9464	4.8577	4.7716	4.6879	4.6065	4.4506	4.3030	4.1633	4.0310
5.7678	5.6502	5.5364	5.4262	5.3195	5.2161	5.1159	5.0188	4.9246	4.8332	4.6586	4.4941	4.3389	4.1925
6.0698	5.9377	5.8102	5.6869	5.5679	5.4527	5.3414	5.2337	5.1295	5.0286	4.8364	4.6560	4.4865	4.3271
6.3406	6.1944	6.0535	5.9177	5.7867	5.6603	5.5383	5.4206	5.3069	5.1971	4.9884	4.7932	4.6105	4.4392
6.5835	6.4236	6.2698	6.1218	5.9794	5.8424	5.7103	5.5832	5.4606	5.3423	5.1183	4.9095	4.7147	4.5327
6.8013	6.6282	6.4620	6.3025	6.1493	6.0021	5.8606	5.7245	5.5936	5.4675	5.2293	5.0081	4.8023	4.6106
6.9967	6.8109	6.6329	6.4624	6.2989	6.1422	5.9918	5.8474	5.7087	5.5755	5.3242	5.0916	4.8759	4.6755
7.1719	6.9740	6.7848	6.6039	6.4308	6.2651	6.1063	5.9542	5.8084	5.6685	5.4053	5.1624	4.9377	4.7296
7.3291	7.1196	6.9198	6.7291	6.5469	6.3729	6.2064	6.0472	5.8947	5.7487	5.4746	5.2223	4.9897	4.7746
7.4700	7.2497	7.0398	6.8399	6.6493	6.4674	6.2938	6.1280	5.9695	5.8179	5.5339	5.2732	5.0333	4.8122
7.5964	7.3658	7.1465	6.9380	6.7395	6.5504	6.3701	6.1982	6.0342	5.8775	5.5845	5.3162	5.0700	4.8435
7.7098	7.4694	7.2414	7.0248	6.8189	6.6231	6.4368	6.2593	6.0902	5.9288	5.6278	5.3528	5.1009	4.8696
7.8115	7.5620	7.3257	7.1016	6.8889	6.6870	6.4950	6.3125	6.1387	5.9731	5.6648	5.3837	5.1268	4.8913
7.9027	7.6447	7.4006	7.1695	6.9506	6.7429	6.5459	6.3587	6.1807	6.0113	5.6964	5.4099	5.1486	4.9094
7.9845	7.7184	7.4672	7.2297	7.0049	6.7921	6.5903	6.3988	6.2170	6.0443	5.7234	5.4321	5.1669	4.9245
8.0578	7.7843	7.5264	7.2829	7.0528	6.8351	6.6291	6.4338	6.2485	6.0726	5.7465	5.4510	5.1822	4.9371
8.1236	7.8431	7.5790	7.3300	7.0950	6.8729	6.6629	6.4642	6.2758	6.0971	5.7662	5.4669	5.1952	4.9476
8.1826	7.8957	7.6258	7.3717	7.1321	6.9061	6.6925	6.4906	6.2994	6.1182	5.7831	5.4804	5.2060	4.9563
8.2355	7.9426	7.6674	7.4086	7.1649	6.9352	6.7184	6.5135	6.3198	6.1364	5.7975	5.4919	5.2151	4.9636
8.2830	7.9844	7.7043	7.4412	7.1937	6.9607	6.7409	6.5335	6.3375	6.1520	5.8099	5.5016	5.2228	4.9697
8.3255	8.0218	7.7372	7.4701	7.2191	6.9830	6.7606	6.5509	6.3528	6.1656	5.8204	5.5098	5.2292	4.9747
8.3637	8.0552	7.7664	7.4957	7.2415	7.0027	6.7779	6.5660	6.3661	6.1772	5.8294	5.5168	5.2347	4.9789
8.3980	8.0850	7.7923	7.5183	7.2613	7.0199	6.7929	6.5791	6.3776	6.1872	5.8371	5.5227	5.2392	4.9825
8.4287	8.1116	7.8154	7.5383	7.2786	7.0350	6.8060	6.5905	6.3875	6.1959	5.8437	5.5277	5.2430	4.9854
8.4562	8.1354	7.8359	7.5560	7.2940	7.0482	6.8175	6.6005	6.3961	6.2034	5.8493	5.5320	5.2463	4.9878
8.4809	8.1566	7.8542	7.5717	7.3075	7.0599	6.8275	6.6091	6.4035	6.2098	5.8541	5.5356	5.2490	4.9898
8.5030	8.1755	7.8704	7.5856	7.3193	7.0701	6.8362	6.6166	6.4100	6.2153	5.8582	5.5386	5.2512	4.9930
8.5229	8.1924	7.8848	7.5979	7.3298	7.0790	6.8439	6.6231	6.4156	6.2201	5.8617	5.5412	5.2531	4.9930
8.5407	8.2075	7.8976	7.6087	7.3390	7.0868	6.8505	6.6288	6.4204	6.2242	5.8647	5.5434	5.2547	4.9941
8.5567	8.2210	7.9090	7.6183	7.3472	7.0937	6.8564	6.6338	6.4246	6.2278	5.8673	5.5453	5.2561	4.9951
8.5710	8.2330	7.9191	7.6268	7.3543	7.0998	6.8615	6.6381	6.4282	6.2309	5.8695	5.5468	5.2572	4.9959
8.5839	8.2438	7.9281	7.6344	7.3607	7.1050	6.8659	6.6418	6.4314	6.2335	5.8713	5.5482	5.2582	4.9966
8.5954	8.2534	7.9361	7.6410	7.3662	7.1097	6.8698	6.6450	6.4341	6.2358	5.8729	5.5493	5.2590	4.9972
8.6058	8.2619	7.9432	7.6469	7.3711	7.1138	6.8732	6.6479	6.4364	6.2377	5.8743	5.5502	5.2596	4.9976
8.6150	8.2696	7.9495	7.6522	7.3754	7.1173	6.8761	6.6503	6.4385	6.2394	5.8755	5.5511	5.2602	4.9980
8.6233	8.2764	7.9551	7.6568	7.3792	7.1205	6.8787	6.6524	6.4402	6.2409	5.8765	5.5517	5.2607	4.9984
8.6308	8.2825	7.9601	7.6609	7.3826	7.1232	6.8810	6.6543	6.4418	6.2421	5.8773	5.5523	5.2611	4.9986
8.6375	8.2880	7.9645	7.6645	7.3855	7.1256	6.8830	6.6559	6.4431	6.2432	5.8781	5.5528	5.2614	4.9989
8.6435	8.2928	7.9685	7.6677	7.3881	7.1277	6.8847	6.6573	6.4442	6.2442	5.8787	5.5532	5.2617	4.9991
8.6489	8.2972	7.9720	7.6705	7.3904	7.1296	6.8862	6.6585	6.4452	6.2450	5.8792	5.5536	5.2619	4.9992
8.6537	8.3010	7.9751	7.6730	7.3925	7.1312	6.8875	6.6596	6.4461	6.2457	5.8797	5.5539	5.2621	4.9993
8.6580	8.3045	7.9779	7.6752	7.3942	7.1327	6.8886	6.6605	6.4468	6.2463	5.8801	5.5541	5.2623	4.9995

Glossary

ABC see activity-based costing

ABM see activity-based management

abnormal loss a decline in units in excess of normal expectations during a production process

absorption costing a cost accumulation and reporting method that treats the costs of all manufacturing components (direct material, direct labor, variable overhead, and fixed overhead) as inventoriable or product costs; it is the traditional approach to product costing; it must be used for external financial statements and tax returns

accepted quality level (AQL) the maximum limit for the number of defects or errors in a process

accounting rate of return (ARR) the rate of earnings obtained on the average capital investment over the life of a capital project; computed as average annual profits divided by average investment; not based on cash flow

accretion an increase in units or volume caused by the addition of material or by factors inherent in the production process

activity a repetitive action performed in fulfillment of business functions

activity analysis the process of detailing the various repetitive actions that are performed in making a product or providing a service, classifying them as value-added and non-value-added, and devising ways of minimizing or eliminating non-value-added activities

activity-based budgeting (ABB) a planning approach applying activity drivers to estimate the levels and costs of activities necessary to provide the budgeted quantity and quality of production

activity-based costing (ABC) a process using multiple cost drivers to predict and allocate costs to products and services; an accounting system collecting financial and operational data on the basis of the underlying nature and extent of business activities; an accounting information and costing system that identifies the various activities performed in an organization, collects costs on the basis of the underlying nature and extent of those activities, and assigns costs to products and services based on consumption of those activities by the products and services

activity-based management (ABM) a discipline that focuses on the activities incurred during the production/performance process as the way to improve the value received by a customer and the resulting profit achieved by providing this value

activity center a segment of the production or service process for which management wants to separately report the costs of the activities performed

activity driver a measure of the demands on activities and, thus, the resources consumed by products and services; often indicates an activity's output

actual cost system a valuation method that uses actual direct material, direct labor, and overhead charges in determining the cost of Work in Process Inventory

ad hoc discount a price concession made under competitive pressure (real or imagined) that does not relate to quantity purchased

administrative department an organizational unit that performs management activities benefiting the entire organization; includes top management personnel and organization headquarters

algebraic method a process of service department cost allocation that considers all interrelationships of the departments and reflects these relationships in simultaneous equations

algorithm a logical step-by-step problem-solving technique (generally requiring the use of a computer) that continuously searches for an improved solution from the one previously computed until the best answer is determined

allocate assign based on the use of a cost driver, a cost predictor, or an arbitrary method

allocation the systematic assignment of an amount to a recipient set of categories

annuity a series of equal cash flows (either positive or negative) per period

annuity due a series of equal cash flows being received or paid at the beginning of a period

applied overhead the amount of overhead that has been assigned to Work in Process Inventory as a result of productive activity; credits for this amount are to an overhead account

appraisal cost a quality control cost incurred for monitoring or inspection; compensates for mistakes not eliminated through prevention activities

appropriation a budgeted maximum allowable expenditure

approximated net realizable value at split-off allocation a method of allocating joint cost to joint products using a simulated net realizable value at the split-off point; approximated value is computed as final sales price minus incremental separate costs

asset turnover a ratio measuring asset productivity and showing the number of sales dollars generated by each dollar of assets

attribute-based costing (ABC II) an extension of activity-based costing using cost-benefit analysis (based on increased customer utility) to choose the product attribute enhancements that the company wants to integrate into a product

authority the right (usually by virtue of position or rank) to use resources to accomplish a task or achieve an objective

autonomation the use of equipment that has been programmed to sense certain conditions

backflush costing a streamlined cost accounting method that speeds up, simplifies, and reduces accounting effort in an environment that minimizes inventory balances, requires few allocations, uses standard costs, and has minimal variances from standard

balanced scorecard (BSC) an approach to performance measurement that weighs performance measures from four perspectives: financial performance, an internal business perspective, a customer perspective, and an innovation and learning perspective

bar code a group of lines and spaces arranged in a special machine-readable pattern by which a scanner measures the intensity of the light reflections of the white spaces between the lines and converts the signal back into the original data

batch-level cost a cost that is caused by a group of things being made, handled, or processed at a single time

benchmarking the process of investigating how others do something better so that the investigating company can imitate, and possibly improve upon, their techniques

benefits-provided ranking a listing of service departments in an order that begins with the one providing the most service to all other corporate areas; the ranking ends with the service department providing service primarily to revenue-producing areas

bill of materials a document that contains information about the product materials components and their specifications (including quality and quantities needed)

bottleneck any object or facility whose processing speed is sufficiently slow to cause the other processing mechanisms in its network to experience idle time

break-even chart a graph that depicts the relationships among revenues, variable costs, fixed costs, and profits (or losses)

break-even point (BEP) the level of activity, in units or dollars, at which total revenues equal total costs

budget a financial plan for the future based on a single level of activity; the quantitative expression of a company's commitment to planned activities and resource acquisition and use

budgeted cost a planned expenditure

budgeting the process of formalizing plans and committing them to written, financial terms

budget manual a detailed set of documents that provides information and guidelines about the budgetary process

budget slack an intentional underestimation of revenues and/or overestimation of expenses in a budgeting process for the purpose of including deviations that are likely to occur so that results will occur within budget limits

budget variance the difference between total actual overhead and budgeted overhead based on standard hours allowed for the production achieved during the period; computed as part of two-variance overhead analysis; also referred to as the controllable variance

build mission a mission of increasing market share, even at the expense of short-term profits and cash flow; typically pursued by a business unit that has a small market share in a high-growth industry; appropriate for products that are in the early stages of the product life cycle

business intelligence (BI) system a formal process for gathering and analyzing information and producing intelligence to meet decision making needs; requires information about internal processes as well as knowledge, technologies, and competitors

business process reengineering (BPR) the process of combining information technology to create new and more effective business processes to lower costs, eliminate unnecessary work, upgrade customer service, and increase speed to market

business-value-added activity an activity that is necessary for the operation of the business but for which a customer would not want to pay

by-product an incidental output of a joint process; it is salable, but the sales value of by-products is not substantial enough for management to justify undertaking the joint process; it is viewed as having a higher sales value than scrap

cafeteria plan a "menu" of fringe benefit options that include cash or nontaxable benefits

capacity a measure of production volume or some other activity base

capital asset an asset used to generate revenues or cost savings by providing production, distribution, or service capabilities for more than one year

capital budget management's plan for investments in long-term property, plant, and equipment

capital budgeting a process of evaluating an entity's proposed long-range projects or courses of future activity for the purpose of allocating limited resources to desirable projects

capital rationing a condition that exists when there is an upper-dollar constraint on the amount of capital available to commit to capital asset acquisition

carrying cost the total variable cost of carrying one unit of inventory in stock for one year; includes the opportunity cost of the capital invested in inventory

CASB see Cost Accounting Standards Board

cash flow the receipt or disbursement of cash; when related to capital budgeting, cash flows arise from the purchase, operation, and disposition of a capital asset

centralization a management style that exists when top management makes most decisions and controls most activities of the organizational units from the company's central headquarters

Certified Management Accountant (CMA) a professional designation in the area of management accounting that recognizes the successful completion of an examination, acceptable work experience, and continuing education requirements

charge-back system a system using transfer prices; see transfer price

coefficient of correlation a measure of dispersion that indicates the degree of relative association existing between two variables

coefficient of determination a measure of dispersion that indicates the "goodness of fit" of the actual observations to the least squares regression line; indicates what proportion of the total variation in y is explained by the regression model

coefficient of variation a measure of risk used when the standard deviations for multiple projects are approximately the same but the expected values are significantly different

committed cost a cost related either to the long-term investment in plant and equipment of a business or to the organizational personnel whom top management deem permanent; a cost that cannot be changed without long-run detriment to the organization

common body of knowledge (CBK) the minimum set of knowledge needed by a person to function effectively in a particular field

compensation committee a company committee comprised mainly of members of the board of directors; is responsible for establishing compensation packages for top management and setting general compensation policies and guidelines

compensation strategy a foundation for the compensation plan that addresses the role compensation should play in the organization

compound interest a method of determining interest in which interest that was earned in prior periods is added to the original investment so that, in each successive period, interest is earned on both principal and interest

compounding period the time between each interest computation

computer-aided design (CAD) a system using computer graphics for product designs

computer-aided manufacturing (CAM) the use of computers to control production processes through numerically controlled (NC) machines, robots, and automated assembly systems

computer integrated manufacturing (CIM) the integration of two or more flexible manufacturing systems through the use of a host computer and an information networking system

concurrent engineering see simultaneous engineering

confrontation strategy an organizational strategy in which company management decides to confront, rather than avoid, competition; an organizational strategy in which company management still attempts to differentiate company products through new features or to develop a price leadership position by dropping prices, even though management recognizes that competitors will rapidly bring out similar products and match price changes; an organizational strategy in which company management identifies and exploits current opportunities for competitive advantage in recognition of the fact that those opportunities will soon be eliminated

constraint a restriction inhibiting the achievement of an objective

contingent pay compensation that is dependent on the achievement of some performance objective

continuous budgeting a process in which there is a rolling twelve-month budget; a new budget month (twelve months into the future) is added as each current month expires

continuous improvement an ongoing process of enhancing employee task performance, level of product quality, and level of company service through eliminating non-value-added activities to reduce lead time, making products (performing services) with zero defects, reducing product costs on an ongoing basis, and simplifying products and processes

continuous loss any reduction in units that occurs uniformly throughout a production process

contract manufacturer an external party that has been granted an outsourcing contract to produce a part or component for an entity

contract vendor an external party that has been granted an outsourcing contract to provide a service activity for an entity

contribution margin the difference between selling price and variable cost per unit or in total for the level of activity; it indicates the amount of each revenue dollar remaining after variable costs have been covered and going toward the coverage of fixed costs and the generation of profits

contribution margin ratio the proportion of each revenue dollar remaining after variable costs have been covered; computed as contribution margin divided by sales

control chart a graphical presentation of the results of a specified activity; it indicates the upper and lower control limits and those results that are out of control

controllable cost a cost over which a manager has the ability to authorize incurrence or directly influence magnitude

controllable variance the budget variance of the two variance approach to analyzing overhead variances

controller the chief accountant (in a corporation) who is responsible for maintaining and reporting on both the cost and financial sets of accounts but does not handle or negotiate changes in actual resources

controlling the process of exerting managerial influence on operations so that they conform to previously prepared plans

conversion the process of transformation or change

conversion cost the total of direct labor and overhead cost; the cost necessary to transform direct material into a finished good or service

core competency a higher proficiency relative to competitors in a critical function or activity; a root of competitiveness and competitive advantage; anything that is not a core competency is a viable candidate for outsourcing

correlation analysis an analytical technique that uses statistical measures of dispersion to reveal the strength of the relationship between variables

cost the cash or cash equivalent value necessary to attain an objective such as acquiring goods and services, complying with a contract, performing a function, or producing and distributing a product

cost accounting a discipline that focuses on techniques or methods for determining the cost of a project, process, or thing through direct measurement, arbitrary assignment, or systematic and rational allocation

Cost Accounting Standards Board (CASB) a body established by Congress in 1970 to promulgate cost accounting standards for defense contractors and federal agencies; disbanded in 1980 and reestablished in 1988; it previously issued pronouncements still carry the weight of law for those organizations within its jurisdiction

cost accumulation the approach to product costing that determines which manufacturing costs are recorded as part of product cost

cost allocation the assignment, using some reasonable basis, of any indirect cost to one or more cost objects

cost avoidance the practice of finding acceptable alternatives to high-cost items and/or not spending money for unnecessary goods or services

cost-benefit analysis the analytical process of comparing the relative costs and benefits that result from a specific course of action (such as providing information or investing in a project)

cost center a responsibility center in which the manager has the authority to incur costs and is evaluated on the basis of how well costs are controlled

cost consciousness a company-wide attitude about the topics of cost understanding, cost containment, cost avoidance, and cost reduction

cost containment the practice of minimizing, to the extent possible, period-by-period increases in per-unit variable and total fixed costs

cost control system a logical structure of formal and/or informal activities designed to analyze and evaluate how well expenditures are managed during a period

cost driver a factor that has a direct cause-effect relationship to a cost; an activity creating a cost

cost driver analysis the process of investigating, quantifying, and explaining the relationships of cost drivers and their related costs

cost leadership strategy a plan to achieve the position in a competitive environment of being the low cost producer of a product or provider of a service; it provides one method of avoiding competition

cost management system (CMS) a set of formal methods developed for planning and controlling an organization's cost-generating activities relative to its goals and objectives

cost object anything to which costs attach or are related

cost of capital (COC) the weighted average cost of the various sources of funds (debt and stock) that comprise a firm's financial structure

cost of goods manufactured (CGM) the total cost of the goods completed and transferred to Finished Goods Inventory during the period

cost of production report a process costing document that details all operating and cost information, shows the computation of cost per equivalent unit, and indicates cost assignment to goods produced during the period

cost-plus contract a contract in which the customer agrees to reimburse the producer for the cost of the job plus a specified profit margin over cost

cost pool a collection of monetary amounts incurred either for the same purpose, at the same organizational level, or as a result of the occurrence of the same cost driver

cost presentation the approach to product costing that determines how costs are shown on external financial statements or internal management reports

cost reduction the practice of lowering current costs, especially those that may be in excess of what is necessary

cost structure the relative composition of an organization's fixed and variable costs

cost table a database providing information about the impact on product costs of using different input resources, manufacturing processes, and design specifications

cost-volume-profit (CVP) analysis a procedure that examines changes in costs and volume levels and the resulting effects on net income (profits)

critical success factors (CSF) any item (such as quality, customer service, efficiency, cost control, or responsiveness to change) so important that, without it, the organization would cease to exist

CVP see cost-volume-profit analysis

cycle time the time between the placement of an order to the time the goods arrive for usage or are produced by the company; it is equal to value-added time plus non-value-added time

data bits of knowledge or facts that have not been summarized or categorized in a manner useful to a decision maker

data mining a form of analysis in which statistical techniques are used to uncover answers to important questions about business operations

decentralization a management style that exists when top management grants subordinate managers a significant degree of autonomy and independence in operating and making decisions for their organizational units

decision making the process of choosing among the alternative solutions available to a course of action or a problem situation

decision variable an unknown item for which a linear programming problem is being solved

defective unit a unit that has been rejected at a control inspection point for failure to meet appropriate standards of quality or designated product specifications; can be economically reworked and sold through normal distribution channels

deferred compensation pay related to current performance that will be received at a later time, typically after retirement

degree of operating leverage a factor that indicates how a percentage change in sales, from the existing or current level, will affect company profits; it is calculated as contribution margin divided by net income; it is equal to (1 ÷ margin of safety percentage)

dependent variable an unknown variable that is to be predicted using one or more independent variables

design for manufacturability (DFM) a process that is part of the project management of a new product; concerned with finding optimal solutions to minimizing product failures and other adversities in the delivery of a new product to customers

differential cost a cost that differs in amount among the alternatives being considered

differentiation strategy a technique for avoiding competition by distinguishing a product or service from that of competitors through adding sufficient value (including quality and/or features) that customers are willing to pay a higher price than that charged by competitors

direct cost a cost that is distinctly traceable to a particular cost object

direct costing see variable costing

direct labor the time spent by individuals who work specifically on manufacturing a product or performing a service; the cost of such time

direct material a readily identifiable part of a product; the cost of such a part

direct method a service department cost allocation approach that assigns service department costs directly to revenue-producing areas with only one set of intermediate cost pools or allocations

discounting the process of reducing future cash flows to present value amounts

discount rate the rate of return used to discount future cash flows to their present value amounts; it should equal or exceed an organization's weighted average cost of capital

discrete loss a reduction in units that occurs at a specific point in a production process

discretionary cost a cost that is periodically reviewed by a decision maker in a process of determining whether it continues to be in accord with ongoing policies; a cost that arises from a management decision to fund an activity at a specified cost amount for a specified period of time, generally one year; a cost that can be reduced to zero in the short run if necessity so dictates

dispersion the degree of variability or difference; it is measured as the vertical distance of an actual point from the estimated regression line in least squares regression analysis

distribution cost a cost incurred to warehouse, transport, or deliver a product or service

dividend growth method a method of computing the cost of common stock equity that indicates the rate of return that common shareholders expect to earn in the form of dividends on a company's common stock

dollar days (of inventory) a measurement of the value of inventory for the time that inventory is held

downsizing any management action that reduces employment upon restructuring operations in response to competitive pressures

dual pricing arrangement a transfer pricing system that allows a selling division to record the transfer of goods or services at one price (e.g., a market or negotiated market price) and a buying division to record the transfer at another price (e.g., a cost-based amount)

dumping selling products abroad at lower prices than those charged in the home country or in other national markets

Du Pont model a model that indicates the return on investment as it is affected by profit margin and asset turnover

e-commerce (electronic commerce) any business activity that uses the Internet and World Wide Web to engage in financial transactions

economic integration the creation of multi-country markets by developing transnational rules that reduce the fiscal and physical barriers to trade as well as encourage greater economic cooperation among countries

economic order quantity (EOQ) an estimate of the number of units per order that will be the least costly and provide the optimal balance between the costs of ordering and the costs of carrying inventory

economic production run (EPR) an estimate of the number of units to produce at one time that minimizes the total costs of setting up production runs and carrying inventory

economically reworked when the incremental revenue from the sale of reworked defective units is greater than the incremental cost of the rework

economic value added (EVA) a measure of the extent to which income exceeds the dollar cost of capital; calculated as income minus (invested capital times the cost of capital percentage)

effectiveness a measure of how well an organization's goals and objectives are achieved; compares actual output results to desired results; determination of the successful accomplishment of an objective

efficiency a measure of the degree to which tasks were performed to produce the best yield at the lowest cost from the resources available; the degree to which a satisfactory relationship of outputs to inputs occurs

electronic data interchange (EDI) the computer-to-computer transfer of information in virtual real time using standardized formats developed by the American National Standards Institute

Employee Stock Ownership Plan (ESOP) a profit-sharing compensation program in which investments are made in the securities of the employer

employee time sheet a source document that indicates, for each employee, what jobs were worked on during the day and for what amount of time

empowerment the process of giving workers the training and authority they need to manage their own jobs

engineered cost a cost that has been found to bear an observable and known relationship to a quantifiable activity base

engineering change order (ECO) a business mandate that changes the way in which a product is manufactured or a service is performed by modifying the design, parts, process, or even quality of the product or service

enterprise resource planning (ERP) system a packaged software program that allows a company to (1) automate and integrate the majority of its business processes, (2) share common data and practices across the entire enterprise, and (3) produce and access information in a real-time environment

environmental constraint any limitation on strategy options caused by external cultural, fiscal, legal/regulatory, or political situations; a limiting factor that is not under the direct control of an organization's management; tend to be fairly long-run in nature

equivalent units of production (EUP) an approximation of the number of whole units of output that could have been produced during a period from the actual effort expended during that period; used in process costing systems to assign costs to production

ethical standard a standard representing beliefs about moral and immoral behaviors

European Union (EU) an economic alliance originally created in 1957 as the European Economic Community by France, Germany, Italy, Belgium, the Netherlands, and Luxembourg and later joined by the United Kingdom, Ireland, Denmark, Spain, Portugal, and Greece; prior to the Maastricht Treaty of 1993 was called the European Community; has eliminated virtually all barriers to the flow of capital, labor, goods, and services among member nations

expatriate a parent company or third-country national assigned to a foreign subsidiary or a foreign national assigned to the parent company

expected capacity a short-run concept that represents the anticipated level of capacity to be used by a firm in the upcoming period, based on projected product demand

expected standard a standard set at a level that reflects what is actually expected to occur in the future period; it anticipates future waste and inefficiencies and allows for them; is of limited value for control and performance evaluation purposes

expired cost an expense or a loss

failure cost a quality control cost associated with goods or services that have been found not to conform or perform to the required standards as well as all related costs (such as that of the complaint department); it may be internal or external

feasible region the graphical space contained within and on all of the constraint lines in the graphical solution to a linear programming problem

feasible solution a solution to a linear programming problem that does not violate any problem constraints

FIFO method (of process costing) the method of cost assignment that computes an average cost per equivalent unit of production for the current period; keeps beginning inventory units and costs separate from current period production and costs

financial accounting a discipline in which historical, monetary transactions are analyzed and recorded for use in the preparation of the financial statements (balance sheet, income statement, statement of owners'/stockholders' equity, and statement of cash flows); it focuses primarily on the needs of external users (stockholders, creditors, and regulatory agencies)

financial budget a plan that aggregates monetary details from the operating budgets; includes the cash and capital budgets of a company as well as the pro forma financial statements

financial incentive a monetary reward provided for performance above targeted objectives

financing decision a judgment made regarding the method of raising funds that will be used to make acquisitions; it is based on an entity's ability to issue and service debt and equity securities

Fisher rate the rate of return that equates the present values of the cash flows of all projects being considered; it is the rate of indifference

fixed cost a cost that remains constant in total within a specified range of activity

fixed overhead spending variance the difference between the total actual fixed overhead and budgeted fixed overhead; it is computed as part of the four-variance overhead analysis

fixed overhead volume variance see volume variance

flexible budget a presentation of multiple budgets that show costs according to their behavior at different levels of activity

flexible manufacturing system (FMS) a production system in which a single factory manufactures numerous variations of products through the use of computer-controlled robots

focused factory arrangement an arrangement in which a vendor (which may be an external party or an internal corporate division) agrees to provide a limited number of products according to specifications or to perform a limited number of unique services to a company that is typically operating on a just-in-time system

Foreign Corrupt Practices Act (FCPA) a law passed by Congress in 1977 that makes it illegal for a U.S. company to engage in various "questionable" foreign payments and makes it mandatory for a U.S. company to maintain accurate accounting records and a reasonable system of internal control

full costing see absorption costing

functional classification a separation of costs into groups based on the similar reason for their incurrence; it includes cost of goods sold and detailed selling and administrative expenses

future value the amount to which one or more sums of money invested at a specified interest rate will grow over a specified number of time periods

General Agreement on Tariffs and Trade (GATT) a treaty among many nations setting standards for tariffs and trade for signees

global economy an economy characterized by the international trade of goods and services, the international movement of labor, and the international flows of capital and information

globalization a changeover in market focus from competition among local or national suppliers to competition among international suppliers

goal a desired abstract achievement

goal congruence a circumstance in which the personal and organizational goals of decision makers throughout a firm are consistent and mutually supportive

golden parachute a benefits package that is triggered by the termination of a manager's employment

grade (of product or service) the addition or removal of product or service characteristics to satisfy additional needs, especially price

grapevine the informal relationships and channels of communication that exist in an organization

growth rate an estimate of the increase expected in dividends (or in market value) per share of stock

harvest mission a mission that attempts to maximize short-term profits and cash flow, even at the expense of market share; it is typically pursued by a business unit that has a large market share in a low-growth industry; it is appropriate for products in the final stages of the product life cycle

high-low method a technique used to determine the fixed and variable portions of a mixed cost; it uses only the highest and lowest levels of activity within the relevant range

historical cost a cost incurred in the past; the recorded purchase price of an asset; a sunk cost

hold mission a mission that attempts to protect the business unit's market share and competitive position; typically pursued by a business unit with a large market share in a high-growth industry

hurdle rate a preestablished rate of return against which other rates of return are measured; it is usually the cost of capital rate when used in evaluating capital projects

hybrid costing system a costing system combining characteristics of both job order and process costing systems

ideal capacity see theoretical capacity

ideal standard a standard that provides for no inefficiencies of any type; impossible to attain on a continuous basis

idle time the amount of time spent in storing inventory or waiting at a production operation for processing

imposed budget a budget developed by top management with little or no input from operating personnel; operating personnel are then informed of the budget objectives and constraints

incremental analysis a process of evaluating changes that focuses only on the factors that differ from one course of action or decision to another

incremental cost the cost of producing or selling an additional contemplated quantity of output

incremental revenue the revenue resulting from an additional contemplated sale

incremental separate cost the cost that is incurred for each joint product between the split-off point and the point of sale

independent project an investment project that has no specific bearing on any other investment project

independent variable a variable that, when changed, will cause consistent, observable changes in another variable; a variable used as the basis of predicting the value of a dependent variable

indirect cost a cost that cannot be traced explicitly to a particular cost object; a common cost

information bits of knowledge or fact that have been carefully chosen from a body of data and arranged in a meaningful way

input-output coefficient a number (prefaced as a multiplier to an unknown variable) that indicates the rate at which each decision variable uses up (or depletes) the scarce resource

inspection time the time taken to perform quality control activities

Institute of Management Accountants (IMA) an organization composed of individuals interested in the field of management accounting; it coordinates the Certified Management Accountant program through its affiliate organization (the Institute of Certified Management Accountants)

integer programming a mathematical programming technique in which all solutions for variables must be restricted to whole numbers

intellectual capital the intangible assets of skill, knowledge, and information that exist in an organization; it encompasses human, structural, and relationship capital

internal control any measure used by management to protect assets, promote the accuracy of records, ensure adherence to company policies, or promote operational efficiency; the totality of all internal controls represents the internal control system

internal rate of return (IRR) the expected or actual rate of return from a project based on, respectively, the assumed or actual cash flows; the discount rate at which the net present value of the cash flows equals zero

Internet business model a model that involves (1) few physical assets, (2) little management hierarchy, and (3) a direct pipeline to customers

interpolation the process of finding a term between two other terms in a series

intranet a mechanism for sharing information and delivering data from corporate databases to the local-area network (LAN) desktops

inventoriable cost see product cost

investment center a responsibility center in which the manager is responsible for generating revenues and planning and controlling expenses and has the authority to acquire, dispose of, and use plant assets to earn the highest rate of return feasible on those assets within the confines and to the support of the organization's goals

investment decision a judgment about which assets will be acquired by an entity to achieve its stated objectives

ISO 9000 a comprehensive series of international quality standards that define the various design, material procurement, production, quality-control, and delivery requirements and procedures necessary to produce quality products and services

ISO 14000 a series of international standards that are designed to support a company's environmental protection and pollution prevention goals in balance with socioeconomic needs

JIT see just-in-time

job a single unit or group of units identifiable as being produced to distinct customer specifications

job cost record see job order cost sheet

job order cost sheet a source document that provides virtually all the financial information about a particular job; the set of all job order cost sheets for uncompleted jobs composes the Work in Process Inventory subsidiary ledger

job order costing system a system of product costing used by an entity that provides limited quantities of products or services unique to a customer's needs; focus of recordkeeping is on individual jobs

joint cost the total of all costs (direct material, direct labor, and overhead) incurred in a joint process up to the split-off point

joint process a manufacturing process that simultaneously produces more than one product line

joint product one of the primary outputs of a joint process; each joint product individually has substantial revenue-generating ability

judgmental method (of risk adjustment) an informal method of adjusting for risk that allows the decision maker to use logic and reason to decide whether a project provides an acceptable rate of return

just-in-time (JIT) a philosophy about when to do something; the when is "as needed" and the something is a production, purchasing, or delivery activity

just-in-time manufacturing system a production system that attempts to acquire components and produce inventory only as needed, to minimize product defects, and to reduce lead/setup times for acquisition and production

just-in-time training a system that maps the skill sets employees need and delivers the training they need just as they need it

kaizen the Japanese word for continuous improvement

kaizen costing a costing technique to reflect continuous efforts to reduce product costs, improve product quality, and/or improve the production process after manufacturing activities have begun

kanban the Japanese word for card; it was the original name for a JIT system because of the use of cards that indicated a work center's need for additional components during a manufacturing process

key variable a critical factor that management believes will be a direct cause of the achievement or nonachievement of the organizational goals and objectives

labor efficiency variance the number of hours actually worked minus the standard hours allowed for the production achieved multiplied by the standard rate to establish a value for efficiency (favorable) or inefficiency (unfavorable) of the work force

labor mix variance (actual mix × actual hours × standard rate) minus (standard mix × actual hours × standard rate); it presents the financial effect associated with changing the proportionate amount of higher or lower paid workers in production

labor rate variance the actual rate (or actual weighted average rate) paid to labor for the period minus the standard rate multiplied by all hours actually worked during the period; it is actual labor cost minus (actual hours × standard rate)

labor yield variance (standard mix × actual hours × standard rate) minus (standard mix × standard hours × standard rate); it shows the monetary impact of using more or fewer total hours than the standard allowed

lead time see cycle time

learning curve a model that helps predict how labor time will decrease as people become more experienced at performing a task and eliminate the inefficiencies associated with unfamiliarity

least squares regression analysis a statistical technique that investigates the association between dependent and independent variables; it determines the line of "best fit" for a set of observations by minimizing the sum of the squares of the vertical deviations between actual points and the regression line; it can be used to determine the fixed and variable portions of a mixed cost

life cycle costing the accumulation of costs for activities that occur over the entire life cycle of a product from inception to abandonment by the manufacturer and consumer

limited liability company an organizational form that is a hybrid of the corporate and partnership organizational forms and used to limit the personal liability of the owners; it is typically used by small professional (such as accounting) firms

limited liability partnership an organizational form that is a hybrid of the corporate and partnership organizational forms and used to limit the personal liability of the owners; it is typically used by large professional (such as accounting) firms

line employee an employee who is directly responsible for achieving the organization's goals and objectives

linear programming a method of mathematical programming used to solve a problem that involves an objective function and multiple limiting factors or constraints

long-term variable cost a cost that was traditionally viewed as a fixed cost

loss an expired cost that was unintentionally incurred; a cost that does not relate to the generation of revenues

make-or-buy decision a decision that compares the cost of internally manufacturing a component of a final product (or providing a service function) with the cost of purchasing it from outside suppliers (outsourcing) or from another division of the company at a specified transfer price

management accounting a discipline that includes almost all manipulations of financial information for use by managers in performing their organizational functions and in assuring the proper use and handling of an entity's resources; it includes the discipline of cost accounting

Management Accounting Guidelines (MAGs) pronouncements of the Society of Management Accountants of Canada that advocate appropriate practices for specific management accounting situations

management control system (MCS) an information system that helps managers gather information about actual organizational occurrences, make comparisons against plans, effect changes when they are necessary, and communicate among appropriate parties; it should serve to guide organizations in designing and implementing strategies so that organizational goals and objectives are achieved

management information system (MIS) a structure of interrelated elements that collects, organizes, and communicates data to managers so they may plan, control, evaluate performance, and make decisions; the emphasis of the MIS is on internal demands for information rather than external demands; some or all of the MIS may be computerized for ease of access to information, reliability of input and processing, and ability to simulate outcomes of alternative situations

management style the preference of a manager in how he/she interacts with other stakeholders in the organization; it influences the way the firm engages in transactions and is manifested in managerial decisions, interpersonal and interorganizational relationships, and resource allocations

manufacturer a company engaged in a high degree of conversion that results in a tangible output

manufacturing cell a linear or U-shaped production grouping of workers or machines

manufacturing cycle efficiency (MCE) a ratio resulting from dividing the actual production time by total lead time; reflects the proportion of lead time that is value-added

manufacturing resource planning (MRP II) a fully integrated materials requirement planning system that involves top management and provides a basis for both strategic and tactical planning

maquiladora a business (typically U.S.-owned on the Mexican side of the United States-Mexico border) that exists under a special trade agreement in which foreign companies import materials into Mexico duty-free for assembly, then export the goods back out of Mexico, and only pay duty on the value added to inventory in the process

margin of safety the excess of the budgeted or actual sales of a company over its breakeven point; it can be calculated in units or dollars or as a percentage; it is equal to (1 ÷ degree of operating leverage)

mass customization personalized production generally accomplished through the use of flexible manufacturing systems; it reflects an organization's increase in product variety from the same basic component elements

master budget the comprehensive set of all budgetary schedules and the pro forma financial statements of an organization

material price variance total actual cost of material purchased minus (actual quantity of material × standard price); it is the amount of money spent below (favorable) or in excess (unfavorable) of the standard price for the quantity of materials purchased; it can be calculated based on the actual quantity of material purchased or the actual quantity used

material quantity variance (actual quantity × standard price) minus (standard quantity allowed × standard price); the standard cost saved (favorable) or expended (unfavorable) due to the difference between the actual quantity of material used and the standard quantity of material allowed for the goods produced during the period

material requisition form a source document that indicates the types and quantities of material to be placed into production or used in performing a service; it causes materials and its cost to be released from the Raw Material Inventory warehouse and sent to Work in Process Inventory

material mix variance (actual mix × actual quantity × standard price) minus (standard mix × actual quantity × standard price); it computes the monetary effect of substituting a nonstandard mix of material

materials requirements planning (MRP) a computer-based information system that simulates the ordering and scheduling of demand-dependent inventories; a simulation of the parts fabrication and subassembly activities that are required, in an appropriate time sequence, to meet a production master schedule

material yield variance (standard mix × actual quantity × standard price) minus (standard mix × standard quantity × standard price); it computes the difference between the actual total quantity of input and the standard total quantity allowed based on output and uses standard mix and standard prices to determine variance

mathematical programming a variety of techniques used to allocate limited resources among activities to achieve a specific objective

matrix structure an organizational structure in which functional departments and project teams exist simultaneously so that the resulting lines of authority resemble a grid

merit pay a pay increment earned by achieving a specific level of performance

method of least squares see least squares regression analysis

method of neglect a method of treating spoiled units in the equivalent units schedule as if those units did not occur; it is used for continuous normal spoilage

mission statement a written expression of organizational purpose that describes how the organization uniquely meets its targeted customers' needs with its products or services

mix any possible combination of material or labor inputs

mixed cost a cost that has both a variable and a fixed component; it varies with changes in activity, but not proportionately

modified FIFO method (of process costing) the method of cost assignment that uses FIFO to compute a cost per equivalent unit but, in transferring units from a department, the costs of the beginning inventory units and the units started and completed are combined and averaged

MRP see materials requirements planning

MRP II see manufacturing resource planning

multiple regression a statistical technique that uses two or more independent variables to predict a dependent variable

multiprocess handling the ability of a worker to monitor and operate several (or all) machines in a manufacturing cell or perform all steps of a specific task

mutually exclusive projects a set of proposed capital projects from which one is chosen, causing all the others to be rejected

mutually inclusive projects a set of proposed capital projects that are all related and that must all be chosen if the primary project is chosen

negotiated transfer price an intracompany charge for goods or services set through a process of negotiation between the selling and purchasing unit managers

net cost of normal spoilage the cost of spoiled work less the estimated disposal value of that work

net present value (NPV) the difference between the present values of all cash inflows and outflows for an investment project

net present value method a process that uses the discounted cash flows of a project to determine whether the rate of return on that project is equal to, higher than, or lower than the desired rate of return

net realizable value approach a method of accounting for by-products or scrap that requires that the net realizable value of these products be treated as a reduction in the cost of the primary products; primary product cost may be reduced by decreasing either (1) cost of goods sold when the joint products are sold or (2) the joint process cost allocated to the joint products

net realizable value at split-off allocation a method of allocating joint cost to joint products that uses, as the proration base, sales value at split-off minus all costs necessary to prepare and dispose of the products; it requires that all joint products be salable at the split-off point

network organization a flexible organization structure that establishes a working relationship among multiple entities, usually to pursue a single function

noncontrollable variance the fixed overhead volume variance; it is computed as part of the two-variance approach to overhead analysis

non-negativity constraint a restriction in a linear programming problem stating that negative values for physical quantities cannot exist in a solution

non-value-added (NVA) activity an activity that increases the time spent on a product or service but that does not increase its worth or value to the customer

normal capacity the long-run (5–10 years) average production or service volume of a firm; it takes into consideration cyclical and seasonal fluctuations

normal cost system a valuation method that uses actual costs of direct material and direct labor in conjunction with a predetermined overhead rate or rates in determining the cost of Work in Process Inventory

normal loss an expected decline in units during the production process

normal spoilage spoilage that has been planned or foreseen; is a product cost

North American Free Trade Agreement (NAFTA) an agreement among Canada, Mexico, and the United States establishing the North American Free Trade Zone, with a resulting reduction in trade barriers

objective a desired quantifiable achievement for a period of time
objective function the linear mathematical equation that states the purpose of a linear programming problem
open purchase ordering a process by which a single purchase order that expires at a set or determinable future date is prepared to authorize a supplier to provide a large quantity of one or more specified items on an as-requested basis by the customer
open-book management a philosophy about increasing a firm's performance by involving all workers and by ensuring that all workers have access to operational and financial information necessary to achieve performance improvements
operating budget a budget expressed in both units and dollars
operating leverage the proportionate relationship between a company's variable and fixed costs
operational plan a formulation of the details of implementing and maintaining an organization's strategic plan; it is typically formalized in the master budget
operations flow document a document listing all operations necessary to produce one unit of product (or perform a specific service) and the corresponding time allowed for each operation
opportunity cost a potential benefit that is foregone because one course of action is chosen over another
opportunity cost of capital the highest rate of return that could be earned by using capital for the most attractive alternative project(s) available
optimal mix of capital the combination of capital sources at which the lowest weighted average cost of capital is achieved
optimal solution the solution to a linear programming problem that provides the best answer to the objective function
ordering cost the variable cost associated with preparing, receiving, and paying for an order
order point the level of inventory that triggers the placement of an order for additional units; it is determined based on usage, lead time, and safety stock
ordinary annuity a series of equal cash flows being received or paid at the end of a period
organizational culture the set of basic assumptions about the organization and its goals and ways of doing business; a system of shared values about what is important and beliefs about how things get accomplished; it provides a framework that organizes and directs employee behavior at work; it describes an organization's norms in internal and external, as well as formal and informal, transactions
organizational-level cost a cost incurred to support the ongoing facility or operations
organizational structure the manner in which authority and responsibility for decision making is distributed in an entity
organization chart a depiction of the functions, divisions, and positions of the people/jobs in a company and how they are related; it also indicates the lines of authority and responsibility
organizational form an entity's legal nature (for example, sole proprietorship, partnership, corporation)
outlier an abnormal or nonrepresentative point within a data set
out-of-pocket cost a cost that is a current or near-current cash expenditure
outsourcing the use, by one company, of an external provider of a service or manufacturer of a component
outsourcing decision see make-or-buy decision
overapplied overhead a credit balance in the Overhead account at the end of a period; when the applied overhead amount is greater than the actual overhead that was incurred
overhead any factory or production cost that is indirect to the product or service; it does not include direct material or direct labor; any production cost that cannot be directly traced to the product
overhead application rate see predetermined overhead rate
overhead efficiency variance the difference between total budgeted overhead at actual hours and total budgeted overhead at standard hours allowed for the production achieved; it is computed as part of a three-variance analysis; it is the same as variable overhead efficiency variance
overhead spending variance the difference between total actual overhead and total budgeted overhead at actual hours; it is computed as part of three-variance analysis; it is equal to the sum of the variable and fixed overhead spending variances

Pareto analysis a method of ranking the causes of variation in a process according to the impact on an objective
Pareto inventory analysis an analysis that separates inventory into three groups based on annual cost-to-volume usage
Pareto principle a rule which states that the greatest effects in human endeavors are traceable to a small number of causes (the *vital few*), while the majority of causes (the *trivial many*) collectively yield only a small impact; this relationship is often referred to as the 20:80 rule
participatory budget a budget that has been developed through a process of joint decision making by top management and operating personnel
payback period the time it takes an investor to recoup an original investment through cash flows from a project
perfection standard see ideal standard
performance evaluation the process of determining the degree of success in accomplishing a task; it equates to both effectiveness and efficiency
performance management system a system reflecting the entire package of decisions regarding performance measurement and evaluation
period cost a cost other than one associated with making or acquiring inventory
periodic compensation a pay plan based on the time spent on the task rather than the work accomplished
perk a fringe benefit provided by the employer
phantom profit a temporary absorption costing profit caused by producing more inventory than is sold
physical measurement allocation a method of allocating a joint cost to products that uses a common physical characteristic as the proration base

piece rate a pay plan in which workers are paid a flat rate for each unit of work accomplished

planning the process of creating the goals and objectives for an organization and developing a strategy for achieving them in a systematic manner

postinvestment audit the process of gathering information on the actual results of a capital project and comparing them to the expected results

practical capacity the physical production or service volume that a firm could achieve during normal working hours with consideration given to ongoing, expected operating interruptions

practical standard a standard that can be reached or slightly exceeded with reasonable effort by workers; it allows for normal, unavoidable time problems or delays and for worker breaks; it is often believed to be most effective in inducing the best performance from workers, since such a standard represents an attainable challenge

predetermined overhead rate an estimated constant charge per unit of activity used to assign overhead cost to production or services of the period; it is calculated by dividing total budgeted annual overhead at a selected level of volume or activity by that selected measure of volume or activity; it is also the standard overhead application rate

predictor an activity measure that, when changed, is accompanied by consistent, observable changes in another item

preference decision the second decision made in capital project evaluation in which projects are ranked according to their impact on the achievement of company objectives

present value (PV) the amount that one or more future cash flows is worth currently, given a specified rate of interest

present value index see profitability index

prevention cost a cost incurred to improve quality by preventing defects from occurring

price fixing a practice by which firms conspire to set a products price at a specified level

prime cost the total cost of direct material and direct labor for a product

probability distribution a range of possible values for which each value has an assigned likelihood of occurrence

process benchmarking benchmarking that focuses on practices and how the best-in-class companies achieved their results

process complexity an assessment about the number of processes through which a product flows

process costing system a method of accumulating and assigning costs to units of production in companies producing large quantities of homogeneous products; it accumulates costs by cost component in each production department and assigns costs to units using equivalent units of production

processing time the actual time consumed performing the functions necessary to manufacture a product

process map a flowchart or diagram indicating every step that goes into making a product or providing a service

process productivity the total units produced during a period using value-added processing time

process quality yield the proportion of good units that resulted from the activities expended

procurement card a card given to selected employees as a means of securing greater control over spending and eliminating the paper-based purchase authorization process

product complexity an assessment about the number of components in a product

product contribution margin the difference between selling price and variable cost of goods sold

product cost a cost associated with making or acquiring inventory

productive capacity the number of total units that could be produced during a period based on available equipment time

productive processing time the proportion of total time that is value-added time; also known as manufacturing cycle efficiency

product- (or process-) level cost a cost that is caused by the development, production, or acquisition of specific products or services

product life cycle a model depicting the stages through which a product class (not necessarily each product) passes

product line margin see segment margin

product variety the number of different types of products produced (or services rendered) by a firm

profit center a responsibility center in which managers are responsible for generating revenues and planning and controlling all expenses

profit margin the ratio of income to sales

profit sharing an incentive payment to employees that is contingent on organizational or individual performance

profit-volume graph a visual representation of the amount of profit or loss associated with each level of sales

profitability index (PI) a ratio that compares the present value of net cash flows to the present value of the net investment

program budgeting an approach to budgeting that relates resource inputs to service outputs

project the purchase, installation, and operation of a capital asset

pseudo microprofit center a center for which a surrogate of market value must be used to measure output revenue

pull system a production system dictated by product sales and demand; a system in which parts are delivered or produced only as they are needed by the work center for which they are intended; it requires only minimal storage facilities

purchasing cost the quoted price of inventory minus any discounts allowed plus shipping charges

push system the traditional production system in which work centers may produce inventory that is not currently needed because of lead time or economic production/order requirements; it requires that excess inventory be stored until needed

quality all the characteristics of a product or service that make it able to meet the stated or implied needs of the buyer; it relates to both performance and value; the pride of workmanship; it is conformance to requirements

quality assurance the process of determining that product or service quality conforms to designated specifications usually through an inspection process

quality audit a review of product design activities (although not for individual products), manufacturing processes and controls, quality documentation and records, and management philosophy

quality control the implementation of all practices and policies designed to eliminate poor quality and variability in the production or service process; it places the primary responsibility for quality at the source of the product or service

raider a firm or individual that specializes in taking over other firms

real microprofit center a center whose output has a market value

realized value approach a method of accounting for byproducts or scrap that does not recognize any value for these products until they are sold; the value recognized upon sale can be treated as other revenue or other income

red-line system an inventory ordering system in which a red line is painted on the inventory container at a point deemed to be the reorder point

regression line any line that goes through the means (or averages) of the set of observations for an independent variable and its dependent variables; mathematically, there is a line of "best fit," which is the least squares regression line

reinvestment assumption an assumption made about the rates of return that will be earned by intermediate cash flows from a capital project; NPV and PI assume reinvestment at the discount rate; IRR assumes reinvestment at the IRR

relevant cost a cost that is logically associated with a specific problem or decision

relevant costing a process that compares, to the extent possible and practical, the incremental revenues and incremental costs of alternative decisions

relevant range the specified range of activity over which a variable cost per unit remains constant or a fixed cost remains fixed in total; it is generally assumed to be the normal operating range of the organization

replacement cost an amount that a firm would pay to replace an asset or buy a new one that performs the same functions as an asset currently held

residual income the profit earned by a responsibility center that exceeds an amount "charged" for funds committed to that center

responsibility the obligation to accomplish a task or achieve an objective

responsibility accounting system an accounting information system for successively higher-level managers about the performance of segments or subunits under the control of each specific manager

responsibility center a cost object under the control of a manager

responsibility report a report that reflects the revenues and/or costs under the control of a particular unit manager

results benchmarking benchmarking in which an end product or service is examined; the focus is on product/service specifications and performance results

return of capital the recovery of the original investment (or principal) in a project

return on capital income; it is equal to the rate of return multiplied by the amount of the investment

return on investment a ratio that relates income generated by an investment center to the resources (or asset base) used to produce that income

revenue center a responsibility center for which a manager is accountable only for the generation of revenues and has no control over setting selling prices, or budgeting or incurring costs

risk uncertainty; it reflects the possibility of differences between the expected and actual future returns from an investment

risk-adjusted discount rate method a formal method of adjusting for risk in which the decision maker increases the rate used for discounting the future cash flows to compensate for increased risk

Robinson-Patman Act a law that prohibits companies from pricing the same products at different amounts when those amounts do not reflect related cost differences

rolling budget see continuous budgeting

routing document see operations flow document

safety stock a buffer level of inventory kept on hand by a company in the event of fluctuating usage or unusual delays in lead time

sales mix the relative combination of quantities of sales of the various products that make up the total sales of a company

sales value at split-off allocation a method of assigning joint cost to joint products that uses the relative sales values of the products at the split-off point as the proration basis; use of this method requires that all joint products are salable at the split-off point

scarce resource a resource that is essential to production activity, but is available only in some limited quantity

scattergraph a graph that plots all known activity observations and the associated costs; it is used to separate mixed costs into their variable and fixed components and to examine patterns reflected by the plotted observations

scrap an incidental output of a joint process; it is salable but the sales value from scrap is not enough for management to justify undertaking the joint process; it is viewed as having a lower sales value than a by-product; leftover material that has a minimal but distinguishable disposal value

screening decision the first decision made in evaluating capital projects; it indicates whether a project is desirable based on some previously established minimum criterion or criteria (see also preference decision)

segment margin the excess of revenues over direct variable expenses and avoidable fixed expenses for a particular segment

sensitivity analysis a process of determining the amount of change that must occur in a variable before a different decision would be made

service company an individual or firm engaged in a high or moderate degree of conversion that results in service output

service department an organizational unit that provides one or more specific functional tasks for other internal units

service time the actual time consumed performing the functions necessary to provide a service

setup cost the direct or indirect cost of getting equipment ready for each new production run

shirking the process of an individual free-riding on a group effort because the individual's share of the group reward is insufficient to compensate for his or her separate effort

shrinkage a decrease in units arising from an inherent characteristic of the production process; it includes decreases caused by evaporation, leakage, and oxidation

simple interest a method of determining interest in which interest is earned only on the original investment (or principal) amount

simple regression a statistical technique that uses only one independent variable to predict a dependent variable

simplex method an iterative (sequential) algorithm used to solve multivariable, multiconstraint linear programming problems

simultaneous engineering an integrated approach in which all primary functions and personnel contributing to a product's origination and production are involved continuously from the beginning of a product's life

six-sigma method a high-performance, data-driven approach to analyzing and solving the root causes of business problems

slack variable a variable used in a linear programming problem that represents the unused amount of a resource at any level of operation; it is associated with less-than-or-equal-to constraints

Society of Management Accountants of Canada the professional body representing an influential and diverse group of Certified Management Accountants; this body produces numerous publications that address business management issues

special order decision a situation in which management must determine a sales price to charge for manufacturing or service jobs outside the company's normal production/service market

split-off point the point at which the outputs of a joint process are first identifiable or can be separated as individual products

spoiled unit a unit that is rejected at a control inspection point for failure to meet appropriate standards of quality or designated product specifications; it cannot be economically reworked to be brought up to standard

staff employee an employee responsible for providing advice, guidance, and service to line personnel

standard a model or budget against which actual results are compared and evaluated; a benchmark or norm used for planning and control purposes

standard cost a budgeted or estimated cost to manufacture a single unit of product or perform a single service

standard cost card a document that summarizes the direct material, direct labor, and overhead standard quantities and prices needed to complete one unit of product

standard cost system a valuation method that uses predetermined norms for direct material, direct labor, and overhead to assign costs to the various inventory accounts and Cost of Goods Sold

standard deviation the measure of variability of data around the average (or mean) value of the data

standard error of the estimate a measure of dispersion that reflects the average difference between actual observations and expected results provided by a regression line

standard overhead application rate a predetermined overhead rate used in a standard cost system; it can be a separate variable or fixed rate or a combined overhead rate

standard quantity allowed the quantity of input (in hours or some other cost driver measurement) required at standard for the output actually achieved for the period

Statement on Management Accounting (SMA) a pronouncement developed and issued by the Management Accounting Practices Committee of the Institute of Management Accountants; application of these statements is through voluntary, not legal, compliance

statistical process control (SPC) the use of control techniques that are based on the theory that a process has natural variations in it over time, but uncommon variations are typically the points at which the process produces "errors," which can be defective goods or poor service

steady-state phase the point at which the learning curve becomes flat and only minimal improvements in performance are achieved

step cost a cost that increases in distinct amounts because of increased activity

step method a process of service department cost allocation that assigns service department costs to cost objects after considering the interrelationships of the service departments and revenue-producing departments

stock appreciation right a right to receive cash, stock, or a combination of cash and stock based on the difference between a specified dollar amount per share of stock and the quoted market price per share at some future date

stock option a right allowing the holder to purchase shares of common stock during some future time frame and at a specified price

stockout the condition of not having inventory available upon need or request

strategic alliance an agreement between two or more firms with complementary core competencies to jointly contribute to the supply chain

strategic planning the process of developing a statement of long-range (5–10 years) goals for the organization and defining the strategies and policies that will help the organization achieve those goals

strategic resource management organizational planning for the deployment of resources to create value for customers and shareholders; key variables in the process include the management of information and the management of change in response to threats and opportunities

strategic staffing an approach to personnel management that requires a department to analyze its staffing needs by considering its long-term objectives and those of the overall company and determining a specific combination of permanent and temporary employees with the best skills to meet those needs

strategy the link between an organization's goals and objectives and the activities actually conducted by the organization

strict FIFO method (of process costing) the method of cost assignment that uses FIFO to compute a cost per equivalent unit and, in transferring units from a department, keeps the cost of the beginning units separate from the cost of the units started and completed during the current period

suboptimization a situation in which an individual manager pursues goals and objectives that are in his/her own and his/her segment's particular interests rather than in the company's best interests

substitute good an item that can replace another item to satisfy the same wants or needs

sunk cost a cost incurred in the past and not relevant to any future courses of action; the historical or past cost associated with the acquisition of an asset or a resource

supply-chain management the cooperative strategic planning, controlling, and problem solving by a company and its vendors and customers to conduct efficient and effective transfers of goods and services within the supply chain

surplus variable a variable used in a linear programming problem that represents overachievement of a minimum requirement; it is associated with greater-than-or-equal-to constraints

synchronous management the use of all techniques that help an organization achieve its goals

tactical planning the process of determining the specific means or objectives by which the strategic plans of the organization will be achieved; it is short-range in nature (usually 1–18 months)

takeover the acquisition of managerial control of the corporation by an outside or inside investor; control is achieved by acquiring enough stock and stockholder votes to control the board of directors and management

target costing a method of determining what the cost of a product should be based on the product's estimated selling price less the desired profit

tax benefit (of depreciation) the amount of depreciation deductible for tax purposes multiplied by the tax rate; the reduction in taxes caused by the deductibility of depreciation

tax deferral postponing taxation of an amount until a future date

tax exemption a tax treatment where income is never subject to income taxation

tax-deferred income current compensation that is taxed at a future date

tax-exempt income current compensation that is never taxed

tax shield (of depreciation) the amount of depreciation deductible for tax purposes; the amount of revenue shielded from taxes because of the depreciation deduction

theoretical capacity the estimated maximum production or service volume that a firm could achieve during a period

theory of constraints (TOC) a method of analyzing the bottlenecks (constraints) that keep a system from achieving higher performance; it states that production cannot take place at a rate faster than the slowest machine or person in the process

third-party logistics outsourcing of the moving and warehousing of finished goods between manufacturer and merchant and sometimes back to the manufacturer

throughput the total completed and sold output of a plant during a period

timeline a representation of the amounts and timing of all cash inflows and outflows; it is used in analyzing cash flow from a capital project

total contribution margin see contribution margin

total cost to account for the sum of the costs in beginning inventory and the costs of the current period

total expected value (for a project) the sum of the individual cash flows in a probability distribution multiplied by their related probabilities

total overhead variance the difference between total actual overhead and total applied overhead; it is the amount of underapplied or overapplied overhead

total quality management (TQM) a structural system for creating organization-wide participation in planning and implementing a continuous improvement process that exceeds the expectations of the customer/client; the application of quality principles to all company endeavors; it is also known as total quality control

total units to account for the sum of the beginning inventory units and units started during the current period

total variance the difference between total actual cost incurred and total standard cost for the output produced during the period

transfer price an internal charge established for the exchange of goods or services between organizational units of the same company

transfer time the time consumed by moving products or components from one place to another

treasurer an individual in a corporation who handles the actual resources of the organization but who does not have access to the accounting records

two-bin system an inventory ordering system in which two containers (or stacks) of raw materials or parts are available for use; when one container is depleted, the removal of materials from the second container begins and a purchase order is placed to refill the first container

underapplied overhead a debit balance in the Overhead account at the end of a period; when the applied overhead amount is less than the actual overhead that was incurred

unexpired cost an asset

unit-level cost a cost caused by the production or acquisition of a single unit of product or the delivery of a single unit of service

units started and completed the difference between the number of units completed for the period and the units in beginning inventory; it can also be computed as the number of units started during the period minus the units in ending inventory

usage the quantity of inventory used or sold each time interval

value the characteristic of meeting the highest number of customer needs at the lowest possible price

value-added (VA) activity an activity that increases the worth of the product or service to the customer

value chain the set of processes that converts inputs into products and services for the firm's customers; it includes the processes of suppliers as well as internal processes

value chart a visual representation indicating the value-added and non-value-added activities and time spent in those activities from the beginning to the end of a process

value engineering a disciplined search for various feasible combinations of resources and methods that will increase product functionality and reduce costs

values statement an organization's statement that reflects its culture by identifying fundamental beliefs about what is important to the organization

variable cost a cost that varies in total in direct proportion to changes in activity; it is constant on a per unit basis

variable costing a cost accumulation and reporting method that includes only variable production costs (direct material, direct labor, and variable overhead) as inventoriable or product costs; it treats fixed overhead as a period cost; is not acceptable for external reporting and tax returns

variable cost ratio the proportion of each revenue dollar represented by variable costs; computed as variable costs divided by sales or as (1 − contribution margin ratio)

variable overhead efficiency variance the difference between budgeted variable overhead based on actual input activity and variable overhead applied to production

variable overhead spending variance the difference between total actual variable overhead and the budgeted amount of variable overhead based on actual input activity

variance a difference between an actual and a standard or budgeted cost; it is favorable if actual is less than standard and is unfavorable if actual is greater than standard

variance analysis the process of categorizing the nature (favorable or unfavorable) of the differences between standard and actual costs and determining the reasons for those differences

vendor-managed inventory a streamlined system of inventory acquisition and management by which a supplier can be empowered to monitor EDI inventory levels and provide its customer company a proposed e-order and subsequent shipment after electronic acceptance

vertex a corner produced by the intersection of lines on a graph

vision a conceptualization of a future state for the organization that is better than the current state

vision statement a written expression about the organization's future upon which all company personnel can base their decisions and behavior so that everyone is working toward the same long-run results

volume variance a fixed overhead variance that represents the difference between budgeted fixed overhead and fixed overhead applied to production of the period; is also referred to as the noncontrollable variance

waste a residual output of a production process that has no sales value and must be disposed of

weighted average cost of capital a composite of the cost of the various sources of funds that comprise a firm's capital structure; the minimum rate of return that must be earned on new investments so as not to dilute shareholder value

weighted average method (of process costing) the method of cost assignment that computes an average cost per equivalent unit of production for all units completed during the current period; it combines beginning inventory units and costs with current production and costs, respectively, to compute the average

working capital total current assets minus total current liabilities

World Trade Organization (WTO) the arbiter of global trade that was created in 1995 under the General Agreement on Tariffs and Trade; each signatory country has one vote in trade disputes

yield the quantity of output that results from a specified input

yield ratio the expected or actual relationship between input and output

zero-base budgeting a comprehensive budgeting process that systematically considers the priorities and alternatives for current and proposed activities in relation to organization objectives; it requires the rejustification of ongoing activities

Author Index

Organization Index

Subject Index

Photo Credits

2 © PhotoDisc, Inc.; **5** © Spencer Grant/PhotoEdit; **47** © Phil Schemeister/Corbis; **76** © Chris Close/Image Bank; **92** © Jim Sugar/Corbis; **130** © Carrier Corporation; **138** © Royalty Free/Corbis; **172** © /Aker Gulf Marine; **191** © Gary A. Conner/PhotoEdit; **218** © /Lumina Candles & Art; **235** © Richard T. Norwitz/Corbis; **260** © Richard Vogel/AP/Wide World Photos; **266** © VCG/FPG International; **302** © /Solectron Corp.; **308** © Morton Beebe/Corbis; **342** © PhotoDisc, Inc.; **350** © Owen Franken/Corbis; **380** © Commerce Bank; **385** © Colin Garratt Milepost/Corbis; **442** © /PNI; **456** © Layne Kennedy/Corbis; **498** © /Image Bank; **501** © Michael Pole/Corbis; **550** © HON Industries; **565** © Phil Banko/Stone; **600** © Barry Sweet/AP/Wide World Photos; **612** © Aaron Horowitz/Corbis; **660** David Toerge/AP/Wide World Photos Courtesy of Lucent Technologies; **674** © Cindy Charles/PhotoEdit; **710** © Courtesy/Alexander Doll Company; **736** © Andy Slacks/Stone; **762** © Max Nash/AP/Wide World Photos; **769** © /Stock Market; **796** © PhotoDisc, Inc.; **810** © Foodpix; **856** © Wachovia; **873** © Laurence Monneret/Stone; **898** © /WMC Limited; **914** © Roger Ressmeyer/Corbis; **928** © PhotoDisc, Inc.; **933** © Paul A. Souders/Corbis